A World of Art

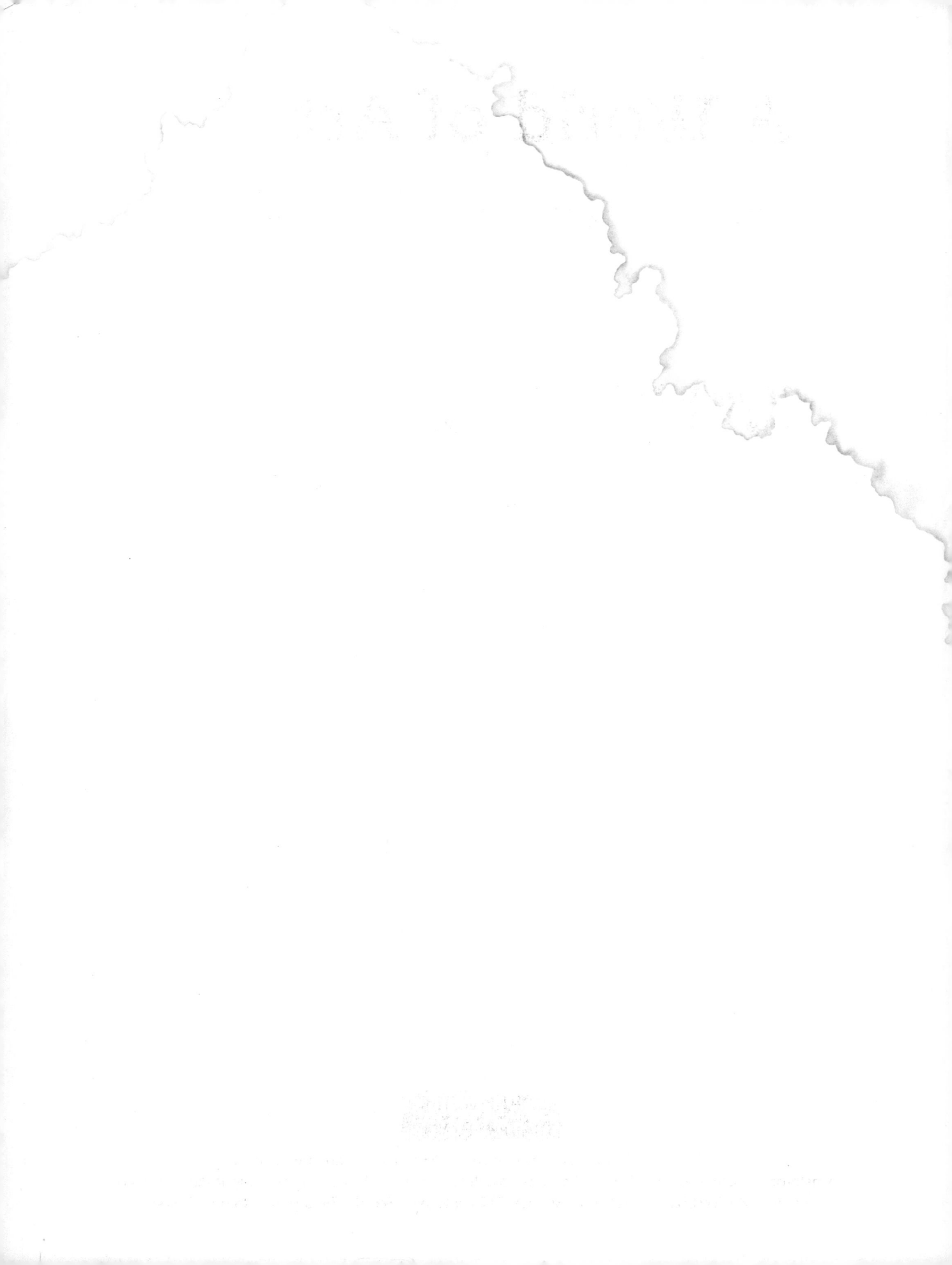

A World of Art

Eighth Edition

Henry M. Sayre
Oregon State University–Cascades Campus

PEARSON

Boston Columbus Indianapolis New York San Francisco
Amsterdam Cape Town Dubai London Madrid Milan Munich Paris Montreal Toronto
Delhi Mexico City São Paulo Sydney Hong Kong Seoul Singapore Taipei Tokyo

Editor in Chief: Sarah Touborg
Senior Editor: Helen Ronan
Editorial Assistants: Victoria Engros and Claire Ptaschinski
Executive Marketing Manager: Wendy Albert
Senior Product Marketer: Jeremy Intal
Marketing Assistants: Frank Alcaron and Paige Patunas
Managing Editor: Melissa Feimer
Senior Program Manager: Barbara Marttine Cappuccio
Project Manager: Joe Scordato
Operations Specialist: Diane Peirano
Senior Digital Project Manager: Rich Barnes
Pearson Imaging Center: Corin Skidds
Full-Service Project Management: Lumina Datamatics
Composition: Lumina Datamatics
Printer/Binder: RR Donnelley
Cover Printer: Phoenix Color
Cover Design: Pentagram
Cover Art Director: Kathryn Foot

Library of Congress Cataloging-in-Publication Data

Sayre, Henry M.,
A world of art / Henry M. Sayre, Oregon State University-Cascades Campus. — EIGHTH Edition.
pages cm
ISBN 978-0-13-408180-9
1. Art. I. Title.
N7425.S29 2015
700—dc23

2015024482

2 16

Student Edition
ISBN 10: 0-13-408180-3
ISBN 13: 978-0-13-408180-9

Instructor's Review Copy
ISBN 10: 0-13-416989-1
ISBN 13: 978-0-13-416989-7

Books à la carte
ISBN 10: 0-13-408226-5
ISBN 13: 978-0-13-408226-4

PEARSON

As always, for my boys, Rob and John, and for Sandy

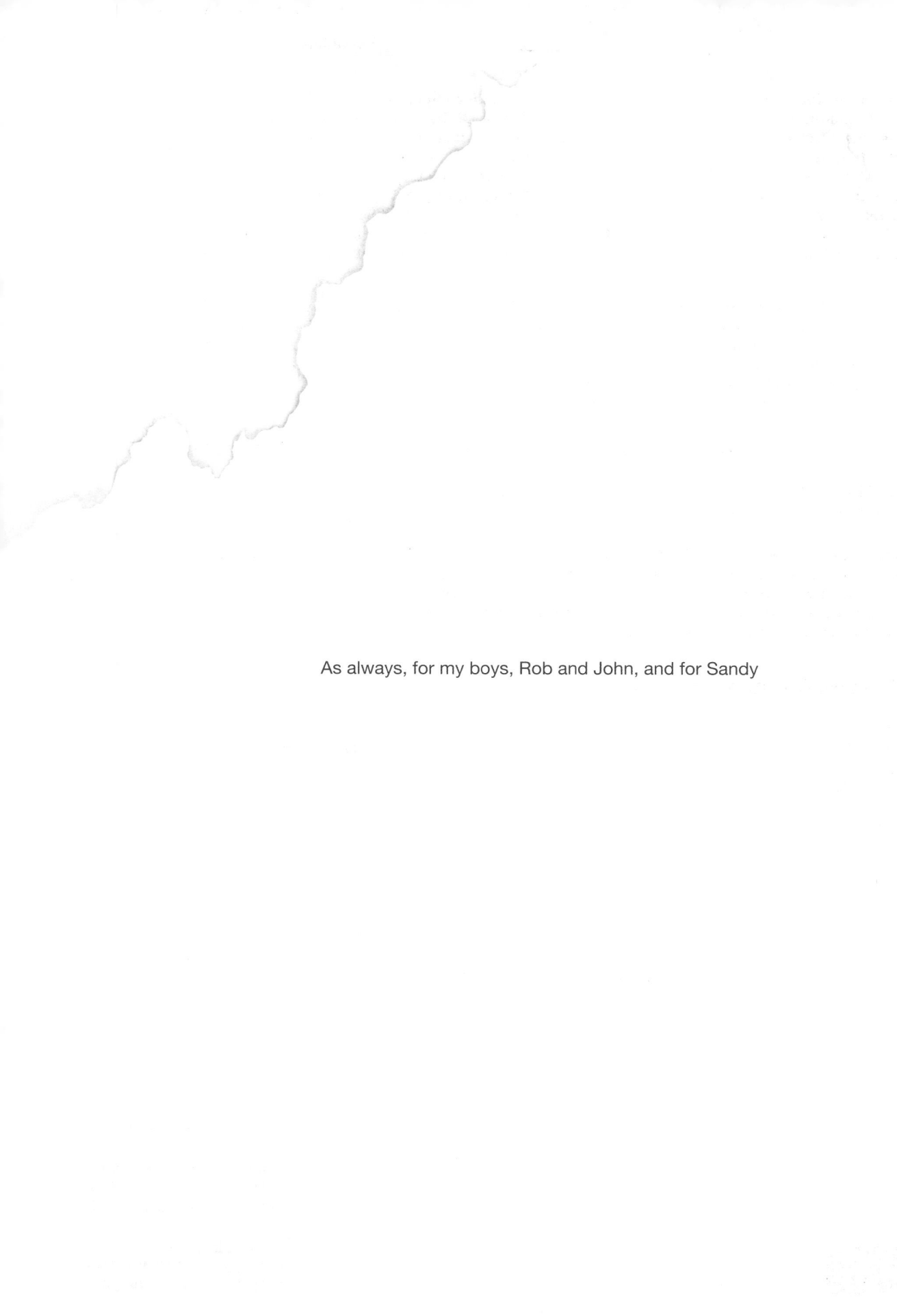

Brief Contents

Dear Student x
Additional Resources & Choices xiv
Student Toolkit xvi

Part 1 The Visual World: Understanding the Art You See 2

- **1** Discovering a World of Art 4
- **2** Developing Visual Literacy 28

Part 2 The Formal Elements and Their Design: Describing the Art You See 46

- **3** Line 48
- **4** Shape and Space 66
- **5** Light and Color 88
- **6** Texture, Time, and Motion 116
- **7** The Principles of Design 132

Part 3 The Fine Arts Media: Learning How Art is Made 158

- **8** Drawing 160
- **9** Painting 182
- **10** Printmaking 212
- **11** Photography and Time-Based Media 238
- **12** Sculpture 274
- **13** The Craft Media 300
- **14** Architecture 328
- **15** The Design Profession 362

Part 4 The Visual Record: Placing the Arts in Historical Context 390

- **16** The Ancient World 392
- **17** The Age of Faith 418
- **18** The Renaissance through the Baroque 444
- **19** The Eighteenth and Nineteenth Centuries 472
- **20** From 1900 to the Present 494

Part 5 The Themes of Art: Seeing Continuity and Change over Time 528

- **21** Spiritual Belief 530
- **22** The Cycle of Life 546
- **23** Love and Sex 564
- **24** The Body, Gender, and Identity 582
- **25** The Individual and Cultural Identity 600
- **26** Power 618
- **27** Science, Technology, and the Environment 638

The Critical Process 658
Glossary 661
Credits 669
Index 674

Contents

Dear Student x
Additional Resources & Choices xiv
Student Toolkit xvi

Part 1

The Visual World: Understanding the Art You See 2

1 Discovering a World of Art 4

The World as We Perceive It 6
The World as Artists See It 8
The Creative Process: From Sketch to Final Vision: Pablo Picasso's *Les Demoiselles d'Avignon* 12
Seeing the Value in Art 20
The Critical Process: Thinking about Making and Seeing Works of Art 26

2 Developing Visual Literacy 28

Words and Images 30
Representation and Abstraction 33
The Creative Process: Abstract Illusionism: George Green's ... *marooned in dreaming: a path of song and mind* 34
Form and Meaning 37
Convention, Symbols, and Interpretation 39
The Critical Process: Thinking about Visual Conventions 44

Part 2

The Formal Elements and Their Design: Describing the Art You See 46

3 Line 48

Varieties of Line 48
Qualities of Line 52
The Creative Process: From Painting to Drawing: Vincent van Gogh's The Sower 54
The Creative Process: The Drip as Line: Hung Liu's *Three Fujins* 60
The Critical Process: Thinking about Line 64

4 Shape and Space 66

Shape and Mass 68
The Creative Process: From Two to Three Dimensions: Umberto Boccioni's *Development of a Bottle in Space* 70
Representing Three-Dimensional Space in Two Dimensions 74
Modern Experiments and New Dimensions 82
The Critical Process: Thinking about Space 86

5 Light and Color 88

Light 89
The Creative Process: The Play of Light and Dark: Mary Cassatt's *In the Loge* 98
Color 100
The Creative Process: The New Pointillism: Chuck Close's *Stanley* 108
Representational and Symbolic Uses of Color 111
The Critical Process: Thinking about Light and Color 114

6 Texture, Time, and Motion 116

Texture 116
Time and Motion 121
The Creative Process: Painting as Action: Jackson Pollock's *No. 32, 1950* 126
The Critical Process: Thinking about the Formal Elements 130

7 The Principles of Design 132

Balance 134
Emphasis and Focal Point 140
The Creative Process: A Multiplication of Focal Points: Diego Velázquez's *Las Meninas* 142
Scale and Proportion 144
Pattern, Repetition, and Rhythm 148
Unity and Variety 153
The Critical Process: Thinking about the Principles of Design 156

Part 3

The Fine Arts Media: Learning How Art is Made 158

8 Drawing 160

From Preparatory Sketch to Finished Work of Art 160
Drawing Materials 165
The Creative Process: Movement and Gesture: Raphael's *Alba Madonna* 166
Innovative Drawing Media 175
The Critical Process: Thinking about Drawing 180

9 Painting 182

Early Painting Media 183

The Creative Process: Preparing to Paint the Sistine Chapel: Michelangelo's *Libyan Sibyl* 190

Oil Painting 193

Watercolor and Gouache 198

Synthetic Media 202

Mixed Media 204

The Creative Process: Political Collage: Hannah Höch's *Cut with the Kitchen Knife* 206

The Critical Process: Thinking about Painting 210

10 Printmaking 212

The Print and its Earliest Uses 214

Relief Processes 216

The Creative Process: Making an Ukiyo-e Print: Kitigawa Utamaro's *Studio* 218

Intaglio Processes 224

The Creative Process: Four-Color Intaglio: Yuji Hiratsuka's *Miracle Grow Hypnotist* 228

Lithography 232

Silkscreen Printing 233

Monotypes 234

The Critical Process: Thinking about Printmaking 236

11 Photography and Time-Based Media 238

The Early History and Formal Foundations of Photography 241

Color and Digital Photography 251

The Creative Process: The Darkroom as Laboratory: Jerry Uelsmann's *Untitled* 252

Film 257

Video Art 261

The Computer and New Media 267

The Creative Process: Revisioning a Painting as Video: Bill Viola's *The Greeting* 268

The Critical Process: Thinking about Photography and Time-Based Media 271

12 Sculpture 274

The Three Forms of Sculptural Space 276

Carving 280

Modeling 282

Casting 283

Assemblage 286

Installations and Earthworks 289

Performance Art as Living Sculpture 295

The Critical Process: Thinking about Sculpture 298

13 The Craft Media 300

The Crafts as Fine Art 302

Ceramics 303

The Creative Process: Ceramics as Politics: Julie Green's *The Last Supper* 308

Glass 310

Fiber 313

The Creative Process: A New Narrative: Fred Wilson's *Mining the Museum* 314

Metal 321

Wood 324

The Critical Process: Thinking about the Crafts as Fine Art 326

14 Architecture 328

Environment 328

Early Architectural Technologies 333

Modern and Contemporary Architectural Technologies 342

The Creative Process: Thinking through Architecture: Frank Lloyd Wright's *Fallingwater* 348

The Creative Process: Discovering Where to Go: Frank Gehry's Guggenheim Museum Bilbao 354

Community Life 356

The Critical Process: Thinking about Architecture 360

15 The Design Profession 362

The Rise of Design in the Nineteenth Century 364

Design in the Modernist Era 371

Streamlining and Organic Design, 1930–60 376

Design Since 1980 381

The Creative Process: April Greiman and Design Technology 384

The Critical Process: Thinking about Design 388

Part 4

The Visual Record: Placing the Arts in Historical Context 390

16 The Ancient World 392

The Earliest Art 394

Mesopotamian Cultures 396

Egyptian Civilization 397

River Valley Societies in India and China 400

Complex Societies in the Americas 402

Aegean and Greek Civilizations 404

The Roman World 410

Developments in Asia 414

17 The Age of Faith 418
Early Christian and Byzantine Art 420
The Rise of Islam 424
Christian Art in Europe 427
Developments in Asia 433
The Cultures of Africa 441

18 The Renaissance through the Baroque 444
The Renaissance 444
The Era of Encounter 455
The Mannerist Style in Europe 461
The Baroque 464

19 The Eighteenth and Nineteenth Centuries 472
The Early Eighteenth Century 474
Cross-Cultural Contact: China and Europe 476
Neoclassicism 477
Romanticism 479
Realism 483
Impressionism 488
Post-Impressionism 490

20 From 1900 to the Present 494
The New "Isms" 496
Dada and Surrealism 500
Politics and Painting 504
American Modernism and Abstract Expressionism 506
Pop Art and Minimalism 508
Cross-Fertilization in Contemporary Art 510
The Critical Process: Thinking about Art Today 526

Part 5
The Themes of Art: Seeing Continuity and Change over Time 528

21 Spiritual Belief 530
Connecting with Spirits and the Divine 532
Giving Gods Human Form 535
Sacred Space 537
Spirituality and Abstraction 542
The Critical Process: Thinking about Art and Spiritual Belief 544

22 The Cycle of Life 546
Birth 548
Youth and Age 550
Contemplating Mortality 554
Burial and the Afterlife 558
The Critical Process: Thinking about the Cycle of Life 562

23 Love and Sex 564
Physical and Spiritual Love 564
Imaging Desire 572
Kisses 577
The Critical Process: Thinking about Love and Sex 580

24 The Body, Gender, and Identity 582
The Body Beautiful 582
Performance: The Body as Work of Art 586
Gender and Identity 589
The Critical Process: Thinking about the Body, Gender, and Identity 598

25 The Individual and Cultural Identity 600
Nationalism and Identity 602
Class and Identity 607
Racial Identity and African-American Experience 611
The Critical Process: Thinking about the Individual and Cultural Identity 616

26 Power 618
Representing Rulers 619
Women and Power 623
Power, Race, and the Colonial Enterprise 627
The Power of the Museum 633
The Critical Process: Thinking about Power 636

27 Science, Technology, and the Environment 638
Technology and the Arts 639
Art and Environmental Understanding 642
Art, the Environment, and the Longer View 653
The Critical Process: Thinking about Science, Technology, and the Environment 656

The Critical Process 658
Glossary 661
Credits 669
Index 674

Dear Student

You might be asking yourself, "Why are they making me take this course? What does art have to do with my engineering, or forestry, or business degree?" In fact, many students come to an art appreciation course thinking of it as something akin to a maraschino cherry sitting atop their education sundae—pretty to look at, but of questionable food value, and of little real use.

But as you come to understand art, I hope you will realize that in studying it, you have learned to *think* better. You might be surprised to learn, for instance, that in 2005 the New York City Police Department began taking newly promoted officers, including sergeants, captains, and uniformed executives, to the Frick Collection, an art museum on New York's Upper East Side, in order to improve their observational skills by having them analyze works of art. Similar classes are offered to New York medical students to help them improve their diagnostic abilities when observing patients, teaching them to be sensitive to people's facial expressions and body language. Art appreciation is not forensic science, but it teaches many of the same skills.

Perhaps more than anything else, an art appreciation course can teach you the art of critical thinking—how to ask the right questions about the visual world that surrounds us, and then respond meaningfully to the complexity of that world. This book is, in fact, unique in its emphasis on the critical thinking process—a process of questioning, exploration, trial and error, and discovery that you can generalize to your own experience and your own chosen field of endeavor. Critical thinking is really a matter of putting yourself in a questioning frame of mind.

We've added seven new chapters to this edition as well. They focus on seven different themes, all of which represent universal concerns that all creative people, in all cultures and at all times, have sought to explore and understand. If different cultures and different eras have inevitably addressed them differently, the quest to understand the world and our place in it is common to us all.

Today, culture is increasingly dominated by images—and I've included a lot of new, very contemporary ones in this eighth edition. The new REVEL digital learning environment available in this edition makes many of these images literally come to life by including some 40 videos of the artists themselves addressing the works at hand. And that's not all that REVEL does. On top of that, nearly every image is pan-zoomable, making it possible for you to study images in detail. Panoramic views of many major monuments allow you explore them both inside and out. All students today must learn to see and interpret the images that surround them. REVEL engages you by asking you questions, creating writing environments, and providing for self-testing. You can no longer just passively "receive" these images, like watching television, or you will never come to understand them. I hope that you'll find this book to be not just a useful, but an indispensable foundation in learning to negotiate your world.

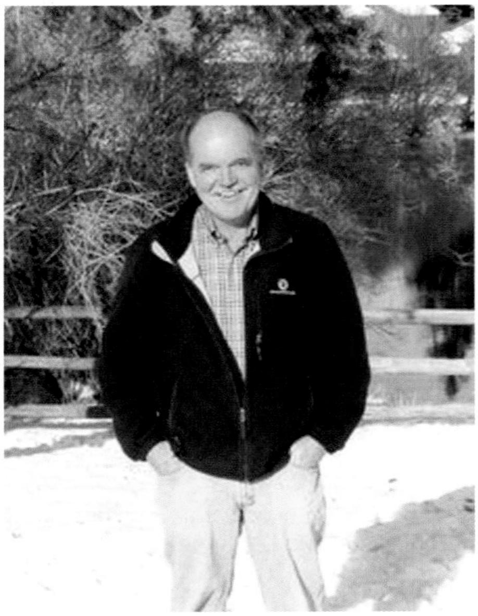

About the Author

Henry M. Sayre is Distinguished Professor of Art History at Oregon State University–Cascades Campus in Bend, Oregon. He is producer and creator of the 10-part television series *A World of Art: Works in Progress*, which aired on PBS in the fall of 1997; and author of seven books: *The Humanities; Writing About Art; The Visual Text of William Carlos Williams; The Object of Performance: The American Avant-Garde since 1970*; and an art history book for children, *Cave Paintings to Picasso*.

What's New to this Edition?

Henry Sayre's *A World of Art* introduces students to art with an emphasis on critical thinking and visual literacy. This new eighth edition further strengthens these key aspects by examining major themes of art and by adding the new **REVEL** digital learning environment, which is designed for the way today's students read, think, and learn (see below).

Seven new chapters focus on major themes in art, each approaching its theme from both an historical and global perspective:

- Spiritual Belief
- The Cycle of Life
- Love and Sex
- The Body, Gender, and Identity
- The Individual and Cultural Identity
- Power
- Science, Technology, and the Environment

These new thematic chapters encourage students to see how artists across time and culture engage with the major questions that connect us as humans today.

Some 40 videos from the award winning PBS-broadcast series art21 in which the artworks reproduced in the text are discussed by the artists themselves, available in REVEL. Over the past decade, art21 has established itself as the preeminent chronicler of contemporary art and artists. These videos from the *Exclusive* series, which showcase art21 and *New York Close Up* artists in previously unreleased archival footage, range in length from 3–8 minutes and focus on aspects of an artist's process, provocative ideas, and biographical anecdotes.

Over 100 new and updated contemporary art images showcase the latest developments in the contemporary art world. *A World of Art* continues its commitment to introducing students to the art of today, while offering them the tools to approach these works with appreciation and understanding.

There are new and updated global art images throughout, including coverage of art in Africa, India, China, and Japan, supporting the text's core goal of introducing students to the world of art. In addition, the new chapters in Part 5 deepen the coverage of world art by showcasing a global range of approaches to universal themes.

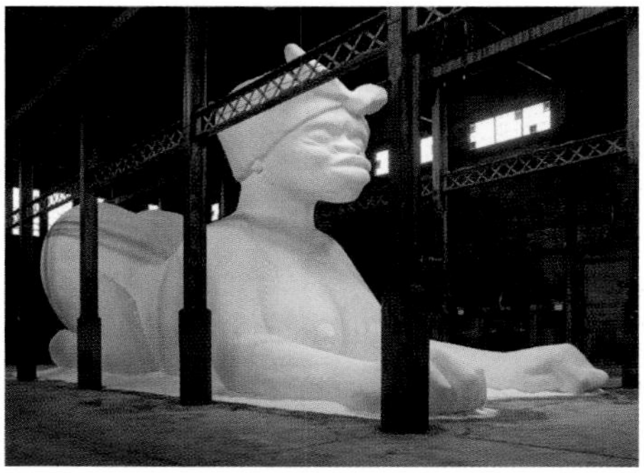

Fig. 7-20 Kara Walker, *A Subtlety: The Marvelous Sugar Baby, an Homage to the unpaid and overworked Artisans who have refined our Sweet tastes from the cane fields to the Kitchens of the New World on the Occasion of the demolition of the Domino Sugar Refining Plant*, 2014. Installation view, Domino Sugar Factory, Williamsburg, Brooklyn, New York. Carved polystyrene coated with 160,000 lb of sugar, 10 × 7 × 75 ft.

Fig. 7-21 Hokusai, *The Great Wave off Kanagawa*, from the series *Thirty-Six Views of Mount Fuji*, 1823–29. Color woodcut, 10 × 15 in.

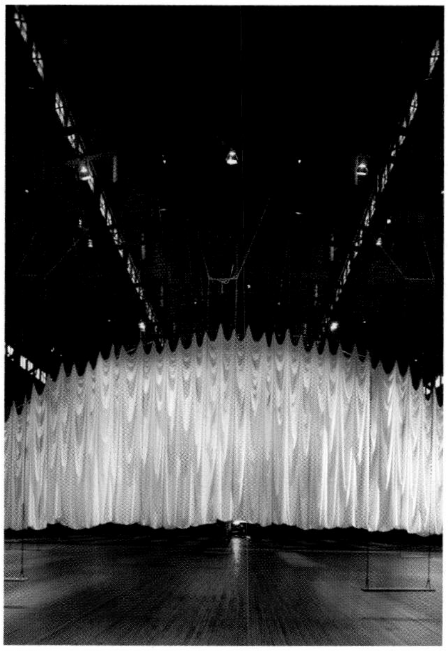

Fig. 13-1 Ann Hamilton, *the event of a thread*, 2012. Large-scale installation, Park Avenue Armory, New York, December 5, 2012–January 6, 2013.

REVEL™

Educational technology designed for the way today's students read, think, and learn

Over the course of the last decade, as technology has increasingly encroached on the book as we know it—with the explosion, that is, of the Internet, digital media, and new forms of publishing, like the iPad and Kindle—I worried that books like A World of Art *might one day lose their relevance. I envisioned them being supplanted by some as-yet-unforeseen technological wizardry, like a machine in a science fiction novel, that would transport my reader into a three- or four-dimensional learning space "beyond the book." Well, little did I know that Pearson Education was developing just such a space, one firmly embedded in the book, not beyond it. From my point of view, REVEL represents one of the most important developments in art publishing and education in decades. I am extremely grateful to the team that has put it together and is continually working to improve it.*

— *Henry Sayre*

When students are engaged deeply, they learn more effectively and perform better in their courses. This simple fact inspired the creation of REVEL: an immersive learning experience designed for the way today's students read, think, and learn. Built in collaboration with educators and students nationwide, REVEL is the newest, fully digital way to deliver respected Pearson content.

REVEL enlivens course content with media interactives and assessments—integrated directly within the author's narrative—that provide opportunities for students to read about and practice course material in tandem. This immersive educational technology boosts student engagement, which leads to better understanding of concepts and improved performance throughout the course.

In REVEL for *A World of Art*, rich media is embedded in the learning path so that students may truly experience and interact with works of art:

- Nearly every image is pan-zoomable, encouraging close looking. Scalemarkers indicate the size of the artwork relative to the human body or human hand.

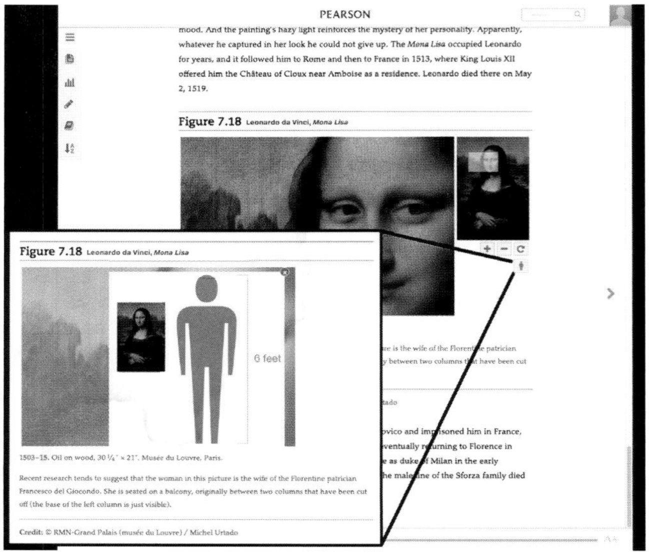

- **Art21 videos** present up-close looks at contemporary artists at work, and **Studio Technique videos** demonstrate the steps involved in processes such as silkscreening, bronze casting, carving, and oil painting.

- **Audio of the text**, read by the author, is an option that frees students' eyes to look at the art while they learn about it.

- **360-degree panoramic views of major monuments as well as video simulations of architectural techniques** help students understand buildings—inside and out.

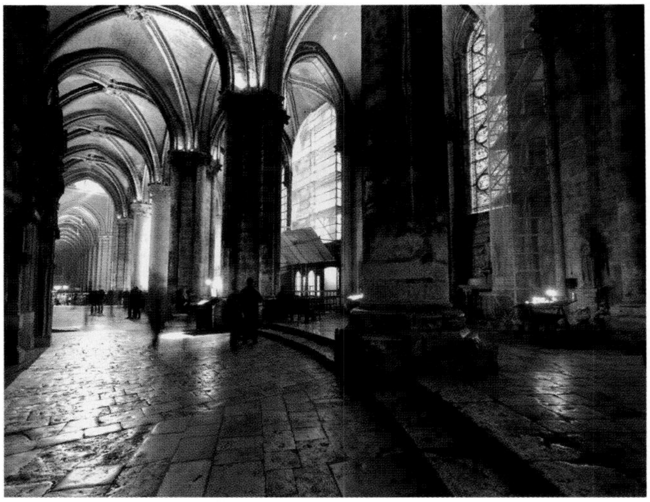

- **Writing prompts,** developed by the author, help foster critical thinking. In every chapter, "Journaling" questions for students to answer are geared toward developing visual analysis skills, while "Shared Writing" prompts that students answer in a discussion space encourage them to articulate opinions and engage in debates about contemporary issues in the arts. A third type of writing assignment, the short essay, is available at the discretion of the instructor in Writing Space, which also includes resources to help students with drafting and editing and to help teachers with grading and responding.

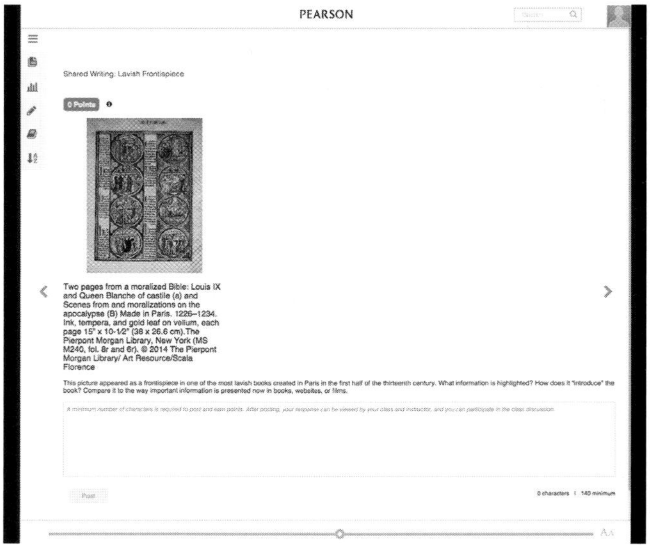

Learn more about REVEL

http://www.pearsonhighered.com/revel/

Additional Resources & Choices

Pearson arts titles are available in the following formats to give you and your students more choices—and more ways to save.

The **Books à la Carte edition** offers a convenient, three-hole-punched, loose-leaf version of the traditional text at a discounted price—allowing students to take only what they need to class. Books à la Carte editions are available both with and without access to REVEL.

Build your own Pearson Custom course material: for enrollments of at least 25, the Pearson Custom Library allows you to create your own textbook by

- combining chapters from best-selling Pearson textbooks in the sequence you want.
- adding your own content, such as a guide to a local worship place, your syllabus, or a study guide you've created.

A Pearson Custom Library book is priced according to the number of chapters and may even save your students money. To begin building your custom text, visit www.pearsoncustomlibrary.com or contact your Pearson representative.

Instructor Resources

LEARNING CATALYTICS

A "bring your own device" student engagement, assessment, and classroom intelligence system. Question libraries for Art Appreciation help generate classroom discussion, guide your lecture, and promote peer-to-peer learning with real-time analytics. Learn more at www.learningcatalytics.com.

INSTRUCTOR'S MANUAL AND TEST ITEM FILE

This is an invaluable professional resource and reference for new and experienced faculty. Each chapter contains the following sections: Chapter Overview, Chapter Objectives, Key Terms, Lecture and Discussion Topics, Resources, and Writing Assignments and Projects. The test bank includes multiple-choice, true/false, short-answer, and essay questions. Available for download from the instructor support section at www.pearsonhighered.com.

MyTest

This flexible online test-generating software includes all questions found in the printed Test Item File. Instructors can quickly and easily create customized tests with MyTest.

Development

Every edition of *A World of Art* has grown over the years, in large part due to the instructors and students who share their feedback, ideas, and experiences with the text. This edition is no different and we are grateful to all who participated in shaping its structure and content. Manuscript reviewers for this eighth edition include:

Rachel Bomze, Passaic County Community College
Sara Clark, Saginaw Valley State University
Chris Coltrin, Shepherd University
Gary Conners, Lone Star College—North Harris
Elizabeth Consavari, San Jose State University
Steve Darnell, Midlands Technical College
Robin Dearing, Colorado Mesa University
Nathan Dolde, Lenoir Community College
Patricia Drew, Irvine Valley College
Tracy Eckersley, University of Louisville
Suzanne Fricke, Central New Mexico Community College
Soo Kang, Chicago State University
Katrina Kuntz, Middle Tennessee State University
Ann Marie Leimer, Missouri Western State University
Jessica Locheed, University of Houston
Fadhili Mshana, Georgia College & State University
Moana Nikou, University of Hawaii, Honolulu Community College
Kate Peaslee, Texas Tech University
Kimberly Riner, Georgia Southern University
Jennifer Robinson, Tallahassee Community College
Sean Russell, College of Southern Nevada
Tom Sale, Hill College
Nicholas Silberg, Savannah State University
Eric Sims, Lone Star College—North Harris
Nancy Stombaugh, Lone Star College—CyFair
Tiffanie Townshend, Georgia Southern University
Paige Wideman, Northern Kentucky University
Kimberly Winkle, Tennessee Technological University

Acknowledgments

Over the years, a great many people have helped make this book what it is today. The contributions of all the people at Oregon State University who originally supported me in getting this project off the ground—Jeff Hale; three chairs of the Art Department, David Hardesty, Jim Folts, and John Maul; three deans of the College of Liberal Arts, Bill Wilkins, Kay Schaffer, and Larry Rodgers; and three university presidents, John Byrne, Paul Risser, and Ed Ray—cannot be forgotten. To this day, and down through this new edition, I owe them all a special debt of gratitude. Finally, in the first edition of this book, I thanked Berk Chappell for his example as a teacher. He knew more about teaching art appreciation than I ever will, and I miss him dearly.

At Pearson, I am especially grateful to the production team who saw this edition through to completion, especially the fine people at Laurence King Publishing in London: including Laurence himself; Editorial Manager Kara Hattersley-Smith; Clare Double, Senior Editor; and the extremely gifted and persistent picture editors Evi Peroulaki and Katharina Gruber. They all made working on the book something of a pleasure. Robert Shore, also in London, was as good a copyeditor as one could ever imagine—and a man of some humor at that. On this shore, Cynthia Ward's help on the new Themes chapters was incisive and invaluable. She has continued to help me fashion the new REVEL environment. At Pearson, I am indebted to Project Manager Joe Scordato, to Ben Ferrini, Image Lead Manager, but most of all to Helen Ronan. Finally, I want to thank, once again, Lindsay Bethoney and the staff at Lumina Datamatics for working so hard to make the book turn out the way I envisioned it.

The marketing and editorial teams at Pearson are beyond compare. On the marketing side, Maggie Moylan, Vice President of Marketing, Wendy Albert, Executive Field Marketer, and Jeremy Intal, Senior Marketing Manager help us all to understand just what students want and need. On the editorial side, my thanks to Sarah Touborg, Editor in Chief, who has supported the ongoing development of this project in every conceivable way; to Helen Ronan, Senior Sponsoring Editor in the Arts, who together with Sarah, has forged the new direction in art publishing that REVEL represents; and to Victoria Engros, the Pearson Editorial Assistant, who has the daunting responsibility of keeping track of everything. Finally, I want to thank the late Bud Therien, who oversaw the development of most of the earlier editions of this book, and a man of extraordinary fortitude, passion, and vision. He is, in many ways, responsible for the way that art appreciation and art history are taught today in this country. I have had no better friend in the business.

Finally, as always, I owe my greatest debt to my colleague and wife, Sandy Brooke. She is present everywhere in this project. It is safe to say she made it possible. I can only say it again: Without her good counsel and better company, I would not have had the will to get this all done, let alone found the pleasure I have had in doing it.

Henry M. Sayre
Oregon State University–Cascades Campus

Student Toolkit

This short section is designed to introduce the over-arching themes and aims of *A World of Art* as well as provide you with a guide to the basic elements of art that you can easily access whenever you interact with works of art—in these pages, in museums, and anywhere else you encounter them. The topics covered here are developed much more fully in later chapters, but this overview brings all this material together in a convenient, quick-reference format.

Why Study the World of Art?

We study art because it is among the highest expressions of culture, embodying its ideals and aspirations, challenging its assumptions and beliefs, and creating new visions and possibilities for it to pursue. That said, "culture" is itself a complex phenomenon, constantly changing and vastly diverse. The "world of art" is composed of objects from many, many cultures—as many cultures as there are and have been. In fact, from culture to culture, and from cultural era to cultural era, the very idea of what "art" even is has changed. It was not until the Renaissance, for instance, that the concept of fine art, as we think of it today, arose in Europe. Until then, the Italian word *arte* meant "guild"—any one of the associations of craftspeople that dominated medieval commerce—and *artista* referred to any student of the liberal arts, particularly grammarians.

But, since the Renaissance, we have tended to see the world of art through the lens of "fine art." We differentiate those one-of-a-kind expressions of individual creativity that we normally associate with fine art—painting, sculpture, and architecture—from craft, works of the applied or practical arts like textiles, glass, ceramics, furniture, metalwork, and jewelry. When we refer to "African art" or "Aboriginal art," we are speaking of objects that, in the cultures in which they were produced, were almost always thought of as applied or practical. They served, that is, ritual or religious purposes that far outweighed whatever purely artistic skill they might evidence. Only in most recent times, as these cultures have responded to the West's ever-more-expansive appetite for the exotic and original, have individual artists in these cultures begun to produce works intended for sale in the Western "fine arts" market.

To whatever degree a given object is more or less "fine art" or "craft," we study it in order to understand more about the culture that produced it. The object gives us insight into what the culture values—religious ritual, aesthetic pleasure, or functional utility, to name just a few possibilities.

The Critical Process

Studying these objects engages us in a critical process that is analogous, in many ways, to the creative process that artists engage in. One of the major features of this text is a series of spreads called The Creative Process. They are meant to demonstrate that art, like most things, is the result of both hard work and, especially, a process of critical thinking that involves questioning, exploration, trial and error, revision, and discovery.

One of the greatest benefits of studying art is that it teaches you to think critically. Art objects are generally "mute." They cannot explain themselves to you, but that does not mean that their meaning is "hidden" or elusive. They contain information—all kinds of information—that can help you explain and understand them if you approach them through the critical thinking process that is outlined below.

Seven Steps to Thinking Critically about Art

1. Identify the artist's decisions and choices.
Begin by recognizing that, in making works of art, artists inevitably make certain decisions and choices—What color should I make this area? Should my line be wide or narrow? Straight or curved? Will I look up at my subject or down on it? Will I depict it realistically or not? What medium should I use to make this object? And so on. Identify these choices. Then ask yourself why these choices were made. Remember, though most artists work somewhat intuitively, every artist has the opportunity to revise or redo each work, each gesture. You can be sure that what you are seeing in a work of art is an intentional effect.

2. Ask questions. Be curious.
Asking yourself why the artist's choices were made is just the first set of questions to pose. You need to consider the work's title: What does it tell you about the piece? Is there any written material accompanying the work? Is the work informed by the context in which you encounter it—by other works around it, or, in the case of sculpture, for instance, by its location? Is there anything you learn about the artist that is helpful?

3. Describe the object.
By carefully describing the object—both its subject matter and how its subject matter is formally realized—you can discover much about the artist's intentions. Pay careful attention to how one part of the work relates to the others.

4. Question your assumptions.
Question, particularly, any initial dislike you might have for a given work of art. Remember that if you are seeing the work in a book, museum, or gallery, then someone likes it. Ask yourself why. Often you'll talk yourself into liking it too. But also examine the work itself to see if it contains any biases or prejudices. It matters, for instance,

in Renaissance church architecture, whether the church was designed for Protestants or Catholics.

5. Avoid an emotional response.
Art objects are supposed to stir up your feelings, but your emotions can sometimes get in the way of clear thinking. Analyze your own emotions. Determine what about the work set them off, and ask yourself if this wasn't the artist's very intention.

6. Don't oversimplify or misrepresent the art object.
Art objects are complex by their nature. To think critically about an art object is to look beyond the obvious. Thinking critically about the work of art always involves walking the line between the work's susceptibility to interpretation and its integrity, or its resistance to arbitrary and capricious readings. Be sure your reading of a work of art is complete enough (that it recognizes the full range of possible meanings the work might possess), and, at the same time, that it doesn't violate or misrepresent the work.

7. Tolerate uncertainty.
Remember that the critical process is an exercise in discovery, that it is designed to uncover possibilities, not necessarily certain truths. Critical thinking is a process of questioning; asking good questions is sometimes more important than arriving at "right" answers. There may, in fact, be no "right" answers.

At the end of each chapter in this book you will find a section called The Critical Process, which poses a series of questions about a work or works of art related to the material in that chapter. These questions are designed both to help you learn to ask similar questions of other works of art and to test your understanding of the chapter materials. Short answers to the questions can be found at the back of the book, but you should try to answer them for yourself before you consult the answers.

A Quick-Reference Guide to the Elements of Art

Basic Terms

Three basic principles define all works of art, whether two-dimensional (painting, drawing, printmaking, and photography) or three-dimensional (sculpture and architecture):

- Form—the overall structure of the work
- Subject matter—what is literally depicted
- Content—what it means

If the subject matter is recognizable, the work is said to be representational. Representational works that attempt to depict objects as they are in actual, visible reality are called realistic. The less a work resembles real things in the real world, the more abstract it is. Abstract art does not try to duplicate the world, but instead reduces the world to its essential qualities. If the subject matter of the work is not recognizable, the work is said to be nonrepresentational, or nonobjective.

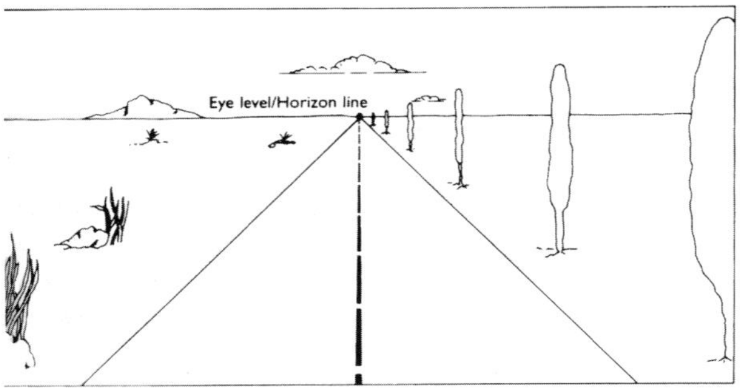

One-point linear perspective Frontal

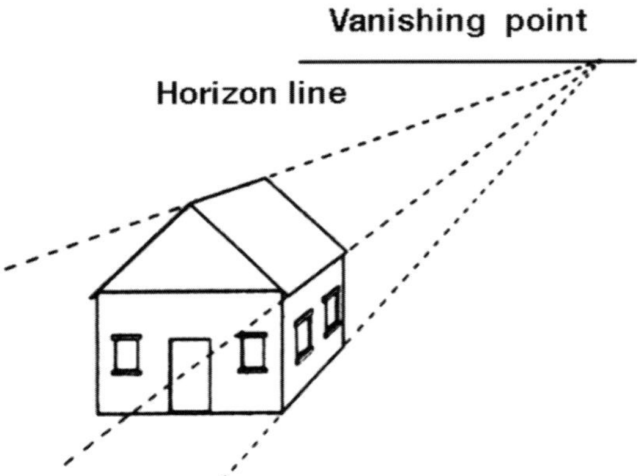

One-point linear perspective Diagonal

The Formal Elements

The term form refers to the purely visual aspects of art and architecture. Line, space, levels of light and dark, color, and texture are among the elements that contribute to a work's form.

LINE is the most fundamental formal element. It delineates shape (a flat two-dimensional area) and mass (a solid form that occupies a three-dimensional volume) by means of outline (in which the edge of a form or shape is indicated directly with a more or less continuous mark) or contour (which is the perceived edge of a volume as it curves away from the viewer). Lines can be implied—as in your line of sight. Line also possesses certain emotional, expressive, or intellectual qualities. Some lines are loose and free, gestural and quick. Other lines are precise, controlled, and mathematically and rationally organized.

SPACE Line is also fundamental to the creation of a sense of deep, three-dimensional space on a two-dimensional surface, the system known as linear perspective. In one-point linear perspective, lines are drawn on the picture plane in such a way as to represent parallel lines receding to a single point on the viewer's horizon, called the vanishing point. When the vanishing point is directly across from the viewer's vantage point, the recession is frontal. When the vanishing point is to one side or the other, the recession is diagonal.

In two-point linear perspective, more than one vanishing point occurs, as, for instance, when you look at the corner of a building.

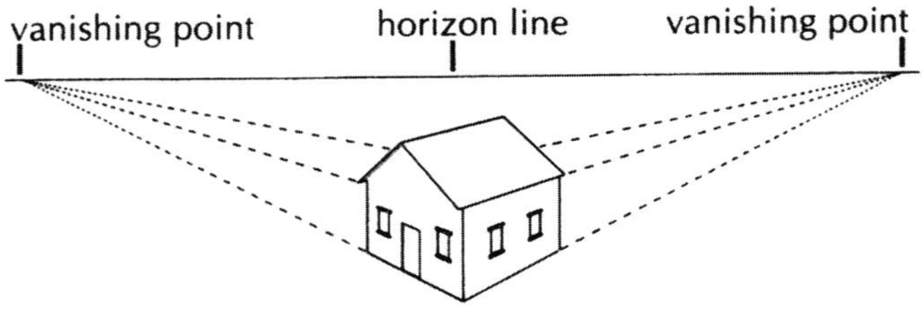

Two-point linear perspective

LIGHT AND DARK are also employed by artists to create the illusion of deep space on a two-dimensional surface. In atmospheric perspective—also called aerial perspective—objects farther away from the viewer appear less distinct as the contrast between light and dark is increasingly reduced by the effects of atmosphere. Artists depict the gradual transition from light to dark around a curved surface by means of modeling. Value is the relative degree of lightness or darkness in the range from white to black created by the amount of light reflected from an object's surface (the gray scale).

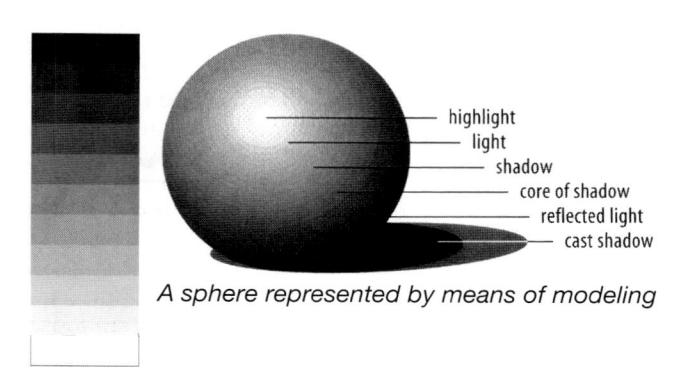

Gray scale

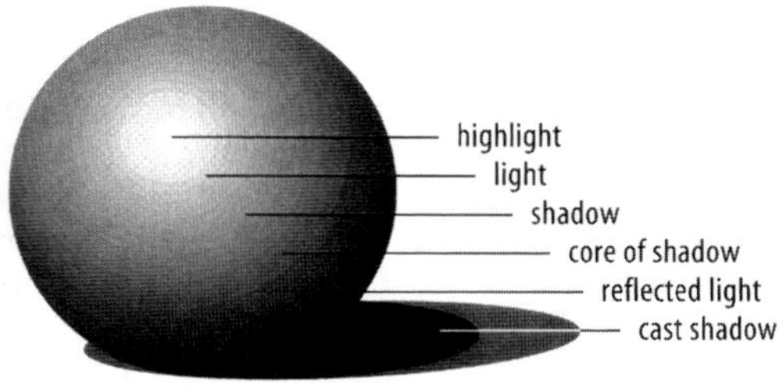

A sphere represented by means of modeling

COLOR has several characteristics. Hue is the color itself. Colors also possess value. When we add white to a hue, thus lightening it, we have a tint of that color. When we add black to a hue, thus darkening it, we have a shade of that color. The purer or brighter a hue, the greater its intensity. Different colors are the result of different wavelengths of light. The visible spectrum—that you see, for instance, in a rainbow—runs from red to orange to yellow (the so-called warm hues) to green, blue, and violet (the so-called cool hues). The spectrum can be rearranged in a conventional color wheel. The three primary colors—red, yellow, and blue (designated by the number 1 on the color wheel)—are those that cannot be made by any mixture of the other colors. Each of the secondary colors—orange, green, and violet (designated by the number 2)—is a mixture of the two primaries it lies between. The intermediate colors (designated by the number 3) are mixtures of a primary and a neighboring secondary. Analogous color schemes are those composed of hues that neighbor each other on the color wheel. Complementary color schemes are composed of hues that lie opposite each other on the color wheel. When the entire range of hues is used, the color scheme is said to be polychromatic.

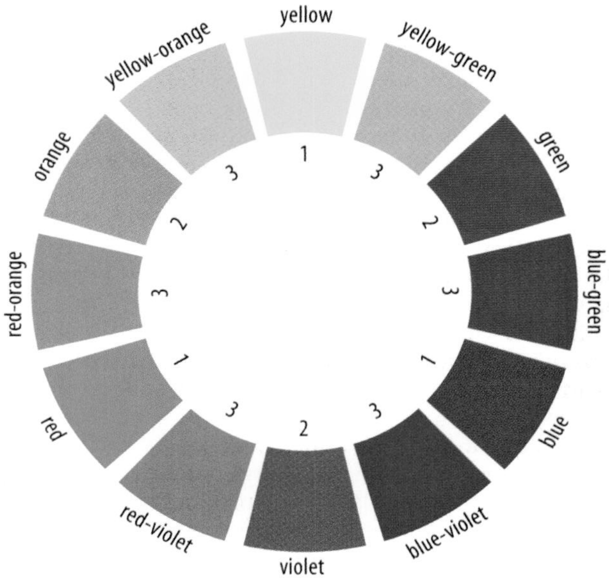

Conventional color wheel

TEXTURE is the tactile quality of a surface. It takes two forms: the actual surface quality—as marble is smooth, for instance; and a visual quality that is a representational illusion—as a marble nude sculpture is not soft like skin.

Visiting Museums

Museums can be intimidating places, but you should remember that the museum is, in fact, dedicated to your visit. Its mission is to help you understand and appreciate its collections and exhibits.

One of the primary functions of museums is to provide a context for works of art—that is, works are grouped together in such a way that they inform one another. They might be grouped by artist (all the sculptures of Rodin might be in a single room); by school or group (the French Cubists in one room, for instance, and the Italian Futurists in the next); by national and historical period (nineteenth-century British landscape); or by some critical theory or theme. Curators—the people who organize museum collections and exhibits—also guarantee the continued movement of people through their galleries by limiting the number of important or "star" works in any given room. The attention of the viewer is drawn to such works by positioning and lighting.

A good way to begin your visit to a museum is to quickly walk through the exhibit or exhibits that particularly interest you in order to gain an overall impression. Then return to the beginning and take your time. Remember, this is your chance to look at the work close at hand, and, especially in large paintings, you will see details that are never visible in reproduction—everything from brushwork to the text of newsprint incorporated in a collage. Take the time to walk around sculptures and experience their full three-dimensional effects. You will quickly learn that there is no substitute for seeing works in person.

A Do-and-Don't Guide to Visiting Museums

DO PLAN AHEAD. Most museums have websites that can be very helpful in planning your visit. The Metropolitan Museum of Art in New York, for instance, and the Louvre in Paris are so large that their collections cannot be seen in a single visit. You should determine in advance what you want to see.

DO HELP YOURSELF to a museum guide once you are at the museum. It will help you find your way around the exhibits.

DO TAKE ADVANTAGE of any information about the collections—brochures and the like—that the museum provides. Portable audio tours can be especially informative, as can museum staff and volunteers—called docents—who often conduct tours.

DO LOOK AT THE WORK BEFORE YOU READ ABOUT IT. Give yourself a chance to experience the work in a direct, unmediated way.

DO READ THE LABELS that museums provide for the artworks they display after you've looked at the work for a while. Almost all labels give the name of the artist (if known), the name and date of the work, its materials and technique (oil on canvas, for instance), and some information about how the museum acquired the work. Sometimes additional information is provided in a wall text, which might analyze the work's formal qualities, or provide some anecdotal or historical background.

DON'T TAKE PHOTOGRAPHS, unless cameras are explicitly allowed in the museum. The light created by flashbulbs can be especially damaging to paintings.

DON'T TOUCH THE ARTWORK. The more texture a work possesses, the more tempting it will be, but the oils in your skin can be extremely damaging, even to stone and metal.

DO TURN OFF YOUR CELL PHONE out of courtesy to others.

DON'T TALK LOUDLY, and be aware that others may be looking at the same piece you are. Try to avoid blocking their line of sight.

DO ENJOY YOURSELF, don't be afraid to laugh (art can be funny), and if you get tired, take a break.

A World of Art

Doug Aitken, *sleepwalkers*, 2007. Installation view. Six-channel video (color, sound), 12 min. 57 sec. Museum of Modern Art, New York.

Dunn Bequest, 212.2008. © Doug Aitken, Courtesy of 303 Gallery, New York; Victoria Miro Gallery, London; Galerie Presenhuber, Zurich; Regen Projects, Los Angeles.

Part 1
The Visual World

Understanding the Art You See

Look at the work of art on the opposite page. What is its purpose? What does it "mean"? Does it even look like "art"? How do the formal qualities of the work—such as its color, its organization, its size and scale—affect my reaction? What do I value in works of art? These are some of the questions that this book is designed to help you address. Appreciating art is never just a question of accepting visual stimuli, but also involves intelligently contemplating why and how works of art come to be made and have meaning. By helping you understand the artist's creative process, we hope to engage your own critical ability, the process by which you create your own ideas as well.

To begin to answer these questions in relation to the accompanying image, you'll need a little context. Just as dark descended on New York City at 5 PM each night between January 16 and February 12, 2007, five 12-minute 57-second films were played on a loop for five hours, until 10 PM, in different combinations across eight different external walls of the Museum of Modern Art. Each film chronicled the nocturnal journeys of five inhabitants of the city from the time they awakened in the evening until dawn the next day—the iconic actors Donald Sutherland and Tilda Swinton as, respectively, a businessman and office worker, the less familiar but still recognizable musicians Chan Marshall (aka Cat Power) and Seu Jorge as a postal worker and an electrician, and a busker discovered in the subway by the work's creator, Doug Aitken, named Ryan Donowho, who plays a bicycle messenger.

Aitken called the work *sleepwalkers*. In a very real sense, he turned the museum inside out, opening his art to the surrounding streets at a time of day when the museum itself is normally closed. As each of Aitken's characters simultaneously awaken, greet the coming evening (their "day"), and move into the city's streets—the businessman into his car, the office worker into a taxi, the postal clerk onto a bus, the electrician into the subway, and the messenger onto his bike—a sense of isolation, loneliness, and introspection pervades, even as their movements reveal an almost uncanny commonality. The pace of Aitken's films slowly crescendos as his characters start their work day until finally, walking down the street, the businessman is hit by a car, and then jumps on its hood to dance a jig, the office worker imagines herself a violinist in the New York Symphony Orchestra, the postal clerk suddenly begins a tight spin as she sorts the mail, the electrician makes a lariat out of a cable and whirls it above his head, and the bike messenger drums frantically on a bucket in the subway. As the films thus move from a state of virtual somnambulism to a fever pitch of motion, they come to parallel "the city's disparate but fused systems of energy," as curator Peter Eleey puts it in his catalogue essay for the MoMA exhibition. Eleey continues:

> We, like each of Aitken's characters, dream into being a wishful, imaginary architecture to connect us, built of the modest hope that others elsewhere are doing the same thing or thinking the same thoughts as we are. We harbor the secret suspicion, the aching desire, that in this hidden choreography someone else, right now, is picking at a sticker on the window of a cab, getting out of bed, listening to the same song, watching the same movie, and most importantly, sharing that same hope about us.

It is worth suggesting, as we begin this book, that this "modest hope" is what all works of art aspire to create, that they aim to connect us in a "hidden choreography," the secret dance of our common desires, played out before us on the walls of a museum—or even out in the streets, where an increasing amount of art, taking increasingly novel and surprising forms, is being made and displayed.

Chapter 1
Discovering a World of Art

Learning Objectives

1.1 Differentiate between passive and active seeing.

1.2 Define the creative process and describe the roles that artists most often assume when they engage in that process.

1.3 Discuss the different ways in which people value, or do not value, works of art.

Is gunpowder a proper artistic medium? New York-based, Chinese-born Cai Guo-Qiang thinks so, and showed off his powers of intervention at the opening of the 2008 Olympic Games in Beijing.

Born in 1957, Cai had left China in 1986 to study in Japan, where he began to explore the properties of gunpowder as a tool for making drawings—drawings that developed, eventually, into large-scale explosion events. Cai was interested in gunpowder as a medium because it seemed to him to have both destructive and constructive properties. It was, after all, a quintessential Chinese medium, used to make fireworks, the display of which, as every American has experienced on the 4th of July, can be stunningly beautiful. Fireworks are set off in celebration of almost every important social event in China, including weddings and funerals, the birth of a child, taking possession of a new home, the election of Communist party officials, and even after one of those officials delivers a speech.

Cai had staged one of the most dramatic of his explosive events in 1993, when, with a band of volunteers, both Japanese and Chinese, he returned to China to lay 10 kilometers (about 6 miles) of fuse and gunpowder clusters, one every 3 meters (10 feet), in the Gobi Desert, beginning at the place where the Great Wall ends, near Dunhuang, the traditional end of the great trade route that had linked China to the Mediterranean since the time of the Roman emperors. At twilight, Cai detonated an explosion that slithered in a red line on the horizon to form an ephemeral extension of the Great Wall (**Fig. 1-1**). He titled the piece *Project to Extend the Great Wall of China by 10,000 Meters: Project for Extraterrestrials No. 10*, understanding full well that it was best viewed from high above the earth. But the event was awe-inspiring from the ground as well. One could only imagine what it might have looked like from on high. Where the Great Wall had originally been built to separate people, Cai's extension brought them together. Where gunpowder was originally a force for destruction, now it was a thing of beauty. These were the same goals that Cai wished to achieve in his pyrotechnic display at the 29th Olympiad.

On August 8, 2008—the eighth day of the eighth month of the eighth year of the twenty-first century—the 29th Olympic Games opened in Beijing, China. The time was 8:08:08 PM. Eight is considered a lucky number in Chinese culture because it sounds like the word for wealth and prosperity. Cai had been chosen by the Chinese government two years earlier to serve as director of visual and special effects for the opening and closing ceremonies of the games. Cai's opening gambit was a trail of 29 firework "footprints of history" (**Fig. 1-2**), representing each of the 29 Olympiads and

Fig. 1-1 Cai Guo-Qiang, *Project to Extend the Great Wall of China by 10,000 Meters: Project for Extraterrestrials No. 10*, realized in the Gobi Desert, February 27, 1993, 7:35 PM.
Photo by Masanobu Moriyama, courtesy of Cai Studio.

fired in succession for 63 seconds across the 9 miles of sky between Tiananmen Square in the center of the city and the Bird's Nest, the Olympic Stadium, designed by the Swiss firm of Herzog & de Meuron (**Fig. 1-3**). Itself a marvel, the stadium consists of a red concrete bowl seating some 91,000 people surrounded by an outer steel frame that structurally resembles the twigs of a bird's nest.

But *Footprints of History* met with almost immediate controversy. Although the pyrotechnic display actually occurred as Cai planned, it was not broadcast live. Television viewers saw instead a 55-second digital film, created from dress-rehearsal footage of the footprint fireworks exploding and sequenced using

Fig. 1-2 Cai Guo-Qiang, *Footprints of History: Fireworks Project for the Opening Ceremony of the 2008 Beijing Olympic Games*, 2008.
Photo by Hiro Ihara, courtesy of Cai Studio.

Fig. 1-3 Herzog & de Meuron, The Bird's Nest—Beijing National Stadium, 2004–08.
© Xiaoyang Liu/Corbis.

computer graphics. Given the climatic conditions in Beijing, where smog often reduces visibility to a few hundred feet, Cai believed the video was necessary. In fact, he considered the video a second work of art. "From my own perspective as an artist," Cai explained in 2008,

> there are two separate realms in which this artwork exists, as two very different mediums have been utilized. First, there is the artwork that exists in the material realm: the ephemeral sculpture. This was viewed by people attending the ceremonies inside the stadium and standing outside on the streets of Beijing. . . . Second, there is a creative digital rendering of the artwork in the medium of video. It is a single version of the event viewed by a large broadcast audience. . . . And perhaps to also take *Footprints of History* into this second realm was necessary because in many of my explosion events, such as *Project to Extend the Great Wall of China by 10,000 Meters*, the very best vantage point is not the human one.

Cai has posted five videos made by audience members of the "ephemeral" event on his website, www.caiguoqiang.com, under Projects for 2008 (a short, 1-minute 7-second video of the *Project to Extend the Great Wall of China by 10,000 Meters* is available for viewing on the same site under Projects for 1993). To some people, Cai's televised video seemed a form of subterfuge. Others wondered whether fireworks even qualified as art. Many people, however, found Cai's work simply magical, a contemporary expression of the most ancient of Chinese traditions.

The World as We Perceive It

What is the difference between passive and active seeing?

Many of us assume, almost without question, that we can trust our eyes to give us accurate information about the world, and many of the objections to Cai's *Footprints of History* were the direct result of his seeming violation of this trust when a 55-second digital film was broadcast instead of the "real thing." Seeing, as we say, is believing. Our word "idea" derives, in fact, from the Greek word *idein*, meaning "to see," and it is no accident that when we say "I see" we often mean "I understand."

The Process of Seeing

But the act of seeing is not a simple matter of our vision making a direct recording of the reality. Seeing is both a physical and psychological process. Physically, visual processing can be divided into three steps:

reception → extraction → inference

In the first step, reception, external stimuli enter the nervous system through our eyes—we "see the light." Next, the retina, which is a collection of nerve cells at the back of the eye, extracts the basic information it needs and sends this information to the visual cortex, the part of the brain that processes visual stimuli. There are approximately 100 million sensors in the retina, but only 5 million channels to the visual cortex. In other words, the retina does a lot of "editing," and so does the visual cortex. There, special mechanisms capable of extracting specific information about such features as color, motion, orientation, and size "create" what is finally seen. What you see is the inference your visual cortex extracts from the information your retina sends it.

Seeing, in other words, is an inherently creative process. The visual system draws conclusions about the world. It represents the world for you by editing out information, deciding what is important and what is not. We all know that our eyes can deceive us, and for centuries artists have taken advantage of this fact. The painter Richard Haas, for instance, is known for his **trompe-l'oeil** architectural murals—that is, murals designed to "trick the eye." In 1989, Haas was commissioned by the Oregon Historical Society to paint the otherwise unappealing, even derelict west facade of their museum and historical center. Haas responded with a trompe-l'oeil rendering of four 35-foot-high sculptures of the Lewis and Clark Expedition of 1804–05, set in an elaborate architectural colonnade rising nine stories—all, of course, an illusion (**Fig. 1-4**).

Fig. 1-4 Richard Haas, Oregon Historical Society, Portland, OR, 1989. Keim silicate paint, 14,000 sq. ft. Architect: Zimmer Gunsel Frasca Partnership. Executed by American Illusion, New York.
Photo courtesy of Richard Haas. Art © Richard Haas/Licensed by VAGA, New York.

But if the eye can be so easily deceived, it is equally true that it does not recall many things it sees even regularly with any measure of accuracy. Consider, for example, what sort of visual information you have stored about the American flag. You know its colors—red, white, and blue—and that it has 50 stars and 13 stripes. You know, roughly, its shape—rectangular. But do you know its proportions? Do you even know, without looking, what color stripe is at the flag's top, or what color is at the bottom? How many short stripes are there, and how many long ones? How many horizontal rows of stars are there? How many long rows? How many short ones? The point is that not only do we each perceive the same things differently, remembering different details, but also we do not usually see things as thoroughly or accurately as we might suppose. As the philosopher Nelson Goodman explains, "The eye functions not as an instrument self-powered and alone, but as a dutiful member of a complex and capricious organism. Not only how but what it sees is regulated by need and prejudice. It selects, rejects, organizes, discriminates, associates, classifies, analyzes, constructs. It does not so much mirror as take and make." In other words, the eye mirrors each individual's complex perceptions of the world.

Active Seeing

Everything you see is filtered through a long history of fears, prejudices, desires, emotions, customs, and beliefs. Through art, we can begin to understand those filters and learn to look more closely at the visual world. Jasper Johns's *Flag* (**Fig. 1-5**) presents an opportunity to look closely at a familiar image. According to Johns, when he created this work, the flag was something "seen but not looked at, not examined." *Flag* was painted at a time when the nation was obsessed with patriotism, spawned by Senator Joseph McCarthy's anti-Communist hearings in 1954, by President Eisenhower's affirmation of all things American, and by the Soviet Union's challenge of American supremacy through the Space Race. Many of the painting's first

Fig. 1-5 Jasper Johns, *Flag*, 1954–55. Encaustic, oil, and collage on fabric mounted on plywood (three panels), 42¼ in. × 5 ft. ⅝ in. Museum of Modern Art, New York.
Gift of Ms. David M. Levy, 28.1942.30. © 2015. Digital image, Museum of Modern Art, New York/Scala, Florence. Art © Jasper Johns/Licensed by VAGA, New York.

audiences were particularly disturbed by the lumps and smears of the painting's surface and the newspaper scraps visible beneath the stars and stripes. While contemporary viewers may not have experienced that Cold War era, the work still asks us to consider what the flag represents. At another level, because we already "know" what a flag is, Johns asks us to consider not what he represents but how he represents it. In other words, he asks us to consider it as a painting.

Faith Ringgold's *God Bless America* (**Fig. 1-6**) has as its historical context the Civil Rights Movement. In it, the American flag has been turned into a prison cell. Painted at a time when white prejudice against African Americans was enforced by the legal system, the star of the flag becomes a sheriff's badge, and its red and white stripes are transformed into the black bars of the jail. The white woman portrayed in the painting is the very image of contradiction: At once a patriot, pledging allegiance to the flag, and a racist, denying blacks the right to vote. She is a prisoner of her own bigotry. While the meaning of the work is open to interpretation, there is no question of its power to draw us into a closer examination of our perceptions and understandings of our world.

Fig. 1-6 Faith Ringgold, *God Bless America*, No. 13 from the series *American People*, 1964. Oil on canvas, 31 × 19 in.

The World as Artists See It

What is the creative process and what roles do artists most often assume when they engage in that process?

Artists, of course, intend to convey their own sense of their world's meaning to us. But if the reactions to Jasper Johns's *Flag* or Cai Guo-Qiang's *Footprints of History* demonstrate how people understand and value the same work of art in different ways, similarly, different artists, responding to their world in different times and places, might see the world in very divergent terms. As it turns out, Cai did not choose to go to the remote oasis of Dunhuang simply because the Great Wall ended there, waiting for him to extend it with fireworks. At the terminus of the Silk Road, since the time of the Han dynasty (206 BCE–220 CE), Dunhuang was the place where the cultures of the East and West first intersected. Western linen, wool, glass, and gold, Persian pistachios, and mustard originating in the Mediterranean were exchanged in the city for Chinese silk, ceramics, fur, lacquered goods, and spices, all carried on the backs of Bactrian camels (**Fig. 1-7**), animals

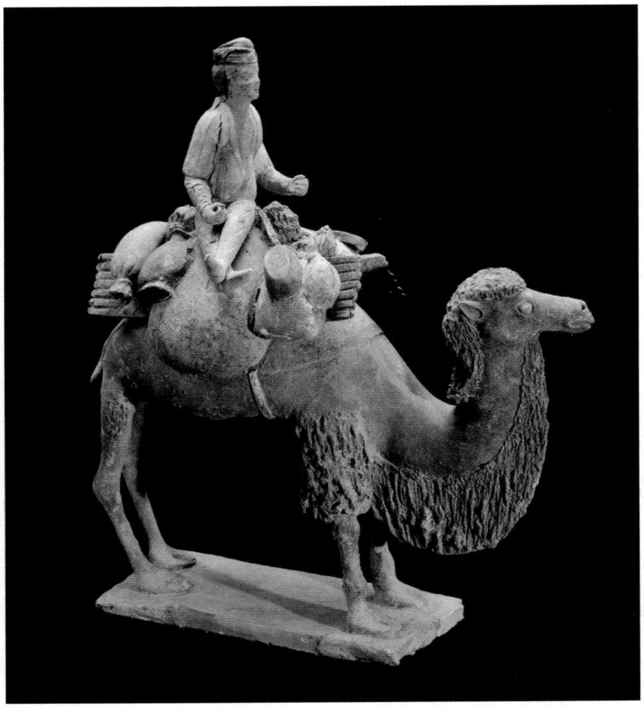

Fig. 1-7 Caravaneer on a camel, China, Tang dynasty (618–907). Polychrome terra-cotta figure, 17⅛ × 14⅛ in. Musée des Arts Asiatiques-Guimet, Paris.

particularly suitable for the cold, dry, and high altitudes of the deserts and steppes of central Asia, which the Silk Road traversed. In fact, they can go for months at a time without water.

Dunhuang is also the site of the greatest collection of early Chinese art to be found anywhere. The story goes that, in 366 CE, a Buddhist monk named Le Sun traveling on the Silk Road had a vision of a thousand Buddhas bathed in a golden, flaming light flickering across the face of a mile-long sandstone cliff near the city. He was inspired to dig a cave-temple on the site. For centuries after, travelers and traders, seeking safety and prosperity, commissioned more caves, decorating them profusely. By the fourteenth century, the resulting Mogao Caves (*Mogaoku* in Chinese, meaning "peerless caves") consisted of some 800 separate spaces chiseled out of the cliff (**Fig. 1-8**). Of these, 492 caves are decorated with murals that cover more that 484,000 square feet of wall space (about 40 times the expanse of the Sistine Chapel in Rome), and some 2,000 sculptures fill the grottoes (**Fig. 1-9**). Today a World Heritage Site—and an increasingly popular tourist destination, despite that fact that it is some 1,150 miles from the Chinese capital of Beijing—the Mogao Caves are a monumental testament to human creativity.

Fig. 1-8 Mogao Caves (Caves of a Thousand Buddhas) in Dunhuang, China.
© Joan Swinnerton/Alamy.

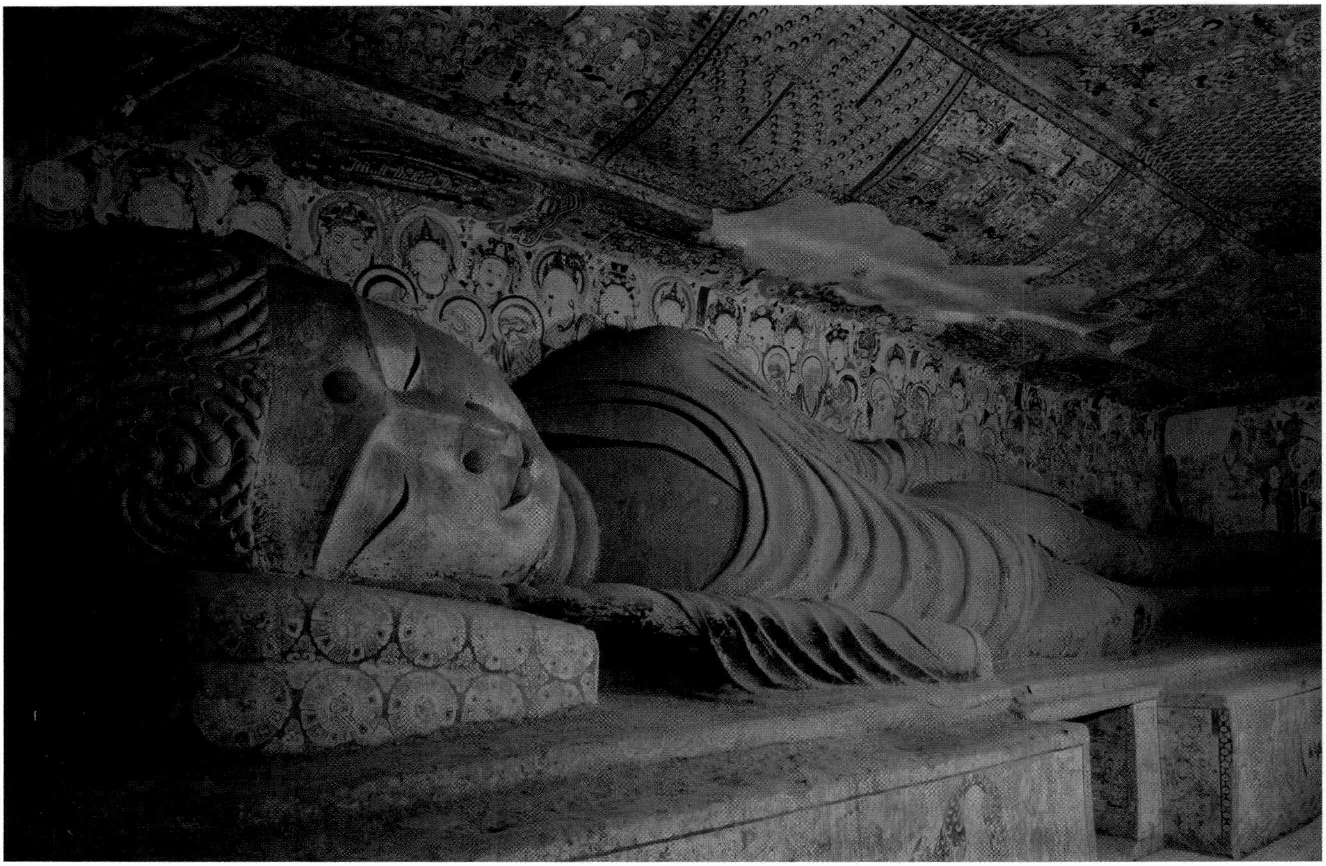

Fig. 1-9 Reclining Buddha, Mogao Caves, Cave 148, Dunhuang, China, Middle Tang dynasty (781–847).
Length: 51 ft.
Photo: Tony Law. © Dunhuang Research Academy.

The Creative Process

All of the innumerable artists who have worked in Dunhuang—from Le Sun to Cai Guo-Qiang—have shared the fundamental desire to *create*, and in order to create, artists have to engage in *critical thinking*. The creative process is, in fact, an exercise in critical thinking. All people are creative, but not all people possess the energy, ingenuity, and courage of conviction that are required to make art. In order to produce a work of art, the artist must be able to respond to the unexpected, the chance occurrences or results that are part of the creative process. In other words, the artist must be something of an explorer and inventor. The artist must always be open to new ways of seeing. The landscape painter John Constable spoke of this openness as "the art of seeing nature." This art of seeing leads to imagining, which leads in turn to making. Creativity is the sum of this process, from seeing to imagining to making. In the process of making a work of art, the artist also engages in a self-critical process—questioning assumptions, revising and rethinking choices and decisions, exploring new directions and possibilities.

Exploring the creative process is the focus of this book. We hope you take from it the knowledge that the kind of creative and critical thinking engaged in by artists is fundamental to every discipline. This same path leads to discovery in science, breakthroughs in engineering, and new research in the social sciences. We can all learn from studying the creative process itself.

Art and the Idea of Beauty

For many people, the main purpose of art is to satisfy our aesthetic sense, our desire to see and experience the beautiful. The question of just what constitutes "beauty" has long been a topic of debate. In fact, it is probably fair to say that the sources of **aesthetic** pleasure—"aesthetic" refers to our sense of the beautiful—differ from culture to culture and from time to time. In Western culture, beauty has long been associated with notions of order, regularity, right proportion, and design—all hallmarks of Classical art and architecture in the Greek Golden Age, the era in which, for instance, the Parthenon in Athens was constructed (see Chapter 16). As a result, for centuries, mountain ranges such as the Alps or the American Rockies, which today rank among our greatest sources of aesthetic pleasure, were routinely condemned. As late as 1681, Thomas Burnet, writing in his *Sacred Theory of the Earth*, could quite easily dismiss them: "They are placed in no Order one with the other. . . . There is nothing in Nature more shapeless or ill-figured. . . . They are the greatest examples of Confusion that we know in Nature." But by the middle of the nineteenth century, great stretches of just such landscapes were being preserved as National Parks in the United States, precisely as testaments to nature's beauty.

The human body has been a similarly contested site. In contrast to the tall, statuesque models we associate with contemporary fashion design, the seventeenth-century artist Peter Paul Rubens preferred fleshier, more rounded models. No one would think of Pablo Picasso's representations of women in the late 1920s and early 1930s as beautiful; rather, they are almost demonic in character. Most biographers believe images such as his *Seated Bather (La Baigneuse)* (**Fig. 1-10**) to be portraits of his wife, the Russian ballerina Olga Koklova, whom he married in 1918. By the late 1920s, their marriage was in a shambles, and Picasso portrays her here as a skeletal horror, her back and buttocks almost crustacean in appearance, her horizontal mouth looking like some archaic mandible. Her pose is ironic, inspired by Classical Greek representations of the nude, and the sea behind her is as empty as the Mediterranean sky is gray. Picasso means nothing in this painting to be pleasing, except our recognition of his extraordinary ability to invent expressive images of tension. Through his entire career, from his portrayal of a brothel in his 1907 *Les Demoiselles d'Avignon* (see *The Creative Process*, pp. 12–13), he represented his relation to women as a sort of battlefield between attraction and repulsion. There can be no doubt which side has won the battle in this painting.

But from a certain point of view, the experience of such dynamic tension is itself pleasing, and it is the ability of works of art to create and sustain such moments that many people value most about them. That is, many people find such moments aesthetically pleasing. The work of art may not itself be beautiful, but it triggers a higher level of thought and awareness in the viewer, and the viewer experiences this intellectual and imaginative stimulus—this higher order of thought—as a form of beauty in its own right.

Roles of the Artist

Most artists think of themselves as assuming one of four fundamental roles—or some combination of the four—as they approach their work: 1) they create a visual record of their time and place; 2) they help us to see the world in new and innovative ways; 3) they make functional objects and structures more pleasurable by imbuing them with beauty and meaning; and 4) they give form to immaterial ideas and feelings.

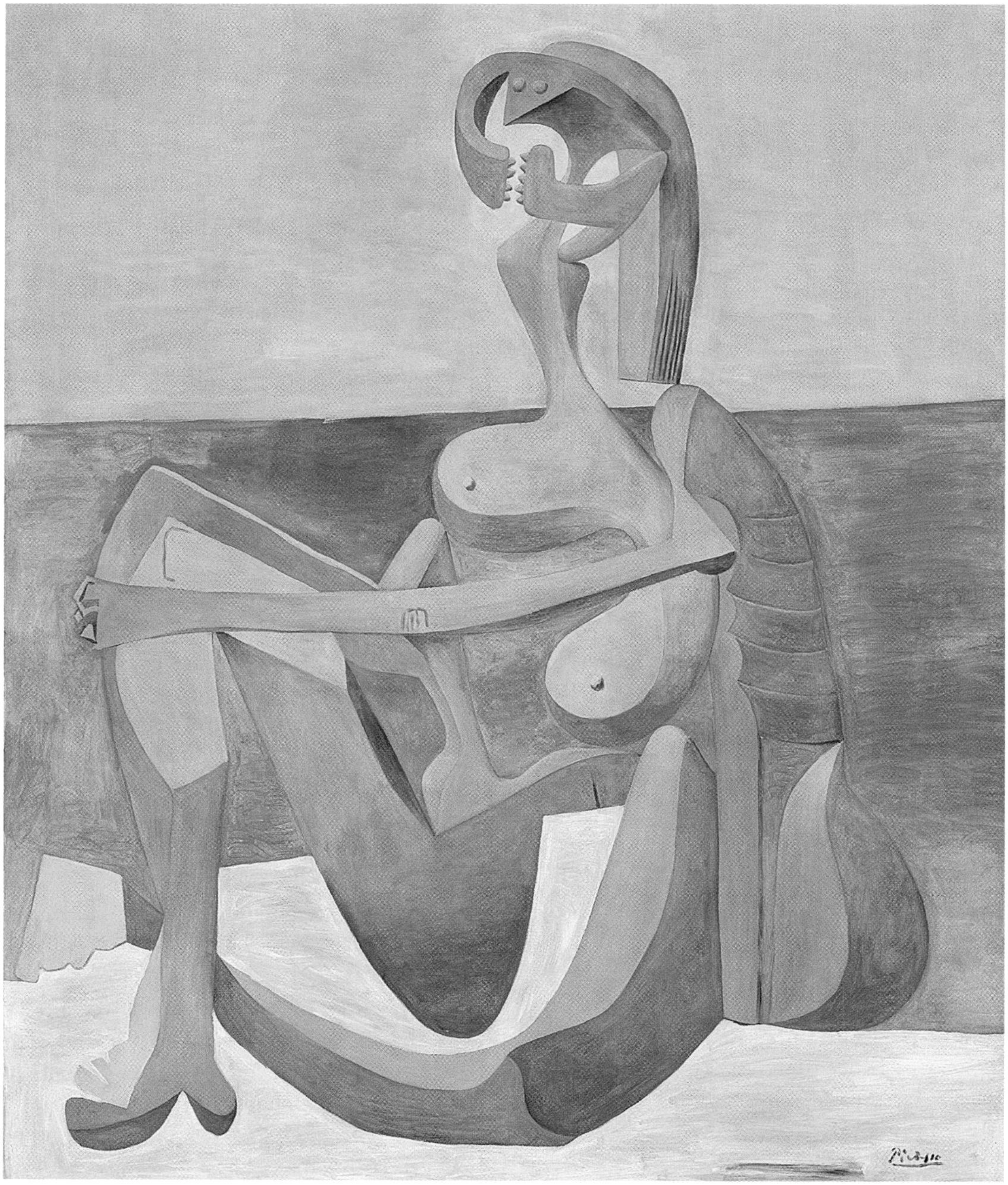

Fig. 1-10 Pablo Picasso, *Seated Bather* (*La Baigneuse*), 1930.
Oil on canvas, 5 ft. 4¼ in. × 4 ft. 3 in. Museum of Modern Art, New York.
Mrs. Simon Guggenheim Fund. (82.1950). © 2015. Digital image, Museum of Modern Art, New York/Scala, Florence. © 2015 Artists Rights Society (ARS), New York. © 2015 Estate of Pablo Picasso/Artists Rights Society (ARS), New York.

1) ARTISTS MAKE A VISUAL RECORD OF THE PEOPLE, PLACES, AND EVENTS OF THEIR TIME AND PLACE Sometimes artists are not so much interested in seeing things anew as they are in simply recording, accurately, what it is that they see. In fact, this was precisely the purpose of the artist who created the Bactrian camel carrying goods across the Silk Road (see Fig. 1-7). The art of portraiture is likewise a direct reflection of this desire, and of all the forms of art portraiture is, in fact, one of the longest-standing traditions. Until the invention of photography, the portrait—whether drawn, painted, or sculpted—was the only way to preserve the physical likeness of a human being.

The Creative Process

From Sketch to Final Vision: Pablo Picasso's *Les Demoiselles d'Avignon*

No one could look at Picasso's large painting of 1907, *Les Demoiselles d'Avignon* (**Fig. 1-13**), and call it aesthetically *beautiful*, but it is, for many people, one of his most aesthetically *interesting* works. Nearly 8 feet square, it would come to be considered one of the first major paintings of the modern era—and one of the least beautiful. The title, chosen not by Picasso but by a close friend, literally means "the young ladies of Avignon," but its somewhat tongue-in-cheek reference is specifically to the prostitutes of Avignon Street, the red-light district of Barcelona, Spain, Picasso's hometown. We know a great deal about Picasso's process as he worked on the canvas from late 1906 into the early summer months of 1907, not only because many of his working sketches survive but also because the canvas itself has been submitted to extensive examination, including X-ray analysis. This reveals early versions of certain passages, particularly the figure at the left and the two figures on the right, which lie under the final layers of paint.

An early sketch (**Fig. 1-11**) reveals that the painting was originally conceived to include seven figures—five prostitutes, a sailor seated in their midst, and, entering from the left, a medical student carrying a book. Picasso probably had in mind some anecdotal or narrative idea contrasting the dangers and joys of both work and pleasure, but he soon abandoned the male figures. By doing so, he involved the viewer much more fully in the scene. No longer does the curtain open up at the left to allow the medical student to enter. Now it is opened by one of the prostitutes as if she were admitting us, the audience, into the bordello. We are implicated in the scene.

And an extraordinary scene it is. Picasso seems to have willingly abdicated any traditional aesthetic sense of beauty. There is nothing enticing or alluring here. Of all the nudes, the two central ones are the most traditional, but their bodies are composed of a series of long lozenge shapes, hard angles, and

Fig. 1-11 Pablo Picasso, *Medical Student, Sailor, and Five Nudes in a Bordello* (Compositional study for *Les Demoiselles d'Avignon*), Paris, early 1907. Black chalk and pastel over pencil on Ingres paper, 18½ × 25 in. Kupferstichkabinett, Kunstmuseum Basel, Switzerland.

Deposited at the Kupferstichkabinett of the Kunstmuseum Basel by the residents of the City of Basel, 1967.106. Photo: Kunstmuseum Basel/Martin Bühler.

Fig. 1-12 Pablo Picasso, Study for *Les Demoiselles d'Avignon: Head of the Squatting Demoiselle,* 1907. Gouache and Indian ink on paper, 24¾ × 18⅞ in. Musée Picasso, Paris.
Inv. MP 539. Photo © RMN-Grand Palais/Thierry Le Mage. © 2015 Estate of Pablo Picasso/Artists Rights Society (ARS), New York.

only a few traditional curves. It is unclear whether the second nude from the left is standing or sitting, or possibly even lying down. (In the early drawing, she is clearly seated.) Picasso seems to have made her position in space intentionally ambiguous.

We know, through X-rays, that all five nudes originally looked like the central two. We also know that, sometime after he began painting *Les Demoiselles*, Picasso visited the Palais du Trocadéro, now the Museum of Man, in Paris, and saw its collection of African sculpture, particularly African masks. He was strongly affected by the experience. The masks seemed to him imbued with power that allowed him, for the first time, to see art, he said, as "a form of magic designed to be a mediator between the strange, hostile world and us, a way of seizing power by giving form to our terrors as well as our desires." As a result, he quickly transformed the faces of three of the five prostitutes in his painting into African masks. The masks freed him from representing exactly what his subjects looked like and allowed him to represent his idea of them instead.

That idea is clearly ambivalent. Picasso probably saw in these masks something both frightening and liberating. They freed him from a slavish concern for accurate representation, and they allowed him to create a much more emotionally charged scene than he would have otherwise been able to accomplish. Rather than offering us a single point of view, he offers us many, both literally and figuratively. The painting is about the ambiguity of experience.

Nowhere is this clearer than in the squatting figure in the lower right-hand corner of the painting. She seems twisted around on herself in the final version, her back to us, but her head is impossibly turned to face us, her chin resting on her grotesque, clawlike hand. We see her, in other words, from both front and back. (Notice, incidentally, that even the nudes in the sketch possess something of this "double" point of view: Their noses are in profile though they face the viewer.) But this crouching figure is even more complex. An early drawing (**Fig. 1-12**) reveals that her face was originally conceived as a headless torso. What would become her hand was initially her arm. What would become her eyes were her breasts. And her mouth began as her bellybutton. Here we are witness to the extraordinary freedom of invention that defines all of Picasso's art, as well as to a remarkable demonstration of the creative process itself.

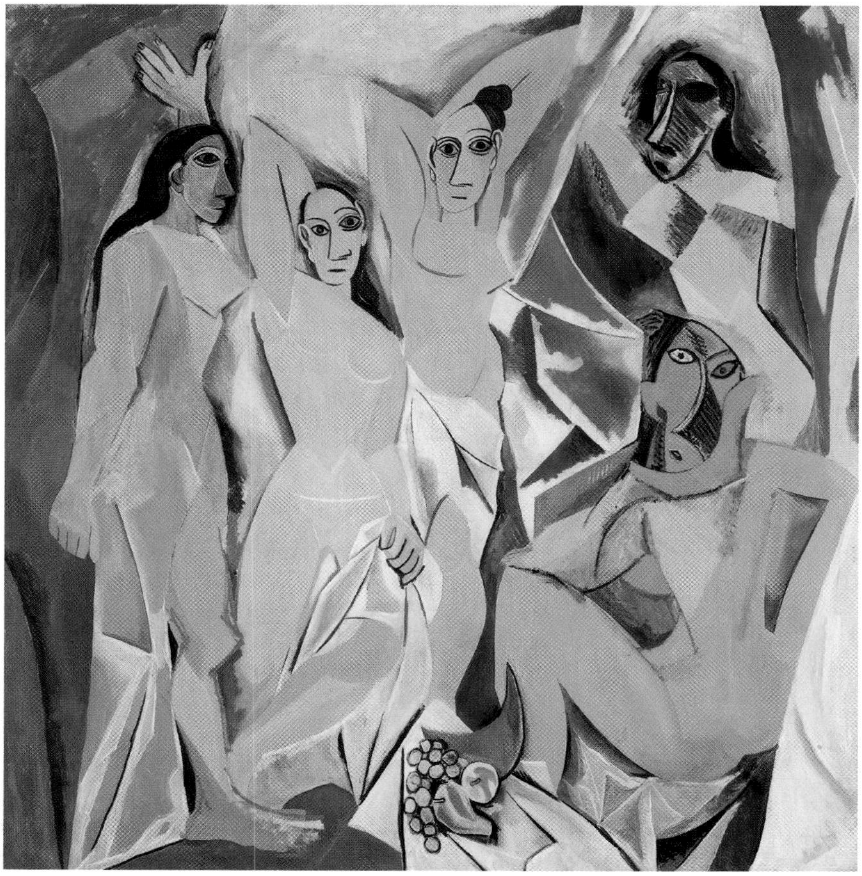

Fig. 1-13 Pablo Picasso, *Les Demoiselles d'Avignon*, 1907. Oil on canvas. 8 ft. × 7 ft. 8 in. Museum of Modern Art, New York.
Acquired through the Lillie P. Bliss Bequest, 333.1939. © 2015 Digital image, Museum of Modern Art, New York/Scala, Florence. © 2015 Estate of Pablo Picasso/Artists Rights Society (ARS), New York.

Mickalene Thomas specializes in portraits of African-American women, often posed in reclining positions amidst décor dating from the 1960s and 1970s (**Fig. 1-14**). (The furniture and textile designs in Thomas's works derive, in fact, from an 18-volume set of books she found in a thrift shop titled *The Practical Encyclopedia of Good Decorating and Home Improvement*, published in 1970.) Her reclining figures are designed to evoke the nineteenth-century paintings of **odalisques**—the Turkish word for "harem slave girl" or "concubine"—such as Édouard Manet's famous portrait of a Parisian courtesan, *Olympia* (**Fig. 1-15**). But where Manet's figure is nude, Thomas's women are clothed. Where most nineteenth-century odalisques are submissive (the forthright stare of Manet's is one of the single exceptions to the rule), Thomas's figures exude a certain authority and self-assurance. They evoke, in fact, the superstar African-American divas of the 1970s, actresses like Tamara Dobson and Pam Grier, who starred in such films such as *Cleopatra Jones* (1973) and *Foxy Brown* (1974), so-called "blaxploitation" films that in the 1970s were in many ways as controversial as hip-hop and rap in the 1980s and 1990s. As Mia Mask described these women in her study of black female film stars, *Divas on Screen*, they "combined brazen sexuality, physical strength, and Black Nationalist sentiment . . . representing black women as both sexually and intellectually self-determined."

Portrait of Mnonja was first exhibited at the U.S. Mission to the United Nations in 2010 as part of the U.S. Department of State's "Art in Embassies" program. Originally, a different portrait had been on display, but when it was sold to the Akron Art Museum, Thomas replaced it with a painting rather appropriately featuring the colors red, white, and blue. Hundreds of rhinestones decorate the surface of *Portrait of Mnonja*. Thomas's model's red high-heel shoes seem perched, notably, on an **anamorphic** projection of a white cat. (Anamorphic representations require the viewer to look at the object from an odd angle—from the far right or left, for instance. From a frontal point of view, the image appears vastly distorted.) Thomas's howling cat is a reverse-image of the black cat hissing at the viewer at Olympia's feet. It is as if over the hundred-plus years since the black maid delivered the bouquet of flowers

Fig. 1-14 Mickalene Thomas, *Portrait of Mnonja*, 2010. Rhinestones, acrylic, and enamel on wood panel, 8 × 10 ft. Smithsonian American Art Museum, Washington, D.C.
Museum purchase through the Luisita L. and Franz H. Denghausen Endowment, 2011.16. © 2015. Digital image, Smithsonian American Art Museum, Washington, D.C./Scala, Florence. Courtesy of Mickalene Thomas and Lehmann Maupin, New York and Hong Kong. © 2015 Mickalene Thomas/Artists Rights Society (ARS), New York.

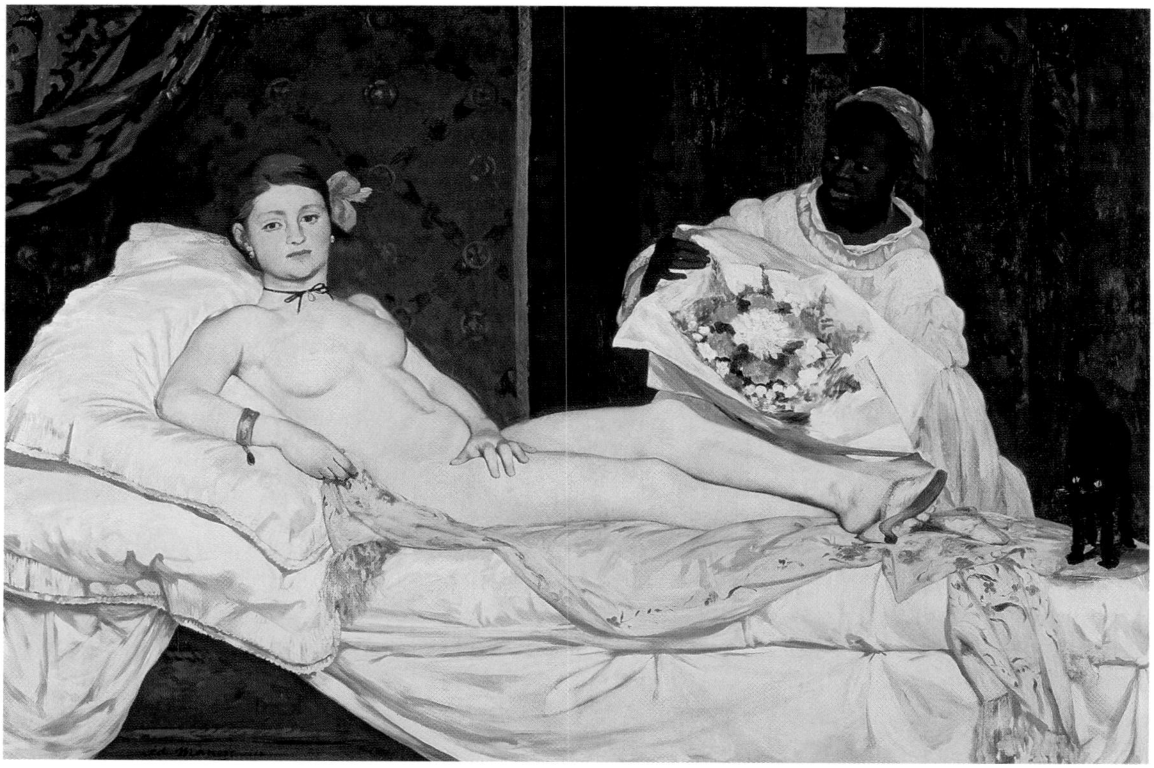

Fig. 1-15 Édouard Manet, *Olympia*, 1863. Oil on canvas, 4 ft. 3 in. × 6 ft. 2¾ in. Musée d'Orsay, Paris.
Inv. RF644. Photo © RMN-Grand Palais (musée d'Orsay)/Hervé Lewandowski.

to Manet's courtesan—brought to her, presumably, by a man (in whose place you, as the viewer, stand and at whom the black cat hisses)—the black maid has displaced the white courtesan to become a contemporary American woman of unmistakable sex appeal but now unburdened by the fetters of sexual and racial exploitation that haunt Manet's earlier work.

For just as surely as Thomas's *Portrait of Mnonja* is a visual record of the artist's own late twentieth-century world, Manet's *Olympia* reflects Parisian life in the 1860s. Manet was something of a professional observer—a famous *flâneur*, a Parisian of impeccable dress and perfect manners who strolled the city, observing its habits and commenting on it with great subtlety, wit, and savoir-faire. Wrote Manet's friend Antonin Proust: "With Manet, the eye played such a big role that Paris has never known a *flâneur* like him nor a *flâneur* strolling more usefully." Nevertheless, as accurately as *Olympia* may reflect its time and place, Manet's audience in the 1860s found the painting appalling. Proust explains that the public at the time thought of "a courtesan in terms of the preconceived idea of an opulent woman displaying her abundant flesh on luxurious sheets," while Manet represented the reality of Parisian brothels which were instead full of girls of desperate and "indigent nudity." Thus, even though Manet believed that he was depicting his time and place with the utmost fidelity, his audience was unwilling to recognize the veracity of his vision.

2) ARTISTS HELP US TO SEE THE WORLD IN NEW OR INNOVATIVE WAYS This is one of the primary roles that Cai Guo-Qiang assumes in creating works like *Project to Extend the Great Wall of China by 10,000 Meters*. In fact, almost all of his work is designed to transform our experience of the world, jar us out of our complacency, and create new ways for us to see and think about the world around us.

This is equally one of the roles assumed by the unknown Tang artist who carved the reclining Buddha in Cave 148 at Mogao (see Fig. 1-9). The Buddha reclines to await his death, when he will pass serenely into nirvana, the perfect peace of mind at which the spirit arrives when it no longer clings to the desires and aversions of worldly life. Standing before the giant reclining form, not only are we made acutely aware of the enormity of the Buddha's achievement, but we also come to recognize how diminutive we are before it. We understand just how small we are in the great scheme of things.

In 2003 Ken Gonzales-Day began researching the history of lynching in nineteenth-century California by assembling as complete a record of the practice in the state that he could. He was particularly interested in revealing how,

Fig. 1-16 Ken Gonzales-Day, *"At daylight the miserable man was carried to an oak . . . ,"* from the series *Searching for California Hang Trees,* 2007. Chromogenic print, 35 × 45 in. Smithsonian American Art Museum, Washington, D.C.

Museum purchase through the Luisita L. and Franz H. Denghausen Endowment, 2012.12.1. © 2015. Digital image, Smithsonian American Art Museum, Washington, D.C./Scala, Florence. © 2015 Ken Gonzales-Day.

when taken collectively, Native Americans, African Americans, Chinese immigrants, and Latinos were lynched more often than persons of Anglo or European descent—and Latinos more than any other group. His goal was to visit as many of the 353 lynching sites he identified as he could. The project resulted in two separate bodies of work—a book, titled *Lynching in the West: 1850–1935*, published in 2006, and a series of photographs titled *Searching for California Hang Trees*. His photograph *"At daylight the miserable man was carried to an oak . . ."* (**Fig. 1-16**), from the series, transforms the way we see the magnificent oak. Shot from below, the tree is represented as a tangle of branches that rise upward to the light as if in testimony to its very longevity (upwards of 300 years). Its gnarled trunk is covered with living moss; in itself it is something of a symbol of the life force. And yet it is the very site of violent death, unseen but—in Gonzales-Day's work—revealed.

3) ARTISTS MAKE FUNCTIONAL OBJECTS AND STRUCTURES (BUILDINGS) MORE PLEASURABLE AND ELEVATE THEM OR IMBUE THEM WITH MEANING This sculpture of a film projector (**Fig. 1-17**) is actually a coffin. It may seem surprising that the family of the deceased should order so elaborately decorative a final resting place, but the African sculptor Kane Kwei and his workshop have been designing and producing coffins such as this one for over 40 years. Trained as a carpenter, Kwei first made a decorative coffin for a dying uncle, who asked him to produce one in the shape of a boat. In Ghana, coffins possess a ritual significance, celebrating a successful life, and Kwei's coffins delighted the community. Soon he was making fish and whale coffins for fishermen, hens with chicks for women with large families, Mercedes-Benz coffins for the wealthy, and cash crops for farmers, such as an 8½-foot replica of a cocoa bean. In 1974, an enterprising San Francisco art dealer brought examples of Kwei's work to the United States, and the artist's large workshop now makes coffins for both funerals and the art market. Today, Kwei's workshop is headed by his grandson, Anang Cedi, and the film-projector coffin illustrated here was photographed in the workshop on August 14, 2013.

Almost all of us apply, or would like to apply, this aesthetic sense to the places in which we live. We decorate our walls with pictures, choose apartments for their

Fig. 1-17 Workshop of Kane Kwei, Coffin in the shape of a film projector, Teshi area, Ghana, Africa, 2013.
© LUC GNAGO/Reuters/Corbis.

visual appeal, ask architects to design our homes, plant flowers in our gardens, and seek out well-maintained and pleasant neighborhoods. We want city planners and government officials to work with us to make our living spaces more appealing.

Public space is particularly susceptible to aesthetic treatments. One of the newest standards of aesthetic beauty in public space is its compatibility with the environment. A building's beauty is measured, in the minds of many, by its self-sufficiency (that is, its lack of reliance on nonsustainable energy sources such as coal), its use of sustainable building materials (the elimination of steel, for instance, since it is a product of iron ore, a nonrenewable resource), and its suitability to the climate and culture in which it is built (a glass tower, however attractive in its own right, would seem out of place rising out of a tropical rainforest). These are the principles of what has come to be known as "green architecture."

The Jean-Marie Tjibaou Cultural Center in Nouméa, New Caledonia, an island in the South Pacific, illustrates these principles (**Fig. 1-18**). The architect is Renzo Piano, an Italian, but the principles guiding his design are anything but Western.

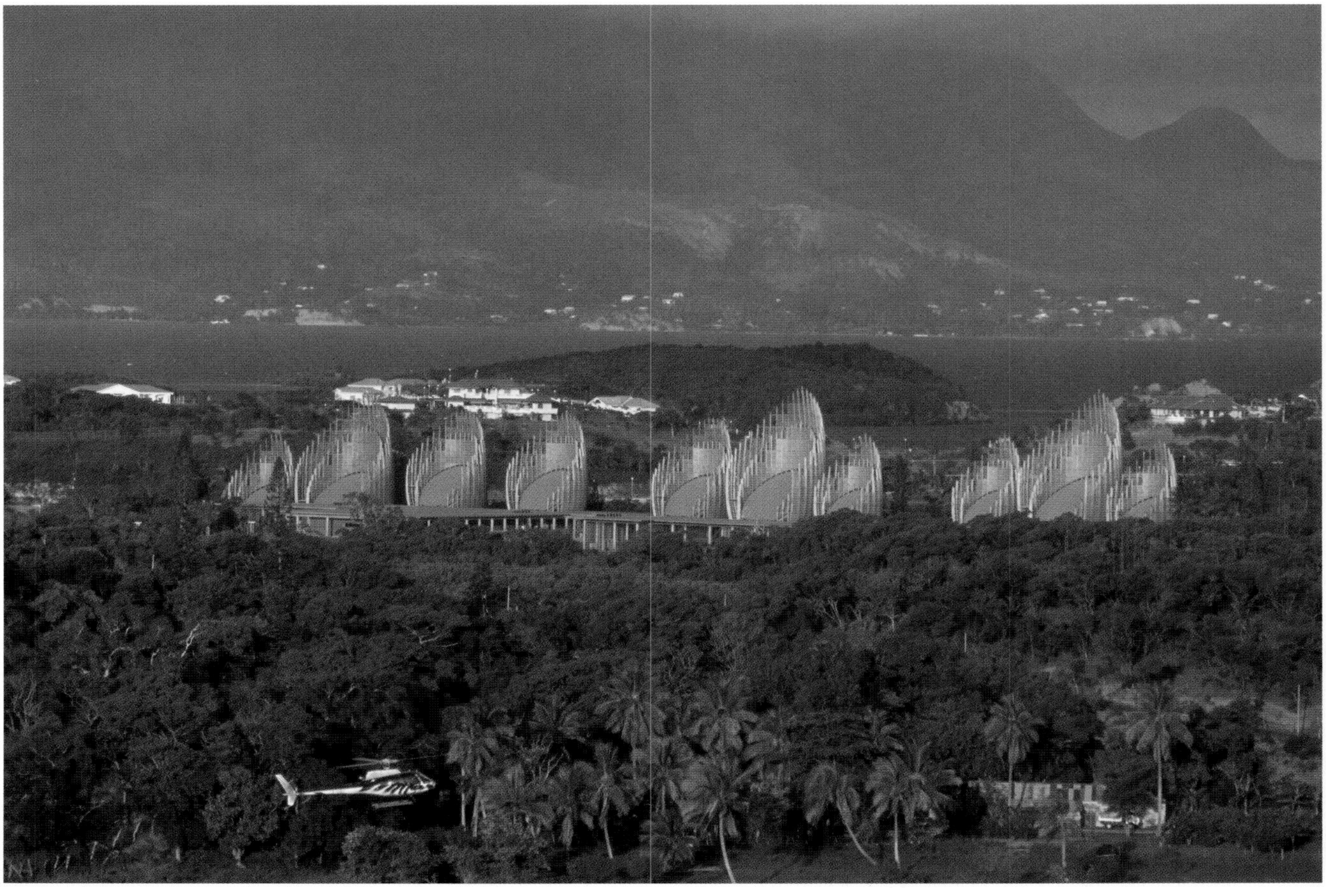

Fig. 1-18 Renzo Piano, Jean-Marie Tjibaou Cultural Center, Nouméa, New Caledonia, 1991–98.
© Giraud-Langevin/Sygma/Corbis.

The Center is named after a leader of the island's indigenous people, the Kanak, and it is dedicated to preserving and transmitting Kanak culture. Piano studied that culture thoroughly, and his design blends Kanak tradition with green architectural principles. The buildings are constructed of wood and bamboo, easily renewable regional resources. Each of the Center's ten pavilions represents a typical Kanak dwelling. In a finished dwelling, however, the vertical staves would rise to meet at the top, and the horizontal elements would weave in and out between the staves, as in basketry. In his version, Piano left the dwelling forms unfinished, as if under construction, but to a purpose—they serve as wind scoops, catching breezes off the nearby ocean and directing them down to cool the inner rooms, the roofs of which face south at an angle that allows them to be lit largely by direct daylight. As in a Kanak village, the pavilions are linked with a covered walkway. Piano describes the project as "an expression of the harmonious relationship with the environment that is typical of the local culture. They are curved structures resembling huts, built out of wooden joists and ribs; they are containers of an archaic appearance, whose interiors are equipped with all the possibilities offered by modern technology."

4) ARTISTS GIVE FORM TO THE IMMATERIAL—HIDDEN OR UNIVERSAL TRUTHS, SPIRITUAL FORCES, PERSONAL FEELINGS Picasso's treatment of women in both *Seated Bather* and *Les Demoiselles d'Avignon* gives form to his own, often tormented, feelings about the opposite sex. In *Les Demoiselles d'Avignon*, the power of these feelings was heightened by his incorporation of African masks into the composition.

When Westerners first encountered African masks in the ethnographic museums of Europe in the late nineteenth and early twentieth centuries, they saw them in a context far removed from their original settings and purposes. In the West, we are used to approaching everyday objects made in African, Oceanic, Native American, or Asian cultures in museums as "works of art." But in their cultures of origin, such objects might serve to define family and community relationships, establishing social order and structure. Or they might document momentous events in the history of a people. They might serve a simple utilitarian function, such as a pot to carry water or a spoon to eat with. Or they might be sacred instruments that provide insight into hidden or spiritual forces believed to guide the universe.

A fascinating example of the latter is a type of magical figure that arose in the Kingdom of Kongo in the late nineteenth century (**Fig. 1-19**). Known as *minkisi* ("sacred medicine"), for the Kongo tribes such figures embodied their own resistance to the imposition of foreign ideas as European states colonized the continent.

Fig. 1-19 ***Nkisi nkonde*, Kongo (Muserongo), Zaire, late 19th century.** Wood, iron nails, glass, resin, 20¼ × 11 × 8 in. The University of Iowa Museum of Art.

Stanley Collection, X1986.573. Image courtesy of the University of Iowa Museum of Art.

Throughout Central Africa, all significant human powers are believed to result from communication with the dead. Certain individuals can communicate with the spirits in their roles as healers, diviners, and defenders of the living. They are believed to harness the powers of the spirit world through *minkisi* (singular *nkisi*). Among the most formidable of *minkisi* is the type known as *minkonde* (singular *nkonde*), which are said to pursue witches, thieves, adulterers, and wrongdoers by night. The communicator activates an *nkonde* by driving nails, blades, and other pieces of iron into it so that it will deliver similar injuries to those worthy of punishment.

Minkonde figures stand upright, as if ready to spring forward. In many figures, one arm is raised and holds a knife or spear (often missing, as here), suggesting that the figure is ready to attack. Other *minkonde* stand upright in a stance of alertness, like a wrestler challenging an opponent. The hole in the stomach of the figure illustrated here contained magical "medicines," known as *bilongo*—sometimes blood or plants, but often kaolin, a white clay believed to be closely linked to the world of the dead, and red ocher, linked symbolically to blood. Such horrific figures—designed to evoke awe in the spectator—were seen by European missionaries as direct evidence of African idolatry and witchcraft, and the missionaries destroyed many of them. More accurately, the *minkonde* represented a form of **animism**, a belief in the existence of souls and conviction that nonhuman things can also be endowed with a soul that serves as the foundation of many religions. However, European military commanders saw them as evidence of an aggressive native opposition to colonial control.

Despite their suppression during the colonial era, such figures are still made today and continue to be used by the Kongo peoples and among Caribbean peoples of African descent. In fact, Cuban performance artist Tania Bruguera dressed up as an *nkonde* in August 1998 (**Fig. 1-20**), standing still in the lobby of the Wifredo Lam Center of Contemporary Art in Havana until she began to wander the city as if in search of those who had broken the promises made to the icon in return for its help, at once asserting the power of the icon even as she revealed the vulnerabilities of her audience. The performance was reenacted at the Neuberger Museum of Art in Purchase, New York, in 2010.

Fig. 1-20 Tania Bruguera, *Displacement*, 1998–99. Cuban earth, glue, wood, nails, textile, dimensions variable. Still from film of the original performance in Havana, Cuba, 1988, exhibited at the Neuberger Museum of Art, New York, January–April 2010.
Courtesy of Tania Bruguera studio.

In the West, the desire to give form to spiritual belief is especially apparent in the traditions of Christian religious art. For example, the idea of daring to represent the Christian God has, throughout the history of the Western world, aroused controversy. In seventeenth-century Holland, images of God were banned from Protestant churches. As one contemporary Protestant theologian put it, "The image of God is His Word"—that is, the Bible—and "statues in human form, being an earthen image of visible, earthborn man, [are] far away from the truth." In fact, one of the reasons that Jesus, for Christians the son of God, is so often represented in Western art is that representing the son, a real person, is far easier than representing the father, a spiritual unknown who can only be imagined.

Nevertheless, one of the most successful depictions of the Christian God in Western culture was painted by Jan van Eyck nearly 600 years ago as part of an altarpiece for the city of Ghent in Flanders (**Figs. 1-21** and **1-22**).

Fig. 1-21 Jan van Eyck, *The Ghent Altarpiece*, ca. 1432. Oil on panel, 11 ft. 5 in. × 15 ft. 1 in. Church of St. Bavo, Ghent, Belgium.

Fig. 1-22 Jan van Eyck, *God*, panel from *The Ghent Altarpiece*, ca. 1432.

Van Eyck's God is almost frail, surprisingly young, apparently merciful and kind, and certainly richly adorned. Indeed, in the richness of his vestments, van Eyck's God apparently values worldly things. The painting seems to celebrate a materialism that is the proper right of benevolent kings. Behind God's head, across the top of the throne, are Latin words that, translated into English, read: "This is God, all-powerful in his divine majesty; of all the best, by the gentleness of his goodness; the most liberal giver, because of his infinite generosity." God's mercy and love are indicated by the pelicans embroidered on the tapestry behind him, which in Christian tradition symbolize self-sacrificing love, for pelicans were believed to wound themselves in order to feed their young with their own blood if other food was unavailable. In the context of the entire altarpiece, where God is flanked by Mary and John the Baptist, choirs of angels, and, at the outer edges, Adam and Eve, God rules over an earthly assembly of worshipers, his divine beneficence protecting all.

Seeing the Value in Art

How does the public come to value art—or not?

On the evening of November 12, 2013, at Christie's auction house in New York City, English painter Francis Bacon's triple portrait *Three Studies of Lucian Freud* (**Fig. 1-23**) sold for $142.4 million, making it the most expensive artwork ever sold at auction. The work had a special place in Bacon's life as well, documenting his lifelong friendship with its subject, the painter Lucian Freud, the grandson of Sigmund Freud: The two painters saw each other virtually every day for a quarter of a century, from the mid-1940s until about the time this work was painted. First exhibited in Italy and then in Bacon's triumphant retrospective in Paris in 1971–72, the three canvases were subsequently separated and sold into three different private collections before an Italian collector reunited the set in the 1990s. The **triptych**—three-paneled—format was crucial to Bacon. It functioned for him as analogous to the filmmaking technique of using three different cameras to shoot the same scene from three different angles. Here the bentwood chair and bedframe serve to ground an unstable, violently convulsive figure, and the perspective lines surrounding both seem to trap the composition as if in the lens of a camera. As in Picasso's *Seated Bather* (see Fig. 1-10), nothing in this painting is meant to be pleasing, except our recognition of the painter's extraordinary ability to invent an expressive image of tension. It is as if the violence of Lucian

Fig. 1-23 Francis Bacon, *Three Studies of Lucian Freud*, 1969. Oil on canvas, each canvas 6 ft. 6 in. × 4 ft. 10 in. Private collection. Photo © Christie's Images/Bridgeman Images. © 2015 Estate of Francis Bacon. All rights reserved. /DACS, London/Artists

Rights Society (ARS), New York.

Freud's inner life is oozing out of his body in the form of Francis Bacon's paint. As interesting as the triptych may be, many people find it hard to like, and they find it almost incredulous that the art market has established it as one of the highest-valued paintings of all time.

In no small part, the extremely high price can be attributed to both the relative rarity of Francis Bacon paintings on the market and the burgeoning post-recession American economy. The art market depends on the participation of wealthy clients through their investment, ownership, and patronage. It is no accident that the major financial centers of the world also support the most prestigious art galleries, auction houses, and museums of modern and contemporary art. Art galleries, in turn, bring artists and collectors together. They usually sign exclusive contracts with artists whose works they believe they can sell. Collectors may purchase work as an investment but, because the value of a given work depends largely upon the artist's reputation, and artists' reputations are finicky at best, the practice is very risky. As a result, what motivates most collectors is the pleasure of owning art and the prestige it confers upon them (the latter is especially important to corporate collectors).

Artistic Value and the "Culture Wars"

It is at auction that the monetary value of works of art is most clearly established. But auction houses are, after all, publicly owned corporations legally obligated to maximize their profits, and prices at auction are often inflated. That said, the value of art is not all about money. Art has intrinsic value as well, and that value is often the subject of intense debate. The fate of the work of two artists, Robert Mapplethorpe and Chris Ofili, offers two clear examples of just what is at stake in what have sometimes been called the "Culture Wars" surrounding artistic expression.

In the summer of 1989, the work of photographer Robert Mapplethorpe was scheduled to be exhibited at the Corcoran Gallery in Washington, D.C. Mapplethorpe had died just a few months earlier of an AIDS-related condition. He was known largely for his photographs of male nudes, and, in a group of works known as the "X Portfolio," for his depictions of sadomasochistic and homoerotic acts. These last, and, in particular, a photograph of a little girl sitting on a bench revealing her genitals, had raised the ire of Senator Jesse Helms of North Carolina who threatened to terminate funding for the National Endowment for the Arts, an independent Federal agency that had partially paid for the exhibition at the Corcoran. Not wanting to jeopardize continued funding of the Endowment, the Corcoran canceled the show. The show was moved to a smaller Washington gallery, Project for the Arts, where nearly 50,000 people visited it in 25 days. After leaving Washington, the exhibition ran without incident in both Hartford, Connecticut, and Berkeley, California, but when it opened at Cincinnati's Contemporary Arts Center, police seized many of the photographs as "criminally obscene" and arrested Dennis Barrie, the Center's director, on charges of pandering and the use of a minor in pornography. The Arts Center, the Robert Mapplethorpe Foundation, and the Mapplethorpe estate together countered the police action by filing suit to determine whether the photographs were obscene under Ohio state law. "We want a decision on whether the work as a whole has serious artistic value," they stated.

In Cincinnati, the judge in the trial of Barrie and the Arts Center ruled, however, that the jury should not consider Mapplethorpe's work "as a whole"; rather, he declared, "the Court finds that each photograph has a separate identity; each photograph has a visual and unique image permanently recorded." Nevertheless, the jury acquitted both Barrie and the Arts Center. They found that each of the images possessed serious artistic value. A good deal of the testimony focused on the formal qualities of Mapplethorpe's work—for example, the way that in his portrait *Ajitto* (**Fig. 1-24**) the human body assumes the geometrical precision of a pentagon. But one of the most compelling witnesses was Robert Sobieszek, senior curator of the International Museum of Photography in Rochester, New York. Mapplethorpe, said Sobieszek, "wanted to document what was beautiful and what was torturous—in his personal experience. If something is truly obscene or pornographic, then it's not art." But in addressing the terms of his own life, he said, Mapplethorpe was "not unlike van Gogh painting himself with his ear cut off."

Thus the jury found that, considered in the context of art as a whole, in the context of art's concern with form, and in the context of the history of art and its tradition of confronting those parts of our lives that give us pain as well as pleasure, Mapplethorpe's work seemed to them to possess "serious artistic value." The Mapplethorpe story makes clear that "value," like beauty, as discussed earlier in this chapter, is a relative term. What some people value, others do not and cannot.

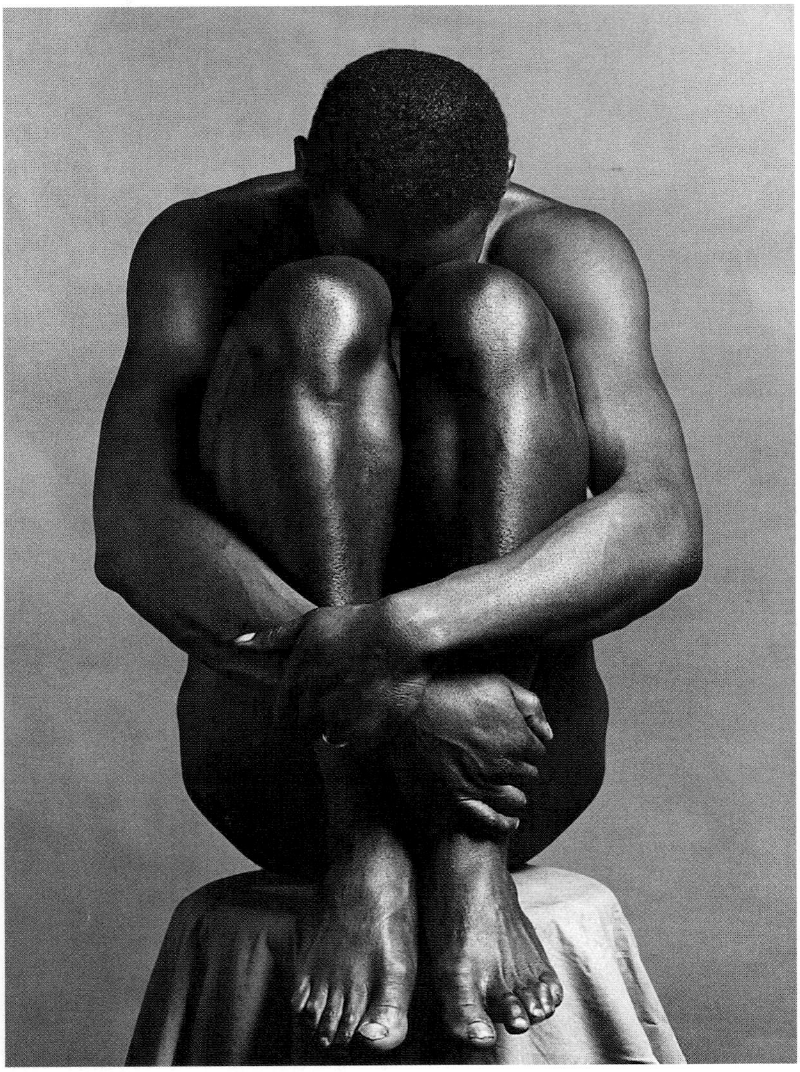

Fig. 1-24 Robert Mapplethorpe, *Ajitto*, 1981. Gelatin silver print, 30 × 40 in.
Used by permission of Art + Commerce. © Robert Mapplethorpe Foundation.

A decade later, this state of affairs was reaffirmed by the controversy surrounding the exhibition *Sensation: Young British Artists from the Saatchi Collection*, which appeared at the Brooklyn Museum from October 2, 1999 through January 9, 2000. At the center of the storm was a painting called *The Holy Virgin Mary* (**Fig. 1-25**) by Chris Ofili, a British-born artist who was raised a Catholic by parents born in Lagos, Nigeria. The work's background gleams with glitter and dabs of yellow resin, a shimmering mosaic evoking medieval icons that contrast with the soft, petal-like texture of the Virgin's blue-gray robes. What at first appears to be black-and-white beadwork turns out to be pushpins. Small cutouts decorate the space—bare bottoms from porn magazines meant to evoke putti, the baby angels popular in Renaissance art. But most controversial of all is the incorporation of elephant dung, acquired from the London Zoo, into the work. Two balls of resin-covered dung, with pins stuck in them spelling out the words "Virgin" and "Mary," support the painting, and another ball of dung defines one of the Virgin's breasts.

Cardinal John O'Connor called the show an attack on religion itself. The

Fig. 1-25 The press surround Chris Ofili's *The Holy Virgin Mary* at the Brooklyn Museum while protesters demonstrate outside, 1999.

Fig. 1-25a (left): © Ruby Washington/New York Times/Redux/eyevine. Fig. 1-25b (right): Sipa Press/REX.

Catholic League for Religious and Civil Rights said people should picket the museum. New York mayor Rudolph W. Giuliani threatened to cut off the museum's city subsidy and remove its board if the exhibition was not canceled, calling Ofili's work, along with that of several other artists, "sick stuff." (Taken to court, the mayor was forced to back down.) Finally, Dennis Heiner, a 72-year-old Christian who was incensed by Ofili's painting, eluded guards and smeared white paint across the work. Charged with second-degree criminal mischief, he was fined a mere $250. The painting has subsequently entered a private collection. For Ofili, the discomfort his work generates is part of the point: His paintings, he says, "are very delicate abstractions, and I wanted to bring their beauty and decorativeness together with the ugliness of shit and make them exist in a twilight zone—you know they're there together, but you can't really ever feel comfortable about it." Ofili works in this same twilight zone, evoking both his African heritage and his Catholic upbringing in his work.

The Avant-Garde and Public Opinion

The Ofili and Mapplethorpe examples demonstrate the many complex factors that go into a judgment of art's value. But it should be clear that the artist's relation to the public depends on the public's understanding of what the artist is trying to say. For one thing, the public tends to receive innovative artwork—work by the **avant-garde**, those who are working in advance of their time—with reservation because it usually has little context, historical or otherwise, in which to view it. It is not easy to appreciate, let alone value, what is not understood. When Marcel Duchamp exhibited his *Nude Descending a Staircase* (**Fig. 1-26**) at the Armory Show in New York City

Fig. 1-26 Marcel Duchamp, *Nude Descending a Staircase, No. 2*, 1912. Oil on canvas, 4 ft. 10 in. × 35 in. Philadelphia Museum of Art.

Louise and Walter Arensberg Collection, 1950. © 2015. Photo: Graydon Wood, 1994, Philadelphia Museum of Art/Art Resource/Scala, Florence. © 2015 Succession Marcel Duchamp/ADAGP, Paris/Artists Rights Society (ARS), New York.

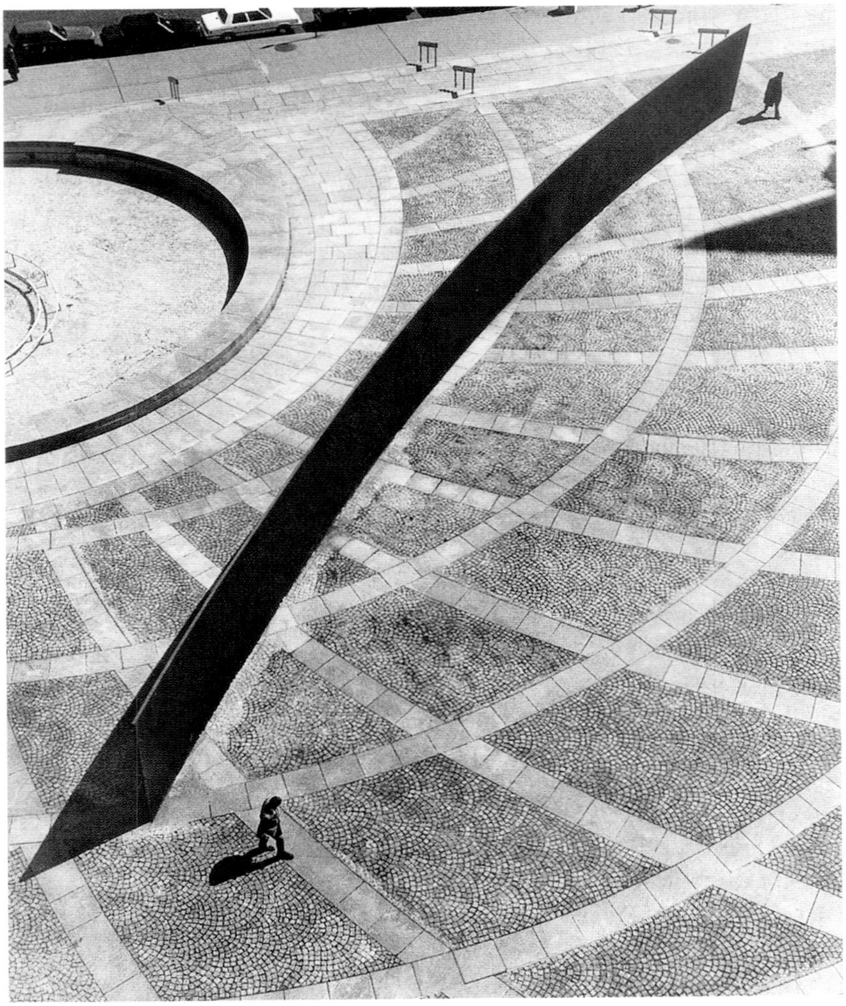

Fig. 1-27 Richard Serra, *Tilted Arc*, 1981. Cor-Ten steel, 12 ft. × 120 ft. × 2½ in. Installed, Federal Plaza, New York City. Destroyed by the U.S. government March 15, 1989.

in 1913, it was a scandalous success, parodied and ridiculed in the newspapers. Former President Teddy Roosevelt told the papers, to their delight, that the painting reminded him of a Navajo blanket. Others called it "an explosion in a shingle factory," or "a staircase descending a nude." *American Art News* held a contest to find the "nude" in the painting. The winning entry declared, "It isn't a lady but only a man."

The Armory Show was most Americans' first exposure to modern art, and more than 70,000 people saw it during its New York run. By the time it closed, after also traveling to Boston and Chicago, nearly 300,000 people had seen it. If not many understood the *Nude* then, today it is easier for us to see what Duchamp was representing. He had read, we know, a book called *Movement*, published in Paris in 1894, a treatise on human and animal locomotion written by Étienne-Jules Marey, a French physiologist who had long been fascinated with the possibility of breaking down the flow of movement into isolated data that could be analyzed. He had also seen studies by the American photographer Eadweard Muybridge of animals and humans in motion (see Fig. 11-2).

Marey, Muybridge, and Duchamp had embarked, we can now see, on the same path, a path that paralleled the development of the motion picture. On December 28, 1895, at the Grand Café on the Boulevard des Capucines in Paris, the Lumière brothers, who knew Marey and his work well, projected motion pictures of a baby being fed its dinner, a gardener being doused by a hose, and a train racing directly at the viewers, causing them to jump from their seats. Duchamp's vision had already been confirmed, but the public had not yet learned to see it.

Teaching the public how to see and appreciate what it called "advanced art" was, in fact, the self-defined mission of the National Endowment for the Arts (NEA) when it was first funded by Congress in 1967. The NEA assumed that teaching people to appreciate art—largely through its Art in Public Places Program, which dedicated a percent of the cost of new public buildings to purchasing art—would enhance the social life of the nation. Public art, the Endowment believed, would make everyone's lives better by making the places in which we live more beautiful, or at least more interesting.

Richard Serra's controversial *Tilted Arc* (**Fig. 1-27**) tested this hypothesis like none other. When it was originally installed in 1981 in Federal Plaza in Lower Manhattan, there was only a minor flurry of negative reaction. However, beginning in March 1985, William Diamond, newly appointed Regional Administrator of the General Services Administration, which had originally commissioned the piece, began an active campaign to have it removed. At the time, nearly everyone believed that the vast majority of people working in the Federal Plaza complex despised the work. In fact, of the approximately 12,000 employees in the complex, only 3,791 signed the petition to have it removed, while nearly as many—3,763—signed a petition to save it. Yet the public perception was that the piece was "a scar on the plaza" and "an arrogant, nose-thumbing gesture," in the words of one observer. Finally, during the night of March 15, 1989, against the artist's vehement protests and after he had filed a lawsuit to block its removal, the sculpture was dismantled and its parts stored in a Brooklyn warehouse. It has subsequently been destroyed.

From Serra's point of view, *Tilted Arc* was destroyed when it was removed from Federal Plaza. He had created it specifically for the site and, once removed, it lost its reason for being. In Serra's words: "Site-specific works primarily engender a dialogue with their surroundings. . . . It is necessary to work in opposition to the constraints of the context, so that the work cannot be read as an affirmation of questionable ideologies and political power." Serra intended his work to be confrontational. It was political. That is, he felt that Americans were divided from their government, and the arc divided the plaza in the same way. Its tilt was ominous—it seemed ready to topple over at any instant. Serra succeeded in questioning political power probably more dramatically than he ever intended, but he lost the resulting battle. He made his intentions known and understood, and the work was judged as fulfilling those intentions. But those in power judged his intentions negatively, which is hardly surprising, considering that Serra was challenging their very position and authority.

Political Visions

One of the reasons that the public has had difficulty, at least initially, accepting so many of the public art projects that have been funded by both the NEA as well as local and state percent-for-art programs modeled after the Federal program is that in many instances people have not found them to be aesthetically pleasing. The negative reactions to Serra's arc are typical. If art must be "beautiful," then Serra's work was evidently not a work of art, at least not in the eyes of the likes of William Diamond. And yet, as the public learned what the piece meant, many came to value the work, not for its beauty but for its insight, for what it revealed about the place they were in. Serra's work teaches us a further lesson about the value of art. If art appears to be promoting a specific political or social agenda, there are bound to be segments of the public that disagree with its point of view.

A classic example is Michelangelo's *David* (**Fig. 1-28**). Today, it is one of the world's most famous sculptures, considered a masterpiece of Renaissance art. But it did not meet with universal approval when it was first

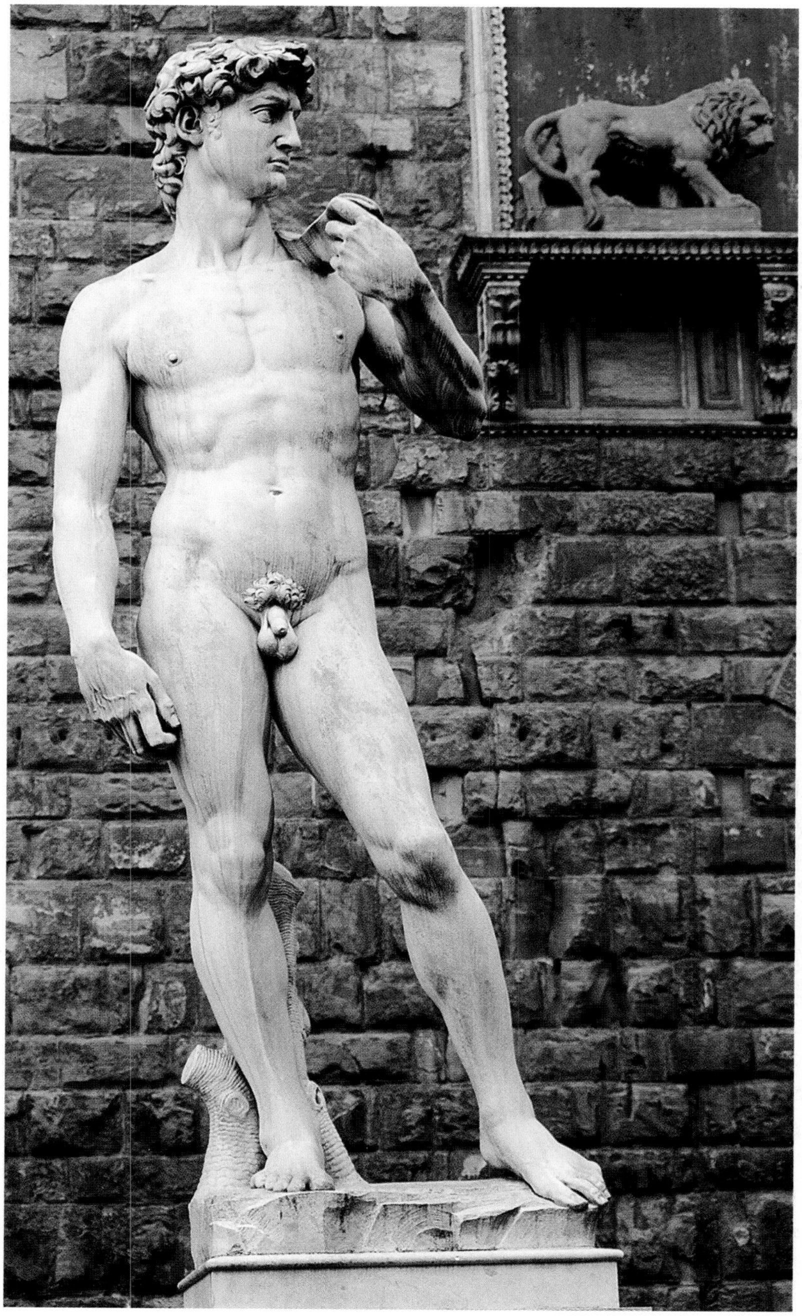

Fig. 1-28 Michelangelo, *David*, 1501–04. Copy of the original as it stands in the Piazza della Signoria, Florence. Original in the Galleria dell'Accademia, Florence. Marble, height 13 ft. 5 in.

displayed in Florence, Italy, in 1504. The sculpture was commissioned three years earlier, when Michelangelo was 26 years old, by the Opera del Duomo ("Works of the Cathedral"), a group founded in the thirteenth century to look after Florence Cathedral and to maintain works of art. It was to be a public piece, designed for outdoor display in the Piazza della Signoria, the plaza where public political meetings took place on a raised platform called the *arringhiera* (from which the English word "harangue" derives). Its political context, in other words, was clear: It represented David's triumph over the tyrant Goliath and was meant to symbolize republican Florence—the city's freedom from foreign and papal domination, as well as from the rule of the Medici family, who had come to be seen as tyrannical.

The *David* was, as everyone in the city knew, a sculptural triumph in its own right. It was carved from a giant 16-foot-high block of marble that had been quarried 40 years earlier. Not only was the block riddled with cracks, forcing Michelangelo to bring all his skills to bear, but earlier sculptors, including Leonardo da Vinci, had been offered the problem stone and refused to use it.

When the *David* was finished, in 1504, it was moved out of the Duomo at eight in the evening. It took 40 men four days to move it the 600 yards to the Piazza della Signoria. It required another 20 days to raise it onto the *arringhiera*. The entire time, its politics hounded it. Each night, stones were hurled at it by supporters of the Medici, and guards had to be hired to keep watch over it. Inevitably, a second group of citizens objected to its nudity, and before its installation a skirt of copper leaves was prepared to spare the general public any possible offense. Today, the skirt is long gone. By the time the Medici returned to power in 1512, the *David* was a revered public shrine, and it remained in place until 1873, when it was replaced by a copy (as reproduced here in order to give the reader a sense of its original context) and moved for protection from a far greater enemy than the Medici—the natural elements themselves. Michelangelo's *David* suggests another lesson about the value of art. Today, we no longer value the sculpture for its politics but rather for its sheer aesthetic beauty and accomplishment. It teaches us how important aesthetic issues remain, even in the public arena.

THE CRITICAL PROCESS

Thinking about Making and Seeing Works of Art

In this chapter, we have discovered that the world of art is as vast and various as it is not only because different artists in different cultures see and respond to the world in different ways, but also because each of us sees and responds to a given work of art in a different way. Artists are engaged in a *creative process*. We respond to their work through a process of *critical thinking*. At the end of each chapter of *A World of Art* is a section like this one titled *The Critical Process* in which, through a series of questions, you are invited to think for yourself about the issues raised in the chapter. In each case, additional insights are provided at the end of the text, in the section titled *The Critical Process*: *Thinking Some More about the Chapter Questions*. After you have thought about the questions raised, turn to the back and see if you are headed in the right direction.

Here, Andy Warhol's *Race Riot* (**Fig. 1-29**) depicts events of May 1963 in Birmingham, Alabama, when police commissioner Bull Connor employed attack dogs and fire hoses to disperse civil rights demonstrators led by Reverend Martin Luther King, Jr. The traditional roles of the artist—to help us see the world in new or innovative ways; to make a visual record of the people, places, and events of their time and place; to make functional objects and structures more pleasurable and elevate them or imbue them with meaning; and to give form to immaterial, hidden, or universal truths, spiritual forces, or personal feelings—are all part of a more general creative impulse that leads, ultimately, to the work of art. Which of these is, in your opinion, the most important for Warhol in creating this work? Did any of the other traditional roles play a part in the process? What do you think Warhol feels about the events (note that the print followed soon after the events themselves)? How does his use of color contribute to his composition? Can you think why there are two red panels, and only one white and one blue? Emotionally, what is the impact of the red panels? In other words, what is the work's psychological impact? What reactions other than your own can you imagine the work generating? These are just a few of the questions raised by Warhol's work, questions to help you initiate the critical process for yourself.

Fig. 1-29 Andy Warhol, *Race Riot*, 1963.
Acrylic and silkscreen on canvas, four panels, each 20 × 33 in.

Thinking Back

1.1 Differentiate between passive and active seeing.

The act of seeing is not a simple matter of making a direct recording of reality. Everything we see is filtered through a long history of fears, prejudices, emotions, customs, and beliefs. Through art, we can begin to understand those filters and learn to look more closely at the visual world. How is the truth of our seeing challenged by trompe-l'oeil works of art? In his painting *Flag*, how does Jasper Johns present an opportunity to look closely at a familiar image? How might the historical context of Faith Ringgold's *God Bless America* influence how we see the work?

1.2 Define the creative process and describe the roles that artists most often assume when they engage in that process.

Artists all share the fundamental desire to create, but artists respond to their world in divergent terms. The artist must be something of an explorer or inventor. What distinguishes artists from other people? What must an artist be able to do to produce a work of art?

Most artists think of themselves as assuming one of four fundamental roles—or some combination of the four—as they approach their work. Artists may help us to see the world in new and innovative ways, create visual records of specific times and places, imbue objects with beauty and meaning, and give form to feelings and ideas. What roles do artists Mickalene Thomas and Édouard Manet assume in their work? What distinguishes the decorative coffins of Kane Kwei's workshop? How does Pablo Picasso give form to the immaterial in his painting *Les Demoiselles d'Avignon*?

1.3 Discuss the different ways in which people value, or do not value, works of art.

The monetary value of a work of art is determined by the art market and is often established at auction houses. But the value of art is not all about money. Art has intrinsic value as well, and that value is often the subject of intense debate. How did this debate manifest itself in the cases of Robert Mapplethorpe and Chris Ofili?

The public tends to receive innovative new artwork with reservation because it usually has little context by which to understand and appreciate it. As Marcel Duchamp's *Nude Descending a Staircase* demonstrates, it is difficult to value that which is not understood. If the National Endowment for the Arts' Art in Public Places Program was designed to teach the public how to appreciate "advanced art," how did Richard Serra's *Tilted Arc* test the NEA's assumptions when it was installed in Federal Plaza in Manhattan? How did political and social issues affect both its reception and, nearly 500 years earlier, the reception of Michelangelo's *David*?

Chapter 2
Developing Visual Literacy

Learning Objectives

2.1 Describe the relationship between words and images.

2.2 Distinguish between representation and abstraction.

2.3 Discuss how form, as opposed to content, might also help us to understand the meaning of a work of art.

2.4 Explain how cultural conventions can inform our interpretation of works of art.

Visual art can be powerfully persuasive, and one of the purposes of this book is to help you to recognize how this is so. Yet it is important for you to understand from the outset that you can neither recognize nor understand—let alone communicate—how visual art affects you without using language. In other words, one of the primary purposes of any art appreciation text is to provide you with a descriptive vocabulary, a set of terms, phrases, concepts, and approaches that will allow you to think critically about visual images. It is not sufficient to say, "I like this or that painting." You need to be able to recognize why you like it, how it communicates to you. This ability is given the name visual literacy.

The fact is, most of us take the visual world for granted. We assume that we understand what we see. Those of us born and raised in the television era are often accused of being nonverbal, passive receivers, like TV monitors themselves. If television, the Internet, movies, and magazines have made us virtually dependent upon visual information, we have not necessarily become visually literate in the process.

What, for instance, is required of us to arrive at some understanding of the painting on the right (**Fig. 2-1**)? In the first place, if we are to make sense of it at all, it is obvious that it requires more of us than just a casual glance. Visual literacy, like scientific inquiry, demands careful observation. Our eyes move over this image looking for clues about what it might mean. We might be tempted to think that there is nothing for us to grasp except for the evident energy of its brushwork, until, finally, the eye comes to rest on what appears to be a sailboat in the middle of the painting, its form reflected in the sea below. *North Atlantic Light*, we note, is the painting's title. Perhaps the yellow ball near the top of the painting is the sun, the painting's brushwork reflecting the turbulence of sky and sea.

As it turns out, in the mid-1960s, the artist responsible for it, Willem de Kooning, had moved to Springs, on the east end of Long Island, and this painting was executed in his studio there. He had moved there, he said in 1972, because "I wanted to get back to a feeling of light in painting. . . . I wanted to get in touch with nature. Not painting scenes from nature, but to get a feeling of that light that was very appealing to me, here particularly." If this piece of biographical information tends to confirm our understanding of the work, our reading still falls short of accounting adequately for much about it, especially the apparent randomness of de Kooning's

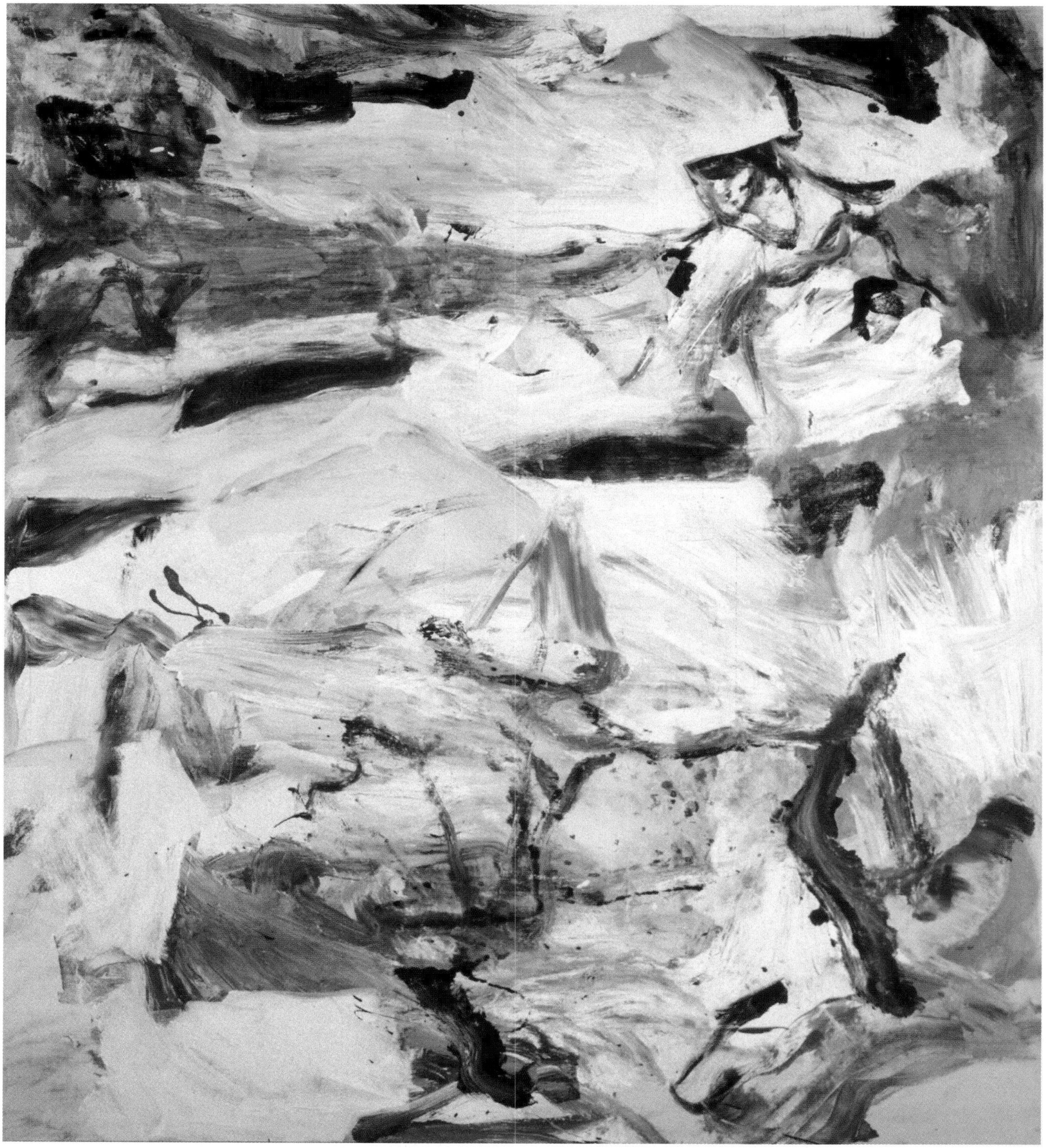

Fig. 2-1 Willem de Kooning, *North Atlantic Light*, 1977. Oil on canvas, 6 ft. 8 in. × 5 ft. 10 in.
Stedelijk Museum, Amsterdam, The Netherlands. Acquired with the support of the Rembrandt Association.

brushwork. If visual literacy first and foremost requires close observation, it also requires the ability to describe and interpret what we see. It is, in other words, a process of critical thinking. To interpret what we observe we need, then, a descriptive vocabulary, and this chapter will introduce you to some of the essential concepts and terms that will help us—the relationships among words, images, and objects in the real world; the ideas of representation and abstraction; the distinctions among form, content, context, and conventions in art.

Words and Images

What is the relationship between words and images?

The Belgian artist René Magritte offered a lesson in visual literacy in his painting *The Treason of Images* (**Fig. 2-2**). Magritte reproduced an image of a pipe similar to that found in tobacco store signs and ads of his time. The caption under the pipe translates into English as "This is not a pipe," which at first seems contradictory. We tend to look at the image of a pipe as if it were really a pipe, but of course it isn't. It is the representation of a pipe. In a short excerpt from the 1960 film by Luc de Heusch, *Magritte, or The Object Lesson*, Magritte himself discussed the arbitrary relation between words and things. Both images and words can refer to things that we see or experience in the world, but they are not the things themselves. Nevertheless, we depend upon words to articulate our understanding of visual culture, and using words well is fundamental to visual literacy.

In a series of photographs focused on the role of women in her native Iran and entitled *Women of Allah*, Shirin Neshat combines words and images in startling ways. In *Rebellious Silence* (**Fig. 2-3**), Neshat portrays herself as a Muslim woman, dressed in a black chador, the traditional covering that extends from head to toe, revealing only hands and face. A rifle divides her face, upon which Neshat has inscribed in ink a Farsi poem by the devout Iranian woman poet Tahereh Saffarzadeh. Saffarzadeh's verses express the deep belief of many Iranian women in Islam. Only within the context of Islam, they believe, are women truly equal to men, and they claim that the chador, by concealing a woman's sexuality, prevents her from becoming a sexual object.

Fig. 2-3 Shirin Neshat, *Rebellious Silence*, from the series *Women of Allah*, 1994. Gelatin silver print and ink, 11 × 14 in.
© Shirin Neshat, courtesy of Gladstone Gallery, New York and Brussels. Photo: Cynthia Preston.

The chador, in this sense, is liberating. It also expresses women's solidarity with men in the rejection of Western culture, symbolized by Western dress. But to a Western audience, unable to read Farsi, the values embodied in the poem are indecipherable, a fact that Neshat fully understands. Thus, because we cannot understand the image, it is open to stereotyping, misreading, misunderstanding—the very conditions of the division between Islam and the West, imaged in the division of Neshat's body and face by the gun. The **subject matter** of the work—what the image literally depicts—barely hints at the complexity of its **content**—what the image means. Indeed, the words that accompany a work of art—it title, for instance, as in de Kooning's *North Atlantic Light*—can go a long way toward helping us understand an image's meaning.

Fig. 2-2 René Magritte, *The Treason of Images, Ceci n'est pas une pipe*, 1929. Oil on canvas, 21½ × 28½ in. Los Angeles County Museum of Art.
© 2015 BI, ADAGP, Paris/Scala, Florence. © 2015 C. Herscovici/Artists Rights Society (ARS), New York.

In Islamic culture, in fact, words take precedence over images, and **calligraphy**—that is, the fine art of handwriting—is the chief form of Islamic art. The Muslim calligrapher does not so much express himself as act as a medium through which Allah (God) can express himself in the most beautiful manner possible. Thus, all properly pious writing, especially poetry, is sacred. This is the case with the page from the poet Firdawsi's *Shahnamah* (**Fig. 2-4**).

Sacred texts are almost always decorated with designs that aim to be visually compelling but not representational. Until recent times, in the Muslim world, every book—indeed, almost every sustained statement—began with the phrase *bismillah al-rahman al-rahim*, which can be translated "In the name of Allah, the Beneficent,

Fig. 2-4 ***Triumphal Entry*, page from a manuscript of Firdawsi's *Shahnamah*, Persian, Safavid culture, 1562–83.** Opaque watercolor, ink, and gold on paper, 18 11/16 × 13 in. Museum of Fine Arts, Boston.

Ever-Merciful," the same phrase that opens the Qur'an. On this folio page from the *Shahnamah*, the *bismillah* is in the top right-hand corner (Arabic texts read from right to left). To write the *bismillah* in as beautiful a form as possible is believed to bring the scribe forgiveness for his sins.

The Islamic emphasis on calligraphic art derives, to a large degree, from the fact that at the heart of Islamic culture lies the word, in the form of the recitations that make up the Qur'an, the messages the faithful believe that God delivered to the Prophet Muhammad through the agency of the Angel Gabriel. The word could be trusted in a way that images could not. In the *hadith*, the collections of sayings and anecdotes about Muhammad's life, Muhammad is quoted as having warned, "An angel will not enter a house where there is a dog or a painting." Thus, images are notably absent in almost all Islamic religious architecture. And because Muhammad also claimed that "those who make pictures will be punished on the Day of Judgment by being told: Make alive what you have created," the representation of "living things," human beings especially, is frowned upon. Such thinking would lead the Muslim owner of a Persian miniature representing a prince feasting in the countryside to erase the heads of all those depicted (**Fig. 2-5**). No one could mistake these headless figures for "living things."

Fig. 2-5 Page from a copy of Nizami's *Khamseh* (*Quintet*) illustrating a princely country feast, Persian, Safavid culture, 1574–75. Illuminated manuscript, 9¾ × 6 in. India Office, London.
© British Library Board, I.O. ISLAMIC 1129, f.29.

The distrust of images is not unique to Islam; at various periods in history Christians have also debated whether it was sinful to depict God and his creatures in paintings and sculpture. In the summer of 1566, for instance, Protestant **iconoclasts** (literally "image breakers," those who wished to destroy images in religious settings) threatened to destroy Jan van Eyck's *Ghent Altarpiece* (see Fig. 1-21), but just three days before all Ghent's churches were sacked, the altarpiece was dismantled and hidden in the tower by local authorities. In Nuremberg, Germany, a large sculpture of Mary and Gabriel hanging over the high altar of the Church of San Lorenz was spared destruction, but only after the town council voted to cover it with a cloth that was not permanently removed until the nineteenth century. The rationale for this wave of destruction, which swept across northern Europe, was a strict reading of the Ten Commandments: "Thou shalt not make any graven image, or any likeness of any thing that is in heaven above, or that is in the earth beneath, or that is in the water under the earth: Thou shalt not bow down thyself to them nor serve them" (Exodus 20:4–5). But whatever the religious justification, it should be equally clear that the distrust of visual imagery is, at least in part, a result of the visual's power. If the worship of "graven images"—that is, idols—is forbidden in the Bible, the assumption is that such images are powerfully attractive, even dangerously seductive.

Representation and Abstraction

What is the difference between representation and abstraction?

In the last section, we began to explore the topic of visual literacy by considering the relationship between words and images. Words and images are two different systems of describing the world. Words refer to the world in the abstract. Images represent the world, or reproduce its appearance. Traditionally, one of the primary goals of the visual arts has been to capture and portray the way the natural world looks. But, as we all know, some works of art look more like the natural world than others, and some artists are less interested than others in representing the world as it actually appears. As a result, a vocabulary has developed that describes how closely, or not, the image resembles visual reality itself. This basic set of terms is where we need to begin in order to talk or write intelligently about works of art.

Generally, we refer to works of art as either representational or abstract. A **representational** work of art portrays natural objects in recognizable form. The more the representation resembles what the eye sees, the more it is said to be an example of **realism**. When a painting is so realistic that it appears to be a photograph, it is said to be **photorealistic** (see *The Creative Process*, pp. 34–35). The less a work resembles real things in the real world, the more it is said to be an example of **abstract** art. When a work does not refer to the natural or objective world at all, it is said to be completely abstract or **nonobjective**.

Albert Bierstadt's painting *Puget Sound on the Pacific Coast* (**Fig. 2-6**) is representational and, from all appearances, highly realistic. However, even when it was painted in 1870, a writer for the *New York Evening Mail*, reporting on his visit to Bierstadt's studio to see the work, worried that it might be more fanciful than realistic: "It is, we are told, in all essential features, a portrait of the place depicted, and we need the assurance to satisfy us that it is not a su-

Fig. 2-6 Albert Bierstadt, *Puget Sound on the Pacific Coast*, 1870. Oil on canvas, 4 ft. 4½ in. × 6 ft. 10 in.
Seattle Art Museum.
Gift of the Friends of American Art at the Seattle Art Museum, with additional funds from the General Acquisition Fund, 2000.70. Photo: Howard Giske.

The Creative Process

Abstract Illusionism: George Green's . . . *marooned in dreaming: a path of song and mind*

Throughout the last three decades of the last century, George Green painted in a distinct style that came to be known as Abstract Illusionism. It was characterized by images of abstract sculptural forms that seemed to float free of the painting's surface in highly illusionistic three-dimensional space. In the last few years of the 1990s, he began to make these paintings on birch, using the wood's natural grain to heighten the illusion, so that it is as if one were looking at a photorealistic painting of an abstract wooden sculpture.

Over the last decade, this process has evolved into a series of canvases of which . . . *marooned in dreaming: a path of song and mind* (**Fig. 2-10**) is exemplary. Like the earlier Abstract Illusionist works of the late 1990s, these paintings begin with a single sheet of raw birch (**Fig. 2-7**). Green then paints a highly illusionistic frame and mat onto the birch (**Fig. 2-8**). The frame is an example of what we call trompe-l'oeil, French for "trick or deceive the eye." As opposed to photorealism, in which the painting is so realistic it appears to be a photograph, trompe-l'oeil effects result in a painting that looks as if it is an actual thing—in this case, an actual frame and mat. If one looks carefully at the lighter wood grain of the birch board at both the left and right edges, it becomes obvious that the shadowing created by the beveled edges and concave surfaces of the molding are painted onto the flat surface of the wood. But Green's frames are so visually convincing that on more than one occasion collectors have asked him if he would mind

Figs. 2-7, 2-8 and 2-9 George Green, . . . *marooned in dreaming: a path of song and mind*, in progress, 2011. Top: Raw birch ground before painting. Middle: Second stage, painted frame and mat. Bottom: Third stage, painted frame and seascape.
Courtesy of the artist.

Fig. 2-10 George Green, . . . *marooned in dreaming: a path of song and mind*, 2011. Acrylic on birch, 4 ft. × 6 ft. 10 in. Courtesy of the artist.

if they changed the frame. (They can't, of course—the frame is an integral part of the painting.)

The third stage of Green's process is to paint a photorealistic seascape into the frame and mat (**Fig. 2-9**). While these seascapes are based on actual photographs taken by the artist, they are, upon further consideration, anything but photographic. In . . . *marooned in dreaming: a path of song and mind*, the clouds are too purple, the sea too garishly green. The aura of the sun behind the clouds lends the scene a quasi-spiritual dimension. And the lightning looks more like airborne jellyfish than an actual atmospheric electrostatic discharge (that said, photographs of actual lightning storms are every bit as unbelievable as these). For all its ostensible realism, in other words, the painting evokes a sort of otherworldliness. Writing about Green's work, the photorealist painter Don Eddy puts it this way: "The totality has the quality of an altered state that I find deeply reminiscent of movies that are heavily dependent on CGI [Computer Generated Imagery]."

Finally, Green overlays the entire composition with a filigree of scrolls and arabesques intertwined with planes of color, globes of wood, and even snapshots of landscapes—all painted on the surface. They are meant to evoke the unrepresentable—the "look" of music, or the flight of the mind. It is as if these elements have been painted on a sheet of glass set atop the painting and frame beneath. They create, at any rate, another surface, closer to the viewer than landscape and frame, and in their total abstraction, they insist on the artificiality of the entire composition. As Green's title suggests, the artist is alone with his own mind, and that mind works between several worlds—the world of actual objects, the imaginative dreamscapes of fantasy, and the unrepresentable sounds of song and music. These are, he suggests, the very layers of imagination.

---

perb vision of that dreamland into which our much admired painter has made at least as many visits as he has made among the material wonders of the West." Bierstadt, in fact, had never visited Puget Sound, and this painting bears no resemblance to the Puget Sound landscape. Bierstadt's painting is naturalistic rather than realistic. **Naturalism** is a brand of representation in which the artist retains apparently realistic elements—in Bierstadt's case, accurate representations of Western flora and fauna, as well as Native American dress and costume—but presents the visual world from a distinctly personal or subjective point of view, in this case, a formula that he used in painting after painting of the American West: a waterfall tumbles down a precipitous mountainside into a lake (in this case, Puget Sound); storm clouds gather; light filters through from above. In fact, the play of light in Bierstadt's *Puget Sound* bears a strong resem-

Fig. 2-11 Wolf Kahn, *Afterglow I*, 1974. Oil on canvas, 41½ in. × 5 ft. 6 in. Whitney Museum of American Art, New York.
Gift of Mr. and Mrs. Harry Kahn. Art © Wolf Kahn/Licensed by VAGA, New York.

blance to that in Willem de Kooning's *North Atlantic Light* (see Fig. 2-1). But where Bierstadt's painting retains strong representational elements, de Kooning's is much more abstract, as if de Kooning is engaged in a sort of dialogue between representation and abstraction.

While still a recognizable image of a landscape, Wolf Kahn's *Afterglow I* (**Fig. 2-11**) is far more abstract than Bierstadt's *Puget Sound*. The painting consists of four bands of color. In the near foreground is the edge of a field, behind it a band of trees in dark shadow, and behind the trees a blue cloud and an orange-hued sunset sky. For Kahn, the less realistic the detail, the better the painting. "When a work becomes too descriptive," the artist told an interviewer in 1995, "too much involved with what's actually out there, then there's nothing else going on in the painting, and it dies on you." In fact, like both de Kooning and Bierstadt, his paintings could be said to be more about light than the actual landscape.

Although Australian Aboriginal artist Old Mick Tjakamarra's *Honey Ant Dreaming* (**Fig. 2-12**) is, in fact, a landscape, it is not immediately recognizable as one. The organizing logic of most Aboriginal art is the so-called Dreaming, a system of belief unlike that of most other religions in the world. The Dreaming is not literally dreaming as we think of it. For the Aborigine, the Dreaming is the presence, or mark, of an Ancestral Being in the world. Images of these Beings—representations of the myths about them, maps of their travels, depictions of the places and landscapes they inhabited—make up the great bulk of Aboriginal art. To the Aboriginal people, the entire landscape is thought of as a series of marks made upon the earth by the Dreaming. Thus, the landscape

Fig. 2-12 Old Mick Tjakamarra, *Honey Ant Dreaming*, 1982. Acrylic on canvas, 36 × 27 in.
© Aboriginal Artists Agency Limited. Photo: Jennifer Steele/Art Resource, New York.

itself is a record of the Ancestral Being's passing, and geography is full of meaning and history. Painting is understood as a concise vocabulary of abstract marks conceived to reveal the ancestor's being, both present and past, in the Australian landscape.

Ceremonial paintings on rocks, on the ground, and on people's bodies were made for centuries by the Aboriginal peoples of Central Australia's Western Desert region. Paintings similar in form and content to these traditional works began to be produced in the region in 1971. In that year, a young art teacher named Geoff Bardon arrived in Papunya Tula—literally "Honey Ant Dreaming" place—a settlement on the edge of the Western Desert organized by the government to provide health care, education, and housing for the Aboriginal peoples. Several of the older Aboriginal men became interested in Bardon's classes, and he encouraged them to make paintings using traditional motifs. At first they painted on small composition boards, but between 1977 and 1979, they moved from these small works to large-scale canvases. Old Mick Tjakamarra's painting *Honey Ant Dreaming* depicts the landscape of Papunya Tula itself, where honey ants live in abundance. The ants store nectar in their distended abdomens, and hang from the ceilings of underground chambers, sometimes for months, until the ant colony needs their stored food. Here, the concentric circles represent three honey ant colony sites and the U-shaped forms around them represent people digging at the sites. The softly curved shapes represent hills or ridges. The black-stemmed plant is native to the region and is used to make pigment for designs etched on the ground during Honey Ant Dreaming ceremonies.

Form and Meaning

How does form contribute to the meaning of a work of art?

As mentioned above, abstract works of art that do not refer to the natural or objective world at all are sometimes called nonobjective. One example, Kazimir Malevich's *Black Square* (**Fig. 2-13**), is concerned primarily with questions of **form**. When we speak of a work's form, we mean everything from the materials used to make it, to the way it employs the various formal elements (discussed in Part 2), to the ways in which those elements are organized into a **composition**. Form is the overall structure of a work of art. Somewhat misleadingly, it is often opposed to **content**, which is what the work of art expresses or means. Obviously, the content of nonobjective art is its form, but all forms, Malevich well knew, suggest meaning. Malevich's painting is really about the relation between the black square and the white ground behind it. By 1912, the Russian artist was engaged, he wrote, in a "desperate attempt to free art from the ballast of objectivity." To this end, he says, "I took refuge in the square." He called his new art Suprematism, defining it as "the supremacy of . . . feeling in . . . art." He opposed feeling, that is, to objectivity, or the disinterested representation of reality.

Fig. 2-13 Kazimir Malevich, *Black Square*, ca. 1923–30. Oil on plaster, 14½ × 14½ in. Musée National d'Art Moderne, Centre Georges Pompidou, Paris.
Inv. AM1978-631. Photo © Centre Pompidou, MNAM-CCI, Dist. RMN-Grand Palais/Jacques Faujou.

Black Square was first exhibited in December 1915 at an exhibition in Petrograd entitled *0.10: The Last Futurist Exhibition of Paintings*. The exhibition's name refers to the idea that each of the ten participating artists were seeking to articulate the "zero degree"—that is, the irreducible core—of painting. What, in other words, most minimally makes a painting? In this particular piece, Malevich reveals that, in relation, these apparently static forms—two squares, a black one set on a white one—are energized in a dynamic tension. At the *0.10* exhibition, *Black Square* was placed high in the corner of the room in the position usually reserved in traditional Russian houses for religious icons. The work is, in part, parodic, replacing images designed to invoke deep religious feeling with what Malevich referred to as "an altogether new and direct form of representation of the world of feeling." As he wrote in his treatise *The Non-Objective World*, "The square = feeling, the white field = the void beyond this feeling." What "feeling" this might be remains unstated—that is, totally abstract.

The work of contemporary Brazilian artist Beatriz Milhazes is likewise founded upon formal relationships.

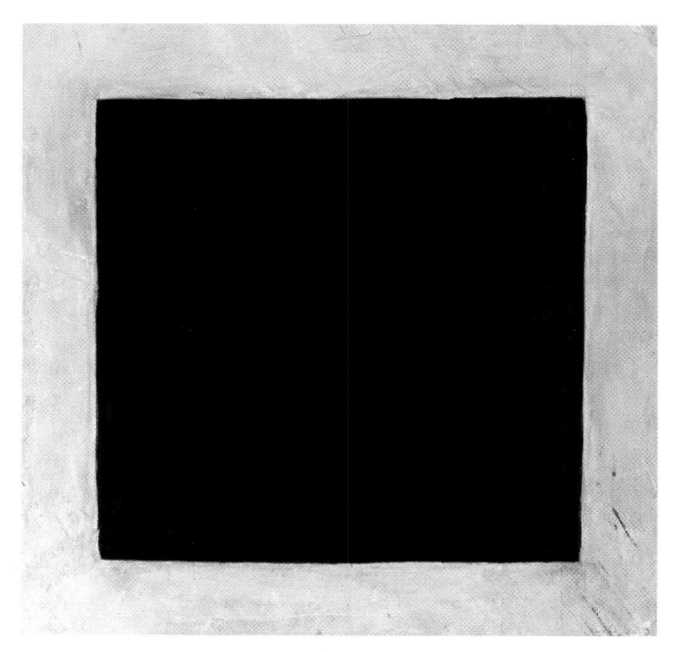

Carambola (**Fig. 2-14**), like all of her work, is based on the square, and, not coincidentally, she counts Malevich among those whose work has most influenced her own. She begins each work with a square, and then, she says, "I build things on top of it. The squares may disappear, but they are still a reference for me to think about composition." In fact, she thinks of the circles that dominate paintings like *Carambola* as containing squares. In essence, she pulls together into a geometrical composition the shapes and forms of Brazilian culture—ornate church facades, the ruffled blouses of Brazilian Mardi Gras costumes, the design of the serpentine walkway that stretches along her native Rio de Janeiro's beachfront, the exotic plants in the botanical garden neighboring her studio in Rio (where, in fact, the carambola tree, from which this painting takes its name, grows). Her color use, too, captures the dizzying kaleidoscope of Brazilian Carnival. "I am interested in conflict," she says, "and the moment you add one more color, you start the conflict, which is endless. So there is a constant movement to your eyes, to your self, to your body, and I like it."

Fig. 2-14 Beatriz Milhazes, *Carambola*, 2008. Acrylic on canvas, 4 ft. 6⅞ in. × 4 ft. 2⅝ in.
Courtesy of James Cohan Gallery, New York and Shanghai.

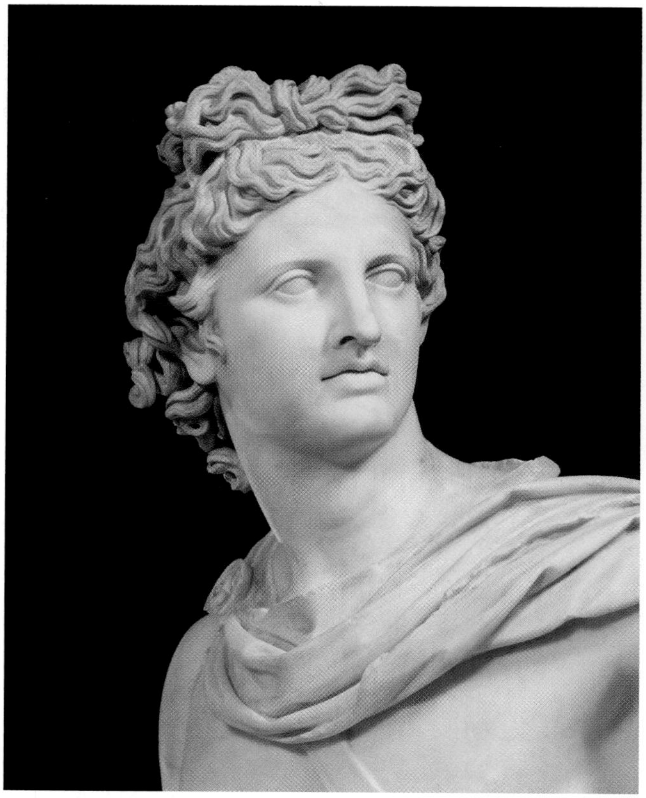

Fig. 2-15 ***Apollo Belvedere*** **(detail), Roman copy after a 4th-century BCE Greek original.** Height of entire sculpture 7 ft. 4 in. Museo Pio-Clementino, Vatican City.
© 2015 Photo Scala, Florence.

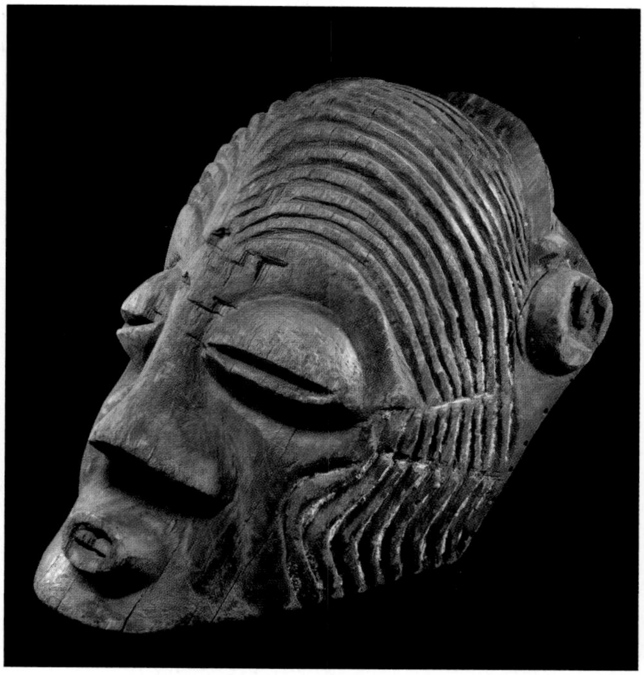

Fig. 2-16 African dancing mask from Ulivira, Lake Tanganyika. Lateral view. Wood, height 24 in.
© The Samuel Courtauld Trust, The Courtauld Gallery, London/Bridgeman Images.

Convention, Symbols, and Interpretation

How do cultural conventions—the use of symbols and iconography—inform the meaning of works of art?

Our understanding of Milhazes's work is highly dependent on understanding its cultural context. Consider another set of examples: an ancient sculpture of the Greek god Apollo and a carved mask from the Sang tribe of Gabon in West Africa (**Figs. 2-15** and **2-16**). In the late 1960s in his television series and book *Civilization*, art historian Kenneth Clark compared the two images through an ethnocentric lens and concluded that the image of the messenger god Apollo demonstrated the superiority of Classical Greek civilization. Clark understood the conventions of Greek sculpture and recognized the meaning of the idealized sculptural form: "To the Hellenistic imagination it is a world of light and confidence, in which the gods are like ourselves, only more beautiful, and descend to earth in order to teach men reason and the laws of harmony." However, his interpretation of the African mask, which he owned, reveals his ignorance of the conventions of the West African nation that created it: "To the Negro imagination it is a world of fear and darkness, ready to inflict horrible punishment for the smallest infringement of a taboo." In fact, the features of the African mask are exaggerated at least in part to separate it from the "real." Clark's ethnocentric reading of it neglects its ritual, celebratory social function in African society. Worn in ceremonies, masks are seen as vehicles through which the spirit world is made available to humankind.

Cultural conventions are often carried forward from one generation to the next by means of **iconography**, a system of visual images the meaning of which is widely understood by a given culture or cultural group. These visual images are **symbols**—that is, they represent something more than their literal meaning. The subject matter of iconographic images is not obvious to any viewer unfamiliar with the symbolic system in use. Furthermore, every culture has its specific iconographic practices, its own system of images that are understood by the culture at large to mean specific things.

Even within our own culture, the meaning of an image may change or be lost over time. When Jan van Eyck

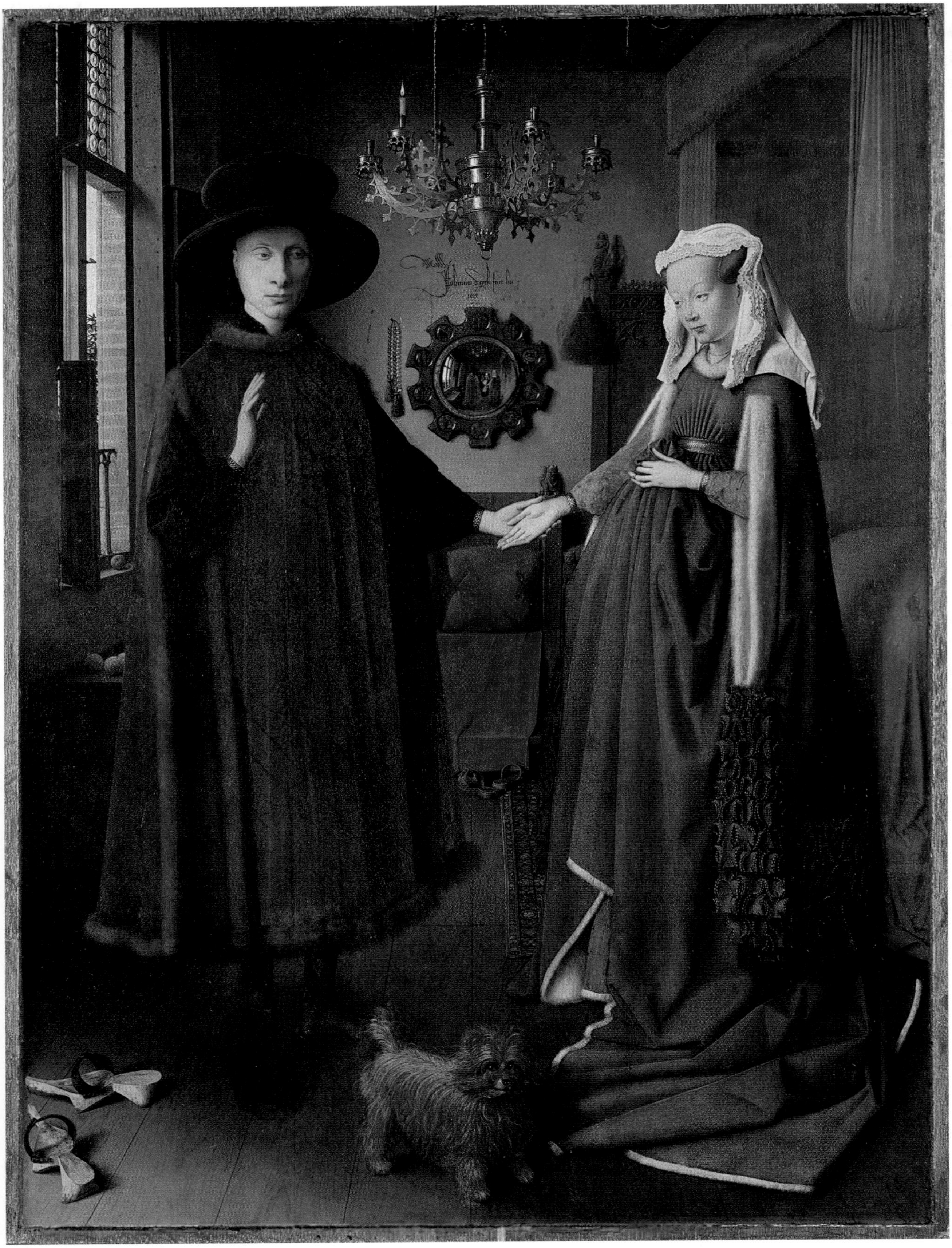

Fig. 2-17 Jan van Eyck, *Giovanni Arnolfini and His Wife Giovanna Cenami*, ca. 1434.
Oil on oak panel, 32¼ × 23½ in. National Gallery, London.

painted his portrait of *Giovanni Arnolfini and His Wife Giovanna Cenami* in ca. 1434 (**Fig. 2-17**), its repertoire of visual images was well understood, but today, much of its meaning is lost to the average viewer. For example, the bride's green dress, a traditional color for weddings, was meant to suggest her natural fertility. She is not pregnant—her swelling stomach was a convention of female beauty at the time, and her dress is structured in a way that accentuates it. The groom's removal of his shoes is a reference to God's commandment to Moses to take off his shoes when standing on holy ground. A single candle burns in the chandelier above the couple, symbolizing the presence of Christ at the scene. And the dog, as most of us recognize even today, is associated with faithfulness and, in this context particularly, with marital fidelity.

But what would Islamic culture make of the dog in the van Eyck painting, as in the Muslim world dogs are traditionally viewed as filthy and degraded? From a Muslim point of view, the painting verges on nonsense. And for almost everyone, viewing van Eyck's work more than 500 years after it was painted, certain elements remain confusing. An argument has recently been made, for instance, that van Eyck is not representing a marriage so much as a betrothal, or engagement. We have assumed for generations that the couple stands in a bridal chamber where, after the ceremony, they will consummate their marriage. It turns out, however, that in the fifteenth century it was commonplace for Flemish homes to be decorated with hung beds with canopies. Called "furniture of estate," these were important status symbols commonly displayed in the principal room of the house as a sign of the owner's prestige and influence. It was also widely understood in van Eyck's time that a touching of the hands, the woman laying her hand in the palm of man, was the sign, especially in front of witnesses, of a mutual agreement to wed.

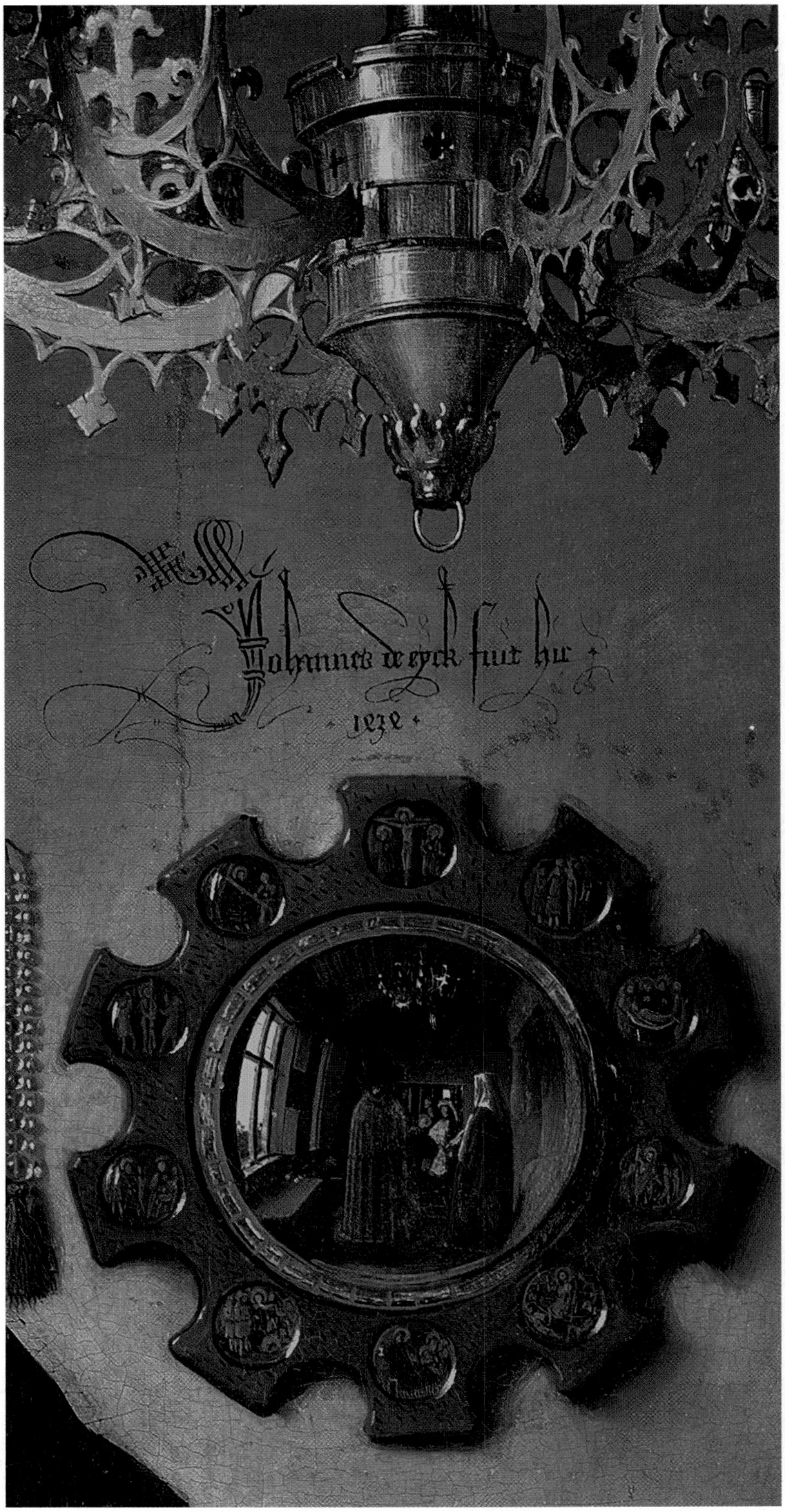

Fig. 2-18 Jan van Eyck, *Giovanni Arnolfini and His Wife* (detail), ca. 1434.
Bridgeman Images.

The painter himself stands in witness to the event. On the back wall, above the mirror, are the words *Jan de Eyck fuit hic, 1434*—"Jan van Eyck was here, 1434" (**Fig. 2-18**). We see the backs of Arnolfini and his wife reflected in the mirror, and beyond them, standing more or less in the same place as we do as viewers, two other figures, one a man in a red turban who is probably the artist himself.

Fig. 2-19 Jean-Michel Basquiat, *Charles the First*, 1982. Acrylic and oil paintstick on canvas, three panels, 6 ft. 6 in. × 5 ft. 2¼ in. overall.

In his painting *Charles the First* (**Fig. 2-19**), Jean-Michel Basquiat employs iconographic systems both of his own and others' making. The painting is an homage to the great jazz saxophonist Charlie Parker, who died in 1955, one of a number of black cultural heroes celebrated by the graffiti-inspired Basquiat. Son of a middle-class Brooklyn family (his father was a Haitian-born accountant, his mother a black Puerto Rican), Basquiat left school in 1977 at age 17, living on the streets of New York for several years during which time he developed the "tag"—or graffiti pen name—SAMO, a combination of "Sambo" and "same ol' shit." SAMO was most closely associated with a three-pointed crown (as self-anointed "king" of the graffiti artists) and the word "TAR," evoking racism (as in "tar baby"), violence ("tar and feathers," a title he would give one of his paintings in 1982), and, through the anagram, the "art" world as well. A number of his paintings exhibited in the 1981 *New York/New Wave* show at an alternative art gallery across the 59th Street Bridge from Manhattan attracted the attention of several art dealers and his career exploded.

Central to his personal iconography is the crown, which is a symbol not only of his personal success, but of the other African-American "heroes" that are the subject of many of his works—jazz artists, such as Parker and Dizzy Gillespie, and "famous Negro athletes," as he calls them, such as boxer Sugar Ray Leonard and baseball's Hank

Aaron. Heroism is, in fact, a major theme in Basquiat's work, and the large "S," which appears three times in the first panel of *Charles the First* and twice in the second, is a symbol for the superhero Superman, as well as for SAMO.

Directly above the triangular Superman logo in the first panel are the letters "X-MN," which refer to the X-Men comic-book series, published by Marvel Comics, whose name appears crossed out at the bottom of the third panel. Marvel describes the X-Men as follows: "Born with strange powers, the mutants known as the X-Men use their awesome abilities to protect a world that hates and fears them." Basquiat clearly means to draw an analogy between the X-Men and his African-American heroes. And, in fact, Basquiat refers to another Marvel Comics hero, the Norse god Thor, whose name appears below the crown in the top left of Basquiat's painting.

The "X" has a special significance in Basquiat's iconography. In the *Symbol Source-book: An Authoritative Guide to International Graphic Symbols*, a book by American industrial designer Henry Dreyfuss first published in 1972, Basquiat discovered a section on "Hobo Signs," marks left, graffitilike, by hobos to inform their brethren about the lay of the local land. In this graphic language, an "X" means "O.K. All right."

The "X" is thus ambiguous, a symbol of both negation (crossed out) and affirmation (all right). This is, of course, the condition in which all of Basquiat's African-American heroes find themselves. The title *Charles the First* is also a reference to King Charles I of England, beheaded by Protestants in the English Civil War in 1649—hence the phrase across the bottom of panels one and two, "Most kings get thier [*sic*] head cut off." Basquiat's reference to Parker's rendering of "Cherokee," in the third panel, evokes not only the beauty of the love song itself, but also the Cherokee Indian Nation's "Trail of Tears," the forced removal of the tribe from Georgia to Oklahoma in 1838 that resulted in the deaths of some 4,000 of their people. Above "Cherokee" are four feathers, a reference at once to Indians, Parker himself, whose nickname was "Bird," and, in the context of Basquiat's work as a whole, the violent practice of tar and feathering. Finally, Basquiat's sense that the price of heroism is high indeed is embedded in two other of his iconographic signs: The "S," especially when lined or crossed out, also suggests dollars, $, and the copyright © sign, which is ubiquitous in his paintings, suggests not just ownership, but the exercise of property rights and control in American society, an exercise and control that Basquiat sees as the root cause of the institution of slavery (to say nothing of the removal of the Cherokee nation to Oklahoma).

In sum, Basquiat's paintings are literally packed with a private, highly ambiguous iconography. But their subject is clear enough. When asked by Henry Geldzahler, curator of contemporary art at the Metropolitan Museum of Art in New York City, just what his subject matter was, Basquiat replied: "Royalty, heroism, and the streets."

If the iconographic program of the Arnolfini double portrait seems remote, and Basquiat's somewhat personal, the iconographic practices of other cultures are even more so. While most of us in the West probably recognize a Buddha when we see one, we do not necessarily understand that the position of the Buddha's hands carries iconographic significance. Buddhism, which originated in India in the fourth century BCE, is traditionally associated with the worldly existence of Sakyamuni, or Gautama, the Sage of the Sakya clan, who lived and taught around 500 BCE. In his 35th year, Sakyamuni experienced enlightenment under a tree at Gaya (near modern Patna) and became the Buddha or Enlightened One.

Buddhism spread to China in the first and second centuries CE. Long before it reached Japan by way of Korea in about 600 CE, it had developed a more or less consistent iconography, especially related to the representation of the Buddha himself. The symbolic hand gestures, or mudras, refer both to general states of mind and to specific events in the life of the Buddha. The mudra best known to Westerners, the hands folded in the seated Buddha's lap, symbolizes meditation. The wooden sculpture of the Amida Buddha illustrated here (**Fig. 2-20**) was assembled from multiple wood blocks and then hollowed out to make it lighter and more portable. The Buddha of Infinite Light, whom the Japanese call Amida, was believed to rule the Pure Land, or the Paradise in the West, into which the faithful might find themselves reborn, thus gaining release from the endless cycle of birth, rebirth, and suffering.

Fig. 2-20 Buddha (Amida), Japan, ca. 1130. Wood with gold lacquer, 37¼ × 27 × 17 in. Seattle Art Museum.
Gift of the Monsen Family, 2011.39. Photo: Elizabeth Mann.

THE CRITICAL PROCESS

Thinking about Visual Conventions

Very rarely can we find the same event documented from the point of view of two different cultures, but two images, one by John Taylor, a journalist hired by *Leslie's Illustrated Gazette* (**Fig. 2-21**), and the other by the Native American artist Howling Wolf (**Fig. 2-22**), son of the Cheyenne chief Eagle Head, both depict the October 1867 signing of peace treaties between the Cheyenne, Arapaho, Kiowa, and Comanche peoples, and the United States government, at Medicine Lodge Creek, a tributary of the Arkansas River, in Kansas. Taylor's illustration is based on sketches done at the scene, and it appeared soon after the events. Howling Wolf's work, actually one of several depicting the events, was done nearly a decade later, after he was taken east and imprisoned at Fort Marion in St. Augustine, Florida, together with his father and 70 other "ringleaders" of the continuing Native American insurrection in the Southern Plains. While in prison, Howling Wolf made many such "ledger" drawings, so called because they were executed on blank accountants' ledgers.

Even before he was imprisoned, Howling Wolf had actively pursued ledger drawing. As Native Americans were introduced to crayons, ink, and pencils, the ledger drawings supplanted traditional buffalo hide art, but in both the hide paintings and the later ledger drawings, artists depicted the brave accomplishments of their owners. The conventions used by these Native American artists differ greatly from those employed by their Anglo-American counterparts. Which, in your opinion, is the more representational? Which is the more abstract?

Both works possess the same overt content—that is, the peace treaty signing—but how do they differ in form? Both Taylor and Howling Wolf depict the landscape, but how are they dissimilar? Can you determine why Howling Wolf might want to depict the confluence of after Medicine Lodge Creek and the Arkansas in his drawing? It is as if Howling Wolf portrays the scene from above, so that simultaneously we can see tipis, warriors, and women in formal attire, and the grove in which the United States soldiers meet with the Indians. Taylor's view is limited to the grove itself. Does this difference in the way the two artists depict space suggest any greater cultural differences? Taylor's work directs our eyes to the center of the image, while Howling Wolf's does not. Does this suggest anything to you?

Perhaps the greatest difference between the two depictions of the events is the way in which the Native Americans are themselves portrayed. In Howling Wolf's drawing, each figure is identifiable—that is, the tribal affiliations and even the specific identities of individuals are revealed through the iconography of the decorations of their dress and tipi. How, in comparison, are the Native Americans portrayed in Taylor's work? In what ways is Taylor's work ethnocentric?

Fig. 2-21 John Taylor, *Treaty Signing at Medicine Lodge Creek*, 1867. Drawing for *Leslie's Illustrated Gazette*, September–December 1867, as seen in Douglas C. Jones, *The Treaty of Medicine Lodge*, page xx, Oklahoma University Press, 1966.

Fig. 2-22 Howling Wolf, *Treaty Signing at Medicine Lodge Creek*, 1875–78. Ledger drawing, pencil, crayon, and ink on paper, 8 × 11 in. New York State Library, Manuscripts and Special Collections, Albany.

One of the most interesting details in Howling Wolf's version is the inclusion of a large number of women. Almost all of the figures in his drawing are, in fact, women. They sit with their backs to the viewer, their attention focused on the signing ceremony before them. Their braided hair is decorated with customary red paint in the part. This convention is of special interest. When the Plains warrior committed himself to a woman, he ceremonially painted her hair to convey his affection for and commitment to her. Notice the absence of any women in Taylor's depiction, as opposed to their prominence in Howling Wolf's. What does this suggest to you about the role of women in the two societies?

Thinking Back

2.1 Describe the relationship between words and images.

Both images and words can refer to things that we see or experience in the world, but they are not the things themselves. Nevertheless, words help us to explain what we see or experience, and are fundamental to visual literacy. If an artwork's subject matter might be readily apparent, articulating its content—what the artwork fully means—requires that we use words. How can the subject matter of Shirin Neshat's *Rebellious Silence* be distinguished from its content? Why do you suppose calligraphy is held in such high esteem in Islam?

2.2 Distinguish between representation and abstraction.

Representational artworks portray recognizable forms. The more the representation resembles what the eye sees, the more it is said to be an example of realism. What does Albert Bierstadt represent in his painting *Puget Sound on the Pacific Coast*? What distinguishes naturalism from other types of realism? How does representational art differ from abstract art?

2.3 Discuss how form, as opposed to content, might also help us to understand the meaning of a work of art.

Form is the overall structure of an artwork. It includes such aspects as the artwork's materials and the organization of its parts into a composition. What role does form typically play in nonobjective art? How does form differ from content? How do Kazimir Malevich and Beatriz Milhazes use form in their works?

2.4 Explain how cultural conventions can inform our interpretation of works of art.

Cultural conventions are often carried from one generation to the next through iconography. Iconography is a system of images whose meaning is understood by a certain cultural group. The images used in iconography represent concepts or beliefs beyond literal subject matter. What cultural conventions used in Jan van Eyck's *Giovanni Arnolfini and His Wife* have we apparently forgotten? How does Jean-Michel Basquiat's *Charles the First* represent a personal iconography? What is a mudra?

Paul Cézanne, ***The Basket of Apples,*** **ca. 1895.** Oil on canvas, 21 7/16 × 31½ in.
The Art Institute of Chicago.

Part 2

The Formal Elements and Their Design

Describing the Art You See

Upon first encountering Paul Cézanne's *The Basket of Apples*, most people sense immediately that it is full of what appear to be visual "mistakes." The painting is a still life, but it is also a complex arrangement of visual elements: Lines and shapes, light and color, space, and—despite the fact that it is a "still" life—time. The edges of the table, both front and back, do not line up. The wine bottle is tilted sideways, and the apples appear to be spilling forward, out of the basket, onto the white napkin, which in turn seems to project forward, out of the picture plane. Indeed, looking at this work, one feels compelled to reach out and catch that first apple as it rolls down the napkin's central fold and falls into our space.

In truth, Cézanne has not made any mistakes at all. Each decision is part of a strategy designed to give back life to the traditional form of the still life—a genre of painting that has as its subject objects of the table, such as food, dishes, and flowers, and which in French is called *nature morte* ("dead nature"). He wants to animate the space of the painting, to make it dynamic rather than static, to engage the imagination of the viewer. He has taken the visual elements of line, space, and texture, and has deliberately manipulated them as part of his composition, the way he has chosen to organize the canvas. As we begin in this section to appreciate how the visual elements routinely function we will better appreciate how Cézanne manipulates them to achieve the wide variety of effects that so animate this painting.

Chapter 3
Line

Learning Objectives

3.1 Distinguish among outline, contour, and implied line.

3.2 Describe the different qualities that lines might possess.

One of the most fundamental elements of nature is **line**. Indeed, lines permeate the universe, a fact that informs almost all the work of London-born painter Matthew Ritchie. Describing his painting *No Sign of the World* (**Fig. 3-1**), he explains: "I use the symbol of the straight line a lot in my drawings and paintings. It usually represents a kind of wound, or a direction. The curved line is like a linking gesture that joins things. But the straight line is usually more like an arrow, or rein, or a kind of rupture." From the bottom of *No Sign of the World*, violet straight lines shoot up into a field of what appear to be broken sticks and branches. Above the horizon line, across the sky, looping lines of this same violet color appear to gather these fragments into circular fields of energy. His work begins with drawings that he then scans into a computer. In that environment, he can resize and reshape them, make them three-dimensional, take them apart, combine them with other drawings, and otherwise transform them. "From the very start, I've been working with digital technology," Ritchie says. "When you make something digital you make it out of little dots. And you can make lines out of particles, but they're really just bits. . . . These are the classic forms of dimensionality—the point, the line, the solid—and then you add time and you've got the universe." Ritchie's project is just that ambitious and vast. He seeks to represent the entire universe and the structures of knowledge and belief through which we seek to understand it. In *No Sign of the World*, it is as if we are at the dawn of creation, at the scene of some original "Big Bang"—as if the world is about to be born but there is no sign of it yet.

Varieties of Line

What are the differences between outline, contour, and implied line?

To draw a line, you move the point of your pencil across paper. To follow a line, your eye moves as well. Lines seem to possess direction—they can rise or fall, head off to the left or to the right, disappear in the distance. Lines can divide one thing from another, or they can connect things. They can be thick or thin, long or short, smooth or agitated. Lines also reflect movement in nature. The patterns of animal and human movement across the landscape are traced in paths and roadways. The flow of water from mountaintop to sea follows the lines etched in the landscape by streams and rivers. Lines, in fact, sometimes play a major role in human history, delineating city limits, county lines, and state and national borders—sometimes contested.

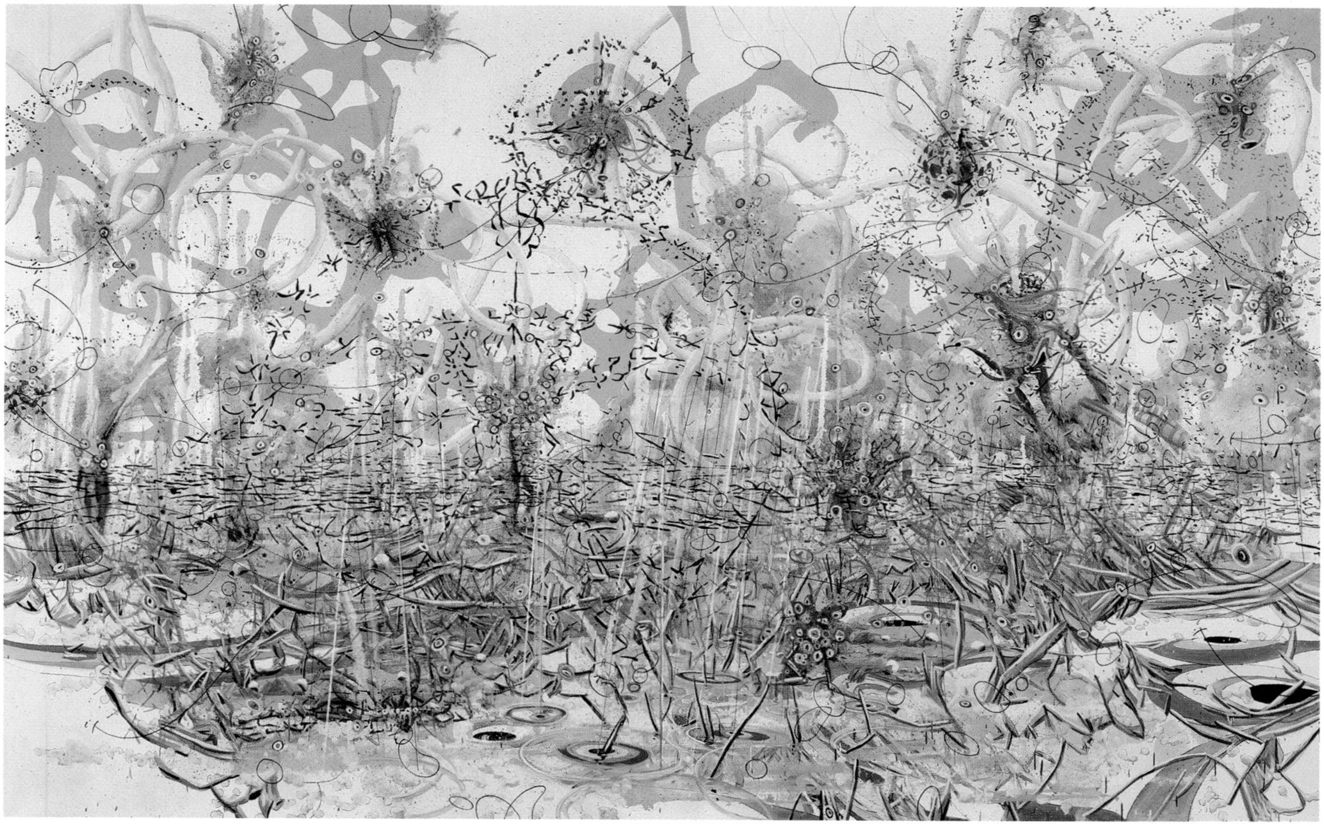

Fig. 3-1 Matthew Ritchie, *No Sign of the World*, 2004. Oil and marker on canvas, 8 ft. 3 in. × 12 ft. 10 in.
© Matthew Ritchie, Image Courtesy of Andrea Rosen Gallery, New York.

Outline and Contour Line

An important feature of line is that it indicates the edge of a two-dimensional (flat) shape or a three-dimensional form. A shape can be indicated by means of an **outline**, as in Yoshitomo Nara's *Dead Flower* (**Fig. 3-2**). In Nara's painting, heavy black outlines delineate both the little girl and the light bulb. This outline style is purposefully juvenile, evoking the Japanese love for *kawaii*, or "cuteness." But, of course, Nara lends his "cute" little girl a kind of menacing punk-rock persona, even if the extent of her violent behavior is limited to cutting off a flower at its stem. The Japanese artist and art historian Takashi Murakami has labeled the style of work reflected in Nara's demonic little girls as "Superflat," an insistence on two-dimensional forms that he sees as a defining characteristic of Japanese culture from eighteenth- and nineteenth-century Japanese prints to present-day animation (*anime*) and comic books (*manga*).

Where outlines tend to emphasize the flatness of a shape, **contour lines** form the outer edge of a three-dimensional shape and suggest its volume, its

Fig. 3-2 Yoshitomo Nara, *Dead Flower*, 1994. Acrylic on canvas, 39¼ × 39¼ in.
© Yoshitomo Nara, courtesy of Pace Gallery. Photograph courtesy of the artist.

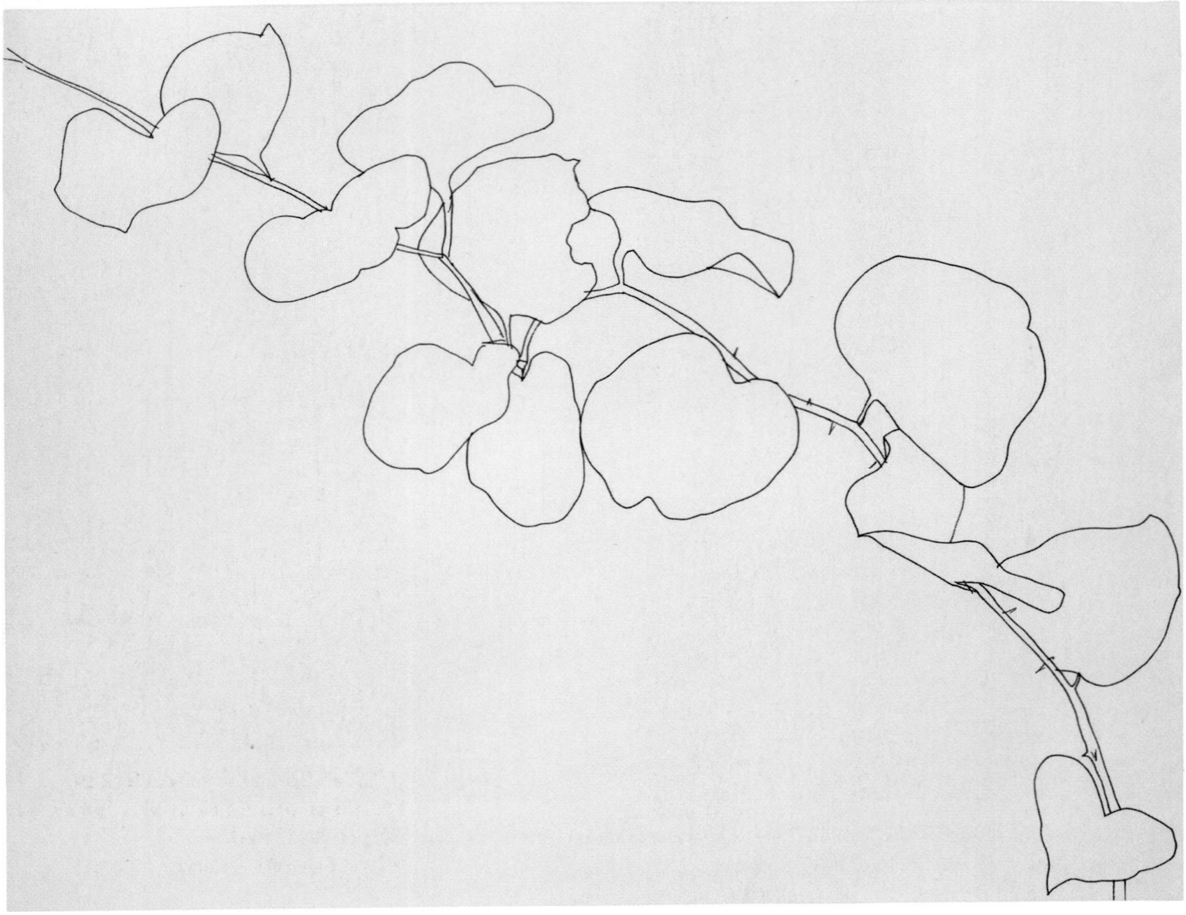

Fig. 3-3 Ellsworth Kelly, *Brier*, 1961. Black ink on wove paper, 22½ × 28½ in.
Wadsworth Atheneum Museum of Art, CT.
Gift of Mr. Samuel Wagstaff in memory of Elva McCormick, 1980.7. © Ellsworth Kelly, all rights reserved.

recession or projection in space. The contour lines in Ellsworth Kelly's *Brier* (**Fig. 3-3**) create the illusion of leaves occupying real space. Lines around the outside of the leaves define the limits of our vision—what we can see of the form from our point of view. As these lines cross each other, or seem to fold and turn, it is as if each line surrounds and establishes each leaf's position in space.

Implied Line

If we point our finger at something, we visually "follow" the line between our fingertip and the object in question. This is an **implied line**, a line where no continuous mark connects one point to another, but where the connection is nonetheless visually suggested. One of the most important kinds of implied line is a function of line of sight, the direction the figures in a given composition are looking. In his *Assumption and Consecration of the Virgin* (**Fig. 3-4**), Titian ties together the three separate horizontal areas of the piece—God the Father above, the Virgin Mary in the middle, and the Apostles below—by implied lines that create simple, interlocking, symmetrical triangles (**Fig. 3-5**) that serve to unify the worlds of the divine and the mortal.

Implied line can also serve to create a sense of directional movement and force, as in *Calvary*, a painting by African artist Chéri Samba (**Fig. 3-6**). Samba began his career before he was 20, working as a signboard painter and newspaper cartoonist in Kinshasa, the capital of Zaire. With their bold shapes and captions (in French and Langala, Zaire's official language), they are, in essence, large-scale political cartoons. *Calvary* places the artist in the position of Christ, not on the cross but splayed out on the ground, a martyr. He is identified as "le peintre," the painter, on the back of his shirt. He lies prostrate before "the house of painting," so identified over the doorway. He is being beaten by three soldiers, identified on the back of one as agents of the Popular Church of Zaire. The caption at the top left reads: "The Calvary of a painter in a country where the rights of man are practically nonexistent." Here, implied lines arc

Fig. 3-4 Titian, ***Assumption and Consecration of the Virgin*****, ca. 1516–18.** Oil on wood, 22 ft. 6 in. × 11 ft. 10 in. Santa Maria Gloriosa dei Frari, Venice.
© 2015. Photo Scala, Florence.

Fig. 3-5 Line analysis of Titian, ***Assumption and Consecration of the Virgin*****, ca. 1516–18.**
© 2015. Photo Scala, Florence.

Fig. 3-6 Chéri Samba, ***Calvary*****, 1992.** Acrylic on canvas, 35 × 45⅝ in.
Photo courtesy of Annina Nosei Gallery, New York. © Chéri Samba.

over the artist—the imminence of the downward thrust of the soldiers' whips—and the political power of the image rests in the visual anticipation of terror that these implied lines convey.

Qualities of Line

What are the different qualities that lines might possess?

Line delineates shape and form by means of outline and contour line. Implied lines create a sense of enclosure and connection as well as movement and direction. But line also possesses certain intellectual, emotional, and expressive qualities.

No one has ever employed line with more consistent expressive force than the seventeenth-century Dutch artist Rembrandt van Rijn. Consider, for instance, the kinds of effects he achieved in *The Three Crosses* (**Fig. 3-7**). As one's eye moves from the center ground beneath Christ on the cross, his line becomes denser and denser, except directly above the cross where line almost disappears altogether, the source, one can only presume, of divine light. Otherwise, Rembrandt's lines seem to envelop the scene, shrouding it in a darkness that moves in upon the crucified Christ like a curtain closing upon a play or a storm descending upon a landscape, and his line becomes more charged emotionally as it becomes denser and darker.

Expressive Qualities of Line

Line, in other words, can express emotion, the feelings of the artist. Such lines are said to be *expressive*. Of the swirling turmoil of line that makes up *The Starry Night* (**Fig. 3-8**), the Dutch painter Vincent van Gogh would

Fig. 3-7 Rembrandt van Rijn, *The Three Crosses*, 1653. Etching, 15¼ × 17¾ in.
1842,0806.139. © The Trustees of the British Museum.

Fig. 3-8 Vincent van Gogh, *The Starry Night*, 1889. Oil on canvas, 29 × 36¼ in. Museum of Modern Art, New York.

write to his brother, Theo, "Is it not emotion, the sincerity of one's feeling for nature, that draws us?" Van Gogh's paintings are, for many, some of the most personally expressive in the history of art. His use of line is loose and free, so much so that it seems almost out of control. He builds his paint up in thick, bold strokes, so that they come to possess a certain "body" of their own—an almost sculptural materiality known as **impasto**. So consistent is he in his application of paint that his style has become essentially autographic: Like a signature, it identifies the artist himself, his deeply anguished and creative genius (see *The Creative Process*, pp. 54–55).

During the 15 months just before *The Starry Night* was painted, while he was living in the southern French town of Arles, van Gogh produced a truly amazing quantity of work: 200 paintings, more than 100 drawings and watercolors, and roughly 200 letters, mostly written to his brother, Theo. Many of these letters help us understand the expressive energies released in this creative outburst. In December 1888, van Gogh's personal turmoil reached a fever pitch when he sliced off a section of his earlobe and presented it to an Arlesian prostitute as a present. After a brief stay at an Arles hospital, he was released, but by the end of January, the city received a petition signed by 30 townspeople demanding his committal. In early May, he entered a mental hospital in Saint-Rémy, and there he painted *The Starry Night*. In this work, life and death—the town and the heavens—swirl as if in a fury of emotion, and they are connected by both the church spire and the swaying cypress, a tree traditionally used to mark graves in southern France and Italy. "My paintings are almost a cry of anguish," van Gogh wrote. On July 27, 1890, a little over a year after *The Starry Night* was painted, the artist shot himself in the chest. He died two days later, at the age of 37.

Sol LeWitt employs a line that is equally autographic, recognizably his own, but one that reveals to us a personality very different from van Gogh's. LeWitt's line is precise, controlled, mathematically rigorous, logical, and rationally organized, where van Gogh's line is

The Creative Process

From Painting to Drawing: Vincent van Gogh's *The Sower*

We know more about the genesis and development of *The Sower* than of almost all of Vincent van Gogh's other paintings, and we can follow the work's progress in some detail. There are four different descriptions of it in his letters, the first on June 17, 1888, in a letter to the Australian painter John Russell (**Fig. 3-9**) that includes a preliminary sketch of his idea. "Am working at a Sower," van Gogh writes in the letter, "the great field all violet the sky & sun very yellow. It is a hard subject to treat."

I heard Rodin had a beautiful
head at the Salon.
I have been to the seaside for a
week and very likely am going thither
again soon. - Flat shore
sands - fine figures there
like Cimabue - straight stylish
Am working at a Sower:
the great field all violet. the sky & sun very
yellow. it is a hard subject to treat.
Please remember me very kindly to
Mrs Russell - and in thought I heartily
shake hands. Yours very truly
Vincent

Fig. 3-9 Vincent van Gogh, Letter to John Peter Russell, June 17, 1888. Ink on laid paper, 8 × 10¼ in. Solomon R. Guggenheim Museum, New York. Thannhauser Collection, Gift, Justin K. Thannhauser, 1978.2514.18. © Solomon R. Guggenheim Foundation, New York. Photo by Robert E. Mates.

The difficulties he was facing in the painting were numerous, having particularly to do with a color problem. As he wrote in a letter to the French painter Émile Bernard on the very next day, June 18, at sunset van Gogh was faced with a moment when the "excessive" contrast between the yellow sun and the violet shadows on the field would necessarily "irritate" the beholder's eye. He had to be true to that contrast and yet find a way to soften it. For approximately eight days he worked on the painting. First, he tried making the sower's trousers white in an effort to create a place in the painting that would "allow the eye to rest and distract it." That strategy apparently failing, he tried modifying the yellow and violet areas of the painting. On June 26, he wrote to his brother, Theo: "Yesterday and today I worked on the sower, which is completely recast. The sky is yellow and green, the ground violet and orange." This plan succeeded (**Fig. 3-10**). Each area of the painting now contained color that connected it to the opposite area, green to violet and orange to yellow.

The figure of the sower was, for van Gogh, the symbol of his own "longing for the infinite," as he wrote to Bernard, and having finished the painting, he remained, in August, still obsessed with the image. "The idea of the Sower continues to haunt me all the time," he wrote to Theo. In fact, he had begun to think of the finished painting as a study that was itself a preliminary work leading to a drawing (**Fig. 3-11**). "Now the harvest, the Garden, the Sower . . . are sketches after painted studies. I think all these ideas are good," he wrote to Theo on August 8, "but the painted studies lack clearness of touch. That is [the] reason why I felt it necessary to draw them."

In the drawing, sun, wheat, and the sower himself are enlarged, made more monumental. The house and tree on the left have been eliminated, causing us to focus more on the sower himself, whose stride is now wider and who seems more intent on his task. But it is the clarity of van Gogh's line that is especially astonishing. Here we have a sort of anthology of line types: short and long, curved and straight, wide and narrow. Lines of each type seem to group themselves into bundles of five or ten, and each bundle seems to possess its own direction and flow, creating a sense of the tilled field's uneven but regular furrows. It is as if, wanting to represent his longing for the infinite as it is contained in the moment of the genesis of life, sowing the field, van Gogh himself returns to the most fundamental element in art—line itself.

Fig. 3-10 Vincent van Gogh, *The Sower*, 1888. Oil on canvas, 25¼ × 31¾ in. Signed, lower left: Vincent.
Collection Kröller-Müller Museum, Otterlo, The Netherlands.

Fig. 3-11 Vincent van Gogh, *The Sower*, 1888. Drawing. Pencil, reed pen, and brown and black ink on wove paper, 9⅝ × 12½ in. Van Gogh Museum, Amsterdam.
Courtesy of Vincent van Gogh Foundation, Amsterdam.

Fig. 3-12 Sol LeWitt, *Wall Drawing No. 681 C, A wall divided vertically into four equal squares separated and bordered by black bands. Within each square, bands in one of four directions, each with color ink washes superimposed*, 1993. Colored ink washes, image: 10 × 37 ft. National Gallery of Art, Washington, D.C.

Dorothy and Herbert Vogel Collection, Gift of Dorothy Vogel and Herbert Vogel, Trustees, 1993.41.1. Photo © Board of Trustees, National Gallery of Art, Washington, D.C. © 2015 LeWitt Estate/Artists Rights Society (ARS), New York.

imprecise, emotionally charged, and almost chaotic. One seems a product of the mind, the other of the heart. And while van Gogh's line is produced by his own hand, LeWitt's often is not.

LeWitt's works are often generated by museum staff according to LeWitt's instructions. Illustrated here is *Wall Drawing No. 681 C* (**Fig. 3-12**), along with two photographs of the work's installation at the National Gallery of Art in Washington, D.C. in 1993, in this instance by his own studio assistants (**Fig. 3-13**). If a museum "owns" a LeWitt, it does not own the actual wall drawing but only the instructions on how to make it. Since LeWitt often writes his instructions so that the staff executing the drawing must make their own decisions about the placement and arrangement of the lines, the work has a unique appearance each time that a museum or gallery produces it.

LeWitt's drawings usually echo the geometry of the room's architecture, lending the work a sense of mathematical precision and regularity. But it is probably the **grid**, the **pattern** of vertical and horizontal lines crossing one another to make squares, that most characteristically dominates compositions of this variety. The grid's geometric regularity lends a sense of order and unity to any composition. Pat Steir's *The Brueghel Series: A Vanitas of Style* (**Fig. 3-14**) is a case in point. The painting is based on a seventeenth-century still-life painting by Jan Brueghel

Fig. 3-13 Installation of *Wall Drawing No. 681 C*, August 25, 1993. National Gallery of Art, Washington, D.C.

Photo © Board of Trustees, National Gallery of Art, Washington, D.C.

Fig. 3-14 Pat Steir, *The Brueghel Series: A Vanitas of Style*, 1983–84. Oil on canvas, 64 panels, each 26½ × 21 in.
Courtesy of the artist and Cheim & Read.

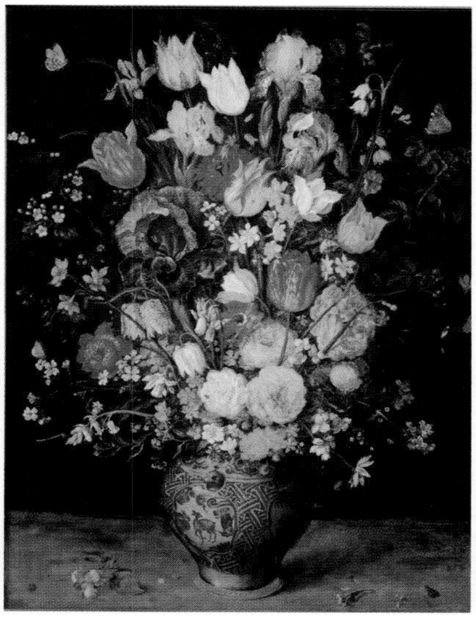

Fig. 3-15 Jan Brueghel the Elder, *Flowers in a Blue Vase*, 1599. Oil on oakwood, 26 × 19⅞ in. Kunsthistorisches Museum, Vienna.
akg-image/Erich Lessing.

the Elder called *Flowers in a Blue Vase* (**Fig. 3-15**). Brueghel's is an example of a ***vanitas*** painting—that is, a reminder that the pleasurable things in life inevitably fade, that the material world is not as long-lived as the spiritual, and, therefore, that the spiritual should command our attention. But the material world is represented in Steir's painting not so much by the standard elements of *vanitas* painting—the fading flowers, for instance—but by painting itself. Steir's *Brueghel Series* is a history of the styles of art. The artist worked for two years to organize her study of style into a series of 64 separate panels, each 26½ × 21 inches. The final composition is approximately 20 feet high. At the top center, one finds an almost perfect reproduction of the original painting by Brueghel. Two panels to the right is a painting in the style of American Abstract Expressionist painter Franz Kline. Jackson Pollock's famous "drip" style is represented in the first panel on the left of the third row. What holds together this variety of styles is the grid, which seems to contain and control them all, as if exercising some sort of rational authority over them. The grid organizes random elements into a coherent system, imposing a sense of logic where none necessarily exists. Steir's history lesson demonstrates that styles come and go, soon fading away only to be replaced by the next. Her painting thus suggests that the pleasures of style are short-lived, even if the pleasures of art might continue on, even without us.

In Steir's *Brueghel Series* some styles are carefully rendered and controlled, others are more loose and free-form—what we call gestural. Often artists use both gestural and controlled lines in the same work.

Fig. 3-16 Hung Liu, *Relic 12*, 2005. Oil on canvas and lacquered wood, 5 ft. 6 in. × 5 ft. 6 in.
Courtesy of Nancy Hoffman Gallery, New York.

In *Relic 12* (**Fig. 3-16**), by the Chinese-born artist Hung Liu, who works today in the United States, the soft, carefully drawn curves of the central figure, and of the butterfly, circles, flowers, and leaves, seem to conspire with the vertical drips of paint that fall softly to the bottom of the canvas like life-giving rain. Hung Liu's work consistently addresses women's place in both pre- and post-revolutionary China (see *The Creative Process*, pp. 60–61). Here, she represents a Chinese courtesan surrounded by symbols from classical Chinese painting, including the circle, or *pi*, the ancient Chinese symbol for the universe, and the butterfly, symbol of change, joy, and love. In front of her, in the red square in the middle of the painting, are Chinese characters meaning "female" and "Nu-Wa." Nu-Wa is the Chinese creation goddess. It was she who created the first humans from the yellow earth, after Heaven and Earth had separated. Since molding each figure individually was too tedious a process, she dipped a rope into mud and then swung it about her, covering the earth around her with lumps of mud. The early handmade figurines became the wealthy and the noble; those that arose from the splashes of mud were the poor and the common. Nu-Wa is worshiped as the intermediary between men and women, as the goddess who grants children, and as the inventor of marriage. Here, Hung Liu's different lines seem to work together to create an image of the wholeness and unity of creation.

With its predominantly vertical and horizontal structures, architecture can lend a sense of order and control to an otherwise chaotic scene. Wenda Gu is known for imaginary calligraphies in which he subverts and abstracts traditional letterforms into scripts that look as if they should be legible but in fact frustrate the viewer's ability to read them. His medium is human hair, which he has collected from around the world and woven into light, semi-transparent calligraphic banners. Beginning in 1993, Gu inaugurated what he has called his *united nations project*, a series of installations at sites around the world designed to challenge notions of distinct national identities and symbolize, through interwoven hair, the compatibility of all people. In 1997 in Hong Kong, a site that for most of the twentieth century the British and Chinese contested to control, he created an installation consisting of a Chinese flag made of Chinese hair, a Union Jack made of British hair, and hair cuttings of Hong Kong citizens scattered across the floor. A year later, at the then PS1 Contemporary Art Center in Brooklyn, New York, he installed *united nations—china monument: temple of heaven* (**Fig. 3-17**). Here, pseudo-script from four different languages—Chinese, English, Hindi, and Arabic—lines the walls and ceiling. The expressive power and gestural freedom of the four calligraphic styles—after all, even English cursive can be expressive, as individual signatures testify—stand in counterpoint to the meaninglessness of the texts themselves. But what organizes this cacophony of languages is the architecture itself. The dimensions of the room, which are readily apparent through the canopy and hanging drapes, are echoed in the vertical and horizontal structure of the tables and chairs, which, in turn, suggest a conference or meeting space in which diverse cultures might communicate—a utopian "united nations" which, as Gu says, "probably can never exist in our reality" but which can "be fully realized in the art world." In fact, this utopian vision is mirrored in the TV monitors embedded in each chair, where a video of the sky—called "heaven" by Gu—constantly plays.

Fig. 3-17 Wenda Gu, *united nations—china monument: temple of heaven*, 1998. Site-specific installation commissioned by the Asia Society, New York for *inside out*, PS1 Contemporary Art Center, New York. Temple of pseudo-English, Chinese, Hindi, and Arabic made of human hair curtains collected from all over the world, 12 Ming-style chairs with television monitors installed in their seats, 2 Ming-style tables, and video film, 13 × 20 × 52 ft. Permanent collection of the Hong Kong Museum of Art, China.
Courtesy of the artist.

The Creative Process

The Drip as Line: Hung Liu's *Three Fujins*

The rainlike drips that fall to the bottom of Hung Liu's *Relic 12* (see Fig. 3-16) are, in fact, a symbol for Liu of her artistic and political liberation. Born in Changchun, China, in 1948, the year that Chairman Mao forced the Nationalist Chinese off the mainland to Taiwan, she lived in China until 1984. Beginning in 1966, during Mao's Cultural Revolution, she worked for four years as a peasant in the fields. Successfully "reeducated" by the working class, she returned to Beijing where she studied, and later taught, painting of a strict Russian Social Realist style—propaganda portraits of Mao's new society that employed a precise and hard-edged line. But this way of drawing and painting constricted Hung Liu's artistic sensibility. In 1980, she applied for a passport to study painting in the United States, and in 1984 her request was granted. An extraordinarily independent spirit, raised and educated in a society that values social conformity above individual identity, Liu depends as a painter on the interplay between the line she was trained to paint and a new, freer line more closely aligned to Western abstraction but tied to ancient Chinese traditions as well.

During the Cultural Revolution, Liu had begun photographing peasant families, not for herself, but as gifts for the villagers. She has painted from photographs ever since, particularly archival photographs that she has discovered on research trips back to China in both 1991 and 1993. "I am not copying photographs," she explains. "I release information from them. There's a tiny bit of information there—the photograph was taken in a very short moment, maybe 1/100 or 1/150 of a second—and I look for clues. The clues give me an excuse to do things." In other words, for Liu, to paint from a photograph is to liberate something locked inside it. For example, the disfigured feet of the woman in *Virgin/Vessel* (**Fig. 3-18**) are the result of traditional Chinese foot-binding. Unable to walk, even upper-class women were forced into prostitution after Mao's Revolution resulted in the confiscation

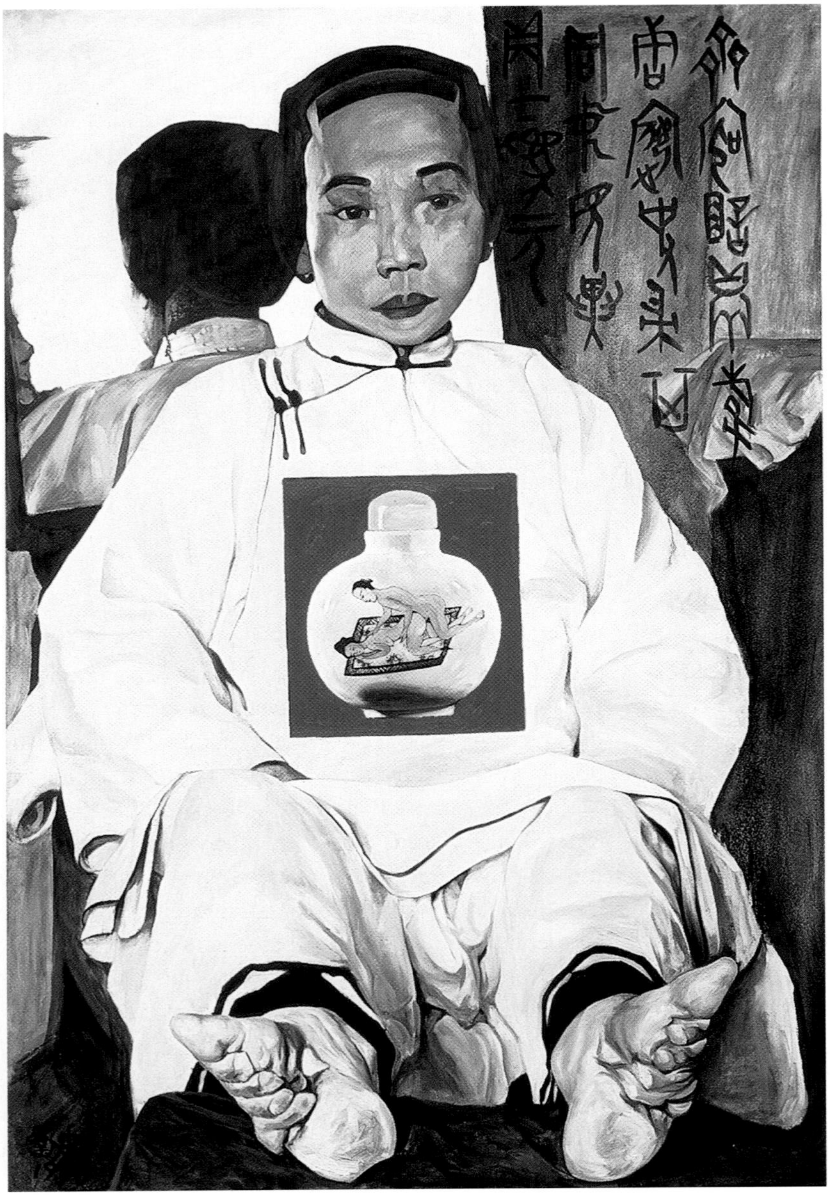

Fig. 3-18 Hung Liu, *Virgin/Vessel*, 1990. Oil on canvas, broom, 6 × 4 ft. Collection of Bernice and Harold Steinbaum.
Courtesy of Nancy Hoffman Gallery, New York.

Fig. 3-19 Hung Liu, *Three Fujins*, 1995. Oil on canvas, bird cages, 8 ft. × 10 ft. 6 in. × 12 in. Private collection, Washington, D.C.
Courtesy of Nancy Hoffman Gallery, New York.

of their material possessions and left them without servants to transport them. In the painting, the woman's body has become a sexual vessel, like the one in front of her. She is completely isolated and vulnerable.

Three Fujins (**Fig. 3-19**) is also a depiction of women bound by the system in which they live. The Fujins were concubines in the royal court at the end of the nineteenth century. Hanging in front of each of them is an actual birdcage, purchased by Liu in San Francisco's Chinatown, symbolizing the women's spiritual captivity. But even the excessively unified formality of their pose—its perfect balance, its repetitious rhythms—belies their submission to the rule of tyrannical social forces. These women have given themselves up—and made themselves up—in order to fit into their proscribed roles. Liu sees the composition of the image as symbolizing "relationships of power, and I want to dissolve them in my paintings."

Speaking of *Three Fujins*, Liu explains how that dissolution takes place, specifically in terms of her use of line: "Contrast is very important. If you don't have contrast, everything just cancels each other thing out. So I draw, very carefully, and then I let the paint drip—two kinds of contrasting line." One is controlled, the line representing power, and the other is free, liberated. "Linseed oil is very thick," Liu goes on, "it drips very slowly, sometimes overnight. You don't know when you leave what's going to be there in the morning. You hope for the best. You plant your seed. You work hard. But for the harvest, you have to wait." The drip, she says, gives her "a sense of liberation, of freedom from what I've been painting. I could never have done this work in China. But the real Chinese traditions—landscape painters, calligraphers—are pretty crazy. My drip is closer to the real Chinese tradition than my training. It's part of me, the deeply rooted traditional Chinese ways."

Fig. 3-20 Jacques-Louis David, *The Death of Socrates*, 1787. Oil on canvas, 4 ft. 3 in. × 6 ft. 5¼ in. Metropolitan Museum of Art, New York.
Catherine Lorillard Wolfe Collection, Wolfe Fund, 1931.45. © 2015. Image copyright Metropolitan Museum of Art/Art Resource/Scala, Florence.

Line Orientation

Most viewers react instinctively to the expressive qualities of line, and these expressive qualities are closely associated with their orientation in the composition. Linear arrangements that emphasize the horizontal and vertical possess a certain architectural stability, that of mathematical, rational control. The deliberate, precise arrangement of Jacques-Louis David's *Death of Socrates* (**Fig. 3-20**) is especially apparent in his charcoal study for the painting (**Fig. 3-21**). David portrays Socrates, the father of philosophy, about to drink deadly hemlock after the Greek state convicted him of corrupting his students, the youth of Athens, by his teaching. In the preliminary drawing, David has submitted the figure of Socrates to a mathematical grid of parallels and perpendiculars that survives into the final painting. The body of the philosopher is turned toward the viewer. This frontal pose is at an angle of 90 degrees to the profile poses of most of the other figures in the composition—at a right angle, that is, that corresponds in three dimensions to the two-dimensional grid structure of the composition. Right angles in fact dominate the painting. Socrates, for instance, points upward with his left hand in a gesture that is at a right angle to his shoulders. Notice especially the gridwork of stone blocks that form the wall behind the figures in the final painting. The human body

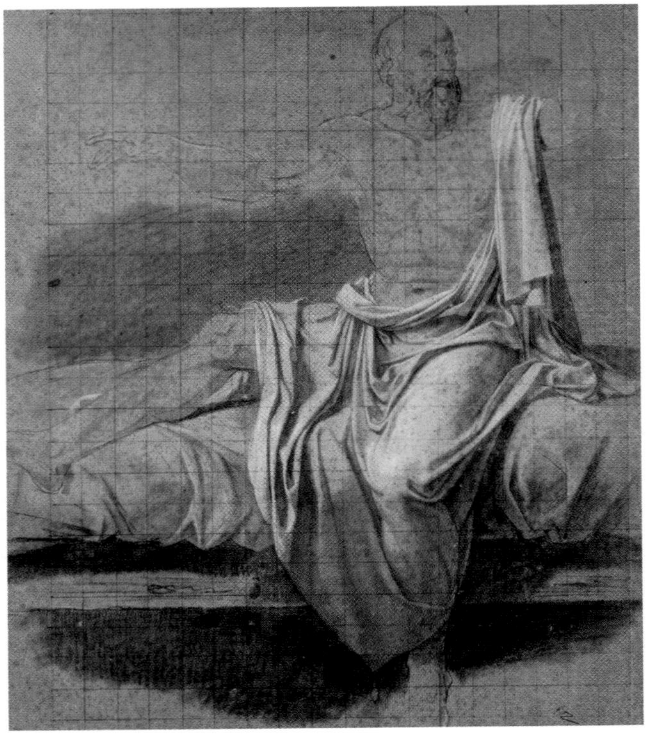

Fig. 3-21 Jacques-Louis David, *Study for the Death of Socrates*, 1787. Charcoal heightened in white on gray-brown paper, 20½ × 17 in. Musée Bonnat, Bayonne, France.
Inv. NI513; AI1890. Photo © RMN.

and the drama of Socrates' suicide are submitted by David to a highly rational order, as if to insist on the rationality of Socrates' actions.

The structure and control evident in David's line are underscored by comparing his work to the diagonal recession and lack of a grid in Eugène Delacroix's much more emotional and Romantic *Study for The Death of Sardanapalus* (**Fig. 3-23**). (The term Romantic, often used to describe nineteenth-century art such as Delacroix's, does not refer just to the expression of love, but also to the expression of all feelings and passions.) The finished painting (**Fig. 3-22**) shows Sardanapalus, the last king of the second Assyrian dynasty at the end of the ninth century BCE, who was besieged in his city by an enemy army. He ordered all his horses, dogs, servants, and wives to be slain before him, and all his belongings destroyed, so that none of his pleasures would survive him when his kingdom was overthrown. The drawing is a study for the

Fig. 3-22 Eugène Delacroix, *The Death of Sardanapalus*, 1827. Oil on canvas, 12 ft. 1½ in. × 16 ft. 2⅞ in. Musée du Louvre, Paris.
Inv. RF2346. Photo © RMN-Grand Palais (musée du Louvre)/Hervé Lewandowski.

Fig. 3-23 Eugène Delacroix, *Study for The Death of Sardanapalus*, 1827.
Pen, watercolor, and pencil, 10¼ × 12½ in. Cabinet des Dessins, Musée du Louvre, Paris.
Inv. RF5274-recto. Photo © RMN-Grand Palais (musée du Louvre)/Thierry Le Mage.

lower corner of the bed, with its elephant-head bedpost, and, below it, on the floor, a pile of jewelry and musical instruments. The figure of the nude leaning back against the bed in the finished work, perhaps already dead, can be seen at the right-hand edge of the study. Delacroix's line is quick, imprecise, and fluid. A flurry of curves and swirls, organized in a diagonal recession from the lower right to the upper left, dominates the study. And this same dynamic quality—a sense of movement and agitation, not, as in David's *Death of Socrates*, stability and calm—is retained in the composition of the final painting. It seems almost chaotic in its accumulation of detail, and its diagonal orientation seems almost dizzyingly unstable. Delacroix's line, finally, is as compositionally disorienting as his subject is emotionally disturbing.

THE CRITICAL PROCESS

Thinking about Line

Line is, in summation, an extremely versatile element. Thick or thin, short or long, straight or curved, line can outline shapes and forms, indicate the contour of a volume, and imply direction and movement. Lines of sight can connect widely separated parts of a composition and direct the viewer's eye across it. Depending on how it is oriented, line can seem extremely intellectual and rational or highly emotional. It is, above all, the artist's most basic tool.

It should come as no surprise, then, that the biases of our culture are, naturally, reflected in the uses artists make of line. Especially in the depiction of human anatomy, certain cultural assumptions have come to be associated with line. Conventionally, vertical and horizontal geometries have been closely identified with the male form—as in David's *Death of Socrates* (see Fig. 3-20). More loose and gestural lines seem less clear, less "logical," more emotional and intuitive, and traditionally have been identified with the female form. In other words, conventional representations of the male and female nude carry with them recognizably sexist implications—man as strong and rational, woman as weak and given to emotional outbursts.

These conventions have been challenged by many contemporary artists. Compare, for instance, a Greek bronze (**Fig. 3-24**), identified by some as Zeus, king of the Greek gods, and by others as Poseidon, Greek god of the sea, and Robert Mapplethorpe's photograph of Lisa Lyon (**Fig. 3-25**), winner of the first IFBB World Women's Bodybuilding Championship in Los Angeles in 1979. The Greek bronze has been submitted to very nearly the same mathematical grid as David's Socrates. The pose that Lyon assumes seems to imitate that of the Greek bronze. In what ways does the orientation of line, in the Mapplethorpe photograph, suggest a feminist critique of Western cultural traditions? How does Lyon subvert our expectations of these traditions, and how does the use of line contribute to our understanding of her intentions?

Fig. 3-24 *Zeus*, or *Poseidon*, ca. 460 BCE. Bronze, height 6 ft. 10 in. National Archaeological Museum, Athens.
Inv. 15161. © Craig & Marie Mauzy, Athens.

Fig. 3-25 Robert Mapplethorpe, *Lisa Lyon*, 1982.
Used by permission of Art + Commerce. © Robert Mapplethorpe Foundation.

Thinking Back

3.1 Distinguish among outline, contour, and implied line.

Line is used to indicate the edge of a two-dimensional (flat) shape or a three-dimensional form. A contour line is the perceived line that marks the border of an object in space. How do contour lines differ from outlines? What is an implied line? How does it function in Titian's *Assumption and Consecration of the Virgin*?

3.2 Describe the different qualities that lines might possess.

Line can also possess intellectual, emotional, and expressive qualities. How does Vincent van Gogh use line in *The Starry Night*? What does it mean for line to be autographic? What qualities are implied by a grid? What function does the drip serve in Hung Liu's work?

Linear arrangements that emphasize the horizontal and vertical tend to possess an architectural stability. How does Wenda Gu take advantage of this? Linear works that emphasize the horizontal and vertical differ from those works that stress expressive line, which, by contrast, inspire the viewer's instinctive reactions. How does Jacques-Louis David's use of line differ from Eugène Delacroix's? What does the term "Romantic" mean when discussing nineteenth-century art?

Chapter 4
Shape and Space

Learning Objectives

4.1 Differentiate between shape and mass.

4.2 Describe how three-dimensional space is represented on a flat surface using perspective.

4.3 Explain why modern artists have challenged the means of representing three dimensions on two-dimensional surfaces.

Berliner Plätze (**Fig. 4-1**), a painting by Julie Mehretu, began, as most paintings do, as a flat shape. In mathematical terms, a **shape** is a two-dimensional area—that is, its boundaries can be measured in terms of height and width. The painter's task is to build up a sense of depth on the flat surface of the canvas shape, and reflected in the depth of Mehretu's painting is her own transitional life. Ethiopian-born, she moved to the United States when she was six, grew up in Michigan, and has since worked in Senegal, Berlin, and New York. Her work thus investigates what she calls "the multifaceted layers of place, space, and time that impact the formation of personal and communal identity." These layers of place, space, and time emerge from the flat shape of the canvas.

In *Berliner Plätze*, she has projected views of the nineteenth-century buildings surrounding various squares (*Plätze*) in Berlin onto the canvas, often layering one over another and sometimes, as at the bottom right, tracing them upside down. These are overlaid in turn with broad white lines that might be, for instance, an aerial view of an airport's runways seen from various heights and points of view. "As the works progress," Mehretu has explained, "the more the information is layered in a way that's hard to decipher what is what. And that's intentional. It's almost like a screening out, creating a kind of skin or layer." In her rendering of the Berlin buildings, Mehretu uses one of the most convincing means of representing actual depth of space on a flat surface—perspective. **Perspective** is a system, known to the Greeks and Romans but not mathematically codified until the Renaissance, that, in the simplest terms, allows the picture plane—the flat surface of the canvas—to function as a window through which a specific scene is presented to the viewer. Thus, Mehretu's painting is not only composed of different layers of painting, but her renderings of Berlin's public squares create the illusion of real space on the flat shape of the canvas.

The painting is one of seven commissioned by Deutsche Bank and the Guggenheim Museum which are known as a group as *Grey Area*, a title that refers to that "in-between" space where things are neither clearly black or white, nor right or wrong, but ambiguous and

Fig. 4-1 Julie Mehretu, *Berliner Plätze*, 2008–09. Ink and acrylic on canvas, 10 × 14 ft. Commissioned by Deutsche Bank AG in consultation with the Solomon R. Guggenheim Foundation for the Deutsche Guggenheim, Berlin.

undefined. (Mehretu talks about working on this series in the art21 *Exclusive* video "Julie Mehretu: Workday.") As a group, the paintings are meant to suggest the sheer complexity of creating and negotiating communal space in the contemporary world.

If we sometimes feel caught up in Mehretu's "grey area," we are at least superficially familiar with the simpler physical parameters of our world, which, together with line, shape and space, are among the most familiar terms we use to describe the physical nature of the world around us. Space is all around us, all the time. We talk about "outer" space (the space beyond our world) and "inner" space (the space inside our own minds). We cherish our own "space." We give "space" to people or things that scare us. But in the twenty-first century, space has become an increasingly contested issue. Since Einstein, we have come to recognize that the space in which we live is fluid. Not only does it take place in time, we are able to move in it and across it with far greater ease than ever before. Today, an even newer kind of space—the space of mass media, the Internet, the computer screen, and cyberspace, as well as the migration of the mind across and through these virtual arenas—is asserting itself. This new kind of space results, as we shall see, in new arenas for artistic exploration. But, first, we need to describe some of the basic tools that artists use in dealing with shape and space in both two- and three-dimensional forms.

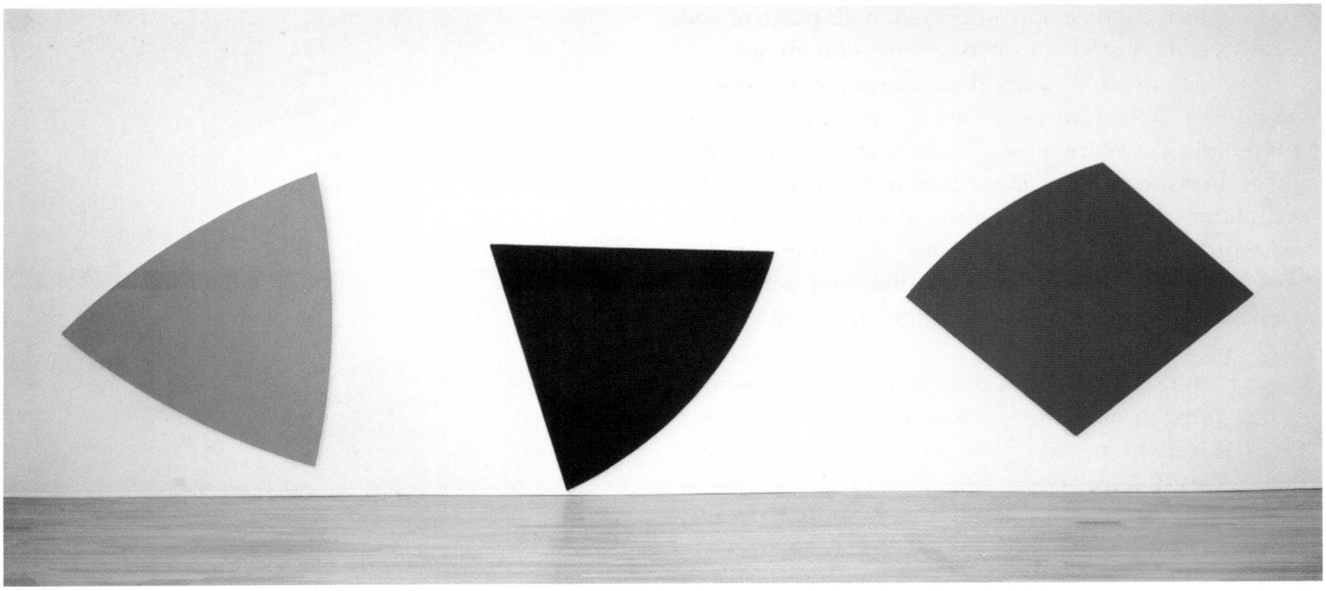

Fig. 4-2 Ellsworth Kelly, *Three Panels: Orange, Dark Gray, Green*, 1986. Oil on canvas, overall 9 ft. 8 in. × 34 ft. 4½ in. Museum of Modern Art, New York.
Gift of Douglas S. Cramer Foundation, 776. 1995.a-c.

Shape and Mass

How does shape differ from mass?

Shape is a fundamental property of two-dimensional art. Ellsworth Kelly's *Three Panels: Orange, Dark Gray, Green* (**Fig. 4-2**) consists of one trapezoidal and two triangular shapes set across the length of a 34-foot stretch of wall. Kelly thought of the wall itself as if it were a large canvas, and of his panels as flat shapes applied to that canvas. The three shapes, composed of both curved and straight lines and spaced unevenly both horizontally and vertically, seem to dance across the wall in a fluid animation.

The instant Kelly placed his shapes on the wall, the wall became what we call the ground, the surface upon which the work is made, and what we call a **figure-ground relation** was established. Of course, the figures here also establish two shapes between them (with implied lines running from the top and bottom corners of each figure serving to define these two shapes). These shapes are known as **negative shapes**, while the figures that command our attention are known as **positive shapes**. Consider, however, this more dynamic figure-ground relationship (**Fig. 4-3**). At first glance, the figure appears to be a black vase resting on a white ground. But the image also contains the figure of two heads resting on a black ground. Such figure-ground rever-

Fig. 4-3 Rubin vase.

sals help us recognize how important both positive and negative shapes are to our perception of an image.

As distinguished from a shape, a **mass**—or form—is a solid that occupies a three-dimensional volume. If shapes are measured in terms of height and width, masses must be measured in terms of height, width, and depth. Though mass also implies density and weight, in the simplest terms, the difference between a shape and a mass is the difference between a square and a cube, a triangle and a cone, and a circle and a sphere.

A photograph cannot quite reproduce the experience of being in the same space as Martin Puryear's *Self* (**Fig. 4-4**), a sculptural mass that stands nearly 6 feet high. Made of wood, it looms out of the floor like a giant basalt outcropping, and it seems to satisfy the other implied meanings of mass—that is, it seems to possess weight and density as well as volume. From Puryear's point of view, the piece looks as if it were a rock worn smooth by the forces of nature—water, sand, and weather—analogous to the idea of a self that has been shaped by the forces of its own history, a history evidenced in its smooth facade, but which remains unstated. In fact, it does not possess the mass it visually announces. It is actually very lightweight, built of thin layers of wood over a hollow core. This hidden, almost secret fragility is the "self" of Puryear's title.

Fig. 4-4 Martin Puryear, *Self*, 1978. Polychromed red cedar and mahogany, 5 ft. 9 in. × 4 ft. × 25 in. Joslyn Art Museum, Omaha.
Museum purchase in memory of Elinor Ashton, 1980.63. © Martin Puryear.

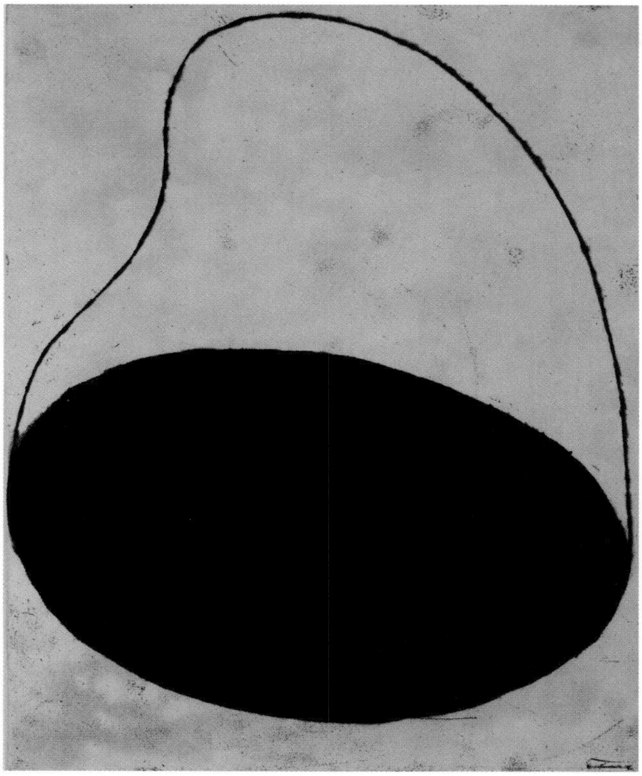

Fig. 4-5 Martin Puryear, *Untitled IV*, 2002. Soft-ground and spitbite etching with drypoint and *Chine-collé* Gampi, 8⅝ × 6⅞ in. Paulson Bott Press, San Francisco.
© Martin Puryear.

Beginning in 2001, Puryear began to work regularly at Paulson Bott Press in San Francisco to recreate his three-dimensional sculptures in the two-dimensional medium of printmaking (for an example of the opposite process, see *The Creative Process*, pp. 70–71). In the art21 *Exclusive* video "Martin Puryear: Printmaking," he describes how different it has been for him to work in two dimensions after have worked for many years solely in sculptural terms. "I try to make work that's about the ideas in the sculpture," he says, "without making pictures of the sculpture." In many ways the black oval form at the base of *Untitled IV* (**Fig. 4-5**), then, is the hidden, hollow core of *Self*.

The Creative Process

From Two to Three Dimensions: Umberto Boccioni's *Development of a Bottle in Space*

In February 1909, an Italian poet named Filippo Marinetti published in the French newspaper *Le Figaro* a manifesto announcing a new movement in modern art, **Futurism**. Marinetti called for an art that would champion "aggressive action, a feverish insomnia, the racer's stride . . . the punch and the slap." He had discovered, he wrote, "a new beauty; the beauty of speed. A racing car whose hood is adorned with great pipes, like serpents of explosive breath . . . is more beautiful than the *Victory of Samothrace*." He promised to "destroy the museums, libraries, academies" and "sing of the multicolored, polyphonic tides of revolution in the modern capitals." These pronouncements proved particularly appealing to Umberto Boccioni, an Italian sculptor who was himself frustrated with the state of sculpture in the first decades of the twentieth century. In all the sculpture of his day, he wrote in his own "Technical Manifesto of Futurist Sculpture" in 1912,

> *we see the perpetuation of the same old kind of misapprehension: an artist copies a nude or studies classical statues with the naive conviction that here he will find a style that equates to modern sensibility without stepping outside the traditional concepts of sculpture. . . . An art that must take all the clothes off a man or woman in order to produce any emotive effect is a dead art!*

"Destroy the systematic nude!" he proclaimed. But he was not quite sure just what should take its place.

Boccioni was, first of all, convinced that no object exists in space on its own. Rather, it is coexistent with its surroundings, and its surroundings determine how it is seen and understood. Two years earlier, in "Futurist Painting: Technical Manifesto," which he co-authored with four other Futurist artists, he had declared:

> *How often have we not seen upon the cheek of the person with whom we are talking the horse which passes at the end of the street. Our bodies penetrate the sofas upon which we sit, and the sofas penetrate our bodies. The motor bus rushes into the houses which it passes, and in their turn the houses throw themselves upon the motor bus and are blended with it.*

To demonstrate this principle, Boccioni made a drawing of a glass bottle resting upon a table, with a drinking glass in front of it (**Fig. 4-6**). The choice of the glass and bottle was a crucial one, for through their semi-transparent surfaces one can see the table behind and beneath them, a large white plate set just to their left, a house in the distance above them and to the left, and most especially the other side of the glass and bottle themselves, which Boccioni has rendered in a series of spiraling lines, as if both bottle and glass were rotating around upon themselves. Boccioni has thus rendered the bottle in volumetric

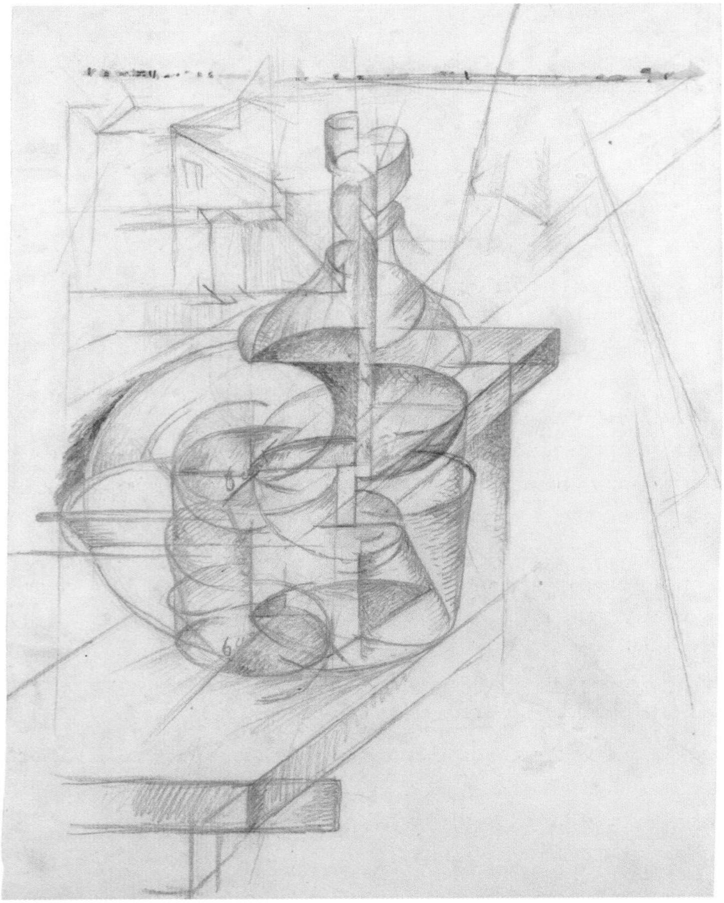

Fig. 4-6 Umberto Boccioni, *Table + Bottle + House*, 1912. Pencil on paper, 13⅛ × 9⅜ in. Civico Gabinetto dei Desegni, Castello Sforzesco, Milan.

Fig. 4-7 Umberto Boccioni, *Development of a Bottle in Space*, 1913. Bronze, 15½ × 23¾ × 15½ in. Metropolitan Museum of Art, New York.
Bequest of Lydia Winston Malbin, 1990.38. © 2015. Image copyright Metropolitan Museum of Art/Art Resource/Scala, Florence.

terms in the two-dimensional medium of pencil on paper. The drawing is a metaphor for "knowing," exposing the limitations of a single point of view. We can only know an object fully if we can see it from all sides, and, as we circle it, we see it against first one backdrop then another and another.

It seems almost inevitable that Boccioni would feel compelled to actually realize his bottle in three-dimensional form (**Fig. 4-7**). In the sculptural version of *Development of a Bottle in Space*, the bottle is splayed open to reveal a series of concentric shells or half-cylinders. Made of solid bronze, it is no longer transparent, as in the drawing, but it invites us to move around it, to see it from all sides. The table on which it rests seems to tilt and lean, suggesting a certain instability at odds with the solidity of the bronze itself.

Boccioni created two versions of the work, a white plaster model titled *Development of a Bottle in Space Through Form*, and an identical plaster model but this time in bright red, titled *Development of a Bottle in Space Through Color*. He evidently felt that our visual experience of the sculpture was radically altered by the addition of color, which also masked something of its form. The original white plaster model belonged to the Marinetti family until 1952 when it was donated to the museum of the University of São Paulo, Brazil. The red model was destroyed in 1917. The numerous extant bronze castings, by which we know the work today, were all executed after Boccioni's death.

Negative Space

Barbara Hepworth's sculpture *Two Figures* (**Fig. 4-8**) invites the viewer to look at it up close. It consists of two standing vertical masses that occupy three-dimensional space in a manner similar to standing human forms. (See, for example, the sculpture's similarity to the standing forms of Fig. 12-9.) Into each of these figures Hepworth has carved **negative spaces**, so called because they are empty spaces that acquire a sense of volume and form by means of the outline or frame that surrounds them. Hepworth has painted these negative spaces white. Especially in the left-hand figure, the negative spaces suggest anatomical features: The top round indentation suggests a head, the middle hollow a breast, and the bottom hole a belly, with the elmwood wrapping around the figure like a cloak.

The negative space formed by the bowl of the ceremonial spoon of the Dan people native to Liberia and the Ivory Coast (**Fig. 4-9**) likewise suggests anatomy. Nearly a foot in length and called the "belly pregnant with rice," the bowl represents the generosity of the most hospitable woman of the clan, who is known as the *wunkirle*. The *wunkirle* carries this spoon at festivals, where she dances and sings. As *wunkirles* from other clans arrive, the festivals become competitions, each woman striving to give away more than the others. Finally, the most generous *wunkirle* of all is proclaimed, and the men sing in her honor. The spoon represents the power of the imagination to transform an everyday object into a symbolically charged container of social good.

The world that we live in (our homes, our streets, our cities) has been carved out of three-dimensional

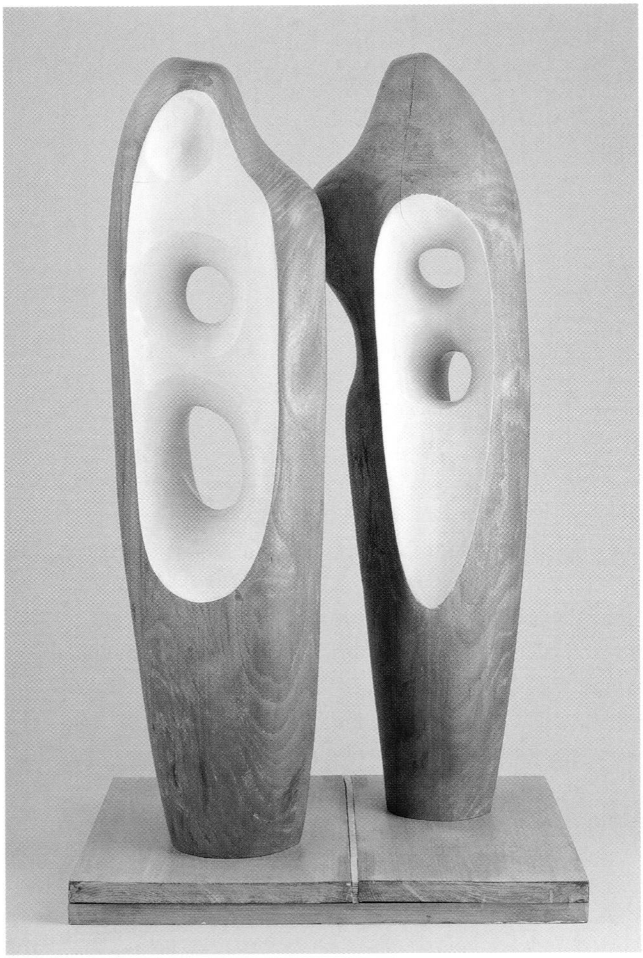

Fig. 4-8 Barbara Hepworth, *Two Figures*, 1947–48. Elmwood and white paint, 38 × 17 in. Frederick R. Weisman Art Museum, University of Minnesota.
Gift of John Rood Sculpture Collection. © Bowness.

Fig. 4-9 Feast-making spoon (*wunkirmian*), Liberia/Ivory Coast. Wood, height 18⅛ in. Private collection.
Photo © Heini Schneebeli/Bridgeman Images.

space, that is, the space of the natural world, which itself possesses height, width, and depth. A building surrounds empty space in such a way as to frame it or outline it. Walls shape the space they contain, and rooms acquire a sense of volume and form. The great cathedrals of the late medieval era were designed especially to elicit from the viewer a sense of awe at the sheer magnitude of the space they contained. Extremely high naves carried the viewer's gaze upward in a gravity-defying flight of vision. The nave of Reims Cathedral in France (**Fig. 4-10**) is 125 feet high. If you were to visit the site, you would not only experience the magnitude of the space, but also see how that magnitude is heightened by the quality of golden light that fills the space. In fact, light can contribute significantly to our sense of space. Think of the space in a room as a kind of negative space created by the architecture. Danish artist Olafur Eliasson seems to fill this space with color in his 1995 installation *Suney* (**Fig. 4-11**). Actually, he has bisected a gallery with a yellow sheet of Mylar (stretched polyester). The side of the gallery in which the viewer stands seems bathed in natural light, while the opposite side seems filled with yellow light. There are separate entrances at each end of the space and, if viewers change sides, their experience of the two spaces is reversed.

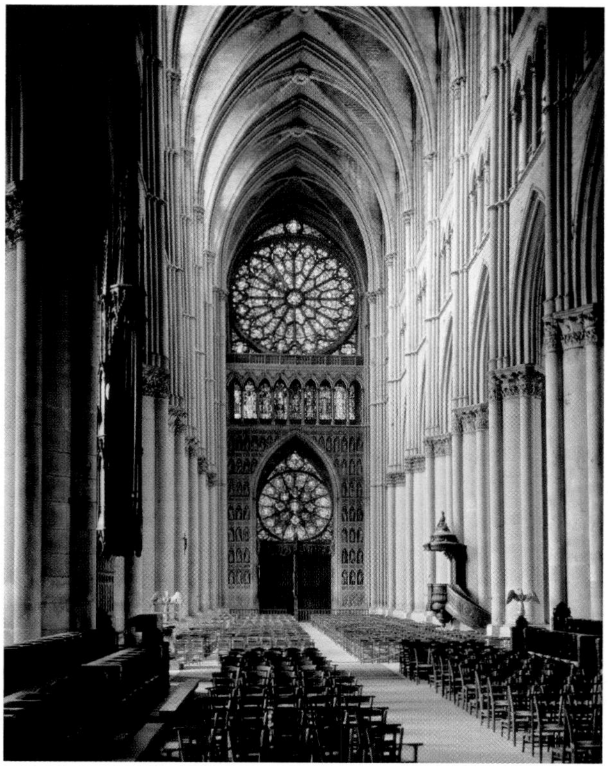

Fig. 4-10 Nave, Reims Cathedral, begun 1211; nave ca. 1220. View to the west.

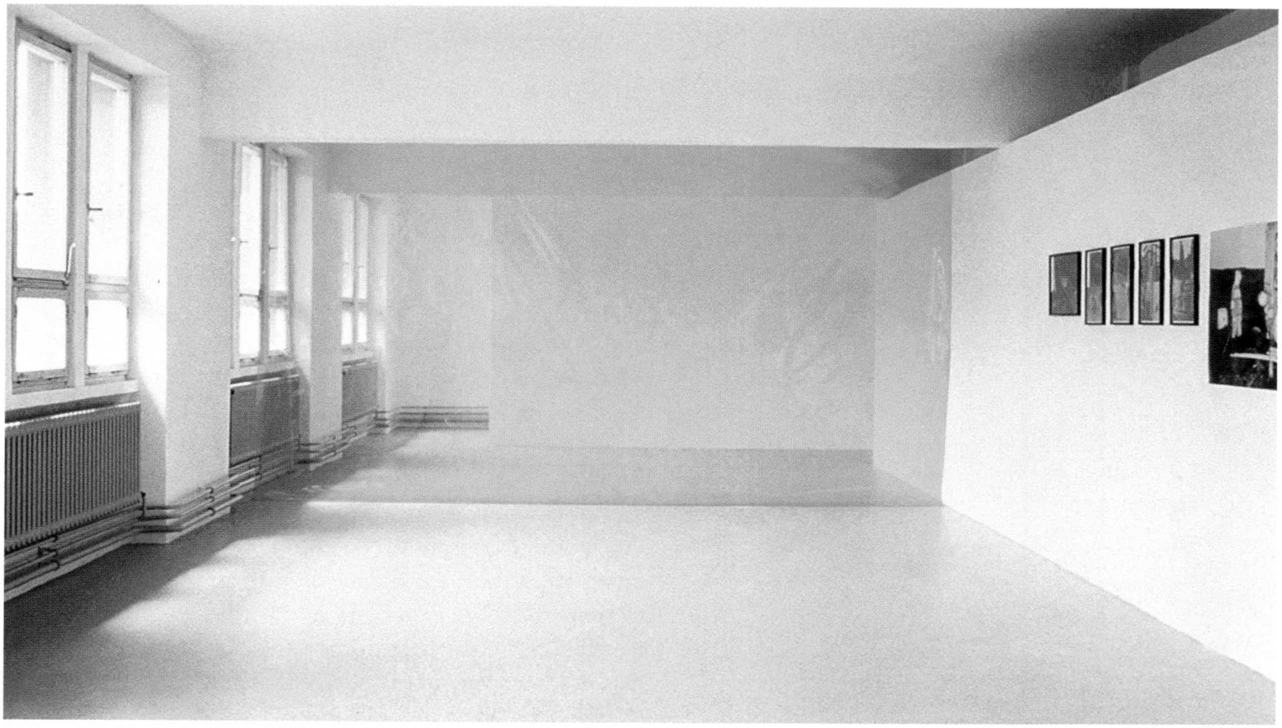

Fig. 4-11 Olafur Eliasson, *Suney*, 1995. Installation view, Künstlerhaus Stuttgart, Germany.
Courtesy of the artist, Tanya Bonakdar Gallery, New York, and Neugerriemschneider, Berlin.

Representing Three-Dimensional Space in Two Dimensions

How do artists use perspective to represent three-dimensional space?

Many artists work in both two- and three-dimensional forms. But in order to create a sense of depth, of three dimensions, on a flat canvas or paper the artist must rely on some form of visual illusion.

There are many ways to create the illusion of deep space, and most are used simultaneously, as in Steve DiBenedetto's *Deliverance* (**Fig. 4-12**). For example, we recognize that objects close to us appear larger than objects farther away, so that the juxtaposition of a large and a small helicopter suggests deep space between them. Overlapping images also create the illusion that one object is in front of the other in space: The helicopters appear to be closer to us than the elaborately decorated red launching or landing pad below. And because we are looking down on the scene, a sense of deep space is further suggested. The use of line also adds to the illusion as the tightly packed, finer lines of the round pad pull the eye inward. The presence of a shadow supplies yet another visual clue that the figures possess dimensionality. (We will look closely at how the effect of light creates believable space in Chapter 5.) Even though the image is highly abstract and decorative, we are still able to read it as representing objects in three-dimensional space.

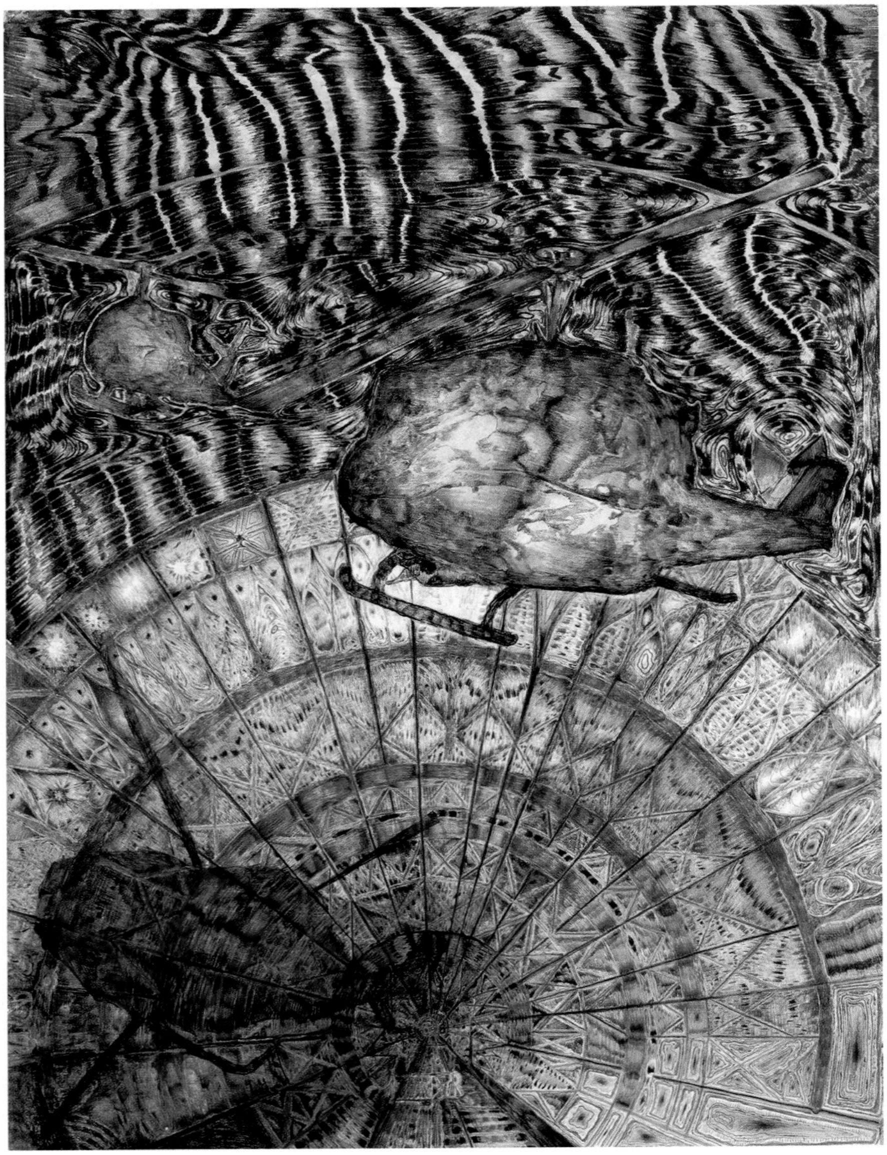

Fig. 4-12 Steve DiBenedetto, *Deliverance*, 2003. Colored pencil and acrylic paint on paper, 30⅛ × 22½ in.

Linear Perspective

The overlapping images in DiBenedetto's work evoke certain principles of perspective, one of the most convincing means of representing three-dimensional space on a two-dimensional surface. In **one-point linear perspective** (**Fig. 4-13**), lines are drawn on the picture plane in such a way as to represent parallel lines receding to a single point on the viewer's horizon, called the **vanishing point**. As the two examples in the diagram make clear, when the vanishing point is directly across from the viewer's **vantage point** (that is, where the viewer is positioned), the recession is said to be **frontal**. If the vanishing point is to one side or the other, the recession is said to be **diagonal**.

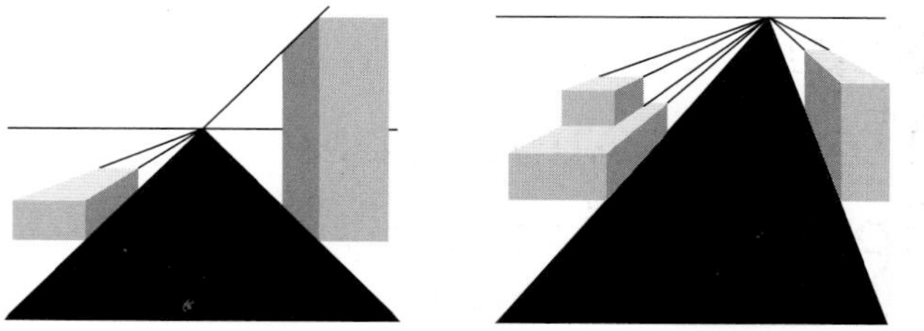

Fig. 4-13 One-point linear perspective. Left: frontal recession, street level. Right: diagonal recession, elevated position.

To judge the effectiveness of linear perspective as a system capable of creating the illusion of real space on a two-dimensional surface, we need only look at an example of a work painted before linear perspective was fully understood and then compare it to works in which the system is successfully employed. Commissioned in 1308, Duccio's *Maestà* ("Majesty") *Altarpiece* was an enormous composition—its central panel alone was 7 feet high and 13½ feet wide. Many smaller scenes depicting the Life of the Virgin and the Life and Passion of Christ appear on both the front and back of the work. In one of these smaller panels, depicting the *Annunciation of the Death of the Virgin* (**Fig. 4-14**), in which the Angel Gabriel warns the Virgin of her impending death, Duccio is evidently attempting to grasp the principles of perspective intuitively. At the top, the walls and ceiling beams all converge at a single vanishing point above the Virgin's head. But the moldings at the base of the arches in the doorways recede to a vanishing point at her hands, while the base of the reading stand, the left side of the bench, and the baseboard at the right converge on a point beneath her hands. Other lines converge on no vanishing point at all. Duccio has attempted to create a realistic space in which to place his figures,

Fig. 4-14 Perspective analysis of Duccio, *Annunciation of the Death of the Virgin*, from the *Maestà Altarpiece*, 1308–11. Tempera on panel, 16⅜ × 21¼ in. Museo dell'Opera del Duomo, Siena.
Canali Photobank, Milan, Italy.

Fig. 4-15 Leonardo da Vinci, *The Last Supper*, ca. 1495–98. Mural (oil and tempera on plaster), 15 ft. 1⅛ in. × 28 ft. 10½ in. Refectory, Monastery of Santa Maria delle Grazie, Milan.

but he does not quite succeed. This is especially evident in his treatment of the reading stand and bench. In true perspective, the top and bottom of the reading stand would not be parallel, as they are here, but would converge to a single vanishing point. Similarly, the right side of the bench is splayed out awkwardly to the right and seems to crawl up and into the wall.

By way of contrast, the space of Leonardo da Vinci's famous depiction of the Last Supper (**Fig. 4-15**) is completely convincing. Leonardo employs a fully frontal one-point perspective system, as the perspective analysis shows (**Fig. 4-16**). This system focuses our attention on Christ, since the perspective lines appear almost as rays of light radiating from Christ's head. During its restoration, a small nail hole was discovered in Christ's temple, just to the left of his right eye. Leonardo evidently drew strings out from this nail to create the perspectival space. *The Last Supper* itself is a wall painting created in the refectory—dining hall—of the monastery of Santa Maria delle Grazie in Milan, Italy. Because the painting's architecture appears to be continuous with the actual architecture of the refectory, it seems as if the world outside the space of the painting is organized around Christ as well. Everything in the architecture of the painting and the refectory draws our attention to him. His gaze controls the world.

Fig. 4-16 Perspective analysis of Leonardo da Vinci, *The Last Supper*, ca. 1495–98.

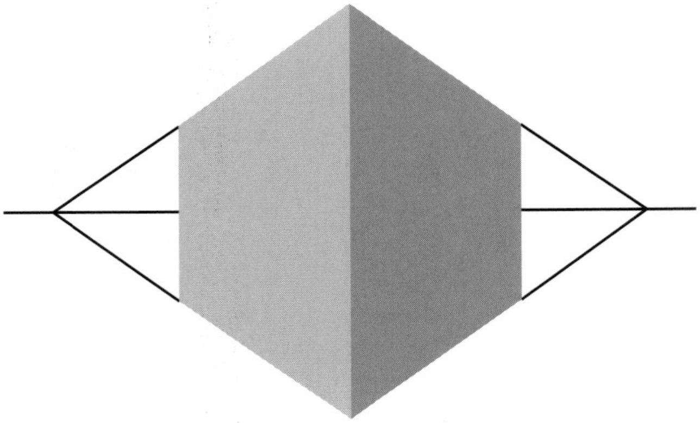

Fig. 4-17 Two-point linear perspective.

Fig. 4-18 Gustave Caillebotte, *Place de l'Europe on a Rainy Day*, 1876–77. Oil on canvas, 6 ft. 11½ in. × 9 ft. ¾ in. The Art Institute of Chicago.
Charles H. and Mary F. S. Worcester Collection, 1964.336. Photo © 2015 Art Institute of Chicago. All Rights Reserved.

When there are two vanishing points in a composition—that is, when an artist uses **two-point linear perspective** (**Fig. 4-17**)—a more dynamic composition often results. The building in the left half of Gustave Caillebotte's *Place de l'Europe on a Rainy Day* (**Fig. 4-18**) is realized by means of two-point linear perspective, but Caillebotte uses perspective to create a much more complex composition. A series of multiple vanishing points organize a complex array of parallel lines emanating from the intersection of the five Paris streets depicted (**Fig. 4-19**). Moving across and through these perspective lines are the implied lines of the pedestrians' movements across the street and square and down the sidewalk in both directions, as well as the line of sight created by the glance of the two figures walking toward the viewer. Caillebotte imposes order on this scene by dividing the canvas into four equal rectangles formed by the vertical lamppost and the horizon line.

Fig. 4-19 Line analysis of Gustave Caillebotte, *Place de l'Europe on a Rainy Day*, 1876–77.
Charles H. and Mary F. S. Worcester Collection, 1964.336. Photo © 2015 Art Institute of Chicago. All Rights Reserved.

Distortions of Space and Foreshortening

The space created by means of linear perspective is closely related to the space created by photography, the medium we accept as representing "real" space with the highest degree of accuracy. The picture drawn in perspective and the photograph both employ a monocular, that is, one-eyed, point of view that defines the picture plane as the base of a pyramid, the apex of which is the single lens or eye. Our actual vision, however, is binocular. We see with both eyes. If you hold your finger up

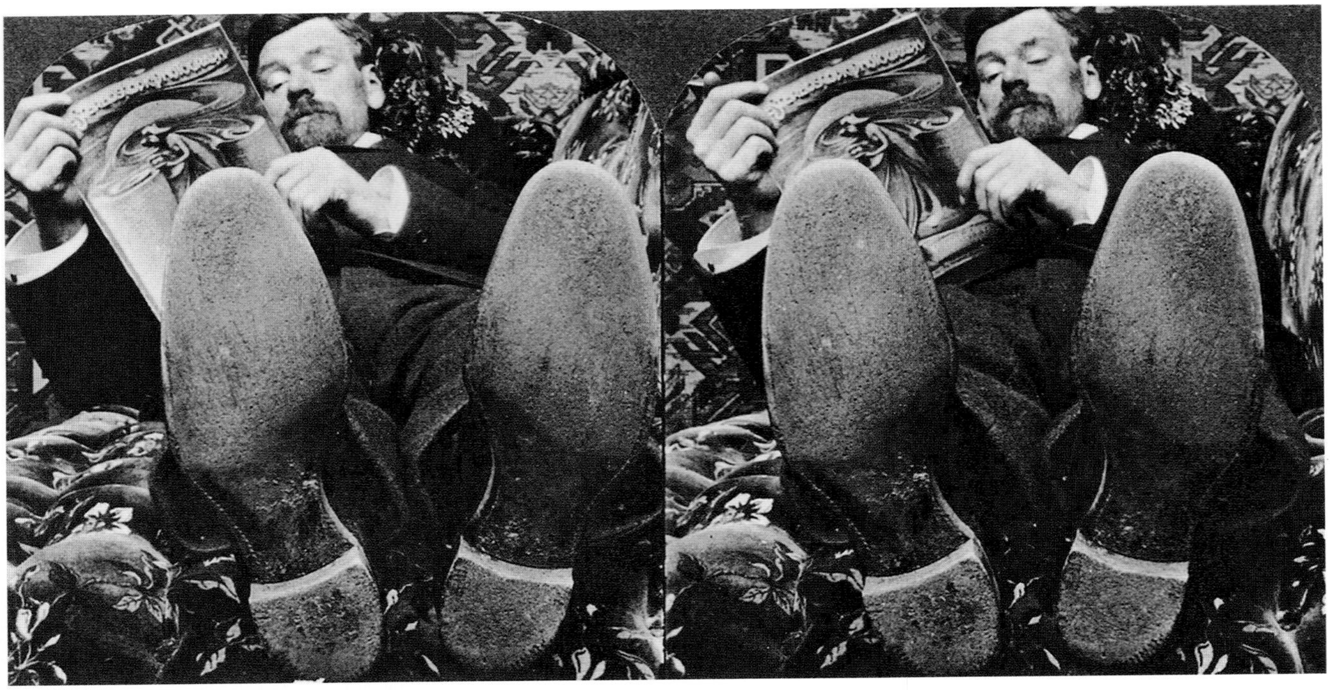

Fig. 4-20 Photographer unknown, *Man with Big Shoes*, ca. 1890. Stereograph. Library of Congress.
Courtesy of Library of Congress.

before your eyes and look at it first with one eye closed and then with the other, you will readily see that the point of view of each eye is different. Under most conditions, the human organism has the capacity to synthesize these differing points of view into a unitary image.

In the nineteenth century, the stereoscope was invented precisely to imitate binocular vision. Two pictures of the same subject, taken from slightly different points of view, were viewed through the stereoscope, one by each eye. The effect of a single picture was produced, with the appearance of depth, or relief, a result of the divergence of the point of view. Usually, the difference between the two points of view is barely discernible, especially if we are looking at relatively distant objects. But if we look at objects that are nearby, as in the stereoscopic view of the *Man with Big Shoes* (**Fig. 4-20**), then the difference is readily apparent.

Painters can make up for such distortions in ways that photographers cannot. If the artist portrayed in Albrecht Dürer's woodcut (**Fig. 4-21**) were to draw

Fig. 4-21 Albrecht Dürer, *Draftsman Drawing a Female Nude*, 1538. Woodcut, second edition, 3 × 8½ in.
One of 138 woodcuts and diagrams in *Underweysung der Messung, mit dem Zirkel und Richtscheyt* (*Teaching of Measurement with Compass and Ruler*). Museum of Fine Arts, Boston.
Horatio Greenough Curtis Fund, 35.53. Photograph © 2015 Museum of Fine Arts, Boston.

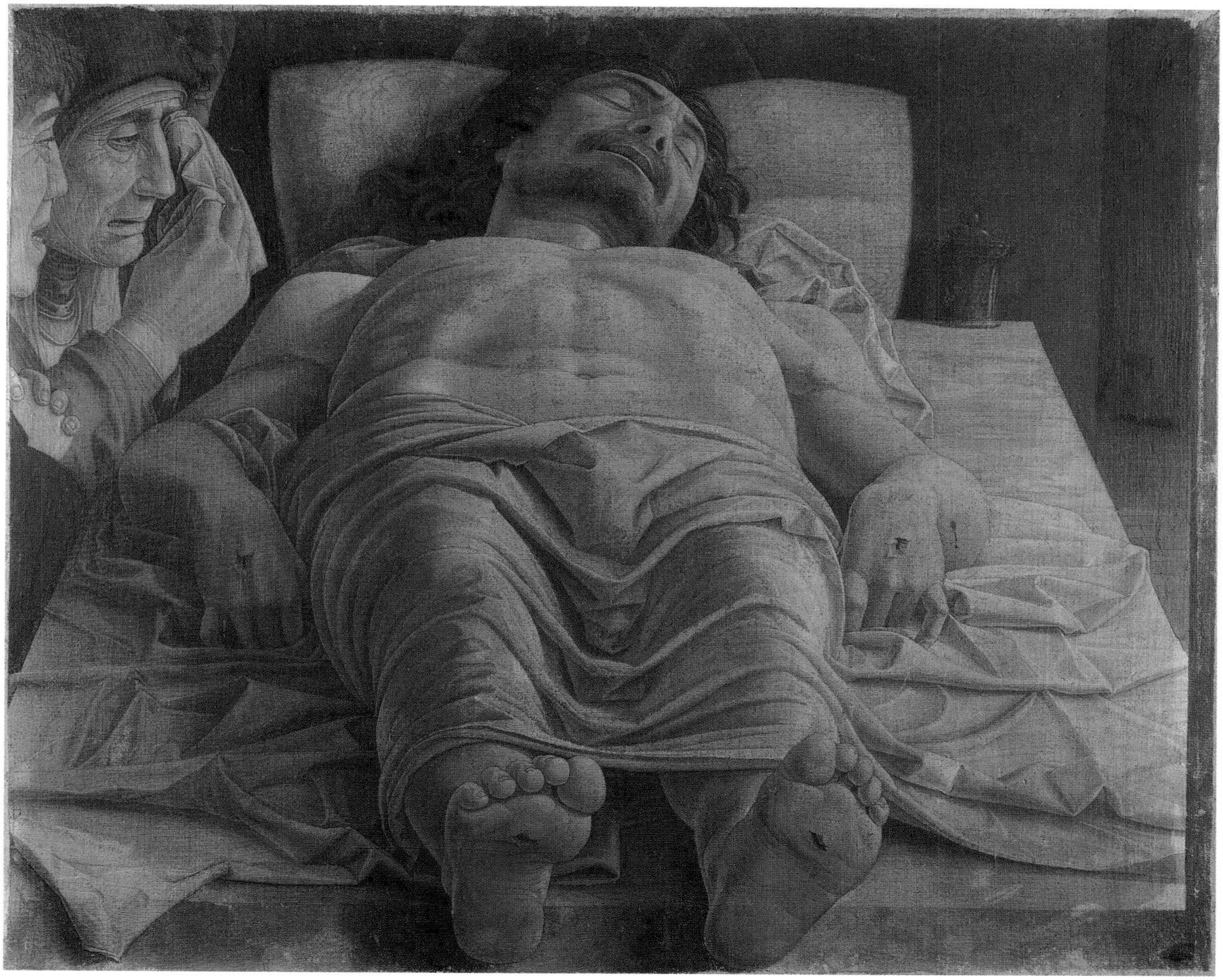

Fig. 4-22 Andrea Mantegna, *The Dead Christ*, ca. 1480.
Tempera on canvas, 26 × 30 in. Brera Gallery, Milan.
DEA/G. CIGOLINI/De Agostini/Getty Images.

exactly what he sees before his eyes, he would end up drawing a figure with knees and lower legs that are too large in relation to her breasts and head. The effect would not be unlike that achieved by the enormous feet that reach toward the viewer in *Man with Big Shoes*. These are effects that Andrea Mantegna would work steadfastly to avoid in his depiction of *The Dead Christ* (**Fig. 4-22**). Such a representation would make comic or ridiculous a scene of high seriousness and consequence. It would be indecorous. Thus, Mantegna has employed foreshortening in order to represent Christ's body. In **foreshortening**, the dimensions of the closer extremities are adjusted in order to make up for the distortion created by the point of view.

The Near and the Far

Foreshortening is a means of countering the laws of perspective, laws which seem perfectly consistent and rational when the viewer's vantage point is sufficiently removed from the foreground, but which, when the foreground is up close, seem to produce oddly weird and disquieting imagery. When Japanese prints entered European markets after the opening of Japan in 1853–54, new possibilities for representing perspectival space presented themselves. Many Japanese prints combined close-up views of things near at hand, such as flowers, trees, or banners, with views of distant landscapes. Rather than worrying about presenting space as a continuous

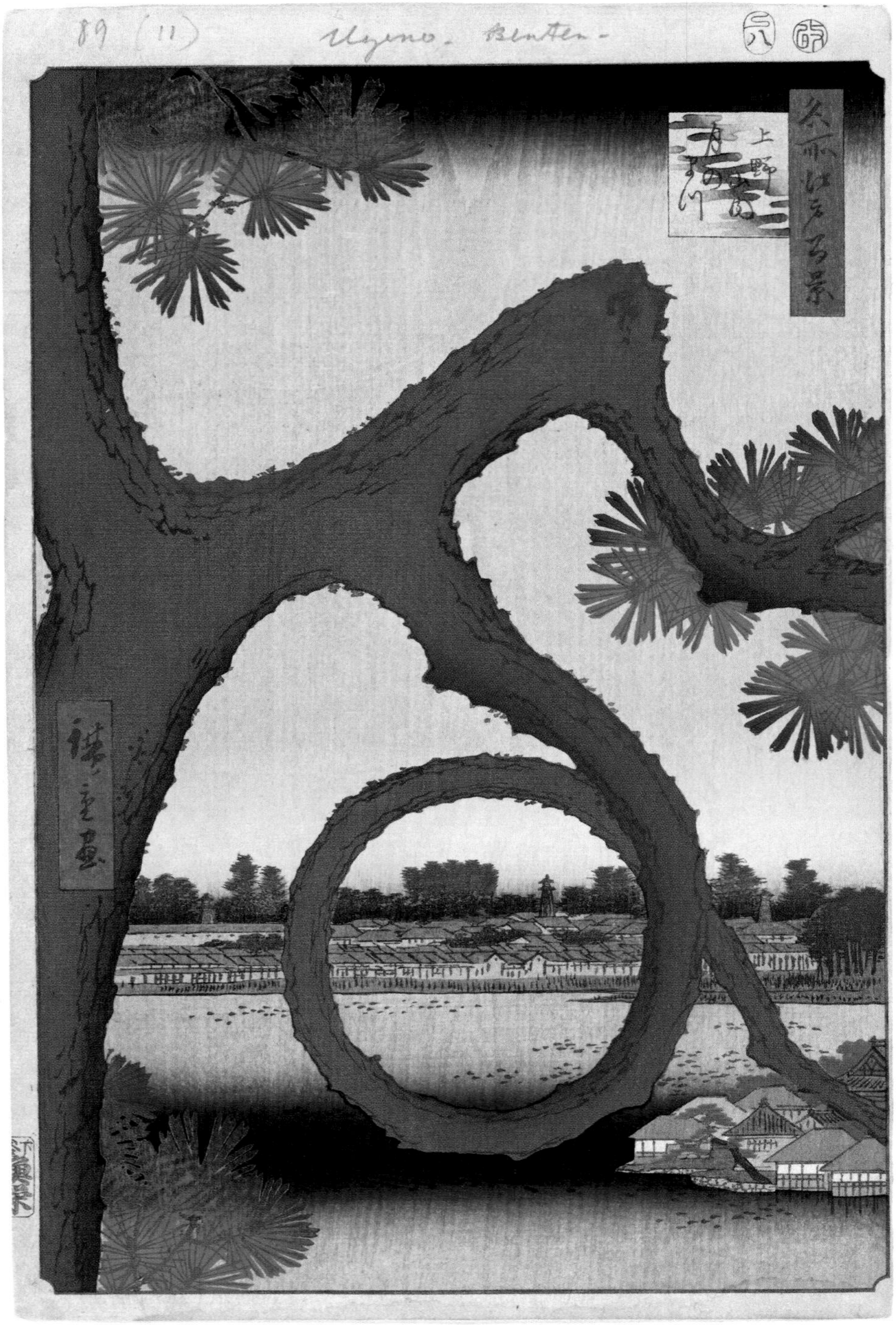

Fig. 4-23 Utagawa Hiroshige (Ando), *Moon Pine, Ueno*, No. 89 from *One Hundred Famous Views of Edo*, 1856. Woodblock print, 14³⁄₁₆ × 9¼ in. The Brooklyn Museum. Gift of Anna Ferris, 30.1478.89.

and consistent recession from the near at hand to the far away, Japanese artists simply elided what might be called the "in between." Thus, in Utagawa Hiroshige's *Moon Pine, Ueno* (**Fig. 4-23**), from his *One Hundred Views of Edo* (Edo was renamed Tokyo in 1868), a giant gap lies between the foreground pine and the city in the distance. The habit in Edo was to give names to trees of great age or particular form, and this pine, renowned for the looping round form of its lower branch, was dubbed "moon pine." Looking at the tree from different angles, one could supposedly see the different phases of the moon as well. The site is a park in the Ueno district of Tokyo, overlooking Shinobazu pond. In the middle of the lake is an island upon which stands the Benten

Shrine, dedicated to the goddess of the fine arts, music, and learning. In the print, the shrine is the red building just above the branch at the lower right. Here, where the branch crosses the island, the gulf between the near and the far seems to collapse, and a certain unity of meaning emerges, as the extraordinary beauty of the natural world (the nearby pine) merges with the best aspects of human productivity (embodied in the distant shrine).

This flattening of space proved to be especially attractive to European modernist painters in the late nineteenth and early twentieth centuries, who, as we will see in the following pages, found the rules of perspective to be limiting and imaginatively cumbersome. But the surprising effects that can be achieved in collapsing the apparent distance between the near and the far have continued to fascinate artists down to the present day. In her video *Touch* (**Fig. 4-24**), Janine Antoni appears to walk along the horizon, an illusion created by her walking on a tightrope stretched between two backhoes on the beach directly in front of her childhood home on Grand Bahama Island. She had learned to tightrope-walk, practicing about an hour a day, as an exercise in bodily control and meditation. As she practiced, she realized, she says, that "it wasn't that I was getting more balanced, but that I was getting more comfortable with being out of balance." This she took as a basic lesson in life. In *Touch*, this sense of teetering balance is heightened by the fact that she appears to be walking on a horizon line that we know can never be reached as it continually moves away from us as we approach it. We know, in other words, that we are in an impossible place, and yet it is a place that we have long contemplated and desired as a culture, the sense of possibility that always seems to lie "just over the horizon." When, in the course of the full-length video, both Antoni and the rope disappear, we are left, as viewers, contemplating this illusory line and just what it means. And we come to understand that the horizon represents what is always in front of us. "It's a very hopeful image," Antoni says; "it's about the future, about the imagination."

Fig. 4-24 Janine Antoni, *Touch*, 2002. Color video, sound (projection), 9 min. 36 sec. loop.
Courtesy of the artist and Luhring Augustine, New York.

Fig. 4-25 Paul Strand, *Abstraction, Porch Shadows*, 1916. Silver platinum print, 12¹⁵⁄₁₆ × 9⅛ in.

Modern Experiments and New Dimensions

Why have modern artists challenged the means of representing three dimensions on two-dimensional surfaces?

One of the most important functions of the means of representing three dimensions on a two-dimensional surface is to make the world more intelligible. Linear perspective provides a way for artists to focus and organize the visual field. Foreshortening makes the potentially grotesque view of objects seen from below or above seem more natural, less disorienting. Modern artists have consistently challenged the utility of these means in capturing the complex conditions of contemporary culture. Very often it is precisely the disorienting and the chaotic that define the modern for them, and perspective, for instance, seems to impose something of a false order on the world.

Experiments in Photographic Space

Even photographers, the truth of whose means was largely unquestioned in the early decades of the twentieth century, sought to picture the world from points of view that challenged the ease of a viewer's recognition. Paul Strand's *Abstraction, Porch Shadows* (**Fig. 4-25**) is an unmanipulated photograph (that is, not altered during the development process) of the shadows of a porch railing cast across a porch and onto a white patio table turned on its side. The camera lens is pointed down and across the porch. The close-up of approximately 9 square feet of porch is cropped so that no single object in the picture is wholly visible. Strand draws the viewer's attention not so much to the scene itself as to the patterns of light and dark that create a visual rhythm across the surface. The picture is more abstraction, as its title suggests, than realistic rendering—a picture of shapes, not things.

It was not until after Strand took this photograph at his family's summer cottage in Twin Lakes, Connecticut, that he was able to see a similar abstraction in the play of shadows in the backyard of his townhouse on West 83rd Street in New York (**Fig. 4-26**). This was a view he had seen hundreds of times before—he had lived in the townhouse for 24 years—but suddenly the abstraction of walls, pavement, and hanging sheets was apparent to him, all animated by the play of light and dark. In fact, such overhead shots were, in 1917, still something of a novelty—few people had even taken photographs from an airplane. The view downward seemed, somewhat startlingly, to flatten the world.

Fig. 4-26 Paul Strand, *Geometric Backyards, New York*, 1917. Platinum print, 10 × 13⅛ in.

Experiments with Space in Painting

Similar effects were achieved by photographers by means of other odd points of view, extreme close-ups, and radical cropping. In painting, modern artists intentionally began to violate the rules of perspective to draw the attention of the viewer to elements of the composition other than its verisimilitude, or the apparent "truth" of its representation of reality. In other words, the artist sought to draw attention to the act of imagination that created the painting, not its overt subject matter. In his large painting *Harmony in Red (The Red Room)* (**Fig. 4-27**), Henri Matisse has almost completely eliminated any sense of three-dimensionality by uniting the different spaces of the painting in one large field of uniform color and design. The wallpaper and the tablecloth are made of the same fabric. Shapes are repeated throughout: The spindles of the chairs and the tops of the decanters echo one another, as do the maid's hair and the white foliage of the large tree outside the window. The tree's trunk repeats the arabesque design on the tablecloth directly below it. Even the window can be read in two ways: It could, in fact, be a window opening to the world outside, or it could be the corner of a painting, a framed canvas lying flat against the wall. In traditional perspective, the picture frame functions as a window. Here, the window has been transformed into a frame.

Fig. 4-27 Henri Matisse, *Harmony in Red (The Red Room)*, 1908–09. Oil on canvas, 5 ft. 10⅞ in. × 7 ft. 2⅝ in. The Hermitage, St. Petersburg.

Fig. 4-28 Paul Cézanne, *Mme. Cézanne in a Red Armchair*, ca. 1877.
Oil on canvas, 28½ × 22 in. Museum of Fine Arts, Boston.
Bequest of Robert Treat Paine II, 44.77.6. Photograph © 2015 Museum of Fine Arts, Boston.

What one notices most of all in Paul Cézanne's *Mme. Cézanne in a Red Armchair* (**Fig. 4-28**) is its very lack of spatial depth. Although the arm of the chair seems to project forward on the right, on the left the painting is almost totally flat. The blue flower pattern on the wallpaper seems to float above the spiraled end of the arm, as does the tassel that hangs below it, drawing the wall far forward into the composition. The line that establishes the bottom of the baseboard on the left seems to ripple on through Mme. Cézanne's dress. Most of all, the assertive vertical stripes of that dress, which appear to rise straight up from her feet parallel to the picture plane, deny Mme. Cézanne her lap. It is almost as if a second, striped vertical plane lies between her and the viewer. By such means Cézanne announces that it is not so much the accurate representation of the figure that interests him as the design of the canvas and the activity of painting itself, the play of its pattern and color.

With the advent of the computer age, a new space for art has opened up, one beyond the boundaries of the frame and, moreover, beyond the traditional boundaries of time and matter. It is the space of information, which in Terry Winters's *Color and Information* (**Fig. 4-29**) seems to engulf us. The painting is enormous, 9 × 12 feet. It is organized around a central pole that rises just to the left of center. A web of circuitrylike squares circle around this pole, seeming to implode into the center or explode out of it—there is no way to tell. Writing in the magazine *Art in America* in 2005, critic Carol Diehl describes her reaction to paintings such as this one:

> At any given moment, some or all of the following impressions may suggest themselves and then quickly fade, to be replaced by others: maps, blueprints, urban aerial photographs, steel girders, spiderwebs, X-rays, molecular structures, microscopic slides of protozoa, the warp and woof of gauzy fabric, tangles or balls of yarn, fishing nets, the interlace of wintry tree branches, magnified crystals, computer readouts or diagrams of the neurological circuits of the brain, perhaps on information overload. That we can never figure out whether what we're looking at depicts something organic or man-made only adds to the enigma.

In fact, the title of this painting refers only to Winters's process, not its enigmatic content. The work began with a series of black-and-white woodcuts generated from small pen-and-ink drawings scanned into a computer so that the blocks could be cut by a laser. Winters wanted to see what would happen if he transformed this digital information into a painting, confounding or amplifying the stark black-and-white contrast of the source images by adding color and vastly magnifying their size. In front of the resulting work, we are suspended between order and chaos, image and abstraction, information and information overload.

Digital Space

Standing in front of Winters's painting is something akin to being immersed in the technological circuitry of contemporary life. But few artists have more thoroughly succeeded in integrating the viewer into digital space than Chinese artist Feng Mengbo. In 1993, having graduated in 1991 from the Printmaking Department of the Central Academy of Fine Arts, Beijing, he created a series of 42 paintings entitled *Game Over: Long March*. They amounted to screenshots of an imaginary video game, and, as one walked by them, one could imagine oneself in a side-scrolling game of the

Fig. 4-29 Terry Winters, *Color and Information*, 1998. Oil and alkyd resin on canvas, 9 × 12 ft.
© Terry Winters, courtesy of Matthew Marks Gallery, New York.

classic Super Mario Bros. variety. When Mengbo finally acquired a computer in 2003, he began transforming his project into an actual video game based on the 8,000-mile, 370-day retreat of the Chinese Communist Party's Red Army, under the command of Mao Zedong in 1934–35. The audience's avatar in Mengbo's work is a small Red Army soldier who, seated on a crushed Coca-Cola can, encounters a variety of ghosts, demons, and deities, in an effort to rescue Princess Toadstool. Now titled *Long March: Restart* (**Fig. 4-30**), the work has become a giant digital space consisting of two walls, each 80 feet long. The viewer is invited to take control of the Red Army avatar who moves through five screens, following the Great Wall into 14 progressively more difficult levels of play. "You go inside this video game," Mengbo explains. "You don't passively sit and play it." The speed at which the avatar moves causes the viewer to move at a frenetic pace down the gallery, then to spin around and move back up the opposite wall. Disembodied, fighting long odds, on the brink of disaster, one realizes that Mengbo's *Long March* is a metaphor for the long march that is contemporary life itself.

Fig. 4-30 Feng Mengbo, *Long March: Restart*, 2008. Video-game installation, one of two screens, each approx. 20 × 80 ft. Museum of Modern Art, New York.
Given anonymously, 1168.2008. © Feng Mengbo. © 2015. Digital image, Museum of Modern Art, New York/Scala, Florence.

THE CRITICAL PROCESS

Thinking about Space

Although it is far more expensive, artists working with time-based media have preferred, given the higher quality of the image, to work with film. One of the most remarkable experiments with the medium of film is the nine-screen installation *Ten Thousand Waves* (**Fig. 4-31**) by British artist and filmmaker Isaac Julien. *Ten Thousand Waves* was inspired by the drowning of 23 Chinese cockle pickers from Fujian province in southeast China in Morecambe Bay, Lancashire, England, on the evening of February 5, 2004. Their tragedy is juxtaposed with a Chinese fable, "The Tale of Yishan Island," in which the Chinese goddess and protector of sailors, the Fujian goddess Mazu—played by Chinese actress Maggie Cheung—saves five boats of fishermen from a storm at sea by directing them to an island that, after they have been rescued, they can never find again. Layered on these two stories is a third story of a contemporary goddess, a sort of reenactment of Wu Yonggang's 1934 silent film *The Goddess* (about a woman who becomes a prostitute to support herself and her son), which tracks her as she moves from the historic Shanghai Film Studio sets of the 1930s into the present-day Pudong district of Shanghai.

Julien's multiscreen images at first seem chaotic, but they underscore that the fixed viewpoint of cinematic experience is highly institutionalized—the onslaught of visual stimulus in Julien's installation is very much like the typical sensory experience of daily life as we are surrounded by sensory input of all kinds. Surrounded by nine screens, viewers find themselves wandering through a disorienting landscape, wanting to see, more or less impossibly, what is on every screen at once. As a result, our sense of space opens to redefinition, and Julien's work suggests that this new perception of space is perhaps as fundamental as that which occurred in the fifteenth century when the laws of linear perspective were finally codified. How would you speak of this space? In what ways is it two-dimensional? In what ways is it three-dimensional? How is space "represented"? How is time incorporated into our sense of space? What are the implications of our seeming to move in and through an array of two-dimensional images? What would you call such new spaces? Digital space? Four-dimensional space? What possibilities do you see for such spaces?

Fig. 4-31 Isaac Julien, *Ten Thousand Waves*, 2010. Installation view, ShanghART Gallery, Shangha. Nine-screen installation, 35 mm film, transferred to High Definition, 9.2 surround sound, 49 min. 41 sec. Edition of 6 plus 1AP.
Courtesy of the Artist and Victoria Miro, London, Metro Pictures, New York, and Galería Helga de Alvear, Madrid. © Isaac Julien. Photography © Adrian Zhou.

Thinking Back

4.1 Differentiate between shape and mass.

A shape is a two-dimensional area, whose boundaries can be measured in height and width. A mass, or form, by contrast, is a solid that occupies a three-dimensional volume. How does Ellsworth Kelly work with shapes in *Three Panels: Orange, Dark Gray, Green*? What are negative shapes and positive shapes? What is figure-ground reversal?

Negative spaces are empty spaces that acquire a sense of volume and form by means of the outline or frame that surrounds them. Negative spaces can be used to suggest forms. How does the sculptor of the feast-making spoon (*wunkirmian*) use negative space to suggest form? How does Barbara Hepworth treat negative spaces in her sculpture *Two Figures*?

4.2 Describe how three-dimensional space is represented on a flat surface using perspective.

By means of illusion, a sense of depth, or three dimensions, can be achieved on a flat surface. There are many ways to create such an illusion, and an artist will often use more than one such technique for creating depth in a single work. Perspective is a system that allows the picture plane to function as a window through which a specific scene is presented to the viewer.

What is a vanishing point? How is two-point linear perspective used? How does Gustave Caillebotte create an illusion of real space in his painting *Place de l'Europe on a Rainy Day*?

What is the difference between monocular and binocular vision? By what means do artists avoid the distortions of the figure inherent in viewing them from near at hand? How do Japanese printmakers modulate between the near and the far?

4.3 Explain why modern artists have challenged the means of representing three dimensions on two-dimensional surfaces.

Modern artists have consistently challenged the utility of perspective and other techniques used to create the illusion of three dimensions on two-dimensional surfaces. Often it is precisely the disorienting and chaotic that define the modern for many artists, and systems such as perspective seem, to them, to present a false sense of order. How have photographers challenged the viewer's recognition of the world? In *Harmony in Red (The Red Room)*, how does Henri Matisse nearly eliminate any illusion of three-dimensionality? How can the illusion of digital space be created?

Chapter 5
Light and Color

Learning Objectives

5.1 Describe the ways in which artists use light to represent space and model form.

5.2 Outline the principles of color theory, and describe the different sorts of color schemes that artists might employ.

5.3 Explain how color might be used both in representational painting and as a symbolic tool.

The manipulation of perspective systems is by no means the only way that space is created in art. Light is at least as important to the rendering of space. For instance, light creates shadow, and thus helps to define the contour of a figure or mass. Architects, particularly, must concern themselves with light. Interior spaces demand lighting, either natural or artificial, and our experience of a given space can be deeply affected by the quality of its light. Color, too, is essential in defining shape and mass. It allows us, for instance, to see a red object against a green one, and thus establish their relation in space.

In 1963, artist Dan Flavin began working exclusively with fluorescent fixtures and tubes. He was, in fact, the first artist to work with fluorescent light, and he quickly came to understand that the light and color specific to the medium were unique. As opposed to the clean, white incandescent light that normally and unobtrusively lit gallery spaces, Flavin's fluorescent lights literally colored the room, both optically and emotionally. They transformed and manipulated the viewer's experience of interior space. One of the results of his research was the creation of the Dan Flavin Art Institute in Bridgehampton, New York, which opened to the public in 1983 (**Fig. 5-1**). The building itself was originally a firehouse, built in 1908, and from 1924 until the mid-1970s it was used as a church. In creating this space, Flavin thought of the fluorescent sculptures that he distributed through the interiors as working together with the architecture to form a single, unified work of art, consisting of the building and its lighting.

Not long after Flavin began working with fluorescent light, the Venezuelan artist Carlos Cruz-Diez began exploring the possible ways in which the medium might radically alter the viewer's normal experience of color. He immerses the visitor in environments saturated by a single color. The viewer's retina, accustomed to seeing a wide range of colors simultaneously, is thus exposed to a completely foreign experience of color. *Chromosaturation* (**Fig. 5-2**) is an interactive space composed of three color chambers—red, green, and blue—that was installed in Paris and Mexico City in 2012–13. It was first installed in 1968, in Dortmund (Germany) and Grenoble (France). As the viewer moves from one chamber to the next, an after-image of the previous visual saturation shocks the retina. "This, in turn," Cruz-Diez has explained, "leads the spectator to the idea that color is a material, physical situation, and to an awareness that color exists in space without the help of form, and in fact with no support at all." Color *is* light.

Light

How do artists use light to represent space and model form?

Since natural light helps us to define spatial relationships, it stands to reason that artists are interested in manipulating it, if not always quite so radically as Flavin and Cruz-Diez. By doing so, they can control our experience of their work.

Atmospheric Perspective

For Leonardo da Vinci, representing the effects of light was at least as important as linear perspective in creating believable space. The effect of the atmosphere on the appearance of elements in a landscape is one of the chief preoccupations of his notebooks, and it is fair to say that Leonardo is responsible for formulating the "rules" of what we call **atmospheric** or **aerial perspective**. Briefly, these rules state that the quality of the atmosphere (the haze and relative humidity) between large objects, such as mountains, and us changes their appearance. Objects farther away from us appear less distinct, often bluer in color, and the contrast between light and dark is reduced.

Fig. 5-1 The Dan Flavin Art Institute, Bridgehampton, New York, 1963–83.
Courtesy of Dia Art Foundation, New York. Photo: Florian Holzherr.

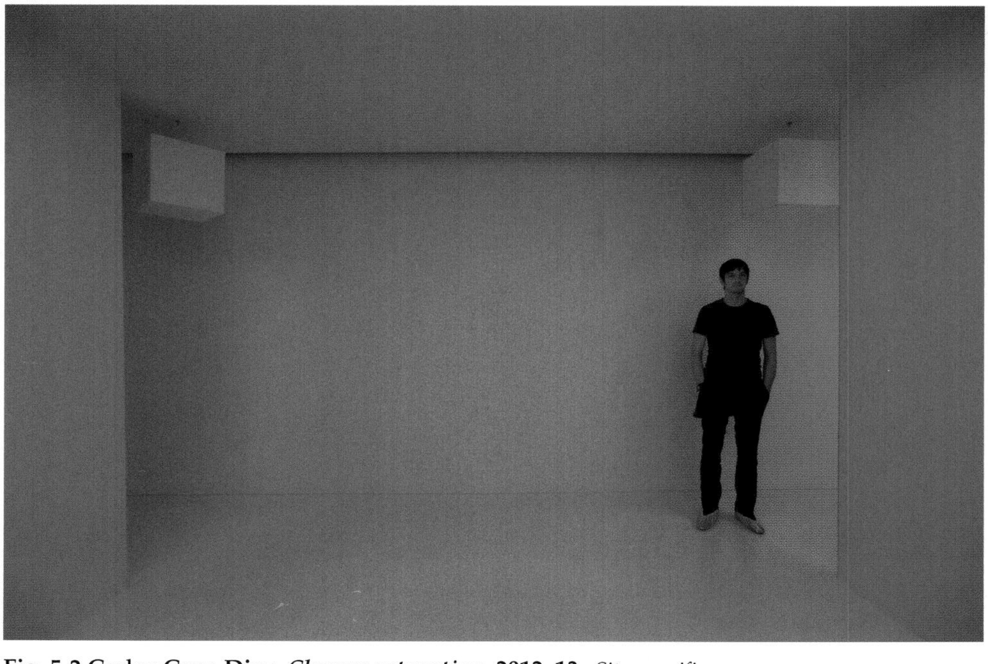

Fig. 5-2 Carlos Cruz-Diez, *Chromosaturation*, 2012–13. Site-specific environment composed of fluorescent lights with blue, red, and green filters.
Courtesy of Americas Society Gallery, New York. Photo © Arturo Sanchez.

Fig. 5-3 Leonardo da Vinci, *Madonna of the Rocks*, ca. 1495–1508. Oil on panel, 6 ft. 3 in. × 47 in. The National Gallery, London.

Clarity, precision, and contrast between light and dark dominate the foreground elements in Leonardo's *Madonna of the Rocks* (**Fig. 5-3**). The Madonna's hand extends over the head of the infant Jesus in an instance of almost perfect perspectival foreshortening. Yet perspective has little to do with the way in which we perceive the distant mountains over the Madonna's right shoulder. We assume that the rocks in the far distance are the same brown as those nearer to us, yet the atmosphere has changed them, making them appear blue. We know that, of these three distant rock formations, the one nearest to us is on the right, and the one farthest away is on the left. Since they are approximately the same size, if they were painted with the same clarity and the same amount of contrast between light and dark, we would be unable to place them spatially. We would see them as a horizontal wall of rock, parallel to the picture plane, rather than as a series of mountains, receding diagonally into space.

By the nineteenth century, aerial perspective had come to dominate the thinking of landscape painters. A painting like J. M. W. Turner's *Rain, Steam, and Speed—The Great Western Railway* (**Fig. 5-4**) certainly employs linear perspective: the diagonal lines of two bridges converge on a vanishing point on the horizon. We stare over the River Thames across the Maidenhead Bridge, which was completed for the railway's new Bristol and Exeter line in 1844, the year Turner painted the scene. But the space of this painting does not depend upon linear perspective. Rather, light and atmosphere dominate it, creating a sense of space that in fact overwhelms the painting's linear elements in luminous and intense light. Turner's light is at once so opaque that it conceals everything behind it and so deep that it seems to stretch beyond the limits of vision. Describing the power of a Rembrandt painting in a lecture delivered in 1811, Turner praised such ambiguity: "Over [the scene] he has thrown that veil of matchless color, that lucid interval of Morning dawn

Fig. 5-4 J. M. W. Turner, *Rain, Steam, and Speed—The Great Western Railway*, 1844. Oil on canvas, 33¾ in. × 4 ft. The National Gallery, London.
akg-image/National Gallery, London.

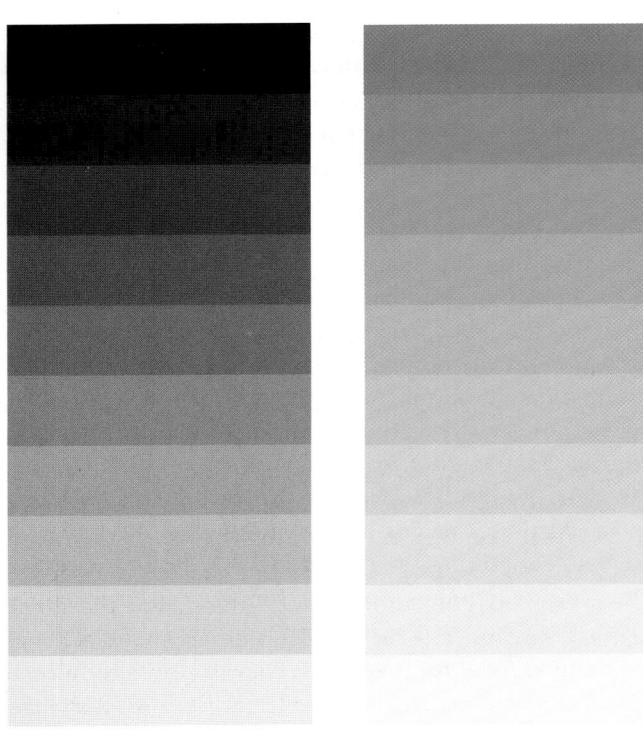

Fig. 5-5 The gray scale.

Fig. 5-6 Blue in a range of values.

and dewy light on which the Eye dwells . . . [and he] thinks it a sacrilege to pierce the mystic shell of color in search of form." With linear perspective one might adequately describe physical reality—a building, for instance—but through light one could reveal a greater spiritual reality.

Value: From Light to Dark

The gradual shift from light to dark that characterizes atmospheric perspective is illustrated by the gray scale (**Fig. 5-5**). The relative level of lightness or darkness of an area or object is traditionally called its relative value. That is, a given area or object can be said to be darker or lighter in value. Colors, too, change value in similar gradients. Imagine, for example, substituting the lightest blue near the bottom of this scale and the darkest cobalt near its top (**Fig. 5-6**). The mountains in the back of Leonardo's *Madonna of the Rocks* (see Fig. 5-3) are depicted in a blue of lighter and lighter value the farther they are away from us.

Likewise, light pink is a lighter value of red, and dark maroon a darker value. In terms of color,

Fig. 5-7 Pat Steir, *Pink Chrysanthemum*, 1984. Oil on canvas, three panels, each 5 × 5 ft.
Courtesy of the artist and Cheim & Read, New York.

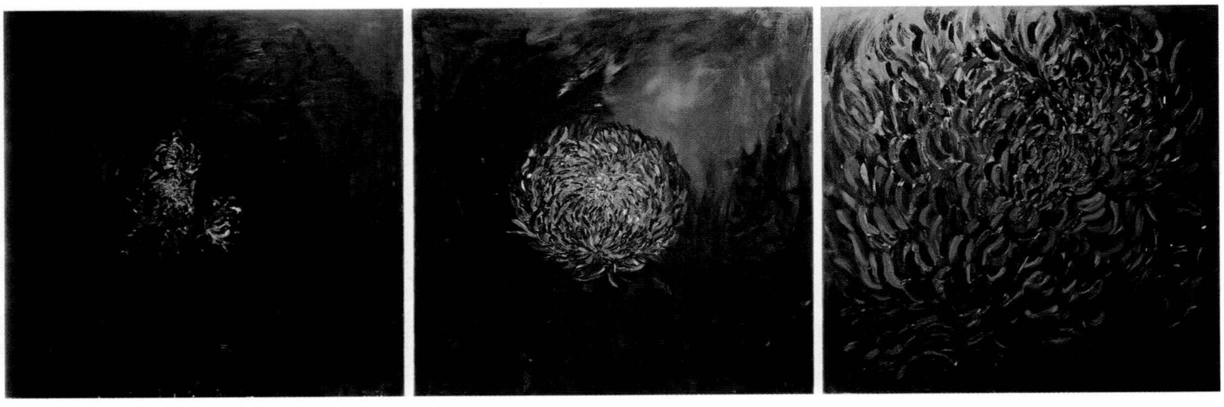

Fig. 5-8 Pat Steir, *Night Chrysanthemum*, 1984. Oil on canvas, three panels, each 5 × 5 ft.
Courtesy of the artist and Cheim & Read, New York.

whenever white is added to the basic hue, or color, we are dealing with a **tint** of that color. Whenever black is added to the hue, we are dealing with a **shade** of that color. Thus, pink is a tint, and maroon a shade, of red. Pat Steir's two large paintings *Pink Chrysanthemum* (**Fig. 5-7**) and *Night Chrysanthemum* (**Fig. 5-8**) are composed of three panels, each of which depicts the same flower in the same light viewed increasingly close up, left to right. Not only does each panel become more and more abstract as our point of view focuses in on the flower, so that in the last panel we are looking at almost pure gestural line and brushwork, but also the feeling of each panel shifts, depending on its relative value. The light painting becomes increasingly energetic and alive. The dark one likewise becomes increasingly less somber but, at the same time, increasingly menacing.

Indeed, Western culture has long associated light with good and dark with evil, as the first lines of the Book of Genesis make clear:

> In the beginning God created the heaven and the earth. And the earth was without form, and void; and darkness was upon the face of the deep. And the Spirit of God moved upon the face of the waters. And God said, Let there be light: and there was light. And God saw the light, that it was good: and God divided the light from the darkness.

In the history of art, this association of light or white with good, and darkness or black with evil, was first fully developed in the late eighteenth- and early nineteenth-century color theory of the German poet and dramatist Johann Wolfgang von Goethe. For Goethe, colors were not just phenomena to be explained by scientific laws. They also had moral and religious significance, existing halfway between the goodness of pure light and the damnation of pure blackness. In heaven there is only pure light, but the fact that we can experience color—which, according to the laws of optics, depends upon light mixing with darkness—promises us at least the hope of salvation.

If, for Goethe, blackness is not merely the absence of color but the absence of good, for African Americans, blackness has come to signify just the opposite. Over the course of the 1960s, as the struggle for civil rights gained intensity, it became a point of pride. As early as 1952, in his novel *Invisible Man*, the African-American author Ralph Ellison had warned African Americans not to allow themselves to be absorbed into white society. The novel was increasingly influential in the African-American community, and by the late 1960s "Black is Beautiful" had become the rallying cry of the Black Power movement, which boldly asserted that black was not only a beautiful color, but a color that was composed of all other colors. Thus the multitude of colors that compose Ben Jones's *Black Face and Arm Unit* (**Fig. 5-9**). Cast life-size from actual hands and arms, the 12-part piece literally embodies an essential blackness. Adorning this essence is a series of bands, ornaments, and scarifications, reminiscent of the facial decorations evident in some of the most ancient African sculpture. The use of line and color here creates a sense of rhythm and exuberance as it celebrates African cultural identity.

Chiaroscuro and Modeling

One of the chief tools employed by artists of the Renaissance to render the effects of light is **chiaroscuro**. In Italian, the

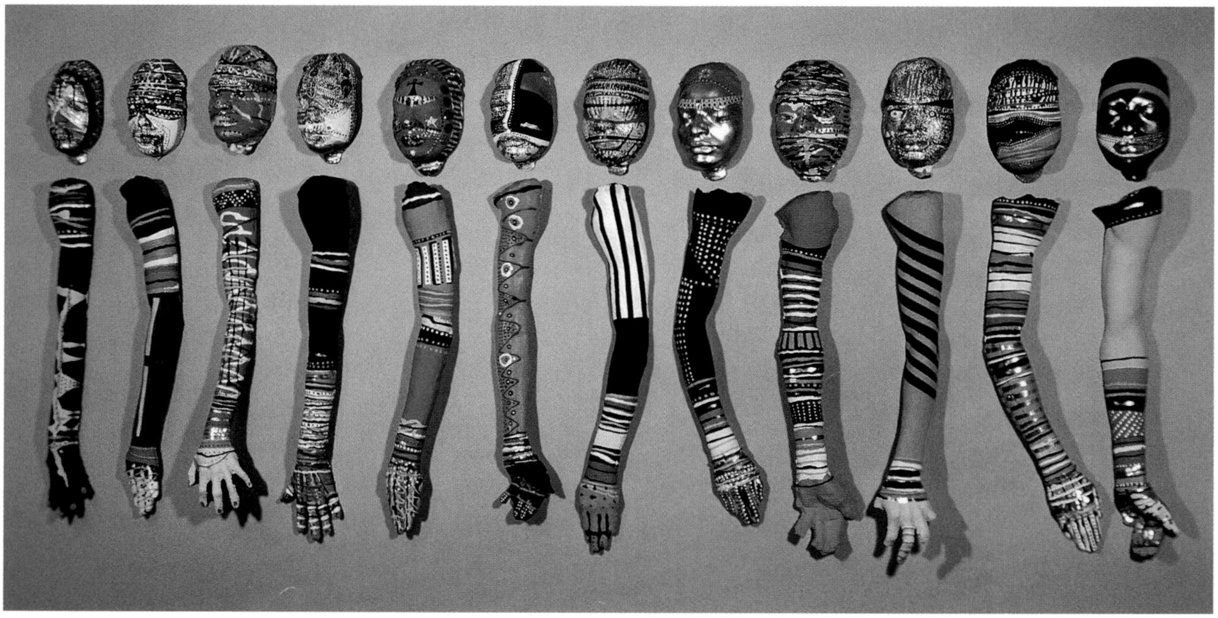

Fig. 5-9 Ben Jones, *Black Face and Arm Unit*, 1971. Acrylic on plaster, life-size plaster casts.
Courtesy of the artist.

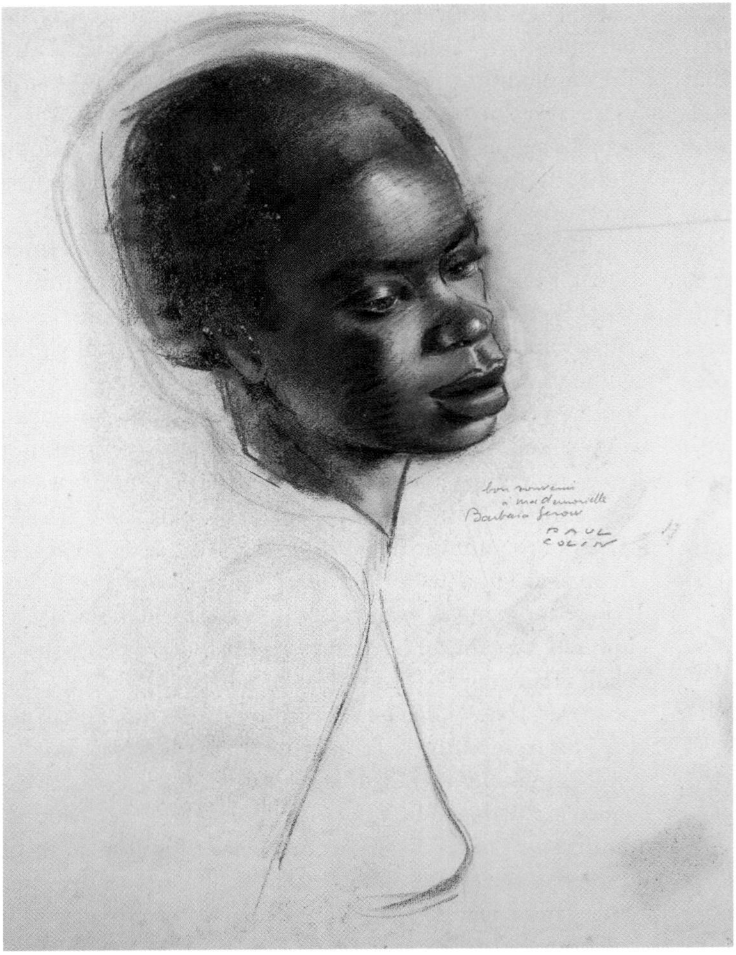

Fig. 5-10 Paul Colin, *Figure of a Woman*, ca. 1930. Black and white crayon on light beige paper, 24 × 18½ in. University of Virginia Art Museum.

word *chiaro* means "light," and the word *oscuro* means "dark." Thus, the word they make when combined refers to the balance of light and shade in a picture, especially its skillful use by the artist in representing the gradual transition around a curved surface from light to dark. The use of chiaroscuro to represent light falling across a curved or rounded surface is called **modeling**.

In his *Figure of a Woman* (**Fig. 5-10**), French artist Paul Colin has employed the techniques of chiaroscuro to model his figure. Drawing on light beige paper, he has indicated shadow by means of black crayon and has created the impression of light with white crayon. Colin made his fame as a poster designer for La Revue Nègre, a troupe of 20 musicians and dancers from Harlem who took the Parisian art world by storm in 1925. It was led by the dancer Josephine Baker, who introduced a new dance, the Charleston, to Parisian audiences, popularized American jazz in Europe, and, most famously, often performed almost completely in the nude. This drawing almost surely derives from Colin's association with Baker and her circle.

The basic types of shading and light employed in chiaroscuro can be observed here (**Fig. 5-11**). **Highlights**, which directly reflect the light source, are indicated by white, and the various degrees of shadow are noted by darker and darker areas of black. There are three basic areas of shadow: the **shadow** proper, which transitions into the **core of the shadow**, the darkest area on the object itself, and the **cast shadow**, the darkest area of all. Finally, areas of reflected light, cast indirectly on the table on which the sphere rests, lighten the underside of shadowed surfaces.

In her *Judith and Maidservant with the Head of Holofernes* (**Fig. 5-12**), Artemisia Gentileschi takes the technique of chiaroscuro to a new level. One of the most important painters of seventeenth-century Europe, Gentileschi utilizes a technique that came to be known as **tenebrism**, from the Italian *tenebroso*, meaning "murky." As opposed to chiaroscuro, a tenebrist style is not necessarily connected to modeling at all. Tenebrism makes use of large areas of dark contrasting sharply with smaller brightly illuminated areas. Competing against the very deep shadows in Gentileschi's painting are dramatic spots of light. Based on the tale in the Book of Judith in the Bible in which the noble Judith seduces the invading general Holofernes and then kills him, thereby saving her people from destruction, the painting is larger than life-size. Its figures are heroic, illuminated in a strong artificial spotlight, and modeled in both their physical features and the folds of their clothing with a skill that lends them astonishing spatial reality and dimension. Not only does Judith's outstretched hand cast a shadow across her face, suggesting a more powerful, revealing source of light off canvas to the left, it also invokes our silence. Like the light itself, danger lurks just offstage. If Judith is to escape, even we must remain still.

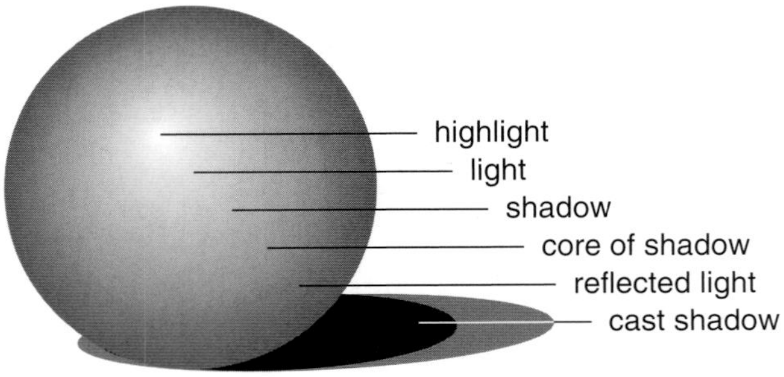

Fig. 5-11 A sphere represented by means of modeling.

Fig. 5-12 Artemisia Gentileschi, *Judith and Maidservant with the Head of Holofernes*, ca. 1625. Oil on canvas, 6 ft. ½ in. × 4 ft. 7¾ in. Detroit Institute of Arts.
Gift of Mr Leslie H. Green. Bridgeman Images.

Hatching and Cross-Hatching

Other techniques used to model figures using effects of light and shade include hatching and cross-hatching. Employed especially in ink-drawing and printmaking, where the artist's tools do not readily lend themselves to creating shaded areas, hatching and cross-hatching are linear methods of modeling. **Hatching** is an area of closely spaced parallel lines, or hatches. The closer the spacing of the lines, the darker the area appears. An example of hatching can be seen in *The Coiffure* (**Fig. 5-13**), a drawing by Mary Cassatt, an artist deeply interested in the play of light and dark (see *The Creative Process*, pp. 98–99). Here, parallel lines, of greater or lesser density, define the relative depth of the shadow in the room. Interestingly, the woman's reflection in the mirror is rendered as untouched white reserve—that is, the original surface of the paper.

Hatching can also be seen in Michelangelo's *Head of a Satyr* (**Fig. 5-14**), at the top and back of the satyr's head and at the base of his neck. The movement of light to dark across a surface creates a sense of volume and form, and in Michelangelo's drawing, this movement is created through **cross-hatching**. In cross-hatching, one set of hatches is crossed at an angle by a second, and sometimes a third, set. As in hatching, the denser the lines, the darker the area appears. The hollows of the satyr's face are tightly cross-hatched. In contrast, the most prominent aspects of the satyr's face, the highlights at the top of his nose and on his cheekbone, are almost completely free of line. Michelangelo employs line to create a sense of volume not unlike that achieved in the sphere modeled above (see Fig. 5-11).

Fig. 5-14 Michelangelo, *Head of a Satyr*, ca. 1620–30. Pen and ink over chalk, 10⅝ × 7⅞ in. Musée du Louvre, Paris.
INV684-recto. Photo © RMN-Grand Palais (musée du Louvre)/Michèle Bellot.

Fig. 5-13 Mary Cassatt, *The Coiffure*, ca. 1891. Graphite with traces of green and brown watercolor, approx. 5⅞ × 4⅜ in. National Gallery of Art, Washington, D.C.
Rosenwald Collection, 1954.12.6. Photo © Board of Trustees, National Gallery of Art, Washington, D.C.

Contrast: Light and Dark

Generally speaking, the greater the contrast between light and dark, as in Artemisia Gentileschi's *Judith and Maidservant with the Head of Holofernes* (see Fig. 5-12), the greater the dramatic impact of the image, an effect exploited particularly by filmmakers, video artists, and photographers working with black-and-white film. A still from Shirin Neshat's black-and-white video *Fervor* is especially evocative (**Fig. 5-15**). Not only are the women and men worshiping at the mosque separated by the screen that cuts down the center of the space, but they are also separated black from white, chador from collared shirt. The power of this image

Fig. 5-15 Shirin Neshat, *Fervor*, 2000. Gelatin silver print, 5 ft. 6 in. × 47 in.

of the separation of female and male worlds (which is, after all, fundamental to Muslim worship) is nothing, however, compared to the contrast between the wall of black chadors and the single white face of the woman who turns toward the camera. Set off from the other women around her, she engages our view with a kind of fierce, almost defiant determination. In the video, it is clear that she is turning to meet the gaze of a man whom she has accidentally met in the street. He is standing on a podium reading the story of Zuleikha and Yusuf, which appears in both the Qur'an and the Bible (where it features as the story of Joseph and the wife of Potiphar). It is a tale of seduction and temptation in which love for the beauty of the physical world is finally understood to be comparable to love for the beauty of God. The drama of Neshat's image depends fully upon the contrast between black and white, which underscores the tension-ridden contrast between physical and spiritual love, as well as the independence of the female gaze from the conformity of the religious practice of those who surround her.

The Creative Process

The Play of Light and Dark: Mary Cassatt's *In the Loge*

Painted in 1878, the year she first exhibited with the Impressionists, Mary Cassatt's *In the Loge (At the Français, a Sketch)* (**Fig. 5-17**) is a study in the contrast between light and dark, as becomes evident when we compare the final work to a tiny sketch, a study perhaps made at the scene itself (**Fig. 5-16**). In the sketch, Cassatt divides the work diagonally into two broad zones, the top left bathed in light, the lower right dominated by the woman's black dress. As the drawing makes clear, this diagonal design is softened by Cassatt's decision to fit the woman's figure into the architectural curve of the loge itself, so that the line running along the railing, then up the woman's arm, continues around the line created by her hat and its strap in a giant compositional arch. Thus, the woman's face falls into the zone of light, highlighted by her single diamond earring and cradled, as it were, in black.

In the final painting, the strict division between light and dark has been somewhat modified, particularly by the revelation of the woman's neck between the hat's strap and her collar, creating two strong light-and-dark diagonals. A sort of angularity is thus introduced into the painting, emphasizing the horizontal quality of the woman's profile and gaze as she stares out at the other loges through her binoculars, at an angle precisely 90 degrees from our point of view.

Across the way, a gentleman, evidently in the company of another woman, leans forward out of his box to stare through his own binoculars in the direction of the woman in black. He is in the zone of light, and the dramatic division between light and dark defines itself as a division between male and female spaces. But Cassatt's woman, in a bold painterly statement, enters the male world. Both her face and her hand holding the binoculars enter the space of light. Giving up the female role as the passive recipient of his gaze, she becomes as active a spectator as the male across the way.

Fig. 5-16 Mary Cassatt, *Study for In the Loge*, 1878. Graphite, 4 × 6 in. Museum of Fine Arts, Boston.
Gift of Dr. Hans Schaeffer, 55.28. Photograph © 2015 Museum of Fine Arts, Boston.

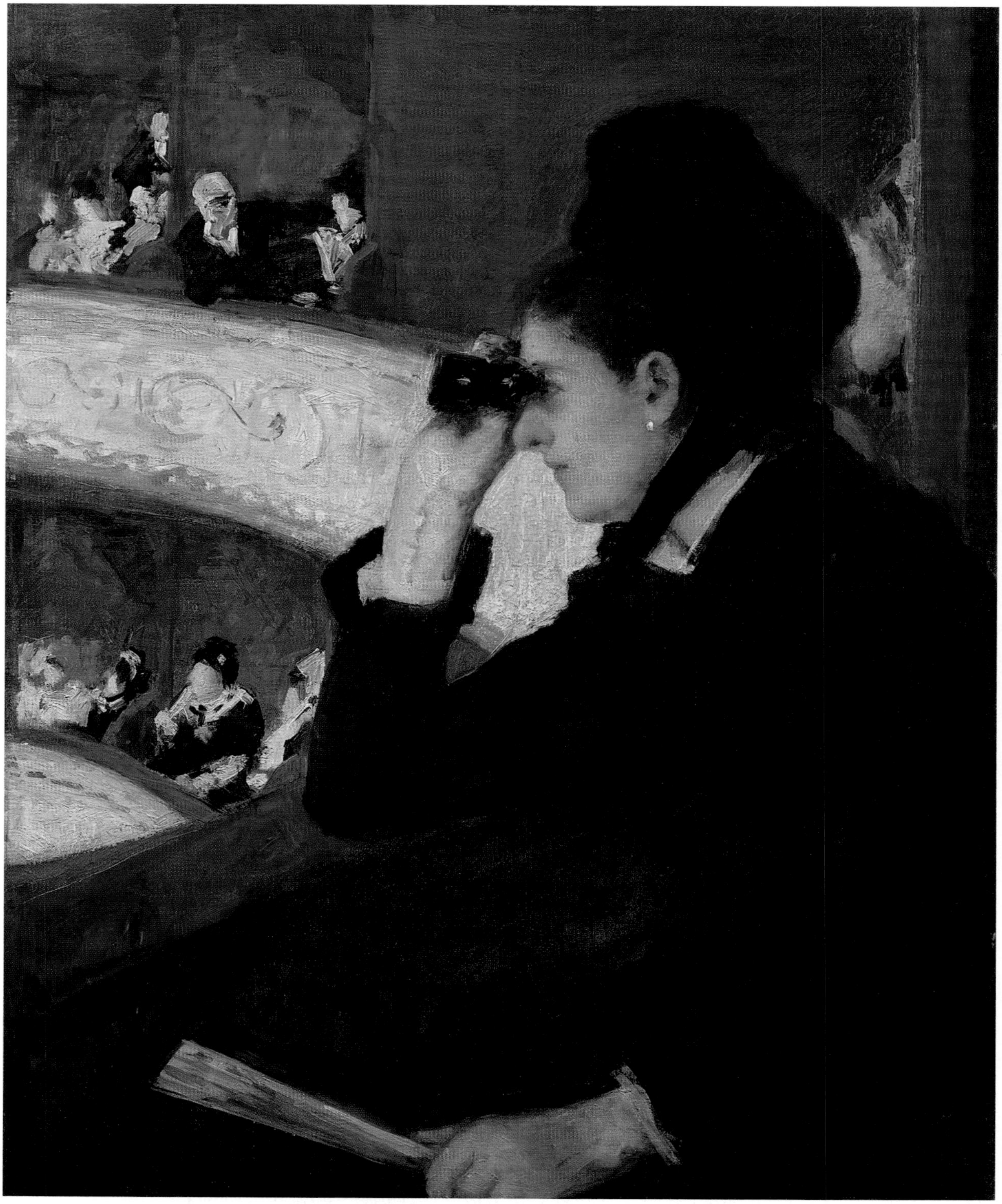

Fig. 5-17 Mary Cassatt, *In the Loge (At the Français, a Sketch)*, 1878. Oil on canvas, 32 × 26 in. Museum of Fine Arts, Boston.

Fig. 5-18 Cai Guo-Qiang, *Transient Rainbow*, realized over the East River, New York, June 29, 2002. One thousand 3-in. multicolor peony fireworks fitted with computer chips, 300 × 600 ft., duration 15 sec. Commissioned by the Museum of Modern Art, New York, for the opening of MoMA Queens.
Photo: Hiro Ihara, courtesy of Cai Studio. © 2015 Cai Guo-Qiang.

Color

What different color schemes might artists use in their work?

When New York City's Museum of Modern Art closed for an extensive redesign and moved to temporary quarters across the river in Queens, it commissioned artist Cai Guo-Qiang, who would later serve as director of visual and special effects at the 29th Olympiad in Beijing (see Fig. 1-2), to celebrate the move with one of his famous explosion projects. His proposal resulted in *Transient Rainbow* (**Fig. 5-18**), a massive fireworks display that extended across the East River, connecting Manhattan and Queens, on the evening of June 29, 2002. For the artist, the rainbow is a sign of hope, renewal, and promise. In Chinese mythology, the rainbow is associated with the goddess Nu-Wa (see Fig. 3-16), who sealed the broken sky after a fight among the gods with stones of seven different colors—the colors of the rainbow. Coming after 9/11, the choice of the rainbow image was similarly designed to heal, at least symbolically, the wounded city. Reflected in the water, the arch created by Cai Guo-Qiang's rainbow creates the circular *pi*, the ancient Chinese symbol for the universe. Nevertheless, since it is by its very nature fleeting and transitory, this work reminds viewers of the fragility and transience of the moment and, by extension, of life itself.

Basic Color Vocabulary

As Sir Isaac Newton first discovered in the 1660s, color is a direct function of light. Sunlight passed through a prism, Newton found, breaks into bands of different colors, in what is known as the **spectrum** (**Fig. 5-19**). By

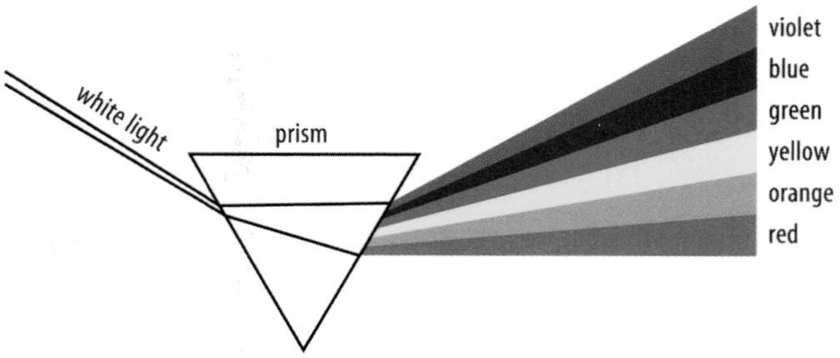

Fig. 5-19 Colors separated by a prism into the spectrum.

reorganizing the visible spectrum into a circle, as Newton himself was the first to do, we have what is recognized as the conventional **color wheel** (**Fig. 5-20**).

The three **primary colors** in this system are red, yellow, and blue (designated by the number 1 on the color wheel). Each of the **secondary colors**—orange, green, and violet (designated by the number 2)—is a mixture of the two primaries that it lies between. Thus, as we all learn in elementary school, green is made by mixing yellow and blue. The **intermediate colors** (designated by the number 3) are mixtures of a primary and a neighboring secondary. If we mix the primary yellow with the secondary orange, for instance, the result is yellow–orange. Theoretically, if we mixed all the colors together, we would end up with black, the absence of color (**Fig. 5-21**)—hence, this color system, which is that of all the colors used in paint, is called a **subtractive process**.

Colored light mixes in a very different way. The primary colors of light are red–orange, green, and blue–violet. The secondaries are yellow, magenta, and cyan.

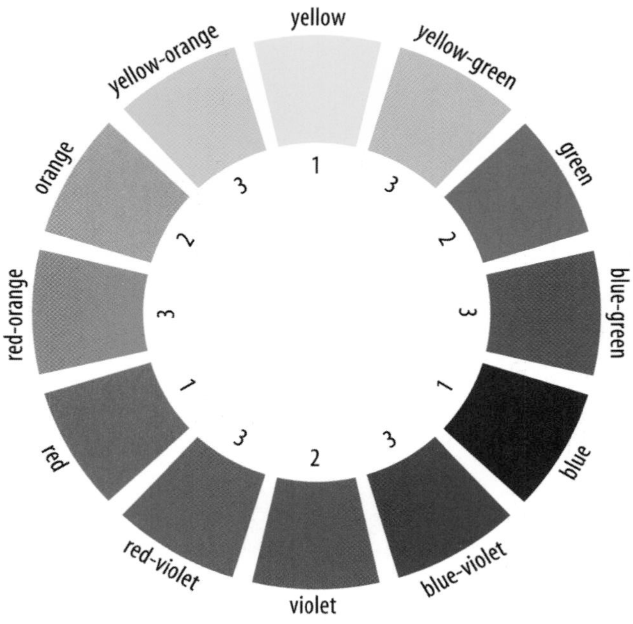

Fig. 5-20 Conventional color wheel.

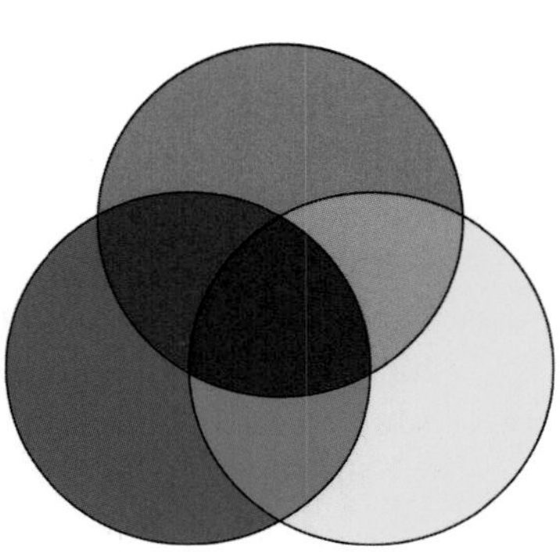

Fig. 5-21 Color mixtures of reflected pigment—subtractive process.

When we mix light, we are involved in an **additive process** (**Fig. 5-22**). Our most common exposure to this process occurs when we watch television or look at a computer monitor. This is especially apparent on a large-screen monitor, where yellow, if viewed close up, can be seen to result from the overlapping of many red and green dots. In the additive color process, as more and more colors are combined, more and more light is added to the mixture, and the colors that result are brighter than either source taken alone. As Newton discovered, when the total spectrum of refracted light is recombined, white light results.

Color is described first by reference to its **hue** as found on the color wheel. There are 12 hues in the color wheel illustrated here (see Fig. 5-20). A color is also described by its relative value, and also by its **intensity** or **saturation**. Intensity is a function of a color's relative brightness or dullness. One lowers the intensity of a hue by adding to it either gray or the hue opposite it on the color wheel (in the case of red, we would add green). Intensity may also be reduced by adding a **medium**—a liquid that makes paint easier to manipulate—to the hue.

There is perhaps no better evidence of the psychological impact that a change in intensity can make than to look at the newly restored frescoes of the Sistine

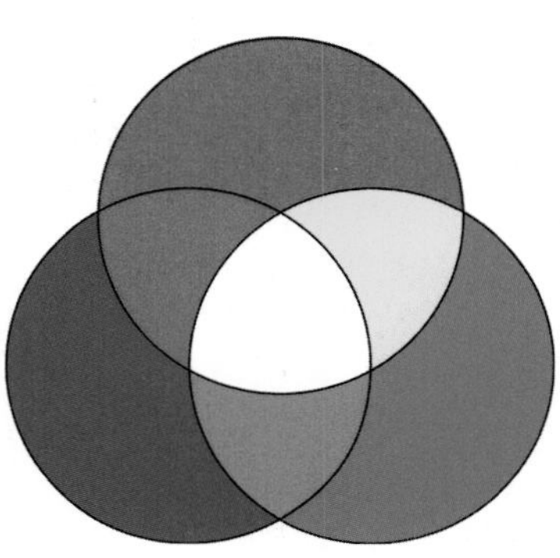

Fig. 5-22 Color mixtures of refracted light—additive process.

Chapel at the Vatican in Rome, painted by Michelangelo between 1508 and 1512 (**Figs. 5-23** and **5-24**). Restorers have discovered that the dull, somber hues always associated with Michelangelo were not the result of his **palette**—the board with a thumb hole at one end used by a painter to hold and mix colors, and, by extension, the range of colors he has chosen to use—but of centuries of accumulated dust, smoke, grease, and varnishes made of animal glue painted over the ceiling by earlier restorers. The colors are in fact much more saturated and intense than anyone had previously supposed. Some experts find them so intense that they seem, beside the golden tones of the unrestored surface, almost garish. As a result, there has been some debate about the merits of the cleaning. But, in the words of one observer: "It's not a controversy. It's culture shock."

Color Schemes

Colors can be employed by artists in different ways to achieve a wide variety of effects. **Analogous color** schemes are those composed of hues that neighbor each other on the color wheel. Such color schemes are often organized on the basis of color **temperature**. Most of us respond to the range from yellow through orange and red as warm, and to the opposite side of the color wheel, from green through violet, as cool. Jane Hammond's *Fallen* (**Fig. 5-25**) is a decidedly warm work of art—just like a sunny fall day. The

Fig. 5-23 Michelangelo, *The Creation of Adam* (unrestored), ceiling of the Sistine Chapel, 1508–12. Fresco. Vatican City. Canali Photobank, Milan, Italy.

Fig. 5-24 Michelangelo, *The Creation of Adam* (restored), ceiling of the Sistine Chapel, 1508–12. Fresco. Vatican City. akg-image/Erich Lessing.

Fig. 5-25 Jane Hammond, *Fallen*, 2004–11. Archival digital inkjet prints on archival paper with acrylic, gouache, matte medium, Jade glue, fiberglass strands, and Sumi ink on a pedestal of high-density foam, cotton, muslin, cotton thread, foam core, and handmade cotton rag paper, 11 in. × 12 ft. 10 in. × 7 ft. 5 in. Whitney Museum of American Art. New York.
2007.6. Courtesy of Galerie Lelong, New York. Photo: Peter Muscato. © Jane Hammond

color scheme consists of yellows, oranges, and reds in varying degrees of intensity and value, punctuated with an occasional touch of green. Even what appears to be brown in this composition is a result of mixing this spectrum of warm colors. Each leaf is in fact a digitally scanned and printed reproduction of an actual leaf that is then painted and dipped into a finish to make it look real. They are subsequently sewn onto the platform on which they are displayed.

But the visual warmth of Hammond's construction is double-edged. Beginning in 2004, Hammond inscribed each of these leaves with the name of a soldier killed in the Iraq War—1,511 names to begin with. As the war wore on, she continued to add new leaves to the pile. As a special exhibition of the work came to a close at New York's FLAG Art Foundation on December 31, 2011, as President Obama officially ended the war, the last leaf was added. The piece was acquired by the Whitney Museum of American Art in 2006, and when it was exhibited there in October 2007, it contained 3,786 leaves. When it opened at FLAG Art in September 2011, it contained 4,455 leaves.

If *Fallen* is a testament to the tragedy of the war in Iraq, it is also a means of healing. Hammond tells the story of a soldier's mother who overheard a conversation about the piece while visiting New York, sought it out at Hammond's gallery, and found her son's name on a leaf—a remarkable coincidence since only about one in six names is visible. The mother was able to find solace in the sheer warmth and beauty of Hammond's field of the fallen.

Just as warm and cool temperatures literally create contrasting physical sensations, when both warm and cool hues occur together in the same work of art they tend to evoke a sense of contrast and tension. Romare Bearden's *She-ba* (**Fig. 5-26**) is dominated by cool blues and greens, but surrounding and accenting these great blocks of color are contrasting areas of red, yellow, and orange.

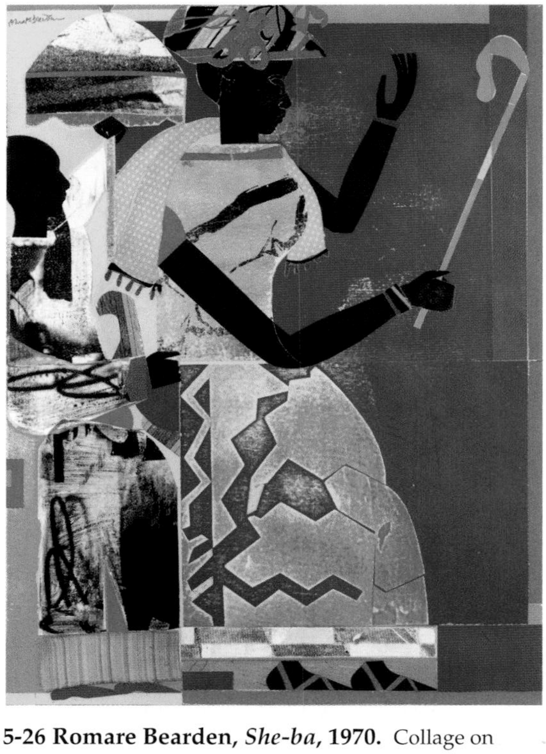

Fig. 5-26 Romare Bearden, *She-ba*, 1970. Collage on paper, cloth, and synthetic polymer paint on composition board, 4 ft. × 35⅞ in. Wadsworth Atheneum, Hartford.
Ella Gallup Sumner and Mary Catlin Sumner Collection Fund, 1971.12. Art © Romare Bearden Foundation/Licensed by VAGA, New York.

"Sometimes, in order to heighten the character of a painting," Bearden wrote in 1969, just a year before this painting was completed, "I introduce what appears to be a dissonant color where the reds, browns, and yellows disrupt the placidity of the blues and greens." Queen of the Arab culture that brought the Muslim religion to Ethiopia, Sheba here imparts a regal serenity to all that surrounds her. It is as if, in her every gesture, she cools the atmosphere, like rain in a time of drought, or shade at an oasis in the desert.

Compositions that employ hues that lie opposite each other on the color wheel, as opposed to next to each other, are called **complementary color** schemes. When two complements appear in the same composition, especially if they are pure hues, each will appear more intense. If placed next to each other, without mixing, complements seem brighter than if they appear alone. This effect, known as **simultaneous contrast**, is due to the physiology of the eye. The cells in the retina that respond to color can only register one complementary color at a time. As the cells respond to one color and then the other, the colors appear to be more intense and highly charged.

The Brazilian feather mask, known as a *Cara Grande* (**Fig. 5-27**), illustrates how complementary colors can intensify each other. The mask is worn during the annual Banana Fiesta in the Amazon Basin; almost 3 feet tall, it is made of wood and covered with pitch to which feathers are attached. The colored feathers are not dyed, but are the natural plumage of tropical birds, and their brilliance

Fig. 5-27 *Cara Grande* feather mask, Tapirapé, Rio Tapirapé, Brazil, ca. 1960.
Height 31 in. National Museum of the American Indian, Washington, D.C.

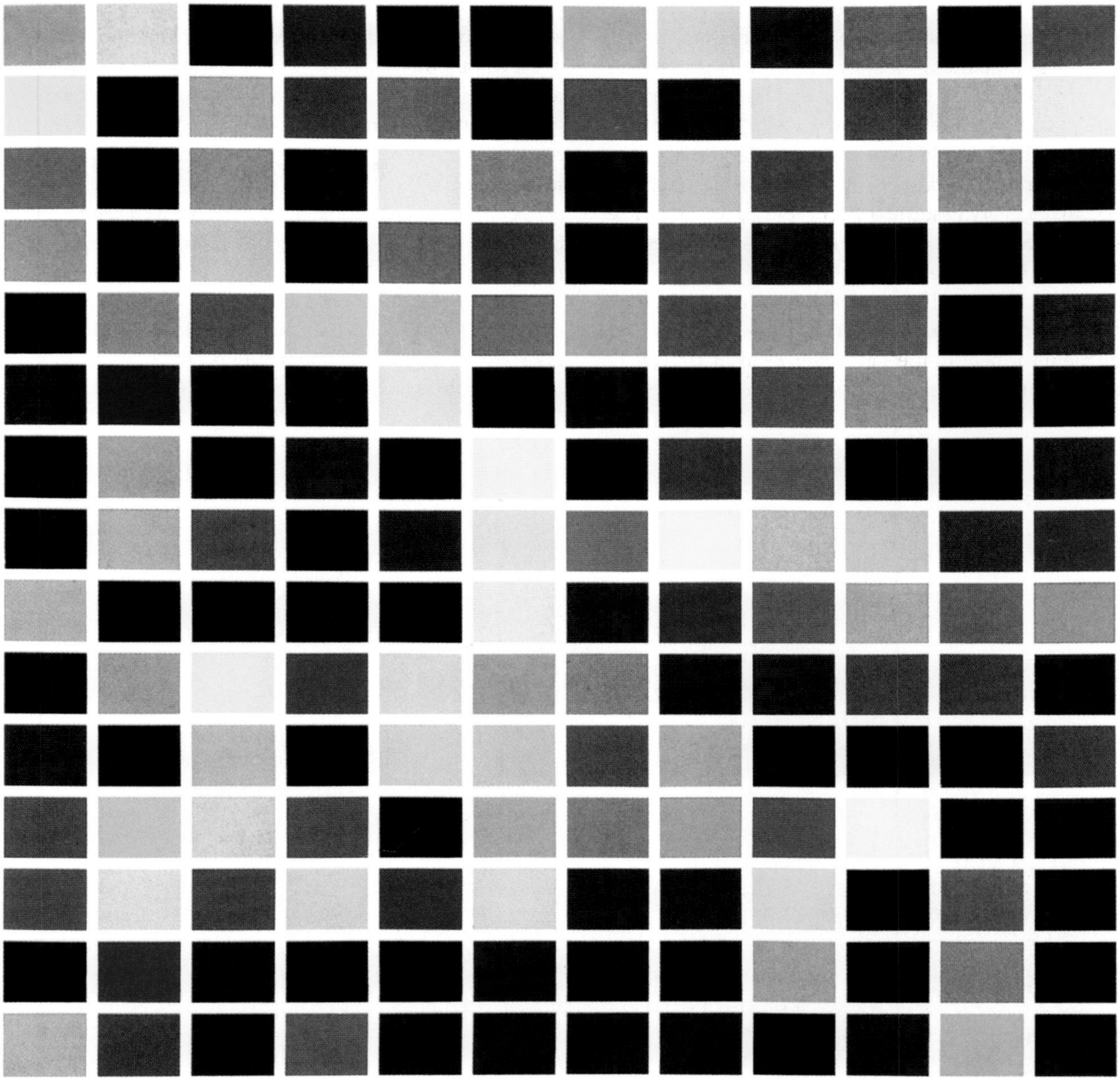

Fig. 5-28 Gerhard Richter, *180 Farben* (*180 Colors*), 1971. Oil on canvas, 6 ft. 6¾ × 6 ft. 6¾ in. Philadelphia Museum of Art.

is heightened by the simultaneous contrast between yellow-orange and blue-violet, which is especially apparent at the outer edge of the mask.

Color interactions can also cause the retina to produce a spot of color where none exists. This is readily demonstrated in Gerhard Richter's *180 Farben* (*180 Colors*) (**Fig. 5-28**). The painting belongs to a series of color charts painted by the artist from the mid-1960s on. The arrangement of the colors on the squares was done by a random process to obtain a diffuse, undifferentiated overall effect, intentionally stripping color of its emotional value. But, to Richter's delight, the paintings are hardly static. Where the vertical and horizontal white lines intersect, a grayish "pop" appears. If the viewer

Fig. 5-29 Georges Seurat, *La Chahut* (*The Can-Can*), 1889–90. Oil on canvas, 5 ft. 6⅛ in. × 4 ft. 7½ in. Museum Kröller-Müller, Otterlo, The Netherlands.

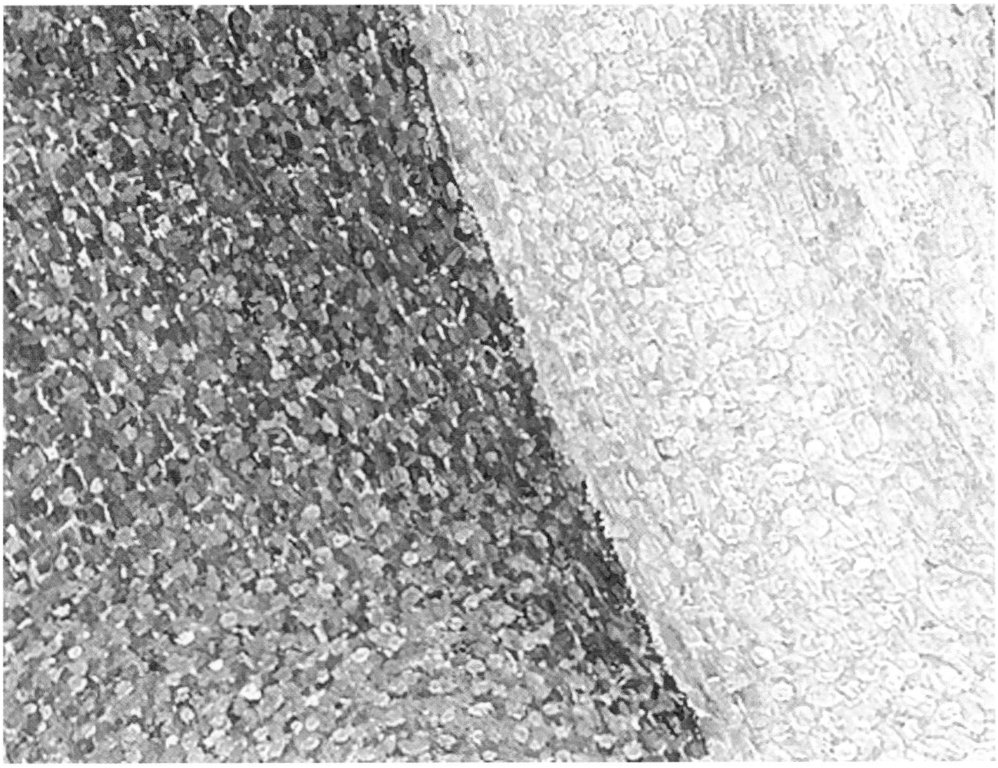

Fig. 5-30 Georges Seurat, *La Chahut* (*The Can-Can*) (detail), 1889–90.

looks at any given "pop" directly, it disappears, suggesting that it exists to the eye only at the edge of vision, a sort of blur or aura that surrounds color.

In his *La Chahut* (*The Can-Can*) (**Fig. 5-29**), Georges Seurat has tried to harmonize his complementary colors rather than create a sense of tension with them. With what almost amounts to fanaticism, Seurat painted this canvas with thousands of tiny dots, or points, of pure color in a process that came to be known as **pointillism**. Instead of mixing color on the palette or canvas, he believed that the eye of the perceiver would be able to mix colors optically. Seurat strongly believed that if he placed complements side by side—particularly orange and blue in the shadowed areas of the painting, as in the detail of the area just above the head of the bass player along the closest dancer's skirt (**Fig. 5-30**)—that the intensity of the color would be dramatically enhanced. He believed that the intensity of his color mixtures would likewise increase the emotional intensity of the work, and thus, in *La Chahut*, the combination of blue and orange, meant to suggest the light from the gas lamps on the wall and ceiling, together with the rising lines of the dancers' skirts and legs, would contribute to a sense of joyousness and festivity in the painting. But, to Seurat's dismay, most viewers found the paintings such as *La Chahut* "lusterless" and "murky." This is because there is a rather limited zone in which the viewer does in fact optically mix the pointillist dots. For most viewers, Seurat's paintings work from about 6 feet away—closer, the painting breaks down into abstract dots; farther away, the colors muddy, turning almost brown. Although Seurat's experiment was not a complete success, the contemporary artist Chuck Close has perfected the technique, as is evidenced in *The Creative Process*, pp. 108–09.

The invention of electric light at the end of the nineteenth century allowed for color to be projected with a brightness and clarity never before seen. Among the artists most taken by this new light and color were Robert and Sonia Delaunay, who explored what their poet friend Guillaume Apollinaire called "the beautiful fruit of light," the colors of the modern world. In the work of both artists, these colors assumed the shape of disks. Robert called these "simultaneous disks" (**Fig. 5-31**), and they were based on his own notions about the simultaneous contrast of colors. He sought to balance complements in giant color wheels. Sonia was less scientific in her approach

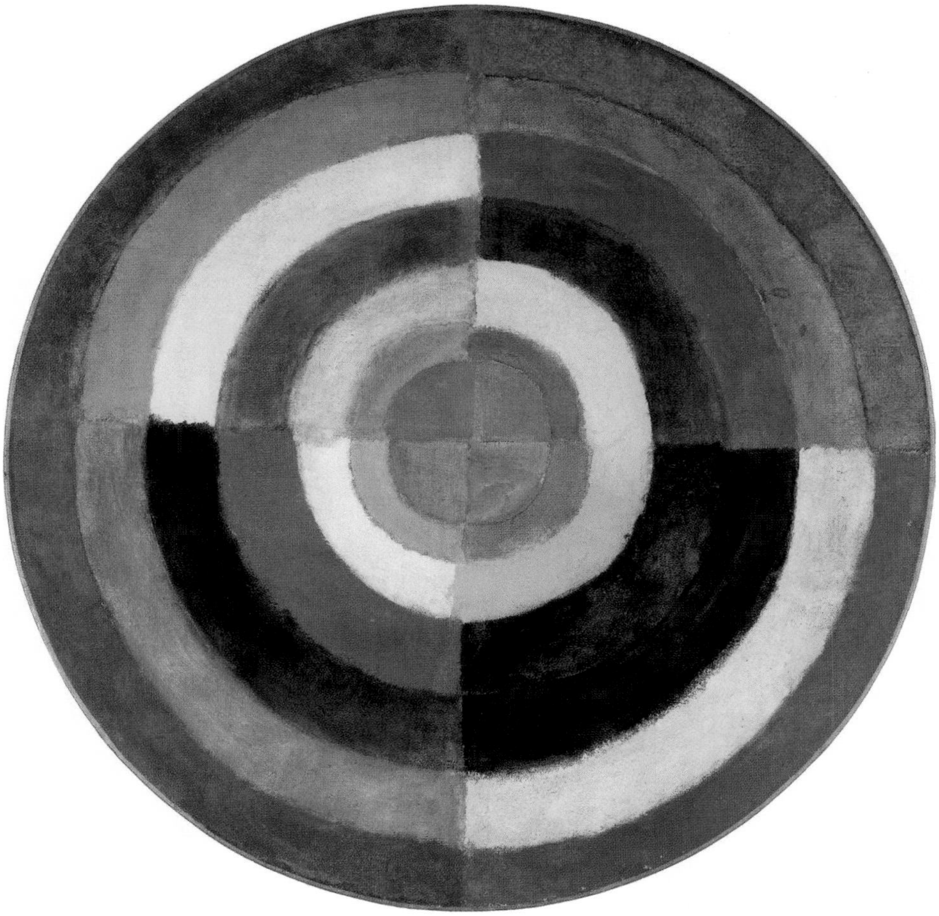

Fig. 5-31 Robert Delaunay, *Premier Disque*, 1912. Oil on canvas, diameter 4 ft. 5 in. Private collection.
Photo © Christie's Images/Bridgeman Images.

The Creative Process

The New Pointillism: Chuck Close's *Stanley*

Chuck Close's 1981 oil painting *Stanley* (**Fig. 5-32**) might best be described as "layered" pointillism (see Fig. 5-29). Like all of his paintings, the piece is based on a photograph. Close's working method is to overlay the original photograph with a grid; then he draws a grid with the same number of squares on a canvas. Close is not so much interested in representing the person whose portrait he is painting as he is in reproducing, as accurately as possible, the completely abstract design that occurs in each square of the photo's grid. In essence, Close's large paintings—*Stanley* is nearly 9 feet high and 7 feet wide—are made up of thousands of little square paintings, as the detail (**Fig. 5-33**) makes clear. Each of these "micro-paintings" is composed as a small target, an arrangement of two, three, or four concentric circles. Viewed up close, it is hard to see anything but the design of each square of the grid. But as the viewer moves farther away, the designs of the individual squares of the composition dissolve, and the sitter's features emerge with greater and greater clarity.

In an interview published in the catalog for his 1990 retrospective exhibition at the Museum of Modern Art in New York, Close describes his working method at some length, comparing his technique to, of all things, the game of golf:

> *When I used to start with the same color in each square, the whole first part of the journey was the same. But now one square will begin as pink and one as blue and one as green and one as orange, so even if the next layer in that area is going in the same part of the spectrum, what is already underneath just makes it more interesting. . . . I want to mix it up. Ultimately it allows me to be intuitive. The system is liberating in that when I used to allow myself to make paintings with any old color, I would use the same color combinations over and over again. I found myself too much a creature of habit. . . .*

Fig. 5-32 Chuck Close, *Stanley II*, 1980–81. Oil on canvas, 9 × 7 ft. Solomon R. Guggenheim Museum, New York.
Purchased with funds contributed by Mr. and Mrs. Barrie M. Damson, 1981, 81.2839. Photo: David Heald. © Solomon R. Guggenheim Foundation, New York. © Chuck Close, courtesy of Pace Gallery.

I try and make decisions in three or four moves. When I mixed paint on a palette and tried to drop it in and get it on the first crack, that was the equivalent of shooting an arrow at a bull's-eye. You hope that you made the right decision, and that it will hit the center in one action. Then, I thought, maybe I could look for some other kind of game, some other kind of process, and it occurred to me that it was possible to do something that's much more like golf. Golf is the only sport in which you move from general to specific in an ideal number of correct moves. The first stroke is just out there, the second stroke corrects that, the third stroke corrects that. By then you are hopefully on the green, and you can try to place the ball in this very specific three-and-a-half-inch diameter circle that you couldn't even have seen from the tee. So it was a different way of thinking about finding what you want, like walking through the landscape rather than going straight for something.

Close's "game" with color is exacting and demanding, requiring a knowledge of the optical effects of color mixing that is virtually unparalleled in the history of art. He is able to achieve, in his work, two seemingly contradictory goals at once. On the one hand, his work is fully representational. On the other, it is fully abstract, even nonobjective in its purely formal interest in color. Close has it both ways.

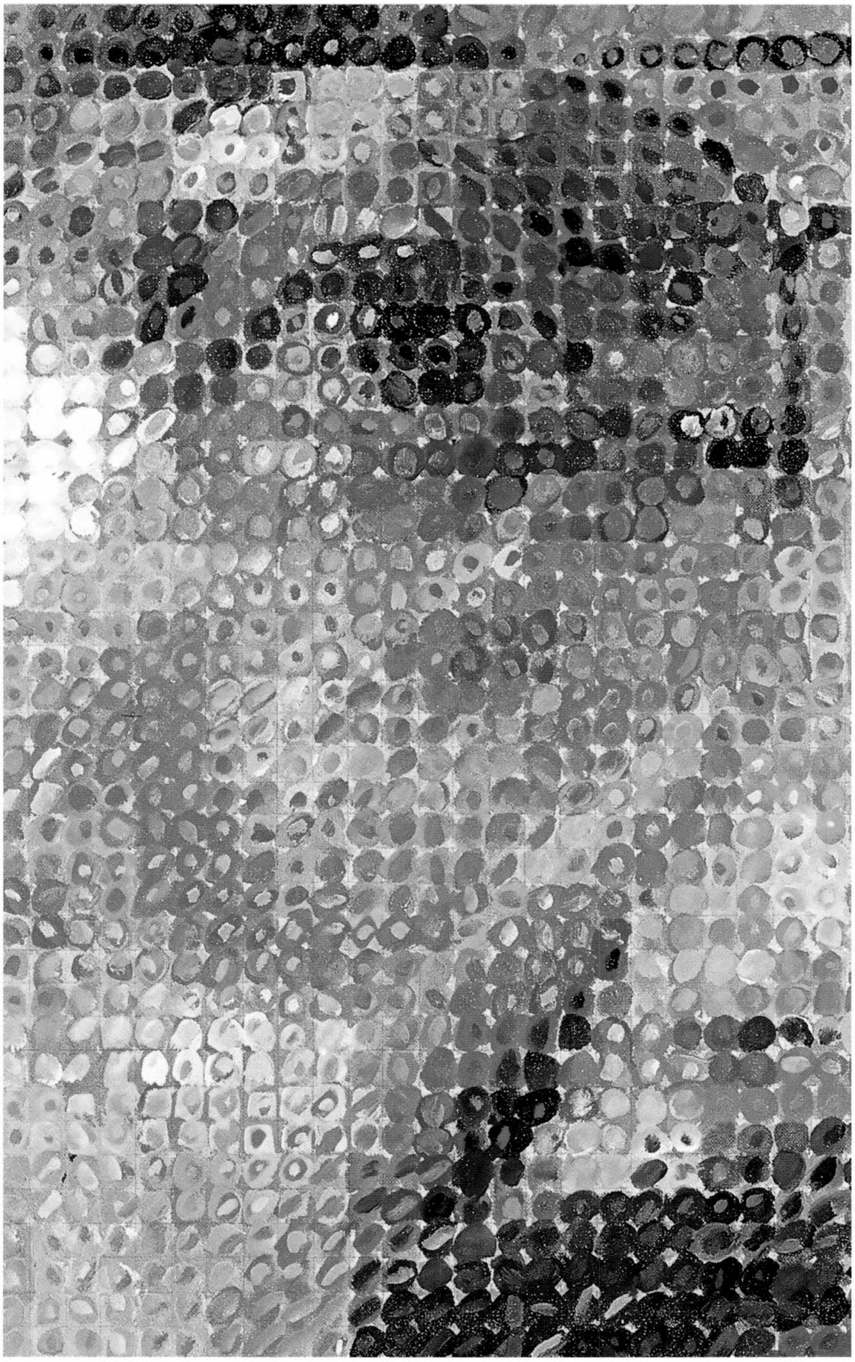

Fig. 5-33 Chuck Close, *Stanley II*, detail, 1980–81.
Purchased with funds contributed by Mr. and Mrs. Barrie M. Damson, 1981, 81.2839. Photo: David Heald. © Solomon R. Guggenheim Foundation, New York (FN 2839). © Chuck Close, courtesy of Pace Gallery.

to the design. Electric streetlights, which were still a relatively new phenomenon, transfixed her: "The halos of the new electric lights made colors and shades turn and vibrate, as if as yet unidentified objects fell out of the sky around us." In *Prismes Electriques* (*Electric Prisms*) (**Fig. 5-34**) she captured the dynamic movement of color and flowing lines that represented for her the flux and flow, the energy and dynamism, of modernity itself.

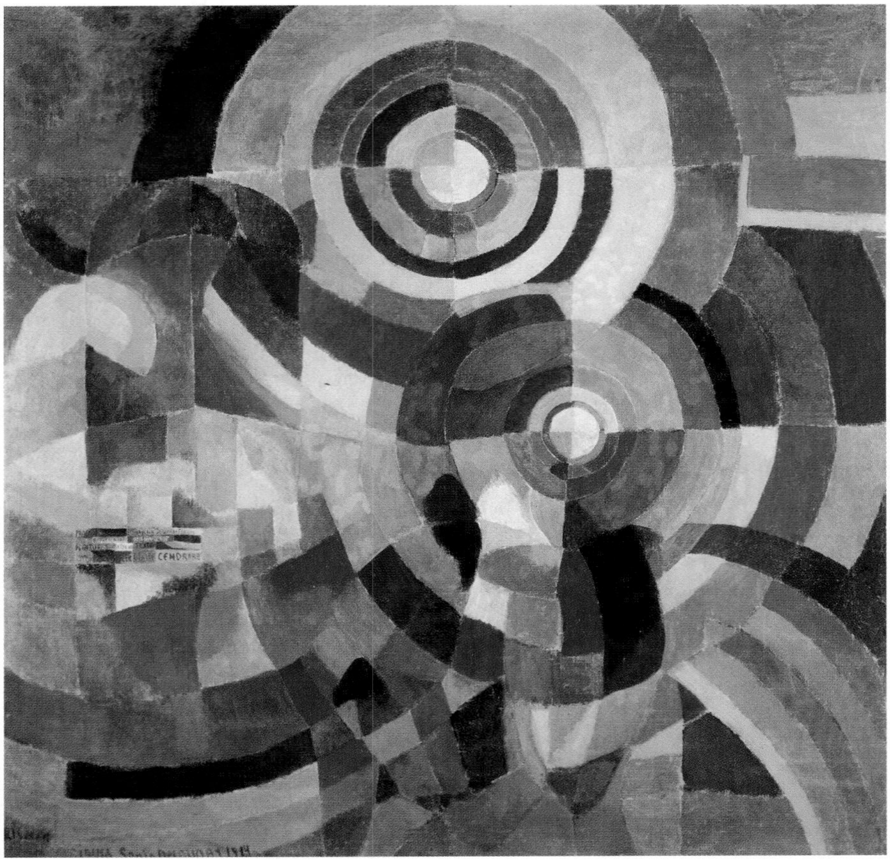

Fig. 5-34 Sonia Delaunay, *Prismes Electriques* (*Electric Prisms*), 1914. Oil on canvas, 8 ft. 2⅜ in. × 8 ft. 2⅜ in. Musée National d'Art Moderne, Paris.
© 2015. Photo Scala, Florence. Pracusa S.A.

Artists working with either analogous or complementary color schemes choose to limit the range of their color selection. Delaunay has rejected such a **closed** or **restricted palette** in favor of an **open palette**, in which she employs the entire range of hues in a wide variety of values and intensities. Such paintings are **polychromatic**. When artists limit their palette to a single color, a **monochromatic** painting results. In the 1960s, Brice Marden created a series of apparently gray monochomatic works, including *The Dylan Painting* (**Fig. 5-35**), so named, Marden says, because "I had told [Bob] Dylan that I wanted to make a painting for him, put it out in the world to help his career, but by the time I got this painting finished, he was very, very famous." To make the painting, Marden combined oil and color (in this case, a sort of eggplant purple and gray) with a mixture of turpentine and beeswax, and then applied the mixture to the canvas. Along a slight strip at the bottom edge short drips of paint mark the history of this painting process. Then, Marden went over all but the bottom strip with a spatula to eliminate all brushstrokes. It is impossible to define the color of the resulting surface, which appears to change with each change of light. The effect of the surface is, in fact, impossible to see in reproduction. From a distance, the painting is decidedly neutral. But, up close, the apparent gray becomes a richly colorful surface, full of texture created by the spatula, that catches all manner of light, and the effect is like looking into an atmosphere of almost infinite space. Marden is one of several painters of the era who, in rejecting polychromatic color and the expressive line, became known as Minimalists. But the richness of Marden's surfaces are, arguably, anything but minimal.

Fig. 5-35 Brice Marden, *The Dylan Painting*, 1966/1986. Oil and beeswax on canvas, 5 ft. ⅜ in. × 10 ft. ½ in. San Francisco Museum of Modern Art.
Helen Crocker Russell Fund purchase and gift of Mrs. Helen Portugal. © 2015 Brice Marden/Artists Rights Society (ARS), New York.

Representational and Symbolic Uses of Color

In what different ways is color used in representational art, and how is it used as a symbolic tool?

There are four different ways of using color in representational art. The artist can employ local color, represent perceptual color, create an optical mix like Seurat, or simply use color arbitrarily for formal or expressive purposes. **Local color** is the color of objects viewed close up in even lighting conditions—the color we "know" an object to be, in the way that we know a banana is yellow or a fire truck is red. Yet while we think of an object as having a certain color, we are also aware that its color can change depending on the light. As we know from the example of atmospheric perspective, we actually see a distant pine-covered hill as blue, not green. That blue is a **perceptual color**, as opposed to the local color of the green trees. The Impressionist painters were especially concerned with rendering such perceptual colors. Monet painted his landscapes outdoors, in front of his subject—*plein-air* painting is the technical term, incorporating the French term for "open air"—so as to be true to the optical colors of the scene before him. He did not paint a grainstack yellow to reflect the fact that he knew hay to be yellow "really." Rather, he painted it in the colors that natural light rendered it to his eyes. Thus, this *Grainstack* (**Fig. 5-36**) is dominated by reds, with after-images of green flashing throughout.

The Impressionists' attempt to render the effects of light by representing perceptual reality is different from Seurat's attempt to reproduce light's effects by means of optical color mixing. Monet mixes color on the canvas. Seurat expects color to mix in your own eye. He put two hues next to each other, creating a third, new hue in the beholder's eye. As we have noted, Seurat's experiment was not a complete success.

Fig. 5-36 Claude Monet, *Grainstack (Sunset)*, 1891. Oil on canvas, 28⅞ × 36½ in.
Museum of Fine Arts, Boston.
Juliana Cheney Edwards Collection, 25.112. Photograph © 2015 Museum of Fine Arts, Boston.

Fig. 5-37 Pierre Bonnard, *The Terrace at Vernonnet*, ca. 1939. Oil on canvas, 4 ft. 9$^{11}/_{16}$ in. × 6 ft. 4½ in. Metropolitan Museum of Art, New York.

Gift of Mrs. Frank Jay Gould, 1968. 68.1. © 2015. Image copyright Metropolitan Museum of Art/Art Resource/Scala, Florence. © 2015 Artists Rights Society (ARS), New York/ADAGP, Paris.

Artists sometimes choose to paint things in colors that are not "true" to either their optical or local colors. Pierre Bonnard's painting *The Terrace at Vernonnet* (**Fig. 5-37**) is an example of the expressive use of **arbitrary color**. No tree is really violet, and yet this large foreground tree is. The woman at the left holds an apple, but the apple is as orange as her dress. Next to her, a young woman carrying a basket seems almost to disappear into the background, painted, as she is, in almost the same hues as the landscape (or is it a hedge?) behind her. At the right, another young woman in orange reaches above her head, melding into the ground around her. Everything in the composition is sacrificed to Bonnard's interest in the play between warm and cool colors, chiefly orange and violet or blue-violet, which he uses to flatten the composition, so that the fore-, middle-, and backgrounds all seem to coexist in the same space. "The main subject," Bonnard would explain, "is the surface which has its color, its laws, over and above those of the objects." He sacrifices both the local and optical color of things to the arbitrary—but not unplanned or random—color scheme of the composition.

Symbolic Color

To different people in different situations and in different contexts, color symbolizes different things. There is no one meaning for any given color, though in a particular cultural environment, there may be a shared understanding of it. So, for instance, when we see a stoplight, we assume that everyone understands that red means "stop" and green means "go." In China, however, this distinction does not exist. In Western culture, in the context of war, red might mean "death" or "blood" or "anger." In the context of Valentine's Day, it means "love." Most Americans, when confronted by the complementary pair of red and green, think first of all of Christmas.

In his painting *The Night Café* (**Fig. 5-38**), Vincent van Gogh employs red and green to his own expressive ends. In a letter to his brother, Theo, written September

8, 1888, he described how the complements work to create a sense of visual tension and emotional imbalance:

> In my picture of the Night Café I have tried to express the idea that the café is a place where one can ruin oneself, run mad, or commit a crime. I have tried to express the terrible passions of humanity by means of red and green. . . . Everywhere there is a clash and contrast of the most alien reds and greens. . . . So I have tried to express, as it were, the powers of darkness in a low wine-shop, and all this in an atmosphere like a devil's furnace of pale sulphur. . . . It is color not locally true from the point of view of the stereoscopic realist, but color to suggest the emotion of an ardent temperament.

While there is a sense of opposition in Wassily Kandinsky's *Black Lines* (*Schwarze Linien*) (**Fig. 5-39**) as well, the atmosphere of the painting is nowhere near so ominous. The work is virtually nonobjective, though a hint of landscape can be seen in the upper left, where three mountainlike forms rise in front of and above what appears to be a horizon line defined by a lake or an ocean at sunset. The round shapes that dominate the painting seem to burst into flowers. Emerging like pods from the red-orange border at the painting's right, they suffuse the atmosphere with color, as if to overwhelm and dominate the nervous black lines that give the painting its title.

Color had specific symbolic meaning for Kandinsky. "Blue," he says, "is the heavenly color." Its opposite is yellow, "the color of the earth." Green is a mixture of the two; as a result, it is "passive and static, and can be compared to the so-called 'bourgeoisie'—self-satisfied, fat, and healthy." Red, on the other hand, "stimulates and excites the heart." The complementary pair of red and green juxtaposes the passive and the active. "In the open air," he writes, "the harmony of red and green is very charming," recalling for him not the "powers of darkness" that van Gogh witnessed in the pair, but the simplicity and pastoral harmony of an idealized peasant life.

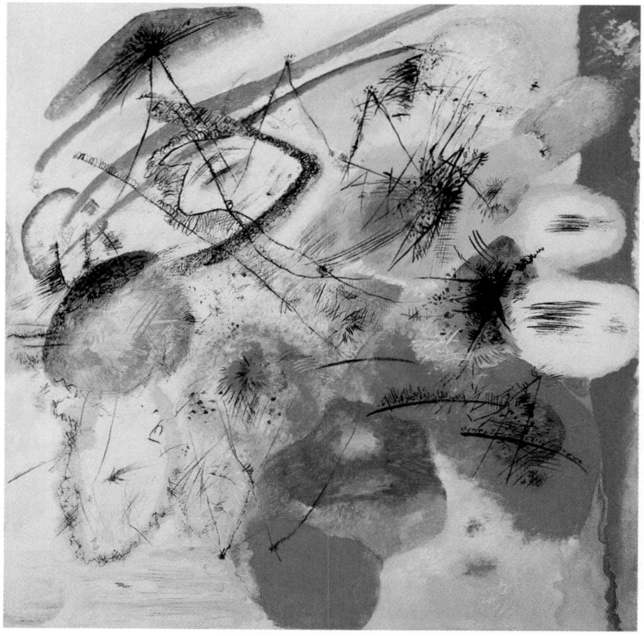

Fig. 5-39 Wassily Kandinsky, *Black Lines* (*Schwarze Linien*), December 1913. Oil on canvas, 4 ft. 3 in. × 4 ft. 3⅝ in. Solomon R. Guggenheim Museum, New York.
Gift, Solomon R. Guggenheim, 1937, 37.241. Photo: David Heald, Solomon R. Guggenheim Foundation/Art Resource, New York. © 2015 Artists Rights Society (ARS), New York/ADAGP, Paris.

Fig. 5-38 Vincent van Gogh, *The Night Café*, 1888. Oil on canvas, 28½ × 36¼ in. Yale University Art Gallery, New Haven.
Bequest of Stephen Carlton Clark, 1961.18.34.

THE CRITICAL PROCESS

Thinking about Light and Color

At first glance, Katharina Grosse's *Cincy* (**Fig. 5-40**) looks as if it might be the product of projected light, but its vibrant swathes of color are, in fact, jets of luminescent spray paint that transform the floor, ceiling, and even the windows of Cincinnati's Rosenthal Center for Contemporary Art (**Fig. 5-41**) into a color field that seems to dissolve the architectural space itself. In fact, the artist has piled dirt into the corner beneath the column and painted it as well. To make such works, Grosse seals the room, dons a full-body suit and protective helmet, grabs an industrial strength spray gun connected by tube to a compressor, and begins to spray. Able to see only a small area in front of her mask, she works intuitively, laying down one fresh band of color over another, exploring the dimensions of the space with jets of spray that reach with unabashed freedom up walls, over windows, and across floors.

Grosse's work is in part a counterstatement to the space in which it was realized. The Rosenthal Center was designed in 2003 by Iraqi-born architect Zaha Hadid, who in 2004 became the first woman and the first Muslim to be awarded the Pritzker Architecture Prize, the field's most prestigious honor. How does Grosse's work contrast with Hadid's? Why do you suppose Grosse responded to Hadid's space in the way she did?

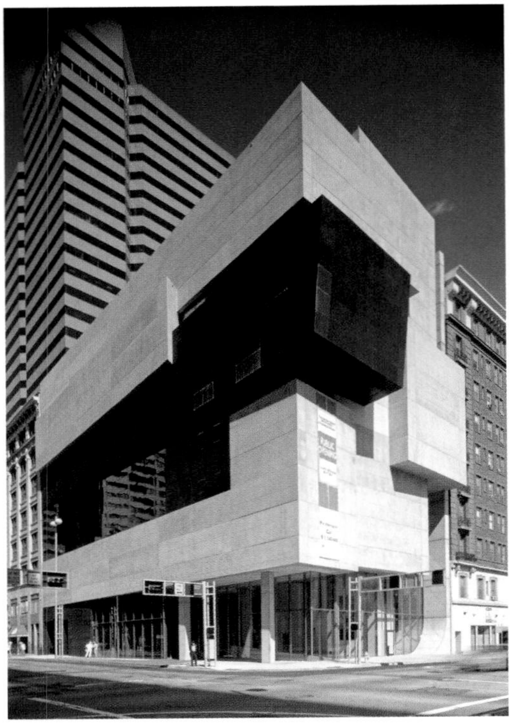

Fig. 5-41 Zaha Hadid, Rosenthal Center for Contemporary Art, Cincinnati, Ohio, 2003. © VIEW Pictures Ltd/Alamy.

Fig. 5-40 Katharina Grosse, *Cincy*, 2006. Installation view, Rosenthal Center for Contemporary Art, Cincinnati, Ohio. Courtesy of the Contemporary Arts Centre (CAC). Photo: Tony Walsh © Katharina Grosse/DACS. © 2015 Artists Rights Society (ARS), New York/VG Bild-Kunst, Bonn.

Thinking Back

5.1 Describe the ways in which artists use light to represent space and model form.

The "rules" of atmospheric, or aerial, perspective state that an object's appearance changes depending on how much atmosphere lies between it and the person viewing it. Objects that lie farther away from the viewer appear less distinct, are generally bluer in color, and have decreased contrast between lights and darks. How does atmospheric perspective differ from linear perspective? How does J. M. W. Turner use atmospheric perspective in his painting *Rain, Steam, and Speed—The Great Western Railway*?

5.2 Outline the principles of color theory, and describe the different sorts of color schemes that artists might employ.

Sir Isaac Newton first discovered that color is a direct function of light. He found that sunlight breaks into bands of different colors, known as the spectrum. Newton reorganized the visible spectrum into a circle known as the color wheel. What are the primary colors, secondary colors, and intermediate colors? What is a subtractive process of color mixing? What is a color's saturation? Colors can be employed to achieve a wide variety of effects. Compositions that employ colors that lie opposite each other on the color wheel are said to have complementary color schemes. How does a complementary color scheme differ from an analogous color scheme? What is color temperature? What is simultaneous contrast?

5.3 Explain how color might be used both in representational painting and as a symbolic tool.

Local color is the color of objects viewed up close, under even lighting conditions. Perceptual color can change depending on the light and surrounding atmosphere. What was Claude Monet's approach to color? What is *plein-air* painting? In what sense is the color in Pierre Bonnard's *The Terrace at Vernonnet* arbitrary? How did Vincent van Gogh and Wassily Kandinsky use color as a symbolic element in their work?

Chapter 6

Texture, Time, and Motion

Learning Objectives

6.1 Explain the difference between actual texture and visual texture.

6.2 Outline some of the ways that time and motion inform our experience of visual art.

To this point, we have discussed some of the most important of the formal elements employed by artists—line, space, light, and color—but several other elements can contribute significantly to an effective work of art. Texture refers to the surface quality of a work. And **time** and **motion** can be introduced into a work of art in a variety of ways.

Commenting on his 2013 project in the California High Desert near Joshua Tree National Park, *Lucid Stead* (**Fig. 6-1**), Phillip K. Smith III has said that "it is about light and shadow, reflected light, projected light, and change." But if light and color appear at first to be its primary elements, texture, time, and motion all contribute significantly to the work's power. It consists of a 70-year-old homesteader's shack—the "stead" of the title—which Smith has transformed by alternating bands of mirror with the weathered planks of the shack's siding: "The reflections, contained within their crisp, geometric bands and rectangles, contrast with the splintering bone-dry wood siding," Smith explains. As the day progresses, the mirrors reflect the surrounding landscape in ever-changing patterns of light, and this textural play seems to animate the structure. The shack appears to be at once transparent and opaque, bright and shadowed—hence the "lucid" of its title, a word that not only means "readily comprehensible," but also "bright" and "shining," or "clear" and "transparent." As night falls, LED lights within the building illuminate the windows and doors in color fields that change from one color to another at a rate that is almost imperceptible. Interior white light reveals the cracks between the structure's horizontal bands (**Fig. 6-2**). Finally, time and motion—the pace of change—are the work's ultimate theme. "This questioning of and awareness of change," Smith explains, "ultimately, is about the alignment of this project with the pace of change occurring within the desert. Through the process of slowing down and opening yourself to the quiet, only then can you really see and hear in ways that you normally could not."

Texture

What differentiates visual from actual texture?

Texture is the word we use to describe a work of art's ability to call forth certain tactile sensations and feelings. It may seem rough or smooth, as coarse as sandpaper or as fine as powder. If it seems slimy, like a slug, it may repel us. If it seems as soft as fur, it may make us want to touch it. In fact, most of us are compelled to touch what we see. It is one of the ways we come to understand our world. That's why signs in museums and galleries saying "Please Do Not Touch" are so necessary: If, for example, every

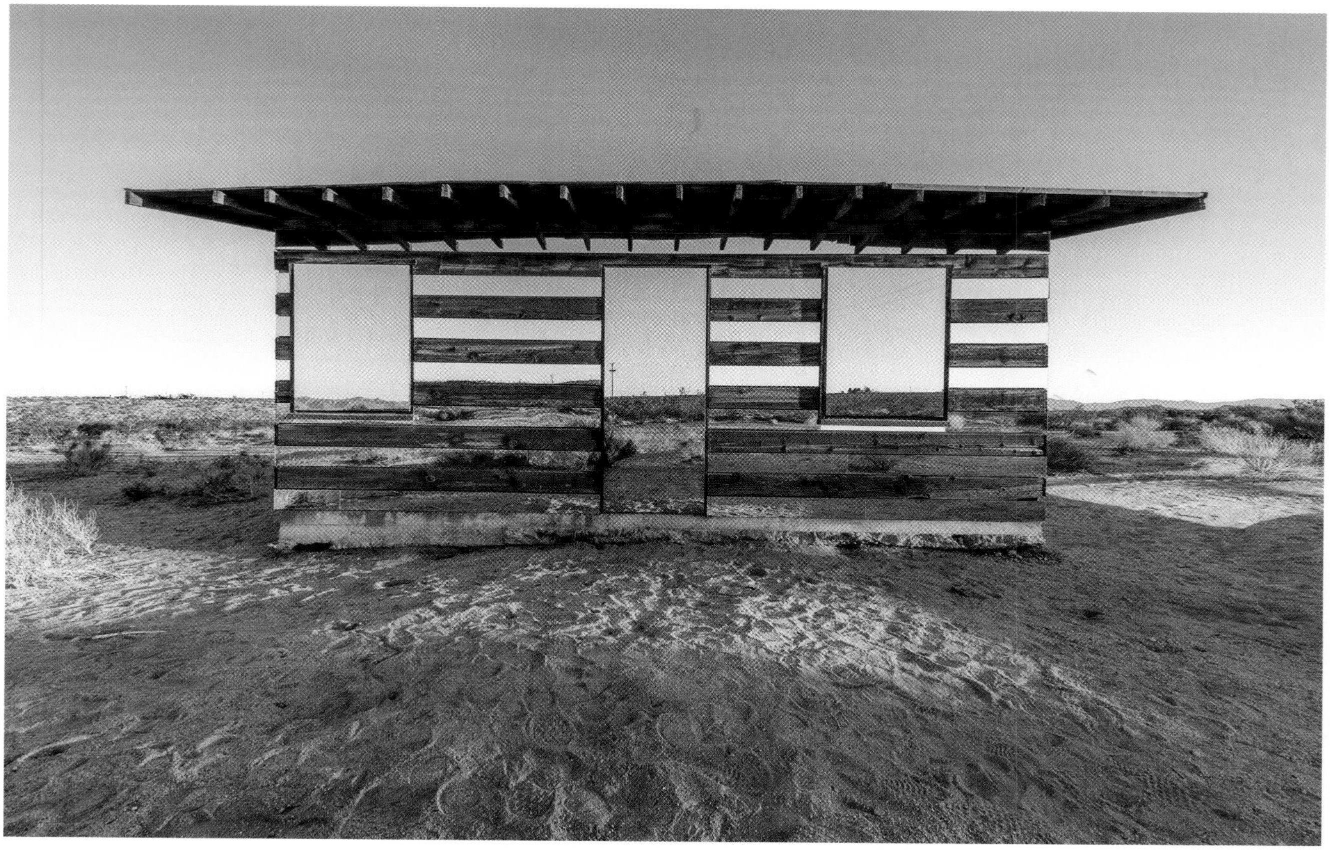

Figs. 6-1 and 6-2 Phillip K. Smith III, *Lucid Stead*, 2013. Seventy-year-old homesteader shack, mirrors, LED lights, custom-built electronic equipment, and Arduino programming.

Photo (top): Steve King. Phillip K. Smith III is represented by Royale Projects: Contemporary Art, CA and all artwork use permissions are courtesy of the gallery.
Photo (bottom): Lance Gerber. Phillip K. Smith III is represented by Royale Projects: Contemporary Art, CA and all artwork use permissions are courtesy of the gallery.

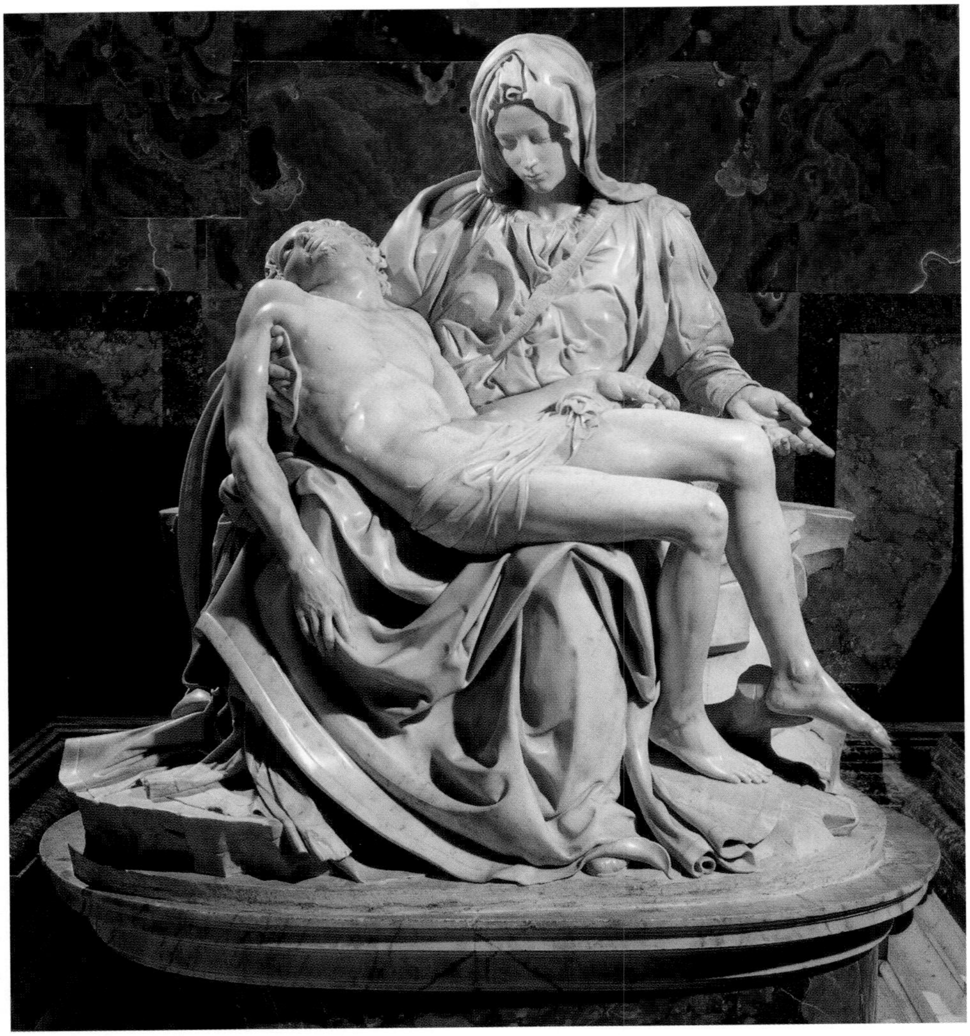

Fig. 6-3 Michelangelo, *Pietà*, 1501. Marble, height 6 ft. 8½ in. Vatican City.
Canali Photobank, Milan, Italy.

visitor to the Vatican in Rome had touched the marble body of Christ in Michelangelo's *Pietà* (**Fig. 6-3**), the rounded, sculptural forms would have been reduced to utter flatness long ago.

Actual Texture

Marble is one of the most tactile of all artistic mediums. Confronted with Michelangelo's almost uncanny ability to transform marble into lifelike form, we are virtually compelled to reach out and confirm that Christ's dead body is made of hard, cold stone and not the real, yielding flesh that the grieving Mary seems to hold in her arms. Even the wound on his side, which Mary almost touches with her own hand, seems real. The drapery seems soft, falling in gentle folds. The visual experience of this work defies what we know is materially true. Beyond its emotional content, part of the work's power derives from the stone's extraordinary texture—from Michelangelo's ability to make stone come to life.

In Manuel Neri's bronze sculpture from the *Mujer Pegada Series* (**Fig. 6-4**), the actual texture of the bronze is both smooth, where it implies the texture of skin on the figure's thigh, for instance, and rough, where it indicates the "unfinished" quality of the work. It is as if Neri can only begin to capture the whole woman who is his subject as she emerges half-realized from the sheet of bronze. Our sense of the transitory nature of the image, its fleeting quality, is underscored by the enamel paint that Neri has applied in broad, loosely gestural strokes to the bronze. This paint adds yet another texture to the piece, the texture of the brushstroke. This brushstroke helps, in turn, to emphasize the work's two-dimensional quality. It is as if Neri's three-dimensional sculpture is attempting to escape the two-dimensional space of the wall—to escape, that is, the space of painting.

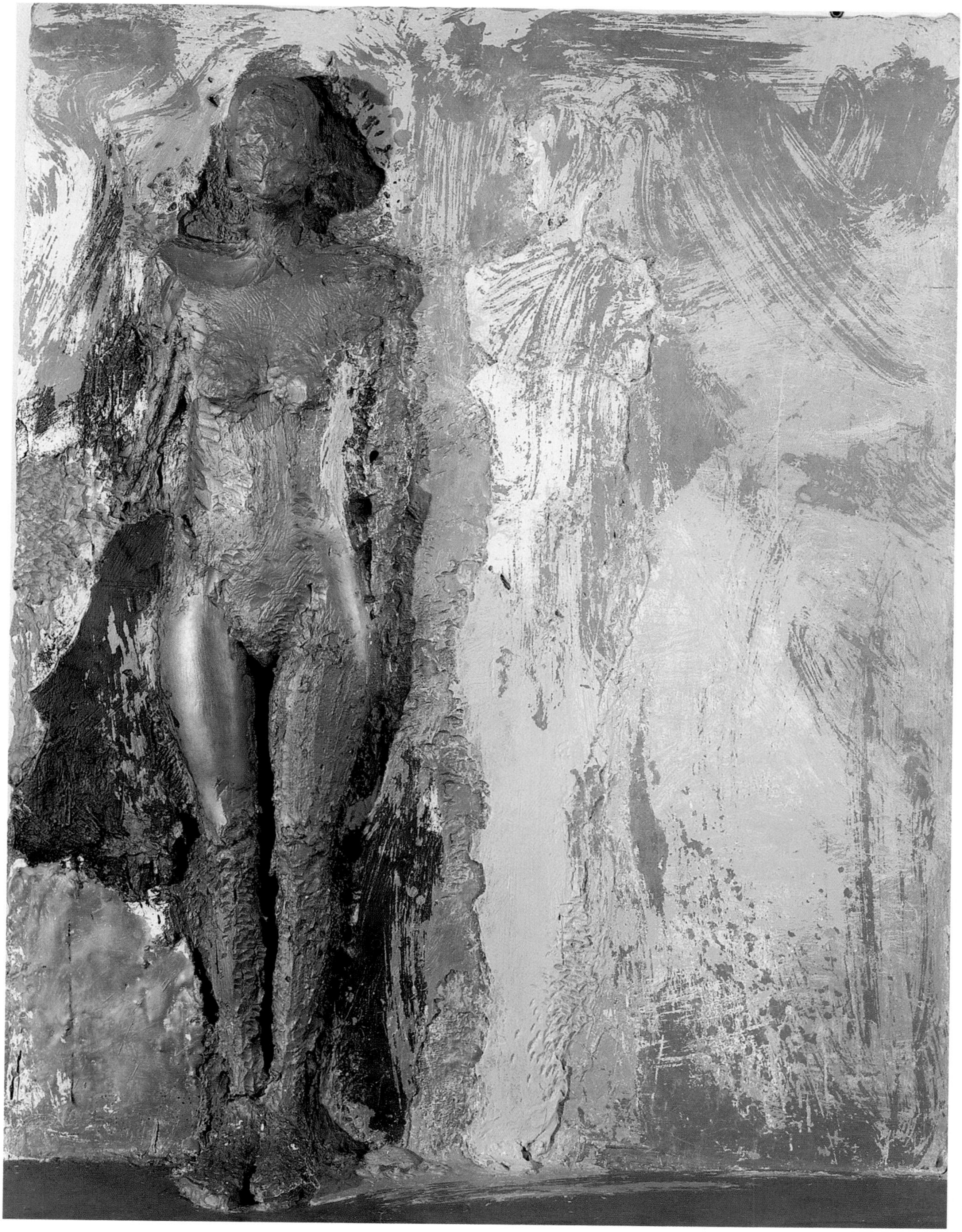

Fig. 6-4 Manuel Neri, *Mujer Pegada Series No. 2*, 1985–86. Bronze with oil-based enamel, 5 ft. 10 in. × 4 ft. 8 in. × 11 in.

Photo: M. Lee Fatheree courtesy of the Manuel Neri Trust.

Fig. 6-5 Max Ernst, *The Horde*, 1927. Oil on canvas, 18⅛ × 21⅝ in. Stedelijk Museum, Amsterdam.

Visual Texture

Visual texture appears to be actual but is not. Like the representation of three-dimensional space on a two-dimensional surface, a visual texture is an illusion. If we were to touch the painting *The Horde* (**Fig. 6-5**), it would feel primarily smooth, despite the fact that it seems to possess all sorts of actual surface texture, bumps and hollows of funguslike growth.

The painting is by Max Ernst, the inventor of a technique called **frottage**, from the French word *frotter*, "to rub." By putting a sheet of paper (painted brown for *Horde*) over textured materials (in this case, an unraveled spool of string) and then rubbing across the paper (sometimes with a pencil, but in *Horde* with an orange crayon), he was able to create a wide variety of textural effects. As he himself described his method:

> I began to experiment indifferently and to question . . . all sorts of materials to be found in my visual field: leaves and their veins, the ragged edges of a bit of linen, the brush strokes of a "modern" painting, the unwound thread of a spool, etc. There my eyes discovered human heads, animals, a battle that ended with a kiss . . . rocks, the sea and the rain, earthquakes, the sphinx in her stable, the little tables around the earth.

In *The Horde*, the lines produced by rubbing the orange crayon over the string created the contour lines of the barbaric creatures. The area above the figures was painted over with blue paint to silhouette the figures against the sky.

William A. Garnett's stunning aerial view of strip farms stretching across an eroding landscape (**Fig. 6-6**) is a study in visual texture. The plowed strips of earth contrast dramatically with the strips that have been left

Fig. 6-6 William A. Garnett, *Erosion and Strip Farms, East Slope of the Tehachapi Mountains*, 1951. Gelatin-silver print, 15⁹⁄₁₆ × 19½ in. Museum of Modern Art, New York.

fallow. And the predictable, geometric textures of the farmed landscape also contrast with the irregular veins and valleys of the unfarmed and eroded landscape in the photograph's upper left. Garnett was, in fact, an avid pilot, deeply interested in American land-use practices even as he was deeply moved by the beauty of the country as seen from the air. Over the course of his career, he logged over 10,000 hours of flight time, photographing the landscape out the window as he traveled over every state and many parts of the world.

The evocation of visual textures is, in fact, one of the primary tools of the photographer. When light falls across actual textures, especially raking light, or light that illuminates the surface from an oblique angle, the resulting patterns of light and shadow emphasize the texture of the surface. In this way, the Garnett photograph reveals the subtlest details of the land surface. But remember: The photograph itself is smooth and flat, and its textures are therefore visual. The textures of its subject, revealed by the light, are actual ones.

Time and Motion

In what ways do time and motion inform our experience of visual art?

One of the most traditional distinctions made between the plastic arts—painting and sculpture—and the written arts—such as music and literature—is that the former are spatial and the latter temporal media. That is, we experience a painting or sculpture all at once; the work of art is before us in its totality at all times. But we experience music and literature over time, in a linear way; a temporal work possesses a distinct beginning, middle, and end.

While there is a certain truth to this distinction, time plays a greater role in the plastic arts than such a formulation might suggest. Some works of art actually move, as, for instance video and film do. Insofar as both tell stories—insofar as they are narrative arts—they might seem closer to a work of literature than to a painting or sculpture. But both video and film rely at

Fig. 6-7 Alexander Calder, *Untitled*, 1976. Aluminum and steel, overall 29 ft. 11⅜ in. × 75 ft. 11⅝ in., gross weight 920 lb. National Gallery of Art, Washington, D.C.

Gift of the Collectors Committee, 1977.76.1 Courtesy of the National Gallery of Art, Washington, D.C. © 2015 Calder Foundation, New York/ Artists Rights Society (ARS), New York.

least as much upon their visual presence as their narrative structure for effect. Sculptures often require us to move around them in order to appreciate them fully (see Chapter 12). And some sculptures actually move. Alexander Calder's mobiles are an example. His untitled mobile that hangs above the lobby of the East Building of the National Gallery of Art in Washington, D.C. (**Fig. 6-7**) is composed of 13 panels and 12 arms that, like a dancer moving through the space of a stage, slowly spin around their points of balance propelled by the currents of air that circulate in the space. We call such works **kinetic art**—art that moves or at least seems to move.

Narratives in Art

Even in the case where the depiction of a given event implies that we are witness to a photographic "frozen moment," an instant of time taken from a larger sequence of events, the single image may be understood as part of a larger narrative sequence: A story. Consider, for instance, Gianlorenzo Bernini's sculpture of *David* (**Fig. 6-8**). As opposed to Michelangelo's *David* (see Fig. 1-28), who rests, fully self-contained, at some indeterminate time before going into battle, Bernini's figure is caught in the midst of action, coiled and ready to launch his stone at the giant Goliath. In a sense, Bernini's sculpture is "incomplete." The figure of Goliath is implied, as is the imminent flight of David's stone across the implicit landscape that lies between the two of them. As viewers, we find ourselves in the middle of this same scene, in a space that is much larger than the sculpture itself. We intuitively back away from David's sling. We follow his eyes toward the absent giant. We are engaged in David's energy, and in his story.

A work of art can also, in and of itself, invite us to experience it in a linear or temporal way. Isidro Escamilla's

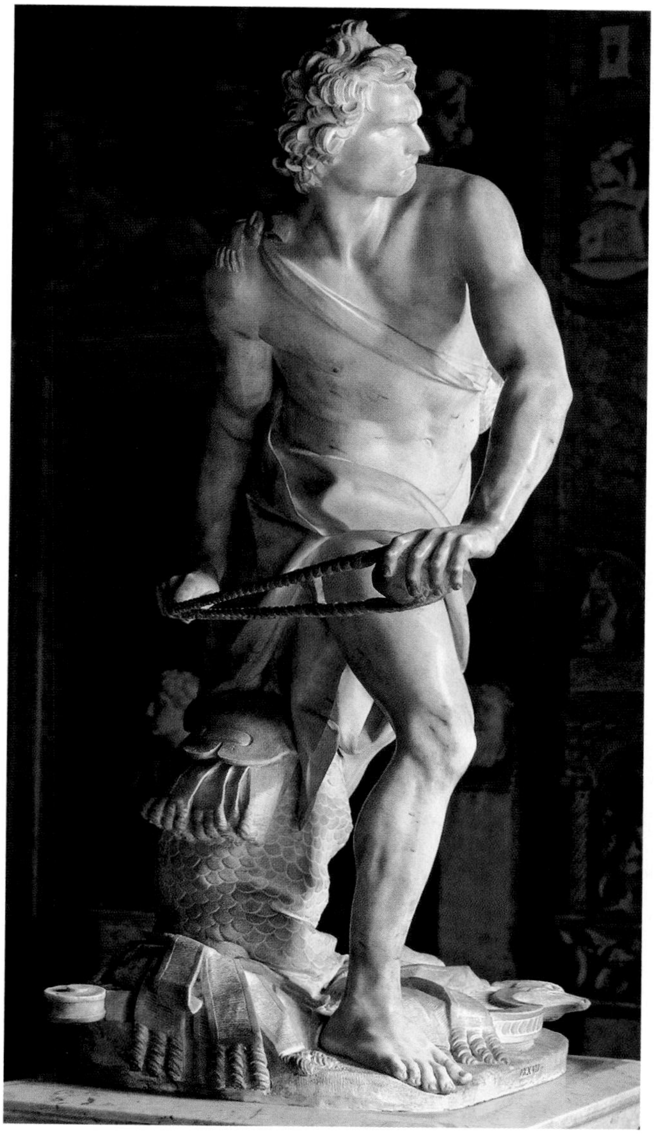

Fig. 6-8 Gianlorenzo Bernini, *David*, 1623. Marble, life-size. Galleria Borghese, Rome.
Canali Photobank, Milan/SuperStock.

Virgin of Guadalupe (**Fig. 6-9**) narrates one of the most famous events in Mexican history. The story goes that in December 1531, on a hill north of Mexico City called Tepeyac, once site of a temple to an Aztec mother goddess, a Christian Mexican Indian named Juan Diego beheld a beautiful dark-skinned woman (in the top left corner of the painting). Speaking in Nahuatl, the native Aztec language, she told Juan Diego to tell the bishop to build a church in her honor at the site, but the bishop doubted Juan Diego's story. So the Virgin caused roses to bloom on the hill out of season and told Juan Diego to pick them and take them to the bishop (represented in the bottom left corner of the painting). When Juan Diego opened his cloak to deliver the roses, an image of the dark-skinned Virgin appeared on the fabric (represented at the bottom right). Soon, miracles were associated with her, and pilgrimages to Tepeyac became increasingly popular. In 1746, the Church declared the Virgin patron saint of New Spain, and in the top right corner of the painting, other saints pay her homage. By the time Escamilla painted this version of the story, the Virgin of Guadalupe had become the very symbol of Mexican identity.

Likewise, we naturally "read" Pat Steir's *Chrysanthemum* paintings (see Figs. 5-7 and 5-8) from left to right, in linear progression. While each of Claude Monet's *Grainstack* paintings (see Fig. 5-36) can be appreciated as a wholly unified totality, each can also be seen as part of a larger whole, a time sequence. Viewed in a series, they are not so much "frozen moments" removed from time as they are about time itself, the ways in which our sense of place changes over time.

Fig. 6-9 Isidro Escamilla, *Virgin of Guadalupe*, September 1, 1864. Oil on canvas, 22⅞ × 15 in. The Brooklyn Museum.
Henry L. Batterman Fund, 45.128.189.

Fig. 6-10 Claude Monet, *Water Lilies, Morning: Willows* (central section and right side), 1916–26.
Triptych, each panel 6 ft. 8 in. × 14 ft. 2 in. Musée de l'Orangerie, Paris.
Bridgeman Images.

Seeing Over Time

To appreciate large-scale works of art, it may be necessary to move around and view them from all sides, or to see them from a number of vantage points—to view them over time. Monet's famous paintings of his lily pond at Giverny, which were installed in the Orangerie museum in Paris in 1927, are also designed to compel the viewer to move (**Fig. 6-10**). They encircle the room, and to be in the midst of this work is to find oneself suddenly in the middle of a world that has been curiously turned inside out: The work is painted from the shoreline, but the viewer seems to be surrounded by water, as if the room were an island in the middle of the pond itself. The paintings cannot be seen all at once. There is always a part of the work behind you. There is no focal point, no sense of unified perspective. In fact, the series of paintings seems to organize itself around and through the viewer's own acts of perception and movement.

According to Georges Clemenceau, the French statesman who was Monet's close friend and who arranged for the giant paintings to hang in the Orangerie, the paintings could be understood not just as a simple representation of the natural world, but also as a representation of a complex scientific fact, the phenomenon of "Brownian motion." First described by the Scottish scientist Robert Brown in 1827, Brownian motion is a result of the physical movement of minute particles of solid matter suspended in fluid. Any sufficiently small particle of matter suspended in water will be buffeted by the molecules of the liquid and driven at random throughout it. Standing in the midst of Monet's panorama, the viewer's eye is likewise driven randomly through the space of the paintings. The viewer is encircled by them, and there is no place for the eye to rest, an effect that Jackson Pollock would achieve later in the century in the monumental "drip" paintings he executed on the floor of his studio (see *The Creative Process*, pp. 126–27).

The Illusion of Movement

Some artworks are created precisely to give us the illusion of movement. In **optical painting**, or "Op Art," as it is more popularly known, the physical characteristics of certain formal elements—particularly line and color—are subtly manipulated to stimulate the nervous system into thinking it perceives movement. Bridget Riley's *Drift No. 2* (**Fig. 6-11**) is a large canvas that seems to wave and roll before our eyes even though it is stretched taut across its support. One of Riley's earliest paintings was an attempt to find a visual equivalent to heat. She had been crossing a wide plain in Italy: "The heat off the plain was quite incredible—it shattered the topographical structure of it and set up violent color vibrations. . . . The important thing was to bring about an equivalent shimmering sensation on the canvas." In *Drift No. 2*, we encounter not heat, but wave action, as though we were, visually, out at sea.

Fig. 6-11 Bridget Riley, *Drift No. 2*, 1966. Acrylic on canvas, 7 ft. 7½ in. × 7 ft. 5½ in. Albright-Knox Art Gallery, Buffalo, New York.

Gift of Seymour H. Knox, Jr., 1967. © 2015. Albright Knox Art Gallery/Art Resource, New York/Scala, Florence. © Bridget Riley 2015. All rights reserved, courtesy of Karsten Schubert, London.

The Creative Process

Painting as Action: Jackson Pollock's *No. 32, 1950*

While not as large as Monet's paintings in the Orangerie, Jackson Pollock's works are still large enough to engulf the viewer. The eye travels in what one critic has called "galactic" space, following first one line, then another, unable to locate itself or to complete its visual circuit through the web of paint. Work such as this has been labeled "action painting," not only because it prompts the viewer to become actively engaged with it, but also because the lines that trace themselves out across the sweep of the painting seem to chart the path of Pollock's own motions as he stood over it. The drips and sweeps of paint record his action as a painter and document it, a fact suggested by Rudy Burckhardt in a photograph taken in June 1950 of Pollock at work on *No. 32, 1950* (**Figs. 6-12** and **6-13**). Painting is not so much a thing—the finished work—as it is an action, the act of painting itself.

Burckhardt had driven from Manhattan to Springs, a village on the eastern end of Long Island, where Pollock lived and worked, painting in a small barn on his property, to photograph the artist at work for a series of articles appearing in *Artnews* titled "'X' Paints a Picture." This photograph would illustrate "Pollock Paints a Picture." But Pollock was reluctant to let Burckhardt photograph him working. "He told me he couldn't paint in front of the camera," Burckhardt remembers. "But he was willing to pretend, so I took pictures of him making the gestures he would make when he actually painted."

Burckhardt's photograph nevertheless tells us much about Pollock's working method. Pollock longed to be completely involved in the process of painting. He wanted to become wholly absorbed in the work. As he had written in a short article called "My Painting," published in 1947, "When I am in

Fig. 6-12 Rudy Burckhardt, Jackson Pollock painting *No. 32, 1950*, 1950.

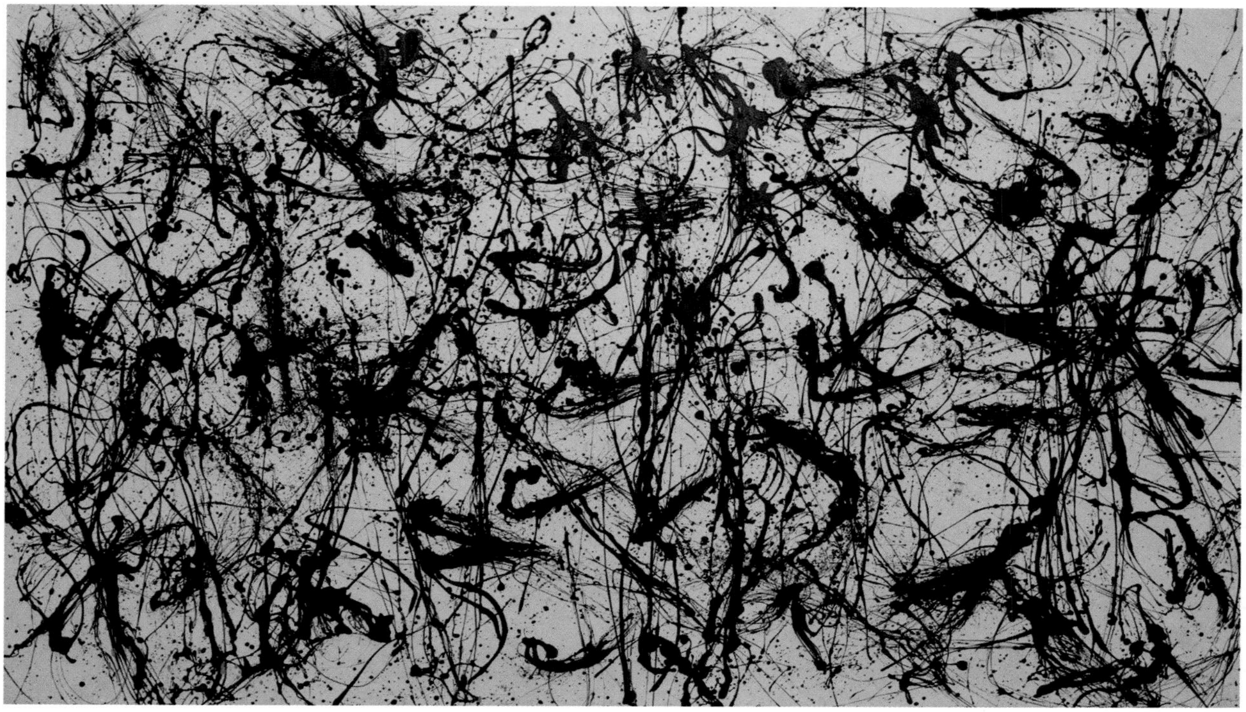

Fig. 6-13 Jackson Pollock, *No. 32, 1950*, 1950. Enamel on canvas, 8 ft. 10 in. × 15 ft. Kunstsammlung Nordrhein-Westfalen, Düsseldorf, Germany.

my painting, I'm not aware of what I'm doing . . . the painting has a life of its own. I try to let it come through. It is only when I lose contact with the painting that the result is a mess. Otherwise there is pure harmony, an easy give and take, and the painting comes out well." Burckhardt was undoubtedly aware of Pollock's statement, but seeing him in his studio reaffirmed it. "Pollock said he liked to be in the painting when he worked," says Burckhardt. "He was submerged, in a way. To see everything he had done, he had to hang the canvas on the wall. Or if he wanted a quick look, he would leave it on the floor and get up on a ladder."

In Burckhardt's photograph, we sense Pollock's absorption in the work. We can imagine the immediacy of his gesture as he flings paint, moving around the work, the paint tracing his path. He worked on the floor, in fact, in order to heighten his sense of being in the work. "I usually paint on the floor," he says in Hans Namuth's film of him at work, also dating from 1950. "I feel more at home, more at ease in a big area, having a canvas on the floor, I feel nearer, more a part of a painting. This way I can walk around it, work from all four sides and be in the painting." According to Namuth, when Pollock was painting, "his movements, slow at first, gradually became faster and more dancelike. . . . Pollock's method of painting suggested a moving picture, the dance around the canvas, the continuous movement, the drama." In fact, the traceries of line on the canvas are like choreographies, complex charts of a dancer's movement. In Pollock's words, the paintings are

energy and motion
made visible—
memories arrested in space.

Fig. 6-14 Grace Ndiritu, *Still Life: White Textiles*, 2005/2007.
Still. Silent video, 4 min. 57 sec.

Time-Based Media

The ways in which time and motion can transform the image itself is one of the principal subjects of Grace Ndiritu, a British-born video and performance artist of Kenyan descent. Ndiritu makes what she calls "hand-crafted videos," solo performances given in front of a camera fixed on a tripod. *Still Life: White Textiles* (**Fig. 6-14**) is one part of the larger four-screen video work *Still Life*, which can be found on Vimeo. Ndiritu's title, *Still Life*, is entirely ironic, for, seated between two sheets of African batik printed fabric, she caresses her thighs, moves her hands beneath the fabric, pulls it, stretches it—in short, she animates the cloth. At once hidden and exposed, Ndiritu creates an image that is at once modestly chaste and sexually charged.

Still Life was inspired by a 2005 exhibition of paintings by Henri Matisse at the Royal Academy in London, *Matisse: The Fabric of Dreams, His Art and His Textiles.* Seeing the show, Ndiritu said,

> reaffirmed the similarity of our working process . . . we share the ritual of assembling textiles and setting up the studio with fabrics as a background to galvanize our artistic practice. Matisse understands and appreciates the beauty and simplicity of working with textiles. The hallucinogenic properties of overlapping patterns, shift and swell in his paintings, override perspective and divorce shape from color.

The effects of which Ndiritu speaks are clearly visible in Matisse's *Harmony in Red (The Red Room)* (see Fig. 4-27), where the textile pattern of the tablecloth is mirrored in the wallpaper, flattening perspective and disorienting the viewer's sense of space. After visiting North Africa in 1911, Matisse often painted female models clothed in African textiles in settings decorated with other textile patterns. But in Ndiritu's work, time and motion transform the textile from decorative pattern into live action. By implication, the female body in Ndiritu's "video painting," as she calls it, is transformed

Fig. 6-15 Teresa Hubbard and Alexander Birchler, *Detached Building*, 2001.
High-definition video with sound transferred to DVD, 5 min. 38 sec. loop.

Fig. 6-16 Teresa Hubbard and Alexander Birchler, *Detached Building*, 2001. High-definition video with sound transferred to DVD, 5 min. 38 sec. loop. Installation photo by Stefan Rohner, courtesy of the artists and Tanya Bonaker Gallery, New York.

from simply a passive object of contemplation—as it was in so many of Matisse's paintings—into an almost aggressive agent of seduction. The power of the work lies in the fact that, simultaneously hidden and exposed as Ndiritu is, that seduction is at once invited and denied.

Video artists Teresa Hubbard and Alexander Birchler think of their videos as "long photographs" to which they have added sound, thus extending the space of the image beyond the frame. In *Detached Building* (**Fig. 6-15**), the camera dollies in one seamless movement around the inside of a tin shed converted into a workshop and rehearsal space, moving to the sound of chirping crickets over a cluttered workbench, a guitar, a chair, a sofa, a drumset, and a power drill, then passing without interruption through the shed's wall into the neglected garden behind it. A young woman enters the garden, picks up stones, and throws them at a nearby house. A window can be heard breaking, and a dog begins to bark. The camera passes back into the interior of the shed, where three young men are now sitting around the room, while a fourth plays a continuous riff on a bass guitar. The camera sweeps around the room again and then passes back outside. The young woman has disappeared. Only the chirping of crickets and the muted sound of the bass guitar can be heard. The camera passes back through the wall, sweeps around the room again, and moves back outside to a view of the guitar player within. The video plays on a continuous 5-minute, 38-second loop, and so, at this point, the camera returns to the empty workshop, and the entire sequence repeats itself. What, the viewer wonders, is the connection between the two scenarios, the boys inside, the girl outside? No plot evidently connects them, only a series of oppositions: Interior and exterior, light and dark, male and female, the group and the individual. The movement of the camera across the boundary of the wall suggests a disruption not only of space but of time. In looped video works such as this, viewers can enter the installation at any point (**Fig. 6-16**), leave at any point, and construct any narrative they want out of what they see.

Finally, one of the most pervasive new forms of viewer involvement in the ongoing temporal space of the image is to be found in interactive online role-playing games such as *World of Warcraft*. Literally thousands of players join either the Alliance or the Horde, creating military agreements with one another or squaring off against each other in epic battles that occur in this virtual world. Since Blizzard Entertainment creates a constant stream of new adventures and territories to explore, occupied by an ever-changing array of new enemies, and since each player becomes his or her own hero, the game space is literally ever-changing.

THE CRITICAL PROCESS

Thinking about the Formal Elements

Bill Viola's video installation *Room for St. John of the Cross* creates a structure of opposition similar to Hubbard and Birchler's *Detached Building*. The work consists, firstly, of a small television monitor in a cubicle that shows a color image of a snow-covered mountain (**Fig. 6-17**). Barely audible is a voice reading poetry. The videotape consists of a single "shot." The camera never moves. The only visible movement is wind blowing through the trees and bushes.

This cubicle is like the cell of the Spanish mystic and poet St. John of the Cross, who was imprisoned in 1577 for nine months in a windowless cell too small to allow him to stand upright. In this cell, he wrote most of the poems for which he is known, poems in which he often imaginatively flies out of captivity, over the city walls and across the mountains. The image on the small monitor is the landscape of which St. John dreams. But in addition, on a large screen, behind the cubicle, Viola has projected a black-and-white video image of snow-covered mountains, shot with an unstable handheld camera (**Fig. 6-18**). These mountains move in wild, breathless flights, image after image flying by in an uneven, rapid rhythm, like the imagination escaping imprisonment on the sound of the loud roaring wind that fills the room, making the voice reading in the cubicle even harder to hear. The meditative stillness of the small cubicle is countered by the fury of the larger space.

Fig. 6-17 Bill Viola, *Room for St. John of the Cross*, 1983. Video/sound installation. Museum of Contemporary Art, Los Angeles.
Bill Viola Studio LLC. Photo: Kira Perov.

As we ourselves move in this installation—and we must move in order to view the piece—we experience many of the formal elements of art all at once. How do you think the architecture of the cell contrasts with the image on the large screen? What conflicting senses of space does Viola employ? How is the play between light and dark, and black-and-white and color imagery, exploited? How does time affect your experience of the piece? These are the raw materials of art, the formal elements, playing upon one another in real time. Viola has set them in motion together, in a single composition.

Fig. 6-18 Bill Viola, *Room for St. John of the Cross*, 1983. Video/sound installation. Museum of Contemporary Art, Los Angeles.
Bill Viola Studio LLC. Photo: Kira Perov.

Thinking Back

6.1 Explain the difference between actual texture and visual texture.

Actual texture refers to the real surface quality of an artwork. Visual texture, by contrast, is an illusion, not unlike the representation of three-dimensional space on a two-dimensional surface. How does Manuel Neri use texture in *Mujer Pegada Series No. 2*? What is the technique of frottage?

6.2 Outline some of the ways that time and motion inform our experience of visual art.

Traditionally, the plastic arts (such as painting and sculpture) have been regarded as spatial, while music and literature have been classified as temporal. However, it is important to recognize the temporal aspect of the plastic arts as well. How is Alexander Calder's *Untitled* an example of kinetic art? An image or object may often be part of a larger story, which is, by definition, sequential. Why might Gianlorenzo Bernini's *David* be called "incomplete"? How do Claude Monet's paintings of water lilies relate to the phenomenon of Brownian motion?

Of all the arts, film and video are probably most naturally concerned with questions of time and motion. What does Grace Ndiritu do in her "hand-crafted videos"? What do Hubbard and Birchler mean when they call their videos "long photographs"? In what ways do online games address questions of time and motion?

Chapter 7

The Principles of Design

Learning Objectives

7.1 Define symmetrical, asymmetrical, and radial balance.

7.2 Explain the relationship between emphasis and focal point.

7.3 Differentiate between scale and proportion.

7.4 Describe the relationship between pattern, repetition, and rhythm.

7.5 Discuss the traditional relationship between unity and variety, and why postmodernist artists have tended to emphasize variety over unity.

The word design is both a verb and a noun. To design something involves organizing the formal elements—line, space, light and color, texture, pattern, time and motion (see Chapters 3–6)—into a unified whole, a composition or design. Design is also a field of study and work within the arts, encompassing graphic, fashion, interior, industrial, and product design (see Chapter 15); here we will focus on design principles that can apply to all works of art.

The principles of design are usually discussed in terms of the qualities of balance; emphasis; proportion and scale; pattern, rhythm, and repetition; and unity and variety. For the sake of clarity, we must discuss these qualities one by one, but artists unite them. For example, Leonardo da Vinci's famous *Study of Human Proportion: The Vitruvian Man* (**Fig. 7-1**) embodies them all. The work's title refers to the ancient Roman architectural historian Vitruvius. For Vitruvius, the circle and the square were ideal shapes. Symmetry, proportion, and ratio, in turn, derive from the perfection of the human figure in all its parts, and the perfectly symmetrical shapes of the circle and square find their source in the figure and are generated by the figure's position in space. Thus, Leonardo's figure is perfectly balanced and symmetrical. The very center of the composition is the figure's navel, a focal point that represents the source of life itself, the fetus's connection by the umbilical cord to its mother's womb. Each of the figure's limbs appears twice, once to fit in the square, symbol of the finite, earthly world, and once to fit in the circle, symbol of the heavenly world, the infinite and the universal. In this way, the various aspects of existence—mind and matter, the material and the transcendental—are unified by the design into a coherent whole.

By way of contrast, the Rasin Building in Prague in the Czech Republic (**Fig. 7-2**) seems anything but unified. Built on the site of a Renaissance structure destroyed in World War II, the building's teetering sense of collapse evokes the postwar cityscape of twisted I-beams, blown-out facades with rooms open to the sky, and sunken foundations, all standing next to a building totally unaffected by the bombing. But that said, the building is also a playful, almost whimsical celebration, among other things, of the marvels of modern engineering—a building made to look as if it is on the brink of catastrophe, even as it is completely structurally sound. So light-hearted is the building that it was called the "Dancing House," or, more specifically, "Fred and Ginger," after the American film stars Fred Astaire and Ginger Rogers. The more solid tower on the corner seems to be leading the transparent tower—Ginger—by the waist, as the two spin around the corner.

The building was the idea of Czech architect Vlado Milunić, who enlisted American architect Frank Gehry to collaborate on the project. To many eyes in Prague, a city renowned for its classical architecture, it seemed an absolutely alien American element dropped into the city. But Milunić conceived of the building as addressing modern Prague even as it engaged the city's past. He wanted the building to consist of two parts: "Like a society that forgot its totalitarian past—a static part—but was moving into a world full of changes. That was the main idea. Two different parts in dialogue, in tension, like plus and minus, like Yang and Yin, like man and woman." It was Gehry who nicknamed it "Fred and Ginger."

Despite the building's startling sense of tension, the architects used many of the traditional principles of design—most notably rhythm and repetition, balance, scale and proportion, and unity and variety—all of which we will consider in more detail later in the chapter. If one side seems about to fall, the other holds it up, in a perfect state of balance. The windows of the more solid tower, connected by sweeping curvilinear lines, move up and down on the facade with an almost musical rhythm. But it was most important to the architects to establish a simultaneous sense of connection and discontinuity between the two towers; they were not meant to blend into a harmonious, unified whole. Rather, it was variety—and change—that most interested them.

Leonardo's study is a remarkable example of the "rules" of proportion, yet the inventiveness and originality of Milunić and Gehry's work teach us, from the outset, that the "rules" guiding the creative process are, perhaps, made to be broken. In fact, the very idea of creativity implies a certain willingness on the part of artists to go beyond the norm, to extend the rules, and to discover new ways to express themselves. As we have seen, artists can easily create visual interest

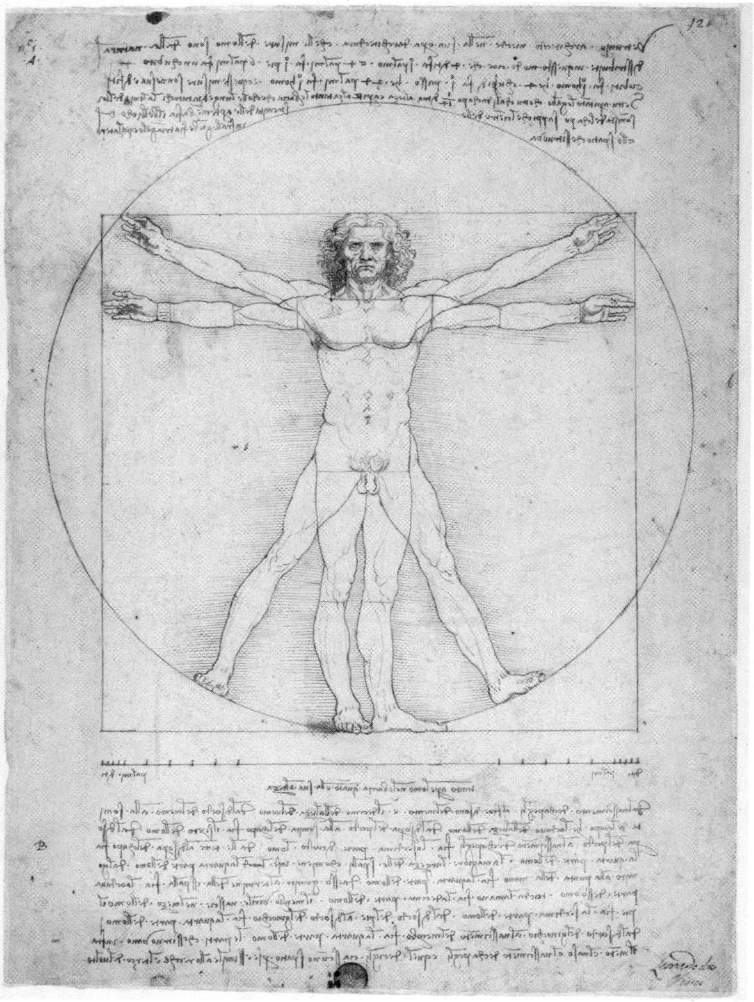

Fig. 7-1 Leonardo da Vinci, *Study of Human Proportion: The Vitruvian Man*, ca. 1492. Pen-and-ink drawing, 13½ × 9⅝ in. Gallerie dell'Accademia, Venice. CAMERAPHOTO Arte, Venice.

Fig. 7-2 Frank Gehry and Vlado Milunić, Rasin Building (a.k.a. the "Dancing House" or "Fred and Ginger"), Prague, Czech Republic. 1992–96.
© Curva de Luz/Alamy.

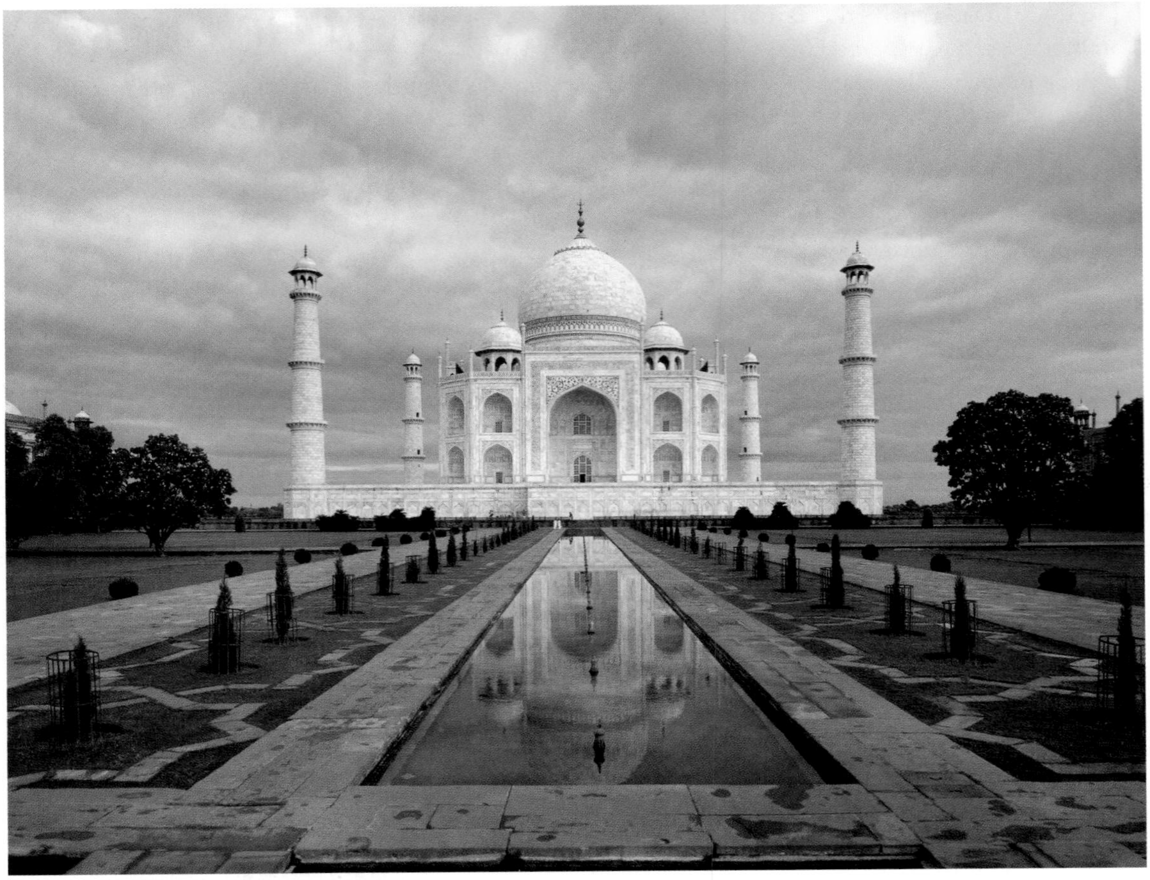

Fig. 7-3 Taj Mahal, Agra, India, Mughal period, ca. 1632–48.

by purposefully breaking with conventions such as the traditional rules of perspective; likewise, any artist can stimulate our interest by purposefully manipulating the principles of design.

In the remainder of this chapter, we discuss the way artists combine the formal elements with design principles to create inventive, original work. Once we have seen how the formal elements and their design come together, we will be ready to survey the various materials, or **media**, that artists employ to make their art.

Balance

What characterizes symmetrical, asymmetrical, and radial balance?

As a design principle, **balance** refers to the even distribution of weight in a composition. In sculpture and architecture, **actual weight**, or the physical weight of materials in pounds, comes into play, but all art deals with **visual weight**, the apparent "heaviness" or "lightness" of the shapes and forms arranged in the composition. Artists achieve visual balance in compositions by one of three means—symmetrical balance, asymmetrical balance, or radial balance. They may also deliberately create a work that appears to lack balance, knowing that instability is threatening and makes the viewer uncomfortable.

Symmetrical Balance

If you were to draw a line down the middle of your body, each side of it would be, more or less, a mirror reflection of the other. When children make "angels" in the snow, they are creating, almost instinctively, **symmetrical** representations of themselves that recall Leonardo's *Study of Human Proportion*. When each side is exactly the same, we have **absolute symmetry**. But even when it is not, as is true of most human bodies, where there are minor discrepancies between one side and the other, the overall effect is still one of symmetry, what we call **bilateral symmetry**. The two sides seem to line up.

One of the most symmetrically balanced—and arguably one of the most beautiful—buildings in the world is the Taj Mahal, built on the banks of the Jumna River at Agra in northern India (**Fig. 7-3**). Conceived as a mausoleum for the favorite wife of Shah Jahan, who died giving birth to their fourteenth child, it is basically a square, although each corner is cut off in order to create a subtle octagon. Each facade is identical, featuring a central arched portal, flanked by two stories of smaller arched openings: These voids contribute to a sense of weightlessness in the building, which rises to a central onion dome. The facades are inlaid with elaborate decorations of semiprecious stones—carnelian, agate, coral, turquoise, garnet, lapis, and jasper—but they are so delicate and lacelike that they emphasize the whiteness of the whole rather than calling attention to themselves. The sense of overall symmetry is further enhanced by the surrounding gardens and reflecting pools.

One of the dominant images of symmetry in Western art is the crucifix, which is, in itself, a construction of absolute symmetry. In Enguerrand Quarton's remarkable *Coronation of the Virgin* (**Fig. 7-4**), the crucifix at the lower center of the composition is a comparatively small detail in the overall composition. Nevertheless, its cruciform shape dominates the whole, and all the formal elements in the work are organized around it. Thus, God, the Father, and Jesus, the Son, flank Mary in almost perfect symmetry, identical in their major features (though the robes of each fall a little differently). On earth below, the two centers of the Christian faith flank the cross, Rome on the left and Jerusalem on the right. And at the very bottom of the painting, below ground level, Purgatory, on the left, out of which an angel assists a newly redeemed soul, balances Hell on the right. Each element balances out another, depicting a unified theological universe.

Fig. 7-4 Enguerrand Quarton, *Coronation of the Virgin*, 1453–54. Panel painting, 6 ft. × 7 ft. 2⅝ in.
Musée de l'Hospice, Villeneuve-lès-Avignon, France.
Bridgeman Images.

Fig. 7-5 Frida Kahlo, *Las Dos Fridas* (*The Two Fridas*), 1939. Oil on canvas, 5 ft. 9⅕ in. × 5 ft. 9⅕ in. Museo de Arte Moderno, Mexico City.

© 2015. Photo Art Resource/Bob Schalkwijk/Scala, Florence. © 2015 Banco de México Diego Rivera Frida Kahlo Museums Trust, Mexico, D.F./Artists Rights Society (ARS), New York.

Perhaps reflecting her own Catholic upbringing, and the predominance of symmetrical altarpieces in Mexican churches, Frida Kahlo's double self-portrait, *Las Dos Fridas* (*The Two Fridas*) (**Fig. 7-5**), is itself symmetrically balanced. Kahlo was married to a successful painter, the Mexican muralist Diego Rivera (see Fig. 20-17), and the portrait represents Rivera's rejection of her. According to Kahlo, the Frida on the right, in native Tehuana costume, is the Frida whom Rivera had loved. The Frida on the left is the rejected Frida. A vein runs between them both, originating in a small photo of Rivera as a child on the once-loved Frida's lap, passing through both hearts, and terminating in the unloved Frida's lap, cut off by a pair of surgical scissors. But the flow of blood cannot be stopped, and it continues to drip, joining the embroidered flowers on her dress.

Asymmetrical Balance

Balance can be achieved even when the two sides of the composition lack symmetry, if they seem to possess the same visual weight. A composition of this nature is said to be **asymmetrically balanced**. You probably remember from childhood what happened when an older and larger child got on the other end of the seesaw. Up you shot, like a catapult. In order to right the balance, the larger child had to move toward the fulcrum of the seesaw, giving your smaller self more leverage and allowing the plank to balance. The illustrations (**Fig. 7-6**) show, in visual terms, some of the ways this balance can be attained (in a work of art, the center axis of the work is equivalent to the fulcrum):

(a) A large area closer to the fulcrum is balanced by a smaller area farther away. We instinctively see something large as heavier than something small.

(b) Two small areas balance one large area. We see the combined weight of the two small areas as equivalent to the larger mass.

(c) A dark area closer to the fulcrum is balanced by a light area of the same size farther away. We instinctively see light-colored areas as light in weight, and dark-colored areas as dense and heavy.

(d) A large light area is balanced by a small dark one. Because it appears to weigh less, the light area can be far larger than the dark one that balances it.

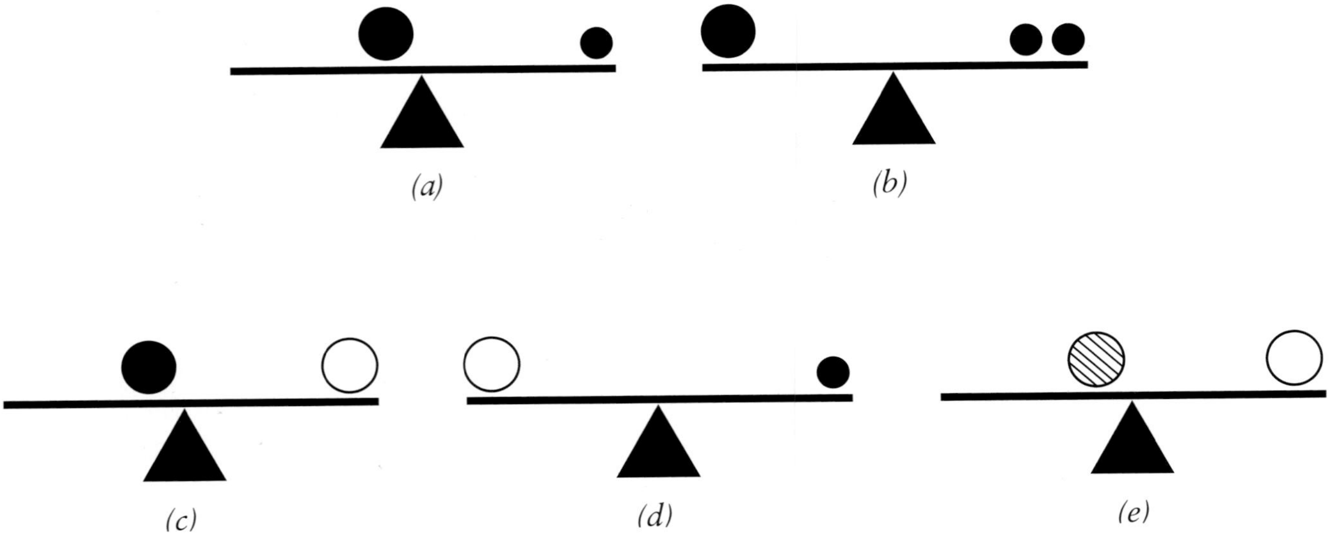

Fig. 7-6 Some different varieties of asymmetrical balance.

(e) A textured area closer to the fulcrum is balanced by a smooth, even area farther away. Visually, textured surfaces appear heavier than smooth ones because texture lends the shape an appearance of added density—it seems "thicker" or more substantial.

These are only a few of the possible ways in which works might appear balanced. There are, however, no "laws" or "rules" about how to go about visually balancing a work of art. Artists generally trust their own eyes. When a work looks balanced, it is balanced.

Johannes Vermeer's *Woman Holding a Balance* (**Fig. 7-7**) is an asymmetrically balanced composition whose subject is the balance between the material and spiritual worlds. The center axis of the composition runs through the fulcrum of the scales that the woman is holding. Areas of light and dark on each side balance the design. The woman is evidently in the process of weighing her jewelry, which is scattered on the table before her. Behind her is a painting depicting the Last Judgment, when Christ weighs the worth of all souls for entry into Heaven. The viewer is invited to think about the connection between the images in the two sides of the painting and how they relate to the woman's life.

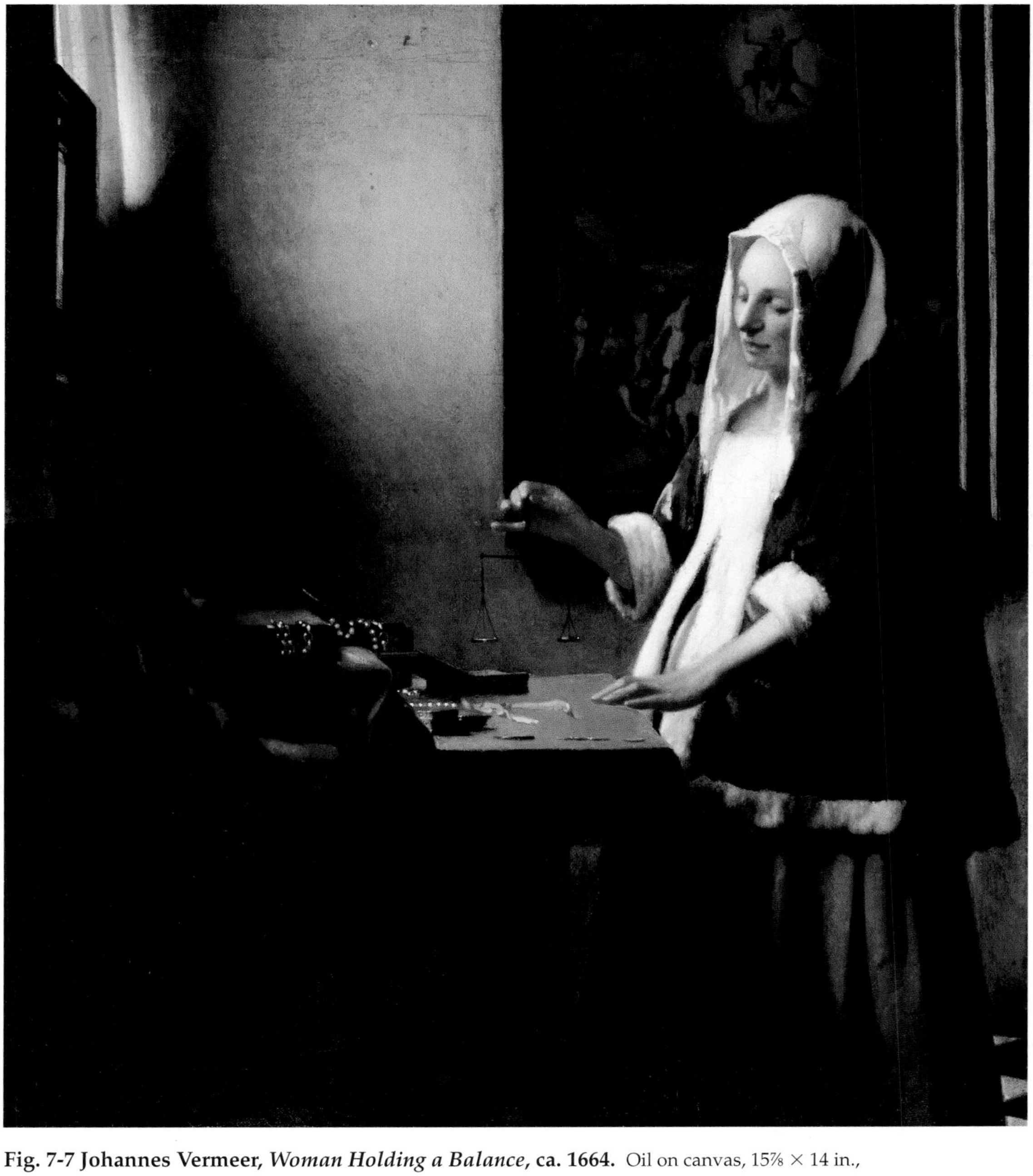

Fig. 7-7 Johannes Vermeer, *Woman Holding a Balance*, ca. 1664. Oil on canvas, 15⅞ × 14 in., framed 24¾ × 23 × 3 in. National Gallery of Art, Washington, D.C.

Fig. 7-8 Childe Hassam, *Boston Common at Twilight*, 1885–86. Oil on canvas, 42 in. × 5 ft. Museum of Fine Arts, Boston. Gift of Miss Maud E. Appleton, 1931.952. Photograph © 2015 Museum of Fine Arts, Boston.

Childe Hassam's *Boston Common at Twilight* (**Fig. 7-8**) is a good example of asymmetrical balance functioning in yet another way. The central axis around which this painting is balanced is not in the middle, but to the left. The setting is a snowy sidewalk on Tremont Street at dusk, as the gaslights are coming on. A fashionably dressed woman and her daughters are feeding birds at the edge of Boston Common. The left side of this painting is much heavier than the right. The dark bulk of the buildings along Tremont Street, along with the horse-drawn carriages and streetcars and the darkly clad crowd walking down the sidewalk, contrast with the expanse of white snow that stretches to the right, an empty space broken only by the dark trunks of the trees rising to the sky. The tension between the serenity of the Common and the bustle of the street, between light and dark—even as night comes on and daylight fades—reinforces our sense of asymmetrical balance. If we were to imagine a fulcrum beneath the painting that would balance the composition, it would in effect divide the street from the Common, dark from light, exactly, as it turns out, below the vanishing point established by the buildings, the street, and the lines of the trees extending down the park. Instinctively, we place ourselves at this fulcrum.

Radial Balance

A final type of balance is **radial balance**, in which everything radiates outward from a central point. The large, dominating, and round stained-glass window above the south portal of Chartres Cathedral in France (**Fig. 7-9**) is a perfect example. Called a "rose window" because of its dominant color and its flowerlike structure, it represents the Last Judgment. At its center is Jesus, surrounded by the symbols of Matthew, Mark, Luke, and John, the writers of the Gospels, and angels and seraphim. The Apostles, depicted in pairs, surround these, and on the outer ring are scenes from the Book of Revelation. In other words, the entire New Testament of the Bible emanates from Jesus in the center.

It is no accident that the house that many think of as one of the great masterpieces of Renaissance architecture, the Villa La Rotonda, designed by Andrea Palladio (**Fig. 7-10**), is defined by its radial balance. Located just outside the city of Vicenza, Italy, and built in the 1560s, its floor plan recalls Leonardo's *Study of Human Proportion* (see Fig. 7-1). Like Leonardo, in fact, Palladio was a careful student of Vitruvius. As in the Vitruvian ideal, the main floor, with its central, domed rotunda surrounded

Fig. 7-9 Rose window, south transept, Chartres Cathedral, ca. 1215.
Chartres, France.
Angelo Hornak.

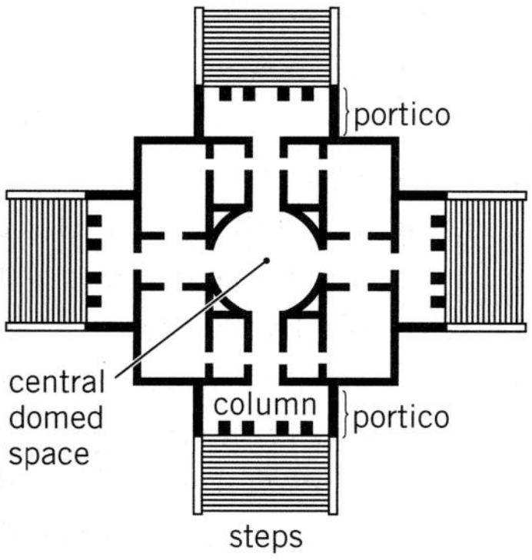

Fig. 7-10 Andrea Palladio, Villa La Rotonda and plan of main floor (*piano nobile*), begun 1560s.
CAMERAPHOTO Arte, Venice.

Fig. 7-11 Anna Vallayer-Coster, *Still Life with Lobster*, 1781. Oil on canvas, 27¾ × 35¼ in. Toledo Museum of Art, Toledo, Ohio. Purchased with funds from the Libbey Endowment, Gift of Edward Drummond Libbey, 1968.1A. Photo: Photography Incorporated, Toledo.

by reception rooms, is perfectly symmetrical. Designed for family life and entertainment, the house looks outward, toward the light of the countryside, rather than inward to the shadow of a courtyard. It is situated on the crest of a hill. On each of its four sides, Palladio has placed a porch, or loggia, approached by a broad staircase, designed to take advantage of the views. In his *Four Books on Architecture*, published near the end of his life, Palladio described the building's site and vistas:

> The site is one of the most pleasing and delightful that one could find because it is on top of a small hill which is easy to ascend; on one side it is bathed by the Bacchiglione, a navigable river, and on the other is surrounded by other pleasant hills which resemble a vast theater and are completely cultivated and abound with wonderful fruit and excellent vines; so, because it enjoys the most beautiful vistas on every side, some of which are restricted, others more extensive, and yet others which end at the horizon, loggias have been built on all four sides; under the floor of these loggias and the hall are the rooms for the convenience and use of the family.

In the words of architectural historian Witold Rybczynski, Palladio's greatness lies in "his equilibrium, his sweet sense of harmony. He pleases the mind as well as the eye. His sturdy houses, rooted in their sites, radiate order and balance, which makes them both of this world and otherworldly." Palladio's houses, in other words, center us both physically and mentally.

Emphasis and Focal Point

What is the relationship between emphasis and focal point?

Artists employ emphasis in order to draw the viewer's attention to one area of the work. We refer to this area as the **focal point** of the composition. The focal point of a radially balanced composition is obvious. The center of the rose window in the south transept of Chartres Cathedral (see Fig. 7-9) is its focal point and, fittingly, an enthroned Christ occupies that spot. The focal point of Quarton's *Coronation of the Virgin* (see Fig. 7-4) is Mary, who is also, not coincidentally, the object of everyone's attention.

One important way that emphasis can be established is by creating strong contrasts of light and color. *Still Life with Lobster* (**Fig. 7-11**) uses a complementary color scheme to focus our attention. The work was painted in the court of the French king Louis XVI by Anna Vallayer-Coster, a female member of the Académie Royale, the official organization of French painters (though it is important to note that after Vallayer-Coster was elected to the Académie in 1770, membership by women was limited to four, perhaps because the male-dominated Académie felt threatened by these women's success). By painting everything else in the composition a shade of green, Vallayer-Coster focuses our attention on the delicious red lobster in the foreground. Lush in its brushwork, and with a sense of luminosity that we can almost feel, the painting celebrates Vallayer-Coster's skill as an artist, her ability to control both color and light. In essence—and the double meaning is intentional—the painting is an exercise in "good taste."

Light can function like a stage spotlight, as in Artemisia Gentileschi's *Judith and Maidservant with the Head of Holofernes* (see Fig. 5-12), directing our gaze to a key place within the frame. The light in Georges de La Tour's *Joseph the Carpenter* (**Fig. 7-12**) draws our attention away from the painting's titular subject, Joseph, the father of Jesus, and to the brightly lit visage of Christ himself. The candlelight here is comparable to the Divine Light, casting an ethereal glow across the young boy's face.

Finally, it is possible, as the earlier example of *Pollock's No. 32, 1950* (see Fig. 6-13) indicates, to make a work of art that is **afocal**—that is, not merely a work in which no single point of the composition demands our attention any more or less than any other, but also one in which the eye can find no place to rest. Your vision seems to want to float aimlessly through the space of this painting, focusing on nothing at all. Alternately, works of art such as Bill Viola's *Room for St. John of the Cross* (see Fig. 6-18) and Diego Velázquez's *Las Meninas* (see *The Creative Process*, pp. 142–43) might have competing focal points, demanding that we divide our attention among them.

Lucas Samaras's *Room No. 2*, the so-called *Mirrored Room* (**Fig. 7-13**), explodes the possibility of the eye ever coming to rest at a single point. The room is an 8-by-8-foot space, lined on the floors, walls, and ceilings with mirrors. Stepping into it (no more than two viewers are allowed into the room at any single time), the viewer's body is fragmented and distributed across space into a seemingly infinite depth stretching in all directions, including, perhaps most disturbingly, below your feet, as if at any moment the

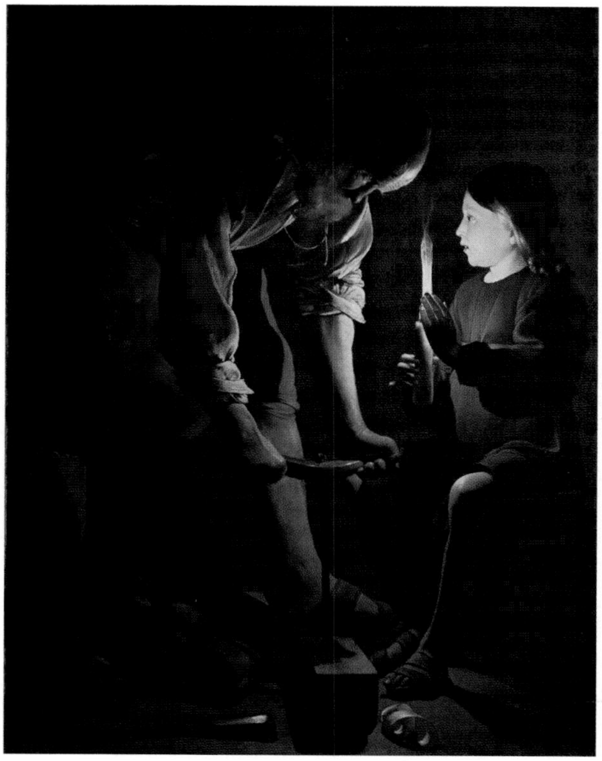

Fig. 7-12 Georges de La Tour, *Joseph the Carpenter*, ca. 1645. Oil on canvas, 18½ × 25½ in. Musée du Louvre, Paris. Inv. RF1948-27. Photo © RMN-Grand Palais (musée du Louvre)/Michel Urtado.

Fig. 7-13 Lucas Samaras, *Room No. 2* (popularly known as the *Mirrored Room*) (detail), 1966. Mirror on wood, 8 × 8 × 10 ft. Albright-Knox Art Gallery, Buffalo, New York. Gift of Seymour H. Knox, Jr., 1966. © Lucas Samaras, courtesy of Pace Gallery.

The Creative Process

A Multiplication of Focal Points: Diego Velázquez's *Las Meninas*

In his masterpiece *Las Meninas* (*The Maids of Honor*) (**Fig. 7-16**), Diego Velázquez creates competing points of emphasis. The scene is the Spanish court of King Philip IV. The most obvious focal point of the composition is the young princess, the *infanta* Margarita, who is emphasized by her position in the center of the painting by the light that shines brilliantly on her alone, and by the implied lines created by the gazes of the two maids of honor who bracket her. But the figures outside this central group, that of the dwarf on the right, who is also a maid of honor, and the painter on the left (a self-portrait of Velázquez), gaze away from the *infanta*. In fact, they seem to be looking at us, and so too is the *infanta* herself. The focal point of their attention, in other words, lies outside the picture plane. In fact, they are looking at a spot that appears to be occupied by the couple reflected in the mirror at the opposite end of the room, over the *infanta*'s shoulder (**Fig. 7-17**)—a couple that turns out to be King Philip IV and Queen Mariana, recognizable from the two portrait busts painted by Velázquez at about the same time as *Las Meninas* (**Figs. 7-14** and **7-15**). It seems likely that they are the subject of the enormous canvas on the left that Velázquez depicts himself as painting, since they are in the position that would be occupied normally by persons sitting for a portrait. The *infanta* Margarita and her maids of honor have come, it would seem, to watch the royal couple have their portrait painted by the great Velázquez. And Velázquez has turned the tables on everyone—the focal point of *Las Meninas* is not the focal point of what he is painting.

Or perhaps the king and queen have entered the room to see their daughter, the *infanta*, being painted by Velázquez, who is viewing the entire room, including himself, in a mirror. Or perhaps the image on the far wall is not a mirror at all, but a painting, a double portrait. It has, in fact, been suggested that both of the single portraits illustrated here are studies for

Fig. 7-14 Diego Velázquez, *Philip IV, King of Spain*, 1652–53. Oil on canvas, 17½ × 14¾ in. Kunsthistorisches Museum, Vienna.
Inv. 324. © 2015. Photo Austrian Archives/Scala, Florence.

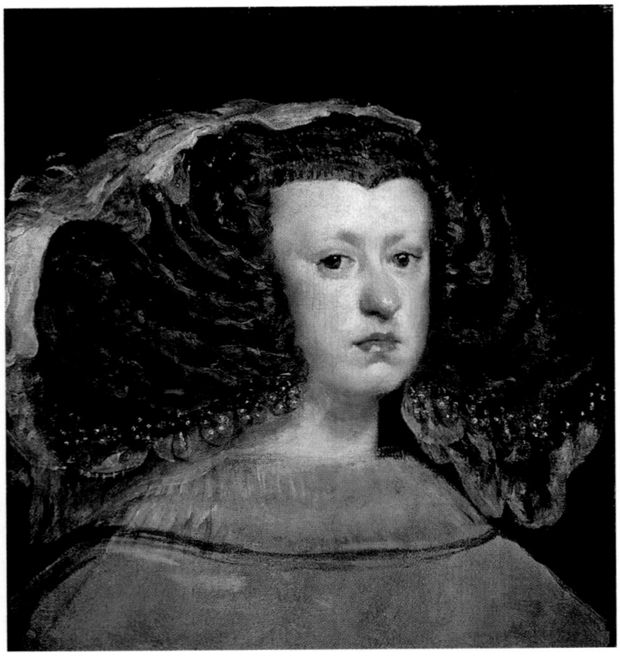

Fig. 7-15 Diego Velázquez, *Portrait of Queen Mariana*, ca. 1656. Oil on canvas, 18⅜ × 17⅛ in. Meadows Museum, Southern Methodist University, Dallas.
Alger H. Meadows Collection. MM.78.01. Photo: Michael Bodycomb.

Fig. 7-16 Diego Velázquez, *Las Meninas* (*The Maids of Honor*), 1656. Oil on canvas, 10 ft. ¾ in. × 9 ft. ¾ in. Museo Nacional del Prado, Madrid.

just such a double portrait (which, if it ever existed, is now lost). Or perhaps the mirror reflects not the king and queen but their double portrait, which Velázquez is painting and which the *infanta* has come to admire.

Whatever the case, Velázquez's painting depicts an actual work-in-progress. We do not know, we can never know, what work he is in the midst of making—a portrait of the king and queen, or *Las Meninas*, or some other work—but it is the working process he describes. And fundamental to that process, it would appear, is his interaction with the royal family themselves, who are not merely his patrons, but the very measure of the nobility of his art.

Fig. 7-17 Diego Velázquez, *Las Meninas* (*The Maids of Honor*) (detail), 1656.

Fig. 7-18 Julie Mehretu, *Mural*, detail, 2010. Acrylic on canvas, 23 × 80 ft. Goldman Sachs headquarters, New York.
Courtesy of the artist and Marian Goodman Gallery, New York.

floor might open up and pull you into its abyss (or, alternately, as if the ceiling might unfold to accept your ascension). Even more important, once you enter the room, you become inseparable from the work (an effect singularly anticipated by Velázquez in *Las Meninas*, as discussed in the previous pages). It is as if you enable it, bring it to life, but in doing so lose all sense of your own singularity as an individual. This stunning ambiguity perhaps accounts for the fact that Samaras's room remains one of the most popular works in the collection of the Albright-Knox Art Gallery in Buffalo, where, in the summer of 2014, it was the focus of the exhibition *Lucas Samaras: Reflections*.

Scale and Proportion

What is the difference between scale and proportion?

Scale is the word we use to describe the dimensions of an art object in relation to the original object that it depicts or in relation to the objects around it. Thus, we speak of a miniature as a "small-scale" portrait, or of a big mural, such as Julie Mehretu's *Mural* at Goldman Sachs's headquarters in New York City (**Fig. 7-18**), as a "large-scale" work. Mehretu's mural, at 80 feet long and 23 feet high, extends the length of the headquarters' lobby, and an art21 *Exclusive* video shows her putting the finishing touches on its installation in 2006.

Scale is an issue that is important when you read a textbook such as this. You must always remember that the reproductions you look at do not usually give you much sense of the actual size of the work. The scale is by no means consistent throughout. That is, a relatively small painting might be reproduced on a full page, and a very large painting on a half-page. In order to make the artwork fit on the book page we must—however unintentionally—manipulate its scale.

In both Do-Ho Suh's *Public Figures* (**Fig. 7-19**) and Kara Walker's *A Subtlety* (**Fig. 7-20**), the artists have intentionally manipulated the scale of the object depicted. In Do-Ho Suh's case, the scale of the people carrying the sculptural pediment has been diminished in relation to the pediment itself, which is purposefully lacking the expected statue of a public hero standing on top of it. "Let's say if there's one statue at the plaza of a hero, who helped or protected our country," Do-Ho Suh explains, "there are hundreds of thousands of individuals who helped him and worked with him, and there's no recognition for them. So in my sculpture, *Public Figures*, I had around six hundred small figures, twelve inches high, six different shapes, both male and female, of different ethnicities"—the "little people" behind the heroic gesture. Walker's *A Subtlety*, in contrast, is gigantic in scale. Subtitled *The Marvelous Sugar Baby, an Homage to the unpaid and overworked Artisans who have refined our Sweet tastes from the cane fields to the Kitchens of the New World on the Occasion of the demolition of the Domino Sugar*

Fig. 7-19 Do-Ho Suh, *Public Figures*, 1998–99. Installation view, MetroTech Center Commons, Brooklyn, New York. Fiberglass/resin, steel pipes, pipe fittings, 10 × 7 × 9 ft.
Courtesy the artist and Lehmann Maupin Gallery, New York.

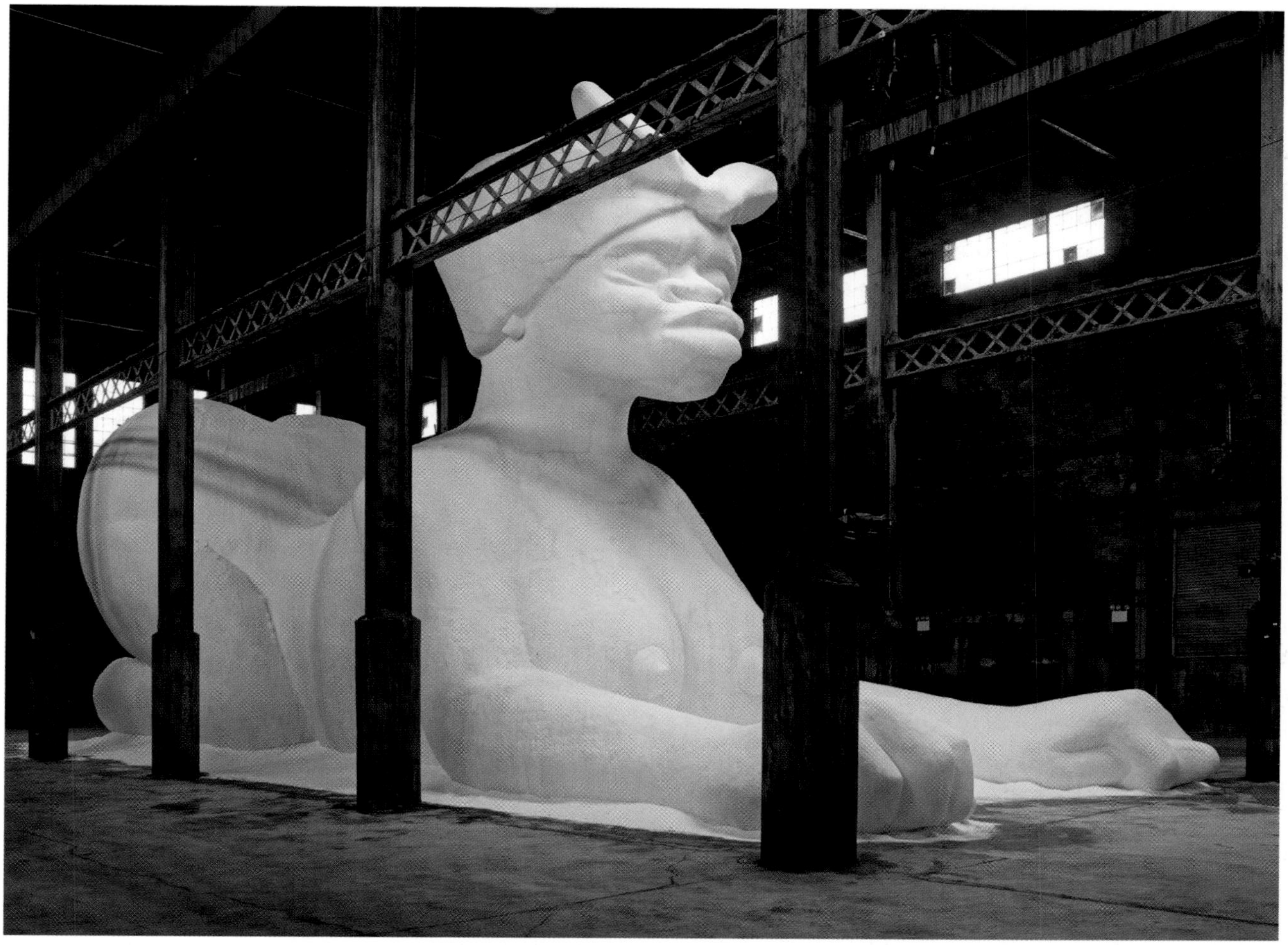

Fig. 7-20 Kara Walker, *A Subtlety: The Marvelous Sugar Baby, an Homage to the unpaid and overworked Artisans who have refined our Sweet tastes from the cane fields to the Kitchens of the New World on the Occasion of the demolition of the Domino Sugar Refining Plant*, 2014. Installation view, Domino Sugar Factory, Williamsburg, Brooklyn, New York. Carved polystyrene coated with 160,000 lb of sugar, 10 × 7 × 75 ft.
Courtesy the artist and Creative Projects, New York.

Fig. 7-21 Hokusai, *The Great Wave off Kanagawa*, from the series *Thirty-Six Views of Mount Fuji*, 1823–29. Color woodcut, 10 × 15 in.

Refining Plant, it is an intentional exaggeration that not-so-subtly parodies the carved sugar centerpieces that graced the tables of the upper classes from medieval to modern times, including those of plantation owners in the antebellum South.

Raw cane sugar, of the kind cultivated in fields throughout the South and Caribbean in the time of slavery, is brown in color. It must be refined—or "whitened"—before it reaches the table. Walker recognized this as a particularly potent metaphor for the pressure to "refine" themselves exerted on the African-American community—the pressure to rise out of slavery into American life or, in other words, the pressure to "integrate" themselves into American society. Thus, Walker's enormous Aunt Jemima-like "Sugar Baby," which purposefully evokes the mysteries of the Great Sphinx that guards the pyramids in Egypt, is designed to draw attention to the magnitude of the sociopolitical crisis that was slavery. She is Walker's ultimate expression of "the Negress" in American society, a theme that she has pursued her entire career (see the art21 *Exclusive* video "Kara Walker: The Negress"). By bringing to light and making large what might otherwise be thought of as a mere "sweet," Walker underscores the human cost of the sugar industry as it developed in the Americas—a kind of "domino effect" at the Domino Sugar factory, beginning with the European desire for sugar, leading to the exploitation of slave labor to produce it, culminating in the subjugation and exploitation of African Americans for generations to come.

Artists also manipulate scale by the way they depict the relative size of objects. As we know from our study of perspective, one of the most important ways to represent recessional space is to depict a thing closer to us as larger than a thing the same size farther away. This change in scale helps us to measure visually the space in the scene before us. When a mountain fills a small percentage of the space of a painting, we know that it lies somewhere in the distance. We judge its actual size relative to other elements in the painting and our sense of the average real mountain's size.

Because everybody in Japan knows just how large Mount Fuji is, many of Hokusai's various views of the mountain take advantage of this knowledge and, by manipulating scale, play with the viewer's expectations. His most famous view of the mountain (**Fig. 7-21**) is a case in point. In the foreground, two boats descend into a trough beneath a great crashing wave that hangs over the scene like a giant, menacing claw. In the distance, Fuji rises above the horizon, framed in a vortex of wave and foam. Hokusai has echoed its shape in the foremost wave of the composition. While the wave is visually larger than the distant mountain, our sense of scale causes us to diminish its importance. The wave will imminently collapse, yet Fuji will remain. For the Japanese, Fuji symbolizes not only the everlasting, but Japan itself, and the print juxtaposes the perils of the moment with the enduring life of the nation.

As opposed to scale, which refers to the relative size of an object, **proportion** refers to the relationship between the parts of an object and the whole. At first glance, all seems right with Jean-Auguste-Dominique Ingres's portrait *Mme. Rivière* (**Fig. 7-22**). But careful observation reveals that the distance from her right shoulder to her right hand is virtually simian—like that of a monkey or ape—in proportion. Ingres has in fact sacrificed the normal proportions of the human body to accommodate the compositional demands of his painting. Her arm echoes the curve of the oval frame, and if, in terms of the painting it seems right, in terms of proportion, its length is vastly exaggerated.

When the proportions of a figure seem normal, however, the representation is more likely to seem harmonious and balanced. The Classical Greeks, in fact, believed that beauty itself was a function of proper proportion. In terms of the human body, these perfect proportions were determined by the sculptor Polyclitus, who not only described them in a now-lost text called *The Canon* (from the Greek *kanon*, meaning "measure" or "rule") but who also executed a sculpture to embody them. This is the *Doryphoros*, or *The Spear Bearer*, the original of which is also lost, although numerous copies survive (**Fig. 7-23**). The perfection of this figure is based on the fact that each part of the body is a common fraction of the figure's total height. According to the **canon**, the height of the head ought to be one-eighth and the breadth of the shoulders one-fourth of the total height of the body.

Fig. 7-22 Jean-Auguste-Dominique Ingres, *Mme. Rivière*, 1805. Oil on canvas, 45⅝ × 35⅜ in. Musée du Louvre, Paris.
Photo © RMN-Grand Palais (musée du Louvre)/Thierry Le Mage.

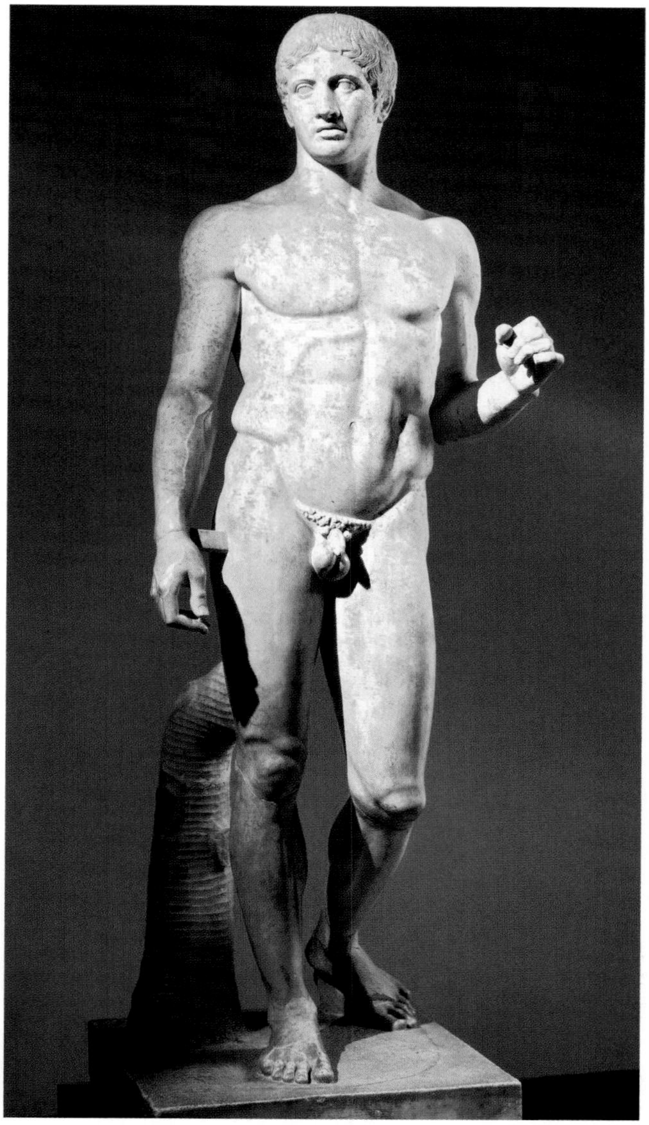

Fig. 7-23 Polyclitus, *Doryphoros* (*The Spear Bearer*), 450 BCE. Marble, Roman copy after lost bronze original, height 7 ft. National Archaeological Museum, Naples.
Art Archive/Musée Archéologique Naples/Collection Dagli Orti.

This sense of mathematical harmony was utilized by the Greeks in their architecture as well. The proportions of the facade of the Parthenon, constructed in the fifth century BCE on the top of the Acropolis in Athens (**Fig. 7-24**), are based on a ratio that can be expressed in the algebraic formula $x = 2y + 1$. The temple's columns, for instance, reflect this formula: There are 8 columns on the short ends and 17 on the sides, because $17 = (2 \times 8) + 1$. The ratio of the length of the top step of the temple's platform, the **stylobate**, to its width is 9:4, because $9 = (2 \times 4) + 1$. That the Parthenon should be constructed with such mathematical harmony is hardly accidental. It is a temple to Athena, not only the protectress of Athens but also the goddess of wisdom, and such mathematical precision represented to the ancient Greeks not merely beauty, but the ultimate wisdom of the universe. Furthermore, this monument to perfection sits atop the Athenian Acropolis, literally "the top of the city." In fact, so commanding is the view from the building's portico that the port of Piraeus can be seen 7½ miles away.

Pattern, Repetition, and Rhythm

What is the relationship between pattern, repetition, and rhythm?

The columns of the Parthenon repeat themselves down each facade, creating a sense of architectural rhythm. Any formal element that repeats itself in a composition—line, shape, mass, color, or texture—creates a recognizable pattern and, through pattern, a sense of rhythm.

In its systematic and repetitive use of the same motif or design, pattern is an especially important decorative tool. Throughout history, decorative patterns have been applied to utilitarian objects in order to make them more pleasing to the eye. Early manuscripts, for instance, such as the page reproduced here from the eighth-century *Lindisfarne Gospels* (**Fig. 7-25**), were illuminated, or elaborately decorated with drawings, paintings, and large capital letters, to beautify the sacred text. This page represents the ways in which Christian imagery—

Fig. 7-24 Parthenon, 447–438 BCE. Pentelic marble, 111 × 237 ft. at base. Athens, Greece.

Fig. 7-25 Cross page from the *Lindisfarne Gospels*, ca. 700. Ink and tempera on vellum, 13½ × 9¼ in.
British Library, London.

the cross—and earlier pre-Christian pagan motifs came together in the early Christian era in the British Isles. The simple design of the traditional Celtic cross, found across Ireland, is almost lost in the checkerboard pattern and the interlace of fighting beasts with spiraling tails, extended necks, and clawing legs that borders the page. These beasts are examples of the pagan "animal style," which consists of intricate, ribbonlike traceries of line that suggest wild and fantastic beasts. The animal style was used not only in England but also in Scandinavia, Germany, and France.

Patterned textiles are closely identified with social prestige and wealth among the Ewe and Asante societies of Ghana. Known as *kente* cloths, these fabrics are designed to be worn at special occasions and ceremonies in the manner of a toga draped around the body (**Fig. 7-26**). The cloths are woven in narrow vertical strips and then sewn together—a man's *kente* prestige cloth is usually made up of 24 such strips. A subtly repetitive pattern results. Before the seventeenth century, *kente* were made of white cotton with designs woven on them in indigo-dyed thread, but after the introduction of richly dyed silks by European traders, the color palette of the *kente* was greatly expanded.

The work of contemporary African sculptor El Anatsui (**Fig. 7-27**) is deeply influenced by the *kente* cloth tradition of his native Ghana, but instead of weaving strips of cloth and then sewing them together, El Anatsui creates his pieces from discarded aluminum caps and seals from liquor bottles, which he flattens, shapes, perforates, and sews together with copper wire. In this way, he brings the traditional patterns associated with African power and prestige into dialogue with the grim realities of African history. Up close, the names of the liquor brands—Dark Sailor, Liquor Headmaster, and Black Gold—all today creations of West African distilleries, reflect the realities of the colonial slave trade when in fact alcohol was introduced to the region.

Repetition often implies monotony. If we see the same thing over and over again, it tends to get boring. Nevertheless, when the same or like elements—shapes, colors, or a regular pattern of any kind—are repeated over and over again in a composition, a certain visual **rhythm** will result. In Jacob Lawrence's *Barber Shop* (**Fig. 7-28**), this rhythm is established through the repetition of both shapes and colors. One pattern is based on the diamond-shaped figures sitting in the barber chairs, each of which is covered with a different-colored

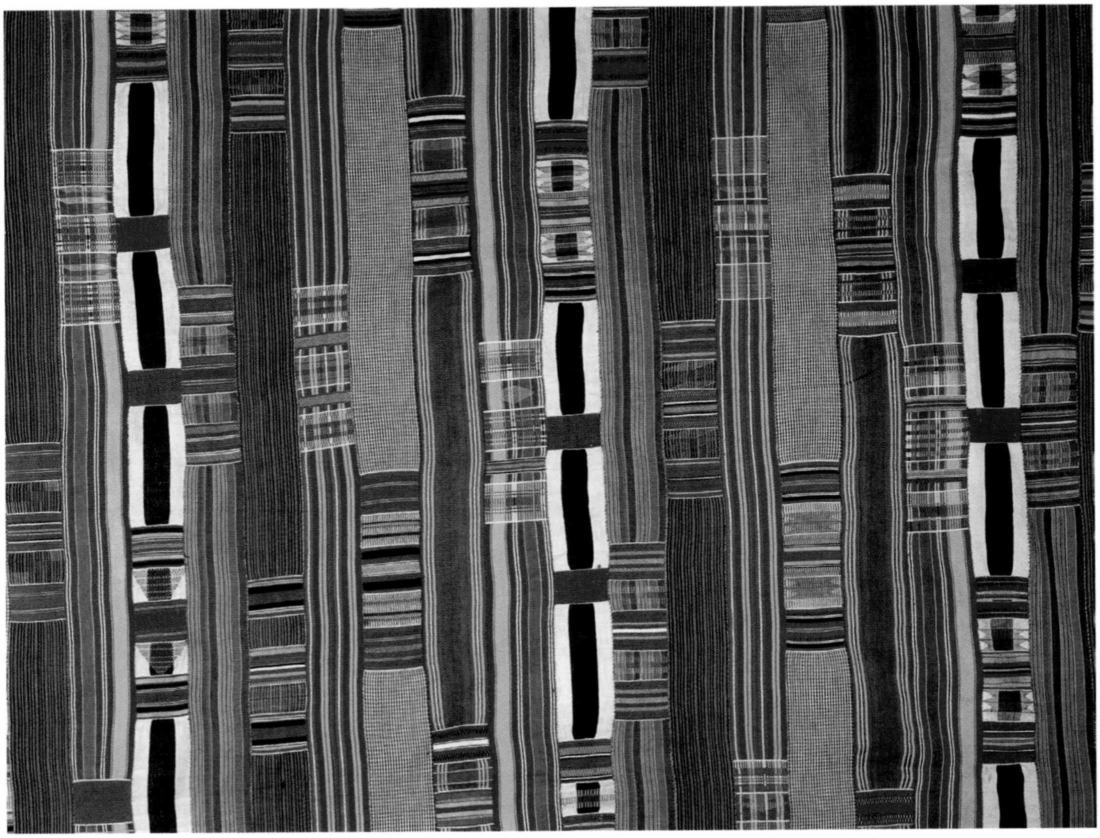

Fig. 7-26 *Kente* prestige cloth (detail), Ghana, Ewe peoples, 19th century. Cotton, silk, warp (vertical threads) 6 ft. 2 in., weft (horizontal threads) 9 ft. 1⅞ in. The British Museum, London.

Fig. 7-27 El Anatsui, *Between Earth and Heaven*, 2006. Aluminum and copper wire, 7 ft. 2¾ in. × 10 ft. 4 in. Metropolitan Museum of Art, New York.

Purchase, Fred M. and Rita Richman, Noah-Sadie K. Wachtel Foundation Inc., David and Holly Ross, Doreen and Gilbert Bassin Family Foundation and William B. Goldstein Gifts, 2007.96. © 2015. Image copyright Metropolitan Museum of Art/Art Resource/Scala, Florence.

Fig. 7-28 Jacob Lawrence, *Barber Shop*, 1946. Gouache on paper, 21⅛ × 29⅜ in. Toledo Museum of Art, Toledo, Ohio.

Purchased with funds from the Libbey Endowment, Gift of Edward Drummond Libbey, 1975.15. Photo: Photography Incorporated, Toledo. © 2015 Jacob and Gwendolyn Knight Lawrence Foundation, Seattle/Artists Rights Society (ARS), New York.

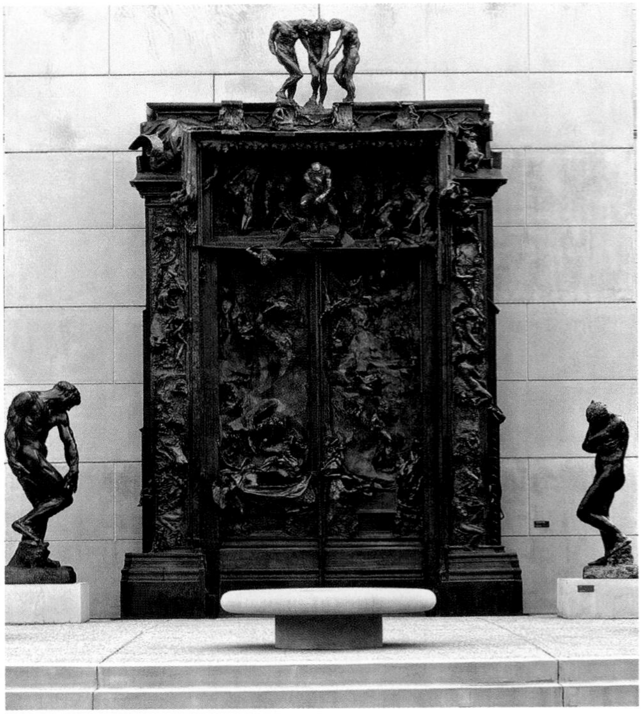

Fig. 7-29 Auguste Rodin, *The Gates of Hell* with *Adam and Eve*, 1880–1917. Bronze, 20 ft. 10¾ in. × 13 ft. 2 in. × 33⅜ in. Stanford University Museum of Art.
Photo: Frank Wing.

Fig. 7-30 Auguste Rodin, *The Three Shades*, 1881–86. Bronze, Coubertin Foundry, posthumous cast authorized by Musée Rodin, 1980, 6 ft. 3½ in. × 6 ft. 3½ in. × 42 in. Iris & B. Gerald Cantor Center for Visual Arts at Stanford University.
Gift of the B. Gerald Cantor Collections.

apron: one lavender and white, one red, and one black and green. The color and pattern of the left-hand patron's apron is echoed in the shirts of the two barbers on the right, while the pattern of the right-hand patron's apron is repeated in the vest of the barber on the left. Hands, shoulders, feet—all work into the triangulated format of the design. "The painting," Lawrence explained in 1979, "is one of the many works . . . executed out of my experience . . . my everyday visual encounters." It is meant to capture the rhythm of life in Harlem, where Lawrence grew up in the 1930s. "It was inevitable," he says,

> that the barber shop with its daily gathering of Harlemites, its clippers, mirror, razors, the overall pattern and the many conversations that took place there . . . was to become the subject of many of my paintings. Even now, in my imagination, whenever I relive my early years in the Harlem community, the barber shop, in both form and content . . . is one of the scenes that I still see and remember.

As we all know from listening to music, and as Lawrence's painting demonstrates, repetition is not necessarily boring. *The Gates of Hell* (**Fig. 7-29**), by Auguste Rodin, was conceived in 1880 as the entry for the Museum of Decorative Arts in Paris, which was never built. The work is based on the *Inferno* section of Dante's *Divine Comedy* and is filled with nearly 200 figures who swirl in hellfire, reaching out as if continually striving to escape the surface of the door. Rodin's famous *Thinker* sits atop the door panels, looking down as if in contemplation of man's fate, and to each side of the door, in its original conception, stand Adam and Eve. At the very top of the door is a group of three figures, the *Three Shades*, guardians of the dark inferno beneath.

What is startling is that *The Three Shades* are not different, but, in fact, all the same (**Fig. 7-30**). Rodin cast his *Shade* three times and arranged the three casts in the format of a semicircle. (As with *The Thinker* and many other figures on the *Gates*, he also exhibited them as a separate, independent sculpture.) Though each figure is identical, thus arranged, and viewed from different sides, each appears to be a unique figure. Furthermore, in the *Gates*, the posture of the figure of Adam, in front and to the left, echoes that of the *Shades* above. This formal repetition, and the downward pull that unites all four figures, implies that Adam is not merely the father of us all, but, in his sin, the very man who has brought us to the Gates of Hell.

In Laylah Ali's most famous and longest-running series of paintings, depicting the brown-skinned and gender-neutral Greenheads (**Fig. 7-31**), repetition plays a crucial role. Her figures are the archetypal "Other," a sort of amalgam of extraterrestrial Martians with their green

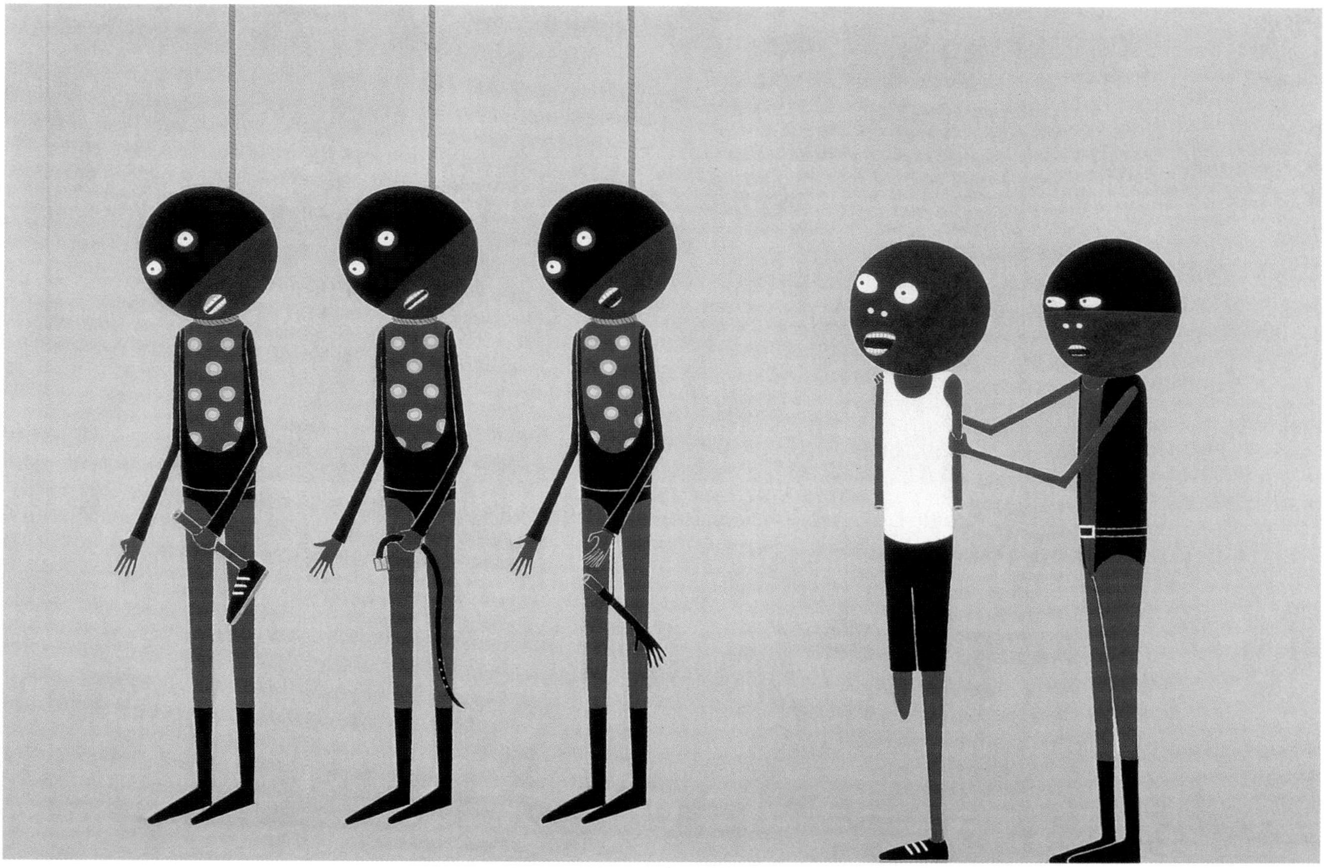

Fig. 7-31 Laylah Ali, *Untitled*, from the series *Greenheads*, 2000. Gouache on paper, 13 × 19 in.
Courtesy of the artist and Paul Kasmin Gallery.

heads and the dark-skinned denizens of the Third World. In the image reproduced here, three almost identical but masked Greenheads are being hanged in front of an unmasked fourth victim. The hanged Greenheads hold in their hands the amputated leg and arm, as well as the belt (for Ali, belts connote power) of the figure awaiting his or her fate. As Ali says, "The repetition is what I think is so striking. It's not like one thing happens and you say, 'Wow! That was just so terrible,' and it will never happen again. You know it will happen again." As she says in the art21 *Exclusive* video "Newspaper Clippings," her images are "never spot-on": "They never follow one conflict directly." The horror of her images, in other words, resides exactly in their repetition and our sense that they could reside anywhere and everywhere.

Unity and Variety

What is the traditional relationship between unity and variety, and why have postmodernist artists tended to emphasize variety over unity?

Repetition and rhythm are employed by artists in order to unify the different elements of their works. In *Barber Shop* (see Fig. 7-28), Jacob Lawrence gives the painting a sense of coherence by repeating shapes and color patterns. Each of the principles of design that we have discussed leads to this idea of organization, the sense that we are looking at a unified whole—balanced, focused, and so on. Even Lawrence's figures, with their strange, clumsy hands, their oversimplified features, and their oddly extended legs and feet, are uniform throughout. Such consistency lends the picture its feeling of being complete.

It is as if, in *Barber Shop*, Lawrence is painting the idea of community itself, bringing together the diversity of the Harlem streets through the unifying patterns of his art. In fact, if everything were the same, in art as in life, there would be no need for us to discuss the concept of "unity." But things are not the same. The visual world is made up of different lines, forms, colors, textures—the various visual elements themselves—and they must be made to work together. Still, Rodin's *Three Shades* atop *The Gates of Hell* (see Fig. 7-30) teaches us an important lesson. Even when each element of a composition is identical, it is variety—in this case, the fact that our point of view changes with each of the *Shades*—that sustains our interest. In general, unity and variety must coexist in a work of art. The artist must strike a balance between the two.

Fig. 7-32 Louise Lawler, *Pollock and Tureen*, 1984. Cibachrome, 16 × 20 in.
Courtesy of the artist and Metro Pictures, New York.

Fig. 7-33 Las Vegas, Nevada, ca. 1985.
Vidler/Mauritius.

In the twentieth century, however, artists have increasingly embraced and exploited tensions between elements rather than trying to balance them. They have sought to expose not just variety, but opposition and contradiction. A photograph by Louise Lawler, *Pollock and Tureen* (**Fig. 7-32**), not only brings two radically contradictory objects into a state of opposition but demonstrates how, by placing them side by side, they influence the ways in which we understand them. Thus, the Pollock painting in this photograph is transformed into a decorative or ornamental object, much like the tureen centered on the table in front of it. Lawler not only underscores the fact that the painting is, like the tureen, a marketable object, but also suggests that the expressive qualities of Pollock's original work have been emptied, or at least nearly so, when looked at in this context.

It is this sense of disjunction, the sense that the parts can never form a unified whole, that we have come to identify with what is commonly called **postmodernism**. The discontinuity between the two parts of Frank Gehry and Vlado Milunić's Rasin building in Prague, Czech Republic (see Fig. 7-2) is an example of this postmodern sensibility, a sensibility defined particularly well by another architect, Robert Venturi, in his important 1972 book, *Learning from Las Vegas*, written with Denise Scott Brown and Steven Izenour. For Venturi, the collision of styles, signs, and symbols that marks the American "strip," especially the Las Vegas strip (**Fig. 7-33**), could be seen in the light of a new sort of unity. "Disorder," Venturi writes, "[is] an order we cannot see. . . . The commercial strip with the urban sprawl . . . [is an order that] *includes*; it includes at all levels, from the mixture of seemingly incongruous land uses to the mixture of seemingly incongruous advertising media plus a system of neoorganic . . . restaurant motifs in Walnut Formica." The strip declares that anything can be put next to anything else. While traditional art has tended to exclude things that it deems unartful, postmodern art lets everything in. In this sense, it is democratic. It could even be said to achieve a unity larger than the comparatively elitist art of high culture could ever imagine.

Elizabeth Murray's shaped canvas *Just in Time* (**Fig. 7-34**) is, at first glance, a two-panel abstract construction of rhythmic curves, oddly and not quite evenly cut in half. But on second glance, it announces its postmodernity. For the construction is also an ordinary teacup, with a pink cloud of steam rising above its rim. In a move that calls to mind Kara Walker's *A Subtlety* (see Fig. 7-20), the scale of this cup—it is nearly 9 feet high—monumentalizes the banal, domestic subject matter. Animal forms seem to arise out of the design—a rabbit on the left, an animated, Disney-like, laughing teacup in profile on the right. The title recalls pop lyrics—"Just in time, I found you just in time." Yet it remains an abstract painting, interesting as painting and as design. It is even, for Murray, deeply serious. She defines the significance of the break down the middle of the painting by citing a stanza from W. H. Auden's poem, "As I walked out one evening":

The glacier knocks in the cupboard,
The desert sighs in the bed,
And the crack in the tea-cup opens
A lane to the land of the dead.

Who knows what meanings are rising up out of this crack in the cup, this structural gap? Murray's painting is at once an ordinary teacup and an image rich in possible meanings, stylistically coherent and physically fragmented. The endless play of unity and variety is what it's about.

Fig. 7-34 Elizabeth Murray, *Just in Time*, 1981. Oil on canvas in two sections, 8 ft. 10 in. × 8 ft. 1 in. Philadelphia Museum of Art.
Purchased: Edward and Althea Budd Fund, the Adele Haas Turner and Beatrice Pastorius Turner Memorial Fund, and funds contributed by Marion Stroud and Lorine E. Vogt, 1981. © 2015. Photo Philadelphia Museum of Art/Art Resource/ Scala, Florence. © 2015 Murray-Holman Family Trust/Artists Rights Society (ARS), New York.

THE CRITICAL PROCESS

Thinking about the Principles of Design

By way of concluding this part of the book, let's consider how the various elements and principles inform a particular work, Claude Monet's *The Railroad Bridge, Argenteuil* (**Fig. 7-35**). Line comes into play here in any number of ways. How would you describe Monet's use of line? Is it classical or expressive? Two strong diagonals—the near bank and the bridge itself—cross the picture. What architectural element depicted in the picture echoes this structure? Now note the two opposing directional lines in the painting—the train's and the boat's. In fact, the boat is apparently tacking against a strong wind that blows from right to left, as the smoke coming from the train's engine indicates. Where else in the painting is this sense of opposition apparent? Consider the relationships of light to dark in the composition and the complementary color scheme of orange and blue that is especially used in the reflections and in the smoke above. Can you detect opposing and contradictory senses of symmetry and asymmetry? What about opposing focal points?

What appears at first to be a simple landscape view, upon analysis reveals itself to be a much more complicated painting. In the same way, what at first appears to be a cloud becomes, rather disturbingly, a cloud of smoke. Out of the dense growth of the near bank, a train emerges. Monet seems intent on describing what larger issues here? We know that when Monet painted it, the railroad bridge at Argenteuil was a new bridge. How does this painting capture the dawn of a new world, a world of opposition and contradiction? Can you make a case that almost every formal element and principle of design at work in the painting supports this reading?

Fig. 7-35 Claude Monet, *The Railroad Bridge, Argenteuil*, 1874. Oil on canvas, 21⅘ × 29⅖ in. Philadelphia Museum of Art.

Thinking Back

7.1 Define symmetrical, asymmetrical, and radial balance.

All art deals with visual weight, the apparent "heaviness" or "lightness" of the shapes and forms arranged in the composition. Actual weight, by contrast, refers to the physical weight in pounds of an artwork's materials. What is asymmetrical balance? How is visual weight balanced in the Taj Mahal? What is radial balance?

7.2 Explain the relationship between emphasis and focal point.

Artists employ emphasis in order to draw the viewer's attention to one area of the work. This area is the focal point of the composition. What is the focal point of a radially balanced artwork? How does Anna Vallayer-Coster create emphasis in *Still Life with Lobster*? How does Diego Velázquez's *Las Meninas* employ multiple focal points? What is an afocal composition?

7.3 Differentiate between scale and proportion.

Scale refers to the dimensions of an art object in relation to the original object that it represents or in relation to the objects around it. Proportion, by contrast, refers to the relationship between the parts of an object and the whole. How does Kara Walker manipulate scale in her sculpture *A Subtlety*? What is the canon? How does Jean-Auguste-Dominique Ingres most obviously violate it? What proportional relationships define the Parthenon?

7.4 Describe the relationship between pattern, repetition, and rhythm.

When the same or similar elements are repeated over and over again to make an observable pattern in a composition, a visual rhythm is established. Artists often use this rhythm in order to unify different elements of a work. How does Laylah Ali depict the Greenheads? How does repetition structure meaning in Jacob Lawrence's *Barber Shop*?

7.5 Discuss the traditional relationship between unity and variety, and why postmodernist artists have tended to emphasize variety over unity.

Unity derives from a sense that the different formal elements—line, form, color, and texture—work together to give the composition a sense of being a consistent and complete whole. In the twentieth century, however, artists have sometimes rejected this sense of elements working together to emphasize, instead, a sense of disjunction and disorder. How does Las Vegas reflect this sensibility?

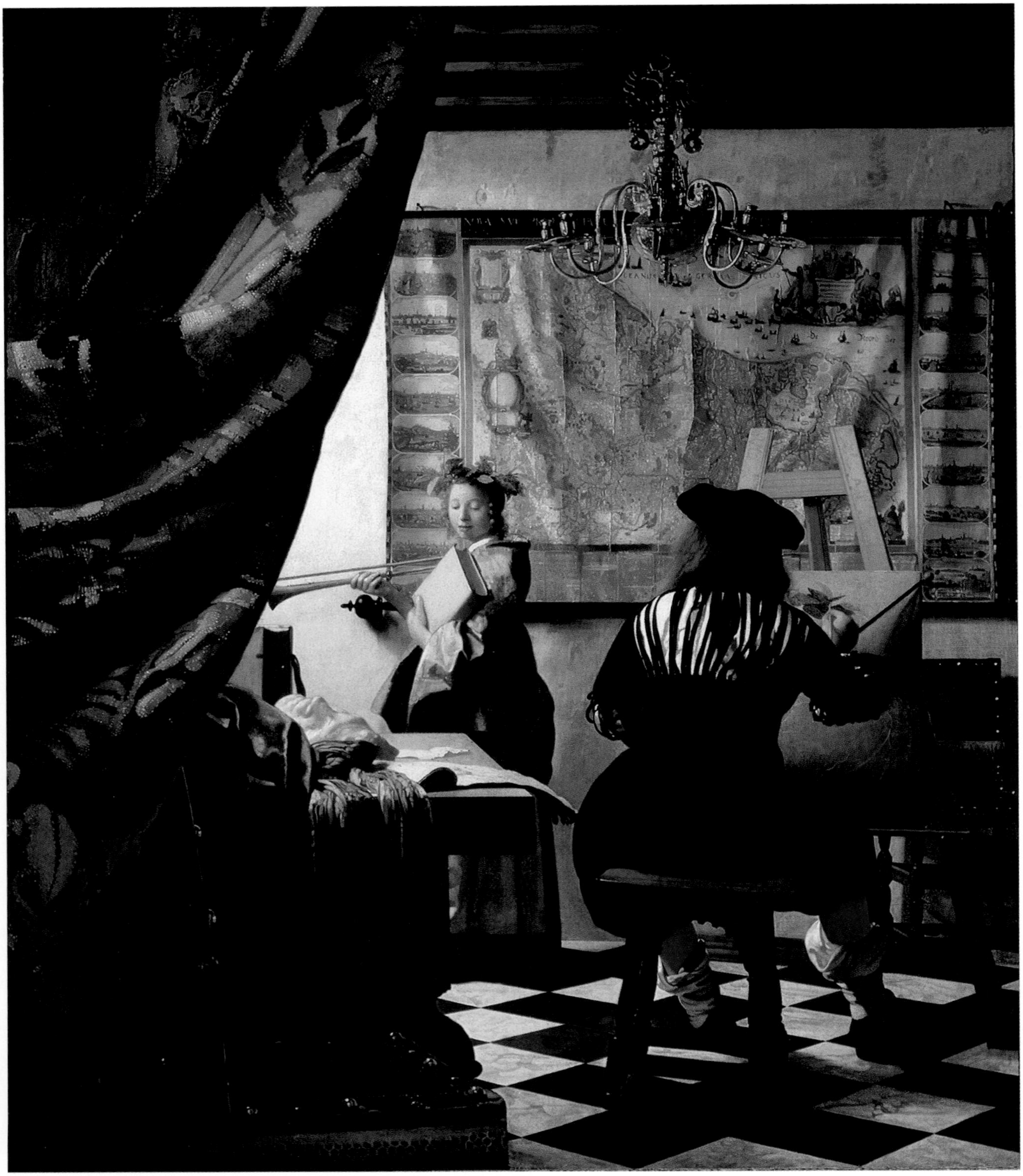

Johannes Vermeer, ***The Allegory of Painting (The Painter and His Model as Klio),*** **1665–66.** Oil on canvas, 4 ft. × 40 in. Kunsthistorisches Museum, Vienna.
Cat. 395, Inv. 9182. akg-image/Erich Lessing.

Part 3

The Fine Arts Media

Learning How Art is Made

In Johannes Vermeer's *The Allegory of Painting*, a stunning variety of media are depicted. The artist, his back to us, is shown painting his model's crown, but the careful observer can detect, in the lower half of the canvas, below his elbow, the white chalk lines of his preliminary drawing. A tapestry has been pulled back at the left, and a beautifully crafted chandelier hangs from the ceiling. A map on the back wall illustrates the art of cartography. Around its edges are a series of landscapes, a type of painting that the Dutch were, even at this moment, beginning to develop as a full-fledged genre. The model herself is posed above a sculpted mask, which lies on the table below her gaze. As the muse of history, she holds a book in one hand, representing writing and literature, and a trumpet, representing music, in the other hand.

Each of the materials in Vermeer's work—painting, drawing, sculpture, tapestry, even the book and the trumpet—represents what we call a medium. The history of the various media used to create art is, in essence, the history of the various technologies that artists have employed. These **technologies** have helped artists both to achieve their desired effects more readily and to discover new modes of creation and expression. A technology, literally, is the "word" or "discourse" (from the Greek *logos*) about a "techne" (from the Greek word for art, which in turn comes from the Greek verb *tekein*, "to make, prepare, or fabricate"). A medium is, in this sense, a techne, a means of making art. In Part 3 we will study all of the various media.

Chapter 8

Drawing

Learning Objectives

8.1 Discuss the history of drawing in the Italian Renaissance and how it came to be considered an art in its own right.

8.2 Distinguish between dry and liquid drawing media and list examples of each.

8.3 Give some examples of how drawing can be an innovative medium.

In 1985, the Norwegian rock band a-ha released a music video of their hit song "Take On Me." Directed by Steve Barron, who in 1990 would direct the first of the Teenage Mutant Ninja Turtles films, it was animated by Michael Patterson and Candace Reckinger, who today are on the faculty of the John C. Hench Division of Animation and Digital Arts at the University of Southern California. To create the video, Patterson and Reckinger appropriated a 1915 invention of the pioneering cartoonist Max Fleischer, creator of Koko the Clown, called the rotoscope, which allows the artist to draw on a transparent easel onto which a movie projector throws frames of live-action film one frame at a time. The two animators rotoscoped approximately 3,000 frames of film over the course of about 16 weeks. The result was one of the most influential pop videos of all time (**Figs. 8-1** and **8-2**).

Viewers were attracted to the video in no small part because it effectively brought a common fantasy to life: A young woman, reading a comic book in a coffee shop, is startled when the comic-book hero—a motorcycle racer, played by a-ha's lead singer, Morten Harket—apparently winks at her. A moment later, he reaches out his hand and draws her into the romantic world of the comic's pages. She is literally *drawn* into the drawing—and into the imaginative world of art. And if the drawings of Patterson and Reckinger seem elementary in comparison, say, to those of Leonardo da Vinci, we nevertheless have come, culturally, to recognize drawing as the starting point of inspiration, the medium in which artists first test out, even discover their ideas. Thus, the heroine of "Take On Me," in literally becoming drawing, also becomes a figure for the power of the human imagination to transcend the conditions of everyday life, to escape, as it were, the coffee shop. This chapter examines drawing as just such a starting point, used by artists across a wide range of media, but also as an end in itself, fully capable of being appreciated as a finished work of art.

From Preparatory Sketch to Finished Work of Art

How did drawings in the Italian Renaissance come to be considered finished works of art?

Drawing has many purposes, but chief among them is preliminary study. Through drawing, artists can experiment with different approaches to their compositions. They illustrate, for themselves, what they are going to do. And, in fact, illustration is another important purpose of drawing. Before the advent of the camera, illustration was the primary way that we recorded our visual history, and

Figs. 8-1 and 8-2 Video for a-ha's "Take On Me," 1985. Two stills. Animation by Michael Patterson and Candace Reckinger. Directed by Steve Barron.

today it provides visual interpretations of written texts, particularly in children's books. Finally, because it is so direct, recording the path of the artist's hand directly on paper, artists also find drawing to be a readymade means of self-expression. It is as if, in the act of drawing, the soul or spirit of the artist finds its way to paper.

Today, we think of drawing as an everyday activity that anyone, both artists and ordinary people, might take up at any time. You doodle on a pad; you throw away the marked-up sheet and start again with a fresh one. We think of artists as making dozens of sketches before deciding on the composition of a major work. But people have not always been able or willing to casually toss out marked-up paper and begin again. Before the late fifteenth century, paper was costly. Look closely at an early Renaissance drawing possibly from the workshop of Maso Finiguerra (**Fig. 8-3**). The young man is sketching on a wooden tablet that he would sand clean after each drawing. The artist who drew him at work, however, worked

Fig. 8-3 Workshop of Maso Finiguerra, *Youth Drawing*, 1450–75. Pen and ink with wash on paper, 7⅝ × 4½ in. The British Museum, London.

in pen and ink on rare, expensive paper. This work thus represents a transition point in Western art—the point at which artists began to draw on paper before they committed their ideas to canvas or plaster.

Paper was not manufactured in the Western world until the thirteenth century in Italy. It was traditionally made out of fiber derived from scraps of cloth—generally hemp, cotton, and linen—and it was less costly than papyrus and parchment, both of which served as the principal writing materials in the West until the arrival of paper. Papyrus (from which our word paper derives, although they are very different) was the invention of the ancient Egyptians (sometime around 4000 BCE) and was made by pounding and pasting together strips of the papyrus plant, which grew in abundance in the marshes of the Nile River. Parchment, popularized by the ancient Romans after the second century BCE, but used around the Mediterranean for many centuries before that, was made from animal skins that had been scraped, soaked, and dried, and was thus more widely available than papyrus, since animals are obviously found outside of the Nile River Basin, but also more expensive, since valuable animals had to be killed to make it. Paper was cheaper than both.

Paper arrived in the West through trade with the Muslim world, which in turn had learned of the process from China. Tradition has it that it was invented in 105 CE by Cai Lun, a eunuch who served in the imperial Han court, but archeologists have found fragments of paper in China that date to before 200 BCE. Papermaking was introduced into the Arabic world sometime in the eighth century CE, where it supported a thriving book trade, centered in Baghdad. It was not until the invention of the printing press by Johannes Gutenberg in fifteenth-century Germany, which itself spurred widespread interest in books, especially the Bible, that papermaking began to thrive in the West. Then publishers, who soon proliferated across the continent, vied for the rag supply. At one point in the early Renaissance, the city of Venice banned the export of rags for fear that its own paper industry might be threatened.

Because it required cloth rags in large quantities, paper remained an expensive, relatively luxury commodity (the technology for making paper from wood pulp was not discovered until the middle of the nineteenth century), and because, until the late fifteenth century, drawing was generally considered a student medium, as the Finiguerra drawing of a student suggests, it was not often done on paper. Copying a master's work was the means by which a student learned the higher art of painting. Thus, in 1493, the Italian religious zealot Savonarola outlined the ideal relationship between student and master: "What does the pupil look for in the master? I'll tell you. The master draws from his mind an image which his hands trace on paper and it carries the imprint of his idea. The pupil studies the drawing, and tries to imitate it. Little by little, in this way, he appropriates the style of

Fig. 8-4 Leonardo da Vinci, *Madonna and Child with St. Anne and Infant St. John the Baptist*, 1499–1500. Black chalk and touches of white chalk on brownish paper, mounted on canvas, 4 ft. 7¾ in. × 41¼ in. National Gallery, London.

Purchased with a special grant and contributions from Art Fund, Pilgrim Trust, and through a public appeal organized by Art Fund, 1962. NG3887. © 2015. Copyright National Gallery, London/Scala, Florence.

his master. That is how all natural things, and all creatures, have derived from the divine intellect." Savonarola thus describes drawing as both the banal, everyday business of beginners and also as equal in its creativity to God's handiwork in nature. For Savonarola, the master's idea is comparable to "divine intellect." The master is to the student as God is to humanity. Drawing is, furthermore, autographic: It bears the master's imprint, his style.

By the end of the fifteenth century, then, drawing had come into its own. It was seen as embodying, perhaps more clearly than even the finished work, the artist's personality and creative genius. As one watched an artist's ideas develop through a series of preparatory sketches, it became possible to speak knowingly about the creative process itself. By the time Giorgio Vasari wrote his famous *Lives of the Painters* in 1550, the tendency was to see in drawing the foundation of Renaissance painting itself. Vasari had one of the largest collections of fifteenth-century—or so-called *quattrocento*—drawings ever assembled, and he wrote as if these drawings were a dictionary of the styles of the artists who had come before him.

In the *Lives*, Vasari recalls how, in 1501, crowds rushed to see Leonardo's *Madonna and Child with St. Anne and Infant St. John the Baptist*, a **cartoon** (from the Italian *cartone*, meaning "paper") or drawing done to scale for a painting or a fresco. "The work not only won the astonished admiration of all the artists," Vasari reported, "but when finished for two days it attracted to the room where it was exhibited a crowd of men and women, young and old, who flocked there, as if they were attending a great festival, to gaze in amazement at the marvels he had created." Though this cartoon apparently does not survive, we can get some notion of it from the later cartoon illustrated here (**Fig. 8-4**). Vasari's account, at any rate, is the earliest recorded example we have of the public actually admiring a drawing.

Leonardo's works illustrate why drawing merits serious consideration as an art form in its own right and why they would so influence younger artists such as Raphael, who based so many of his paintings on quickly realized preparatory sketches (see *The Creative Process*, pp. 166–67). In Leonardo's *Study for a Sleeve* (**Fig. 8-5**), witness the extraordinary fluidity and spontaneity of the master's line. In contrast to the stillness of the resting arm (the hand, which is comparatively crude, was probably added later), the drapery is depicted as if it were a whirlpool or vortex. The directness of the medium, the ability of the artist's hand to move quickly over paper, allows Leonardo to bring out this turbulence. Through the intensity of his line, Leonardo imparts a degree of emotional complexity to the sitter, which is revealed in the part as well as in the whole. But the drawing also reveals the movements of the artist's own mind. It is as if the still sitter were at odds with the turbulence of the artist's imagination, an imagination that will not hold still whatever its object of contemplation. The fact is that in drawings like this one we learn something important not only about Leonardo's technique but also about what drove his imagination. More than any other reason, this was why, in the sixteenth century, drawings began to be preserved by artists and, simultaneously, collected by connoisseurs, experts on and appreciators of fine art.

Fig. 8-5 Leonardo da Vinci, *Study for a Sleeve*, ca. 1510–13.
Pen, lampblack, and chalk, 3⅛ × 6¾ in. The Royal Collection.

Drawing Materials

What is the difference between dry and liquid drawing media and what are some examples of each?

Just as the different fine arts media produce different kinds of images, different drawing materials produce different effects as well. Drawing materials are generally divided into two categories—dry media and liquid media.

Dry Media

The dry media, which include metalpoint, chalk, charcoal, graphite, and pastel, consist of coloring agents, or **pigments**, that are sometimes ground or mixed with substances that hold the pigment together, called **binders**. Binders, however, are not necessary if the natural pigment—for instance, charcoal made from vine wood heated in a hot kiln until only the carbon charcoal remains—can be applied directly to the surface of the work.

METALPOINT One of the most common techniques used in drawing in late-fifteenth- and early-sixteenth-century Italy was **metalpoint**. A stylus (point) made of gold, silver, or some other metal is applied to a sheet of paper prepared with a mixture of powdered bones (or lead white) and gumwater (when the stylus was silver, as it often was, the medium was called silverpoint). Sometimes, pigments other than white were added to this preparation in order to color the paper. When the metalpoint stylus is applied to this ground, a chemical reaction results, and line is produced.

A metalpoint line, which is pale gray, is very delicate and cannot be widened by increasing pressure upon the point. To make a thicker line, the artist must switch to a thicker point. Often, the same stylus would have a fine point on one end and a blunt one on the other. Since a line cannot be erased without resurfacing the paper, drawing with a metalpoint stylus requires extreme patience and skill. Leonardo's metalpoint drawing of a woman's head (**Fig. 8-6**) shows this skill. Shadow is rendered here by means of careful hatching. At the same time, a sense of movement and energy is evoked not only by the directional force of these parallels, but also by the freedom of Leonardo's line, the looseness of the gesture even in this most demanding of formats.

Fig. 8-6 Leonardo da Vinci, *Study of a Woman's Head or of the Angel of the Vergine delle Rocce*, 1473. Silverpoint with white highlights on prepared paper, 7⅛ × 6¼ in. Biblioteca Reale, Turin, Italy.
Alinari/Bridgeman Images.

The Creative Process

Movement and Gesture: Raphael's *Alba Madonna*

In a series of studies for *The Alba Madonna* (**Fig. 8-9**), the great Renaissance draftsman Raphael demonstrates many of the ways that artists use drawings to plan a final work. It is as if Raphael, in these sketches, had been instructed by Leonardo himself. We do know, in fact, that when Raphael arrived in Florence in 1504, he was stunned by the freedom of movement and invention that he discovered in Leonardo's drawings. Leonardo admonished his students to sketch subjects quickly: "Rough out the arrangement of the limbs of your figures and first attend to the movements appropriate to the mental state of the creatures that make up your picture rather than to the beauty and perfection of their parts."

In the studies illustrated here, Raphael worked on both sides of a single sheet of paper (**Figs. 8-7** and **8-8**). On one side he has drawn a male model from life and posed him as the Madonna. In the sweeping cross-hatching below the figure in the sketch, one can already sense the circular format of the final painting, as these lines rise and turn up the arm and shoulder and around to the model's head. Inside this curve is another, extending up the model's thigh and curving across his chest to his neck and face. Even the folds of the drapery under his extended arm echo this curvilinear structure.

On the other side of the paper, all the figures present in the final composition are included. The major difference between this and the final painting is that the infant St. John offers up a bowl of fruit in the drawing and Christ does not yet carry a cross in his hand. But the circular format of the final painting is fully realized in this drawing. A hastily drawn circular frame encircles the group (outside this frame, above it, are first ideas for yet another Madonna and Child, and below it, in the bottom right corner,

Figs. 8-7 and 8-8 Raphael, Studies for *The Alba Madonna* (recto and verso), ca. 1511. Left: red chalk; right: red chalk and pen and ink; both $16\frac{5}{8} \times 10\frac{3}{4}$ in. Left: Musée des Beaux Arts, Lille, France. Right: Private collection.

Fig. 8-9 Raphael, *The Alba Madonna*, ca. 1510. Oil on panel transferred to canvas, diameter 37¼ in., framed 4 ft. 6 in. × 4 ft. 5½ in. National Gallery of Art, Washington, D.C.

an early version of the Christ figure for this one). The speed and fluency of this drawing's execution are readily apparent, and if the complex facial expressions of the final painting are not yet indicated here, the emotional tenor of the body language is. The postures are both tense and relaxed. Christ seems to move away from St. John even as he turns toward him. Mary reaches out, possibly to comfort the young saint, but equally possibly to hold him at bay. Raphael has done precisely as Leonardo directed, attending to the precise movements and gestures that will indicate the mental states of his subjects in the final painting.

CHALK AND CHARCOAL Metalpoint is a mode of drawing that is chiefly concerned with **delineation**—that is, with a descriptive representation of the drawing's subject through an outline or contour drawing. Effects of light and shadow are essentially "added" to the finished drawing by means of hatching or heightening. With the softer media of chalk and charcoal, however, it is much easier to give a sense of the volumetric—that is, of three-dimensional form—through modulations of light and dark. By the middle of the sixteenth century, artists like Raphael used natural chalks, derived from red ocher hematite, white soapstone, and black carbonaceous shale, which were fitted into holders and shaved to a point (see Figs. 8-7 and 8-8). With these chalks, it became possible to realize gradual transitions from light to dark, either by adjusting the pressure of one's hand or by merging individual strokes by gently rubbing over a given area with a finger, cloth, or eraser. Charcoal sticks are made from burnt wood, and the best are made from hardwood, especially vines. They can be either hard or soft, sharpened to so precise a point that they draw like a pencil, or held on their sides and dragged in large bold gestures across the surface of the paper.

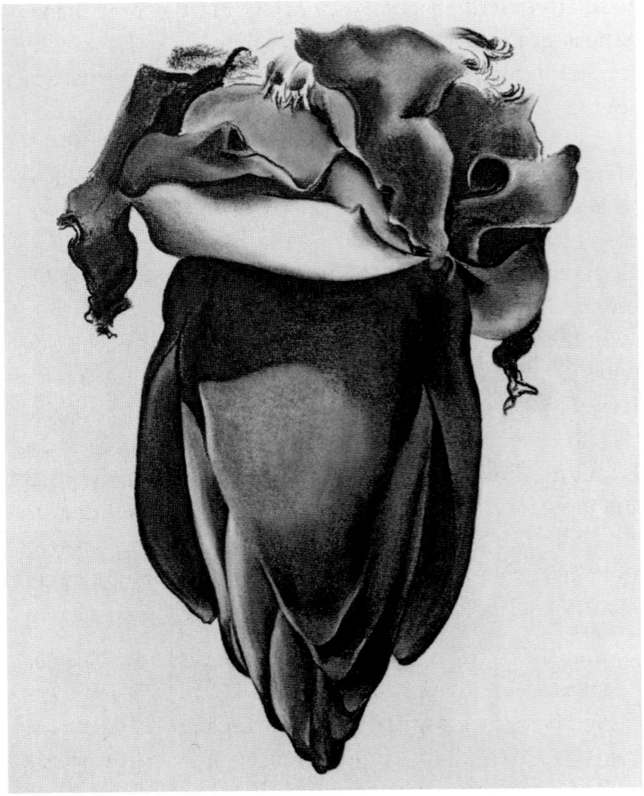

Fig. 8-10 **Georgia O'Keeffe, *Banana Flower*, 1933.** Charcoal and black chalk on paper, 21¾ × 14¾ in. Museum of Modern Art, New York.

Given anonymously (by exchange), 21.1936. © 2015. Digital image, Museum of Modern Art, New York/Scala, Florence. © 2015 Georgia O'Keeffe Museum/Artists Rights Society (ARS), New York.

In her charcoal drawing of a *Banana Flower* (**Fig. 8-10**), Georgia O'Keeffe achieves a sense of volume and space comparable to that realized by means of chalk. Though she is noted for her stunning oil paintings of flowers, this is a rare example in her work of a colorless flower composition. O'Keeffe's interest here is in creating three-dimensional space with a minimum of means, and the result is a study in light and dark in many ways comparable to a black-and-white photograph.

Because of its tendency to smudge easily, charcoal was not widely used during the Renaissance except in **sinopie**, tracings of the outlines of compositions drawn on the wall before the painting of frescoes. Such sinopie have come to light only recently, as frescoes have been removed from their plaster supports—usually walls or ceilings—for conservation purposes. Drawing with both charcoal and chalk requires a paper with tooth—a rough surface to which the media can adhere. Today, charcoal drawings can be kept from smudging by spraying synthetic resin fixatives over the finished work.

In the hands of modern artists, charcoal has become one of the more popular drawing media, in large part because of its expressive directness and immediacy. In her *Self-Portrait, Drawing* (**Fig. 8-11**), Käthe Kollwitz has revealed the extraordinary expressive capabilities of charcoal as a medium. Much of the figure was realized by dragging the stick up and down in sharp angular gestures along her arm from her chest to her hand. It is as if this line, which

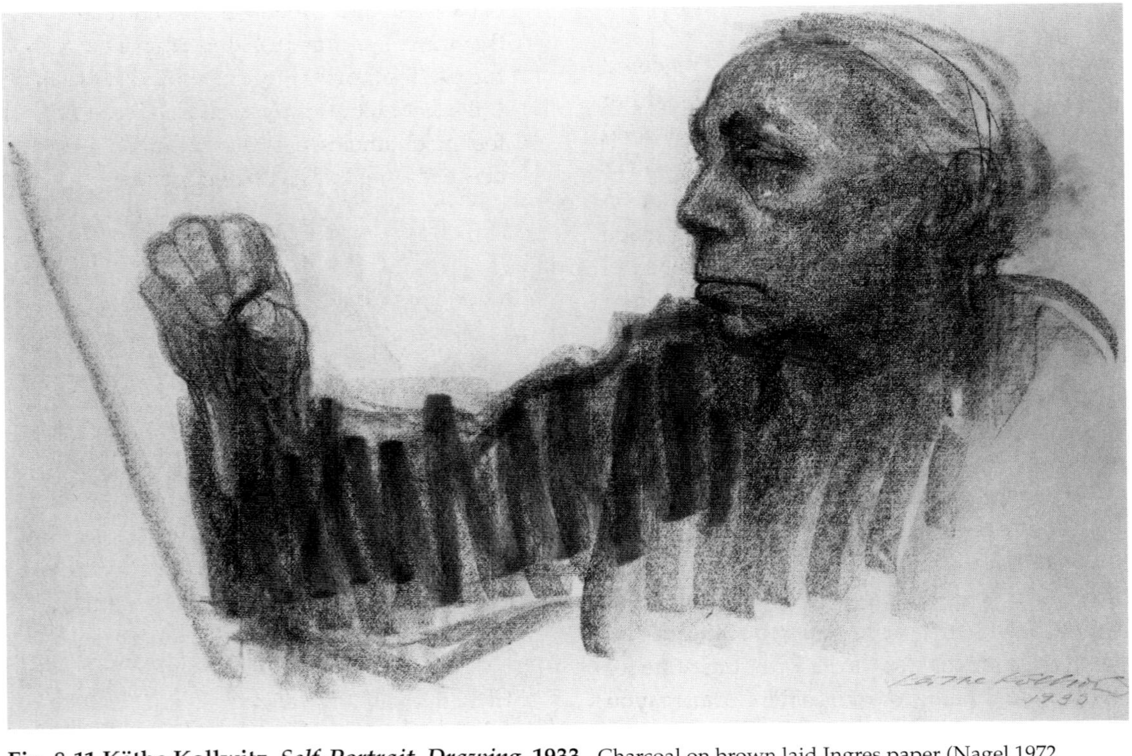

Fig. 8-11 Käthe Kollwitz, *Self-Portrait, Drawing*, 1933. Charcoal on brown laid Ingres paper (Nagel 1972 1240), 18¾ × 25 in. National Gallery of Art, Washington, D.C.

Rosenwald Collection, 1943.3.5217. © 2015 Board of Trustees, National Gallery of Art. © 2015 Artists Rights Society (ARS), New York/VG Bild-Kunst, Bonn.

Fig. 8-12 Georges Seurat, *The Artist's Mother*, 1882–83. Conté crayon on Michallet paper, 12 5/16 × 9 7/16 in. Metropolitan Museum of Art, New York.

Joseph Pulitzer Bequest, 1951; acquired from the Museum of Modern Art, Lillie P. Bliss Collection, 55.21.1. © 2015. Digital image Metropolitan Museum of Art/Art Resource/Scala, Florence.

mediates between the two much more carefully rendered areas of hand and face, embodies the dynamics of her work. This area of raw drawing literally connects her mind to her hand, her intellectual and spiritual capacity to her technical facility. It embodies the power of the imagination. She seems to hold the very piece of charcoal that has made this mark sideways between her fingers. She has rubbed so hard, and with such fury, that it has almost disappeared.

GRAPHITE Graphite, a soft form of carbon similar to coal, was discovered in 1564 in Borrowdale, England. As good black chalk became more and more difficult to obtain, the lead **pencil**—graphite enclosed in a cylinder of soft wood—increasingly became one of the most common of all drawing tools. It became even more popular during the Napoleonic Wars early in the nineteenth century. Then, because supplies of English graphite were cut off from the continent, the Frenchman Nicholas-Jacques Conté invented, at the request of Napoleon himself, a substitute for imported pencils that became known as the **Conté crayon** (not to be confused with the so-called Conté crayons marketed today, which are made with chalk). Conté substituted clay for some of the graphite. This technology was quickly adapted to the making of pencils generally. Thus, the relative hardness of the pencil could be controlled—the less graphite, the harder the pencil—and a greater range of lights (hard pencils) and darks (soft pencils, employing more graphite) became available.

Georges Seurat's Conté crayon study (**Fig. 8-12**) indicates the powerful range of tonal effects afforded by the new medium. As Seurat pressed harder, in the lower areas of the composition depicting his mother's dress, the coarse texture of his Michallet paper was filled by the crayon. Pressing less firmly, Seurat created a sense of light filling the room and lighting his mother's sewing. Where he has not drawn on the surface at all—on her collar—the glare of the white paper is almost as intense as light itself.

Vija Celmins's *Untitled (Ocean)* (**Fig. 8-13**) is an example of a highly developed photorealist graphite drawing. A little larger than a sheet of legal paper, the drawing is an extraordinarily detailed rendering of ocean waves as seen from Venice Pier in Venice, California. "I had a realization," Celmins recalled in 2002,

> that the surface of the ocean was somehow like the surface of the paper and that I could combine the images and have the image and the drawing unfold together.
>
> I really didn't fudge around or erase or smear. The graphite went on quite clear. I usually started actually at the right hand corner and moved straight up, like a kind of record of a double consciousness. A consciousness of the surface of the paper and also the surface of the image. It's about a kind of double reality of seeing what's there in a most ordinary way, a flat piece of paper and then seeing the double reality of an image that implies a different kind of space which is laid on top of the other image, but which really isn't there. . . . I like to think of it like a ghost of an ocean. There is a feeling of timelessness that's implied in an image of an ocean that really has no boundaries.

Fig. 8-13 Vija Celmins, *Untitled (Ocean)*, 1970. Graphite on acrylic ground on paper, 14 1/8 × 18 7/8 in. Museum of Modern Art, New York.

Mrs. Florene M. Schoenborn Fund, 585.1970. © 2015. Digital image, Museum of Modern Art, New York/Scala, Florence. © 2015 Vija Celmins.

This is one of a long series of drawings based on small 3½ × 5-inch photographs, and the sense of infinite space that Celmins's drawings evoke is in no small part a function of the arbitrary frame of the camera lens which always suggests the continuance of space beyond its edges. Celmins used a pencil of differing hardness for each drawing in the series, exploring the range of possibilities offered by the medium. In the process, she learned a great deal about the expressive potential of the medium. "I began to see," she says, "that the graphite itself had a certain life to it."

PASTEL **Pastel** is essentially a chalk medium with colored pigment and a nongreasy binder added to it. Pastels come in sticks the dimension of an index finger and are labeled soft, medium, and hard, depending on how much binder is incorporated into the medium—the more binder, the harder the stick. Since the pigment is, in effect, diluted by increased quantities of binder, the harder the stick, the less intense its color. This is why we tend to associate the word "pastel" with pale, light colors. Although the harder sticks are much easier to use than the softer ones, some of the more interesting effects of the medium can only be achieved with the more intense colors of the softer sticks. The lack of binder in pastels makes them extremely fragile. Before the final drawing is fixed, the marks created by the chalky powder can literally fall off the paper, despite the fact that, since the middle of the eighteenth century, special ribbed and textured papers have been made that help hold the medium to the surface.

Of all artists who have ever used pastel, perhaps Edgar Degas was the most proficient and inventive. He was probably attracted to the medium because it was more direct than painting, and its unfinished quality seemed particularly well suited to his artistic goal of capturing the reality of the contemporary scene, especially

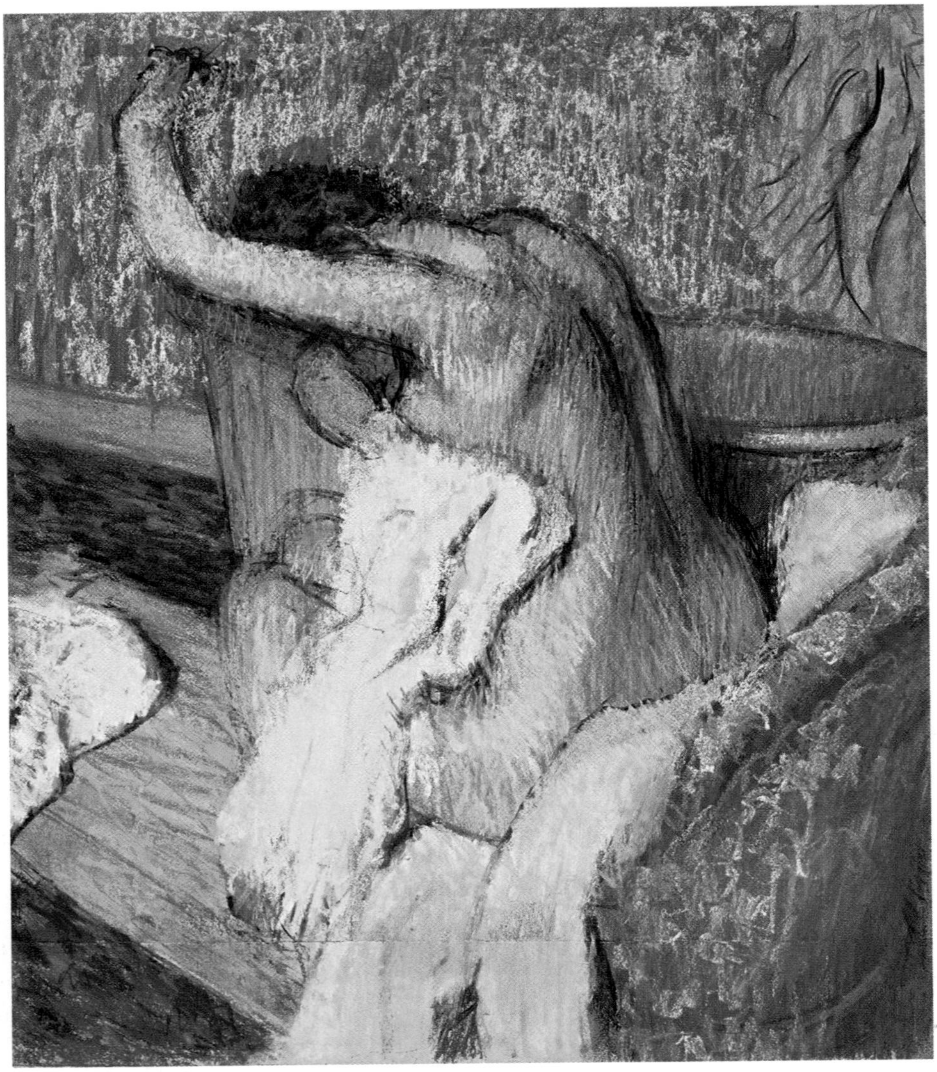

Fig. 8-14 Edgar Degas, *After the Bath, Woman Drying Herself*, ca. 1889–90. Pastel on paper, 26⅝ × 22¾ in. The Courtauld Institute of Art, London.

Fig. 8-15 Mary Cassatt, *Young Mother, Daughter, and Son*, 1913. Pastel on paper, 43¼ × 33¼ in. Memorial Art Gallery of the University of Rochester. Marion Stratten Gould Fund. mag.rochester.edu/

in a series of pastel drawings of women at their bath (**Fig. 8-14**). Degas's use of his medium is unconventional, incorporating into the "finished" work both improvised gesture and a loose, sketchlike drawing. Degas invented a new way to use pastel, building up the pigments in successive layers. Normally, this would not have been possible because the powdery chalks of the medium would not hold to the surface. But Degas worked with a fixative, the formula for which has been lost, that allowed him to build up layers of pastel without affecting the intensity of their color. Laid on the surface in hatches, these successive layers create an optical mixture of color that shimmers before the eyes in a virtually abstract design.

The American painter Mary Cassatt met Degas in Paris in 1877, and he became her artistic mentor. Known for her pictures of mothers and children, Cassatt learned to use the pastel medium in even bolder terms than Degas. In this drawing, *Young Mother, Daughter, and Son* (**Fig. 8-15**), one of Cassatt's last works, the gestures of her pastel line again and again exceed the boundaries of the forms that contain them, and loosely drawn, arbitrary blue strokes extend across almost every element of the composition.

The owner of this work, Mrs. H. O. Havemeyer, Cassatt's oldest and best friend, saw in works such as this one an almost virtuoso display of "strong line, great freedom of technique and a supreme mastery of color." When Mrs. Havemeyer organized a benefit exhibition of Cassatt's and Degas's works in New York in 1915, its proceeds to be donated to the cause of women's suffrage, she included works such as this one because Cassatt's freedom of line was, to her, the very symbol of the strength of women and their equality to men. Seen beside the works by Degas, it would

Fig. 8-16 Sandy Brooke, *Fate and Luck: Eclipse*, 2011. Oilstick on linen, 30 × 24 in.
Courtesy of the artist. © 2011 Sandy Brooke. Photo: Gary Alvis.

be evident that the pupil had equaled, and in many ways surpassed, the achievement of Degas himself.

OILSTICK Oilsticks are oil paint manufactured with enough wax for the paint to be molded into stick form. They allow the painter to draw directly onto a surface without brushes, palettes, paint tubes, or solvents. Although related to pastel sticks, which are too soft to permit long and continuous strokes across the surface, the density of oilsticks allows the artist more gestural freedom and a sense of direct engagement with the act of drawing itself. Sandy Brooke's oilstick drawing *Fate and Luck: Eclipse* (**Fig. 8-16**) is one of a series of paintings and drawings on the theme announced in the title. As Brooke says, "Things we cannot explain are often written off as Fate, and when things go well, we might feel we just got Lucky. Much of life is a complete mystery; it's the same in painting." Here, the helicopters are simultaneously symbols of rescue and agents of war. The eclipse of the title, imaged in a horizontal band about one-quarter the way up the painting, is, in some cultures, an omen of good things to come, in others just the opposite. The forces of nature—the dragonfly, the hummingbirds, the sea, and the eclipse—collide here with the forces of civilization. With oilstick—often smeared and diluted—Brooke is able to create particularly transparent effects. "For me," Brooke says,

> *the act of looking at the surface of this work is comparable to looking into water. Images behind and above the viewer*

are reflected off the semi-transparent surface beneath which other forms appear and disappear, fragment and coalesce, depending on the degree of surface turbulence. As we look into the painting, the possibility arises that what we see there, in the flow of the current, in the shadow of the storm, is a reflection of ourselves, and a reflection of history itself, the disasters and triumphs of our age.

Liquid Media

In liquid media, pigments are suspended in liquid binders that flow much more easily onto the surface than dry media such as chalk. In fact, because liquid media are so fluid, they can also be applied with a brush.

PEN AND INK During the Renaissance, as paper became more and more widely available, most drawings were done with iron-gall ink, which was made from a mixture of iron salts and an acid obtained from the nutgall, a swelling on an oak tree caused by disease. The characteristic brown color of most Renaissance pen-and-ink drawings results from the fact that this ink, though black at application, browns with age.

The quill pen used by most Renaissance artists, which was most often made from a goose or swan feather, allows for far greater variation in line and texture than is possible with a metalpoint stylus or even with a pencil. As we can see in this drawing by Elisabetta Sirani (**Fig. 8-17**), one of the leading artists in Bologna during the seventeenth century, the line can be thickened or thinned, depending on the artist's manipulation of the flexible quill and the absorbency of the paper (the more absorbent the paper, the more freely the ink will flow through its fibers). Diluted to a greater or lesser degree, ink also provides her with a more fluid and expressive means to render light and shadow than the elaborate and tedious hatching that was necessary when using stylus or chalk. Drawing with pen and ink is fast and expressive. Sirani, in fact, displayed such speed and facility in her compositions that, according to a story that most women will find familiar, she was forced to work in public in order to demonstrate that her work was her own and not done by a man.

In this example from Jean Dubuffet's series of drawings *Corps de Dame* (**Fig. 8-18**) (in French, the title means both a group of women and the bodies of women), the

Fig. 8-17 Elisabetta Sirani, *The Holy Family with a Kneeling Monastic Saint*, ca. 1660. Pen and brown ink, black chalk, on paper, 10⅜ × 7⅜ in. Private collection.

Photo © Christie's Images/Bridgeman Images.

Fig. 8-18 Jean Dubuffet, *Corps de Dame*, June–December 1950. Pen, reed pen, and ink, 10⅝ × 8⅜ in. Museum of Modern Art, New York.

Jean and Lester Avnet Collection, 54.1978. © 2015 Digital image, Museum of Modern Art, New York/Scala, Florence. © 2015 Artists Rights Society (ARS), New York/ADAGP, Paris.

whorl of line, which ranges from the finest hairline to strokes nearly a half-inch thick, defines a female form, her two small arms raised as if to ward off the violent gestures of the artist's pen itself. Though many see Dubuffet's work as misogynistic—the product of someone who hates women—it can also be read as an attack on academic figure drawing, the pursuit of formal perfection and beauty that has been used traditionally to justify drawing from the nude. Dubuffet does not so much render form as flatten it and, in a gesture that insists on the modern artist's liberation from traditional techniques and values, his use of pen and ink threatens to transform drawing into scribbling, or conscious draftsmanship into automatism, that is, unconscious and random automatic marking. In this, his work is very close to Surrealist experiments designed to make contact with the unconscious mind.

Fig. 8-19 Giovanni Battista Tiepolo, *The Adoration of the Magi*, 1740s. Pen and brown wash over graphite sketch, 11⅗ × 8⅕ in. Iris & B. Gerald Cantor Center for Visual Arts at Stanford University. Mortimer C. Leventritt Fund, 1950.392.

WASH AND BRUSH When ink is diluted with water and applied by brush in broad, flat areas, the result is called a **wash**. Giovanni Battista Tiepolo's *Adoration of the Magi* (**Fig. 8-19**) is essentially three layers deep. Over a preliminary graphite sketch is a pen-and-ink drawing, and over both Tiepolo has laid a brown wash. The wash serves two purposes here: It helps to define volume and form by adding shadow, but it also creates a visual pattern of alternating light and dark elements that helps to make the drawing much more dynamic than it would otherwise be. As we move from right to left across the scene, deeper and deeper into its space, this alternating pattern leads us to a central moment of light, which seems to flood from the upper right, falling on the infant Jesus himself.

Many artists prefer to draw with a brush. It not only affords them a sense of immediacy and spontaneity, but the soft brushtip allows artists to control the width of their lines. Drawing with a brush is a technique with a long tradition in the East, perhaps because the brush is used there as a writing instrument. Chinese calligraphy requires that each line in a written character begin very thinly, then broaden in the middle before tapering again to a point. Thus, in the same gesture, a line can move from broad and sweeping to fragile and narrow, and back again. Such ribbons of line are extremely expressive. In his depiction of the Tang poet Li Bo (**Fig. 8-20**), Liang Kai juxtaposes the quick strokes of diluted ink that form the robe with the fine, detailed brushwork of his face. This opposition contrasts the fleeting materiality of the poet's body—as insubstantial as his chant, which drifts away on the wind—with the enduring permanence of his poetry.

Fig. 8-20 Liang Kai, *The Poet Li Bo Walking and Chanting a Poem*, Southern Song dynasty, ca. 1200. Hanging scroll, ink on paper, 31¾ × 11⅞ in. Tokyo National Museum, Japan.
Image: TNM Image Archives.

Innovative Drawing Media

In what ways can drawing be an innovative medium?

Drawing is by its nature an exploratory medium. It invites experimentation. Taking up a sheet of heavy prepainted paper of the brightest colors, Henri Matisse was often inspired, beginning in the early 1940s, to cut out a shape in the paper with a pair of wide-open scissors, using them like a knife to carve through the paper. He considered working with scissors a kind of drawing. "Scissors," he says, "can acquire more feeling for line than pencil or charcoal." Sketching with the scissors, Matisse discovered what he considered to be the essence of a form. Beginning in 1951, confined to a wheelchair and unable to stand to paint, and continuing until his death in 1954, Matisse turned almost exclusively to cutouts. He cut very large swathes of color freehand, and then had them pinned loosely to the white studio walls. Studying them from his wheelchair, he later rearranged them, recut and recombined them, until their composition

Fig. 8-21 Henri Matisse, *Venus*, 1952. Paper collage on canvas, 39⅞ × 30⅛ in. National Gallery of Art, Washington, D.C.

satisfied him. In their color, they were like painting. In their cutting, they were a kind of drawing. And in the process of subtracting paper from the original sheets of color, they were like sculpting from a large block of wood or marble. Finally, the shapes were glued to large white paper backgrounds for shipping and display. In this *Venus* (**Fig. 8-21**), the figure of the goddess is revealed in the negative space of the composition. It is as if the goddess of love—and hence love itself—were immaterial. In the blue positive space to the right we discover the profile of a man's head, as if love springs, fleetingly, from his very breath.

In his installation *Whispers from the Walls* (**Fig. 8-22**), a full-scale recreation of what a 1920s North Texas one-room house lived in by an African-American family working the fields might have looked like, Whitfield Lovell has used charcoal drawing in a particularly evocative way. On the shack's plank walls—salvaged from abandoned buildings around Denton, Texas, where the piece was first installed at the University of North Texas—he has drawn life-size figures based on actual photographs of the Texas African Americans, especially those who lived in the thriving Denton African-American community in the 1920s. The very fragility of the medium lends the drawings an almost ghostlike presence, an eerie sense of the past rising through and in the collection of period artifacts—blankets, a rag carpet, a trunk, a gas lamp, pots and pans, the hat on the bed—that he has assembled in the room. The room smells of must. "Rising River Blues" seems to play on an old phonograph. The sound of soft voices can be overheard, as if emanating from the drawings themselves.

Lovell says that the inspiration for drawing on walls came from a 1993 visit to an Italian villa that had been owned by a slave trader: "Somehow the experience of being in the villa and knowing its history was so haunting that I could not work the way I was accustomed to working. . . . I wanted to leave some dignified images of black people in that space." *Whispers from the Walls* is, in this sense, Lovell's attempt to restore to contemporary America—and Denton, Texas in particular—that dignity.

One of the great drawing innovators of the day is South African artist William Kentridge, who employs his drawings to create his own animated films. These films are built up from single drawings in charcoal and pastel on paper that are successively altered through erasure, additions, and redrawings that are photographed at each stage of evolution. Instead of being constructed, as in normal animation, out of hundreds

Fig. 8-22 Whitfield Lovell, *Whispers from the Walls*, 1999. Mixed-media installation, varying dimensions. Courtesy of DC Moore Gallery, New York.

of separate drawings, Kentridge's films are made of hundreds of photographs of drawings in process. A week's drawing might add up to around 40 seconds of animation.

The process of erasure, and the smudged layering that results, is for Kentridge a kind of metaphor for memory, and it is memory that concerns the artist, especially the memory of **apartheid** in South Africa and, by extension, the memory of the forces that mark the history of modernity as a whole. The films chronicle the rise and fall of a white Johannesburg businessman, Soho Eckstein. Always dressed in a pinstripe suit, Soho buys land and then mines it, extracting the resources and riches of the land and creating an empire based upon his own exploitation of miners and landscape. He is emotionally the very embodiment of the industrial infrastructure he has helped to create—dark, somber, virtually dehumanized. Over time, as the films have followed his career, he has come to understand the high price that he and his country have paid for his actions.

Made shortly after the establishment in South Africa of the Truth and Reconciliation Commission, headed by Archbishop Desmond Tutu, *History of the Main Complaint* (**Fig. 8-23**) is the sixth film in Kentridge's exploration of the meaning of Eckstein's life. Just as in the hearings of the Commission, where individuals told their stories of personal suffering and abuse in order to encourage those responsible to admit their guilt, the theme of this film is Eckstein's recognition of his own, and white South Africa's, responsibility. The film opens with Eckstein lying in a hospital bed in a coma—that he is wearing a suit gives away the fact that his "coma" is a metaphor for his inability to recognize his own complicity. In his unconscious state, he drives down a road in which he witnesses atrocity after atrocity until he himself hits a woman with his car. A red cross appears at the point of impact, and he wakens from his stupor, finally aware of what he and other white South Africans have done. Extended segments of Kentridge's *History of the Main Complaint* are included in the art21 *Exclusive* video "William Kentridge: Pain and Sympathy," in which the artist also discusses the difficulty and purpose of drawing the horrors of apartheid.

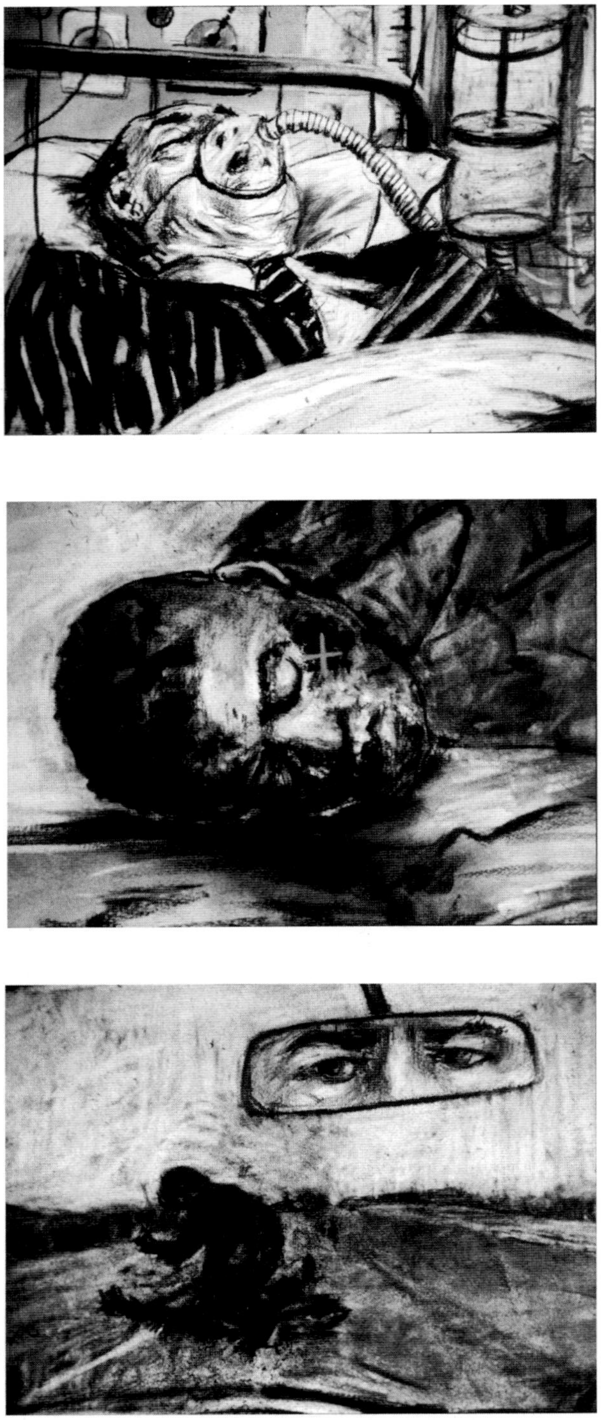

Fig. 8-23 William Kentridge, *History of the Main Complaint*, 1996. Stills. Film, 35 mm, shown as video, projection, black and white, and sound (mono), 5 min. 50 sec.
Courtesy of Marion Goodman Gallery, New York.

Drawing has always held an important place in popular culture, particularly in the world of the comic book and that version of the comic-book genre generally intended for more mature audiences, the graphic novel. Among the most popular of the latter have been Frank Miller's *Batman: The Dark Knight Returns* (1986) and Art Spiegelman's *Maus: A Survivor's Tale* (1986), a tale recounting his own parents' experience as Polish Jews during World War II, in which Jews are portrayed as mice, Germans as cats, and Americans as dogs. The latter made a lasting impression on Iranian artist Marjane Satrapi, who created her own graphic novel, *Persepolis*, while living in exile in Paris in 2001. Named after the capital of ancient Persia, in what is now modern-day Iran, *Persepolis* tells the story of Satrapi's own childhood as she grew up in Iran. Born in 1969, she was ten years old

Fig. 8-24 Marjane Satrapi, Page from the "Kim Wilde" chapter of the graphic novel *Persepolis*, 2001. Ink on paper, $16\frac{9}{16} \times 11\frac{11}{16}$ in.

when the king of Iran, Shah Mohammed Reza Pahlavi, was forced to flee the country as Islamic fundamentalists under the spiritual leadership of Ayatollah Khomeini took over. The page from the novel illustrated here takes place in 1983 (**Fig. 8-24**). Unsympathetic to the revolution, and in some measure proud of their 13-year-old daughter's defiance of its dismissal of all things Western as morally corrupt, her parents have smuggled into the country a denim jacket, a pair of Nike tennis shoes, a Michael Jackson button, and posters of the heavy metal band Iron Maiden and pop star Kim Wilde, whose New Wave hit "Kids in America" had reached the top of the charts in 1981. Here, Satrapi dresses up in her new gear in preparation for heading out into the streets to buy bootleg tapes of Kim Wilde and the English band Camel. "For an Iranian mother," Satrapi writes in French at the bottom of the page (*Persepolis* was originally published in France), "my mother was very permissive. Apart from me, I only knew two or three other girls who were allowed to go out alone at the age of 13." Satrapi's drawing style subtly but effectively supports this narrative. In revolutionary Iran, all is black and white. From the point of view of the guardians of the revolution, there is no moral middle ground, only right and wrong, as plain and simple as Satrapi's drawing itself. It should come as no surprise, finally, that in 2007 Satrapi turned *Persepolis* into an animated feature film, which was nominated for an Academy Award for Best Animated Feature in 2008. As a form, the graphic novel lends itself to precisely the kind of animation that distinguishes Kentridge's art.

THE CRITICAL PROCESS

Thinking about Drawing

As we have seen, drawing is one of the most basic and one of the most direct of all media. Initially, drawing was not considered an art in its own right, but only a tool for teaching and preliminary study. By the late Renaissance, it was generally acknowledged that drawing possessed a vitality and immediacy that revealed significant details about the artist's personality and style.

Frank Auerbach's *Head of Catherine Lampert VI* (**Fig. 8-25**) began with a series of drawings that were rubbed and wiped out—perhaps over a period of a couple of years, given the drawing's dates. In the process, he created a light-gray charcoal ground. With an eraser, he carved into this ground, establishing the light planes of the face, and then built up her features with a much darker, loosely gestural line.

A year or two before this drawing was made, Auerbach met Lampert when she was curating the 1978 exhibition of his work at the Hayward Gallery in London. She has since curated numerous exhibitions by the artist and has been sitting for his portraits for over 30 years, visiting his Camden studio always for two hours at a time, usually in the evening. Drawings such as this one are studies for the numerous painted portraits of Auerbach's sitters, always made from life in preparation for, and often during the process of, making a painting.

Fig. 8-25 Frank Auerbach, *Head of Catherine Lampert VI*, 1979–80. Charcoal and chalk on canvas, 30⅜ × 23 in. Museum of Modern Art, New York.
Purchase, 436.1981. © 2015. Digital image, Museum of Modern Art, New York/Scala, Florence. © Frank Auerbach.

In her introduction to the exhibition catalogue of Auerbach's exhibition at the Venice Biennale in 1986, Lampert described the artist's process: "[He] moves noisily around the room . . . continuously active, drawing in the air, talking to himself, hardly pausing, much less contemplating in the usual sense of the word." The drawings and paintings, Lampert's co-author Isabel Carlisle adds, represent an effort "to celebrate life through the energy specific to all individuals through their changing moods and to fuse those energies with his own furious energy during the painting's execution." How is that energy reflected in Auerbach's line? Does anything about the drawing suggest repose? How would you compare it to Delacroix's study for *The Death of Sardanapalus* (see Fig. 3-23)? How does Auerbach achieve a sense of three-dimensional depth in this drawing? If his purpose is to capture something of the sitter's personality, what does this drawing suggest about her temperament?

Thinking Back

8.1 Discuss the history of drawing in the Italian Renaissance and how it came to be considered an art in its own right.

Paper was first manufactured in Italy in the thirteenth century. How does paper differ from papyrus and parchment, which had been used earlier? Apprentices, such as the youth in Finiguerra's workshop, drew on wooden tablets because paper was so expensive. What accounts for the high cost of paper?

By the end of the fifteenth century, drawing had come into its own as an artistic medium since it was considered to embody the artist's personality and creative genius. What is a cartoon? What accounts for the power of Leonardo's drawings?

8.2 Distinguish between dry and liquid drawing media and list examples of each.

The dry media, which include metalpoint, chalk, charcoal, graphite, and pastel, consist of coloring agents, or pigments, that are sometimes ground or mixed with substances that hold the pigment together, called binders. Metalpoint was one of the most common drawing techniques in late fifteenth- and early sixteenth-century Italy. In this technique, a stylus (point) made of metal is applied to a sheet of prepared paper. When the point touches the prepared ground, a chemical reaction results, producing marks on the paper. What is delineation? How do softer dry media, such as chalk, charcoal, graphite, and pastel, differ from metalpoint?

Liquid media consist of a pigment, which is the coloring agent, and a binder, which holds the pigment together. In wet media, such as ink, the pigment is held in a liquid binder. How was ink typically made during the Renaissance? What is a wash? What qualities does a brush afford in drawing?

8.3 Give some examples of how drawing can be an innovative medium.

Drawing is, by nature, an exploratory medium, inviting experimentation. Many modern and contemporary artists have pushed traditional boundaries of drawing, using new techniques and materials, working at a large scale, and integrating drawing with film. How did Henri Matisse work in an innovative manner to make his *Venus*? How did William Kentridge create his *History of the Main Complaint*?

Chapter 9
Painting

Learning Objectives

9.1 Distinguish among the early painting media—encaustic, fresco, and tempera.

9.2 Describe what is distinctive about oil painting as a medium.

9.3 Explain why watercolor is perhaps the most expressive of the painting media.

9.4 Discuss some of the advantages offered the artist by synthetic painting media.

9.5 Outline some of the ways that painting has combined itself with other media.

From the earliest times, one of the major concerns of Western painting has been representing the appearance of things in the natural world. There is a famous story told by the historian Pliny about a contest between the Greek painters Parrhasius and Zeuxis as to who could make the most realistic image:

> Zeuxis produced a picture of grapes so dexterously represented that birds began to fly down to eat from the painted vine. Whereupon Parrhasius designed so lifelike a picture of a curtain that Zeuxis, proud of the verdict of the birds, requested that the curtain should now be drawn back and the picture displayed. When he realized his mistake, with a modesty that did him honor, he yielded up the palm, saying that whereas he had managed to deceive only birds, Parrhasius had deceived an artist.

This tradition, which views the painter's task as rivaling the truth of nature, has survived to the present day.

But until sometime early in the fifteenth century, painting was not regarded as a particularly important practice. Around that time, a figure known as *La Pittura*—literally, "the picture"—began to appear in Italian art (**Fig. 9-1**). As art historian Mary D. Garrard has noted, the emergence of this figure, the personification of painting, could be said to announce the cultural arrival of painting as an art. In the Middle Ages, painting was never included among the liberal arts—those areas of knowledge that were thought to develop general intellectual capacity—which included rhetoric, arithmetic, geometry, astrology, and music. While the liberal arts were understood to involve inspiration and creative invention, painting was considered merely a mechanical skill, involving, at most, the ability to copy. The emergence of *La Pittura* announced that painting was finally something more than mere copywork, that it was an intellectual pursuit equal to the other liberal arts, all of which had been given similar personifications early in the Middle Ages.

In her *Self-Portrait as the Allegory of Painting* (**Fig. 9-2**), Artemisia Gentileschi presents herself as both a real person and as the personification of *La Pittura*. Iconographically speaking, Gentileschi may be recognized as *La Pittura* by virtue of the pendant around her neck which symbolizes imitation. And Gentileschi can imitate the appearance of things very well—she presents us with a portrait of herself as she really looks. Still, in Renaissance terms, imitation means more than simply

Fig. 9-1 Giorgio Vasari, *The Art of Painting*, 1542. Fresco of the vault of the Main Room, Casa Vasari, Arezzo, Italy.
Canali Photobank, Milan, Italy.

Fig. 9-2 Artemisia Gentileschi, *Self-Portrait as the Allegory of Painting*, 1630. Oil on canvas, 35¼ × 29 in.
The Royal Collection.
Bridgeman Images. Photo: C. Cooper Ltd. © Her Majesty Queen Elizabeth II, 2015.

copying appearances: It is the representation of nature as seen by and through the artist's imagination. On the one hand, Gentileschi's multicolored garment alludes to her craft and skill as a copyist—she can imitate the effects of color—but, on the other hand, her unruly hair stands for the imaginative frenzy of the artist's temperament. Thus, in this painting, she portrays herself both as a real woman and as an idealized personification of artistic genius, possessing all the intellectual authority and dignity of a Leonardo or a Michelangelo. Though in her time it was commonplace to think of women as intellectually inferior to men—"women have long dresses and short intellects" was a popular saying—here Gentileschi transforms painting from mere copywork and, in the process, transforms her own possibilities as a creative person.

In this chapter, we will consider the art of painting, paying particular attention to how its various media developed in response to artists' desires to imitate reality and express themselves more fluently. But before we begin our discussion of these various painting media, we should be familiar with a number of terms that all the media share and that are crucial to understanding how paintings are made.

Early Painting Media

What differentiates each of the early painting media—encaustic, fresco, and tempera—from one another?

From prehistoric times to the present day, the painting process has remained basically the same. As in drawing, artists use pigments, or powdered colors, suspended in a medium or binder that holds the particles of pigment together. The binder protects the pigment from changes and serves as an adhesive to anchor the pigment to the **support**, or the surface on which the artist paints—a wall, a panel of wood, a sheet of paper, or a canvas. Different binders have different characteristics. Some dry more quickly than others. Some create an almost transparent paint, while others are opaque—that is, they cannot be seen through. The same pigment used in different binders will look different because of the varying degrees of each binder's transparency.

Since most supports are too absorbent to allow the easy application of paint, artists often prime (pre-treat) a support with a paintlike material called a **ground**. Grounds also make the support surface smoother or more uniform in texture. Many grounds, especially white grounds, increase the brightness of the final picture.

Finally, artists use a **solvent** or **vehicle**, a thinner that enables the paint to flow more readily and that also cleans brushes. All water-based paints use water for a vehicle. Other types of paints require a different thinner—in the case of oil-based paint, turpentine.

Each painting medium has unique characteristics and has flourished at particular historical moments. Though many media have been largely abandoned as new media have been discovered—media that allow the artist to create a more believable image or that are simply easier to use—almost all media continue to be used to some extent, and older media, such as encaustic and fresco, sometimes find fresh uses in the hands of contemporary artists.

Encaustic

Encaustic, made by combining pigment with a binder of hot wax, is one of the oldest painting media. It was widely used in Classical Greece, most famously by Polygnotus, but his work, as well as all other Greek painting except that on vases, has entirely perished. (The contest between Zeuxis and Parrhasius was probably conducted in encaustic.)

Most of the surviving encaustic paintings from the ancient world come from Faiyum in Egypt, which, in the second century CE, was a thriving Roman province about 60 miles south of present-day Cairo. The Faiyum paintings are funeral portraits, which were attached to the mummy cases of the deceased, and they are the only indication we have of the painting techniques used by the Greeks. A transplanted Greek artist may, in fact, have been responsible for *Mummy Portrait of a Man* (**Fig. 9-3**), though we cannot be sure.

Fig. 9-3 *Mummy Portrait of a Man*, Faiyum, Egypt, ca. 160–70 CE. Encaustic on wood, 14 × 18 in. Albright-Knox Art Gallery, Buffalo, New York.
Charles Clifton Fund, 1938. © 2015. Albright Knox Art Gallery/Art Resource, New York/Scala, Florence.

What is clear, though, is the artist's remarkable skill with the brush. The encaustic medium is a demanding one, requiring the painter to work quickly so that the wax will stay liquid. Looking at *Mummy Portrait of a Man*, we notice that, while the neck and shoulders have been rendered with simplified forms, giving them a sense of strength that is almost tangible, the face has been painted in a very naturalistic and sensitive way. The wide, expressive eyes and the delicate modeling of the cheeks make us feel that we are looking at a "real" person, which was clearly the artist's intention.

The extraordinary luminosity of the encaustic medium has led to its revival in recent years. Of all contemporary artists working in the medium, no one has perfected its use more than Jasper Johns in works such as his encaustic *Flag* (see Fig. 1-5).

Fresco

Wall painting was practiced by the ancient Egyptians, Greeks, and Romans, as well as by Italian painters of the Renaissance. Numerous examples survive from the Aegean civilizations of the Cyclades and Crete (see Fig. 16-18), to which later Greek culture traced its roots. In the eighteenth century, a great many frescoes were discovered at Pompeii and nearby Herculaneum, where they had been buried under volcanic ash since the eruption of Mount Vesuvius in 79 CE. A series of still-life paintings was unearthed in 1755–57 that proved so popular in France that they led to the renewed popularity of the still-life genre. This *Still Life with Eggs and Thrushes* (**Fig. 9-4**), from the Villa of Julia Felix, is particularly notable, especially the realism of the dish of eggs, which seems to hang over the edge of the painting and push forward into our space. The fact that all the objects in the still life have been painted life-size adds to the work's sense of realism.

The preferred medium for wall painting for centuries was **fresco**, in which pigment is mixed with limewater (a solution containing calcium hydroxide, or slaked lime) and then applied to a lime plaster wall that is either still wet or hardened and dry. If the paint is applied to a wet wall, the process is called ***buon fresco*** (Italian for "good" or "true fresco"), and if it is applied to a dry wall, it is called ***fresco secco***, or "dry fresco." In *buon fresco*, the wet plaster absorbs the wet pigment, and the painting literally becomes part of the wall. The artist must work quickly, plastering only as much wall as can be painted before the plaster dries, but the advantage of the process is that it is extremely durable. In *fresco secco*, on the other hand, the pigment is combined with binders such as egg yolk, oil, or wax and applied separately, at virtually any pace the artist desires. As a result, the artist can render an object with extraordinary care and meticulousness. The disadvantage of the *fresco secco* technique is that moisture can creep in between the plaster and the paint, causing the paint to flake off the wall. This is what happened to Leonardo da Vinci's *Last Supper* in Milan (see Fig. 4-15), which peeled away to such a tragic degree that the image almost disappeared. Beginning in 1979, it underwent careful restoration, a job finally completed in 1999.

Nevertheless, in extremely dry environments, such as the Buddhist caves at Ajanta, India, *fresco secco* has

Fig. 9-4 ***Still Life with Eggs and Thrushes*, Villa of Julia Felix, Pompeii, before 79 CE.**
Fresco, 35 in. × 4 ft. National Archaeological Museum, Naples.

proven extremely durable (**Fig. 9-5**). Painting in the fifth century CE, the artists at Ajanta covered the walls of the caves with a mixture of mud and cow dung, bound together with straw or animal hair. Once dry, this mud mixture was smoothed over a layer of gypsum or lime plaster, which served as the ground for the painting. The artists' technique is fully described in the *Samarangana Sutra Dhara*, an encyclopedic work on Indian architecture written in the early eleventh century CE. The artist first outlined his subject in iron ore, then filled in the outline with color, building up the figure's features from darker to lighter tones to create the subtle gradations of modeling required to achieve the sense of a three-dimensional body. Protruding features, such as shoulders, nose, brow, and, on this figure especially, the right hand, thus resonate against the dark background of the painting, as if reaching out of the darkness of the cave into the light.

This figure is a bodhisattva, an enlightened being who, in order to help others achieve enlightenment, postpones joining the Buddha in nirvana—not exactly heaven, but the state of being freed from suffering and

Fig. 9-5 ***Bodhisattva*, detail of a fresco wall painting in Cave I, Ajanta, Maharashtra, India, ca. 475 CE.**

Fig. 9-6 Giotto, *Lamentation*, ca. 1305. Fresco, approx. 5 ft. 10 in. × 6 ft. 6 in. Scrovegni Chapel, Padua, Italy.

the cycle of rebirth. It is one of two large bodhisattvas that flank a Buddha shrine at the back of the large hall in Cave 1 at Ajanta, which was cut into the mountainside and features monks' cells around its sides. Lavishly adorned with jewelry, including long strands of pearls and an ornate crown, the delicate gesture of the right hand forming what is known as the teaching mudra (see Chapter 2), the figure seems intended to suggest to the viewer the joys of following the path of the Buddha.

In Europe, the goal of creating the illusion of reality dominates fresco painting from the early Renaissance in the fourteenth century through the Baroque period of the late seventeenth century. It is as if painting at the scale of the wall invites, even demands, the creation of "real" space. In one of the great sets of frescoes of the early Renaissance, painted by Giotto in the Scrovegni Chapel in Padua, Italy, this realist impulse is especially apparent. (Because it stands at one end of an ancient Roman arena, it is sometimes called the Arena Chapel.)

The Scrovegni Chapel was specially designed for the Scrovegni family, possibly by Giotto himself, to house frescoes, and it contains 38 individual scenes that tell the stories of the lives of the Virgin and Christ. In the *Lamentation* (**Fig. 9-6**), the two crouching figures with their backs to us extend into our space in a manner similar to the bowl of eggs in the Roman fresco. Here, the result is to involve us in the sorrow of the scene. As the hand of the leftmost figure with its back to us cradles Christ's head, we are invited to imagine ourselves in that figure's place, as if the hand were our own. One of the more remarkable aspects of this fresco, however, is the placement of its focal point—Christ's face—in the lower-left-hand corner of the composition, at the base of the diagonal formed by the stone ledge. Just as the angels in the sky seem to be plummeting toward the fallen Christ, the tall figure on the right leans forward in a sweeping gesture of grief that mimics the angels' descending flight.

Lines dividing various sections of Giotto's fresco are clearly apparent, especially in the sky. In the lower half of the painting these divisions tend to follow the contours of the various figures. These sections, known as ***giornata***, literally a "day's work" in Italian, are the areas that Giotto was able to complete in a single session. Since in *buon fresco* the paint had to be applied on a wet wall, Giotto could only paint an area that he could complete before the plaster coat set. If the area to be painted was complex—a face, for instance—painting it might require the entire *giornata*. Extremely detailed work would be added later, as in *fresco secco*.

Fig. 9-7 Fra Andrea Pozzo, *The Glorification of St. Ignatius*, 1691–94.
Ceiling fresco. Nave of Sant' Ignazio, Rome.

The fresco artists' interest in illusionism culminated in Michelangelo's frescoes for the Sistine Chapel (see *The Creative Process*, pp. 190–91) and in the Baroque ceiling designs of the late seventeenth century. Among the most remarkable of these is *The Glorification of St. Ignatius* (**Fig. 9-7**), which Fra Andrea Pozzo painted for the Church of Sant' Ignazio in Rome. Standing in the nave, or central portion of the church, and looking upward, the congregation had the illusion that the roof of the church had been removed, revealing the glories of Heaven. A master of perspective, about which he wrote an influential treatise, Pozzo realized his effects by extending the architecture in paint one story above the actual windows in the vault. St. Ignatius, the founder of the Jesuit order, is shown being transported on a cloud toward the waiting Christ. The foreshortening of the many figures, becoming ever smaller in size as they rise toward the center of the ceiling, greatly adds to the realistic, yet awe-inspiring, effect.

Tempera

Most artists in the early Renaissance who painted frescoes also worked in **tempera**, a medium made by combining water, pigment, and some gummy material, usually egg yolk. The paint was meticulously applied with the point of a fine red sable brush. Colors could not readily be blended, and, as a result, effects of chiaroscuro were accomplished by means of careful and gradual hatching. In order to use tempera, the painting surface, often a wood panel, had to be prepared with a very smooth ground, not unlike the smooth plaster wall prepared for *buon fresco*. **Gesso**, made from glue and plaster of Paris or chalk, is the most common ground, and, like wet plaster, it is fully absorbent, combining with the tempera paint to create an extremely durable and softly glowing surface unmatched by any other medium.

To early Renaissance eyes, Giotto's *Madonna and Child Enthroned* (**Fig. 9-8**) represented, like his frescoes in the Scrovegni Chapel, a significant "advance" in the era's increasingly insistent desire to create increasingly realistic work. It is possible, for instance, to feel the volume of the Madonna's knee in Giotto's altarpiece, to sense actual bodies beneath the draperies that clothe his models. The neck of Giotto's Madonna is modeled and

Fig. 9-8 Giotto, *Madonna and Child Enthroned*, ca. 1310.
Tempera on panel, 10 ft. 8 in. × 6 ft. 8¼ in. Galleria degli Uffizi, Florence.

curves round beneath her cape. Her face is sculptural, as if real bones lie beneath her skin.

What motivated this drive toward realism? Painting, it should be remembered, can suggest at least as much, and probably more, than it portrays. Another way to say this is that painting can be understood in terms of its **connotation** as well as its **denotation**. What a painting denotes is clearly before us: Giotto has painted a Madonna and Child surrounded by angels. But what this painting connotes is something else. To a thirteenth- or fourteenth-century Italian audience, the altarpiece would have been understood as depicting the ideal of love that lies between mother and child—and, by extension, the greater love of God for humanity. Although the relative realism of Giotto's painting is what secures its place in art history, its **didacticism**—that is, its ability

The Creative Process

Preparing to Paint the Sistine Chapel: Michelangelo's *Libyan Sibyl*

On May 10, 1506, Michelangelo received an advance payment from Pope Julius II to undertake the task of frescoing the ceiling of the Sistine Chapel at the Vatican in Rome. By the end of July, a scaffolding had been erected. By September 1508, Michelangelo was painting and, for the next four and a half years, he worked almost without interruption on the project.

According to Michelangelo's later recounting of events, Julius had originally envisioned a design in which the central part of the ceiling would be filled with "ornaments according to custom" (apparently a field of geometric ornaments) surrounded by the 12 Apostles in the 12 spandrels. Michelangelo protested, assuring Julius that it would be "a poor design" since the Apostles were themselves "poor too." Apparently convinced, the pope then freed Michelangelo to paint anything he liked. Instead of the Apostles, Michelangelo created a scheme of 12 Old Testament prophets alternating with 12 sibyls, or women of Classical antiquity said to possess prophetic powers. The center of the ceiling would be filled with nine scenes from Genesis.

As the scaffolding was erected, specially designed by the artist so that he could walk around and paint from a standing position, Michelangelo set to work preparing hundreds of drawings for the ceiling. These drawings were then transferred to full-size cartoons, which would be laid up against the moist surface of the fresco as it was prepared, their outlines traced through with a stylus. None of these cartoons, and surprisingly few of Michelangelo's drawings, have survived.

One of the greatest, and most revealing, of the surviving drawings is a *Study for the Libyan Sibyl* (**Fig. 9-9**). Each of the sibyls holds a book of prophecy—though not Christian figures, they prophesy the revelation of the New Testament in the events of the Old Testament that they surround. *The Libyan Sibyl* (**Fig. 9-10**) is the last sibyl that Michelangelo would paint. She is positioned next to the *Separation of Light from Darkness*, the last of the central panels, which is directly over the altarpiece. The Libyan Sibyl herself turns to close her book and place it on the desk behind her. Even as she does so, she steps down from her throne, creating a stunning opposition of directional forces, an exaggerated, almost spiral *contrapposto*. She abandons her book of prophecy as she turns to participate in the celebration of the Eucharist on the altar below.

The severity of this downward twisting motion obviously developed late in Michelangelo's work on the figure. In the drawing, the sibyl's hands are balanced evenly, across an almost horizontal plane. But the idea of dropping the left hand, in order to emphasize more emphatically the sibyl's downward movement, came almost immediately, for just below her left arm is a second variation, in which the upper arm drops perceptibly downward and the left hand is parallel to the face instead of the forehead, matching the positions of the final painting. In the drawing, the sibyl is nude, and apparently Michelangelo's model is male, his musculature more closely defined than in the final painting. Furthermore, in

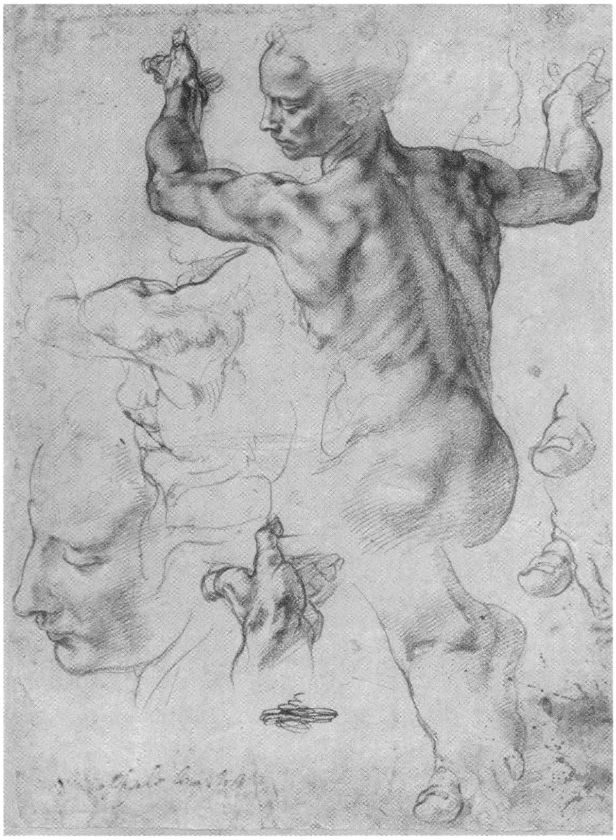

Fig. 9-9 Michelangelo, *Study for the Libyan Sibyl*, ca. 1510. Red chalk on paper, 11⅜ × 8⁷⁄₁₆ in. Metropolitan Museum of Art, New York.

Fig. 9-10 Michelangelo, *The Libyan Sibyl*, 1511–12. Fresco, detail of the Sistine Chapel Ceiling, Vatican City.

the drawing, the model's face is redone to the lower left, the lips made fuller and feminized, the severity of the original model's brow and cheek softened. The magnificently foreshortened left hand is redone in larger scale, as if in preparation for the cartoon, and so is the lower-left foot. There are, in fact, working upward from the bottom of the drawing, three versions of the model's big toe, and, again, the top two are closer to the final painted version than the toe on the bottom, with its more fully realized foot. In the middle version, especially, the second toe splays more radically backward, again to emphasize downward pressure and movement. In the final painting, Michelangelo directs our attention to this foot and toe, illuminating them like no other portion of the figure, the fulcrum upon which the sibyl turns from her pagan past to the Christian present.

Fig. 9-11 Sandro Botticelli, *Primavera*, ca. 1482. Tempera on a gesso ground on poplar panel, 6 ft. 8 in. × 10 ft. 3¼ in. Galleria degli Uffizi, Florence.

to teach, to elevate the mind, in this case, to the contemplation of salvation—was at least as important to its original audience. Its truth to nature was, in fact, probably inspired by Giotto's desire to make an image with which its audience could readily identify. It seemed increasingly important to capture not the spirituality of religious figures, but their humanity.

Sandro Botticelli's *Primavera* (**Fig. 9-11**), painted for a chamber next to the bedroom of his patron Lorenzo di Pierfrancesco de' Medici, is one of the greatest tempera paintings ever made. As a result of its restoration in 1978, we know a good deal about how it was painted. The figures and trees were painted on an undercoat—white for the figures, black for the trees. The transparency of the drapery was achieved by layering thin yellow washes of transparent medium over the white undercoat. As many as 30 coats of color, transparent or opaque, depending on the relative light or shadow of the area being painted, were required to create each figure.

Julie Green takes full advantage of the possibility of creating transparent washes of color with egg tempera in her painting *Don't Name Fish after Friends* (**Fig. 9-12**), a painting she worked on for over a decade. It began as a portrait of a Hasidic Jewish man whose well-made and somewhat flamboyant clothing

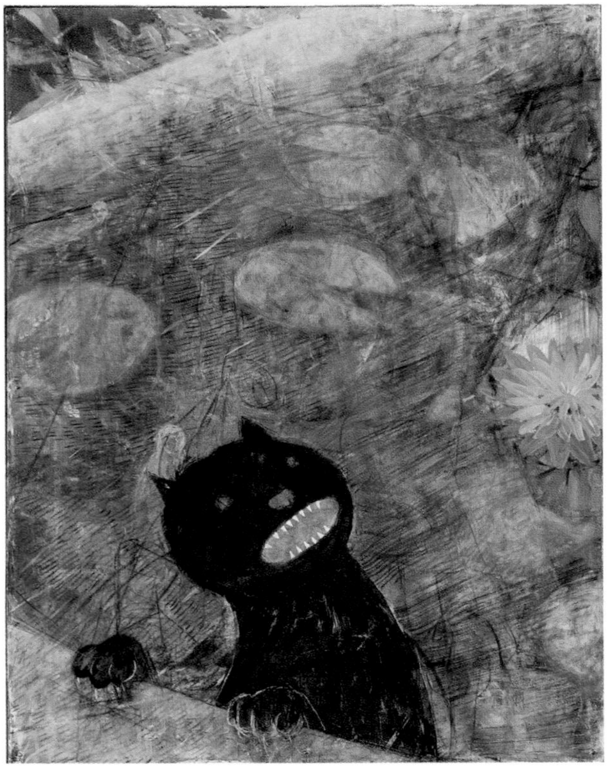

Fig. 9-12 Julie Green, *Don't Name Fish after Friends*, 1999–2009. Egg tempera on panel, 24 × 18 in.

attracted Green's interest. Traces of the herringbone pattern of his jacket can still be seen at the water's edge, but he has been erased. The painting then underwent a dozen transformations, including, at one point, a depiction of an armadillo crossing the basketball court across from Green's house in Norman, Oklahoma, now, like the flamboyantly dressed man who first inspired the painting, also erased. It is as if, looking into the water, traces of these earlier paintings shimmer beneath the surface, all scraped away but leaving some mark behind.

The final painting memorializes the fate of the koi living in the pond behind her house. Named after two close friends, Roger and Janet, Green dreamed one night that her one-eyed cat, Rio, had eaten Janet. When she awoke, the pond was in a shambles, its water lilies knocked over, and Janet was missing. Janet II was purchased, but the new Janet and Roger did not seem to get along. A wire cover was put over the pond, and a year passed without incident, but when Green returned from a brief vacation, Janet II was discovered belly-up, having probably succumbed to overfeeding by a neighbor. "With plans to paint a *memento mori*," Green says, "I set departed Janet II on top of the compost pile and went off for paint supplies. Twenty minutes later I returned to find a lovely white fish bone, nothing else." Today, Janet III swims happily beside the original Roger in the pond. The painting, of course, stands on its own and requires no knowledge of its history, but its surface, and the layers of paint half-visible beneath it, suggest precisely such a history.

Oil Painting

What are the distinctive properties of oil painting as a medium?

Even as Botticelli was creating stunning effects by layering transparent washes of tempera on his canvases, painters in northern Europe were coming to the realization that similar effects could be both more readily and more effectively achieved in **oil paint**. Oil paint is a far more versatile medium than tempera. It can be blended on the painting surface to create a continuous scale of tones and hues, many of which, especially darker shades, were not possible before oil paint's invention. As a result, the painter who uses oils can render the subtlest changes in light and achieve the most realistic three-dimensional effects, rivaling sculpture in this regard. Thinned with turpentine, oil paint can become almost transparent. Used directly from the tube, with no thinner at all, it can be molded and shaped to create three-dimensional surfaces, a technique referred to as impasto. Perhaps most important, because its binder is linseed oil, oil painting is slow to dry. Whereas with other painting media artists had to work quickly, with oil they could rework their images almost endlessly.

The ability to create such a sense of reality is a virtue of oil painting that makes the medium particularly suitable for the celebration of material things. By glazing the surface of the painting with thin films of transparent color, the artist creates a sense of luminous materiality. Light penetrates this glaze, bounces off the opaque underpainting beneath, and is reflected back up through the glaze (**Fig. 9-13**). Painted objects thus seem to reflect light as if

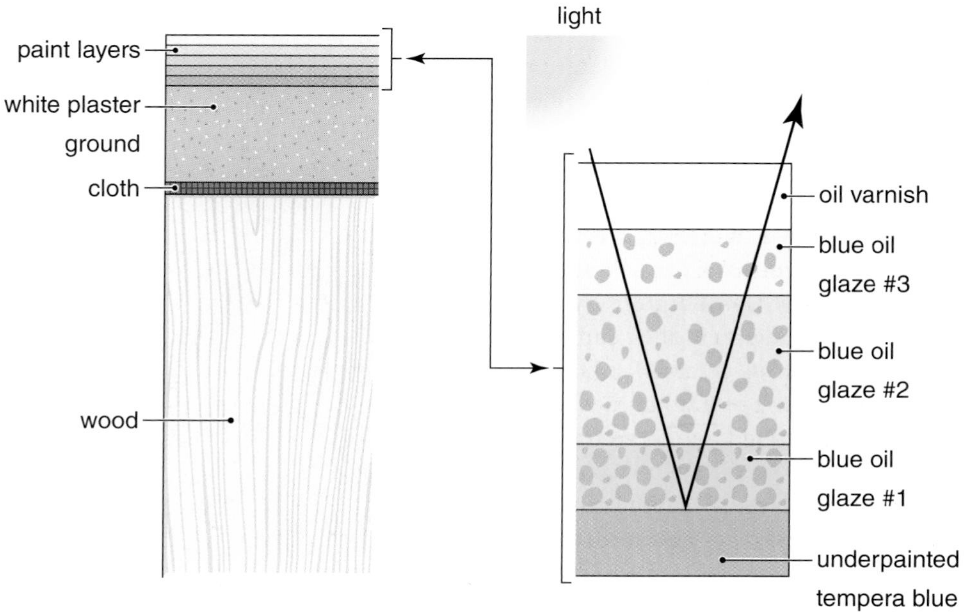

Fig. 9-13 Diagram of a section of a 15th-century oil painting, demonstrating the luminosity of the medium.

Fig. 9-14 Robert Campin and workshop, *The Annunciation* (*The Mérode Altarpiece*), ca. 1425–30. Oil on wood, triptych, central panel 25¼ × 24⅞ in., each wing 25⅜ × 10¾ in. Metropolitan Museum of Art, New York. Cloisters Collection, 1956.70. © 2015. Image © Metropolitan Museum of Art/Art Resource/Scala, Florence.

they were real, and the play of light through the painted surfaces gives them a sense of tangible presence.

Although the ancient Romans had used oil paint to decorate furniture, the medium was first used in painting in the early fifteenth century in Flanders. The artist Robert Campin, in all likelihood working with other artists in his workshop, was among the first to recognize the realistic effects that could be achieved with the new medium. In *The Mérode Altarpiece* (**Fig. 9-14**), the Christian story of the Annunciation of the Virgin, the revelation to Mary that she will conceive a child to be born the Son of God, takes place in a fully realized Flemish domestic interior. The Archangel Gabriel approaches Mary from the left, almost blocking the view of the altarpiece's two donors, the couple who commissioned it, dressed in fashionable fifteenth-century clothing and standing outside the door at the left. Seven rays of sunlight illuminate the room and fall directly on Mary's abdomen. On one of the rays, a miniature Christ, carrying a cross, flies into the scene (**Fig. 9-15**). Campin is telling the viewers that the entire life of Christ, including the Passion itself, enters Mary's body at the moment of conception. The scene is not idealized. In the right-hand panel, Joseph the carpenter works as a real fifteenth-century carpenter might have. In front of him is a recently completed mousetrap. Another mousetrap sits outside on the window ledge, apparently for sale. These are real people with real daily concerns. The objects in the room—from the vase and flowers to the book and candle—seem to possess a material reality that lends a sense of reality to the story of the Annunciation itself. In fact, the Archangel Gabriel appears no less (and no more) "real" than the brass pot above his head.

Another noteworthy aspect of Campin's altarpiece is its astonishingly small size. If its two side panels are closed

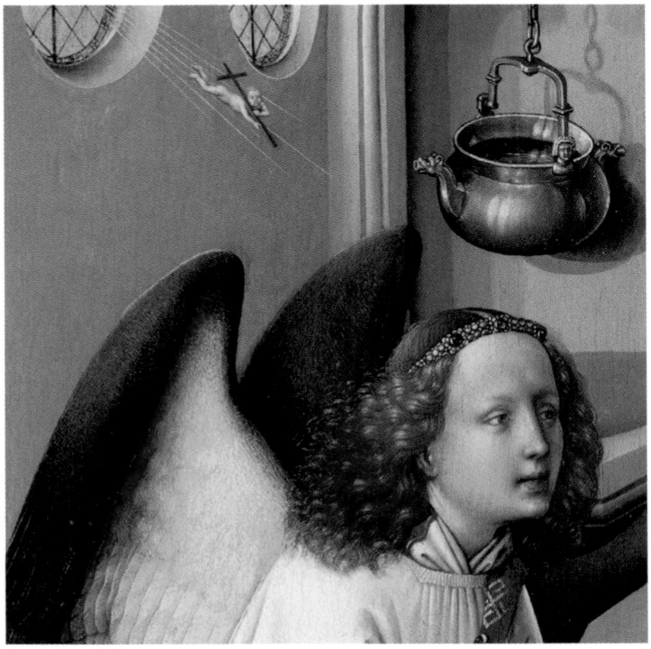

Fig. 9-15 Robert Campin and workshop, *The Annunciation* (*The Mérode Altarpiece*) (detail), ca. 1425–30.
© 2015. Image © Metropolitan Museum of Art/Art Resource/Scala, Florence.

over the central panel, as they are designed to, the altarpiece is just over 2 feet square—making it entirely portable. This little altarpiece is itself a material object, so intimate and detailed that it functions more like the book that lies open on the table than a painting. It is very different from the altarpieces being made in Italy during the same period. Most of those were monumental in scale and painted in fresco, permanently embedded in the wall, and therefore not portable. Campin's altarpiece is made to be held up close, in the hands, not surveyed from afar, suggesting its function as a private, rather than public, devotional object.

By 1608, the Netherlands freed itself from Spanish rule and became, by virtue of its almost total dominance of world trade, the wealthiest nation in the world. By that time, artists had become extremely skillful at using the medium of oil paint to represent these material riches. One critic has called the Dutch preoccupation with still life "a dialogue between the newly affluent society and its material possessions." In a painting such as Jan de Heem's *Still Life with Lobster* (**Fig. 9-16**), we are witness to the remains of a most extravagant meal, most of which has been left uneaten. This luxuriant and conspicuous display of wealth is deliberate. Southern fruit in a cold climate is a luxury, and the peeled lemon, otherwise untouched, is a sign of almost wanton consumption. For de Heem, the painting was at least in part a celebration, an invitation to share, at least visually and thus imaginatively, in its world. The feast on the table was a feast for the eyes.

But de Heem's painting was also a warning, an example of a ***vanitas*** painting. The *vanitas* tradition of still-life painting is specifically designed to induce in the spectator a higher order of thought. *Vanitas* is the Latin term for "vanity," and *vanitas* paintings, especially popular in northern Europe in the seventeenth century, remind us of the vanity, or frivolous quality, of human existence. If one ordinarily associates the contemplation of the normal subjects of still-life paintings with the enjoyment of the pleasurable things in life, here they take on another connotation as well. The overturned goblet, the half-peeled lemon, the oyster on the half-shell (which spoils quickly), the timepiece beside it, all remind the viewer that the material world celebrated in the painting is not as

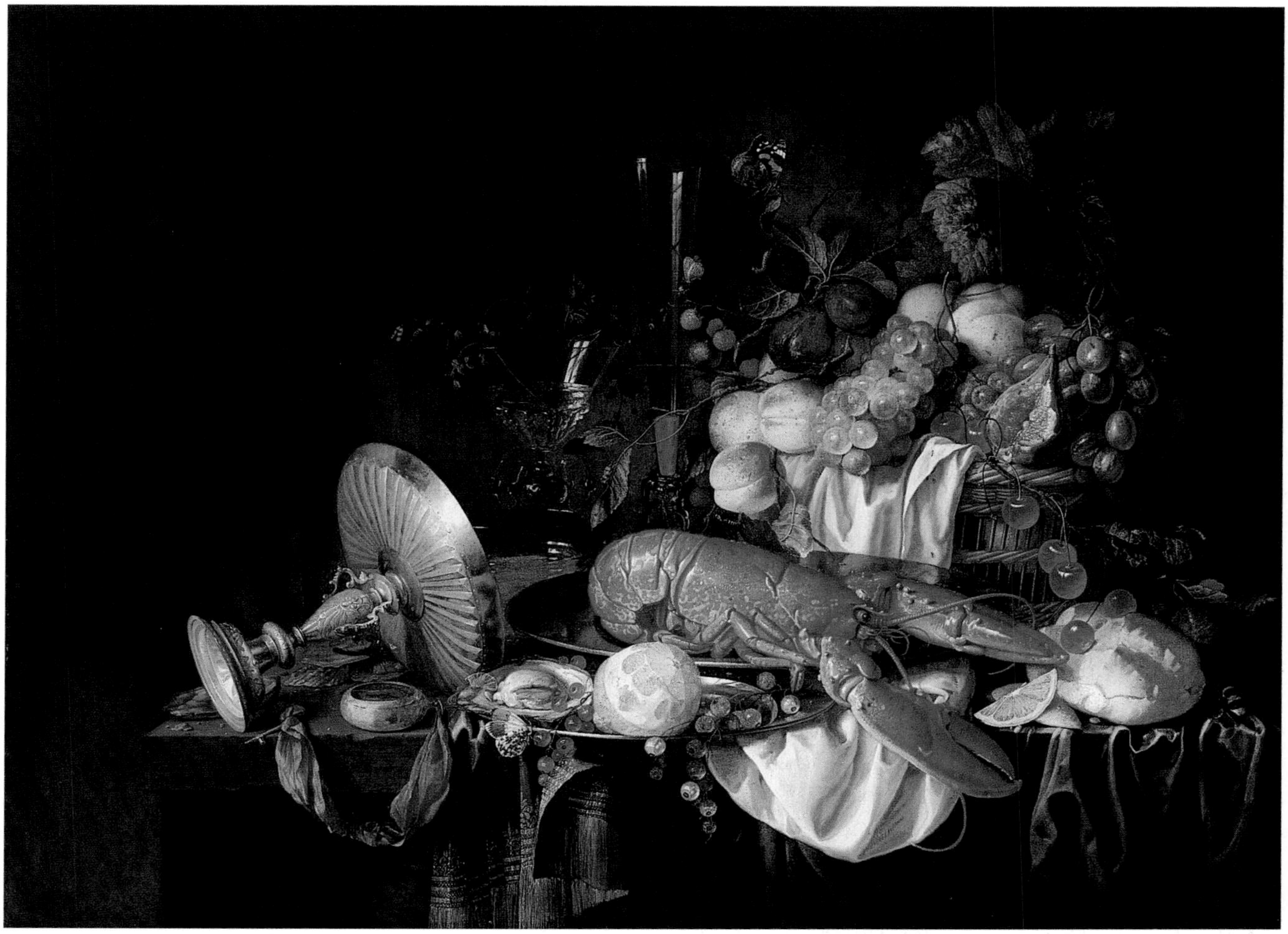

Fig. 9-16 Jan de Heem, *Still Life with Lobster*, late 1640s. Oil on canvas, 25⅛ × 33¼ in. Toledo Museum of Art, Toledo, Ohio.
Photo: Photography Incorporated, Toledo.

long-lasting as the spiritual, and that spiritual well-being may be of greater importance than material wealth.

Contemporary Spanish artist Antonio López García has revisited the *vanitas* tradition in many of his highly realistic still lifes and interiors. *New Refrigerator* (**Fig. 9-17**) is a modern still life, the objects of traditional still life removed from the tabletop into the refrigerator. Of particular note in López García's painting is the contrast between the extreme attention he pays to capturing the light in the room—note the light reflecting off the white tiled floor and the tiled wall behind the refrigerator—and the way he has rendered the objects in the open refrigerator, which are simply abstract blotches of local color. In fact, the abstraction of the still-life objects is echoed in the white blotch on the upper wall, which appears to be a highly realistic rendering of a plaster patch. In this painting, the complex interchange between reality and spirituality that the *vanitas* still-life painting embodies is transformed into an interchange between the objective and the subjective, between the material world and the artist's mental or emotional conception of that world.

Virtually since its inception, oil painting's expressive potential has been recognized as fundamental to its power. Much more than in fresco, where the artist's gesture was lost in the plaster, and much more than in tempera, where the artist was forced to use brushes so small that gestural freedom was absorbed by the scale of the image, oil paint could record and trace the artist's presence before the canvas.

The expressive potential of the medium lies at the heart of Josephine Halvorson's *Carcass* (**Fig. 9-18**). Halvorson travels widely, scouring the world for small, usually overlooked objects—shuttered windows, plaster patches not unlike that above the refrigerator in López García's painting, sections of stone walls, forgotten

Fig. 9-17 Antonio López García, *New Refrigerator*, 1991–94.
Oil on canvas, 7 ft. 10½ in. × 6 ft. 2¹³⁄₁₆ in. Collection of the artist.
Photo © Francisco Fernández, Unidad Móvil Fotografía Especializada. © 2015 Artists Rights Society (ARS), New York/VEGAP, Madrid.

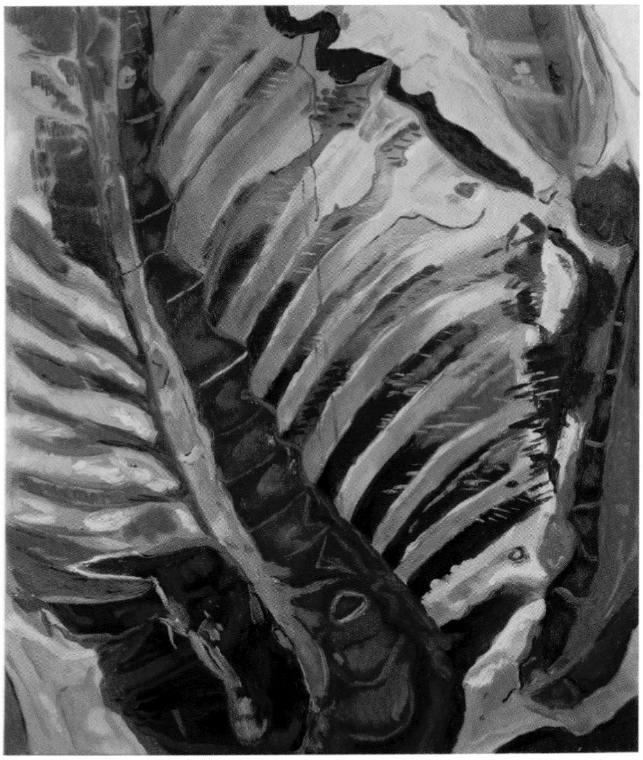

Fig. 9-18 Josephine Halvorson, *Carcass*, 2011. Oil on linen, 34 × 28 in.
Courtesy of the artist and Sikkema Jenkins & Co., New York.

machine parts—which she paints in single, usually day-long sittings on site. Her intention is to convey to the viewer something of the same feelings that drew her to the object in first place, and thereby bring to the object a new life. In 2011, while visiting a friend in Iceland, she walked past a slaughterhouse. "I thought, well maybe in Iceland because the community is so small and intimate, I could have access to the slaughterhouse and maybe even do a painting there," she explains in an episode of art21's documentary series *New York Close Up*, "Close Encounters with Josephine Halvorson." "I saw eight cows get skin taken off. I remember at one point a head was thrown onto a table. And it landed with such weight and force that the blood continued and splattered all over me. It was that visceral; you know, it was right there. I think those feelings come through in the painting." Halvorson's feelings are embodied in the painting's sometimes violent brushwork (which can be studied in detail by zooming in on the image). "Every brushstroke counts," she says, because every brushstroke conveys—as in a Jackson Pollock painting (see Fig. 6-13), and in Pollock's words—"memories arrested in space."

Like Halvorson, British-born painter Rackstraw Downes has traveled widely looking for material that interests him. In 2002, he first visited West Texas, drawn to what he calls the "sparseness and extreme clarity" of the landscape. *Presidio in the Sand Hills Looking East with ATV Tracks and Water Tower* (**Fig. 9-19**) was painted just outside Presidio, Texas, on the Mexico/U.S. border south of Marfa, Texas, and west of Big Bend National Park, where he now lives part of each year. Like Claude Monet (see Fig. 5-36)—and like Halvorson—Downes paints ***en plein air***, moving between New York and Texas on a seasonal basis so that he can work on site, outdoors; he lives in Presidio from November to April. In the art21 *Exclusive* video "Rackstraw Downes: Texas Hills," Downes explains what attracted him to the view of the Presidio hills with their ATV tracks and water tower:

> The towers are enigmatic. That white tower up there is such a wacky shape, popping out of that mound. These things appeal to me. And then I love the fact that the kids ride around here in their ATVs. The thought of somebody riding around on one of these machines like this, with absolutely no rules and laws governing them, and so forth and so on. I think it's very wonderful. I think it's a lovely bit of youth having its own good time, in its own way.

Downes is, of course, simultaneously conscious of the environmental impact of the ATVs, just as he is conscious of the environmental impact of cement factories, garbage dumps, oil refineries, radio towers, and drainage ditches—all of which he has painted at one time or

Fig. 9-19 Rackstraw Downes, *Presidio in the Sand Hills Looking East with ATV Tracks and Water Tower*, 2012. Oil on canvas, 16½ in. × 5 ft. 5¼ in.
Courtesy of Betty Cuningham Gallery, New York.

another. His subject matter, after all, is man's impact on nature. "I don't think of myself as a landscape painter," he has said. "I like to say I paint my environment, my surroundings." And the fact is, his surroundings are a degraded environment. And his paintings literally surround the viewer. They dismiss perspective, resorting instead to a sort of bird's-eye, 180-degree view. "Everything changes as you make the minutest movement of your head, and still more when you turn your shoulders," he explains. Looking at a Rackstraw Downes painting, it is as if the landscape envelops you, as if you are almost inevitably implicated in its space.

Watercolor and Gouache

Why is watercolor at least potentially the most expressive of the painting media?

The ancient Egyptians used watercolor to illustrate papyrus scrolls, and it was employed intermittently by other artists down through the centuries, notably by Albrecht Dürer and Peter Paul Rubens. The medium, it quickly became evident, was especially suitable for artists who wished to explore the expressive potential of painting, rather than pursue purely representational ends.

Watercolor paintings are made by applying pigments suspended in a solution of water and gum arabic to dampened paper. Historically, they have often been used as a sketching tool. Certainly, as a medium, watercolor can possess all of the spontaneity of a high-quality sketch. Working quickly, it is possible to achieve gestural effects that are very close to those possible with brush and ink.

Depending on the absorbency of the paper and the amount of watercolor on the brush, watercolor spreads along the fibers of the paper when it is applied. Thin solutions of pigment and binder have the appearance of soft, transparent washes, while dense solutions can become almost opaque. The play between the transparent and the opaque qualities of the medium is central to Winslow Homer's *A Wall, Nassau* (**Fig. 9-20**). Both the wall and the sky behind it are transparent washes, and the textural ribbons and spots of white on the coral limestone wall are actually

Fig. 9-20 Winslow Homer, *A Wall, Nassau*, 1898. Watercolor and graphite on off-white wove paper, 14¾ × 21½ in. Metropolitan Museum of Art, New York.
Amelia B. Lazarus Fund, 1910.228.90. © 2015. Image copyright Metropolitan Museum of Art/Art Resource/Scala, Florence.

Fig. 9-21 John Marin, *Untitled (The Blue Sea)*, ca. 1921. Watercolor and charcoal on paper, 16½ × 19⅝ in. Smithsonian American Art Museum, Washington, D.C.
Museum Purchase, 1964.2V. © 2015. Photo Smithsonian American Art Museum/Art Resource/Scala, Florence.
© 2015 Estate of John Marin/Artists Rights Society (ARS), New York.

unpainted paper. Between these two light bands of color lies the densely painted foliage of the garden and, to the right, the sea, which becomes a deeper and deeper blue as it stretches toward the horizon. A white sailboat heads out to sea on the right. Almost everything of visual interest in this painting takes place between the sky above and the wall below. Even the red leaves of the giant poinsettia plant that is the painting's focal point turn down toward this middle ground. Pointing up from the top of the wall, framing this middle area from below, is something far more ominous—dark, almost black shards of broken glass. Suddenly, the painting is transformed. No longer just a pretty view of a garden, it begins to speak of privacy and intrusion, and of the divided social world of the Bahamas at the turn of the last century, the islands given over to tourism and its associated wealth at the expense of the local black population. The wall holds back those outside it from the beauty and luxury within, separating them from the freedom offered, for instance, by the boat as it sails away.

The expressive potential of watercolor became especially apparent in the early years of the twentieth century as artists began to abandon the representational aims of painting in favor of realizing more abstract ends. Influenced by developments in Europe, where the likes of Georges Braque and Pablo Picasso (see Fig. 1-10) were creating more and more abstract works of art, American painters like John Marin, who lived in Paris from 1905 to 1911 and witnessed this shift firsthand, began to explore the possibilities of abstraction themselves. A painting like Marin's *Untitled (The Blue Sea)* (**Fig. 9-21**) is the result. Rather than a visual recording of the Maine coast where he lived, it is an evocation of the feelings that the coast engendered in him. Writing in 1913, Marin explained:

> We have been told somewhere that a work of art is a thing alive. You cannot create a work of art unless the things you behold respond to something within you. . . . It is this "moving of me" that I try to express so that I may recall the spell I have been under and behold the expression of the different emotions that have been called into being.

In *Untitled (The Blue Sea)*, the basic forms of the landscape are still visible—the rocky coastline moving in a diagonal from left to right in the foreground, a peninsula jutting out into the ocean at the horizon line, the blue sky, the yellow light of a setting sun—but the gestural sweep of Marin's line, the sense of immediacy and energy in his application of washes of watercolor, realizes precisely that "moving of me" he seeks to capture. In fact, it is very likely that this painting is one that he exhibited in a retrospective exhibition at the Museum of Modern Art in New York in 1936 under the title *Movement, the Blue Sea*.

Unlike watercolor, which is transparent, **gouache**—the term is derived from the Italian word *guazzo*, meaning "puddle"—is opaque. Its opacity is the result of mixing what is essentially watercolor with Chinese white chalk. While gouache colors display a light-reflecting brilliance, it is difficult to blend brushstrokes of gouache together. Thus, the medium lends itself to the creation of large, flat, colored forms. It is this abstract quality that attracted Jacob Lawrence to it. Everything in the painting *You can buy bootleg whiskey for twenty-five cents a quart* (**Fig. 9-22**) tips forward. This not only creates a sense of disorienting, drunken imbalance, but also emphasizes the flat two-dimensional quality of the painting's space. Lawrence's dramatically intense complementary colors blare like the jazz we can almost hear coming from the radio.

Artists sometimes combine both watercolor and gouache in the same painting. John Singer Sargent's *Rushing Brook* (**Fig. 9-23**) is an example. The opaque gouache here has the advantage of burying Sargent's underdrawing beneath it, but perhaps more important is the effect that he is able to achieve in setting the transparent values of watercolor against the more intense and flat dabs of gouache—for example, in the contrast between the transparent blues of the water and the gray and white gouache that suggest the tumbling foam of the brook itself. Sargent often applied his gouache over a layer of wax resist (a clear wax crayon), which may well account for the texture so apparent in much of the white gouache areas.

Fig. 9-22 Jacob Lawrence, *You can buy bootleg whiskey for twenty-five cents a quart*, from the *Harlem Series*, 1942–43. Gouache on paper, 15½ × 22½ in. Portland Art Museum, Oregon.

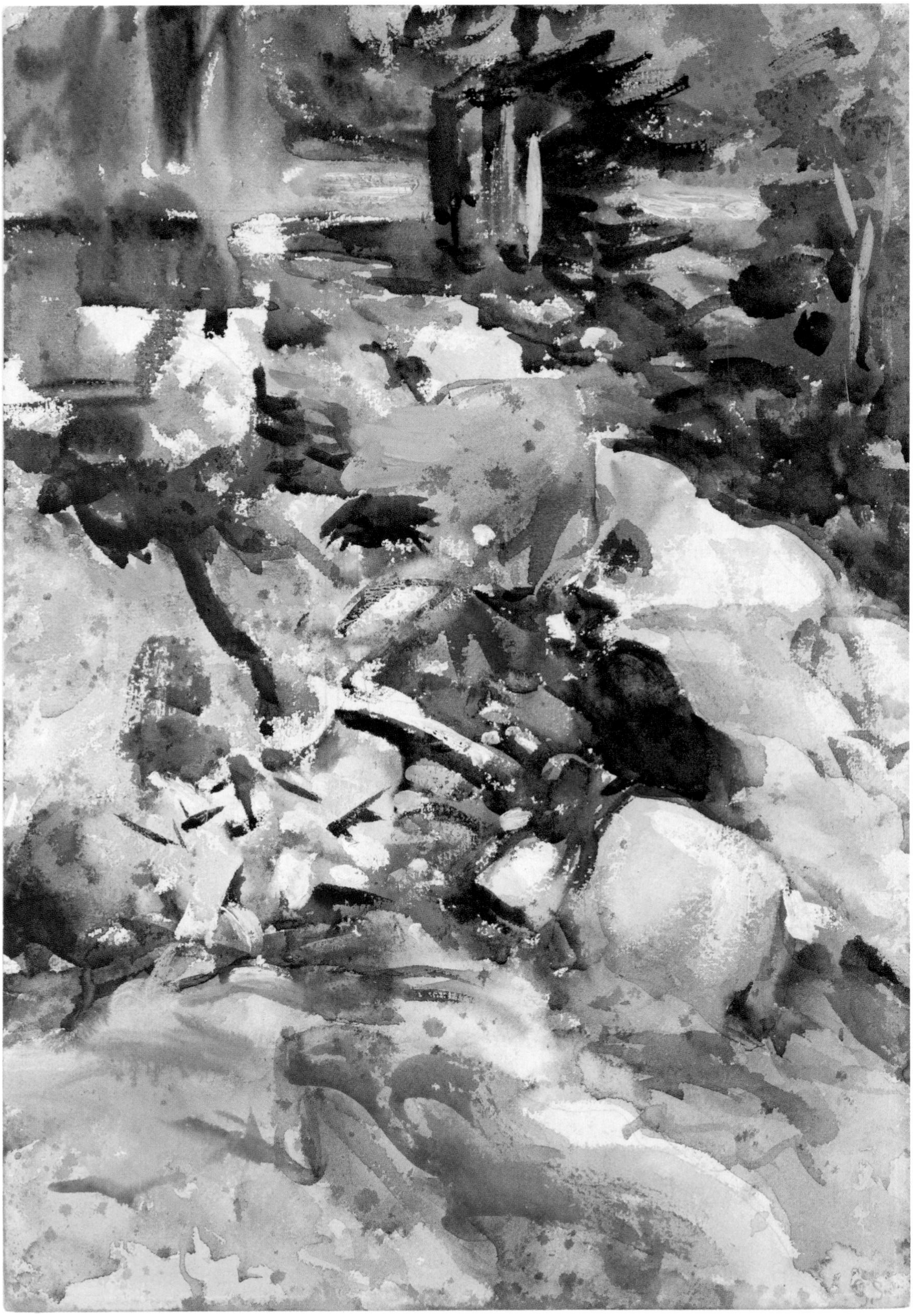

Fig. 9-23 John Singer Sargent, *Rushing Brook*, ca. 1904–11. Watercolor, gouache, and graphite underdrawing on off-white wove paper, 18⅜ x 12⅜ in. Metropolitan Museum of Art, New York.

Synthetic Media

What are some of the advantages of synthetic painting media?

Many artists have found oil paint to be a frustrating medium. Because of its slow-drying characteristics and the preparation necessary to ready the painting surface, it lacks the sense of immediacy so readily apparent in more direct media like drawing or watercolor. For the same reasons, the medium is not particularly suitable for painting out-of-doors, where one is continually exposed to the elements. When chemically created pigments and paints—synthetic media—began to become available in the twentieth century, they were quickly adopted by artists who wanted the "look" of oil paint but none of its frustrating characteristics.

The first artists to experiment with synthetic media were a group of Mexican painters, led by David Alfaro Siqueiros and Diego Rivera, whose goal was to create large-scale revolutionary mural art (see Fig. 20-17). Painting outdoors, where their celebrations of the struggles of the working class could easily be seen, Siqueiros, Rivera, and José Clemente Orozco—*Los Tres Grandes*, as they are known—worked first in fresco and then in oil paint, but the sun, rain, and humidity of Mexico quickly ruined their efforts. In 1937, Siqueiros organized a workshop in New York, closer to the chemical industry, expressly to develop and experiment with new synthetic paints. One of the first media used at the workshop was pyroxylin, commonly known as Duco, a lacquer developed as an automobile paint.

In the early 1950s, Helen Frankenthaler gave up the gestural qualities of the brush loaded with oil paint

Fig. 9-24 Helen Frankenthaler, *The Bay*, 1963. Acrylic on canvas, 6 ft. 8¾ in. × 6 ft. 9½ in. Detroit Institute of Arts.

Founders Society Purchase, Dr. & Mrs. Hilbert H. Delawter Fund. Bridgeman Images. © 2015 Helen Frankenthaler Foundation, Inc./Artists Rights Society (ARS), New York.

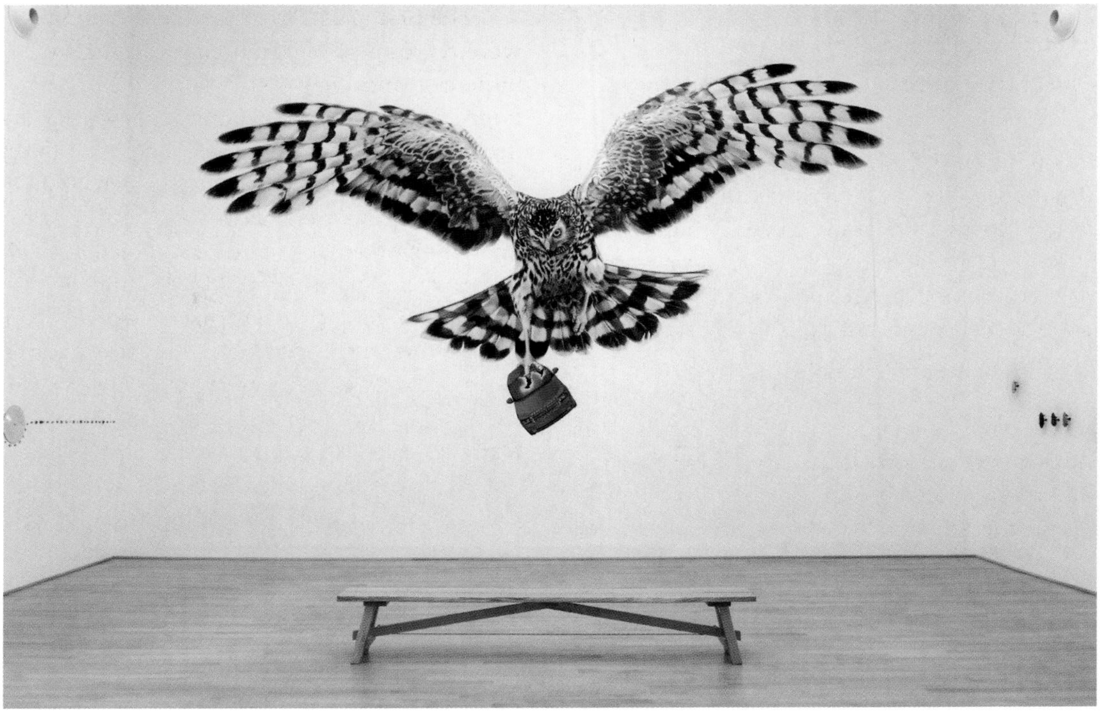

Fig. 9-25 Jeremy Deller, *A Good Day for Cyclists* (painted by Sarah Tynan), 2013. Acrylic on wall, as installed in Jeremy Deller's *English Magic*, British Pavilion, 55th Venice Biennale.
Photo: Cristiano Corte.

and began to stain raw, unprimed canvas with greatly thinned oil pigments, soaking color into the surface in what has been called an art of "stain-gesture" by moving the unprimed, unstretched canvas around to allow the paint to flow over it. Her technique soon attracted a number of painters who were themselves experimenting with Magna, a paint made from **acrylic** resins—materials used to make plastic—mixed with turpentine. Staining canvas with oil created a messy, brownish "halo" around each stain or puddle of paint, but the painters realized that the "halo" disappeared when they stained the canvas with Magna, the paint and canvas really becoming one.

At almost exactly this time, researchers in both Mexico and the United States discovered a way to mix acrylic resins with water and, by 1956, water-based acrylic paints were on the market. These media were inorganic and, as a result, much better suited to staining raw canvas than turpentine or oil-based media, since no chemical interaction could take place that might threaten the life of the painting.

Inevitably, Frankenthaler gave up staining her canvases with oil and moved to acrylic in 1963. With this medium, she was able to create such intensely atmospheric paintings as *The Bay* (**Fig. 9-24**). Working on the floor and pouring paint directly on the canvas, the artist was able to make the painting seem spontaneous, even though it is quite large. "A really good picture," Frankenthaler says, "looks as if it's happened at once. . . . It looks as if it were born in a minute."

The usefulness of acrylic for mural painting was immediately apparent. Once dried, outdoors, the acrylic surface was relatively immune to the vicissitudes of weather. This durability also recommends the medium for murals painted indoors in public spaces. For his six-room installation in the British Pavilion at the 2013 Venice Biennale, entitled *English Magic*, Jeremy Deller, who might best be described as, at once, author, artist, producer, director, social critic, and historian, commissioned a mural by Sarah Tynan to grace the back wall of the pavilion's foyer. Titled *A Good Day for Cyclists* (**Fig. 9-25**), it features a hen harrier, one of the rarest birds of prey in the UK, and a bird universally detested by devotees of traditional country sports in England because of its proclivity for dining on grouse, sinking its talons into a red Range Rover. Placed nearly 20 feet high on the starkly white wall, it almost seemed to be flying directly at the visitor. The exhibition brochure, distributed at the door, explained:

> On 24 October 2007, a wildlife officer and two members of the public observed a pair of hen harriers being shot out of the sky as they flew over the Sandringham Estate. The only people known to be shooting that day were Prince Harry and his

Fig. 9-26 Kenny Scharf, Mural on Houston Street, SoHo, Manhattan, New York, as it appeared on May 31, 2011.

friend William van Cutsem. The police investigated the incident and questioned the prince, his friend and a Sandringham gamekeeper, but the case was later dropped as the carcasses of the birds could not be found.

The Range Rover, which can cost upwards of $200,000, has most recently been the British royal family's car of choice.

Acrylic paint in aerosol cans is, of course, the very foundation of the graffiti writer's craft. Aerosol spray paint was first invented in 1949 by Ed Seymour, the owner of a Sycamore, Illinois, paint company, who used it to spray aluminum coating on radiators. By the early 1970s, the home-decorating companies Krylon and Rust-Oleum were producing hundreds of millions of cans of acrylic spray paint a year. Not only small and easy to carry, these cans were also easy to steal, and graffiti writing exploded onto the scene in the 1970s, born of the same cultural climate that produced the popular poetry/music/performance/dance phenomenon known as rap, or hip-hop. While still considered a criminal activity by many, graffiti has entered the mainstream art world in, for instance, the work of Jean-Michel Basquiat (see Fig. 2-19) or even on the walls of art spaces such as the former Deitch Projects space, now curated by Hole Gallery, on Houston Street in New York's SoHo district (**Fig. 9-26**), where, beginning in 2008, the wall's owner has invited numerous artists to create work. Pictured here is a mural by Kenny Scharf, which he painted without a predetermined plan in five days in late November 2010. It required over 200 cans of spray paint and was in place until late June 2011.

Mixed Media

In what ways has painting combined itself with other media?

All of the painting media we have so far considered can be combined with other media, from drawing to fiber and wood, as well as found objects, to make new works of art. In the twentieth century in particular, artists purposefully and increasingly combined various media: The result is **mixed-media** work. The motives for working with mixed media are many, but the primary formal one is that mixed media violate the integrity of painting as a medium. They do this by introducing into the space of painting materials from the everyday world.

Collage and Photomontage

The two-dimensional space of the canvas was first challenged by Pablo Picasso and his close associate Georges Braque when they began to utilize collage in their work. **Collage** is the process of pasting or gluing fragments of printed matter, fabric, natural material—anything that is relatively flat—onto the two-dimensional surface of a canvas or panel. Collage creates, in essence, a low-relief assemblage.

A good example of collage is one created soon after Picasso and Braque began using the new technique, by their colleague Juan Gris. Although no one would mistake *The Table* (**Fig. 9-27**) for an accurate rendering of reality, it is designed to raise the question of just what, in art, is "real" and what is "false" by bringing elements from the real world into the space of the painting. The woodgrain of the tabletop is both woodgrain-printed wallpaper and paper with the woodgrain drawn on it by hand. Thus, it is both "false" wood and "real" wallpaper, as well as "real" drawing. The fragment of the newspaper headline—it's a "real" piece of newspaper, incidentally—reads "*Le Vrai et le Faux*" ("The True and the False"). A novel lies open at the base of the table. Is it any less "real" as a novel just because it is a work of fiction? The key in the table drawer offers us a witty insight into the complexity of the work, for in French the word for "key," *clé*, also means "problem." In this painting, the problematic interchange between art and reality that painting embodies is fully highlighted. If painting is, after all, a mental construction, an artificial reality and not reality itself, are not mental constructions as real as anything else?

Fig. 9-27 Juan Gris, *The Table*, 1914. Colored papers, printed matter, charcoal on paper mounted on canvas, 23½ × 17½ in. Philadelphia Museum of Art.

A. E. Gallatin Collection, 1952. © 2015 Photo Philadelphia Museum of Art/Art Resource/Scala, Florence.

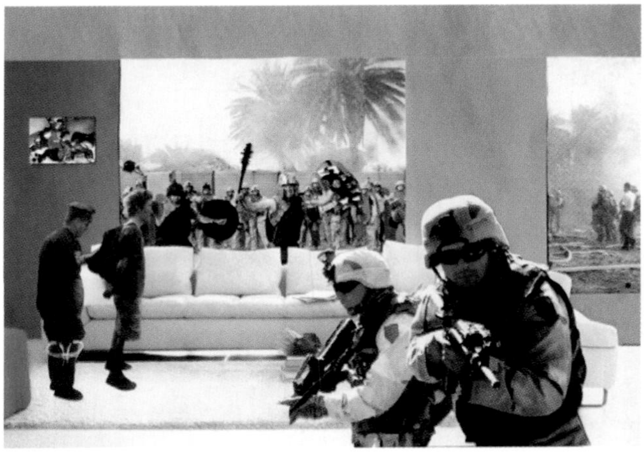

Fig. 9-28 Martha Rosler, *Gladiators*, from the series *House Beautiful: Bringing the War Home*, New Series, 2004. Photomontage, dimensions variable.

Courtesy of Martha Rosler and Mitchell-Innes & Nash, New York.

Because it brings "reality"—often photographs of real events and people—into the framed space of the artwork, collage offers artists a direct means of commenting on the social or political environment in which they work (for an example of a Nazi-era political collage, see *The Creative Process*, pp. 206–07). When the collage consists entirely of photographs, we call the resulting work **photomontage**—a direct reference to the groundbreaking filmic practices of the Russian filmmaker Sergei Eisenstein (see Fig. 11-29). In her two series of photomontage images, *Bringing the War Home*, the first dating from the Vietnam era and the second from the years of the war in Iraq (**Fig. 9-28**), Martha Rosler combines news photographs of the war with advertisements from architecture, lifestyle, and design magazines. As surely as during the Vietnam era, when, for the first time, the day's battle could be seen on television in the comfort of our living rooms, the uncanny reality of her images suggests a comfort level with violence, as if what was, 45 years ago, a television image has now, in the new world of high-definition digital 3D animation, assumed a virtual presence. And yet her technique—the antiquated cut-and-paste routine of collage—belies the sense of reality achieved in the image, undermining it and forcing us to question any level of comfort we might feel. What real difference, as wars go on and on, she seems to ask, does technological advancement really make? At what cost comes a "house beautiful"?

The Creative Process

Political Collage: Hannah Höch's *Cut with the Kitchen Knife*

Given collage's inclusiveness, it is hardly surprising that it is among the most political of media. In Germany, after World War I, as the forces that would lead to the rise of Hitler's Nazi party began to assert themselves, a number of artists in Berlin, among them Hannah Höch, began to protest against the growing nationalism of the country in their art. Reacting to the dehumanizing speed, technology, industrialization, and consumerism of the modern age, they saw in collage, and in its more representational cousin, photomontage—collage constructed of photographic fragments—the possibility of reflecting the kaleidoscopic pace, complexity, and fragmentation of everyday life. Höch was particularly friendly with Raoul Hausmann, whose colleague Richard Huelsenbeck had met a group of so-called Dada artists in Zurich, Switzerland, in 1916. The anarchic behavior of these "anti-artists" had impressed both men, and with Höch and others they inaugurated a series of Dada evenings in Berlin, the first such event occurring on April 12, 1918. Huelsenbeck read a manifesto, others read sound or noise poetry, and all were accompanied by drums, instruments, and audience noise. On June 20, 1920, they opened a Dada Fair in a three-room apartment covered from floor to ceiling with a chaotic display of photomontages, Dada periodicals, drawings, and assemblages, one of which has been described as looking like "the aftermath of an accident between a trolley car and a newspaper kiosk." On one wall was Hannah Höch's photomontage *Cut with the Kitchen Knife Dada through the Last Weimar Beer Belly Cultural Epoch of Germany* (**Fig. 9-30**).

We are able to identify many of the figures in Höch's work with the help of a preparatory drawing (**Fig. 9-29**). The top right-hand corner is occupied by the forces of repression. The recently deposed emperor Wilhelm II, with two wrestlers forming his mustache, gazes out below the words "*Die anti-dadistische Bewegung*," or "the anti-Dada movement," the leader of what Höch calls in her title "the Weimar beer belly." On Wilhelm's shoulder rests an exotic dancer with the head of General Field Marshal Friedrich von Hindenburg. Below them are other generals and, behind Wilhelm, a photograph of people waiting in line at a Berlin employment office.

The upper left focuses on Albert Einstein, out of whose brain Dada slogans seem to burst, as if the theory of relativity, overturning traditional physics as it did, was a proto-Dada event. In the very center of the collage is a headless dancer, and above her floats the head of printmaker Käthe Kollwitz. To the right of her are the words "*Die grosse Welt dada*," and then, further down, "*Dadaisten*": "the great dada World," and "Dadaists." Directly above these words are Lenin, whose head tops a figure dressed in hearts, and Karl Marx, whose head seems to emanate from a machine. Raoul Hausmann stands just below in a diver's suit. A tiny picture of Höch herself is situated at the bottom right, partially on the map of Europe that depicts the progress of women's enfranchisement. To the left, a figure stands above the crowd shouting "*Tretet Dada bei*"—"Join Dada."

Fig. 9-29 Hannah Höch, *Study for "Cut with the Kitchen Knife Dada through the Last Weimar Beer Belly Cultural Epoch of Germany,"* 1919. Ballpoint pen sketch on white board, 10⅝ × 8⅝ in. Staatliche Museen, Berlin, Preussischer Kulturbesitz Nationalgalerie. bpk/Nationalgalerie, SMB/Jörg P. Anders. © 2015 Artists Rights Society (ARS), New York/VG Bild-Kunst, Bonn.

Fig. 9-30 Hannah Höch, *Cut with the Kitchen Knife Dada through the Last Weimar Beer Belly Cultural Epoch of Germany*, 1919. Collage, 44⅞ × 35 7⁄16 in. Nationalgalerie Staatliche Museen, Berlin.

Inv. NG 57/91. Photo: Jorg P. Anders, Berlin. © 2015 Photo Scala, Florence/bpk, Bildagentur fuer Kunst, Kultur und Geschichte, Berlin. © 2015 Artists Rights Society (ARS), New York/VG Bild-Kunst, Bonn.

Painting Beyond the Frame

One of the most important results of mixed media has been to extend what might be called "the space of art." If this space was once defined by the picture frame—if art was once understood as something that was contained within that boundary and hung on a wall—that definition of space was extended in the hands of mixed-media artists, out of the two-dimensional and into the three-dimensional space.

At first glance, Kara Walker's installations, such as *Insurrection! (Our Tools Were Rudimentary, Yet We Pressed On)* (**Figs. 9-31** and **9-32**), seem almost doggedly unsculptural. Her primary tool, after all, is the silhouette, a form of art that was popularized in the courts of Europe in the early eighteenth century. It takes its name from Étienne de Silhouette, an ardent silhouette artist who, as Louis XV's finance minister in the 1750s and 1760s, was in charge of the king's merciless taxation of the French people. Peasants, in fact, took to wearing only black in protest: "We are dressing à la Silhouette," so the saying went. "We are shadows, too poor to wear color. We are Silhouettes!"

Walker's silhouette works reflect the political context of the medium's origins, except that she has translated it to the master–slave relationship in the nineteenth-century antebellum U.S. South. In fact, throughout the nineteenth century, silhouette artists traveled across the United States catering especially to the wealthy, Southern plantation owners chief among them. In *Insurrection!*, a series of grisly scenes unfolds across three walls. On the back wall, a plantation owner propositions a naked slave who hides from him behind a tree. A woman with a tiny baby on her head escapes a lynching. In the corner, on the right wall (in a scene barely visible in Fig. 9-31, but reproduced in its entirety in Fig. 9-32), slaves disembowel a plantation owner with a soup ladle, as another readies to strike him with a frying pan, and another at the right—perhaps the "Negress" that Simpson refers to in her art21 *Exclusive* video "Kara Walker: Negress"—raises her fist in defiance.

But what really transforms this installation into a sculptural piece are light projections from the ceiling that throw light onto the walls. These projections are not only metaphoric—as viewers project their own fears and desires onto other bodies—they also activate the space by projecting the viewers' shadows onto the walls so that they themselves become implicated in the scene.

This movement is nowhere more forcefully stated than in the work of Robert Rauschenberg. Rauschenberg's painting *Monogram* (**Fig. 9-33**) literally moves "off the wall"—the title of Calvin Tomkins's biography of the artist—onto the floor. A **combine-painting**, or high-relief collage, Rauschenberg worked on the canvas over a five-year period from 1955 to 1959.

The composer John Cage once defined Rauschenberg's combine-paintings as "a situation involving multiplicity." They are a kind of collage, but more lenient than other collages about what they will admit into their space. They will, in fact, admit anything, because unity is not something they are particularly interested in. They bring together objects of diverse and various kinds and simply allow them to coexist beside one another in the same space. In Rauschenberg's words, "A pair of socks is no less suitable to make a painting with than wood, nails, turpentine, oil, and fabric." Nor, apparently, is a stuffed Angora goat.

Rauschenberg discovered the goat in a secondhand office-furniture store in Manhattan. The problem it presented, as Tomkins has explained, was how "to make the

Figs. 9-31 and 9-32 Kara Walker, *Insurrection! (Our Tools Were Rudimentary, Yet We Pressed On)*, 2000. Installation views, Solomon R. Guggenheim Museum, New York. Cut paper silhouettes and light projections, site-specific dimensions.
Purchased with funds contributed by the International Director's Council and Executive Committee Members, 2000. Photo: Ellen Labenski. © Solomon R. Guggenheim Museum, New York. © Kara Walker. Courtesy of Sikkema Jenkins.

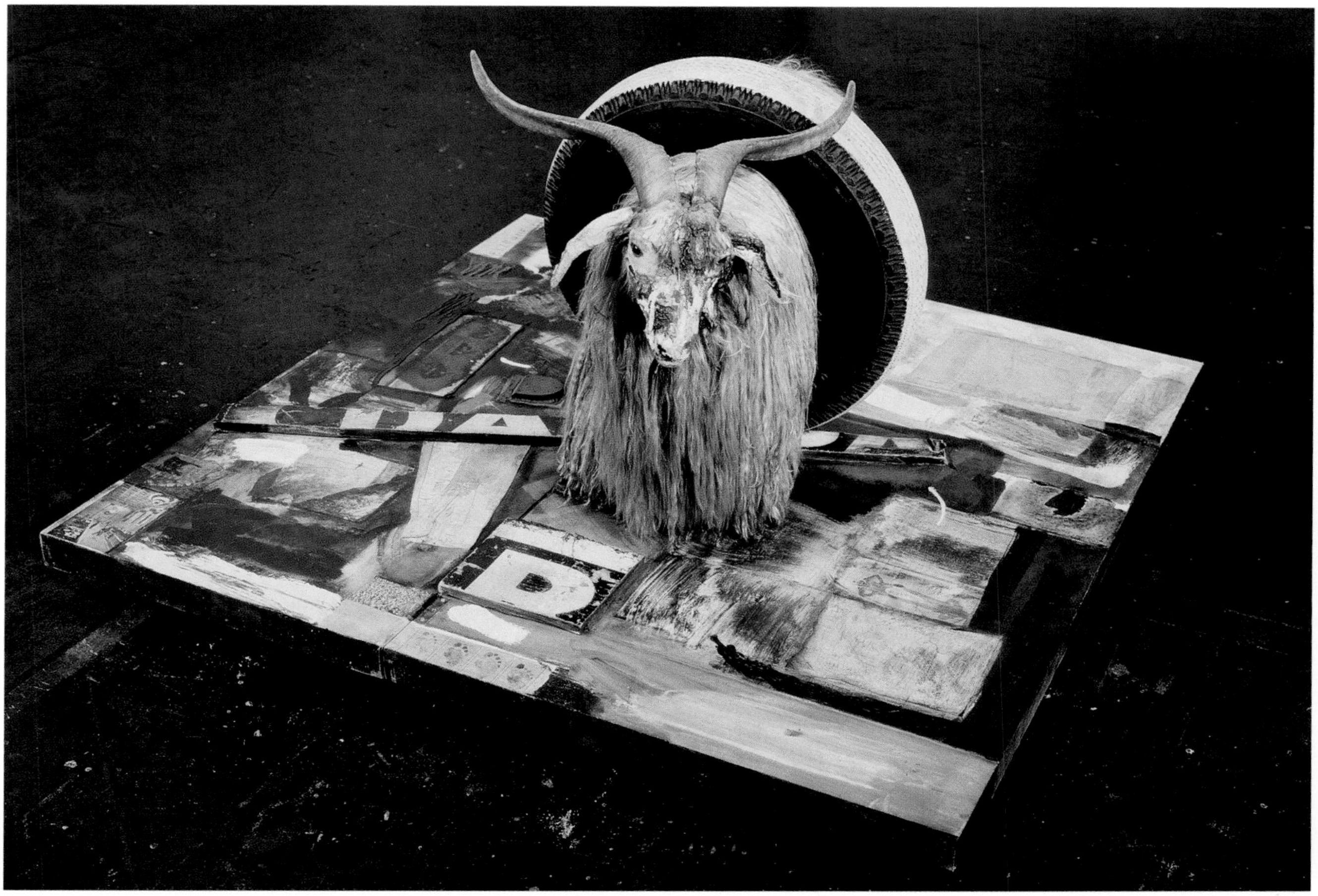

Fig. 9-33 Robert Rauschenberg, *Monogram*, 1955–59. Freestanding combine: oil, fabric, wood, on canvas and wood, rubber heel, tennis ball, metal plaque, hardware, stuffed Angora goat, rubber tire, mounted on four wheels, 42 in. × 5 ft. 3¼ in. × 5 ft. 4½ in.

animal look as if it belonged in a painting." In its earliest recorded state, the goat is mounted on a ledge in profile in the top half of a 6-foot painting. It peers over the edge of the painting and casts a shadow on the wall. Compared to later states of the work, the goat is integrated into the two-dimensional surface, or as integrated as an object of its size could be.

In the second state, Rauschenberg brought the goat off its perch and set it on a platform in front of another combine-painting, this one nearly 10 feet high. Now it seemed about to walk forward into our space, dragging the painting behind it. At this point, Rauschenberg also placed an automobile tire around the goat's midsection, which asserted the volume and three-dimensionality of the goat.

But Rauschenberg was not happy with this design, either. Finally, he put the combine-painting flat on the floor, creating what he called a "pasture" for the goat. Here, Rauschenberg manages to accomplish what seems logically impossible: The goat is at once fully contained within the boundaries of the picture frame and totally liberated from the wall. Painting has become sculpture.

One of the most interesting extensions of painting into new media is the use of matte painting in cinema. Matte paintings represent landscapes or locations, real or imaginary, that free filmmakers to create environments that would otherwise be too expensive to visit or impossible to build. They were traditionally made by artists using paints or pastels on large sheets of glass in front of which live-action footage, such as Dorothy's approach to the Emerald City in *The Wizard of Oz*, might be filmed.

In the digital age matte painting has acquired new levels of sophistication. For the film *The Bucket List*, Ron Crabb created a matte painting of the Taj Mahal. In the film, Jack Nicholson and Morgan Freeman walk around a pool in front of the iconic building in India. But the scene was actually shot at the Los Angeles Arboretum. The pool in the matte painting is much wider than the actual Taj Mahal (see Fig. 7-3). Everything from the reflecting pool back was painted by Crabb in multiple layers—hundreds, actually—so that as the camera tracked Nicholson and Freeman as they walked around the pool, the resulting shifts in perspective could be matched in the painted backdrop, thus creating a seamless sense of reality. The wider LA Arboretum pool allowed Crabb to reflect the Taj Mahal in its entirety.

THE CRITICAL PROCESS

Thinking about Painting

In this chapter, we have considered all of the painting media—encaustic, fresco, tempera, oil paint, watercolor, gouache, acrylic paints, and mixed media—and we have discussed not only how these media are used but also why artists have favored them. One of the most important factors in the development of new painting media has always been the desire of artists to represent the world more and more faithfully. But representation is not the only goal of painting. If we recall Artemisia Gentileschi's *Self-Portrait* at the beginning of this chapter (see Fig. 9-2), she is not simply representing the way she looks but also the way she feels. In her hands, paint becomes an expressive tool. Some painting media—oil paint, watercolor, and acrylics—are better suited to expressive ends than others because they are more fluid or can be manipulated more easily. But the possibilities of painting are as vast as the human imagination itself. In painting, anything is possible.

And, as we have seen in the last section of this chapter, the possibilities of painting media can be extended even further when they are combined with other media. The art of Fred Tomaselli is a case in point. In the late 1980s, Tomaselli began producing mixed-media works that combine pills (over-the-counter medicines, prescription pharmaceuticals, and street drugs), leaves (including marijuana leaves), insects, butterflies, and various cutout elements, including floral designs, representations of animals, and body parts. The resulting images constitute for Tomaselli a kind of cartography—he sees them as "maps" describing his place in the world. *Airborne Event* (**Fig. 9-34**) might well be considered an image of a psychedelic high. But Tomaselli, born in the late 1950s, is well aware of the high price first hippie and then punk cultures have paid for their hallucinogenic indulgences. Another way to read this painting is as a critique of what has been called "the jewel-like nature of a pill." That is, Tomaselli's work might also be considered an essay on the toxic nature of beauty or "airborne events" such as disease or disaster. How does it suggest that the world it depicts is as artificial as it is visionary? In order to answer this question, it might be useful to compare Tomaselli's mixed-media work to Fra Andrea Pozzo's *Glorification of St. Ignatius* (see Fig. 9-7).

Fig. 9-34 Fred Tomaselli, *Airborne Event*, 2003. Mixed media, acrylic, and resin on wood, 7 ft. × 5 ft. × 1½ in.

Thinking Back

9.1 Distinguish among the early painting media—encaustic, fresco, and tempera.

One of the oldest painting media is encaustic, noted for its luminosity and made by combining pigment with a binder of hot wax. The painter must work quickly so that the wax will stay liquid. For centuries, the preferred medium for wall painting was fresco, in which pigment, mixed with limewater, is applied to a plaster wall. In *buon fresco*, the pigment is applied to a wet wall, while in *fresco secco*, the pigment is applied to a dry wall. Why has *fresco secco* been particularly durable at the Buddhist caves at Ajanta? What is a *giornata*? Most artists in the Renaissance who painted frescoes also worked in tempera, made by combining water, pigment, and some gummy material, usually egg yolk. As in fresco, colors cannot be readily blended, and tempera must be used on a smooth painting surface called gesso, made from glue and plaster of Paris or chalk.

9.2 Describe what is distinctive about oil painting as a medium.

Oil paint is a highly versatile medium. It can be blended on the painting's surface to create a continuous scale of tones and hues, fostering a superior illusion of three dimensions. It can also be applied in thin layers called glazes, which promote luminosity. What is impasto? Why does oil paint have superior *expressive* potential?

9.3 Explain why watercolor is perhaps the most expressive of the painting media.

Watercolor paint is made from pigment suspended in gum arabic, and it flows so readily that it is possible to achieve dramatic gestural effects. To make a watercolor painting, this paint is combined with water and applied to paper. How does Winslow Homer create visual interest in his watercolor *A Wall, Nassau*? How does John Marin's *Untitled (The Blue Sea)* express movement?

9.4 Discuss some of the advantages offered the artist by synthetic painting media.

Synthetic media allow painters to both paint more quickly, since they dry far more rapidly than oil paint, and—because they are able to withstand the natural elements to a far greater degree than oil paint—to use them out-of-doors. Thus, the Mexican muralists used Duco, a lacquer developed as an automobile paint, to paint on walls exposed to the weather. Helen Frankenthaler began experimenting with Magna, a paint made from acrylic resins in the early 1950s, and when researchers discovered a way to mix acrylic resins with water in 1956, acrylic paints reached the mass market, culminating with their availability in aerosol cans. What made these aerosols attractive to graffiti writers?

9.5 Outline some of the ways that painting has combined itself with other media.

Painting media can often be used in combination with each other and with other media, such as drawing, fiber, found objects, and film. Many artists, particularly beginning in the twentieth century, have been interested in challenging tradition by violating the integrity of painting. What is collage, and why is it often used for political goals? How can mixed media be used to extend the "space of art"? What is combine-painting? What is matte painting?

Chapter 10
Printmaking

Learning Objectives

10.1 Define what a print is and discuss its earliest uses.

10.2 Characterize relief processes in printmaking.

10.3 Characterize intaglio processes in printmaking.

10.4 Describe the lithographic process and its invention.

10.5 Describe the silkscreen process.

10.6 Differentiate monotypes from other kinds of print.

A **print** is an image or design printed from an engraved plate, wooden block, or similar surface. In 2000, soon after her cat Ginzer died, Kiki Smith brought the body to Harlan & Weaver, a print publisher and workshop in New York City, and traced its form onto an etching plate. For several weeks, Smith worked on the print, slowly developing it in a series of **states**, or stages in the process, until she considered it finished. (These various states of the image can be seen in the art21 *Exclusive* video "Kiki Smith: Printmaking," along with footage of her working on a related print, *Two*, at Harlan & Weaver) Along the way, Smith restored the cat to a kind of life, lending it a ferocious, animated glare, and, as if to affirm her pet's feral roots, she made a second print of a bird skeleton to place beside it (**Fig. 10-1**). The result is a kind of dialogue between the forces of life, death, and even resurrection that speaks not only to the raw realities of the animal world but also to the fragility of our own place in that world. If Smith's print is a kind of memorial to Ginzer, it is also an act of identification with both Ginzer's and the bird's fate.

Since the nineteenth century, and increasingly since World War II, the art world has witnessed what might well be called an explosion of artists like Smith making prints. The reasons for this are many. For one thing, the fact that prints exist in multiple numbers seems to many artists absolutely in keeping with an era of mass production and distribution. The print allows the contemporary artist, in an age increasingly dominated by the mass media and mechanical modes of reproduction such as photography, to investigate the meaning of mechanically reproduced imagery. An even more important reason is that the unique work of art—a painting or a sculpture—has become, during the twentieth century, too expensive for the average collector, even though the size of the purchasing public has grown exponentially. Far less expensive than unique paintings, prints are an avenue through which artists can more readily reach a wider audience.

Fig. 10-1 Kiki Smith, *Ginzer* and *Bird Skeleton*, 2000. Set of two prints, aquatint, drypoint, and etching on Hahnemühle bright white paper; ***Ginzer***: paper size 22½ × 31 in., image size 18 × 24 in.; ***Bird Skeleton***: paper size 12 × 12 in., image size 6 × 6 in. Edition of 24.

Courtesy of the artist and Harlan & Weaver, New York.

The Print and its Earliest Uses

What is a print and what motivated the earliest prints to be made?

There are five basic processes of printmaking—relief, intaglio, lithography, silkscreen, and monotype—and we will consider them all in this chapter. In each case, the process results in an **impression**, or example, of an image that has been transferred through pressure onto paper from a **matrix**, the surface upon which the design has been created. A single matrix can be used to make many virtually identical impressions. Taken together, these multiple impressions, made on paper from the same matrix, are called an **edition**. As collectors have come to value prints more and more highly, the somewhat confusing concept of the **original print** has come into being. How, one wonders, can an image that exists in multiple be considered "original"? By and large, an original print can be distinguished from the reproductive print—one printed mechanically—by the fact that it has been printed by the artist or under the artist's supervision. Since the late nineteenth century, artists have signed and numbered each impression—for example, the number 3/35 at the bottom of a print means that this is the third impression in an edition of 35. Often, artists reserve a small number of additional **proofs**—trial impressions made before the final edition is run—for personal use. These are usually designated "AP," meaning "artist's proof." After the edition is made, the original plate is destroyed or canceled by incising lines across it. This is done to protect the collector against a misrepresentation about the number of prints in a given edition.

Fig. 10-2 Frontispiece, *Diamond Sutra*, from Cave 17, Dunhuang, printed in the ninth year of the Xiantong Era of the Tang dynasty, 868 CE. Ink on paper, woodblock handscroll. British Library. © British Library Board, Or. 8210/P.2, frontispiece and text.

The medium of printmaking appears to have originated in China in the ninth century CE with the publication of the world's earliest known printed book, the *Diamond Sutra*, one of Buddhism's more important texts. Discovered in 1907 in a cave at Dunhuang among hundreds of other paper and silk scrolls, all perfectly preserved by the dry desert air (see Chapter 1), the 18-foot-long handscroll begins with a print showing the Buddha preaching to his followers (**Fig. 10-2**). Although only a single copy of the scroll survives (in the British Library in London), the image was apparently intended for wide-scale distribution—an inscription at the end of the scroll reads: "Reverently [caused to be] made for universal free distribution by Wang Jie on behalf of his two parents on the 13th of the 4th moon of the 9th year of Xiantong [11 May 868 CE]." This postscript reveals one of the most important characteristics of the print (as opposed to painting or sculpture)—that is, its vital role in the mass distribution of ideas, especially the popularization of iconographic and stylistic traditions, the conventions of a shared visual culture.

The art of printmaking in Europe seems to have spread, like paper itself, westward from China. Of course, the basic principles of printmaking had existed for centuries before the publication of the *Diamond Sutra*. In the ancient world, from China to Greece, signature seals—small engraved carvings pressed into wax to confirm receipt or ownership—were widely used to confirm receipt, authorship, or ownership of a letter or document. Before the widespread use of paper, pictorial designs were being printed onto fabric across the European continent. As paper became more and more widely used in the fifteenth century, producers inscribed signature watermark designs on their paper by attaching bent wire to the molds used in production. Among the earliest paper prints to receive widespread distribution across Europe, among even the illiterate, were playing cards, the designs of which have changed little since late medieval times.

But printmaking developed rapidly after the appearance of the first printed book. Sometime between 1435 and 1455, in the German city of Mainz, Johannes Gutenberg discovered a process for casting individual letterforms by using an alloy of lead and antimony. The letterforms could be composed into pages of type and then printed on a wooden standing press using ink made of lampblack and oil varnish. Although the Chinese alchemist Pi Sheng had invented movable type in 1045 CE, now, for the first time, the technology was available in the West, and identical copies of written works could be reproduced over and over again.

In 1455, Gutenberg published his first major work, the *Forty-Two-Line Bible* (**Fig. 10-3**)—so named because each column of type contains 42 lines—the first substantial book to be published from movable type in Europe. An artist added the colorful decorative design of the marginalia and capitals by hand after the book was printed. By the middle of the sixteenth century, roughly one hundred years after this Bible was published, 3,830 editions of the Bible had been published in Europe—altogether about 1 million copies.

Meanwhile, printing presses were churning out a wide variety of books throughout Europe, and many were illustrated. *The Nuremberg Chronicle*, published in 1493 by one of the first professional book publishers in history, Anton Koberger, contains many prints. Appearing in two editions, one in black-and-white (**Fig. 10-4**) and another much more costly edition with hand-colored illustrations, *The Nuremberg Chronicle* was intended as a history of the world. A bestseller in its day, it contained more than 1,800 pictures, though only 654 different blocks were employed. Forty-four images of men and women were repeated 226 times to represent different famous historical characters, and depictions of many different cities utilized the same woodcut.

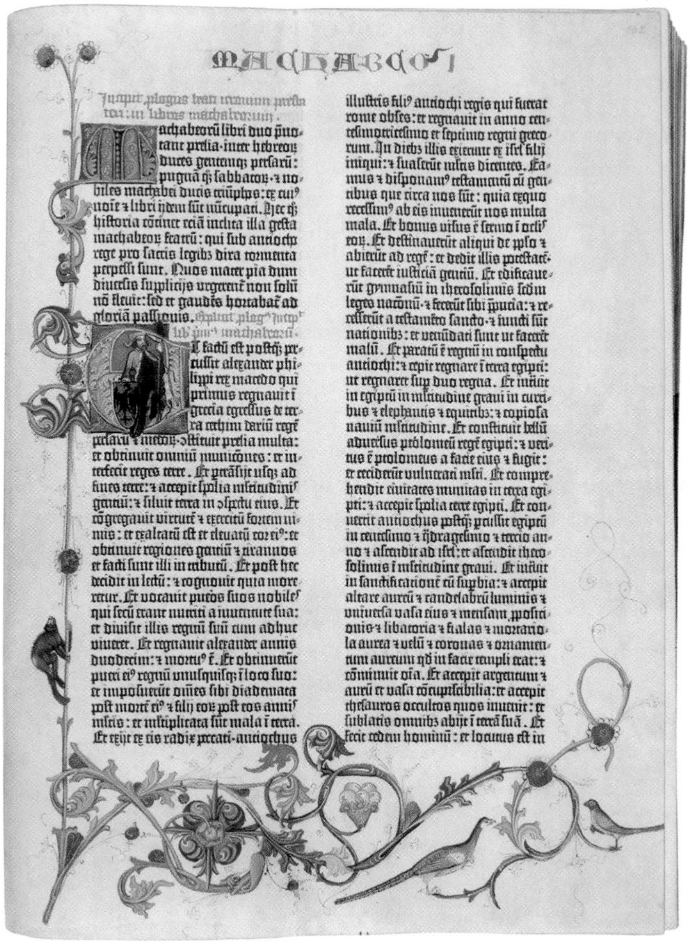

Fig. 10-3 Johannes Gutenberg, Page from the *Forty-Two-Line Bible*, Mainz, 1455–56. Page 162 recto with initials "M" and "E" and depiction of Alexander the Great; text printed with movable letters and hand-painted initials and marginalia. Staatsbibliothek zu Berlin.

Photo: Ruth Schacht. © 2015. Photo Scala, Florence/bpk, Bildagentur fuer Kunst, Kultur und Geschichte, Berlin.

Fig. 10-4 Hartmann Schedel, *The Nuremberg Chronicle: View of Venice*, 12 July 1493. Woodcut, illustration size approx. 10 × 20 in. Metropolitan Museum of Art, New York.

Rogers Fund, 1921.36.145. Image © Metropolitan Museum of Art/Art Resource/Scala, Florence.

Relief Processes

What characterizes the relief processes of printmaking?

The term **relief** refers to any printmaking process in which the image to be printed is raised off the background in reverse. Common rubber stamps use the relief process. If you have a stamp with your name on it, you will know that the letters of your name are raised off it in reverse. You press the letters into an ink pad, and then to paper, and your name is printed right side up. All relief processes rely on this basic principle.

Woodcut

The earliest prints, such as the illustrations for the *Diamond Sutra* and *The Nuremberg Chronicle*, were **woodcuts**. A design is drawn on the surface of a woodblock, and the parts that are to print white are cut or gouged away, usually with a knife or chisel. This process leaves the areas that are to be black elevated. A black line is created, for instance, by cutting away the block on each side of it. This elevated surface—like the elevated letterform of the printing press—is then rolled with a relatively viscous ink, thick and sticky enough that it will not flow into the hollows (**Fig. 10-5**). Paper is then rolled through a press directly against this inked and raised surface.

The woodcut print offers the artist a means of achieving great contrast between light and dark, and, as a result, dramatic emotional effects. In the twentieth century, the expressive potential of the medium was recognized, particularly by the German Expressionists. In his *Fränzi Reclining* (**Fig. 10-6**), Erich Heckel gouged out the figure of his model, the 12-year-old Fränzi, whose unassuming poses Heckel and his colleagues greatly

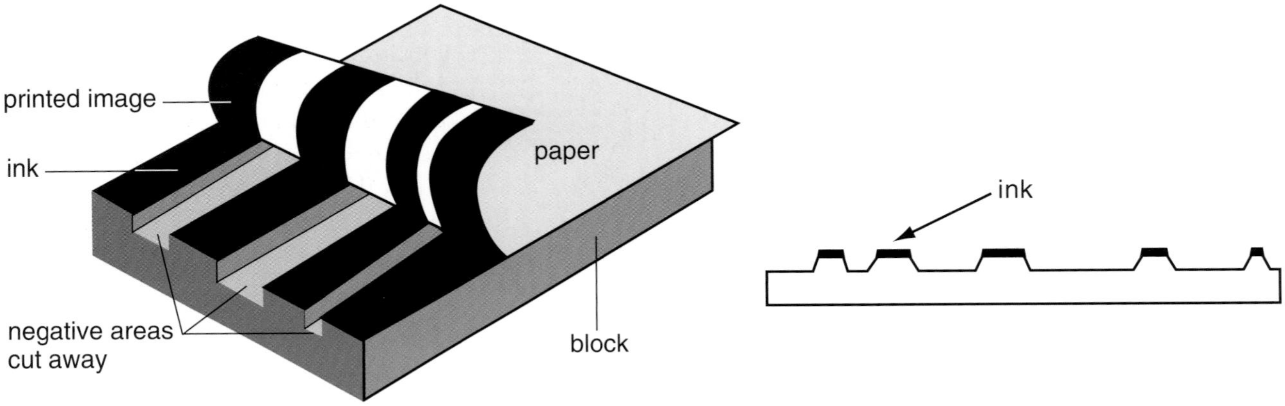

Fig. 10-5 Relief-printing technique.

Fig. 10-6 Erich Heckel, *Fränzi Reclining*, 1910. Woodcut, printed in color, block $8\frac{15}{16} \times 16\frac{9}{16}$ in., sheet $13\frac{15}{16} \times 21\frac{7}{8}$ in. Museum of Modern Art, New York.

Gift of Mr. and Mrs. Otto Gerson, 40.1958. Image © 2015 Metropolitan Museum of Art/Art Resource/Scala, Florence. © 2015 Artists Rights Society (ARS), New York/VG Bild-Kunst, Bonn.

preferred to the more sophisticated ones of professional models, rendering the adolescent awkwardness of her body as a simple, flat form. Then, Heckel sawed the woodblock into pieces, inked each piece separately, and reassembled it like a jigsaw for printing. The jagged rawness of his forms reflects the directness of his knife and saw cutting into the block.

But the rough gouging and cutting of the block evident in the Heckel woodcut do not reflect the historical refinement of the medium. By the mid-eighteenth century, technology developed by the Chinese for making color woodblock prints from multiple blocks was beginning to be popularized in Japan. The resulting images, known as *nishiki-e*, or "brocade pictures"—so named because they were felt to resemble brocade fabrics—were, at first, commissioned by a group of wealthy Japanese who, among various other intellectual pursuits, routinely exchanged elaborately decorated calendars on New Year's Day. Since the government held a monopoly on the printing of all calendars, the artists making these *nishiki-e* calendars went to elaborate lengths to disguise their efforts, and the symbols for the months were introduced into the compositions in the subtlest ways.

The first and most prominent of the artists to produce *nishiki-e* calendars was Suzuki Harunobu. So admired were his designs that, by 1766, they were widely distributed commercially—minus, of course, their calendar symbols. Before his death in 1770, Harunobu produced hundreds of *nishiki-e* prints, many of them dedicated to illustrating the most elegant aspects of eighteenth-century Japanese life, and his prints were, if not the first, then certainly the most influential early examples of what would soon become known as ***ukiyo-e***, "pictures of the transient world of everyday life" (see *The Creative Process*, pp. 218–19). He was especially renowned for his ability to portray women of great beauty, and some of his favorite subjects were the beautiful courtesans in the Yoshiwara pleasure district of Edo (modern Tokyo): *Two Courtesans, Inside and Outside the Display Window* (**Fig. 10-7**) is a striking example. The display window, or *harimise*, is the lattice-windowed area in the front of a brothel where the potential client might choose the courtesan of his pleasure. This print is remarkable for both its graphic simplicity and its subtle evocation of traditional Japanese culture and values. Instead of showing the entirety of the window, Harunobu depicts just one section, creating a powerfully realized grid structure into which he has placed his figures. In other words, the delicate, rounded lines of the courtesans' features and clothing contrast dramatically with the broad two-dimensional structure of the *harimise*. This graphic contrast, equally realized in the contrast between the inside and outside of the *harimise*, as well as the fact that one courtesan stands while the other sits, reflects the philosophy embodied in the traditional Japanese principle of complementarity, which itself originates in Chinese Taoist philosophy. Representing unity within diversity, opposites organized in perfect harmony, the ancient symbol for this principle is the famous yin and yang:

Yin is generative, nurturing, soft, and passive, and is associated with feminine principles. Yang is active, hard, and aggressive, and is associated with the masculine. Thus, Harunobu's print is not merely a depiction of everyday life in the Yoshiwara pleasure district, but a subtle philosophical defense of the era's sexual mores.

European artists became particularly interested in the woodblock process in the nineteenth century through their introduction to the Japanese woodblock print. Woodblock printing had essentially died as an art form in Europe as early as the Renaissance,

Fig. 10-7 Suzuki Harunobu, *Two Courtesans, Inside and Outside the Display Window*, Japanese, Edo period, about 1768–69. Woodblock print (*nishiki-e*), ink and color on paper, 26⅜ × 5¹⁄₁₆ in. Museum of Fine Arts, Boston.
Denman Waldo Ross Collection, 1906.1248. Photograph © 2015 Museum of Fine Arts, Boston.

The Creative Process

Making an *Ukiyo-e* Print: Kitagawa Utamaro's *Studio*

Most Japanese prints are examples of what is called *ukiyo-e*, or "pictures of the transient world of everyday life." Inspired in the late seventeenth century by a Chinese manual on the art of painting entitled *The Mustard-Seed Garden*, which contained many woodcuts in both color and black-and-white, *ukiyo-e* prints were commonplace in Japan by the middle of the eighteenth century. Between 1743 and 1765, Japanese artists like Suzuki Harunobu (see Fig. 10-7) developed their distinctive method for color printing from multiple blocks.

The subject matter of these prints is usually concerned with the pleasures of contemporary life—hairdos and wardrobes, daily rituals such as bathing, theatrical entertainments, life in the Tokyo brothels, and so on, in endless combination. Kitagawa Utamaro's depiction of *The Fickle Type*, from his

Fig. 10-8 Kitagawa Utamaro, *The Fickle Type*, from the series *Ten Physiognomies of Women*, ca. 1793. Woodcut, 14 × 9⅞ in.
Courtesy of Library of Congress.

Fig. 10-9 Kitagawa Utamaro, *Utamaro's Studio, Eshi . . . dosa-hiki* (the three primary steps in producing a print from drawing to glazing), from the series *Edo meibutsu nishiki-e kosaku*, ca. 1803. Oban triptych, ink and color on paper, 24¾ × 9⅝ in. Published by Tsuruya Kiemon. The Art Institute of Chicago.

series *Ten Physiognomies of Women* (**Fig. 10-8**), embodies the sensuality of the world that the *ukiyo-e* print so often reveals. Hokusai's view of the eternal Mount Fuji in *The Great Wave off Kanagawa* (see Fig. 7-21) was probably conceived as a commentary on the self-indulgence of the genre of *ukiyo-e* as a whole. The mountain—and, by extension, the values it stood for, the traditional values of the nation itself—is depicted in Hokusai's famous series as transcending the fleeting pleasures of daily life.

Traditionally, the creation of a Japanese print was a team effort, and the publisher, the designer (such as Utamaro), the carver, and the printer were all considered essentially equal in the creative process. The head of the project was the publisher, who often conceived of the ideas for the prints, financing individual works or series of works that the public would, in his estimation, be likely to buy. Utamaro's depiction of his studio in a publisher's establishment (**Fig. 10-9**) is a *mitate*, or fanciful picture. Each of the workers in the studio is a pretty girl—hence, the print's status as a *mitate*—and they are engaged, according to the caption on the print, in "making the famous Edo [present-day Tokyo] color prints." Utamaro depicts himself at the right, dressed in women's clothing and holding a finished print. His publisher, also dressed as a woman, looks on from behind his desk. On the left of the triptych is a depiction of workers preparing paper. They are **sizing** it—that is, brushing the surface with an astringent crystalline substance called alum that reduces the absorbency of the paper so that ink will not run along its fibers—then hanging the sized prints to dry. The paper was traditionally made from the inside of the bark of the mulberry tree mixed with bamboo fiber, and, after sizing, it was kept damp for six hours before printing.

In the middle section of the print, the block is actually prepared. In the foreground, a worker sharpens her chisel on a stone. Behind her is a stack of blocks upon which brush drawings made by Utamaro have been placed face down and secured on each block with a weak rice-starch dissolved in water. The woman seated at the desk in the middle rubs the back of the drawing to remove several layers of fiber. She then saturates what remains with oil until it becomes transparent. At this point, the original drawing looks as if it were drawn on the block.

Next, the workers carve the block, and we can see here large white areas being chiseled out of the block by the woman seated in the back. Black-and-white prints of this design are made and then returned to the artist, who indicates the colors for the prints, one color to a sheet. The cutter then carves each sheet on a separate block. The final print is, in essence, an accumulation of the individually colored blocks, requiring a separate printing for each color.

but not long after Commodore Matthew C. Perry's arrival in Japan in July 1853, ending 215 years of isolation from the rest of the world, Japanese prints flooded the European market, and they were received with enthusiasm. Part of their attraction was their exotic subject matter, but artists were also intrigued by the range of color in the prints, their subtle and economical use of line, and their novel use of pictorial space.

Impressionist artists such as Édouard Manet, Edgar Degas, and Mary Cassatt were particularly influenced by Japanese prints. But the artist most enthusiastic about them was Vincent van Gogh. He owned prints by the hundreds, and on numerous occasions copied them directly. *Japonaiserie: The Courtesan (after Kesai Eisen)* (**Fig. 10-10**) is an example. The central figure in the painting is copied from a print by Kesai Eisen that van Gogh saw on the cover of a special Japanese issue of *Paris Illustré* published in May 1886 (**Fig. 10-11**). All the other elements of the painting are derived from other Japanese prints, except perhaps the boat at the very top, which appears Western in conception. The frogs were copied from Yoshimaro's *New Book of Insects*, and both the cranes and the bamboo stalks are derived from prints by Hokusai (see Fig. 7-21). Van Gogh's intentions in combining all these elements become clear when we recognize that the central figure is a courtesan (her tortoiseshell hair ornaments signify her profession), and that the words *grue* (crane) and *grenouille* (frog) were common Parisian words for prostitutes. Van Gogh explained his interest in Japanese prints in a letter written in September 1888: "Whatever one says," he wrote, "I admire the most popular Japanese

Fig. 10-10 Vincent van Gogh, *Japonaiserie: The Courtesan (after Kesai Eisen)*, 1887. Oil on canvas, 41⅜ × 24 in. Van Gogh Museum, Amsterdam.
Courtesy of Vincent van Gogh Foundation.

Fig. 10-11 "Le Japon," cover of *Paris Illustré*, May 1886. Van Gogh Museum, Amsterdam.
Courtesy of Vincent van Gogh Foundation.

Fig. 10-12 Kitagawa Utamaro, *Shaving a Boy's Head*, ca. 1795. Color woodblock print, $15\frac{1}{8} \times 10\frac{1}{4}$ in. The Minneapolis Institute of Arts.
Bequest of Richard P. Gale, 74.1.153. Bridgeman Images.

Fig. 10-13 Mary Cassatt, *The Bath*, 1890–91. Drypoint and aquatint on laid paper, plate $12\frac{5}{8} \times 9\frac{3}{4}$ in., sheet $17\frac{3}{16} \times 12$ in. National Gallery of Art, Washington, D.C.
Rosenwald Collection. Photo © Board of Trustees, National Gallery of Art, Washington, D.C. Photo: Dean Beasom.

prints, colored in flat areas, and for the same reasons that I admire Rubens and Veronese. I am absolutely certain that this is no primitive art."

Of all the Impressionists, perhaps the American Mary Cassatt, who exhibited with the group beginning in 1867, was most taken with the Japanese tradition. She was especially impressed with its interest in the intimate world of women, the daily routines of domestic existence. She consciously imitated works like Utamaro's *Shaving a Boy's Head* (**Fig. 10-12**). Cassatt's *Bath* (**Fig. 10-13**), one of ten prints inspired by an April 1890 exhibition of Japanese woodblocks at the École des Beaux-Arts in Paris, exploits the same contrasts between printed textiles and bare skin, between colored fabric and the absence of color in space. Her whole composition is made up of flatly silhouetted shapes against a bare ground, the whole devoid of the traditional shading and tonal variations that create the illusion of depth in Western art.

Wood Engraving

By the late nineteenth century, woodcut illustration had reached a level of extraordinary sophistication. Illustrators commonly employed a method known as **wood engraving**. Wood engraving is a "white-line" technique in which the fine, narrow grooves cut into the block do not hold ink. The grainy end of a section of wood—comparable to the rough end of a 4 × 4—is utilized instead of the smooth side of a board, as it is in woodcut proper. The end grain can be cut in any direction without splintering, and thus extremely delicate modeling can be achieved by means of careful hatching in any direction.

Fig. 10-14 ***Noon-Day Rest in Marble Canyon*****, after an original sketch by Thomas Moran, from J. W. Powell,** ***Exploration of the Colorado River of the West and its Tributaries*****, 1875.** Wood engraving, 6½ × 4⅜ in.
New York Public Library.

The wood engraving used to illustrate Captain J. W. Powell's 1875 *Exploration of the Colorado River of the West* (**Fig. 10-14**) was copied by a professional wood engraver from an original sketch, executed on the site, by American painter Thomas Moran (his signature mark, in the lower left-hand corner, is an "M" crossed by a "T" with an arrow pointing downward). A narrative of the first exploration of the Colorado River canyon from Green River, in Wyoming, to the lower end of the Grand Canyon, the book—together with a number of paintings executed by Moran from the same sketches—presented America with its first views of the great Western canyonlands.

Linocut

A **linocut** is similar to a woodcut, except, as its name suggests, the block is made of linoleum instead of wood. Softer than wood, linoleum is easier to cut but wears down more quickly under pressure, resulting in smaller editions. As in woodcut, color can also be added to a print by creating a series of different blocks, one for each color, each of which is aligned with the others in a process known as **registration** (the same process used, incidentally, by Japanese *ukiyo-e* printers to align the different-colored blocks of their prints).

Fig. 10-15 Elizabeth Catlett, *Sharecropper*, 1952, printed 1970. Color linocut on cream Japanese paper, image 17¾ × 17 in. The Art Institute of Chicago.
Restricted gift of Mr. and Mrs. Robert S. Hartman, 1992.182. Art © Catlett Mora Family Trust/Licensed by VAGA, New York.

African-American artist Elizabeth Catlett's's linocut *Sharecropper* (**Fig. 10-15**) is comprised of three separate linoleum blocks printed in black, dark green (for the jacket), and burnt sienna (for the neck and face). The practice of sharecropping, which was introduced soon after the emancipation of the slaves in the last half of the nineteenth century, essentially reinstated the conditions of slavery itself as white landlords exploited former slaves by contracting for a share of the crops produced on their small plots of land in return for the dubious privilege of working the land. We look up at Catlett's sharecropper as if we are her children, and what we see is anything but a visage defeated by a lifetime of indentured servitude. Instead we are witness to a determined strength, a will to endure. She is entirely representative of Catlett's own lifetime dedication to create art that promotes social change. The artist died in 2012 at the age of 96.

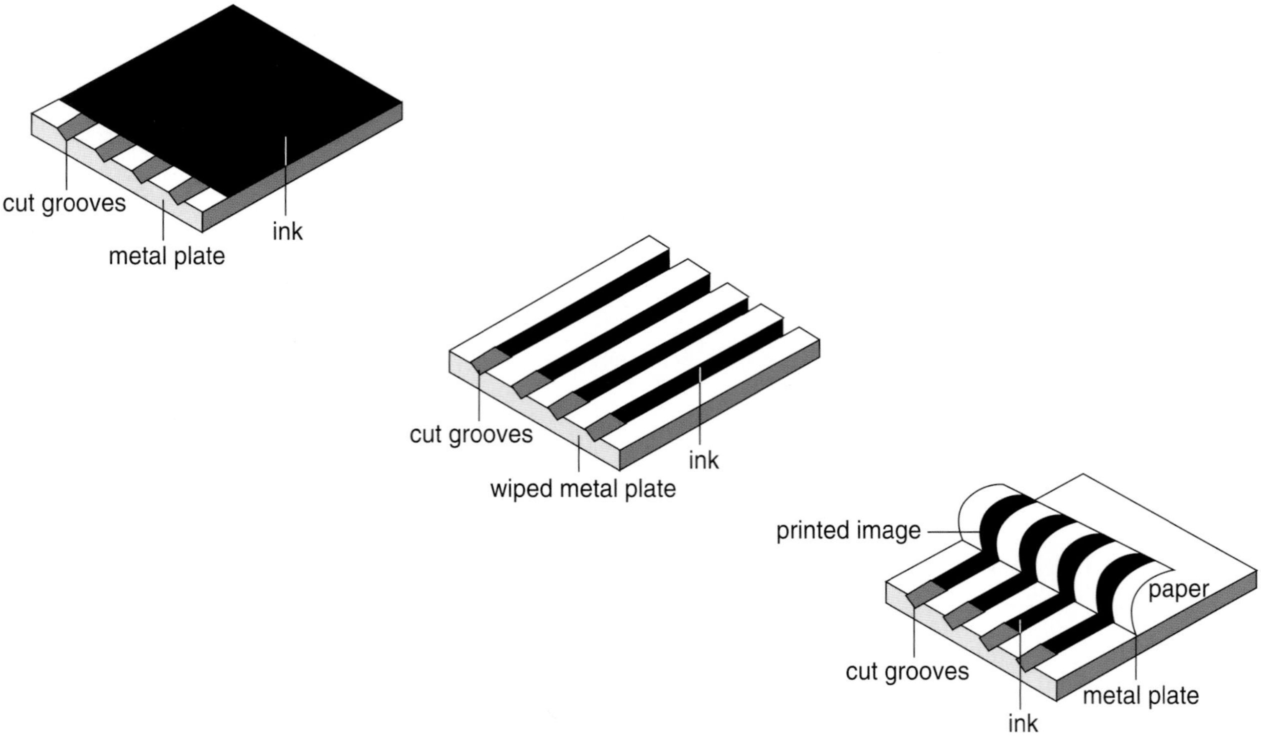

Fig. 10-16 Intaglio printmaking technique, general view.

Intaglio Processes

What characterizes the intaglio processes of printmaking?

Relief processes rely on a raised surface for printing. With the **intaglio** process, on the other hand, the areas to be printed are below the surface of the plate. *Intaglio* is the Italian word for "engraving," and the method itself was derived from engraving techniques practiced by goldsmiths and armorers in the Middle Ages. In general, intaglio refers to any process in which the cut or incised lines on the plate are filled with ink (**Figs. 10-16** and **10-17**). The surface of the plate is wiped clean, and a sheet of dampened paper is pressed into the plate with a very powerful roller so that the paper picks up the ink in the depressed grooves. Since the paper is essentially pushed into the plate in order to be inked, a subtle but detectable elevation of the lines that result is always evident in the final print. Modeling and shading are achieved in the same way as in drawing, by hatching, cross-hatching, and often **stippling**—where, instead of lines, dots are employed in greater and greater density the deeper and darker the shadow.

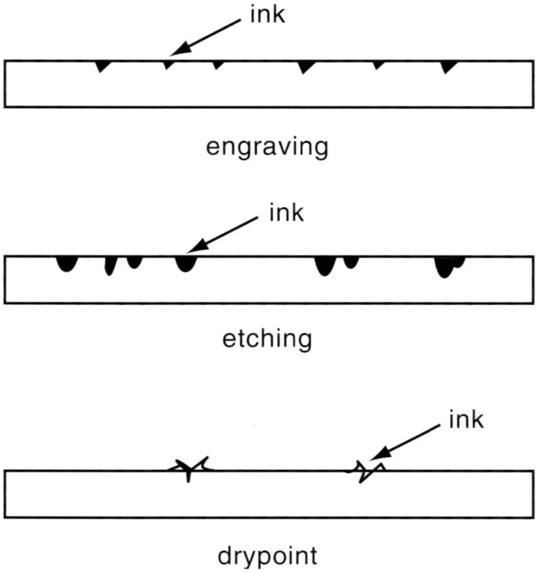

Fig. 10-17 Intaglio printmaking techniques, side views.

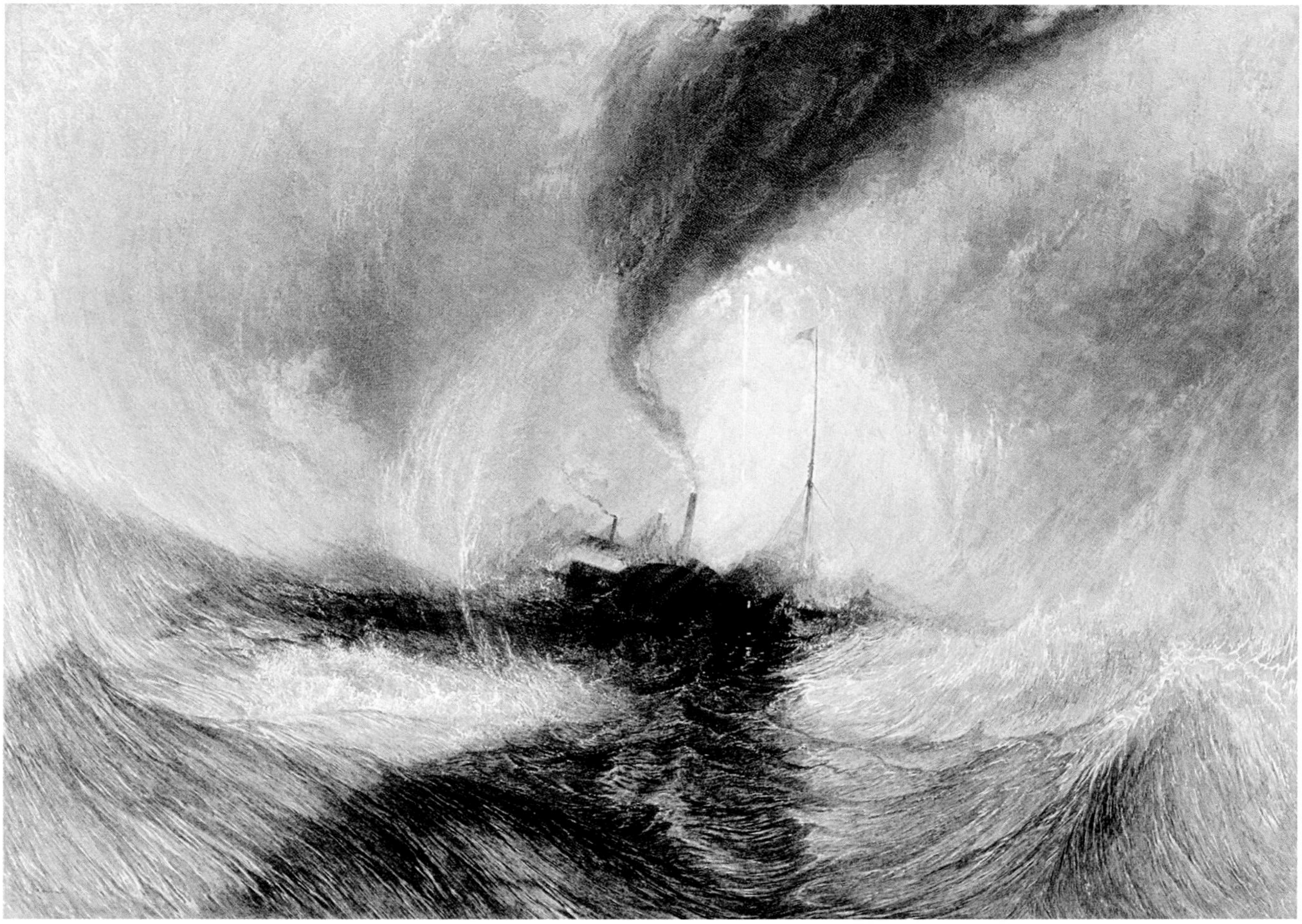

Fig. 10-18 After J. M. W. Turner, *Snow Storm: Steamboat off a Harbor's Mouth* (1842), engraved by R. Brandard, published 1859–61. Engraving on steel.

Engraving

Engraving is accomplished by pushing a small V-shaped metal rod, called a **burin**, across a metal plate, usually of copper or zinc, forcing the metal up in slivers in front of the line. These slivers are then removed from the plate with a hard metal scraper. Depending on the size of the burin used and the force with which it is applied to the plate, the results can range from almost microscopically fine lines to ones so broad and coarse that they can be felt with a fingertip.

Line engravings were commonly used to illustrate books and reproduce works of art in the era before the invention of photography, and for many years after. Illustrated here is an engraving done on a steel plate (steel was capable of producing many more copies than either copper or zinc) of J. M. W. Turner's painting *Snow Storm: Steamboat off a Harbor's Mouth* (**Fig. 10-18**). The anonymous engraver captures the play of light and dark in the original by using a great variety of lines of differing width, length, and density.

Etching

Etching is a much more fluid and free process than engraving and is capable of capturing something of the same sense of immediacy as the sketch. As a result, master draftsmen, such as Rembrandt, readily took to the medium. It satisfied their love for spontaneity of line. Yet the medium also requires the utmost calculation and planning, an ability to manipulate chemicals that verges, especially in Rembrandt's greatest etchings, on wizardry, and a certain willingness to risk losing everything in order to achieve the desired effect.

Creating an etching is a twofold process, consisting of a drawing stage and an etching stage. The metal plate is first coated with an acid-resistant substance called a **ground**, and this ground is drawn upon. If a hard ground is chosen, then an etching needle is required to break through it and expose the plate. Hard grounds are employed for finely detailed linear work. Soft grounds, made of tallow or petroleum jelly, can also be used, and virtually any tool, including the artist's finger, can be used to expose the plate. The traditional soft-ground technique is often called crayon manner or pencil manner because the final product so closely resembles crayon and pencil drawing. In this technique, a thin sheet of paper is placed on top of the ground and is drawn on with a soft pencil or crayon. When the paper is removed, it lifts the ground where the drawing instrument was pressed into the paper.

Whichever kind of ground is employed, the drawn plate is then set in an acid bath, and those areas that have been drawn are eaten into, or etched, by the acid. The undrawn areas of the plate are, of course, unaffected by the acid. The longer the exposed plate is left in the bath, and the stronger the solution, the greater the width and depth of the etched line. The

Fig. 10-19 Rembrandt van Rijn, *The Angel Appearing to the Shepherds*, 1634. Etching, 10¼ × 8½ in. Rijksmuseum, Amsterdam.
Mr and Mrs De Bruijn-van der Leeuw Bequest, Muri, Switzerland.

strength of individual lines or areas can be controlled by removing the plate from the bath and **stopping out** a section by applying a varnish or another coat of ground over the etched surface. The plate is then resubmerged into the bath. The stopped-out lines will be lighter than those that are again exposed to the acid. When the plate is ready for printing, the ground is removed with solvent, and the print is made according to the intaglio method.

Rembrandt's *The Angel Appearing to the Shepherds* (**Fig. 10-19**) is one of the most fully realized etchings ever printed, pushing the medium to its very limits. (Although Rembrandt worked exclusively with brown and black inks, it is possible to work with colored inks as well—see *The Creative Process*, pp. 228–29). For this print, Rembrandt altered the usual etching process. Fascinated by the play of light and dark, he wanted to create the feeling that the angel, and the light associated with her, were emerging out of the darkness. Normally, in etching, the background is white, since it is unetched and there are no lines on it to hold ink. Here, Rembrandt wanted a black background, and he worked first on the darkest areas of the composition, creating an intricately cross-hatched landscape of ever-deepening shadow. Only the white areas bathed in the angel's light remained undrawn. At this point, the plate was placed in acid and bitten as deeply as possible. Finally, the angel and the frightened shepherds in the foreground were worked up in a more traditional manner of etched line on a largely white ground. It is as if, at this crucial moment of the New Testament, when the angel announces the birth of Jesus, Rembrandt reenacts, in his manipulation of light and dark, the opening scenes of the Old Testament—God's pronouncement in Genesis, "Let there be light."

Drypoint

A third form of intaglio printing is known as **drypoint**. The drypoint line is scratched into the copper plate with a metal point that is pulled across the surface, not pushed as in engraving. A ridge of metal, called a **burr**, is pushed up along each side of the line, giving a rich, velvety, soft texture to the print when inked, as is evident in Mary Cassatt's *The Map* (*The Lesson*) (**Fig. 10-20**). The softness of line generated by the drypoint process is especially appealing. Because this burr quickly wears off in the printing process, it is rare to find a drypoint edition of more than 25, and the earliest numbers in the edition are often the finest.

Fig. 10-20 Mary Cassatt, *The Map* (*The Lesson*), 1890. Drypoint, 6³⁄₁₆ × 9³⁄₁₆ in. The Art Institute of Chicago.
Joseph Brooks Fair Collection, 1933.537. Photo © 1999 Art Institute of Chicago. All rights reserved.

The Creative Process

Four-Color Intaglio: Yuji Hiratsuka's *Miracle Grow Hypnotist*

Like woodcut prints, colored etchings require separate printings for each color, but whereas Utamaro used separate, individually colored blocks for each color (see Fig. 10-9), in etching any section not requiring the new color can be stopped out or simply printed over the colors previously applied, or a combination of both. Yuji Hiratsuka's *Miracle Grow Hypnotist* (**Fig. 10-23**) is a four-color print produced by this means. He inks four separate copper plates, printing black first, then yellow, red, and blue, in that order, on very thin Japanese Kozo paper, the delicate surface of which allows the printmaker to pull finer details off the plate. Reproduced here are the black and red plates of *Miracle Grow Hypnotist* (**Figs. 10-21** and **10-22**). Hiratsuka finishes his prints with a French technique known as *Chine-collé* (from the French *chine*, "tissue," and *collé*, "glued"), in which glue is applied to the back of the completed work before it is passed through the press again with a heavier rag paper beneath, thus creating a much less fragile work.

Hiratsuka creates prints that might be called contemporary *ukiyo-e*, revealing "the transient world of everyday life" in parodic terms. In his work, he often explores the coexistence of Western and Eastern influences in Japanese society. Here, Hiratsuka's enigmatic figure seems to invoke the creationary forces of the universe embodied in the traditional *kami*, or spirits, of the indigenous Shinto religion still practiced widely in Japan—note the black lines of force that surround her hands. At the same time, Hiratsuka's title invokes the American company Miracle-Gro, which actually manufactures a liquid cactus plant food. Hiratsuka's hypnotist, his image suggests, is perhaps something of a charlatan, promising the red-robed figure behind her to make the cactus grow with a magic spell, a deed she will actually accomplish with the aid of a commercial fertilizer.

Figs. 10-21 and 10-22 Yuji Hiratsuka, *Miracle Grow Hypnotist*, black and red plates, 2005. Four-color intaglio (etching, aquatint) and *Chine-collé* on Japanese Kozo (mulberry) paper, 18 × 13 in. Edition of 26.

Fig. 10-23 Yuji Hiratsuka, *Miracle Grow Hypnotist*, 2005. Four-color intaglio (etching, aquatint) and *Chine-collé* on Japanese Kozo (mulberry) paper, 18 × 13 in. Edition of 26.

Fig. 10-24 J. M. W. Turner, *Ship in a Storm*, from the *Little Liber*, engraved by the artist, ca. 1826.
Mezzotint, 7½ × 9⅞ in. Fitzwilliam Museum, University of Cambridge, UK.
Bridgeman Images.

Mezzotint and Aquatint

Two other intaglio techniques should be mentioned—mezzotint and aquatint. **Mezzotint** is, in effect, a negative process. That is, the plate is first ground all over using a sharp, curved tool called a **rocker**, leaving a burr over the entire surface that, if inked, would result in a solid black print. The surface is then lightened by scraping away the burr to a greater or lesser degree. One of the great masters of the mezzotint process was J. M. W. Turner, who between 1823 and 1826 executed 12 mezzotint engravings for a project he called the *Little Liber*, which he evidently intended to publish. But the project was never accomplished in his lifetime, and the plates were found in his studio after his death. Each of the engravings reveals Turner's interest in mezzotint's ability to modulate between the darkest blacks, from which the image has been scraped—in *Ship in a Storm* (**Fig. 10-24**) the black hull of the ship itself—to an almost luminescent white in the flash of lightning to the ship's right. The richness of the dark tones that distinguishes mezzotint as a process is readily apparent if one compares the mezzotint to an image treating a similar theme: The steel engraving of Turner's *Snow Storm: Steamboat off a Harbor's Mouth* (see Fig. 10-18). The linear qualities of the latter line engraving give way, in the mezzotint, to broad swathes of light and shadow, washes rather than lines of ink.

Like mezzotint, **aquatint** also relies for its effect not on line but on tonal areas of light and dark. Invented in France in the 1760s, the method involves coating the surface of the plate with a porous ground through which acid can penetrate. Usually consisting of particles of resin or powder, the ground is dusted onto the plate, then set in place by heating it until it melts. The acid bites around each particle into the surface of the plate, creating a sandpaperlike texture: The denser the resin, the lighter the tone of the resulting surface. Line is often added later, usually by means of etching or drypoint.

Fig. 10-25 Jane Dickson, *Stairwell*, 1984. Aquatint on Rives BFK paper, 35¾ × 22¾ in. Mount Holyoke College Art Museum, South Hadley, Massachusetts. Henry Rox Memorial Fund for the Acquisition of Works by Contemporary Women Artists.

Jane Dickson's *Stairwell* (**Fig. 10-25**) is a pure aquatint, printed in three colors, in which the roughness of the method's surface serves to underscore the emotional turmoil and psychological isolation embodied in her subject matter. "I'm interested," Dickson says, "in the ominous underside of contemporary culture that lurks as an ever-present possibility in our lives. . . . I aim to portray psychological states that everyone experiences." In looking at this print, one can almost feel the acid biting into the plate, as if the process itself is a metaphor for the pain and isolation of the figure leaning forlornly over the banister.

Lithography

What is lithography and how was it invented?

Lithography—meaning, literally, "stone writing"—is the chief **planographic printmaking process**, meaning that the printing surface is flat. There is no raised or depressed surface on the plate to hold ink. Rather, the method depends on the fact that grease and water don't mix.

The process was discovered accidentally by a young German playwright named Alois Senefelder in the 1790s in Munich. Unsuccessful in his occupation, Senefelder was determined to reduce the cost of publishing his plays by writing them backwards on a copper plate in a wax and soap ground and then etching the text. But with only one good piece of copper to his name, he knew he needed to practice writing backwards on less expensive material, and he chose a smooth piece of Kelheim limestone, the material used to line the Munich streets and thus abundantly available. As he was practicing one day, his laundry woman arrived to pick up his clothes and, with no paper or ink on the premises, he jotted down what she had taken on the prepared limestone slab. It dawned on him to bathe the stone with nitric acid and water, and when he did so, he found that the acid had etched the stone and left his writing raised in relief above its surface.

Recognizing the commercial potential of his invention, he abandoned the theater to perfect the process. By 1798, he had discovered that if he drew directly on the stone with a greasy crayon, and then treated the entire stone with nitric acid, water, and gum arabic (a very tough substance obtained from the acacia tree which attracts and holds water), then ink would stick to the grease drawing but not to the treated and dampened stone. He also discovered that the acid and gum arabic solution did not actually etch the limestone. As a result, the same stone could be used again and again. The essential processes of lithography had been invented.

Possibly because it is so direct a process, actually a kind of drawing on stone, lithography was the favorite printmaking medium of nineteenth- and twentieth-century artists. In the hands of Honoré Daumier, who turned to lithography to depict current events, the feeling of immediacy that the lithograph could inspire was most fully realized. From the early 1830s until his death in 1872, Daumier was employed by the French press as an illustrator and political caricaturist. Recognized as the greatest lithographer of his day, Daumier did some of his finest work in the 1830s for the monthly publication *L'Association Mensuelle*, each issue of which contained an original lithograph. His famous print *Rue Transnonain* (**Fig. 10-26**) is direct reportage of the

Fig. 10-26 Honoré Daumier, *Rue Transnonain, April 15, 1834*, 1834. Lithograph, 11½ × 17⅝ in.
The Art Institute of Chicago.
Rosenwald Collection, 1943.3.2957. Photo © Board of Trustees, National Gallery of Art, Washington, D.C.

outrages committed by government troops during an insurrection in the Parisian workers' quarters. He illustrates what happened in a building at 12 rue Transnonain on the night of April 15, 1834, when police, responding to a sniper's bullet that had killed one of their number and had appeared to originate from the building, revenged their colleague's death by slaughtering everyone inside. The father of a family, who had evidently been sleeping, lies dead by his bed, his child crushed beneath him, his dead wife to his right and an elder parent to his left. The foreshortening of the scene draws us into the lithograph's visual space, making the horror of the scene all the more real.

While lithography flourished as a medium throughout the twentieth century, it enjoyed a marked increase in popularity after the late 1950s. In 1957, Tatyana Grosman established Universal Limited Art Editions (ULAE) in West Islip, New York. Three years later, June Wayne founded the Tamarind Lithography Workshop in Los Angeles with a grant from the Ford Foundation. While Grosman's primary motivation was to make available to the best artists a quality printmaking environment, one of Wayne's main purposes was to train the printers themselves. Due to her influence, workshops sprang up across the country, including Gemini G.E.L. in Los Angeles, Tyler Graphics in Mount Kisco, New York, Landfall Press in Chicago, Cirrus Editions in Los Angeles, and Derrière l'Étoile in New York City.

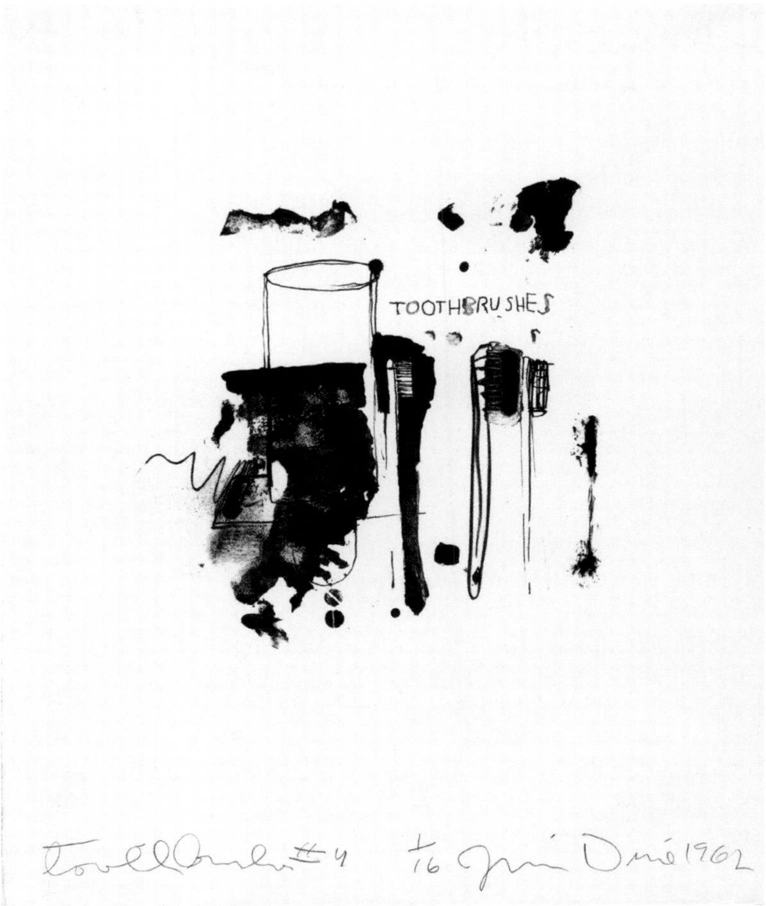

Fig. 10-27 Jim Dine, *Toothbrushes #4*, 1962. Lithograph, image (irregular) $13\frac{7}{16} \times 13\frac{7}{16}$ in., sheet $25\frac{1}{4} \times 19\frac{15}{16}$ in. Museum of Modern Art, New York. Gift of the Celeste and Armand Bartos Foundation, 353.1963. © 2015. Digital image, Museum of Modern Art, New York/Scala, Florence. © 2015 Jim Dine/Artists Rights Society (ARS), New York.

Among the earliest artists to print at ULAE was Jim Dine, who, when he went to West Islip in 1962 at Grosman's invitation, was undergoing intense psychoanalysis. His first prints depicted tools and common household items. The tools were personal symbols of his youth, when he had worked in his family's hardware stores in Ohio and Kentucky. A series of lithographs representing toothbrushes (**Fig. 10-27**) are recollections of his childhood as well, as if responding to the perennial parental question, "Have you brushed your teeth this morning?" Dine's images are drawn directly on the stone with **tusche**, a greasing liquid that also comes in a hardened crayonlike form, made of wax tallow, soap shellac, and lampblack, which is the best material for drawing on a lithographic stone. The sense of immediacy in these abstract gestures—the blotches and smudges of black ink that in fact recall the Abstract Expressionist gestures of Jackson Pollock (see Fig. 6-13)—stands in direct counterpoint to the realistic renderings of toothbrushes, glass, and printed word, as if Dine is literally blotting out his memories. In fact, the printed word "TOOTHBRUSHES" likewise contrasts with the handwritten title and autographic signature at the bottom of the print.

Silkscreen Printing

How are silkscreens made?

Silkscreens are more formally known as **serigraphs**, from the Greek *graphos*, "to write," and the Latin *seri*, "silk." Unlike other printmaking media, no expensive, heavy machinery is needed to make a serigraph. (That said, although simple silkscreens are often used to print T-shirts, even T-shirt printers have developed relatively sophisticated silkscreen machinery, and elaborate serigraphy studios containing extremely sophisticated machinery also exist.) The principles of the silkscreen process are essentially the same as those required for stenciling, where a shape is cut out of a piece of material and that shape is reproduced over and over on other surfaces by spreading ink or paint over the cutout. In serigraphy proper, shapes are not actually cut out. Rather, the fabric—silk or, more commonly today, nylon and polyester—is stretched tightly on a frame, and a stencil is made by painting a substance such as glue across the fabric in the areas where the artist does not want ink to pass through. Alternately, special films can be cut out and stuck to the fabric, or tusche can be used. This last method allows the artist a freedom of drawing that is close to the lithographic process. The areas that are left uncovered are those that will print. Silkscreen inks are very thick, so that they will not run beneath the edge of the cutout, and must be pushed through the open areas of the fabric with the blade of a tool called a squeegee.

Serigraphy is the newest form of printmaking, although related stencil techniques were employed in textile printing in China and Japan as early as 550 CE. Until the 1960s, serigraphy was used primarily in commercial printing, especially by the advertising industry. In fact, the word "serigraphy" was coined in 1935 by the curator of the Philadelphia Museum of Art in order to differentiate the work of artists using the silkscreen in creative ways from that of their commercially oriented counterparts.

In *Enter the Rice Cooker* (**Fig. 10-28**), Roger Shimomura addresses the tension between the two cultures within and between which he lives, the American culture in which he was raised, and the Japanese culture that is his heritage. A *shoji* screen, a Japanese room partition or sliding panel made of squares of translucent rice paper framed in black lacquered wood, divides the image. Behind the screen is a 1950s-type American woman, wearing a red evening glove and applying lipstick. On this side of the screen is a samurai warrior holding a modern electric rice cooker, a figure at once ferocious and, given the rice cooker, oddly domesticated. The title of the print is deliberately vague: Does it refer to the rice cooker he holds, or is he, in something of a racial slur, the "rice cooker"? (It is worth pointing out, in this context, that an electric rice cooker was the very first product of the Sony Corporation, introduced soon after World War II.) The print, in other words, addresses both racial and sexual stereotypes, even as it parodies the *ukiyo-e* tradition, especially *shunga*, or erotic, *ukiyo-e* prints. At the same time, Shimomura has used the silkscreen technique to evoke the banal world of Pop Art, which itself parodied the crass commercialism of Hollywood sexuality.

Fig. 10-28 Roger Shimomura, *Enter the Rice Cooker*, 1994.
Color screenprint on Saunders 410 gram HP, image 36 × 41 in. Edition of 170.
Spencer Museum of Art, University of Kansas.
Gift of the artist, 2005.0072.

Monotypes

How does the monotype process differ from other printmaking processes?

There is one last kind of printmaking for us to consider, one that has much in common with painting and drawing. However, **monotypes** are generally classified as a kind of printmaking because they use both a plate and a press in the making of the image. Unlike other prints, however, a monotype is a unique image. Once it is printed, it can never be printed again.

In monotypes, the artist forms an image on a plate with printer's ink or paints, and the image is transferred to paper under pressure, usually by means of an etching press. Part of the difficulty and challenge of the process is that if a top layer of paint is applied over a bottom layer of paint on the plate, when printed, the original bottom layer will be the top layer and vice versa. Thus, the foreground elements of a composition must be painted first on the plate, and the background elements over them. The process requires considerable planning.

One of the most prolific masters of the medium was Maurice Prendergast, who between 1892 and 1902 created about 200 works using the process. In a letter to a student and friend in 1905, he offered instructions about how to proceed with the process: "Paint on copper in oils, wiping

Fig. 10-29 Maurice Prendergast, *The Picnic*, ca. 1895–97.
Monotype, $8^{15}/_{16} \times 5^{13}/_{16}$ in. San Diego Museum of Art.
San Diego Museum of Art, USA/Museum purchase/Bridgeman Images.

parts to be white. When the picture suits you, place on it Japanese paper and either press in a press or rub with spoon till it please you." In fact, Prendergast's Boston studio was too small to accommodate a press, and he made his monotypes on the floor using a large spoon to transfer paint to paper. His characteristic subjects were young well-to-do women strolling on the seashore or relaxing in fields and parks, such as in *The Picnic* (**Fig. 10-29**). Quite evidently, what appealed to him about the process was the way in which the marks of his brushwork survive in the print—the finished print is clearly the result of energetic painting—and yet, in transferring the paint to paper, a kind of atmospheric haze results, in which drawing and line give way to patterns of light and color. The technique also possesses an element of surprise and discovery that fascinated Prendergast. His brother would recall that, "as he rubbed with the spoon, he would grow more and more excited, lifting up the paper at one of the corners to see what effects the paint was making." In some sense Prendergast's excitement summarizes the appeal of printmaking as a whole. As new techniques have been invented—from relief to intaglio to lithograph, silkscreen printing, and monotypes—the artist's imagination has been freed to discover ever-new means of representation and expression.

THE CRITICAL PROCESS

Thinking about Printmaking

Like Roger Shimomura, Andy Warhol is a Pop artist who recognized in silkscreen printing possibilities not only for making images but for commenting on American culture in general. In his many silkscreen images of Marilyn Monroe, almost all made within three or four years of her death in 1962, he depicted her in garish, conflicting colors (**Fig. 10-30**). Twenty years later, he created a series of silkscreen prints, commissioned by New York art dealer Ronald Feldman, of endangered species. What do the Marilyn silkscreens and images like *San Francisco Silverspot* (**Fig. 10-31**) from the *Endangered Species* series have in common? Think of Marilyn as both a person and a Hollywood image. What does it mean to be an "image"? How, in the case of the endangered species, might existing as an "image" be more useful than not? Consider the quality of color in both silkscreens. How does color affect the meaning of both works? Why do you think that Warhol resorts to such garish, bright coloration? Finally, how do both images suggest that Warhol was something of a social critic intent on challenging the values of mainstream America?

Fig. 10-30 Andy Warhol, *Marilyn Monroe*, 1967. Silkscreen print, 37½ × 37½ in. Chazen Museum of Art, University of Wisconsin–Madison.
Robert Gale Doyon Fund and Harold F. Bishop Fund Purchase, 1978-252. © 2015 Andy Warhol Foundation for the Visual Arts, Inc./Artists Rights Society (ARS), New York.

Fig. 10-31 Andy Warhol, *San Francisco Silverspot*, from the series *Endangered Species*, 1983. Screenprint, 38 × 38 in.
Courtesy of Ronald Feldman Fine Arts, New York. Photo: Dr. James Dee. © 2015 Andy Warhol Foundation for the Visual Arts, Inc./Artists Rights Society (ARS), New York.

Thinking Back

10.1 Define what a print is and discuss its earliest uses.

A print is a single impression of an image that has been transferred through pressure to a surface (usually paper). The image is transferred from a matrix, where the design has originally been created. A single matrix can be used to make many impressions, which are typically almost identical. What is an edition? How does an original print differ from a reproductive print? What are proofs?

Printmaking appears to have originated in China to illustrate the *Diamond Sutra*, and from the outset it was understood as a vehicle for the mass distribution of ideas and the popularization of iconographic and stylistic traditions. In Europe, printmaking developed rapidly after the appearance of the first printed book.

10.2 Characterize relief processes in printmaking.

Relief refers to any printmaking process in which the image to be printed is raised from the background in reverse. Woodcuts and rubber stamps are examples of relief printmaking processes. What are *nishiki-e* prints? What defines the method known as wood engraving? What is a linocut?

10.3 Characterize intaglio processes in printmaking.

The term intaglio comes from the Italian word for "engraving." In intaglio processes, the areas to be printed are below the surface of the plate. The matrix is a plate on which incised lines are filled with ink. Pressure transfers this ink to a surface, typically paper. What is stippling? How does engraving differ from etching? What defines the process known as mezzotint?

10.4 Describe the lithographic process and its invention.

Lithography means "stone writing." It is the chief planographic printmaking process, meaning that the surface of the matrix is flat. In lithography, the method for creating a printable image involves writing on a stone with a greasy crayon, which holds ink. Who invented lithography and for what purpose? What is tusche?

10.5 Describe the silkscreen process.

In silkscreen printing, or serigraphy, fabric is stretched tightly on a frame, and a stencil is made by painting a substance such as glue across the fabric in the areas where the artist does not want ink to pass through, or, alternately, special films can be cut out and stuck to the fabric. The areas left uncovered are those that will print. How does Roger Shimomura's *Enter the Rice Cooker* create a dialogue between American and Japanese cultures?

10.6 Differentiate monotypes from other kinds of print.

Monotypes differ from other kinds of print because they are unique images. In monotypes, the artist forms an image on a plate with printer's ink or paint, and the image is transferred to paper under pressure. What attracted Maurice Prendergast to the process?

Chapter 11

Photography and Time-Based Media

Learning Objectives

11.1 Describe the origins of photography and the formal principles that most inform it.

11.2 Describe how color and digital technologies have transformed photographic practice.

11.3 Outline the basic principles of film editing, including montage, as well as the technological developments that advanced the medium.

11.4 Outline some of the ways that video art has exploited the immediacy of the medium while at the same time critiquing popular culture.

11.5 Discuss some of the technological innovations that have advanced time-based art into the digital age.

In 2010, photographer Catherine Opie was asked to propose a permanent installation for a long corridor of the Cleveland Clinic's Hillcrest Hospital in Mayfield Heights, Ohio, not far from where the artist grew up, in Sandusky, Ohio, on the shores of Lake Erie. Opie, who is famous, among other things, for her ongoing studies of the horizon line, wanted to capture the inherent beauty of the lake shore in northern Ohio—the special qualities of its light—as well as provide a space for patients, visitors, doctors, and other hospital employees to find in her work an uplifting, perhaps even transcendent experience during what might well be a difficult time of their lives. (Opie talks about the work as it was being installed in the art21 *Exclusive* video "Catherine Opie: Cleveland Clinic.")

To make the piece, Opie traveled six times to Ohio over the course of 12 months, photographing along the Lake Erie shoreline from Cleveland to Port Clinton, across Sandusky Bay. The finished work, titled *Somewhere in the Middle* (a reference both to "Middle America" and to the horizon line that divides the photographs in half), consists of 22 photographs, beginning and ending with images of the Cleveland shoreline, the city rising behind it, but the central 17 document the four seasons as they are reflected on the lake itself. "In spring I came in," she recalls, speaking of four photographs of which *Untitled #13 (Spring)* (**Fig. 11-1**) is the second, "the ice was just starting to melt, and by the fifth day the ice had completely melted. So in those four images you have the sequence of the lake going back to water." At first glance, the water seems to reflect clouds in the sky above, until one recognizes that the billowy white forms are actually ice breaking up on the lake. But like stills from a film, these four photographs capture progress across five days, and the sequence as a whole, a year's passing. Opie's sequence, in fact, illustrates one of the fundamental characteristics of her medium. Photography is addressed to time. It captures time, holding the moment in its grasp in perpetuity.

Photography began, in about 1838, with still images, but the still image almost immediately generated the thought that it might be possible to capture the object in

Fig. 11-1 Catherine Opie, *Untitled #13 (Spring)*, from *Somewhere in the Middle*, suite of 22 photographs installed at the Cleveland Clinic's Hillcrest Hospital, 2011. Inkjet print, 50 × 37½ in.

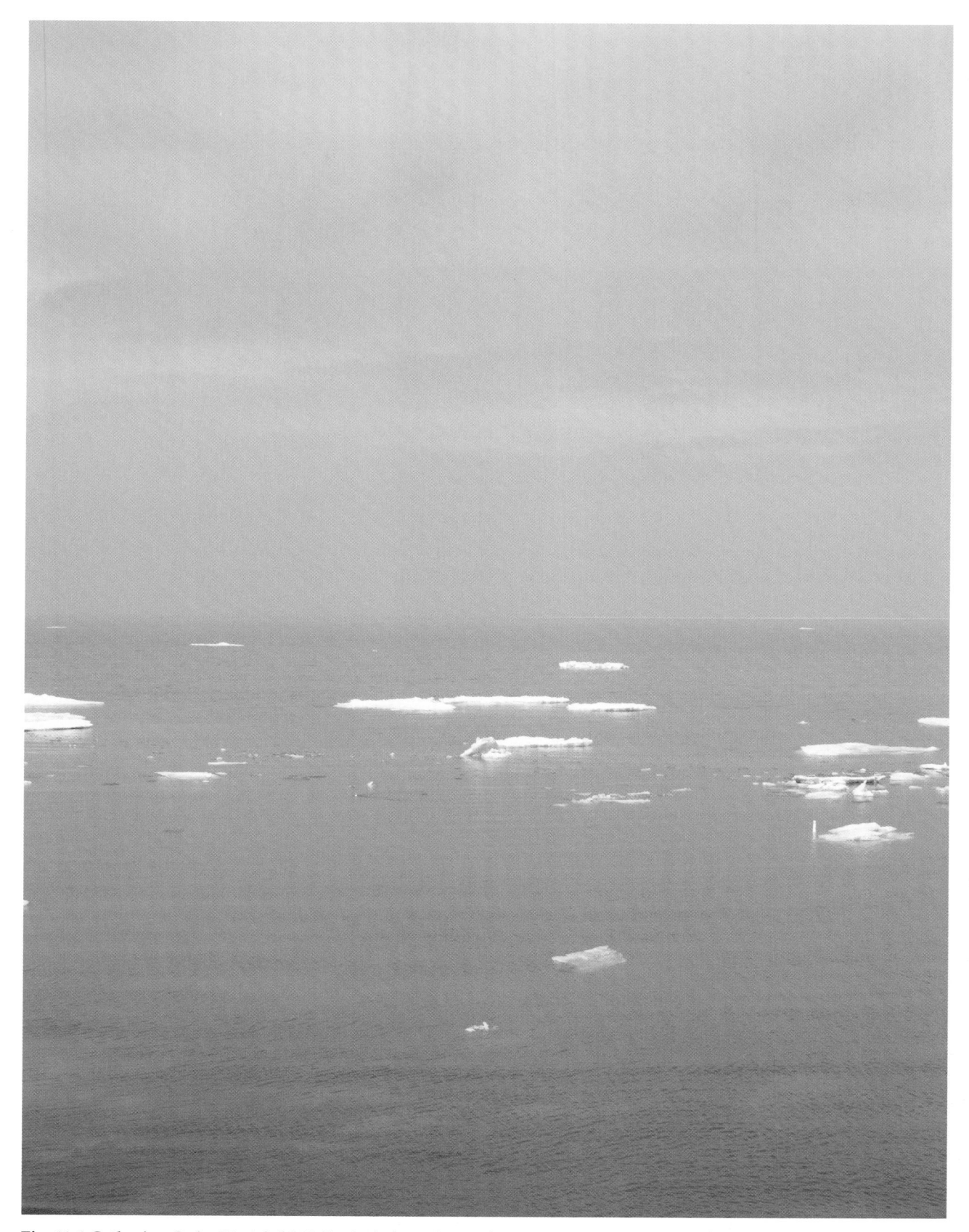

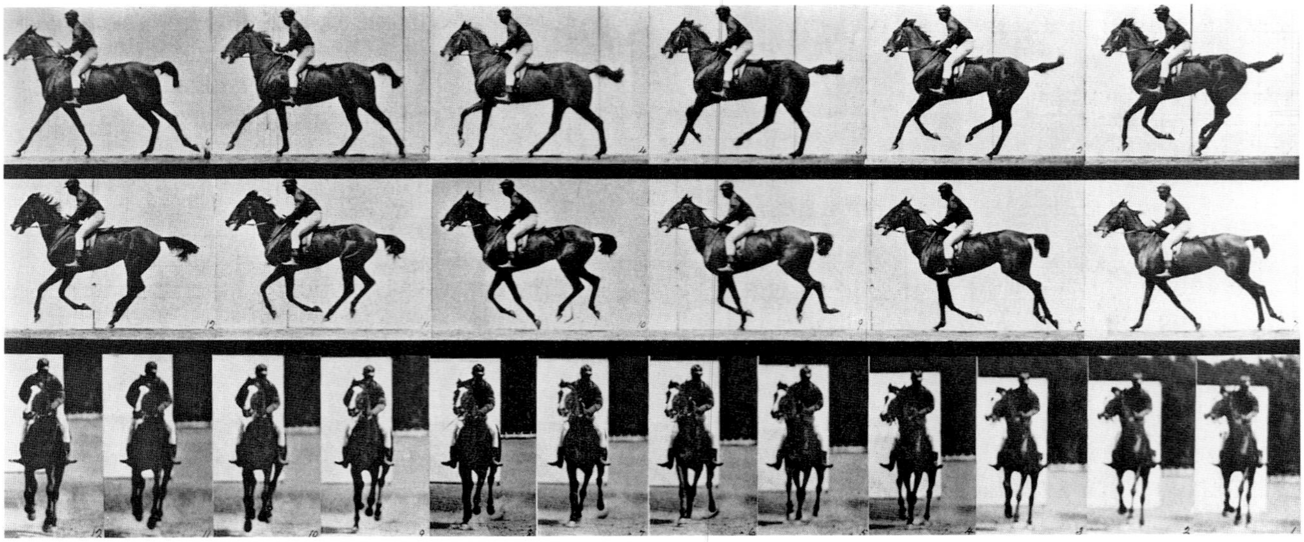

Fig. 11-2 Eadweard Muybridge, *Annie G., Cantering, Saddled*, December 1887. Collotype print, sheet 19 × 24⅛ in., image 7¼ × 16¼ in. Philadelphia Museum of Art.
1962-135-280. © 2015. Photo Philadelphia Museum of Art/Art Resource/Scala, Florence.

motion as well. Such a dream seemed even more possible when photographs of a horse trotting were published by Eadweard Muybridge in *La Nature* in 1878 (**Fig. 11-2**). Muybridge had used a trip-wire device in an experiment commissioned by California governor Leland Stanford to settle a bet about whether there were moments in the stride of a trotting or galloping horse when it was entirely free of the ground.

Work such as Muybridge's soon inspired Thomas Edison and W. K. Laurie Dickson to invent, between 1888 and 1892, the Kinetoscope, the first continuous-film motion-picture viewing machine, itself made possible by George Eastman's introduction of celluloid film that came on a roll, produced expressly for his new camera, the Kodak. Dickson devised a sprocket wheel that would advance the regularly perforated roll of film, and Edison decided on a 35 mm width for the strip of film (eventually the industry standard). But Edison's films were only viewable on the Kinetoscope through a peephole, one person at a time.

The first projected motion pictures available to a large audience had their public debut on December 28, 1895, in Paris, when August and Louis Lumière showed ten films, projected by their Cinématographe, the first motion-picture apparatus, that lasted for about 20 minutes. Among the most popular of their early films was *L'Arroseur Arrosé* (*Waterer and Watered*) (**Fig. 11-3**), in which a boy steps on a gardener's hose, stopping the flow of water. When the gardener looks at the nozzle, the boy steps off the hose, and the gardener douses himself. A brief chase ensues, with both boy and gardener leaving the frame of the stationary camera for a full two seconds. Audiences howled with delight.

To the silent moving image, sound was soon added. To the "talkie" was added color. And film developed in its audience a taste for "live" action, a taste satisfied by live television transmission, video images that allow us to view anything happening in the world as it happens. Thus, not unlike the history of painting, the history of time-based media is a history of increasing immediacy and verisimilitude, or semblance to the truth. In this chapter, we will survey that history, starting with still photography, moving to film and, finally, to video. Our focus will be on these media in relation to art.

Fig. 11-3 Poster for the Cinématographe, with the Lumière Brothers film *L'Arroseur Arrosé* (*Waterer and Watered*) on screen, 1895. British Film Institute.
Mary Evans/Iberfoto.

The Early History and Formal Foundations of Photography

How did photography develop and what formal concerns most define it?

Photography (from the Greek *phos*, "light," and *graphos*, "writing," literally "writing with light") is, like collage, at least potentially an inclusive rather than an exclusive medium. You can photograph anything you can see. As one historian of American photography has put it: "The world is essentially a storehouse of visual information. Creation is the process of assemblage. The photograph is a process of instant assemblage, instant collage." Walker Evans's photograph *Roadside Stand near Birmingham, Alabama* (**Fig. 11-4**) is an example of just such "instant collage." Evans's mission as a photographer was to capture every aspect of American visual reality, and his work has been called a "photographic equivalent to the Sears, Roebuck catalog of the day." But the urge to make such instant visual assemblages—to capture a moment in time—is as old as the desire to represent the world accurately. We will begin our discussion of photography by considering the development of the technology itself, and then we will consider the fundamental aesthetic problem photography faces—the tension between form and content, the tension between the way a photograph is formally organized as a composition and what it expresses or means.

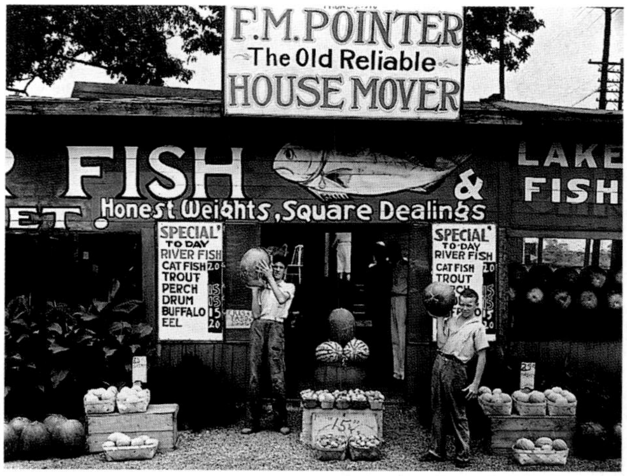

Fig. 11-4 Walker Evans, *Roadside Stand near Birmingham, Alabama*, 1936. Library of Congress.

Early History

Camera is the Latin word for "room." And, in fact, by the sixteenth century, a darkened room, called a camera obscura, was routinely used by artists to copy nature accurately. The scientific principle employed is essentially the same as that used by the camera today. A small hole on the side of a light-tight room admits a ray of light that projects a scene, upside down, directly across from the hole onto a white wall. The camera obscura depicted here (**Fig. 11-5**) was an invention of necessity, designed to allow for the observation of an eclipse of the sun without looking directly at its potentially blinding light.

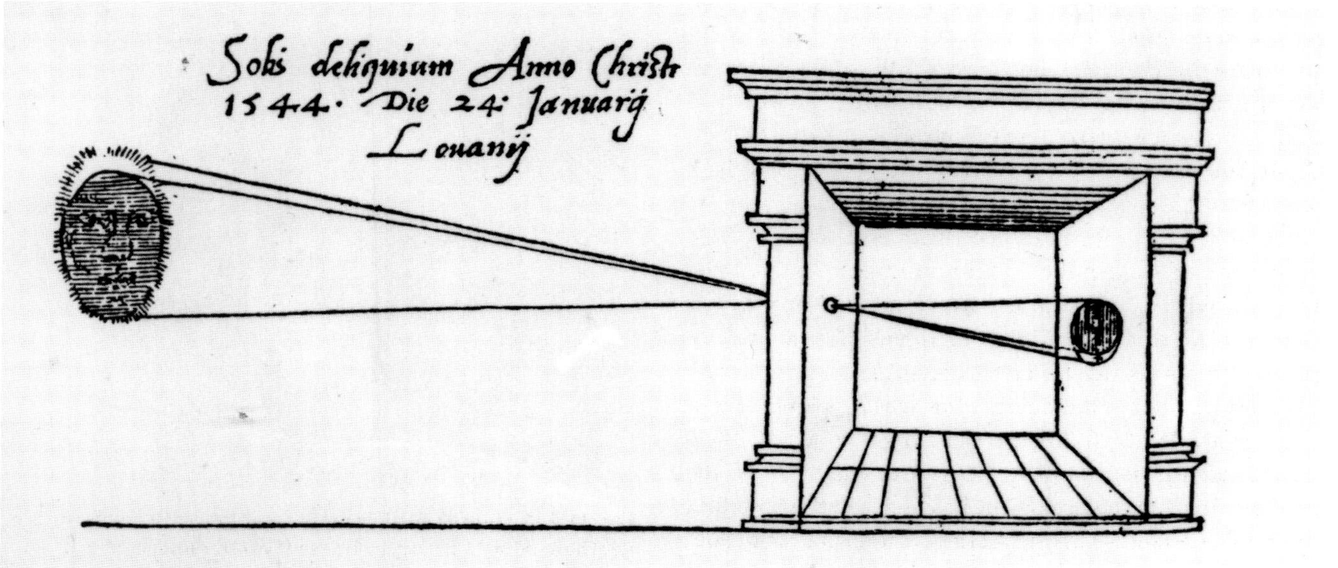

Fig. 11-5 The first published illustration of a camera obscura observing a solar eclipse, published in 1544 by Dutch cartographer and mathematician Gemma Frisius. Woodcut. Bridgeman Images.

Fig. 11-6 William Henry Fox Talbot, *Mimosoidea Suchas, Acacia*, ca. 1841. Photogenic drawing. National Media Museum, Bradford, UK.
1937-366/14. National Media Museum/Science & Society Picture Library.

But working with the camera obscura was a tedious proposition, even after small portable dark boxes came into use. The major drawback was that while it could capture the image, it could not independently preserve it. Artists had to trace its projections onto paper or canvas. In 1839, that problem was solved simultaneously in England and France, and the public was introduced to a new way of representing the world.

In England, William Henry Fox Talbot presented a process for fixing negative images on paper coated with light-sensitive chemicals, a process that he called **photogenic drawing** (**Fig. 11-6**). In France, a different process, which yielded a positive image on a polished metal plate, was named the **daguerreotype** (**Fig. 11-7**), after one of its two inventors, Louis-Jacques-Mandé Daguerre (Nicéphore Niépce had died in 1833, leaving Daguerre to perfect the process and garner the laurels). Public reaction was wildly enthusiastic, and the French and English press faithfully reported every development in the greatest detail.

When he saw his first daguerreotype, the French painter Paul Delaroche is reported to have exclaimed, "From now on, painting is dead!" Delaroche may have overreacted, but he nevertheless understood the potential of the new medium of photography to usurp painting's historical role of representing the world. In fact,

Fig. 11-7 Louis-Jacques-Mandé Daguerre, *Le Boulevard du Temple*, 1839. Daguerreotype. Bavarian National Museum, Munich.
© Corbis.

photographic portraiture quickly became a successful industry. As early as 1841, a daguerreotype portrait could be had in Paris for 15 francs (approximately $225 today). That same year in London, Richard Beard opened the first British portrait studio, bringing a true sense of showmanship to the process. One of his first customers, the novelist Maria Edgeworth, described having her portrait done at Beard's in a breathless letter dated May 25, 1841:

> It is a wonderful mysterious operation. You are taken from one room into another upstairs and down and you see various people whispering and hear them in neighboring passages and rooms unseen and the whole apparatus and stool on a high platform under a glass dome casting a snapdragon blue light making all look like spectres and the men in black gliding about.

In the face of such a "miracle," the art of portrait painting underwent a rapid decline. Of the 1,278 paintings exhibited at the Royal Academy in London in 1830, more than 300 were miniatures, the most popular form of the portrait; in 1870, only 33 miniatures were exhibited. In 1849 alone, 100,000 daguerreotype portraits were sold in Paris. Not only had photography replaced painting as the preferred medium for portraiture, it had democratized the genre as well, making portraits available not only to the wealthy, but also to the middle class, and even, with some sacrifice, to the working class.

The daguerreotype itself had some real disadvantages as a medium, however. In the first place, it required considerable time to prepare, expose, and develop the plate. Iodine was vaporized on a copper sheet to create light-sensitive silver iodide. The plate then had to be kept in total darkness until the camera lens was opened to expose it. At the time Daguerre first made the process public in 1839, imprinting an image on the plate took from 8 to 10 minutes in bright summer light. His own view of the Boulevard du Temple (see Fig. 11-7) was exposed for so long that none of the people in the street, going about their business, left any impression on the plate, save for one solitary figure at the lower left, who is having his shoes shined. By 1841, the discovery of so-called chemical "accelerators" had made it possible to expose the plate for only one minute, but a sitter could not move in that time for fear of blurring the image. The plate was finally developed by suspending it face down in heated mercury, which deposited a white film over the exposed areas. The unexposed silver iodide was dissolved with salt. The plate then had to be rinsed and dried with the utmost care.

An even greater drawback of the daguerreotype was that it could not be reproduced. Using paper instead of a metal plate, Talbot's photogenic process made multiple prints a possibility. Talbot quickly learned that he could reverse the negative image of the photogenic drawings by placing sheets of sensitized paper over them and exposing both again to sunlight. Talbot also discovered that sensitized paper, exposed for even a few seconds, held a latent image that could be brought out and developed by dipping the paper in gallic acid. This **calotype** process is the basis of modern photography.

In 1843, Talbot made a picture, which he called *The Open Door* (**Fig. 11-8**), that convinced him that the calotype could not only document the world as we know it,

Fig. 11-8 William Henry Fox Talbot, *The Open Door*, 1843. Calotype. National Museum of Photography, London.
Digital image courtesy of Getty's Open Content Program.

but also become a work of art in its own right. When he published the image in his book *The Pencil of Nature*, the first book of photographs ever produced, he captioned it as follows: "A painter's eye will often be arrested where ordinary people see nothing remarkable. A casual gleam of sunshine, or a shadow thrown across his path, a time-withered oak, or a moss-covered stone may awaken a train of thoughts and feelings, and picturesque imaginings." For Talbot, at least, painters and photographers saw the world as one.

In 1850, the English sculptor Frederick Archer introduced a new **wet-plate collodion** photographic process that was almost universally adopted within five years. In a darkened room, he poured liquid collodion—made of pyroxyline dissolved in alcohol or ether—over a glass plate bathed in a solution of silver nitrate. The plate had to be prepared, exposed, and developed all within 15 minutes and while still wet. The process was cumbersome, but the exposure time was short and the rewards were quickly realized.

On her forty-ninth birthday, in 1864, Julia Margaret Cameron, the wife of a high-placed British civil servant and friend to many of the most famous people of her day, was given a camera and collodion-processing equipment by her daughter and son-in-law. "It may amuse you, Mother, to photograph," the accompanying note said. Cameron set up a studio in a chicken coop at her home on the Isle of Wight, and over the course of the next ten years convinced almost everyone she knew to pose for her, among them the greatest men of British art, literature, and science. She often blurred their features slightly, believing this technique drew attention away from mere physical appearance and revealed more of her sitter's inner character. Commenting on her photographs of famous men like Thomas Carlyle (**Fig. 11-9**), she wrote, "When I have had such men before my camera, my whole soul has endeavored to do its duty towards them in recording faithfully the greatness of the inner man as well as the features of the outer man. The photograph thus taken has been almost the embodiment of a prayer."

More than anything else, the ability of the portrait photographer to expose, as it were, the "soul" of the sitter led the French government to give photography the legal status of art as early as 1862. But from the beginning, photography served a documentary function as well—it recorded and preserved important events. Photographs of war, which initially startled audiences, were first published during the Crimean War, fought between Russia and an alliance of European countries and the declining Ottoman Empire in 1854–56. At the outbreak of the American Civil War, in 1861, Mathew Brady spent the entirety of his considerable fortune to outfit a band of photographers to document the war. When Brady insisted that he owned the copyright for every photograph taken by anyone in his

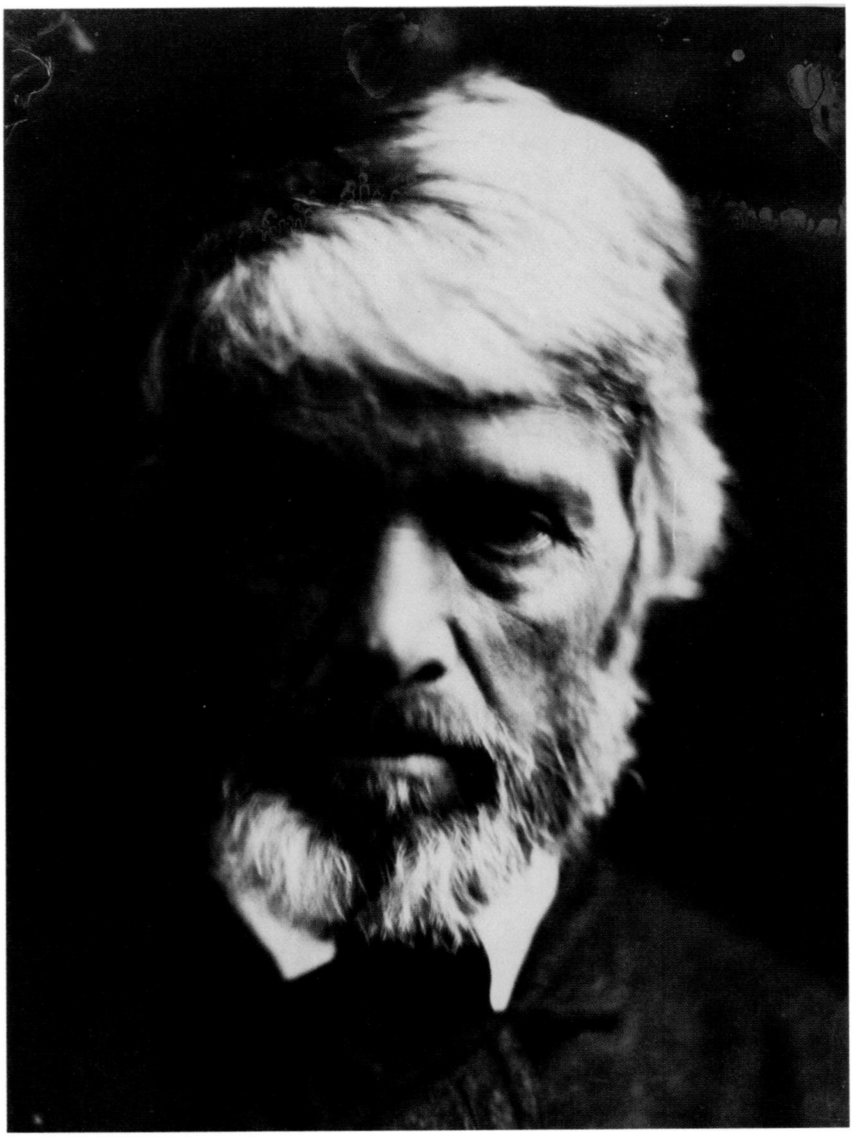

Fig. 11-9 Julia Margaret Cameron, *Portrait of Thomas Carlyle*, 1863.
Albumen print, 14 7/16 × 10 3/16 in. The J. Paul Getty Museum.
Digital image courtesy of Getty's Open Content Program.

employ, whether it was made on the job or not, several of his best photographers quit, among them Timothy O'Sullivan and Alexander Gardner. *A Harvest of Death, Gettysburg, Pennsylvania, July 1863* (**Fig. 11-10**) was published after the war in 1866 in *Gardner's Photographic Sketchbook of the War*, probably the first book-length photo-essay. It is a condemnation of the horrors of war, with the Battle of Gettysburg at its center. O'Sullivan's matter-of-fact photograph is accompanied by the following caption:

> The rebels represented in the photograph are without shoes. These were always removed from the feet of the dead on account of the pressing need of the survivors. The pockets turned inside out also show that appropriation did not cease with the coverings of the feet. Around is scattered the litter of the battlefield, accoutrements, ammunitions, rags, cups and canteens, crackers, haversacks, and letters that may tell the name of the owner, although the majority will surely be buried unknown by strangers, and in a strange land.

In O'Sullivan's photograph, both foreground and background are intentionally blurred to draw attention to the central corpses. Such focus was made possible by the introduction of albumen paper, which retained a high degree of sharpness on its glossy surface. "Such a picture," Gardner wrote, "conveys a useful moral: It shows the blank horror and reality of war, in opposition to the pageantry. Here are the dreadful details! Let them aid in preventing such another calamity falling upon the nation." One of the first great photojournalists, O'Sullivan is reported to have photographed calmly

Fig. 11-10 Timothy O'Sullivan (negative) and Alexander Gardner (print), *A Harvest of Death, Gettysburg, Pennsylvania, July 1863*, from *Gardner's Photographic Sketchbook of the War*, 1866. Albumen silver print (also available as a stereocard), 6¼ × 7$^{13}/_{16}$ in. Library of Congress, Washington, D.C.

during the most horrendous bombardments, twice having his camera hit by shell fragments.

Form and Content

It might be said that every photograph is an abstraction, a simplification of reality that substitutes two-dimensional for three-dimensional space, an instant of perception for the seamless continuity of time, and, in black-and-white work at least, the gray scale for color. By emphasizing formal elements over representational concerns, the artist further underscores this abstract side of the medium (see, for instance, the photographs by Paul Strand, Figs. 4-25 and 4-26). One of the greatest sources of photography's hold on the popular imagination lies in this ability to aestheticize the everyday—to reveal as beautiful that which we normally take for granted. When he shot his groundbreaking photograph *The Steerage* (**Fig. 11-11**) in 1907, American photographer Alfred Stieglitz was transfixed not by the literal figures and objects in his viewfinder, but by the spatial relations. "There were men, women, and children," he wrote,

> on the lower level of the steerage [the lower class deck of a steamship]. . . . The scene fascinated me: A round straw hat; the funnel leaning left, the stairway leaning right; the white drawbridge, its railings made of chain; white suspenders crossed on the

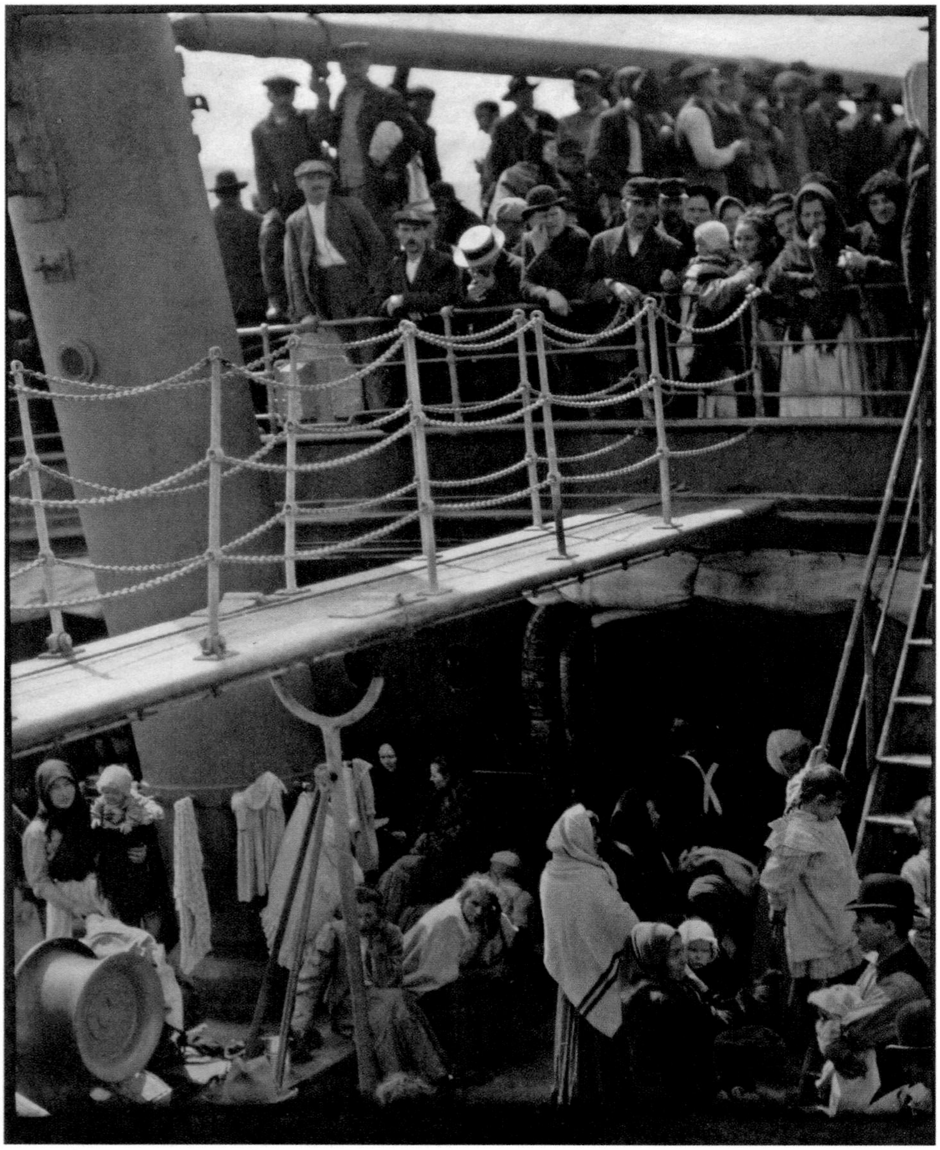

Fig. 11-11 Alfred Stieglitz, *The Steerage*, 1907. Photogravure, 12⅝ × 10$^{3}/_{16}$ in. Museum of Modern Art, New York.

Provenance unknown, 526.1986. © 2015. Digital image, Museum of Modern Art, New York/Scala, Florence. © 2015 Georgia O'Keeffe Museum/Artists Rights Society (ARS), New York.

> back of a man below; circular iron machinery; a mast that cut into the sky, completing a triangle. I stood spellbound for a while. I saw shapes related to one another—a picture of shapes, and underlying it, a new vision that held me.

It is no coincidence, given this point of view, that Stieglitz was the first to reproduce the photographs of Paul Strand—*Abstraction, Porch Shadows* in particular (see Fig. 4-25)—in his photography magazine *Camera Work*, which he published from 1903 to 1916. And the geometric beauty of Stieglitz's work deeply influenced Charles Sheeler, who was hired by Henry Ford to photograph the new Ford factory at River Rouge in the late 1920s (**Fig. 11-12**). Sheeler's precise task was to aestheticize Ford's plant. His photographs, which were immediately recognized for their artistic merit and subsequently exhibited around the world, were designed to celebrate industry. They revealed, in the smokestacks, conveyors, and iron latticework of the factory, a grandeur and proportion not unlike that of the great Gothic cathedrals of Europe.

Even when the intention is simply to bring the facts to light, as is often true in photojournalism, the power of the photograph frequently comes from the aesthetic charge of the work lent to it by its formal composition. In the 1930s, in the wake of the Great Depression, the Federal government's Farm Security Administration (FSA) initiated a photographic project employing some 15 photographers to document the plight of America's famers. During its eight-year existence, the Farm Security Administration created over 77,000 black-and-white documentary photographs. Of them all, the most well known today are those by Walker Evans, which were first published in *Let Us Now Praise Famous Men*, a book produced in 1941 with writer James Agee. The book's title is ironic, for its subjects are the least famous, the poorest of the poor: sharecroppers, the men, women, and children of Depression-ridden central Alabama in the summer of 1936 when Agee and Evans lived among them. But again, it is the simple life and inherent nobility of these poor people that form Evans and Agee's theme. Their almost stoic heroism is captured in the rich textures and clean lines of Evans's photograph of a sharecropper's humble dwelling (**Fig. 11-13**). The photo is a revelation of stark beauty in the middle of sheer poverty.

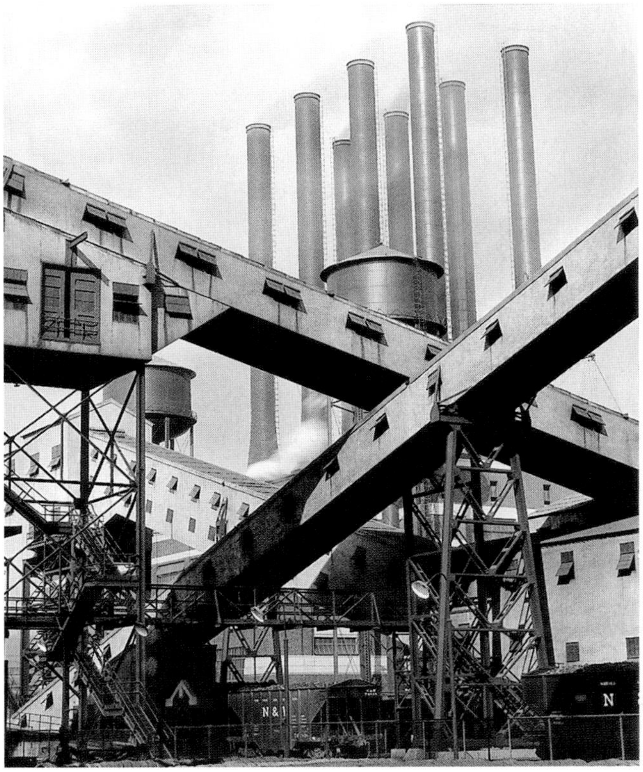

Fig. 11-12 Charles Sheeler, *Criss-Crossed Conveyors—Ford Plant*, 1927. Gelatin silver print, 10 × 8 in. Museum of Fine Arts, Boston.

© Lane Collection. Courtesy Museum of Fine Arts, Boston.

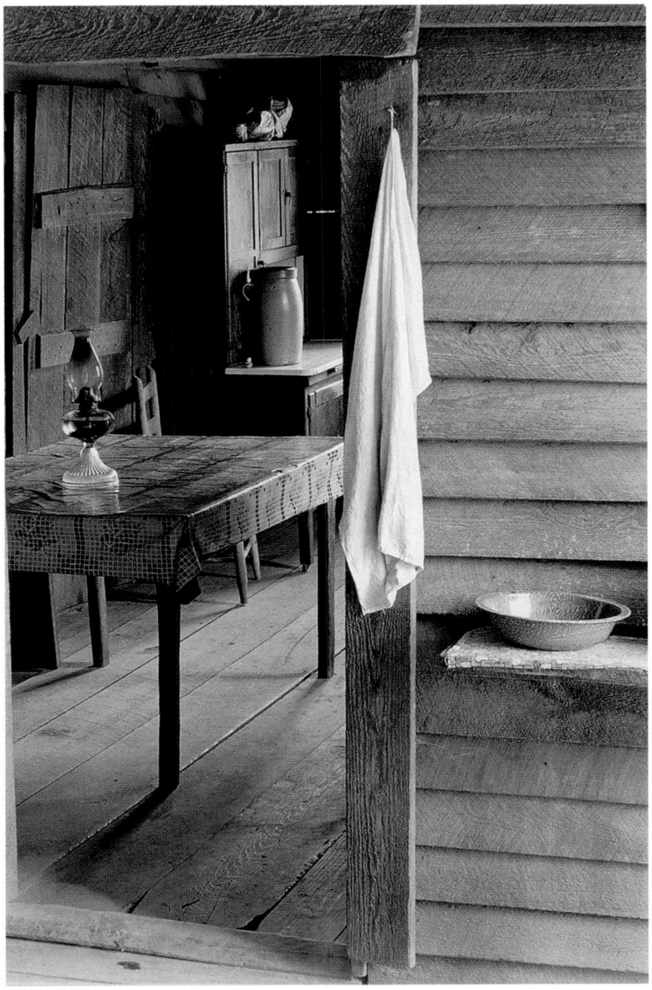

Fig. 11-13 Walker Evans, *Alabama Tenant Farmer's Kitchen (Washstand with View into Dining Area of Burroughs' Home, Hale County, Alabama)*, 1936. 35 mm photograph.

Courtesy of Library of Congress. Image copyright Walker Evans Archive, Metropolitan Museum of Art, New York.

Fig. 11-14 An-My Lê, *29 Palms: Night Operations III*, 2003–04. Gelatin silver print, 26 × 37½ in.

Evans's work depends for much of its power not only on the elegance of its formal composition but on our own certainty that the image is authentic and unmediated. Vietnamese-born but American-educated An-My Lê's work contests the boundaries of the actual. Her 2003 series of photographs *29 Palms* (**Fig. 11-14**) depicts the training maneuvers of personnel preparing for deployment to Afghanistan and Iraq at the 29 Palms, California, Marine Air Ground Task Force Training Command. She is as interested in the landscape that she photographs, in this case the Mojave Desert near Joshua Tree National Park, as she is in the actual events, which are themselves staged reenactments. Her work describes, in fact, the relationship of war—even "fake" war—with the landscape itself. She explains:

> I'm fascinated by the military structure, by strategy, the idea of a battle, the gear. But at the same time, how do you resolve the impact of it? What it is meant to do is just horrible. But war can be beautiful. I think it's the idea of the sublime—moments that are horrific but, at the same time, beautiful—moments of communion with the landscape and nature. And it's that beauty that I wanted to embrace in my work. I think that's why the work seems ambiguous. And it's meant to be.

Her work, in other words, captures something of the feeling of Timothy O'Sullivan's *Harvest of Death* (see Fig. 11-10). It turns out that O'Sullivan and his fellow photographers working for Mathew Brady often staged their photographs, not out of any sense of deceit but in order to heighten the dramatic effect of the image. O'Sullivan may or may not have moved the bodies of the soldiers in his photograph to heighten its visual impact, but he did lower the camera angle and raise the horizon line to fill as much of the image as possible with the dead. It was not factual but emotional truth that was O'Sullivan's object. Likewise, if the "battle" in the Mojave Desert that Lê has photographed is staged, with the result that the images are akin to black-and-white film stills from, say, Francis Ford Coppola's *Apocalypse Now*, the work nonetheless embodies something of the national psyche. It represents at some level who Lê believes the American people are.

The ambiguity of An-My Lê's images is analogous, in fact, to the chief characteristic of their formal compositions. Talking about the ways in which he arrived at the photographic image, the great French photographer Henri Cartier-Bresson described the relationship between form and content in the following terms:

> We must place ourselves and our camera in the right relationship with the subject, and it is in fitting the latter into the frame of the viewfinder that the problems of composition begin. This recognition, in real life, of a rhythm of surfaces, lines, and values is for me the essence of photography. . . . We compose almost at the moment of pressing the shutter. . . . Sometimes one remains motionless, waiting for something to happen; sometimes the situation is resolved and there is nothing to photograph. If something should happen, you remain alert, wait a bit, then shoot and go off with the sensation of having got something. Later you can amuse yourself by tracing out on the photo the geometrical pattern, or spatial relationships, realizing that, by releasing the shutter at that precise instant, you had instinctively selected an exact geometrical harmony, and that without this the photograph would have been lifeless.

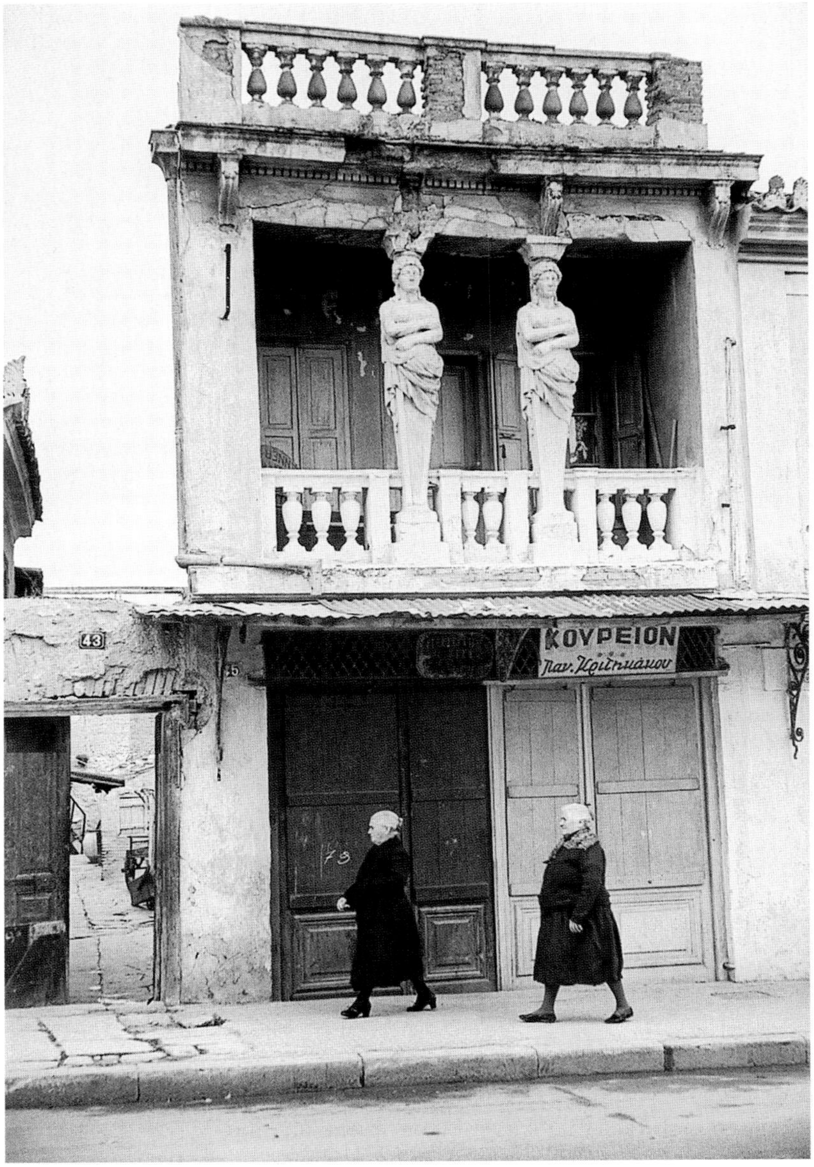

Fig. 11-15 Henri Cartier-Bresson, *Athens*, 1953.
Magnum Photos, Inc.

Thus, in looking at this photograph (**Fig. 11-15**), we can imagine Cartier-Bresson walking down a street in Athens, Greece, one day in 1953, and coming across the second-story balcony with its references to the Classical past. Despite the doorways behind the balcony, the second story appears to be a mere facade. Cartier-Bresson stops, studies the scene, waits, and then spies two women walking up the street in his direction. They pass beneath the two female forms on the balcony above and, at precisely that instant, he releases the shutter. Cartier-Bresson called this "the decisive moment." Later, in the studio, the parallels and harmonies between street and balcony, antiquity and the present moment, youth and age, white marble and black dresses, stasis and change—all captured in this photograph—become apparent to him, and he prints the image.

The Photographic Print and its Manipulation

For many photographers, the real art of photography takes place not behind the viewfinder but in the darkroom (see *The Creative Process*, pp. 252–53, for an example of Jerry Uelsmann's darkroom techniques). Among the masters of darkroom techniques was Ansel Adams who, with colleague Fred Archer, developed the **Zone System** in the late 1930s.

Fig. 11-16 Ansel Adams, *Moonrise, Hernandez, New Mexico*, 1941. Gelatin silver print, 18½ × 23 in.

Adams defined the Zone System as "a framework for understanding exposures and development, and visualizing their effect in advance." A zone represents the relation of the image's (or a portion of the image's) brightness to the value or tone that the photographer wishes it to appear in the final print. Thus each picture is broken up into zones ranging from black to white with nine shades of gray in between—a photographic gray scale (see Fig. 5-5).

Over the course of his career, Adams became adept at anticipating the zonal relationships that he desired in the final print, even as he was first exposing his negatives to light. As a result, just in setting his camera's **aperture**—the size of the opening of the lens—he could go a long way toward establishing the luminescence of the scene that he wanted.

Fig. 11-17 Gary Alvis, *The Painted Hills*, John Day Fossil Beds National Monument, Oregon, 2008. Six-stitch Cibachrome print, dimensions variable.

"I began to think about how the print would appear and if it would transmit any of the feeling of the . . . shape before me in terms of its expressive-emotional quality," he wrote in his autobiography. "I began to see in my mind's eye the finished print I desired." He called this a process of "visualization," a process never fully completed until he was working in the darkroom. He often spent hours and hours in the darkroom creating the image that he felt represented his initial visualization. There, he employed the techniques of dodging and burning to attain the finish he desired. **Dodging** decreases the exposure of selected areas of the print that the photographer wishes to be lighter; **burning** increases the exposure to areas of the print that should be darker. To dodge an area of a print, he might hold a piece of cardboard over it. To burn an area, he might hold a thick piece of paper with a hole cut out of it over the area that he wished to darken.

In one of his most famous prints, *Moonrise, Hernandez, New Mexico* (**Fig. 11-16**), large parts of the sky are burned, while the village, which was fast falling into darkness as the sun set on the afternoon that he took this photograph, is dodged to bring out more of its detail. If the sky was actually never this dark against the rising moon, and if the village was more in shadow, the stunning contrast between light and dark, as if we stand in this photograph at the very cusp of day's transition into night, captures the emotional feeling that Adams first visualized when he saw the scene, drove his car into the deep shoulder of the road, and hauled his equipment into place to take the photograph. It represents the essence, he felt, of a changing world.

Color and Digital Photography

How have color and digital technologies transformed photographic practice?

Until the late 1960s, color was largely ignored by fine art photographers, who associated it with advertising. In fact, until the 1960s, color could only be processed in commercial labs and the images tended to discolor rapidly, and so most photographers worked with the technology they could control—black-and-white. But, in the 1970s, Kodak introduced new color technologies that allowed for far greater fidelity, control, luminosity, and durability.

In color photography, the formal tensions of black-and-white photography are not necessarily lost. Throughout his career, Gary Alvis has worked in both black-and-white and color. In *The Painted Hills* (**Fig. 11-17**), the cool blues of mountain and sky contrast dramatically with the warm ochers and oranges of the desert landscape. Alvis actually constructed this photograph by digitally stitching together six different shots of the place, taken over the course of several years, visiting the site at the same time of year each time.

The Creative Process

The Darkroom as Laboratory: Jerry Uelsmann's *Untitled*

Jerry Uelsmann considers his camera "a license to explore." In many ways, for him photography is not so much the act of capturing a "decisive moment" on film, but the activity that occurs afterward, in the darkroom. The darkroom is a laboratory, where the real implications of what he has photographed can be explored. Uelsmann calls this process "post-visualization."

Uelsmann begins by photographing both the natural world and the human figure. Sometimes, though not always, the two come together in the finished work. He examines his contact sheets, looking for material that interests him and that somehow, in his imagination, might fit together—a rock with a splattering of bird excrement (**Fig. 11-18**), a grove of trees (**Fig. 11-19**), hands about to touch each other (**Fig. 11-20**). He then covers over all the other information in the photograph, framing the material of interest. Each image rests on its own enlarger, and moving from one enlarger to the next, he prints each part in sequence on the final print. The resulting image possesses something of the character of a Surrealist landscape (see Chapter 20). As Uelsmann explains:

> I am involved with a kind of reality that transcends surface reality. More than physical reality, it is emotional, irrational,

Figs. 11-18, 11-19, and 11-20 Jerry Uelsmann, *Untitled*.

Fig. 11-21 Jerry Uelsmann, *Untitled* (first version).

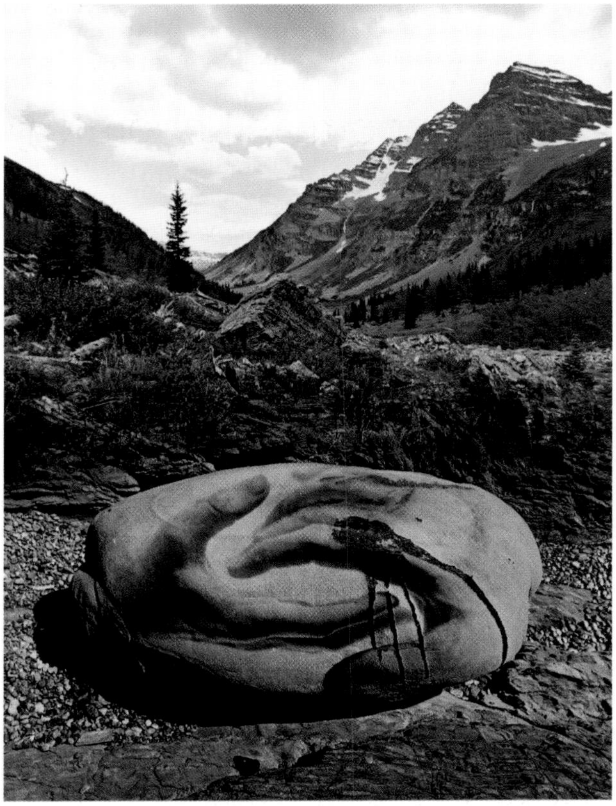

Fig. 11-22 Jerry Uelsmann, *Untitled* (second version).

> intellectual, and psychological. It is because of the fact that these other forms of reality don't exist as specific, tangible objects that I can honestly say that subject matter is only a minor consideration which proceeds after the fact and not before.

In other words, what drives Uelsmann first and foremost is the formal relations among the elements—the formal similarity between, say, the shape of the hands and that of the rock—the way in which the images seem to work together whatever their actual content.

One of the most powerful transformations generated in the post-visualization process is the effect of a wound on one of the two hands, and with it the suggestion of a healing touch or at least a helpful hand being offered by one hand to the other. In the first version of the print (**Fig. 11-21**), the stone containing the hands thus becomes an egglike symbol of nurturing, a sort of life force lying beneath the roots of nature itself. But Uelsmann was by no means satisfied with the image, and he returned to his contact sheets. In a second version (**Fig. 11-22**), he placed the hands and stone in the foreground of a mountain landscape. Here, the lines of the hands formally echo the lines of the mountains beyond. The final print seems more mysterious than the earlier version. It is, as Uelsmann is fond of saying, "obviously symbolic, but not symbolically obvious."

People began to notice the work of Nan Goldin in the late 1970s, when she began to mount slideshows of her photographic portraits (and sometimes self-portraits) in the New York clubs that she frequented. Color slides were her primary medium because she could not afford to have prints made of her work, nor could she get access to a darkroom. As Goldin repeatedly showed the series, often to audiences composed of the lovers and friends featured in the slides themselves, she created an accompanying soundtrack that itself constantly evolved. But a few songs always remained the same, among them the opening song, *The Ballad of Sexual Dependency*, a Bertolt Brecht/Kurt Weill piece from *The Threepenny Opera*, Dean Martin's *Memories*, at the end, Dionne Warwick's *Don't Make Me Over*, Petula Clark's *Downtown*, and Yoko Ono's *She Fights Back*. The opening song eventually gave her slideshow its name, and in 1986 a selection of the works was published under that title by Aperture.

Goldin's world was by no means glamorous. She and her friends frequented places like Tin Pan Alley, a Times Square basement bar in the era before Times Square, in those days the center of the city's sex trade, was gentrified. In fact, Goldin is herself featured as a Tin Pan Alley bartender in Bette Gordon's now infamous 1983 indie film, *Variety*, about a young woman, Christine, who takes a job selling tickets at a pornographic theater in the neighborhood. Tin Pan Alley is a prominent location in the film, and, indeed, some of Goldin's photographs decorate the walls of Christine's apartment, including *Vivienne in the green dress* (**Fig. 11–23**). Like the majority of her work in these years, Goldin shot the photograph indoors in an artificial light that tends to intensify the color. Here Goldin's use of a flash bulb causes Vivienne to cast a shadow on the corner of the room behind her. The blues and greens of the wall, the dress, and the small portable radio on the windowsill all contrast dramatically with Vivienne's red lipstick, the red plastic bangle on her wrist, and the red–orange leaves in the vase. Above all, the interior light seems to set itself off from the darkness outside with an intensity that is at once warming and alarming.

We tend to forget today that color photography was once a new technology, introduced to the public at large in the 1950s and 1960s. The rise of color photography in the 1960s coincided with the growing popularity of color television. On February 17, 1961, when NBC first aired all of its programs in color, only 1 percent of American homes possessed color sets. By 1969, 33 percent of American homes had color TVs, and today they command 100 percent of the market. The advent of the Polaroid camera and film, and inexpensive color processing for Kodak film, both contributed to a growing cultural taste for color images. In fact, in the course of Goldin's career, Kodak ceased to manufacture color slide film, which she initially used to create her work. Today, Goldin, like almost all color photographers, has moved into the digital age. But in the proliferation of portraits that she made in the 1980s and 1990s, she anticipates the age of the selfie, Facebook, and Instagram.

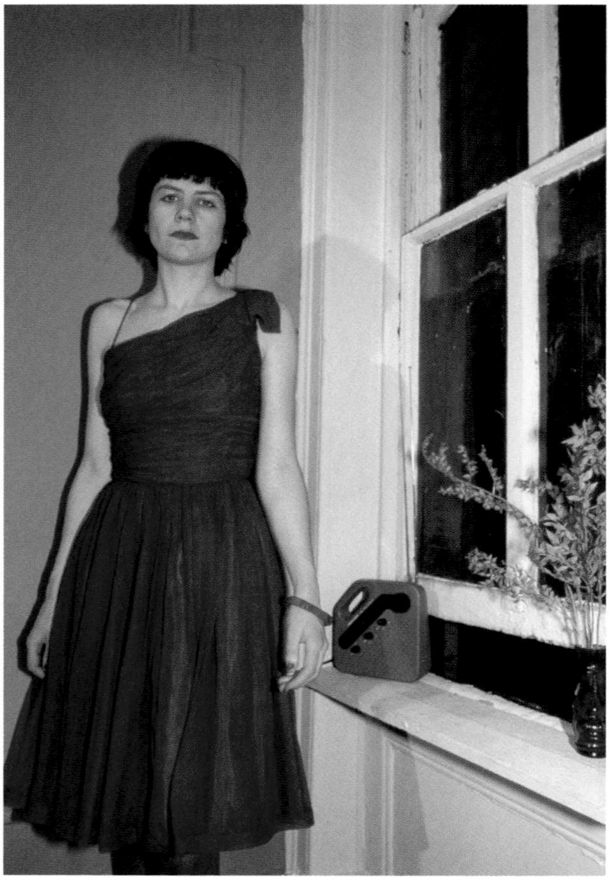

Fig. 11-23 Nan Goldin, *Vivienne in the green dress, NYC*, 1980.

Today, digital technologies have transformed the world of photography, not only rendering film obsolete but transforming photography into a highly manipulable medium. One of the most renowned masters of the digital medium is Andreas Gursky, whose *Ocean II* (**Fig. 11-24**) is one of six similarly large views of the world's oceans. To the left is the Labrador/Newfoundland coast, Greenland is at the center top, Iceland is at the top right, and, at the bottom right, are the northwest coast of Africa and the Cape Verde Islands. The works were inspired by the flight monitor on a jet one night when Gursky was flying from Dubai to Melbourne. Over the Indian Ocean he saw, on the monitor, the Horn of Africa to the far left, a

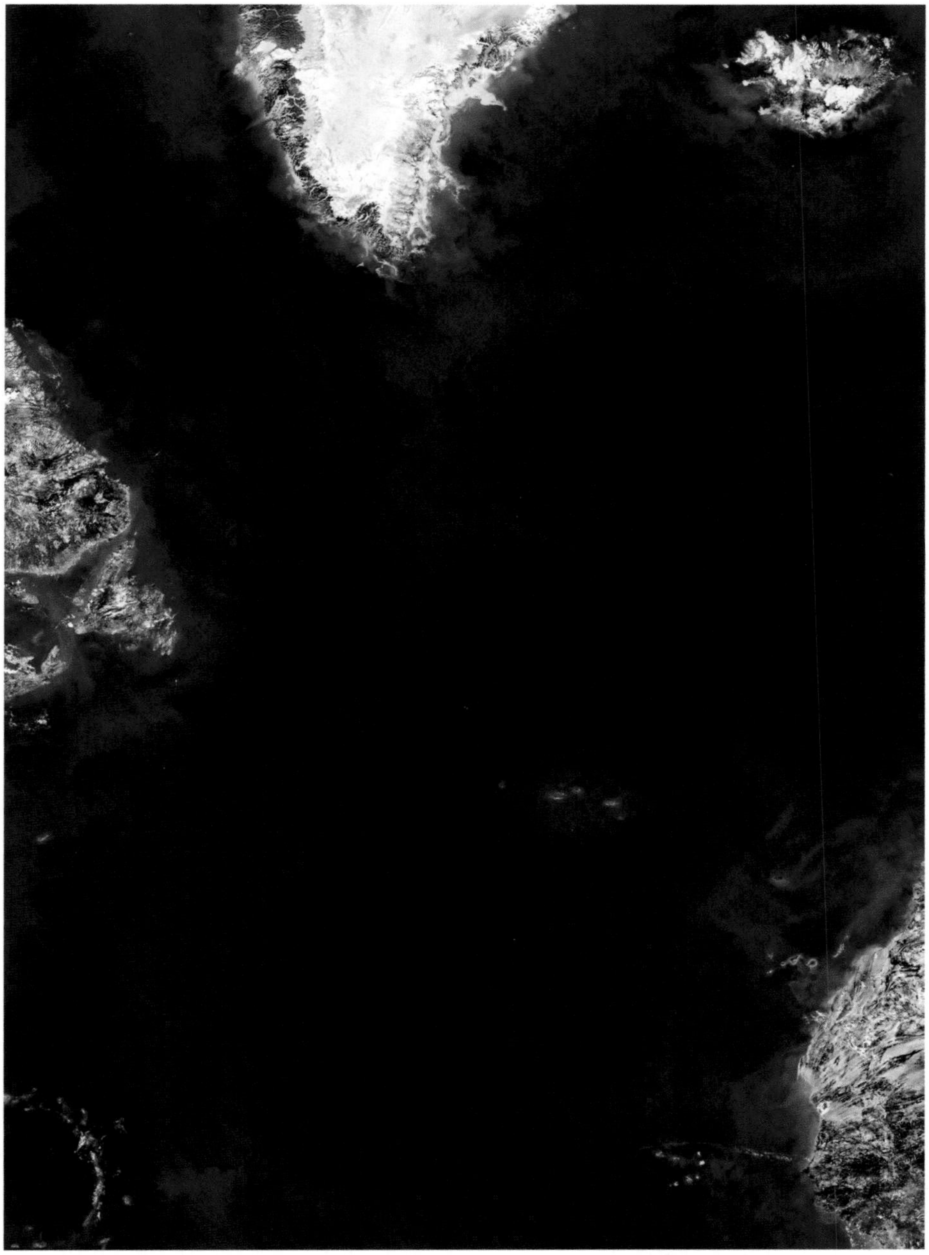

Fig. 11-24 Andreas Gursky, *Ocean II*, 2010. Chromogenic print, 11 ft. 2¼ in. × 8 ft. 2⅛ in. × 2½ in.

tip of Australia to the far right—and in between, the vast blue expanse of the sea. To make these pictures, Gursky used high-definition satellite photographs which he augmented from various picture sources on the Internet. The satellite photos were restricted, however, to exposures of sharply contoured land masses. Consequently, the transitional zones between land and water—as well as the oceans themselves, which are cloudless—had to be generated digitally. That all these pieces nevertheless convey the feeling of real subaquatic depths is due solely to the precision of Gursky's visual work. He even consulted shoal maps to get the right color nuances for the water surfaces.

The images are very disconcerting, something like an inside-out atlas where, instead of land masses edged by oceans, we see oceans edged by fingers of land. And the remarkable depth and density of Gursky's blue contrasts

Fig. 11-25 Eleanor Antin, *Constructing Helen*, from the series *Helen's Odyssey*, 2007.
Chromogenic print, 5 ft. 8 in. × 16 ft. 7 in.
Courtesy of the artist and Ronald Feldman Fine Arts, New York.

vividly with mapping's standard robin's-egg blues. The pictures are large enough that, in standing front of them, one feels surrounded by water. We do not float above the ocean, like human satellites, but instead float in it. We are immersed in it, swallowed up in its vast expanse. The immensity of the photographs somehow manages to convey the immensity of the oceans themselves, and their centrality to our life on the planet.

Eleanor Antin's *Constructing Helen* (**Fig. 11-25**), which the artist discusses in the art21 *Exclusive* video "Eleanor Antin: Helen's Odyssey," is the final photograph in her series *Helen's Odyssey*. Here, we are witness to the history of Helen as the monumental creation of a patriarchal culture—from Homer to the nineteenth century—that Antin parodies from the vantage point of contemporary feminist thought. In spirit, this Helen—an actual model transformed digitally into a gigantic sculpture—is a parody of late nineteenth-century academic paintings like Alexandre Cabanel's *Birth of Venus* (**Fig. 11-26**), which, at the Salon of 1863, was purchased by no less an admirer than Napoleon III. The series *Helen's Odyssey* is, in fact, designed to revise our sense of Greek history by focusing not on the heroes of the Homeric epic, but on Helen herself: "Her story comes down to us from European literature's founding epic," Antin says. "But what do we know of her? After three thousand years of notoriety she remains strangely silent as the most beautiful and disastrous objectification of male anxiety and desire." Antin calls her images "historical takes," by which she means both her own "take" on history and a cinematic "take," the filming of a scene. Like a filmmaker, Antin is the director and producer of the digital scene before us.

Fig. 11-26 Alexandre Cabanel, *The Birth of Venus*, 1863. Oil on canvas, 4 ft. 4 in. × 7 ft. 6 in. Musée d'Orsay, Paris.
Inv. RF273. Photo © RMN-Grand Palais (musée d'Orsay)/Hervé Lewandowski.

Fig. 11-27 Fernand Léger, *Ballet Mécanique*, 1924.
The Humanities Film Collection, Oregon State University.

Film

What are the basic principles of film editing, including montage, and what technological developments have advanced the medium over the years?

As we noted at the beginning of the chapter, almost as soon as photography was invented, people sought to extend its capacities to capture motion. Eadweard Muybridge captured the locomotion of animals and human beings (see Fig. 11-2) in sequences of rapidly exposed photos. It was, in fact, the formal revelations of film that first attracted artists to it. As forms and shapes repeated themselves in time across the motion-picture screen, the medium seemed to invite the exploration of rhythm and repetition as principles of design. In his 1924 film *Ballet Mécanique* (**Fig. 11-27**), the Cubist painter Fernand Léger chose to study a number of different images—smiling lips, wine bottles, metal discs, working mechanisms, and pure shapes such as circles, squares, and triangles. By repeating the same image again and again at separate points in the film, Léger was able to create a visual rhythm that, to his mind, embodied the beauty—the ballet—of machines in the modern world.

Assembling a film, the process of **editing**, is a sort of linear collage, as Léger plainly shows. Although the movies may seem true to life, as if they were occurring in real time and space, this effect is only an illusion accomplished by means of editing. It is perhaps not coincidental that, as film began to come into its own in the second decade of the twentieth century, collage, constructed by cutting and pasting together a variety of fragments, was itself invented.

The first great master of editing was D. W. Griffith who, in *The Birth of a Nation* (**Fig. 11-28**), essentially invented the standard vocabulary of filmmaking. Griffith

Fig. 11-28 Battle scene from *The Birth of a Nation*, directed by D. W. Griffith, 1915.
Courtesy of the Library of Congress.

sought to create visual variety in the film by alternating between and among a repertoire of **shots**, each one a continuous sequence of film frames. A **full shot** shows the actor from head to toe, a **medium shot** from the waist up, a **close-up** the head and shoulders, and an **extreme close-up** a portion of the face. The image of the battle scene reproduced here is a **long shot**, a shot that takes in a wide expanse and many characters at once. Griffith makes use of another of his techniques in this shot as well—the frame slowly opens in a widening circle as a scene begins or slowly blacks out in a shrinking circle to end a scene. This is called an **iris shot**.

Related to the long shot is the **pan**, a name given to the panoramic vista, in which the camera moves across the scene from one side to the other. Griffith also invented the **traveling** or **tracking shot**, in which the camera, mounted and moved on tracks, moves parallel to the action. In editing, Griffith combined these various shots in order to tell his story. Two of his more famous editing techniques are cross-cutting and flashbacks. The **flashback**, in which the editor cuts to narrative episodes that are supposed to have taken place before the start of the film, is now standard in film practice, but it was entirely new to film practice when Griffith first used it. **Cross-cutting** is an editing technique meant to create high drama. The editor moves back and forth between two separate events in ever-shorter sequences, the rhythm of shots increasing to a furious pace. Griffith borrowed these techniques from fiction writing to tell a visual story in film.

A film about the Civil War and Reconstruction, *The Birth of a Nation* is unrepentant in its racism, culminating in a tightly edited cross-cut sequence in which a white woman tries to fend off the sexual advances of a black man as the Ku Klux Klan rides to her rescue, which led the NAACP (National Association for the Advancement of Colored People), newly formed in 1915 when the film was released, to seek to have it banned. Riots broke out in Boston and Philadelphia, while Denver, Pittsburgh, St. Louis, Minneapolis, and eight states denied it a release. But Griffith's film remains one of the highest-grossing movies in film history, in no small part due to its inventive editing.

One of the other great innovators of film editing was the Russian filmmaker Sergei Eisenstein. Eisenstein did his greatest work in Bolshevik Russia after the 1917 Revolution, in a newly formed state whose leader, Vladimir Lenin, had said, "Of all the arts, for us the cinema is the most important." In this atmosphere, Eisenstein created what he considered a revolutionary new use of the medium. Rather than concentrating on narrative sequencing, he sought to create a sense of shock that would ideally lead the audience to a new perception and knowledge. He called his technique **montage**—the sequencing of widely disparate images to create a fast-paced, multifaceted image. In the famous "Odessa Steps Sequence" of his 1925 film *Battleship Potemkin*, four frames of which are reproduced here (**Fig. 11-29**), Eisenstein used 155 separate shots in 4 minutes 20 seconds of film, which equates to an astonishing average rate of 1.6 seconds per shot (the sequence is widely available on the Internet). The movie is based on the story of an unsuccessful uprising against the Russian monarchy in 1905, and the sequence depicts the moment when the crowd pours into the port city of Odessa's harbor to welcome the liberated ship *Potemkin*. Behind them, at the top of the steps leading down to the pier, soldiers appear. In the scene, the soldiers fire on the crowd, a mother lifts her dead child to face the soldiers, women weep, and a baby carriage careens down the steps. For Eisenstein, the assemblage of all these shots makes for a single film "image." "The strength of montage resides in this," he wrote, "that it involves the creative process—the emotions and mind of the spectator . . . assemble the image."

The thrust of Eisenstein's work is to emphasize action and emotion through enhanced time sequencing. Just the opposite effect is created by Douglas Gordon

Fig. 11-29 Sergei Eisenstein, *Battleship Potemkin*, 1925. Four stills.
Goskino/Kobal Collection.

Fig. 11-30 Douglas Gordon, *24 Hour Psycho*, 1993.
Photo: Studio lost but found (Bert Rossi), Courtesy of Gagosian Gallery © Douglas Gordon. From Psycho, 1960, USA. Directed and produced by Alfred Hitchcock, Distributed by Paramount Pictures Universal City Stuidoes, Inc.

in his 1993 *24 Hour Psycho* (**Fig. 11-30**). Gordon's work is an extreme-slow-motion video projection of Alfred Hitchcock's 1960 classic film *Psycho*. As opposed to the standard 24 frames per second, Gordon projects the film at 2 frames per second, extending the playing time of the movie to a full 24 hours. Hitchcock's original in fact utilizes many of Eisenstein's time sequencings to create a film of uncanny tension. But Gordon's version so slows Hitchcock's pace that each action is extended, sometimes excruciatingly so—as in the famous shower scene. To view either film is to understand the idea of duration in terms one might never before have experienced.

The Popular Cinema

However interesting Gordon's *24 Hour Psycho* might be on an intellectual level, and however much it might transform our experience of and appreciation for Hitchcock's film, it is not the kind of movie that most audiences would appreciate. Audiences expect a narrative, or story, to unfold, characters with whom they can identify, and action that thrills their imaginations. In short, they want to be entertained. After World War I, American movies dominated the screens of the world like no other mass media in history, precisely because they entertained audiences so completely. And the name of the town where these entertainments were made became synonymous with the industry itself—Hollywood.

The major players in Hollywood were Fox and Paramount, the two largest film companies, followed by Universal and Metro-Goldwyn-Mayer (MGM). With the introduction of sound into the motion-picture business in 1926, Warner Brothers came to the forefront as well. In addition, a few well-known actors, notably Douglas Fairbanks, Mary Pickford, and Charlie Chaplin, maintained control over the financing and distribution of their own work by forming their own company, United Artists. Their ability to do so, despite the power of the other major film companies, is testimony to the power of the **star** in Hollywood.

The greatest of these stars was Charlie Chaplin, who, in his famous role of The Tramp, managed to merge humor with a deeply sympathetic character who could pull the heartstrings of audiences everywhere. In *The Gold Rush*, an 80-minute film made in 1925, much of it filmed on location near Lake Tahoe in the Sierra Nevada mountains of California, he portrayed the abysmal conditions faced by miners working in the Klondike gold fields during the Alaska gold rush of 1898. One scene in this movie is particularly poignant—and astonishingly funny: Together with a fellow prospector, Big Jim, a starving Charlie cooks and eats, with relish and delight, his old leather shoe (**Fig. 11-31**).

The Gold Rush is a silent film, but a year after it was made, Warner Brothers and Fox were busy installing speakers and amplification systems in theaters as they perfected competing sound-on-film technologies. On October 6, 1927, the first words of synchronous speech uttered by a performer in a feature film were spoken by Al Jolson in *The Jazz Singer*: "Wait a minute! Wait a minute!

Fig. 11-31 Charlie Chaplin in *The Gold Rush*, 1925.
United Artists.
Everett Collection.

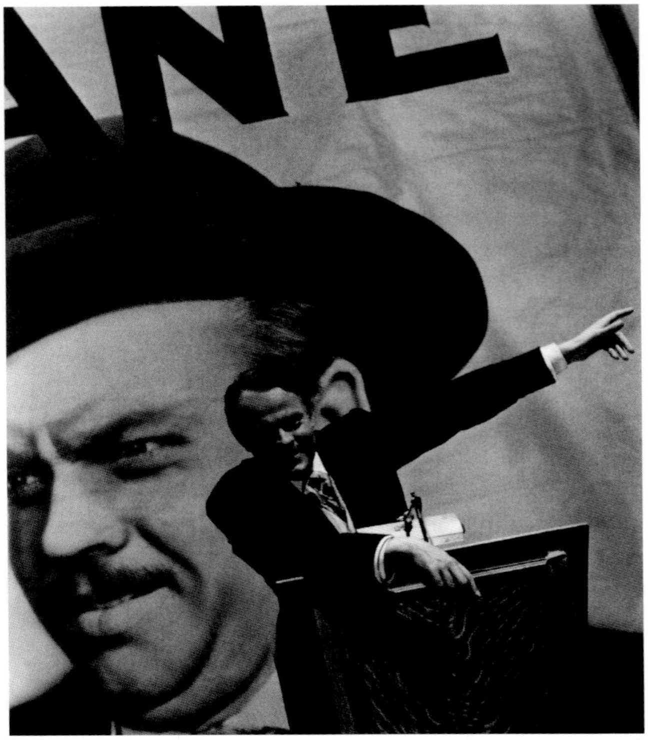

Fig. 11-32 Orson Welles in *Citizen Kane*, 1941.
Kobal Collection.

You ain't heard nothing yet." By 1930, the conversion to sound was complete.

For the next decade, the movie industry produced films in a wide variety of **genres**, or narrative types—comedies, romantic dramas, war films, horror films, gangster films, and musicals. By 1939, Hollywood had reached a zenith. Some of the greatest films of all time date from that year, including the classic western *Stagecoach*, starring John Wayne, *Gone with the Wind*, starring Vivien Leigh and Clark Gable, and *Mr. Smith Goes to Washington*, starring Jimmy Stewart. But perhaps the greatest event of the year was the arrival of 24-year-old Orson Welles in Hollywood. Welles had made a name for himself in 1938 when his Halloween-night radio broadcast of H. G. Wells's novel *War of the Worlds* convinced many listeners that Martians had invaded New Jersey. Gathering the most talented people in Hollywood around him, he produced, directed, wrote, and starred in *Citizen Kane*, the story of a media baron modeled loosely on newspaper publisher William Randolph Hearst. Released in 1941 to rave reviews, the film used every known trick of the filmmaker's trade, with high-angle and low-angle shots (**Fig. 11-32**), a wide variety of editing effects, including dissolves between scenes, and a narrative technique, fragmented and consisting of different points of view, unique to film at the time. All combined to make a work of remarkable total effect that still stands as one of the greatest achievements of American popular cinema.

The year 1939 also marked the emergence of color as a major force in the motion-picture business. The first successful full-length Technicolor film had been *The Black Pirate*, starring Douglas Fairbanks, released in 1926, but color was considered an unnecessary ornament, and audiences were indifferent to it. However, when, in *The Wizard of Oz*, Dorothy arrives in a full-color Oz, having been carried off by a tornado from a black-and-white Kansas, the magical transformation of color become stunningly evident. And audiences were stunned by the release of *Gone with the Wind*, with its four hours of color production. Much of that film's success can be attributed to art director William Cameron Menzies. Menzies had worked for years in Hollywood, and for such an ambitious project, he realized he needed to start working far in advance of production. Two years before shooting began, he started creating **storyboards**—panels of rough sketches outlining the shot sequences—for each of the movie's scenes. These storyboards helped to determine camera angles, locations, lighting, and even the editing sequence well in advance of actual shooting. His panoramic overviews, for which the camera had to pull back above a huge railway platform full of wounded Confederate soldiers, required the building of a crane, and they became famous as a technological achievement. For the film's burning-of-Atlanta sequence (**Figs. 11-33** and **11-34**), Menzies's storyboard shows seven shots, beginning and ending with a panoramic overview, with cuts to close-ups of both Rhett Butler and Scarlett O'Hara fully indicated.

Meanwhile, Walt Disney had begun to create feature-length animated films in full color. The first was *Snow White and the Seven Dwarfs*, in 1937, which was followed, in 1940, by both *Pinocchio* and *Fantasia*. **Animation**, which means "bringing to life," was suggested to filmmakers from the earliest days of the industry when it became evident that film itself was a series of "stills" animated by their movement in sequence. Obviously, one could draw these stills as well as photograph them. But in order for motion to appear seamless, and not jerky, literally thousands of drawings need to be executed for each film, up to 24 per second of film time.

In the years after World War II, the idea of film as a potential art form resurfaced, especially in Europe. Fostered in large part by international film festivals, particularly in Venice and Cannes, this new "art cinema" brought directors to the fore, seeing them as the **auteurs**, or "authors," of their works. Chief among these was the Italian director Federico Fellini, whose film about the decadent lifestyle of 1960s Rome, *La Dolce Vita*, earned him an international reputation. Close on

Fig. 11-33 William Cameron Menzies, Storyboard for the burning-of-Atlanta scene from *Gone with the Wind*, 1939.
MGM/Photofest.

his heels came the Swedish director Ingmar Bergman and the French "New Wave" directors Jean-Luc Godard and Alain Resnais.

By the end of the 1960s, Hollywood had lost its hold on the film industry, and most films had become international productions. But, a decade later, it regained control of the medium when, in 1977, George Lucas's *Star Wars* swept onto the scene. In many ways an anthology of stunning special effects, the movie had made over $200 million even before its highly successful twentieth-anniversary rerelease in 1997, and it inaugurated an era of "blockbuster" Hollywood attractions, including *E.T.*, *Titanic*, *The Lord of the Rings* trilogy, and series like the *Harry Potter* and *Twilight* films.

Fig. 11-34 Burning-of-Atlanta scene from *Gone with the Wind*, 1939.
MGM/Photofest.

Video Art

How has video art exploited the immediacy of the medium, even as it has critiqued popular culture?

One of the primary difficulties faced by artists who wish to explore film as a medium is the sheer expense of using it. The more sophisticated a film is in terms of its camera work, lighting, sound equipment, editing techniques, and special effects, the more expensive it is to produce. With the introduction in 1965 of the relatively inexpensive handheld video camera, the Sony Portapak, artists were suddenly able to explore the implications of seeing in time. Video is not only cheaper than film but it is also more immediate—that is, what is seen on the recorder is simultaneously seen on the monitor. While video art tends to exploit this immediacy, commercial television tends to hide it by attempting to make videotaped images look like film.

Korean-born Nam June Paik was one of the first people in New York to buy a Portapak. His video installations explore the limits and defining characteristics of the medium. By the mid-1960s, Paik's "altered TVs"

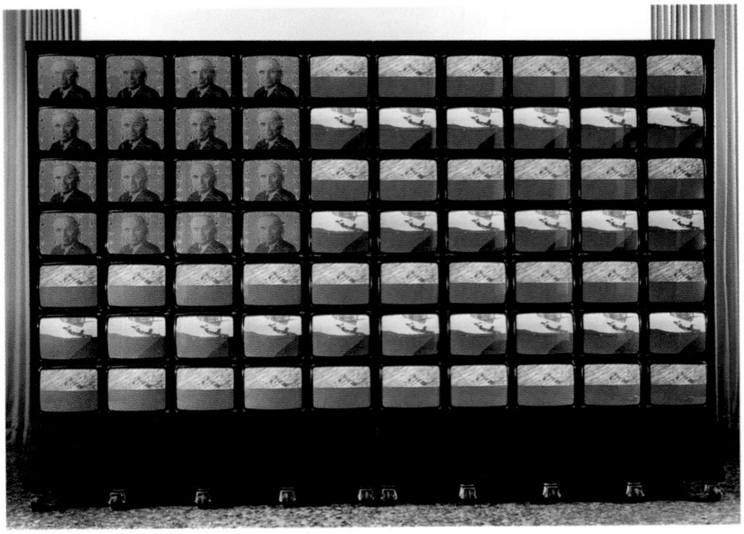

Fig. 11-35 Nam June Paik, *Video Flag*, 1985–96. Seventy video monitors, 4 laser-disk players, computer, timers, electrical devices, wood and metal housing on rubber wheels, 7 ft. 10⅜ in. × 11 ft. 7¾ in. × 47¾ in. Hirshhorn Museum and Sculpture Garden, Smithsonian Institution, Washington, D.C. Holenia Purchase Fund, in memory of Joseph H. Hirshhorn, 1996. Photo: Lee Stalsworth. © Estate of Nam June Paik.

displayed images altered by magnets combined with video feedback and other technologies that produced shifted patterns of shape and color. Until his death in 2006, he continued to produce large-scale video installations, including the 1995 work *Megatron/Matrix*, which consisted of 215 monitors programmed with both live video images from the Seoul Olympic Games and animated montages of nudes, rock concert clips, national flags, and other symbolic imagery. In 1985–86, he began to use the American flag as the basis for computer sculpture, making three separate flag sculptures: *Video Flag X* (Chase Manhattan Bank collection), *Video Flag Y* (The Detroit Institute of Arts), and *Video Flag Z* (Los Angeles County Museum of Art).

Today, *Video Flag Z*, a 6-foot-high grid of 84 white Quasar monitors that once flashed a pulsating montage of red, white, and blue images across its surface, is packed away in the Los Angeles County Museum's warehouse. "We can't find replacement parts anymore," the museum's curator explains. And this is a danger most electronic media face as they fall victim to the ever-increasing rate of technological change. Jon Ippolito, the Guggenheim Museum's associate curator of media arts, warns, "There's a looming threat of mass extinction on the media-arts landscape." One solution is for media artists to reengineer their works, which is precisely what Paik did for his *Video Flag* (**Fig. 11-35**) at the Hirshhorn Museum in Washington, D.C. The monitors incorporate a face that morphs through every U.S. president of the Information Age, from Harry S. Truman to Bill Clinton. Built a decade after the earlier flags, the Hirshhorn's *Video Flag* incorporates what were then (1996) the latest advances in technology, such as laser disks, automatic switchers, 13-inch monitors (rather than the 10-inch monitors used in previous versions), and other devices. But today, as the electronics industry has ceased producing both video equipment and videotape itself, it too is threatened by the obsolescence of its working parts.

From the outset, one of the principal attractions of video as a medium for artists was its immediacy, the fact that the image was transmitted instantaneously in "real" time. Installations such as Bruce Nauman's *Live-Taped Video Corridor* (**Fig. 11-36**) were designed precisely to underscore the sometimes startling effects of such immediacy. The piece consisted of two floor-to-ceiling panels forming a tunnel the length of

Fig. 11-36 Bruce Nauman, *Live-Taped Video Corridor*, 1970. Wallboard, video camera, two video monitors, videotape player, and videotape, dimensions variable. Solomon R. Guggenheim Museum, New York. Installation view: 1970 Annual Exhibition of Contemporary American Sculpture, Whitney Museum of American Art, New York, December 12, 1970–February 7, 1971. Panza Collection, Gift, 92.4165.

a room. At the far end were two video monitors stacked on top of one another. As viewers inched their way down the corridor one at a time, it gradually became clear that they were walking toward their own image, shot from a surveillance camera mounted on the ceiling. The experience was tantamount to suddenly finding oneself in some sinister surveillance operation, the possibility of which had become increasingly real by the early 1970s as closed-circuit television (CCTV) systems proliferated across the country—in 1969, police cameras had been installed in the New York City Municipal Building near City Hall, and other cities soon followed suit, their CCTV systems constantly monitored by officers.

On the other hand, such immediacy seemed, at least superficially, to guarantee that the video image was authentic, that it recorded a "live" moment with a certain truth. The videotape of Chris Burden's 1971 performance *Shoot* (**Fig. 11-37**) exploited this "truth factor" as no artist had before (and few have since). On November 19, 1971, Burden stood before a small audience of friends at F Space, an alternative gallery in Santa Ana, California, run by students in the MFA program at UC-Irvine. Burden had one of his fellow students, a trained sharpshooter, fire a rifle at him from about halfway across the gallery. Burden had intended that the shooter just graze the skin of his left arm, but the wound was more severe and Burden had to receive emergency medical attention. Burden did not produce his video of the event until three years later (and the final video contains only 8 seconds of actual film—the remainder is composed of black-screen audio-recording with titles and still photography), in no small part to affirm that the event, known only through photographs to that point in time, had indeed taken place.

Fig. 11-37 Chris Burden, *Shoot*, 1974. Still. Videotape of a 1971 performance, approx. 2 min. 15 sec.
Courtesy of Electronic Arts Intermix (EAI), New York. © Chris Burden.

Artists also saw video art as a way to challenge and critique popular culture, particularly television. In her video *Technology/Transformation: Wonder Woman* (**Fig. 11-38**), Dara Birnbaum pirated an episode of the Linda Carter TV series *Wonder Woman*, which ran for three seasons from 1976 to 1979, and by repeating short

Fig. 11-38 Dara Birnbaum, *Technology/Transformation: Wonder Woman*, 1978–79.
Still. Video, approx. 5 min. 16 sec.
Courtesy of Electronic Arts Intermix (EAI), New York.

sequences from the episode again and again—Wonder Woman running through the woods, her breasts bouncing heavily, or the explosion that marks the moment when Wonder Woman is transformed from the "real" secretary, Diana Prince, into her superhero self—revealed just how sexist (and banal) the show's representation of women really was. The video concludes with two minutes of the Wonderland Disco Band's 1978 "Wonder Woman Disco," its lyrics scrolling by on a blue ground, the sexual implications of the song's chorus—"Shake thy wonder maker"—fully exposed.

Perhaps no artist in the 1970s challenged the expectations of art audiences more hilariously than William Wegman, whose series of short videos has also recently been reissued on DVD (*William Wegman: Video Works 1970–1999*). In one, called *Deodorant*, the artist simply sprays an entire can of deodorant under one armpit while he extolls its virtues. The video, which is about the same length as a normal television commercial, is an exercise in consumerism run amok. In *Rage and Depression* (**Fig. 11-39**), Wegman sits smiling at the camera as he speaks the following monologue:

> I had these terrible fits of rage and depression all the time. It just got worse and worse and worse. Finally my parents had me committed. They tried all kinds of therapy. Finally they settled on shock. The doctors brought me into this room in a straitjacket because I still had this terrible, terrible temper. I was just the meanest cuss you could imagine, and when they put this cold, metal electrode, or whatever it was, to my chest, I started to giggle and then when they shocked me, it froze on my face into this smile, and even though I'm still incredibly depressed—everyone thinks I'm happy. I don't know what I'm going to do.

Fig. 11-39 William Wegman, *Rage and Depression, Reel 3*, 1972–73. Still. Video, approx. 1 min.
Courtesy of the artist.

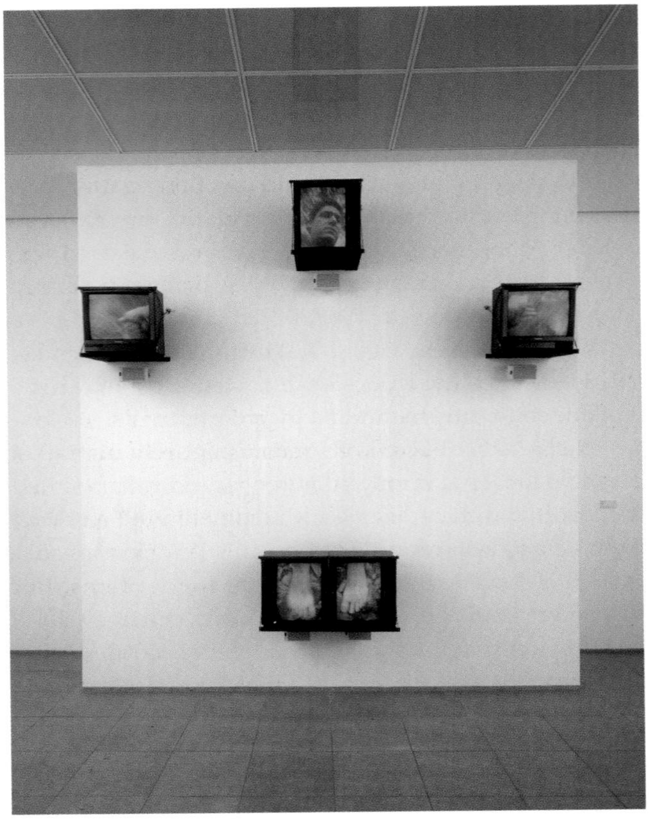

Fig. 11-40 Gary Hill, *Crux*, 1983–87. Five-channel video installation (NTSC, color, sound), 5 video monitors, 5 speakers, 1 synchronizer. Hamburger Bahnhof–Museum für Gegenwart, Nationalgalerie, Berlin.
Inv. FNG 68/93. Photo: Jens Ziehe. © 2015. Photo Scala, Florence/bpk, Bildagentur für Kunst, Kultur und Geschichte, Berlin. © 2015 Gary Hill/Artists Rights Society (ARS), New York.

Wegman completely undermines the authority of visual experience here. What our eyes see is an illusion. He implies that we can never trust what we see, just as we should not trust television's objectivity as a medium.

Gary Hill's video installation *Crux* (**Fig. 11-40**), made in the mid-1980s, transforms the traditional imagery of the Crucifixion. The installation consists of five television monitors mounted on a wall in the shape of a cross. Hill shot the piece on a deserted island in the middle of the Hudson River in New York. Attached to his body were five video cameras, one on each shin facing his feet, one braced in front of his face and pointed directly back at him, and one on each arm aimed at his hands, which he extended out from his body. On his back he carried all the necessary recording equipment and power packs. The cameras recorded his bare-footed trek across the island, through the woods and an abandoned armory to the river's edge. The 26-minute journey captures all the agony and pain of Christ's original ascent of Golgotha, as he carried his own cross to the top of the hill where he was crucified. But all we see of Hill's walk are his two bruised and stumbling feet, his two hands groping for balance, and his exhausted face. The body that connects them is absent, a giant blank spot on the gallery wall. This absence not only suggests the disappearance of Christ's body after the Resurrection, but it is also the "crux" of the title. A "crux" is a cross, but it is also a vital or decisive point (as in "the crux of the matter"), or something that torments by its puzzling nature. By eliminating his body, Hill has discovered a metaphor for the soul—that puzzling energy which is spiritually present but physically absent.

While archival video footage is becoming increasingly available, the work of most contemporary artists working with time-based media (*video* art per se no longer exists—the medium has become entirely digital) is available for viewing only at museums and galleries. Artists tend to produce their work in very limited editions, designed to maximize competition among museum collectors for copies. There are some exceptions. Bill Viola has released a number of his early works on DVD including *Selected Works 1976–1981; Hatsu-Yume (First Dream)* (1981), a visual foray into the nature of light and darkness as metaphors for life and death; *I Do Not Know What It Is I Am Like* (1986), an investigation of humanity's relation to nature; and *The Passing* (1991), a meditation on the endless cycle of birth and death like *Hatsu-Yume*, but focused on Viola's own family. (One of the video installations he created as the American representative to the Venice Biennale in 1995 is the subject of *The Creative Process* on pp. 268–69.)

Viola's short video *The Reflecting Pool* (**Fig. 11-41**) demonstrates his technical prowess. It lasts for seven minutes. The camera is stationary, overlooking a pool that fills the foreground. Light filters through the forest behind the pool. Throughout the tape there is the sound of water gently streaming into the pool, and then, covering it during the opening shots, a drone that resembles the sound of a truck or plane passing by. Viola emerges from the forest wearing a shirt and trousers. He walks up to the edge of the pool, where he is reflected in the water. Then suddenly, with a grunt, he jumps out over the pool, but his body freezes in the fetal position in midair above the water. In the pool the light changes

Fig. 11-41 Bill Viola, *The Reflecting Pool*, 1977–79. Four stills. Video, color, mono sound, 7 min.
Bill Viola Studio LLC. Photos: Kira Perov.

Fig. 11-42 Peter Fischli and David Weiss, *Der Lauf der Dinge* (*The Way Things Go*), 1987. Stills. 16 mm color film, 30 min.

and the water stills before it is then animated in three successive sequences by concentric circles of ripples as if a fish has risen to the surface or something (invisible) has dropped into it from the feet of the suspended figure above. A reflected figure walks along the pool from left to right and as he does so the frozen figure suspended above the pool gradually fades into the landscape. Two reflected figures, a woman and a man, move along the right edge of the pool and then across the far side until they stop at the far left corner. The circles of water implode inward in backward motion. The water turns black, as if in the bottom half of the image it is night, reflecting the single figure again, now bathed in light. He moves off to the right. Then the pool returns to daylight, and suddenly Viola emerges from the water naked, his back to us. He climbs onto the edge of the pool and walks away, in small fragmented segments, into the forest.

The stationary camera is key to the work. It allows Viola to work with three separate recordings of the space and recombine them within the (apparently) coherent space of the frame by registering them much in the manner that a printmaker registers the different colors in pulling a single print. First is a series of recordings made by using very slow dissolves between each action (throwing things into the water to create the rippling effects, the reflection of himself walking around the edge of the pool). Some of these actions were recorded in real time, but others, like the changing light on the pool surface, are time-lapse, and still others, like the imploding circle of concentric ripples, are in reverse motion. The second recording consists of Viola walking out of the forest to the edge of the pool and then jumping into the air. This recording ends in a freeze-frame of about three or four minutes' duration, during which it undergoes a slow fade so that the figure appears to dissolve into the background. The final recording consists simply of the empty scene in real time. It is this space that comprises the forest background into which the leaping figure disappears. What Viola offers the viewer is a quasi-mysterious space of reflection, a reflecting pool removed from the fractious realities of modern life, into which the viewer might dive like Viola himself.

As it turns out, one of the seminal time-based works of the late twentieth century, *Der Lauf der Dinge* (*The Way Things Go*), is widely available on DVD. Created by Swiss artists Peter Fischli and David Weiss, the film was first screened in 1987 at Documenta, the international art exhibition that takes place every five years in Kassel, Germany. There it caused an immediate sensation, and since then it has been screened in museums around the world. It consists of a kinetic sculptural installation inside a 100-foot-long warehouse that begins when a black plastic bag (full of who knows quite what), suspended from the ceiling, spins downward until it hits a tire on top of a slightly inclined orange-colored board and nudges it over a small strip of wood down the shallow slope. This initiates a series of physical and chemical, cause-and-effect chain reactions in which ordinary household objects slide, crash, spew liquids onto, and ignite one another in a linear 30-minute sequence of self-destructing interactions (**Fig. 11-42**). In part a metaphor for the history of Western culture, in part a hilarious slapstick comedy of errors, for many viewers *The Way Things Go* captures the spirit of modern life.

The Computer and New Media

What sorts of effects has computer technology made possible in art?

If the image on a computer monitor is literally two-dimensional, the screen space occupied by the image is, increasingly, theatrical, interactive, and time-based. In his groundbreaking 1999 study of the global digital network, *E-topia*, William J. Mitchell, dean of the School of Architecture and Planning at the Massachusetts Institute of Technology, put it this way:

> In the early days of PCs, you just saw scrolling text through the rectangular aperture [of your personal computer], and the theatrical roots of the configuration were obscured. . . . [But] with the emergence of the PC, the growth of networks, and ongoing advances in display technology, countless millions of glowing glass rectangles scattered through the world have served to construct an increasingly intricate interweaving of cyberspace and architecture. . . . As static tesserae [pieces of glass or ceramic used to make mosaics] were to the Romans, active pixels are to us. Signs and labels are becoming dynamic, text is jumping off the page into three-dimensional space, murals are being set in motion, and the immaterial is blending seamlessly with the material.

The advances in technology are startling. To make *The Reflecting Pool*, Bill Viola used the new CMX 600 nonlinear editing system at the WNET Television Laboratory in New York, the first system to free video editors from working chronologically from the beginning of the tape to the end, giving them the ability to retrieve any segment of original video footage at any time and place it anywhere in the sequence. It was not until ten years later, in 1989, that Avid's Media Composer system was launched, a digital nonlinear editing program that provided editors with the ability to copy videotape footage in real time to digital hard disks. This invention allowed a video editor to use a computer to easily view shots, make cuts, and rearrange sequences faster than traditional tape-based methods. The cost was about $100,000. Today, comparable software costs less than $300. In 1990, when Steven Spielberg began discussions about transforming Michael Crichton's novel *Jurassic Park* into a movie, CGI, computer-generated imaging, did not exist. Three years later, the movie made its stunning animated dinosaurs come to life. Today, software with far greater capabilities is available for use on your laptop and, as we have seen, artists such as Isaac Julien have integrated CGI technology into their video works (see Fig. 4-31).

Fig. 11-43 David Claerbout, *Sections of a Happy Moment*, 2007. Stills. Single-channel video projection, 1920 × 1600 hd progressive, black-and-white, stereo audio, 25 min. 57 sec.

David Claerbout's 2007 single-channel video installation *Sections of a Happy Moment* (**Fig. 11-43**) is a tour de force of computer-generated imagery. Nearly 26 minutes long, the video depicts a single moment in the life of a Chinese family, who are grouped in a circle in the

The Creative Process

Revisioning a Painting as Video: Bill Viola's *The Greeting*

When video artist Bill Viola first saw a reproduction of Jacopo da Pontormo's 1528 painting *The Visitation* (**Fig. 11-45**), he knew that he had to do something with it. Asked to be the American representative at the 1995 Venice Biennale, perhaps the oldest and most prestigious international arts festival, he decided to see if he could create a piece based on Pontormo's painting for the exhibition. He therefore converted the United States Pavilion into a series of five independent video installations, which he called, as a whole, *Buried Secrets*. By "buried secrets" he meant to refer to our emotions, which have for too long lain hidden within us. "Emotions," he says, "are precisely the missing key that has thrown things out of balance, and the restoration to their right place as one of the higher orders of the mind of a human being cannot happen fast enough."

What fascinated Viola about Pontormo's painting was, first of all, the scene itself. Two women meet each other in the street. They embrace as two other women look on. An instantaneous knowledge and understanding seems to pass between their eyes. The visit, as told in the Bible by Luke (1:36–56), is of the Virgin Mary to Elizabeth. Mary has just been told by the Angel Gabriel: "You shall conceive and bear a son, and you shall give him the name Jesus," the moment of the Annunciation. In Pontormo's painting, the two women, one just pregnant with Jesus, the other six months pregnant, after a lifetime of barrenness, with the child who would grow to be John the Baptist, share each other's joy. For Viola, looking at this work, it is their shared intimacy—that moment of contact in which the nature of their relationship is permanently changed—that most fascinated him: Here is the instant when we leave the isolation of ourselves and enter into social relations with others. Viola decided that he wanted to recreate this encounter, to try to capture in media such as film or video—media that can depict the passing of time—the emotions buried in the moment of the greeting itself.

In order to recreate the work, Viola turned his attention to other aspects of Pontormo's composition. He was particularly interested in how the piece depicted space. There seemed to him to be a clear tension between the deep space of the street behind the women and the space occupied by the women themselves. He thus made a series of sketches of the hypothetical street behind the women (**Fig. 11-44**); then, working with a set designer, recreated it. The steep, odd perspective of the buildings had to fit into a 20-foot-deep sound stage. He discovered that if he filled the foreground with four women, as in the Pontormo painting, much of the background would be lost. Furthermore, the fourth woman in the painting presented dramatic difficulties. Removed from the main group as she is, there was really little for her to do in a recreation of the scene involving live action.

A costume designer was hired; actors auditioned, were cast, and then rehearsed. On Monday, April 3, 1995, on a sound stage in Culver City, California, Viola shot *The Greeting*. He had earlier decided to shoot the piece on film, not video,

Fig. 11-44 Bill Viola, Sketch for the set of *The Greeting*, 1995.
Bill Viola Studio LLC.

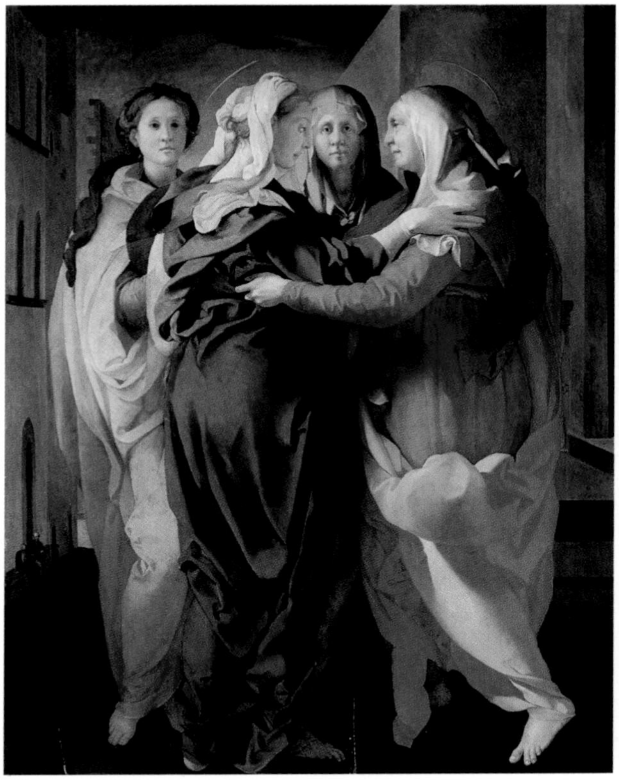

Fig. 11-45 Jacopo da Pontormo, *The Visitation*, 1528. Oil on canvas, 6 ft. 7½ in. × 5 ft. 1⅜ in. Pieve di S. Michele, Carmignano, Italy.
Canali Photobank, Milan, Italy.

Fig. 11-46 Bill Viola, *The Greeting*, 1995. Video/sound installation for the exhibition *Buried Secrets*. United States Pavilion, Venice Biennale, 1995. Arizona State University Art Museum, Tempe.
Bill Viola Studio LLC. Performers: Angela Black, Suzanne Peters, Bonnie Snyder. Photo: Kira Perov.

because he wanted to capture every nuance of the moment. On an earlier project, he had used a special high-speed 35 mm camera that was capable of shooting an entire roll of film in about 45 seconds at a rate of 300 frames per second. The camera was exactly what he needed for this project. The finished film would run for more than ten minutes. The action it would record would last for 45 seconds.

"I never felt more like a painter," Viola says of the piece. "It was like I was moving color around, but on film." For ten slow-motion minutes, the camera never shifts its point of view. Two women stand talking on a street, and a third enters from the left to greet them. An embrace follows (**Fig. 11-46**).

Viola knew, as soon as he saw the unedited film, that he had what he wanted, but questions still remained. How large should he show the piece—on a table monitor, or larger than life-size, projected on a wall? He could not decide at first, but at the last minute he determined that he would project it. On the day of the Venice Biennale opening, he saw it in its completed state for the first time, and for the first time since filming it, he saw it with the other key element in video—sound. It seemed complete as it never had before. Gusts of wind echo through the scene. Then the woman in red leans across to the other and whispers, "Can you help me? I need to talk with you right away." Joy rises to their faces. Their emotions surface. The wind lifts their dresses, and they are transformed.

courtyard of an urban housing complex, gazing up at a ball hanging in midair. At first, it seems to be a slideshow of shots of the scene apparently taken simultaneously by myriad cameras positioned all around the courtyard at different heights and focal lengths, but it is nothing of the sort. Claerbout, in fact, used a multitude of cameras simultaneously to photograph the 11 characters in the scene in front of a blue background, each time concentrating on one or two people. In the process he generated more than 50,000 images, finally choosing 180 of them to insert digitally into the background scenes, themselves shot from a number of different angles and digitally manipulated, of a social housing complex designed by the Belgian modernist architect Renaat Braem and built in 1950–57 in the Kiel district of Antwerp. The slideshow moves at a pace of about one every eight or nine seconds, and is accompanied by an altogether unremarkable solo piano soundtrack that underscores, as it were, the movement of the slides. The viewer is caught up in a paradoxical representation of time, which is simultaneously suspended, like the ball, and ongoing, in the continuous loop of the slideshow and score.

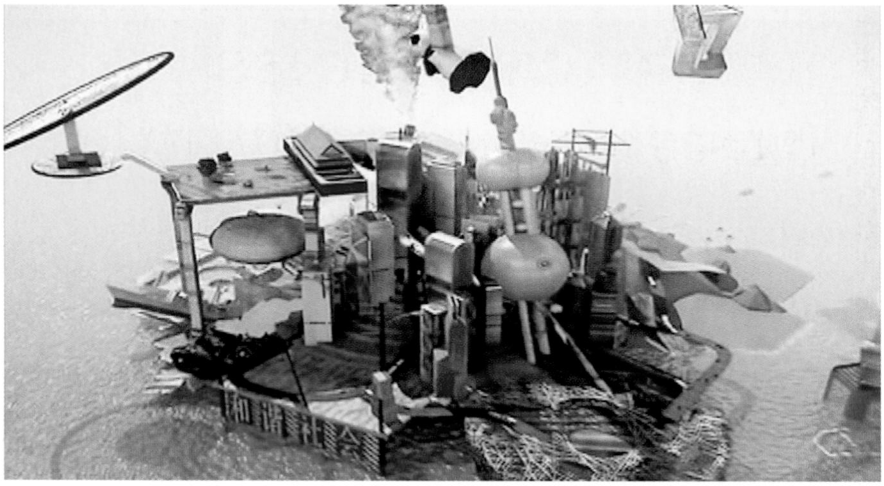

Fig. 11-47 Cao Fei, *RMB City*, in *Art in the Twenty-First Century*, season 5 episode, "Fantasy," 2009. Production still. Segment: Cao Fei.

It is, finally, in the virtual space of the computer that Chinese artist Cao Fei worked on her online virtual *RMB City* (**Fig. 11-47**), a sort of Beijing gone mad. Named for the Chinese unit of currency (RMB/Renminbi), the city is an amalgamation of such historical and contemporary landmarks as the People's Palace Hotel in Beijing, Rem Koolhaas's CCTV building in Beijing (see Fig. 14-44), and the "Bird's Nest" stadium built for the 2008 Beijing Summer Olympics (see Fig. 1-3). Cao Fei herself inhabited it as her avatar, China Tracy, who, across a period of two years, invited the public and various artists to explore issues, ranging from art and architecture to literature, cinema, and politics, while functioning not as themselves but as their avatar personalities, the interaction between whom Cao describes in the art21 *Exclusive* video "Cao Fei: Avatars." Cao designed the space in her home studio in Guangzhou, China, and then had the online virtual-world company Linden Lab, headquartered in San Francisco, create and host the interactive three-dimensional space of the city on its virtual world platform. Thus, *RMB City* was a digital art space in which the viewer's avatar could actively participate and interact with others.

THE CRITICAL PROCESS

Thinking about Photography and Time-Based Media

Jeff Wall's *A Sudden Gust of Wind* (**Fig. 11-48**) is a large, backlit photographic image modeled on a nineteenth-century Japanese print by Hokusai, *Sunshu Ejiri* (**Fig. 11-49**), from the series *Thirty-Six Views of Mount Fuji*, which also includes *The Great Wave off Kanagawa* (see Fig. 7-21). Wall's interest lies, at least in part, in the transformations contemporary culture has worked on traditional media. Thus his billboardlike photograph creates a scene radically different from the original. What sorts of transformations can you see? Consider, first of all, the content of Wall's piece. What does it mean that businessmen inhabit the scene rather than Japanese in traditional dress? How has the plain at Ejiri—considered one of the most beautiful locations in all of Japan—been translated by Wall? And though Hokusai indicates Mount Fuji with a simple line drawing, why has Wall eliminated the mountain altogether? (Remember that Fuji is, for the Japanese, a national symbol, and it is virtually held in spiritual reverence.)

But perhaps the greatest transformation of all is from the print to the photograph. Wall's format, in fact, is meant to invoke cinema, and the scene is anything but the result of some chance photographic encounter. Wall employed professional actors, staged the scene carefully, and shot it over the course of nearly five months. The final image consists of 50 separate pieces of film spliced together through digital technology to create a completely artificial but absolutely realistic scene. For Wall, photography has become "the perfect synthetic technology," as conducive to the creation of propaganda as art. What is cinematic about this piece? What does this say about the nature of film as a medium—not only photographic film but motion-picture film? Where does "truth"

Fig. 11-48 Jeff Wall, *A Sudden Gust of Wind (after Hokusai)*, 1993. Transparency in lightbox, 7 ft. 6$\frac{3}{16}$ in. × 12 ft. 4$\frac{7}{16}$ in. Tate Gallery, London.
Courtesy of the artist.

Fig. 11-49 Hokusai, *Sunshu Ejiri*, from the series *Thirty-Six Views of Mount Fuji*, ca. 1830–32. Polychrome woodblock print, ink and color on paper, $9\frac{7}{8} \times 14\frac{3}{4}$ in. Metropolitan Museum of Art, New York.
Henry L. Phillips Collection, Bequest of Henry L. Phillips, 1939, JP2953. © 2015. Image copyright Metropolitan Museum of Art/Art Resource/Scala, Florence.

lie? Can we—indeed, should we—trust what we see? If we can so easily create "believable" imagery, what are the possibilities for belief itself? And, perhaps most important of all, why must we, engaged in the critical process, consider not just the image itself, but also the way the image is made, the artistic process?

Thinking Back

11.1 Describe the origins of photography and the formal principles that most inform it.

In 1839, Englishman William Henry Fox Talbot presented a process for fixing negative images on paper coated with light-sensitive chemicals. This process, which Talbot called photogenic drawing, resulted in some of the first photographs. How does photogenic drawing differ from daguerreotype photography? What is the calotype process? What new process did Julia Margaret Cameron use, and why did she sometimes blur the features of her subjects? What was the intended effect of photographing the American Civil War?

Why did photographers like Alfred Stieglitz and Paul Strand emphasize the formal elements of composition? How do An-My Lê's photographs mediate between the factual and the beautiful? What is the "decisive moment"? For many photographers, the real art of photography takes place not behind the viewfinder but in the darkroom. What is the Zone System? What is a camera's aperture? What is involved in the techniques of dodging and burning?

11.2 Describe how color and digital technologies have transformed photographic practice.

In color photography, the formal tensions of black-and-white photography are not necessarily lost. Gary Alvis relies on the contrast between warm and cool colors to achieve his effects, and Nan Goldin on the sometimes jarring interaction of bright, complementary colors. Today, digital technologies have transformed the world of photography, not only rendering film obsolete but transforming photography into a highly manipulable medium. How do both Andreas Gursky and Eleanor Antin use digital technologies to manipulate scale?

11.3 Outline the basic principles of film editing, including montage, as well as the technological developments that advanced the medium.

Editing is the process of arranging the sequences of a film after it has been shot in its entirety. The first great master of editing was D. W. Griffith, who, in *The Birth of a Nation*, essentially invented the standard vocabulary of filmmaking. How does a full shot differ from a medium shot? What is a flashback? What is cross-cutting? Montage is the sequencing of widely disparate images. What, for its creator, Sergei Eisenstein, was its intended effect?

The history of popular cinema is a history of technological advances in the medium. To the silent film was added sound, to sound color. Why is 1939 such a pivotal year in the history of cinema?

11.4 Outline some of the ways that video art has exploited the immediacy of the medium while at the same time critiquing popular culture.

With the introduction in 1965 of the Sony Portapak, artists were suddenly free to explore the medium of video. If video was eventually threatened by rapid technological change, rendering the medium extinct surprisingly quickly as digital media supplanted it, when first introduced, it was attractive to artists for the sense of immediacy it embodied. How did Bruce Nauman's *Live-Taped Video Corridor* exploit the medium's sense of immediacy? Video can be instrumental in documenting otherwise ephemeral performances, such as Chris Burden's *Shoot*. How was Burden's video an important addition to the performance itself? Dara Birnbaum used the medium to critique popular television, and William Wegman tested the medium's visual authority. How do *The Reflecting Pool* and *The Greeting* reflect Bill Viola's technological prowess?

11.5 Discuss some of the technological innovations that have advanced time-based art into the digital age.

Today, video art per se no longer exists—the medium has become entirely digital, and the advances in technology are startling. Nonlinear editing systems and CGI technologies, once innovative and very expensive, are now affordable and available to almost anyone with a computer. How does David Claerbout's *Sections of a Happy Moment* belie the seeming simplicity of its slideshow format? Describe the space that defines Cao Fei's *RMB City*.

Chapter 12
Sculpture

Learning Objectives

12.1 Differentiate among relief, sculpture in-the-round, and sculpture as an environment.

12.2 Describe carving as a method of sculpture and account for its association with spiritual life.

12.3 Account for the popularity of molded ceramic sculpture.

12.4 Describe the casting process, and the lost-wax process in particular.

12.5 Define assemblage and account for its association with the idea of transformation.

12.6 Compare and contrast installations and earthworks as environments.

12.7 Describe how the body becomes sculptural in performance art.

Sculpture is one of the oldest and most enduring of all the arts. The types of sculpture considered in this chapter—carving, modeling, casting, construction and assemblage, installation art, and earthworks—employ two basic processes: They are either subtractive or additive in nature. In **subtractive processes**, the sculptor begins with a mass of material larger than the finished work and removes material, or subtracts from that mass until the work achieves its finished form. Carving is a subtractive process. In **additive processes**, the sculptor builds the work, adding material as the work proceeds. Sarah Sze's installation *Triple Point (Pendulum)* (**Fig. 12-1**), which she created as the American representative at the fifty-fifth Venice Biennale in 2013, is an example of an additive work. Sze is notorious for her densely arranged groupings of the most common objects, stepladders and tripods, plastic water bottles and Styrofoam cups, cinder blocks and pillows, live cacti and saltine crackers, nature photographs and rocks bound with string, a pillow, a fan, a pile of books (including a McMaster-Carr catalog containing some 555,000 mechanical, electrical, plumbing, and utility products), a swing arm lamp, and a bucket of paint. These objects—and many, many more—are arranged in a circle around a compass inscribed on the floor displaying the orientation of the cardinal directions, above the center of which hangs a pendulum, its erratic and unpredictable motion driven by a small motor on the ceiling. These things come together with what appears to be a sense, at once, of both purpose and randomness. As Sze states in the art21 *Exclusive* video "Sarah Sze: Improvisation": "Improvisation is crucial. I want the work to be sort of an experience of something alive—to have this feeling that it was improvised, that you can see decisions happening on site, the way you see a live sports event, the way you hear jazz." This mass of things, which operate, as she says, at "the edge between life and art," suggest a kind of dystopian potential in the proliferation of "stuff," as if ecological catastrophe threatens to spread in every direction as things increasingly accumulate.

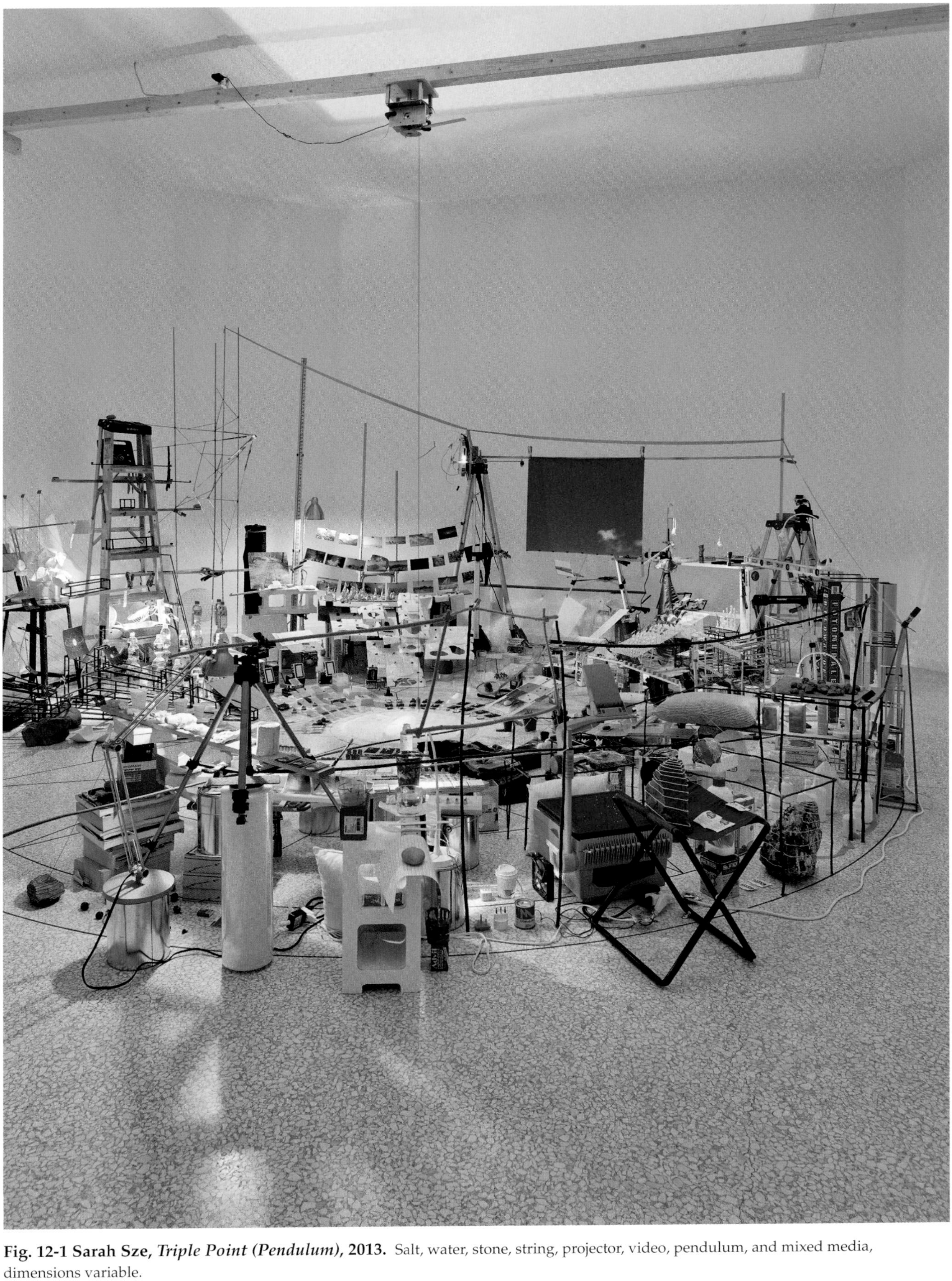

Fig. 12-1 Sarah Sze, *Triple Point (Pendulum)*, 2013. Salt, water, stone, string, projector, video, pendulum, and mixed media, dimensions variable.

The Three Forms of Sculptural Space

How do relief, sculpture in-the-round, and sculpture as environment differ?

Sculptures occupy the same physical, three-dimensional space that we inhabit. They could even be said to intrude into our space, demanding that we interact with them, and we experience them in three distinct ways—as relief, in-the-round, and as environments. And each of these, in turn, makes very different demands upon the viewer. We might look at them on a wall, rather as we look at a painting. We might walk around them. Or we might enter into them, so that we, in effect, become part of them. Finally, as we will see at the end of this chapter, in performance art the body itself can become a kind of living sculpture.

Relief

The raised portion of a woodblock plate stands out in relief against the background (see Chapter 10). The woodblock plate is, in essence, a carved **relief** sculpture, a sculpture that has three-dimensional depth but is meant to be seen from only one side. In other words, it is **frontal**, meant to be viewed from the front—and it is very often used to decorate architecture.

The Greeks, for instance, used the sculptural art of relief as a means to decorate and embellish the beauty of their great architectural achievements. Forms and figures carved in relief are spoken of as done in either **low relief** or **high relief**. (Some people prefer the corresponding French terms, *bas-relief* and *haut-relief*.) The very shallow depth of Egyptian raised reliefs is characteristic of low relief, though technically any sculpture that extends from the plane behind it less than 180 degrees is considered low relief. High-relief sculptures project forward from their base by at least half their depth, and often several elements will be fully in the round. Thus, even though it possesses much greater depth than, say, a carved woodblock plate, the fragment from the **frieze**, or sculptural band, on the Parthenon called the *Maidens and Stewards* (**Fig. 12-2**) projects only a little distance from the background, and no sculptural element is detached entirely from it. It is thus still considered low relief.

The naturalism of the Parthenon frieze is especially worth noting. Figures overlap one another and are shown in three-quarter view, making the space seem far deeper than it actually is. The figures themselves seem almost to move in slow procession, and the garments they wear reveal real flesh and limbs beneath them. The carving of this drapery invites a play of light and shadow that further activates the surface, increasing the sense of movement.

Two of the most famous examples of high-relief sculpture in the history of art were designed in 1401–02 by Filippo Brunelleschi and Lorenzo Ghiberti as part of a competition to win the commission from the city of Florence for the doors of the city's baptistery, a building standing in front of Florence Cathedral and used for the

Fig. 12-2 ***Maidens and Stewards*, fragment of the *Panathenaic Procession*, from the east frieze of the Parthenon, Acropolis, Athens, 447–438 BCE.** Marble, height approx. 43 in. Musée du Louvre, Paris.
Bridgeman Images.

Christian rite of baptism. The judges requested a panel depicting the story of how God tested the faith of the patriarch Abraham by commanding him to sacrifice Isaac, his only son. Abraham took Isaac into the wilderness to perform the deed, but at the last moment an angel stopped him, implying that God was convinced of Abraham's faith and would be satisfied with the sacrifice of a ram instead. Brunelleschi and Ghiberti both depicted the same aspect of the story, the moment when the angel intervenes. Rather than placing their figures on a shallow platform, as one might expect in the shallow space available in a relief sculpture, both sought to create a sense of a deep, receding space, enhancing the appearance of reality. Brunelleschi placed Isaac in the center of the panel and the other figures, whose number and type were probably prescribed by the judges, all around (**Fig. 12-3**). The opposition between Abraham and the angel, as the angel grabs Abraham's arm to stop him from plunging his knife into his son's breast, is highly dramatic and realistic, an effect achieved in no small part by Brunelleschi's rendering of them as almost fully realized 360-degree forms. Ghiberti, in contrast, set the sacrifice to one side of the panel (**Fig. 12-4**). He replaced a sense of physical strain with graceful rhythms, so that Isaac and Abraham are unified by the bowed curves of their bodies, Isaac's nude body turning on its axis to face Abraham. The angel in the upper right-hand corner is represented in a more dynamic manner than in Brunelleschi's panel. This heavenly visitor seems to have rushed in from deep space. The effect is achieved by foreshortening (see Chapter 4). In addition, the strong diagonal of the landscape, which extends from beneath the sacrificial altar and rises up into a large rocky outcrop behind the other figures, creates a more vivid sense of real three-dimensional space than Brunelleschi's scene, and this must have played a role in the judges' decision to award the commission to Ghiberti.

Fig. 12-4 Lorenzo Ghiberti, *Sacrifice of Isaac*, competition relief commissioned for the doors of the Baptistery, Florence, 1401–02.
Parcel-gilt bronze, 21 × 17½ in. Museo Nazionale del Bargello, Florence.

Fig. 12-3 Filippo Brunelleschi, *Sacrifice of Isaac*, competition relief commissioned for the doors of the Baptistery, Florence, 1401–02.
Parcel-gilt bronze, 21 × 17½ in. Museo Nazionale del Bargello, Florence.

Sculpture In-the-Round

Perhaps because the human figure has traditionally been one of the chief subjects of sculpture, movement is one of the defining characteristics of the medium. Even in relief sculptures, it is as if the figures want to escape the confines of their base. **Sculpture in-the-round**—or freestanding sculpture—literally demands movement. It is meant to be seen from all sides, and the viewer must move around it. Giambologna's *Capture of the Sabine Women* (**Figs. 12-5 and 12-6**) is impossible to represent in a single photograph. Its figures rise in a spiral, and the sculpture changes dramatically as the viewer walks around it and experiences it from each side. It is in part the horror of the scene that lends the sculpture its power, for as it draws us around it, in order to see more of what is happening, it involves us both physically and emotionally in the scene it depicts.

It was, in fact, simply to demonstrate his inventive skill that Giambologna undertook to carve the sculpture. He conceived of it as three serpentine, or spiraling, figures, lacking a single predominant view, without specific reference, let alone title. But when the head of the Florentine government decided to place it in the Loggia della Signoria, a focal point of Florentine life, Giambologna was asked to name it. He suggested that the woman might be Andromeda, wife of Perseus, a statue of whom already graced the space. Somebody else, however, suggested the Sabines as a subject, and the sculpture has been known as *The Capture of the Sabine Women* ever since. (According to legend, the founders of ancient Rome, unable to find wives among their neighbors, the Sabines, tricked the entire tribe into visiting Rome for a

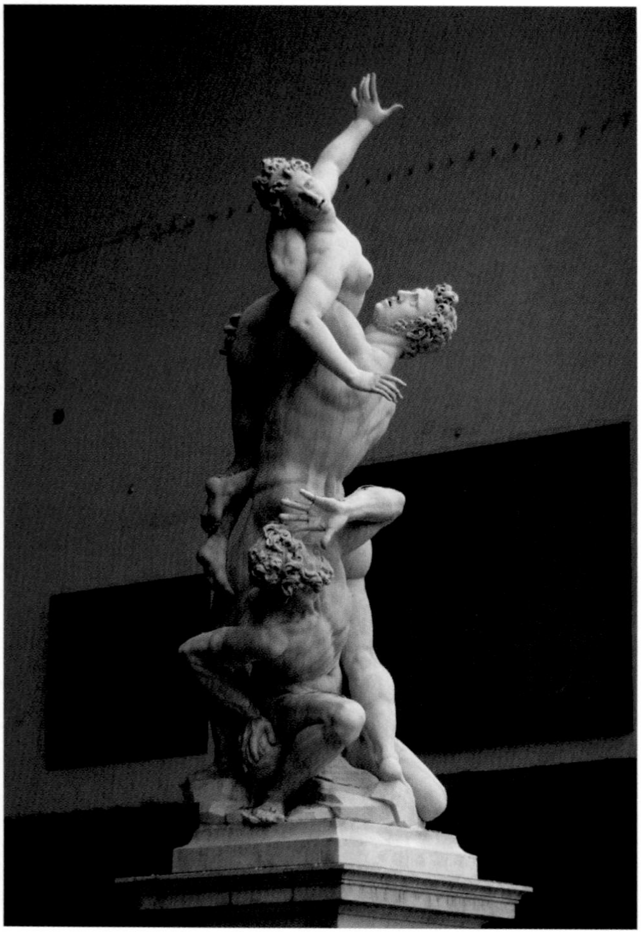

Figs. 12-5 and 12-6 Giambologna, *The Capture of the Sabine Women*, 1583.
Marble, height 13 ft. 6 in. Loggia dei Lanzi, Florence.

festival and then took its women by force.) What mattered was not the piece's subject, however, but its sculptural genius in uniting three figures in a single successful spiral composition.

Environments

The viewer is even more engaged in the other sculptural media we will discuss in this chapter—environments. **Environments** are sculptural spaces which you can physically enter into or explore either indoors or in a contained space out-of-doors, such as a plaza, where they are generally referred to as **installations**. **Earthworks**, by contrast, are large-scale outdoor environments made in and of the land itself. An environment can be **site-specific**—that is, designed for a particular place in such a way that the space is transformed by its presence—or, like Sol LeWitt's instructions for installing his drawings (see Fig. 3-12), it can be modified to fit into any number of potential sites.

For his large-scale environment *TorusMacroCopula* (**Fig. 12-7**), one of four sculptures installed in the gallery space of Louis Vuitton's Tokyo store in 2012–13, Brazilian sculptor Ernesto Neto suspended thousands of plastic balls in expanses of netting hung from the ceiling to form a long, circuitous pathway above the floor of the gallery which visitors were invited to traverse. The plastic balls are "macro" reproductions of fish eggs—or roe—contained in tightly woven egg sacs. The entire structure is a "torus"—that is, a surface generated by revolving a circle around a central axis (a doughnut would be an example), but in this case the torus has been cut and its ends unlinked. By way of contrast, a "copula" is a link, usually between the subject of a sentence and its predicate, as in "the man is tall," where "is" is the copula. Indeed, the verb *to be* is among the most common copulas, and here Neto uses it in his title to suggest that the idea of "being" is central to the work. For Neto, body and mind are inextricably linked—body is mind and mind is body—and it is as "body-minds that we connect the things in this world, in life—the way we touch, the way we feel, the way we think and the way we deal." Thus, as we walk precariously along the catwalk, suspended in space, tottering, grasping for balance, our body-mind becomes acutely aware of itself. The title of Neto's installation as a whole was *Madness Is Part of Life*, and the state of imbalance in which viewers find themselves immersed is, for Neto, a metaphor for madness itself, an experience outside the rules of "being" by which we normally—and more or less unconsciously—operate.

Fig. 12-7 Ernesto Neto, *TorusMacroCopula*, one of four sculptures in *Madness Is Part of Life*, 2012.
Installation view, Espace Louis Vuitton, Tokyo, 2012–13. Polypropylene, polyester string, and plastic balls, length 25 ft. 7 in.
Courtesy of the artist, Tanya Bonakdar Gallery, New York, and Galeria Fortes Vilaça, São Paolo.

Carving

What is carving and why is stone carving associated with spiritual life?

With these terms in mind—relief sculpture, sculpture in-the-round, and environments—we can now turn to the specific methods of making sculpture. The first of these is carving, a subtractive process in which the material being carved is chipped, gouged, or hammered away from an inert, raw block of material. Wood and stone are the two most common carving materials. Both present problems for the artist to solve. Sculptors who work in wood must pay attention to the wood's grain, since wood is only easily carved in the direction it grew. To work "against the grain" is to risk destroying the block. Sculptors who work in stone must take into account the different characteristics of each type of stone. Sandstone is gritty and coarse, marble soft and crystalline, granite dense and hard. Each must be dealt with differently. For Michelangelo, each stone held within it the secret of what it might become as a sculpture. "The best artist," he wrote, "has no concept which some single marble does not enclose within its mass. . . . Taking away . . . brings out a living figure in alpine and hard stone, which . . . grows the more as the stone is chipped away." But carving is so difficult that even Michelangelo often failed to realize his concept. In his *"Atlas" Slave* (**Fig. 12-8**), he has given up. The block of stone resists Michelangelo's desire to transform it, as if refusing to release the figure it holds enslaved within it. Yet, arguably, the power of Michelangelo's imagination lies in his willingness to leave the figure unrealized. Atlas, condemned to bearing the weight of the world on his shoulders forever as punishment for challenging the Greek gods, is literally held captive in the stone.

From the earliest times, because of its permanence, stone has borne a certain connection to ideas of

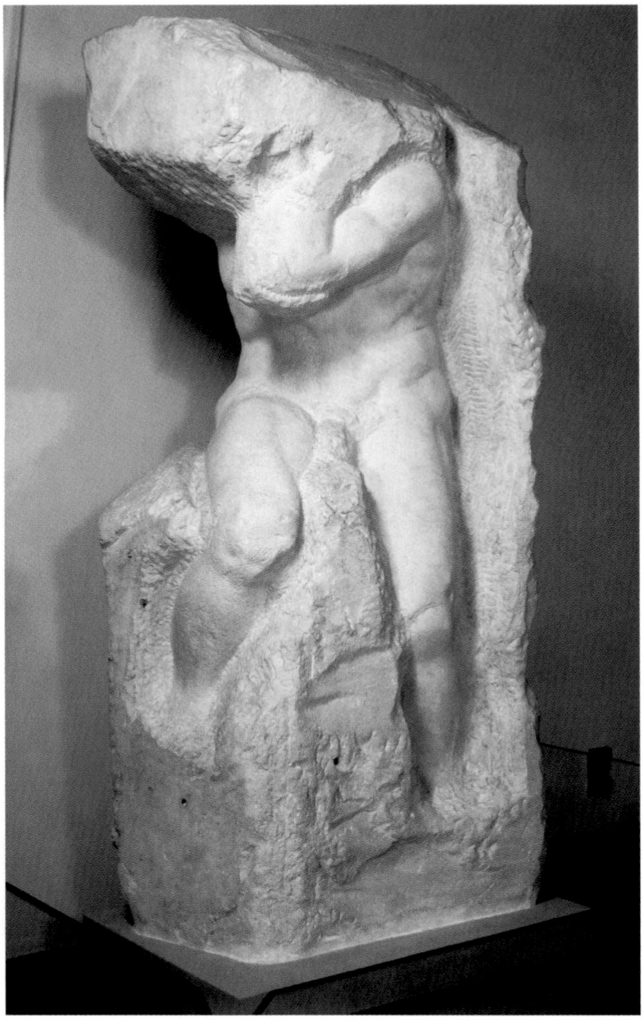

Fig. 12-8 Michelangelo, *"Atlas" Slave*, ca. 1513–20. Marble, 9 ft. 2 in. Galleria dell'Accademia, Florence.

© 2015. Photo Scala, Florence, courtesy of the Ministero Beni e Att. Culturali.

Fig. 12-9 *Menkaure with a Woman*, probably Khamerernebty, from valley temple of Menkaure, Giza, Dynasty 4, ca. 2480 BCE. Schist, height 4 ft. 8 in. Museum of Fine Arts, Boston.

Boston Museum Fine Art Expedition, 11.1738. Photograph © 2015 Museum of Fine Arts, Boston.

immortality and the spiritual world. In Egypt, for example, stone funerary figures (**Fig. 12-9**) were carved to bear the ***ka***, or individual spirit, of the deceased into the eternity of the afterlife. The permanence of the stone was felt to guarantee the *ka*'s immortality. For the ancient Greeks, only the gods were immortal. What tied the world of the gods to the world of humanity was beauty itself, and the most beautiful thing of all was the perfectly proportioned, usually athletic, male form.

Egyptian sculpture was known to the Greeks as early as the seventh century BCE, and Greek sculpture is indebted to it, but the Greeks quickly evolved a much more naturalistic style. In other words, compared with the rigidity of the Egyptian figures, this *Kouros*, or youth (**Fig. 12-10**), is both more at ease and more lifelike. Despite the fact that his feet have been lost, we can see that the weight of his body is on his left leg, allowing his right leg to relax completely. This youth, then, begins to move. The sculpture begins to be animated, to portray not just the figure but also its movement. It is as if the stone has begun to come to life. Furthermore, the *Kouros* is much more anatomically correct than his Egyptian forebear. In fact, by the fifth century BCE, the practice of medicine had established itself as a respected field of study in Greece, and anatomical investigations were commonplace. At the time that the *Kouros* was sculpted, the body was an object of empirical study, and its parts were understood to be unified in a single, flowing harmony.

This flowing harmony was further developed by Praxiteles, without doubt the most famous sculptor of his day. In works such as *Hermes and Dionysus* (**Fig. 12-11**), he shifted the weight of the body even more dynamically, in a pose known as ***contrapposto***, or counterbalance. In *contrapposto*, the weight falls on one foot, raising the corresponding hip. This shift in weight is countered by a turn of the shoulders, so that

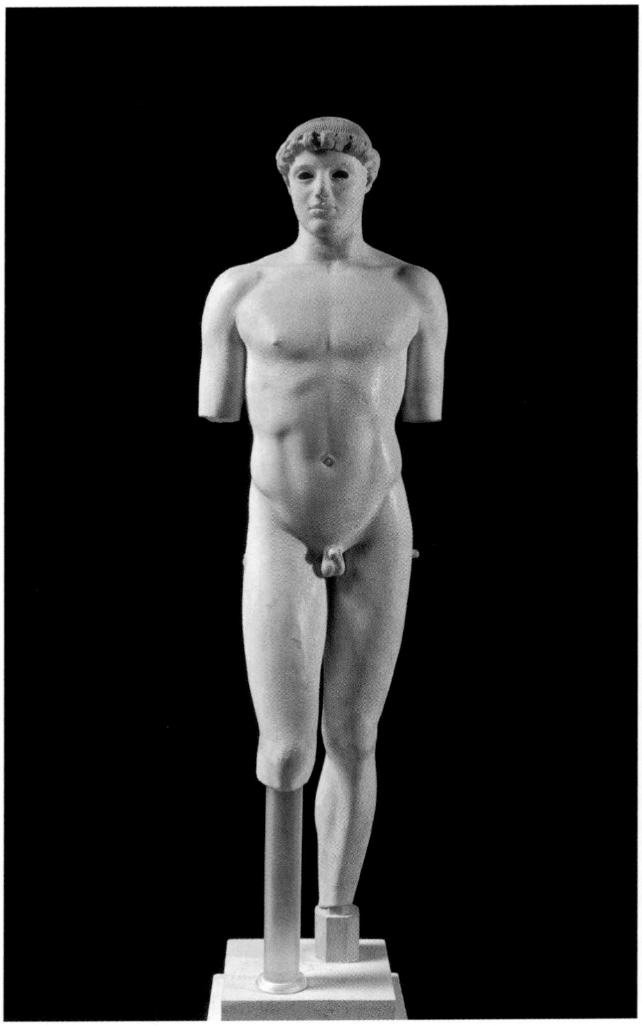

Fig. 12-10 *Kouros* (a.k.a. *The Kritios Boy*), ca. 480 BCE.
Marble, height 36 in.
Inv. no. 698 akg-image/De Agostini/G. Nimatallah.

Fig. 12-11 Praxiteles, *Hermes and Dionysus*, ca. 330 BCE.
Marble, height 7 ft. 1 in. National Archaeological Museum, Athens.
© Craig & Marie Mauzy, Athens.

the figure stands in a sort of S-curve. The result is an even greater sense of naturalism and movement.

Modeling

Why is clay such a popular medium for modeled sculpture?

When you pick up a handful of clay, you almost instinctively know what to do with it. You smack it with your hand, pull it, squeeze it, bend it, pinch it between your fingers, roll it, slice it with a knife, and shape it. Then you grab another handful, repeat the process, and add it to the first, building a form piece by piece. These are the basic gestures of the additive process of modeling, in which a pliant substance, usually clay, is molded.

Clay, a natural material found worldwide, has been used by artists to make everything from pots to sculptures since the earliest times. Its appeal is largely due to its capacity to be molded into forms that retain their shape. Once formed, the durability of the material can be ensured by **firing** it—that is, baking it—at temperatures normally ranging between 1,200 and 2,700 degrees Fahrenheit in a **kiln**, or oven, designed especially for the process. This causes it to become hard and waterproof. We call all works made of clay **ceramics**.

Throughout history, the Chinese have made extraordinary ceramic works, including the finest porcelains of fine, pure white clay. We tacitly acknowledge their expertise when we refer to our own "best" dinner plates as "china." But the most massive display of the Chinese mastery of ceramic art was discovered in 1974 by well diggers who accidentally drilled into the tomb of Qin Shihuangdi, the first emperor of China (**Fig. 12-12**). In 221 BCE, Qin Shihuangdi united the country under one rule and imposed order, establishing a single code of law and requiring the use of a single written language. Under his rule, the Great Wall was built, and construction of his tomb required a force of more than 700,000 men. Qin Shihuangdi was buried near the central Chinese city of Xian, or Chin (the origin of the name China), and his tomb contained more than 6,000 life-size, and extraordinarily lifelike, ceramic figures of soldiers and horses, immortal bodyguards for the emperor. More recently, clerks, scribes, and other court figures have been discovered, as well as a set of magnificent bronze horses and chariots.

Fig. 12-12 Tomb of Emperor Qin Shihuangdi, 221–206 BCE. Painted ceramic figures, life-size.

Casting

What is casting and what, in particular, is the lost-wax process?

The body parts of the warriors in Qin Shihuangdi's tomb were all first modeled by the emperor's army of artisans. Then, molds were made of the various parts, and they were filled with liquid clay and fired over high heat, a process repeated over and over again. Artisans then assembled the soldiers, choosing different heads, bodies, arms, and legs in order to give each sculpture a sense of individual identity. In other words, each piece was first cast, and then later assembled.

Casting employs a mold into which some molten material is poured and allowed to harden. It is an invention of the Bronze Age (beginning in approximately 2500 BCE), when it was first used to make various utensils by simply pouring liquid bronze into open-faced molds. The technology is not much more complicated than that of a gelatin mold. You pour gelatin into the mold and let it harden. When you remove the gelatin, it is shaped like the inside of the mold. Small figures made of bronze are similarly produced by making a simple mold of an original modeled form, filling the mold with bronze, and then breaking the mold away.

As the example of gelatin demonstrates, bronze is not the only material that can be cast. In the kingdom of Benin, located in southern Nigeria, on the coastal plain west of the Niger River, brass casting reached a level of extraordinary accomplishment as early as the late fourteenth century. Brass, which is a compound composed of copper and zinc, is similar to bronze but contains less copper and is yellower in color. When, after 1475, the people of Benin began to trade with the Portuguese for copper and brass, an explosion of brass casting occurred. A brass head of an oba, or king of a dynasty, which dates from the eighteenth century (**Fig. 12-13**), is an example of a cast brass sculpture. When an oba dies, one of the first duties of the new oba—the old oba's son—is to establish an altar commemorating his father and to decorate it with newly cast brass heads. The heads are not portraits. Rather, they are generalized images that emphasize the king's coral-bead crown and high bead collar, the symbols of his authority. The head has a special significance in Benin ritual. According to British anthropologist R. E. Bradbury, the head

> symbolizes life and behavior in this world, the capacity to organize one's actions in such a way as to survive and prosper. It is one's Head that "leads one through life." . . . On a man's Head depends not only his own well-being but that of his wives and children. . . . At the state level, the welfare of the people as a whole depends on the Oba's Head which is the object of worship at the main event of the state ritual year.

The oba head is an example of one of the most enduring, and one of the most complicated, processes for casting metal. The **lost-wax process**, also known as ***cire-perdue***, was perfected by the Greeks, if not actually invented by them. Because metal is both expensive and heavy, a technique had to be developed to create hollow

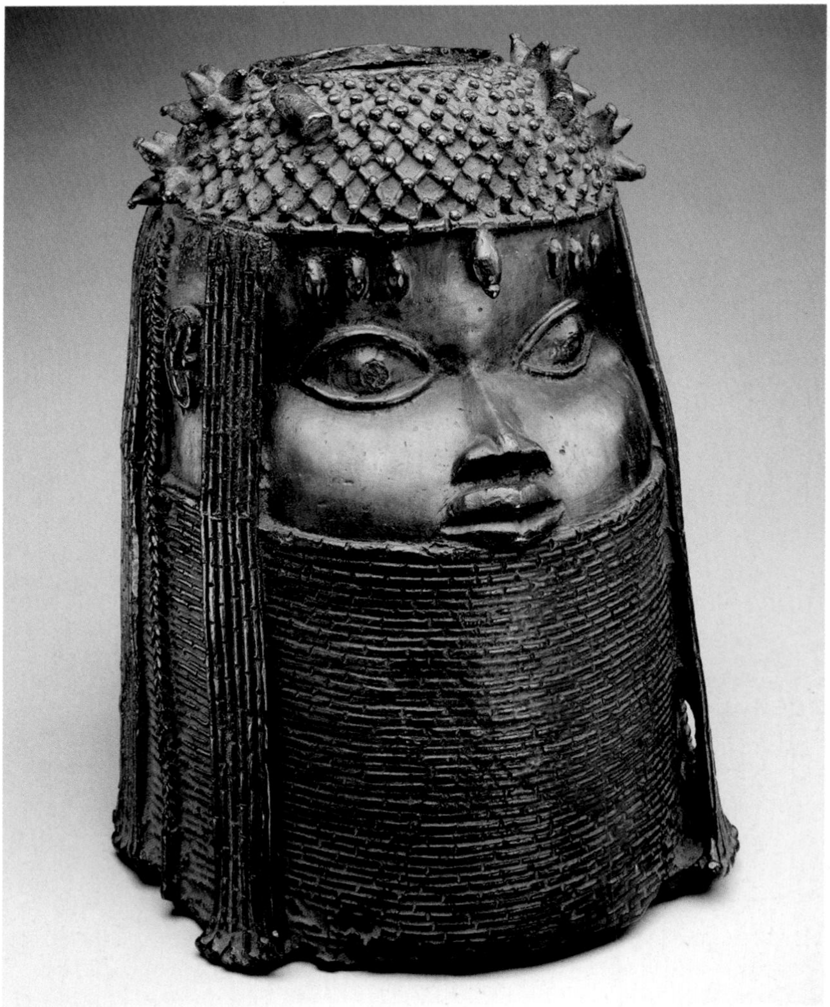

Fig. 12-13 *Head of an Oba*, Nigeria, Africa, Edo, Court of Benin, 18th century. Brass and iron, height 13⅛ in. Metropolitan Museum of Art, New York. Gift of Mr. and Mrs. Klaus G. Perls, 1991.17.2. © 2015. Image copyright Metropolitan Museum of Art/Art Resource/Scala, Florence.

images rather than solid ones, a process schematized in simplified terms here (**Fig. 12-14**).

In the lost-wax method, the sculpture is first modeled in some soft, pliable material, such as clay, wax, or plaster in a putty state. This model looks just like the finished sculpture but the material of which it is composed is of course nowhere near as durable as metal. As the process proceeds, this core is at least theoretically disposable, though many sculptors, including Auguste Rodin (see Fig. 7-29), have habitually retained these cores for possible recasting.

A mold is then made of the model (today, synthetic rubber is most commonly used to make this mold). When it is removed, we are left with a negative impression of the original—in other words, something like a gelatin mold of the object. Molten wax is then poured or brushed into this impression to the same thickness desired for the final sculpture—about an eighth of an inch. The space inside this wax lining is filled with an **investment**—a mixture of water, plaster, and powder made from ground-up pottery. The mold is then removed, and we are left with a wax casting, identical to the original model, that is filled with the investment material. Rods of wax are then applied to the wax casting; they stick out from it like giant hairs. They will carry off melted wax during baking and will eventually provide channels through which the molten bronze will be poured. The sculpture now consists of a thin layer of wax supported by the investment. Sometimes bronze pins are driven through the wax into the investment in order to hold investment, casting, and channels in place.

This wax cast, with its wax channels, is ready to be covered with another outer mold of investment. When this outer mold cures, it is then baked in a kiln at a temperature of 1,500 degrees Fahrenheit, with the wax replica inside it. The wax rods melt, providing channels for the rest of the wax to run out as well—hence the term "lost-wax process." A thin space where the wax once was now lies empty between the inner core and the outer mold, the separation maintained by the bronze pins.

Molten bronze is poured into the casting gate, an opening in the top of the mold, filling the cavity where the wax once was. Hence, many people refer to casting as a **replacement process**—bronze replaces wax. When the bronze has cooled, the mold and the investment are removed, and we are left with a bronze replica of the wax form, complete with the latticework of rods. The rods are cut from the bronze cast, and the surface is smoothed and finished.

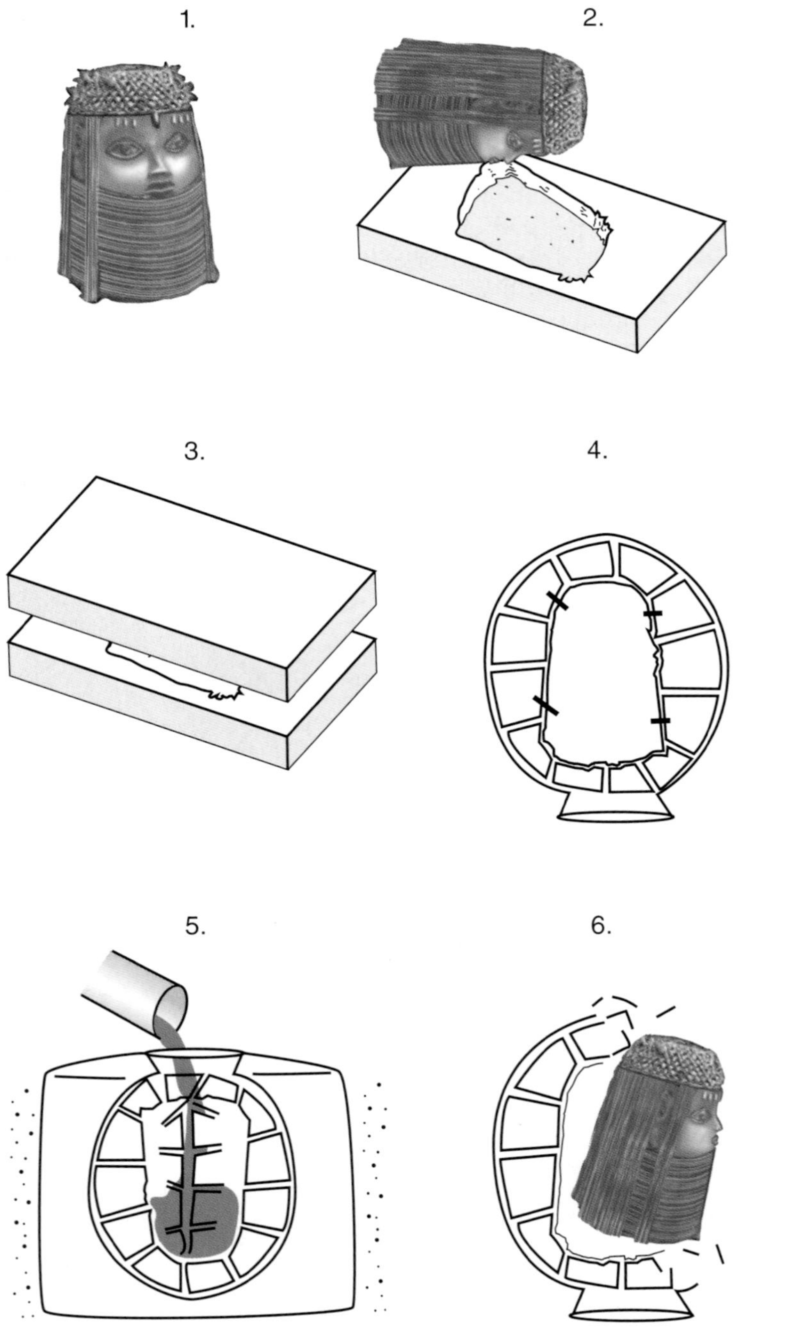

Fig. 12-14 The lost-wax casting process. A positive model (1), often created with clay, is used to make a negative mold (2). The mold is coated with wax, the wax shell is filled with a cool fireclay, and the mold is removed (3). Metal rods, to hold the shell in place, and wax rods, to vent the mold, are then added (4). The whole is placed in sand, and the wax is burned out (5). Molten bronze is poured in where the wax used to be. When the bronze has hardened, the whole is removed from the sand, and the rods and vents are removed (6).

Bronze is so soft and malleable that the individual pieces can easily be joined in either of two ways: pounded together with a hammer, the procedure used in Greek times, or welded, the more usual procedure today. Finally, the shell is reassembled to form a perfect hollow replica of the original model. Auguste Rodin's large *Burghers of Calais* (**Fig. 12-15**) was, in fact, cast in several pieces and then welded together. Rodin's sculpture was commissioned by the city of Calais to commemorate six of its leading citizens (or burghers) who, during the Hundred Years' War in 1347, agreed to sacrifice themselves and free the city of siege by the English by turning themselves over to the enemy for execution. Rodin depicts them, dressed in sackcloth with rope halters, about to give themselves up to the English. Each is caught up in his own thoughts—they are, alternately, angry, resentful, resigned, distraught, and fearful. Their hands and feet are deliberately elongated, exaggerating their pathos. Rodin felt that the hand was capable of expressing the full range of human emotion. In this work, the hands give, they suffer, they hold at bay, they turn inward. The piece, all told, is a remarkable example of sculpture in-the-round, an assemblage of individual fragments that the viewer can only experience by walking around the whole and taking in each element from a different point of view. As it turns out, the story has a happy ending. The English queen, upon seeing the courage of the burghers, implored her husband to have mercy on them, and he agreed. Still, Rodin depicts them as they trudge toward what they believe will be their final destiny. In fact, the Calais city fathers wanted to raise the sculpture on a pedestal, but Rodin insisted that it remain on level ground, where citizens could identify with the burghers' sacrifice and make their heroism at least potentially their own.

Although, because of its durability, bronze is a favorite material for casting sculptures meant for the out-of-doors, other materials have become available to artists in recent years, including aluminum and fiberglass. Because it is a material light enough to hang on a brick wall in high relief, fiberglass became the preferred medium of John Ahearn. In 1980, Ahearn moved to the South Bronx and began to work with the neighborhood's people, sometimes in collaboration with his friend and local resident Rigoberto Torre. He had learned the art of plaster casting from his uncle, who had cast plaster statues for churches and cemeteries. The figures in *Homage to the People of the South Bronx: Double Dutch at Kelly Street 1:*

Fig. 12-15 Auguste Rodin, *The Burghers of Calais*, 1884–85. Bronze, 6 ft. 7⅜ in. × 6 ft. 8⅞ in.
Place de l'Hôtel de Ville, Calais, France.
© imageBROKER/Alamy.

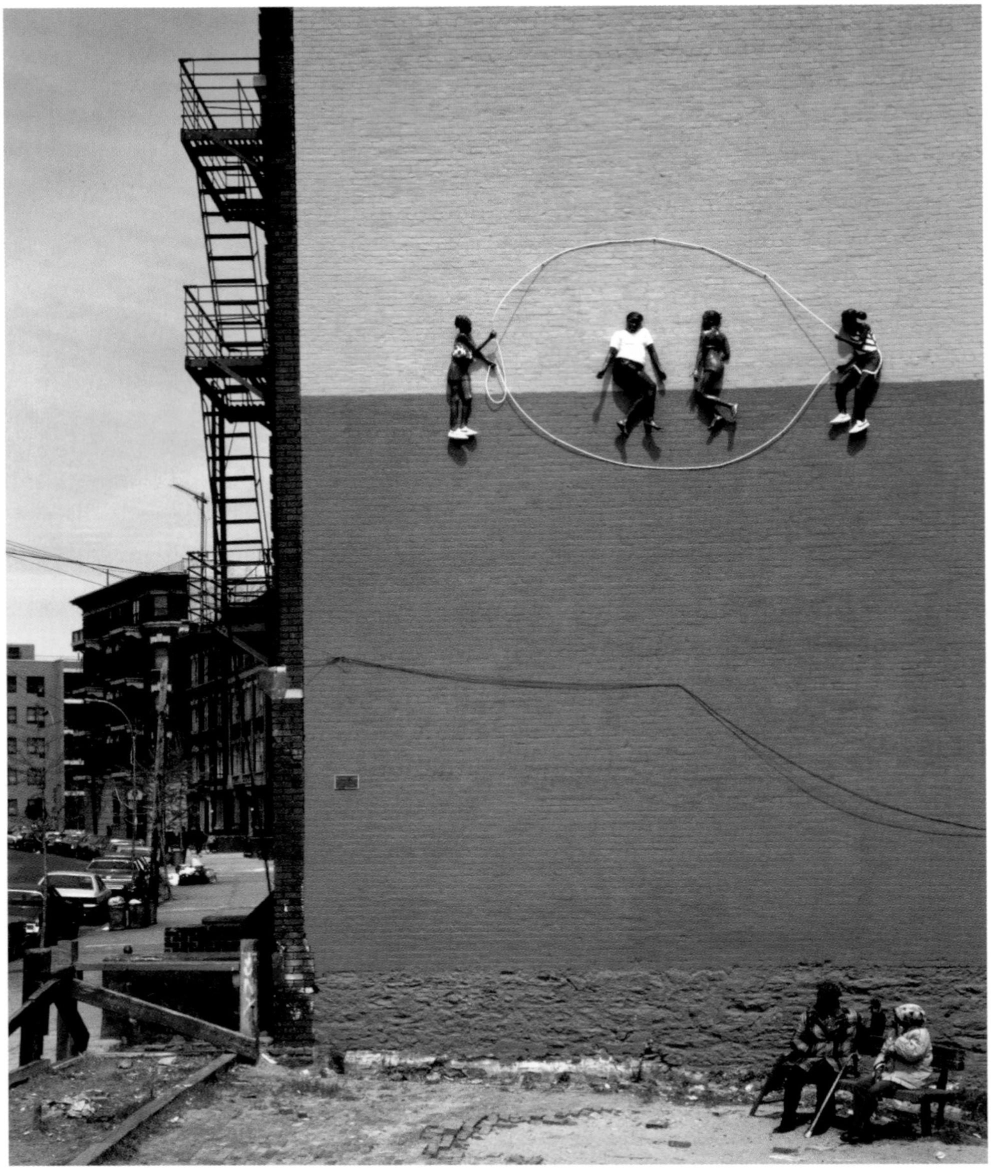

Fig. 12-16 John Ahearn, *Homage to the People of the South Bronx: Double Dutch at Kelly Street 1: Frieda, Jevette, Towana, Stacey*, 1981–82. Cast fiberglass, oil, and cable, each figure 4 ft. 6 in. × 4 ft. 6 in. × 12 in.
Image courtesy of Alexander and Bonin, New York.

Frieda, Jevette, Towana, Stacey (**Fig. 12-16**) almost look as if they are alive, save for the fact that they are jump-roping some 20 feet up the side of a building in which one of the girls actually lived. In fact, Frieda, Jevette, Towana, and Stacey were all cast from life in plaster, a process that required Ahearn's subjects to lie still and breathe through straws while the plaster set on their faces and bodies. Then, in a manner quite similar to the lost-wax bronze process, the plaster figures were realized in fiberglass. "The key to my work is life—lifecasting," says Ahearn. "The people I cast know that they are as responsible for my work as I am, even more so. The people make my sculptures." In works like *Homage to the People of the South Bronx*, Ahearn managed to capture the spirit of a community that was financially impoverished but that possessed real, if unrecognized, dignity.

Assemblage

Why is assemblage so often associated with the idea of transformation?

To the degree that they are composed of separately cast pieces later welded or grouped together, works like Rodin's *Burghers of Calais* and Ahearn's *Homage to the People of the South Bronx* are examples of **assemblage**, the process of bringing individual objects or pieces together to form a larger whole. But as a process, assemblage is more often associated with the transformation of common materials into art, in which the artist brings together parts found in the world and puts them together in a new composition. For instance, Louise Nevelson's *Sky Cathedral* (**Fig. 12-17**) is a giant assemblage of wooden boxes, woodworking remnants and scraps, and found objects. It is entirely frontal and functions like a giant high-relief altarpiece—hence its name—transforming and elevating its materials to an almost spiritual dimension. Nevelson manages to make a piece of almost endless variety and difference appear unified and coherent through the asymmetrical balance of its grid structure, the repetition of forms and shapes, and, above all, its overall black coloring. The black lends the piece a certain mystery, which is heightened by the way in which it is lit in the museum, with diffuse light from the sides which deepens the work's shadows. For Nevelson, black is itself simply powerful. It represents a kind of totality since it, indeed, contains all colors. And thus, for her, it is essentially aristocratic, lending whatever it adorns a sense of presence and authority that approaches greatness.

Many African cultures use assemblage to create objects of sacred or spiritual significance. The *nkisi* figure from the Kongo (see Fig. 1-19) is an example. In the Yoruba cultures of western Nigeria and southern Benin, the artworks produced for the king and his court—particularly crowns and other display pieces—are composed of a variety of materials. The display piece commissioned in the early twentieth century by the king of a small Yoruba kingdom combines beadwork, cloth, basketry, and other fiber in a sculptural representation of a royal wife (**Fig. 12-18**). With crested hairdo and child on her back, she is portrayed presenting a lidded offering bowl,

Fig. 12-17 Louise Nevelson, *Sky Cathedral*, 1958. Wood, painted black, 9 ft. 7 in. × 11 ft. 3 in. × 28 in. Albright-Knox Art Gallery, Buffalo, New York.

Gift of Mr. and Mrs. Ben Mildwoff, 136.1958.1-57. © 2015. Digital image, Museum of Modern Art, New York/Scala, Florence. © 2015 Estate of Louise Nevelson/Artists Rights Society (ARS), New York.

Fig. 12-18 Display piece, Yoruba culture, early 20th century. Cloth, basketry, beads, and fiber, height 41¼ in. The British Museum, London.

Af1924,-.136. © The Trustees of the British Museum.

which she holds below her conical breasts. Attendants are attached to her body, one of whom helps her hold the offering bowl by balancing it on her head. Around the bottom of her body, four male figures, wearing top hats, offer their protection, guns at their sides. The beadwork defining all of the sculpture's various elements is itself an assemblage of various geometric designs and patterns. For the Yoruba, geometric shapes, divided into smaller geometric shapes, suggest the infinitude of forces in the cosmos. As in all Yoruba beadwork, the play between different geometric patterns and elements creates a sense of visual dynamism and movement, which the Yoruba call the principle of "shine." Shine not only refers to the shiny characteristics of the glass beadwork itself, but suggests as well the idea of completeness or wholeness. On the one hand, the sculpture is meant to reflect the power of the king, but it is, simultaneously, an acknowledgment, on the king's part, of the power of women, and his incompleteness without them. The Yoruba, in fact, have a deep belief in the powers of what they call "Our Mothers," a term that refers to all Yoruba female ancestors. Kings cannot rule without drawing upon the powers of Our Mothers.

Many assemblages, like Nevelson's *Sky Cathedral*, are made from the throwaway remnants of contemporary commodity culture, transforming them into art. Jeff Koons's sculptures are recreations of commodity culture itself, ranging from three basketballs floating in a half-filled tank of water (*Three Ball Total Equilibrium Tank [Two Dr J Silver Series, Spalding NBA Tip-Off]*, 1985) to a life-size porcelain and gold-plated statue of Michael Jackson cuddling his pet chimpanzee (*Michael Jackson and Bubbles*, 1988). By taking the basketballs out of circulation, in the former, he transforms them into fetish objects, commenting wryly on the culture's adulation of athletic prowess. The latter culminated his *Banality* series, which also included *Pink Panther*, a life-size porcelain sculpture of the Pink Panther in the arms of a bare-breasted blond. But one of his most audacious works—and one of his most popular—is *Puppy* (**Fig. 12-19**), shown here installed in front of the Guggenheim Bilbao museum. An assemblage consisting of an armature of stainless steel, an irrigation system, and live flowering plants, it is nothing other than a Chia Pet grown large. In the art21 *Exclusive* video "Jeff Koons: Versailles," Koons comments that,

Fig. 12-19 Jeff Koons, *Puppy*, 1992. Stainless steel, soil, geotextile fabric, internal irrigation system, and live flowering plants, 40 ft. 6 in. × 40 ft. 6 in. × 21 ft. 4 in. The Solomon R. Guggenheim Foundation, New York.

Fig. 12-20 Robert Gober, *Untitled*, 1999. Plaster, beeswax, human hair, cotton, leather, aluminum pull tabs, and enamel paint, 33½ × 40 × 24¾ in. Philadelphia Museum of Art.

Gift (by exchange) of Mrs. Arthur Barnwell, 1999. © 2015. Photo Philadelphia Museum of Art/Art Resource/Scala, Florence. Photo: Graydon Wood. © Robert Gober. Courtesy of Matthew Marks Gallery.

when he conceived of *Puppy*, he was thinking of Louis XIV of France, whose palace at Versailles, outside Paris, was the most magnificent royal residence in Europe. "It's the type of work," Koons says of *Puppy*,

> that Louis would have had the fantasy for. You know, he'd wake up in the morning . . . and think, "What do I want to see today? I want to see a puppy. I want to see it made out of 60,000 plants, and I want to see it by this evening." And he would come home that night, and *voilà*, there it would be."

It is an image, in other words, that reflects the taste of arguably the most profligate king in history, a taste for extravagance appealing equally, it would seem, to the public today. But however kitsch, *Puppy* insists on its status as art, even as it causes us to reflect on the commodity status of art itself.

Robert Gober's sculptural assemblages evolve from fragments of our everyday domestic lives that are juxtaposed with one another to create haunting objects that seem to exist halfway between reality and the fitful nightmare of a dreamscape. Gober repeatedly returns to the same fundamental repertoire of objects—body parts (made of plaster and beeswax for skin), particularly lower legs, usually graced with actual body hair, shoes, and socks; storm drains; pipes; doors; children's furniture; and, his most ubiquitous image, a common domestic sink. His work, in essence, does not include, as the saying goes, "everything but the kitchen sink"; it includes everything *and* the kitchen sink. *Untitled* (**Fig. 12-20**) is, in this sense, standard Gober fare. But despite the repetition of certain objects across the body of his work, each new sculpture seems entirely fresh.

Part of the power of Gober's works is that their meaning is open-ended, even as they continually evoke a wide range of American clichés. His objects invite multiple interpretations, none of which can ever take priority over any of the others. Consider, for instance, a sink. A sink is, first of all, a place for cleansing, its white enamel sparkling in a kind of hygienic purity. But this one is nonfunctional, its drain leading nowhere—a sort of "sinkhole." While looking at it, the viewer begins to get a "sinking" feeling that there is more to this image than might have been apparent at first. Of course, the two legs suspended over the basin instead of water spigots has suggested this to even the unthoughtful viewer all along.

They are, evidently, the legs of a young girl. Although not visible in a photograph, they are covered with a light dusting of actual human hair. Oddly enough, they are both left feet, suggesting adolescent awkwardness (a person who can't dance is said to have "two left feet"). More to the point, hanging over the sink, they evoke something akin to bathroom humor even as they seem to suggest the psychological mire of some vague sexual dread.

Installations and Earthworks

What do installations and earthworks have in common and how do they differ?

Obviously, the introduction of any work of art into a given space changes it. Encountered in an environment where the viewer expects to see works of art—in a museum or gallery—the work might surprise or, even, cause us to reevaluate the space itself. But in other kinds of space—in the streets or landscape—to suddenly encounter a work of art can be transformative, causing us to rethink just what our expectations for art might be.

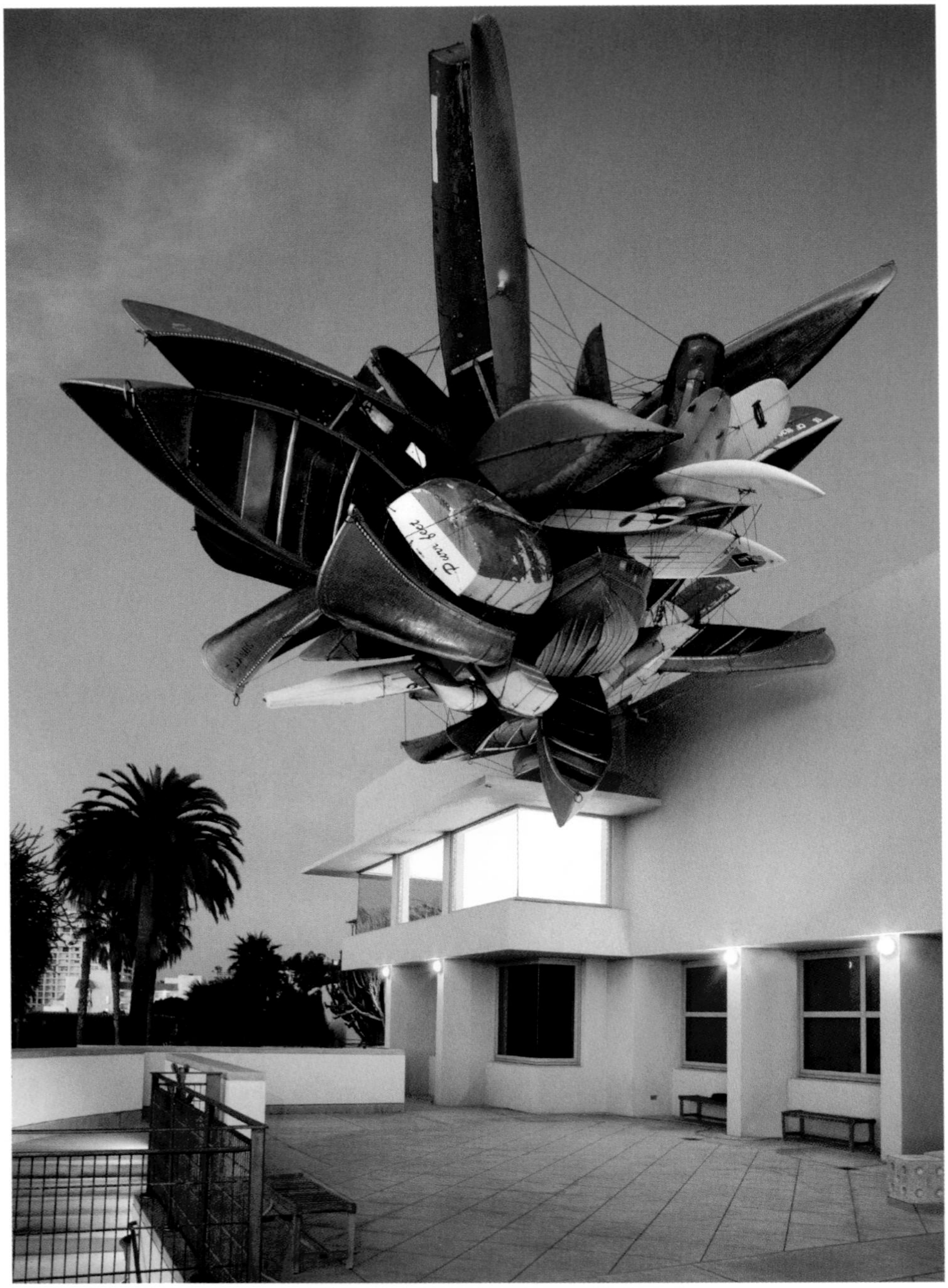

Fig. 12-21 Nancy Rubins, *Pleasure Point*, 2006. Nautical vessels, stainless steel, stainless-steel wire, and boats, 25 ft. 4 in. × 53 ft. 1 in. × 24 ft. Museum of Contemporary Art, San Diego.
Museum Purchase, International and Contemporary Collectors Funds. © Nancy Rubins. Collection Photo: Pablo Mason. Courtesy of the artist and Gagosian Gallery.

Installations

Installation art does this radically by introducing sculptural and other materials into a space in order to transform our experience of it. Nancy Rubins's *Pleasure Point* (**Fig. 12-21**) is just such a work. *Pleasure Point* was commissioned by the Museum of Contemporary Art, San Diego, for the ocean side of its building in La Jolla. An assemblage of rowboats, canoes, jet skis, and surfboards, it is attached to the roof of the museum by high-tension stainless-steel wire. As it cantilevers precariously out over the oceanfront plaza of the museum, it seems to draw, as if by some unseen magnetic force, the various seacraft that compose it into a single point. Rubins has worked with the discarded refuse of consumer culture, such as water heaters, mattresses, and airplane parts, since the mid-1970s. Boats have a special appeal for her. The inspiration for this work, in fact, derives from her witnessing a cache of boats at Pleasure Point Marina in a Southern California resort community. Rubins is fascinated by the simple structure and functionality of boats, and by their presence throughout human history. Her sculpture, of course, confronts that functionality, transforming the boats—literally elevating them out of their element, the ocean—into the space of art. They are no longer just boats, but an exuberant composition of color and form.

Cloud Gate (**Fig. 12-22**) is a site-specific sculpture designed by Indian-born British artist Anish Kapoor expressly for the City of Chicago's Millennium Park. Shaped like a giant bean, its underlying structure is covered with 168 highly polished stainless-steel plates seamlessly welded together. "What I wanted to do in Millennium Park," Kapoor explains,

> is make something that would engage the Chicago skyline . . . so that one will see the clouds kind of floating in, with those very tall buildings reflected in the work. And then, since it is in the form of a gate, the participant, the viewer, will be able to enter into this very deep chamber that does, in a way, the same thing to one's reflection as the exterior of the piece is doing to the reflection of the city around.

Reflected across its surface is the Chicago skyline, the skyscapers along Michigan Avenue to the west and those north of Randolph Avenue to the north. Although *Cloud Gate* weighs some 100 tons, its reflective surface, as well as its poised balance on the two ends, renders it almost weightless to the eye. In fact, in the right light, and standing in the right position, it is sometimes difficult to distinguish where the sculpture ends and the sky begins. This sense of ethereal reflection is countered when the viewer walks under the 12-foot arch beneath the piece—into what Kapoor calls its "navel"—where the sculpture seems to draw its outside surroundings into itself in a kind of vortex of reflection.

Many installations incorporate film and video in a sculptural or architectural setting. Eleanor Antin's 1995 *Minetta Lane—A Ghost Story* consists of a recreation of three buildings on an actual street in New York City's Greenwich Village that runs for two blocks between

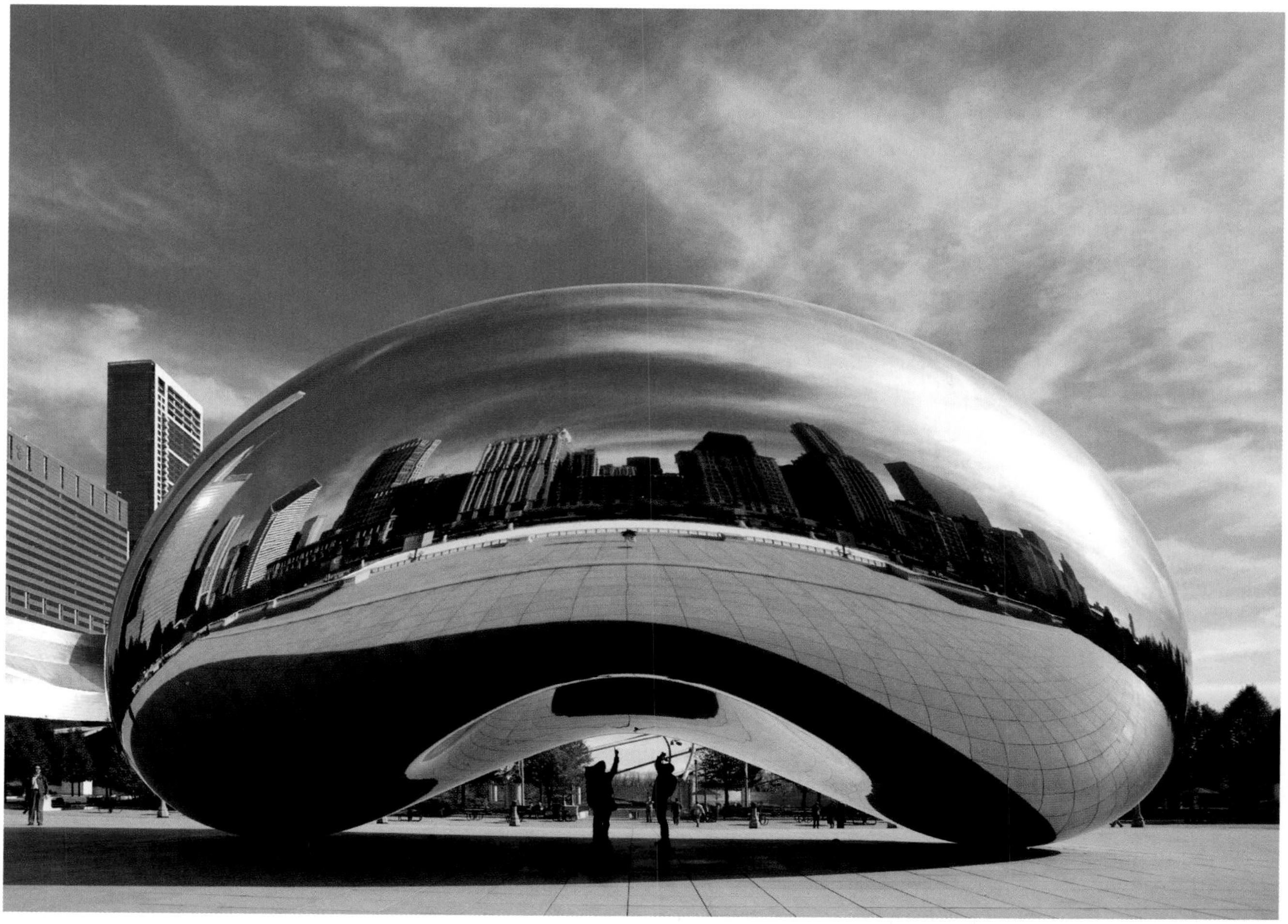

Fig. 12-22 Anish Kapoor, *Cloud Gate*, 2004. Stainless steel, 33 × 66 × 42 ft. Millennium Park, Chicago.
© Arcaid Images/Alamy. Courtesy of the City of Chicago and Gladstone Gallery, New York and Brussels. © Anish Kapoor.

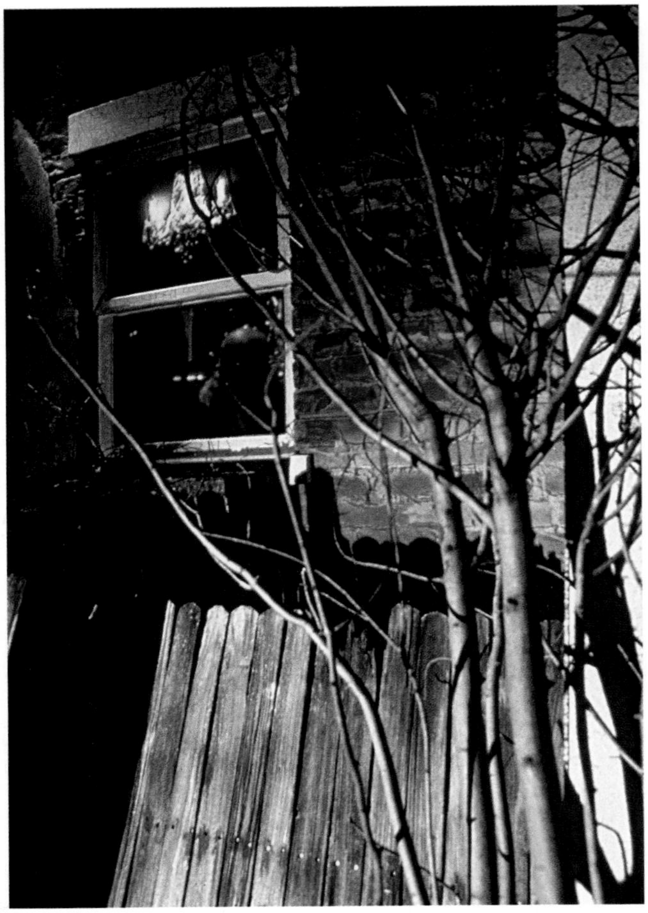

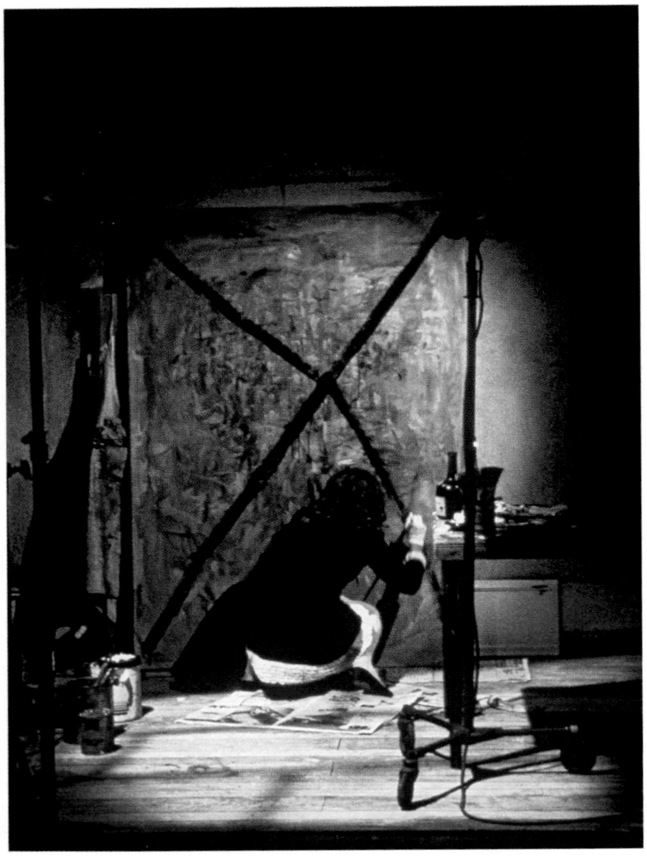

Figs. 12-23, 12-24, and 12-25 Eleanor Antin, *Minetta Lane—A Ghost Story*, 1995. Mixed-media installation. Installation view (top left), two video projections (top right and bottom right). Top right: actors Amy McKenna and Joshua Coleman. Bottom right: artist's window with Miriam (the Ghost). Courtesy of the artist and Ronald Feldman Fine Arts, New York.

MacDougal Street and Sixth Avenue (**Fig. 12-23**). In the late 1940s and early 1950s, it was the site of a low-rent artists' community, and Antin seeks to recreate the bohemian scene of that lost world. For the installation, Antin prepared three narrative films, transferred them onto video disc, and back-projected them onto tenement windows of the reconstructed lane. The viewer, passing through the scene, thus voyeuristically sees in each window what transpires inside. In one window (**Fig. 12-24**), a pair of lovers sport in a kitchen tub. In a second (**Fig. 12-25**), an Abstract Expressionist painter is at work. And in a third, an old man tucks in his family of caged birds for the night. These characters are the ghosts of a past time, but their world is inhabited by another ghost. A little girl, who is apparently invisible to those in the scene but clearly visible to us, paints a giant "X" across the artist's canvas and destroys the relationship of the lovers in the tub. She represents a destructive force that, in Antin's view, is present in all of us. The little girl is to the film's characters as they are to us. For the artist, the lovers and the old man represent the parts of us that we have lost—like our very youth. They represent ideas about art, sexuality, and life that, despite our nostalgia for them, no longer pertain.

Earthworks

The larger a work, the more our visual experience of it depends on multiple points of view. Since the late 1960s, one of the focuses of modern sculpture has been the creation of large-scale out-of-doors environments, generally referred to as earthworks. Robert Smithson's

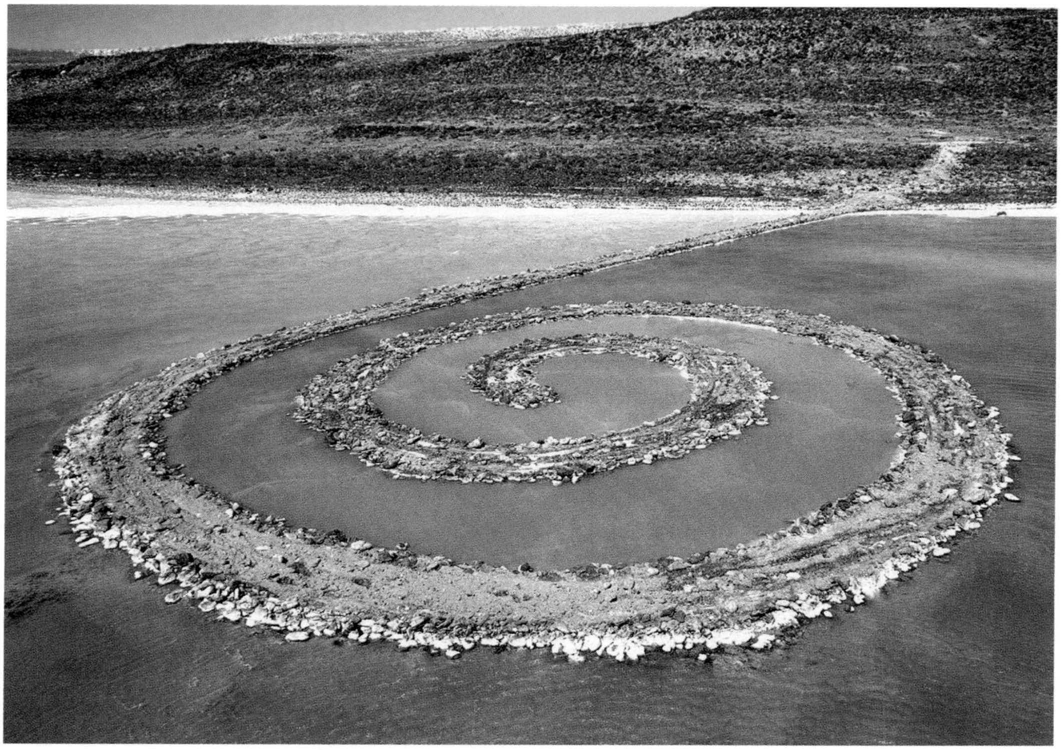

Fig. 12-26 Robert Smithson, *Spiral Jetty*, April 1970. Great Salt Lake, Utah.
Black rock, salt crystals, earth, red water (algae), 3 ft. 6 in. × 15 ft. × 1,500 ft.
Collection: Dia Art Foundation, New York. Courtesy of James Cohan Gallery, New York and Shanghai.

Spiral Jetty (**Fig. 12-26**) is a classic example of the medium. Stretching into the Great Salt Lake at a point near the Golden Spike monument, which marks the spot where the rails of the first transcontinental railroad were joined, *Spiral Jetty* literally *is* landscape. Made of mud, salt crystals, rocks, and water, it is a record of the geological history of the place. But it is landscape that has been created by man. The spiral form makes this clear. The spiral is one of the most widespread of all ornamental and symbolic designs on earth. In Egyptian culture, it designated the motion of cosmic forms and the relationship between unity and multiplicity, in a manner similar to the Chinese yin and yang. The spiral is, furthermore, found in three main natural forms: expanding like a nebula, contracting like a whirlpool, or ossified like a snail's shell. Smithson's work suggests the way in which these contradictory forces are simultaneously at work in the universe. Thus the *Jetty* gives form to the feelings of contradiction he felt as a contemporary inhabitant of his world. Motion and stasis, expansion and contraction, life and death, all are simultaneously suggested by the 1,500-foot coil, the artist's creation extending into the Great Salt Lake, America's Dead Sea.

Smithson also understood that, in time, this monumental earthwork would be subject to the vast changes in water level that characterize the Great Salt Lake. In fact, not long after its completion, *Spiral Jetty* disappeared as the lake rose, only to reappear in 2003 as the lake fell again. The work was now completely transformed, encrusted in salt crystals (**Fig. 12-27**), recreated,

Fig. 12-27 Robert Smithson, *Spiral Jetty*, as it appeared in August 2003.
Photo: Sandy Brooke.

as it were, by the slow workings of nature itself.

Spiral Jetty was directly inspired by the Great Serpent Mound, an ancient Native American earthwork in Adams County, Ohio (**Fig. 12-28**). Built by the Hopewell culture sometime between 600 BCE and 200 CE, it is nearly a quarter of a mile long. And though almost all other Hopewell mounds contain burials, this one does not. Its "head" consists of an oval enclosure that may have served some ceremonial purpose, and its tail is a spiral. The spiral would, in fact, become a favorite decorative form of the later Mississippian cultures. The monumental achievement of Smithson's *Spiral Jetty*, made with dump trucks and bulldozers, is dwarfed by the extraordinary workmanship and energy that must have gone into the construction of this prehistoric earthwork.

Fig. 12-28 Great Serpent Mound, Adams County, Ohio, Hopewell culture, ca. 600 BCE–200 CE. Length approx. 1,254 ft.
Tony Linck/SuperStock.

Art Parks

Over the last several decades, art parks—a sort of cross between installations and earthworks that incorporate works of art into the natural landscape—have become increasingly popular. Part of the power of such work consists in the relationship they establish and the tension they embody between the natural world and civilization. A series of interventions conceived by sculptor Karen McCoy for Stone Quarry Hill Art Park in Cazenovia, New York, including the grid made of arrowhead leaf plants in a small pond, illustrated here (**Figs. 12-29** and **12-30**), underscores this. The work was guided by a concern for land use and was designed to respond to the concerns of local citizens who felt their rural habitat was rapidly falling victim to the development and expansion of nearby Syracuse, New York. Thus, McCoy's grid deliberately evokes the orderly and regimented forces of civilization, from the fence lines of early white settlers to the street plans of modern suburban developers, but it represents these forces benignly. The softness and fragility of the grid's flowers, rising delicately from the quiet pond, seem to argue that the acts of man can work at one with nature, rather than in opposition to it.

One of the most extensive collections of large-scale sculpture in the world can be found an hour north of New York City in the lower Hudson Valley

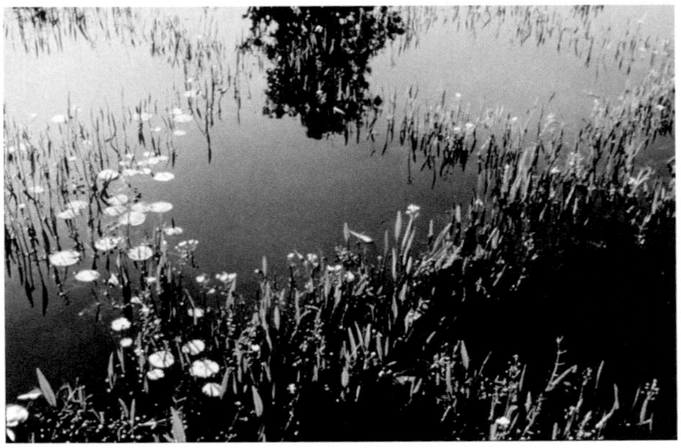

Figs. 12-29 and 12-30 Karen McCoy, *Considering Mother's Mantle*, project for Stone Quarry Hill Art Park, Cazenovia, New York, 1992. View of gridded pond made by transplanting arrowhead leaf plants, 40 × 50 ft. Detail (below).
Photo courtesy of the artist.

at Storm King Art Center. Scattered across its 500 acres are some 100 sculptures by many of the most acclaimed artists of the late twentieth and early twenty-first centuries. A recent addition is Chinese artist Zhang Huan's *Three-Legged Buddha* (**Fig. 12-31**). Zhang began his career as a performance artist in Beijing, but he moved to New York in 1998, where he continued an artistic practice that explored issues of cultural difference and nomadism. Drawn to more traditional aspects of Chinese culture, he returned to his country of birth in 2005, where he visited the Longhua Temple to burn incense before a sculpture of the Buddha. Incense ash was scattered across the floors, and he recognized in this ash the hopes and dreams of generations of Chinese Buddhists. When he discovered that the ash was treated as garbage he began to collect it, eventually making extremely fragile sculptures, as much as 13 feet high, out of the material. *Three-Legged Buddha* was conceived as a tribute to all the Buddha sculptures destroyed during the Cultural Revolution in China in the 1960s and 1970s. The legs are modeled on actual Buddha statue fragments, but the face rising out of the ground beneath them is a self-portrait. Small perforations dot the sculpture's surface, and there are hatches in each of the piece's parts that allow people to gain entrance to the interior. Incense burns inside the sculpture, the smoke rising out of the perforations as well as out of the nostrils and eyes of the self-portrait.

Performance Art as Living Sculpture

How is the body treated as sculpture in performance art?

If installations are works created to fill an interior architectural space and earthworks to occupy exterior spaces, both are activated by the presence of human beings in the space. Zhang Huan's *Three-Legged Buddha* not only invites viewers to walk beneath and around it, the smoky incense emanating from it lends it a kinetic quality, a sort of "liveness." It should come as no surprise that many performance artists have come to concern themselves with the live human activity that goes on in space. Many have even conceived of themselves, or other people in their works, as something akin to live sculptures.

Zhang Huan, in fact, explored this idea in many of the performances he engaged in before coming to America in 1998. In his 1997 *To Raise the Water Level in a Fishpond*, he invited immigrant workers in Beijing who had lost their jobs in the government's relentless

Fig. 12-31 Zhang Huan, *Three-Legged Buddha*, 2007. Steel and copper, 28 ft. 2½ in. × 42 ft. × 22 ft. 7⅝ in. Storm King Art Center, Hudson Valley, New York.
Photograph by Jerry L. Thompson © Zhang Huan Studio, courtesy of Pace Gallery.

Fig. 12-32 Zhang Huan, *To Raise the Water Level in a Fishpond*, August 15, 1997. Performance documentation (middle-distance detail), Nanmofang fishpond, Beijing, China. C-print on Fuji archival paper, 60 × 90 in. Courtesy of Zhang Huan Studio.

modernization of Chinese industry to stand in a pond (**Fig. 12-32**). By raising the level of the water by one meter, they would assert their presence even as they ideally, but unrealistically, might raise the government's consciousness of their needs as well. As a political act, Zhang Huan acknowledged that raising the water in the pond one meter higher was "an action of no avail." But as an act of human poetry—the human mass serving as a metaphor for the Chinese masses—it verges on the profound.

One of the innovators of **performance art** was Allan Kaprow, who, in the late 1950s, "invented" what he called **Happenings**, which he defined as "assemblages of events performed or perceived in more than one time and place. . . . A Happening . . . is art but seems closer to life." It was, in fact, the work of Jackson Pollock that inspired Kaprow to invent the form. The inclusiveness of paintings containing whatever Pollock chose to drop into them, not only paint but nails, tacks, buttons, a key, coins, cigarettes, and matches, gave Kaprow the freedom to bring everything, including the activity of real people acting in real time, into the space of art. "Pollock," Kaprow wrote in 1958, two years after the former's death, "left us at the point where we must become preoccupied with and even dazzled by the space and objects of our everyday life, either our bodies, clothes, rooms, or, if need be, the vastness of Forty-Second Street. . . . Objects of every sort are materials for the new art: paint, chairs, food, electric and neon signs, smoke, water, old socks, a dog, movies, a thousand other things will be discovered by the present generation of artists. . . . The young artist of today need no longer say, 'I am a painter,' or 'a poet' or 'a dancer.' He is simply an 'artist.' All of life will be open to him."

In *Household* (**Fig. 12-33**), there were no spectators, only participants, and the event was choreographed in advance by Kaprow. The site was a dump near Cornell University in Ithaca, New York. At 11 AM on the day of the Happening, the men who were participating built a wooden tower of trash, while the women built a nest of saplings and string. A smoking, wrecked car was towed onto the site, and the men covered it with strawberry jam. The women, who had been screeching inside the nest, came out to the car and licked the jam as the men destroyed their nest. Then the men returned to the wreck and, slapping white bread over it, began to eat the jam themselves. As the men ate, the women destroyed their tower. Eventually, as the men took sledgehammers to the wreck and set it on fire, the animosity between the two groups began to wane. Everyone gathered and watched until the car was burned up, and then left quietly. What this Happening means, precisely, is not entirely clear, but it does draw attention to the violence of relations between men and women in our society and the frightening way in which violence can draw us together as well as drive us apart.

Fig. 12-33 Allan Kaprow, *Household*, 1964. Licking jam off a car hood, near Ithaca, New York. Cornell University Library. Division of Rare and Manuscript Collections. Photo: Sol Goldberg.

Fig. 12-34 Marina Abramović and Ulay, *Imponderabilia*, 1977. Performance at the Galleria Communale d'Arte Moderna, Bologna, Italy.

In much performance art, the physical presence of the body in space becomes a primary concern. The performance team of Marina Abramović and Uwe Laysiepen (known as Ulay) made this especially clear in works such as *Imponderabilia*, performed in 1977 at a gallery in Milan, Italy (**Fig. 12-34**). They stood less than a foot apart, naked and facing each other, in the main entrance to the gallery, so that people entering the space had to choose which body—male or female—to face as they squeezed between them. A hidden camera filmed each member of the public as he or she passed through the "living door," and their "passage" was then projected on the gallery wall. Choosing which body to face, rub against, and literally feel, forced each viewer to confront their own attitudes and feelings about sexuality and gender. Abramović and Ulay's bodies composed the material substance of the work and so did the bodies of the audience members, who suddenly found themselves part of the artwork itself—at least they did for 90 minutes, until the police stopped the performance. For Abramović's 2010 retrospective exhibition at the Museum of Modern Art in New York, *Imponderabilia* was reperformed continuously in shifts by four couples for the duration of the exhibition—about 700 hours.

Working on her own, Abramović has continued to explore a similar terrain, what she calls "the space in-between, like airports, or hotel rooms, waiting rooms, or lobbies . . . all the spaces where you are not actually at home"—not least of all, the space between her and Ulay in her earlier work. She feels that we are most vulnerable in such spaces, and vulnerability, for her, means that "we are completely alive." *The House with the Ocean View* (**Fig. 12-35**) was performed on November 15–26, 2002, at the Sean Kelly Gallery in New York. Abramović lived in three rooms, situated 6 feet above the gallery floor, a toilet and shower in one, a chair and table in another, and clothes and a mattress in the third. The three rooms were connected to the floor by three ladders with butcher's knives for rungs. For 12 days she did not eat, read, write, or speak. She drank water, relieved herself, and sang and hummed as she chose. She slept in the gallery every night, and during the day the public was invited to participate in what she called an "energy dialogue" with the artist. What lay "in-between" the artist and her audience were those ladders. She could stare across at her audience, and her audience back at her, feelings could even be transmitted, but the space "in-between" could not be bridged except at unthinkable risk. At once a metaphor for geopolitical and daily domestic realities, the work is a sobering realization of our separation from one another, and a call for us to exert the energy necessary to change.

Fig. 12-35 Marina Abramović, *The House with the Ocean View—Nov. 22 9:54 AM*, 2002. Living installation, November 15–26, 2002. Sean Kelly Gallery, New York.

THE CRITICAL PROCESS
Thinking about Sculpture

In 1992, the artists Christo and Jeanne-Claude announced plans for a project called *Over the River*, a proposal to drape nearly 6 miles of silvery, luminous fabric panels above the Arkansas River along a 42-mile stretch of the river between Salida and Cañon City in south-central Colorado. The fabric panels, the husband-and-wife duo proposed, would be suspended for two weeks at eight distinct points along the river that were selected by the artists for their aesthetic merits and technical viability. As with all Christo and Jeanne-Claude projects, the proposal met with immediate, and sustained, criticism.

What impact, environmentalists quickly retaliated, would the project have on bighorn sheep populations in the area? What about fish and birds? How, people asked, could Christo and Jeanne-Claude justify the expense—a projected $50 million that, many argued, could be far better spent? Why "desecrate" the already beautiful Arkansas River canyon? Why, in fact, pick the Arkansas River canyon at all?

For Christo, the process of preparing the environmental statements necessary for getting the project approved—even the work of those opposed to Christo's plans—caused people to think, not only about the project itself but also about what constitutes a work of art in the first place. Christo's was, in fact, the first Environmental Impact Statement ever required of a work of art. In November of 2011, Federal regulators with the Bureau of Land Management (BLM) approved the artists' plan. Since then, a group known as ROAR (Rags Over the Arkansas River) has filed legal proceedings against the BLM and Colorado State Parks challenging their authorizing the project to move forward, and Christo will identify a future August date for the exhibition when the legal process is finally resolved.

As for the cost: Christo and Jeanne-Claude have always funded the costs associated with their projects through the sale of artworks such as the one illustrated here (**Fig. 12-36**). The project requires no public subsidy or taxpayer support, nor have Christo and Jeanne-Claude ever accepted sponsorship or endorsement fees.

Why the Arkansas River? Christo and Jeanne-Claude, who passed away in November 2009, traveled 14,000 miles and visited 89 rivers in seven Rocky Mountain States looking for the right site. The Arkansas between Salida and Cañon City was chosen for several reasons: The east–west orientation of the river, which will allow the fabric panels to better reflect sunlight from morning to evening; high river banks suitable for the suspension of steel cables; the fact that U.S. Route 50 runs continuously along the river to facilitate viewing; the presence of a nearby railroad that can provide essential access and supply lines; and rafting conditions that allow for viewers to see the work of art from the river.

Over the River involves two different viewing experiences: one from the highway, where the fabric will reflect the colors of the sky and clouds from sunrise to sunset; the other at water level, where rafters, kayakers, and canoeists will be able to view the clouds, sky, and mountains through the translucent fabric. How is *Over the River*, then, similar to sculpture in-the-round? In what more specific ways is it similar to Anish Kapoor's *Cloud Gate* (see Fig. 12-22)? Obviously, one of the ways *Over the River* differs most dramatically from *Cloud Gate* is in its temporary, two-week period of display. Why do you suppose Christo prefers temporary installations rather than permanent ones? Christo also enjoys the controversy that his projects inevitably generate. Why? What important issues does a work like *Over the River* raise other than environmental ones?

Fig. 12-36 Christo, *Over the River, Project for the Arkansas River, State of Colorado*, 2010. Drawing in two parts (detail), pencil, charcoal, pastel, wax crayon, enamel paint, wash, fabric sample, hand-drawn topographic map, and technical data, detail size 19 × 96 in. and 42 × 96 in. Courtesy of Christo and Jeanne-Claude.

Thinking Back

12.1 Differentiate among relief, sculpture in-the-round, and sculpture as an environment.

Relief sculpture has three-dimensional depth but is attached to a surface, and it is typically meant to be seen frontally. Sculpture in-the-round, by contrast, is unattached to any surfaces, and it is typically meant to be viewed from all sides. How does low relief differ from high relief? What is a frieze? Environments are physical spaces into which the viewer can enter. How do installations differ from earthworks?

12.2 Describe carving as a method of sculpture and account for its association with spiritual life.

Carving is a subtractive process in which material is chipped, gouged, or hammered away from a raw block of material. Because of their permanence, stone carvings have long been associated with immortality and the afterlife. What is the Egyptian *ka*? In what ways did *contrapposto* contribute to the naturalism of Greek sculpture?

12.3 Account for the popularity of molded ceramic sculpture.

Molding is an additive process. Clay has been the most popular material for molding since the earliest times, largely due to its capacity to be molded into forms that retain their shape. How does firing contribute to the medium's durability?

12.4 Describe the casting process, and the lost-wax process in particular.

Casting is a replacement process. It involves the creation of a form (often made using modeling), then building a mold around the form and pouring a material into the mold, which dries in the form of the original form. The poured material is often a molten metal, as in the lost-wax process. How is an investment used in casting?

12.5 Define assemblage and account for its association with the idea of transformation.

Assemblage is the process of bringing individual objects together to form a larger whole. As a process, assemblage is often associated with transformation because it turns common materials into art. How is Jeff Koons's work indicative of this? How does Robert Gober use a combination of materials to create meaning in *Untitled*?

12.6 Compare and contrast installations and earthworks as environments.

Installations introduce sculptural and other materials into a space in order to transform our experience of it. They are generally indoors, although they can also exist outdoors in contained spaces such as plazas. Earthworks are made in and of the land. But both invite the viewer to participate in the spaces they create. How do art parks encourage this?

12.7 Describe how the body becomes sculptural in performance art.

The introduction of human beings into the space of art suggested to some artists that their own bodies, or the bodies of others, could have a sculptural presence in a given space. How does the body alter the experience of space in both Zhang Huan's *To Raise the Water Level in a Fishpond* and in Abramović and Ulay's *Imponderabilia*? In what ways does Abramović explore the vulnerability of the body in her other work?

Chapter 13
The Craft Media

Learning Objectives

13.1 Characterize the difference between craft and fine art.

13.2 Describe the different ceramic methods and materials.

13.3 Outline some ways in which glass has become an artistic medium.

13.4 Describe some of the different uses of fiber in the arts.

13.5 Explain why gold has been a favored material since ancient times.

13.6 Describe the uses and limitations of wood as an art material.

The many so-called "craft" media—ceramics, glass, fiber, metal, and wood in particular—have traditionally been distinguished from the fine arts because they are employed to make **functional objects**, from the utensils with which we eat, to the clothes we wear. In the hands of an artist, however, these media can be employed to make objects that are not only of great beauty but that also must be appreciated as works of art in their own right.

Consider how contemporary artist Ann Hamilton has made use of a line that closes the Preface to *On Weaving*, published in 1965 by one of the greatest weavers of the twentieth century, Anni Albers (see Fig. 13-24): The "thoughts" that compose her book, Albers wrote, "can, I believe, be traced back to the event of a thread." For Hamilton, whose work has consistently addressed the relationship between texts and textiles (both derive from the same Latin root, *texo*, to weave or compose), Albers's phrase inspired a large-scale installation in the Drill Hall of New York's Park Avenue Armory called *the event of a thread* (**Fig. 13-1**). If weaving is defined as one thread crossing another, the crossings of threads making a whole cloth, Hamilton's work is a sort of compendium of crossings, most especially of texts and textiles. A white silk cloth hangs on an interconnected system of pulleys and ropes supporting swings suspended from the hall's arched iron trusses some 70 feet above the floor. As the audience members swing, at different speeds and velocities, the silk fabric responds in ever-shifting waves and billows. At the same time, two people read from scrolls at the front of the Drill Hall, their voices being broadcast on radios that audience members carry into the space in paper bags. At the other end of the hall, a writer responds to the activity in the room. As Hamilton describes it, "the field of swings is bracketed by reading and writing. . . . If on a swing, we are alone, we are together in a field. This condition of the social is *the event of a thread*. Our crossings with its motions, sounds, and textures is its weaving; is a social act."

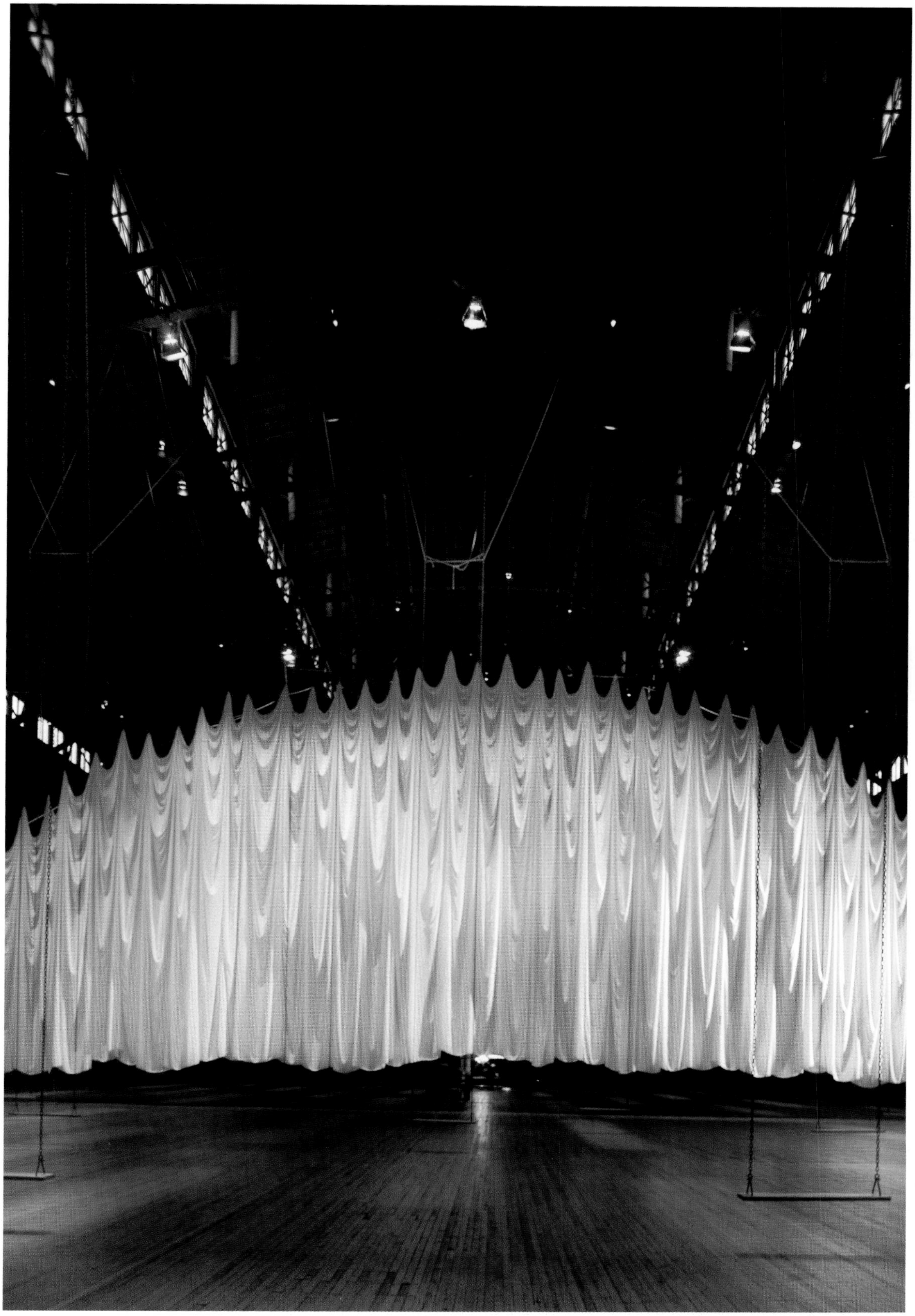

Fig. 13-1 Ann Hamilton, *the event of a thread*, 2012. Large-scale installation, Park Avenue Armory, New York, December 5, 2012–January 6, 2013.
Courtesy of Ann Hamilton Studio.

The Crafts as Fine Art

How do we distinguish between craft and fine art?

Hamilton obviously transforms the idea of weaving in *the event of a thread*, and in making this transformation defines, rather precisely (although radically), how traditional craft media cross over into fine art. The crafts are works of expert handiwork or craftsmanship, done by the maker's own hand with extraordinary skill. But despite the fact that painters and sculptors and printmakers are all expert with their hands as well, we don't call their work "craft." Indeed, many artists feel insulted if their work is described as being "craftful." These artists probably feel that a craft must be functional. But the distinction between craft and artwork is not that clear-cut. Perhaps the only meaningful distinction we can draw between art and craft is this: If a work is primarily made to be used, it is craft, but if it is primarily made to be seen or, in Hamilton's case, experienced, it is art. However, the maker's intention may be irrelevant. If you buy an object because you enjoy looking at it, then whatever its usefulness, it is, for you at least, a work of art.

Historically, the distinction between the crafts and fine arts can be traced back to the beginnings of the Industrial Revolution, when, on May 1, 1759, in Staffordshire, England, a 28-year-old man by the name of Josiah Wedgwood opened his own pottery manufacturing plant. With extraordinary foresight, Wedgwood chose to make two very different kinds of pottery: one he called "ornamental ware" (**Fig. 13-2**), the other "useful ware" (**Fig. 13-3**). The first consisted of elegant handmade luxury items, the work of highly skilled craftsmen. The second was described in his catalogue as "a species of earthenware for the table, quite new in appearance . . . manufactured with ease and expedition, and consequently cheap." And it was the "useful ware" (dubbed "Queen's Ware" because the English royal family quickly became interested in it) that made Wedgwood's reputation. In fact, he depended upon it to support his business. This new cream-colored earthenware was made mechanically by casting liquid clay in molds instead of by throwing individual pieces and shaping them by hand. Designs were chosen from a pattern book and printed by mechanical means directly on the

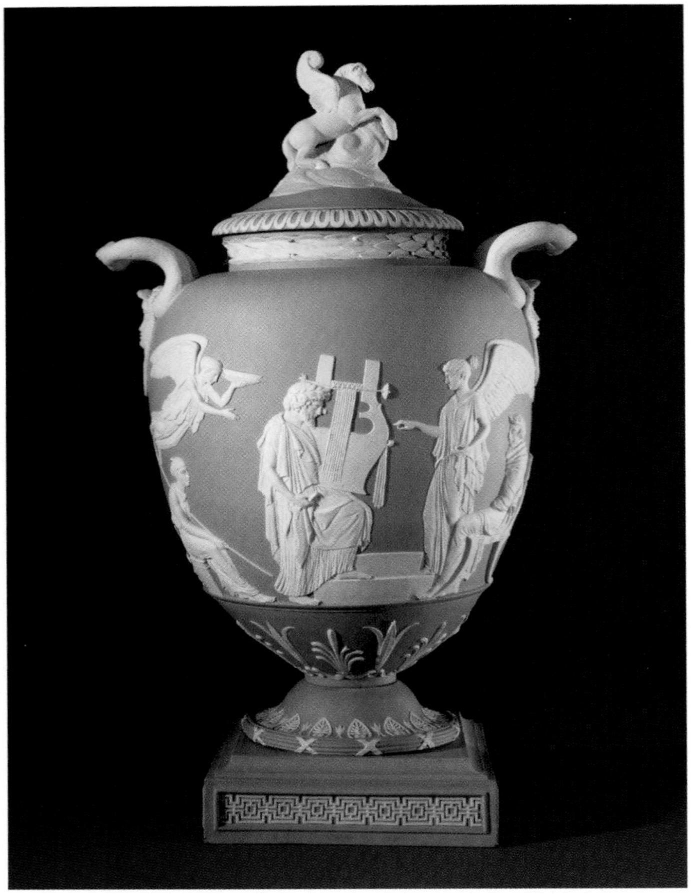

Fig. 13-2 Josiah Wedgwood, *Pegasus Vase*, ca. 1785. Jasper quartz, height 18 in. The British Museum, London.
1786,0527.1 © The Trustees of the British Museum.

Fig. 13-3 Josiah Wedgwood, Queen's Ware dinner service (detail), ca. 1790. Private collection.
Photo © Christie's Images/Bridgeman Images.

pottery. Because Wedgwood could mass-produce his earthenware both quickly and efficiently, a reliable, quality tableware was made available to the middle-class markets of Europe and America. Until this moment, almost everything people used was handmade, and thus unique. With the advent of machine mass-manufacturing, the look of the world changed forever.

But Wedgwood considered his ornamental ware to be works of art. Like the artist, producers of ornamental ware had a hands-on relation to the objects they made. Wedgwood's ornamental ware was almost always decorated with low-relief Greek figures intended to evoke both the white marble statuary of the ancient Greeks and their ceramic vases, in this case (see Fig. 13-2) a particular vase depicting the Apotheosis of Homer (that is, the great poet's ascension to the heavens), with the winged horse Pegasus on top resting on a pale blue cloud. The original Greek vase was acquired by the British Museum in 1772 (**Fig. 13-4**) and Wedgwood knew it well. In fact, when he completed the *Pegasus Vase*, Wedgwood was so proud of his work that he donated it immediately to the British Museum, so that it might take its rightful place beside the Greek vase that inspired it.

Fig. 13-4 Attributed to the Manner of the Peleus Painter, Red-figure calyx-krater, ca. 450–440 BCE. Height 18 in., diameter 18½ in. The British Museum, London.

Ceramics

What different methods and materials are used in ceramics?

The Greek vase and both Wedgwood's ornamental and useful wares are examples of ceramics. These are objects that are formed out of clay and then hardened by firing, or baking in a very hot oven, called a kiln (see Chapter 12). Ceramic objects are generally either flat and relieflike (think of a plate or a square of tile), or hollow, like cast sculpture (think of a pitcher). Unlike metal casts, the hollowness of ceramic objects is not a requirement of weight or cost as much as it is of utility (ceramic objects are made to hold things), and of the firing process itself. Solid clay pieces tend to hold moisture deep inside, where it cannot easily evaporate, and during firing, as this moisture becomes super-heated, it can cause the object to explode. In order to make hollow ceramic objects, a number of techniques have been developed.

Most ceramic objects are created by one of three means—slab construction, coiling, or throwing on a potter's wheel, as discussed below. Pieces made by any one of these techniques are then painted with **glazing**. Ceramic glazes consist of powdered minerals suspended in water, which are applied to the object after the first firing. When the object is fired a second time, the minerals dissolve and fuse into a glassy, nonporous coating that bonds to the ceramic clay. Glazes serve many purposes. They were probably first created to seal clay vessels, which might otherwise absorb food or drink, thus stimulating the growth of bacteria (if in the ancient world the existence of bacteria per se was unknown, the odor they produced was well understood). But the chemical reaction of firing the glaze also produces colors, and these colors have become an important aesthetic element in the creation of ceramics as works of art.

Fig. 13-5 Hon'ami Koetsu, *Raku tea bowl*, Momoyama or early Edo period, early 17th century. Hand-built black raku-type high-fired earthenware with black glaze, 3⅗ × 5 × 4½ in. Victoria and Albert Museum, London.

Slab Construction

An unnamed tea bowl by Hon'ami Koetsu (**Fig. 13-5**) is similar to one named *Shichiri* (literally "Seven Leagues") in the collection of the Goho Museum, Tokyo, a name derived from the Seven Leagues Beach near Fujisawa, some 30 miles south of Tokyo, noted for its dark sands, rich in iron ore. It is an example of **slab construction**, where clay is rolled out flat, rather like a pie crust, and then shaped by hand. The tea bowl has a special place in the Japanese tea ceremony, the Way of the Tea, a highly formalized ritual that developed in the sixteenth century. In small tea rooms specifically designed for the purpose and often decorated with calligraphy on hanging scrolls or screens, the guest was invited to leave the concerns of the daily world behind and enter a timeless world of ease, harmony, and mutual respect. Koetsu was an accomplished tea master. At each tea ceremony, the master assembles a variety of different objects and utensils used to make tea, together with a collection of painting and calligraphy works. Through this ensemble the master expresses his artistic sensibility, a sensibility shared with his guest, so that guest and host collaborate to make the ceremony itself a work of art.

This tea bowl, shaped perfectly to fit the hand, was made in the early seventeenth century at one of the "Six Ancient Kilns," the traditional centers of wood-fired ceramics in Japan. These early kilns, known as *anagamas*, were narrow underground tunnels, dug out following the contour of a hillside. The pit was filled with pottery, and heat moved through the tunnel from the firebox at the lower end to the chimney at the upper end. The firing would take an average of seven days, during which time temperatures would reach 2,500 degrees Fahrenheit. The coloration that distinguished these pieces results from wood ash in the kiln melting and fusing into glass on the pottery. The simplicity of these wood-fired pieces appealed to the devotee of the tea ceremony, and tea masters such as Koetsu often named their pieces after the accidental effects of coloration achieved in firing. The most prized effect is a scorch, or *koge*, when the firing has oxidized the natural glass glaze completely, leaving only a gray-black area. Such a *koge* dominates the surface of this tea bowl, and its similarity to the *Shichiri* tea bowl in Tokyo suggests that this *koge* represents a similar beach, its sands darkened by the incoming tide.

In 1976, a young American ceramic artist by the name of Peter Callas built the first traditional Japanese *anagama*, or wood-burning kiln, in the United States in Piermont, New York. Three years later, California artist Peter Voulkos was regularly firing his work in Callas's kiln. Voulkos's work is particularly suited to the wood-firing process, in which the artist must give up control of his creations and resign himself to the accidental effects that

Fig. 13-6 Peter Voulkos, *The Eagle Has Landed*, 1999. Wood-fired stoneware stack, height 34½ in., diameter 23 in. Museum of Fine Arts, Houston.

Beatrice S. and Melvin B. Eagle Collection, gift of Beatrice and Melvin Eagle. Bridgeman Images. © Voulkos Family Trust.

result from submitting them to a heat of 2,500 degrees Fahrenheit over the course of a seven-day firing. His "stacks" (**Fig. 13-6**), giant bottlelike pyramids of clay that average about 250 pounds, are so named because Voulkos literally stacks clay cylinders one on top of the other to create his form. Before they are quite dry, he gouges them, draws on them with various tools, and drags through the clay in giant sweeps across the form's surface. Then he fires it in the *anagama*. Anything can happen in the firing. Depending on such factors as how the pieces in the kiln are stacked, the direction of the flame, where ash is deposited on the surface of the work, how a section near the flame might or might not melt, and undetectable irregularities in the clay itself, each stack will turn out differently. The Japanese call this a "controlled accident." For Voulkos, it is the source of excitement in the work, "the expectancy of the unknown" that is fundamental to the process.

Coiling

María Martinez's black jar (**Fig. 13-7**) is an example of a second technique often used in ceramic construction, **coiling**, in which the clay is rolled out in long, ropelike strands that are coiled on top of each other. As the potter builds the coils up in a continuous spiral, each strand is smoothed and blended one to the next, eliminating any trace of the original ropes of clay and making pot walls of uniform thickness. Before firing, the pot is burnished or polished to a high gloss, usually with a stone.

This pot is a specific example of a technique developed by María and her husband, Julián, in about 1919 at San Ildefonso Pueblo, 20 miles northwest of Santa Fe, New Mexico. The red clay pot was smoothed to an extreme sheen and then a design was painted on it with liquid clay—a **slip**, as it is known. The pot was smothered in dung part way through the firing, the resulting smoke blackening the clay, the areas painted with the slip remaining matte, or dull, and the other areas taking on a highly glossed, shiny finish. So distinctive was María's style that she was encouraged to sign her pots, becoming the first potter in the Southwest to do so and thus leading the way to the acceptance of Native American pottery as a fine art.

The Potter's Wheel

Native American cultures relied on coiling techniques, whereas peoples of most other parts of the world used the potter's wheel. Egyptian potters employed a wheel by about 4000 BCE, and their basic invention has remained

Fig. 13-7 María and Julián Martinez, *Jar*, San Ildefonso Pueblo, New Mexico, ca. 1939. Blackware, 11⅛ × 13 in. The National Museum of Women in the Arts, Washington, D.C. Gift of Wallace and Wilhelmina Holladay. Photo: Lee Stalsworth. Courtesy of National Museum of Women in the Arts.

Fig. 13-8 Pottery wheel-throwing, from *The Craft and Art of Clay*.

in use ever since. The ancient Greeks became particularly skillful with the process (the calyx-krater, Fig. 13-4, is an example), which has the advantage over hand-building of allowing the potters to create works with far greater speed, as well as giving them far greater control of a pot's thickness and shape. The potter's wheel is a flat disk attached to a flywheel below it, which is kicked by the potter (or, in modern times, driven by electricity) to make the upper disk turn. A slab of clay, from which air pockets have been removed by slamming it against a hard surface, is centered on the wheel (**Fig. 13-8**). As the slab turns, the potter pinches the clay between fingers and thumb, sometimes using both hands at once, and pulls it upward in a round, symmetrical shape, making it wider or narrower as the form demands, and shaping both the inside and outside simultaneously. The most skilled potters apply even pressure on all sides of the pot as it is thrown.

Porcelain

There are three basic types of ceramics. **Earthenware**, made of porous clay and fired at low temperatures, must be glazed if it is to hold liquid. **Stoneware** is impermeable to water because it is fired at high temperatures, and it is commonly used for dinnerware today. Finally, **porcelain**, fired at the highest temperatures of all, is a smooth-textured clay that becomes virtually translucent and extremely glossy in finish during firing. The first true porcelain was made in China during the Tang

Fig. 13-9 Plate, Ming dynasty, late 16th–early 17th century, *Kraakporselein*, probably from the Ching-te Chen kilns. Porcelain, painted in underglaze blue, diameter 14¼ in. Metropolitan Museum of Art, New York.

Rogers Fund, 1916.13. © 2015. Image copyright Metropolitan Museum of Art/Art Resource/Scala, Florence.

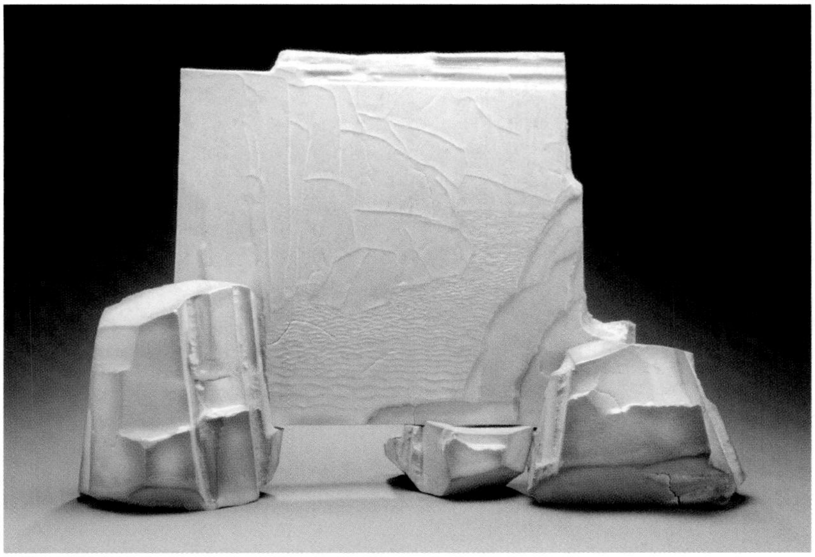

Fig. 13-10 Wayne Higby, *Lake Powell Memory—Seven Mile Canyon*, 1996. Glazed porcelain, 16¾ × 22 × 10 in. Los Angeles County Museum of Art. Smits Ceramics Purchase Fund, AC1997.91.1.1-.4. © 2015. Digital Image Museum Associates/ LACMA/Art Resource New York/Scala, Florence. © Wayne Higby.

dynasty (618–906 CE). By the time of the Ming dynasty (1368–1644), the official kilns at Jingdezhen had become a huge industrial center, producing ceramics for export. Just as the Greek artist painted Homer on the red-orange vase (see Fig. 13-4), Chinese artists painted elaborate designs onto the glazed surface of the porcelain. Originally, Islamic countries were the primary market for the distinctive blue-and-white patterns of Ming porcelain (**Fig. 13-9**), but as trade with Europe increased, so too did Europe's demand for Ming design. (For a contrasting set of blue-and-white plates, see Julie Green's *The Last Supper* in *The Creative Process*, pp. 308–09.)

One of the masters of contemporary ceramic sculpture working in porcelain is Wayne Higby. Widely known for his bowls, boxes, and slabs that reference the American landscape, Higby visited the Jingdezhen kilns in 1992, and a year later Lake Powell in Arizona. The result is a series of porcelain sculptures that evoke the flooded canyon walls of the lake. *Lake Powell Memory—Seven Mile Canyon* (**Fig. 13-10**) consists of a thick slab of clay onto the surface of which he inscribed a design representing canyon and lake; then the slab was fired at an intense enough heat to cause it to crack. At both the bottom right and left, the slab is held in place by porcelain blocks fashioned to look like rocks fallen from the cliffs to the water's edge. The result is a translucent landscape through which light seems to pass in an almost spiritual way.

The *Lake Powell* slabs inspired what is perhaps the largest porcelain sculpture ever created, *EarthCloud* (**Fig. 13-11**), a two-part panoramic installation that runs through two adjacent performing arts buildings

Fig. 13-11 Wayne Higby, *EarthCloud*, 2006–12 (detail). Twelve thousand hand-cut glazed porcelain tiles, approx. 5,000 sq. ft., connecting two buildings. Miller Performing Arts Center, Alfred University, New York.
Photo: Brian Oglesbee. © Wayne Higby.

The Creative Process

Ceramics as Politics: Julie Green's *The Last Supper*

If the business of storing and serving foodstuffs has traditionally fallen to ceramic wares, modern and contemporary artists have often abandoned this functionality in favor of more aesthetic concerns. But artist Julie Green has transformed the traditional role of ceramics into a powerful aesthetic—and political—statement.

In 2000, Green began a project called *The Last Supper* (**Fig. 13-12**). In order to draw attention to the number of Americans executed each year under various death-penalty laws from state to state, as well as to the basic humanity of each of these individuals living on death row, Green began querying the states about the menu each requested for his or her "last meal." Each of these meals she depicted on a different plate, blue on white, in the traditional manner of Chinese porcelain (see Fig. 13-9). But the blue color has specific religious connotations as well. In the sixteenth century, Pope Pius V reserved the color blue (made predominantly from the relatively rare and certainly expensive gemstone lapis lazuli) for depictions of the Virgin Mary. Thus, her color scheme recalls not only the Last Supper of Christ—"Do this in remembrance of me," Christ said to the Apostles—but also Christ's mother and, by extension, the mothers of all her subjects. But the choice of blue is even more complex than that: "The blue in *The Last Supper*," Green explains, "refers to the blues, blue-plate specials, heavenly blue, and old-style prison uniforms and mattresses of navy and white striped fabric. Also there is something cartoon-like and absurd about blue tacos, blue pizza, blue ketchup, blue bread."

Each of the plates is titled by the state of execution and date—no inmates' names are given. But each tells us something remarkably personal about the inmate in question. Consider the three plates illustrated here (**Fig. 13-13**). At the top left is *Georgia, 26 June 2007*: "Four fried pork chops, collard greens with boiled okra, fried fatback, fried green tomatoes, cornbread, lemonade, one pint of strawberry ice cream, and three glazed donuts." Below it is *Texas, 22 January 2009*: "Twenty-four bbq chicken wings, two cheeseburgers with everything, four slices of pizza with jalapeños, three slices of buttered toast, one sweet potato pie, sherbet rainbow ice cream, and twelve cans of Dr. Pepper/Big Red." The oval-shaped plate on the right is *Indiana, 5 May 2007*: "Pizza and birthday cake shared with fifteen family and friends." Quoted on the plate are the words of a prison official—"He never had a birthday cake so we ordered a birthday cake for him."

When Green first began painting the plates over a decade ago—they now number over 500—she wanted them to be "institutional-looking and awkward, lacking in richness," but over the years, they have become much more complex and painterly. In part, this is because she has mastered the

Fig. 13-12 Julie Green, *The Last Supper*, 2000–ongoing. Installation view of 283 plates in the 2008 exhibition *Criminal*, San Francisco State University.
Photo: Andrew Bird.

technique of applying the thick and oily mineral-based paint to the porcelain plates, but it also reflects her growing understanding of the complexities of the inmates themselves, as well as the complex feelings that the death penalty itself generates. Thus, some of her plainest plates—*Virginia 27 April 2006* simply states: "Requested that last meal not be released to the public"—are among the most poignant. All of the plates are viewable online at greenjulie.com.

Fig. 13-13 Julie Green, *The Last Supper*, 2000–ongoing. Three details. Top left: *Georgia, 26 June 2007*. Bottom left: *Texas, 22 January 2009*. Right: *Indiana, 5 May 2007*.
Photo courtesy of the artist.

on the campus of Alfred University in upstate New York. As its title implies, it simultaneously evokes the geological strata of the region's landscape and bands of cumulus clouds wind-blown across the sky. Inset among these porcelain tiles—of which there are some 12,000, in six different structures and depths of relief—are 500 tiles covered in gold leaf, in turn evoking both the mineral veins of the earth and the golden light of the sun. At night, especially, when the facility is in use, viewers see the fields of porcelain reflected in the glass walls of the building even as they look through from one building to another, or out past the buildings to the valley beyond. The viewer is literally caught up in this landscape, both abstract and real, surrounded by light and its reflection.

Glass

What are some of the ways in which glass has been used as an artistic medium?

Since ancient times, glassware was made either by forming the hot liquid glass, made principally of silica, or sand, mixed with soda ash, on a core or by casting it in a mold. The invention of glassblowing techniques late in the first century BCE so revolutionized the process that, in the Roman world, glassmaking quickly became a major industry. To blow glass, the artist dips the end of a pipe into molten glass and then blows through the pipe to produce a bubble. While it is still hot, the bubble is shaped and cut.

This glass bowl (**Fig. 13-14**) was probably made near Rome in the second quarter of the first century CE, before glassblowing took hold. It is made of opaque chips of colored glass. These chips expanded and elongated in the oven as they were heated over a core ceramic form. As the glass chips melted, they fused together and fell downward over the form, creating a decorative patchwork of dripping blobs and splotches. By the time this vase was made, demand for glass was so great that many craftsmen had moved from the Middle East to Italy to be near the expanding European markets.

In twelfth-century Europe, blown glass was used to make the great stained-glass windows that decorated the era's cathedrals. Stained glass is made by adding metallic salts to the glass during manufacture. A variety of different colors were blown by artisans and rolled out into square pieces. These pieces were then broken or cut into smaller fragments and assembled over a drawing marked out in chalk dust. Features of people and other figures

Fig. 13-14 Mosaic glass bowl, fused and slumped, Roman, 25 BCE–50 CE. Height 4½ in. Victoria and Albert Museum, London.

were painted on the glass in dark pigments, and the fragments were joined by strips of lead. The whole window was then strengthened with an armature of iron bands, at first stretched over the windows in a grid, but later shaped to follow the outlines of the design itself.

Among the very first stained-glass windows were those commissioned by Abbot Suger for the royal abbey of Saint-Denis just north of Paris, dedicated by King Louis VII and his queen, Eleanor of Aquitaine, on June 11, 1144. Suger had long dreamed of making his abbey the most beautiful in all of France. In preparing his plans, he read what he believed to be the writings of the original St. Denis. (We now know that he was reading the mystical tracts of a first-century Athenian follower of St. Paul known as Pseudo-Dionysius.) Light, these writings instructed, was the physical and material manifestation of the Divine Spirit. And so stained glass became a fundamental component of his design (**Fig. 13-15**). Suger would later survey the accomplishments of his administration and explain his religious rationale for his beautification of Saint-Denis:

> Marvel not at the gold and the expense but at the craftsmanship of the work.
> Bright is the noble work; but being nobly bright, the work
> Should brighten the minds, so that they may travel, through the true lights,
> To the True Light where Christ is the true door.

As beautiful as the church might be, it was designed to elevate the soul to the realm of God.

Today, the Pilchuck Glass School in Washington State is one of the leading centers of glassblowing in the world, surpassed only by the traditional glassblowing industry of Venice, Italy. Dale Chihuly, one of Pilchuck's cofounders, has been instrumental in transforming the medium from its utilitarian origins to more sculptural ends. Chihuly's floating, hanging, and standing glass works are extraordinary installation pieces designed to animate large interior spaces. Chihuly has been influential in establishing glass as a viable art medium, even inspiring the construction of a new Museum of Glass in his native Tacoma, Washington, which opened to the public in 2002. The first of several installations titled *Mille Fiori*,

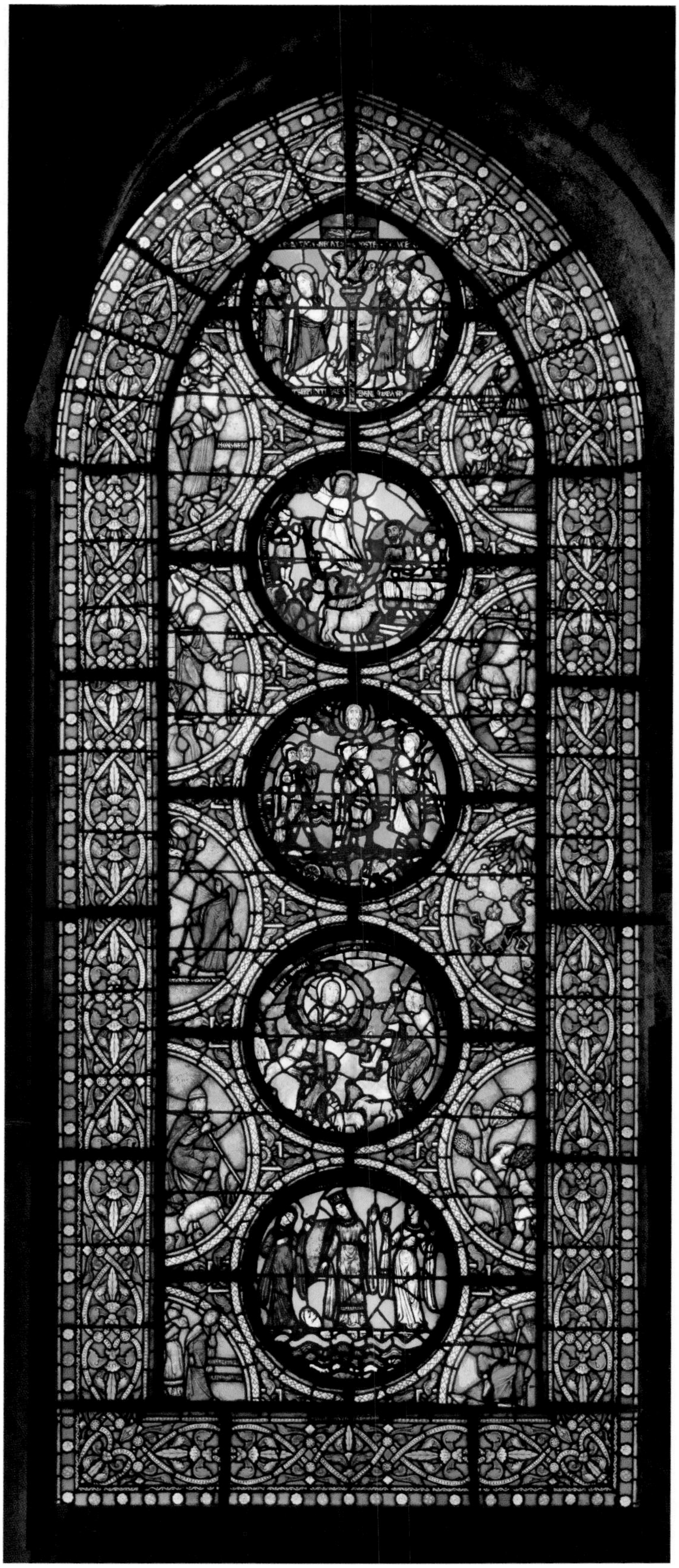

Fig. 13-15 Moses window, Abbey church of Saint-Denis, Saint-Denis, France, 1140–44.

Fig. 13-16 Dale Chihuly, *Mille Fiori*, 2003. On display at the Tacoma Art Museum, Washington, May 3–January 4, 2004. Glass, dimensions variable.
Photo by Teresa Nouri Rishel.

"a thousand flowers" (**Fig. 13-16**), was exhibited at the Tacoma Art Museum in 2003. The inspiration, as with so much of his work, was at once the sea, especially the waters of Puget Sound near his boyhood home in Tacoma, and flowers, which thrived in his mother's garden when he was a child. For Chihuly, the distinction between art and craft is irrelevant. "I don't really care if they call it art or craft," he says, "it really doesn't make any difference to me, but I do like the fact that people want to see it."

Fig. 13-17 Fred Wilson, *Drip Drop Plop*, 2001. Glass, approx. 8 ft. 3 in. × 6 ft. × 5 ft. 2 in.
Photograph by Ellen Labenski, courtesy of Pace Gallery New York. © Fred Wilson, courtesy of Pace Gallery.

Fred Wilson is an artist and curator who has spent much of his career looking at and thinking about the arts and crafts of American society. He is especially adept at sifting through existing museum collections, reorganizing some objects and bringing others out of storage, in order to create commentaries on the history of American racism and the sociopolitical realities of the American museum system (see *The Creative Process*, pp. 314–15, for an exhibit he created from the collections of the Maryland Historical Society). In 2001, Wilson began working with glass as he prepared to be the American representative at the 2003 Venice Biennale. Given Venice's preeminence as a glass-manufacturing city, glass seemed a natural choice, and he hired the famed glassworkers on the island of Murano to create the pieces that he designed. But it was a difficult medium for him to work with. With glass, he says, "it's hard to make anything that has a lot of meaning—or where the meaning is at least as strong as the beauty of the material. Infusing meaning is what I'm really interested in."

Wilson chose to work with black glass, because black as a color is so obviously a metaphor for African Americans, but also because it refers to the long history of black Africans in Venice, epitomized in Western consciousness by Shakespeare's *Othello: The Moor of Venice*. Inspired by the watery canals and lagoons of Venice, he shaped the glass so that it appeared to be liquid—ink, oil, tar. In *Drip Drop Plop* (**Fig. 13-17**), what appear to be glass tears descend the wall to form puddles of black liquid on the floor. Some of the tears and puddles have eyes: "Because of 1930s cartoons that were recycled in my childhood in the 1960s, these cartoon eyes on a black object represent African Americans in a very derogatory way. . . . So I sort of view them as black tears." But the glass tears suggest other things as well—the degradation of the environment, for one, as they fall off the wall like a spill from an oil tanker. They also take on the appearance of sperm, suggesting an almost masturbatory ineffectuality. All these meanings are at least partially at work, and they underscore the ways in which art and craft differ. Art, in essence, goes far beyond mere utility. It provokes thought, and it produces meaning.

Fiber

What are some of the different uses of fiber in the arts?

We do not usually think of fiber as a three-dimensional medium. However, fiber arts are traditionally used to fill three-dimensional space, in the way that a carpet fills a room or that clothing drapes across a body. In the Middle Ages, tapestry hangings such as *The Unicorn in Captivity* (**Fig. 13-18**) were hung on the stone walls of huge mansions and castles to soften and warm the stone. Fiber is an extraordinarily textural medium, and, as a result, it has recently become an increasingly favored medium for sculpture.

Fig. 13-18 ***The Hunt of the Unicorn, VII: The Unicorn in Captivity*, Franco-Flemish, 16th century, ca. 1500.** Silk and wool, silver and silver-gilt threads, 12 ft. 1 in. × 8 ft. 3 in. Metropolitan Museum of Art, New York.

Cloisters Collection, Gift of John D. Rockefeller, Jr. 1937.80.6. © 2015. Image copyright Metropolitan Museum of Art/Art Resource/Scala, Florence.

The Creative Process

A New Narrative: Fred Wilson's *Mining the Museum*

In his work as a museum curator, Fred Wilson has transformed exhibition design by exposing the cultural, political, and socioeconomic assumptions that underlie the modern museum space. Traditionally, museums have tried to create coherent, even homogeneous, spaces in which to view exhibitions. The "white room" effect is one such design principle—that is, the walls of the space are uniform and white so as not to detract from the work on the walls. Even when more elaborate design ideas come into play—for instance, when an architectural setting is recreated in order to reconstruct the original era or setting of the works on display—the principle of an intellectually coherent space, one that helps the viewer to understand and contextualize the work, predominates.

Wilson believes that this traditional curatorial stance has caused most museums to "bury" or ignore works that do not fit easily into the dominant "story" that the museum tells. In 1992, The Contemporary, a museum exhibiting in temporary spaces in Baltimore, Maryland, arranged for Wilson to install an exhibition at the Maryland Historical Society. Wilson saw it as an opportunity to reinterpret the Historical Society's collection and present a larger story about Maryland history than the museum was used to telling.

Wilson begins all of his projects with a research phase—in this case, into the history of Baltimore and its people. "When I go into a project," he says, "I'm not looking to bring something to it. I'm responding more than anything else. You can still get a very personal emotional response from a situation or an individual who lived a hundred years ago. It's connecting over time that I'm responding to." In the archives and collections of the museum, Wilson was able to discover a wealth of material that the museum had never exhibited, not least because it related to a part of Maryland history that embarrassed and even shamed many viewers—the reality of slavery. Wilson brought these materials to light by juxtaposing them with elements of the collection that viewers were used to seeing.

Behind a "punt gun" ostensibly used for hunting game birds on Chesapeake Bay, Wilson placed reward notices for runaway slaves. A document discovered in the archives, an inventory of the estate of one Caleb Goodwin (**Fig. 13-19**), lists all his slaves and animals together with their estimated value. What jars the contemporary reader is the fact that least valuable of all, valued at a mere dollar, is the "negro woman Hannah seventy-three years of age." Even the "old Mule called Coby" is worth five times as much. In the middle of a display of silver repoussé objects made by Maryland craftsmen in the early 1800s (**Fig. 13-21**), Wilson placed a set of iron slave shackles, underscoring the fact that Maryland's luxury

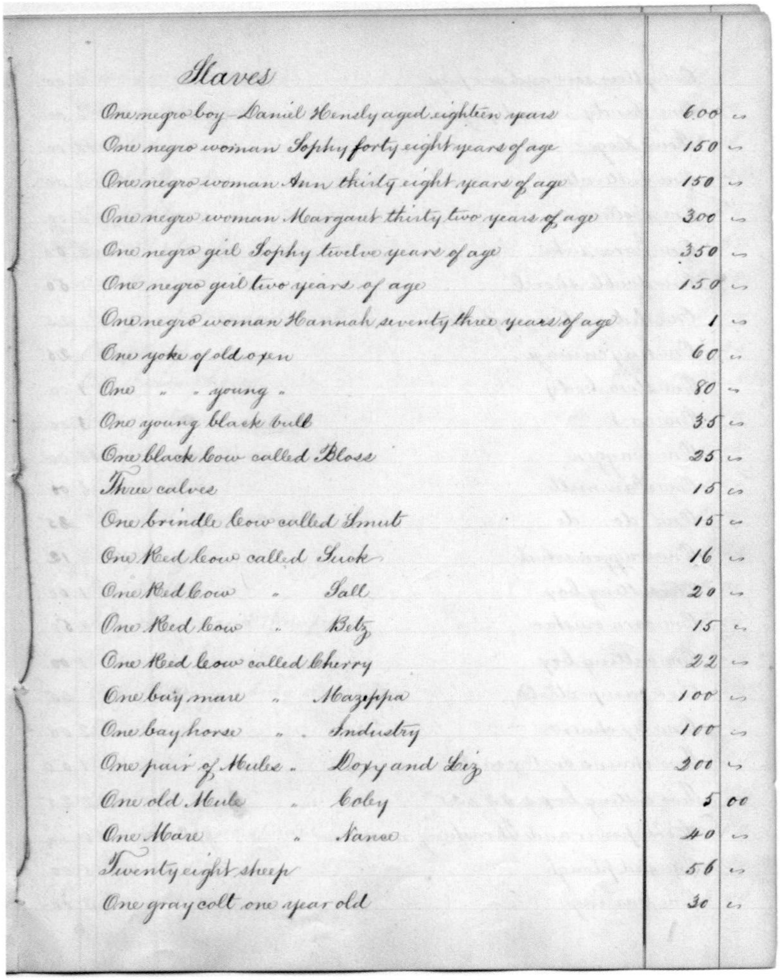

Slaves

One negro boy Daniel Hensly aged eighteen years	600	
One negro woman Sophy forty eight years of age	150	
One negro woman Ann thirty eight years of age	150	
One negro woman Margaret thirty two years of age	300	
One negro girl Sophy twelve years of age	350	
One negro girl two years of age	150	
One negro woman Hannah seventy three years of age	1	
One yoke of old oxen	60	
One " " young "	80	
One young black bull	35	
One black Cow called Bloss	25	
Three calves	15	
One brindle Cow called Smut	15	
One Red Cow called Suck	16	
One Red Cow " Sall	20	
One Red Cow " Betz	15	
One Red Cow called Cherry	22	
One bay mare " Mazeppa	100	
One bay horse " Industry	100	
One pair of Mules " Doxy and Liz	200	
One old Mule " Coby	5	00
One Mare " Nance	40	
Twenty eight sheep	56	
One gray colt one year old	30	

Fig. 13-19 Caleb Goodwin, *Inventory of Slaves and Livestock*, ca. 1855. Manuscript. Maryland Historical Society Library.

Johnston & Donaldson Papers, 1767-1891, MS.1564. Special Collections. Courtesy of Maryland Historical Society, Baltimore, Maryland.

economy was built on slavery. Similarly, in a display of Maryland cabinetmaking, he placed a whipping post (**Fig. 13-20**) that was used until 1938 in front of the Baltimore city jail, and that the museum had ignored for years, storing it with its collection of fine antique cabinets. (The whipping post is discussed by Wilson in the art21 *Exclusive* video "Fred Wilson: Beauty and Ugliness.")

Wilson was equally struck by what was missing from the museum's collection. While the museum possessed marble busts of Henry Clay, Napoleon Bonaparte, and Andrew Jackson, none of whom had any particular impact on Maryland history, it possessed no busts of three great black Marylanders—Harriet Tubman, Frederick Douglass, and the astronomer and mathematician Benjamin Banneker. Thus, at the entrance to the museum, across from the three marble busts in the museum's collection, he placed three empty pedestals, each identified with the name of its "missing" subject.

"Objects," Wilson says, "speak to me." As an artist, curator, and exhibition designer, he translates what these objects say to him for all of us to hear. "I am trying to root out . . . denial," he says. "Museums are afraid of what they will bring to the surface and how people will feel about issues that are long buried. They keep it buried, as if it doesn't exist, as though people aren't feeling these things anyway, instead of opening that sore and cleaning it out so it can heal."

Figs. 13-20 and 13-21 Fred Wilson, *Cabinetmaking 1820–1960* and *Metalwork 1793–1880*, from *Mining the Museum: An Installation by Fred Wilson*,
The Contemporary and Maryland Historical Society, Baltimore, 1992–1993.
Photograph by Jeff D. Goldman. © Fred Wilson, courtesy Pace Gallery.

But all fiber arts, sculptural or not, trace their origins back to **weaving**, a technique for constructing fabrics by means of interlacing horizontal and vertical thread—the very "event of a thread," with all its "crossing," upon which Ann Hamilton based her work at New York's Park Avenue Armory (see Fig. 13-1). The vertical threads—called the **warp**—are held taut on a loom or frame, and the horizontal threads—the **weft** or **woof**—are woven loosely over and under the warp. A **tapestry** is a special kind of weaving in which the weft yarns are of several colors and the weaver manipulates the colors to make an intricate design.

In 2002, Kiki Smith (see Fig. 10-1) began working with textiles at the Fabric Workshop in Philadelphia (the art21 *Exclusive* video "Kiki Smith: The Fabric Workshop" explores her work there). As Wendy Weitman writes in *Kiki Smith: Prints, Books & Things*, "Smith thrives on collaboration. . . . Sculpture and printmaking share this collaborative attribute, each often requiring specialized artisans to achieve the finished object. Not surprisingly, Smith excels at both." Thus, in 2011, she turned her attention to tapestry, working together with the tapestry experts at Magnolia Editions in Oakland, California. Magnolia uses a Jacquard loom, invented by Joseph-Marie Jacquard, who in 1804 took the ancient technique of card weaving to a new level. Weavers threaded different colors of yarn through holes in cards and then twisted the cards back and forth as they wove the weft to form the design. Jacquard created perforated cards, like those later used in player pianos or early computers, and Magnolia has refined the process by incorporating digital programming into the process. Smith has taken advantage of Magnolia's tapestry technique, especially its ability to record and weave into the tapestry the subtlest and most minute shifts in color. The result is tapestries like the almost 10-foot high *Guide* (**Fig. 13-22**). A celebration of the wonder and power of nature, the tapestry is not at all unrelated to the celebration of spring realized in the thousands of flowers that fill the *Unicorn Tapestry* in New York (see Fig. 13-18).

Fig. 13-22 Kiki Smith, *Guide*, 2012. Jacquard tapestry, approximately 9 ft. 11 in. × 6 ft. 4½ in. Edition of 10.

In **embroidery**, a second traditional fiber art, the design is made by needlework. From the early eighteenth century onward, the town of Chamba was one of the centers of the art of embroidery in India. It was known, particularly, for its *rumals*, embroidered muslin textiles that were used as wrappings for gifts (**Fig. 13-23**). If an offering was to be made at a temple, or if gifts were to be exchanged between families of a bride and groom, an embroidered *rumal* was always used as a wrapping.

The composition of the Chamba *rumals* is consistent. A floral border encloses a dense series of images, first drawn in charcoal and then embroidered, on a plain white muslin background. For a wedding gift, as in the *rumal* illustrated here, the designs might depict the wedding itself. The designs were double-darned, so that

Fig. 13-23 Embroidered *rumal*, late 18th century. Muslin and colored silks. Victoria and Albert Museum, London.

an identical scene appeared on both sides of the cloth. Because of its location in the foothills and mountains of the Himalayas, offering relief from the heat of the Indian plains, the region around Chamba was a favorite summer retreat for British colonists, and its embroidery arts became very popular in nineteenth-century Britain.

One of the most important textile designers of the twentieth century was Anni Albers. This wall hanging (**Fig. 13-24**) was done on a 12-harness loom, each harness capable of supporting a 4-inch band of weaving. Consequently, Albers designed a 48-inch-wide grid composed of 12 of the 4-inch-wide units. Each unit is a vertical rectangle, variable only in its patterning, which is either solid or striped. The striped rectangles are themselves divided into units of 12 alternating stripes. Occasional cubes are formed when two rectangles of the same pattern appear side by side.

Anni Albers regarded such geometric play as rooted in nature. Inspired by reading *The Metamorphosis of Plants* by Johann Wolfgang von Goethe, the eighteenth-century German poet and philosopher, she was fascinated by the way a simple basic pattern could generate, in nature, infinite variety. There is, in the design here, no apparent pattern in the occurrence of solid or striped rectangles or in the colors employed in them. This variability of particular detail within an overall geometric scheme is, from Albers's point of view, as natural and as inevitable as the repetition itself.

Fig. 13-24 Anni Albers, Wall hanging, 1926. Silk (two-ply weave), 6 × 4 ft. The Busch-Reisinger Museum, Harvard University Art Museums, Cambridge, Massachusetts.

Inv. BR48.132. Photo: Michael Nedzweski. © President and Fellows of Harvard College, Harvard University. © 2015 Josef and Anni Albers Foundation/Artists Rights Society (ARS), New York.

Fig. 13-25 Faith Ringgold, *Tar Beach*, Part I of the series *Woman on a Bridge*, 1988.
Acrylic on canvas bordered with printed, painted, quilted, and pieced cloth, 6 ft. 2⅝ in. × 5 ft. 8½ in.
Solomon R. Guggenheim Museum, New York.
Gift, Mr. and Mrs. Gus and Judith Lieber, 1988. Photo © Solomon R. Guggenheim Foundation/Art Resource, New York.
© Faith Ringgold.

In the early 1970s, Faith Ringgold (see Fig. 1-6) began to paint on soft fabrics and frame her images with decorative quilted borders made by her mother. After her mother's death in 1981, Ringgold created the quilt borders herself, and she began writing an autobiography, published in 1995 as *We Flew Over the Bridge: The Memoirs of Faith Ringgold*, which she incorporated into her painting/quilts. *Tar Beach* (**Fig. 13-25**) is one of these. "Tar Beach" refers to the roof of the apartment building where Ringgold's family would sleep on hot summer nights when she was growing up. The fictional narrator of this story is an eight-year-old girl named Cassie, shown lying on a quilt (within the quilt) with her brother at the lower right while her parents sit at a nearby table playing cards. A second Cassie flies over the George Washington Bridge at the top of the painting, a manifestation of the child's dreams. In the accompanying story, she imagines she can fly, taking the bridge for her own, claiming a union building for her father (half-black, half-Indian, he had helped to build it, but because of his race could not join the union himself), and an ice-cream factory for her mother, who deserved to eat "ice cream every night for dessert." The painting is a parable of the African-American experience, portraying at once the hopes and aspirations of their community even as it embodies the stark reality of their lives.

The principles of quiltmaking are quite simple. Quiltmaker Clay Lohmann, who as a male quiltmaker remains something of a rarity in the art world, points out that most modern athletic shoes are made like quilts and basic home construction uses the same principles as well—an interior wall, an exterior wall, wall studs serving as the quilting pattern, and most often fiberglass insulation as the batting between them. Lohmann makes what he calls "anatomy" quilts, which take advantage of his training in drawing and anatomy. *Black Lung* (**Fig. 13-26**) refers to the lung disease that develops from inhaling coal dust. The profile of a stern-looking man rises from the neckline of what appears to be a dress, but may well be a hospital robe. The black bands at top and bottom lend the quilt the aura of a funeral shroud. The quilting at the bottom of the lavender and gold bands suggests perspectival space, as if the figure is fading away. The pattern in the gold band is, incidentally, composed of the numbers 1–9, the alphabet, and an address. All suggests a history, something of a tragic story. "I grew up around and slept under quilts made by family members," Lohmann says. "All of my quilting is an homage to the unsung, underappreciated and most often women quilters who, no matter what level of artist achievement, simply are not recognized as 'artists.' I incorporate bits of lace, embroidered tea towels, pillowcases, tablecloths, and in a nod to punk fashion, safety pins."

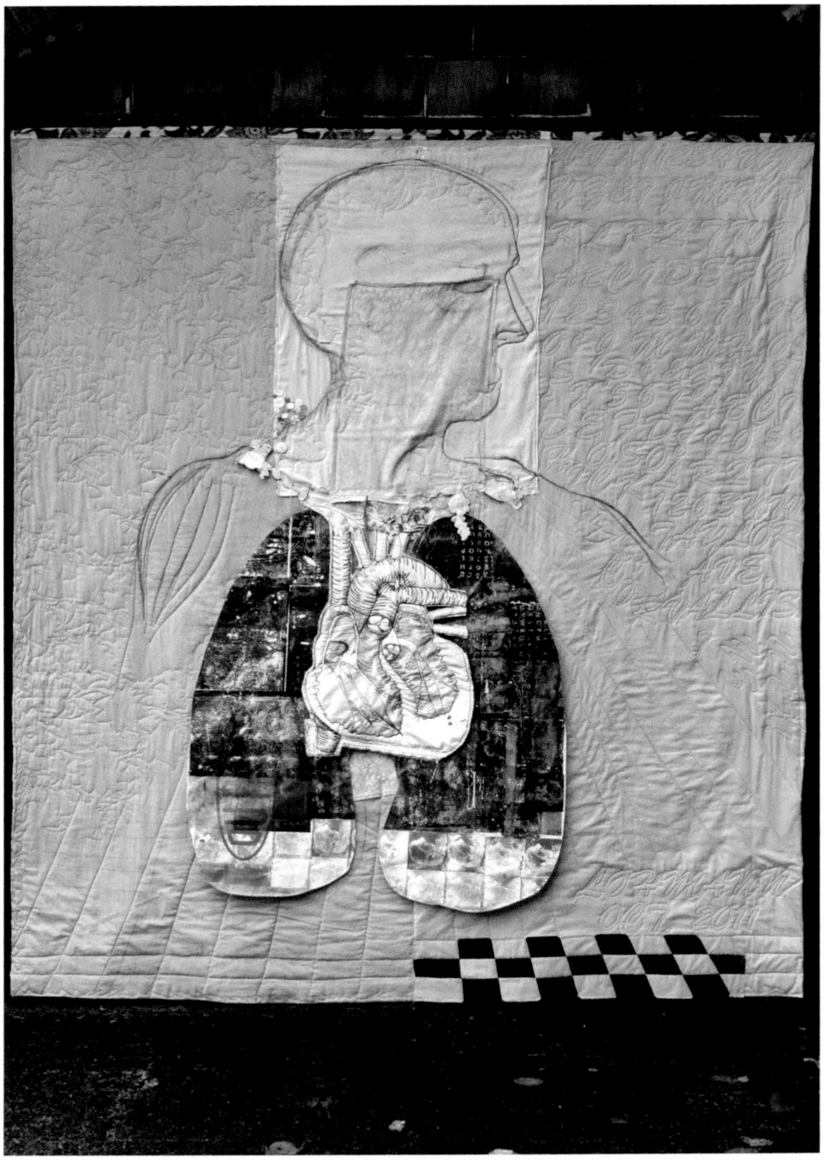

Fig. 13-26 Clay Lohmann, *Black Lung*, 2011. Cotton cloth, thread, silk batting, inflatable lung, buttons, tubing, safety pins, 7 ft. 6 in. × 6 ft. 8 in. Courtesy of the artist.

It was in the hands of Magdalena Abakanowicz, in the last century, that

Fig. 13-27 Magdalena Abakanowicz, *Backs in Landscape*, 1978–81. Eighty sculptures of burlap and resin molded from plaster casts, overlife-size. Marlborough Gallery, New York.
Photo: Dirk Bakker, 1982. © Magdalena Abakanowicz, courtesy of Marlborough Gallery, New York.

fiber became a tool of serious artistic expression, freed of any associations with utilitarian crafts. In the early 1970s, using traditional fiber materials such as burlap and string, Abakanowicz began to make forms based on the human anatomy (**Fig. 13-27**). She presses these fibers into a plaster mold, creating a series of forms that, though generally uniform, are strikingly different from piece to piece, the materials lending each figure an individual identity.

As Anni Albers's work also demonstrates, pattern and repetition have always played an important role in textile design. Abakanowicz brings new meaning to the traditional functions of repetitive pattern. These forms, all bent over in prayer, or perhaps pain, speak to our condition as humans, our spiritual emptiness—these are hollow forms—and our mass anxiety.

The textile wrappings also remind us of the traditional function of clothing—to protect us from the elements. Here, huddled against the sun and rain, each figure is shrouded in a wrap that seems at once clothing and bandage. It is as if the figures are wounded, cold, impoverished, homeless—the universal condition. As Abakanowicz reminds us:

> It is from fiber that all living organisms are built—the tissues of plants, and ourselves. Our nerves, our genetic code, the canals of our veins, our muscles. We are fibrous structures. Our heart is surrounded by the coronary plexus, the plexus of most vital threads. Handling fiber, we handle mystery. . . . When the biology of our body breaks down, the skin has to be cut so as to give access to the inside. Later it has to be sewn, like fabric. Fabric is our covering and our attire. Made with our hands, it is a record of our souls.

This, too, is the subject for artist Yinka Shonibare. Like Chris Ofili (see Fig. 1-25), Shonibare was born in England to Nigerian parents, but unlike Ofili he was raised in Nigeria before returning to art school in London. In the mid-1990s, he began making works out of the colorful printed fabrics that are worn throughout West Africa (**Fig. 13-28**), all of which are created by English and Dutch designers, manufactured in Europe, then exported to Africa, whence they are in turn remarketed to the West as authentic African design. In this sense, the fabrics are the very record of Shonibare's soul, traveling back and forth, from continent to continent. "By making hybrid clothes," Shonibare explains,

> I collapse the idea of a European dichotomy against an African one. There is no way you can work out where the opposites are. There is no way you can work out the precise

Fig. 13-28 Yinka Shonibare, MBE, *Victorian Couple*, 1999. Wax-printed cotton textile, left approx. 5 ft. × 36 in. × 36 in., right approx. 5 ft. × 24 in. × 24 in.
Courtesy James Cohan Gallery, New York and Shanghai © 2015 Yinka Shonibare MBE. All Rights Reserved, DACS/ARS, New York.

Fig. 13-29 Joana Vasconcelos, *Contamination* (*Contaminação*), 2008–10. Handmade woolen knitting and crochet, felt appliqués, industrial knitted fabric, fabrics, ornaments, polystyrene, polyester, steel cables. Dimensions variable. Palazzo Grassi, Venice, Italy.

> nationality of my dresses, because they do not have one. And there is no way you can work out the precise economic status of the people who would've worn those dresses because the economic status and the class status are confused in these objects.

In fact, even the era of these costumes is drawn into question. The bustle on the woman's dress is distinctly nineteenth-century, while the man's entire wardrobe seems distinctly out of the 1960s American hippie movement, especially given the decorative effect of the trumpets on his trouser legs.

In 2008, Portuguese artist Joana Vasconcelos installed her work *Contamination* (**Fig. 13-29**) at the Pinacoteca do Estado in São Paolo, Brazil, and then, subsequently, at the Berardo Museum in Lisbon and the Centre Culturel Calouste Gulbenkian in Paris. In the summer of 2011, it was installed at the Palazzo Grassi in Venice, Italy. As it moved, from country to country, it morphed as Vasconcelos continued to add new elements to it—fabric samples, jeweled insects, children's toys, sequins, pom-poms, beach towels—the detritus of consumer culture that proliferates and contaminates contemporary life. All this, she and her assistants sewed, knitted, and crocheted in place, allowing its amoebalike forms to spread like a viral contagion, as if reproducing in wild sexual abandon across, around, and through whatever architectural space it found itself inhabiting.

Metal

Why has gold been a favored material since ancient times?

Perhaps the most durable of all craft media is metal, and, as a result, it has been employed for centuries to make vessels for food and drink, tools for agriculture and building, and weapons for war. We have discussed traditional metal-casting techniques (see Chapter 12), but it is worth remembering that Chinese artisans had developed a sophisticated bronze-casting technique as early as the sixteenth century BCE, many centuries before the advent of the lost-wax technique in the West. The Chinese apparently constructed two-piece "sandwich" molds that did not require wax to hold the two sides apart. (For an example, see Fig. 16-14.)

Of all metals, gold is the easiest to work, being relatively soft and occurring as it does in an almost pure state. Since the earliest times, its brilliance has been linked to royalty. In ancient Egyptian culture, it was closely associated with both the sun god, Re, and the king himself, who was considered the son of Re. Because of its permanence—it neither corrodes nor tarnishes—it was further associated with the *ka*, the eternal life of the ruler, similar to the "soul" or "life force" in other

Fig. 13-30 *Tutankhamun Hunting Ostriches from His Chariot*, base of the king's ostrich-feather fan, ca. 1335–1327 BCE. Beaten gold, 4 × 7¼ in. Egyptian Museum, Cairo.
akg-image/Erich Lessing.

Fig. 13-31 Griffin bracelet, from the Oxus treasure, ca. 500–400 BCE. Gold and stones, diameter 5 in. British Museum, London.
De Agostini/Bridgeman Images.

religions. A representation of King Tutankhamun hunting, found in his grave, is typical of Egyptian gold ornamentation (**Fig. 13-30**). The work is an example of gold **repoussé**—that is, its design was realized by hammering the image from the reverse side. The design on the front was then refined by means of **embossing**—the reverse of repoussé.

Over the years, metals, especially gold and silver, have also been lavishly used in the creation of jewelry. The Persian griffin bracelet pictured here (**Fig. 13-31**) was discovered in 1877 as part of the Oxus treasure, named after the river in Central Asia where it was found. The griffin is a mythological beast, half-eagle, half-lion, that symbolized vigilance and courage, and was believed by the Persians to guard the gold of India, and the story associated with the discovery of this bracelet is indeed one of heroism and courage. Originally sold to Muslim merchants, the Oxus treasure was soon stolen by bandits, who were intent on dividing the loot evenly by melting it

Fig. 13-32 Benvenuto Cellini, *Saltcellar: Neptune (Sea) and Tellus (Earth)*, 1540–43. Gold, niello work, and ebony base, height 10¼ in. Kunsthistorisches Museum, Vienna.
akg-image/Erich Lessing.

down. Captain F. C. Burton, a British officer in Pakistan, heard of the robbery, rescued the treasure, and returned it to the merchants, asking only that he be given one of two griffin bracelets as his reward. He subsequently donated it to the Victoria and Albert Museum in London, while its companion piece, illustrated here, eventually found its way to the British Museum. Considered one of the most beautiful works of jewelry ever made, the bracelet was originally inlaid with colored stones. The minute detail of the griffins—especially the feathers on wings and necks, as well as the clawed feet—must have suggested, inlaid with stone, the finest Asian silk drapery.

The Oxus treasure was almost surely a royal hoard and, throughout history, the most elaborate metal designs have always been commissioned by royalty. In 1539, Benvenuto Cellini designed a saltcellar (**Fig. 13-32**) for Francis I of France. Made of gold and enamel, it is actually a functional salt and pepper shaker. Salt is represented by the male figure, Neptune, god of the sea, and hence overlord of the sea's salt. Pepper is the provenance of earth, represented by the female figure. Along the base of the saltcellar is a complex array of allegorical figures depicting the four seasons and four times of day (dawn, day, twilight, and night), embodying both seasonal festivities and the daily meal schedule. In his autobiography, Cellini described the work as follows:

> I first laid down an oval framework and upon this ground, wishing to suggest the interminglement of land and ocean, I modeled two figures, one considerably taller than a palm in height, which were seated with their legs interlaced, suggesting those lengthier branches of the sea which run up into the continents. The sea was a man, and in his hand I placed a ship, elaborately wrought in all its details, and well adapted to hold a quantity of salt. Beneath him I grouped the four sea-horses, and in his right hand he held his trident. The earth I fashioned like a woman, with all the beauty of form, the grace, and charm of which my art was capable. She had a richly decorated temple firmly based upon the ground at one side; and here her hand rested. This I intended to receive the pepper. In her other hand I put a cornucopia, overflowing with all the natural treasures I could think of. Below the goddess, on the part which represented earth, I collected the fairest animals that haunt our globe. In the quarter presided over by the deity of ocean, I fashioned such choice kinds of fishes and shells as could be properly displayed in that small space.

While Cellini apparently later changed the positions of the hands and what they were holding, the description, which must have been written some 20 years after the fact, is accurate. When a Vatican cardinal saw the model,

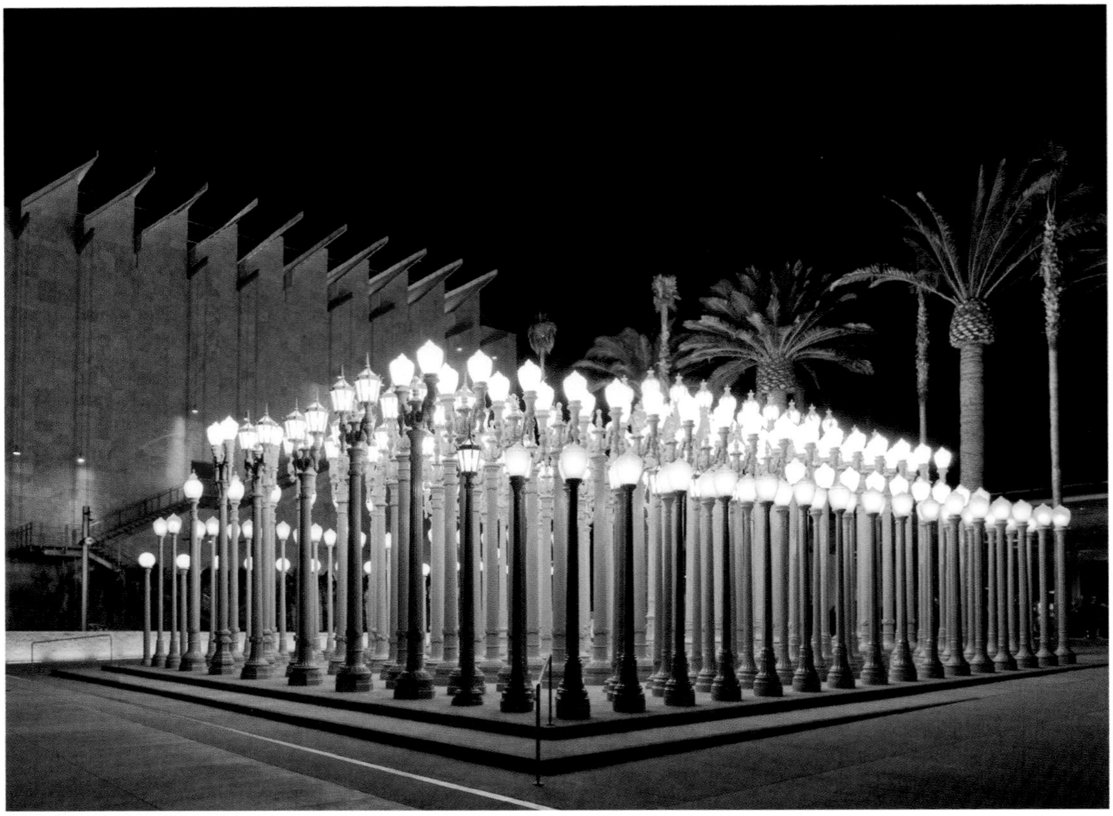

Fig. 13-33 Chris Burden, *Urban Light*, 2000–07. Two hundred and two restored cast-iron antique street lamps, 26 ft. 8½ in. × 57 ft. 2½ in. × 58 ft. 8½ in. Los Angeles County Museum of Art.
Gordon Family Foundation's gift to "Transformation: LACMA Campaign," M.2007.147.1-.202. © 2015. Digital Image Museum Associates/LACMA/Art Resource New York/Scala, Florence. © Chris Burden.

he told Cellini: "Unless you make it for the King, to whom I mean to take you, I do not think that you will make it for another man alive."

Of course, not all metalwork is done in gold. In the nineteenth and the early twentieth century cast iron was frequently used for decorative benches and railings, and larger projects such as bridges. In 2000, artist Chris Burden (see Fig. 11-37) began collecting cast-iron street lamps made in the 1920s and 1930s. Gradually, over the years, he collected more and more of them—sandblasting them, recasting missing parts, rewiring them to code, and then painting them all a uniform gray—until, by 2006, he owned some 150, which he installed in tight rows around his studio in Topanga Canyon in western Los Angeles County. He saw in them some iconic quality, as if they captured a spirit related to the rise of the modern era. "Street lamps," he says, "are one of the fundamental building blocks of an urban metropolis. The richly detailed fluted lamps are an ornate totem to industrialism and represent a form of public art. My artwork *Urban Light*, is ultimately a statement about what constitutes a civilized and sophisticated city, safe after dark and beautiful to behold." In 2006, he offered them for sale, and by the time they were purchased by the Los Angeles County Museum of Art, where they came to serve as a kind of entryway on Wilshire Boulevard into the newly refurbished museum complex, their number had grown to 202 (**Fig. 13-33**). Powered by solar cells, they are turned on each evening at dusk, creating a soft glow that animates the entire complex. Where once they served a purely utilitarian purpose, lighting the streets of Los Angeles, Hollywood, Anaheim, and even Portland, Oregon, they have become, in Burden's hands, a kind of temple to the urbanization of the world.

Wood

What are some uses and limitations of wood as a material?

Because it is so easy to carve, and because it is so widely available, artisans have favored wood as a medium throughout history. Yet because it is an organic material, wood is also extremely fragile, and few wood artifacts survive from ancient cultures.

Of all woods, cedar, native to the Northwest American coast, is a particular favorite of Native American artists in that region because of its relative impermeability by the weather, its resistance to insect attack, and its protective, aromatic odor. Chests such as this Heiltsuk

Fig. 13-34 Heiltsuk, *Bent-Corner Chest* (*Kook*), ca. 1860. Yellow and red cedar, and paint, 21¼ × 35¾ × 20½ in. Seattle Art Museum.
Gift of John H. Hauberg and John and Grace Putnam. 86.278. Photo: Paul Maciapia.

example (**Fig. 13-34**) were designed to contain family heirlooms and clan regalia, and were opened only on ceremonial occasions. Often such a chest also served as the ceremonial seat of the clan leader, who sat upon it, literally supported by his heritage.

Wood has also been a favorite, even preferred, material for making furniture, and, in the hands of accomplished artists, a piece of furniture can be transformed into a work of art in its own right. The earliest Americans understood this from the outset. Some of the most magnificent furniture designed in the newly founded American colonies in the seventeenth century came from Ipswich, Massachusetts. There, by the 1660s, two "joiners," or furniture-makers, William Searle and his son-in-law Thomas Dennis, were crafting some of the most beautiful trunks and chests produced in seventeenth-century New England. The panels of the chest illustrated here (**Fig. 13-35**) are carved in a design popular in Searle and Dennis's native Devonshire, England. Stalks of flowers and leaves emerge from an urn, only the opening of which is visible at the bottom of each of the three panels. Formally, the chest is notable for the symmetry of its design, the two outside panels bracketing the center one. But perhaps more striking is the very richness of the design, its elaborate, even exuberant celebration of the natural world.

Americans, raised with the story of the *Mayflower* and Plymouth Plantation, most especially the image of that first winter of 1620–21, when nearly half the population of that first settlement succumbed to the harshness of their circumstances, rarely appreciate the feelings that the Puritans had for the natural beauty—and bounty—of the place they now called home. At the time of their arrival, most of the eastern United States was covered in tall forests of oak, pine, hemlock, maple, ash, and birch. It was in fact the ready availability of high-quality wood scoured from the landscape, oak in particular, that so attracted Searle and Dennis to Ipswich in the first place. There they could still search the nearby forests for a good tree. The oaks they cut were at least 200 years old, many much older, and they were very close-ringed, as many as 15 to 20 rings per inch (a modern-day oak would be notable if it possessed 10 per inch). This chest is an image of that bounty.

Fig. 13-35 Attributed to Thomas Dennis or William Searle, Chest, made in Ipswich, Massachusetts, 1660–80. Red oak, white oak, 29¾ in. × 4 ft. 1⅛ in. × 21⅜ in. Metropolitan Museum of Art, New York.
Gift of Mrs. Russell Sage, 1909, 10.125.685. © 2015.Image copyright Metropolitan Museum of Art/Art Resource/Scala, Florence.

THE CRITICAL PROCESS
Thinking about the Crafts as Fine Art

A fascinating intervention of the crafts into the worlds of both art and science is *Crochet Coral Reef* (**Fig. 13-36**), a project sponsored by the Institute for Figuring in Los Angeles, an organization that explores the aesthetic dimensions of science, mathematics, and the arts, according to their website, "from the physics of snowflakes and the hyperbolic geometry of sea slugs, to the mathematics of paper folding and graphical models of the human mind." It was founded in 2003 by sisters Margaret Wertheim, a science writer, and Christine Wertheim, an artist. The two grew up in Queensland, Australia, where the Great Barrier Reef, one of the natural wonders of the world, has undergone severe environmental damage in the last few decades as vast sections of the coral reef have died. In order to draw attention to the devastation, the sisters inaugurated the *Crochet Coral Reef* project.

The installation is based on the findings of mathematician Daina Taimina, who in 2001 argued that crocheting offered one of the best ways to model hyperbolic geometry, and that, in turn, coral was a hyperbolic geometric structure in its own right. Thousands of people—by and large women, but a number of men as well—have contributed to the *Crochet Coral Reef* project, and *Crochet Coral and Anemone Garden,* pictured below, is but one of a number of installations, among them *Toxic Reef*, crocheted from yarn and plastic trash.

As "women's work," crocheting is a traditional craft done at one remove from "high art." That in its structure it symbolizes, even mirrors, what we might call "high mathematics" was particularly attractive to the Wertheims, not because this fact elevated crocheting to the level of "high art," but because it suggested something about the nature of political and economic power in modern society. Can you articulate what commentary on society they may have recognized in the analogy between crocheting and hyperbolic geometry? Normally, crocheting is done for utilitarian purposes—for clothing, for instance—but here it serves a purely aesthetic function. Or does it? What utilitarian purpose does it still serve? What traditional role of the artist do the many people who have worked on the *Crochet Coral Reef* project play?

Fig. 13-36 Institute For Figuring, *Crochet Coral Reef* project, 2005–ongoing. Created and curated by Margaret and Christine Wertheim.
Photo: Alyssa Gorelick.

Thinking Back

13.1 Characterize the difference between craft and fine art.

The line between the arts and the crafts is a fine one. For many, a craft object is defined by the fact that it is functional, but many functional objects have artistic qualities. How did Josiah Wedgwood distinguish between craft and art objects? Many artists have taken the craft media to innovative and new ends. How has Ann Hamilton done this? Fred Wilson?

13.2 Describe the different ceramic methods and materials.

Ceramics are objects that are formed out of clay and then hardened by firing in a very hot oven called a kiln. Ceramic objects can be formed in a few different ways: slab construction, coiling, and throwing on a potter's wheel. How does a ceramic artist use slip? What distinguishes earthenware, stoneware, and porcelain?

13.3 Outline some ways in which glass has become an artistic medium.

Around the first century BCE, glassblowing techniques were developed, turning glass into a major industry. In this process, the glassblower dips the end of a pipe into molten glass and then blows through the pipe to produce a bubble, which is then shaped and cut. How is stained glass made? What role has Dale Chihuly played in redefining the medium of glass today?

13.4 Describe some of the different uses of fiber in the arts.

Weaving is a technique for constructing fabrics in which vertical threads (the warp) are interlaced with horizontal threads (the weft, or woof). The warp threads are held tightly on a frame, and the weft threads are continuously pulled above and below. What distinguishes a tapestry? What defines the technique of embroidery? What are *rumals*? What is a quilt? Describe some of the ways that contemporary artists have extended the use of fiber into more sculptural forms and installations.

13.5 Explain why gold has been a favored material since ancient times.

Perhaps the most durable of all craft media is metal. Of all metals, gold is the easiest to work. It is relatively soft, occurs in an almost pure state, and has consequently, since ancient times, been linked with royalty. How does repoussé differ from embossing? What features of the Oxus treasure would point to it coming from a royal hoard? How did Chris Burden transform the functional street lamp into a work of art?

13.6 Describe the uses and limitations of wood as an art material.

Because it is so easy to carve, and because it is so widely available, artisans have favored wood as a medium throughout history. Yet because it is organic, wood is also extremely fragile, and few wood artifacts survive from ancient cultures. It remains, however, one of the most preferred media for furniture, where it can be carved to artistic effect.

Chapter 14
Architecture

Learning Objectives

14.1 Describe the relationship between architecture and its environment.

14.2 Outline the architectural technologies that predate the modern era.

14.3 Describe the technological advances that have contributed to modern and contemporary architecture.

14.4 Describe how the idea of community serves as a driving force in architecture.

In the early 1980s, the president of France, François Mitterrand, embarked on a program of *Grands Projets* designed to transform and revitalize the French capital, Paris. Among the most important of these was a plan to expand the Louvre Museum by creating a central entryway, in the middle of the Cour Napoléon, the courtyard contained by the Old Louvre palace, to the east, and two later wings, the Richelieu wing to the north, and the Denon wing to the south, the latter completed by Louis XIII in the early seventeenth century but begun by Catherine de Medici in 1550. American architect I. M. Pei was awarded the commission. His plan was simple but elegant. The entire Cour Napoléon and the Place du Carrousel to its west were excavated, creating a vast underground visitor's center with entries on three sides into the collections and surmounted, at the center of the Cour Napoléon, by Pei's today iconic shimmering glass pyramid (**Fig. 14-1**). Pei's pyramid is distinctly contemporary, but it adds just one more historical layer to a building that originated in the thirteenth century as a defensive fortress and was subsequently enlarged by major additions that incorporated, in succession, Renaissance, Baroque, and Neoclassical styles.

In this chapter, we will consider how our built environment has developed in ways comparable to the Louvre itself—how we have traveled, in effect, from the fortresses of the past to skyscrapers and postmodernist designs. We will see that the "look" of our buildings and our communities depends on two different factors and their interrelation—environment, or the distinct landscape characteristics of the local site, including its climatic features, and **technology**, the materials and methods available to a given culture. The site has had a considerable influence on the design. In Pei's case at the Louvre, he had to find a way to respond to its very history. Thus, the key to understanding and appreciating architecture always involves both technology and environment. We will consider environment first.

Environment

How does the environment affect architecture?

The built environment reflects the natural world and the conception of its inhabitants of their place within the natural scheme of things. A building's form might echo the world around it, or it might contrast with it. It also might respond to the climate of the place. In each case,

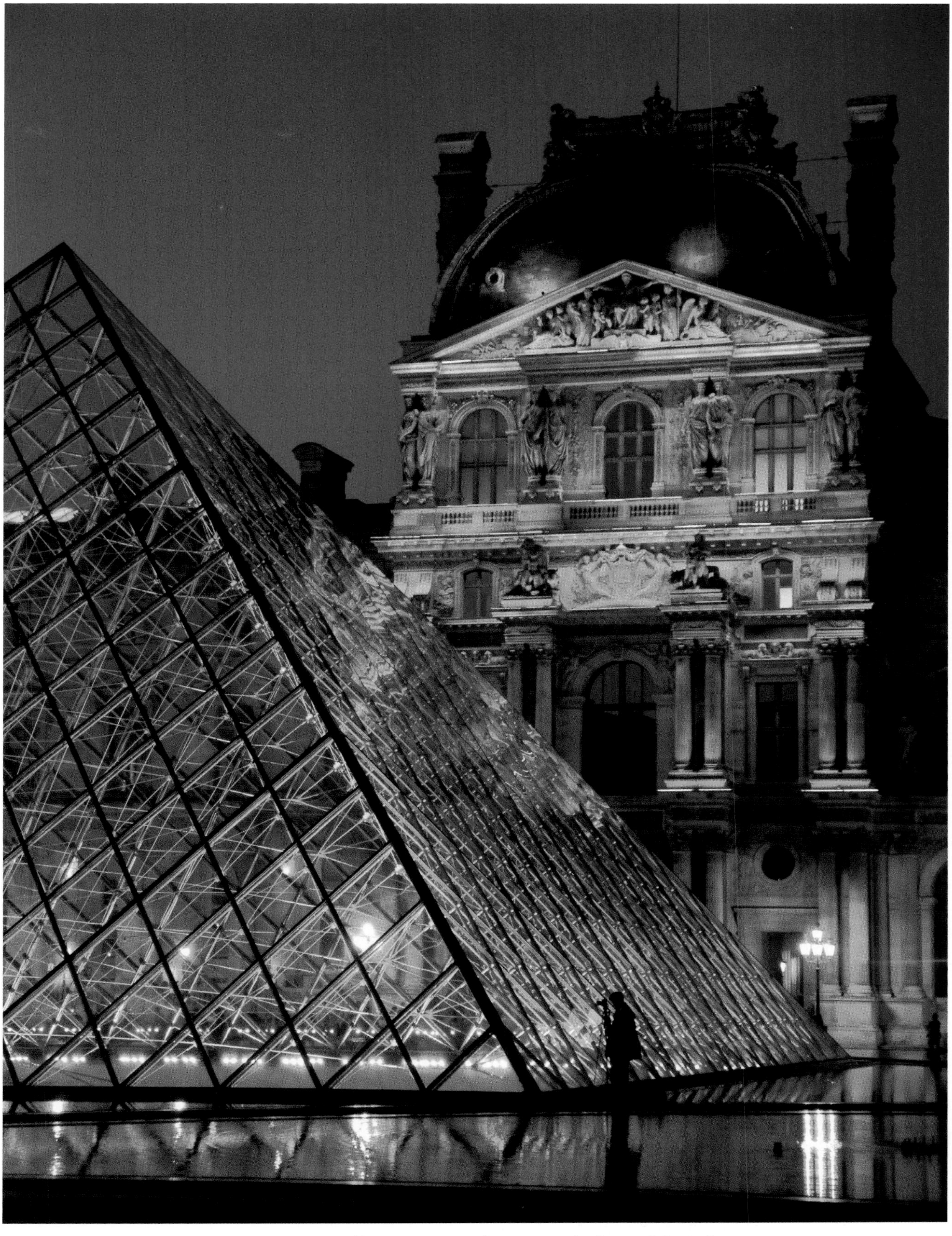

Fig. 14-1 I. M. Pei, Glass Pyramid, Cour Napoléon, Louvre, Paris, 1983–89; in front of the 17th-century Denon wing of the museum. Pyramid height 69 ft., width 108 ft.

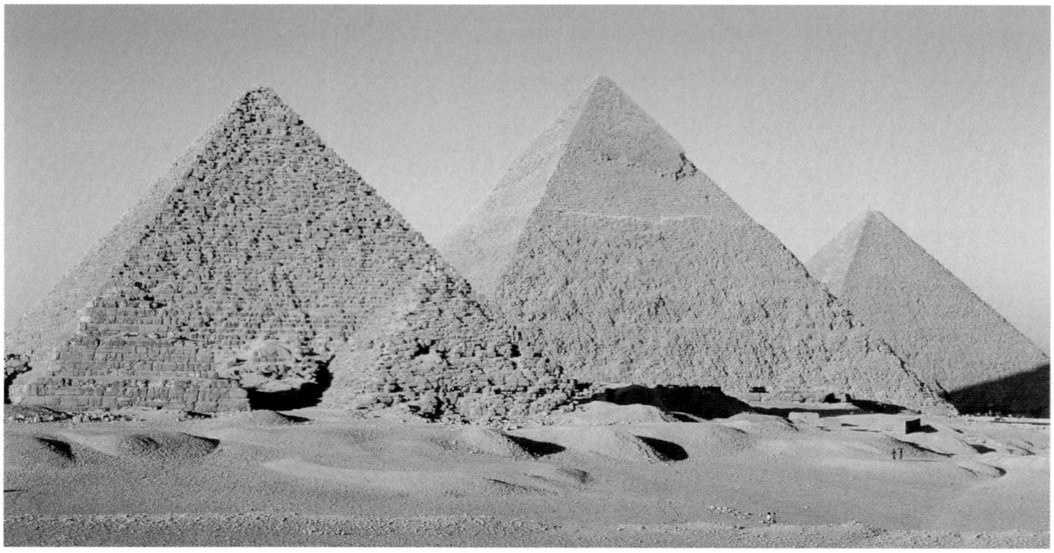

Fig. 14-2 Pyramids of Menkaure (ca. 2470 BCE), Khafre (ca. 2500 BCE), and Khufu (ca. 2530 BCE). Original height of Pyramid of Khufu 480 ft., length of each side at base 755 ft.
© Free Agents Limited/CORBIS. Photo: Dallas and John Heaton.

the choices builders make reveal their attitudes toward the world around them.

The architecture of the vast majority of early civilizations was designed to imitate natural forms. The significance of the pyramids of Egypt (**Fig. 14-2**) is the subject of much debate, but their form may well derive from the image of the god Re, who in ancient Egypt was symbolized by the rays of the sun descending to earth. A text in one pyramid reads: "I have trodden these rays as ramps under my feet." As one approached the mammoth pyramids, covered in limestone to reflect the light of the sun, the eye was carried skyward to Re, the Sun itself, who was, in the desert, the central fact of life.

The Impact of Climate

The designs of many buildings, in fact, reflect the climatic conditions of environments. When African slaves arrived in the Americas in the eighteenth century, they found themselves living in a climate very much like that they had left in Africa. A late eighteenth-/early nineteenth-century painting of the Mulberry Plantation in South Carolina (**Fig. 14-3**) depicts slave houses with steeply pitched roofs similar to the thatched-roof houses of the same era found in West Africa. The roof comprises over half the height of the house, allowing warm air to rise in the interior and trap cooler air beneath it—a distinct advantage in the hot and humid climates of both Africa and the Carolinas.

The Anasazi cliff dwelling known as Spruce Tree House (**Fig. 14-4**) at Mesa Verde National Park in southwestern Colorado reflects a similar relation between humans and their environment. The Anasazi lived in these cliffside caves for hundreds, perhaps thousands, of years. The cave provided security, but to live there was also to be closer to the people's origin and, therefore, to the source of their strength. For unknown reasons, the Anasazi abandoned their cliff dwellings in about 1300 CE. One possible cause was a severe drought that lasted from 1276 to 1299. It is also possible that disease, a shortened growing season, or war with Apache and Shoshone tribes caused the Anasazi to leave the highland mesas and migrate south into Arizona and New Mexico.

At the heart of the Anasazi culture was the **kiva**, a round, covered hole in the center of the communal plaza in which all ceremonial life took place. The roofs of two underground kivas on the north end of the ruin have been restored. They are constructed of horizontally

Fig. 14-3 Thomas Coram, *View of Mulberry House and Street*, ca. 1800. Oil on paper. Gibbes Museum of Art, Charleston, South Carolina.
Carolina Art Association, 1968.18.0001. © Image courtesy of the Gibbes Museum of Art/Carolina Art Association.

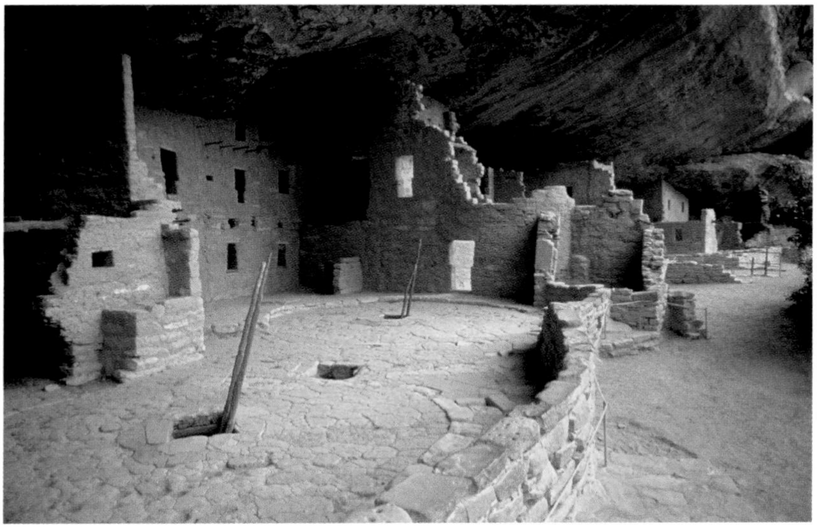

Fig. 14-4 Spruce Tree House, Mesa Verde, ca. 1200–1300 CE. Courtyard formed by restoration of the roofs over two underground kivas.
Photo: John Deeks/Photo Researchers, Inc.

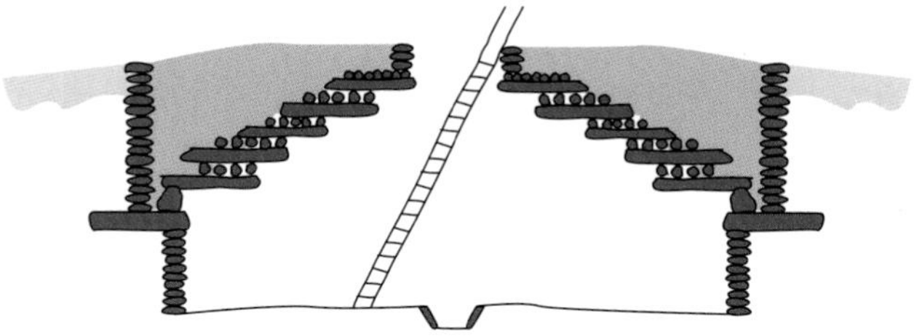

Fig. 14-5 Cribbed roof construction of a kiva.

laid logs built up to form a dome with an access hole (**Fig. 14-5**). The people utilized these roofs as a common area. Down below, in the enclosed kiva floor, was a *sipapu*, a small, round hole symbolic of the Anasazi creation myth, which told of the emergence of the Anasazi's ancestors from the depths of the earth. In the parched Southwestern desert country it is equally true that water, like life itself, also seeps out of small fissures in the earth. Thus, it is as if the entire Anasazi community, and everything necessary to its survival, emerges from Mother Earth.

"Green" Architecture

Both the slave houses at Mulberry Plantation and the cliff dwellings at Mesa Verde are attempts to allay, in some measure, the heat of their environments. In the face of climate change, architects have been challenged to engage in a different, more environmentally friendly and sustainable, practice—so-called **green architecture**.

One of the masterpieces of green architecture is Renzo Piano's Jean-Marie Tjibaou Cultural Center in New Caledonia. As Piano's design suggests, green architecture is characterized by a number of different principles, but usually only some of these principles are realized in a given project:

1) *Smaller buildings*. This represents an attitude that is the very opposite of the Dubai model (see Fig. 14-49), and it is no accident that residential architecture, such as the 2,800-square-foot Brunsell Residence designed by Obie Bowman at Sea Ranch, California (**Fig. 14-6**), has led the way in the development of sustainable, green architecture.
2) *Integration and compatibility with the natural environment*. Although only portions of Bowman's structure are 4 feet underground, he has created a rooftop meadow of the same grass species as the surrounding headlands, thus creating the feeling that the structure is almost entirely buried in the earth. As Bowman explains: "The places we make emphasize their connectedness to the character and quality of the setting and are designed as part of the landscape

Fig. 14-6 Obie Bowman, Brunsell Residence, Sea Ranch, California, 1987.

rather than as isolated objects placed down upon it."

3) *Energy efficiency and solar orientation*. The rooftop meadow on the Sea Ranch house helps to stabilize interior temperatures. In addition, solar collectors capture the sunlight to heat the residence's water, and the architect sited the house specifically to protect it from the prevailing winds. A south-facing solarium provides winter warmth.
4) *Use of recycled, reusable, and sustainable materials*. Brockholes Visitor Center, near Preston, Lancashire, in the United Kingdom, designed by architect Adam Kahn (**Fig. 14-7**), is clad in oak shake tiles formed out of tree stumps, which would otherwise be burned as waste. Insulation in the walls of the building consists of recycled newspapers. Set in the middle of a low-lying wildlife refuge, the building floats (thereby foregoing the need for concrete foundations). Beds of reeds have been planted around the steep-pitched roofs so that, in time, the roofs will appear to emerge from them.

These principles are, of course, more difficult to implement in densely populated urban environments. But faced with the prospect of climate change, in 2010 the Museum of Modern Art in New York sponsored a workshop-exhibition, *Rising Currents: Projects for New York's Waterfront*, that brought together five architectural teams tasked with reinventing New York's urban infrastructure in the light of rising sea levels—as much as 6 feet by 2100—the prospect of which threatens the very habitability of the city (when Hurricane Sandy struck in October 2012, the exhibition turned out to be remarkably prescient).

The team of Eric Bunge and Mimi Hoang, of nARCHITECTS, proposed a project entitled *New Aqueous City* (**Fig. 14-8**), which introduces, in their words, "a novel urban paradigm: a city that can control and absorb rising sea levels even as it accommodates an expected spike in population over the next century." To that end, in areas less than 20 feet above sea level—that is, areas subject to flooding during a Category 3 storm—buildings constructed of lightweight materials are hung from bridges that rise on vertical support structures. The buildings, in fact, are accessed from above, and the bridges themselves not only serve as "streets" but as safe evacuation pathways during storms. At the same time, waterways extend into the city in a network of infiltration basins, swales, and culverts designed to absorb storm surge. As this project makes clear, as the environment—that is to say, nature itself—increasingly impinges upon the urban infrastructure, new solutions and innovative approaches to architecture will be required.

Fig. 14-7 Adam Kahn, Brockholes Visitor Center, Lancashire Wildlife Trust reserve, Preston, U.K., 2011.

© Ashley Cooper/Corbis.

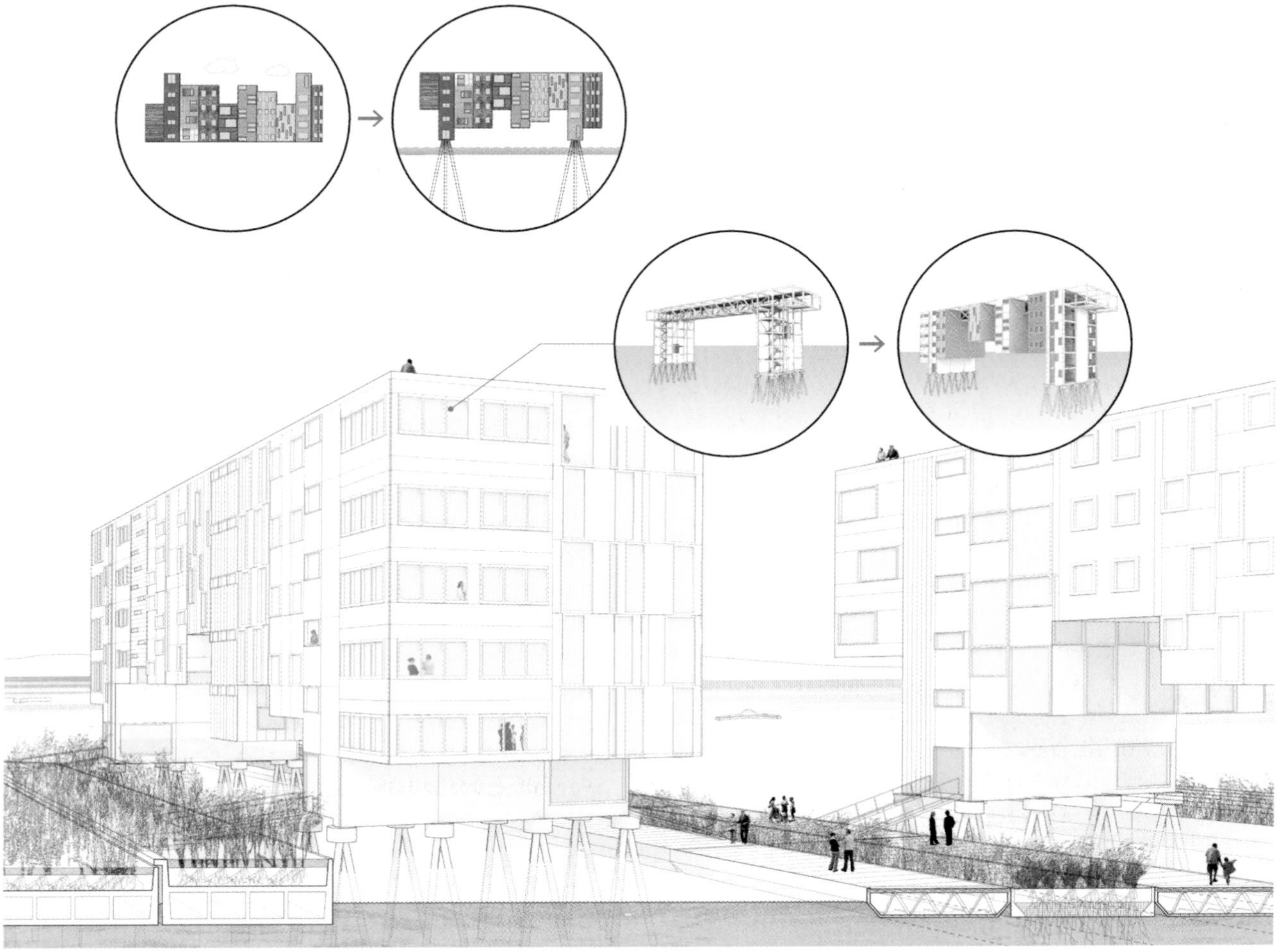

Fig. 14-8 Eric Bunge and Mimi Hoang, nARCHITECTS, *New Aqueous City*, 2010. From *Rising Currents: Projects for New York's Waterfront*, a workshop-exhibition sponsored by the Museum of Modern Art, New York, March 24–October 11, 2010.
Courtesy of nARCHITECTS.

Early Architectural Technologies

What are the architectural technologies that predate the modern era?

Green architecture of necessity requires architects to pursue new technologies as they seek to solve problems heretofore largely unanticipated. But the basic technological challenge faced by architecture since the earliest times is to construct upright walls and put a roof over the empty space they enclose. Walls may employ one of two basic structural systems: the **shell system**, in which one basic material provides both the structural support and the outside covering of the building, and the **skeleton-and-skin system**, which consists of a basic interior frame, the skeleton, that supports the more fragile outer covering, the skin.

In a building that is several stories tall, the walls or frame of the lower floors must also support the weight of the upper floors. The ability of a given building material to support weight is thus a determining factor in how high the building can be. The walls or frame also support the roof. The span between the elements of the supporting structure—between, for instance, stone walls, columns, or steel beams—is determined by the tensile strength of the roof material. **Tensile strength** is the ability of a building material to span horizontal distances without support and without buckling in the middle: The greater the tensile strength of a material, the wider its potential span. Almost all technological advances in the history of architecture depend on either the invention of new ways to distribute weight or the discovery of new materials with greater tensile strength. We begin our survey with the most basic technology and move forward to the most advanced.

Load-Bearing Construction

The simplest method of making a building is to make the walls **load-bearing**—make the walls themselves bear the weight of the roof. One does this by piling and stacking any material—stones, bricks, mud, and straw—right up to roof level. Many load-bearing structures, such as the Egyptian pyramids, are solid almost all the way through, with only small open chambers inside them.

Although the Anasazi cliff dwelling contains more livable space than a pyramid, it too is a load-bearing construction. The kiva is built of **adobe** bricks—bricks made of dried clay—piled on top of one another, and the roof is built of wood. The complex roof of the kiva spans a greater circumference than would be possible with just wood, and it supports the weight of the community in the plaza above. This is achieved by the downward pressure exerted on the wooden beams by the stones and fill on top of them above the outside wall, which counters the tendency of the roof to buckle.

Post-and-Lintel Construction

The walls surrounding the Lion Gate at Mycenae in Greece (**Fig. 14-9**) are of load-bearing construction. But the gate itself represents another form of construction: post-and-lintel. **Post-and-lintel construction** consists of a horizontal beam supported at each end by a vertical post or a wall. In essence, the downward force of the horizontal bridge holds the vertical posts in an upright position, and, conversely, the posts support the stone above in a give-and-take of directional force and balance. So large are the stones used to build this gate—both the length of the lintel and the total height of the post-and-lintel structure are roughly 13 feet—that later Greeks believed it could only have been built by the mythological race of one-eyed giants, the Cyclopes.

Post-and-lintel construction is fundamental to all Greek architecture. As can be seen in the First Temple of Hera, at Paestum, Italy (**Fig. 14-10**), the columns, or posts, supporting the structure were placed relatively close together. This was done for a practical reason: If stone lintels, especially of marble, were required to span too great a distance, they were likely to crack and eventually collapse. Each of the columns in the temple is made of several pieces of stone, called **drums**. Grooves carved in the stone, called **fluting**, run the length of the column and unite the individual drums into a single unit. Each column tapers dramatically toward the top and slightly toward the bottom, an architectural feature known as **entasis**. Entasis deceives the eye and makes the column look absolutely vertical. It also gives the column a sense of almost human musculature and strength. The columns suggest the bodies of human beings, holding up the roof like miniature versions of the giant Atlas, who carried the world on his shoulders.

Fig. 14-9 Lion Gate, Mycenae, Greece, 1250 BCE.

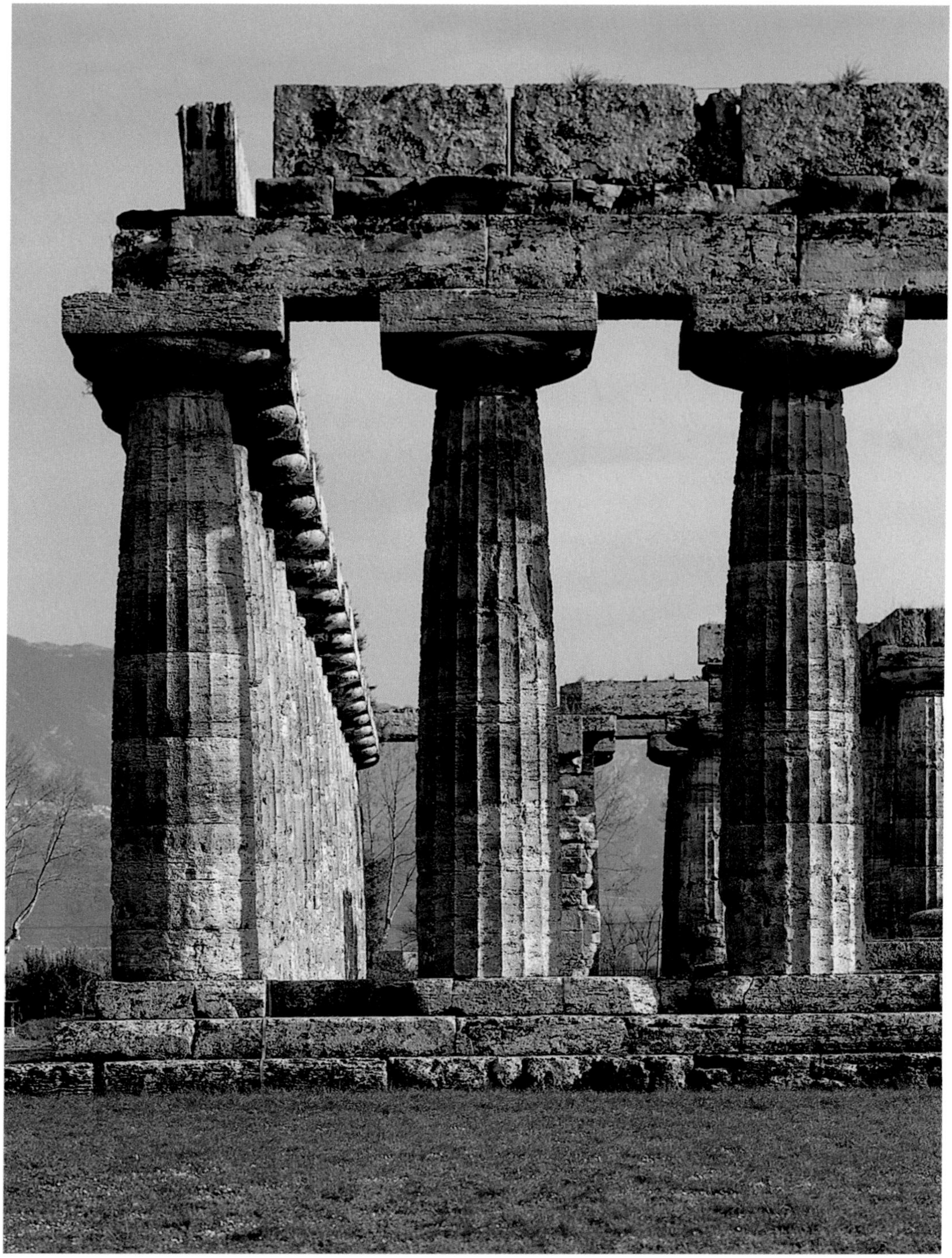

Fig. 14-10 First Temple of Hera, Paestum, Italy, ca. 550 BCE.
Canali Photobank, Milan, Italy.

The values of the Greek city-state were embodied in its temples. The temple was usually situated on an elevated site above the city—an **acropolis**, from *akros*, meaning "top," of the *polis*, "city"—and was conceived as the center of civic life. Its **colonnade**, or row of columns set at regular intervals around the building and supporting the base of the roof, was constructed according to the rules of geometry and embodied cultural values of equality and proportion. So consistent were the Greeks in developing a generalized architectural type for their temples that it is possible to speak of them in terms of three distinct architectural types—the Doric, the Ionic,

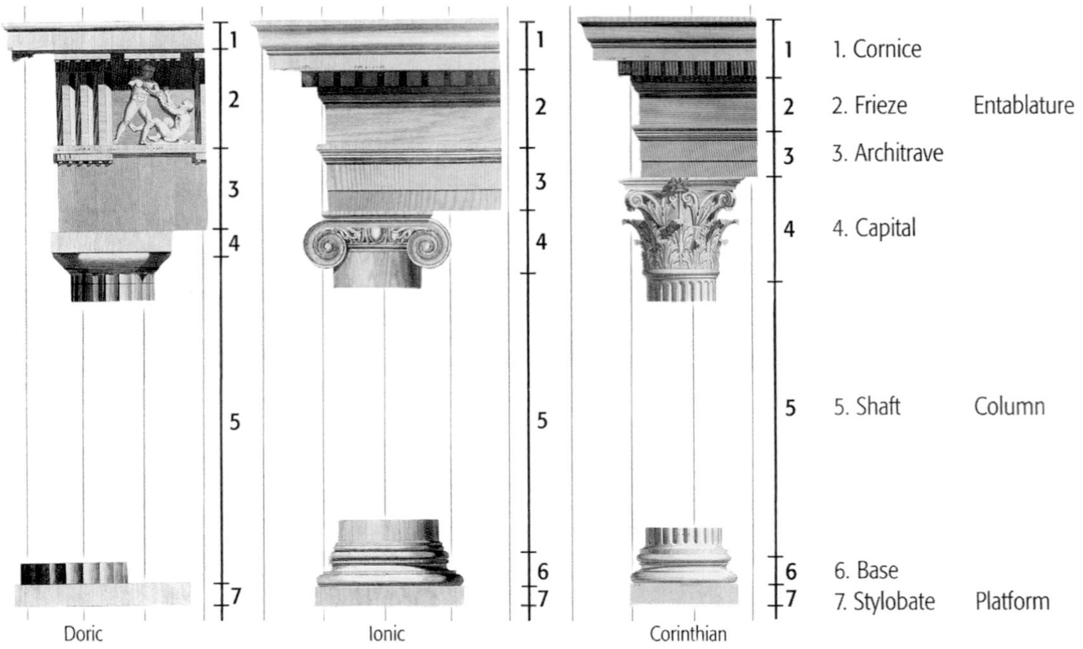

Fig. 14-11 The Greek orders, from James Stuart, *The Antiquities of Athens*, London, 1794.
Courtesy of Library of Congress.

and the Corinthian, the last of which was rarely used by the Greeks themselves but later became the standard order in Roman architecture (**Fig. 14-11**). In ancient times, the heavier Doric order was considered masculine, and the more graceful Ionic order feminine. It is true that the Ionic order is slimmer and much lighter in feeling than the Doric.

The vertical design, or **elevation**, of the Greek temple is composed of three elements—the **platform**, the **column**, and the **entablature**. The relationship among these three units is referred to as its **order**. The Doric, the earliest and plainest of the three, is used in the temple at Paestum. The Ionic is later, more elaborate, and organic, while the Corinthian is more organic and decorative still. The elevation of each order begins with its floor, the **stylobate**, or the top step of the platform on which the building rests. The column in the Doric order consists of two parts, the **shaft** and the **capital**, to which both the Ionic and Corinthian orders add a base. The orders are most quickly distinguished by their capitals. The Doric capital is plain, marked only by a subtle outward curve. The Ionic capital is much more elaborate and is distinguished by its scroll. The Corinthian capital is decorated with stylized acanthus leaves. The entablature consists of three parts: the **architrave**, or weight-bearing and weight-distributing element; the frieze, the horizontal band just above the architrave that is generally decorated with relief sculptural elements; and the **cornice**, the horizontal molded projection that crowns or completes the wall.

Arches, Vaults, and Domes

The geometrical order of the Greek temple suggests a conscious desire to control the natural world. So strong was this impulse that Greek architecture seems defiant in its belief that the intellect is superior to the irrational forces of nature. We can read this same

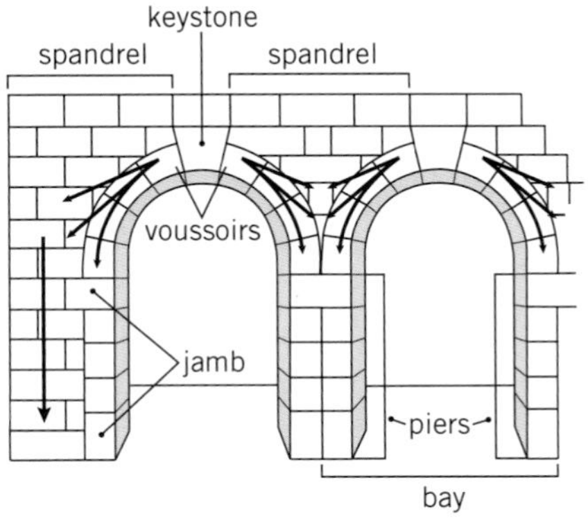

Fig. 14-12 Round arch.

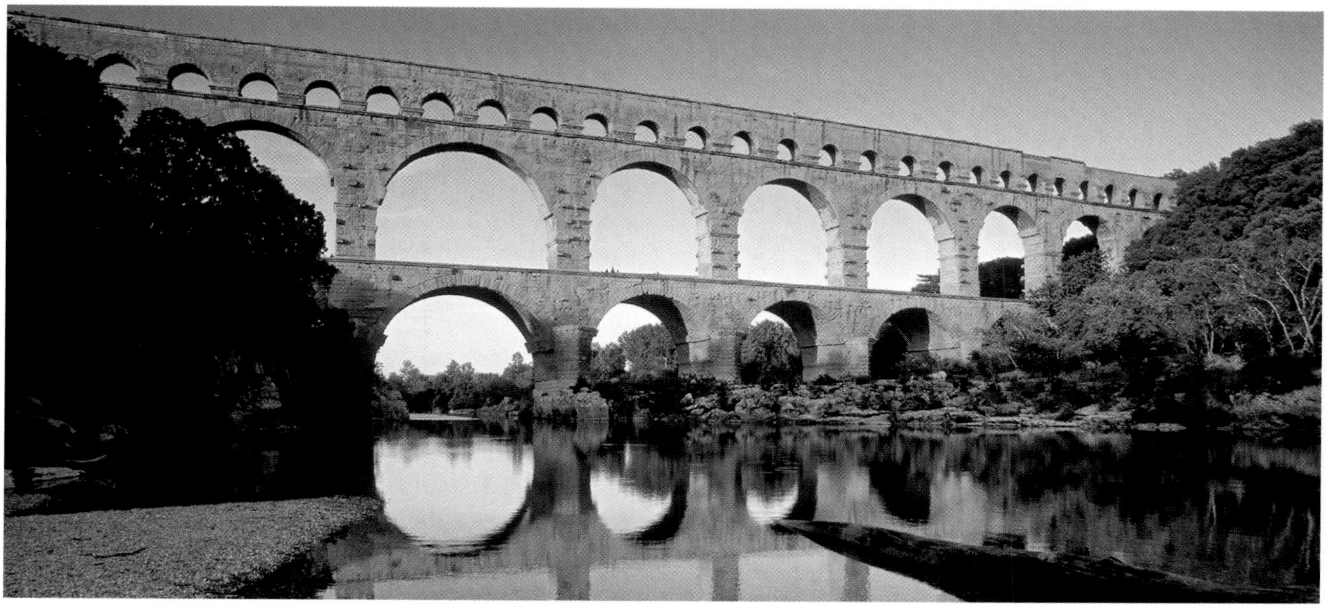

Fig. 14-13 Pont du Gard, near Nîmes, France, late 1st century BCE–early 1st century CE. Height 164 ft.

impulse in Roman architecture—the will to dominate the site. Though the Romans made considerable use of colonnades—rows of columns—they also perfected the use of the **round arch** (**Fig. 14-12**), an innovation that revolutionized the built environment. The Romans recognized that the arch would allow them to make structures with a much larger span than was possible with post-and-lintel construction. Made of wedge-shaped stones, called **voussoirs**, each cut to fit into the semicircular form, an arch is not stable until the **keystone**, the stone at the very top, has been put into place. At this point, equal pressure is exerted by each stone on its neighbors, and the scaffolding that is necessary to support the arch while it is under construction can be removed. The arch supports itself, with the weight of the whole transferred downward to the posts. A series of arches could be made to span a wide canyon with relative ease. One of the most successful Roman structures is the Pont du Gard (**Fig. 14-13**), an aqueduct used to carry water from the distant hills to the Roman compound in Nîmes, France. Still intact today, it is an engineering feat remarkable not only for its durability, but also, like most examples of Roman architecture, for its incredible size.

With the development of the **barrel vault**, or **tunnel vault** (**Fig. 14-14,** left), which is essentially an extension in depth of the single arch by lining up one arch behind another, the Romans were able to create large, uninterrupted interior spaces. The strength of the vaulting structure of the Roman Colosseum

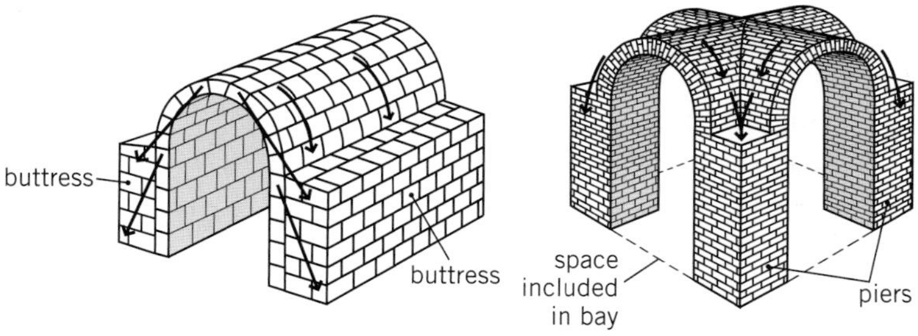

Fig. 14-14 Barrel vault (left) and groin vault (right).

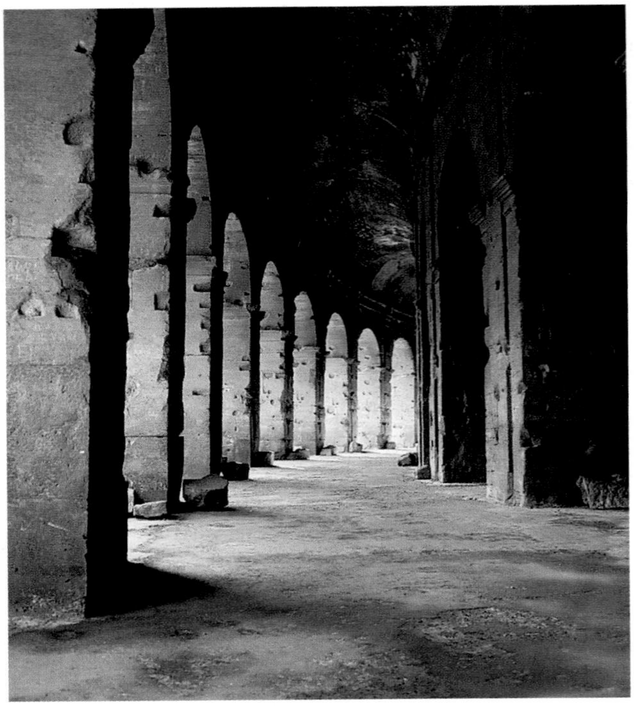

Fig. 14-15 Barrel-vaulted gallery, ground floor of the Colosseum, Rome, 72–80 CE.

(**Figs. 14-15** and **14-16**) allowed more than 50,000 spectators to be seated in it. The Colosseum is an example of an **amphitheater** (literally meaning a "double theater"), in which two semicircular theaters are brought face to face, a building type invented by the Romans to accommodate large crowds. Built for gladiatorial games and other "sporting" events, including mock naval battles and fights to the death between humans and animals, the Colosseum is constructed both with barrel vaults and with **groin vaults** (**Fig. 14-14,** right), the latter created when two barrel vaults are made to meet at right angles. These vaults were made possible by the Roman invention of concrete. The Romans discovered that if they added volcanic aggregate, such as that found near Naples and Pompeii, to the concrete mixture, it would both set faster and be stronger. The Colosseum is constructed of these concrete blocks, held together by metal cramps and dowels. They were originally covered with stone and elaborate stucco decorations.

The Romans were also the first to perfect the **dome**, which takes the shape of a hemisphere, sometimes defined as a continuous arch rotated 360 degrees on its axis. Conceived as a temple to celebrate all their gods,

Fig. 14-16 Aerial view, Colosseum, Rome, 72–80 CE.

Fig. 14-17 Interior, Pantheon, Rome, 117–25 CE.
Photo: Hemera Technologies.

the Roman Pantheon (**Fig. 14-17**)—from the Greek words *pan* ("every") and *theos* ("god")—consists of a 142-foot-high dome set on a cylindrical wall 140 feet in diameter. Every interior dimension appears equal and proportionate, even as its scale overwhelms the viewer. The dome is concrete, which was poured in sections over a huge mold supported by a complex scaffolding. Over 20 feet thick where it meets the walls—the **springing**, or the point where an arch or dome rises from its support—the dome thins to only 6 feet at the circular opening, 30 feet in diameter, at its top. Through this **oculus** (Latin for "eye"), the building's only source of illumination, worshipers could make contact with the heavens. As the sun shone through it, casting a round spotlight into the interior, it seemed as if the eye of Jupiter, king of the gods, shone upon the Pantheon walls. Seen from the street (**Fig. 14-18**), where it was originally approached between parallel colonnades that culminated in a podium now lost to the rise of the area's street level, its interior space could only be intuited. Instead, the viewer was confronted by a portico composed of eight mammoth Corinthian columns made of polished granite rising to a pediment some 121 feet wide.

Even though their use of concrete was forgotten, the architectural inventions of the Romans provided the basis for building construction in the Western world for nearly 2,000 years. The idealism, even mysticism, of the Pantheon's vast interior space, with its evocation of the

Fig. 14-18 Exterior, Pantheon, Rome, 117–25 CE.
© Vincenzo Pirozzi, Rome.

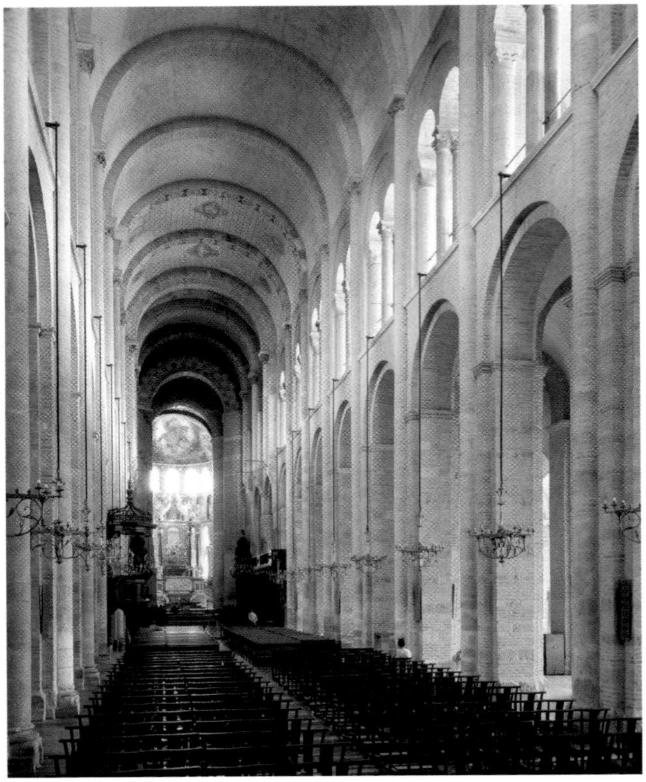

Fig. 14-19 Nave, St. Sernin, Toulouse, France, ca. 1080–1120.

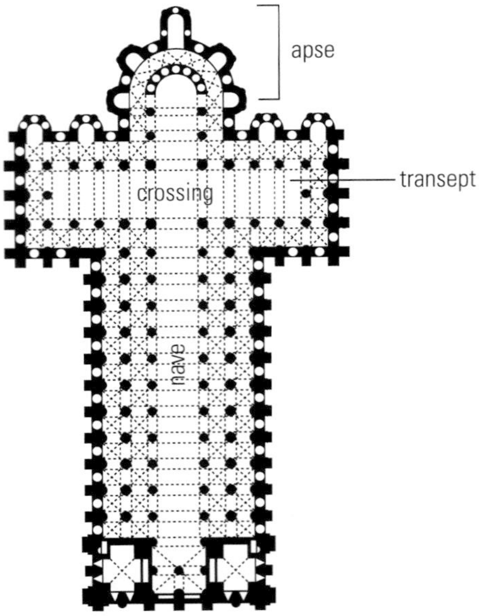

Fig. 14-20 Plan, St. Sernin, Toulouse, France, ca. 1080–1120.

Fig. 14-21 Amiens Cathedral, begun 1220.

symbolic presence of Jupiter, found its way into churches as the Christian religion came to dominate the West. Large congregations could gather beneath the high barrel vaults of churches, which were constructed on Roman architectural principles. Vault construction in stone was employed especially in Romanesque architecture—so called because it used so many Roman methods and architectural forms.

The barrel vault at St. Sernin, in Toulouse, France (**Fig. 14-19**), is a magnificent example of Romanesque architecture. The plan of this church is one of great symmetry and geometric simplicity (**Fig. 14-20**). It reflects the Romanesque preference for rational order and logical development. Every measurement is based on the central square at the **crossing**, where the two **transepts**, or side wings, cross the length of the **nave**, the central aisle of the church used by the congregation, and the **apse**, the semicircular projection at the end of the church that is topped by a Roman half-dome. Each square in the aisles, for instance, is one-quarter the size of the crossing square. Each transept extends two full squares from the center. The tower that rises over the crossing, incidentally, was completed in later times and is taller than it was originally intended to be.

The immense interior space of the great Gothic cathedrals, which arose throughout Europe beginning in about 1150 CE, is the culmination of this direction in architecture. A building such as the Pantheon, with a 30-foot hole in its roof, was simply impractical in the severe climates of northern Europe. As if in response to the dark and dreary climate outside, the interior of the Gothic cathedral rises to an incredible height, lit by stained-glass windows that transform a dull day with a warm and richly radiant light. The enormous interior space of Amiens Cathedral (**Fig. 14-21**), with an interior height of 142 feet and a total interior surface of more than 26,000 square feet, leaves any viewer in awe. At the

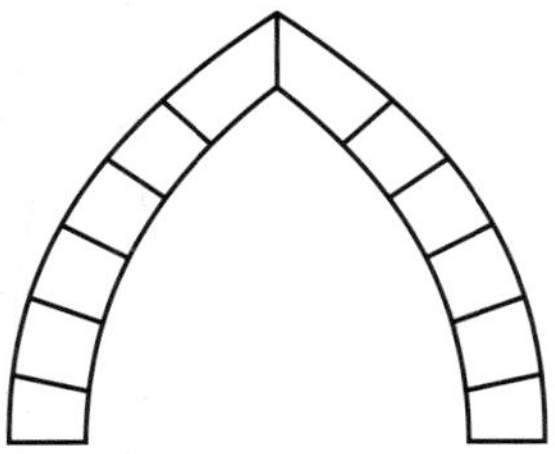

Fig. 14-22 Pointed arch.

center of the nave is a complex maze, laid down in 1288, praising the three master masons who built the complex, Robert de Luzarches, and Thomas and Renaud de Cormont, who succeeded in creating the largest Gothic cathedral ever built in northern Europe.

The great height of the Gothic cathedral's interior space is achieved by means of a system of pointed, rather than round, arches. The height of a rounded arch is determined by its width, but the height of a **pointed arch** (**Fig. 14-22**) can readily be extended by straightening the curve of the sides upward to a point, the weight descending much more directly down the wall. By using the pointed arch in a scheme of groin vaults, the almost ethereal space of the Gothic cathedral, soaring upward as if toward God, is realized.

All arches tend to spread outward, creating a risk of collapse; early on, the Romans learned to support the sides of the arch to counteract this lateral thrust. In the great French cathedrals, the support was provided by building a series of arches on the outside whose thrusts would counteract the outward force of the interior arches. Extending inward from a series of columns or piers, these **flying buttresses** (**Figs. 14-23** and **14-24**), so named because they lend to the massive stone architecture a sense of lightness and flight, are an aesthetic response to a practical problem. Together with the stunning height of the nave allowed by the pointed arch, the flying buttresses reveal the desire of the builder to elevate the cathedral above humdrum daily life in the medieval world. The cathedral became a symbol not only of the divine, but also of the human ability to exceed, in art and in imagination, our own limitations and circumstances.

Fig. 14-23 Flying buttresses, Cathedral of Notre-Dame, Paris, 1211–90.
© Bednorz-images, Cologne.

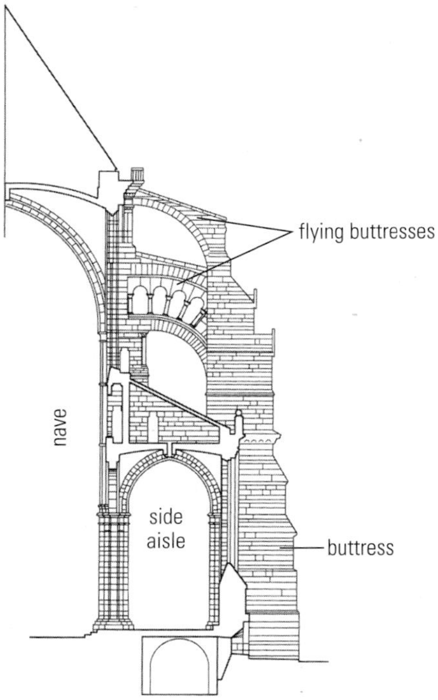

Fig. 14-24 Flying buttress. Diagram (after Acland).

Modern and Contemporary Architectural Technologies

What technological advances have contributed to modern and contemporary architecture?

Until the nineteenth century, the history of architecture was determined by innovations in the ways the same materials—mostly stone—could be employed. In the nineteenth century, iron, a material that had been known for thousands of years, but never employed in architecture, absolutely transformed the built environment.

Cast-Iron Construction

Wrought iron was soft and flexible, and, when heated, it could be easily turned and twisted into a variety of forms. But engineers discovered that, by adding carbon to iron, they could create a much more rigid and strong material—**cast iron**. The French engineer Gustave Eiffel used cast iron in his new lattice-beam construction technique, which produces structures of the maximum rigidity with the minimum weight by exploiting the way in which girders can be used to brace one another in three dimensions.

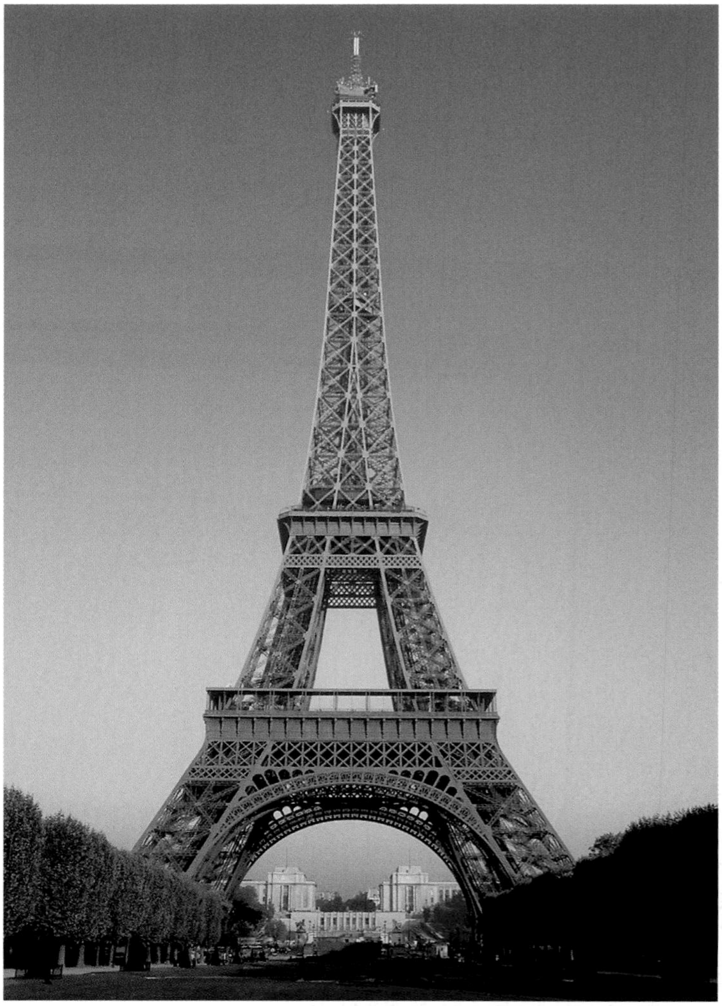

Fig. 14-25 Gustave Eiffel, Eiffel Tower, 1887–89. Seen from the Champ de Mars. Height of tower 1,051 ft.
Alain Evrard/Globe Press. Photo Researchers, Inc.

The most influential result was the Eiffel Tower (**Fig. 14-25**), designed as a monument to industry and the centerpiece of the international Paris Exposition of 1889. Over 1,000 feet high, and at that time by far the tallest structure in the world, the tower posed a particular problem—how to build a structure of such a height, yet one that could resist the wind. Eiffel's solution was simple but brilliant: Construct a skeleton, an open lattice-beam framework that would allow the wind to pass through it. Though it served for many years as a radio tower—on July 1, 1913, the first signal transmitted around the world was broadcast from its top, inaugurating the global electronic network—the tower was essentially useless, nothing more than a monument. Many Parisians hated it at first, feeling that it was a blight on the skyline. Newspapers jokingly held contests to "clothe" it. The French writer Guy de Maupassant often took his lunch at the restaurant in the tower, despite the fact that the food was not particularly appealing: "It's the only place in Paris," he said, "where I don't have to see it." But by the early years of the twentieth century the tower had become the symbol of Paris itself, probably the most famous structure in the world. Most important, it demonstrated the possibility of building to very great heights without load-bearing walls. The tower gave birth to the skeleton-and-skin system of building. And the idea of designing "clothes" to cover such a structure soon became a reality.

Frame Construction

The role of iron and steel in changing the course of architecture in the nineteenth century cannot be overestimated—and we will consider steel in even more detail in a moment—but two more humble technological innovations had almost as significant an impact, determining the look of our built environment down to the present day. The mass production of the common nail, together with improved methods and standardization in the process of milling lumber, led to a revolution in home-building techniques.

Lumber cannot easily support structures of great height, but it is perfect for domestic architecture. In 1833, in Chicago, the common **wood-frame** construction (**Fig. 14-26**), a true

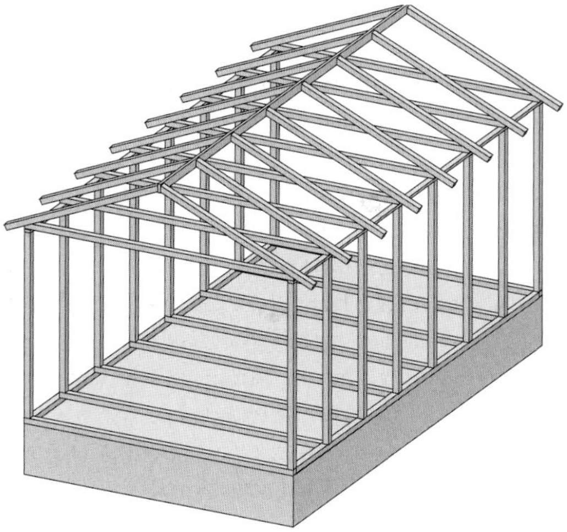

Fig. 14-26 Wood-frame construction.

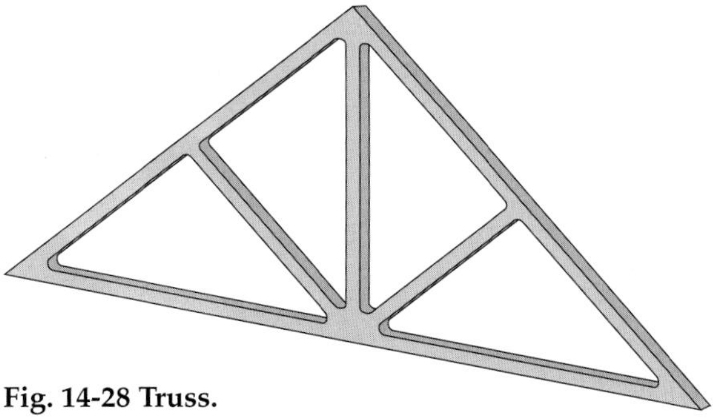

Fig. 14-28 Truss.

skeleton-and-skin building method, was introduced. Sometimes called **balloon-frame** construction, because early skeptics believed houses built in this manner would explode like balloons, the method is both inexpensive and relatively easy. A framework skeleton of, generally, 2 × 4-inch beams is nailed together. Windows and doors are placed in the wall using basic post-and-lintel design principles, and the whole is sheathed with planks, clapboard, shingles, or any other suitable material. The roof is somewhat more complex, but as early as the construction of Old St. Peter's Basilica in Rome in the fourth century CE (**Fig. 14-27**), the basic principles were in use. The walls of St. Peter's were composed of columns and arches made of stone and brick, but the roof was wood. And notice the angled beams supporting the roof over the aisles. These are elementary forms of the **truss**, prefabricated versions of which most home-builders today use for the roofs of houses. One of the most rigid structural forms in architecture, the truss (**Fig. 14-28**) is a triangular framework that, because of its rigidity, can span much wider areas than a single wooden beam.

Wood-frame construction is, of course, the foundation of American domestic architecture, and it is

Fig. 14-27 Reconstruction drawing of Old St. Peter's Basilica, Rome, ca. 320–27.

Fig. 14-29 Charles Bulfinch, Harrison Gray Otis House, Boston, Massachusetts, 1795–96.
Photo courtesy of Historic New England.

versatile enough to accommodate a variety of styles. Compare, for instance, two residences built near the end of the eighteenth century, the Harrison Gray Otis House in Boston, Massachusetts (**Fig. 14-29**), and the Parlange Mansion, built on an indigo plantation north of Baton Rouge, Louisiana (**Fig. 14-30**). The Otis House was designed by Charles Bulfinch, America's first native-born professional architect, and its simple, clearly articulated exterior brick-clad facade with its five window bays set a stylistic standard for the city. Brick was chosen to cover the wood-frame construction beneath to provide insulation and protection against New England's severe winter weather. The Parlange Mansion likewise uses brick, made in this case by the plantation's slaves. The upper floor rests above a half-buried brick basement with brick pillars supporting the open-air gallery which surrounds the second story. The walls, both inside and out, are plastered with a mixture of mud, sand, Spanish moss, and deer hair, and are painted white, providing cooling insulation in the hot and humid Louisiana summers. The upper level contains the main living quarters. Each room in the house, on both the upper and lower levels, opens onto the surrounding galleries, which serve as hallways for the house, protecting the inner rooms from direct sunlight.

Early in the twentieth century, wood-frame construction formed the basis of a widespread "bungalow" style of architecture, which has enjoyed a revival in the last decade and which is characterized by a gabled roof, overhanging eaves, exposed rafters and decorative brackets under the eaves, and a covered porch or veranda fronting the house (**Fig. 14-31**). It became popular when furniture designer Gustav Stickley

Fig. 14-30 Architect unknown, Mansion at Parlange Plantation, New Roads, Louisiana. ca. 1785–95.
© Philip Gould/Corbis.

Fig. 14-31 Christian Gladu, The Bungalow Company, *The Birch*, North Town Woods, Bainbridge Island, Washington, 1998.
Photo courtesy of Bungalow Company.

began publishing bungalow designs in his magazine *The Craftsman*. From the beginning, the bungalow was conceived as a form of domestic architecture available to everyone. Like Stickley's furniture, which he thought of as "made" for bungalows, it was democratic. It embodied, from Stickley's point of view, "that plainness which is beauty." The hand-hewn local materials—stone and shingles—employed in the construction tied the home to its natural environment. And so did its porches, which tied the interior to the world outside, and which, with their sturdy, wide-set pillars, bespoke functional solidity. By the late 1920s, as many as 100,000 stock plans had been sold by both national architectural companies and local lumber and building firms, and, across America, bungalows popped up everywhere. In the popular imagination, the word "bungalow" was synonymous with "quality."

Steel-and-Reinforced-Concrete Construction

It was in Chicago that frame construction began, and it was Chicago that most impressed C. R. Ashbee, a representative of the British National Trust, when he visited America in 1900: "Chicago is the only American city I have seen where something absolutely distinctive in the aesthetic handling of material has been evolved out of the Industrial system." A young architect named Frank Lloyd Wright impressed him most, but it was Wright's mentor, Louis Sullivan, who was perhaps most responsible for the sense of vitality to which Ashbee was responding.

For Sullivan, the foremost problem that the modern architect had to address was how the building might transcend the "sinister" urban conditions out of which, of necessity, it had to rise. The development of steel construction techniques, combined with what Sullivan called "a system of ornament," offered him a way to mitigate the urban malaise. A fireproof steel skeletal frame, suggested by wood-frame construction, freed the wall of load-bearing duties and opened it both to ornament and to large numbers of exterior windows. The vertical emphasis of the building's exterior lines echoed the upward sweep of the steel skeleton. As a result, the exterior of the tall building no longer seemed massive; rather, it might rise with an almost organic lightness into the skies.

The building's real identity depended on the ornamentation that could now be freely distributed across its facade. Ornament was, according to Sullivan, "spirit." The inorganic, rigid, and geometric lines of the steel frame would flow, through the ornamental detail that covered it, into "graceful curves," and angularities would "disappear in a mystical blending of surface." Thus, at the top

Fig. 14-32 Louis H. Sullivan, Bayard-Condict Building, New York, 1897–98.
© Angelo Hornak/Corbis.

Fig. 14-33 Louis H. Sullivan, Bayard-Condict Building (detail), New York, 1897–98.
© Nathan Benn/Ottochrome/CORBIS.

of Sullivan's Bayard Building (**Figs. 14-32** and **14-33**)—a New York, rather than a Chicago, building—the vertical columns that rise between the windows blossom in an explosion of floral decoration.

Such ornamentation might seem to contradict completely the dictum for which Sullivan is most famous—"Form follows function." If the function of the urban building is to provide a well-lit and ventilated place in which to work, then the steel-frame structure and the abundance of windows on the building's facade make sense. But what about the ornamentation? How does it follow from the structure's function? Isn't it simply an example of purposeless excess?

Down through the twentieth century, Sullivan's original meaning has largely been forgotten. He was not promoting a notion of design akin to the sense of practical utility that can be discovered in, for instance, a Model T Ford. For Sullivan, "The function of all functions is the Infinite Creative Spirit," and this spirit could be revealed in the rhythm of growth and decay that we find in nature. Thus, the elaborate, organic forms that cover his buildings were intended to evoke the Infinite. For Sullivan, the primary function of a building was to elevate the spirit of those who worked in it.

Almost all of Sullivan's ornamental exuberance seems to have disappeared in the architecture of Frank Lloyd Wright, whom many consider the first truly modern architect. But from 1888 to 1893, Wright worked as chief draftsman in Sullivan's Chicago firm, and Sullivan's belief in the unity of design and nature can still be understood as instrumental in Wright's work. In an article written for the *Architectural Record* in 1908, Wright emphasized that "a sense of the organic is indispensable to an architect," and, as early as the 1890s, he was routinely "translating" the natural and the organic into what he called "the terms of building stone."

The ultimate expression of Wright's intentions is the so-called Prairie House, the most notable example of which is the Robie House in Chicago, designed in 1906 and built in 1909 (**Figs. 14-34** and **14-35**). Although the house is contemporary in feeling—with its wide overhanging roof extending out into space, its fluid, open interiors, and its rigidly geometric lines—it was, from Wright's point of view, purely "organic" in conception.

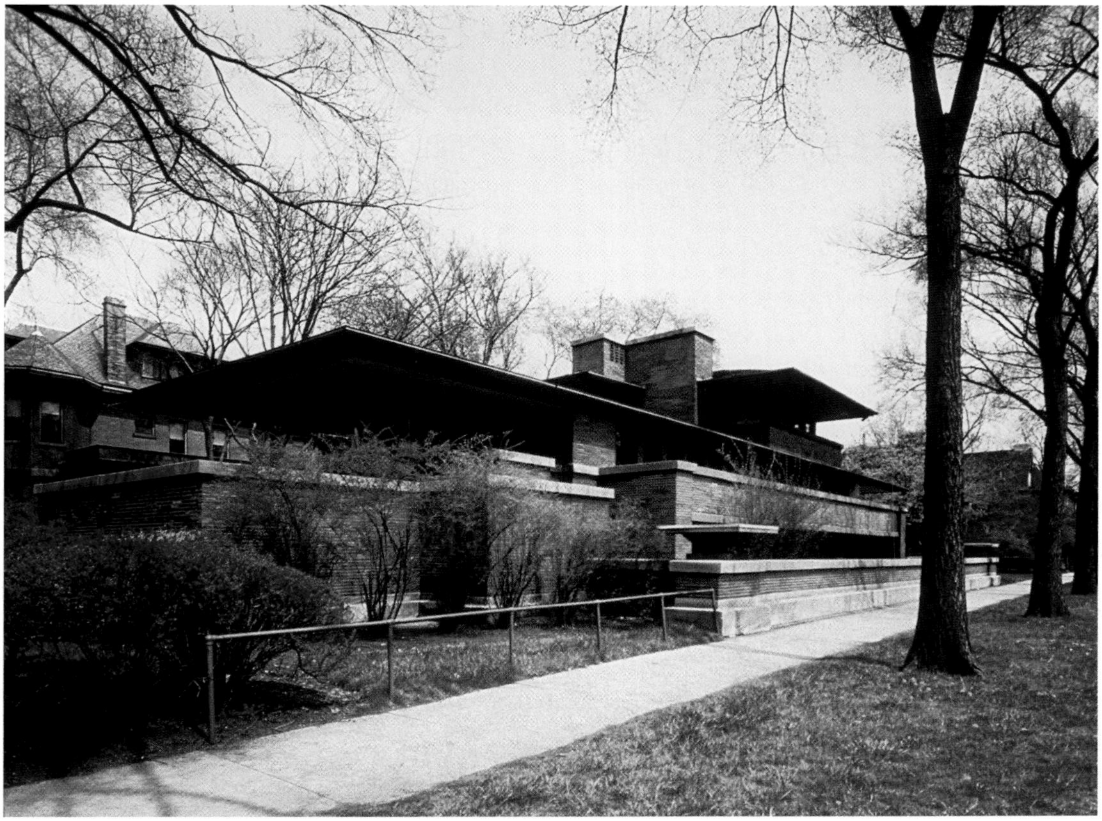

Fig. 14-34 Frank Lloyd Wright, Robie House, South Woodlawn, Chicago, Illinois, 1909.
Photo: Hedrich Blessing Photographers/Chicago Historical Society/UIG via Getty Images.

Wright spoke of the Prairie House as being "of" the land, not "on" it, and the horizontal sweep of the roof and the open interior space reflect the flat expanses of the Midwestern prairie landscape. Alternatively, in a different environment, a house might reflect the cliffs of a Pennsylvania ravine (see *The Creative Process*, pp. 348–49). The **cantilever**, a horizontal form supported on one end and jutting out into space on the other, was made possible by newly invented steel-and-reinforced-concrete construction techniques. Under a cantilevered roof, one could be simultaneously outside and protected. The roof thus ties together the interior space of the house and the natural world outside. Furthermore, the house itself was built of materials—brick, stone, and wood, especially oak—native to its surroundings.

The architectural innovations of Wright's teacher, Louis Sullivan, led directly to the skyscraper. It is the sheer strength of steel that makes the modern skyscraper a reality. Structures with stone walls require thicker walls on the ground floor as they rise higher. A 16-story building, for instance, would require ground-floor walls approximately 6 feet thick. But the

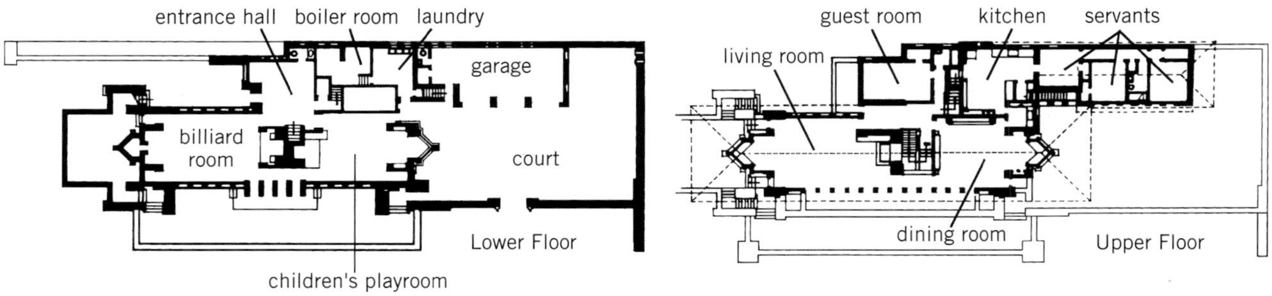

Fig. 14-35 Frank Lloyd Wright, Plan of the Robie House, South Woodlawn, Chicago, Illinois, 1909.

The Creative Process

Thinking through Architecture: Frank Lloyd Wright's *Fallingwater*

Fallingwater (**Fig. 14-37**), Frank Lloyd Wright's name for the house he designed for Edgar and Lillian Kaufmann in 1935, is arguably the most famous modern house in the world. Edgar Kaufmann was owner of Kaufmann's Store in Pittsburgh, the largest readymade men's clothing store in the country, and his son had begun to study with Wright in 1934. In November of that year, Wright first visited the site. There are no known design drawings until the following September. Writing a few years before about his own design process, Wright stated that the architect should

> *conceive the building in the imagination, not on paper but in the mind, thoroughly—before touching paper. Let it live there—gradually taking more definite form before committing it to the draughting board. When the thing lives for you, start to plan it with tools. Not before. . . . It is best to cultivate the imagination to construct and complete the building before working on it with T-square and triangle.*

The first drawings were done in two hours when Kaufmann made a surprise call to Wright and told him he was in the neighborhood and would like to see something. Using a different colored pencil for each of the house's three floors on the site plan, Wright completed not only a floor plan, but also a north–south cross-section and a view of the exterior from across the stream (**Fig. 14-36**). The drawings were remarkably close to the final house.

Wright thought of the house as entirely consistent with his earlier Prairie Houses. It was, like them, wedded to its site, only the site was markedly different. The reinforced-concrete cantilevers mirrored the natural cliffs of the hillside down and over which the stream, Bear Run, cascades. By the end of 1935, Wright had opened a quarry on the site to extract local stone for the house's construction.

Meanwhile, the radical style of the house had made Kaufmann nervous. He hired engineers to review Wright's plan, and they were doubtful that reinforced concrete could sustain

Fig. 14-36 Frank Lloyd Wright, Drawing for *Fallingwater*, Kaufmann House, Bear Run, Pennsylvania, 1936. Color pencil on tracing paper, 15⅜ × 27¼ in. The Frank Lloyd Wright Foundation, Scottsdale, Arizona.

the 18-foot cantilevers that Wright proposed. When Kaufmann sent the engineers' reports to Wright, Wright told him to return the plans to him "since he did not deserve the house." Kaufmann apologized for his lack of faith, and work on the house proceeded.

Still, the contractor and engineer didn't trust Wright's plans for reinforcing the concrete for the cantilevers, and before the first slab was poured, they put in nearly twice as much steel as Wright had called for. As a result, the main cantilever droops to this day. Wright was incensed that no one trusted his calculations. After the first slab was set, but still heavily braced with wooden framing, Wright walked under the house and kicked a number of the wooden braces out.

The house, finally, is in complete harmony with its site. "I began to see a building," Wright wrote in 1936, as the house was nearing completion, "primarily . . . as a broad shelter in the open, related to vista; vista without and vista within. You may see in these various feelings, all taking the same direction, that I was born an American, child of the ground and of space."

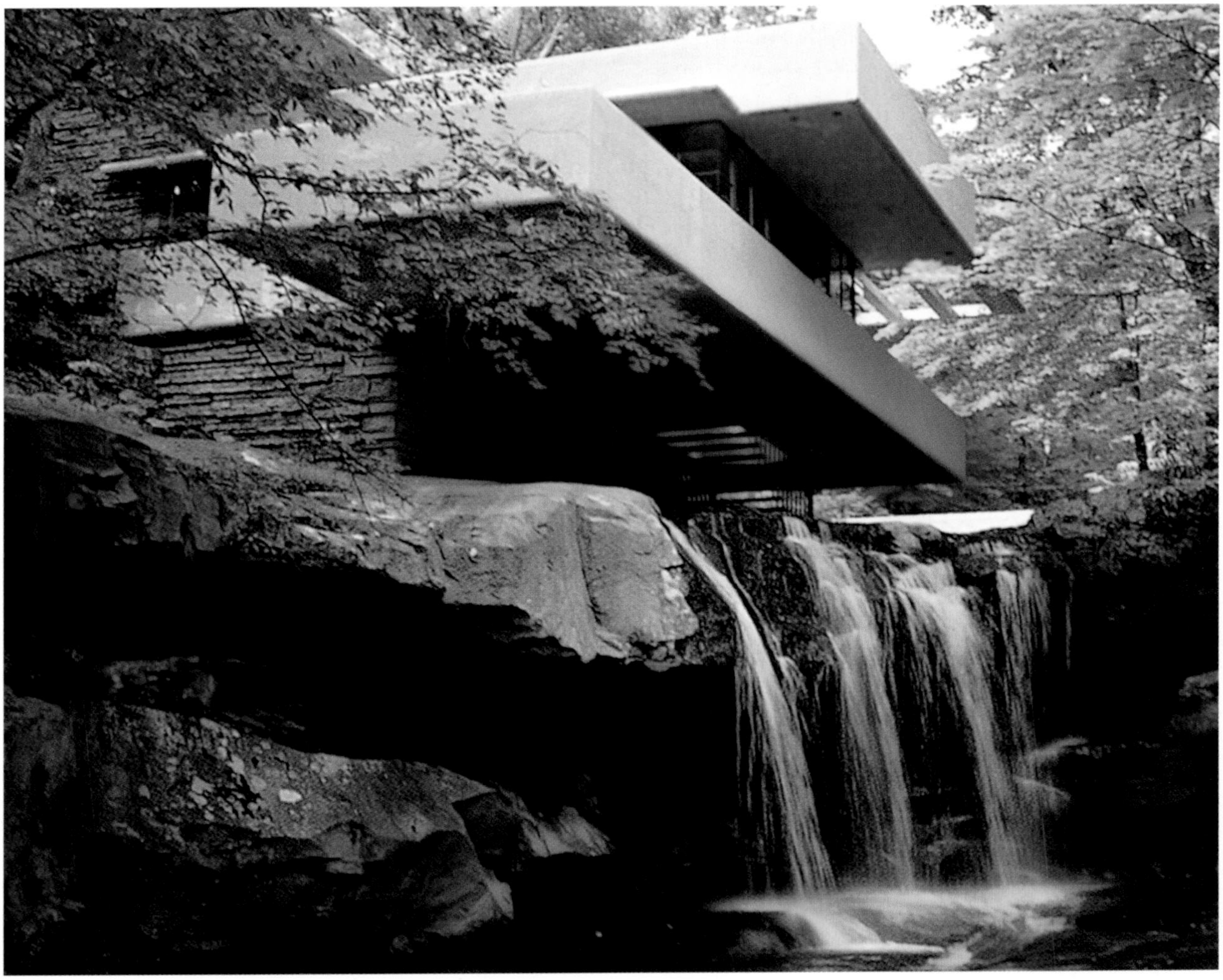

Fig. 14-37 Frank Lloyd Wright, *Fallingwater*, Kaufmann House, Bear Run, Pennsylvania, 1936.

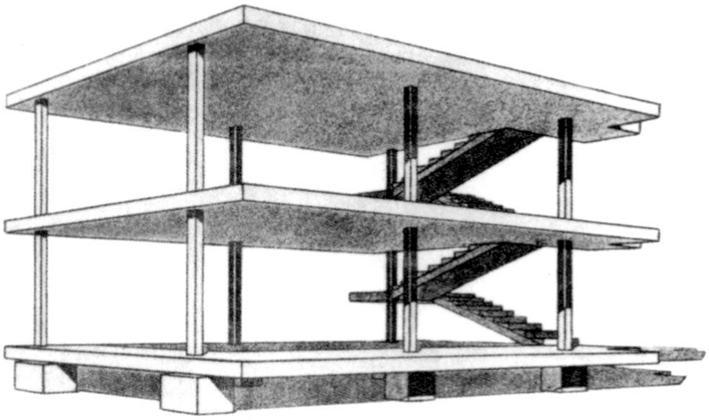

Fig. 14-38 Le Corbusier, Perspective drawing for the Domino Housing Project, 1914. French Embassy.

steel cage, connected by floors made of **reinforced concrete**—concrete in which steel reinforcement bars, or **rebars**, are placed to both strengthen and make concrete less brittle—overcomes this necessity. The simplicity of the resulting structure can be seen clearly in French architect Le Corbusier's 1914 drawing for the Domino Housing Project (**Fig. 14-38**). The design is almost infinitely expandable, both sideways and upward. Any combination of windows and walls can be hung on the frame. Internal divisions can be freely designed in an endless variety of ways, or, indeed, the space can be left entirely open. Even the stairwell can be moved to any location within the structural frame.

In 1932, Alfred H. Barr, Jr., a young curator at the Museum of Modern Art in New York City, who would later become one of the most influential historians of modern art, identified Le Corbusier as one of the founders of a new "International Style." In the catalogue for the exhibition *Modern Architecture*, Barr wrote:

> Slender steel posts and beams, and concrete reinforced by steel have made possible structures of skeleton-like strength and lightness. The modern architect working in the new style conceives of his building . . . as a skeleton enclosed by a thin light shell. He thinks in terms of volume—of space enclosed by planes and surfaces—as opposed to mass and solidity. This principle of volume leads him to make his walls seem thin flat surfaces by eliminating moldings and by making his windows and doors flush with the surface.

Taking advantage of the strength of concrete-and-steel construction, Le Corbusier lifted his houses on stilts (**Fig. 14-39**), thus creating, out of the heaviest of materials, a sense of lightness, even flight. The entire structure is composed of primary forms (that is, rectangles, circles, and so on). Writing in his first book, *Towards a New Architecture*, translated into English in 1925, Le Corbusier put it this way: "Primary forms are beautiful forms because they can be clearly appreciated." "A house," he said, "is a machine for living in!"—functional and precise, with no redundant parts.

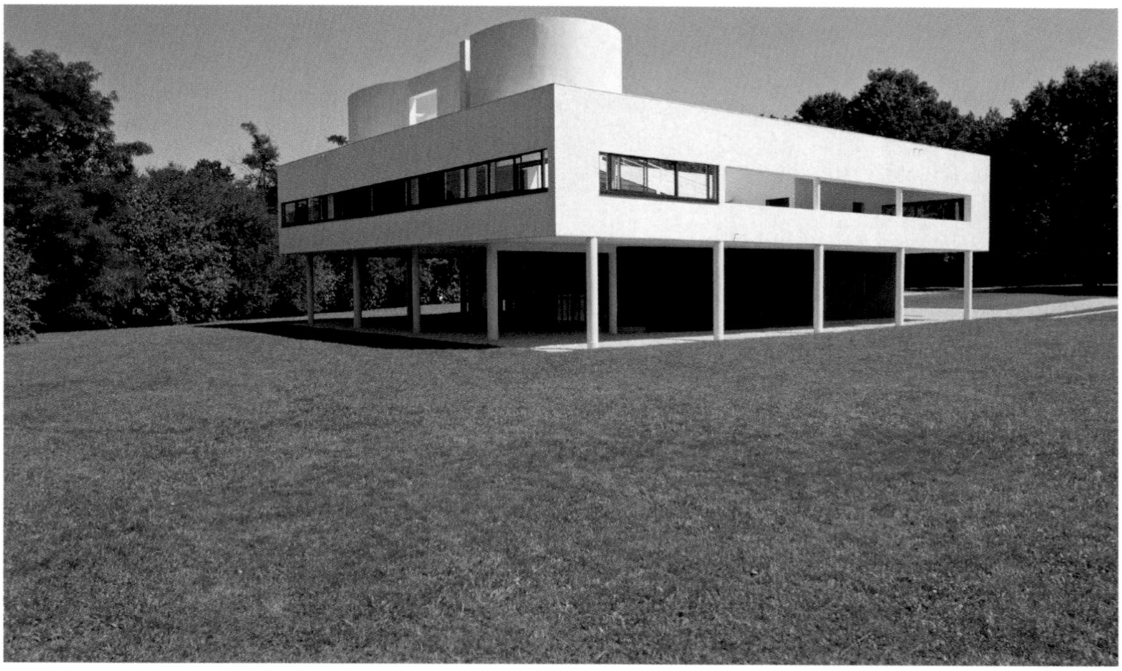

Fig. 14-39 Le Corbusier and Pierre Jeanneret, Villa Savoye, Poissy-sur-Seine, France, 1928–30.

Fig. 14-40 Ludwig Mies van der Rohe, Farnsworth House, Fox River, Plano, Illinois, 1950.
akg-image/VIEW Pictures/Grant Smith.

For Barr, Ludwig Mies van der Rohe was the other great innovator of the International Style. His Farnsworth House (**Fig. 14-40**), which was built in 1950, opens itself to its surroundings. An homage to Le Corbusier's Villa Savoye, the house is virtually transparent—both opening itself out into the environment and inviting it in.

But the culmination of Le Corbusier's steel-and-reinforced-concrete Domino plan is the so-called International Style skyscraper, the most notable example of which is the Seagram Building in New York City (**Fig. 14-41**), a collaboration between Mies van der Rohe and Philip Johnson. In 1932, Johnson had written the foreword to Barr's *Modern Architecture* catalogue. The **International Style** is marked by its austere geometric simplicity, and the design solution presented by the Seagram Building is extremely elegant. The exposed structural I-beams (that is, steel beams that, seen in cross-section, look like the capital letter "I") are finished in bronze to match the amber-tinted glass sheath. At the base, these exterior beams drop, unsheathed, to the courtyard, creating an open-air steel colonnade around a recessed glass lobby. New York law requires that buildings must conform to a "setback" restriction: Buildings that at ground level occupy an entire site must stagger-step inward as they rise in order to avoid "walling-in" the city's inhabitants. But the Seagram Building occupies less than one-half its site; as a result, it is free to rise vertically out of the plaza at its base. At night, the lighted windows activate the building's exterior, and by day, the surface of the opaque glass reflects the changing world around the building.

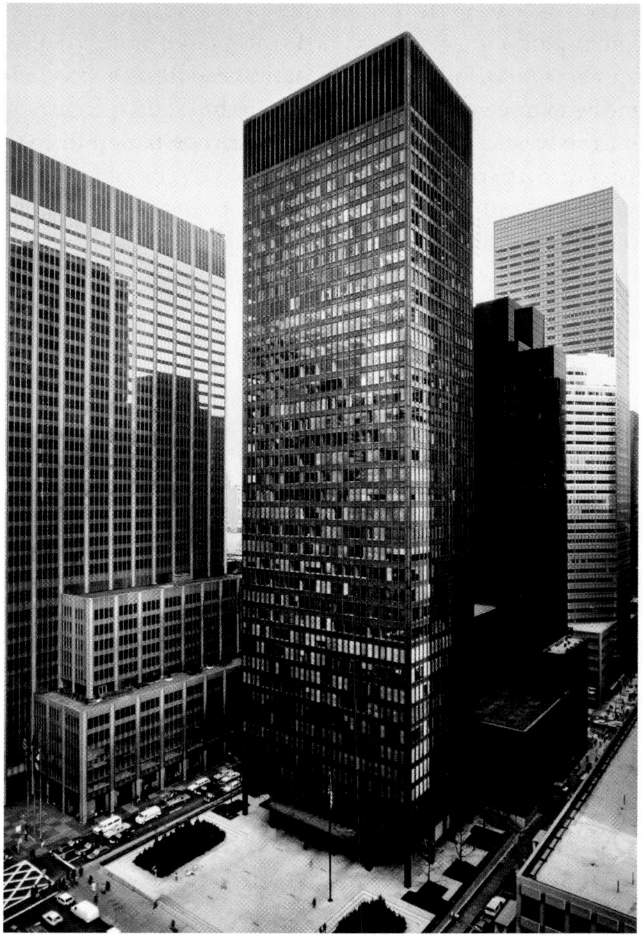

Fig. 14-41 Ludwig Mies van der Rohe and Philip Johnson, Seagram Building, New York City, 1958.
© Andrew Gam.

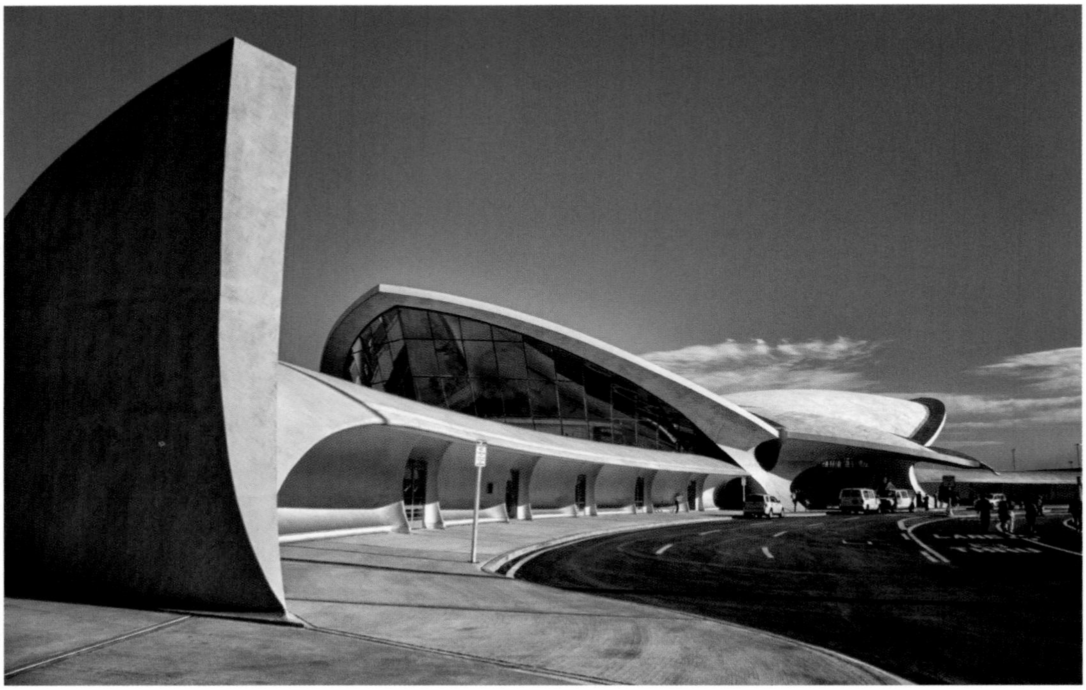

Fig. 14-42 Eero Saarinen, TWA Terminal, John F. Kennedy International Airport, New York, 1962.

Rejecting the International Style's emphasis on primary geometric forms, the architecture of Eero Saarinen demonstrates how steel-and-reinforced-concrete construction can be utilized in other ways. One of his most successful buildings is the TWA Terminal at Kennedy International Airport in New York (**Figs. 14-42** and **14-43**), designed in 1956 and completed after his death in 1961. It is defined by a contrast between the openness provided by the broad expanses of window and the sculptural mass of the reinforced-concrete walls and roof. What results is a constant play of light and shadow throughout the space. The exterior—two huge concrete wings that appear to hover above the runways—is a symbolic rendering of flight.

Fig. 14-43 Eero Saarinen, TWA Terminal, John F. Kennedy International Airport, interior, New York, 1962.

Increasingly, contemporary architecture has largely become a question of creating distinctive buildings that stand out in the vast sameness of the "world metropolis," the massive interconnected fabric of places where people "do business," and among which they travel, the hubs (all served by airports) of today's mobile society. It is also a question of creating buildings of distinction—contemporary architecture is highly competitive. Most major commissions are competitions, and most cities compete for the best, most distinctive architects.

The Asian city is particularly intriguing to postmodern architects because, much more than the American city, where, by and large, people don't live where they work, Asian cities possess a much greater "mix" of functions and scales, tall buildings that rise in the midst of jumbled smaller structures that seem to change rapidly, almost from one day to the next. One of the most intriguing new projects in Asia is the work of the Rotterdam-based Office for Metropolitan Architecture (OMA), headed by Rem Koolhaas. Since 1995, Koolhaas has been a professor at Harvard University, where he is

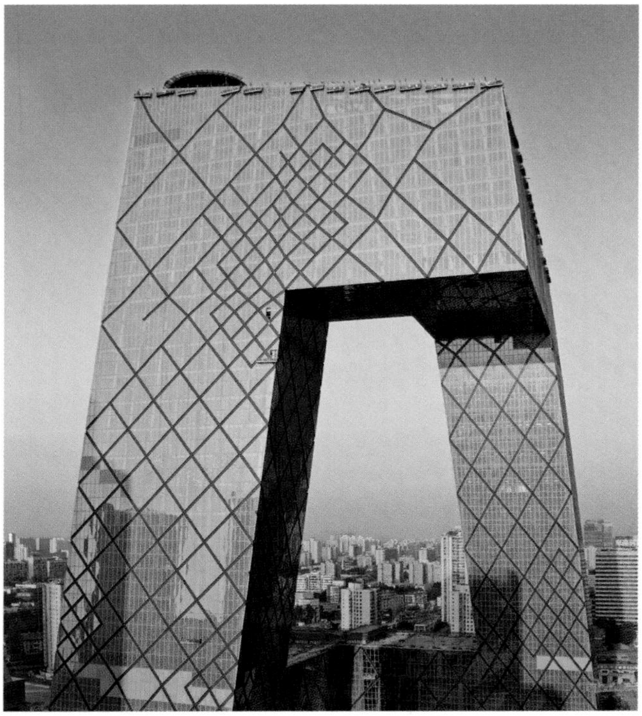

Fig. 14-44 Rem Koolhaas and Ole Scheeren, OMA, New Headquarters, Central Chinese Television (CCTV), Beijing, China, 2008.
© Keren Su/Corbis. Photo courtesy of OMA/Ole Scheeren and Rem Koolhaas.

leading a series of research projects for Harvard's "Project on the City," a student-based research group whose recent projects include a study of five cities in the Pearl River Delta of China, and "Shopping," an analysis of the role of retail consumption in the contemporary city. His OMA firm's most recent work includes the new Museum of Modern Art extension in New York, the new Seattle Public Library, and Central China Television's headquarters (**Fig. 14-44**), completed for the Beijing Olympics in 2008. The CCTV tower is 750 feet high, an icon for the Olympics themselves. But, perhaps in keeping with the international spirit of the Games, it possesses many identities. As Koolhaas explained to an interviewer in 2008, just as the tower was coming to completion: "It looks different from every angle, no matter where you stand. Foreground and background are constantly shifting. We didn't create a single identity, but 400 identities. That was what we wanted: To create ambiguity and complexity, so as to escape the constraints of the explicit."

Probably no two countries in the world, however, have defined themselves more as centers of international architectural experimentation than Spain and the United Arab Emirates. Drawing on the talents of architects from around the world—to say nothing of the possibilities for design offered these architects by computer technologies—Spain has capitalized on the momentum generated by the 1992 Olympics in Barcelona, which required a massive building effort, and the excitement generated by Frank Gehry's computer-designed Guggenheim Museum in Bilbao (see *The Creative Process*, pp. 354–55), completed in 1997. Jean Nouvel's Torre Agbar (**Fig. 14-45**), completed in 2005 in Barcelona, is just one example of the new innovative architecture that is erupting across the country. Thirty-one stories high, the bullet-shaped building is the centerpiece of a new commercial district planned by the city. The reinforced-concrete structure, crowned by a glass-and-steel dome, has a multicolored facade of aluminum panels, behind glass louvers, in 25 different colors. There are 4,400 windows and 56,619 transparent and translucent glass plates. The louvers are tilted at different angles calculated to deflect the direct sunlight. At night, 4,500 yellow, blue, pink, and red lights, placed over the facade, illuminate the entire tower.

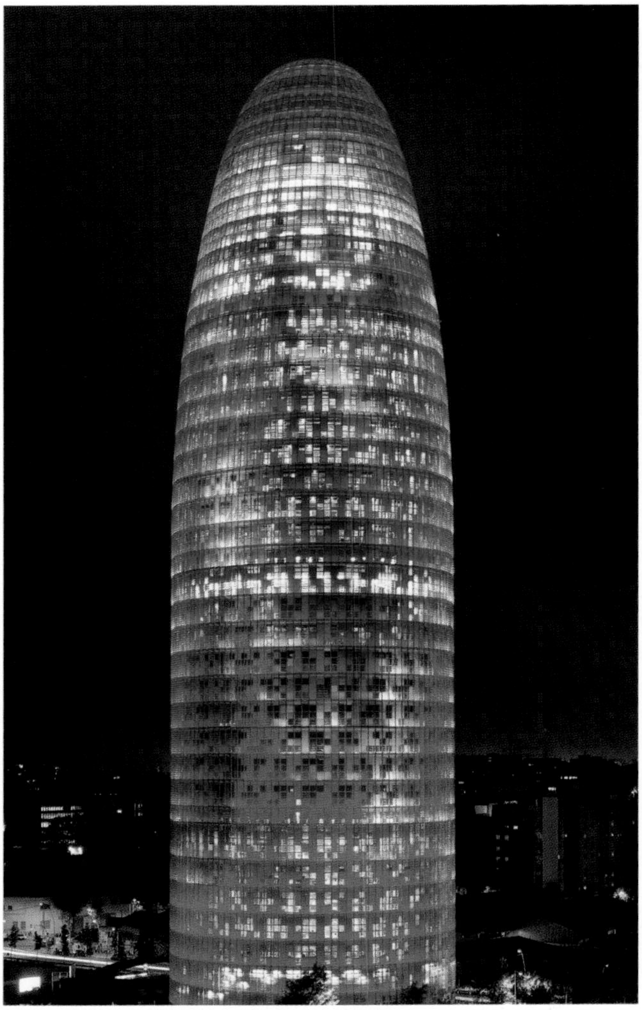

Fig. 14-45 Ateliers Jean Nouvel with b720 Arquitectos, Torre Agbar, Barcelona, 2005. Lighting design by Yann Kersalé.
Photo: Roland Halbe.

The Creative Process

Discovering Where to Go: Frank Gehry's Guggenheim Museum Bilbao

Just as I. M. Pei's expansion of the Louvre, with its glass pyramid, was designed to revitalize the French capital itself, in the 1990s American architect Frank Gehry's design for the Guggenheim Museum Bilbao (**Fig. 14-47**) was a project conceived as part of a plan to reinvigorate the Basque fishing port and industrial city of Bilbao in northern Spain. Set along the riverfront, at the site of an old dock and warehouse, it is linked to the downtown historic district across the river (itself largely a pedestrian zone) by a footbridge designed by Santiago Calatrava (see Fig. 14-55), completed the same year as the museum, and known as the Zubizuri (Basque for "white bridge"). The museum itself is enormous—260,000 square feet, including 19 gallery spaces connected by ramps and metal bridges. It is covered in titanium, a material chosen because it reflects light with stunning clarity. Thus, at night it seems gilded in gold, by day it is silvery, and at noon virtually translucent.

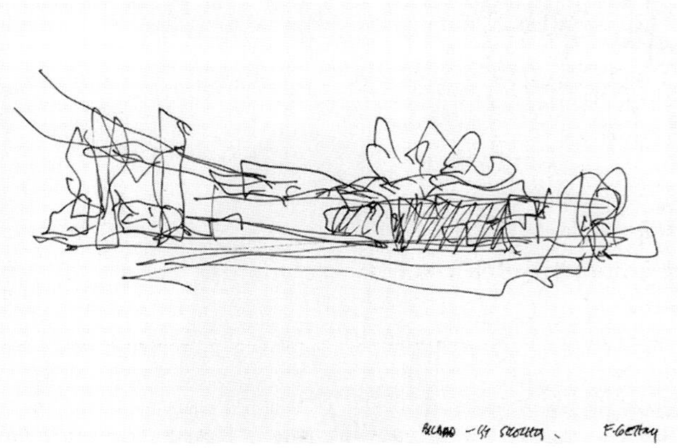

Fig. 14-46 Frank Gehry, *Guggenheim Museum Bilbao, North Elevation,* October 1991. Sketch by Frank Gehry.

Gehry's early drawings of the north, riverfront facade for the museum (**Fig. 14-46**), executed only three months after he had won the competition to design the building in 1991, reveal his process of searching for the form his buildings eventually take. "I start drawing sometimes," Gehry has said,

> *not knowing where it is going. I use familiar strokes that evolve into the building. Sometimes it seems directionless, not going anywhere for sure. It's like feeling your way along in the dark, anticipating that something will come out usually. I become voyeur of my own thoughts as they develop, and wander about them. Sometimes I say "boy, here it is, here it is, it's coming." I understand it, I get all excited.*

His semi-automatic "doodles," then, result in explorations that are surprisingly close to Gehry's finished building. They anticipate the fluidity of its lines, the flowing movement of the building along the riverfront space.

Fig. 14-47 Frank Gehry, Guggenheim Museum Bilbao, 1997.

Gehry moves quickly from such sketches to actual scale models. The models, for Gehry, are like sculpture: "You forget about it as architecture, because you're focused on this sculpting process." The models, finally, are transformed into actual buildings by means of CATIA, a computer program originally developed for the French aerospace industry (**Fig. 14-48**). And it turns out that the digital design models produced by the CATIA program were not only useful for envisioning the shapes of "sculpted" buildings. The data produced by such computerized designs was also critical in estimating construction costs and budgets. The program demonstrated to builders, contractors—and the client—that Gehry's plan was not only buildable, but affordably so.

Gehry's design for the Guggenheim in Bilbao was stunningly successful, drawing rave reviews, massive numbers of visitors, and even the critical reservation that the architecture was so noteworthy that it overshadowed the art within the structure.

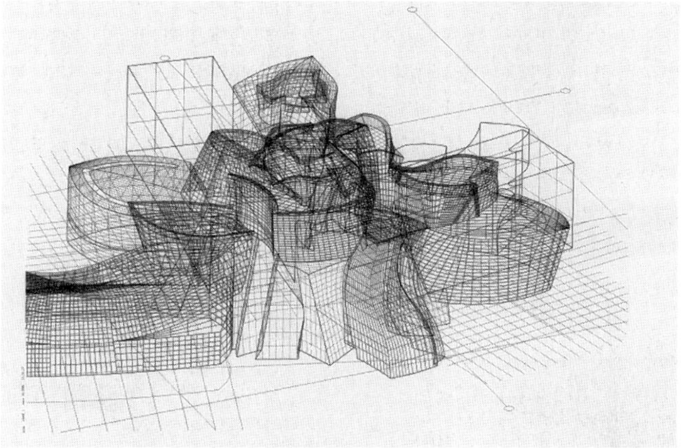

Fig. 14-48 Frank Gehry, Guggenheim Museum Bilbao, ca. 1994.
© Gehry Partners, LLP.

Dubai, in the United Arab Emirates, is the most rapidly growing city in the world, so much so that, in 2008, Rem Koolhaas was commissioned by a Dubai-based developer to propose a 1.5-billion-square-foot Waterfront City that would approximate the density of Manhattan on an artificial island surrounded by water from the Persian Gulf channeled into canals dug out of the desert. Koolhaas has conceived of the island as a perfect square, with the tallest towers concentrated along its southern edge to shield the interior blocks from the hot desert sun.

Koolhaas's extravagant project is in keeping with the architectural ambitions of Dubai itself. As of 2012 the city boasted 911 completed high-rise buildings, 18 of which top out at over 984 feet (300 meters), more than any other city in the world. The tallest of these—indeed, the tallest freestanding structure in the world at 2,684 feet (more than twice as high as the Empire State Building)—is the Burj Khalifa (**Fig. 14-49**). *Burj* is Arabic for "tower," and this tower is the centerpiece of yet another real-estate

Fig. 14-49 Adrian Smith, Skidmore, Owings & Merrill, Burj Khalifa, Dubai, United Arab Emirates, 2010.
© Blaine Harrington III/Corbis.

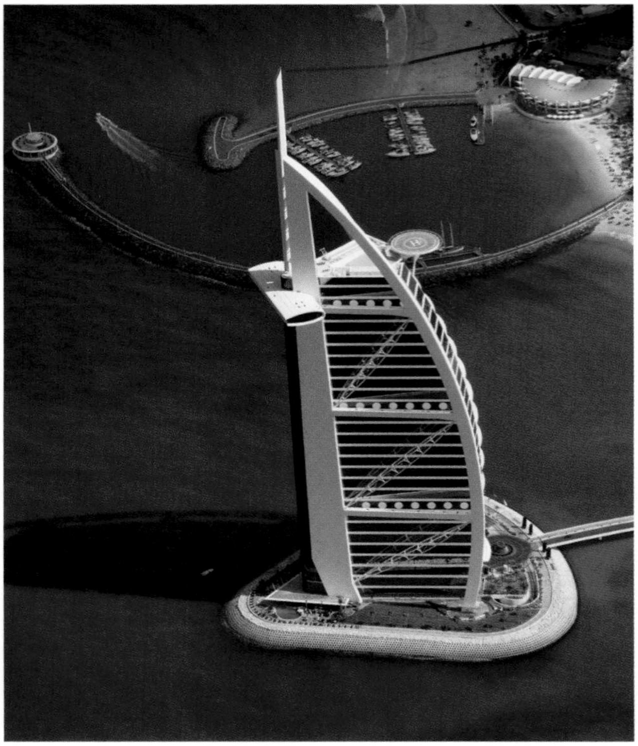

Fig. 14-50 Tom Wills-Wright, Burj Al-Arab, Dubai, United Arab Emirates, 1999.
© Tim Griffith/Arcaid/Corbis.

development that will include 30,000 homes, 9 hotels, over 7 acres of parkland, at least 19 residential towers, the Dubai Mall, and a 30-acre manmade lake. Designed by Adrian Smith of the New York architecture firm Skidmore, Owings & Merrill, the structure opened in January 2010.

But perhaps the gem of Dubai is the Burj Al-Arab (**Fig. 14-50**), a luxury hotel perched on its own island like some enormous wind-filled sail in the blue waters of the Persian Gulf. Designed by British architect Tom Wills-Wright, the hotel rises some 1,053 feet over the Gulf. Its main lobby rises over 500 feet, high enough to accommodate the Statue of Liberty. Essentially a glass tower, its windows are covered by a double-knit Teflon fabric that reflects over 70 percent of the light and heat from the outside. A round cantilevered helipad, which also serves as the world's highest tennis court, extends off the front of the building from the twenty-eighth floor.

Community Life

How does the idea of community serve as a driving force in architecture?

However much we might respect a building like Mies van der Rohe and Philip Johnson's Seagram Building (see Fig. 14-41), the dark uniformity of its gridlike facade, in the hands of less skillful architects, came to represent, for many, the impersonality and anonymity of urban life. The skyscraper became, by the 1960s, the embodiment of conformity and mediocrity in the modern world. Rather than a symbol of community, it became a symbol of human anonymity and loneliness.

Nevertheless, the idea of community remains a driving impulse in American architecture and design. Richard Meier's Atheneum (**Fig. 14-51**), in New Harmony, Indiana, is a tribute to this spirit. New Harmony is the site of two of America's great utopian communities. The first, Harmony on the Wabash (1814–24), was founded by the Harmony Society, a group of Separatists from the German Lutheran Church. In 1825, Robert Owen, a Welsh-born industrialist and social philosopher, bought their Indiana town and the surrounding lands for his own utopian experiment. Owen's ambition was to create a more perfect society through free education and the abolition of social classes and personal wealth. World-renowned scientists and educators settled in New Harmony. With the help of William Maclure, the Scottish geologist and businessman, they introduced vocational education, kindergarten, and other educational reforms.

Meier's Atheneum serves as the Visitors Center and introduction to historic New Harmony. It is a building oriented, on the one hand, to the orderly grid of New Harmony itself, and, on the other, to the Wabash River, which swings at an angle to the city. Thus, the angular wall that the visitor sees on first approaching the building points to the river, and the uncontrollable forces of nature. The glass walls and the vistas they provide serve to connect the visitor to the surrounding landscape. But overall, the building's formal structure recalls Le Corbusier's Villa Savoye (see Fig. 14-39) and the International Style as a whole. It is this tension between man and nature upon which all "harmony" depends.

Since the middle of the nineteenth century, there have been numerous attempts to incorporate the natural world into the urban context. New York's Central Park (**Fig. 14-52**), designed by Frederick Law Olmsted and Calvert Vaux after the city of New York acquired the 840-acre tract of land in 1856, is an attempt to put city-dwelling humans back in touch with their roots in nature. Olmsted developed a system of paths, fields, and wooded areas modeled after the eighteenth-century gardens of English country estates. These estate gardens appeared wholly natural, but they were in actuality extremely artificial, with manmade lakes, carefully planted forests, landscaped meadows, meandering paths, and fake Greek ruins.

Olmsted favored a park similarly conceived, with, in his words, "gracefully curved lines, generous spaces, and the absence of sharp corners, the idea being to suggest and imply leisure, contemplativeness and happy tranquility." In such places, the rational eighteenth-century

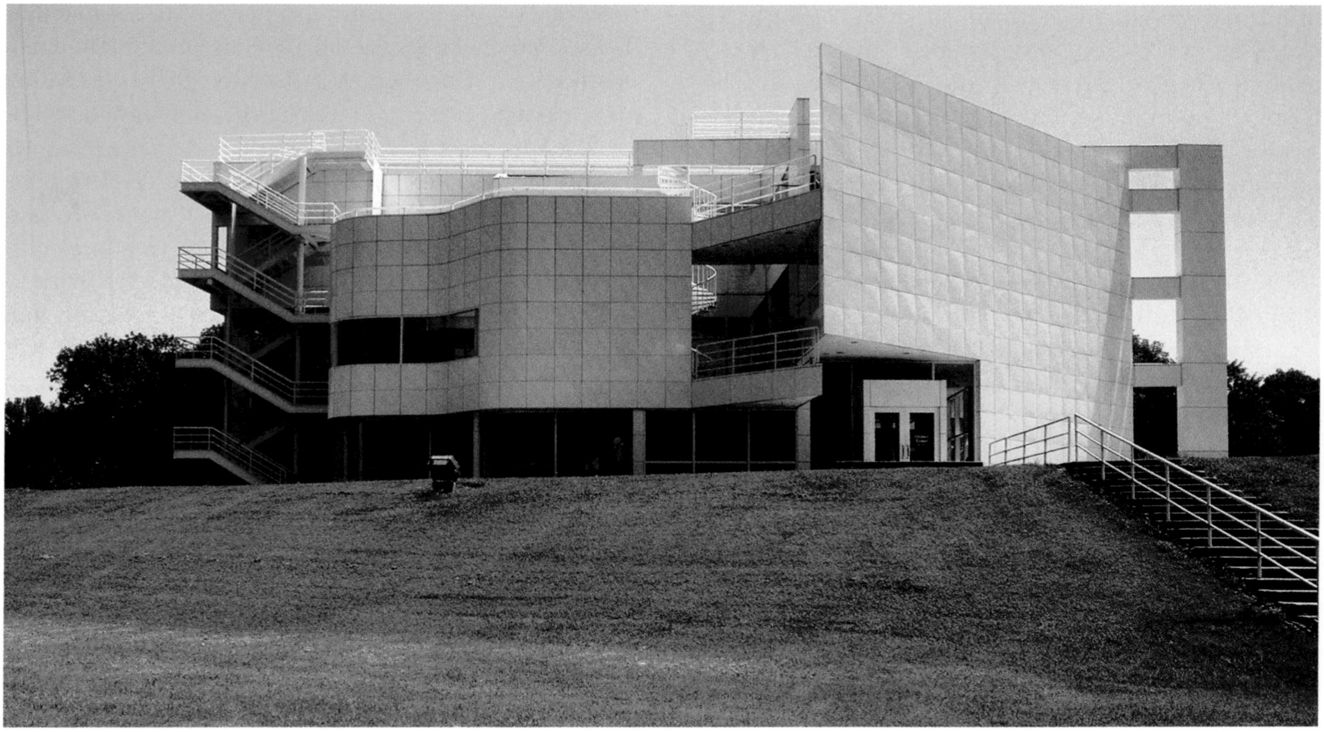

Fig. 14-51 Richard Meier, Atheneum, New Harmony, Indiana, 1979.
Digital imaging project.
Photo © Mary Ann Sullivan.

Fig. 14-52 Frederick Law Olmsted and Calvert Vaux, Central Park, New York City, 1857–87.
© Ball Miwako/Alamy.

mind had sought refuge from the trials of daily life. Likewise, in Central Park, Olmsted imagined the city dweller escaping the rush of urban life. "At every center of commerce," he wrote, "more and more business tends to come under each roof, and, in the progress of building, walls are carried higher and higher, and deeper and deeper, so that now 'vertical railways' [elevators] are coming in vogue." For Olmsted, both the city itself and Neoclassical Greek and Roman architectural features in the English garden offer geometries—emblems of reason and practicality—to which the "gracefully curved" lines of the park and garden stand in counterpoint.

Suburbia

So successful was Olmsted's plan for Central Park that he was subsequently commissioned to design many other parks, including South Park in Chicago and the parkway system of the City of Boston, Mont Royal in Montreal, and the grounds at Stanford University and the University of California at Berkeley. But he perhaps showed the most foresight in his belief that the increasing density of the city demanded the growth of what would later become known as the suburb, a residential community lying outside but within commuting distance of the city. "When not engaged in business," Olmsted wrote, the worker

> has no occasion to be near his working place, but demands arrangements of a wholly different character. Families require to settle in certain localities which minister to their social and other wants, and yet are not willing to accept the conditions of town-life . . . but demand as much of the luxuries of free air, space, and abundant vegetation as, without loss of town-privileges, they can be enabled to secure.

As early as 1869, Olmsted laid out a general plan for the city of Riverside, Illinois, one of the first suburbs of Chicago (**Fig. 14-53**), which was situated along the Des Plaines River. The plan incorporated the railroad as the principal form of transportation into the city. Olmsted strived to create a communal spirit by subdividing the site into small "village" areas linked by drives and walks, all situated near common areas that were intended to have "the character of informal village greens, commons, and playgrounds."

Together with Forest Hills in New York, Llewellyn Park in New Jersey, and Lake Forest, also outside of Chicago, Olmsted's design for Riverside set the standard for suburban development in America. The pace of that development was steady but slow until the 1920s, when suburbia exploded. During that decade, the suburbs grew twice as fast as the central cities. Beverly Hills in Los Angeles grew by 2,500 percent, and Shaker Heights outside of Cleveland by 1,000 percent. The Great Depression and World War II slowed growth temporarily, but, by 1950, the suburbs were growing at a rate ten times faster than the cities. Between 1950 and 1960, American cities grew by 6 million people or 11.6 percent. In that same decade, the suburban population grew by 19 million, a rate of 45.6 percent. And, for the first time, some cities actually began to lose population: The populations of both Boston and St. Louis declined by 13 percent.

There were two great consequences of this suburban emigration: First, the development of the highway system, aided as well by the rise of the automobile as the primary means of transportation; and, second, the collapse of the financial base of the urban center itself. As early as 1930, there were 800,000 automobiles in Los Angeles—two for every five people—and the city quite consciously decided not to spend public monies on mass transit but to support instead a giant freeway system (**Fig. 14-54**). The freeways essentially overlaid the rectilinear grid of the city's streets with continuous, streamlined ribbons of highway. Similarly, in 1940, Pennsylvania opened a turnpike that ran the length of the state. Public enthusiasm was enormous, and traffic volume far exceeded expectations. That same year, the first stretches of the Pasadena Freeway opened. Today

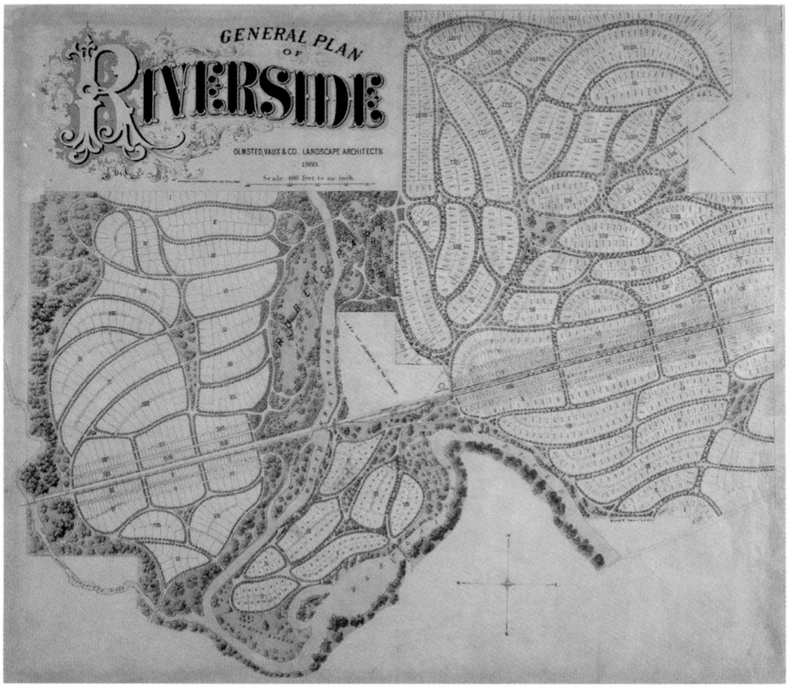

Fig. 14-53 Olmsted, Vaux & Co., General plan of Riverside, Illinois, 1869.
Courtesy of United States Department of the Interior, National Park Service, Frederick Law Olmsted National Historc Site.

Fig. 14-54 Los Angeles Freeway Interchange.
© Chad Ehlers/Alamy.

it is estimated that roads and parking spaces for cars occupy between 60 and 70 percent of the total land area of Los Angeles.

Infrastructure

However, not only automobiles but also money—the wealth of the middle class—drove down these highways, out of the core city and into the burgeoning suburbs. The cities were faced with discouraging and destructive urban decline. Most discouraging of all was the demise of the **infrastructure**, the systems that deliver services to people—water supply and waste removal, energy, transportation, and communications. The infrastructure is what determines the quality of city life. If we think about many of the works of art we have studied in this chapter, we can recognize that they were initially conceived as part of the infrastructure of their communities. For example, the Pont du Gard (see Fig. 14-13) is a water-supply aqueduct. Public buildings such as temples, churches, and cathedrals provide places for people to congregate. Even skyscrapers are integral parts of the urban infrastructure, providing centralized places for people to work. As the infrastructure collapses, businesses close down, industries relocate, the built environment deteriorates rapidly, and even social upheaval can follow. To this day, downtown Detroit has never recovered from the 1967 riots and the subsequent loss of jobs in the auto industry in the mid-1970s. Block after block of buildings that once housed thriving businesses lie decayed and unused.

Perhaps one of the most devastating assaults on a city's infrastructure occurred on September 11, 2001, when terrorists brought down the twin towers of the World Trade Center in New York City. Almost immediately after the tragedy, plans were put in place to rebuild the site at Ground Zero, highlighted by an architectural competition. Problems of urban planning were paramount. Transportation issues involving the city's street and subway systems vied with retail, office, and other commercial interests for consideration. But all designs had to address the heavy weight of the site's symbolic significance—the memory of the World Trade Center itself and the people who had worked there.

One of the most successful designs submitted for the site is by Spanish architect Santiago Calatrava. His plan for the Port Authority Trans Hudson (PATH) train station (**Fig. 14-55**) is based on a sketch that he drew of a child's hands releasing a bird into the air. Calatrava said that the goal of his design was to "use light as a construction material." At ground level, the station's steel, concrete, and glass canopy functions as a skylight that allows daylight to penetrate 60 feet to the tracks below. On nice days, the canopy's roof retracts to create a dome of sky above the station. A total of 14 subway lines will be accessible from the station, and it will also connect to ferry services and airport transportation. The Port Authority sees it as the centerpiece of a new regional transportation infrastructure designed to rejuvenate lower Manhattan.

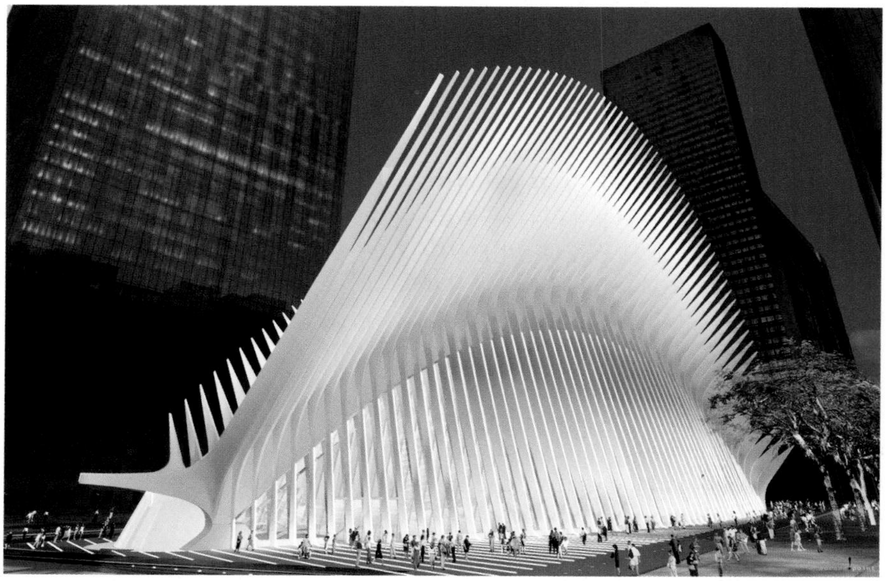

Fig. 14-55 Santiago Calatrava, Port Authority Trans Hudson (PATH) station, World Trade Center site, 2004. Digital three-dimensional model.
© 2015 Santiago Calatrava/Artists Rights Society (ARS), New York/VEGAP, Madrid.

THE CRITICAL PROCESS

Thinking about Architecture

Fig. 14-56 Multistory apartment block, Taos Pueblo, New Mexico, originally built 1000–1450.
© Karl Weatherly/Corbis.

Perhaps because developments in architecture are so closely tied to advances in technology, this chapter is exceptionally historical in emphasis, moving as it does from rudimentary post-and-lintel construction to advanced architectural accomplishments made possible by both computer technologies and the ability of architects themselves to move physically and communicate virtually on a global scale.

That said, it must be admitted, as the saying goes, that the more things change, the more things stay the same. The need of humans to dwell in suitable habitats and their desire to congregate in livable communities are timeless impulses. Consider, for instance, a kind of dwelling that has survived from prehistoric times to the present, the apartment block. By 7000 BCE, across the Middle East, houses consisting of mud brick and timber stood side by side with abutting walls, often terraced in ways that probably resembled the Native American pueblos of the American Southwest. The main parts of the Taos Pueblo (**Fig. 14-56**) were most likely constructed between 1000 and 1450, and look today much as they did when Spanish explorers and missionaries first arrived in the area in the sixteenth century. The Pueblo is divided into two apartment blocks, which rise on either side of a vast dance plaza bisected by a stream. The Pueblo's walls, which are several feet thick, are made of adobe, a mixture of earth, water, and straw formed into sun-dried mud bricks. The roofs are supported by large wooden beams which are topped by smaller pieces of wood, and the whole roof is then covered with packed dirt. Each of the five stories is set back from the one below, thus forming terraces that serve as patios and viewing areas for ceremonial activities in the dance plaza below.

Taos Pueblo has much in common with Israeli architect Moshe Safdie's Habitat (**Fig. 14-57**), designed as an experimental housing project for Expo 67, the Montreal World's Fair, but today still serving a community of content residents,

Fig. 14-57 Moshe Safdie, Habitat, Montreal, Canada, 1967.
© Michael Harding/Arcaid/Corbis.

most of whom think of themselves as living in Montreal's "most prestigious apartment building." Safdie's design is based on modular prefabricated concrete blocks stacked in what Safdie called "confused order" and connected by internal steel cables. Safdie used 354 uniform blocks to make up 158 apartments of from one to four bedrooms. Each apartment has an outdoor living space, generally on the roof of the apartment directly below. The stacks are arranged to maximize privacy, access to views of the St. Lawrence River, and protection from the weather.

In what ways does Safdie's design evoke Southwest Native American pueblos? How does it differ? In what ways is Safdie's design reminiscent of Le Corbusier's Domino Housing Project (see Fig. 14-38)? How does it differ?

Thinking Back

14.1 Describe the relationship between architecture and its environment.

The designs of many buildings reflect the climatic conditions of their environments. Why did the houses of Mulberry Plantation have steeply pitched roofs? How do Anasazi cliff dwellings reflect the Anasazi culture?

Environmental concerns have provoked a new "green" architecture. Green architecture is defined by its environmentally friendly and sustainable approach to building. Its principles include smaller buildings, integration and compatibility with the natural environment, energy efficiency, and the employment of recycled, reusable, and sustainable materials. How is the prospect of climate change affecting urban architecture?

14.2 Outline the architectural technologies that predate the modern era.

The simplest method of making a building is to make the walls load-bearing by stacking any material—stones, bricks, mud, and straw—right up to roof level. Just a step more sophisticated is post-and-lintel construction, which is fundamental to all Greek architecture. Why are the columns—or posts—in Greek temples placed so closely together?

The relationship between the units of a Greek temple is known as its order. Columns in the Doric order are the plainest, while those of the Ionic order have a distinctive scroll, and those in the Corinthian order are decorated with stylized acanthus leaves. What is an elevation? What is entasis?

The ancient Romans developed the arch, an innovation in which wedge-shaped voussoirs were cut to fit into a semicircular form, which was locked by a keystone at the top. The arch revolutionized the built environment, allowing the Romans to span much larger spaces than post-and-lintel construction would allow. What is a barrel vault, or tunnel vault? How are groin vaults created?

14.3 Describe the technological advances that have contributed to modern and contemporary architecture.

The sheer strength of steel was a major enabling factor in skyscraper construction, as it dispensed with the need for the thick walls required in the lower levels of stone buildings. Reinforced concrete (concrete with steel bars embedded) significantly promoted strength in skyscrapers. What is a cantilever? What characterizes the International Style?

14.4 Describe how the idea of community serves as a driving force in architecture.

The idea of community has spawned such utopian communities as New Harmony, Indiana. How does Richard Meier's Atheneum reflect that spirit? What was the driving force behind New York's Central Park, and how is that park related to the rise of the suburb? How has the idea of community been affected by the decline of the urban infrastructure?

Chapter 15
The Design Profession

Learning Objectives

15.1 Describe how the Arts and Crafts Movement and Art Nouveau gave rise to design as a profession.

15.2 Explain how modernist avant-garde movements impacted the design profession.

15.3 Discuss the appeal of streamlining and the ways in which the organic continued to influence design after World War II.

15.4 Explain how the rise of numerous and diverse markets in the late twentieth century impacted design.

During the 1920s in the United States, many people who had once described themselves as involved in the graphic arts, the industrial arts, the craft arts, or the arts allied to architecture, and even architects themselves, began to be referred to as designers. They were seen as serving industry. They could take any object or product—a shoe, a chair, a book, a poster, an automobile, or a building—and make it appealing, and thereby persuade the public to buy it or a client to build it. People find products appealing for two reasons—their functionality and their style. Obviously, a product needs to work, and work well, to attract buyers. But it also has to look good, and this "look," or style, is a stimulus for consumption and show. It implies not only aesthetic appeal but good taste. Most successful product design embodies both functionality and a distinctive stylistic appearance.

A good recent example is Knoll's Toboggan Chair (**Fig. 15-1**). Designed by Masamichi Udagawa and Sigi Moeslinger, of New York-based Antenna Design, the chair is a response to a shift in office design from individual workstations, often isolated in cubicles, to a more casual shared space that encourages conversation and collaborative interaction. Whether they work in an ad agency or financial services firm, employees can use the Toboggan as a lightweight, movable chair, or turn it around so that the backrest becomes a surface for a tablet, small laptop, or sketchbook. Or if they choose to sit sideways in it, the backrest transforms itself into an armrest. This flexibility lies at the heart of Knoll's sense that the new work environment requires functional "activity spaces." But functionality is not the only driving force of the Toboggan. Its lightweight sled design, available in an array colors, is also meant to be visually stimulating—it references, as we will see, some of the more important innovations in modern furniture design—while subtly suggesting, in its multiple uses, the kind of flexible thinking that is required in the new office environment, where innovation is increasingly valued above all else.

Fig. 15-1 Masamichi Udagawa and Sigi Moeslinger, Antenna Design, Knoll Toboggan Chair, 2012.
Courtesy of Knoll, Inc.

The Rise of Design in the Nineteenth Century

How did the Arts and Crafts Movement and Art Nouveau contribute to the rise of design as a profession?

While it would be possible to approach design by analyzing individual media—graphic design and typography, furniture design, transportation design, and so on—since the start of the Arts and Crafts Movement and the related rise of Art Nouveau in the last half of the nineteenth century, the profession has been defined more by a series of successive movements and styles than by the characteristic properties of any given medium.

The Arts and Crafts Movement

The Arts and Crafts Movement was itself a reaction to the fact that, during the first half of the nineteenth century, as mass production increasingly became the norm in Britain, the quality and aesthetic value of mass-produced goods declined. In order to demonstrate to the British the sorry state of modern design in their country, Henry Cole, a British civil servant who was himself a designer, organized the Great Exhibition of 1851. The industrial production on exhibit showed, once and for all, just how bad the situation was. Almost everyone agreed with the assessment of Owen Jones: "We have no principles, no unity; the architect, the upholsterer, the weaver, the calico-painter, and the potter, run each their independent course; each struggles fruitlessly, each produces in art novelty without beauty, or beauty without intelligence."

The building that housed the exhibition in Hyde Park was an altogether different proposition. A totally new type of building, which became known as the Crystal Palace (**Figs. 15-2** and **15-3**), it was designed by Joseph Paxton, who had once served as gardener to the duke of Devonshire and had no formal training as an architect. Constructed of more than 900,000 square feet of glass set in prefabricated wood and cast iron, it was three stories tall and measured 1,848 × 408 feet. It required only nine months to build, and it ushered in a new age in construction. As one architect wrote at the time, "From such beginnings what glories may be in reserve. . . . We may trust ourselves to dream, but we dare not predict."

Not everyone agreed. A. W. N. Pugin, who had collaborated on the new Gothic-style Houses of Parliament, called the Crystal Palace a "glass monster," and, moved by its resemblance to a greenhouse, the essayist and reformer John Ruskin, who likewise had championed a return to a pre-industrial Gothic style in his book *The Stones of Venice*, called it a "cucumber frame." Under their influence, William Morris, a poet, artist, and ardent socialist, dedicated himself to the renewal of British design through the renewal of medieval craft traditions. In his own words: "At this time, the revival of Gothic architecture was making great progress in England. . . . I threw myself into these movements with all my heart; got a friend [Philip Webb] to build me a house very medieval in spirit . . . and set myself to decorating it." Built of traditional red brick, the house was called the

Fig. 15-2 Joseph Paxton, Crystal Palace, Great Exhibition, London, 1851. Iron, glass, and wood, 1,848 × 408 ft. Lithograph by Charles Burton, *Aeronautic View of the Palace of Industry for All Nations, from Kensington Gardens*, published by Ackerman (1851). London Metropolitan Archives, City of London, UK.

Bridgeman Images.

Fig. 15-3 Joseph Paxton, Interior, Crystal Palace, Great Exhibition, London, 1851.
Institute for the History and Theory of Architecture, Zurich.
© Historical Picture Archive/Corbis.

Red House (**Fig. 15-4**), and nothing could be further in style from the Crystal Palace. Where the latter reveals itself to be the product of manufacture—engineered out of prefabricated, factory-made parts and assembled, with minimal cost, by unspecialized workers in a matter of a few months—the former is an intentionally rural—even archaic—building that rejects the industrial spirit of Paxton's Palace. It signaled, Morris hoped, a return to craft traditions in which workers were intimately tied, from start to finish, to the design and manufacture of their products.

Morris longed to return to a handmade craft tradition for two related reasons. He felt that the mass-manufacturing process alienated workers from their labor, and he also missed the quality of handmade items. Industrial laborers had no stake in what they made, and thus no pride in their work. The result, he felt, was both shoddy workmanship and unhappy workers.

Fig. 15-4 Philip Webb, The Red House, Bexleyheath, U.K., 1859.
Photo: Charlotte Wood.

As a result of the experience of building the Red House and attempting to furnish it with objects of a medieval, handcrafted nature, a project that was frustrated at every turn, Morris decided to take matters into his own hands. In 1861, he founded the firm that would become Morris & Co. It was dedicated "to undertake any species of decoration, mural or otherwise, from pictures, properly so-called, down to the consideration of the smallest work susceptible of art beauty." To this end, the company was soon producing stained glass, painted tiles, furniture, embroidery, table glass, metalwork, chintzes, wallpaper, woven hangings, tapestries, and carpets.

In his designs, Morris constantly emphasized two principles: simplicity and utility. Desire for simplicity—"simplicity of life," as he put it, "begetting simplicity of taste"—soon led him to create what

Fig. 15-5 Morris and Company, Sussex Rush-Seated Chairs, ca. 1865. Wood with black varnish. Musée d'Orsay, Paris. Inv. OAO1318, OAO1319. Photo ©RMN-Grand Palais (musée d'Orsay)/ Hervé Lewandowski.

he called "workaday furniture," the best example of which is the company's line of Sussex rush-seated chairs (**Fig. 15-5**). Such furniture was meant to be "simple to the last degree" and to appeal to the common man. As Josiah Wedgwood had done 100 years earlier (see Chapter 13), Morris quickly came to distinguish this "workaday" furniture from his more costly "state furniture," for which, he wrote, "we need not spare ornament . . . but [may] make them as elaborate and elegant as we can with carving or inlaying or paintings; these are the blossoms of the art of furniture." An adjustable reclining chair (the forefather of all recliners) designed by Morris's friend, Philip Webb (**Fig. 15-6**), is the "state" version of the Sussex rush-seated chair. Covered in rich, embossed velvet, the chair quickly became a symbolic standard of good living. As Morris's colleague Walter Crane put it:

> The great advantage . . . of the Morrisian method is that it lends itself to either simplicity or splendor. You might be almost plain enough to please Thoreau, with a rush-bottomed chair, piece of matting, and oaken trestle-table; or you might have gold and luster . . . gleaming from the side-board, and jeweled light in your windows, and walls hung with rich arras tapestry.

Perhaps nothing underscores Morris's aesthetic taste more than his work as bookmaker and typographer at the Kelmscott Press. On November 15, 1888, Morris went to a slide lecture by the typographer Emery Walker at a meeting of the Arts and Crafts Exhibition Society. That night he saw a series of brilliantly colored magic-lantern photographic slides of illuminated books, projected through one of the newly powerful gas lanterns that would soon revolutionize the study of art history as well. He was so moved by the slide show that the next morning he sat down with Walker and drew up plans for the Kelmscott Press.

Among the most remarkable aspects of the Walker/ Morris collaboration is that no one had ever before used a magic lantern to blow up letterforms on the wall in order to study—and then modify—their particular characteristics. Morris's daughter, May Morris, writing in 1912 in the introduction to volume 15 of *The Collected Works of William Morris* describes the process as follows:

> Mr. Walker got his people to photograph upon an enlarged scale some pages from Aretino's "Historia fiorentina" printed in Venice by Jacques le Rouge in 1476 and pages of all the more important fifteenth century Roman types. These enlargements enabled

Fig. 15-6 The Morris Adjustable Chair, designed by Philip Webb, made by Morris, Marshall, Faulkner & Co., ca. 1880. Ebonized wood, covered with Utrecht velvet. Victoria and Albert Museum, London.

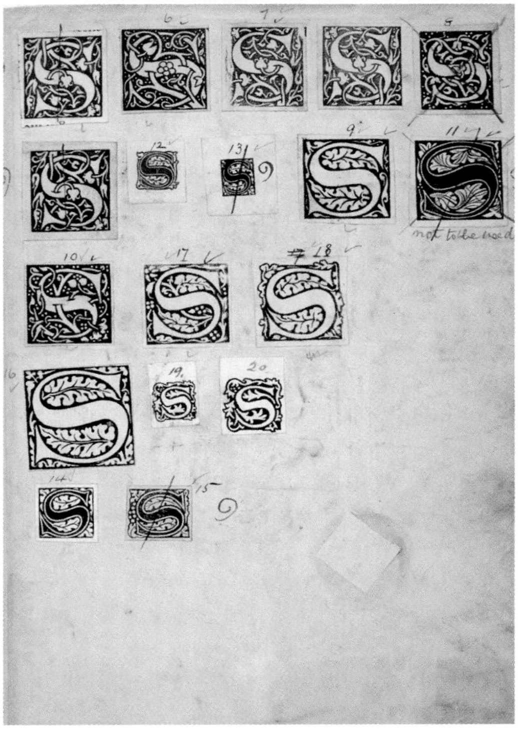

Fig. 15-7 William Morris, Page from a specimen book with sample proof letters, Kelmscott Press, ca. 1896. The Wilson, Cheltenham Art Gallery & Museum, Gloucestershire, U.K.
© Cheltenham Art Gallery & Museums, Gloucestershire, UK/Bridgeman Images.

> Father [i.e., Morris] to study the proportions and peculiarities of the letters. Having thoroughly absorbed these, so to speak, he started designing his own type on this big scale. When done, each letter was photographed down to the size the type was to be.

These photographs were in turn transferred to woodblocks and collected in specimen books (**Fig. 15-7**), which allowed Morris to compare various iterations of a given letter's design.

Morris's edition of Chaucer's works (**Fig. 15-8**) is a direct expression of his belief in the values and practices of the fifteenth-century typographers who so interested him. In their spirit, he commissioned handmade, wire-molded, linen paper similar to that used in fifteenth-century Bologna. He designed a font, appropriately called "Chaucer," which was based on Gothic script. In order to make it more legible, he widened most letterforms, increased the differences between similar characters, and made curved characters rounder. "Books should be beautiful," he argued, "by force of mere typography." But he stopped at nothing to make the Chaucer beautiful in every detail. He set his type by hand, insisting upon a standard spacing between letters, words, and lines. He positioned material on the page in the manner of medieval bookmakers, designed 14 large borders, 18 different frames for the illustrations, and 26 large initial words for the text. Finally, he commissioned 87 illustrations from the English painter Sir Edward Burne-Jones. The book, he felt, should be like architecture, every detail—paper, ink, type, spacing, margins, illustrations, and ornament—all working together as a single design unit.

Morris claimed that his chief purpose as a designer was to elevate the circumstances of the common man. "Every man's house will be fair and decent," he wrote, "all the works of man that we live amongst will be in harmony with nature . . . and every man will have his share of the best." But common people were in no position to afford the elegant creations of Morris & Co. Unlike Wedgwood (see Chapter 13), whose common, "useful" ware made the most money for the firm, it was the more expensive productions—the state furniture, tapestries, and embroideries—that kept Morris & Co. financially afloat. Inevitably, Morris was forced to confront the inescapable conclusion that to handcraft an object made it prohibitively expensive. With resignation

Fig. 15-8 William Morris (design) and Edward Burne-Jones (illustration), Opening page of Geoffrey Chaucer, *The Works of Geoffrey Chaucer Newly Augmented*, Kelmscott Press, 1896. Sheet 16¾ × 11½ in. Edition of 425 copies. Yale Center for British Art.
Paul Mellon Collection/Bridgeman Images.

Fig. 15-9 Gustav Stickley, Settee, 1905–09. Oak, upholstery (replaced), 4 ft. ⅞ in. × 47½ in. × 25³⁄₁₆ in., seat 19 in. × 5 ft. 2 in. Los Angeles County Museum of Art.

Gift of Max Palevsky, AC1993.1.8. © 2015. Digital Image Museum Associates/LACMA/Art Resource New York/Scala, Florence.

and probably no small regret, he came to accept the necessity of mass manufacture.

In the United States, Gustav Stickley's magazine *The Craftsman*, first published in 1901 in Syracuse, New York, was the most important supporter of the Arts and Crafts tradition. The magazine's self-proclaimed mission was "to promote and to extend the principles established by [William] Morris," and its first issue was dedicated exclusively to Morris. Likewise, the inaugural issue of *House Beautiful* magazine, published in Chicago in 1896, included articles on Morris and the English Arts and Crafts Movement. Stickley, recognizing the expense of Morris's handcrafted furniture and the philosophical dilemma that Morris faced in continuing to make it, accepted the necessity of machine-manufacturing his own work. Massive in appearance, lacking ornamentation, its aesthetic appeal depended, instead, on the beauty of its wood, usually oak (**Fig. 15-9**).

By the turn of the century, architect Frank Lloyd Wright was also deeply involved in furniture design. Like Morris before him, Wright felt compelled to design furniture for the interiors of his Prairie Houses that matched the design of the building as a whole (see Fig. 14-34). "It is quite impossible," Wright wrote, "to consider the building as one thing, its furnishings another, and its setting and environment still another. The Spirit in which these buildings are conceived sees these all together at work as one thing." The table lamp designed for the Susan Lawrence Dana House in Springfield, Illinois (**Fig. 15-10**), is meant to reflect the dominant decorative feature of the house—a geometric rendering of the sumac plant that is found abundantly in the neighboring Illinois countryside, chosen because the site of the house itself was particularly lacking in vegetation. Given a very large budget, Wright designed 450 glass panels and 200 light fixtures for the house, which are variations on the basic sumac theme. Each piece is unique and individually crafted.

The furniture designs of Morris, Stickley, and Wright point out the basic issues that design faced in the twentieth century. The first dilemma, to which we have been paying particular attention, was whether the product should be handcrafted or mass-manufactured. But formal issues arose as well. If we compare Wright's designs to Morris's, we can see that they use line completely differently. Even though both find the source of their forms in nature, Wright's forms are rectilinear and geometric, Morris's curvilinear and organic. Both believed in "simplicity," but the word meant different things to the two men. Morris, as we have seen, equated simplicity with the natural. Wright, on the other hand, designed furniture for his houses because, he said, "simple things . . . were nowhere at hand. A piece of wood without a moulding was an anomaly, plain fabrics were nowhere to be found in stock." To Wright, simplicity meant plainness. The history of design continually confronts the choice between the geometric and the organic. The major design movement at the turn of the century, Art Nouveau, chose the latter.

Fig. 15-10 Frank Lloyd Wright, Table lamp, executed for the Linden Glass Co. for the Susan Lawrence Dana House, 1903. Bronze, leaded glass.

Photo © Christie's Images/Bridgeman Images.© 2015 Frank Lloyd Wright Foundation, Scottsdale, AZ/Artists Rights Society (ARS), New York.

Art Nouveau

The day after Christmas in 1895, a shop opened in Paris named the Galeries de l'Art Nouveau. It was operated by one S. Bing, whose first name was Siegfried, though art history has almost universally referred to him as Samuel, perpetuating a mistake made in his obituary in 1905. Bing's new gallery was a success, and in 1900, at the Universal Exposition in Paris, he opened his own pavilion, Art Nouveau Bing. By the time the Exposition ended, the name **Art Nouveau** had come to designate not merely the work he displayed but a decorative arts movement of international dimension.

Bing had visited the United States in 1894. The result was a short book titled *Artistic Culture in America*, in which he praised America's architecture, painting, and sculpture, but most of all its arts and crafts. The American who fascinated him most was the glassmaker Louis Comfort Tiffany, son of the founder of the famous New York jewelry firm Tiffany and Co. The younger Tiffany's work inspired Bing to create his new design movement, and Bing contracted with the American to produce a series of stained-glass windows designed by such French artists as Henri de Toulouse-Lautrec and Pierre Bonnard. Because oil lamps were at that very moment being replaced by electric lights—Thomas Edison had startled the French public with his demonstration of electricity at the earlier Universal Exposition in Paris, in 1889—Bing placed considerable emphasis on new, modern modes of lighting. From his point of view, a new light and a new art went hand in hand. And Tiffany's stained-glass lamps (**Fig. 15-11**), backlit by electric light, brought a completely new sense of vibrant color to interior space.

Even more than his stained glass, Bing admired Tiffany's iridescent Favrile glassware, which was named after the obsolete English word for handmade, "fabrile." The distinctive feature of this type of glassware is that nothing of the design is painted, etched, or burned into the surface. Instead, every detail is built up by the craftsperson out of what Tiffany liked to call "genuine glass." In the vase illustrated here (**Fig. 15-12**), we can see many of the design characteristics most often associated with Art Nouveau, from the wavelike line of the peacock feathers to the self-conscious asymmetry of the whole. In fact, the formal vocabulary of Art Nouveau could be said to consist of young saplings and shoots, willow trees, buds, vines—anything organic and undulating, including snakes

Fig. 15-11 Louis Comfort Tiffany, Tiffany Studios, Water-lily table lamp, ca. 1904–15. Leaded Favrile glass, and bronze, height 26½ in. Metropolitan Museum of Art, New York.

Gift of Hugh J. Grant, 1974.214.15ab. © 2015. Image copyright Metropolitan Museum of Art/Art Resource/Scala, Florence.

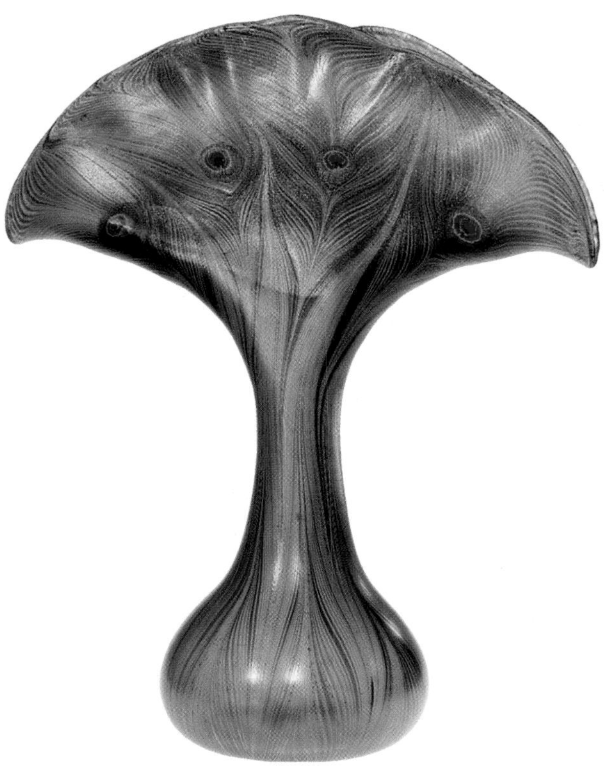

Fig. 15-12 Louis Comfort Tiffany, Tiffany Glass & Decorating Co. (1893–1902), Corona, New York, Peacock Vase, ca. 1893–96. Favrile glass, height 41⅛ in., width 11½ in. Metropolitan Museum of Art, New York.

Gift of H. O.Havemeyer, 1896.17.10. © 2015. Image copyright Metropolitan Museum of Art/Art Resource/Scala, Florence.

Fig. 15-13 Jan Toorop, Poster for *Delftsche Slaolie* (Delft Salad Oil), 1894.
Dutch advertisement poster, 36¼ × 24⅜ in.
Acquired by exchange, 684.1966. © 2015. Digital image, Museum of Modern Art, New York/Scala, Florence.

and, especially, women's hair. The Dutch artist Jan Toorop's advertising poster for a peanut-based salad oil (**Fig. 15-13**) flattens the long, spiraling hair of the two women preparing salad into a pattern very like the elaborate wrought-iron grillework also characteristic of Art Nouveau design. Writing about Bing's installation at the 1900 Universal Exposition, one writer described Art Nouveau's use of line this way: "[In] the encounter of the two lines . . . the ornamenting art is born—an indescribable curving and whirling ornament, which laces and winds itself with almost convulsive energy across the surface of the [design]!"

Yet, for many, Art Nouveau seemed excessively subjective and personal, especially for public forms such as architecture. Through the example of posters like Toorop's, Art Nouveau became associated with an interior world of aristocratic wealth, refinement, and even emotional and sexual abandon. It seemed the very opposite of the geometric and rectilinear design practiced by the likes of Frank Lloyd Wright, and a new geometric design gradually replaced it. By the time of the Exposition Internationale des Arts Décoratifs et Industriels Modernes—the International Exposition of Modern Decorative and Industrial Arts—in Paris in 1925, geometric design held sway.

Design in the Modernist Era

How did the modernist avant-garde art movements affect the design profession?

The Exposition Internationale des Arts Décoratifs et Industriels Modernes was planned as early as 1907, during the height of Art Nouveau, but logistical problems—especially the outbreak of World War I—postponed it for almost 20 years. A very influential event, the exposition was the most extensive international showcase of the style of design then called Art Moderne and, since 1968, better known as **Art Deco**.

Art Deco designers tended to prefer more up-to-date materials—chrome, steel, and Bakelite plastic—and sought to give expression to everyday "moderne" life. The *Skyscraper* bookcase by the American designer Paul T. Frankl (**Fig. 15-14**), made of maple wood and Bakelite, is all sharp angles that rise into the air, like the brand-new skyscrapers that were beginning to dominate America's urban landscape.

Influenced in no small part by Frankl's ideas, and associated with what, by 1920, was considered the most avant-garde of all modern art movements, the Cubism of Pablo Picasso and Georges Braque (see Chapter 20), Art Deco designers turned increasingly to geometric forms, as opposed to the free-flowing lines of Art Nouveau. Even the leading fashion magazines of the day reflect this in their covers and layouts. In Eduardo Benito's *Vogue* magazine cover (**Fig. 15-15**), we can see an impulse toward simplicity and rectilinearity comparable to Frankl's bookcase. The world of fashion embraced the new geometric look. During the 1920s, the boyish silhouette became increasingly fashionable. The curves of the female body were suppressed (**Fig. 15-16**), and the waistline disappeared in tubular, "barrel"-line skirts. Even long, wavy hair, one of the defining features of Art Nouveau style, was abandoned, and the schoolboyish "Eton crop" became the hairstyle of the day.

Fig. 15-14 Paul T. Frankl, *Skyscraper* bookcase, ca. 1927. Maple wood and Bakelite, height 6 ft. 7⅞ in., width 34⅜ in., depth 18⅞ in. Metropolitan Museum of Art, New York.

Purchase: Theodore R. Gamble, Jr. Gift in honor of his mother, Mrs. Theodore Robert Gamble, 1982.30ab. © 2015. Image copyright Metropolitan Museum of Art/Art Resource/Scala, Florence.

Fig. 15-15 Eduardo Benito, Cover of *Vogue*, May 25, 1929.
Eduardo Garcia Benito/Vogue. © Conde Nast.

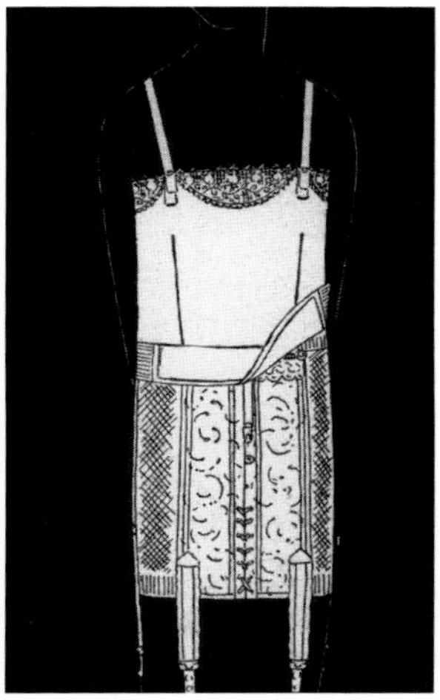

Fig. 15-16 Harriet Meserole, Corset, *Vogue*, October 25, 1924.
Harriet Meserole/Vogue. © Conde Nast.

The Modern Avant-Gardes and Design

At the 1925 Paris Exposition, one designer's pavilion stood apart from all the rest, not because it was better than the others, but because it was so different. As early as 1920, the architect Le Corbusier (see Figs. 14-38 and 14-39) had written in his new magazine *L'Esprit Nouveau* (The New Spirit) that "decorative art, as opposed to the machine phenomenon, is the final twitch of the old manual modes; a dying thing." He proposed a *Pavillon de l'Esprit Nouveau* (Pavilion of the New Spirit) for the exposition that would contain "only standard things created by industry in factories and mass-produced; objects truly of the style of today."

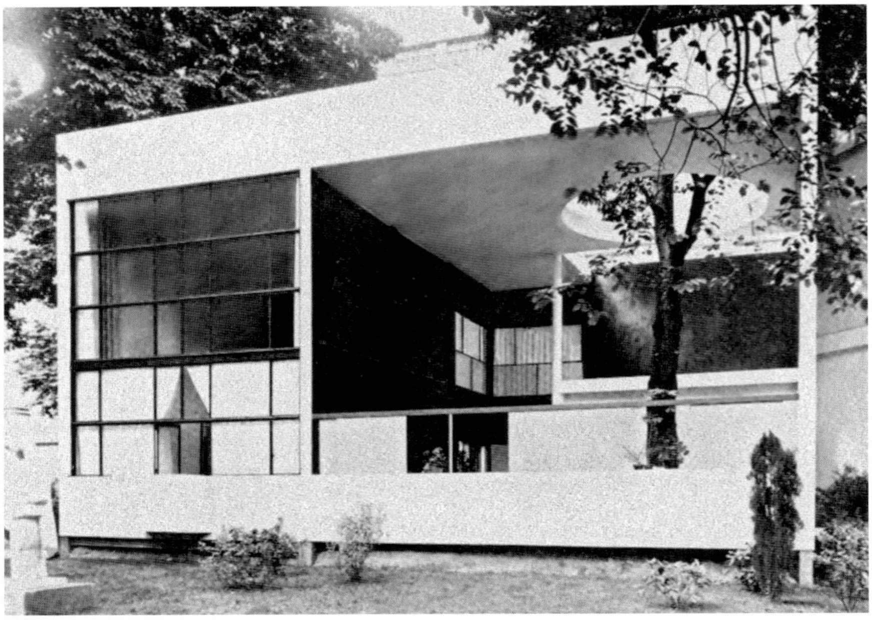

Fig. 15-17 Le Corbusier, *Pavillon de l'Esprit Nouveau*, Exposition Internationale des Arts Décoratifs et Industriels Modernes, Paris, 1925. Copied from Le Corbusier, *My Work* (London: Architectural Press, 1960), p. 72.

Le Corbusier: © F.L.C./ADAGP, Paris/Artists Rights Society (ARS), New York 2015. Pierre Jeanneret: © 2015 Artists Rights Society (ARS), New York/ADAGP, Paris.

For Le Corbusier, making expensive, handcrafted objects amounted to making antiques in a contemporary world. From his point of view, the other designers at the 1925 exposition were out of step with the times. The modern world was dominated by the machine, and though designers had shown disgust for machine manufacture ever since the time of Morris & Co., they did so at the risk of living forever in the past. "The house," as Le Corbusier had declared, "is a machine for living."

Le Corbusier's "new spirit" horrified the exposition's organizers, and, accordingly, they gave him a parcel of ground for his pavilion between two wings of the Grand Palais, with a tree, which could not be removed, growing right in the middle of it. Undaunted, Le Corbusier built a modular version of his Domino Housing Project design (see Fig. 14-38) right around the tree, cutting a hole in the roof to accommodate it (**Fig. 15-17**). So distressed were the exposition officials that they ordered a high fence to be built completely around the site in order to hide it from public view. Le Corbusier appealed to the Ministry of Fine Arts, and, finally, the fence was removed. "Right now," Le Corbusier announced in triumph, "one thing is sure: 1925 marks the decisive turning point in the quarrel between the old and the new. After 1925, the antique lovers will have virtually ended their lives, and productive industrial effort will be based on the 'new.'"

The geometric starkness of Le Corbusier's design had been anticipated by developments in the arts that began to take place in Europe before World War I. A number of new avant-garde (from the French, meaning "advance guard") groups had sprung up, often with radical political agendas, and dedicated to overturning the traditional and established means of art-making through experimental techniques and styles.

Among these was the De Stijl movement in Holland. **De Stijl**, which is Dutch for "The Style," took its lead, like all the avant-garde styles, from the painting of Picasso and Braque, in which the elements of the real world were simplified into a vocabulary of geometric forms. The De Stijl artists simplified the vocabulary of art and design even further, employing only the primary colors—red, blue, and yellow—plus black and white. Their design relied on a vertical and horizontal grid, often dynamically broken by a curve, circle, or diagonal line. Rather than enclosing forms, their compositions seemed to open out into the space surrounding them.

Fig. 15-18 Gerrit Rietveld, *Red and Blue Chair*, ca. 1918. Wood, painted, height 34⅛ in., width 26 in., depth 26½ in., seat height 13 in. Museum of Modern Art, New York.

Gift of Philip Johnson, 487.1953. © 2015. Digital image, Museum of Modern Art, New York/Scala, Florence. © 2015 Artists Rights Society (ARS), New York/c/o Pictoright Amsterdam.

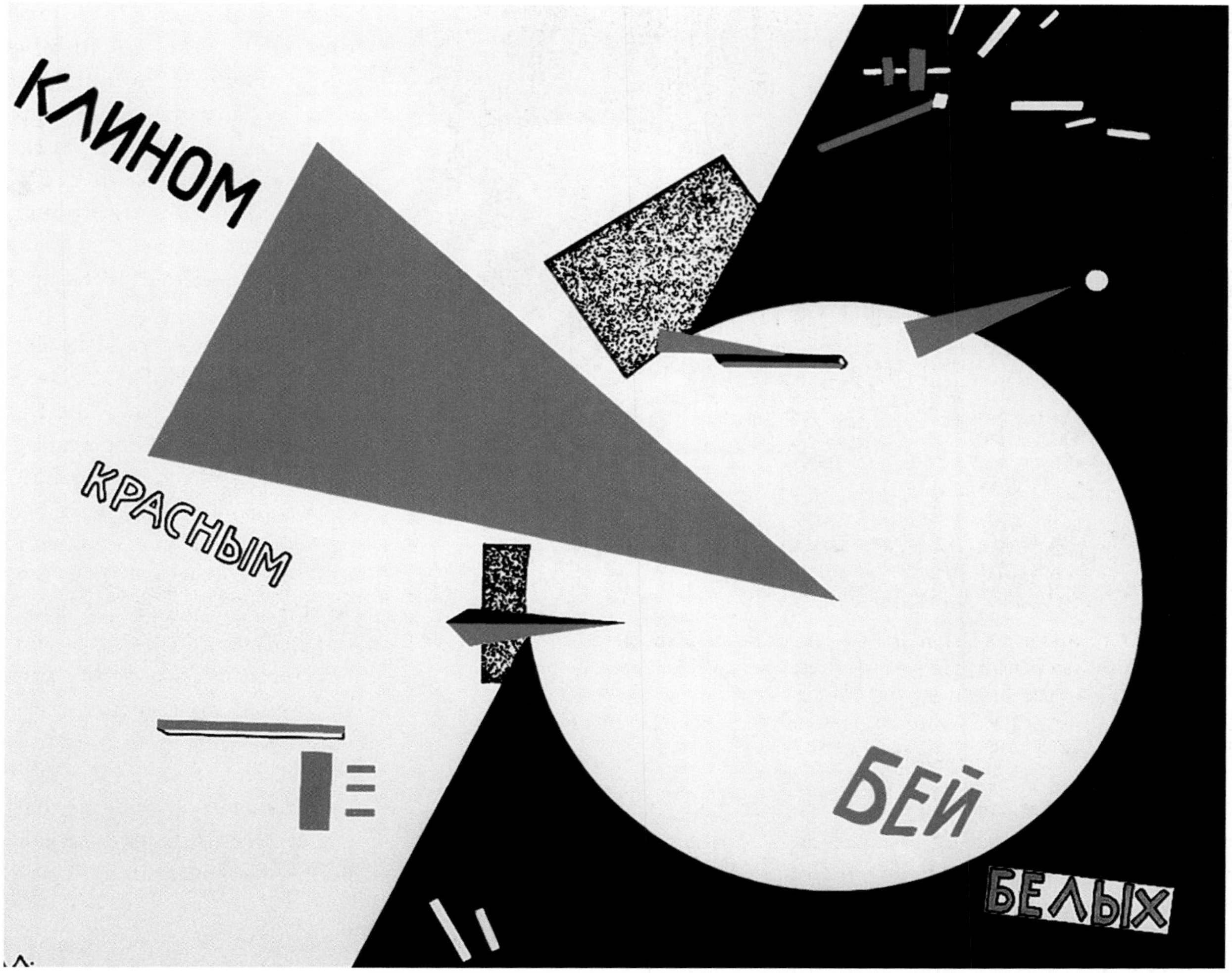

Fig. 15-19 El Lissitzky, *Beat the Whites with the Red Wedge*, 1919.
Lithograph. Van Abbemuseum, Eindhoven, Holland.
© 2015 Artists Rights Society (ARS), New York/VG Bild-Kunst, Bonn.

Gerrit Rietveld's famous chair (**Fig. 15-18**) is a summation of these De Stijl design principles. The chair is designed against, as it were, the traditional elements of the armchair. Both the arms and the base of the chair are insistently locked in a vertical and horizontal grid. But the two planes that function as the seat and the back seem almost to float free from the closed-in structure of the frame. Rietveld dramatized their separateness from the black grid of the frame by painting the seat blue and the back red. All in all, Rietveld's design is meant to engage its sitters in a dynamic situation that might, idealistically, release their own creative energies.

This notion of dynamic space can also be found in Russian **Constructivism**, a movement in the new post-revolutionary Soviet state that dreamed of uniting art and everyday life through mass production and industry. The artists, the Constructivists believed, should "go into the factory, where the real body of life is made." They believed, especially, in employing nonobjective formal elements in functional ways. El Lissitzky's design for the poster *Beat the Whites with the Red Wedge* (**Fig. 15-19**), for instance, is a formal design with propagandistic aims. It presents the "Red" Bolshevik cause as an aggressive red triangle attacking a defensive and static "White" Russian circle. Although the elements employed are starkly simple, the implications are disturbingly sexual—as if the Reds are male and active, while the Whites are female and passive—and the sense of aggressive action, originating both literally and figuratively from "the left," is unmistakable.

Typography, too, reflected this emphasis on standardization and simplicity. Gone were the ornamental effects of **serif type** styles—that is, letterforms, such as the font used in this text, which have small lines at the end of the letter's main stroke—and in their place plain and geometric **sans serif** ("without serif") fonts came to the fore. One of the great proponents of this new typography

Fig. 15-20 Cassandre (Adolphe Mouron), *L'Intrans*, poster for the French daily newspaper *L'Intransigeant*, 1925. Kunstbibliothek, Staatliche Museen zu Berlin.

was the French poster designer Cassandre. "A poster . . . is not meant to be a . . . unique specimen conceived to satisfy a single art lover," Cassandre wrote, but "a mass-produced object" that "must have a commercial function. . . . Designing a poster means solving a technical and commercial problem . . . in a language that can be understood by the common man." The poster campaign Cassandre created for the French newspaper *L'Intransigeant* (**Fig. 15-20**) combines the flat letterforms of the first half of the newspaper's name (it was commonly referred to by its readers simply as "*L'Intrans*") with flat geometric images of Marianne, the symbolic voice of France, as she shouts out the news that she is receiving over the telegraph wires that feed into her ear. Note that the fragment from the newspaper's masthead slogan "*Le Plus Fort . . .*"—"The Largest [Circulation of Any Evening Newspaper]"—remains in serif font, underscoring, in fact, the clarity of the cleaner, sans-serif type of the larger name. This typographic style, viewed by millions, helped to popularize the geometric simplicity championed by the avant-gardes.

The Bauhaus

One of the most important of the modern avant-garde movements in terms of its contribution to the design profession was the **Bauhaus**, a school of arts and crafts founded in Weimar, Germany, by Walter Gropius in 1919. At the German Pavilion at the 1925 Paris Exposition, one could see a variety of new machines designed to make the trials of everyday life easier, such as an electric washing machine and an electric armoire in which clothes could be tumble-dried. When asked who could afford such things, Gropius replied, "To begin with, royalty. Later on, everybody."

Like Le Corbusier, Gropius saw in the machine the salvation of humanity. And he thoroughly sympathized with Le Corbusier, whose major difficulty in putting together his *Pavillon de l'Esprit Nouveau* had been the unavailability of furniture that would satisfy his desire for "standard things created by industry in factories and mass-produced; objects truly of the style of today." Ironically, at almost exactly that moment, Marcel Breuer,

Fig. 15-21 Marcel Breuer, Armchair, Model B3, late 1927 or early 1928.
Chrome-plated tubular steel with canvas slings, height 28⅛ in., width 30¼ in., depth 27¾ in. Museum of Modern Art, New York.
Gift of Herbert Bayer, 229.1934. © 2015. Digital image, Museum of Modern Art, New York/ Scala, Florence.

a furniture designer working at Gropius's Bauhaus, was applying himself to just that question.

In the spring of 1925, Breuer purchased a new bicycle, manufactured out of tubular steel by the Adler company. Impressed by the bicycle's strength—it could easily support the weight of two riders—its lightness, and its apparent indestructibility, Breuer envisioned furniture made of this most modern of materials. "In fact," Breuer later recalled, speaking of the armchair that he began to design soon after his purchase (**Fig. 15-21**), "I took the pipe dimensions from my bicycle. I didn't know where else to get it or how to figure it out."

The chair is clearly related to Rietveld's *Red and Blue Chair* (see Fig. 15-18), consisting of two diagonals for seat and back set in a cubic frame. It is easily mass-produced—and, in fact, is still in production today. But its appeal was due, perhaps most of all, to the fact that it looked absolutely new, and it soon became an icon of the machine age. Gropius quickly saw how appropriate Breuer's design would be for the new Bauhaus building in Dessau. By early 1926, Breuer was at work designing modular tubular-steel seating for the school's auditorium, as well as stools and side chairs to be used throughout the educational complex. As a result, Breuer's furniture became identified with the Bauhaus.

But the Bauhaus was much more than a furniture design operation. In 1919, Gropius was determined to break down the barriers between the crafts and the fine arts, and to rescue each from its isolation by training craftspeople, painters, and sculptors to work on cooperative ventures. There was, Gropius said, "no essential difference" between the crafts and the fine arts. There were no "teachers," either; there were only "masters, journeymen, and apprentices." All of this led to what Gropius believed was the one place where all of the media could interact and all of the arts work cooperatively together. "The ultimate aim of all creative activity," Gropius declared, "is the building," and the name of the school itself is derived from the German words for building (*Bau*) and house (*Haus*).

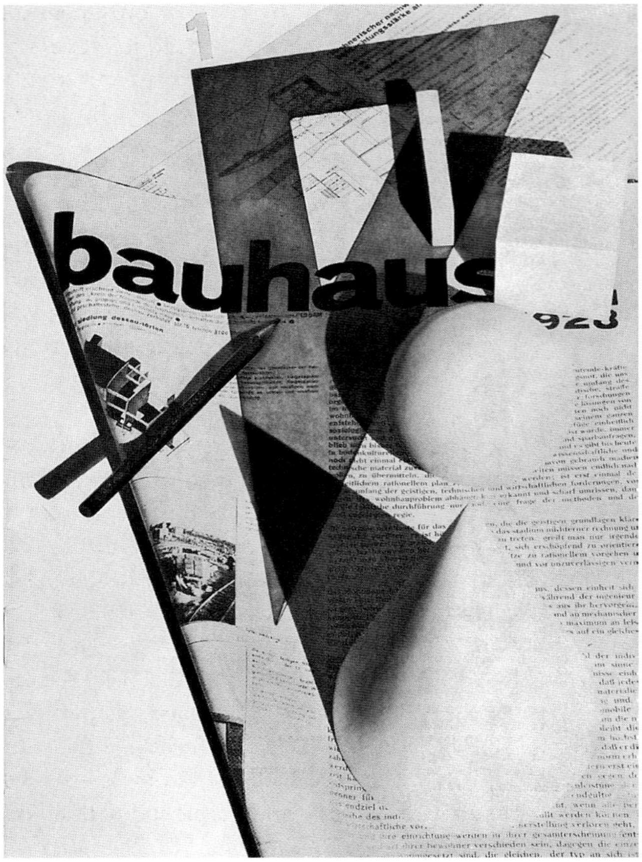

Fig. 15-22 Herbert Bayer, Cover for *Bauhaus 1*, 1928.
Photomontage. Bauhaus–Archiv, Berlin.
Photo: Bauhaus–Archiv, Berlin. © 2015 Artists Rights Society (ARS), New York/VG Bild-Kunst, Bonn.

We can understand Gropius's goals if we look at Herbert Bayer's design for the cover of the first issue of *Bauhaus* magazine, which was published in 1928 (**Fig. 15-22**). Each of the three-dimensional forms—cube, sphere, and cone—casts a two-dimensional shadow. The design is marked by the letterforms Bayer employs in the masthead. This is Bayer's Universal Alphabet, which he created to eliminate what he believed to be needless typographical flourishes, including capital letters. Bayer, furthermore, constructed the image in the studio and then photographed it, relying on mechanical reproduction instead of the handcrafted, highly individualistic medium of drawing. The pencil and triangle suggest that any drawing to be done is mechanical drawing, governed by geometry and mathematics. Finally, the story on the cover of the first issue of *Bauhaus* is concerned with architecture—to Gropius, the ultimate creative activity.

Streamlining and Organic Design, 1930–60

What was the appeal of streamlining and how did designers after World War II continue in the direction of organic design?

Even as the geometry of the machine began to dominate design, finding particular favor among the architects of the International Style (see Chapter 14), in the ebb and flow between the organic and the geometric that dominates design history, the organic began to flow back into the scene as a result of advances in scientific knowledge. In 1926, the Daniel Guggenheim Fund for the Promotion of Aeronautics granted $2.5 million to the Massachusetts Institute of Technology, the California Institute of Technology, the University of Michigan, and New York University to build wind tunnels. Designers quickly discovered that by eliminating extraneous detail on the surface of a plane, boat, automobile, or train, and by rounding its edges so that each subform merged into the next by means of smooth transitional curves, air would flow smoothly across the surface of the machine. Drag would thereby be dramatically reduced, and the machine could move faster with less expenditure of energy. "Streamlining" became the transportation cry of the day.

The nation's railroads were quickly redesigned to take advantage of this new technological information. Since a standard train engine would expend 350 horsepower more than a streamlined one operating at top speed, at 70 to 110 m.p.h., streamlining would increase pulling capacity by 12 percent. It was clearly economical for the railroads to streamline.

At just after 5 o'clock on the morning of May 26, 1934, a brand-new streamlined train called the Burlington *Zephyr* (**Fig. 15-23**) departed Union Station in Denver bound for Chicago. Normally, the 1,015-mile trip

Fig. 15-23 Burlington Northern Co., *Zephyr #9900*, 1934.
© Bettmann/CORBIS. Photo: Philip Gendreau.

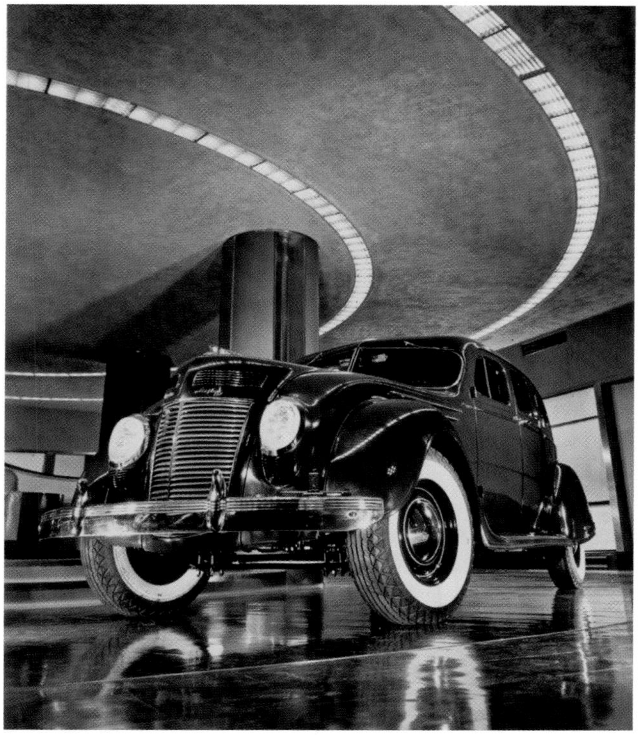

Fig. 15-24 ***Chrysler Salon, N. Y. C.*****, showing the 1937 Chrysler** ***Airflow*** **four-door sedan on display in the Chrysler Building, New York City, 1937.**
Library of Congress, Washington, D.C.
Inv. LC-USZC4-4839. Photo: F. S. Lincoln. Courtesy of Library of Congress Prints and Photographs Division Washington, D.C. 20540.

took 26 hours, but this day, averaging 77.61 miles per hour and reaching a top speed of 112 miles per hour, the *Zephyr* arrived in Chicago in a mere 13 hours and 5 minutes. The total fuel cost for the haul, at 5¢ per gallon, was only $14.64. When the train arrived later that same evening at the Century of Progress Exposition on the Chicago lakefront, it was mobbed by a wildly enthusiastic public. If the railroad was enthralled by the streamlined train's efficiency, the public was captivated by its speed. It was, in fact, through the mystique of speed that the Burlington Railroad meant to recapture dwindling passenger revenues. Ralph Budd, president of the railroad, deliberately chose not to paint the *Zephyr*'s stainless-steel sheath. To him it signified "the motif of speed" itself.

But the *Zephyr* was more than its sheath. It weighed one-third less than a conventional train, and its center of gravity was so much lower that it could take curves at 60 miles per hour that a normal train could only negotiate at 40. Because regular welding techniques severely damaged stainless steel, engineers had invented and patented an electric welding process to join its stainless-steel parts. All in all, the train became the symbol of a new age. After its trips to Chicago, it traveled more than 30,000 miles, visiting 222 communities. Well over 2 million people paid a dime each to tour it, and millions more viewed it from the outside. Late in the year, it became the feature attraction of a new film, *The Silver Streak*, a somewhat improbable drama about a high-speed train commandeered to deliver iron lungs to a disease-stricken Nevada town.

Wind-tunnel testing had revealed that the ideal streamlined form most closely resembled a teardrop. A long train could hardly achieve such a shape—at best it resembled a snake. But the automobile offered other possibilities. The first production-model streamlined car was the Chrysler *Airflow* (**Fig. 15-24**), which abandoned the teardrop ideal and adopted the look of the new streamlined trains. The man who inspired Chrysler to develop the automobile was Norman Bel Geddes. Bel Geddes was a poster and theatrical designer when he began experimenting, in the late 1920s, with the design of planes, boats, automobiles, and trains—things he thought of as "more vitally akin to life today than the theatre." After the stock market crash in 1929, his staff of 20 engineers, architects, and draftsmen found themselves with little or nothing to do, so Bel Geddes turned them loose on a series of imaginative projects, including the challenge to dream up some way to transport "a thousand luxury lovers from New York to Paris fast. Forget the limitations." The specific result was his *Air Liner Number 4* (**Fig. 15-25**), designed with the assistance of Dr. Otto Koller, a veteran airplane designer. With a wingspan of 528 feet, Bel Geddes estimated that it could carry 451 passengers and 115 crew members from Chicago to London in 42 hours. Its passenger decks included a dining room, game deck, solarium, barber shop and beauty salon, nursery, and private suites for all

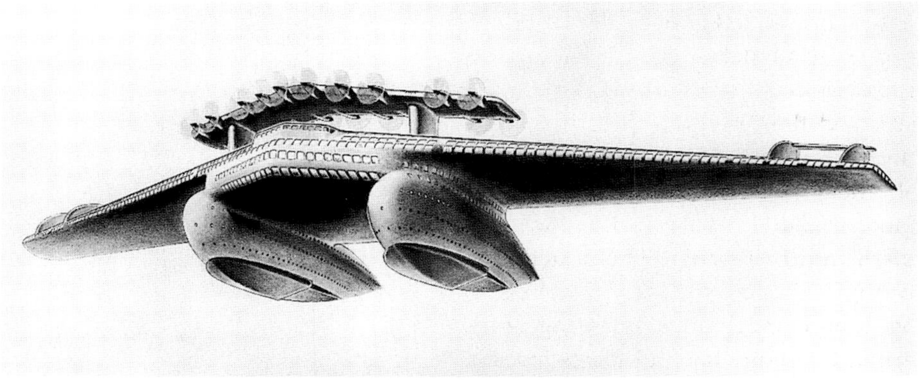

Fig. 15-25 Norman Bel Geddes, with Dr. Otto Koller, ***Air Liner Number 4*****, 1929.** Harry Ransom Humanities Research Center, The University of Texas at Austin.
Norman Bel Geddes Collection, Theatre Arts Collection. Courtesy of Edith Lutyens and Norman Bel Geddes Foundation, Inc.

on board. Among the crew were a nursemaid, a physician, a masseuse and a masseur, wine stewards, waiters, and an orchestra.

Although Bel Geddes insisted that the plane could be built, it was the theatricality and daring of the proposal that really captured the imagination of the American public. Bel Geddes was something of a showman. In November 1932, he published a book entitled *Horizons* that included most of the experimental designs he and his staff had been working on since the stock market collapse. It was wildly popular. And its popularity prompted Chrysler to go forward with the *Airflow*. Walter P. Chrysler hired Bel Geddes to coordinate publicity for the new automobile. In one ad, Bel Geddes himself, tabbed "America's foremost industrial designer," was the spokesman, calling the *Airflow* "the first sincere and authentic streamlined car . . . the first real motor car." Despite this, the car was not a success. Though it drew record orders after its introduction in January 1934, the company failed to reach full production before April, by which time many orders had been withdrawn, and serious production defects were evident in those cars the company did manage to get off the line. The *Airflow* attracted more than 11,000 buyers in 1934, but in 1937 only 4,600 were sold, and Chrysler dropped the model.

However, streamlining had caught on, and other designers quickly joined the rush. One of the most successful American designers, Raymond Loewy, declared that streamlining was "the perfect interpretation of the modern beat." To Russel Wright, the designer of the tableware illustrated here (**Fig. 15-26**), streamlining captured the "American character." It was the essence of a "distinct American design." And it seemed as if almost everything, from pencil sharpeners to vacuum cleaners to meat slicers (**Fig. 15-27**), had to be streamlined. To be modern was to be streamlined. Even more important, to be streamlined was to be distinctly American in style. Thus, to be

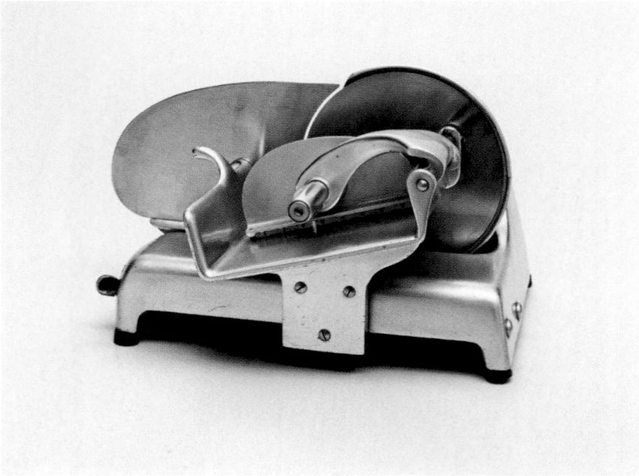

Fig. 15-27 Theodore C. Brookhart and Egmont Arens, "Streamliner" Meat Slicer, Model 410, 1940. Manufactured by Hobart Manufacturing Co. Aluminum, steel, rubber, 13 × 21¼ × 16½ in. Museum of Modern Art, New York.
Gift of Eric Brill in memory of Abbie Hoffman, 99.1989. © 2015. Digital image, Museum of Modern Art, New York/Scala, Florence.

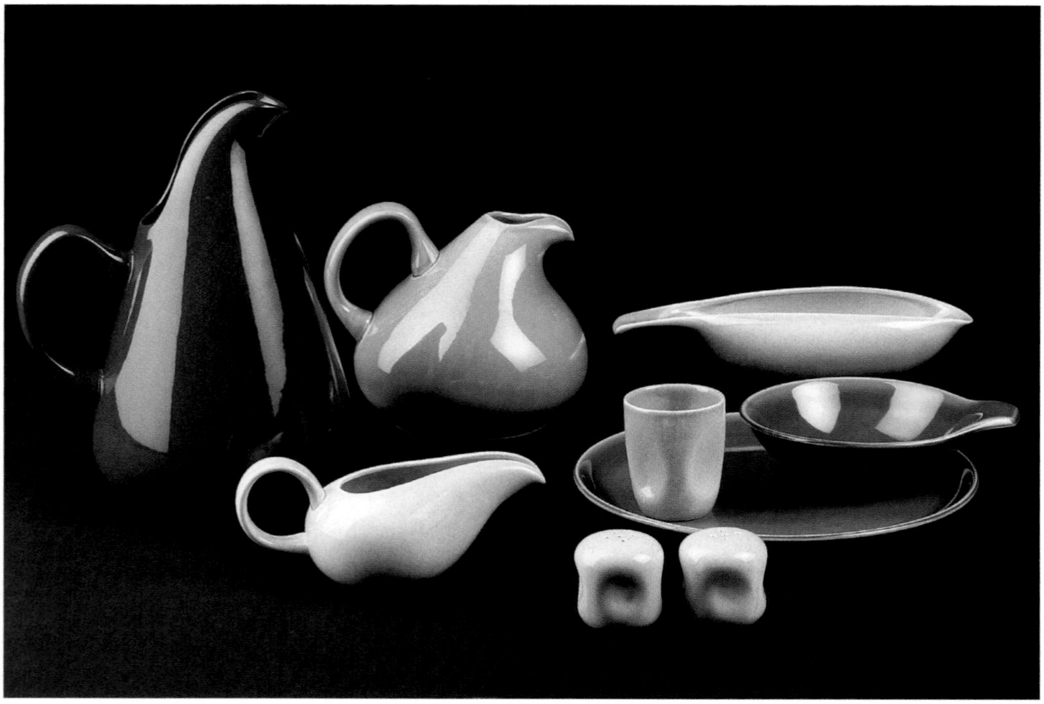

Fig. 15-26 Russel Wright, American Modern dinnerware, designed 1937, introduced 1939. Glazed earthenware. Syracuse University Library, New York.
Russel Wright Papers, Special Collections Research Center.

Fig. 15-28 General Motors, Cadillac Fleetwood, 1959.
Photo: General Motors Media Archives.

modern was to be American, an equation that dominated industrial and product design worldwide through at least the 1960s, until Japanese industrial design began to dominate, especially in the electronics industry.

The end of World War II heralded an explosion of new American design, particularly attributable to the rapid expansion of the economy, as 12 million military men and women were demobilized. New home starts rose from about 200,000 in 1945 to 1,154,000 in 1950. These homes had to be furnished, and new products were needed to do the job. Passenger-car production soared from 70,000 a year in 1945 to 6,665,000 in 1950, and, in the following ten years, Americans built and sold more than 58 million automobiles. The fully organic forms of streamlining had announced a major shift in direction away from design dominated by the right angle and toward a looser, more curvilinear style, and many of the new cars soon sported fins, suggesting both that they moved as gracefully as fish and that their streamlined speed was so great that they needed stabilizers (**Fig. 15-28**). The fins were, in fact, inspired by the tail fins on the U.S. Air Force's P-38 "Lightning" fighter plane (**Fig. 15-29**), which Harley Earl, chief stylist at General Motors, had seen during the war. He designed them into the 1948 Cadillac as an aerodynamic symbol. But by 1959, when the craze hit its peak, fins no longer had anything to do with aerodynamics. As the Cadillac made clear, it had simply become a matter of "the bigger, the better." And, in many ways, the Cadillac's excess defines American style in the 1950s. This was the decade that brought the world fast food (both the McDonald's hamburger and the TV dinner), Las Vegas, *Playboy* magazine, and a TV in almost every home.

In 1940, before the war, which in effect halted all product development in the United States, the Museum of Modern Art in New York held a competition titled "Organic Design in Home Furnishings." The first prize was awarded jointly to Charles Eames and Eero Saarinen, both young instructors at the Cranbrook Academy of Art in Michigan. Under the direction of the architect Eliel Saarinen, Eero's father, Cranbrook was similar in many respects to the Bauhaus, especially in terms of its

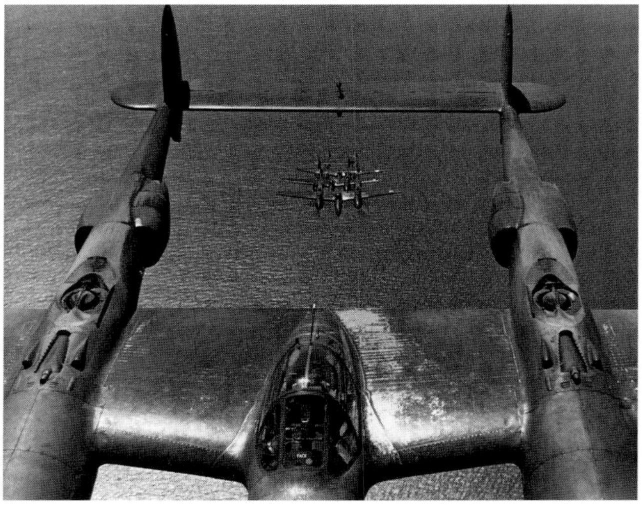

Fig. 15-29 Four Lockheed P-38 Lightning fighters in formation, ca. 1942–45.
© Museum of Flight/Corbis.

Fig. 15-30 Charles and Ray Eames, Side Chair, Model DCM, 1946. Molded walnut-veneered plywood, steel rods, and rubber shock mounts, height 25⅝ in., width 17⅜ in., depth 22¼ in. Museum of Modern Art, New York.

Gift of Herman Miller Furniture, 156.1973. © 2015. Digital image, Museum of Modern Art, New York/Scala, Florence.

emphasis on interdisciplinary work on architectural environments. It was, however, considerably more open to experiment and innovation than the Bauhaus, and the Eames/Saarinen entry in the Museum of Modern Art competition was the direct result of the elder Saarinen encouraging his young staff to rethink entirely just what furniture should be.

All of the furniture submitted to the show by Eames and Saarinen used molded plywood shells in which the wood veneers were laminated to layers of glue. The resulting forms almost demand to be seen from more than a single point of view. "The problem," as Saarinen said of the chair, "becomes a sculptural one." The furniture was very strong, comfortable, and reasonably priced. Because of the war, production and distribution were necessarily limited, but, in 1946, the Herman Miller Company made 5,000 units of a chair Eames designed with his wife, Ray Eames, also a Cranbrook graduate (**Fig. 15-30**). Instantly popular and still in production today, the chair consists of two molded-plywood forms that float on elegantly simple steel rods. The effect is amazingly dynamic: The back panel has been described as "a rectangle about to turn into an oval," and the seat almost seems to have molded itself to the sitter in advance.

Eero Saarinen, who would later design the TWA Terminal at John F. Kennedy International Airport (see Figs. 14-42 and 14-43), took the innovations he and Eames had made in the "Organic Design in Home Furnishings" competition in a somewhat different direction. Unlike Eames, who in his 1946 chair had clearly abandoned the notion of the one-piece unit as impractical, Saarinen continued to seek a more unified design approach, feeling that it was more economical to stamp furniture from a single piece of material in a machine. His *Tulip Pedestal* furniture (**Fig. 15-31**)—a design that quickly found its place in the new "patio" culture of the 1950s—is one of his most successful solutions. Saarinen had planned to make the pedestal chair entirely out of plastic, in keeping with his unified approach, but he discovered that a plastic stem would not take the necessary strain. Forced, as a result, to make the base out of cast aluminum, he painted

Fig. 15-31 Eero Saarinen, *Tulip Pedestal* furniture, 1955–57. Chairs: plastic seat, painted metal base; tables: wood or marble top, plastic laminate base.

Courtesy of Knoll Inc.

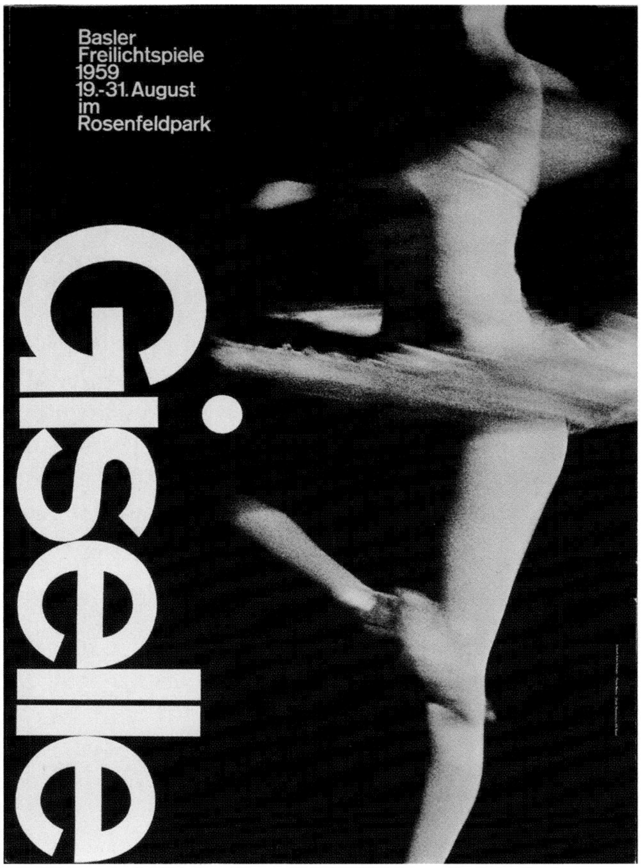

Fig. 15-32 Armin Hofmann, Poster for *Giselle, Basler Freilichtspiele*, 1959. Photolithograph, 4 ft. 2¼ in. × 35½ in. Printed at Wassermann A. G., Basel. Museum of Modern Art, New York. Gift of the designer, 330.1963. © 2015. Digital image, Museum of Modern Art, New York/Scala, Florence.

it the same color as the plastic in order to make the chair at least appear uniform throughout.

But the unity of the design image so valued by Saarinen was almost simultaneously being challenged by the Swiss graphic designer Armin Hofmann, whose practice as both a teacher at the Basel School of Arts and Crafts and as the designer of numerous posters for cultural clients would influence the next generation of graphic designers, in both the United States and Europe, perhaps more than any other. Like Herbert Bayer before him (see Fig. 15-22), he freely incorporated photographs into his poster designs. Like Saarinen, whose *Tulip Pedestal* furniture evoked the backyard garden just as his TWA air terminal evoked a wing, Hofmann placed his emphasis on finding a symbolic form or image appropriate to the content that his posters were trying to convey. The poster for the ballet *Giselle* (**Fig. 15-32**), for instance, immediately conveys the idea of dance. It does this through the studied contrast between light and dark, between the blurred, turning form of the dancer and the static clarity of the type, and between, finally, the geometry of the design and the organic movement of the body. By these means, Hofmann arrives at a synthesis of the competing stylistic forces at work in the history of modern design—the organic and curvilinear versus the geometric and linear.

Design Since 1980

How did the design profession react to the rise of numerous and diverse markets in the late twentieth century?

One way to view the evolution of design since 1960 is to recognize a growing tendency to accept the tensions between the organic and the geometric, and the natural and the mechanical, that dominate its history as not so much an either/or situation but as a question of both/and. In its unification of competing and contrasting elements, the Eames chair, with its contrasting steel-support structure and molded-plywood seat and back, is the forerunner of this trend.

The contemporary has been marked by a willingness to incorporate anything and everything into a given design. This is not simply a question of the organic versus the geometric. It is, even more, a question of the collisions of competing cultures of an almost incomprehensible diversity and range. On our shrinking globe, united by television and the telephone, by the fax machine and the copier, email, and the Internet, and especially by increasingly interdependent economies, we are learning to accept, perhaps faster than we realize, a plurality of styles.

This tendency to embrace a plurality of styles stood, by the early 1980s, in direct contradiction to received wisdom about the necessity of "branding" and maintaining a uniform corporate identity. As much as its product has changed over the years, from the Model T at the start of the twentieth century to the Model A in the 1930s, and, after the war, the Fairlaine, the Thunderbird, and the Mustang, to say nothing of trucks and, more recently, SUVs, Ford's logo (**Fig. 15-33**) has remained virtually the same (although in

Fig. 15-33 The Ford logo on display at the 2009 New York International Auto Show, Jacob Javits Center, New York. © Ramin Talaie/Corbis.

the mid-1900s it was supplanted by model logos for a period of time). Originally created in 1903 by Ford executive Childe Harold Wills from his own business cards, it is rendered in Spencerian script (also used in the Coca-Cola logo), a style of penmanship named for its creator, Platt Rogers Spencer, and widely taught in schools throughout the last half of the nineteenth century as a particularly clear and suitable cursive script for doing business. The blue oval shield was an addition of 1907.

There are many other corporate identity programs that share similar longevity—General Electric's Art Nouveau "GE," the CBS eye, Apple's apple. Such logos are designed to be recognized by the widest possible audience, but in the 1980s designers began to address "niche," or more narrowly specialized, groups. Television had recognized the possibility of successfully attracting a niche audience with the series *St. Elsewhere*, which aired from 1982 to 1988, but which had very low overall ratings, never higher than forty-ninth in the annual Nielsen ratings. Nevertheless, the show attracted large numbers of married, young, upper-middle-class professionals—yuppies—with enough disposable income to attract, in turn, major advertising accounts.

One of the first groups of designers to take advantage of this realization was the so-called Memphis Group in Milan, Italy, founded in December 1980 when Ettore Sottsass organized a meeting of designers to form a collaborative furniture manufacturing company. The name "Memphis" came from the fact that throughout that first meeting Bob Dylan's "Stuck Inside of Mobile with the Memphis Blues Again" played repeatedly throughout the meeting—"mobile," in Italian, means "furniture." One of those present, the architect Andrea Branzi, has described what motivated the new group's practice:

> Very briefly, the new situation at the sociological level can be outlined as follows. The vast mass markets, toward which design has always aspired, have disappeared. In their place, in this post-industrial scenario, we find numerous and diverse partial markets, concentrated around what Charles Jencks calls "semantic groups," new cultural sets that make up the society, traversing old social classes diagonally. . . . Today design is operating in a context that demands . . . merchandise capable of selecting its own user, not just able to promote itself generically to everyone.

The resulting "New Design" was, as a result, wildly eclectic. Its products deliberately challenged the limits and assumptions of "good taste." Although intended for a luxury market, Sottsass's "Carlton" Room Divider (**Fig. 15-34**) is a bookcase made of cheap,

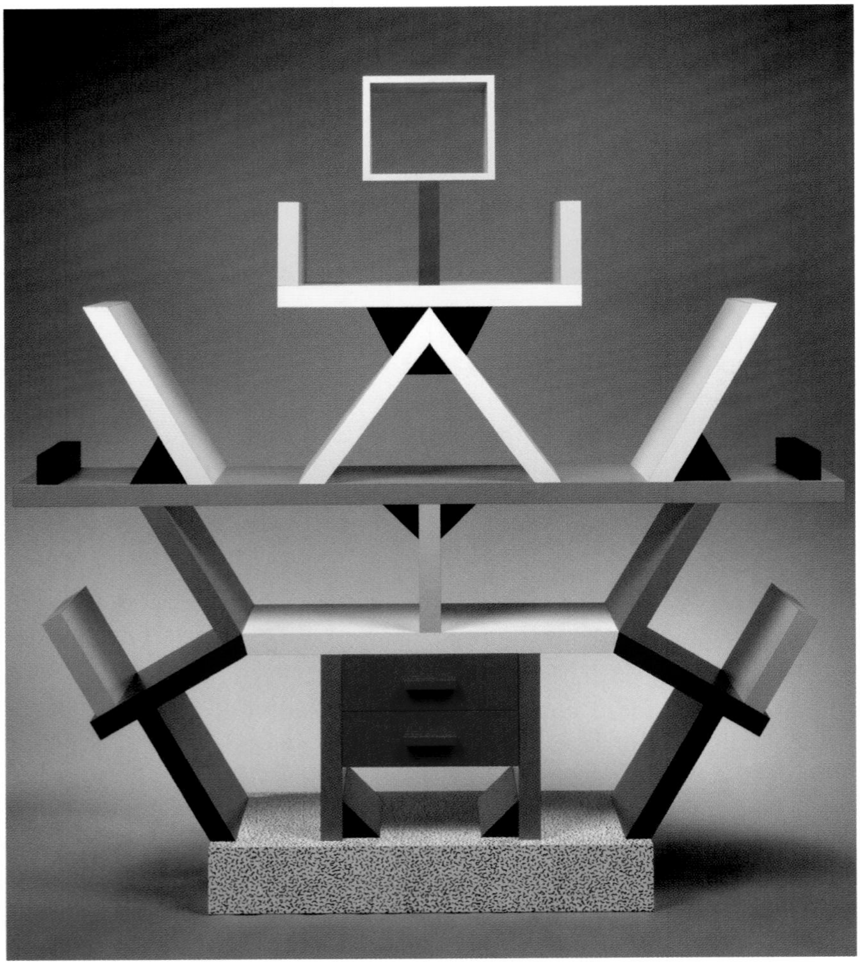

Fig. 15-34 Ettore Sottsass, "Carlton" Room Divider, 1981.
Manufacturer: Memphis Milano. Wood, plastic laminate, height 6 ft. 4¾ in., width 6 ft. 2¾ in., depth 15¾ in. Metropolitan Museum of Art, New York.
John C. Waddell Collection, Gift of John C. Waddell, 1997.460.1a-d. Image © Metropolitan Museum of Art/Art Resource/Scala, Florence © Ettore Sottsass © 2015 Artists Rights Society (ARS), New York/ADAGP, Paris.

brightly colored plastic laminates, in which books themselves would rest at odd, precarious-feeling angles. Yet, these angles are themselves part of an entirely simple structural system defined by real and implied equilateral triangles.

It seems hardly coincidental that almost simultaneously, in 1981, MTV first aired its ever-mutating company logo (**Fig. 15-35**), which made it abundantly clear that it was no longer necessary to standardize a corporate identity. MTV's instant success in fact suggested that it may not even be desirable. The logo was commissioned from Manhattan Design, a New York-based firm noted for its radical experimentation, and it was the brainchild of partners Pat Gorman and Frank Olinsky. The network's working name at the time was "The Music Channel," and Olinsky had initially sketched out a large sans-serif, three-dimensional "M" for the new network's logo. Gorman, however, felt that the "M" was too static and uninteresting so she wrote "tv" across its face in a kind of painterly scrawl. Almost immediately the designers realized that their logo could be almost infinitely altered through variations in color and pattern. In fact, it could become other objects—a birthday cake, a billboard, or a takeout carton of Chinese food. The two convinced the network finally to change its name to Music Television in order to accommodate the logo, and throughout the network's early years, a new logo appeared for ten seconds at the top of every hour.

Suddenly, the logo had a sort of life and personality. It was no longer static but animated. And it introduced to the design world the idea of motion graphics that would soon come to dominate cable television, video gaming, and computer animation. In fact, perhaps nothing transformed the design profession more than the computer itself (see *The Creative Process*, pp. 384–85, for a discussion of the work of April Greiman, a graphic designer who led the way in the computer revolution). Before the introduction of Apple Corporation's Macintosh

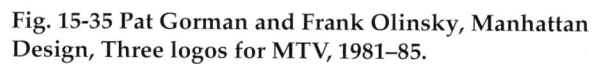

Fig. 15-35 Pat Gorman and Frank Olinsky, Manhattan Design, Three logos for MTV, 1981–85.

© 2014 Viacom International Inc. All Rights Reserved. MTV's "Logo" used with permission by MTV. ©2014 Viacom Media Networks. All Rights Reserved. MTV, all related titles, characters and logos are trademarks owned by Viacom Media Networks, a division of Viacom International Inc.

The Creative Process

April Greiman and Design Technology

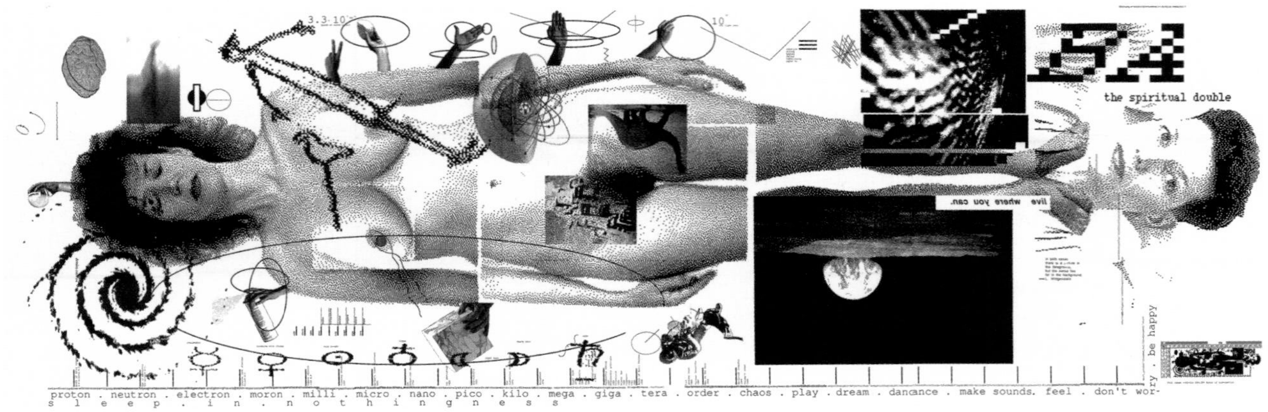

Fig. 15-36 April Greiman, *Does It Make Sense?*, 1985. *Design Quarterly* #133, Walker Art Center and MIT Press Publishers.

The design career of April Greiman—who studied, incidentally, with Armin Hofmann (see Fig. 15-32)—might best be looked at as a continual work-in-progress. Perhaps no other designer has more consistently recognized and utilized the possibilities offered by computer technologies for innovation in design, and, as these technologies have developed over the past 30 or 35 years, her design has developed with them.

Among her earliest works is a groundbreaking 1985 project comprising an entire issue of *Design Quarterly* entitled *Does It Make Sense?* (**Fig. 15-36**). The piece was composed and assembled as a single document on MacDraw—if not the first use in magazine production of this early vector-based drawing program, meaning that an object's properties and placement could be changed at any time, then certainly in 1985 by far the largest. The magazine unfolded into a life-size single-page self-portrait of a digitalized nude Greiman, measuring some 2 × 6 feet, surrounded by images of a dinosaur and Stonehenge (on each side of her pubis), the earth rising over a lunar horizon and a cirrus cloud (on her legs), a prehistoric cave painting (floating over her breast), a brain above her head, a spiral galaxy below it, across the top, mudralike hand gestures, and, across the bottom, astrological symbols. A timetable runs the length of the poster, marking the dates of such events as the invention of electricity, Greiman's birthday, and, at the bottom right, her poster/magazine issue itself, reproduced in miniature. All deeply personal images, they announced Greiman's belief that design should "think with the heart" and reach its audience on an emotional level.

As digital technologies have advanced into increasingly interactive modes of communication, Greiman's work has moved with them. An example is her innovative Web design, including the website of her own design consultancy, Made in Space (**Fig. 15-37**). By and large Web design is standardized. The most commonly repeated design elements include a logo in the upper left-hand corner of the page, a search box on the homepage, breadcrumbs listed horizontally, a shopping-cart link in the upper

Fig. 15-37 April Greiman, madeinspace.la website, screen capture, 2014. © 2015 April Greiman.

right-hand corner, and so on. As Greiman explains,

> *That's the thing about HTML, you can just copy all that code and paste it into your desktop and then just add your own images, it all looks very* templated. . . . *Part of it is you know you can make websites in Photoshop or in Illustrator, so everybody is doing that. But, to a certain extent, they are primitive technologies; in terms of the potential of what can be done. It's just repeating tasks and cut-and-paste and not really thinking. We are sort of subscribing then, to what engineers of the software have thought about this medium of communication. Because, keep in mind, designers like us are not designing the software. We're not writing code. We're just using the code.*

The Made in Space website (at madeinspace.la), to the contrary, consists of several semi-transparent screen images of the designer's studio that bleed into one another. As the user's cursor floats over the images various breadcrumbs come into and out of focus as they float in and out of the screen.

Greiman's innovative approach to design is further displayed in her 2001 book *Something from Nothing*. Her fascination with digital photography and masterful sense of exhibition design were evident in a 2006 exhibition, *Drive-by Shooting*, at the Pasadena Museum of California Art, in which low-resolution digital images were blown up to large scale, creating extraordinarily rich images and color palettes that were cantilevered from the wall (**Figs. 15-38** and **15-39**), involving the viewer in their almost dizzying sense of speed and motion (see the text-and-image video of the work at drive-byshooting.com). "With technology today," Greiman says, "we can float ideas, text, and images in time and space."

Figs. 15-38 and 15-39 April Greiman, *Guardrail to Sevilla*, 2006, and installation view of the exhibition *Drive-by Shooting: April Greiman Digital Photography*, Pasadena Museum of California Art, 2006. Digital photograph, 42 in. × 4 ft. 8 in.

Fig. 15-40 Apple Corporation, Macintosh computer, Cupertino, California, 1984.
Photo: malerapaso.

Fig. 15-41 Apple iPhone 3G, as displayed in Toronto, July 11, 2008.
© MARK BLINCH/Reuters/Corbis.

computer in 1984 (**Fig. 15-40**), most graphic design curricula emphasized the importance of craftsmanship and traditional drawing skills. But the Macintosh's Graphical User Interface (GUI), with its handheld mouse that transformed the screen into a desktop and the cursor into a pointer, together with the introduction of compatible software programs—at first MacWrite and MacPaint, but soon followed by Aldus Pagemaker, QuarkXPress and Adobe Photoshop, Illustrator, and InDesign—soon allowed for desktop publishing to become a reality, and computer-generated design began to be the focus of a generation of younger designers who worked in almost open defiance of mainstream design itself. The scanner and printer quickly supplanted the ruler, the Exacto knife, hand-drawn calligraphy, the drafting table, and the light box. The laborious pace of handcrafted design was replaced by the speed of electronic media. Speed, in turn, allowed for greater experimentation and freedom. And within a generation, computer-literate students had revolutionized the design processes that they had inherited from their professors, who in turn were forced to catch up with the students who were fast leaving them behind. By the start of the twenty-first century, the laptop was capable of performing at a level only realized in large mainframe environments ten years earlier, and by the end of the new century's first decade, the iPhone (**Fig. 15-41**) was capable of storing 66 GBs of data versus the original Macintosh's 64 KB—that is, roughly 64 million times as much.

Faster, smaller, more memory, and greater versatility—these have been the factors driving the design process of the computer industry over the last 30 years. In this context, an image can suddenly "go viral," as Shepard Fairey's poster of Barack Obama did during the 2008 election campaign (**Fig. 15-42**). Fairey was a skateboard artist and trained graphic designer who first achieved notoriety in 1989 with a street sticker campaign, *Andre the Giant Has a Posse*. Inspired by Barack Obama's 2008 presidential campaign, Fairey designed and distributed the Obama *Hope* poster, at first without authorization of a campaign staff nervous about a street artist's participation in grassroots electioneering. But when all was said and done, Fairey had distributed over 300,000 stickers and 500,000 posters, and Obama had officially written to thank him for his work. "Your images have a profound effect on people, whether seen in a gallery or on a stop sign," the President wrote. Such a convergence of street art and high art is almost completely a function of the mass distribution of idea and image on

Fig. 15-42 Shepard Fairey, Barack Obama *Hope* poster, 2008. Screenprint, 36 × 24 in.
Photo flab/Alamy. © Shepard Fairey/ObeyGiant.com.

the Internet. And it challenges notions of copyright and ownership as well. In fact, Associated Press photographer Mannie Garcia sued Fairey for copying his photograph of the President. The case was settled out of court.

The new computer-based design makes it possible to create imagery that might be used in a variety of media contexts. English graphic designer Chris Ede's illustration for the iTunes App store for Clear Channel (**Fig. 15-43**) digitally blends hand-drawn and photographic representations of sports and music—the two main focuses of his client. The piece works both as a still, one-frame image, as illustrated here, and as an animated Web banner (for the iheartradio section of their website), in which music flows from the speaker flower with iPhone petals in abstract colorful waves carrying the various graphic elements of the design. The desire of Ede's client for an image that can, as it were, transform itself from still into movement speaks to a change not only in design but in the very way we conceive of the human imagination. As the image increasingly manifests itself as no longer static but moving—in the video and film arts as well as Web design—perhaps the ways in which we think and create are changing as well.

Fig. 15-43 Chris Ede, Illustration for Clear Channel Online Music & Radio, 2008.
Josh Klenert, creative director.
Courtesy of Chris Ede.

THE CRITICAL PROCESS

Thinking about Design

In 1964, the Herman Miller Company, who first produced and distributed the Eames side chair in 1946 (see Fig. 15-30), introduced what it called the Action Office, the first iteration of what would develop before the end of the decade into the modular and customizable system of semi-enclosed cubicles that remains the standard design of office space to this day. By 1998, 40 million office workers in the U.S. alone were working in 42 different versions of Herman Miller's Action Office.

The Action Office was the brainchild of graphic designer and sculptor, Robert Propst, who became president of Herman Miller Research Corp. in 1960. As Propst put it in a 1964 Herman Miller brochure: "Today's office is a wasteland. It saps vitality, blocks talent, frustrates accomplishment. It is the daily scene of unfulfilled intentions and failed efforts." His 1968 book *The Office: A Facility Based on Change* promoted the cubicle as the answer to these woes. He believed that as each worker adapted the space to his or her individual needs, efficiency, productivity, and creativity would blossom. In a 1974 Herman Miller promotional film for the Action Office that concludes the art21 *New York Close Up* segment "Mika Tajima Versus the Cubicle," a secretary works away in her properly personalized cubicle as the narrator sums up the company's vision: "She needs decor, color, warmth, vitality, and something as basic and all-inclusive as dignity. She's an action secretary! And she needs Action Office!"

In 2010, the focus of the art21 film, Mika Tajima found 26 Action Office wall panels dating from 1971 for sale at a telemarketing office in Bayonne, New Jersey, and purchased them to use as "readymades" in a sculptural installation named after Propst's book and meant to underscore the bleak realities of the dehumanizing work spaces that Propst's modernist aesthetic created (**Fig. 15-44**). She created enclosed cubes, non-functioning cubicles that no one can enter (or, if somehow trapped inside, leave), metaphors for the confinement and isolation of the modern office itself. The fabric on a number of the Action Office panels was worn thin and torn. Tajima replaced the original fabric with canvas and painted the panels as monochrome, pseudo-Minimalist paintings of the 1960s and 1970s which, in the Minimalist artists' confidence that they were producing works of timeless beauty and eloquence, parallel the utopian vision of Propst and Herman Miller in their belief that they were creating a truly ideal, rather than dysfunctional, work space.

Tajima's critique of modernist design implicitly valorizes a different kind of design. What do you think that would be? Would it surprise you to discover that Tajima finds the idea of manufactured products and "beauty" to be somewhat at odds? Why might she feel this way? How do Knoll's new Toboggan office furnishings (see Fig. 15-1) and the Action Office compare?

Fig. 15-44 Mika Tajima, *A Facility Based on Change*, 2011. Panels, canvas, acrylic, silkscreen, paper, pins, clips, Balans chair, dimensions variable. Courtesy of the artist.

Thinking Back

15.1 Describe how the Arts and Crafts Movement and Art Nouveau gave rise to design as a profession.

The people who first began, in the 1920s, to call themselves "designers" were seen as serving industry. In fact, design is so intimately tied to industry that its origins as a profession can be traced back only to the beginnings of the industrial age. What was the role of Morris & Co. in furthering the design movement? How did Art Nouveau reflect Morris's ideas?

15.2 Explain how modernist avant-garde movements impacted the design profession.

Art Deco designers sought to give expression to everyday life in the twentieth century. They tended to prefer up-to-date materials such as chrome, steel, and Bakelite plastic. Movement toward the geometric, reflecting the impact of Cubism, is perhaps the defining characteristic of Art Deco. How does Eduardo Benito's 1929 cover of *Vogue* reflect the impulses of Art Deco? How did fashion express the interests of Art Deco? How did Le Corbusier's *Pavillon de l'Esprit Nouveau* at the 1925 Art Deco Exposition in Paris reflect the art of avant-garde groups such as Dutch De Stijl and Russian Constructivism?

The artists of De Stijl simplified the vocabulary of art and design, employing only the primary colors—red, yellow, and blue—plus black and white. Their designs relied on vertical and horizontal grids and compositions that seemed to open to the surrounding space. How does Gerrit Rietveld go against the traditional elements of the armchair in his *Red and Blue Chair*?

How did typography come to reflect these same tendencies? If Le Corbusier claimed that a house "is a machine for living," how did the Bauhaus artists reflect this same spirit?

15.3 Discuss the appeal of streamlining and the ways in which the organic continued to influence design after World War II.

Streamlining is a direct response to the growing importance of speed—in the transportation industry in particular—in modern culture, and it seemed to many to embody the very idea of the modern. As designer Raymond Loewy put it, streamlining was "the perfect interpretation of the modern beat." How were the organic lines of the streamlined train or automobile realized in the furniture design of Charles and Ray Eames? Or in Eero Saarinen's?

15.4 Explain how the rise of numerous and diverse markets in the late twentieth century impacted design.

In an increasingly united world in the age of the Internet, we are exposed to a plurality of styles, and as a society, we are learning to accept this. The social condition of plurality has increasingly led to designers focusing on widely diverse "niche" markets. How does the MTV logo reflect this condition? How does it compare to the Ford automobile logo? How did the Memphis Group respond to this situation? What has been the impact of computer technologies on the design profession?

Maurice Jarnoux, ***André Malraux preparing*** **Le Musée Imaginaire, 1947**.
Maurice Jarnoux/Paris Match via Getty Images.

Part 4

The Visual Record

Placing the Arts in Historical Context

In 1947, the French intellectual André Malraux came to recognize how photography might make possible what he called, in French, a *musée imaginaire*, an "imaginary museum," or, as the title of the book in English had it, a *Museum Without Walls*. Before photography, one might visit the Louvre in Paris or the Uffizi in Florence, study the great works of art in their galleries, and memorize what one saw as best one could. But photography made a great many more works available to the lover of art, and made it possible, furthermore, to compare them. In a real sense, photography made art history possible. But at some cost:

> In our Museum Without Walls, picture, fresco, miniature, and stained-glass window seem of one and the same family. For all alike—miniatures, frescoes, stained glass, tapestries, Scythian plaques, pictures, Greek vase paintings, "details" and even statuary—have become "color plates." In the process they have lost their properties as objects. . . . [I]n reproduction [they] lose both their original significance as objects and their function (religious or other).

Of course, museums fashioned this same transformation on the objects they housed. They removed them from the context in which they were made (religious or other), and placed them next to one another in the new sacred space of the gallery. If it is the task of art history to restore for the viewer some sense of the object's original significance, the proliferation of images that Malraux's Museum Without Walls envisions makes the art historian's task that much more urgent.

For Malraux's Museum Without Walls is in many ways the forebear of the digital archives that are today made available to viewers by museums and other art websites around the world—a virtual museum without walls consisting of literally hundreds of thousands of images. If Malraux faced an enormous task in arranging the images for his Museum Without Walls, covering the floor of his apartment with photograph after photograph, today the task of arranging the images we find on the Internet is more daunting yet. But the manner in which we organize these images remains the same as it was even before the invention of photography, let alone the rise of the digital archive. We organize images in roughly two ways—historically and culturally or thematically. The chapters that follow represent an historical and cultural organization of art objects. They are designed to help you place the works of art so far discussed in *A World of Art*—and others you might find on the Internet—into a broader historical and cultural context.

Chapter 16
The Ancient World

Learning Objectives

16.1 Describe some ways in which prehistoric art reflects the social aspirations of early peoples.

16.2 Discuss the relationship between the gods and the people in Mesopotamian art.

16.3 Account for the stability of Egyptian art and culture.

16.4 Describe the growing technological sophistication of the river valley societies of India and China.

16.5 Explain the large size of so many artworks and cultural sites in the Americas.

16.6 Differentiate between Minoan and Mycenaean culture and describe how the Greek *polis* and its art differ from its Aegean predecessors.

16.7 Discuss how the art and architecture of Rome suggest the empire's power.

16.8 Compare and contrast Chinese militarism with Buddhist pacifism.

On a cold December afternoon in 1994, Jean-Marie Chauvet and two friends were exploring the caves in the steep cliffs along the Ardèche River gorge in southern France. After descending into a series of narrow passages, they entered a large chamber. There, beams from their headlamps lit up a group of drawings that would astonish the three explorers—and the world (**Fig. 16-1**). Most remarkably, the artists responsible for making them seem to have understood and practiced a kind of perspectival drawing—that is, they were able to convey a sense of three-dimensional space on a two-dimensional surface. In the painting reproduced here, several horses appear to stand one behind the other. The head of the top horse overlaps a black line, as if peering over a branch or the back of another animal. In no other cave yet discovered do drawings show the use of shading, or modeling, so that the horses' heads seem to have volume and dimension. And yet these cave paintings, rendered over 30,000 years ago, predate other cave paintings by at least 10,000 years, and in some cases by as much as 20,000 years.

Since the late nineteenth century, we have known that prehistoric peoples—peoples who lived before the time of writing and so of recorded history—drew on the walls of caves. The Chauvet Cave, as it has come to be known, may have served as some sort of ritual space, in which a rite or ceremony is habitually practiced by a group, often in a religious or quasi-religious context. The cave, for instance, might be understood as a gateway to the underworld and death, or as a symbol of the womb and birth. The general arrangement of the animals in the paintings by species or gender, often in distinct areas of the cave, suggests to some that

120,000 BCE

Modern humans begin world migration
100,000 BCE

Cave paintings in France and Spain
30,000 BCE

120,000 BCE
Modern humans emerge in Africa

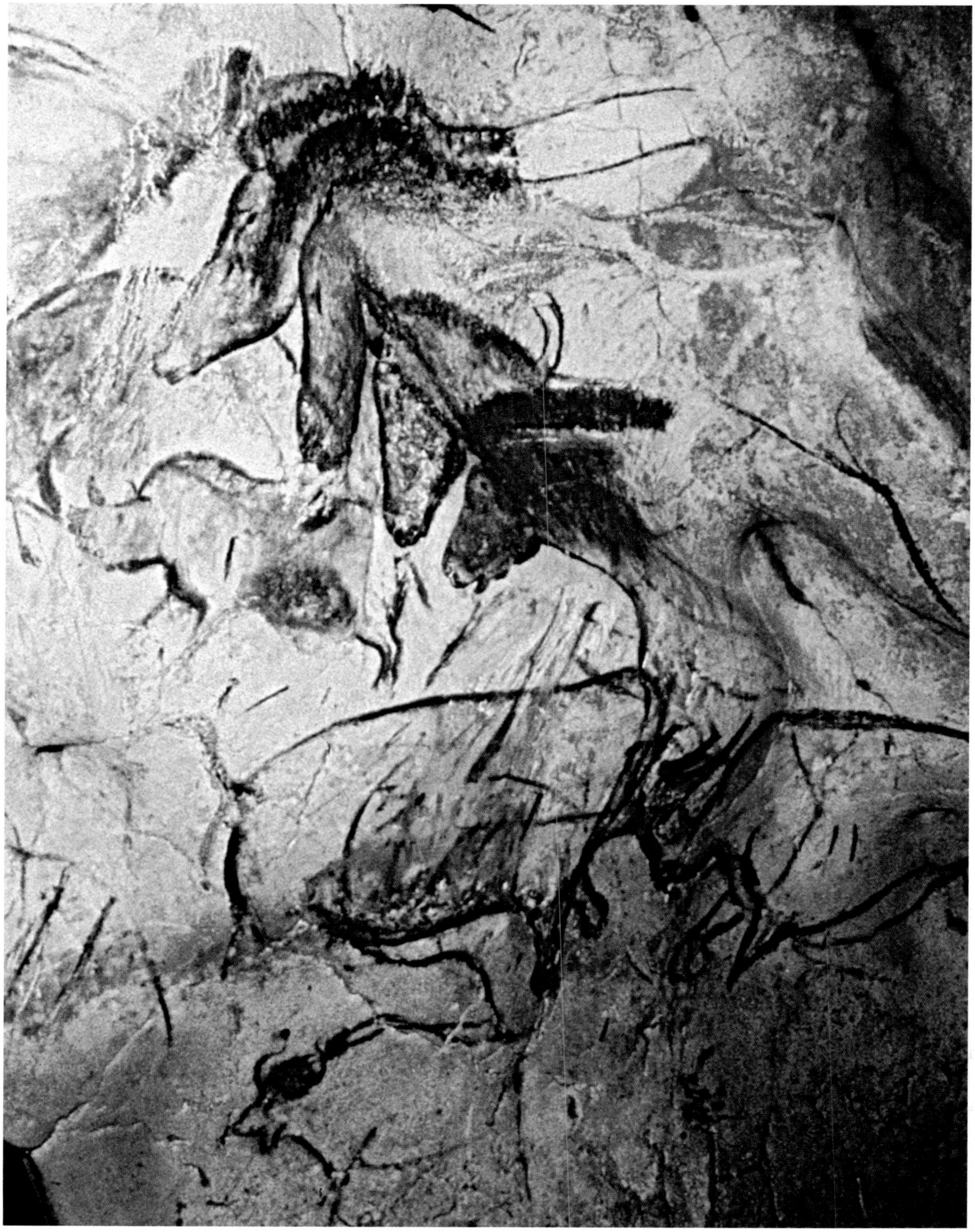

Fig. 16-1 Wall painting with horses, Chauvet Cave, Vallon-Pont-d'Arc, Ardèche gorge, France, ca. 30,000 BCE. Paint on limestone, height approx. 6 ft.

Ministère de la Culture et de la Communication. Direction Régionale des Affaires Culturelles de Rhône-Alpes. Service Régional de l'Archéologie/akg-images.

the paintings may have served as lunar calendars for predicting the seasonal migration of the animals. Whatever the case, surviving human footprints indicate that the cave was a ritual gathering place and in some way served the common good.

From the earliest times, people have gathered together in just such cooperative ventures. As these groups become more and more sophisticated, we call them **civilizations**—social, economic, and political entities distinguished by their ability to express themselves through images and, later, written language. This chapter outlines the rise of civilizations up through the Roman Empire.

The Earliest Art

How do prehistoric artworks reflect the social aspirations of the earliest peoples?

Besides cave paintings, early artists also created sculptural objects—small carved figures of people (mostly women) and animals. These reflect a more abstract and less naturalistic approach to representation, as illustrated in a limestone statuette of a woman found at Willendorf, in modern Austria (**Fig. 16-2**). (Archeologists originally named it the *Venus* of Willendorf, but its makers obviously had no knowledge of the Roman goddess.) Here, the breasts, belly, and genitals are exaggerated and the face lacks defining features, suggesting a connection to fertility and child-bearing. We know, too, that the figurine was originally painted in red ocher, symbolic of menses. And her navel is not carved; rather, it is a natural indentation in the stone. Whoever carved her seems to have recognized, in the raw stone, a connection to the origins of life. But such figures may have served other purposes as well. Perhaps they were dolls, guardian figures, or images of beauty in a cold, hostile world, where having body fat might have made the difference between survival and death.

Fig. 16-2 *Woman* (formerly a.k.a. the *Venus of Willendorf*), Lower Austria, ca. 25,000–20,000 BCE. Limestone, height 4½ in. Naturhistorisches Museum, Vienna.
akg-image/Erich Lessing.

As the Ice Age waned, around 8000 BCE, humans began to domesticate animals and cultivate food grains, practices that started in the Middle East and spread slowly across Greece and Europe for the next 6,000 years, reaching Britain last. Agriculture also developed in the southern part of China and spread to Japan and Southeast Asia; it arose independently in the Americas; and in Africa, herding, fishing, and farming communities dotted the continent. Gradually, Neolithic—or New Stone Age—peoples abandoned temporary shelters for permanent structures built of wood, brick, and stone. Religious rituals were regularized in shrines dedicated to that purpose. Crafts—pottery and weaving, in particular—began to flourish.

The Neolithic cultures that flourished along the banks of the Yellow River in China beginning in about 5000 BCE also produced large quantities of pottery (**Fig. 16-3**). These cultures were based on growing rice

Fig. 16-3 Basin, Majiayao culture, Majiayao phase, Gansu province, China, ca. 3000–2700 BCE. Earthenware with painted decoration, diameter 11 in. Metropolitan Museum of Art, New York.
Anonymous Loan, L. 1996.55.6. Dorling Kindersley Media Library. © Judith Miller/Doris Kindersley/Wallis and Wallis.

Fig. 16-4 Beaker with ibex, dogs, and long-necked birds, from southwest Iran, ca. 5000–4000 BCE. Baked clay with painted decoration, height 11¼ in.
Inv. SB3174. Photo © RMN-Grand Palais (musée du Louvre)/Droits réservés.

Fig. 16-5 Stonehenge, Salisbury Plain, Wiltshire, England, ca. 2000 BCE.
© Spencer Grant/Photo Edit.

and millet (grains from the Near East would not be introduced for another 3,000 years), and this agricultural emphasis spawned towns and villages. In Gansu province, Neolithic potters began to add painted decoration to their work. The flowing, curvilinear forms painted on the shallow basin illustrated here include "hand" motifs on the outside, and round, almost eyelike forms that flow into each other on the inside.

Some of the most remarkable Neolithic painted pottery comes from Susa, on the Iranian plateau. The patterns on one particular beaker (**Fig. 16-4**) from around 5000 to 4000 BCE are highly stylized animals, the largest of which is an ibex, a popular decorative feature of prehistoric ceramics from Iran. Associated with the hunt, the ibex may have been a symbol of plenty. The front and hind legs are rendered by two triangles, the tail hangs behind it like a feather, the head is oddly disconnected from the body, and the horns rise in a large, exaggerated arc to encircle a decorative circular form. Hounds race around the band above the ibex, and wading birds form a decorative band across the beaker's top.

In northern Europe, especially in Britain and France, a distinctive kind of monumental stone architecture made its appearance late in the Neolithic period. Known as **megaliths**, or "big stones," these works were constructed without the use of mortar and represent the most basic form of architectural construction. Without doubt, the most famous megalithic structure in the world is the cromlech—from the Celtic *crom*, "circle," and *lech*, "place"—known as Stonehenge (**Fig. 16-5**), on Salisbury Plain, about 100 miles west of present-day London. A henge is a circle surrounded by a ditch with built-up embankments, presumably for fortification. The site at Stonehenge reflects four major building periods, extending from about 2750 to 1500 BCE. By about 2100 BCE, most of the elements visible today were in place—but many elements remain invisible, as was revealed by archeologist Vince Gaffney in 2014, whose Stonehenge Hidden Landscapes Project has produced an underground survey revealing more than 15 previously unknown monuments, including two large pits thousands of feet from the henge itself, but like the henge, aligned with sunrise and sunset at the summer solstice.

Other archeologists have uncovered a second cromlechlike circle at Durrington Wells, about 2 miles north of Stonehenge, consisting of a circular ditch surrounding a ring of postholes out of which very large timber posts would have risen. The circle was the center of a village consisting of as many as 300 houses. The two sites are connected by the River Avon. Archeologists speculate that Stonehenge was, in effect, one half of a huge monument complex, one made of timber and representing the transience of life, the other made of stone and signifying the eternity of ancestral life. The orientation of Stonehenge toward the rising sun at the summer solstice also indicates a connection to planting and harvest and the passing of time. The fact remains that the effort required for the construction of Stonehenge suggests that the late Neolithic peoples who built it were extremely social beings, capable of great cooperation. They worked together not only to find the giant stones that rise at the site, but also to quarry, transport, and raise them. Theirs was, in other words, a culture of some magnitude and no small skill. It was a culture capable of both solving great problems and organizing itself in the name of creating a great social center.

Mesopotamian Cultures

How does Mesopotamian art portray the relationship between the gods and the people?

Between 4000 and 3000 BCE, irrigation techniques were developed on the Tigris and Euphrates rivers in Mesopotamia, allowing for more intensive agriculture and population growth. In the southern plains of Mesopotamia, a people known as the Sumerians developed writing, schools, libraries, and written laws. Ancient Sumer consisted of a dozen or more city-states, each with a population of between 10,000 and 50,000, and each with its own reigning deity. Each of the local gods had the task of pleading the case of their particular communities with the other gods, who controlled the wind, the rain, and so on.

Communication with the god occurred in a ziggurat, a pyramidal temple structure consisting of successive platforms with outside staircases and a shrine at the top. An early Mesopotamian text calls the ziggurat "the bond between heaven and earth." Visitors—almost certainly limited to members of the priesthood—might bring an offering of food or an animal to be sacrificed to the resident god and often placed a statue in the temple that represented themselves in a state of perpetual prayer. We know this from inscriptions on many of the statues. One, dedicated to the goddess Tarsirsir, protector of Girsu, a city-state near the mouth of the Tigris River, reads in part, "May the statue, to which let my mistress turn her ear, speak my prayers." A group of such statues, found in the shrine room of the ziggurat at Tell Asmar, near present-day Baghdad, includes seven men and two women (**Fig. 16-6**). The men wear belted, fringed skirts. The two women wear robes. They all have huge eyes,

Fig. 16-6 Worshipers and deities from the Abu Temple, Tell Asmar, Iraq, ca. 2900–2600 BCE. Limestone, alabaster, and gypsum, height of tallest figure 30 in. Excavated by the Iraq Expedition of the Oriental Institute of the University of Chicago, February 13, 1934.

Courtesy of Oriental Institute of the University of Chicago. Photo: Anna Ressman.

Fig. 16-8 *Assurnasirpal II Killing Lions*, **from the palace complex of Assurnasirpal II, Kalhu (modern Nimrud, Iraq), ca. 850 BCE.** Alabaster, height approx. 39 in. The British Museum, London.
The Trustees of the British Museum/Art Resource, NY.

Fig. 16-7 ***Stele of Hammurabi*****, ca. 1760 BCE.** Basalt, height of stele approx. 7 ft., height of relief 28 in. Musée du Louvre, Paris.
Photo © RMN-Grand Palais (musée du Louvre)/Franck Raux.

inlaid with lapis lazuli (a blue semiprecious stone) or shell. Their wide-eyed appearance is probably meant to suggest that they are gazing in perpetual awe at the deity. The figures clasp their hands in front of them, suggestive of prayer when empty and of making an offering when holding a cup. Some scholars believe that the two tallest figures represent Abu, god of vegetation, and his consort, due to their especially large eyes, but all of the figures are probably worshipers.

One of the most influential Mesopotamian cultures was that of Babylon, which rose to power under the leadership of Hammurabi in the eighteenth century BCE. The so-called Law Code of Hammurabi is inscribed on a giant stele—an upright stone slab, carved with a commemorative design or inscription. It is a record of decisions and decrees made by Hammurabi (**Fig. 16-7**) over the course of some 40 years of his reign. In 282 separate "articles," which cover both sides of the basalt monument, the stele celebrates Hammurabi's sense of justice and the wisdom of his rule. Atop the stele, Hammurabi receives the blessing of Shamash, the sun god, notable for the rays of light that emerge from his shoulders. The god is much larger than Hammurabi; in fact, he is to Hammurabi as Hammurabi is to his people. Hammurabi's Code was repeatedly copied for over a thousand years, establishing the rule of law in Mesopotamia for a millennium.

After the fall of Babylon in 1595 BCE, victim of a sudden invasion of Hittites from Turkey, only the Assyrians, who lived around the city of Assur in the north, managed to maintain a continuing cultural identity. By the time Assurnasirpal II came to power, in 883 BCE, the Assyrians dominated the entire region. Assurnasirpal II built a magnificent capital at Kalhu, on the Tigris River. Designed to assert the power and authority of the king, it was surrounded by nearly 5 miles of walls, 120 feet thick and 42 feet high. A surviving inscription tells us that 69,574 people were invited by Assurnasirpal to celebrate the city's dedication. Many of its walls were decorated with alabaster reliefs, including a series of depictions of *Assurnasirpal II Killing Lions* (**Fig. 16-8**). The scene depicts several consecutive actions at once: As soldiers drive the lion toward the king from the left, he shoots it.

Egyptian Civilization

How do we account for the stability of Egyptian art and culture?

At about the same time that Sumerian culture developed in Mesopotamia, Egyptian society began to flourish along the Nile River. The Nile flooded almost every year, leaving behind rich deposits of fertile soil that could be easily

2500 BCE
Cities of Harappa and Mohenjo-daro flourish in India

Fig. 16-9 *Palette of King Narmer* (front and back), Hierakonpolis, Upper Egypt, ca. 3000 BCE.
Slate, height 25 in.
akg-image/Erich Lessing.

planted once the floodwater receded. The cycle of flood and sun made Egypt one of the most productive cultures in the ancient world and one of the most stable. For 3,000 years, from 3100 BCE until the defeat of Mark Antony and Cleopatra by the Roman general Octavian in 30 BCE, Egypt's institutions and culture remained remarkably unchanged. Its stability contrasted sharply with the conflicts and shifts in power that occurred in Mesopotamia.

Egyptian culture was dedicated to providing a home for the *ka*, that part of the human being that defines personality and that survives life on earth after death. The enduring nature of the *ka* required that artisans decorate tombs with paintings that the spirit could enjoy after death. Small servant figures might be carved from wood to serve the departed in the afterlife. The *ka* could find a home in a statue of the deceased. Mummification—the preservation of the body by treating it with chemical solutions and then wrapping it in linen—provided a similar home, as did the elaborate coffins in which the mummy was placed. The pyramids (see Fig. 14-2) were, of course, the largest of the resting places designed to house the *ka*.

The enduring quality of the *ka* accounts for the unchanging way in which, over the centuries, Egyptian figures, especially the pharaohs, were represented. A canon of ideal proportions was developed that was almost universally applied. The figure is, in effect, fitted into a grid. The feet rest on the bottom line of the grid, the ankles are placed on the first horizontal line, the knee on the sixth, the navel on the thirteenth (higher on the female), elbows on the fourteenth, and the shoulders on the nineteenth. These proportions are used in the *Palette of King Narmer* (**Fig. 16-9**). A palette was an object designed for grinding pigments and making body or eye paint, but this particular example was not meant for actual use but rather was a gift to a deity placed in a temple. The tablet celebrates the victory of Upper Egypt, led by King Narmer, over Lower Egypt, in a battle that united the country. Narmer is depicted holding an enemy by the hair, ready to finish him off. On the other side, he is seen reviewing the beheaded bodies of his foes. Narmer's pose is typical of Egyptian art. The lower body is in profile, his torso and shoulders

Fig. 16-10 ***King Khafre*, Giza, Egypt, ca. 2530 BCE.** Diorite, height 5 ft. 6⅛ in. Egyptian Museum, Cairo.
© Jürgen Liepe, Berlin.

fully frontal, his head in profile again, though a single eye is portrayed frontally.

The rigorous geometry governing Egyptian representation is apparent in the statue of Khafre (**Fig. 16-10**). Khafre's frontal pose is almost as rigid as the throne upon which he sits. It is as if he has been composed as a block of right angles. If it was the king's face that made his statue recognizable, it is also true that his official likeness might change several times during his reign, suggesting that the purpose of the royal sculpture was not just portraiture but also the creation of the ideal image of kingship.

For a brief period, in the fourteenth century BCE, under the rule of the emperor Akhenaten, the conventions of Egyptian art and culture were transformed. Akhenaten declared an end to traditional Egyptian religious practices, relaxing especially the longstanding preoccupation with the *ka*, and introducing a form of monotheism (the worship of a single god) into polytheistic Egypt. The sun god, manifested as a radiant sun disk—the Aten—embodied all the characteristics of the other Egyptian deities, and thus made them superfluous. Though the traditional standardized proportions of the human body were only slightly modified, artists seemed more intent on depicting special features of the human body—hands and fingers, the details of a face. Nowhere is this attention to detail more evident than in the famous bust of Akhenaten's queen, Nefertiti (**Fig. 16-11**). Both the graceful curve of her neck and her almost completely relaxed look make for what seems to be a stunningly naturalistic piece of work, though it remains impossible to say if this is a true likeness or an idealized portrait.

Fig. 16-11 ***Queen Nefertiti*, Tell el Amarna, ca. 1365 BCE.** Painted limestone, height 19⅝ in. Ägyptisches Museum, Berlin.
Acc. No. AM21300. Photo: Margarete Buesing. © 2015. Photo Scala, Florence/bpk, Bildagentur fuer Kunst, Kultur und Geschichte, Berlin.

3000 BCE

Menes unites Upper and Lower Egypt
3000 BCE

2500 BCE
Great Sphinx and Pyramids at Giza

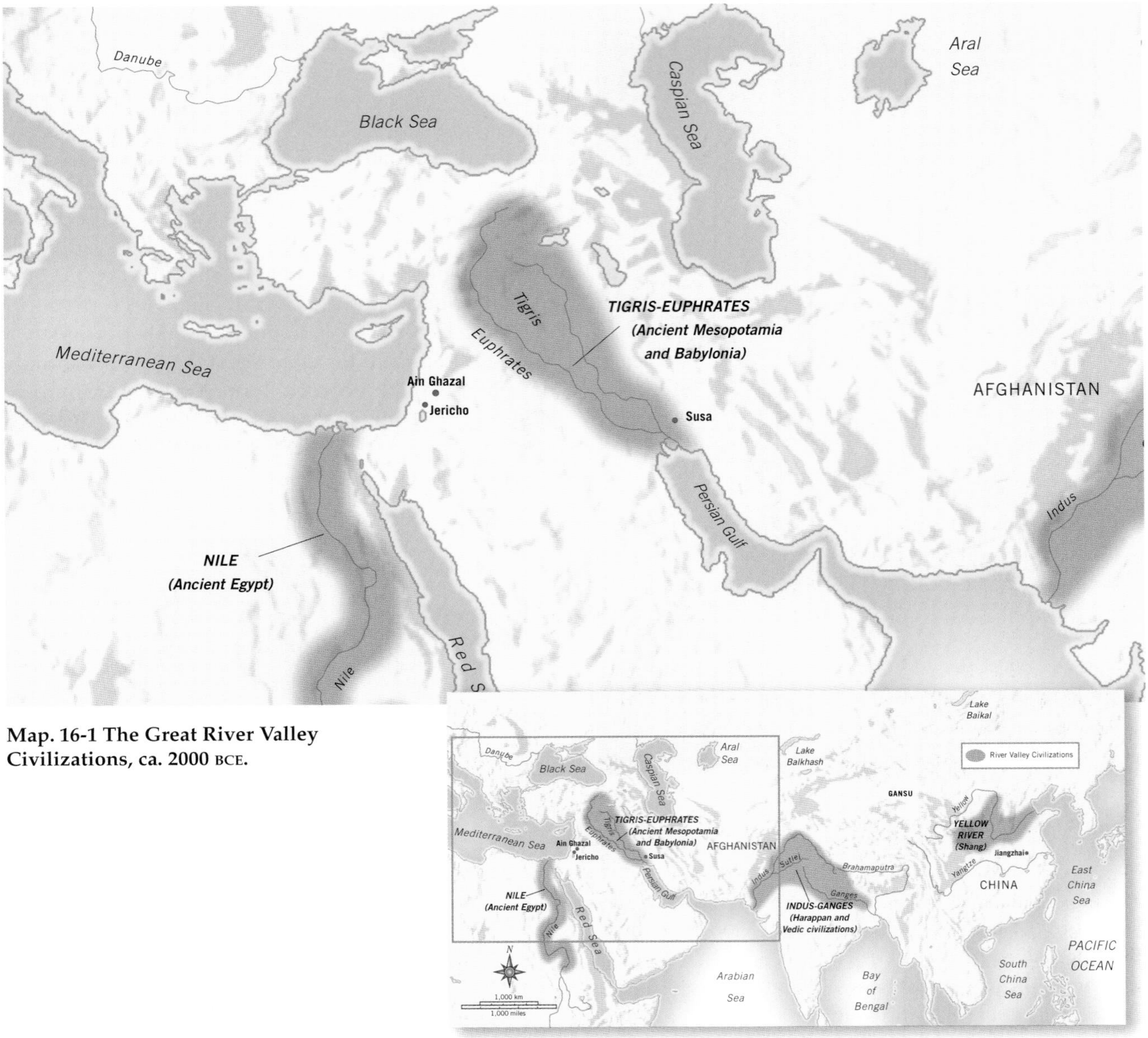

Map. 16-1 The Great River Valley Civilizations, ca. 2000 BCE.

River Valley Societies in India and China

What technological innovations reflect the growing sophistication of the river valley societies of India and China?

Indian civilization was born along the Indus River around 2700 BCE in an area known as Sind—from which the words India and Hindu originate. The earliest Indian peoples lived in at least two great cities in the Indus Valley, Harappa and Mohenjo-daro, the best preserved of the two. Built atop a citadel is a complex of buildings, presumably a governmental or religious center, surrounded by a wall 50 feet high. Set among the buildings on the citadel is a giant pool (**Fig. 16-12**). Perhaps a public bath or a ritual space, its finely fitted bricks, laid on edge and bound together with gypsum plaster, made it watertight. Outside the wall and below the citadel, a city of approximately 6 to 7 square miles, with broad avenues and narrow side streets, was laid out in a rough grid. It appears to have been home to a population of

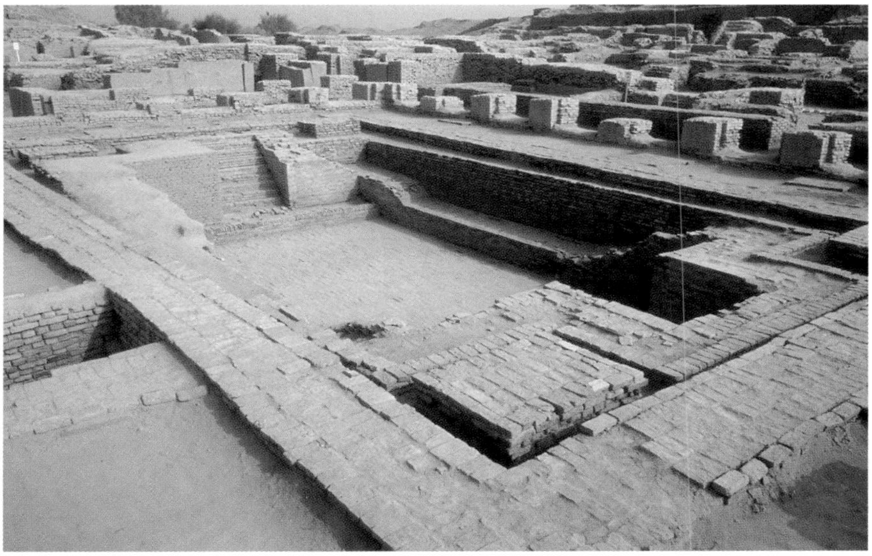

Fig. 16-12 Large water tank, possibly a public or ritual bathing area, from Mohenjo-Daro, Indus Valley civilization, ca. 2600–1900 BCE. akg-images/Gerard Degeorge.

between 20,000 and 50,000. A network of covered drainage systems ran through the streets, channeling waste and rainwater into the river. The houses were built with standard sizes of baked brick, each measuring 2¾ × 5½ × 11 inches, a ratio of 1:2:4. A brick of identical ratio but larger—4 × 8 × 16 inches—was used in the building of platforms and city walls. Unlike the sun-dried bricks used in other cultures at the time, Mohenjo-daro's bricks were fired, which made them much more durable. All of this suggests a civilization of considerable technological know-how and sophistication. As the stone sculpture torso of a "priest-king" (**Fig. 16-13**) found at Mohenjo-daro demonstrates, the people of the city were also accomplished artists. This figure, with his neatly trimmed head, is a forceful representation of a powerful personality, although his half-closed eyes suggest that this might have been made to commemorate the figure's death.

The Indus Valley civilizations began to collapse around 1800 BCE, perhaps as the result of a prolonged drought, and by 1000 BCE its cities had been abandoned. During its decline, the Vedic people, who called themselves Aryans, moved into the Indus Valley. Over time, their numbers increased and they spread east to the Ganges River Valley as well as north and south. Their cultural heritage would provide the basis for the development of Hinduism and Hindu art (see Chapter 17).

The North China Plain lies in the large, fertile valley of the Yellow River (see **Map 16-1**). Around 7000 BCE, when the valley's climate was much milder and the land more forested than it is today, the peoples inhabiting this fertile region began to cultivate the soil, growing

Fig. 16-13 Torso of a "priest-king," from Mohenjo-daro, Indus Valley civilization, ca. 2000–1900 BCE. Steatite, height 7⅞ in. National Museum of Pakistan, Karachi, Pakistan. Photo Scala, Florence.

primarily millet. Archeologists recognize at least three separate cultural groups in this region during this period, distinguished by their different pottery styles and works in jade. As Neolithic tribal people, they used stone tools, and although they domesticated animals very early on, they maintained the shamanistic practices of their hunter-gatherer heritage. Later inhabitants of this region would call this area the "Central Plain" because they believed it was the center of their country. During the ensuing millennia, Chinese culture in the Central Plain coalesced in ways that parallel developments in the Middle East and Greece during the same period, as China transformed itself from an agricultural society into a more urban-centered state.

For most of the second millennium BCE, the Shang dynasty ruled the Yellow River Valley. Shang kings displayed their power with treasures made of jade, shells, bone, and lacquer. Through the manufacture of ritual vessels such as the *guang*, or wine vessel, illustrated here (**Fig. 16-14**), the Shang developed an extremely sophisticated bronze-casting technology, as advanced as any ever used. Coiled serpents emerge from the vessels wings, with tiger-dragons just above them. Serving as a handle is a horned bird that is transformed into a dragon-serpent—all figures symbolizing royal authority and strength. Made for offerings of food, water, and wine during ceremonies of ancestor worship, these bronze vessels were kept in the ancestral hall and brought out for banquets. Leaders made gifts of bronze as tokens of political patronage, and strict rules governed the number of bronzes a family might possess according to its rank and social position.

Fig. 16-14 Spouted ritual wine vessel (*Guang*), Shang dynasty, early Anyang period, 13th century BCE. Bronze, height 8½ in. Metropolitan Museum of Art, New York.
Rogers Fund, 1943. 43.25.4. Photo: Lynton Gardiner. © 2015. Image copyright Metropolitan Museum of Art/Art Resource/Scala, Florence.

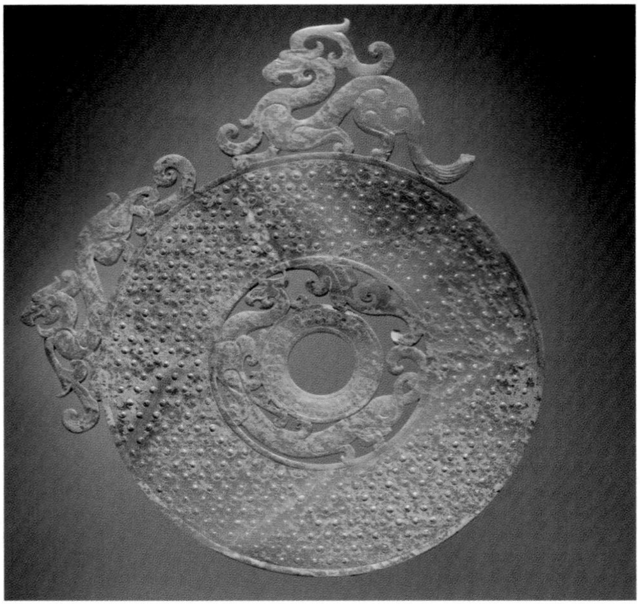

Fig. 16-15 Ritual disk (*bi*) with dragon and phoenix motif, from Jincun, Henan province, Eastern Zhou dynasty (771–256 BCE). Jade, diameter 6¼ in. The Nelson-Atkins Museum of Art, Kansas City, Missouri.
Purchase: William Rockhill Nelson Trust, 33-81. Photo: Matthew Pearson.

This ritual jade disk, or *bi*, made sometime in the fourth or third century BCE (**Fig. 16-15**), is emblematic of the continuity of Chinese historical traditions and ethnic identity. The earliest *bi* disks are found in burials dating from around 4000 BCE, and are thought to be part of the archaic paraphernalia of the shaman. While their original significance is unknown, by the time this one was made they were said to symbolize heaven. This example is decorated with a dragon and two tigers, auspicious symbols likewise emerging from China's prehistoric past.

Complex Societies in the Americas

What is the reason for the giant size of so many artworks and cultural sites in the Americas?

As early as 1500 BCE, a group known as the Olmec came to inhabit most of the area that we now refer to as Mesoamerica, from the southern tip of Mexico to Honduras and El Salvador. They built huge ceremonial precincts in the middle of their communities and developed many of the characteristic features of later Mesoamerican culture, such as pyramids, ball courts, mirror-making, and a calendar system.

The Olmec built their cities on great earthen platforms, probably designed to protect their ceremonial centers from rain and flood. On these platforms, they erected giant pyramidal mounds, where an elite group of ruler-priests lived, supported by the general population that farmed the rich, sometimes swampy land that surrounded them. These pyramids may have been an architectural reference to the volcanoes that dominate Mexico, or they may have been tombs—excavations may eventually tell us. At La Venta, very near the present-day city of Villahermosa, three colossal stone heads stood guard over the ceremonial center on the south end of the platform (**Fig. 16-16**), and a fourth guarded the north end by itself. Each head weighs between 11 and 24 tons, and each bears a unique emblem on its headgear, which is similar to old-style American leather football helmets. At other Olmec sites, as many as eight of these heads have been found, some up to 12 feet tall. They are carved of basalt, although the nearest basalt quarry is 50 miles to the south in the Tuxtla Mountains. They were evidently at least partially carved at the quarry, then loaded onto rafts and floated downriver to the Gulf of Mexico before going back upriver to their final positions. The stone heads are generally believed to be portraits of Olmec rulers, and they all share the same facial features, including wide, flat noses and thick lips. They suggest that the ruler was the culture's principal mediator with the gods, literally larger than life.

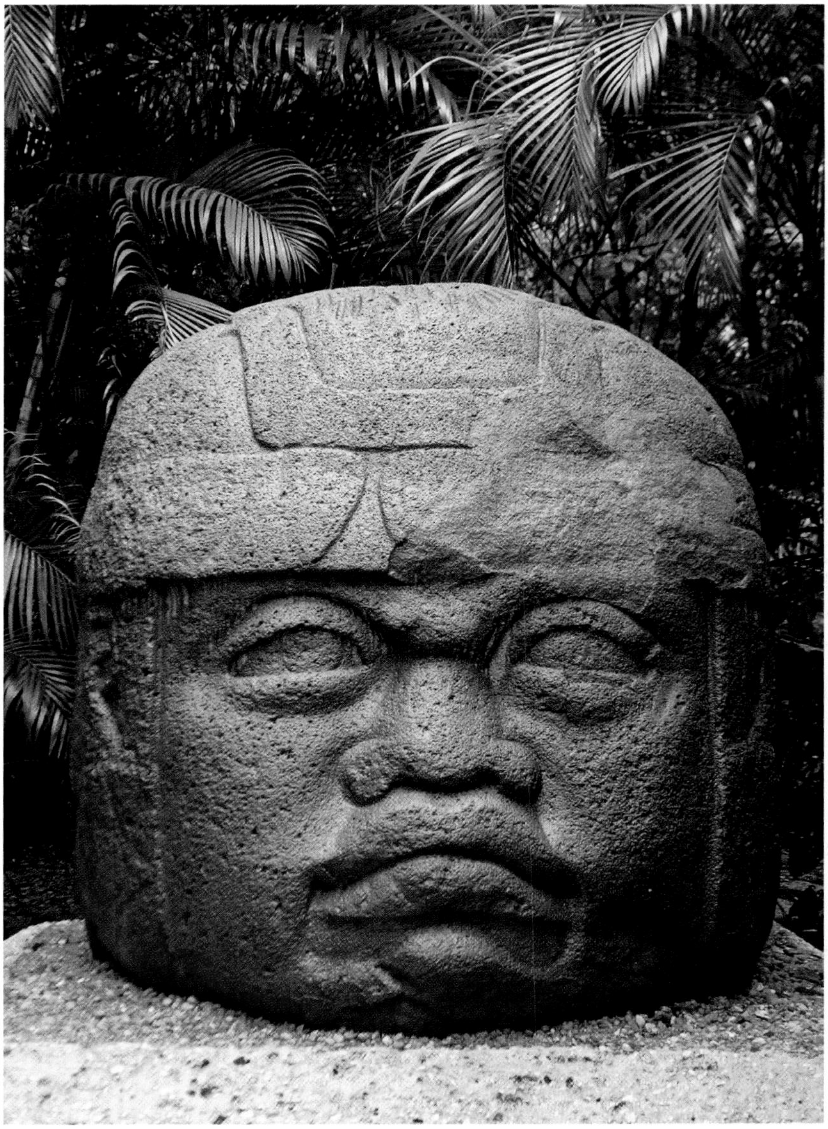

Fig. 16-16 Colossal head, Olmec culture, ca. 900–500 BCE.
Basalt, height 7 ft. 5 in. La Venta Park, Villahermosa, Tabasco, Mexico.
© Carlos S. Pereyra/age Fotostock.

Equally large and complex cultures arose later in the Mississippi Basin in North America. The great mound at Cahokia (**Fig. 16-17**), near the juncture of the Illinois, Missouri, and Mississippi rivers at present-day East St. Louis, Illinois, required the moving of over 22 million cubic feet of earth and probably three centuries to construct, beginning about 900 CE. It was the focal point of a ritual center that contained as many as 120 mounds, some of which were aligned with the position of the sun at the equinoxes, as well as nearly 400 other platforms, wooden enclosures, and houses. A stockade, or fence, surrounded the mound and a large area in front of it, suggesting that warfare probably played an important

Fig. 16-17 Monks Mound, the centerpiece of Cahokia Mounds State Historic Site, Illinois, Mississippian culture, ca. 1150 CE–1650 CE.
Art Archive/Ira Block/NGS Image Collection.

role in Mississippian life. Evidence also suggests that the Mississippians worshiped the sun: The Natchez people, one of the Mississippian peoples who survived contact with European culture, called their chief the Great Sun, and their highest social class the Suns.

Aegean and Greek Civilizations

What distinguishes Minoan from Mycenaean culture and the culture of the Greek polis *from both these predecessors?*

The later Greeks thought of the Bronze Age Aegean peoples as their ancestors—particularly those who inhabited the island of Crete, and Mycenae, on the Peloponnese—and considered their activities and culture part of their own prehistory. They even had a word for the way they knew them—*archaiologia*, "knowing the past." They did not practice archeology as we do today, excavating ancient sites and scientifically analyzing the artifacts discovered there. Rather, they learned of their past through legends passed down, at first orally and then in writing, from generation to generation. Interestingly, the modern practice of archeology has confirmed much of what was legendary to the Greeks.

Aegean Cultures

The early Aegean cultures were impressive centers of power and wealth. The origins of the Minoan peoples on the island of Crete are unclear—they may have arrived there as early as 6000 BCE—but their culture reached its peak between 1600 and 1450 BCE. The so-called "*Toreador*" fresco (**Fig. 16-18**) does not actually depict a bullfight, as its modern title suggests. Instead, a youthful acrobat can be seen vaulting over the bull's back as one maiden holds the animal's horns and another waits to catch him (traditionally, as in Egyptian art, women are depicted with light skin, men with a darker complexion). The three almost nude figures appear to be toying with a charging bull in what may be a ritual activity, connected perhaps to a rite of passage, or in what may simply be a sporting event, designed to entertain the royal court.

In Minoan culture, the bull was an animal of sacred significance. Legend has it that the wife of King Minos, after whom the culture takes its name, gave birth to

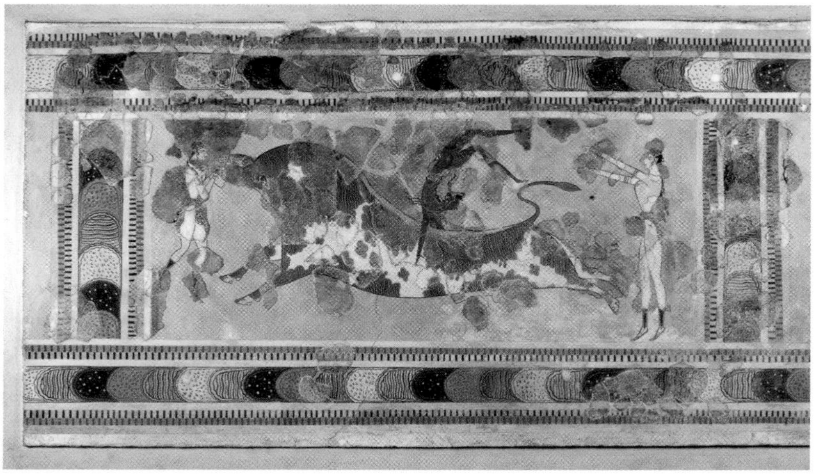

Fig. 16-18 The "*Toreador*" fresco, Knossos, Crete, ca. 1500 BCE. Height, including upper border, approx. 24½ in. Archaeological Museum, Iraklion, Crete.
© Craig & Marie Mauzy, Athens.

Fig. 16-19 Snake Goddess or Priestess, from the palace at Knossos, Crete, ca. 1500 BCE. Faience, height 11⅝ in. Archaeological Museum, Iraklion, Crete.
© Craig & Marie Mauzy, Athens.

a creature half-human and half-bull—the Minotaur. Minos had a giant labyrinth, or maze, constructed to house the creature, to whom Athenian youths and maidens were sacrificed until it was killed by the hero Theseus. The legend of the labyrinth probably arose in response to the intricate design of the palaces built for the Minoan kings.

Ample archeological evidence tells us that the Minoans worshiped female deities. We do not know much more than that, but some students of ancient religions have proposed that the Minoan worship of one or more female deities is evidence that in very early cultures the principal deity was a goddess rather than a god.

It has long been believed that one of the Minoan female deities was a snake goddess, but, recently, scholars have questioned the authenticity of most of the existing snake-goddess figurines. Sir Arthur Evans (1851–1941), who first excavated at the Palace of Minos on Crete, identified images of the Cretan goddess as "Mountain Goddess," "Snake Goddess," "Dove Goddess," "Goddess of the Caves," "Goddess of the Double Axes," "Goddess of the Sports," and "Mother Goddess." He saw all of these as different aspects of a single deity, or Great Goddess. A century after Evans introduced the Snake Goddess (**Fig. 16-19**) to the world, scholars are still debating its authenticity. In his book *Mysteries of the Snake Goddess* (2002), Kenneth Lapatin makes a convincing case that craftspeople employed by Evans manufactured artifacts for the antiquities market. He believes that the body of the statue is an authentic antiquity, but the form in which we see it is largely the imaginative fabrication of Evans's restorers. Many parts were missing when the figure was unearthed, and so an artist working for Evans fashioned new parts and attached them to the figure. The snake in the goddess's right hand lacked a head, leaving its identity as a snake open to question. Most of the goddess's left arm, including the snake in her hand, was absent and fabricated later. When the figure was discovered, it lacked a head, and this one is completely fabricated. The cat on the goddess's head is original, although it was not found with the statue. Lapatin believes that Evans, eager to advance his own theory that Minoan religion was dedicated to the worship of a Great Goddess, never questioned the manner in which the figures were restored. As interesting as the figure is, its identity as a snake goddess is at best questionable. We cannot even say with certainty that the principal deity of the Minoan culture was female, let alone that she was a snake goddess. There are no images of snake goddesses in surviving Minoan wall frescoes, engraved gems, or seals, and almost all of the statues depicting her are fakes or imaginative reconstructions.

It is unclear why Minoan culture abruptly ended in approximately 1450 BCE. Great earthquakes and volcanic eruptions may have destroyed the civilization, or perhaps it fell victim to the warlike Mycenaeans from the mainland, whose culture flourished between 1400 and 1200 BCE. The Mycenaeans built stone fortresses on the hilltops of the Peleponnese (see Fig. 14-9), and theirs was a culture dominated by military values. In *The Warrior Vase* (**Fig. 16-20**), we see Mycenaean soldiers marching to war, perhaps to meet the Dorian invaders who destroyed their civilization soon after 1200 BCE. The Dorian weapons were made of iron and therefore were superior to the softer bronze Mycenaean spears. But it was representatives of Mycenaean culture, immortalized by Homer in *The Iliad* and *The Odyssey*, who sacked the great Trojan city of Troy. They buried their dead in so-called beehive tombs, which, dome-shaped, were full of gold and silver, including masks of the royal dead, a burial practice similar to that of the Egyptians. One of the most famous of these masks was believed to be the funerary mask of Agamemnon (**Fig. 16-21**), the Mycenaean king who led the Greeks to Troy in pursuit of Helen, the wife of his brother King Menelaus of Sparta. Helen had eloped with Paris, son of King Priam of Troy. Scholars have subsequently determined that the mask predates the Trojan War by some 300 years.

In about 1200 BCE, just after the fall of Mycenae, the Greek world consisted of various tribes separated by the geographical features of the peninsula, with its deep bays, narrow valleys, and jagged mountains (see **Map 16-2** of Greece and its city-states). These tribes soon developed into independent and often warring city-states, with their own constitutions, coinage, and armies. We know that in 776 BCE these feuding states declared a truce in order to hold the first Olympic Games. Although the Greeks thought of the Aegean peoples, particularly

Fig. 16-20 *The Warrior Vase*, Mycenae, ca. 1200 BCE. Ceramic, height 16 in. National Archaeological Museum, Athens.

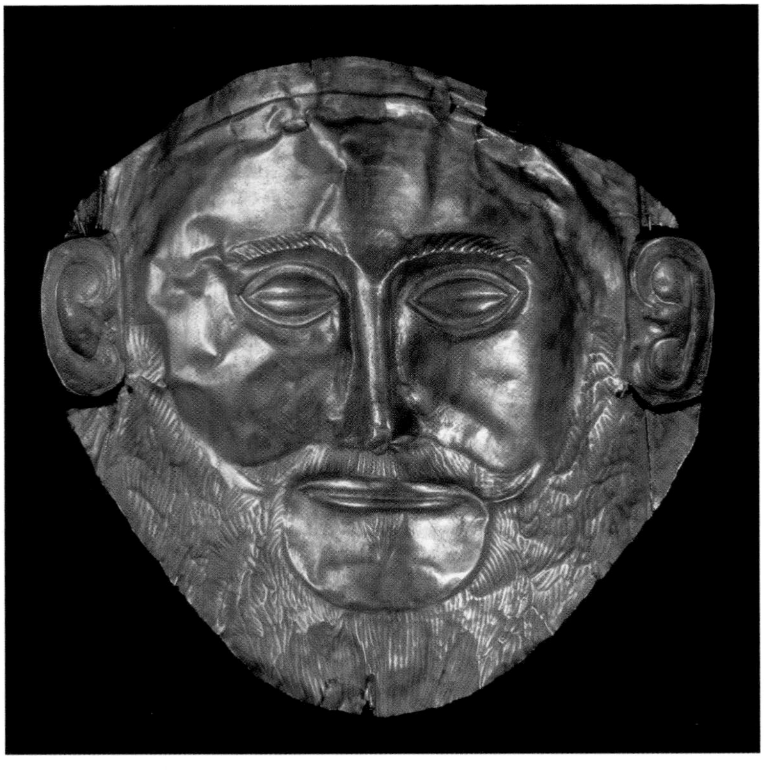

Fig. 16-21 Funerary mask (Mask of Agamemnon), from Grave Circle A, Mycenae, Greece, ca. 1600–1550 BCE. Gold, height approx. 12 in. National Archaeological Museum, Athens.

539 BCE
Cyprus the Great establishes the Persian Empire

500 BCE

551–479 BCE
Confucius in China

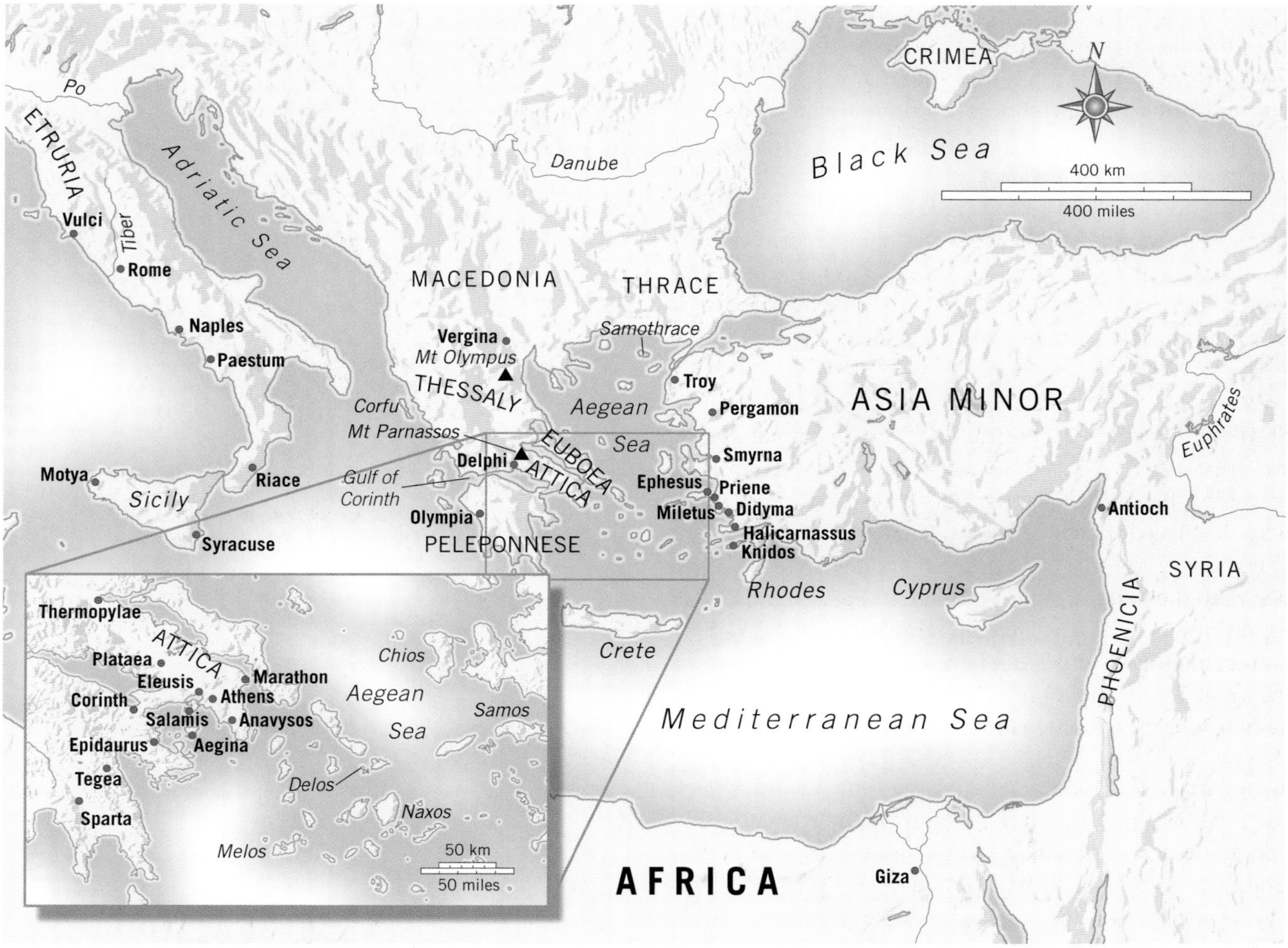

Map 16-2 The City-States of Ancient Greece.

the Minoans and Mycenaeans, as their ancestors and considered their activities and cultures part of their own prehistory, the Olympic Games represented a moment so significant that the Greeks later took it as the starting point of their history.

Greek Civilization

The rise of the Greek city-state, or *polis*, marks the moment when Western culture begins to celebrate its own human strengths and powers—the creative genius of the mind itself—over the power of nature. The Western world's gods now became personified, taking human form and assuming human weaknesses. Though immortal, they were otherwise versions of ourselves, no longer angry beasts or natural phenomena such as the earth, the sun, or the rain. In fact, if their gods looked and acted like people, that is because the Greeks were great students of human behavior and of the human form as well, which they portrayed in highly naturalistic detail. By the fifth century BCE, this interest in all aspects of the human condition was reflected throughout Greek culture. The physician Hippocrates systematically studied human disease, and the historian Herodotus, in his account of the Persian Wars, began to chronicle human history. Around 500 BCE in Athens, all free male citizens were included in the political system, and democracy—from *demos*, meaning "people," and *kratia*, meaning "power"—was born. It was not quite democracy as we think of it today: Slavery was considered natural, and women were excluded from political life. Nevertheless, the concept of individual

Fig. 16-22 The Acropolis, Athens, Greece, rebuilt in the second half of the 5th century BCE.

freedom was cherished. And by the fourth century BCE, the philosopher Plato had developed theories not only about social and political relations but also about education and aesthetic pleasure.

The values of the Greek city-state were embodied in its temples. The temple was usually situated on an elevated site above the city, and the acropolis, from *akros*, meaning "top," and *polis*, "city," was conceived as the center of civic life. The crowning achievement of Greek architecture is the complex of buildings on the Acropolis in Athens (**Fig. 16-22**), designed to replace those destroyed by the Persians in 480 BCE. Construction began in about 450 BCE under the leadership of the great Athenian statesman Pericles. The central building of the new complex, designed by Ictinos and Callicrates, was the Parthenon, dedicated to the city's namesake, Athena Parthenos, the goddess of wisdom. A Doric temple of the grandest scale, it is composed entirely of marble. At its center was an enormous ivory and gold statue of Athena, sculpted by Phidias, who was in charge of all the ornamentation and sculpture for the project. The Athena is long since lost, and we can imagine his achievement only by considering the sculpture on the building's pediment (see Fig. 12-2) and its friezes, all of which reflect Phidias' style and maybe his design.

Fig. 16-23 *Nike*, from the balustrade of the Temple of Athena Nike, ca. 410–407 BCE. Marble, height 42 in. Acropolis Museum, Athens.

The Phidian style is marked by its naturalness. The human figure often assumes a relaxed, seemingly effortless pose, or it may be caught in the act of movement, athletic or casual. In either case, the precision with which the anatomy has been rendered is remarkable. The relief of *Nike* (**Fig. 16-23**), goddess of victory, from the balustrade of the Temple of Athena Nike on the Acropolis in Athens, is a perfect example of the Phidian style. As Nike bends to take off her sandal, the drapery both reveals and conceals the body beneath. Sometimes appearing to be transparent, sometimes dropping in deep folds and hollows, it contributes importantly to the sense of reality conveyed by the sculpture. It is as if we can see the body literally push forward out of the stone and press against the drapery.

The Greek passion for individualism, reason, and accurate observation of the world continued even after the disastrous defeat of Athens in the Peloponnesian War in 404 BCE, which led to a great loss of Athenian power. In 338 BCE, the army of Philip, King of Macedon, conquered Greece, and after Philip's death two years later, his son, Alexander the Great, came to power. Because Philip greatly admired Athenian culture, Alexander was educated by the philosopher Aristotle, who persuaded the young king to impose Greek culture throughout his empire. **Hellenism**, or the culture of Greece, thus came to dominate the Western world. The court sculptor to Alexander the Great was Lysippus, known to us only through later Roman copies of his work. Lysippus challenged the Classical canon of proportion created by Polyclitus (see Fig. 7-23), creating sculptures with smaller heads and slenderer bodies that lent his figures a sense of greater height. In a Roman copy of a lost original by Lysippus known as the *Apoxyomenos* (**Fig. 16-24**), or *The Scraper*, an athlete removes oil and dirt from his body with an instrument called a strigil. He seems detached from his circumstances, as if recalling his victory, both physically and mentally uncontained by the space in which he stands.

In the sculpture of the fourth century BCE, we discover a graceful, even sensuous, beauty marked by *contrapposto* and three-dimensional realism (see Fig. 12-11). The depiction of physical beauty becomes an end in itself, and sculpture increasingly seems to be more about the pleasures of seeing than anything else. At the same time, artists strove for an ever-greater degree of realism, and in the sculpture of the Hellenistic Age, we find an increasingly animated and dramatic treatment of the figure. The *Nike of Samothrace* (**Fig. 16-25**) is a masterpiece of Hellenistic realism. The goddess has been depicted as she alights on the prow of a victorious war galley, and one can almost feel the wind as it buffets her, and the surf spray that has soaked her garment so that it clings revealingly to her torso.

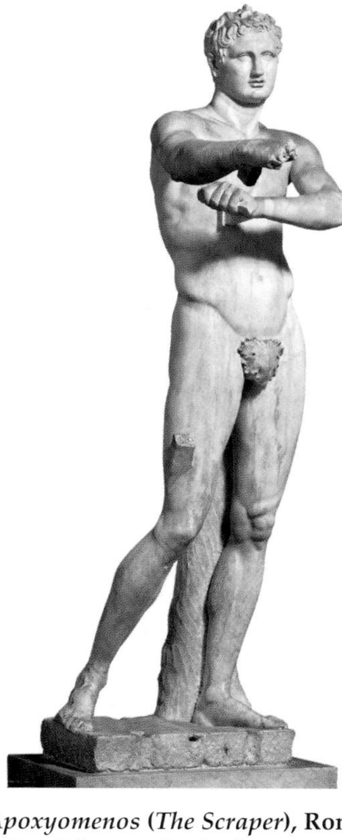

Fig. 16-24 ***Apoxyomenos* (*The Scraper*), Roman copy of an original Greek bronze by Lysippus, ca. 350–325 BCE.** Marble, height 6 ft. 8½ in. Vatican Museums, Vatican City.

Fig. 16-25 ***Nike of Samothrace*, ca. 190 BCE.** Marble, height approx. 8 ft. Musée du Louvre, Paris.

Fig. 16-26 The Laocoön Group, Roman copy, perhaps after Agesander, Athenodorus, and Polydorus of Rhodes, 1st century CE. Marble, height 7 ft. Vatican Museums, Vatican City. © 2015 Photo Scala, Florence.

The swirl of line that was once restricted to drapery overwhelms the entire composition of The Laocoon Group (Fig. 16-26), in which Laocoön, a Trojan priest, and his two sons are overwhelmed by serpents sent by the sea god Poseidon. We are caught in the midst of the Trojan War. The Greeks have sent the Trojans a giant wooden horse as a "gift." Inside it are Greek soldiers, and Laocoön suspects as much. And so Poseidon, who favors the Greeks, has chosen to silence Laocoön forever. So theatrical is the group that to many eyes it verges on melodrama, but its expressive aims are undeniable. The sculptor is no longer content simply to represent the figure realistically; sculpture must convey emotion as well.

The Roman World

How do Roman art and architecture suggest the empire's power?

Although the Romans conquered Greece (in 146 BCE), like Philip of Macedon and Alexander, they regarded Greek culture and art as superior to any other. Thus, like the Hellenistic Empire before it, the Roman Empire possessed a distinctly Greek character. The Romans imported thousands of original Greek artworks and had them copied in even greater numbers. In fact, much of what we know today about Greek art we know only through Roman copies. The Greek gods were adapted to the Roman religion, Jupiter bearing a strong resemblance to Zeus, Venus to Aphrodite, and so on. The Romans used the Greek architectural orders in their own buildings and temples, preferring especially the highly decorative Corinthian order. Many, if not most, of Rome's artists were of Greek extraction, though they were "Romanized" to the point of being indistinguishable from the Romans themselves. In making Greek culture their own, they in essence asserted their power and domination over it.

Roman art derives, nevertheless, from at least one other source. Around 750 BCE, at about the same time as the Greeks first colonized the southern end of the Italian

Fig. 16-27 Portrait of a Boy, early 3rd century BCE. Bronze, height 9 in. Museo Archeologico Nazionale, Florence. Nicolo Orsi Battaglini/Ikona.

Fig. 16-28 *She-Wolf*, ca. 500 BCE. Bronze, height 33½ in. Museo Capitolino, Rome.

peninsula, the Etruscans, whose language has no relation to any known tongue, and whose origin is somewhat mysterious, established a vital set of city-states in the area between present-day Florence and Rome. Little remains of the Etruscan cities, which were destroyed and rebuilt by Roman armies in the second and third centuries BCE, and we know the Etruscans' culture largely through their sometimes richly decorated tombs. At Veii, just north of Rome, the Etruscans established a sculptural center that gave them a reputation as the finest metalworkers of the age. They traded widely, and from the sixth century on, a vast array of bronze objects, from statues to hand mirrors, were made for export. Etruscan art was influenced by the Greeks, as this life-size bronze head (**Fig. 16-27**), with its almost melancholy air, makes clear.

The Romans traced their ancestry to the Trojan prince Aeneas, who escaped after the sack of Troy and who appears in Homer's *Iliad*. The city of Rome itself was founded early in Etruscan times—in 753 BCE, the Romans believed—by Romulus and Remus, twins nurtured by a she-wolf (**Fig. 16-28**). Though the figures of Romulus and Remus are Renaissance additions to the bronze, the image served as the totem of the city of Rome from the day on which a statue of a she-wolf was dedicated on the Capitoline Hill in Rome in 296 BCE—although almost certainly not this one, which scholars now believe dates from medieval times. The she-wolf reminded the Romans of the fiercely protective loyalty and power of their motherland.

Fig. 16-29 *Augustus of Primaporta*, ca. 20 BCE. Marble, height 6 ft. 8 in. Vatican Museums, Vatican City.

Beginning in the fifth century BCE, Rome dedicated itself to conquest and created an empire that included all areas surrounding the Mediterranean and that stretched as far north as present-day England (see **Map 16-3** of the Roman Empire). By the time the Romans conquered Greece, their interest in the accurate portrayal of human features was long established, and Hellenistic art only supported this tendency. A great ruler was fully capable of idealizing himself as a near-deity, as is evident in the *Augustus of Primaporta* (**Fig. 16-29**), so known because it was discovered at the home of Augustus' wife, Livia, at Primaporta, on the outskirts of Rome. The pose is directly

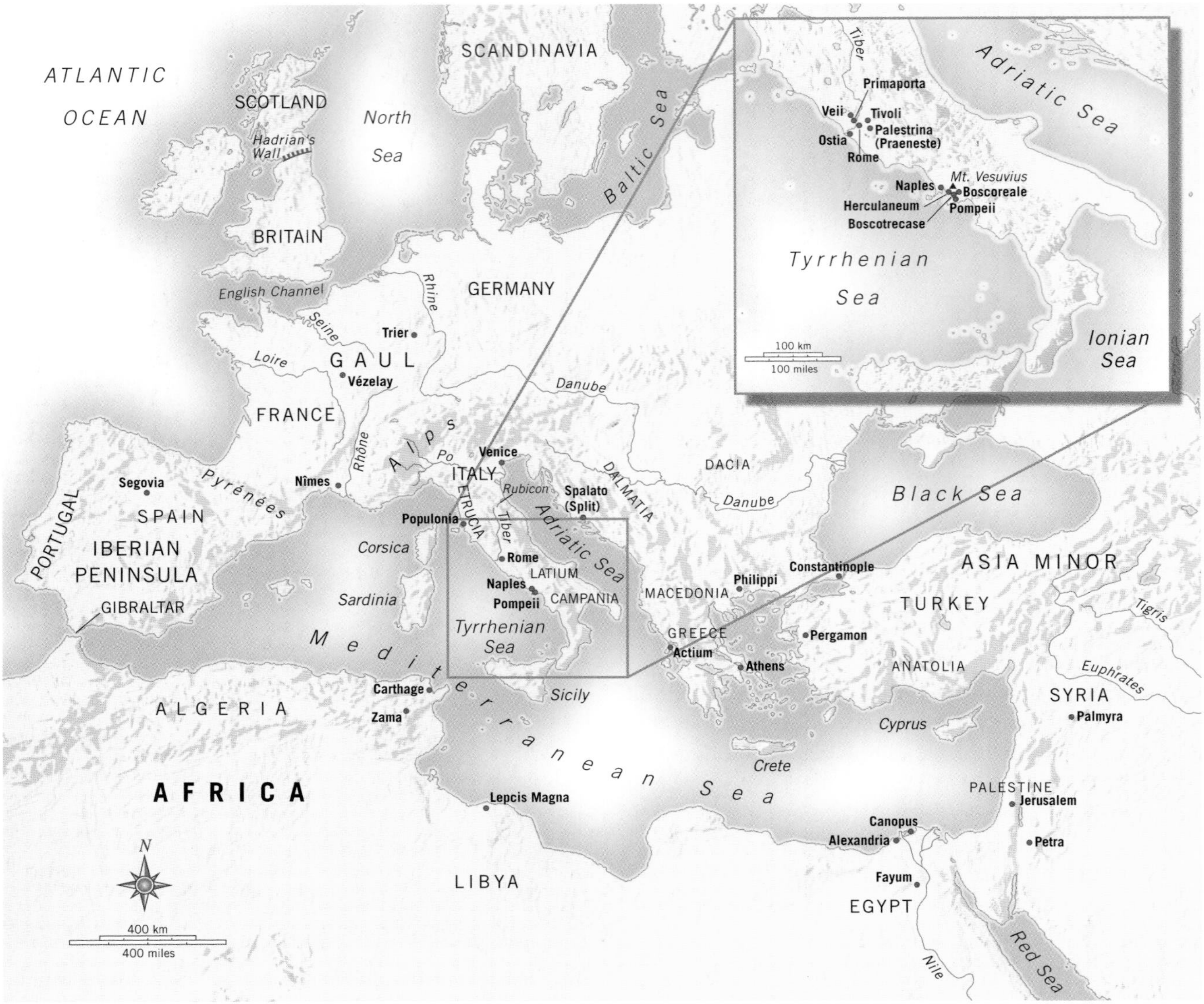

Map 16-3 The Roman Empire at its Greatest Extent, ca. 180 CE.

indebted to the *Doryphoros* (*The Spear Bearer*) of Polyclitus (see Fig. 7-23). The extended arm points toward an unknown, but presumably greater, future—a symbol of the empire's political aspirations. The military garb announces his role as commander-in-chief. The small Cupid riding a dolphin at his feet makes claim to Augustus' divine descent from Venus.

The perfection of the arch and dome and the development of structural concrete were the Romans' major architectural contributions (see Chapter 14). But they were also extraordinary monument-builders. Upon the death of the emperor Titus, who defeated rebellious Jews in Palestine and sacked the Second Temple of Jerusalem in 70 CE, his brother, Domitian, constructed a memorial arch at the highest point on the Sacred Way in Rome to honor his victory (**Fig. 16-30**). Originally, this Arch of Titus was topped by a statue of a four-horse chariot and driver. Such **triumphal arches**, as they were called since triumphant armies marched through them, composed of a simple barrel vault enclosed within a rectangle, and enlivened with sculpture and decorative engaged columns, would deeply influence later architecture of the Renaissance, especially the facades of Renaissance cathedrals.

Another remarkable symbol of Roman power is the Column of Trajan (**Figs. 16-31** and **16-32**). Encircled by a spiraling band of relief sculpture 50 inches high and,

The Edict of Milan grants religious freedom to all and ends persecution of Christians
313 CE

313 CE

180 CE
Pax Romana begins to break down

Fig. 16-30 Arch of Titus, Rome, ca. 81 CE. Concrete with marble facade, height 50 ft., width 44 ft. 4 in.
Canali Photobank, Milan, Italy.

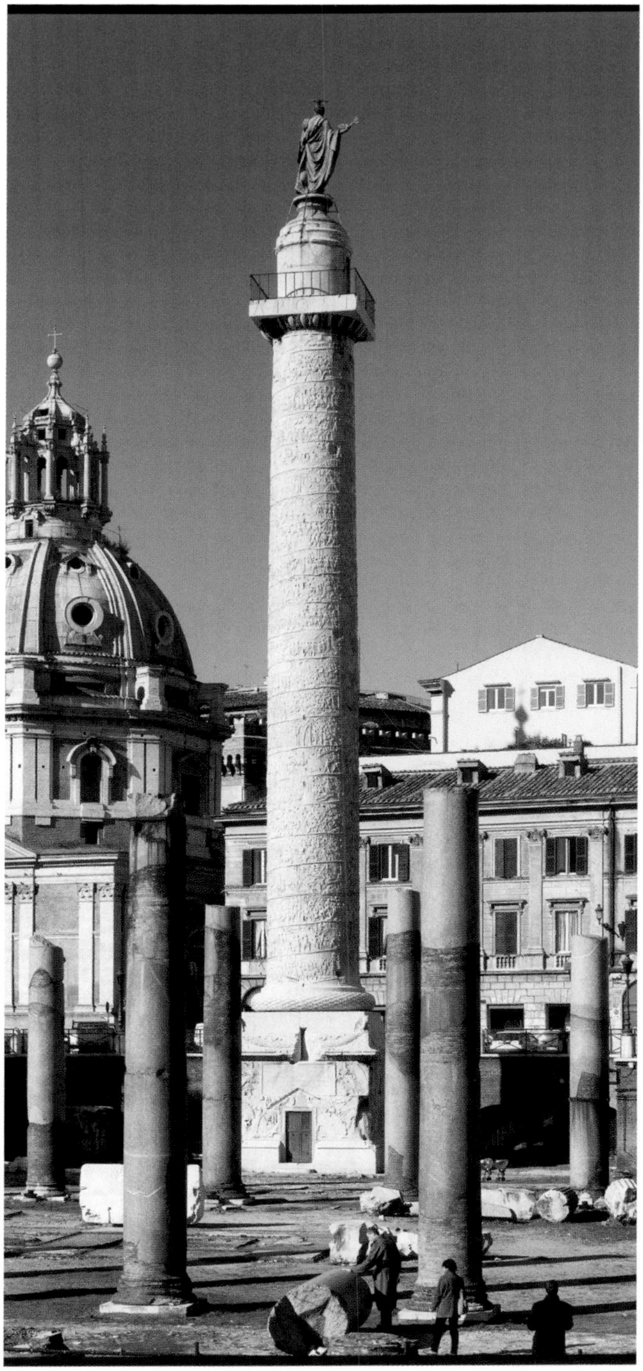

Figs. 16-31 and 16-32 Attributed to Apollodorus, Column of Trajan, Rome, 113 CE, and detail. Marble, height originally 128 ft., length of frieze approx. 625 ft.
Fig. 16-31: © Vincenzo Pirozzi, Rome.
Fig. 16-32: © 2015. Photo Scala, Florence, courtesy of the Ministero Beni e Att. Culturali.

if it were unwound and stretched out, 625 feet long, the column details the emperor Trajan's two successful campaigns in present-day Hungary and Romania in the first century BCE. The 150 separate episodes celebrate not only military victories, but Rome's civilizing mission as well.

As the empire solidified its strength under the *Pax Romana*—150 years of peace initiated by Augustus in 27 BCE—a succession of emperors celebrated its glory in a variety of elaborate public works and monuments, including the Colosseum and the Pantheon (see Figs. 14-16 and 14-18). By the first century CE, Rome's population approached 1 million, with most of its inhabitants living in apartment buildings (an archival record indicates that, at this time, there were only 1,797 single-family homes in the city). They congregated daily at the Forum, a site originally developed by the Etruscans as a marketplace, but which, in a plan developed by Julius Caesar and implemented by Augustus, became a civic center symbolic of Roman power and grandeur, paved in marble and dominated by colonnaded public spaces, temples, basilicas, and state buildings such as the courts, the archives, and the Curia, or senate house.

Although Rome became extraordinarily wealthy, the empire began to falter after the death of the emperor Marcus Aurelius in 180 CE. Invasions of Germanic tribes from the north, Berbers from the south, and Persians from the east wreaked havoc upon the empire's economic, administrative, and military structure. By the time the emperor Constantine decided to move the capital to Byzantium in 323 CE—renaming it Constantinople, today's Istanbul—the empire was hopelessly divided, and the establishment of the new capital only underscored the division.

Developments in Asia

How would you compare Chinese militarism to Buddhist pacifism?

At about the same time that Rome began establishing its imperial authority over the Mediterranean world, one of several warring states in China, the Qin (the origin of our name for China), conquered the other states and unified them under the leadership of Qin Shihuangdi, who declared himself "First Emperor" in 221 BCE. The Qin worked very quickly to achieve a stable society. To discourage nomadic invaders from the north, particularly the Huns, they built the Great Wall of China (**Fig. 16-33**). The wall was constructed by soldiers, augmented by criminals, civil servants who found themselves in disfavor, and conscripts from across the countryside. Each family was required to provide one able-bodied adult male to work on the wall each year. It was made of rammed earth, reinforced by continuous horizontal courses of brushwood, and faced with stone. Watchtowers were built at high points, and military barracks were built in the valleys below. At the same time, the Chinese constructed nearly 4,350 miles of roads, linking even the farthest reaches of the country to the Central Plain. By the end of the second century CE, China had some 22,000 miles of roads serving a country of nearly 1.5 million square miles.

Fig. 16-33 The Great Wall, near Beijing, begun late 3rd century BCE.
© Steve Bloom Images/Alamy.

Soon after the death of Qin Shihuangdi, whose tomb was another massive undertaking (see Fig. 12-12), the Qin collapsed and the Han dynasty came to power, inaugurating over 400 years of intellectual and cultural growth. What we know of everyday life in Han society comes mostly from surviving poetry, but our understanding of domestic architecture derives from ceramic models such as that of a house found in a tomb, presumably created for use by the departed in the afterlife (**Fig. 16-34**). It is four stories high and topped by a watchtower. The family lived in the middle two stories, while livestock, probably pigs and oxen, were kept in the lower level with its courtyard extending in front of the house.

We know through surviving literary descriptions that the Han emperors built lavish palaces, richly decorated with wall paintings. The prosperity of the Han dynasty was due largely to the expansion of trade, particularly the export of silk. The silk-trading routes reached all the way to Imperial Rome. The quality of Han silk is evident in a silk banner from the tomb of the wife of the marquis of Dai discovered on the outskirts of present-day Changsha in Hunan (**Fig. 16-35**). Painted with scenes representing on three different levels the underworld, the earthly realm, and the heavens, it represents the Han conception of the cosmos. Long, sinuous, tendril-like lines describing dragons' tails, coiling serpents, long-tailed birds, and flowing draperies unify the three realms. In the right-hand corner of the heavenly realm, above the crossbar of the T, is an image of the sun containing a crow, and in the other corner is a crescent moon supporting a toad. The deceased noblewoman herself stands on the white platform in the middle region of the banner. Three attendants stand behind her and two figures bearing gifts kneel before her. On the white platform of the bottom realm, bronze vessels contain food and wine for the deceased.

Fig. 16-34 Model of a Multi-Storied Tower, Eastern Han dynasty, 1st century CE. Earthenware with unfired pigments, 4 ft. 4 in. × 33½ in. × 27 in. The Nelson-Atkins Museum of Art, Kansas City, Missouri.

Fig. 16-35 ***Lady of Dai with Attendants*****, Han dynasty, after 168** BCE. Painted silk banner from the tomb of Dai Hou Fu-ren, Mawangdui Tomb I, Changsha, Hunan, China. Silk, height 6 ft. 8¼ in. Hunan Museum, Changsha, China.

Han prosperity was constantly threatened by incursions of nomadic peoples to the north, chiefly the Huns, whom the Chinese called Xiongnu, and whose impact would later be felt as far away as Rome. In 138 BCE, Emperor Wu attempted to forge military alliances with the Huns, sending General Zhang Qian with 100 of his best fighting men into the northern territories. The Huns held the general captive for ten years. When he returned, he spoke of horses that were far stronger and faster than those in China. A small bronze horse found in his tomb at Wuwei in

Gansu represents the kind of horse he so admired (**Fig. 16-36**). Its power is captured in the energetic lines of its composition, its flaring nostrils, and barreled chest. But it is, simultaneously, perfectly, almost impossibly, balanced on one leg, as if defying gravity, having stolen the ability to fly from the bird beneath its hoof. Any army using such horses, Zhang believed, would be unbeatable.

Elsewhere in Asia, the philosophy of the Buddha, or the Enlightened One, was taking hold. Its founder, Shakyamuni Buddha, lived from about 563 to 483 BCE. He was born Prince Siddhartha Gautama, child of a ruler of the Shakya clan—Shakyamuni means "sage of the Shakyas"—and was raised to be a ruler himself. Troubled by what he perceived to be the suffering of all human beings, he abandoned the luxurious lifestyle of his father's palace to live in the wilderness. For six years he meditated, until, sitting under a banyan tree at Bodh Gaya, he attained complete enlightenment—nirvana, the release from worldly desires that ends the cycle of death and reincarnation and begins a state of permanent bliss.

The philosophy of the Buddha is based on a message of self-denial and meditation, which he preached across northern India, attracting converts from all levels of Indian society. The religion gained strength for centuries after the Buddha's death and finally became institutionalized in India under the rule of Ashoka (273–232 BCE). Deeply saddened by the horrors of war, and believing that his power rested ultimately in religious virtue and not military force, Ashoka became an ardent pacifist and a great patron of the Buddhist monks, erecting some 84,000 shrines, called stupas, throughout India, all elaborately decorated with sculpture and painting. The **stupa** is literally a burial mound, dating from prehistoric times, but by the time the Great Stupa at Sanchi was made (**Fig. 16-37**)—it is the earliest surviving example of the form—it had come to house important relics of the Buddha himself or the remains of later Buddhist holy persons. This stupa is made of rubble, piled on top of the original shrine, which has been faced with brick to form a hemispherical dome that symbolizes the earth itself. A railing—in this case, made of white stone and clearly visible in this photograph—encircles the sphere. Ceremonial processions moved along the narrow path behind this railing. Pilgrims would circle the stupa in a clockwise direction on another wider path, at ground level, retracing the path of the sun, thus putting themselves in harmony with the cosmos and symbolically walking the Buddhist Path of Life around the World Mountain.

All the ancient centers of civilization underwent wars, conquests, and dramatic cultural changes. And all produced great philosophers, great art, and great writing, much of which we still find current and useful today. All were organized around religion, and with the dawn of the Christian era, religion continued to play a central role in defining culture.

Fig. 16-37 The Great Stupa, Sanchi, Madhya Pradesh, India, view of the West Gateway, founded 3rd century BCE, enlarged ca. 150–50 BCE. Shrine height 50 ft., diameter 105 ft.
© Atlantide Phototravel/Corbis. Photo: Massimo Borchi.

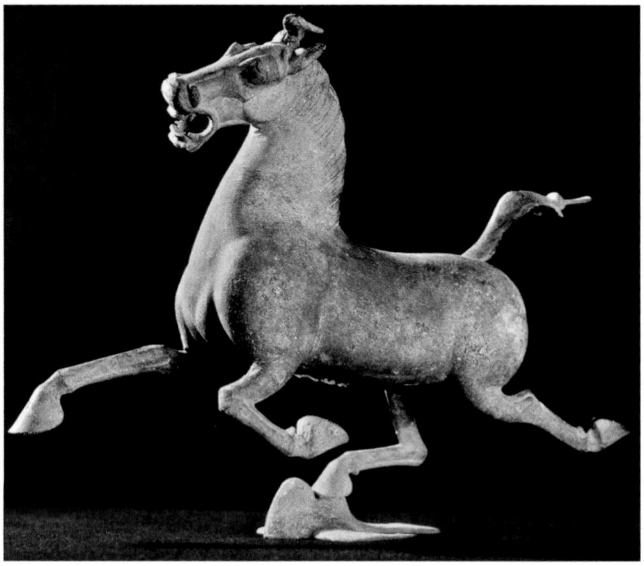

Fig. 16-36 *Flying Horse Poised on One Leg on a Swallow*, from the tomb of Governor-General Zhang at Wuwei, Gansu, Late Han dynasty, 2nd century CE. Bronze, 13½ × 17¾ in. Gansu Provincial Museum.
Art Archive/Genius of China Exhibition.

Thinking Back

16.1 Describe some ways in which prehistoric art reflects the social aspirations of early peoples.

The paintings discovered in caves in Spain and France suggest that prehistoric people gathered for ritual or ceremonial purposes, probably in the interest of serving the common good. In Britain and France, a distinctive kind of monumental stone architecture was produced. Known as megaliths, meaning “big stones,” these works required significant organization and problem-solving skills to create. What do we know of the original purpose of Stonehenge?

16.2 Discuss the relationship between the gods and the people in Mesopotamian art.

Ancient Sumer consisted of a dozen or more city-states, each with a population of between 10,000 and 50,000, and each with its own reigning deity. Communication with the god occurred in a ziggurat. Visitors—almost certainly limited to members of the priesthood—might bring an offering of food or an animal to be sacrificed to the resident god and often placed a statue in the temple that represented themselves in a state of perpetual prayer. These statues are remarkable for their large eyes. What do these eyes suggest? What does the carving at the top of the *Stele of Hammurabi* suggest about the relationship of the god Shamash to the king, and, in turn, about that of the king to his people? Why do you think Assurnasirpal II built such a large capital for his Assyrian empire?

16.3 Account for the stability of Egyptian art and culture.

Egyptian culture was dedicated to providing a home for the *ka*, the part of the human being believed to define personality. Egyptians believed that the *ka* survived after death. The enduring quality of the *ka* accounts for the unchanging way in which, over the centuries, Egyptian figures, especially the pharaohs, were represented. They extensively decorated tombs and preserved bodies through mummification to appease the *ka*. What purpose did Egyptian pyramids serve? How were Egyptian pharaohs represented?

16.4 Describe the growing technological sophistication of the river valley societies of India and China.

The earliest Indian peoples lived in at least two great cities in the Indus Valley, Harappa and Mohenjo-daro. Unlike the sun-dried bricks used in other cultures at the time, Mohenjo-daro’s bricks were of a standard size and were fired, which made them much more durable, suggesting a civilization of considerable technological know-how and sophistication. The Shang dynasty in the Yellow River Valley of China developed an extremely sophisticated bronze-casting technology, as advanced as any ever used.

16.5 Explain the large size of so many artworks and cultural sites in the Americas.

In Mesoamerica, the Olmec built cities on great earthen platforms, probably designed to protect their ceremonial centers from rain and flood. What does the size of the heads that guard these platforms suggest? What does the size of the Mississippian complexes in North America suggest?

16.6 Differentiate between Minoan and Mycenaean culture and describe how the Greek *polis* and its art differ from its Aegean predecessors.

Minoan culture on the island of Crete thrived between 1600 and 1450 BCE, when it abruptly ended. Evidence suggests that the Minoans worshiped female goddesses, but why is their worship of a “Snake Goddess” today suspect? Perhaps Minoan culture fell victim to the warlike Mycenaeans from the mainland, whose culture flourished between 1400 and 1200 BCE. Theirs was a culture dominated by military values, as Homer described it in his *Iliad*. The rise of the Greek city-state, or *polis*, marks the moment when Western culture begins to celebrate its own human strengths and powers—the creative genius of the mind itself and the concept of individual freedom. How are these values reflected in the architecture of the Parthenon and in Greek sculpture?

16.7 Discuss how the art and architecture of Rome suggest the empire’s power.

By making Greek culture their own, the Romans in essence asserted their power over it. As it dedicated itself to the conquest of the entire Mediterranean, the empire built monuments—arches, amphitheaters, and columns—celebrating its own power. How does the *Augustus of Primaporta* demonstrate Greek influence? What is distinctly Roman about it?

16.8 Compare and contrast Chinese militarism with Buddhist pacifism.

After the Qin united all of China in 221 BCE, the task of defending the country from invading nomadic tribes to the north required China to build the Great Wall. The succeeding Han dynasty thrived for 400 years, but it too was threatened from the north. Held captive by the Huns for ten years, the Han general Zhang Qian recognized the beauty of Hun horses. How does the Chinese defensive posture compare to Ashoka’s acceptance of Buddhism?

Chapter 17
The Age of Faith

Learning Objectives

17.1 Describe the principal architectural and decorative features of early Christian and Byzantine places of worship.

17.2 Explain the origins of the mosque and describe its chief features.

17.3 Describe the chief characteristics of the Carolingian, Romanesque, and Gothic styles.

17.4 Describe how Indian art and architecture reflect the Hindu religion, and how the Buddhist faith is evident in the arts of China and Japan.

17.5 Describe some of the characteristic works of the Ife, Shona, and Zagwe cultures.

Our study of the ancient world—from ancient fertility statues, to the Egyptian *ka*, to the rise of Buddhism—shows how powerful religion can be in setting the course of a culture, and the advent of Christianity in the Western world makes this abundantly clear. So powerful was the Christian story that in the West the common calendar changed. From the sixth century on, time was recorded in terms of years "BC" (before Christ) and years "AD" (*anno Domini*, the year of Our Lord, with the number indicating the years since his birth). Today, usage has changed somewhat—the preferred terms, as we use them in this text, are BCE (before the common era) and CE (the common era)—but the West's calendar remains Christian.

At the Dome of the Rock in Jerusalem (**Fig. 17-1**), all three of the great Western faiths—Judaism, Christianity, and Islam—intersect. In Jewish tradition, it was here that Abraham prepared to sacrifice his son Isaac. The Jewish Temple of Solomon originally stood here, and the site is further associated, in all three religions, with God's creation of Adam. The Second Temple of Jerusalem also stood on this spot until it was destroyed by Roman soldiers when they sacked the city in 70 CE to put down a Jewish revolt. Only the Wailing Wall remains, part of the original retaining wall for the platform supporting the Temple Mount and, for Jews, the most sacred site in Jerusalem. To this day, the plaza in front of the wall functions as an open-air synagogue where daily prayers are recited and other Jewish rituals are performed. On Tisha B'Av, the ninth day of the month of Av, which occurs either in July or August, a fast is held commemorating the destruction of the successive temples on this site, and people sit on the ground before the wall reciting the Book of Lamentations.

One of the earliest examples of Muslim architecture, built in the 680s, the Dome of the Rock's **ambulatory**—its circular, colonnaded walkway—encloses a projected rock that lies directly beneath its golden dome. By the sixteenth century, Islamic faithful claimed that the Prophet Muhammad ascended to heaven from this spot, on a winged horse named Buraq, but there is no evidence that this story was in circulation when the Dome was originally built. Others thought that it represented the ascendency of Islam over Christianity in the Holy Land. Still others believed the rock to be the

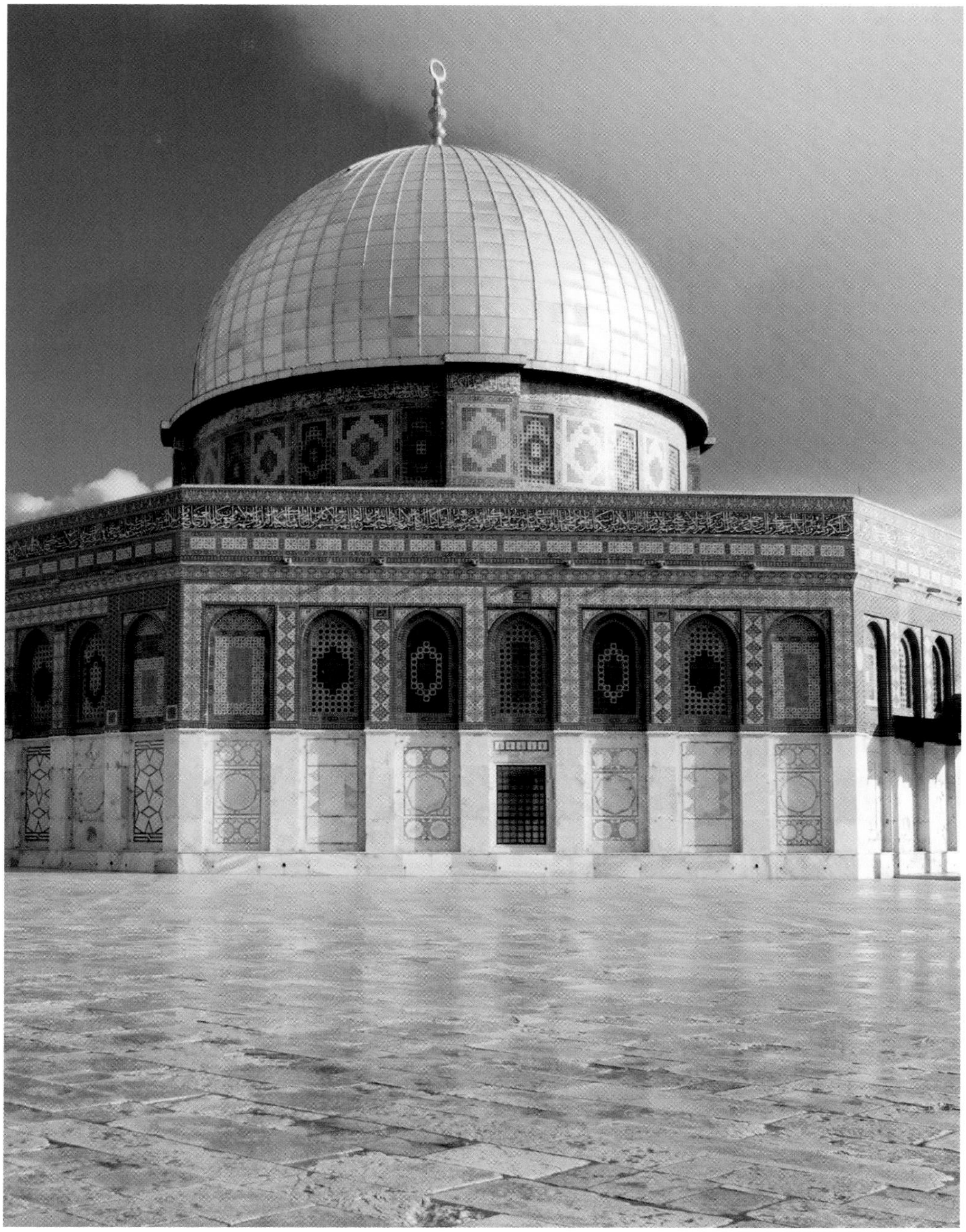

Fig. 17-1 The Dome of the Rock, Jerusalem, late 680s–91.

center of the world, or that it could refer to the Temple of Solomon, the importance of which is fully acknowledged by Muslims, who consider Solomon a founding father of their own faith. All of this suggests that the Dome was meant to proselytize, or convert both Jews and Christians to the Muslim faith. The sanctity of the spot, then, in the heart of Jerusalem, is recognized by Jews, Christians, and Muslims alike, and the intersection of these three religions, together with the spread of Buddhism in Asia and the growth of the Hindu faith in Southeast Asia, is the subject of this chapter. The powerful influence of all these religions throughout the first millennium and well into the second gave rise to an age of faith.

400

ca. 400–500 Germanic tribes invade Rome

Augustus writes *The City of God* **426**

Last Roman emperor dethroned **476**

Early Christian and Byzantine Art

What are the principal architectural and decorative features of early Christian and Byzantine churches?

Christianity spread through the Roman world at a very rapid pace, in large part due to the missionary zeal of St. Paul. By 250 CE, fully 60 percent of Asia Minor had converted to the religion, and when the Roman emperor Constantine legalized Christianity in the Edict of Milan in 313 CE, Christian art became imperial art. The Classical art of Greece and Rome emphasized the humanity of its figures, their corporeal reality. But the Christian God was not mortal and could not even be comfortably represented in human terms. Though His Son, Jesus, was human enough, the mystery of both Jesus' Virgin Birth and his rising from the dead most interested early Christian believers. The world that the Romans had celebrated on their walls in fresco—a world of still lifes and landscapes—was of little interest to Christians, who were more concerned with the spiritual and the heavenly than with their material surroundings.

Constantine chose to make early Christian places of worship as unlike Classical temples as possible. The building type that he preferred was the rectangular **basilica**, which the Romans had used for public buildings, especially courthouses. The original St. Peter's in Rome, constructed around 333–90 CE but destroyed in the sixteenth century to make way for the present building, was a basilica (see Fig. 14-27). Equally important for the future of Christian religious architecture was Santa Costanza (**Fig. 17-2**), the small mausoleum built around 354 CE for the tomb of Constantine's daughter, Constantia. Circular in shape and topped with a dome supported by a barrel vault, the building defines the points of the traditional Greek cross, which has four equal arms. Surrounding the circular space is an ambulatory, similar to that found in the Dome of the Rock, that was used for ceremonial processions.

The circular form of Santa Costanza appears often in later Byzantine architecture. By the year 500, most of the Western Empire, traditionally Catholic, had been overrun by barbarian forces from the north. When the emperor Justinian assumed the throne in Constantinople in 527, he dreamed of restoring the lost empire. His armies quickly recaptured the Mediterranean world, and he began a massive program of public works. Justinian attached enormous importance to architecture, believing that nothing better served to underscore the power of the emperor. The church of Hagia Sophia, meaning "Holy Wisdom," was his imperial place of worship in Constantinople (**Figs. 17-3** and **17-4**). The huge interior,

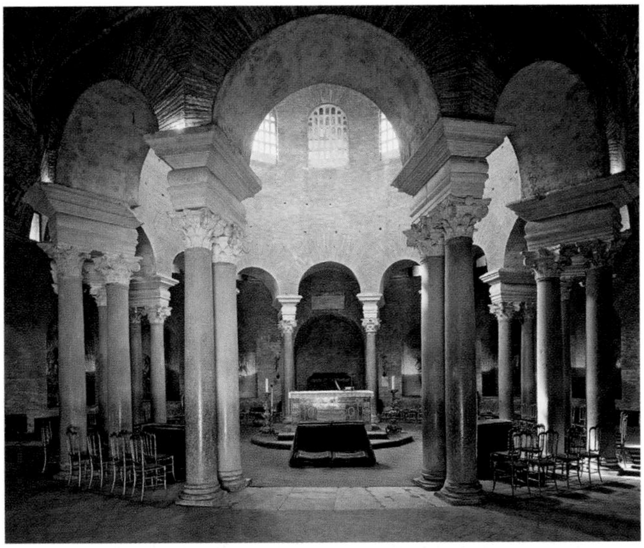

Fig. 17-2 Santa Costanza, Rome, ca. 354 CE.

Fig. 17-3 Anthemius of Tralles and Isidorus of Miletus, Hagia Sophia, Istanbul, and plan, 532–37.

Photo: Ayhan Altun/Altunimages.

Fig. 17-4 Anthemius of Tralles and Isidorus of Miletus, Interior, Hagia Sophia, Istanbul, 532–37.
Photo: Ayhan Altun/Altunimages.

crowned by a dome, is reminiscent of the circular, central plan of Ravenna's San Vitale (see Fig. 17-6), but this dome is abutted at either end by half-domes that extend the central core of the church along a longitudinal axis reminiscent of the basilica, with the apse extending in another smaller half-dome out one end of the axis. These half-domes culminate in arches that are repeated on the two sides of the dome as well. The architectural scheme is, in fact, relatively simple—a dome supported by four **pendentives**, the curved, inverted triangular shapes that rise up to the rim of the dome between the four arches themselves. This dome-on-pendentive design was so enthusiastically received that it became the standard for Byzantine church design.

The interior of Hagia Sophia was decorated with **mosaics**—small pieces of stone, glass, or tile arranged in a pattern or image. Many were later destroyed or covered over in the eighth and ninth centuries when **iconoclasts**, meaning "image-breakers," who believed literally in the Bible's commandment against the worship of "graven" images, destroyed much Byzantine art. Forced to migrate westward, Byzantine artists discovered Hellenistic naturalism and incorporated it into later Byzantine design. The mosaic of Christ from Hagia Sophia (**Fig. 17-5**) is representative of that later synthesis.

Mosaics are made of small pieces of stone called **tesserae**, from the Greek word *tesseres*, meaning "square." In ancient Rome, they were a favorite decorative element, used because of their durability, especially to embellish villa floors. But the Romans rarely used mosaic on their walls, where they preferred the more refined and naturalistic effects that were possible with fresco. For no matter how skilled the mosaic artist, the naturalism of the original drawing would inevitably be lost when the small stones were set in cement.

Fig. 17-5 *Christ*, from *Deësis* mosaic, 13th century.
Hagia Sophia, Istanbul.
Photo: Ayhan Altun/Altunimages.

The Byzantine mosaic artists, in fact, had little interest in naturalism. Their intention was to create a symbolic, mystical art, something for which the mosaic medium was perfectly suited. Gold tesserae were made by sandwiching gold leaf between two small squares of glass, and polished glass was also used. By setting the tesserae unevenly, at slight angles, a shimmering and transcendent effect was realized, which was heightened by the light from the church's windows.

Though only a few of the original mosaics at Hagia Sophia have been restored, and later mosaics were few, the light in the interior is still almost transcendental in feeling, and one can only imagine the heavenly aura when gold and glass reflected the light that entered the nave through the many windows that surround it. In Justinian's own words:

> The sun's light and its shining rays fill the temple. One would say that the space is not lit by the sun without, but that the source of light is to be found within, such is the abundance of light. . . . The scintillations of the light forbid the spectator's gaze to linger on the details; each one attracts the eye and leads it on to the next. The circular motion of one's gaze reproduces itself to infinity. . . . The spirit rises toward God and floats in the air.

At Ravenna, Italy, from where Justinian could exercise control over the Adriatic Sea, he built a new church modeled on the churches of Constantinople—San Vitale (**Fig. 17-6**). Although its exterior is octagonal, the interior space is essentially circular, like Santa Costanza before it. Only in the altar and the apse, which lie to the right of the central domed area in the floor plan, is there any reference to the basilica structure that dominates Western church architecture. But if the facade of San Vitale is very plain, more or less unadorned, local brick, inside it is elaborately decorated with marble and glittering mosaics, including two elaborate mosaics that face each other on the side walls of the apse, one depicting Theodora, the wife of Justinian (**Fig. 17-7**), and the other Justinian himself (**Fig. 17-8**). Theodora had at one time been a circus performer, but she became one of the emperor's most trusted advisors, sharing with him a vision of a Christian Roman Empire. In the mosaic, she carries a golden cup of wine, and Justinian, on the opposite wall, carries a bowl containing bread. Together they are bringing to the Church an offering of bread and wine for the celebration of the Eucharist. The haloed Justinian is to be identified with Christ, surrounded as he is by 12 advisors, like the 12 Apostles. And the haloed Theodora, with the three Magi bearing gifts to the Virgin and newborn Christ embroidered on the hem of her skirt, is to be understood as a figure for Mary. In this image, Church and State become one and the same.

These mosaics bear no relation to the naturalism that dominated Greek and Roman culture. Here, the human figures are depicted wearing long robes that hide the musculature and cause a loss of individual identity. Although each face has unique features—some of Justinian's attendants, for example, are bearded, while others are not, and the hairstyles vary—all have identical wide-open eyes, curved brows, and long noses. The feet of the figures turn outward, as if to flatten the space in which they stand. They are disproportionately long and

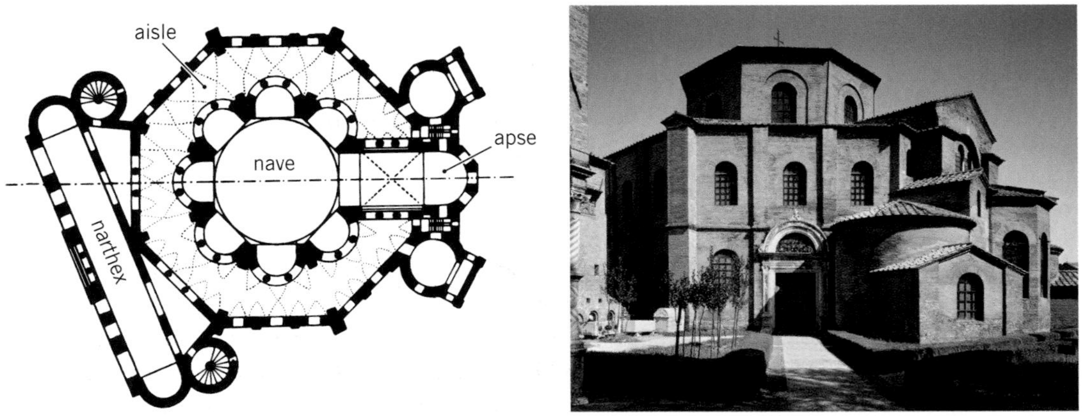

Fig. 17-6 Plan and exterior, San Vitale, Ravenna, dedicated 547.
Canali Photobank, Milan, Italy.

Visigoths in Spain adopt Western Christianity
589

597
St. Augustine in England

600

Figs. 17-7 and 17-8 ***Theodora and Her Attendants*** **(top),** ***Justinian and His Attendants*** **(bottom), San Vitale, ca. 547.** Mosaic, each 8 ft. 8 in. × 12 ft.
CAMERAPHOTO Arte, Venice.

thin, a fact that lends them a heavenly lightness. And they are motionless, standing before us without gesture, as if eternally still. The Greek ideal of sculpture in the round, with its sense of the body caught in an intensely personal, even private moment—Nike taking off her sandal (see Fig. 16-23), for instance, or Laocoön caught in the intensity of his torment (see Fig. 16-26)—is gone. All sense of drama has been removed from the idea of representation.

Justinian's reign marked the apex of the early Christian and Byzantine era. By the seventh century, barbarian invaders had taken control of the Western Empire, and the new Muslim Empire had begun to expand to the east. Reduced in area to the Balkans and Greece, the Byzantine

Empire nevertheless held on until 1453, when the Turks finally captured Constantinople and renamed it Istanbul, converting Hagia Sophia into a mosque.

The Rise of Islam

What is the origin of the mosque and what are its chief features?

Born in Mecca on the Arabian Peninsula in about 570 to a prominent family, Muhammad, the founder of the Islamic faith, was orphaned at age six and received little formal education. He worked in the caravan trade in the Arabian Desert, first as a camel driver for his uncle, and then, after marrying a wealthy widow 15 years his senior at age 25, as head of his wife's flourishing caravan firm. But at the age of 40, in 610, he heard a voice in Arabic—the Archangel Gabriel's, as the story goes—urging him, "Recite!" He responded, "What shall I recite?" And for the next 22 years, he claimed to receive messages, or "recitations," from God through the agency of Gabriel. These he memorized and, probably later, scribes collected them to form the scriptures of Islam, the Qur'an (or Koran), which means "recitations." Muhammad also claimed that Gabriel commanded him to declare himself the "Seal of the Prophets," that is, the messenger of the one and only Allah (the Arab word for God) and the final prophet in a series of God's prophets on earth, extending from Abraham and Moses to Jesus.

At the core of Muhammad's revelations is the concept of submission to God—the word Islam, in fact, means "submission" or "surrender." God, or Allah, is all—all-powerful, all-seeing, all-merciful. Because the universe is his creation, it is necessarily good and beautiful, and the natural world reflects Allah's own goodness and beauty. To immerse oneself in nature is thus to be at one with God. But the most beautiful creation of Allah is humankind. As in Christianity, Muslims believe that human beings possess immortal souls and that they can live eternally in heaven if they surrender to Allah and accept him as the one and only God.

In 622, Muhammad was forced to flee Mecca when its polytheistic leadership became irritated at his insistence on the worship of only one God. In a journey known as the *hijra* (or *hegira*, "emigration"), he and his followers fled to the oasis of Yathrib, 200 miles north, which they renamed al-Medina, meaning "the city of the Prophet." There, Muhammad created a community based not on kinship, the traditional basis of Arab society, but on common submission to the will of God.

At Medina, Muhammad also built a house that surrounded a large open courtyard, which served as a community gathering place, on the model of the Roman forum. There, the men of the community would gather on Fridays to pray and listen to a sermon delivered by Muhammad. It thus became known as the *masjid*, the Arabic word for **mosque**, or "place of prostration." On the north and south ends of the courtyard, covered porches were erected, supported by palm tree trunks and roofed by thatched palm fronds, which protected the community from the hot Arabian sun. This many-columned covered area, known as a **hypostyle space** (from the Greek *hupostulos*, "resting upon pillars"), would later become a required feature of all Muslim mosques. Another required feature was the ***qibla***, a wall that indicated the direction of Mecca. On this wall were both the ***minbar***, or stepped pulpit for the preacher, and the ***mihrab***, a niche commemorating the spot at Medina where Muhammad planted his lance to indicate the direction in which people should pray.

The Prophet's Mosque in Medina has been rebuilt so many times that its original character has long since been lost. But not so at Damascus, where, in 705, the Muslim community had grown so large that radical steps had to be taken to accommodate it, and a Byzantine church was torn down, leaving a large courtyard (**Fig. 17-9**), the

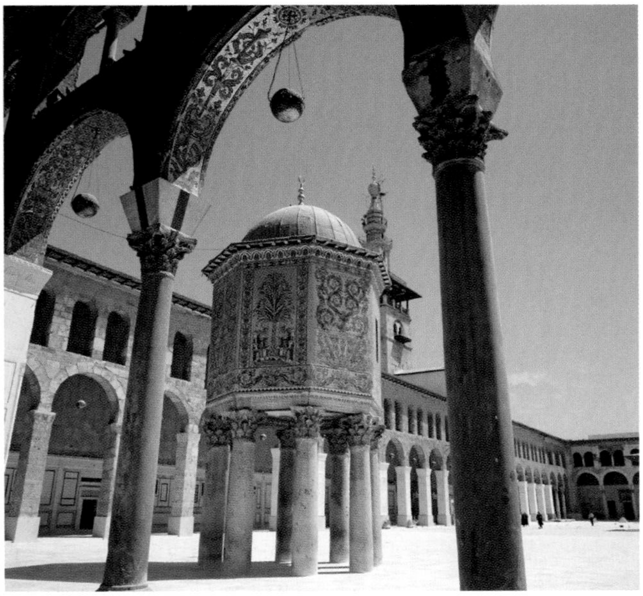

Fig. 17-9 Courtyard of the Great Mosque of Damascus, 705–16.
Photo: Christopher Rennie, Robert Harding World Imagery.

Fig. 17-10 Tile mosaic *mihrab*, from the Madrasa Imami, Isfahan, Persia (Iran), ca. 1354 (restored). Glazed and cut ceramic, 11 ft. 3 in. × 7 ft. 6 in. Metropolitan Museum of Art, New York.

compound walls of which were transformed into the walls of a new mosque. A large prayer hall was constructed against the *qibla* wall and decorated with an elaborate mosaic facade, some of which is visible in the illustration, facing into the courtyard, while the street side of the mosque was left relatively plain.

One of the most important characteristics of Islamic culture is its emphasis on calligraphy (see Fig. 2-4), and the art of calligraphy was incorporated into Islamic architecture from the beginning. By the mid-ninth century, the walls of palaces and mosques were covered by it, and throughout the following centuries, the decoration became more and more elaborate. The mosaic *mihrab*, originally from a *madrasa*, or teaching college, in Iran, contains three different inscriptions from the Qur'an (**Fig. 17-10**). The outer frame is a description of the duties of true believers and the heavenly rewards in store for those who build mosques. The next contains the Five Pillars of Islam, the duties every believer must perform, including, at least once in a lifetime, a pilgrimage to Mecca. And, finally, in the center of the inner wall, the reminder: "The mosque is the house of every pious person." All of this is contained in a beautifully balanced and symmetrical design.

After the Prophet Muhammad fled Mecca for Medina in 622, the Muslim Empire had expanded rapidly (see **Map 17-1**, showing the expansion of Islam). By 640, Muhammad's successors, the Caliphs, had conquered Syria, Palestine, and Iraq. Two years later, they defeated the army of Byzantium at Alexandria, and, by 710, they had captured all of northern Africa and had moved into Spain. They advanced north until 732, when Charles Martel, grandfather of Charlemagne, defeated them at Poitiers, France. But the Caliphs' foothold in Europe remained strong, and they did not leave Spain until 1492. Even the Crusades failed to reduce their power. During the First Crusade, 50,000 men were sent to the Middle East, where they managed to hold Jerusalem and much of Palestine for a short while. The Second Crusade, in 1146, failed to regain control and, in 1187, the Muslim warrior Saladin reconquered Jerusalem. Finally, in 1192, Saladin defeated King Richard I of England in the Third Crusade.

The Muslim impact on the culture of North Africa cannot be overstated. Beginning in about 750, not long after Muslim armies had conquered most of North Africa, Muslim traders, following the routes created by the Saharan Berber peoples, began trading for salt, copper, dates, and especially gold with the sub-Saharan peoples of the Niger River drainage. Gradually they came to dominate the trans-Saharan trade routes, and Islam became the dominant faith of West Africa.

In 1312, a devout Muslim named Mansa Moussa came to the throne of Mali. He built magnificent mosques throughout his empire, including the Djingareyber Mosque in Timbuktu (**Fig. 17-11**). Still standing today and made of burnt brick and mud, it dominates the city. Under Moussa's patronage, the city of Timbuktu grew in wealth and prestige and became a cultural focal point for the finest poets, scholars, and artists of Africa and the Middle East. To draw further attention to Timbuktu, and to attract more scholars and poets to it, Moussa embarked on a pilgrimage to Mecca in 1334. He arrived in Cairo at the head of a huge caravan of 60,000 people, including 12,000 servants, with 80 camels carrying more than 2 tons of gold to be distributed among the poor. In fact, Moussa distributed so much gold in Egypt that the value of the precious metal fell dramatically and did not recover for a number of years.

Islam penetrates sub-Saharan Africa **1000–1100**	Beginning of First Crusade **1096**

1000

1071 Turks capture Jerusalem

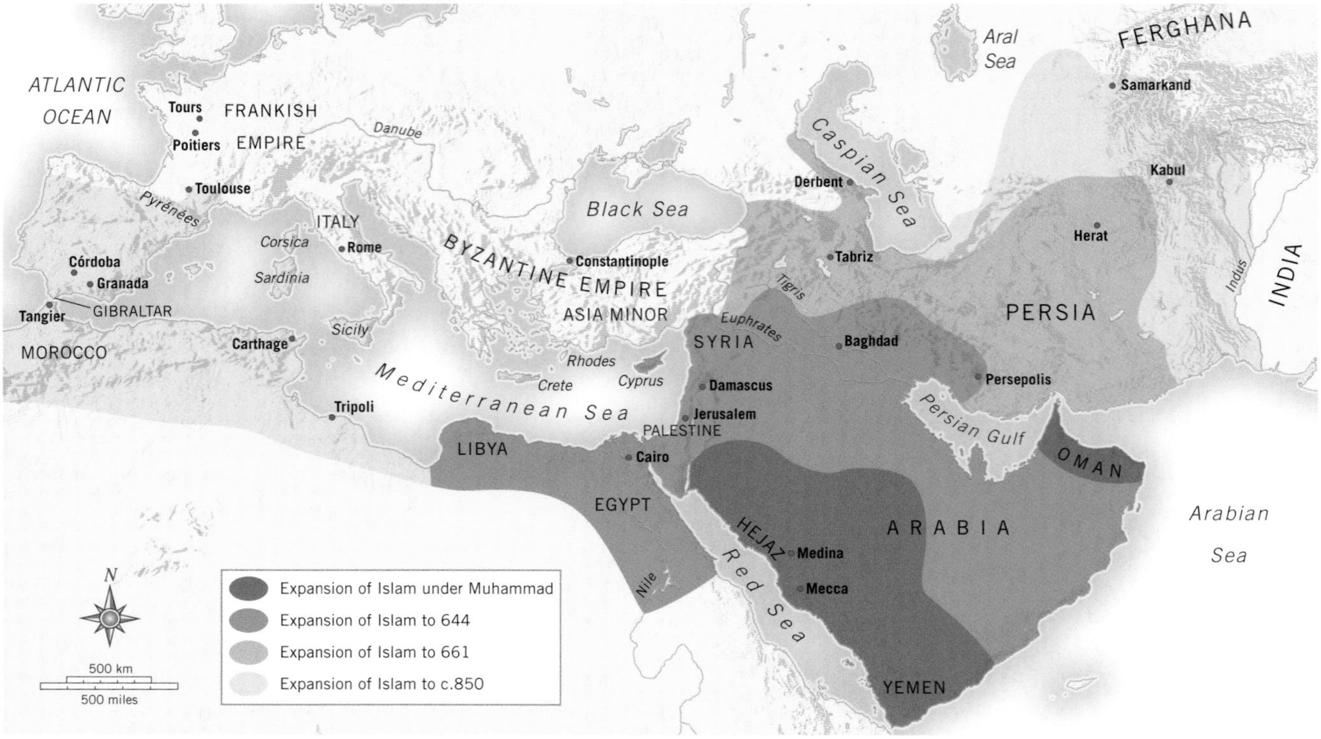

Map 17-1 The Expansion of Islam to 850 CE.

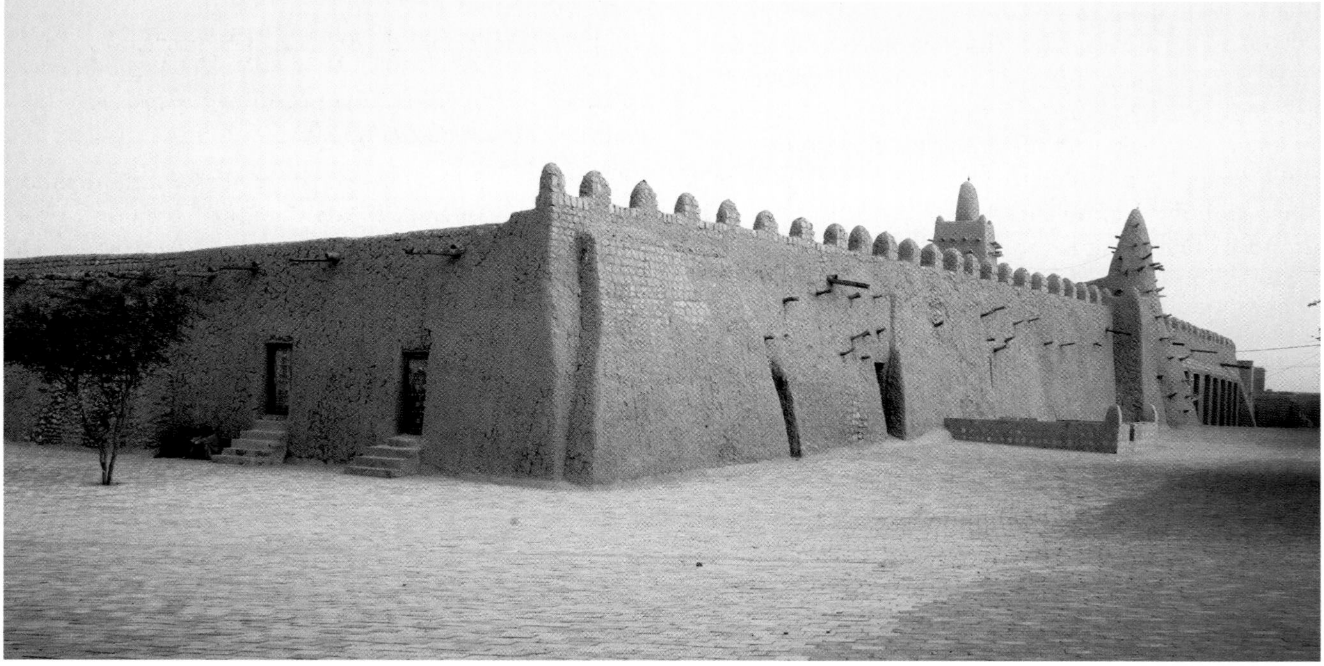

Fig. 17-11 Djingareyber Mosque, Timbuktu, ca. 1312.

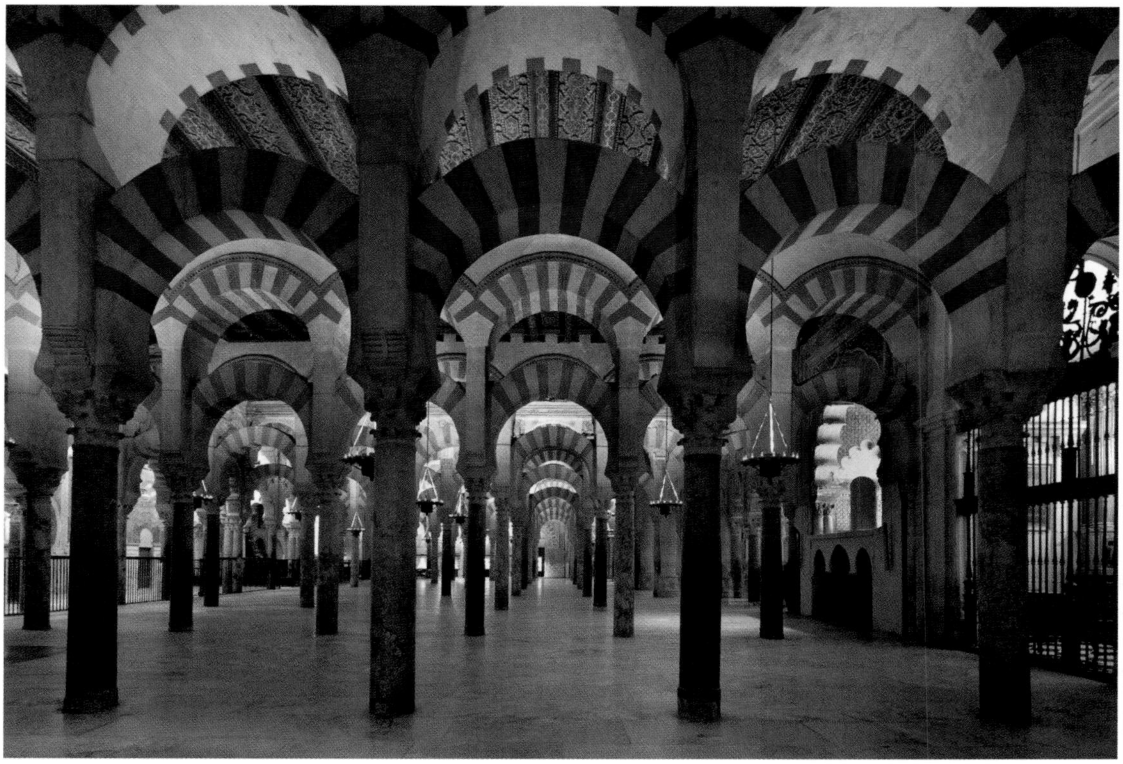

Fig. 17-12 Interior, Sanctuary of the mosque at Córdoba, Spain, 786–987.

In Spain, the center of Muslim culture was originally Córdoba. For its mosque, Islamic rulers converted an existing Visigoth church. The Visigoths, a Christianized Germanic tribe who had invaded Spain three centuries earlier, had built their church with relatively short, stubby columns. To create the loftier space required by the mosque, the architects superimposed another set of columns on top, creating two tiers of arches, one over the other, using a distinctive alternation of stone and red brick voussoirs (**Fig. 17-12**). The use of two different materials is not only decorative but also functional, combining the flexibility of brick with the strength of stone. Finally, the hypostyle plan of the mosque was, in essence, infinitely expandable, and subsequent Caliphs enlarged the mosque in 852, 950, 961–76, and 987, until it was over four times the size of the original and incorporated 1,200 columns. As in all Muslim design, where a visual rhythm is realized through symmetry and repetition of certain patterns and motifs, the rhythm of arches and columns unifies the interior of the Córdoba mosque.

Christian Art in Europe

What are the chief characteristics of the Carolingian, Romanesque, and Gothic styles?

Until the year 1000, the center of Western civilization was located in the Middle East, at Constantinople. In Europe, tribal groups with localized power held sway: The Lombards in what is now Italy, the Franks and the Burgundians in regions of France, and the Angles and Saxons in England. Though it possessed no real political power, the papacy in Rome had begun to work hard to convert the pagan tribes and to reassert the authority of the Church. As early as 496, the leader of the Franks, Clovis, was baptized into the Church. Even earlier (ca. 430), St. Patrick had undertaken an evangelical mission to Ireland, establishing monasteries and quickly converting the native Celts. These new monasteries were designed to serve missionary as well as educational functions. At a time when only priests and monks could read and write, the sacred texts they produced came to reflect native Celtic designs. These

Fig. 17-13 Purse cover, from the Sutton Hoo burial ship, ca. 625. Gold with Indian garnets and cloisonné enamels, originally on an ivory or bone background (now lost), length 8 in. The British Museum, London.
1939,1010.3. © The Trustees of the British Museum.

designs are elaborately decorative, highly abstract, and contain no naturalistic representation. Thus, Christian art fused with the native traditions, which employed the so-called "animal style." Some of the best examples of this animal style, such as this purse cover (**Fig. 17-13**), have been found at Sutton Hoo, northeast of present-day London, in the grave of an unknown seventh-century East Anglian king. In this design two pairs of animals and birds, facing each other, are elongated into serpentine ribbons of decoration, a common Scandinavian motif. Below this, two Swedish hawks with curved beaks attack a pair of ducks. On each side of this design, a male figure stands between two animals. Note particularly the design's symmetry, its combination of interlaced organic and geometric shapes, and, of course, its animal motifs. Throughout the Middle Ages, this style was imitated in manuscripts, stone sculpture, church masonry, and wood sculpture.

In 597, Gregory the Great, the first monk to become pope, sent an emissary, later known as St. Augustine of Canterbury, on a mission to convert the Anglo-Saxons. This mission brought Roman religious and artistic traditions into direct contact with Celtic art, and, slowly but surely, Roman culture began to dominate the Celtic-Germanic world.

Carolingian Art

When Charlemagne (Charles, or Carolus, the Great) assumed leadership of the Franks in 771, this process of Romanization was assured. At the request of the pope, Charlemagne conquered the Lombards, becoming their king, and on Christmas Day 800, he was crowned Holy Roman emperor by Pope Leo III at St. Peter's Basilica in Rome. The fusion of Germanic and Mediterranean styles that reflected this new alliance between Church and state is known as **Carolingian art**, a term referring to the art produced during the reign of Charlemagne and his immediate successors.

The transformation in style that Charlemagne effected is evident if we compare the work of an artist trained in the linear Celtic tradition to one created during Charlemagne's era. In the former (**Fig. 17-14**), copied from an earlier Italian original, the image is flat, the figure has not been modeled, and the perspective is completely askew. It is pattern—and the animal style—that really interests the artist, not accurate representation. But Charlemagne was intent on restoring the glories of Roman civilization. He actively collected and had copied the oldest surviving texts of the Classical Latin authors. He created schools in monasteries and cathedrals across

ca. 800–1000
England and Europe invaded by Vikings, Magyars, and Muslims

Cluny monastery founded
910

Rise of Inca Empire in South America
ca. 1000

1000

Fig. 17-14 ***St. Matthew*, from the *Lindisfarne Gospels*, ca. 700.** Manuscript page, approx. 11 × 9 in. British Library, London. © British Library Board, Cotton Nero D. IV, f.25v.

Fig. 17-15 ***St. Matthew*, from the *Gospel Book of Charlemagne*, ca. 800–810.** Manuscript page, 12$\frac{3}{4}$ × 9$\frac{7}{8}$ in. Kunsthistorisches Museum, Vienna. Inv. SK XIII18.

Europe in which Classical Latin was the accepted language. A new script, with Roman capitals and new lowercase letters, the basis of modern type, was introduced. A second depiction of St. Matthew (**Fig. 17-15**), executed 100 years after the one on the left, demonstrates the impact of Roman realism on northern art. Found in Charlemagne's tomb, this illustration looks as if it could have been painted in Classical Rome.

Romanesque Art

After the dissolution of the Carolingian state in the ninth and tenth centuries, Europe disintegrated into a large number of small feudal territories. The emperors were replaced by an array of rulers of varying power and prestige who controlled smaller or larger fiefdoms (areas of land worked by persons under obligation to the ruler) and whose authority was generally embodied in a chateau or castle surrounded by walls and moats. Despite this atomization of political life, a recognizable style that we have come to call **Romanesque** developed throughout Europe beginning in about 1050. Although details varied from place to place, certain features remained constant for nearly 200 years.

Romanesque architecture is characterized by its easily recognizable geometric masses—rectangles, cubes, cylinders, and half-cylinders. The wooden roof that St. Peter's Basilica had used was abandoned in favor of fireproof stone and masonry construction, apparently out of bitter experience with the invading nomadic tribes, who burned many of the churches of Europe in the ninth and tenth centuries. Flat roofs were replaced by vaulted ceilings. By structural necessity, these were supported by massive walls that often lacked windows sufficient to provide adequate lighting. The churches were often built along the roads leading to pilgrimage centers, usually monasteries that housed Christian relics, and they had to be large enough to accommodate large crowds of the faithful. For instance, St. Sernin, in Toulouse, France (see Figs. 14-19 and 14-20), was on the pilgrimage route to Santiago de Compostela, in Spain, where the body of St. James was believed to rest.

Thanks in large part to Charlemagne's emphasis on monastic learning, monasteries had flourished since the Carolingian period, many of them acting as feudal landlords as well. The largest and most powerful was Cluny, near Maçon, France. Until the building of the new St. Peter's in Rome, the church at Cluny was the largest in the Christian world. It was 521 feet in length, and its nave vaults rose to a height of 100 feet. The height of the nave was made possible by the use of pointed arches. The church was destroyed in the French Revolution, and only part of one transept survives.

With the decline of the Roman Empire, the art of sculpture had largely declined in the West, but in the Romanesque period it began to reemerge. It is certain that the idea of educating the masses in the Christian message through architectural sculpture on the facades of the pilgrimage churches contributed to the art's rebirth. The most important sculptural work was usually located on the **tympanum** of the church, the semicircular arch above the lintel on the main door. It often showed Christ with His 12 Apostles. Another favorite theme was the Last Judgment, full of depictions of sinners suffering the horrors of hellfire and damnation. To the left of Gislebertus's *Last Judgment* at Autun, France (**Fig. 17-16**), the blessed arrive in heaven, while on the right, the damned are seized by devils. Combining all manner of animal forms, the monstrosity of these creatures recalls the animal style of the Germanic tribes.

Fig. 17-16 Gislebertus, *Last Judgment*, tympanum and lintel, west portal, cathedral, Autun, France, ca. 1125–35. Stone, approx. 12 ft. 6 in. × 22 ft.
© Bednorz-images, Cologne.

Gothic Art

The great era of **Gothic** art begins in 1137 with the rebuilding of the choir of the abbey church of Saint-Denis, located just outside Paris (see Fig. 13-15). Abbot Suger of Saint-Denis saw his new church as both the political and the spiritual center of a new France, united under King Louis VI. Although he was familiar with Romanesque architecture, which was then at its height, Suger chose to abandon it. The Romanesque church was difficult to light, because the structural need to support the nave walls from without meant that windows had to be eliminated. Suger envisioned something different. He wanted his church flooded with light as if by the light of Heaven itself. After careful planning, he began work in 1137, painting the old walls of the original abbey, which were nearly 300 years old, with gold and precious colors. Then he added a new facade with twin towers and a triple portal. Around the back of the ambulatory he added a circular string of chapels, all lit with large stained-glass windows, "by virtue of which," Suger wrote, "the whole would shine with the wonderful and uninterrupted light."

It was this light that proclaimed the new Gothic style. Light, he believed, was the physical and material manifestation of the Divine Spirit. Suger wrote: "Marvel not at the gold and the expense but at the craftsmanship of the work. Bright is the noble work; but being nobly bright, the work should brighten the minds, so that they may travel, through the true lights, to the True Light where Christ is the true door." As beautiful as the church might be, it was designed to elevate the soul to the realm of God.

Fig. 17-17 West facade, Chartres Cathedral, France, ca. 1134–1220; south spire, ca. 1160; north spire 1507–13.
© Bednorz-images, Cologne.

As the Gothic style developed, French craftsmen became increasingly accomplished in working with stained glass, creating windows such as Chartres Cathedral's famous rose window (see Fig. 7-9). Important architectural innovations also contributed to this goal (**Fig. 17-17**). The massive stonework of the Romanesque style was replaced by a light, almost lacy, play of thin columns and patterns of ribs and windows all pointing upward in a rising crescendo that seems to defy gravity, even as it carries the viewer's gaze toward the heavens. Compare, for instance, the Romanesque south tower of Chartres Cathedral to the fully Gothic north tower, which rises high above its starkly symmetrical neighbor. Extremely high naves—the nave at Chartres is 120 feet high, Reims 125, and highest of all is Beauvais at 157 (the equivalent of a 15-story building)—made possible by flying buttresses (see Figs. 14-23 and 14-24) add to this emphasis on verticality. They contribute a sense of elevation that is at once physical and spiritual, as does the preponderance of pointed rather than rounded arches.

In Germany's Cologne Cathedral (**Fig. 17-18**), the width of the nave has been narrowed to such a degree that the vaults seem to rise higher than they actually do. The cathedral was not finished until the nineteenth century, though built strictly in accordance with thirteenth-century plans. The stonework is so slender, incorporating so much glass into its walls, that the effect is one of almost total weightlessness.

Fig. 17-18 Choir of Cologne Cathedral, Germany, 13th and 14th centuries. Caisse Nationale des Monuments Historiques.
© Svenja-Foto/Corbis.

The Gothic style in Italy is unique. For instance, the exterior of Florence Cathedral (**Fig. 17-19**) is hardly Gothic at all. It was, in fact, designed to match the dogmatically Romanesque octagonal Baptistry that stands in front of it. But the interior space is completely Gothic in character. Each side of the nave is flanked by an arcade that opens almost completely into the nave by virtue of four wide pointed arches. Thus nave and arcade become one, and the interior of the cathedral feels more spacious than any other. Nevertheless, rather than the mysterious and transcendental feelings evoked by most Gothic churches, Florence Cathedral produces a sense of tranquility and of measured, controlled calm. This sense of measured space is in large part a function of the enormous size of the dome above the crossing, the architectural feat of Filippo Brunelleschi.

The Gothic style in architecture inspired an outpouring of sculptural decoration. There was, for one thing, much more room for sculpture on the facade of the Gothic church than had been available on the facade of the Romanesque church. There were now three doors where there had been only one before, and doors were added to the transepts as well. The portal at Reims (**Fig. 17-20**), which notably substitutes a stained-glass rose window for the Romanesque tympanum and a pointed for a round arch, is sculpturally much lighter than, for instance, the tympanum at Autun, France (see Fig. 17-16). The elongated bodies of the Romanesque figures are distributed in a very shallow space. In contrast, the sculpture of the Gothic cathedral is more naturalistic. The proportions of the figures are more natural, and the figures assume more natural poses as well. The space they occupy is

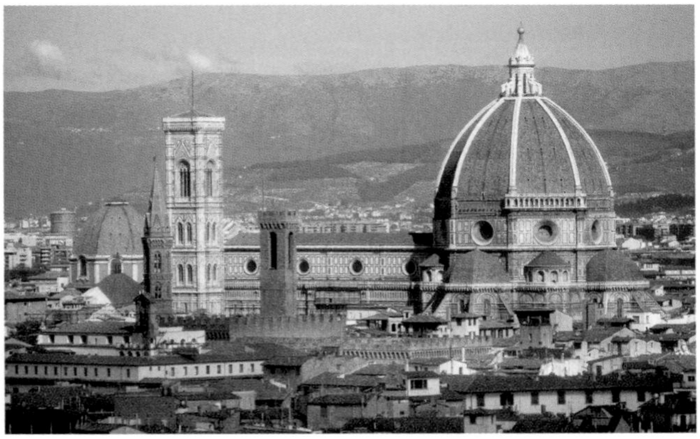

Fig. 17-19 Florence Cathedral (Santa Maria del Fiore), begun by Arnolfo de Cambio, 1296; dome by Filippo Brunelleschi, 1420–36.
© Vanni Archive/CORBIS. Photo: Ruggero Vanni.

Fig. 17-20 Central portal of the west facade, Reims Cathedral, France, ca. 1225–90.

deeper—so much so that they appear to be fully realized sculpture in-the-round, freed of the wall behind them. Most important of all, many of the figures seem to assert their own individuality, as if they were actual persons. The generalized "types" of Romanesque sculpture are beginning to disappear. The detail of figures at the bottom of the Reims portal (**Fig. 17-21**) suggests that each is

Fig. 17-21 ***Annunciation and Visitation*** **(detail), west portal, Reims Cathedral, France, ca. 1225–45.**

engaged in a narrative scene. The angel on the left smiles at the more somber Virgin. The two at the right seem about to step off their pedestals. What is most remarkable is that the space between the figures is bridged by shared emotion, as if feeling can unite them in a common space.

Developments in Asia

How do Indian art and architecture reflect the Hindu religion, and how is the Buddhist faith evident in the arts of China and Japan?

In Asia, Buddhism spread out of India and into China in the first century CE. By 600 CE, it had found its way into Japan. It would not take root in Southeast Asia until the thirteenth century. There, the dominant religion was Hinduism.

India

As early as 1500 BCE, Aryan tribesmen from northern Europe arrived in India, bringing a religion that would have as great an impact on the art of India as Islam had on the art of the Middle East. The Vedic traditions of the light-skinned Aryans, written in religious texts called the *Vedas*, allowed for the development of a class system based on racial distinctions. Status in one of the four classes—the priests (*Brahmans*), the warriors and rulers (*kshatriyas*), the farmers and merchants (*vaishayas*), and the serfs (*shudras*)—was determined by birth, and one could escape one's caste only through reincarnation. Buddhism, which began about 563 BCE, was in many ways a reaction against the Vedic caste system, allowing for salvation by means of individual self-denial and meditation, and it gained many followers.

From the *Vedas* in turn came the *Upanishads*, a book of mystical and philosophical texts that date from sometime after 800 BCE. Taken together, the *Vedas* and the *Upanishads* form the basis of the Hindu religion, with Brahman, the universal soul, at its center. The religion has no single body of doctrine, nor any standard set of practices. It is defined above all by the diversity of its beliefs and deities.

As Hinduism developed, the functions of Brahman, the divine source of all being, were split among three gods—Brahma, the creator; Vishnu, the preserver; and Shiva, the destroyer—as well as various female deities. Vishnu was one of the most popular. In his role as preserver, he is the god of benevolence, forgiveness, and love, and like the other two main Hindu gods, he was believed capable of assuming human form, which he did more often than the other gods due to his great love for humankind. Among his most famous incarnations are his appearance as Rama, the ideal son, brother, husband, warrior, and king, who provides a model of righteous conduct, and as Krishna, a warrior who probably accounts in large part for Vishnu's popularity, since in the *Vishnu Puranas* (the "old stories" of Vishnu), collected about 500 CE, he is depicted as seducing one after another of his devotees. His celebration of erotic love symbolizes the mingling of the self and the absolute spirit of Brahman.

If Brahma is the creator of the world, Shiva takes what Brahma has made and embodies the world's cyclic rhythms. Since in Hinduism the destruction of the old world is followed by the creation of a new world, Shiva's role as destroyer is required, and a positive one. In this sense, he possesses reproductive powers, and in this manifestation of his being, he is often represented as a *lingam* (phallus), often carved in stone on temple grounds or at shrines. As early as the tenth and eleventh centuries, artists in the Tamil Nadu region of southern India began making large bronze and copper editions of Shiva in his manifestation as Shiva Nataraja, Lord of the Dance (**Fig. 17-22**). Such images were commissioned as

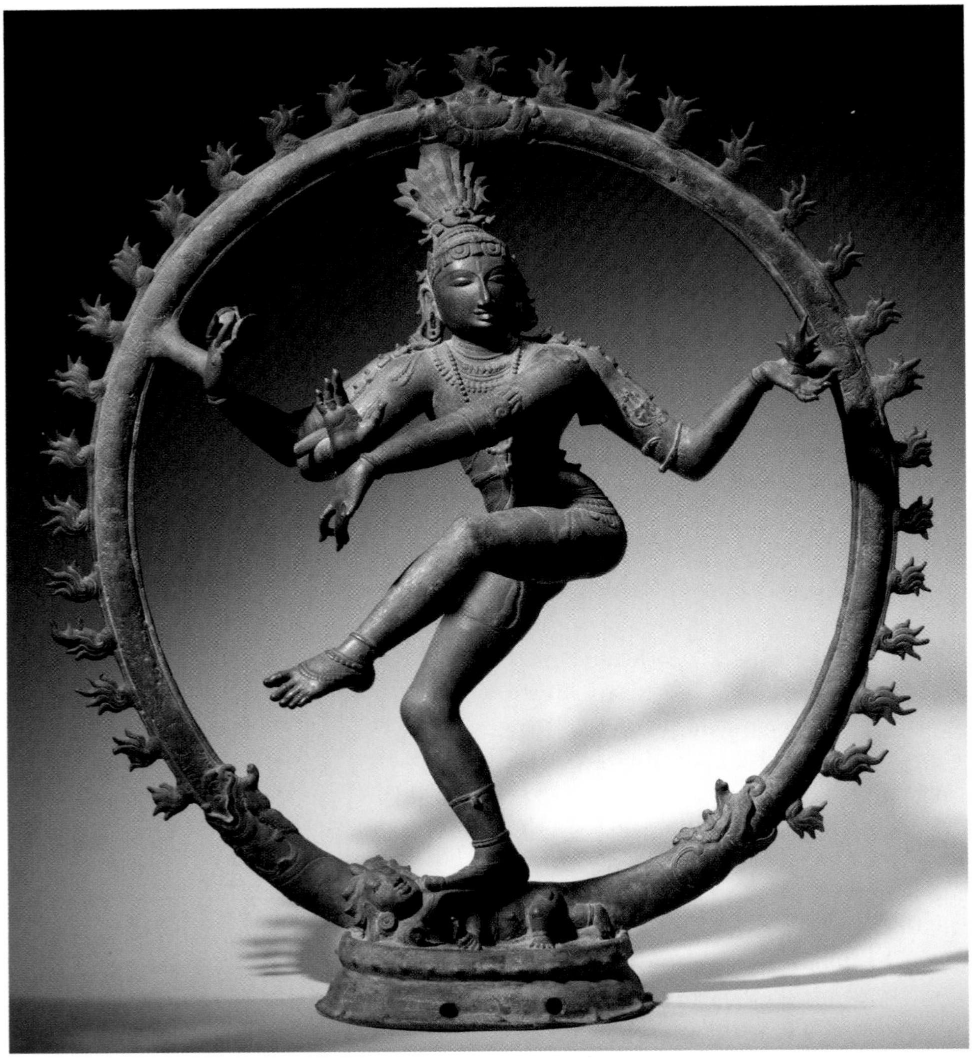

Fig. 17-22 ***Shiva as Lord of the Dance (Nataraja)*, Tamil Nadu, India, Chola period (880–1279), ca. 11th century.** Bronze, 44½ × 40 × ¾ in. The Cleveland Museum of Art. Purchase from the J. H. Wade Fund, 1930.331. Photo © Cleveland Museum of Art.

icons for the region's many temples. Since Shiva embodies the rhythms of the universe, he is also a great dancer. It is said that all the gods were present when Shiva first danced, and they begged him to dance again. Shiva promised to do so in the hearts of his devotees as well as in a sacred grove in Tamil Nadu itself. As he dances, he is framed in a circle of fire, symbolic of both creation and destruction, the cycle of birth, death, and reincarnation.

Goddess worship is fundamental to the Hindu religion. Villages usually recognize goddesses as their protectors, and the goddess Devi is worshiped in many forms throughout India. She is the female aspect without whom the male aspect, which represents consciousness or discrimination, remains impotent and void. She is also synonymous with Shakti, the primordial cosmic energy, and represents the dynamic forces that move through the entire universe. Shaktism, a particular brand of Hindu faith that regards Devi as the Supreme Brahman itself, believes that all other forms of divinity, female or male, are themselves simply forms of Devi's diverse manifestations. But she has a number of particular manifestations. In an extraordinary miniature carving from the twelfth century, Devi is seen in her manifestation as Durga (**Fig. 17-23**), portrayed as the 16-armed slayer of a buffalo inhabited by the fierce demon Mahisha. Considered invincible, Mahisha threatens to destroy the world, but Durga comes to the rescue. In this image, she has just severed the buffalo's head and Mahisha, in the form of a tiny, chubby man, his hair composed of snake heads, emerges from the buffalo's decapitated body and looks up admiringly at Durga even as his toes are being bitten by her lion. Durga smiles serenely as she hoists Mahisha by his hair and treads gracefully on the buffalo's body.

Fig. 17-23 *The Goddess Durga Killing the Buffalo Demon, Mahisha (Mahishasuramardini)*, Bangladesh or India, Pala period, 12th century. Argillite, height. 5⁵⁄₁₆ in. Metropolitan Museum of Art, New York.

Diana and Arthur G. Altschul Gift, 1993.7. Image copyright Metropolitan Museum of Art/Art Resource/Scala, Florence.

The Hindu respect for sexuality is evident even in its architecture. The Kandariya Mahadeva temple (**Fig. 17-24**) represents the epitome of northern Hindu architecture. Its rising towers are meant to suggest the peaks of the Himalayas, home of the Hindu gods, and this analogy would have been even clearer when the temple was painted in its original white gesso. In the center of the temple is the *garbhagriha*, or "womb chamber," the symbolic sacred cavern at the heart of the sacred mountain/temple. Here rests the cult image of the Brahman, in this case the *lingam* of Shiva. Although it is actually almost completely dark, the *garbhagriha* is considered by Hindu worshipers to be filled with the pure light of Brahman.

Fig. 17-24 Kandariya Mahadeva temple, Khajuraho, Madhya Pradesh, India, Chandella dynasty, ca. 1025–50.

© Neil Grant/Alamy.

By the twelfth century, Hinduism had spread from India southeast into present-day Cambodia, where

Fig. 17-25 Angkor Wat, Cambodia, early 12th century.
Andrew Gunners/Digital Vision/Getty Images.

Hindu art achieved a monumental imperial grandeur. In Cambodia, the Khmer monarchy established its capital at Angkor, about 150 miles northwest of present-day Phnom Penh. Covering about 70 square miles, the city was crossed by broad avenues and canals and filled with royal palaces and temples. The largest of these temples, Angkor Wat (**Fig. 17-25**), was created by Suryavarman II in the twelfth century. Five central towers, representing the five peaks of Mount Meru, the center of the Hindu cosmos, rise above a moat surrounding the complex. The approach to the galleries at the towers' base is from the west, crossing a long bridge over the moat, which symbolizes the oceans surrounding the known world. On June 21, the summer solstice and the beginning of the Cambodian solar year, a visitor to the temple arriving through the western gate would see the sun rise directly over the central tower. In this way, the symbolic evocation of the cosmos, so fundamental to Hindu temple architecture, is further elaborated in astronomical terms.

China

In China, and throughout much of Asia, Buddhism exerted the same power to stir the human imagination as Christianity did in the West. And as images of Christ became a central feature of art in the West, so too did images of the Buddha in the East.

The first Chinese Buddhist monk to set out on the Silk Road in search of Buddhist scripture to translate into Chinese was Zhu Shixing of Hunan province. His journey dates from about 260 CE. At the same time, far away on the Silk Road, a resident of Dunhuang (see Chapter 1) began his life's work as a translator of Buddhist texts. One of the most telling manifestations of the religion's spread is the appearance everywhere of images of the Buddha (**Fig. 17-26**). In early Buddhist art, the Buddha was never shown in figural form. It was believed to be impossible to represent the Buddha, since he had already passed to nirvana. Instead, his presence was symbolized by such things as his footprints, the banyan tree, the wheel (representing *dharma*, or the Wheel of Law), or elephants, symbols of mental strength. By the fourth century, during the reign of the Gupta rulers in India, the Buddha was commonly represented in human form. Typically his head is oval, framed by a halo. Atop his head is a mound, symbolizing his spiritual wisdom, and on his forehead is a "third eye," symbolizing his spiritual vision. His demeanor is gentle, reposed, and meditative. His elongated ears refer to his royal origins, and his

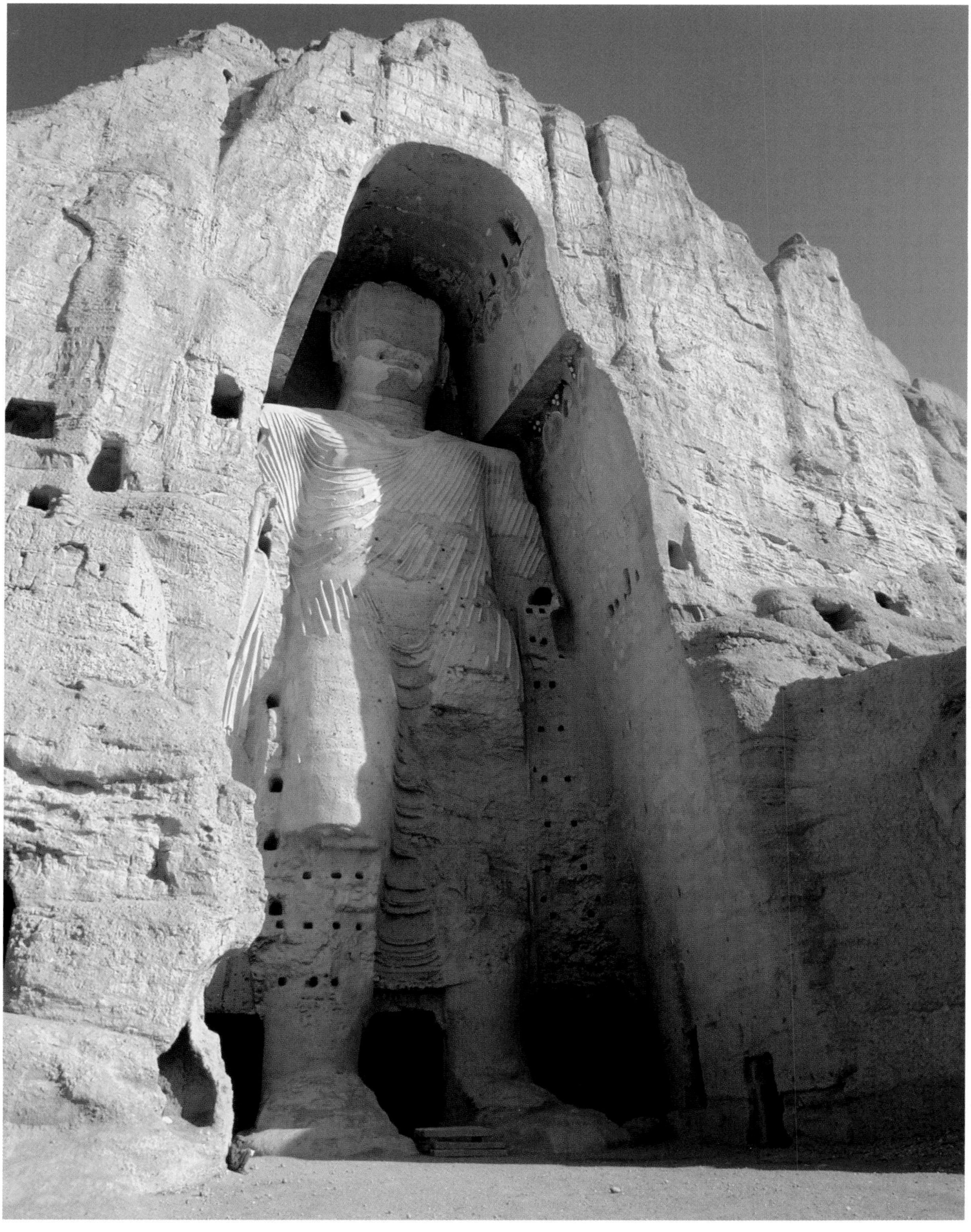

Fig. 17-26 Colossal Buddha, Bamiyan, Afghanistan, ca. 3rd century CE. Stone, height 175 ft.
© Ian Griffiths/Robert Harding World Imagery/Corbis.

The *Tale of Genji*, arguably the first novel, appears in the Heian court in Japan
1010–30

First use of movable type in China
1090

1040

ca. 1040
A Chinese writer describes three forms of gunpowder

Fig. 17-27 Great Wild Goose Pagoda at Ci'én Temple, Xi'an, Shanxi, Tang dynasty, first erected 645 CE.
© Jean-Pierre De Mann/Robert Harding World Imagery.

Fig. 17-28 Guo Xi, *Early Spring*, Northern Song dynasty, 1072. Hanging scroll, ink, and slight color on silk, length 60 in. Collection of the National Palace Museum, Taipei, Taiwan, R.O.C. © Corbis.

hands are set in one of several symbolic gestures, called mudras. At Bamiyan, on the Silk Road in present-day Afghanistan, two massive Buddhas, 175 and 120 feet tall, were carved into a cliff face in the third century CE. These figures were completely destroyed by the fundamentalist Islamic Taliban in 2001. However, many surviving replicas from the Silk Road era suggest that the hands of these Buddhas, which succumbed to natural forces long ago, were held up in the *Dharmachakra* mudra, the teaching pose, which symbolizes intellectual debate and is often associated with Buddhist centers of learning. Painted gold and studded with jewels, and surrounded by caves decorated with Buddhist wall paintings, these enormous images reflect the magnitude of the Buddha's eternal form, at which the earthly body can barely hint.

Beginning in 618, at about the same time that Islam arose in the Middle East, the Tang dynasty reestablished a period of peace and prosperity in China that, except for a brief period of turmoil in the tenth century, would last 660 years. During this period, the **pagoda** became a favored architectural form in China. A pagoda is a multistoried structure of successively smaller, repeated stories, with projecting roofs at each story. The design derives from Indian stupas, which had grown increasingly towerlike by the sixth century CE, as well as Han watchtowers. In fact, the pagoda was understood to offer the temple a certain protection. The Great Wild Goose Pagoda (**Fig. 17-27**) was built in 645 for the monk Xuanzang, who taught and translated the materials he brought back with him from a 16-year pilgrimage to India. In its simplicity and symmetry, it represents the essence of Tang architecture.

Since the time of the Song dynasty, which ruled the empire from 960 until it was overrun by Kublai Khan in 1279, the Taoists in China had emphasized the importance of self-expression, especially through the arts. Poets, calligraphers, and painters were appointed to the most important positions of state. After calligraphy, the Chinese valued landscape painting as the very highest form of artistic endeavor. For them, the activity of painting was a search for the absolute truth embodied in nature, a search that was not so much intellectual as intuitive. They sought to understand a concept shared by both Confucian and Buddhist thought, the *li*, or "principle," upon which the universe is founded, and thus to understand the symbolic meaning and feeling that underlies every natural form. The symbolic meanings of Guo Xi's *Early Spring* (**Fig. 17-28**), for instance, were recorded in a book authored by his son, Guo Si, titled *The Lofty Message of the Forests and Streams*. According to this book, the central peak here symbolizes the emperor, and its tall pines the gentlemanly ideals of the court. Around the emperor, the masses assume their natural place, just as around the mountain, the trees and hills fall, like the water itself, in the order and rhythms of nature.

Japan

Until the sixth century CE, Japan was a largely agricultural society that practiced Shinto, an indigenous system of belief involving the worship of *kami*, or deities believed to inhabit many different aspects of nature, from trees and rocks to deer and other animals. But during the Asuka period (552–646 CE), the philosophy, medicine, music, food, and art and architecture of China and Korea were introduced to the culture. At about this same time, Buddhism was introduced into the country. According to the *Kojiki*, or *Chronicles of Japan*, a collection of myths and stories dating from about 700 CE, a statue of the Buddha and a collection of sacred Buddhist texts were given to Japanese rulers by a Korean king in 552. By 708, the Fujiwara clan had constructed a new capital at Nara and officially accepted Buddhism as the state religion. Magnificent temples and monasteries were constructed, including what would remain, for a thousand years, the largest wooden structure in the world, the Todaiji temple (**Fig. 17-29**). It houses a giant bronze, known as the Great Buddha, over 49 feet high and weighing approximately 380 tons. According to ancient records, as many as 2.6 million people were required to aid in the temple's construction, although that number represents close to half of Japan's population at the time and is probably an exaggeration. The original temple was twice destroyed by warring factions, in 1180 and again in 1567. The current Buddha is in fact a 1691 reconstruction of the original, and the Todaiji temple is itself a reconstruction of 1709. The restored temple is considerably smaller than the original, approximately two-thirds its size, and now stands 188 feet in width and 156 feet high.

As early as the seventh century, Buddhist doctrine and Shinto had begun to influence each other. In the eighth century, the Great Buddha at Nara became identified with the principal Shinto goddess Amaterasu, from whom all Japanese emperors are said to have descended, and Buddhist ceremonies were incorporated into Shinto court ritual. But, between 784 and 794, the

Fig. 17-29 Todaiji temple, Nara, Japan, 752, reconstructed 1709.
© Sakamoto Photo Research Laboratory/Corbis.

Fig. 17-30 ***Night Attack on the Sanjo Palace*** **(detail), from the** ***Scrolls of Events of the Heiji Period*****, Kamakura period, late 13th century.** Handscroll, ink and colors on paper, 16¼ in. × 22 ft. 11½ in. Museum of Fine Arts, Boston. Fenollosa-Weld Collection, 11.4000. Photo © 2015 Museum of Fine Arts, Boston.

capital of Japan was moved to Heiankyo—modern-day Kyoto—inaugurating the great elegance and refinement of the Heian period. Heiankyo quickly became the most densely populated city in the world. According to records, the move occurred because the secular court needed to distance itself from the religious influence of the Buddhist monks at Nara.

During the Heian period, the emperors had increasingly relied on regional warrior clans—samurai (literally, "those who serve")—to exercise military control, especially in the countryside. Over time, these clans became more and more powerful, until, by 1100, they had begun to emerge as a major force in Japanese military and political life, inaugurating the Kamakura period, which takes its name from the capital city of the most prominent of these clans, the Minamoto.

The Kamakura period actually began when the Minamoto clan defeated its chief rival, the Taira, in 1185, but the contest for power between the two dominated the last years of the Heian period. The complex relationship between the Fujiwara of the Heian era and the samurai clans of the Kamakura is embodied in a long handscroll narration of an important battle of 1160, from the *Scrolls of Events of the Heiji Period*, painted by an unknown artist in the thirteenth century, perhaps 100 years after the events themselves. In 1156, Go Shirakawa ascended to the head of the Fujiwara to serve in what had become their traditional role as regent to the emperor, the highest position in the government. But Go Shirakawa resisted the Fujiwara attempt to take control of the government, and in 1157, they recruited one of the two most powerful samurai clans, the Minamoto, to help them stage a coup and imprison the emperor. *Night Attack on the Sanjo Palace* (**Fig. 17-30**) depicts the moment troops led by Fujiwara Nobuyori attacked the emperor's palace, taking him prisoner and burning his palace to the ground. This is the central scene of the scroll, which begins with the army moving toward the palace from the right and ends with it leaving in

Fig. 17-31 Armor (*yoroi*), late Kamakura period, early 14th century. Lacquered iron and leather, silk, stenciled leather, copper-gilt, height 37½ in., weight 38 lb. 3 oz. Metropolitan Museum of Art, New York. Gift of Bashford Dean, 1914.100.121. Image copyright Metropolitan Museum of Art/Art Resource/Scala, Florence.

triumph to the left. The chaos and violence of the events are captured by the sweeping linear ribbons of flame and smoke rising to the upper right and the confusion of horsemen, warriors, fleeing ladies, the dead, and the dying in the foreground, all framed by an architecture that falls at a steep diagonal to the bottom left.

The samurai warriors, dressed in elaborate iron armor, were master horsemen and archers. In this scene, many hold their bows, the lower portions of which are smaller than the top in order that they might pass over a horse's neck. They wore a special armor, known as *yoroi*, made of overlapping iron and lacquered leather scales (**Fig. 17-31**). A breastplate and backplate were strapped together with leather thongs, and a separate piece of armor protected the right side, particularly vulnerable when the archer raised his arm to draw his bow. A four-sided skirt was attached to the armor to protect the upper legs. And the helmet was made of iron plates from which a neckguard flared sharply outward. Diagonal bands of multicolored lacings originally decorated this *yoroi*, a symbol of the rainbow and a reminder that both beauty and good fortune are fleeting. Stenciled in the leather breastplate is an image of Fudo Myo-o ("The Immovable"), one of the five great guardians of the Buddhist faith. Because he is unshakable in his duty, fierce in his demeanor, and exercises strict mental discipline, Fudo Myo-o was a figure venerated by the samurai.

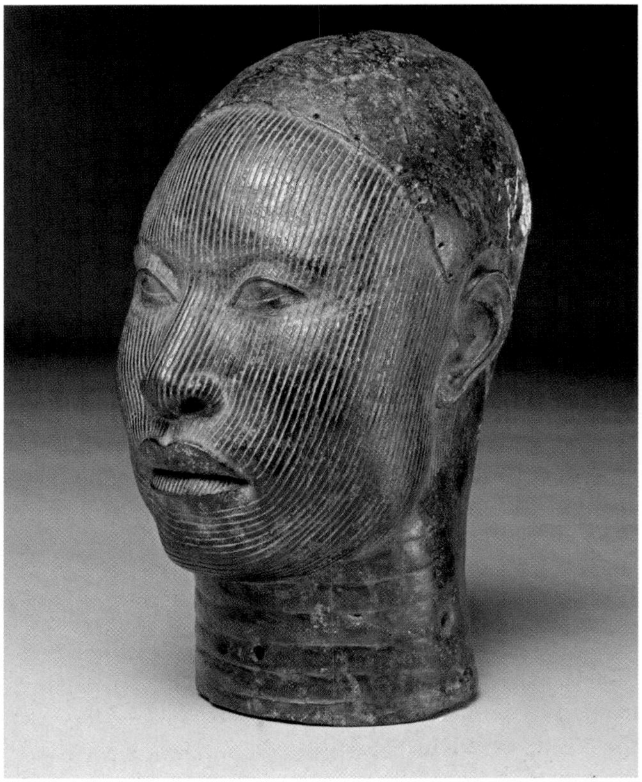

Fig. 17-32 *Head of a King* (*Oni*), Ife culture, Nigeria, ca. 13th century. Brass, height 11⁷⁄₁₆ in. Museum of Ife Antiquities, Ife, Nigeria.
Photo © Dirk Bakker/Bridgeman Images.

The Cultures of Africa

What are some of the characteristic works of the Ife, Shona, and Zagwe cultures?

Just as in Europe and Asia, powerful kingdoms arose across Africa in the early centuries of the second millennium. As we have seen, the influence of Islam helped to establish a powerful culture in the kingdom of Mali (see Fig. 17-11). Farther south, along the western coast of central Africa, the Yoruba state of Ife developed along the Niger River. Near the southeastern tip of Africa, the Shona civilization produced urban centers represented today by the ruins of "Great Zimbabwe." On the eastern side of Africa, the Zagwe dynasty maintained a long Christian heritage introduced in the first millennium from the Middle East.

By the middle of the twelfth century, Ife culture was producing highly naturalistic brass sculptures depicting its rulers. An example is the *Head of a King* (or *Oni*) (**Fig. 17-32**). The parallel lines that run down the face represent decorative effects made by scarring—**scarification**. The hole in the lower neck suggests that the head may have been attached to a wooden mannequin, and in memorial services the mannequin may well have worn the royal robes of the Ife court. Small holes along the scalp line suggest that hair, or perhaps a veil of some sort, also adorned the head. But the head itself was, for the Ife, of supreme importance. It was the home of the spirit, the symbol of the king's capacity to organize the world and to prosper. Ife culture depended for its welfare on its kings' heads.

Inland from the southwestern coast of Africa, the Shona people built an entirely indigenous African civilization in the region of today's Zimbabwe beginning in about 1100. As trade developed along the African coast, the Shona positioned themselves as an inland hub where coastal traders could travel to procure goods for export. From surrounding regions they mined or imported copper and gold, and received in return exotic goods such as porcelain and glass from Asia and the Middle East.

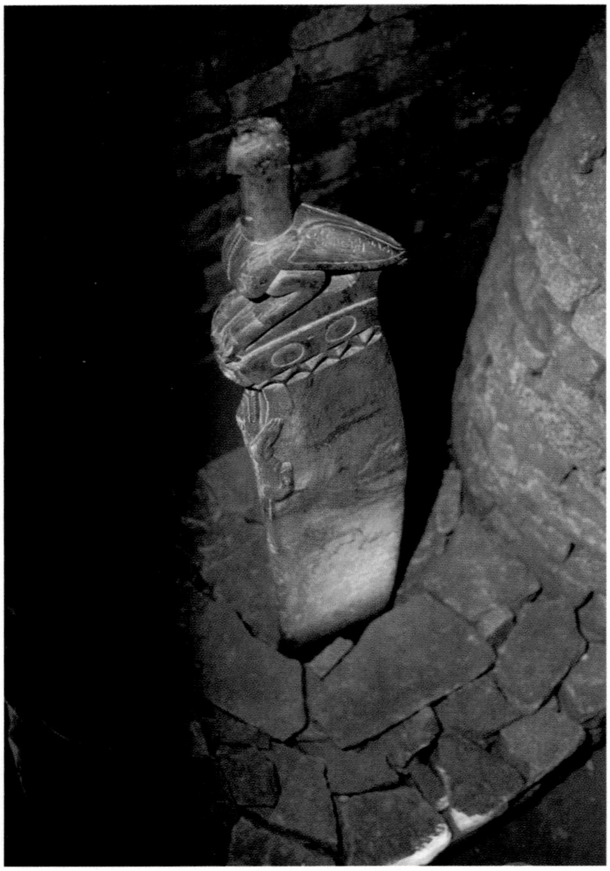

Fig. 17-33 Bird carved from soapstone, Great Zimbabwe, Zimbabwe, ca. 1200–1400. Height 13½ in., atop a stone monolith, total height 5 ft. 4 in. Great Zimbabwe Site Museum, Zimbabwe.

Between the thirteenth and fifteenth centuries, the Shona erected the massive stone buildings and walls of a city known today as Great Zimbabwe. The origin of the Shona word *zimbabwe* is debated, but a composite of various meanings suggests that it referred to the "palaces of stone" in this city. A huge city for its time, the ruins cover 1 square mile and are believed to have housed a population of somewhere between 10,000 and 20,000. Great Zimbabwe has several distinct, separately enclosed areas with ceremonial platforms decorated with carved geometric patterns and tall rock monoliths topped by carved birds (**Fig. 17-33**). The bird topping this monolith is not a recognizable species and includes certain human features, such as toes instead of talons. This has led to speculation that the figure may represent deceased Shona rulers who were believed to have the power to move between the spirit and human worlds. A crocodile, possibly another symbol of royalty, climbs up the front of the monolith.

One of the dynasties of greatest cultural importance in medieval East Africa was that of the Zagwe, who reigned for approximately 150 years, from the early twelfth century to 1270. They carved massive churches into the soft rock of the region (**Fig. 17-34**). The most famous of these was commissioned by the emperor Lalibela. In the town now known by his name, he ordered the construction of a series of these sunken rock churches. Engineers had to conceive of the completed building in advance, including decorative details, because subtractive techniques such as carving do not allow for repair of mistakes. Once the shell of the building was carved, the interior was hollowed out into rooms for use in Christian worship and study.

Fig. 17-34 Beta Ghiorghis (House of St. George), Lalibela, Ethiopia, 13th century.

Thinking Back

17.1 Describe the principal architectural and decorative features of early Christian and Byzantine places of worship.

The emperor Constantine chose to make early Christian places of worship as unlike Classical temples as possible. He chose a rectangular building type called the basilica, which the ancient Romans had used for secular public functions. Early Christians and, later, Byzantines also used circular buildings, which derived from mausoleum architecture. What is an ambulatory? What was most notable about the worshiper's experience of Hagia Sophia? How is San Vitale decorated?

17.2 Explain the origins of the mosque and describe its chief features.

At Medina, Muhammad built a house that surrounded a large open courtyard, which served as a community gathering place, on the model of the Roman forum. There, the men of the community would gather on Fridays to pray and listen to a sermon delivered by Muhammad. It thus became known as the *masjid*, the Arabic word for mosque, or "place of prostration." Covered porches were erected to protect the community from the hot Arabian sun. This many-columned area, known as a hypostyle space, would become a standard feature of mosques. Mosques are required to have a *qibla*, a wall that indicates the direction of Mecca. What is a *minbar*? What is a *mihrab*?

17.3 Describe the chief characteristics of the Carolingian, Romanesque, and Gothic styles.

Soon after Charlemagne assumed leadership of the Franks in 771, he was crowned Holy Roman emperor by Pope Leo III at St. Peter's Basilica in Rome. The fusion of Germanic and Mediterranean cultures reflected a new alliance between Church and State that resulted in a Carolingian style of art. How does the illustration of St. Matthew from the *Gospel Book of Charlemagne* reflect this new style?

Romanesque architecture is characterized by its easily recognizable geometric masses—rectangles, cylinders, and half-cylinders. Romanesque buildings have large vaulted ceilings, which require massive walls, typically lacking windows. The art of sculpture began to reemerge in the Romanesque period. What role did the pilgrimage route play in church-building? What is a tympanum, and how would it be used in church decoration?

Light is a defining feature of Gothic buildings. Unlike Romanesque structures, Gothic buildings are well lit. Light was believed to serve as a manifestation of the divine. Gothic buildings are defined by an emphasis on verticality. What role did Abbot Suger play in the development of the Gothic style? How does the Gothic style in Italy differ from the French Gothic style?

17.4 Describe how Indian art and architecture reflect the Hindu religion, and how the Buddhist faith is evident in the arts of China and Japan.

Hinduism is defined above all by the diversity of its beliefs and deities, all of which were, together with lesser gods, often depicted in sculpture. How is the Hindu respect for sexuality reflected in its architecture? By the fourth century, the Buddha was commonly represented in human form. How does the Great Goose Pagoda reflect a Buddhist heritage? What is *li*, and how is it manifest in Guo Xi's *Early Spring*? By 600 CE, Buddhism had reached Japan. How did it merge with the indigenous Shinto religion? How did the samurai reflect its values?

17.5 Describe some of the characteristic works of the Ife, Shona, and Zagwe cultures.

Ife art is distinguished by its brass sculptures depicting its rulers. What importance do the Ife attach to these heads? The Shona people of Zimbabwe were great traders, and between the thirteenth and fifteenth centuries they built a great city known as Great Zimbabwe. What is unique about the churches of Lalibela?

Chapter 18

The Renaissance through the Baroque

Learning Objectives

18.1 Explain how humanism informs the art of both the Early and High Renaissance.

18.2 Discuss some of the ways that the encounter with other cultures impacted the long-established artistic traditions of China and Japan, the Americas, and Africa.

18.3 Describe how the Mannerist style is different from that of the High Renaissance.

18.4 Define the Baroque as it manifests itself in both art and architecture.

During the period extending from about 1400 to 1500—that is, as the Gothic era waned—Western European culture experienced a rebirth of Classical learning and values. For this reason we call the period the **Renaissance**, from the Italian *rinascita*, "rebirth." By the middle of the fourteenth century, the Italian poet Dante Alighieri had picked the ancient Roman poet Virgil as his guide through his fictional Inferno and Purgatory, another Italian poet Petrarch was busy amassing his own Classical library, and the author of what might be thought of as the first short stories in Western literature—the Florentine writer Boccaccio, who, like Dante, wrote in the vernacular Italian instead of Latin—was also learning Greek. Where the Romans had once copied many of the greatest Greek sculptures from antiquity, now those same sculptures were being unearthed in Rome, and served as models for a new generation of Renaissance artists.

But in many ways, the Gothic era might in fact best be seen not so much as a coda to the Middle Ages but rather as a long overture to the Renaissance, and we can see, perhaps, in the sculptures at Reims Cathedral (see Fig. 17-21), which date from the first half of the thirteenth century, the beginnings of the spirit that would develop into the Renaissance sensibility. These figures are no longer archetypal and formulaic representations; they are almost real people, displaying real emotions. This tendency toward increasingly naturalistic representation in many ways defines Gothic art, but it is even more pronounced in Renaissance art. If the figures in the Reims portal seem about to step off their columns, Renaissance figures seem to share our space as if part of our world. By the time of the Limbourg Brothers' early fifteenth-century manuscript illumination for *Les Très Riches Heures du Duc de Berry* (**Fig. 18-1**), human beings are represented, for the first time since Classical antiquity, as casting actual shadows upon the ground. The architecture is also rendered with some measure of perspectival accuracy. The scene is full of realistic detail, and the potential of landscape to render a sense of actual space is fully realized.

The Renaissance

How does humanism inform the painting of both the Early and the High Renaissance?

In December 1347, rats infested with fleas carrying bubonic plague arrived on the island of Sicily. Within months, the disease spread northward, through the ports

Construction of the Duomo, Florence Cathedral, begins
1296

1345
Petrarch discovers the letters of Cicero

Bubonic plague introduced to Europe, and the "Black Death" sweeps the continent
1347

1400

Fig. 18-1 The Limbourg Brothers, *October*, from *Les Très Riches Heures du Duc de Berry*, 1413–16. Manuscript illumination. Musée Condé, Chantilly, France.
Photo © RMN-Grand Palais (domaine de Chantilly)/René-Gabriel Ojéda.

of Venice, Genoa, and Pisa, across Italy, southern France, and eastern Spain. The disease began in the lymph glands of the groin or armpits, which slowly filled with pus and turned black. The inflammations were called buboes—hence the name bubonic plague—and their black color lent the plague its other name, the Black Death. Since it was carried by rodents, which were commonplace even in wealthy homes, hardly anyone was spared. In Tuscany, the death rate in the cities was near 60 percent. In Florence, on June 24, 1348, the feast day of the city's patron saint, John the Baptist, 1,800 people reportedly died, and another 1,800 the next day—about 4 percent of the city's population in the space of two days.

After the Black Death, it seemed possible, even necessary, to begin again. In politics, feudal rule gave way to centralized forms of government. City-states flourished, strengthened by the influx of workers migrating from the countryside, as manufacture and trade supplanted agriculture as the basis of the European economy. The Church, which in medieval times had been the very foundation of Western culture, found itself challenged on all fronts. Politically, European monarchs questioned its authority. Philosophically, a growing class of intellectuals challenged its long-held doctrines. Morally, many of these same intellectuals denounced the behavior of its clergy and called for reform.

The Early Renaissance

But perhaps above all, the Renaissance was the era of the individual. As early as the 1330s, the poet and scholar Petrarch had conceived of a new **humanism**, a belief in the unique value of each person. Petrarch argued that the birth of Christ had ushered in an "age of faith," which had blinded the world to learning and thus condemned it to darkness. The study of Classical languages, literature, history, and philosophy—what we call the "humanities"—could lead to a new, enlightened stage of history. People should be judged, Petrarch felt, by their actions. It was not God's will that determined who they were and what they were capable of; rather, glory and fame were available to anyone who dared to seize them.

Embodying this belief is a sculpture by Donatello, which turns its attention directly to the Classical past. His *David* (**Fig. 18-2**) was, in fact, the first life-size nude sculpture since antiquity. He is posed in perfectly Classical *contrapposto* fashion. But the young hero—almost anti-heroic in the youthful fragility of his physique—is also fully self-conscious, his attention turned, in what appears to be full-blown self-adoration, upon himself as an object of physical beauty. Writing in 1485, the philosopher Giovanni Pico della Mirandola—Pico, as he is known—addressed himself to every ordinary (male) person: "Thou, constrained by no limits, in accordance with

Fig. 18-2 Donatello, *David*, ca. 1425–30. Bronze, height 5 ft. 2¼ in. Museo Nazionale del Bargello, Florence.

thine own free will . . . shalt ordain for thyself the limits of thy nature. We have set thee at the world's center . . . [and] thou mayst fashion thyself in whatever shape thou shalt prefer." Out of such sentiments Donatello's *David* was born, as were the archetypal Renaissance geniuses—men like Michelangelo and Leonardo da Vinci—but also Niccolò Machiavelli's wily and pragmatic Prince, for whom the ends justify any means, and the legendary Faust, who sold his soul to the devil in return for youth, knowledge, and magical power.

Donatello had traveled to Rome in 1402 with his friend Filippo Brunelleschi, the inventor of geometric, linear perspective (see Fig. 4-13), a system Brunelleschi probably developed as he studied the ruins of ancient Rome. It was Brunelleschi who accepted a commission to design and build a dome over the crossing of Florence Cathedral (see Fig. 17-19). The other great innovator of the day was the painter Masaccio, who died in 1428 at the age of 27, having worked only six years. He was 15 years younger than Donatello and 24 years younger than Brunelleschi, and learned from them both, translating Donatello's naturalism and Brunelleschi's sense of proportion into the art of painting. In his *The Tribute Money* (**Fig. 18-3**), painted around 1427, Christ's disciples, especially St. Peter, wonder whether it is proper to pay taxes to the Roman government when, from their point of view, they owe allegiance to Christ, not Rome. But Christ counsels them to separate their earthly affairs from spiritual obligations—"Render therefore unto Caesar the things which are Caesar's; and unto God the things that are God's" (Matthew 22:21). To that end, Christ tells St. Peter and the other disciples that they will find the coin necessary to pay the imperial tax collector, whose back is to us, in the mouth of a fish. At the left, St. Peter extracts the coin from the fish's mouth, and, at the right, he pays the required tribute money to the tax collector. The figures here are modeled by means of chiaroscuro in a light that falls upon the scene from the right (notice their cast shadows). We sense the physicality of the figures beneath their robes. The landscape is rendered through atmospheric perspective, and the building on the right is rendered in a one-point-perspective scheme, with a vanishing point behind the head of Christ. All of these artistic devices are in themselves innovations; together, they constitute one of the most remarkable achievements in the history of art, an extraordinary change in direction from the flat, motionless figures of the Middle Ages toward a fully realistic representation.

In the north of Europe, in Flanders particularly, a flourishing merchant society promoted artistic developments that in many ways rivaled those of Florence. The Italian revival of Classical notions of order and measure was, for the most part, ignored in the north. Rather, the

Fig. 18-3 Masaccio, *The Tribute Money*, ca. 1427. Fresco. Brancacci Chapel, Santa Maria del Carmine, Florence.

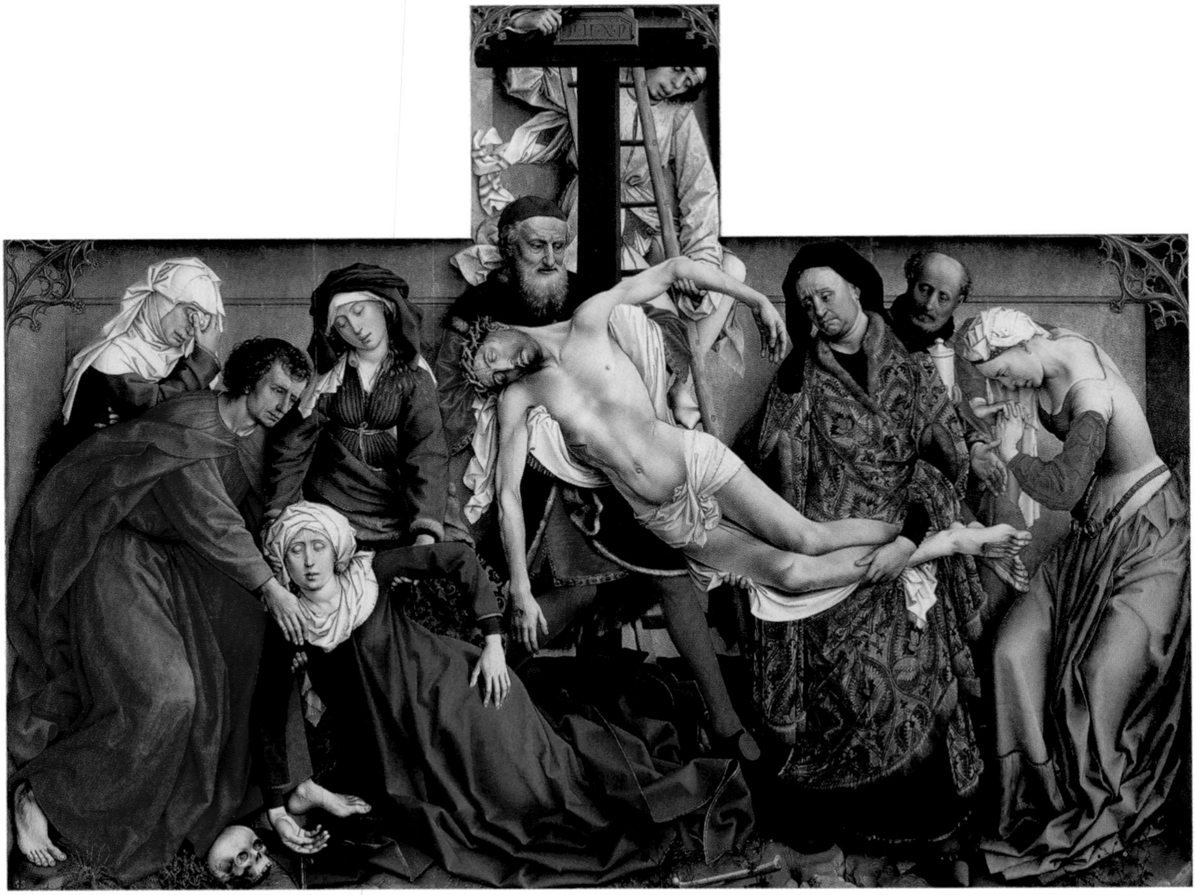

Fig. 18-4 Rogier van der Weyden, *The Deposition*, ca. 1435–38. Oil on wood, 7 ft. 1⅝ in. × 8 ft. 7⅛ in. Museo Nacional del Prado, Madrid.

northern artists were deeply committed to rendering believable space in the greatest and most realistic detail. *The Mérode Altarpiece*, executed by Robert Campin (see Fig. 9-14), is almost exactly contemporary with Masaccio's *Tribute Money*, but in the precision and clarity of its detail—in fact, an explosion of detail—it is radically different in feel. The chief reason for the greater clarity relates to medium. Northern painters developed oil paint in the first half of the fourteenth century. With oil paint, painters could achieve dazzling effects of light on the surface of the painting—as opposed to the matte, or nonreflective, surfaces of both fresco and tempera. These effects recall, on the one hand, the Gothic style's emphasis on the almost magical light of the stained-glass window. In that sense, the effect achieved seems transcendent. But it also lends the depicted objects a sense of material reality, and thus caters to the material desires of the north's rising mercantile class.

If we compare Rogier van der Weyden's *The Deposition* (**Fig. 18-4**) to Piero della Francesca's *The Flagellation of Christ* (**Fig. 18-5**), the differences between northern (Flemish) and southern (Italian) sensibilities become evident. Virtually a demonstration of the rules of linear perspective, Piero's scene depicts Pontius Pilate watching as executioners whip Christ. Although it is much more architecturally unified, the painting pays homage to Masaccio's *Tribute Money*. Emotionally speaking, Rogier's *Deposition* has almost nothing in common with Piero's *Flagellation*. It is as if Piero has controlled the violence of his emotionally charged scene by means of mathematics, while Rogier has emphasized instead the pathos and human feeling that pervade his scene of Christ being lowered from the cross. While Piero's composition is essentially defined by a square and a rectangle, with figures arranged in each in a basically triangular fashion, Rogier's composition is controlled by two parallel,

Fig. 18-5 Piero della Francesca, *The Flagellation of Christ*, ca. 1455. Tempera on wood, 32¾ × 23⅓ in. Palazzo Ducale, Galleria Nazionale delle Marche, Urbino.

deeply expressive, sweeping curves, one defined by the body of Christ and the other by the swooning figure below him. Next to the high drama of Rogier's painting, Piero's seems almost static, but the understated brutality of Christ's flagellation in the background of Piero's painting is equally compelling.

But all in all, the Early Renaissance, in Italy at least, could be said to be the work of the Medici family. For 76 years, from 1418, when they became bankers to the papacy, until 1494, when irate citizens removed them from power, they molded and manipulated, controlled and cajoled, persuaded and provoked the Florentines into becoming a citizenry befitting the city they envisioned, a city founded on humanist values. The family's power was fully cemented by Cosimo de' Medici, who, as banker to the papacy, secured Florence's domination over rival Siena. Cosimo surrounded himself with humanists. He collected ancient Greek and Roman art, bringing to Florence the finest examples of sculpture he could find. He also sought the humanists' guidance about what books and manuscripts of the ancients he ought to collect, and commissioned translations of Greek philosophy and literature, since he himself could not master the language. But it was his grandson Lorenzo, known as *il Magnifico*—"the Magnificent"—who fully transformed Florence into a model humanist city, the envy of all Italy, after assuming responsibility for leading the family and the city in 1469.

Cosimo had founded a Platonic Academy of Philosophy in Florence and Lorenzo continued to champion it. There, Lorenzo and his close friend and contemporary, the painter Sandro Botticelli, studied a brand of Neoplatonic thought that transformed the philosophic writings of Plato almost into a religion. According to

Fig. 18-6 Sandro Botticelli, *The Birth of Venus*, ca. 1482. Tempera on canvas, 5 ft. 8⅞ in. × 9 ft. 1⅞ in. Galleria degli Uffizi, Florence.

the Neoplatonists, in the contemplation of beauty, the inherently corrupt soul could transform its love for the physical and material into a purely spiritual love of God. Thus, Botticelli uses mythological themes to transform his pagan imagery into a source of Christian inspiration and love. His *Birth of Venus* (**Fig. 18-6**), the first monumental representation of the nude goddess since ancient times, represents innocence itself, a divine beauty free of any hint of the physical and the sensual. It was this form of beauty that the soul, aspiring to salvation, was expected to contemplate. But such meanings were by no means clear to the uninitiated, and when the Dominican monk Girolamo Savonarola denounced the Medicis as pagan, the majority of Florentines agreed. In 1494, the family was banished.

The High Renaissance

Still, for a short period at the outset of the sixteenth century, Florence was again the focal point of artistic activity. The three great artists of the High Renaissance—Leonardo, Michelangelo, and Raphael—all lived and worked in the city. As a young man, Michelangelo had been a member of Lorenzo de' Medici's circle, but with the Medicis' demise in 1494, he fled to Bologna. He returned to Florence seven years later to work on a giant piece of marble left over from an abandoned commission. Out of this, while still in his twenties, he carved his monolithic *David* (see Fig. 1-28). But, in 1505, Michelangelo was commanded to leave Florence for Rome by Pope Julius II to serve in the pope's plans for rebuilding St. Peter's Basilica and the Vatican. It was for Pope Julius II that Michelangelo painted his Sistine Chapel ceiling (see Figs. 5-24 and 9-10), one of the masterpieces of the High Renaissance.

Leonardo, some 23 years older than Michelangelo, had left Florence as early as 1481 for Milan. There, he offered his services to the great duke of Milan, Ludovico Sforza, first as a military engineer and, only secondarily, as an architect, sculptor, and painter. Ludovico was embroiled in military matters, and Leonardo pronounced himself the military engineer

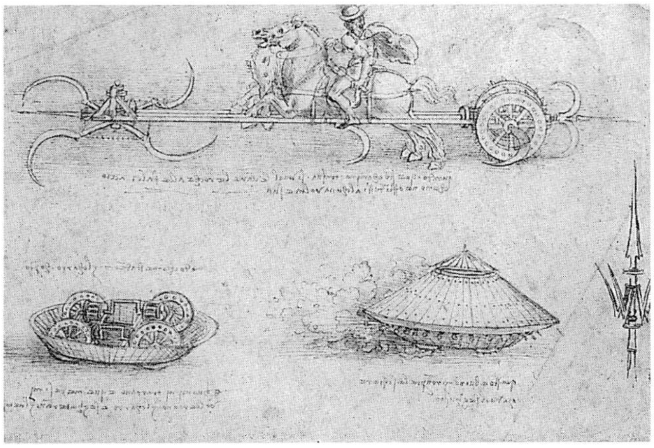

Fig. 18-7 Leonardo da Vinci, *A Scythed Chariot, Armored Car, and Pike*, ca. 1487. Pen and ink and wash, 6⅜ × 9¾ in. The British Museum, London.
1860,0616.99. © The Trustees of the British Museum.

Ludovico was looking for, capable of constructing great "machines of war." Leonardo's restless imagination, in fact, led him to the study of almost everything: natural phenomena like wind, storms, and the movement of water; anatomy and physiology; physics and mechanics; music; mathematics; plants and animals; geology; and astronomy, to say nothing of painting and drawing. His drawing of *A Scythed Chariot, Armored Car, and Pike* (**Fig. 18-7**) is indicative of his work for Sforza. "I will make covered vehicles," he wrote to the duke, "which will penetrate the enemy and their artillery, and there is no host of armed men so great that they will not be broken down by them." The chariot in the drawing is equipped with scythes to cut down the enemy, and the armored car, presented in an upside-down view as well as scooting along in a cloud of dust, was to be operated by eight men. But Leonardo's work for Sforza was not limited to military operations. From 1495 to 1498, he painted his world-famous fresco *The Last Supper* (see Fig. 4-15), which many consider to be the first painting of the High Renaissance, in Santa Maria delle Grazie, a monastic church under the protection of the Sforza family. Leonardo left Milan soon after the French invaded in October 1499, and by April he had returned to Florence, where he concentrated his energies on a life-size cartoon for *Madonna and Child with St. Anne and Infant St. John the Baptist* (see Fig. 8-4). This became so famous that Florentines flocked to see it. At about this time he also painted the *Mona Lisa* (**Fig. 18-8**). Perhaps a portrait of the wife of the Florentine banker Zanobi del Giocondo, the painting conveys a psychological depth that has continued to fascinate viewers up to the present day. Its power derives, at least in part, from a manipulation of light and shadow that imparts a blurred imprecision to the sitter's features, lending her an aura of ambiguity and mystery. This interest in the psychology, not just the physical looks, of the sitter is typical of the Renaissance imagination.

When Raphael, then 21 years old, arrived in Florence in 1504, he discovered Leonardo and Michelangelo locked in a competition over who would get the commission to decorate the city council chamber in the Palazzo Vecchio with pictures celebrating the Florentine past. Leonardo painted a *Battle of Anghiari* and Michelangelo a *Battle of Cascina*, neither of which survives. The young Raphael was immediately con-

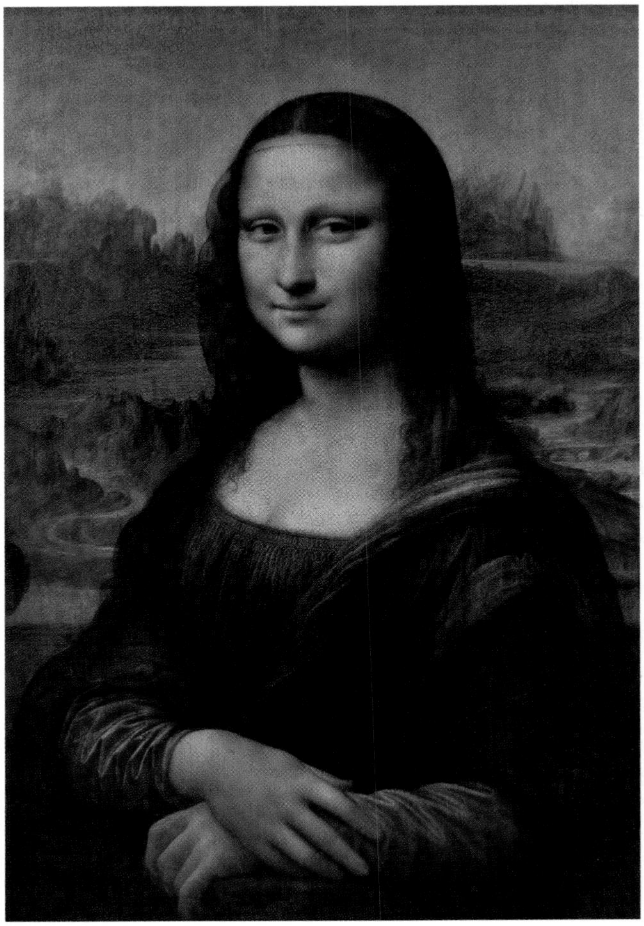

Fig. 18-8 Leonardo da Vinci, *Mona Lisa*, ca. 1503–05. Oil on wood, 30¼ × 21 in. Musée du Louvre, Paris.
Photo © RMN-Grand Palais (musée du Louvre)/Michel Urtado.

Fig. 18-9 Raphael, *The School of Athens*, 1510–11. Fresco. Stanza della Segnatura, Vatican Palace, Vatican City.
Photo Fine Art Images/Heritage Images/Scala, Florence.

fronted by the cult of genius that in many ways has come to define the High Renaissance. Artists of inspiration were considered different from everyone else, and guided in their work by an insight that, according to the Neoplatonists, was divine in origin. The Neoplatonists believed that the goals of truth and beauty were not reached by following the universal rules and laws of Classical antiquity—notions of proportion and mathematics. Nor, given the fallen condition of the world, would fidelity to visual reality guarantee beautiful results. Instead, the artist of genius had to rely on subjective and personal intuition—what the Neoplatonists called the "divine frenzy" of the creative act—to transcend the conditions of everyday life. Plato had argued that painting was mere slavish imitation of an already existing thing—it was a diminished reality. The Neoplatonists turned this argument on its head. Art now exceeded reality. It was a window, not upon nature, but upon divine inspiration itself.

Raphael learned much from both Leonardo and Michelangelo, and, in 1508, he was awarded the largest commission of the day, the decoration of the papal apartments at the Vatican in Rome. On the four walls of the first room, the Stanza della Segnatura, he painted frescoes representing the four domains of knowledge—Theology, Law, Poetry, and Philosophy. The most famous of these is the last, *The School of Athens* (**Fig. 18-9**). Raphael's painting depicts a gathering of the greatest philosophers and scientists of the ancient world. The symmetry of the composition is reminiscent of Leonardo's *Last Supper*, but the perspectival rendering of space is much deeper. Where, in Leonardo's masterpiece, Christ is situated at the vanishing point, in Raphael's work, Plato and Aristotle occupy that position. These two figures represent the two great, opposing schools of philosophy: the Platonists, who were concerned with the spiritual world of ideas (thus, Plato points upward), and the Aristotelians, who were concerned with the matter-of-factness of material reality (thus, Aristotle points over the ground upon which he walks). The expressive power of the figures owes much to Michelangelo, who, it is generally believed, Raphael portrayed as the philosopher Heraclitus, the brooding, self-absorbed figure in the foreground.

Raphael's work in Rome is typical of the rapid spread of the ideals of the Italian Renaissance culture to the rest of Italy and Europe. In Venice, however, painting developed somewhat independently of the Florentine manner. The emphasis in Venetian art is on the sensuousness of light and color and the pleasures of the senses. The closest we have come to it so far is in the mysterious glow that infuses Leonardo's *Mona Lisa*, but what is only hinted at in Leonardo's work explodes in Venetian painting as full-blown theatrical effect. Building up color by means of glazing, as Leonardo did in his soft, luminous landscapes (see Fig. 5-3), their paintings, like the great palaces of Venice whose reflections shimmered on the Grand Canal, demonstrate an exquisite sensitivity to the play of light and shadow and to the luxurious display of detail and design.

The mysterious qualities of Leonardo's highly charged atmospheric paintings are fully realized in Giorgione's *The Tempest* (**Fig. 18-10**). The first known mention of the painting dates from 1530, when it surfaced in the collection of a Venetian patrician. We know almost nothing else about it, which contributes to its mystery. At the right, an almost nude young woman nurses her child. At the left, a somewhat disheveled young man, wearing the costume of a German mercenary soldier, gazes at the woman and child with evident pride. Between them, in the foreground, stands a pediment topped by two broken columns. A creaky wooden bridge crosses the estuary in

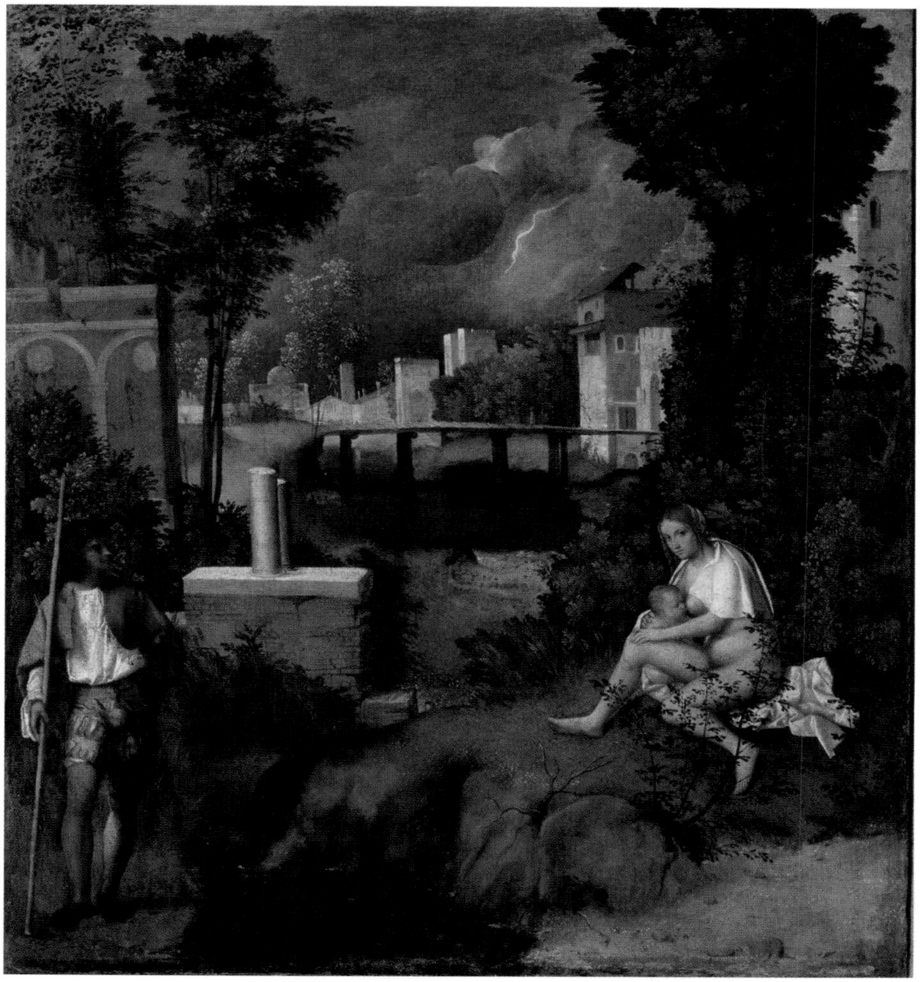

Fig. 18-10 Giorgione, *The Tempest*, ca. 1509. Oil on canvas, 31¼ × 28¾ in.
Gallerie dell'Accademia, Venice.
CAMERAPHOTO Arte, Venice.

Fig. 18-11 Titian, *Venus of Urbino*, 1538. Oil on canvas, 47 in. × 5 ft. 5 in. Galleria degli Uffizi, Florence.
© Studio Fotografico Quattrone, Florence.

the middle ground, and lightning flashes in the distance, illuminating a densely built cityscape. What, we must ask, is the relationship between the two figures? Are they husband and wife? Or are they lovers, whose tempestuous affair has resulted in the birth of a child? These are questions that remain unanswered, but which the deeply atmospheric presentation of the scene sustains.

The almost comfortable sensuality of the scene—even its suggestion of outright sexuality—would become one of the chief subjects of Venetian art. When Giorgione died of the plague in 1510, at only 32 years of age, it seems likely that his friend Titian, ten years younger, finished several of his paintings. While lacking the sense of intrigue that his mentor captured in *The Tempest*, Titian's *Venus of Urbino* (**Fig. 18-11**) is more frankly addressed to the sexual appetites of its viewers. Painted for Duke Guidobaldo della Rovere of Urbino in 1538, this "Venus"—more a real woman than an ethereal goddess, and referred to by Guidobaldo as merely a "nude woman"—is frankly available. She stares out at the viewer, Guidobaldo himself, with a matter-of-factness that suggests she is totally comfortable with her nudity. (Apparently the lady-in-waiting and maid at the rear of the palatial rooms are searching for suitably fine clothing in which to dress her.) Her hand both covers and draws attention to her genitals. Her dog, a traditional symbol of both fidelity and lust, sleeps lazily on the white sheets at her feet. She may be, ambiguously, either a courtesan or a bride. (The chest from which the servant is removing clothes is a traditional reference to marriage.) In either case, she is, primarily, an object of desire.

In the north of Europe, the impact of the Italian Renaissance is perhaps best understood in the work of the German artist Albrecht Dürer. As a young man, he had copied Italian prints, and, in 1495, he traveled to Italy to study the Italian masters. From this point on, he strove to establish the ideals of the Renaissance in his native country. The first artist to be fascinated by his own image, Dürer painted self-portraits throughout his career. In this act, he asserts his sense of the importance of the individual, especially the individual of genius and talent, such as he. Meaning to evoke his own spirituality, he presents himself almost as if he were Christ (**Fig. 18-12**). Yet not even Dürer could quite synthesize the northern love for precise and accurate naturalism—the desire to render the world of real things—with the southern idealist desire to transcend that same world.

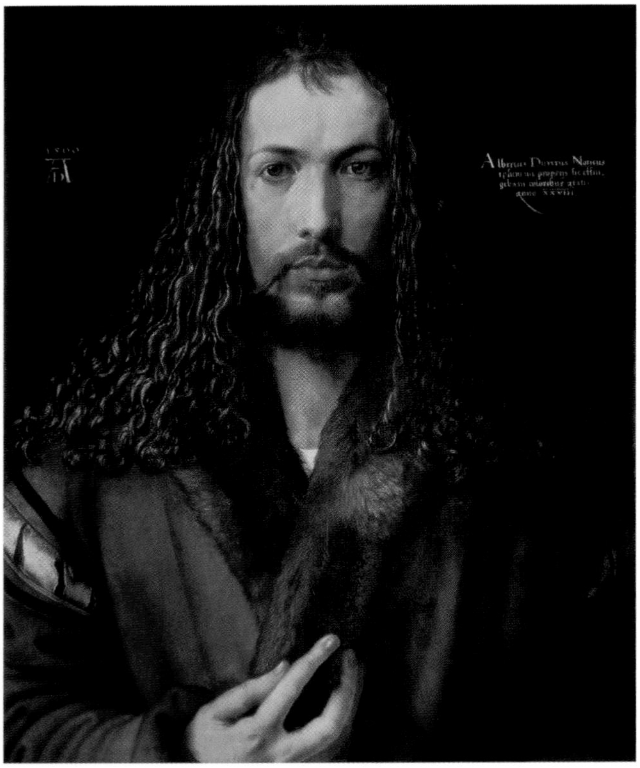

Fig. 18-12 Albrecht Dürer, *Self-Portrait*, 1500. Oil on panel, 26¼ × 19¼ in. Alte Pinakothek, Munich.
Inv. 537. © 2015. Photo Scala, Florence/bpk, Bildagentur fuer Kunst, Kultur und Geschichte, Berlin.

1260 — 1264–1368 Beijing thrives as Chinese capital under Mongol rule — 1274 First Mongol invasion of Japan — 1300

The Era of Encounter

In what ways did the encounter with other cultures impact the long-established artistic traditions of China and Japan, the Americas, and Africa?

When, in 1488, Bartolomeu Dias, investigating the coast of West Africa, was blown far south by a sudden storm and, turning northeast, found that he had rounded what would later be called the Cape of Good Hope and entered the Indian Ocean, and when, four years later, Christopher Columbus sailed westward, into the Atlantic Ocean, fully anticipating that he would soon arrive in Japan, an era of cultural encounter like none previously known was inaugurated. In China and Japan, the Americas, and Africa strong cultural traditions were already in place, but they were transformed by their encounters with European culture, even as Europe was itself transformed by contact with them.

Art in China and Japan

Already, in 1275, a young Venetian by the name of Marco Polo had arrived in Beijing, China, and quickly established himself as a favorite of the Mongol ruler Kublai Khan, first emperor of the Yuan dynasty. Polo served in an administrative capacity in Kublai Khan's court and for three years ruled the city of Yangchow. Shortly after his return to Venice in 1295, he was imprisoned after being captured by the army of Genoa in a battle with his native Venice. While there, he dictated an account of his travels. His description of the luxury and magnificence of the Far East, by all accounts reasonably accurate, was virtually the sole source of information about China available in Europe until the nineteenth century.

At the time of Marco Polo's arrival, many of the scholar-painters of the Chinese court, unwilling to serve under the foreign domination of Kublai Khan, were retreating into exile from public life. In exile, they conscientiously sought to keep traditional values and arts alive by cultivating earlier styles in both painting and calligraphy. According to the inscription on Cheng Sixiao's *Ink Orchids* (**Fig. 18-13**), this painting was done to protest the "theft of Chinese soil by invaders," referring to the Mongol conquest of China. The orchids, therefore, have been painted without soil around their roots, showing an art flourishing, even though what sustains it has been taken away.

In 1368, Zhu Yuanzhang drove the Mongols out of China and restored Chinese rule in the land, establishing

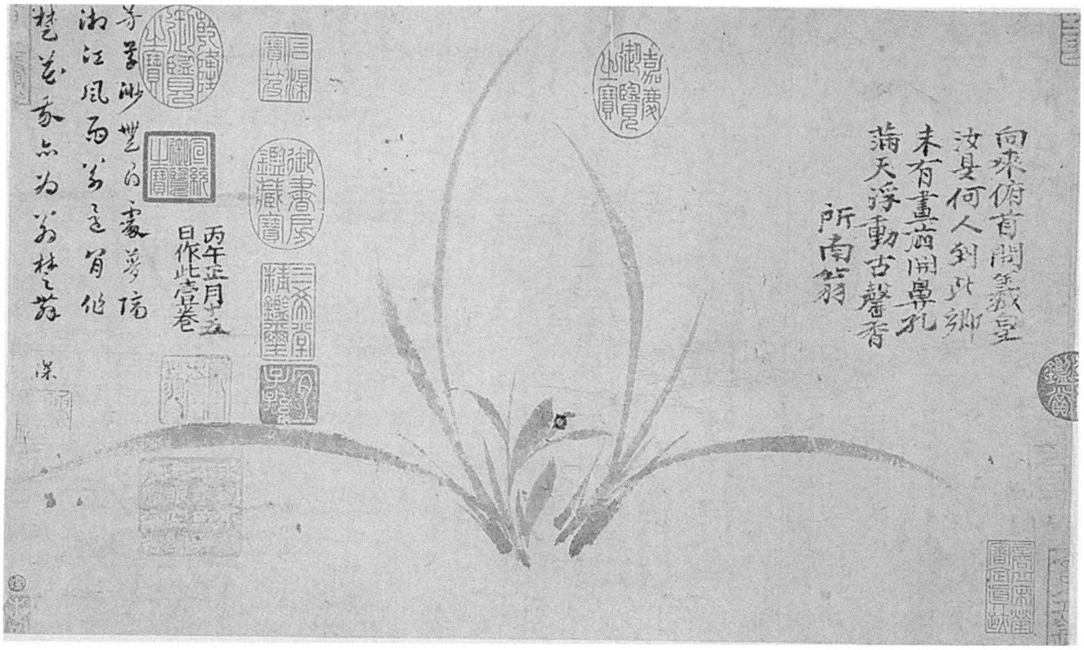

Fig. 18-13 Cheng Sixiao, *Ink Orchids*, Yuan dynasty, 1306. Handscroll, ink on paper, 10⅛ × 16¾ in. Municipal Museum of Fine Arts, Osaka.
Galileo Picture Services, LLC, New York/PPS.

Fig. 18-15 Shen Zhou, *Poet on a Mountaintop*, leaf from an album of landscapes, painting mounted as part of a handscroll, Ming dynasty, ca. 1500. Ink and color on paper, 15¼ × 23¾ in. The Nelson-Atkins Museum of Art, Kansas City, Missouri.
Purchase: William Rockhill Nelson Trust, 46-51/2. Photo: John Lamberton.

the dynasty called the Ming ("bright" or "brilliant"), which lasted until 1644. Late in the Ming dynasty, an artist, calligrapher, theorist, and high official in the government bureaucracy, Dong Qichang, wrote an essay that has affected the way we have looked at the history of Chinese painting ever since, although many scholars, even in Dong Qichang's time, viewed it as oversimplistic. It divided the history of Chinese painting into two schools, northern and southern, although geography had little to do with it. It was not place but the spirit in which the artist approached his painting that determined to which school he belonged.

Hundreds of Birds Admiring the Peacocks (**Fig. 18-14**) by Yin Hong, a court artist active in the late fifteenth and early sixteenth centuries, is an example of the northern school, conservative and traditional in its approach. It is defined by its highly refined decorative style, which emphasizes the technical skill of the painter, the rich use of color, and reliance on traditional Chinese painting—in this case the birds-and-flowers genre extremely popular in the Song dynasty. Like Guo Xi's Song dynasty painting *Early Spring* (see Fig. 17-28), Yin Hong's painting also takes on a symbolic meaning that refers directly to the emperor. Just as the central peak in Guo Xi's painting symbolizes the emperor himself, with the lower peaks and trees assuming a place of subservience to him, here the emperor is symbolized by the peacock around whom "hundreds of birds"—that is, court officials—gather in obeisance.

Fig. 18-14 Yin Hong, *Hundreds of Birds Admiring the Peacocks*, Ming dynasty, ca. late 15th–early 16th century. Hanging scroll, ink and color on silk, 7 ft. 10½ in. × 6 ft. 5 in. The Cleveland Museum of Art.
Purchase from the J. H. Wade Fund, 1974.31. Photo © Cleveland Museum of Art.

The southern style was unorthodox, radical, and inventive. Thus, a painting like *Poet on a Mountaintop* (**Fig. 18-15**) by Shen Zhou radicalizes the traditional Chinese landscape. For the southern artist, reality rested in the mind, not the physical world, and thus self-expression is the ultimate aim. Here, the poet stands as the central figure in the painting, facing out over an airy void in which hangs the very image of his mind, the poem inscribed in the top left of the painting:

White clouds like a belt encircle the mountain's waist
A stone ledge flying in space and the far thin road.
I lean alone on my bramble staff and gazing contented into space
Wish the sounding torrent would answer to your flute.

Fig. 18-17 School of Kano, *Namban* six-panel screen, 1593–1600. Kobe City Museum of Namban Art, Japan.
Galileo Picture Services, LLC, New York/PPS.

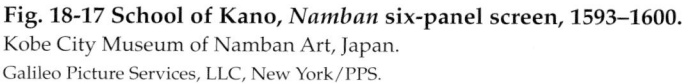

Fig. 18-16 Sesshu Toyo, *Haboku Landscape*, 1400s–early 1500s. Hanging scroll, ink on paper, 28¼ × 10½ in. The Cleveland Museum of Art.
Gift of the Norweb Foundation, 1955.43.
Photo © Cleveland Museum of Art.

The southern style ideally synthesizes the three areas of endeavor that any member of the cultural elite—or literati, the literary intelligentsia—was expected to master: poetry, calligraphy, and painting.

In the thirteenth century in Japan, Zen Buddhism, the Japanese version of Chinese Chan Buddhism, began to take hold. The question of the extent of the influence of Zen on Japanese art is a problematic one. As has often been pointed out, the features normally associated with Zen (Chan) Buddhism in the arts—simplicity of design, suggestion rather than description, and controlling balance through irregularity and asymmetry—are also characteristic of indigenous Japanese taste. Still, a number of Japanese artists, usually Zen monks themselves, turned to China and its Chan traditions for inspiration. In order to acquaint himself more fully with Chinese traditions, for instance, Sesshu Toyo, a Zen priest-painter, traveled to China in 1468–69, copying the Song dynasty masters and becoming adept at the more abstract forms of representation practiced by the Chinese Buddhists. *Haboku Landscape* (**Fig. 18-16**) is painted in the Zen Buddhist manner known as *haboku*, meaning "broken or splashed ink," the application of one layer of ink over another "breaking" the initial surface or description. No mark on this painting could actually be thought of as representational. Rather, the denser ink suggests trees and rocks, while the softer washes evoke tall mountains in the distance, water, and mist.

The presence of foreign traders in Japan, principally Portuguese and Dutch, soon made itself felt in Japanese painting, particularly in a new genre of screen painting known as *namban*, literally, "southern barbarian," referring to the "barbarian" Westerners who arrived from the south by ship. In the most popular theme of this genre, a foreign galleon arrives in Kyoto harbor (**Fig. 18-17**). The ship's crew unloads goods, and the captain and his men proceed through the streets of the city to Nambanji, the Jesuit church in Kyoto. The priests themselves are Japanese converts to Christianity.

The uniqueness of these paintings is that they present a convergence of cultures—encouraged by the prospect of trade, not only with Europeans but with the peoples of other Asian countries—unparalleled in world history. The Portuguese, with the help of slave labor from Africa, had established a base in Macao, which they had been ceded by the Chinese in return for suppressing piracy on the Chinese coast, and they served as the conduit between China and Japan, exchanging Japanese silver for Chinese raw silk, which the Japanese processed into textiles, particularly kimonos, of remarkable quality.

Art in Mexico and South America

By the time Christopher Columbus arrived in what he dubbed the "New World" in 1492, many significant cultures, like that of the Olmec (see Fig. 16-16), had already come and gone. By the fourth century CE, Teotihuacán (**Figs. 18-18** and **18-19**) had become an important commercial center inhabited by a people of unknown ethnic identity. As opposed to the later Mayan cities, many of which were quickly forgotten and overgrown in the jungle, Teotihuacán remained, a thousand years after it flourished, the mythic center of Mesoamerican civilization, the site of pilgrimages by even the most important Aztec rulers.

The city is laid out in a grid system, the basic unit of which is 614 square feet, and every detail is subjected to this scheme—the very image of power and mastery. A great broad avenue, known as the Avenue of the Dead, runs through the city. It links two great pyramids, the Pyramids of the Moon and the Sun, each surrounded by about 600 smaller pyramids, 500 workshops, numerous plazas, 2,000 apartment complexes, and a giant market area. The Pyramid of the Sun is oriented to mark the passage of the sun from east to west and the rising of the stellar constellation, the Pleiades, on the days of the equinox. Each of its two staircases contains 182 steps, which, when the platform at its apex is added, together total 365. The pyramid is thus an image of time. This representation of the solar calendar is echoed in another pyramid at Teotihuacán, the Temple of Quetzalcóatl, which is decorated with 364 serpent fangs.

At its height, in about 500 CE, the population of Teotihuacán was perhaps 200,000, making it one of the largest cities in the world. Scholars believe that a female deity, associated with the moon, as well as cave and mountain rituals, played an important role in Teotihuacán culture. The placement of the Pyramid of the Moon in front of the dead volcano Cerro Gordo (see Fig. 18-19) supports this theory. It is as if the mountain, seen from a vantage point looking north up the Avenue of the Dead, embraces the pyramid in its flanks. And the pyramid, in turn, seems to channel the forces of nature—the water abundant on the mountain in particular—into the heart of the city.

To the south, another culture, that of the Maya, both predated and postdated that of Teotihuacán. The Maya occupied several regions: the highlands of Chiapas and Guatemala; the Southern Lowlands of Guatemala, Honduras, El Salvador, Belize, and the Mexican states of Chiapas; and the Northern Lowlands in the states of Yucatán, Campeche, and Quintana Roo. They were never unified into a single political entity, but rather consisted of many small kingdoms that engaged in warfare with one another over land and resources. An elaborate calendar system enabled them to keep track of their history—and, evidence suggests, predict the future. It consisted of two interlocking ways of recording time, a 260-day calendar and a 365-day calendar. The 260-day calendar probably derives from the length of human gestation, from a pregnant woman's first missed menstrual period to birth. When both calendars were synchronized, it took exactly 52 years of 365 days for a given day to repeat itself—the so-called calendar round—and the end of each cycle was widely celebrated.

Fig. 18-18 Teotihuacán, Mexico, as seen from the Pyramid of the Moon, looking south down the Avenue of the Dead, the Pyramid of the Sun at the left, ca. 350–650 CE.

© Gina Martin/National Geographic Image Collection.

Fig. 18-19 The Pyramid of the Moon, looking north up the Avenue of the Dead.

© Frandesca Yorke/Dorling Kindersley.

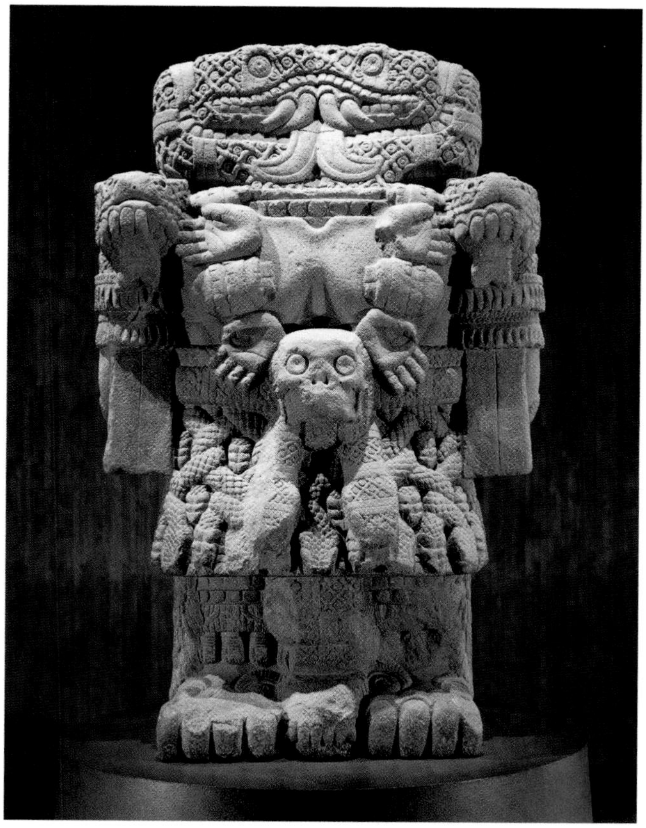

Fig. 18-20 ***Coatlicue*, Aztec, 15th century.** Basalt, height 8 ft. 3 in. National Museum of Anthropology, Mexico City.
De Agostini/G. Dagli Orti/Bridgeman Images.

Fig. 18-21 Aztecs confront the Spaniards, from Diego de Durán's *History of the Indies of New Spain*, 1581. Biblioteca Nacional, Madrid.
Bridgeman Images.

Particularly among the Aztecs, who traced their ancestry to the merging of Mayan and Toltec cultures at Chichen Itzá, on the Yucatán Peninsula, the calendar's tie to the menstrual cycle required blood sacrifice. Coatlicue was the Aztec goddess of life and death. In this sculpture (**Fig. 18-20**), her head is composed of two fanged serpents, which are symbolic of flowing blood. She wears a necklace of human hearts, severed hands, and a skull. Her skirt is made of interwoven serpents which, to the Aztecs, represented both childbirth and blood—that is, fertility and decapitation.

In 1519–21, the Aztec Empire of Mexico was conquered by the Spanish *conquistador* ("conqueror") Hernán Cortés and his army of 600 men through a combination of military technology (gunpowder, cannon, and muskets), disease inadvertently introduced by his troops, and a series of lies and violations of trust. The Aztecs possessed neither guns nor horses, nor much in the way of clothing or armor, all of which made them appear, if not uncivilized, then completely vulnerable. They were also vulnerable because other native populations in Mexico deeply resented the fact that the Aztecs regularly raided their villages to obtain victims for blood sacrifice.

Anthropological evidence suggests that just before Cortés's arrival, in about 1450, the Aztecs, in their thirst for blood sacrifice, had wiped out the entire population of Casas Grandes, near present-day Chihuahua in northern Mexico, a trading center containing over 2,000 pueblo apartments. Given such Aztec behavior, other tribes were willing to cooperate with Cortés. One of the most important documents of the Spanish conquest, the 1581 *History of the Indies of New Spain*, by Diego de Durán, a Dominican priest fluent in Nahuatl, the Aztec language, includes an illustration depicting Cortés's technological superiority (**Fig. 18-21**). Here, an army led by Pedro de Alvarado, one of Cortés's generals, confronts the Aztec military orders of the Eagle and the Jaguar. The Spanish wear armor and fight with crossbows and firearms, while the Aztecs have only spears. Durán's *History* is the product of extensive interviews and conversations with the Aztecs themselves. It represents a concerted effort to preserve Aztec culture, recounting Aztec history from its creation story through the Spanish conquest.

As in Mesoamerica, complex cultures developed in South America during the period corresponding to the Middle Ages in Europe, particularly in the area of present-day Peru. Moche culture flourished there for a thousand years, from about 200 BCE to 800 CE. The Moche built large mound temples made entirely of adobe bricks, sun-baked blocks of clay mixed with straw. The largest, located in the Moche Valley, from which

Fig. 18-22 ***Moche Lord with a Feline*, from Moche Valley, Peru, Moche culture, ca. 100 BCE–500 CE.** Painted ceramic, height 7½ in. The Art Institute of Chicago.

the culture takes its name, is the so-called Pyramid of the Sun. It is over 1,000 feet long and 500 feet wide, and rises to a height of 59 feet. In these pyramids, people buried their dead, accompanied by gold earrings, pendants, necklaces, and other ornaments, as well as elaborately decorated ceramic bowls, pots, and bottles. The most distinctive bottles depict scenes representative of Moche culture as a whole (**Fig. 18-22**), usually on bottles with distinctive stirrup spouts that curve elegantly away from the body of the vessel. The list of the subjects depicted is almost endless—animals of all kinds, from seals to owls, warriors, plants, musicians, homes, children at play, women weaving, couples engaged in sex, a man washing his hair—as if the culture were intent on representing every facet of its daily life. Recent research suggests, however, that every one of these scenes has a ritual or symbolic function. The image shown here, for instance, may well represent the warrior-priest who presided over Moche sacrifice ceremonies, in which prisoners captured in battle were sacrificed and their blood drunk by elaborately dressed warriors.

About 800 CE, the Moche suddenly vanished, many believe as a result of floods brought about by a series of weather events related to El Niño. This major temperature fluctuation of the waters of the eastern Pacific Ocean causes substantial changes in rainfall levels both regionally and worldwide. The resulting political vacuum lasted for over 400 years until, around 1300, the Inca culture emerged. The Inca were, above all, sublime masons. Working with stone tools and without mortar, they crafted adjoining granite blocks that fit so snugly together that their walls have, for centuries, withstood earthquakes that have destroyed many a later structure.

Original Inca walls are still visible at one of the most elaborately decorated of all Inca sites, Cuzco's Coricancha (literally, "the corral of gold"), the Inca Temple of the Sun facing the main plaza (**Fig. 18-23**). Dedicated to Inti, the sun god, the original temple was decorated with 700 sheets of gold studded with emeralds and turquoise, and designed to reflect the sunlight admitted through its windows. Its courtyard was filled with golden statuary. After their conquest of Peru, the Spanish quickly adapted the foundations of the Inca temple to their own purposes, constructing a Dominican church and monastery on them. The Inca traditionally gathered to worship at the curved, circular wall of the Coricancha, and thus

Fig. 18-23 Original Inca stone wall of the Coricancha with a Dominican monastery rising above it, Cuzco, Peru, Inca culture.

the apse of Santo Domingo was deliberately constructed above it to emphasize Christian control of the native site.

African Art of the Encounter

After Portugal began to explore the west coast of Africa, starting in 1488, evidence of their presence quickly appeared in African art. The Portuguese enjoyed a certain status as divine visitors from the watery world, the realm of Olokun, god of the sea. They were considered to be the equivalent of the mudfish, because they could both "swim" (in their boats) and walk on land. The mudfish was sacred to the Benin people, who lived in the Niger River basin just south of the Ife, and who saw it as a symbol of both transformation (it lies dormant all summer on dry mudflats and is seemingly "reborn" each fall when the rains come) and power (it can deliver strong electric shocks and possesses fatal spines). Likewise, the Portuguese seemed to be born of the sea and possessed fatal "spines" of their own—rifles and musketry. A remarkable example of this association of the mudfish with the Portuguese is an alternating mudfish/Portuguese decorative design that forms the tiara of an ivory mask worn as a hip pendant by a West African queen (**Fig. 18-24**).

Fig. 18-24 Mask of an *iyoba* (queen mother), probably Idia, Court of Benin, Nigeria, ca. 1550. Ivory, iron, and copper, height 9⅜ in. Metropolitan Museum of Art, New York.
Michael C. Rockefeller Collection, Gift of Nelson A. Rockefeller, 1972, 1978.412.323. © 2015. Image copyright Metropolitan Museum of Art/Art Resource/Scala, Florence.

Fig. 18-25 *Portuguese Warrior Surrounded by* Manillas, Court of Benin, Nigeria, 16th century. Bronze. Kunsthistorisches Museum, Vienna.

At first Benin had traded gold, ivory, rubber, and other forest products for beads and, particularly, brass. The standard medium of exchange was a horseshoe-shaped copper or brass object called a *manilla*, five of which appear in an early sixteenth-century Benin plaque portraying a Portuguese warrior (**Fig. 18-25**). Such metal plaques decorated the palace and royal altar area particularly, and here the soldier brings with him the very material out of which the plaque is made. If his weapons—trident and sword—suggest his power, it is a power in the service of the Benin king, at least from the Benin point of view.

The Mannerist Style in Europe

How does Mannerist painting differ from that of the High Renaissance?

Shortly after the Spanish conquest of separatist states within Spain in 1519 and the death of Raphael in 1520, many Italian painters embarked on a stylistic course that came to be known as **Mannerism**. Highly individualistic and *mannered*, or consciously artificial, this style was dedicated to "invention," and the technical and imaginative virtuosity of the artist became of paramount importance. Each Mannerist artist may, therefore, be identified by his own "signature" style. Where the art of the High Renaissance sought to create a feeling of balance and proportion, quite the opposite is the goal of Mannerist art. In the later work of Michelangelo, for example, particularly the great fresco of *The Last Judgment* on the altar wall of the Sistine Chapel (**Fig. 18-26**), executed in the years 1534 to 1541, we find figures of grotesque proportion arranged in an almost chaotic, certainly athletic, swirl of line. Mannerist painters represented space in unpredictable and ambiguous ways,

Fig. 18-26 Michelangelo, *The Last Judgment*, on altar wall of Sistine Chapel, 1534–41.
Fresco. Vatican Museums, Vatican City.
Vatican Museums,Vatican City/Bridgeman Images.

Fig. 18-27 Tintoretto, *The Miracle of the Slave*, 1548. Oil on canvas, approx. 14 × 18 ft. Gallerie dell'Accademia, Venice.
Cameraphoto Arte Venezia/Bridgeman Images.

so that bodies sometimes seem to fall out of nowhere into the frame of the painting, as in Tintoretto's *The Miracle of the Slave* (**Fig. 18-27**). The drama of Tintoretto's painting is heightened by the descent of the vastly foreshortened St. Mark, who hurtles in from above to save the slave from his executioner. The rising spiral line created by the three central figures—the slave, the executioner holding up his shattered instruments of torture, and St. Mark—is characteristic of Mannerism, but the theatricality of the scene, heightened by its dramatic contrast of light and dark, anticipates the Baroque style which soon followed.

Often, the space of a Mannerist painting seems too shallow for what is depicted, a feeling emphasized by the frequent use of radical foreshortening, as in the Tintoretto. Or the figure itself may be distorted or elongated, as in Bronzino's *An Allegory with Venus and Cupid* (**Fig. 18-28**). The colors are often bright and clashing. At the upper right of Bronzino's painting, Time, and, at the upper left, Truth part a curtain to reveal the shallow space in which Venus is fondled by her son, Cupid. Folly is about to shower the pair in rose petals. Envy tears her hair out at center left. The Mannerist distortion of space is especially evident in the distance separating Cupid's shoulders and head.

As in El Greco's *The Burial of Count Orgaz* (**Fig. 18-29**), Mannerist painting often utilizes more than one focal point, and these often seem contradictory. Born in Crete

Fig. 18-28 Bronzino, *An Allegory with Venus and Cupid*, ca. 1540–50. Oil on wood, approx. 5 ft. 1 in. × 4 ft. 8¾ in. National Gallery, London.
Bought, 1860, Inv. 4993. © 2015. Copyright National Gallery, London/Scala, Florence.

Fig. 18-29 El Greco, *The Burial of Count Orgaz*, 1586. Oil on canvas, 16 ft. × 11 ft. 10 in. Church of Santo Tomé, Toledo, Spain.
© 2015. Photo Scala, Florence.

and trained in Venice and Rome, where he studied the works of Titian, Tintoretto, and the Italian Mannerists, El Greco moved to Toledo, Spain, in 1576, and lived there for the rest of his life. In the painting we see here, the realism of the lower ensemble, which includes local Toledo nobility and clergy of El Greco's day (even though the painting represents a burial that took place more than 200 years earlier, in 1323), gives way in the upper half to a much more abstract and personal brand of representation. El Greco's elongated figures—consider St. Peter, in the saffron robe behind Mary on the upper left, with his long piercing fingers on a longer, almost drooping hand—combine with oddly rolling clouds that rise toward an astonishingly small representation of Christ. So eclectic and individual is this painter's style that it is difficult to label it even as Mannerist.

Fig. 18-30 St. Peter's, Rome; nave and facade by Carlo Maderno, 1607–15; colonnade by Gianlorenzo Bernini, 1657.
Ikona.

The Baroque

How does the Baroque manifest itself in both art and architecture?

The **Baroque** style, which is noted particularly for its theatricality and drama, was, in many respects, a creation of the papacy in Rome. Around 1600, faced in the north with the challenge of Protestantism, which had grown steadily more powerful ever since Martin Luther's first protests in 1517, the Vatican took action. It called together as many talents as it could muster with the clear intention of turning Rome into the most magnificent city in the world, "for the greater glory of God and the Church." At the heart of this effort was an ambitious building program. In 1603, Carlo Maderno was assigned the task of adding an enormous nave to Michelangelo's central plan for St. Peter's, converting it back into a giant basilica (**Fig. 18-30**). Completed in 1615, the scale of the new basilica was even more dramatically emphasized when Gianlorenzo Bernini added a monumental oval piazza surrounded by colonnades to the front of the church. Bernini conceived of his colonnade as an architectural embrace, as if the church were reaching out its arms to gather in its flock. The wings that connect the facade to the semicircular colonnade tend to diminish the horizontality of the facade and emphasize the vertical thrust of Michelangelo's dome. The enormous scale of the space can hardly be inferred from a photograph such as the one reproduced here.

As vast as Bernini's artistic ambitions were, he was comparatively Classical in his tastes. If we compare Bernini's colonnade at St. Peter's to Francesco Borromini's facade for San Carlo alle Quattro Fontane in Rome (**Fig. 18-31**), we notice immediately how symmetrical Bernini's design appears— despite its magnificent scale, it is positively conservative by comparison. Borromini's extravagant design was immediately popular. The head of the religious order for whom San Carlo alle Quattro Fontane was built wrote with great pride, "Nothing similar can be found anywhere in the world. This is attested by the foreigners who . . . try to procure copies of the plan. We have been asked for them by Germans, Flemings, Frenchmen, Italians, Spaniards, and even Indians." We can detect in these remarks the Baroque tendency to define artistic genius increasingly in terms of originality, the creation of things never before seen. Bernini's colonnade makes clear that Classical virtues were upheld, but emerging for the first time, often in the work of the same artist, is a countertendency, a sensibility opposed to tradition and dedicated to invention.

One of the defining characteristics of the Baroque is its insistence on bringing together various media to achieve the most theatrical effects. Bernini's Cornaro Chapel in Santa Maria della Vittoria (**Figs. 18-32** and **18-33**) is perhaps the most highly developed of these dynamic and theatrical spaces. The altarpiece depicts the ecstasy of St. Teresa. St. Teresa, a nun whose conversion took place after the death of her father, experienced visions, heard voices, and felt a persistent and piercing pain in her side. This was caused, she believed, by the flaming arrow of Divine Love, shot into her by an angel: "The pain was so great I screamed aloud," she wrote, "but at the same time I felt such infinite sweetness that I wished the pain to last forever. . . . It was the sweetest caressing of

Fig. 18-31 Francesco Borromini, Facade, San Carlo alle Quattro Fontane, Rome, 1665–67.

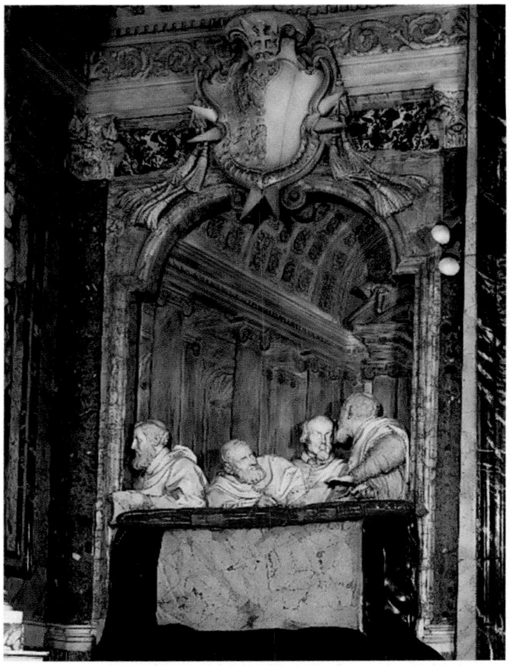

Fig. 18-32 Gianlorenzo Bernini, *The Cornaro Family in a Theater Box*, 1647–52. Marble, life-size. Cornaro Chapel, Santa Maria della Vittoria, Rome.

the soul by God." The paradoxical nature of St. Teresa's feelings is typical of the complexity of Baroque sentiment. Bernini fuses the angel's joy and St. Teresa's agony into an image that depicts what might be called St. Teresa's "anguished joy." Even more typical of the Baroque sensibility is Bernini's use of every device available to him to dramatize the scene. The sculpture of St. Teresa is illuminated by a hidden window above, so that the figures seem to glow in a magical white light. Gilded bronze rays of heavenly light descend upon the scene as if from the burst of light painted high on the frescoed ceiling of the vault. To the left and right of the chapel are theater boxes containing marble spectators, witnesses—like us—to this highly charged, operatic moment.

The Baroque style quickly spread beyond Rome and throughout Europe. Elaborate Baroque churches were constructed, especially in Germany and Austria. In the early years of the seventeenth century, furthermore, a number of artists from France, Holland, and Flanders were strongly influenced by the work of the Italian painter Caravaggio. Caravaggio openly disdained the

Fig. 18-33 Gianlorenzo Bernini, *The Ecstasy of St. Teresa*, 1647–52. Marble, life-size. Cornaro Chapel, Santa Maria della Vittoria, Rome.

great masters of the Renaissance, creating instead a highly individualistic brand of painting that sought its inspiration not in the proven styles of a former era but literally in the streets of contemporary Rome. When viewing his work, it is often difficult to tell that his subject is a religious one, so ordinary are his people and so dingy and commonplace his settings. Yet despite Caravaggio's desire to secularize his religious subjects, their light imbues them with a spiritual reality. It was, in fact, the contrast in his paintings between light and dark, mirroring the contrast between the spiritual content of the painting and its representation in the trappings of the everyday, that so powerfully influenced painters across Europe.

Caravaggio's naturalism is nowhere so evident as in *The Calling of St. Matthew* (**Fig. 18-34**), which was painted, somewhat surprisingly, for a church. The scene is a tavern. St. Matthew, originally a tax collector, sits counting the day's take with a band of his agents, all of them apparently prosperous, if we are to judge from their attire. From the right, two barefoot and lowly figures, one of whom is Christ, enter the scene, calling St. Matthew to join them. He points at himself in some astonishment. Except for the undeniably spiritual quality of the light, which floods the room as if it were revelation itself, the only thing telling us that this is a religious painting is the faint indication of a halo above Christ's head.

Fig. 18-34 Caravaggio, *The Calling of St. Matthew*, ca. 1599–1602. Oil on canvas, 11 ft. 1 in. × 11 ft. 5 in. Contarelli Chapel, San Luigi dei Francesci, Rome.
Canali Photobank, Milan, Italy.

Though not directly influenced by Caravaggio, Rembrandt, the greatest master of light and dark of the age, knew Caravaggio's art through Dutch artists who had studied it. Rembrandt extends the sense of dramatic opposition Caravaggio achieved by manipulating light across a full range of tones, changing its intensity and modulating its brilliance, so that every beam and shadow conveys a different emotional content. In his *Resurrection of Christ* (**Fig. 18-35**), he uses the contrast between light and dark to underscore emotional difference. He juxtaposes

Fig. 18-35 Rembrandt van Rijn, *The Resurrection of Christ*, ca. 1635–39.
Oil on canvas, 36¼ × 26⅜ in. Alte Pinakothek, Munich.

the chaotic world of the Roman soldiers, sent reeling into a darkness symbolic of their own ignorance by the angel pulling open the lid of Christ's sepulcher, with the quiet calm of Christ himself as He rises in a light symbolic of true knowledge. Light becomes, in Rembrandt's hands, an index to the psychological meaning of his subjects, often hiding as much as it reveals, endowing them with a sense of mystery even as it reveals their souls.

In northern Europe, where strict Protestant theology had purged the churches of religious art and Classical subjects were frowned upon as pagan, realism thrived. Works with secular, or nonreligious, subject matter—still-life painting (see Fig. 9-16), representations of everyday people living out their lives (genre painting), and landscapes—became extremely popular. In Spain, where the royal family had deep historical ties to the north, the visual realism of Diego Velázquez came to dominate painting (see Fig. 7-16). Spurred on by the great wealth it had acquired in its conquest of the New World, Spain helped to create a thriving market structure in Europe. Dutch artists quickly introduced their own goods—that is, paintings—into this economy, with the Spanish court as one of its most prestigious buyers. No longer working for the Church, but instead for this new international market, artists painted the everyday things that they thought would appeal to the bourgeois tastes of the new consumer.

Of all the new secular subject matter that arose during the Baroque Age, the genre of landscape perhaps most decisively marks a shift in Western thinking. In Annibale Carracci's *Landscape with Flight into Egypt* (**Fig. 18-36**), the figure and the story have become incidental to the landscape. Joseph has dreamed that King Herod is searching for the infant Jesus to kill him, and he flees into Egypt with Mary and the child, to remain there until after Herod's death. But this landscape is hardly Egypt. Rather, Carracci has transferred the story to a highly civilized Italian setting. This is the pastoral world, a middle ground between civilization and wilderness, where people can live free of both the corruption and decadence of city and court life and the uncontrollable forces of nature.

Fig. 18-36 Annibale Carracci, *Landscape with Flight into Egypt*, ca. 1603. Oil on canvas, 4 ft. ¼ in. × 8 ft. 2½ in. Galleria Doria Pamphilj, Rome.
Canali Photobank, Milan, Italy.

Fig. 18-37 Claude, *A Pastoral Landscape*, ca. 1650. Oil on copper, 15½ × 21 in.
Yale University Art Gallery, New Haven.
Bequest of Leo C. Hanna, 1959.47. Image courtesy of Yale University Art Gallery.

One of the most idyllic of all landscape painters goes even further. Claude Lorrain—or just Claude, as he is usually known—casts the world in an eternally poetic light. In his *Pastoral Landscape* (**Fig. 18-37**), he employs atmospheric perspective to soften all sense of tension and opposition and to bring us to a world of harmony and peace. In this painting, and many others like it, the best civilization has to offer has been melded with the best of a wholly benign and gentle nature.

Landscape painters felt that, because God made the earth, one could sense the majesty of his soul in his handiwork, much as one could sense emotion in a painter's gesture upon canvas. The grandeur of God's vision was symbolically suggested in the panoramic sweep of the extended view. Giving up two-thirds of the picture to the infinite dimensions of the heavens, Jacob van Ruisdael's *View of Haarlem from the Dunes at Overveen* (**Fig. 18-38**) is not so much about the land as it is about the sky—and the light that emanates from it, alternately casting the earth in light and shadow, knowledge and ignorance. It is significant that rising to meet the light is the largest building in the landscape, the church. The beam of light that in Caravaggio's painting suggests the spiritual presence of Christ becomes, in landscape, a beam of light from the "Sun/Son," a pun popular among English poets of the period, including John Donne. By

Native American population reduced to about 70,000
1675

— 1675 —

Fig. 18-38 Jacob van Ruisdael, *View of Haarlem from the Dunes at Overveen*, ca. 1670. Oil on canvas, 22 × 24⅜ in. Royal Cabinet of Painting, Mauritshuis, The Hague.

the last half of the seventeenth century, it is as if the real space of the Dutch landscape had become so idealized that it is almost Edenic.

The example of landscape offers us an important lesson in the direction art took from the late seventeenth century. The spiritual is no longer found exclusively in the church. It can be found in nature, in light, in form—even, as we progress toward the modern era, in the artist's very self. And by the end of the seventeenth century, the Church is no longer the major patron of art it had been for centuries before. From Spanish kings, to wealthy Dutch merchants, to an increasingly large group of middle-class bourgeoisie with disposable incomes and the desire to refine their tastes, the patrons of art changed until, by the middle of the twentieth century, art came to be bought and sold in an international "art market."

Thinking Back

18.1 Explain how humanism informs the art of both the Early and High Renaissance.

The term "Renaissance" refers to a period of revived interest in the arts and sciences of Classical antiquity. The Renaissance began at the turn of the fifteenth century, but was anticipated in the preceding Gothic period. How does Donatello draw upon Classical traditions in his *David*? How does Early Renaissance painting in the north differ from that of the south? What did the Neoplatonists believe? How do these beliefs manifest themselves in the paintings of Botticelli?

Although Michelangelo, Leonardo, Raphael, and the Venetian painters Giorgione and Titian all worked in distinctive ways, what humanist values did they share? What role did the idea of "genius" play in their art?

18.2 Discuss some of the ways that the encounter with other cultures impacted the long-established artistic traditions of China and Japan, the Americas, and Africa.

While Marco Polo's arrival at the court of Kublai Chan in China in 1275 did not significantly change Chinese society, his reports of his journey fueled interest in the region in Europe. How does Cheng Sixiao's *Ink Orchids* reflect the attitude of Chinese scholar-painters to Kublai Khan's court? What two different approaches to painting did Dong Qichang see as defining the art of the Ming dynasty? How did Chinese Chan Buddhism impact Japanese Zen Buddhist art? What is *namban* painting?

In Mexico, the city of Teotihuacán, which was flourishing by the fourth century, became a mythic center of Mesoamerican civilization and a sacred site of the Aztecs. To the south, the Maya created elaborate cultural centers, although they were never unified into a single political entity. They did, however, share a remarkable calendar system. How would you describe it? How are its values reflected in the Aztec sculpture of *Coatlicue*? In Peru, the Inca culture followed that of the Moche, which suddenly vanished around 800. The Inca were extraordinary masons. How did the Spanish take advantage of the Inca Coricancha temple in Cuzco?

The Benin peoples regarded the Portuguese as divine visitors because they could both "swim" (in their boats) and walk on land. How are the Portuguese represented in the mask of an *iyoba* (queen mother)? What is a *manilla*?

18.3 Describe how the Mannerist style is different from that of the High Renaissance.

Individualistic and artificial, the Mannerist style is dedicated to technical and imaginative virtuosity. Mannerist artists use bright, clashing colors and represent space in ambiguous ways, departing from the balance of High Renaissance art. How does Bronzino's painting *An Allegory with Venus and Cupid* typify the Mannerist style? How does El Greco represent the human figure?

18.4 Define the Baroque as it manifests itself in both art and architecture.

The Baroque style is noted for its theatricality, drama, extravagance, emotionalism, and originality. The integration of various media in a single work is characteristic of the Baroque. In Baroque painting, naturalism and strong contrast are common. How does Francesco Borromini's San Carlo alle Quattro Fontane typify the Baroque? How does Rembrandt demonstrate Caravaggio's influence in his *Resurrection of Christ*?

Chapter 19

The Eighteenth and Nineteenth Centuries

Learning Objectives

19.1 Describe the two styles of art that vied for favor in the court of Louis XIV and the style that came to dominate the court of Louis XV.

19.2 Explain how contact between China and Europe influenced the art of both.

19.3 Define Neoclassicism and describe how it reflected the political aspirations of the age.

19.4 Outline the beliefs that unify Romanticism as a movement.

19.5 Explain how Realism replaced the idealizing tendencies of the Romantic movement.

19.6 Define Impressionism in terms of both its stylistic techniques and its subject matter.

19.7 Explain some of the ways that the Post-Impressionists extended and redirected the Impressionist enterprise.

Louis XIV, who ruled France from 1643 to 1715, thought of himself as *Le Roi Soleil*, "the Sun King," because like the sun (associated with Apollo, the ancient Greek god of peace and the arts) he saw himself dispensing bounty across the land. His ritual risings and retirings (the *levée du roi* and the *couchée du roi*) symbolized the actual rising and setting of the sun. They were essentially state occasions, attended by either the entire court or a select group of fawning aristocrats who eagerly entered their names on waiting lists.

Louis's sense of his own authority—to say nothing of his notorious vanity—is wonderfully captured in Hyacinthe Rigaud's official state portrait of 1701 (**Fig. 19-1**). The king has flung his robes over his shoulder in order to reveal his white stockings and shoes with high, red heels. He designed the shoes himself to compensate for his 5-foot-4-inch height. He is 63 years old in this portrait, but he means to make it clear that he is still a dashing courtier.

Louis also established his authority through his control of the arts. He was the absolute judge of taste at the French court and a great patron of the arts. He inherited some 200 paintings from his father but increased the royal collection tenfold during his reign. His motives were simple enough: Championing the greatest in art would establish him as the greatest of kings. "Gentlemen," he is reputed to have said to members of the Royal Academy (artists working for the French court), "I entrust to you the most precious thing on earth—my fame."

But Louis's own tastes were eclectic, and the self-indulgence of the French court, so obvious in Rigaud's portrait, precipitated not merely artistic counterreaction but eventually political revolution. Against the grandiose power of the court, the individual began to arise as a force; not the humanist individual of the Renaissance, but the common man himself. In the nineteenth century, after the French Revolution of 1789, the Romantics explored the individual psyche, the Realists the plight

Fig. 19-1 Hyacinthe Rigaud, *Louis XIV, King of France*, 1701. Oil on canvas, 9 ft. 1 in. × 6 ft. 4⅜ in. Château de Versailles et du Trianon, Versailles, France.

Inv. MV2041. Photo © RMN-Grand Palais (Château de Versailles)/Daniel Arnaudet/Gérard Blot.

of common folk, and the Impressionists the joys of everyday life.

The Early Eighteenth Century

What two styles of art vied for favor at the court of Louis XIV and what style came to dominate the court under Louis XV?

By the start of the eighteenth century, almost every royal court in Europe modeled itself on Louis XIV's. Louis's aesthetic standards modulated between the balance, harmony, and proportions of Classical art and the decorative exuberance of the Italian Baroque. Louis was, after all, a product of the seventeenth century. He had assumed the throne in 1643, and he would hold sway over European taste until his death in 1715.

Poussin versus Rubens

In the 1640s, the head of Louis's Royal Academy of Painting and Sculpture, Charles Le Brun, had studied in Rome with the Classical painter Nicolas Poussin. Poussin believed that the aim of painting was to represent the noblest human actions with absolute clarity. To this end, distracting elements—particularly color, but anything that appeals primarily to the senses—had to be suppressed. In Poussin's *Landscape with St. John on Patmos* (**Fig. 19-2**), the small figure of St. John is depicted writing the biblical Book of Revelation. Not only do the architecture and the architectural ruins lend a sense of Classical geometry to the scene, but even nature has been submitted to Poussin's Classicizing order. Notice, for instance, how the tree on the left bends just enough as it crosses the horizon to form a right angle with the slope of the distant mountain.

Fig. 19-2 Nicolas Poussin, *Landscape with St. John on Patmos*, 1640. Oil on canvas, 40 in. × 4 ft. 5½ in. The Art Institute of Chicago.

A. A. Munger Collection, 1930.500. Photo © 2015 Art Institute of Chicago.

Le Brun installed Poussin's views as an official, royal style. By Le Brun's standards, the greatest artists were the ancient Greeks and Romans, followed closely by Raphael and Poussin; the worst painters were the Flemish and Dutch, who not only "overemphasized" color and appealed to the senses, but also favored "lesser" genres, such as landscape and still life.

But Le Brun's hold on the French Academy was questioned by a large number of painters who championed the work of the great Flemish Baroque painter Peter Paul Rubens over that of Poussin. Rubens, who had painted a cycle of 21 paintings celebrating the life of Marie de' Medici, Louis XIV's grandmother, was a painter of extravagant Baroque tastes. Where the design of Poussin's *Landscape with St. John on Patmos* is based on horizontal and vertical elements arranged parallel to the picture plane, Rubens's forms in *The Disembarkation of Marie de' Medici* (**Fig. 19-3**) are dispersed across a pair of receding diagonals. In this painting, which depicts Marie's arrival in France as the new wife of King Henri IV, our point of view is not frontal and secure, as it is in the Poussin, but curiously low, perhaps even in the water. Poussin, in his design, focuses on his subject, St. John, who occupies the center of the painting, whereas Rubens creates a multiplicity of competing areas of interest. Most of all, Poussin's style is defined by its linear clarity. Rubens's work is painterly, dominated by a play of color, dramatic contrasts of light and dark, and sensuous, rising forms. Poussin is restrained, Rubens exuberant.

The Rococo

With the death of Louis XIV in 1715, French life itself became exuberant. This was an age whose taste was formed by society women with real, if covert, political power, especially Louis XV's mistress Mme. de Pompadour. The **salons**, gatherings held by particular hostesses on particular days of the week, were the social events of the day. Artists and art lovers would always gather at Mme. Geoffrin's on Mondays, while a famous musician might appear at another salon. A highly developed sense of wit, irony, and gossip was necessary to succeed in this society.

Fig. 19-3 Peter Paul Rubens, *The Disembarkation of Marie de' Medici at the Port of Marseilles on November 3, 1600*, 1621–25. Oil on canvas, 13 × 10 ft. Musée du Louvre, Paris. akg-image/Erich Lessing.

Fig. 19-4 Jean-Honoré Fragonard, *Bathers*, ca. 1765. Oil on wood, 25¼ × 31½ in. Musée du Louvre, Paris. © 2015. Photo Scala, Florence.

So skilled was the repartee in the salons that the most biting insult could be made to sound like the highest compliment. Sexual intrigue was not merely commonplace but expected. The age was obsessed with sensuality, and one can easily trace the origins of Fragonard's *Bathers* (**Fig. 19-4**) back to the mermaids at the bottom of Rubens's painting. Fragonard was Mme. de Pompadour's favorite painter, and the *Bathers* was designed to appeal to the tastes of the eighteenth-century French court.

This was the age of the **Rococo**, a word derived from the French *rocaille*, referring to the small stones and shells that decorate the interiors of grottoes, the artificial caves popular in landscape design at the time. The Rococo was deeply indebted to the Baroque sensibility of Rubens, as Fragonard's *Bathers* demonstrates. It was, in some sense, the Baroque eroticized, conceived to lend an erotic tone to its environment. Marie-Louise-Élisabeth Vigée-Lebrun's portrait of *The Duchess of Polignac* (**Fig. 19-5**) combines in exquisite fashion all of

Fig. 19-5 Marie-Louise-Élisabeth Vigée-Lebrun, *The Duchess of Polignac*, 1783. Oil on canvas, 38¾ × 28 in. Private Collection/Bridgeman Images.

the tools of the Baroque sensibility, from Rembrandt's dramatic lighting to Rubens's sensual curves and, given the musical score in the duchess's hand, even Bernini's sense of the theatrical moment.

Cross-Cultural Contact: China and Europe

How did contact between China and Europe influence the art of both?

Ever since the first Portuguese trading vessels had arrived in China in 1514, Chinese goods—porcelain, wallpapers, carved ivory fans, boxes, lacquerware, and patterned silks—had flooded European markets. By 1715, every major European trading nation had an office in Canton, and Europeans themselves developed a taste for a style of art that became known as **chinoiserie** (meaning "all things Chinese"). Blue-and-white porcelain ware—"china," as it came to be known in the West—was especially desirable, and before long, ceramists at Meissen, near Dresden, Germany, had learned to make their own porcelain. This allowed for almost unbounded imitation and sale of Chinese designs on European-manufactured ceramic wares. Even a Rococo painter like François Boucher imitated the blue-on-white Chinese style in oil paint (**Fig. 19-6**). The scene depicts a Chinese man bending to kiss the hand of his lady, who sits with her parasol beneath a statue, not of Venus (as might be appropriate in a European setting), but of the Buddha. A blue-on-white Chinese vase of the kind Boucher is imitating rests on a small platform behind the lady, and the whole scene is set in an elaborate Rococo frame.

Fig. 19-6 François Boucher, *Le Chinois galant*, 1742. Oil on canvas, 41 in. × 4 ft. 9 in. The David Collection, Copenhagen, Denmark.
Inv. B 275. Photo: Pernille Klemp.

Since 1644, China had been ruled by Qing ("clear" or "pure") Manchus, or Manchurians, who had invaded China from the north and captured Beijing. By 1680, the Qing rulers had summoned many Chinese artists to the Beijing court, and the imperial collection of art grew to enormous size. (Today the collection is divided between the National Palace Museum in Taipei and the Palace Museum in Beijing.) While many court artists modeled their work on the earlier masterpieces collected by the Qing emperors, others turned to the study of Western techniques introduced by the Jesuits.

But it was not at court that Western conventions were most fully expressed. In the port cities such as Yangzhou and Guangzhou, throughout the eighteenth century, Chinese artists created images for export to both the West and Japan. At the same time, Westernized ceramics became very popular with the increasingly wealthy Chinese mercantile class. Local commercial artists decorated ceramic wares with images provided by European traders. As Western trading companies placed large orders to meet the European demand for ceramics, Chinese artists mastered the art of perspective. Especially popular were views of cities, often sold as woodblock prints, but even created to decorate ceramic bowls (**Fig. 19-7**). This example depicts the Hongs at Canton (present-day Guangzhou), the 13 trading posts where the Chinese allowed foreigners to reside. Perspectival space appealed to the Chinese audience because it was both novel and exotic. The Western audience, used to perspective, found the views of urban China exotic in themselves.

Fig. 19-7 Punch bowl with view of Canton, 1783–86. Enameled ceramic, porcelain. The British Museum, London.

Neoclassicism

What is Neoclassicism and how did it reflect the political aspirations of the age?

Despite the Rococo sensibility of the age, the seventeenth-century French taste for the Classical style that Le Brun had championed did not disappear. When Herculaneum and Pompeii were rediscovered, in 1738 and 1748, respectively, interest in Greek and Roman antiquity revived as well. The discovery fueled an increasing tendency among the French to view the Rococo style as symptomatic of a widespread cultural decadence, epitomized by the luxurious lifestyle of the aristocracy. The discovery also caused people to identify instead with the public-minded values of Greek and Roman heroes, who placed moral virtue, patriotic self-sacrifice, and "right action" above all else. A new Classicism—a **Neoclassicism**—soon supplanted the Rococo.

Virtue is, in fact, the subject of much Neoclassical art—a subject matter distinctly at odds with the early Rococo sensibility. Women are no longer seen cavorting like mermaids, or even luxuriously dressed like the duchess of Polignac. Angelica Kauffmann's *Egeria Handing Numa Pompilius His Shield* (**Fig. 19-8**), painted in 1794, depicts the water-nymph Egeria advising Numa Pompilius, second king of Rome. In the Ovidian myths associated with her, Egeria counseled Numa in the establishment of the rules and rituals of the Roman state. Here, Egeria hands Numa his shield, but reminds him of the higher value of peace, as she raises her hand to the heavens, a gesture that formally underscores the Neoclassical geometry of the composition.

The most accomplished of the Neoclassical painters was Jacques-Louis David (see Figs. 3-20 and 3-21). David took an active role in the French Revolution in 1789, recognizing as an expression of true civic duty and virtue the desire to overthrow the irresponsible monarchy that had, for two centuries at least, squandered France's wealth. His *Death of Marat* (**Fig. 19-9**) celebrates a fallen hero of the Revolution. Slain in his bath by a monarchist—a sympathizer with the overthrown king—Marat is posed by David as Christ is traditionally posed in Deposition scenes (see Fig. 18-4), his arm draping over the edge of the tub. A dramatic Caravaggesque light falls over the revolutionary hero, his virtue embodied in the Neoclassical simplicity of David's design.

Fig. 19-8 Angelica Kauffmann, *Egeria Handing Numa Pompilius His Shield*, 1794. Oil on canvas, 17 × 18¾ in. Private collection.

Photo: © Christie's Images/Bridgeman Images.

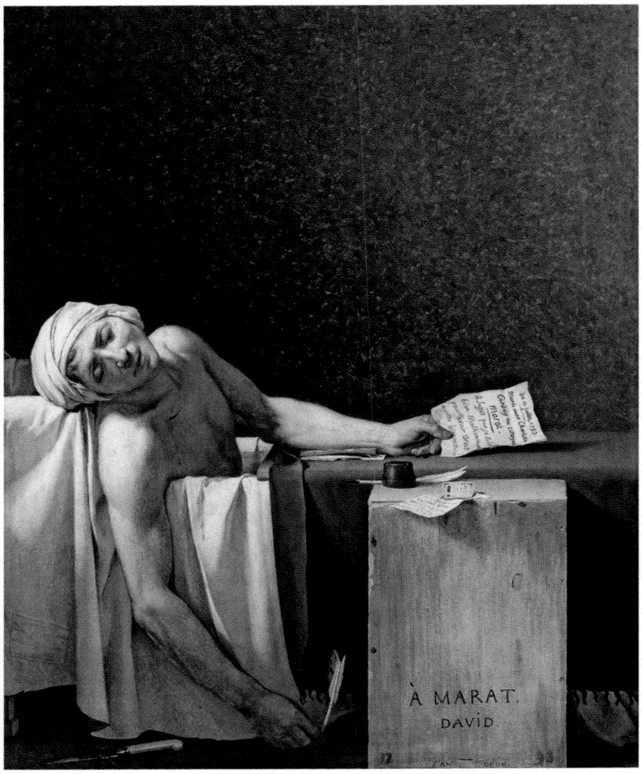

Fig. 19-9 Jacques-Louis David, *The Death of Marat*, 1793. Oil on canvas, 5 ft. 5 in. × 4 ft. 2½ in. Musées Royaux des Beaux-Arts de Belgique, Brussels.

© Musées Royaux des Beaux-Arts de Belgique, Brussels. Photo: J. Geleyns/Ro scan.

Napoleon crowns himself Emperor of France **1804**

Wars of Independence in Latin America begin **1808**

—1800

1803 Louisiana Purchase

1807 Serfdom abolished in Prussia

The same sensibility informs the Neoclassical architecture of Thomas Jefferson. For Jefferson, the Greek orders embodied democratic ideals, possessing not only a sense of order and harmony but also a moral perfection deriving from measure and proportion. He utilized these themes in the facade of his own home at Monticello (**Fig. 19-10**). The colonnade thus came to be associated with the ideal state, and, in the United States, Jefferson's Neoclassical architecture became an almost official Federal style.

Neoclassicism found official favor in France with the rise of Napoleon Bonaparte. In 1799, Napoleon brought the uncertain years that followed the French Revolution to an end when he was declared First Consul of the French Republic. As this title suggests, Napoleon's government was modeled on Roman precedents. He established a centralized government and instituted a uniform legal system. He invaded Italy and brought home with him many examples of Classical sculpture, including *The Laocoön Group* (see Fig. 16-26) and the *Apollo Belvedere* (see Fig. 2-15). In Paris itself, he built triumphal Roman arches, including the famous Arc de Triomphe, a column modeled on Trajan's in Rome, and a church, La Madeleine, modeled after the temples of the first Roman emperors (**Fig. 19-11**). In 1804, Napoleon was himself crowned emperor of the largest European empire since Charlemagne's in the ninth century.

Neoclassical art was used to legitimate this empire. David saw Napoleon as the salvation of France (so chaotic had revolutionary France been that David himself had been imprisoned, a sure sign, he thought, of the confusion of the day), and he received important commissions from the new emperor. But it was David's finest pupil,

Fig. 19-11 Pierre-Alexandre Vignon, La Madeleine, Paris, 1806–42. Length 350 ft., width 147 ft., height of podium 23 ft., height of columns 63 ft.

Jean-Auguste-Dominique Ingres, who became the champion of Neoclassical ideals in the nineteenth century. In 1806, he was awarded the Prix de Rome, a scholarship that allowed him to depart for Italy, where he remained for 18 years, studying Raphael in particular and periodically sending new work back to France.

Ingres's Neoclassicism was "looser" than his master's. In a painting such as the *Grande Odalisque* (**Fig. 19-12**), with its long, gently curving limbs, we are more clearly in the world of Mannerist painting than that of the Greek nude. Ingres's color is as rich as Bronzino's in *An Allegory with Venus and Cupid* (see Fig. 18-28), and, in fact, his theme is much the same. His odalisque—a harem slave—seems more decadent than not, deeply involved in a world of satins, peacock feathers, and, at the right, hashish. Certainly, it is not easy to detect much of the high moral tone of earlier Neoclassical art.

Beside Eugène Delacroix's own *Odalisque* (**Fig. 19-13**), Ingres's Classicism becomes more readily apparent. To Ingres, Delacroix, who was a generation younger, represented a dangerous and barbaric Neo-Baroque sensibility in contrast to his own Neoclassicism.

Ingres and Delacroix became rivals. Each had his critical champions, each his students and followers. For Ingres, drawing was everything. Therefore, his painting was, above all, linear in style. Delacroix, however, was fascinated by the texture of paint itself, and in his painterly

Fig. 19-10 Thomas Jefferson, Monticello, Charlottesville, Virginia, 1770–84; 1796–1806.

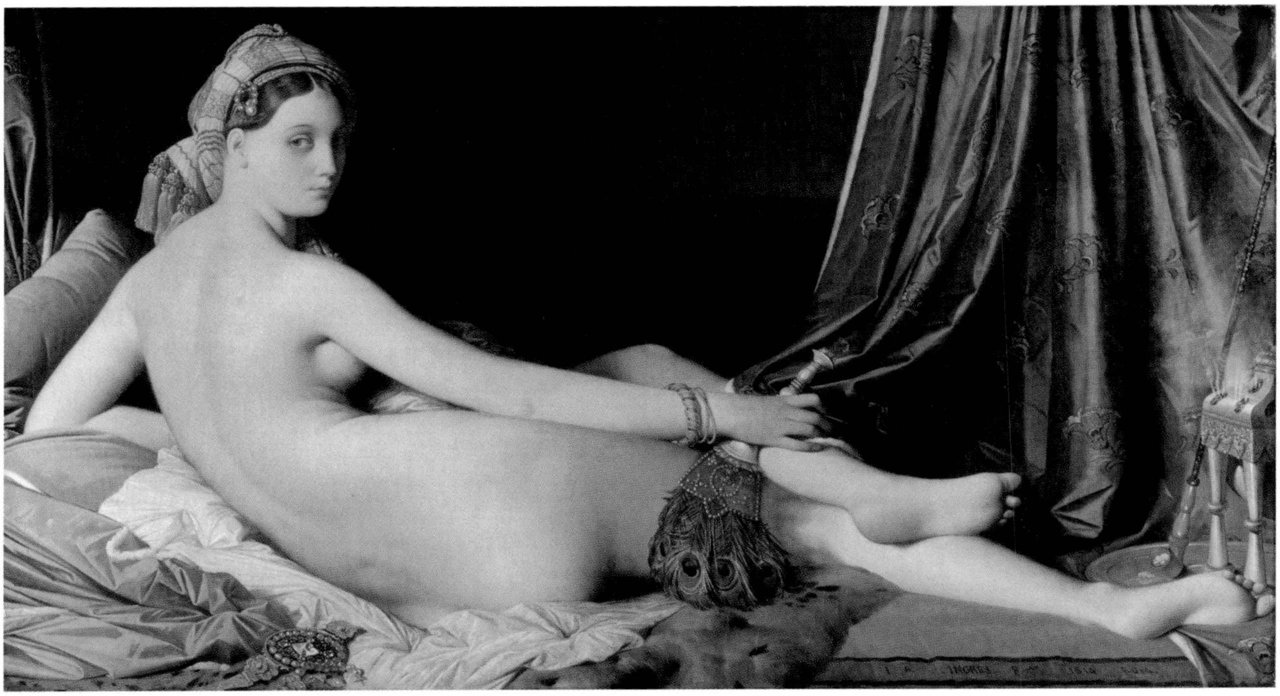

Fig. 19-12 Jean-Auguste-Dominique Ingres, *Grande Odalisque*, 1814. Oil on canvas, 35¼ in. × 5 ft. 3¾ in. Musée du Louvre, Paris.
Inv. RF1158. Photo © RMN-Grand Palais (musée du Louvre)/Thierry Le Mage.

attack upon the canvas, we begin to sense the artist's own passionate temperament. Viewed beside the Delacroix, the pose of the odalisque in Ingres's painting is positively conservative. In fact, Ingres felt he was upholding traditional values in the face of the onslaught represented by the uncontrolled individualism of his rival.

Fig. 19-13 Eugène Delacroix, *Odalisque*, 1845–50. Oil on canvas, 14⅞ × 18¼ in. Fitzwilliam Museum, University of Cambridge, England.
Bridgeman Images.

Romanticism

What beliefs unify Romanticism as a movement?

We have come to call the kind of art exemplified by Delacroix **Romanticism**. At the heart of this style is the belief that reality is a function of each individual's singular point of view, and that the artist's task is to reveal that point of view. Individualism reigned supreme in Romantic art. For this reason, Romanticism sometimes seems to have as many styles as it has artists. What unifies the movement is more a philosophical affirmation of the power of the individual mind than a set of formal principles.

In England, the Romantic movement was defined by the poets William Wordsworth, Samuel Taylor Coleridge, and John Keats, but the painters John Constable and Joseph Mallord William Turner explored its many possibilities. The tension between the timeless and the more fleeting aspects of nature deeply informs the paintings of Constable. He focused most of his efforts on the area around the valley of the Stour River in his native East Bergholt, Suffolk. At the left of *The Hay Wain* (**Fig. 19-14**) is the house of Willie Lott, a farmer, who lived in this house his entire 80 years, spending only four nights of his life away from it. For Constable, the house symbolized a stability and permanence that contrasts dramatically with the impermanence of the weather, the constant flux of light and shadow, sun and cloud. The final painting is thus a testament to both Lott's permanence and the patterns of constant change that define nature. The passing storm, indicated by the darkened clouds on the left, contrasts with the brightly lit field below the billowing clouds at the right; the longevity of the tree behind the house with its massive trunk contrasts with the distant freshly cut hay at the right; the gentleman fisherman contrasts with the hard-working cart drivers.

Turner, the other great English landscape painter of the day, freely explored what he called "the colors of the imagination." More than anything else he was interested in light, not the thing seen but the medium through which it is seen. In Turner's paintings, earth and vegetation seem to dissolve into light and water, into the very medium—gleaming oil or translucent watercolor—in which he paints them. In *The Upper Falls of the Reichenbach*, for instance, Turner's depiction of the falls, among the highest in the Swiss Alps, seems to animate the rocky precipice (**Fig. 19-15**). Turner draws our attention not to the rock, cliff, and mountain, but to the mist and light through which we see them.

Perhaps the best way to understand the difference between Constable and Turner is to consider the scale of their respective visions. Constable's work is "close," nearby and familiar, with an abundance of human associations. Turner's is exotic, remote, and even alienating. The human figure in Constable's paintings is an essential and elemental presence, uniting mankind and nature. The human figure in Turner's paintings is minuscule, almost irrelevant to the painting except insofar as its minuteness underscores nature's very indifference to human existence. Not only is *The Upper Falls of the Reichenbach* removed from the close-at-hand world of Constable's paintings, but the cowherd and his dog, barely visible at the lower left of the painting, are dwarfed by the immensity of the scene. Cattle graze on the rise at the bottom middle, and another herd is on the ridge across the gorge.

Fig. 19-14 John Constable, *The Hay Wain*, 1821. Oil on canvas, 4 ft. 3⅜ in. × 6 ft. 1 in. The National Gallery, London.
Presented by Henry Vaughan, 1886. Inv. 5387. © 2015. Copyright National Gallery, London/Scala, Florence.

Fig. 19-15 J. M. W. Turner, *The Upper Falls of the Reichenbach*, ca. 1810–15.
Watercolor, 10⅞ × 15⁷⁄₁₆ in. Yale Center for British Art.
Paul Mellon Collection, B1977.14.4702.

The vast scale of Turner's painting suggests his interest in representing the **sublime**. Theories of the sublime had first appeared in the eighteenth century, most notably in Edmund Burke's *A Philosophical Inquiry into the Origin of Our Ideas of the Sublime and Beautiful* (1756). For Burke, it was a feeling of awe experienced before things that escaped the ability of the human mind to comprehend them—mountains, chasms, storms, and catastrophes. The sublime exceeded reason; it presented viewers with something vaster than themselves, thereby making them realize their smallness, even their insignificance, in the face of the infinite. The sublime evokes the awe-inspiring forces of nature, as opposed to the beautiful, which is associated with nature at her most harmonious and tranquil. A pastoral landscape may be beautiful; a vast mountain range, sublime.

No painting of the period more fully captures the terrifying prospect of the sublime than Caspar David Friedrich's *Monk by the Sea* (**Fig. 19-16**). It indicates just how thoroughly the experience of the infinite—that is, the experience of God—can be found in nature. But the God faced by this solitary monk is by no

Fig. 19-16 Caspar David Friedrich, *Monk by the Sea*, 1809–10.
Oil on canvas, 42½ in. × 5 ft. 7 in. Nationalgalerie, Staatliche Museen zu Berlin.
Inv. NG 9/85. Photo: Joerg P. Anders. © 2015. Scala, Florence/bpk, Bildagentur fuer Kunst, Kultur und Geschichte, Berlin.

means benign. The infinite becomes, in this painting, a vast, dark, and lonely space—so ominous that it must surely test the monk's faith. The real terror of this painting lies in its sense that the eternal space stretching before this man of faith may not be salvation but, instead, a meaningless void. And with his back to us, he stands in for us all.

The terror suggested by the precarious position, both physical and psychological, of Friedrich's monk is characteristic of Romantic individualism—that is, of a mind that turns inward and does not like what it finds. One of the most individual of the Romantics, and one of the most terrifyingly obsessed, was the Spanish painter Francisco de Goya y Lucientes. After a serious illness in 1792, Goya turned away from a late Rococo style and began to produce a series of paintings depicting inmates of a lunatic asylum and a hospital for wounded soldiers. When Napoleon invaded Spain in 1808, Goya recorded the atrocities both in paintings and in a series of etchings, *The Disasters of War*, which remained unpublished until long after his death. His last, so-called "Black Paintings" were brutal interpretations of mythological scenes that revealed a universe operating outside the bounds of reason, a world of imagination unchecked by a moral force of any kind. In one of these, *Saturn Devouring One of His Sons* (**Fig. 19-17**), which was painted originally on the wall of the dining room in Goya's home, Saturn is allegorically a figure for Time, which consumes us all. But it is the incestuous cannibalism of the scene, the terrible monstrosity of the vision itself, that tells us of Goya's own despair. The inevitable conclusion is that, for Goya, the world was a place full of terror, violence, and horror.

This sense of the terrible is by no means unique to Goya. Compare, for instance, Théodore Géricault's *The Raft of the Medusa* (**Fig. 19-18**). On July 2, 1816, the French frigate *Medusa* was wrecked on a reef off the African coast. The overloaded ship had been carrying soldiers and settlers to Senegal. The captain and other senior officers escaped in lifeboats, leaving 150 behind to fend for themselves on a makeshift wooden raft for 12 harrowing days, at the end of which only 15 survived. The incident infuriated Géricault. The captain's appointment had depended on his connections with the French monarchy, which had been restored after Napoleon's defeat at Waterloo. Here, therefore, was clear evidence of the nobility's decadence. To illustrate his beliefs and feelings, Géricault planned a giant canvas, showing the raft just at the moment that the rescue ship, the *Argus*, was spotted on the horizon. He went to the Normandy coast to study the movement of water. He even had a model of the raft constructed in his studio and arranged wax figures upon it. His student, Delacroix, posed face down for the central nude. The final painting positions the raft on a diagonal axis, creating two contradictory pyramidal points of tension. On the left, the mast not only suggests the crucifix but also reveals that the raft is sailing away from its rescuers, while, on the right, the survivors climb desperately in their attempt to be seen. Géricault's horrifying picture, exhibited only a few months after it was conceived, fueled the Romantic movement with the passion of its feelings.

Fig. 19-17 Francisco Goya, *Saturn Devouring One of His Sons*, 1820–22. Fresco, transferred to canvas, 4 ft. 9⅞ in. × 32⅝ in. Museo Nacional del Prado, Madrid.

Fig. 19-18 Théodore Géricault, *The Raft of the Medusa*, 1819. Oil on canvas, 16 ft. 1¼ in. × 23 ft. 6 in. Musée du Louvre, Paris.
Inv. RF2229. Photo © RMN-Grand Palais (musée du Louvre)/Martine Beck-Coppola.

Realism

How did Realism replace the idealizing tendencies of the Romantic movement?

When Géricault was preparing *The Raft of the Medusa*, he regularly visited morgues to study and draw the bodies and limbs of the dead. This urge for realism runs counter to, but exists alongside, the imaginative and idealizing tendencies of the Romantic sensibility. If we compare two history paintings from the first half of the nineteenth century, we can see how the idealizing tendency of the Romantic sensibility gradually faded away. Faced with the reality of war, idealism seemed absurd. Eugène Delacroix's *Liberty Leading the People* (**Fig. 19-19**) represents Liberty as an idealized allegorical figure, but the battle itself, which took place during the July Revolution of 1830, is depicted in a highly realistic manner, with figures lying dead on the barricades beneath Liberty's feet, and

Fig. 19-19 Eugène Delacroix, *Liberty Leading the People*, 1830. Oil on canvas, 8 ft. 6⅜ in. × 10 ft. 8 in. Musée du Louvre, Paris.
Louvre-Lens, France/Bridgeman Images.

Fig. 19-20 Ernest Meissonier, *Memory of Civil War (The Barricades)*, 1849. Oil on canvas, 11½ × 8¾ in. Musée du Louvre, Paris.
Inv. RF1942-31. Photo © RMN-Grand Palais (musée du Louvre)/Droits réservés.

Notre-Dame Cathedral at the distant right shrouded in smoke. In Ernest Meissonier's *Memory of Civil War (The Barricades)* (**Fig. 19-20**), painted from a sketch made at the scene during the 1848 Revolution, all the nobility of war has been drained from the picture. The blue, white, and red of the French flag have been reduced to piles of tattered clothing and blood, what one contemporary gruesomely described as an "omelet of men."

So thoroughly did the painter Gustave Courbet come to believe in recording the actual facts of the world around him that he declared, in 1861, "Painting is an essentially concrete art and can only consist of the presentation of real and existing things. It is a completely physical language, the words of which consist of all visible objects." Courbet and others aspiring to such realism believed artists should confine their representations to accurate observations and notations of the phenomena of daily life. No longer was there necessarily any "greater" reality beyond or behind the facts that lay before their eyes. Courbet's gigantic painting *Burial at Ornans* (**Fig. 19-21**) seems, at first glance, to hold enormous potential for symbolic and allegorical meaning, but just the opposite is the case. In the foreground is a hole in the ground, the only "eternal reward" Courbet's scene appears to promise. No one, not even the dog, seems to be focused on the event itself. The artist offers us a panorama of distraction, of common people performing their everyday duties, in a landscape

Fig. 19-21 Gustave Courbet, *Burial at Ornans*, 1849. Oil on canvas, 10 ft. 3½ in. × 21 ft. 9 in. Musée d'Orsay, Paris.
Inv. RF325. Photo © RMN-Grand Palais (musée d'Orsay)/Gérard Blot/Hervé Lewandowski.

Fig. 19-22 Honoré Daumier, *Fight between Schools, Idealism and Realism*, 1855.
Bridgeman Images.

whose horizontality reads like an unwavering line of monotony. If the crucifix rises into the sky over the scene, it does so without deep spiritual significance. In fact, its curious position, as if it were set on the horizon line, lends it a certain comic dimension, a comedy that the bulbous faces of the red-cloaked officers of the parish also underscore. The painting was rejected by the jury of the Universal Exposition of 1855, where Courbet had hoped to display it. To emphasize his disdain for the values of the establishment, Courbet opened a one-person exhibition outside the Exposition grounds, calling it the Pavilion of Realism. Honoré Daumier immediately responded with a cartoon depicting the *Fight between Schools, Idealism and Realism* (**Fig. 19-22**). The Courbet-like Realist, with his square palette, house painter's brush, and wooden shoes, battles the aged, Classically nude idealist, who wears the helmet of a Greek warrior.

It was, at least in part, the realist impulse that led to the invention of photography in the 1830s (see Figs. 11-6 and 11-7). And it was also in this spirit that Karl Marx, in *The Communist Manifesto*, declared: "All that was solid and established crumbles away, all that was holy is profaned, and man is at last compelled to look with open eyes upon his conditions of life and true social relations." Marx's sentiments, written in response to the wave of revolutions that swept Europe in 1848, are part and parcel of the realist enterprise. Rosa Bonheur's *Plowing in the Nivernais* (**Fig. 19-23**) was commissioned in response to the French Revolution of 1848. It reveals her belief in the virtue of toil and the common life of the French peasant. But it was her realism, her extraordinary ability to depict animals, that made her the most famous female artist of her day. Suddenly, it was socially and aesthetically important, even imperative, to paint neither the sublime nor the beautiful nor the picturesque, but the everyday, the commonplace, the low, and the ugly. Painters, it was felt, must represent the reality of their time and place, whatever it might look like.

As Daumier's cartoon makes clear, the art of the past, exemplified by the Classical model, was felt to be worn out, incapable of expressing the realities of contemporary life. *"Il faut être de son temps"*—"it is necessary to be of one's own time"—was the rallying cry of

Fig. 19-23 Rosa Bonheur, *Plowing in the Nivernais*, 1849. Oil on canvas, 5 ft. 9 in. × 8 ft. 8 in. Musée d'Orsay, Paris.
Inv. RF64. Photo © RMN-Grand Palais (musée d'Orsay)/Michel Urtado.

the day. The modern world was marked by change, by the uniqueness of every moment, each instant, like a photograph, different from the last. Painting had to accommodate itself to this change. There were no longer any permanent, eternal truths.

The painter whose work came to represent this new direction was Édouard Manet, whose *Olympia* (see Fig. 1-15) caused an outcry when it was first exhibited in 1865 and who had already outraged the public two years earlier with *Le Déjeuner sur l'herbe*, or *Luncheon on the Grass* (**Fig. 19-24**). Manet was the consummate *flâneur* (see Chapter 1), and the *flâneur* is distinguished by an important trait: his attitude toward the bourgeoisie. He holds their vulgar, materialistic lifestyle in contempt, and his greatest devotion is to shocking them. Thus, it came as no surprise to Manet when *Le Déjeuner sur l'herbe* was rejected in 1863 by the jury for the annual exhibition sponsored by the Académie des Beaux-Arts, known as the Salon. It was not designed to please them. The Salon drew tens of thousands of visitors a day to the Louvre and was the world's most prominent art event. The public then reacted with outrage when Manet's painting appeared at the Salon des Refusés, an exhibition hurriedly ordered by Napoleon III after numerous complaints arose about the large number of rejected artworks. While many of the paintings included in the Salon des Refusés were of poor quality, others, including *Le Déjeuner sur l'herbe*, were vilified because of their supposedly scandalous content or challenging style. The Paris newspapers lumped them all together: "There is something cruel about this exhibition: people laugh as they do at a farce. As a matter of

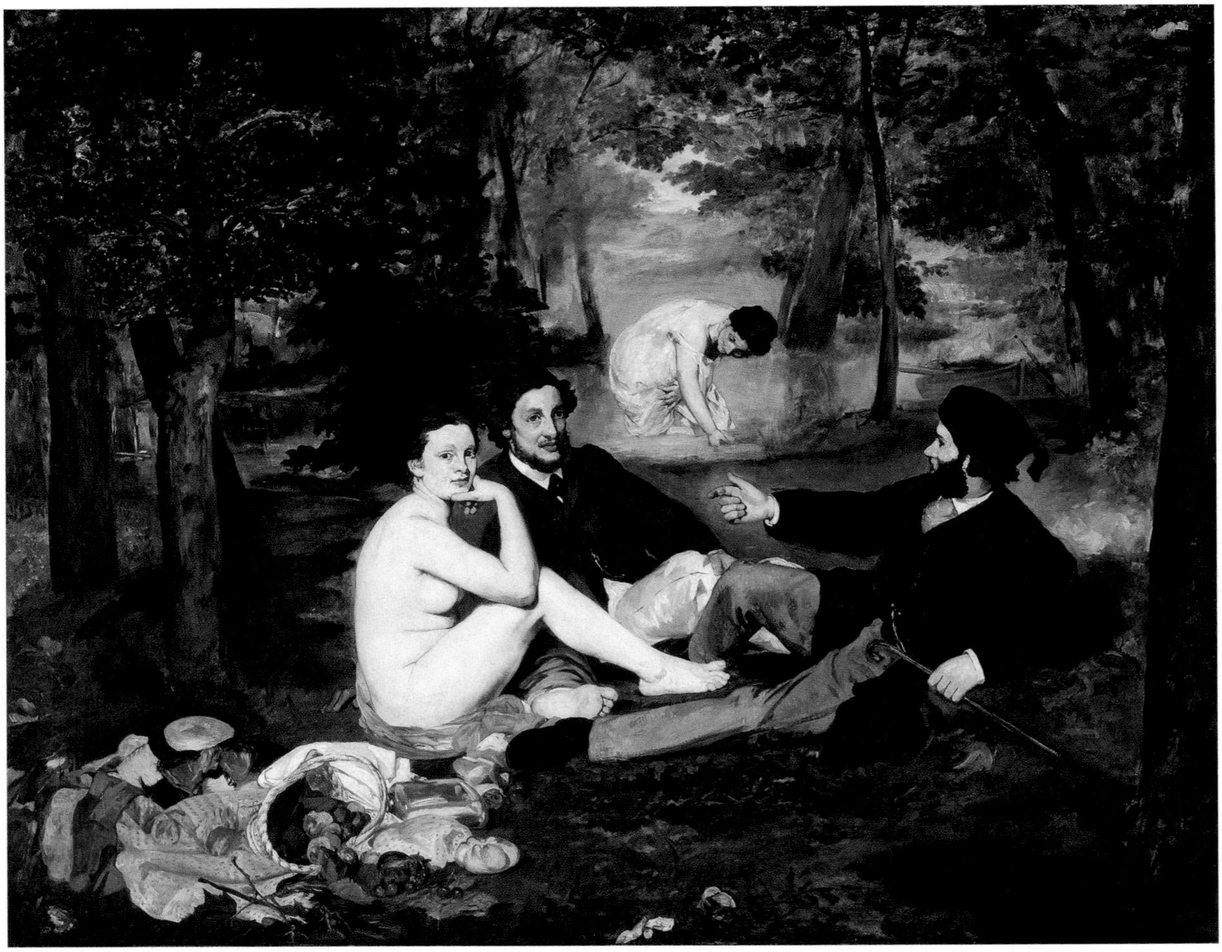

Fig. 19-24 Édouard Manet, *Le Déjeuner sur l'herbe* (*Luncheon on the Grass*), 1863. Oil on canvas, 7 ft. × 8 ft. 10 in. Musée d'Orsay, Paris.
Inv. RF1668. Photo © RMN-Grand Palais (musée d'Orsay)/Hervé Lewandowski.

fact it is a continual parody, a parody of drawing, of color, of composition."

Although it was not widely recognized at the time, Manet had by no means abandoned tradition completely in favor of the depiction of everyday life in all its sordid detail. *Le Déjeuner sur l'herbe* was directly indebted to a Renaissance engraving executed by Marcantonio Raimondi (**Fig. 19-25**) after a lost painting by Raphael, *The Judgment of Paris*. Manet's three central figures assume the same poses as the wood nymphs seated at the lower right of the engraving. No one noticed, even though a copy of the print was housed at the Louvre. Manet's audience could only see a brazen nude, inexplicably unruffled by the arrival upon the scene of the audience itself—with whom else could she be exchanging her gaze? In fact, what most irritated both critics and the public was the apparently "slipshod" nature of Manet's painting technique. He painted in broad visible strokes. The body of the seated nude in *Le Déjeuner* was flat. The painting's sense of space was distorted, and the bather in the background and the stream she stands in both seemed about to spill forward into the picnic.

Manet's rejection of traditional painting techniques was intentional: He was drawing attention to his very modernity, to the fact that he was breaking with the past. His manipulation of his traditional sources supported the same intentions. In the words of his contemporary, Karl Marx, Manet was looking "with open eyes upon his conditions of life and true social relations." Raphael had depicted the Judgment of Paris, the mythological contest in which Paris chose Venus as the most beautiful of the goddesses, a choice that led to the Trojan War. In his depiction of a decadent picnic in the Bois de Boulogne, Manet passed judgment upon a different Paris, the modern city in which he lived. His world had changed. It was less heroic, its ideals less grand.

Edgar Degas's *The Glass of Absinthe* (**Fig. 19-26**) was painted a decade after Manet's *Le Déjeuner*, and was directly influenced by Manet's example. Degas's wandering eye has caught the underside of Parisian café society. Absinthe was an alcoholic drink that attacked the nerve centers, eventually causing severe cerebral damage. Especially popular among the working classes, it was finally banned in France in 1915. In the dazed, absent look of this young woman, Degas reveals the consequences of absinthe consumption with a shockingly direct realism worthy of Courbet.

Fig. 19-25 Marcantonio Raimondi, *The Judgment of Paris* (detail), ca. 1510–20. Oil engraving, after Raphael. Clipped impression, plate line 11⅝ × 17¼ in. Metropolitan Museum of Art, New York.

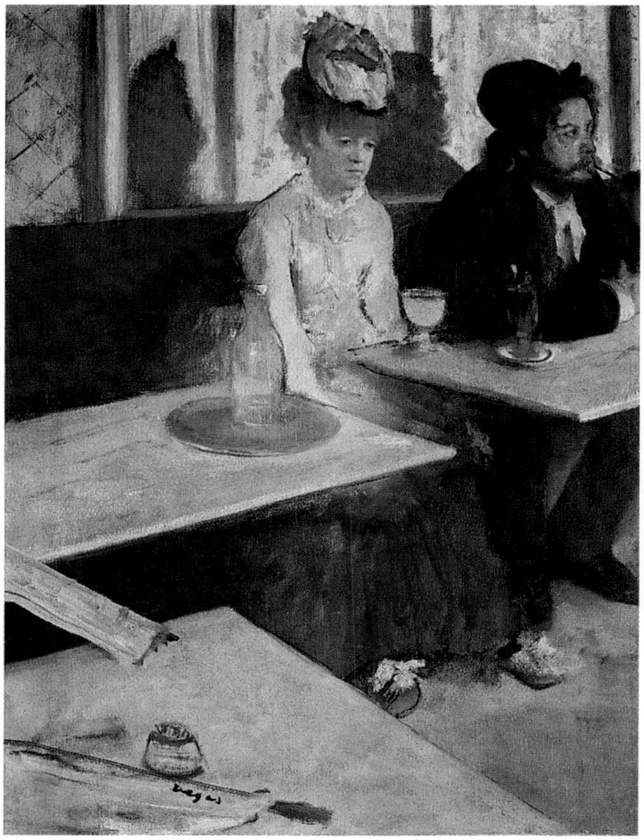

Fig. 19-26 Edgar Degas, *The Glass of Absinthe*, 1875–76. Oil on canvas, 36 × 27 in. Musée d'Orsay, Paris.

Fig. 19-27 Édouard Manet, *Chez le Père Lathuille*, 1879. Oil on canvas, 36⅝ × 44 in. Musée des Beaux-Arts, Tournai, Belgium.

Fig. 19-28 Claude Monet, *Impression—Sunrise*, 1872. Oil on canvas, 19½ × 25½ in. Musée Marmottan, Paris.

Manet himself would continue to scour the Paris streets and cafés for subject matter. *Chez le Père Lathuille* (**Fig. 19-27**) is set at a famous café-restaurant in the Batignolles district of Paris, just to the west of Montmartre. Its subject is ostensibly a late luncheon—the other tables in the restaurant are empty and the waiter stands patiently by, ready to serve coffee when the very prim and proper lady at the table finishes her fruit. But there is no place set for the young man beside her, nor, evidently, a chair. His open collar, sideburns, and mustache suggest he is a gigolo—at best a bohemian student. He crouches beside the lady, who stiffly purses her lips, his arm reaching behind her back, his hand fondling her glass of wine, quite clearly trying to seduce her. This is Manet at this wittiest and most observant.

Impressionism

What characterizes Impressionism in terms of both stylistic technique and subject matter?

In the late 1860s, the young painter Claude Monet began to employ the same rich, thick brushstrokes Manet was already using, but with an even looser hand. Combining two or more pigments on a single wide brush, he allowed them to blend as they were brushed onto the canvas. He would paint "wet on wet"—with wet pigment over and through an already-painted surface that had not yet dried. Most of all, he painted with the intense hues made possible by the development of synthetic pigments.

Others followed his lead, and together, in April 1874, they held a group exhibition. They called themselves "Painters, Sculptors, Engravers, etc. Inc.," but before long they were known as the **Impressionists**. The painting that gave them their name was Monet's *Impression—Sunrise* (**Fig. 19-28**). Monet, the critic Théodore Duret wrote in 1878, "is the Impressionist painter par excellence. . . . [He] has succeeded in setting down the fleeting impression which his predecessors had neglected or considered impossible to render with the brush . . . the fleeting appearances which the accidents of atmosphere present to him . . . a singularly lively and striking sensation of the observed scene. His canvases really do communicate impressions." Impressionist paintings, in fact, have the feel of sketches, as if they were executed spontaneously, even instantaneously, in the manner of photographic snapshots.

Impression—Sunrise was exhibited at the first Impressionist exhibition, which opened on April 15, 1874. In another painting exhibited by Monet at that same exhibition, *Boulevard des Capucines*, we look out over the *grands boulevards* of Paris with the two top-hatted men who lean forward out the window at the right (**Fig. 19-29**). The building at the left is the Grand Hôtel, and between it and the next building, the space compressed by Monet's perspective, is the Place de l'Opéra. We are, in fact, standing in the exhibition space of the first Impressionist

Fig. 19-29 Claude Monet, *Carnival on the Boulevard des Capucines*, 1873. Oil on canvas, 24 × 31½ in. Pushkin Museum of Fine Arts, Moscow.
© 2015. Photo Scala, Florence.

show, and this is a work of art about its own marketplace. Monet's brushwork, capturing the play of light on the leaves of the trees and the crowds in the street, is even looser and freer than in *Impression—Sunrise*. Writing in the *Paris-Journal* in May 1874, the critic Ernest Chesneau recognized the painting's significance:

> The extraordinary animation of the public street, the crowd swarming the sidewalks, the carriages on the pavement, and the boulevard's trees waving in dust and light—never has the elusive, fugitive, instantaneous quality of movement been captured and fixed in all its tremendous fluidity as it has in this extraordinary, marvelous sketch. . . . At a distance, one salutes a masterpiece in this stream of life, this trembling of great shadow and light, sparkling with ever darker shadows and brighter lights. But come closer, and it all vanishes. Only an indecipherable chaos of palette scrapings remains. . . . It is necessary to go forward and transform the sketch into a finished work. But what a bugle call for those who listen carefully, how it resounds far into the future!

Chesneau failed to understand that this "sketch" was already "finished." But he was right that it was a painting of the future. It would not take long for the public to understand that this "chaotic" brushwork was the very mark of a new sensibility, one dedicated to capturing what the French call *le temps*, a word that suggests "the time," "the weather," and "the age" all at once.

The Impressionists' subject matter sets them apart from their predecessors at least as much as their technique does. Unlike the Realist painters of a generation earlier, the Impressionists were less interested in social criticism than in depicting in their work the pleasures of life, including the pleasures of simply seeing. If Impressionism is characterized by a way of seeing—by the attempt to capture the fleeting effects of light by applying paint in small, quick strokes of color—it is also defined by an intense interest in images of leisure. The Realists would have rejected these images as unworthy of their high moral purposes. (The exception is Manet, who would befriend the Impressionists, Monet and Pierre-Auguste Renoir especially, and would, in later works such as *Chez le Père Lathuille*, adopt their subject matter.)

The Impressionists painted life in the Parisian theaters and cafés, the *grands boulevards* teeming with shoppers, country gardens bursting with flowers, the racetrack and seaside, the suburban pleasures of boating and swimming on the Seine. Renoir's *Bal du Moulin de la Galette* (**Fig. 19-30**) is typical. All of the figures

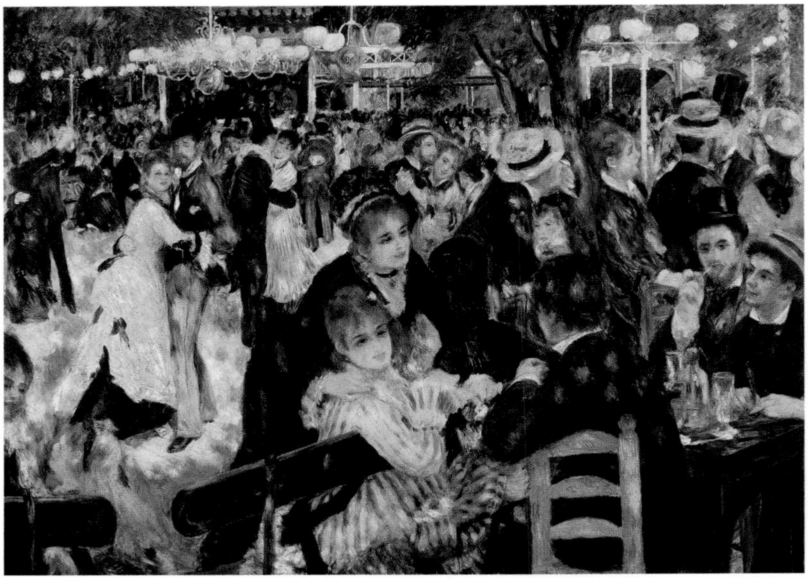

Fig. 19-30 Pierre-Auguste Renoir, *Bal du Moulin de la Galette*, 1876. Oil on canvas, 4 ft. 3½ in. × 5 ft. 9 in. Musée d'Orsay, Paris.
Bridgeman Images.

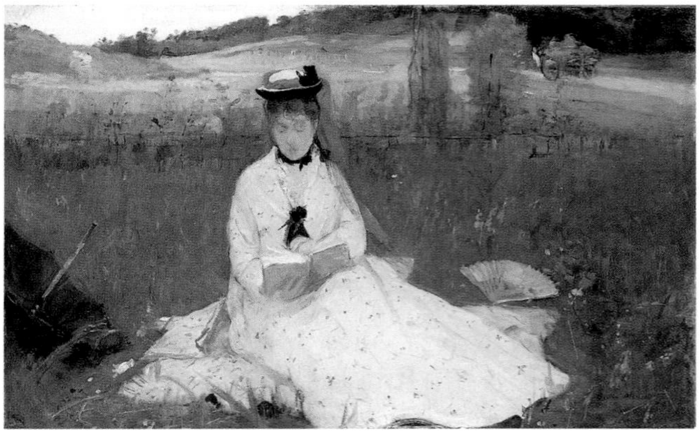

Fig. 19-31 Berthe Morisot, *Reading*, 1873. Oil on canvas, 17¾ × 28½ in. The Cleveland Museum of Art.
Gift of the Hanna Fund, 1950.89. Photo © Cleveland Museum of Art.

in the painting are Renoir's friends. One of his closest, Georges Rivière, seated at the table at the far right, described the painting soon after it was shown at the third Impressionist exhibition in 1877: "It is a page of history, a precious monument to Parisian life, done with rigorous exactitude. No one before Renoir had thought of portraying an event in ordinary life on a canvas of such big dimensions."

The distance of Impressionist painting from its Realist predecessors is summed up in Berthe Morisot's *Reading* (**Fig. 19-31**), probably one of four paintings Morisot exhibited at the first Impressionist exhibition in 1874. In the background, a farmer's cart heads down the road, the proper subject matter of the Realist. But Morisot's sister, depicted in the painting, has no interest in what passes behind her, and neither, really, does the painter herself. The cart is rendered in a few loose, rapid brushstrokes, as is the entire landscape. Leisure is Morisot's subject.

Increasingly, this urge to observe the world in its most minute particulars led to the investigation of optical reality in and for itself. As early as the 1870s, in his paintings of boats on the river at Argenteuil (see Fig. 7-35), Monet began to paint the same subjects over and over again, studying the ways in which the changing light transformed his impressions. This working method led to his later serial studies of grainstacks (see Fig. 5-36), Rouen Cathedral, and his garden at Giverny (**Fig. 19-32**), where he moved in 1883. By the turn of the century, he had given up painting "modern life" altogether, concentrating instead on capturing the "presentness" of his garden, the panoramic views that would be installed in the Orangerie in Paris in 1927 (see Fig. 6-10).

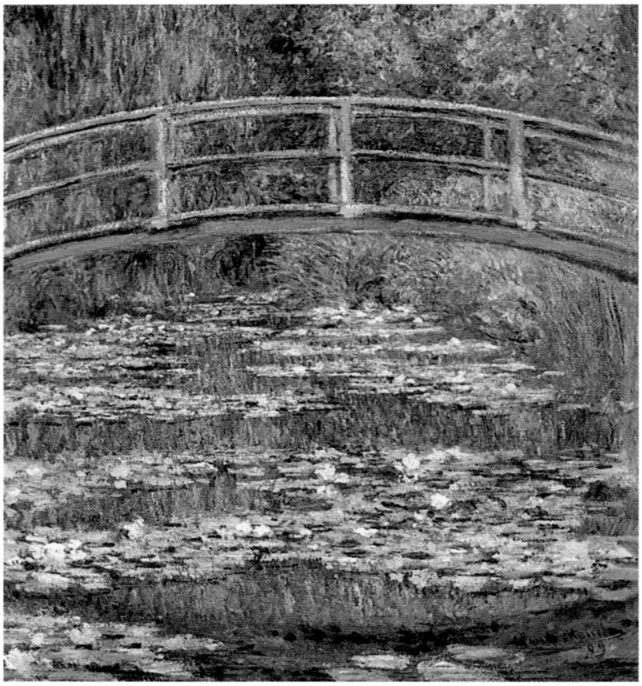

Fig. 19-32 Claude Monet, *Bridge over a Pool of Water Lilies*, 1899. Oil on canvas, 36½ × 29 in. Metropolitan Museum of Art, New York.
H. O. Havemeyer Collection. Bequest of Mrs. H. O. Havemeyer, 1929.100.113. © 2015. Image copyright Metropolitan Museum of Art/Art Resource/Scala, Florence.

Post-Impressionism

How did the Post-Impressionists both extend and redirect the Impressionist enterprise?

Although by the 1880s many artists had come to see Impressionism's subject matter as trivial, they were still interested in investigating and extending its formal innovations and in reexamining the symbolic possibilities of painting. Monet's work at Giverny can be seen as an example of just such an ongoing formal exploration. So can Vincent van Gogh's—in paintings such as *The Starry Night* (see Fig. 3-8) and *The Night Café* (see Fig. 5-38), he explored the symbolic possibilities of both line and color. A number of other painters—among them Paul Gauguin, Georges Seurat, and Paul Cézanne—embarked on a similar brand of **Post-Impressionism**, each dedicated to redirecting the Impressionist enterprise.

Paul Gauguin criticized the conditions of modern life, but he did so by leaving Europe and seeking out a new life in the South Seas. There, in paintings such as *The Day of the Gods (Mahana no Atua)* (**Fig. 19-33**), he tried to

Kodak camera invented
1888

1889
Eiffel Tower built in Paris

1891
Thomas Edison patents the radio

Ellis Island opens as East Coast immigration center
1892

1895

Fig. 19-33 Paul Gauguin, *The Day of the Gods (Mahana no Atua)*, 1894. Oil on canvas, 26⅞ × 36⅛ in. The Art Institute of Chicago.
Helen Birch Bartlett Memorial Collection, 1926.198. © 2015 Art Institute of Chicago.

capture the mystery and magic of the "primitive" culture, a world of unity, peace, and naked innocence far removed from the turmoil of "civilized" life. The perfect balance of the painting's composition and the brilliant color of the scene are structural realizations of paradise on earth.

In paintings such as *La Chahut* (*The Can-Can*) (see Fig. 5-29), Georges Seurat sought to impose a formal order upon the world, and in the process, he revealed its rigidity, its lack of vitality. Though Seurat's subject matter in *The Bathers* (**Fig. 19-34**) is Impressionist, his composition is not. It is architectural, intentionally returning to the seventeenth-century compositional principles of Poussin (see Fig. 19-2). And it subtly critiques the image of Impressionist leisure. These are not well-to-do middle-class Parisians, but workers (their costume gives them away) swimming in the Seine just downriver from the factory town of Asnières. Smokestacks belch soot in the distance. The spot, as observant Parisians knew, was directly across from the outlet of the great collective sewer from Paris. In the summer of 1884, according to the local press, "more than 120,000 cubic feet of solids had accumulated at the sewer's mouth; several hundred square meters of which are covered with a bizarre vegetation, which gives off a disgusting smell." Suddenly, the green material floating in the water is transformed.

Of all the Post-Impressionist painters, Paul Cézanne, working alone in the South of France, most thoroughly emphasized the formal aspects of painting at the expense of subject matter, and in this he looked forward most to the direction of art in the twentieth century. Cézanne pushed toward an idea of painting that established for the picture an independent existence, to be judged in terms of the purely formal interrelationships of line, color, and plane. In his *Still Life with Cherries and Peaches* (**Fig. 19-35**), he

Fig. 19-34 Georges Seurat, *The Bathers*, 1883–84. Oil on canvas, 6 ft. 7½ in. × 9 ft. 10½ in. The National Gallery, London.
National Gallery, London/akg.

Fig. 19-35 Paul Cézanne, *Still Life with Cherries and Peaches*, 1885–87. Oil on canvas, 19¾ × 24 in. Los Angeles County Museum of Art.
Photo © 2005 Museum Associates/LACMA.

Fig. 19-36 Paul Cézanne, *Mont Sainte-Victoire and the Viaduct of the Arc River Valley*, 1882–85. Oil on canvas, 25¾ × 32⅛ in. Metropolitan Museum of Art, New York.

H. O. Havemeyer Collection. Bequest of Mrs. H. O. Havemeyer, 1929 (29.100.64). Photo: Malcom Varon. © 2015. Image copyright Metropolitan Museum of Art/Art Resource/Scala, Florence.

Fig. 19-37 Paul Cézanne, *The Large Bathers*, 1906. Oil on canvas, 6 ft. 10 in. × 8 ft. 3 in. Philadelphia Museum of Art.

Purchased with the W. P. Wilstach Fund, W 1937-1-1. © 2015. Photo Philadelphia Museum of Art/Art Resource/Scala, Florence

emphasizes the act of composition itself, the process of seeing. It is as if he has rendered two entirely different views of the same still life simultaneously. The peaches on the right are seen from a point several feet in front of the table, while the cherries on the left have been painted from directly above. As a consequence, the table itself seems to broaden out behind the cherries.

Similarly, *Mont Sainte-Victoire and the Viaduct of the Arc River Valley* (**Fig. 19-36**) collapses the space between foreground and background by making a series of formal correspondences between them, by the repetition of the shape of the lower right-hand branch of the tree, for instance, the road below it, and the shape of the mountain itself. Finally, in *The Large Bathers* (**Fig. 19-37**), the pyramidal structure of the composition draws attention to the geometry that dominates even the individual faceting of the wide brushstrokes, which he laid down as horizontals, verticals, and diagonals. The simplification of the human body evident here, as well as Cézanne's overall emphasis on form, had a profound effect on painting in the twentieth century. It is in Cézanne that the art of the twentieth century dawns.

Thinking Back

19.1 Describe the two styles of art that vied for favor at the court of Louis XIV and the style that came to dominate the court of Louis XV.

Louis XIV's aesthetic tastes modulated between the balance, harmony, and proportions of Nicolas Poussin and the decorative and sensual exuberance of Peter Paul Rubens. How did his head of the Royal Academy of Painting, Charles Le Brun, rate the two painters? Upon Louis XIV's death, the Rococo came to dominate court taste. How would you describe it?

19.2 Explain how contact between China and Europe influenced the art of both.

Europeans developed a style of art called "chinoiserie," meaning "all things Chinese." In turn, Chinese artists learned the art of perspective from trade with Europeans. How does François Boucher typify "chinoiserie" in his *Le Chinois galant*? What was the Western reaction to Chinese porcelain and how did the Chinese accommodate it?

19.3 Define Neoclassicism and describe how it reflected the political aspirations of the age.

Neoclassicism is a new Classicism, championing the balance, harmony, and proportions of Classical art. Jacques-Louis David used Neoclassicism to portray the virtue of a fallen revolutionary, Marat. Later, David and Jean-Auguste-Dominique Ingres used Neoclassicism to legitimize Napoleon's rule. In America, Thomas Jefferson used a Neoclassical style in his home at Monticello to embody democratic ideals. How does Jean-Auguste-Dominique Ingres's style differ from Eugène Delacroix's? Why is Neoclassicism regarded as being at odds with the styles of both the Rococo before it and Romanticism after it?

19.4 Outline the beliefs that unify Romanticism as a movement.

Romanticism may seem to have as many styles as it has artists. The movement is unified by a philosophical affirmation of the power of the individual mind. At its heart is the belief that reality is a function of each individual's point of view. What does Francisco Goya express in his "Black Paintings"? What is the sublime?

19.5 Explain how Realism replaced the idealizing tendencies of the Romantic movement.

The urge for realism runs counter to, but exists alongside, the imaginative and idealizing tendencies of the Romantic sensibility. So much did Gustave Courbet come to believe in recording the actual facts of the world around him that he declared, in 1861, "Painting is an essentially concrete art and can only consist of the presentation of real and existing things." In the mind of a painter like Édouard Manet, this meant recording the facts of bourgeois life in Paris as seen through his *flâneur* sensibilities. Why, then, did *Le Déjeuner sur l'herbe* offend the French public?

19.6 Define Impressionism in terms of both its stylistic techniques and its subject matter.

The Impressionists departed from their predecessors both in technique and subject. They painted so that their work should at least appear to have been done spontaneously, recording fleeting appearances and the effects of light. They were less interested in social criticism than the Realist painters of the previous generation, instead favoring the pleasures of life as subject matter. How did the name "Impressionism" originate? Why did Claude Monet paint the same subject repeatedly?

19.7 Explain some of the ways that the Post-Impressionists extended and redirected the Impressionist enterprise.

Monet's work at Giverny can be seen as an example of an ongoing formal exploration of the possibilities of painting, while Vincent van Gogh explored the symbolic possibilities of line and color. A number of other painters—among them Paul Gauguin, Georges Seurat, and Paul Cézanne—embarked on a similar brand of exploration, each dedicated to redirecting the Impressionist enterprise. Gauguin sought to express what he saw as the mystery and magic of Tahitian culture. What defines the Post-Impressionist projects of Seurat and Cézanne?

Chapter 20
From 1900 to the Present

Learning Objectives

20.1 Distinguish between Cubism, Fauvism, German Expressionism, and Futurism.

20.2 Explain the rise of Dada and the emergence of Surrealism.

20.3 Discuss how politics impinged on the art of Diego Rivera and Pablo Picasso in the 1930s.

20.4 Describe the reaction of both American modernist and Abstract Expressionist painters to European modernism.

20.5 Explain how Pop Art and Minimalism both responded to the example of Abstract Expressionism.

20.6 Outline some of the major trends in contemporary art.

At the dawn of the twentieth century, the world was in motion. As early as 1880, one French advertising company boasted that it could post a billboard ad in 35,937 municipalities in the space of just five days—a billboard of the kind advertising Astra Construction in *L'Équipe de Cardiff* (*The Cardiff Team*) (**Fig. 20-1**), a painting by Robert Delaunay. The painting depicts the men of the Cardiff (Wales) rugby team leaping up at a rugby ball in the center of the painting. They represent the internationalization of sport; the first modern Olympic Games had taken place in 1896 in Athens, followed by the 1900 Games in Paris, staged in conjunction with the Universal Exposition, and rugby was a medal sport in each. The rugby ball is framed by the famous Grande Roue de Paris. Built for the 1900 Universal Exposition, at 100 meters (328 feet) in height, it was the tallest Ferris wheel in the world. On July 1, 1913, the year that Robert Delaunay painted *The Cardiff Team*, a signal was broadcast from the top of the Eiffel Tower, seen dominating Delaunay's work, establishing worldwide Standard Time. By 1903, Orville Wright had been airborne for 59 seconds, and by 1908, he would fly for 91 minutes. A year later, Louis Blériot crossed the English Channel by plane (though it would be another 18 years until Charles Lindbergh would cross the Atlantic by air). The airplane in Delaunay's painting is a "box kite" design, built in a Paris suburb beginning in 1907 by the Voisin brothers, Gabriel and Charles, the first commercial airplane manufacturers in Europe. Finally, the signboard "MAGIC" refers to Magic City, an enormous dance hall near the Eiffel Tower. Delaunay called his work Simultanism, a term that refers to the immediacy of vision, suggesting that in any given instant an infinite number of states of being simultaneously exist. This is the thrust of the painting and it is equally the thrust of twentieth-century art—speed, motion, change, culminating in the twenty-first century in the almost instantaneous global reach of the Information Age.

First radio message sent across the Atlantic
1901

Wright Brothers invent the airplane
1903

1905

1901
Ragtime jazz develops in the U.S.

1905
Revolution in Russia

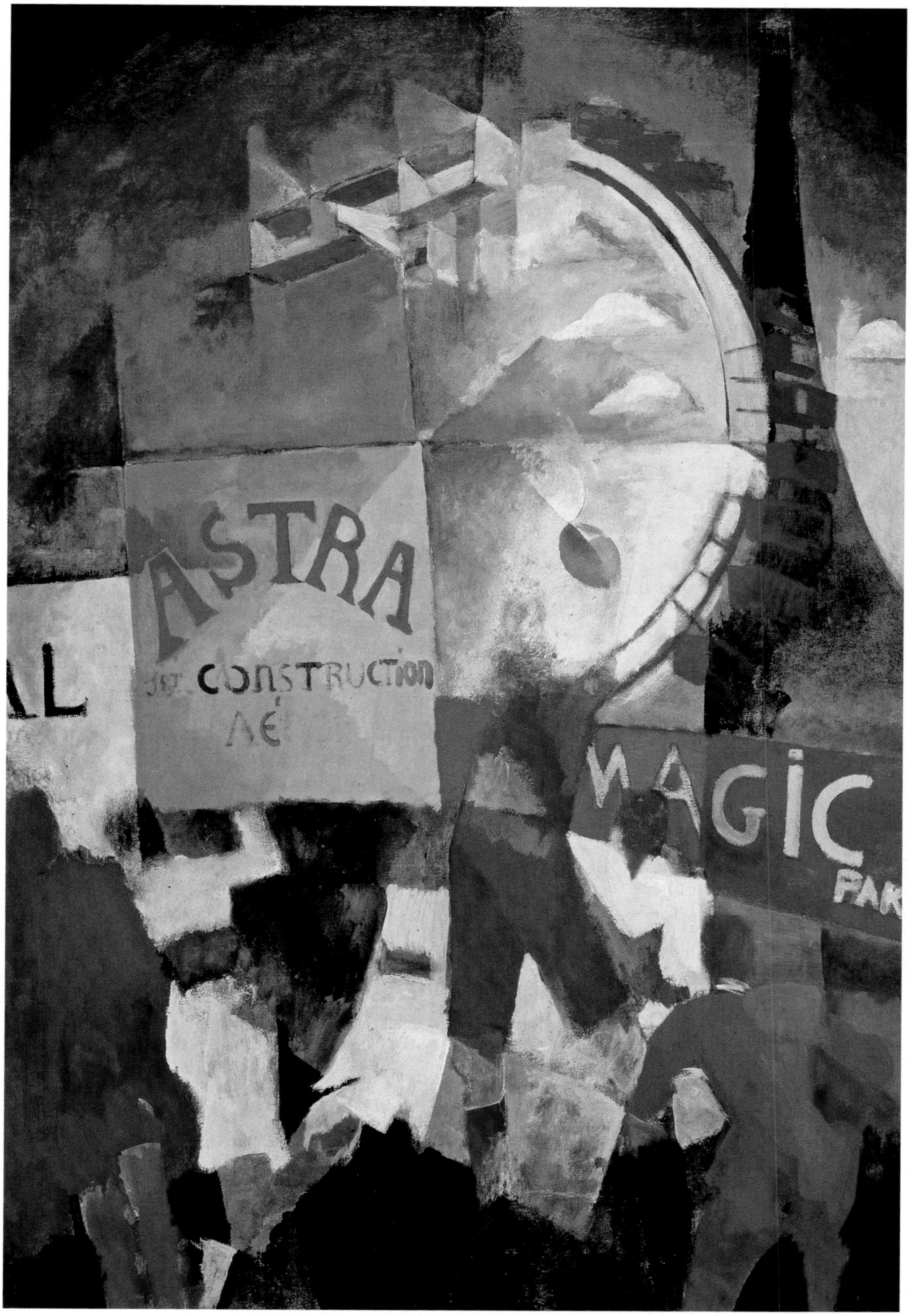

Fig. 20-1 Robert Delaunay, *L'Équipe de Cardiff* (*The Cardiff Team*), 1913. Oil on canvas, 10 ft. 8⅜ in. × 6 ft. 10 in. Van Abbemuseum, Eindhoven, Holland.
Inv. 84. De Agostini/Bridgeman Images.

The New "Isms"

What are Cubism, Fauvism, German Expressionism, and Futurism?

At the center of the new spirit of change and innovation that is the subject of this chapter stood the Spanish-born Pablo Picasso. Picasso's studio in Paris was quickly recognized by other artists and intellectuals as the center of artistic innovation in the new century. From around Europe and America, artists flocked to see *Les Demoiselles d'Avignon* (see Fig. 1-13), which by 1910 had come to symbolize the modernist break from tradition, and they carried his spirit—and the spirit of French painting generally—back with them to Italy, Germany, and America, where it influenced the arts there. "Make it new!" was something of the mantra of the day, and new art movements—new "isms," including Delaunay's Simultanism—rapidly succeeded one another.

Fig. 20-2 Georges Braque, *Houses at l'Estaque*, 1908. Oil on canvas, 28¾ × 23¾ in. Hermann and Margit Rupf Foundation.

Cubism

Soon after Georges Braque first saw *Les Demoiselles d'Avignon*, he began to paint a series of landscapes based on its formal innovations. His *Houses at l'Estaque* (**Fig. 20-2**) takes Paul Cézanne's manipulation of space even further than the master did (see Fig. 19-36). The tree that rises from the foreground seems to meld into the roofs of the distant houses near the top of the painting. At the right, a large, leafy branch projects out across the houses, but its leaves appear identical to the greenery that is growing between the houses behind it. It becomes impossible to tell what is foreground and what is not. The houses descending down the hill before us are themselves spatially confusing. Walls bleed almost seamlessly into other walls, walls bleed into roofs, roofs bleed into walls. Braque presents us with a design of triangles and cubes as much as he does a landscape.

Together, over the course of the next decade, Picasso and Braque created the movement known as **Cubism**, of which Braque's *Houses at l'Estaque* is an early example. The name derived from a comment made by the critic Louis Vauxcelles in a short review that appeared directly above a headline announcing the "conquest of the air" by the Wright brothers: "Braque . . . reduces everything, places and figures and houses, to geometrical schemes, little cubes." It was, as the accidental juxtaposition of Cubism and the Wright brothers suggested, a new world, and when Picasso returned to Paris from Spain in the fall of 1909, he brought with him landscapes that showed just how much he had learned from Braque (**Fig. 20-3**).

Fig. 20-3 Pablo Picasso, *Houses on the Hill, Horta de Ebro*, 1909. Oil on canvas, 25⅝ × 31⅞ in. Nationalgalerie, Museum Berggruen, Staatliche Museen zu Berlin.

Photo: Jens Ziehe. © 2015. Photo Scala, Florence/bpk, Bildagentur für Kunst, Kultur und Geschichte, Berlin. © 2015 Estate of Pablo Picasso/ Artists Rights Society (ARS), New York.

Fig. 20-4 Georges Braque, *Violin and Palette*, September 1, 1909. Oil on canvas, 36⅛ × 16⅞ in. Solomon R. Guggenheim Museum, New York.
54.1412. Photo © Solomon R. Guggenheim Foundation, New York. Photo by David Heald. © 2015 Artists Rights Society (ARS), New York/ADAGP, Paris.

Fig. 20-5 Pablo Picasso, *Guitar, Sheet Music, and Wine Glass*, 1912. Charcoal, gouache, and papiers-collés, 18⅞ × 14¾ in. The McNay Art Museum, San Antonio, Texas.
Bequest of Marion Koogler McNay, 1950.112. © 2015. McNay Art Museum/Art Resource, New York/Scala, Florence. © 2015 Estate of Pablo Picasso/Artists Rights Society (ARS), New York.

Other artists soon followed the lead of Picasso and Braque, and the impact of their art could be felt everywhere. For the Cubist, art was primarily about form. Analyzing the object from all sides and acknowledging the flatness of the picture plane, the Cubist painting represented the three-dimensional world in increasingly two-dimensional terms, emphasizing the flatness of the picture plane and the design realized upon it rather than any illusion of depth. The curves of the violin in Braque's *Violin and Palette* (**Fig. 20-4**) are flattened and cubed, so much so that in places the instrument seems as flat as the sheets of music above it. The highly realistic, almost trompe-l'oeil nail at the painting's top—obviously three-dimensional, but thereby underscoring the flatness of the rest of the painting—introduces another characteristic of Cubist work. Casting its own shadow, it can be seen either as part of the painting, holding up the palette, or as real, holding the painting to the wall. Such play between the reality of painting and the reality of the world soon led both Picasso and Braque to experiment with collage (see Chapter 9). In *Guitar, Sheet Music, and Wine Glass* (**Fig. 20-5**), Picasso includes a newspaper fragment in the painting. At the bottom of the image, the headline of *Le Journal* reads, "*La bataille s'est engagée*"—"Battle is joined." Literally, it refers to a battle in the Balkans, where Bulgaria attacked the Turks, November 17 through 19. But the "battle" is also metaphorical, the battle between art and reality. Similarly, the background's trellis-and-rose wallpaper is no more or less real than the fragment of the actual musical score, the *faux-bois* ("false wood") guitar, and the Cubist drawing of a goblet, cut out of some preexisting source like the other elements in the work. By admitting these things into the space of art, Picasso and Braque redefined painting as

Fig. 20-6 Henri Matisse, *Woman with a Hat*, 1905.
Oil on canvas, 31¼ × 23½ in. San Francisco Museum of Modern Art.
Bequest of Elise S. Haas.© 2015 Succession H. Matisse/Artists Rights Society (ARS), New York.

Fig. 20-7 Wassily Kandinsky, *Sketch I for "Composition VII,"* 1913.
Indian ink, 30¾ × 39⅜ in. Felix Klee Collection, Kunstmuseum, Bern. 1979.222. © 2007 Artists Rights Society (ARS), New York.

the setting in which the forces of the high and low, art and the real world, must engage one another.

Fauvism

Though the Cubists tended to deemphasize color in order to emphasize form, Henri Matisse favored the expressive possibilities of color. Matisse, in a sense, synthesized the art of Cézanne and Georges Seurat, taking the former's broad, flat zones of color and the latter's interest in setting complementary hues beside one another. Under the influence of van Gogh, whose work had not been seen as a whole until an exhibition at the Bernheim-Jeune Gallery in 1901, Matisse felt free to use color arbitrarily. A number of other young painters joined him, and at the Autumn Salon of 1905 they exhibited together—and were promptly labeled **Fauves** ("Wild Beasts"). It was Matisse's *Woman with a Hat* (**Fig. 20-6**) that caused the greatest uproar. The public could not fathom how he could so willfully transform an otherwise traditional portrait with such a violent and nonrepresentational use of color. The broad brushstrokes of green paint that define his model's forehead and nose were the particular object of ridicule. But some critics saw in this work the promise of great things to come. The painter Maurice Denis wrote of them: "One feels completely in the realm of abstraction. Of course, as in the most extreme departures of van Gogh, something still remains of the original feeling of nature. But here one finds, above all in the work of Matisse, the sense of . . . painting in itself, the act of pure painting." Gertrude Stein and her brother Leo agreed, and they soon bought the painting.

German Expressionism

It was in Germany that Denis's idea of "pure painting" fully took hold. In Dresden, a group of artists known as *Die Brücke* ("The Bridge"), among them Ernst Kirchner, Emil Nolde, and Erich Heckel (see Fig. 10-6), advocated a raw and direct style, epitomized by the slashing gouges of the woodblock print. A group of artists known as *Der Blaue Reiter* ("The Blue Rider") formed in Munich around the Russian Wassily Kandinsky. They believed that through color and line alone works of art could express the feelings and emotions of the artist directly to the viewer—hence the name **Expressionism**.

In the 1890s, Kandinsky had seen an exhibition of Claude Monet's *Grainstacks* (see Fig. 5-36). Noting how the grainstacks themselves seemed to disintegrate in the diffuse light, Kandinsky was convinced that "the importance of an 'object' as the necessary element in painting" was suspect. Nothing of the geometry of Cubism can be detected in Kandinsky's early paintings such as *Sketch I for "Composition VII"* (**Fig. 20-7**). Kandinsky considered his painting to be equivalent to music, and his works are alive in nonfigurative movement and color. Each color and each line carried, for Kandinsky, explicit expressive meaning (see Fig. 5-39). He believed that paintings like his had "the power to create [a] spiritual atmosphere" that would "lead us away from the outer to the inner basis."

The paintings of the Fauves convinced Kandinsky that through color he could eliminate the object altogether. "Color," Kandinsky wrote in his 1911 treatise *Concerning the Spiritual in Art*, "is a power which directly influences the soul."

Kandinsky's ideas find remarkable expression in the work of another member of the Blue Rider group, Franz Marc, who adopted Kandinsky's color symbolism in his depiction of animals. "I try to heighten my feeling for the organic rhythm of all things," Marc wrote, "to feel myself pantheistically into the trembling and flow of the blood of nature." More than any other German painter, Marc understood the sensuality of Matisse's line and employed it in his work. His use of color, which echoes, of course, the name of the movement to which he belonged, is liberated from the world of appearance, but it is highly emotional. He painted horses over and over again (**Fig. 20-8**). Sometimes they were blue—Marc associated blue with masculinity, strength, and purity—sometimes red, sometimes yellow, depending on his emotions as he was painting. Marc never fulfilled his promise as a painter. He was killed fighting in World War I in 1916.

Fig. 20-8 Franz Marc, *Die grossen blauen Pferde* (*The Large Blue Horses*), 1911.
Oil on canvas, 41 5/16 in. × 5 ft. 11 1/4 in. Walker Art Center, Minneapolis.
Gift of the T. B. Walker Foundation, Gilbert M. Walker Fund, 1942. De Agostini/Bridgeman Images.

— 1928

Discovery of penicillin 1928

1928 First television broadcast

First Soviet Five-Year Plan 1928

1929 U.S. stock market crash; Great Depression begins

Futurism

If abstraction was the hallmark of the new century, certain thematic concerns defined it as well. The world had become, quite literally, a new place. In the summer of 1900, with the opening of the Universal Exposition, Paris found itself electrified, its nights almost transformed to day. The automobile, a rarity before the new century, dominated the city's streets by 1906. People were flying airplanes. Albert Einstein proposed a new theory of relativity and Niels Bohr a new model for the atom. Many people felt that there could be no tradition, at least not one worth imitating, in the face of so much change.

When, in February 1909, Filippo Marinetti published his manifesto announcing the advent of Futurism (see Chapter 4), there were, in fact, no Futurist painters. Marinetti had to leave Paris, go back to Italy, and recruit them. But when they subsequently exhibited their show of Futurist painting around Europe from 1912 until the outbreak of World War I in 1914, outraging as many as they pleased, these painters—Umberto Boccioni, Carlo Carrà, Luigi Russolo, Giacomo Balla, and Gino Severini—embodied the spirit of the machine and of rapid change that seemed to define the century itself. Balla's *Dynamism of a Dog on a Leash* (**Fig. 20-9**) captures the Futurist fascination with movement. It demonstrates, as well, its debt to new technological media—in particular, photography and the new art of film (see Figs. 11-2 and 11-3).

Fig. 20-10 Umberto Boccioni, *Unique Forms of Continuity in Space*, 1913. Bronze, 43⅞ × 34⅞ × 15¾ in. Museum of Modern Art, New York.

Acquired through the Lillie P. Bliss Bequest, 231.1948. © 2015 Digital image, Museum of Modern Art, New York/Scala, Florence.

Fig. 20-9 Giacomo Balla, *Dynamism of a Dog on a Leash*, 1912. Oil on canvas, 35⅜ × 43½ in. Albright-Knox Art Gallery, Buffalo, New York.

Bequest of A. Conger Goodyear and Gift of George F. Goodyear, 1964. © 2015. Albright Knox Art Gallery/Art Resource, New York/Scala, Florence. © 2015 Artists Rights Society (ARS), New York/SIAE, Rome.

Boccioni's *Unique Forms of Continuity in Space* (**Fig. 20-10**) gives the sense of a figure striding forward, clothing flapping in the wind, a sort of new *Nike of Samothrace* (see Fig. 16-25). Boccioni probably means to represent a nude, its musculature stretched and swollen to reveal its dynamic movement through space and time in the same way that he stretched the form of a bottle, exposing its volumetric dimensions in his *Development of a Bottle in Space* (see Fig. 4-7). "What we want to do," he explained, "is show the living object in its dynamic growth."

Dada and Surrealism

How do you explain the rise of Dada and the emergence of Surrealism?

World War I more than dampened this exuberance. The war was catastrophic. As many as 10 million people were killed and 20 million wounded, most in grueling trench warfare on the western front, a battle line that remained virtually stationary for three years and ran from Oostende on the Dutch coast, past Reims and Verdun, to Lunéville in France. World War I represented to many the bankruptcy of Western thought, and it served notice that all that had come before needed to be swept away.

Founded simultaneously in Zurich, Berlin, Paris, and New York during the war, **Dada** took up Futurism's call for the annihilation of tradition but, as a result of the war, without its sense of hope for the future. Its name referred, some said, to a child's first words; others claimed it was a reference to a child's hobbyhorse; and still others celebrated it as a simple nonsense sound. As a movement, it championed senselessness, noise, and illogic. Dada was, above all, against art, or at least art in the traditional sense of the word. Its chief strategy was insult and outrage. Perhaps Dada's chief exponent, Marcel Duchamp always challenged tradition in a spirit of fun. His *L.H.O.O.Q.* (**Fig. 20-11**) is an image of Leonardo's *Mona Lisa* (see Fig. 18-8) with a mustache drawn on her upper lip. Saying the letters of the title with French pronunciation reveals it to be a pun, *elle a chaud au cul*, roughly translated as "she's hot in the pants." Such is the irreverence of Dada.

In New York, in 1917, Duchamp submitted a common urinal to the annual Exhibition of the Society of Independent Artists, titled it *Fountain*, signed it R. Mutt, and claimed for it the status of sculpture (**Fig. 20-12**). At first it was rejected, but when Duchamp let it be known that he and R. Mutt were one and the same, it was accepted. Thus, whether something was art depended on who made it—or found it, in this case. It also depended on where it was seen—in the museum, it was one thing, in the plumbing store, quite another. Furthermore, on its pedestal, in the context of the museum, Duchamp's "fountain" looked to some as if it were indeed sculpture.

Fig. 20-11 Marcel Duchamp, *L.H.O.O.Q.*, 1919. Rectified Readymade (reproduction of Leonardo da Vinci's *Mona Lisa* altered with pencil), 7¾ × 4⅛ in. Philadelphia Museum of Art.

Louise and Walter Arensberg Collection, 1950. © 2015. Photo Philadelphia Museum of Art/Art Resource/Scala, Florence. © 2015 Succession Marcel Duchamp/ADAGP, Paris/Artists Rights Society (ARS), New York.

Fig. 20-12 Marcel Duchamp, *Fountain*, 1917. Glazed sanitary china with black print. Photo by Alfred Stieglitz in *The Blind Man*, No. 2 (May 1917); original lost. Philadelphia Museum of Art.

Louise and Walter Arensberg Collection, 1950, 1998-74-1. Photo Philadelphia Museum of Art/Art Resource/Scala, Florence. © 2015 Succession Marcel Duchamp/ADAGP, Paris/Artists Rights Society (ARS), New York.

Duchamp did not so much invalidate art as authorize the art world to consider all manner of things in aesthetic terms. His logic was not without precedent. Cubist collage had brought "real things" like newspaper clippings into the space of painting, and photography, especially, often revealed aesthetic beauty in common experience. But Duchamp's move, like Dada generally, was particularly challenging and provocative. "I was interested," he explained, "in ideas—not merely in visual products."

The art of **Surrealism** was born of Dada's preoccupation with the irrational and the illogical, as well as its interest in ideas. When the French writer André Breton issued the First Surrealist Manifesto in 1924, the nihilist spirit of Dada was clearly about to be replaced by something more positive. Breton explained the direction his movement would take: "I believe in the future resolution of these two states, dream and reality, which are seemingly so contradictory, into a kind of absolute reality, a surreality." To these ends, the new art would rely on chance operations, automatism (or random, thoughtless, and unmotivated notation of any kind), and dream images—the expressions of the unconscious mind. Two different sorts of imagery resulted. The first contained recognizable, if fantastic, subject matter. It was typified by the work of René Magritte (see Fig. 2-2), Giorgio de Chirico, who was acknowledged as an important precursor to the Surrealist movement by the Surrealists themselves, and Salvador Dalí. De Chirico claimed not to understand his own paintings. They were simply images that obsessed him, and they conveyed, Breton felt, the "irremediable anxiety" of the day. Thus, in *Melancholy and Mystery of a Street* (**Fig. 20-13**), the little girl rolls her hoop toward the ominous black shadow of a figure lurking behind the wall. Dalí called paintings such as *The Persistence of Memory* (**Fig. 20-14**) "hand-painted dream photographs." The limbless figure lying on the ground like a giant slug is actually a self-portrait of the artist, who seems to have moved into a landscape removed from time and mind.

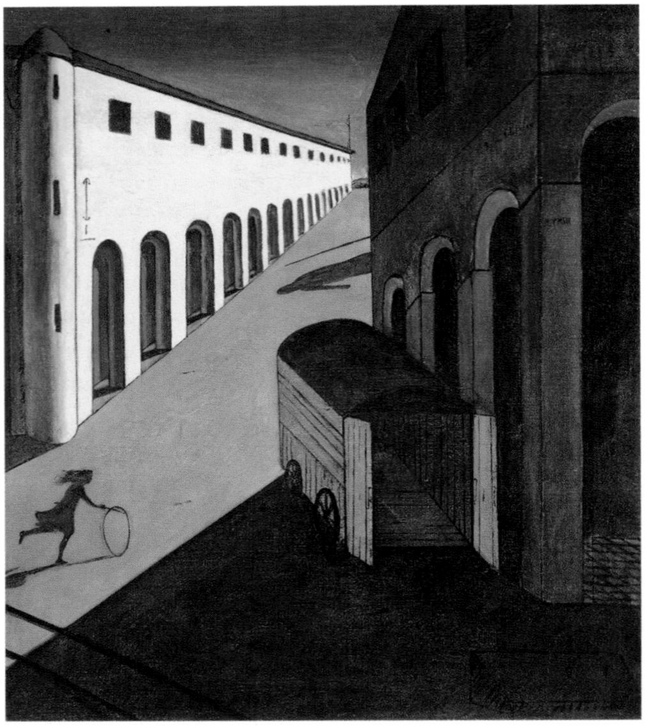

Fig. 20-13 Giorgio de Chirico, *Melancholy and Mystery of a Street*, 1914. Oil on canvas, 24¼ × 28½ in. Private collection.
© 2015 Artists Rights Society (ARS), New York/SIAE, Rome.

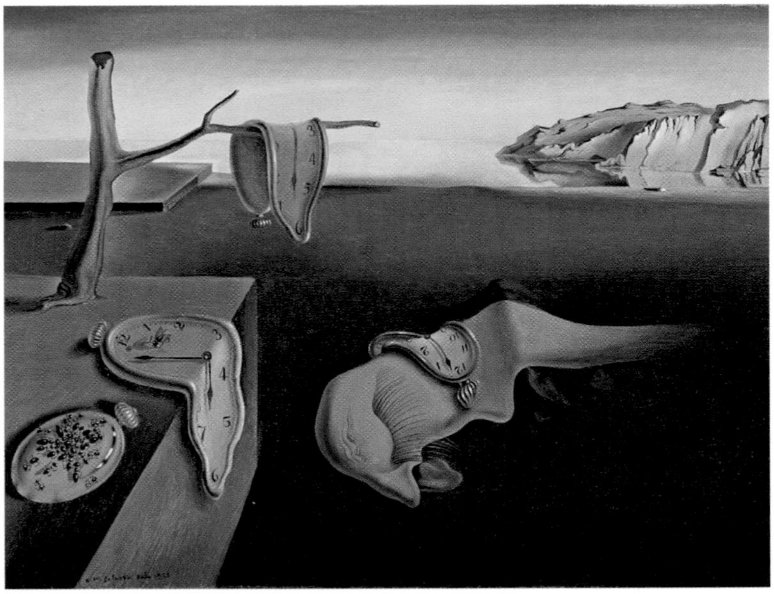

Fig. 20-14 Salvador Dalí, *The Persistence of Memory*, 1931. Oil on canvas, 9½ × 13 in. Museum of Modern Art, New York.
Given anonymously, 162.1934. © 2015 Digital image, Museum of Modern Art, New York/Scala, Florence. © 2015 Salvador Dalí, Fundació Gala-Salvador Dalí, Artists Rights Society (ARS), New York.

The other type of Surrealist painting was virtually abstract, presenting us with a world of indecipherable visual riddles. The painting of the Spanish artist Joan Miró and many of the early mobiles of Alexander Calder (see Fig. 6-7) fall into this category. In Miró's

Fig. 20-15 Joan Miró, *Painting*, 1933. Oil on canvas, 4 ft. 3⅜ in. × 5 ft. 4⅛ in. Wadsworth Atheneum, Hartford.

Ella Gallup Sumner and Mary Catlin Sumner Collection Fund. Photo Wadsworth Atheneum, Hartford. © 2015 Successió Miró/Artists Rights Society (ARS), New York/ADAGP, Paris.

Painting (**Fig. 20-15**), biomorphic, amoebalike forms float in a space that suggests a darkened landscape. If we look closely, however, faces, hair, and hands begin to appear. Everything in this composition seems fluid, susceptible to continuing and ongoing mutation, moving back and forth between representation and abstraction.

Although never officially a member of the movement, in the late 1920s and early 1930s Picasso worked in a distinctly Surrealist mode and contributed regularly to Surrealist publications. Breton, in fact, argued that Picasso led the way to Surrealist art with *Les Demoiselles d'Avignon*. Picasso's Surrealism would assert itself most fully in a series of monstrous bonelike figures (see Fig. 1-10) that alternated with sensuous portraits of his mistress Marie-Thérèse Walter, whom he had met when she was only 17, in January 1927. For eight years, until 1935, he led a double life, married to Olga Koklova while conducting a secret affair with Marie-Thérèse. Since Marie-Thérèse is so readily identifiable in her portraits, it is tempting to see the more monstrous figures as portraits of Olga. Picasso was indeed obsessed in these years with the duality of experience. His 1932 double portrait of Marie-Thérèse, *Girl before a Mirror* (**Fig. 20-16**), expresses this—she is the moon, or night, at the right, and the sun, or light, on

Fig. 20-16 Pablo Picasso, *Girl before a Mirror*, 1932. Oil on canvas, 5 ft. 4 in. × 4 ft. 3¼ in. Museum of Modern Art, New York.

Gift of Mrs. Simon Guggenheim, 2.1938. © 2015. Digital image, Museum of Modern Art, New York/Scala, Florence. © 2015 Estate of Pablo Picasso/Artists Rights Society (ARS), New York.

the left, where her own face appears in both profile and three-quarter view. Her protruding belly on the left suggests her fertility (indeed, she gave birth to their child, Maya, in 1935, soon after Picasso finally separated from Olga), though in the mirror, in typical Picasso fashion, we see not her stomach but her buttocks. She is the conscious self on the left, her subconscious self revealing itself in the mirror. Picasso's work addresses Surrealism's most basic theme—the self in all its complexity.

Politics and Painting

How did the art of the 1930s reflect the politics of the era?

The era between World War I and World War II marks the period in Western history when, in Germany, Italy, Spain, and the Soviet Union, totalitarian and nationalistic regimes—fascist dictatorships—rose to power. It was also a time of political upheaval in Latin America, particularly in Mexico, where guerilla groups led by Emiliano Zapata and Pancho Villa demanded "land, liberty, and justice" for Mexico's peasant population. Their primary purpose was to give back to the people land that the government had deeded to foreign investors in the hope that they might modernize the country. In light of such events, politics impinged mightily on the arts. The Mexican Revolution, which started in 1910, fueled a wave of intense nationalism to which artists responded by creating art that from their point of view was true to the aspirations of the people of Mexico. When the government initiated a massive building campaign, a new school of muralists arose to decorate these buildings. It was led by Diego Rivera, David Siquieros, and José Clemente Orozco.

From 1930 to 1934, Rivera received a series of commissions in the United States. They included one from Edsel B. Ford and the Detroit Institute of Arts to create a series of frescoes for the museum's Garden Court on the subject of *Detroit Industry*, and another from the Rockefellers to create a lobby fresco entitled *Man at the Crossroads Looking with Hope and High Vision to a New and Better Future* for the RCA Building in Rockefeller Center in New York. When Rivera included a portrait of Communist leader Lenin in the lobby painting, Nelson A. Rockefeller insisted that he remove it. Rivera refused, and Rockefeller, after paying Rivera his commission, had the painting destroyed.

Rivera reproduced the fresco soon after in Mexico City and called it *Man, Controller of the Universe* (**Fig. 20-17**). At the center, Man stands below a telescope with a microscope in his hand. Two ellipses of light

Fig. 20-17 Diego Rivera, *Man, Controller of the Universe*, 1934. Fresco, main panel 15 ft. 11 in. × 37 ft. 6 in. Palacio de Bellas Artes, Mexico City, D.F. Mexico.

emanate from him, one depicting the cosmos, the other the microscopic world. Beneath him is the earth, with plants growing in abundance, the products of scientific advancements in agriculture. To the right, between healthy microbes and a starry cosmos, is Lenin, holding the hands of workers of different cultures. On the left, between microscopic renderings of syphilis and other diseases and a warring cosmos, is New York society, including Nelson Rockefeller enjoying a cocktail. At the top left, armed figures wearing gas masks and marching in military formation evoke World War I, while at the upper right, workers wearing Communist red scarves raise their voices in solidarity. Man must steer his course between the evils of capitalism and the virtues of Communism, Rivera appears to be saying.

One of the greatest political paintings of the era is Pablo Picasso's *Guernica* (**Fig. 20-18**). It represents an event in the Spanish Civil War that occurred on April 26, 1937. That day, Republican Basque troops, who were fighting the Fascist forces of General Francisco Franco, were retreating toward Bilbao on the northern Spanish coast. A bridge over the Mandaca River, at the edge of a town of 7,000 people called Guernica, was the last escape route for vehicles in the area, and the German air force, which had come to the aid of Franco, was determined to destroy it. The attack was planned by Wolfram von Richthofen, the cousin of the almost-mythical German ace of World War I, Manfred von Richthofen, the Red Baron, and a man eager to create his own legend. The strike force consisted of three squadrons—a total of 33 planes. Each was loaded with 3,000 pounds of bombs, as well as several hundred small incendiary cylinders. The attack, a type of sudden coordinated strike that soon was known as a blitzkrieg, commenced at 4:30 in the afternoon and lasted for three-and-a-quarter hours. The first bombs were dropped near the railroad station—the bridge was ignored—and, from that point on, the planes released their bombs indiscriminately into the smoke and dust raised by the first explosions. By the time the fires subsided three days later, the entire central part of the town—15 square blocks—was totally destroyed. Nearly 1,000 people had been killed.

Picasso, who was sympathetic to the Republican side and who considered himself exiled in Paris, was outraged at the events. Many elements of the painting refer to Surrealist dream symbolism. The horse,

Fig. 20-18 Pablo Picasso, *Guernica*, 1937. Oil on canvas, 11 ft. 5½ in. × 25 ft. 5¼ in. Museo Nacional Centro de Arte Reina Sofía, Madrid.

at the center left, speared and dying in anguish, represents the fate of the dreamer's creativity. The entire scene is surveyed by a bull, which represents at once Spain itself, the simultaneous heroism and tragedy of the bullfight, and the Minotaur, the bull-man who for the Surrealists stood for the irrational forces of the human psyche. The significance of the electric light bulb, at the top center of the painting, and the oil lamp, held by the woman reaching out the window, has been much debated, but they represent, at least, old and new ways of seeing.

American Modernism and Abstract Expressionism

How did American artists react to the example of European modernism?

With the outbreak of World War II, Picasso decided that *Guernica* should stay in the United States. He arranged for it to be kept at the Museum of Modern Art in New York, where it was to be held until the death of Franco and the reestablishment of public liberty in Spain. Franco, however, did not die until 1975, two years after Picasso himself. The painting was returned to Spain, finally, in 1981. It hangs today in a special annex of the Museo Nacional Centro de Arte Reina Sofía in Madrid.

The painting profoundly affected American artists. "Picasso's *Guernica* floored me," Lee Krasner reported. "When I saw it first . . . I rushed out, walked about the block three times before coming back to look at it. And then I used to go to the Modern every day to see it." Krasner's own *Untitled* painting (**Fig. 20-19**), done soon after *Guernica*'s arrival in New York in 1939, reflects *Guernica*'s angular forms and turbulent energy. But it differs in important ways from *Guernica*. It is totally abstract, and where *Guernica* is a monochrome gray-brown, like burnt newsprint, Krasner's painting is vibrant with color. Probably more than any other artist of her day, Krasner understood how to integrate the competing aesthetic directions of European abstraction, fusing the geometric and Expressionist tendencies of modern art in a single composition.

Until 1940, abstraction such as Krasner's was not very well accepted in the United States. To be sure, American **modernism** had been responsive to trends in European painting since the early years of the century, but instead of pushing toward abstraction, as had happened in Europe, American modernists tended to utilize European painting's formal innovations in more realist painting. Many artists preferred a realist approach, which was supported, on the one hand, by the growing popularity of photography, and, on the other, by an increasing conviction that art, in the face of the harsh realities of the Great

Fig. 20-19 Lee Krasner, *Untitled*, ca. 1940. Oil on canvas, 30 × 25 in.

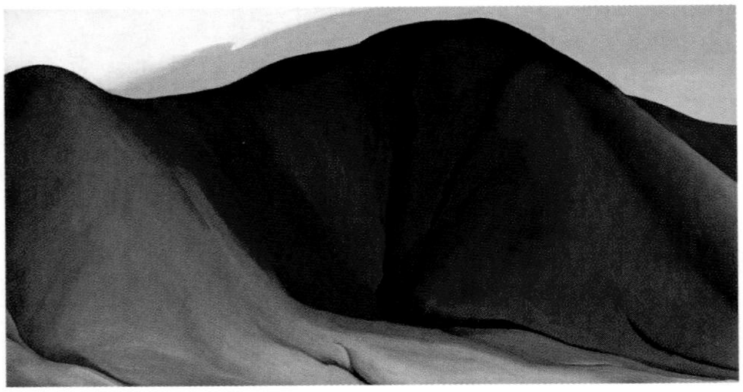

Fig. 20-20 Georgia O'Keeffe, *Purple Hills near Abiquiu*, 1935. Oil on canvas, 16 × 30 in. San Diego Museum of Art.
Gift of Mr. and Mrs. Norton S. Walbridge, 1976.216. 2015 Georgia O'Keeffe Foundation/Artists Rights Society (ARS), New York.

Depression of the 1930s, should deal with the problems of daily life. Still, these artists were willing to learn from the formal discoveries of their more abstraction-oriented contemporaries, and we are often as attracted to the form of their work as to their subject matter. In her *Purple Hills near Abiquiu* (**Fig. 20-20**), Georgia O'Keeffe utilizes the sensuous line of the German Expressionist painter Franz Marc (see Fig. 20-8) to create a landscape that almost seems to be alive, a body capable of moving and breathing like one of Marc's animals. In a painting like *Nighthawks* (**Fig. 20-21**), Edward Hopper depicts the emotional isolation of the average American. But the composition is powerfully supported by the visual simplicity of his design, a geometry inspired by the example of European modernism. It is as if his figures are isolated from one another in the vast horizontal expanse of the canvas. The Great Depression and the outbreak of World War II, nevertheless, provided the impetus for the development of abstract painting in the United States. President Roosevelt's WPA (Works Progress Administration) had initiated, in 1935, a Federal Art Project that supported artists financially and thus allowed them to work as they pleased. Furthermore, many leading European artists emigrated to the United States to escape ever-worsening conditions in Europe. Suddenly, in New York, American painters could not only see Picasso's *Guernica*, but also found themselves in the company of Fernand Léger, Piet Mondrian, Yves Tanguy, Marcel Duchamp, and André Breton. A style of painting referred to as **Abstract Expressionism** soon developed. It harkened back to Kandinsky's nonobjective work of 1910 to 1920, but it was not unified in its stylistic approach. Rather, the term grouped together a number of painters dedicated to the expressive capacities of their own individual gestures and styles.

Fig. 20-21 Edward Hopper, *Nighthawks*, 1942. Oil on canvas, 30 in. × 5 ft. The Art Institute of Chicago.
Friends of American Art Collection, 1942.51. © 2015 Art Institute of Chicago.

Jackson Pollock was deeply influenced by the Surrealist notion of automatism, the direct and unmediated expression of the self. Pouring and flinging paint onto canvas, usually on the floor, he created large "all-over"—completely covered, large-scale—surfaces with no place for the eye to rest (see Figs. 6-12 and 6-13). Because of the energy and movement of such paintings, the Abstract Expressionism of Pollock has been labeled "action painting." Willem de Kooning's work, with its visible application of paint to the surface, is the definitive example of this approach. Though his paintings of female subjects, including *Woman and Bicycle* (**Fig. 20-22**), are often seen

Fig. 20-22 Willem de Kooning, *Woman and Bicycle*, 1952–53. Oil on canvas, 6 ft. 4½ in. × 4 ft. 1 in. Whitney Museum of American Art, New York.
Purchase 55.35. © 2015 Willem de Kooning Foundation/Artists Rights Society (ARS), New York.

as an attack upon women, de Kooning's hashed-out, scribbled-over, loosely gestural painting is equally a celebration of his own freedom from the conventions of figural representation. "I do not think . . . of art," he explained, "as a situation of comfort."

The monumental quietness of Mark Rothko's canvases (**Fig. 20-23**) conveys almost the opposite feeling. To call this "action painting" would be a misnomer. The painting produces a meditative, not active, space. In place of action, we find a carefully modulated field of color that suggests the luminous space and light of Monet's *Grainstacks* (see Fig. 5-36), only without the realistic image. However, because Rothko emphasizes the horizontal band and the horizon line, his paintings often suggest the point where land meets sky. The bands of color bleed mysteriously into one another or into the background, at once insisting on the space they occupy by the richness of their color and dissolving at the edges like mist. "I am interested only in expressing the basic human emotions—tragedy, ecstasy, doom, and so on," Rothko explained, "and the fact that lots of people break down and cry when confronted with my pictures shows that I communicate with those basic human emotions. The people who weep before my pictures are having the same religious experience I had when I painted them." Viewers find themselves enveloped in Rothko's so-called "color fields," so that they become stage sets, in a sense, for the human dramas that unfold before them.

Pop Art and Minimalism

How did Pop Art and Minimalism react to the example of Abstract Expressionism?

In the 1960s, a group of younger artists, led by Andy Warhol, Claes Oldenburg, and Roy Lichtenstein, invented a new American form of realism, **Pop Art**. It was in part a reaction to the supposed authenticity of Abstract Expressionist gesture, and it reflected a sense that genuine American experience was not so much heartfelt as it was determined by the culture machine of Wall Street finance and Madison Avenue advertising. Pop represented life as America lived it, a world of Campbell's soup cans, Coca-Cola bottles, comic strips, and movie stars (see Fig. 10-30). Based on an actual Sunday cartoon strip, Lichtenstein's 4-by-4-foot painting *Oh, Jeff . . . I Love You, Too . . . But . . .* (**Fig. 20-24**) suggests, by its very size, the powerful role of popular culture in our emotional lives. This is an image of modern love, which appears to say that, even as adults, Americans are still mired in the superficial world of teenage crushes. Most important, perhaps, Pop Art left behind traditional artistic media like

Fig. 20-23 Mark Rothko, *Four Darks in Red*, 1958. Oil on canvas, 9 ft. 4 in. × 9 ft. 8 in. Whitney Museum of American Art, New York.
Purchase with funds from the Friends of the Whitney Museum of American Art, Mr. and Mrs. Eugene M. Schwartz, Mrs. Samuel A. Seaver, and Charles Simon, 68.9. © 2015 Kate Rothko Prizel & Christopher Rothko/Artists Rights Society (ARS), New York.

Fig. 20-24 Roy Lichtenstein, *Oh, Jeff . . . I Love You, Too . . . But . . .*, 1964. Oil on magma on canvas, 4 × 4 ft.
© Estate of Roy Lichtenstein.

painting. Artists turned instead to slick renderings made by mechanical reproduction techniques, such as photolithography, that evoked commercial illustration more than fine art.

Another reaction against Abstract Expressionism led, in the same period, to a style of art known as **Minimalism**. The ultimate question Minimalist art asks is "What, minimally, makes a work of art?" This was not a new question. Marcel Duchamp had posed it with his "Readymades" (see Fig. 20-12). In many ways, Pop itself was asking the same question: What, after all, made a picture of a soup can or a comic strip "art"? But Minimalist artists stressed the aesthetic quality of their works; they were confident that they were producing works of (timeless) beauty and eloquence. Perhaps most of all, Minimalism invites the viewer to contemplate its sometimes seductively simple beauty. It invites, in other words, the active engagement of the viewer in experiencing it.

This is precisely the point of a room installation at the Massachusetts Museum of Contemporary Art (Mass MoCA) by Sol LeWitt, one of 105 wall drawings installed at the museum in 2008 as part of a survey exhibition of LeWitt's work that will be on display until 2033 (**Fig. 20-25**). The piece literally surrounds the viewer, covering every wall of a 26-by-46-foot room. Like the other wall drawings in the exhibition, which cover over 1 acre of interior walls in a 27,000-square-foot, three-story historic old mill building situated at the heart of Mass MoCA's campus, the drawing began as a set of instructions to be followed by workers who would execute the work independently of the artist. "The idea," LeWitt said, in one of his most famous statements, "becomes the machine that makes the art." The instructions are comparable to a composer's musical score—notations designed to guide those executing the piece as if it were a performance. For *Wall Drawing #146A*, LeWitt proposed a "vocabulary" of 20 different kinds of lines to be combined into 192 different pairs. His inspiration was the work of photographer Eadweard Muybridge, who in the late nineteenth century created photographic sequences of animals and humans in motion (see Fig. 11-2). "I've long had a strong affinity toward Muybridge," LeWitt declared. "A lot of his ideas appear in my work." In this case, LeWitt captures the sense of a logical, serial movement through space. Nevertheless, the "art" in works such as LeWitt's is extremely matter-of-fact—unmediated, that is, by concerns outside itself. One hardly needs to know of LeWitt's interest in Muybridge to find oneself totally immersed in and engaged by the work. The wall drawing is about the simple beauty of its form, insisting specifically that we pay attention to its order and arrangement.

Fig. 20-25 Sol LeWitt, *Wall Drawing #146A: All two-part combinations of arcs from corners and sides, and straight, not straight, and broken lines within a 36-in. (90-cm) grid*, June 2000.
White crayon on blue wall. LeWitt Collection, Chester, Connecticut. Mass MoCA, North Adams, Massachusetts.

Cross-Fertilization in Contemporary Art

What are some of the major trends in contemporary art?

By the end of the 1960s, artists felt free to engage in a wide spectrum of experimental approaches to painting, ranging from the stylized imagery introduced by Pop artists to the street style of graffiti writers, and from full-blown abstraction to startlingly naturalistic realism. Indeed, the exchange of ideas between proponents of realism and those of abstraction during the post-World War II era had far-reaching effects. Rather than an either/or proposition, there is abundant cross-fertilization between the approaches.

A Plurality of Styles

We can witness this dialogue between realism and abstraction in the work of the contemporary German artist Gerhard Richter, who moves freely between the two—sometimes repainting photographs, black-and-white and color, and sometimes creating large-scale abstract works. This willfully ambivalent aesthetic position informs one of Richter's more provocative paintings, *September* (**Fig. 20-26**). It is an abstraction, in keeping with his sense that "with abstract painting we create a better means of approaching what can be neither seen nor understood"—that is, in this case, the inexplicable horror of the events of September 11, 2001. That day, Richter was on Lufthansa flight 408 en route from Cologne, Germany, to Newark, New Jersey. Richter's flight was scheduled to land at 12:30 PM, but at 10:24, the Federal Aviation Administration closed airspace over the United States, and Richter's plane was diverted to Halifax, Nova Scotia. He returned to Germany two days later.

This "abstraction" is, in fact, a painting of the Twin Towers, the North Tower rising at the right, and the South Tower in the middle right as seen at 9:03 AM, when United Airlines flight 175 from Boston crashed into it.

Fig. 20-26 Gerhard Richter, *September*, 2005. Oil on canvas, 20½ × 28⅜ in. Museum of Modern Art, New York.

Smoke billows from its side. Debris seems to fill the air. "The little picture of the two towers was very colorful to start with," Richter told an interviewer, "with the garish explosion beneath the wonderful blue sky and the flying rubble. That couldn't work; only when I destroyed it, so to speak, scratched it off, was it fit to be seen." It is fit to be seen largely because it remains just at the edge of the graspable, as if it presents itself to us as an image, not so much of the events themselves, but of our memory of them. As Robert Storr has put it in his small, but eloquent, book on the painting, "the farther away my experience of that day seems to become, the more remote and . . . the less sharply defined even my most vivid recollections become."

The forms that Elizabeth Murray uses in creating her paintings are likewise simultaneously recognizable and abstract. Discussing paintings like *Bop* (**Fig. 20-27**), which Murray can be seen working on in the art21 *Exclusive* video "Elizabeth Murray: 'Bop'," she explains: "I want both. I want all things. I want everything. I want to be able to say, 'Oh, that's a cloud with windows, or that's just this floating, weird, bloopy shape with cutouts.' Because I enjoy that: I enjoy the possibilities of all of these forms." The organizational logic of putting these forms together is likewise open to almost endless possibility. "For a couple of years," she told an interviewer in 2003, "I've been working with cutting out shapes and kind of glomming them together and letting it go where it may. Like basically making a zigzag shape and making a rectangular shape and a circular, bloopy, fat, cloudy shape and just putting them all together and letting the cards fall where they may." Her project, in fact, is to work until the forms do seem to come together into a unified whole.

Fig. 20-27 Elizabeth Murray, *Bop*, 2002–03. Oil on canvas, 9 ft. 10 in. × 10 ft. 10½ in.
Photograph by Ellen Page Wilson, courtesy of Pace Gallery. © 2015 Murray-Holman Family Trust/Artists Rights Society (ARS), New York.

Fig. 20-28 Diana al-Hadid, *Nolli's Orders*, 2012. Steel, polymer gypsum, fiberglass, wood, foam, paint, plaster, aluminum foil, pigment, 22 ft. × 19 ft. × 10 ft. 2 in.
Image courtesy of the artist and Marianne Boesky Gallery. © Diana Al-Hadid. Photo Credit: Dennis Harvey.

The collision of diverse and seemingly irreconcilable forms lies at the heart of Syrian-born sculptor Diana al-Hadid's work. *Nolli's Orders* (**Fig. 20-28**) is a monumental construction, 22 feet high and 19 feet wide, that incorporates human forms into a pyramidal structure, the base of which consists of architectural blocks and colonnades, seemingly embedded in flows of water or lava, rising to its apex in a latticelike, stair-step grid of small open-sided boxes. (See the artist at work on the piece in her New York studio, in the art21 *New York Close Up* episode "Diana al-Hadid's Studio Boom.") The figures themselves (all headless) are based on figures that al-Hadid has found in various Mannerist and northern Renaissance paintings. Placed as they are in the architecture of the piece, they create an odd disjunction of scale. It is as if al-Hadid has rendered in sculpture the bodies in the foreground of a painting at something close to life-size, at the same time that she has brought forward the painting's background landscape and cityscape, much smaller in the painting because reduced by perspective, without changing their relative size. In other words, the near and the far are collapsed into a single space. The work in fact takes its title from Giambattista Nolli, the eighteenth-century Italian surveyor who in 1748 created a map of Rome that, even as it demarcated the streets, squares, and buildings of the city, revealed the interior spaces of major public buildings like churches and palaces. For Nolli, the city was a series of enclosed spaces—the open street or square as enclosed as the church interior or monastery courtyard. And perhaps it is this sense of containment, the body trapped in a multiplicity of spaces—physical, historical, and perhaps psychological—that is al-Hadid's subject.

In fact, in the contemporary world we are bombarded by a multiplicity of discontinuous and contradictory experiences of the kind that Robert Venturi, Denise Scott Brown, and Steven Izenour identified as central to contemporary life in their book *Learning from Las Vegas*

Fig. 20-29 Fiona Rae, *I'm Learning to Fly!!*, 2006. Oil and acrylic on canvas, 7 ft. × 5 ft. 9 in.

(see Fig. 7-33). It is just this very plurality of things that British artist Fiona Rae incorporates into her paintings. She is especially fond of images of the transfer decals popular among Japanese schoolgirls—in the case of *I'm Learning to Fly!!* (**Fig. 20-29**), 11 multicolored Bambi-like deer and 18 black hearts. These pop-culture images climb over and around an array of brushmarks in almost every idiom—Abstract Expressionist drips, Baroque ribbons, feathery gestures, heavily layered impasto, cartoonish outlines, a grid of narrow vertical and horizontal lines, and an area of apparent airbrushing. In the end, her painting reflects an all-inclusiveness and heterogeneity, admitting into the surface anything and everything.

The Global Present

"Language is a virus," declared American author William S. Burroughs, referring, at least in part, to the fact that American English had by then become the international language of business, politics, the media, and culture—a plague upon indigenous languages that threatened their

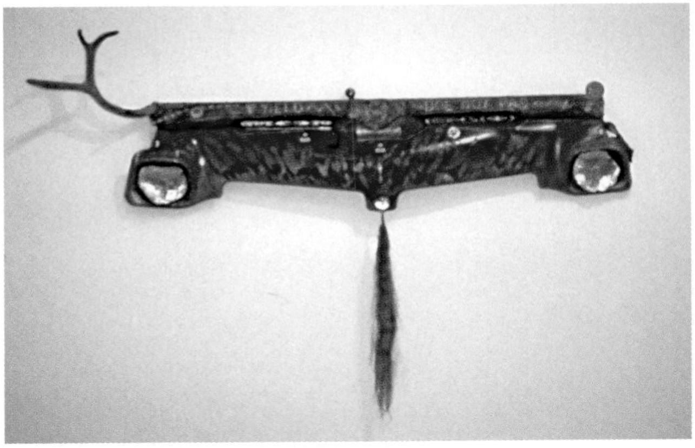

Fig. 20-30 Jimmie Durham, *Headlights*, 1983. Car parts, antler, shell, etc. Private collection.

extinction. In Asia and Africa, in the Latino, Hispanic, and Native American worlds, and in Muslim societies, artists have responded by acknowledging that life in a global culture increasingly demands that they accept multiple identities.

Although we normally think of the Western world's impact on these other cultures in negative terms—in the process of Westernization, ancient customs are lost, and cultural artifacts are looted and carried off for display in Western museums—many non-Western artists have incorporated the art of the West into their own art in positive ways. As Native American artist Jimmie Durham has put it, "We took glass beads, horses, wool blankets, wheat flour for frybread, etc., very early, and immediately made them identifiably 'Indian' things. We are able to do that because of our cultural integrity and because our societies are dynamic and able to take in new ideas." Similarly, the aboriginal painters of Australia have adopted the use of acrylic paint, integrating the medium into their own cultural traditions (see Fig. 2-12). Durham himself makes what he calls "fake Indian artifacts." Categorically non-Native American materials, such as the bright chrome automobile fender depicted here (**Fig. 20-30**), are transformed into something that looks completely Indian. But the cultural forces at work are highly complex. As much as Native American culture has the ability to absorb Western materials and make them its own, anything a Native American makes, Durham knows, is always seen by the dominant Anglo-American culture as an "artifact," a surviving fragment of a "lost" people that does not quite qualify as "art" proper. His "fake" artifacts expose this assumption.

1973

1973–74
Energy crisis in Western countries

South Vietnam falls to Vietcong
1975

Fig. 20-31 David P. Bradley (White Earth Oijbwe, and Mdewakaton Dakota), *Indian Country Today*, 1996–97. Acrylic on canvas, 6 × 5 ft. Peabody Essex Museum, Salem, Massachusetts.

Museum Purchase through the Mr. and Mrs. James Krebs Fund, E300409. © Peabody Essex Museum, Salem, Massachusetts, USA/Bridgeman Images. © David P. Bradley.

In his *Indian Country Today* (**Fig. 20-31**), Native American artist David Bradley depicts a traditional kachina dance taking place in the plaza of the pueblo. Performed by male dancers who impersonate kachinas, the spirits who inhabit the clouds, rain, crops, animals, and even ideas such as growth and fertility, the dances are sacred and, although tourists are allowed to view them, photography is strictly prohibited. The actual masks worn in ceremonies are not considered art objects by the Pueblo people. Rather, they are thought of as active agents in the transfer of power and knowledge between the gods and the men who wear them in the dance. Kachina figurines are made for sale to tourists, but they are considered empty of any ritual power or significance (see Fig. 21-3). This commercialization of native tradition is further

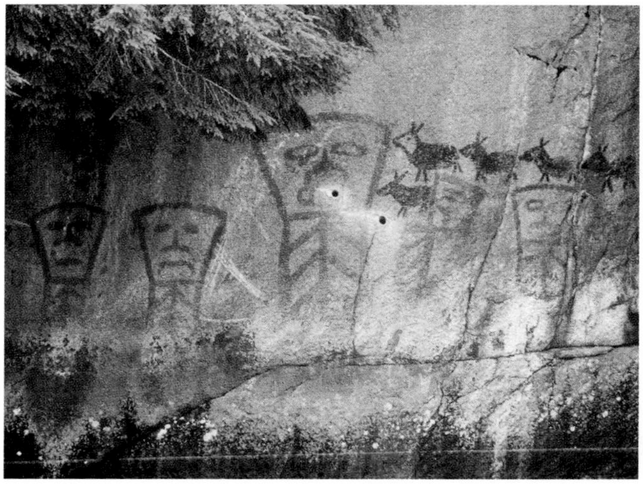

Fig. 20-32 Mollie Wilson, Kwakwaka'wakw pictograph recording a 1927 potlatch showing coppers and cows, Kingcome Inlet, 1927. Wall painting, 6 × 30 ft.

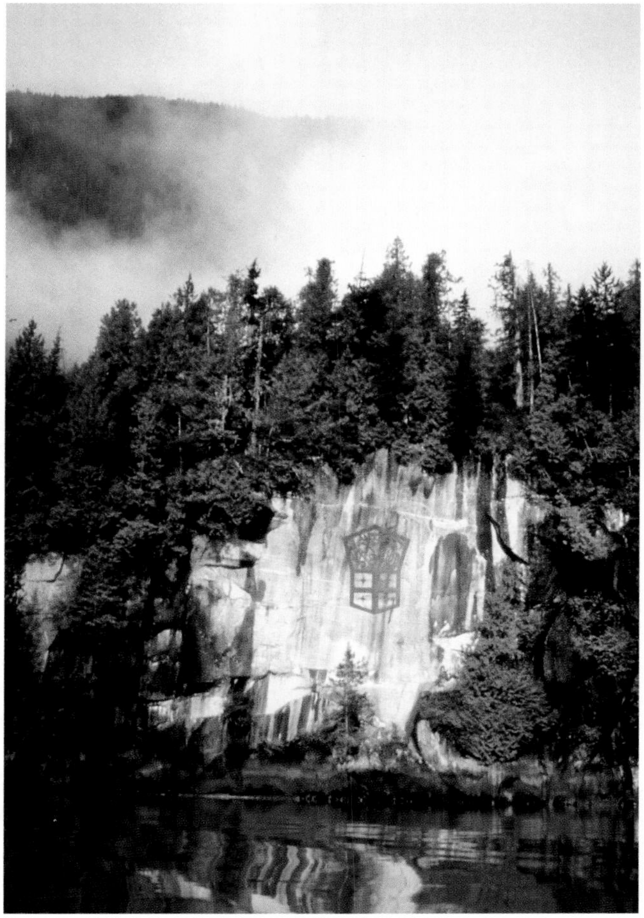

Fig. 20-33 Marianne Nicholson, Kwakwaka'wakw pictograph of a copper on a cliff near Kingcome, 1998. Red oxide paint, 28 × 38 ft.

imaged by the train passing behind the pueblo—the Santa Fe Railroad's *Chief*. Behind the train, at the right, is the Four Corners Power Plant, in northwestern New Mexico, one of the largest coal-fired generating stations in the United States and one of the greatest polluters, spewing smoke into the air. Behind the power plant is an open-pit strip mine. The city of Santa Fe—a major tourist attraction—and a Native American-run casino, its parking lot full of buses, occupy the left side of the image. But overlooking all is a giant mesa, with kachina-like eyes and mouth, suggesting that even in the contemporary world, where tradition and progress appear to be in a state of constant tension, the spirits still oversee and protect their peoples.

The return to tradition has, in fact, become a central theme of Native American art. This is especially true in the Pacific Northwest, where for generations cultural traditions were systematically suppressed by both the United States and Canadian governments. In 1884, for instance, the Canadian government banned the potlatch ceremonies long practiced by Northwest tribes. These ceremonies, hosted by a chief, revolved around major life events such as marriage, assumption of leadership, or death. The presentation and consumption of food was an important part of the ceremony, and so was the display of art—carved bowls and spoons for the food, masks, garments, and headdresses for performances—all designed to underscore the chief's wealth, the principal symbol of which was the copper. A copper is a shield-shaped plaque made of beaten metal (originally from the Copper River, across the Gulf of Alaska from Anchorage). A pictographic representation of a 1927 Kwakwaka'wakw potlatch, conducted in defiance of Canadian law in Kingcome Inlet, off Queen Charlotte Strait across from the north end of Vancouver Island, contains a series of coppers, as well as another symbol of wealth, cows purchased from white settlers that were cooked at the feast (**Fig. 20-32**). In 1998, Kwakwaka'wakw artist Marianne Nicholson received permission from the Kingcome community to stencil a giant copper on the face of a cliff that falls into the Inlet near her ancestral village of Gwayi (**Fig. 20-33**). The images on the copper include an image of the supernatural figure Wolf with a treasure chest, based on a Kwakwaka'wakw

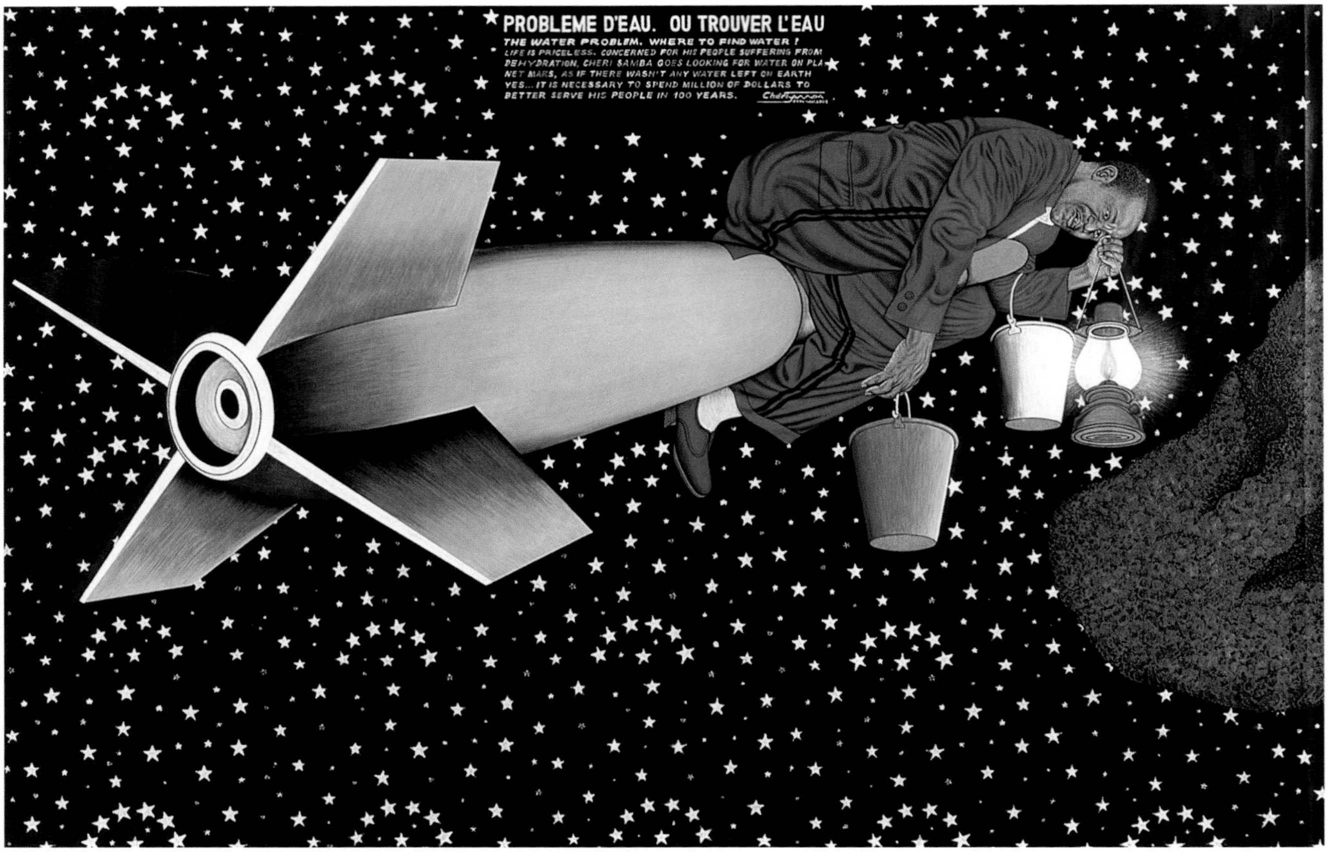

Fig. 20-34 Chéri Samba, *Problème d'eau. Où trouver l'eau?* (*The Water Problem. Where to Find Water?*), 2004. Acrylic on canvas, 4 ft. 5⅛ in. × 6 ft. 6¾ in. The Pigozzi Collection, Geneva.

story of the origins of the village of Gwayi itself, in which two wolves, transformed into humans, journey up Wakeman and Kingcome Inlets where they build houses, make canoes, and receive treasures of supernatural power. The first pictograph painted in the Inlet for over 60 years, it celebrates the continuing tradition of the potlatch by directly referencing the small 1927 coppers nearby. As Aldona Jonaitis, director of the University of Alaska Museum of the North, has put it in her book *Art of the Northwest Coast*, "This enormous representation of an image imbued with such cultural meaning makes a clear statement: this land is ours."

The political and social challenges facing indigenous populations worldwide are also the subject of Chéri Samba, whose narrative paintings of the despotic Mobutu regime in his native Zaire were treated earlier (see Fig. 3-6). In *Problème d'eau. Où trouver l'eau?* (*The Water Problem. Where to Find Water?*) (**Fig. 20-34**), a text block at the top of the painting reads: "Life is priceless. Concerned for his people suffering from dehydration, Chéri Samba goes looking for water on Planet Mars, as if there wasn't any water left on Earth. Yes . . . it is necessary to spend million [*sic*] of dollars to better serve his people in 100 years." Samba's self-appointed superhero status, emphasized by the phallic missile that he straddles, is blatantly absurd in light of the thousands of refugees who died of dehydration on the Rwanda/Zaire border during the Rwanda civil war in the mid-1990s, and subsequent war between Ugandan and Rwandan forces in Zaire itself. He assumes the attitude, that is, of the United States, spending millions upon millions of dollars for space exploration—to discover only trace particles of water on Mars—while millions die for lack of water in Africa.

Fig. 20-35 Shahzia Sikander, *Pleasure Pillars*, 2001. Watercolor, dry pigment, vegetable color, tea, and ink on wasli paper, 12 × 10 in. Collection of Amita and Purnendu Chatterjee.
Courtesy of the artist.

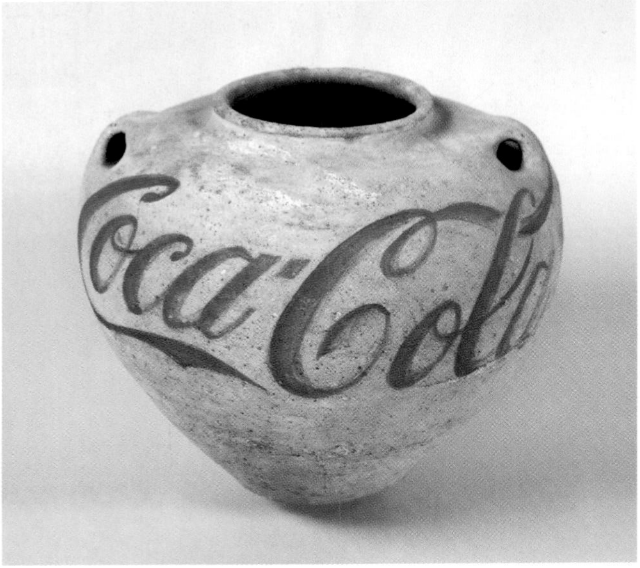

Fig. 20-36 Ai Weiwei, *Han Dynasty Urn with Coca-Cola Logo*, 1994. Paint and Han dynasty urn, 10 × 11 × 11 in.
© Ai Weiwei. Courtesy of Mary Boone Gallery, New York.

Combining her training as a miniature artist in her native Pakistan with her graduate studies at the Rhode Island School of Design, Shahzia Sikander addresses the heterogeneity of her own background in works such as *Pleasure Pillars* (**Fig. 20-35**). In the center of the composition is a self-portrait with spiraling horns. Below it are two bodies, one a Western Venus, the other the Hindu goddess of fertility, rain, health, and nature, Devi, who is said to hold the entire universe in her womb (see Fig. 17-23). Between them two hearts pump blood—perhaps a reference to Frida Kahlo's *Las Dos Fridas* (*The Two Fridas*) (see Fig. 7-5), her Western inspiration, just as the dancers surrounding her self-portrait are her Eastern inspiration. Western and Eastern images of power also inform the image—the fighter jet at the top of the image and the image of a lion killing a deer at the bottom left, copied from an Iranian miniature of the Safavid dynasty (1499–1736).

The rapid economic expansion of China in the new global economy has been the subject of many works by Ai Weiwei. Ai first came to the United States in 1981, and lived in New York's East Village, absorbing particularly the critique of commodity fetishism implied in the work of the Pop artists and a younger generation of American artists that included Jeff Koons (see Fig. 12-19). Since returning to China in 1993, he has worked as a political activist, focusing particularly on the government's censorship of the Internet. In 2009, the government shut down his blog; in 2011, it held him under arrest for 81 days, ostensibly for "economic crimes"; and in 2012, just before his major retrospective at the Smithsonian Institution's Hirshhorn Museum (which he was not allowed to attend), it closed his Beijing company, through which he makes and distributes most of his work. One of his principal strategies as an artist has been to transform historical artifacts in gestures that traditional Chinese historians consider vandalism. In 1994, for instance, he carved and painted the Coca-Cola logo on a 2,000-year-old Han dynasty urn (**Fig. 20-36**). The gesture is an ironic commentary on the tension between cultural and economic values in contemporary society.

Japanese artist Kohei Nawa addresses the interface between technology and nature, specifically the digital

Fig. 20-37 Kohei Nawa, *PixCell-Deer #24*, 2011. Mixed media; taxidermied deer with artificial crystal glass, 6 ft. 8$^{11}/_{16}$ in. × 4 ft. 11⅛ in. × 6 ft. 6¾ in. Metropolitan Museum of Art, New York.
2011.493a–j. Purchase, Acquisitions Fund and Peggy and Richard M. Danziger Gift, 2011. © 2015 Kohei Nawa. Image copyright Metropolitan Museum of Art/Art Resource/Scala, Florence.

and the organic, in works such as his *PixCell-Deer 24* (**Fig. 20-37**). Nawa's "pixcells" are transparent glass beads of various sizes that he applies over the entire surface of objects—quite often, as in this case, taxidermied deer—purchased from the Internet, where he first encountered them digitally as pixels. When the taxidermied animal actually arrives at his studio, it insists, somewhat disturbingly, on the actuality of its skin and bones—on the integrity, that is, of its organic, molecular cell structure. By covering the animal with his "pixcell" beads, the animal's form is fragmented into myriad surfaces of light and reflection, a thousand microvisions in which the natural body is both magnified and distorted into a new organism from which emanates a translucent—and transcendent—light, reminiscent of the deer's role, in the Japanese cultural tradition, as sacred companion to the ancient sages.

Revisioning History

As the world of art has become increasingly diverse and plural in character, African-American voices have become increasingly prominent, and among the most influential have been Kara Walker (see Figs. 7-20, 9-31, and 9-32), Carrie Mae Weems, and Kerry James Marshall. Each has, in different ways, consciously engaged with the past, in order to more fully articulate the parameters of African-American experience in the United States.

In the early 1990s, Weems came across a series of photographs of African-American slaves housed in Harvard University's Peabody Museum of Archaeology and Ethnology. Their history proved at once tragic and revealing. In 1850, four years after moving to the United States in order to assume the position of professor of zoology and geology at Harvard University, Louis Agassiz, arguably the most respected scientific figure of the day, whose studies of glaciology, for instance, had led him to be the first to propose that the earth had once endured an Ice Age, commissioned J. T. Zealy to take a series of photographs of slaves on a plantation in South Carolina to use as scientific visual evidence to support his theories on the physical differences among the races. Agassiz believed that the different races arose separately in the different climatic zones of the world, and that they were by no means equal. "It

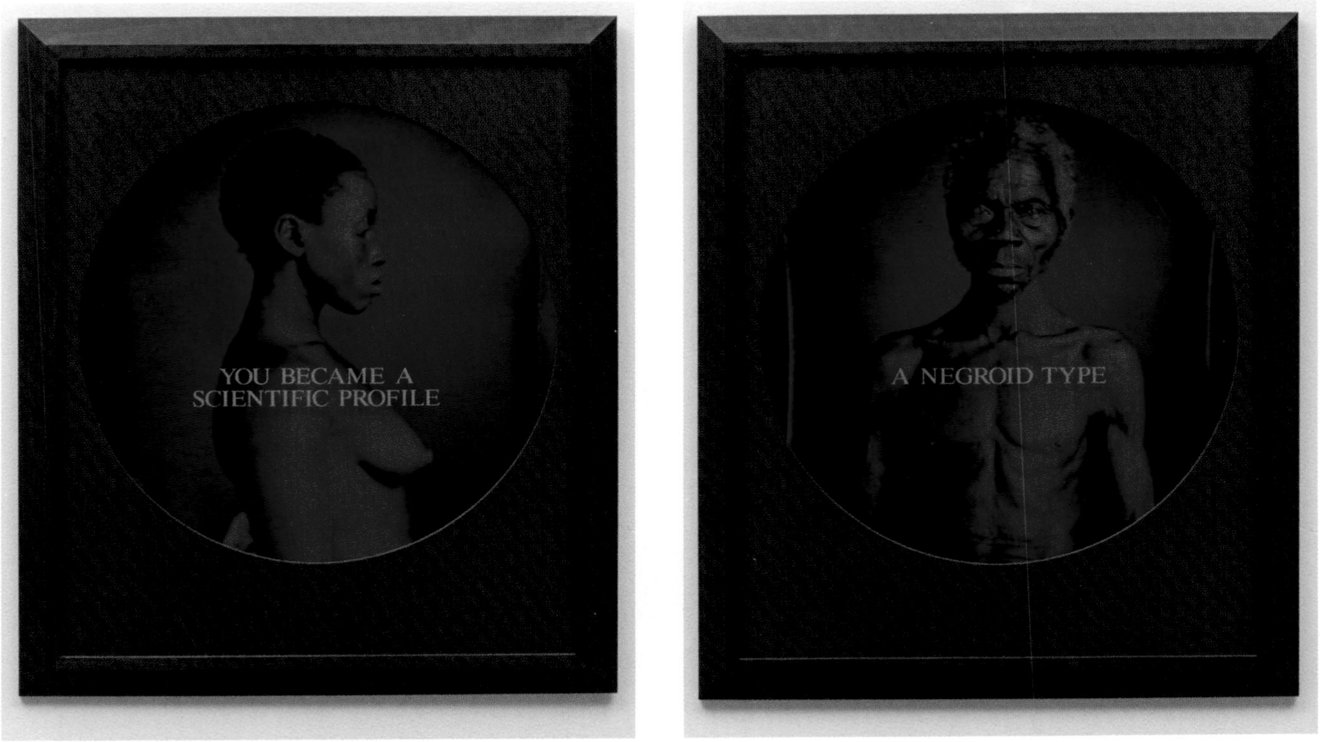

Fig. 20-38 Carrie Mae Weems, *You Became a Scientific Profile & A Negroid Type*, from the series *From Here I Saw What Happened and I Cried*, 1995. Chromographic color prints with sandblasted text on glass, 25⅝ × 22¾ in. Museum of Modern Art, New York.
Courtesy of the artist and Jack Shainman Gallery, New York.

is impossible for me to repress the feeling," he wrote in 1846, upon seeing African Americans for the first time in Philadelphia,

> that they are not the same blood as us. In seeing their black faces with their thick lips and grimacing teeth, the wool on their head, their bent knees, their elongated hands, the large curved nails, and especially the livid color of the palms of their hands, I could not take my eyes off their faces in order to tell them to stay far away.

Weems appropriated these images, enlarged them, reshot them through a red lens, placed them in circular mats to echo the camera lens, and put them behind glass onto which she etched words that revealed Agassiz's intentions (**Fig. 20-38**). The two images reproduced here are the second and third in the series, identified in the Peabody's files as "Delia, born in the USA of enslaved African parents, daughter of Renty, Congo," and "Renty, Congo, Plantation of B. F. Taylor, Esq."—in other words, the daughter and her father. "When we're looking at these images," Weems has said, "we're looking at the ways in which Anglo America—white America—saw itself in relationship to the black subject. I wanted to intervene in that by giving a voice to a subject that historically has had no voice." A photographer herself, Weems is exploring in these works something of the power of the camera lens and the authority that the photograph can assert for itself as seemingly "objective" evidence. But there is nothing "objective" about these photographs. Rather, they played a key role in supporting and arguably prolonging slavery.

Kerry James Marshall has concentrated on depicting African-American life and history throughout his career. (In two different art21 *Exclusive* videos, "Being an Artist" and "Black Romantic," Marshall discusses what it means to be a black artist.) His *Many Mansions* (**Fig. 20-39**), one of a series of paintings inspired by Marshall's observation that so many public housing projects in the United States have "garden" in their names, is a meditation on African-American experience. This painting depicts

1990

Nelson Mandela released from prison in South Africa **1990**

Reunification of East and West Germany; Berlin Wall torn down **1990**

Operation Desert Storm in Iraq **1991**

Collapse of the Soviet Union **1991**

World Trade Center bombed **1993**

Nelson Mandela becomes president of South Africa **1994**

Fig. 20-39 Kerry James Marshall, *Many Mansions*, 1994. Acrylic and collage on unstretched canvas, 9 ft. 6 in. × 11 ft. 3 in.
Courtesy of Jack Shainman Gallery, New York.

Chicago's Stateway Gardens (officially known as IL2-22, as inscribed at the top right of Marshall's work), an immense complex of eight high-rise apartment buildings on Chicago's South Side. Three young men in white shirts and ties are working in the garden in what is at once an ironic commentary on the virtual impossibility of transforming the concrete urban environment into a garden and a sincere attempt on Marshall's part to contradict the false, negative image of the African-American male. At the left, two bluebirds support a banner that reads "Bless Our Happy Home." Floating above the entire scene is a red ribbon that reads "In My Mother's House There Are Many Mansions." An adaptation of a biblical passage from the Gospel of John that begins "In my father's house . . .", it is a reference to the matriarchal structure of urban African-American culture. Easter baskets embody the promise of hope and renewal even as they project a crass materialism. As is typical of his work, Marshall is unwilling to adopt a single point of view, and he embraces the ironies sustained in the painting's very contradictions.

Such ironies are also the subject of Enrique Chagoya's *Crossing I* (**Fig. 20-40**), which draws on pop imagery to address the cultural, political, and psychological "borderland" that lies between Mexico and the United States. Born in Mexico in 1953, Chagoya immigrated to the

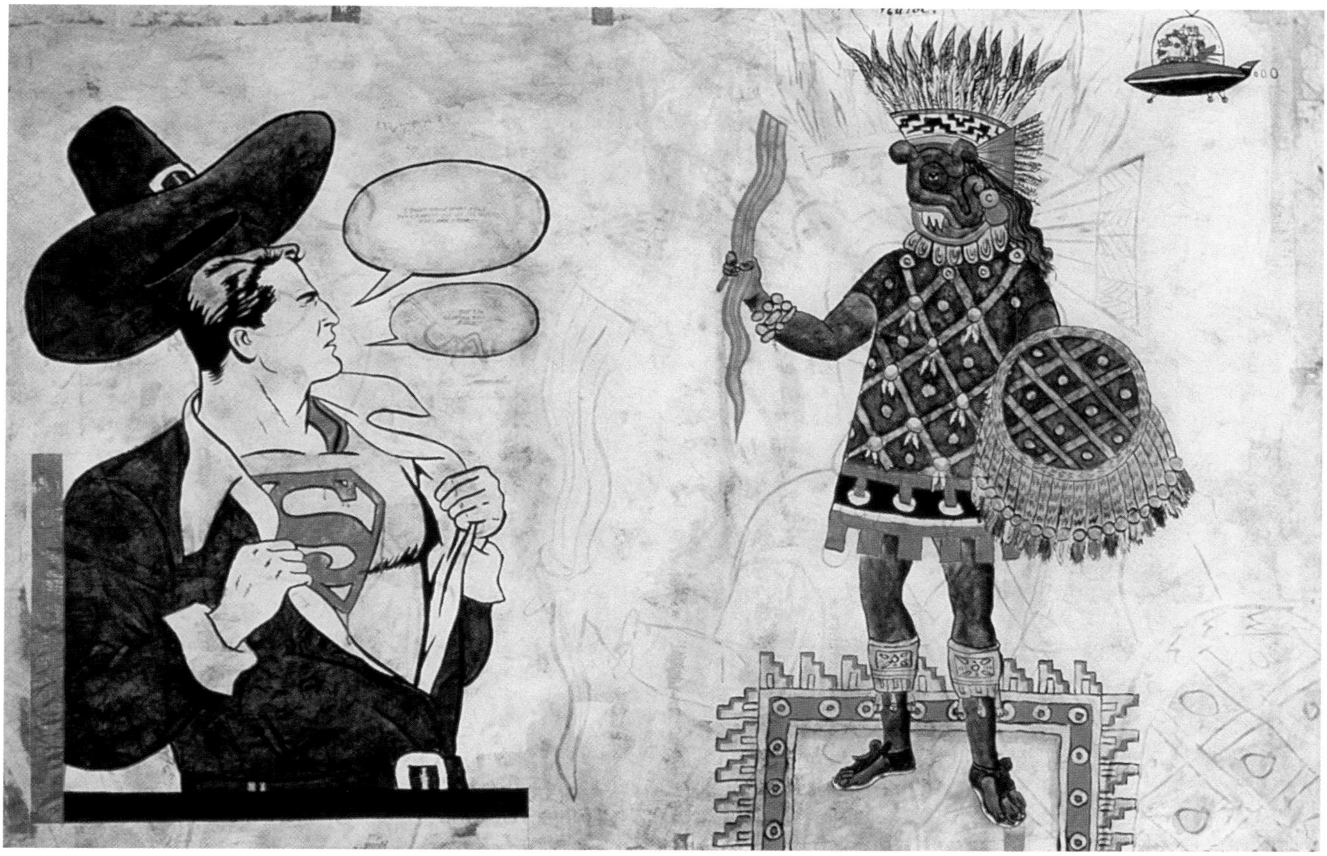

Fig. 20-40 Enrique Chagoya, *Crossing I*, 1994. Acrylic and oil on paper, 4 × 6 ft. Collection of Julia and Thomas Lanigan, Upper Monclair, New Jersey.
Photo: Rubén Guzmán; © Enrique Chagoya.

United States when he was 24 years of age, and became a United States citizen in 2000. "I integrate diverse elements," Chagoya says, "from pre-Columbian mythology, Western religious iconography, ethnic stereotypes, ideological propaganda from various times and places, American popular culture, etc. The art becomes a product of [these] collisions." Here, the gods of two cultures confront each other—Superman, shedding his Puritan outerwear, and Tlaloc, the Aztec god of fertility and rain, lightning bolt in hand. Superman exclaims, in the top bubble, "I don't know what hole you crawled out of or where you came from . . ." and in the bottom bubble, beside the faint outline of Clark Kent's glasses, ". . . but I'm sending you back!" An "alien" spacecraft, occupied by Quetzalcóatl, the Aztec god whom, in 1519, Motecuhzoma believed the invading Hernán Cortés to be—a devastating case of mistaken identity—backs Tlaloc up. Pop Art meets the indigenous Aztec style, itself largely destroyed by zealous missionaries intent on Christianizing the native population. While the outcome of this confrontation is hardly in doubt—the modern world will overcome the traditional one—Chagoya's design underscores the fact that it was the Puritans (and the Spanish) who were the first "alien" invaders of the Americas.

Identity, Media, and the Art Market

One of the most important of the political voices to emerge in the last half of the twentieth century was that of feminism. Since the early 1970s, when the feminist movement began to take hold in this country, women had played an increasingly vital role in defining the issues and directions of contemporary art. An important aspect of feminist art has been its critique of traditional ways of seeing—ways of seeing prescribed and institutionalized by men. As our assumptions and expectations have become increasingly

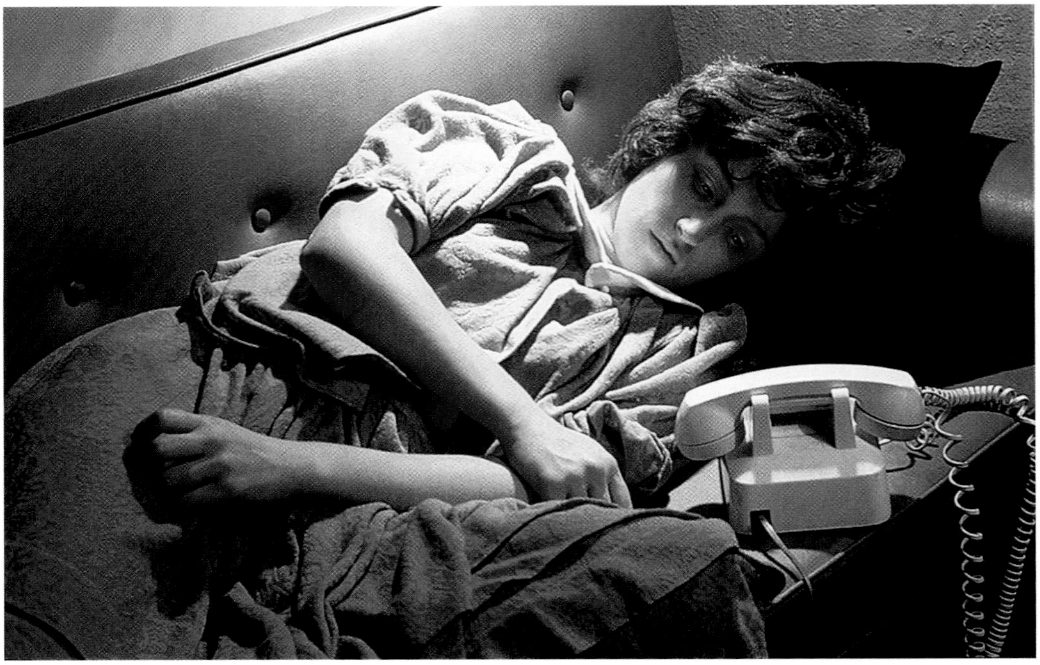

Fig. 20-41 Cindy Sherman, *Untitled #96*, 1981. Chromogenic color print, 24 in. × 4 ft.
Courtesy of the artist and Metro Pictures, New York.

challenged, the art world has become increasingly unbound by any rules or by any ruling "isms." Artists can draw on personal experiences or stylistic trends and address their work to a wide audience or a relatively narrow one. But one overriding characteristic of contemporary art is its struggle with the question of identity. Cindy Sherman's untitled photographs, for instance, are self-portraits (**Fig. 20-41**), sometimes presented at the scale of the film still and other times at the scale of a large poster. They are actually performances that address the ways in which our culture "views" women. In this case, we are witness to a highly ironic, if empathetic, display of female passivity.

The implication is that Sherman's life, and by extension our own, is a series of performances; that, chameleonlike, we change identities as readily as we change our clothes, picking and choosing who we are from media images. The mass media—from television and video to electronic signboards and commercial photography—are increasingly not only the means of contemporary art but its subject. Barbara Kruger's word-and-photograph pieces relate to billboard imagery, but they continue the feminist imperative of contemporary art, addressing issues of gender. In *Untitled (We won't play nature to your culture)* (**Fig. 20-42**), Kruger exposes the traditional nature/culture dichotomy for what it is—a strategy that authorizes the cultural and

Fig. 20-42 Barbara Kruger, *Untitled (We won't play nature to your culture)*, 1983. Photograph, 6 × 4 ft.
Courtesy of Mary Boone Gallery, New York.

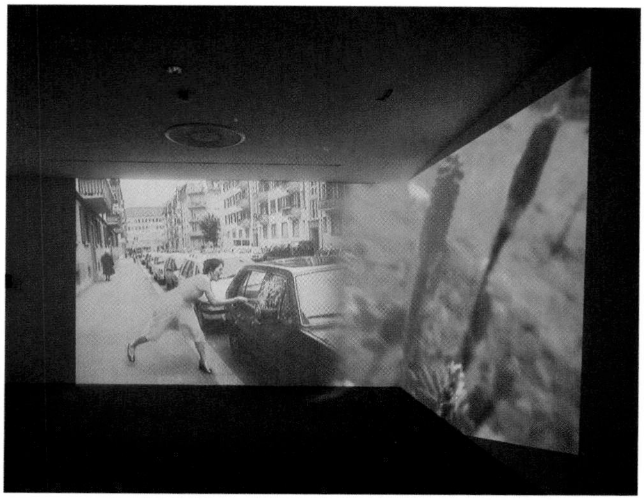

Fig. 20-43 Pipilotti Rist, *Ever Is Over All*, 1997. Two-channel video with overlapping projections (color, sound with Anders Guggisberg). Museum of Modern Art, New York.

Fractional gift offered by Donald L. Bryant, Jr., 241.2000.b. © 2015. Digital image, Museum of Modern Art, New York/Scala, Florence. © 2014 Pipilotti Rist.

Fig. 20-44 Raymond Pettibon, *No Title (The bright flatness)*, 2003. Watercolor on paper, 39 × 38½ in. Museum of Modern Art, New York.

Judith Rothschild Foundation Contemporary Drawings Collection Gift, 2736.2005. © 2015. Digital image, Museum of Modern Art, New York/Scala, Florence. © 2015 Raymond Pettibon. Courtesy of David Zwirner, New York.

intellectual domination of the male over a passive and yielding female nature.

But there is nothing passive and yielding about the female character in the video installation *Ever Is Over All* (**Fig. 20-43**), made in 1997 by Swiss-born Pipilotti Rist. First screened at the Venice Biennale in 1997, one side of the double-projection video portrays a field of kniphofia, more commonly known as red-hot pokers. On the other side of the projection, a woman walks down a street, wearing a conservative blue dress and bright red shoes à la Dorothy in *The Wizard of Oz*. She is carrying a single stem of kniphofia. A soft, even soothing "la, la, la" of song accompanies her. With a broad smile on her face, she lifts the long-stemmed flower in her hand and smashes it into the passenger window of a parked car. Glass shatters. She moves on, smashing more car windows. Up from behind her comes a uniformed woman police officer, who passes by with a smiling salute. Her stroll down the boulevard plays in a continuous loop in the gallery. This is, apparently, the new Oz, the Emerald City that we discover "somewhere over the rainbow," where the tensions between nature and culture, violence and pleasure, the legal and the criminal, impotence and power, all seem to have dissolved.

One way to think of Rist's video installation is to recognize in it the collapse of any meaningful distinction between high and low culture. Not only have artists mined popular culture for subject matter, generally to critique it, but popular culture has convincingly asserted its place in the art world on its own terms. Based in southern California, Raymond Pettibon began his career in the late 1970s publishing self-designed "zines," small-circulation magazines—at first printed offset and later with Xerox—a form he has continued to practice. At about the same time he began to design album covers and 8½ × 11-inch concert flyers, at first for the punk band Black Flag, for which his brother, Greg Ginn, played lead guitar, and then for nearly every important punk band on the West Coast. Soon his repertoire included skateboards, surfboards, T-shirts, posters, and stickers, and he developed a vast following in the Los Angeles punk scene. In 1992, curator Paul Schimmel included him in the exhibition *Helter Skelter: L.A. Art in the 1990s* at the Los Angeles Museum of Contemporary Art, and his artworld career took off from there. His subjects are often deeply political, even dark in their critique of current events, but surfing is a recurring theme, one in which he seems to find a modicum of peace. Below the giant breaking wave in this drawing (**Fig. 20-44**), dwarfing the surfer on his red board beneath, he has written: "The bright flatness of the California landscape needs a dark vaulted interior." That interior space lies in the barrel or tube of the wave.

Fig. 20-45 Banksy, *Kissing Coppers*, ca. 2005. Spray paint on wall, various sites, Brighton and London, U.K.
© Michael Shuttleworth/Alamy.

Fig. 20-46 Jennifer Allora and Guillermo Calzadilla, *Algorithm*, 2011. ATM, pipe organ, and computer, 19 ft. 4⅜ in. × 10 ft. ⅛ in. × 4 ft. 11⅛ in.
© Allora&Calzadill, courtesy of Gladstone Gallery, New York and Brussels.

Perhaps no popular art style has more thoroughly entered the art world than graffiti. The example of Jean-Michel Basquiat (see Fig. 2-19) is a case in point. But the pseudonymous British graffiti artist Banksy has taken the form to a new level, stenciling his work on walls across Great Britain (**Fig. 20-45**). "Despite what they say," he writes in his 2006 book *Banksy: Wall and Piece*, "graffiti is not the lowest form of art . . . it's actually one of the more honest art forms available. There is no elitism of hype, it exhibits on the best walls a town has to offer and nobody is put off by the price of admission." The lowest form of art, he says, is corporate: "The people who truly deface our neighborhoods are the companies that scrawl giant slogans across buildings and buses trying to make us feel inadequate unless we buy their stuff." Banksy's exact identity remains a matter of speculation, but his work is so widely revered that all London art museum bookstores stock Martin Bull's *Banksy Locations & Tours: A Collection of Graffiti Locations and Photographs in London, England*, first published in 2006, with a new edition being issued almost yearly since.

A large part of Banksy's popularity lies in the fact that he eschews the art marketplace altogether. In fact, in the fall of 2013, Banksy had an elderly man tend a stall in New York's Central Park offering the artist's works for $60 each. But the market is a driving force in today's art world, a fact reinforced by the Puerto Rico-based team of Jennifer Allora and Guillermo Calzadilla. When the two were chosen to represent the United States at the 2011 Venice Biennale, they proposed what has been called a "neo-surrealistic" installation of six works under the overall title *Gloria*, referencing, according to the accompanying catalogue, "military, religious, Olympic, economic, and cultural grandeur, as well as the numerous pop songs the word has inspired." They took a number of "everyday" objects—a tank, a sunbed, a copy of Thomas Crawford's 1855 *Statue of Freedom* that crowns the dome of the Capitol building

Fig. 20-47 Phil Collins, Part one of The Smiths karaoke trilogy, *The World Won't Listen*, 2004–07. Still. Color video projection with sound, 58 min.
Courtesy of Shady Lane Productions, Berlin, and Tanya Bonakdar Gallery, New York.

in Washington, D.C., state-of-the-art business-class seats from Delta and American Airlines, an ATM, and a pipe organ—and transformed them into absurd and strange objects that force viewers to reconsider these markers of "cultural grandeur." *Algorithm* (**Fig. 20-46**) consists of a working ATM attached to the pipe organ so that every time a visitor uses the machine to get cash, make a deposit, check a balance, or transfer funds, a unique musical score is generated, based on an algorithmic procedure developed by composer Jonathan Bailey, and quoting, according to Bailey, "a wide variety of musical motifs from short individual notes to complex sequences of chords, melodies, as well as instructions to modify the tonality of the organ itself." Each transaction becomes a kind of surreal version of Beethoven's *Ode to Joy*, celebrating, to the generally perverse delight of the visitor, his or her participation in the global network of international commerce.

It is, finally, this sense of an increasingly global culture that defines the art world a decade into the twenty-first century, a fact underscored by English artist Phil Collins's video trilogy *The World Won't Listen*. Beginning in 2004, Collins created posters inviting people to perform karaoke renditions of all the songs from The Smiths' classic 1987 album *The World Won't Listen*, first in Bogotá, Colombia, then in Istanbul, Turkey, and finally in Jakarta and Bandung, Indonesia. From November 2007 through March 2008, the three 58-minute videos of the performances were screened simultaneously in three connected rooms at the Dallas Museum of Art.

"In all the locations," Collins told the Dallas Museum's curator of contemporary art, Suzanne Weaver, "some people had a very rudimentary grasp of English. But they knew the songs so devastatingly well through repetition, every breath and every ad lib, which, considering the importance of lyrics in the songs . . . is pretty amazing." The performers sing in front of travelogue leisure-world backdrops (**Fig. 20-47**) ranging from lakeside villas to tropical resorts to American national parks, each entering, as they sing, even if only for a moment, the glamorous world of pop idolatry. "Other people sometimes find karaoke embarrassing, or laughable, or delusional," Collins explains, "but I find it moving and incredibly courageous. . . . It's like a mild form of heroism." What Collins's trilogy suggests, finally, is a human community of far-flung "fans," but believers, too, in lyrics like those that conclude the song "Rubber Ring", in which, The Smiths remind us, we should never forget the songs that have saved our lives.

THE CRITICAL PROCESS

Thinking about Art Today

What is the role of art today? What does the museum offer us? Is it merely a repository of cultural artifacts? Or can it help us to understand not only our past, but our present and our future? These are questions that museum professionals are asking themselves, and questions that students of art might well ask themselves as well.

Consider Olafur Eliasson's installation *The Weather Project* (**Fig. 20-48**). When it was installed in the mammoth Turbine Hall of the Tate Modern, London, in the winter of 2003, it was roundly criticized as "mere" entertainment, in no small part because it attracted over 2 million visitors. At the end of the 500-foot hall hung a giant yellow orb, 90 feet above the floor. The ceiling itself was covered with mirrors, thus doubling the size of the space. The "sun" was actually a semicircle of some 200 yellow sodium streetlights, which, when reflected in the ceiling mirrors, formed a circle. Artificial mist machines filled the hall with a dull, wintry fog. What was the attraction?

Fig. 20-48 Olafur Eliasson, *The Weather Project*, 2003. Installation view, Tate Modern, London. Monofrequency lights, projection foil, haze machine, mirror oil, aluminum, and scaffolding.
Courtesy of the artist, Tanya Bonakdar Gallery, New York, and neugerriemschneider, Berlin.

In no small part, it seemed to reside in the very artificiality of the environment. Visitors to the top floor of the gallery could easily see the trussing supporting the mirrored ceiling as well as the means by which Eliasson had constructed the sun shape. The extraordinary visual effects of Eliasson's installation were, in the end, created by rather ordinary means. But this ordinariness, in turn, suggested profound and somewhat disturbing truths about our world. If Eliasson could create this almost post-apocalyptic environment—with its dead, heatless sun, perpetual fog, and cold stone ground—with such minimal means, what might we, as a world, create with the advanced technologies so readily at our disposal? In other words, as viewers lay on the floor of the museum and saw themselves reflected on the ceiling above, were they viewing themselves in the present, or seeing themselves in the future? What hath humanity wrought?

The Weather Project was, then, something of a chilling experience, both literally and figuratively. "I prefer to regard the institution," Eliasson has said, "as a place where one steps even deeper into society, from where one can scrutinize society." It is perhaps relevant for you to consider writings about art of the kind you are reading now as such spaces too. To conclude, what is it about your world that you have come to understand and appreciate more deeply and fully?

Thinking Back

20.1 Distinguish between Cubism, Fauvism, German Expressionism, and Futurism.

For the Cubist, art was primarily about form. Analyzing the object from all sides and acknowledging the flatness of the picture plane, the Cubist painting represented the three-dimensional world in increasingly two-dimensional terms. How did Cubism free painting?

The Fauves, led by Henri Matisse, emphasized the expressive possibilities of color freed of representational ends, while the German Expressionists believed that through color and line works of art could express the feelings and emotions of the artist directly to the viewer. How did Kandinsky's work move toward abstraction?

In the words of its leader Filippo Marinetti, Futurism called for a new movement that would champion "a new beauty; the beauty of speed," which would replace traditional ideals of beauty. How did Futurist artists reflect the new art of film?

20.2 Explain the rise of Dada and the emergence of Surrealism.

Dada took up Futurism's call for the annihilation of tradition, but, as a result of World War I, without its sense of hope for the future. How did Marcel Duchamp's *Fountain* comment on the status of sculpture when it was first exhibited in 1917? The art of Surrealism was born of Dada's preoccupation with the irrational and the illogical, but the nihilist spirit of Dada was replaced by something more positive as the Surrealists turned to chance operations, automatism, and dream imagery—the expressions of the unconscious mind. What two types of imagery resulted?

20.3 Discuss how politics impinged on the art of Diego Rivera and Pablo Picasso in the 1930s.

Diego Rivera first responded to the events of the Mexican Revolution in his mural art, but, in 1930 to 1934, he worked in the United States. Why did Nelson Rockefeller destroy his mural *Man at the Crossroads*? In France, Picasso was deeply affected by the Fascists' bombing of the Basque city of Guernica. How does the painting titled *Guernica* reflect his interest in Surrealism?

20.4 Describe the reaction of both American modernist and Abstract Expressionist painters to European modernism.

How did painters like Lee Krasner react to Picasso's *Guernica*? Why did many American modernist painters retain a realist direction in their art? Nevertheless, a forceful brand of abstraction, Abstract Expressionism, developed in the United States in the early 1940s and 1950s. The term Abstract Expressionism groups together a number of painters dedicated to the expressive capacities of their individual gestures and styles. It is not stylistically unified in its approach. What is "action painting"? How did Mark Rothko approach painting?

20.5 Explain how Pop Art and Minimalism both responded to the example of Abstract Expressionism.

Pop Art was at least in part a reaction to the supposed authenticity of Abstract Expressionist gesture, and it reflected a sense that genuine American experience was not so much heartfelt as it was determined by the culture machine of Wall Street finance and Madison Avenue advertising. Pop represented life as America lived it, a world of Campbell's soup cans, Coca-Cola bottles, comic strips, and movie stars. Minimalist artworks address notions of space—how objects take up space and how the viewer relates to them spatially. Minimalist art directly reacts to the unmediated expression of action painting. How does Minimalist art contrast with Pop Art? How did Sol LeWitt regard his practice of painting?

20.6 Outline some of the major trends in contemporary art.

Contemporary art is distinguished by its acceptance of a plurality and heterogeneity of styles, sometimes even within the practice of a single artist, like Gerhard Richter, or in a single work. The art of the last 30 years has also focused on the collision of cultures that the increasingly global economy has fostered. How have Native American artists responded to the demands of a global culture? What forces in this global culture most interest Ai Weiwei? African Americans and Latino Americans have increasingly revisited and revisioned their own histories in the Americas. How have artists variously confronted questions of identity and the forces of the art market?

Left: **Statue of a discus thrower (*discobolus*), known as the *Townley Discobolus*, Roman period, 2nd century CE, after a lost Greek original of about 450–440 BCE by Myron, from the villa of the emperor Hadrian at Tivoli, Italy.** Marble, 5 ft. 6½ × 41$\frac{5}{16}$ × 24$\frac{13}{16}$ in. The British Museum, London. Right: **Sui Jianguo, *Discobolus*, 2012**. Bronze, painted white, height 6 ft. 8⅛ in. The British Museum, London.

Left: GR 1805,0703.43. © The Trustees of the British Museum. Right: 2012,5014.1. © Sui Jianguo Studio, courtesy Pace Gallery. Photo credit © The Trustees of the British Museum. © Sui Jianguo Studio, courtesy of Pace Gallery.

Part 5
The Themes of Art

Seeing Continuity and Change over Time

At the Olympic Games, which the Greeks first held in 776 BCE, all athletes performed nude, and these athletic contests gave rise to what might best be called a "cult of the body." The physically fit male not only won accolades in athletic contests; he also represented the conditioning and strength of the military forces of his particular city-state. The writings attributed to the so-called father of medicine, Hippocrates, who lived in Athens in the fifth century BCE, insist on the relationship between cause and effect in physical illness, the mind's ability to influence the physical body for good or ill, and the influence of diet and environment on physical health. In fact, for the Greeks, the beautiful body came to reflect not only physical but also mental superiority.

The body and its representation has been one of the most consistent themes in the history of art, and changes in the way that different cultures represent the body—or any other major theme, for that matter—can tell us much about the values of a particular time and place. The appearance of Sui Jianguo's *Discobolus* (*The Discus Thrower*) in the British Museum in the summer of 2012—the Classical *Townley Discobolus* resides in the Great Court of the museum—drives this point home. During Mao's Cultural Revolution in China virtually the only statues carved in China were of Mao himself. On June 4, 1989, when a group of young sculptors placed a "Goddess of Democracy" in Tiananmen Square facing Mao's portrait above the Tiananmen Gate, tanks cleared the square of protestors and crushed the sculpture. That same year, Sui Jianguo graduated from the Central Academy with a degree in sculpture, and, as China opened up to Western traditions (and capitalist economics) during the 1990s, he turned his attention to the gradual shift in Chinese culture that was taking place. A nude *discobolus* would still be a problematic proposition in China, but one wearing a *zhongshan* jacket—or Mao suit—captures the difficult transition that China is undergoing, even though his apparent dig at Mao's image might prove equally problematic.

This section focuses on seven major themes that reveal the same patterns of continuity and change:

- Spiritual Belief
- The Life Cycle
- Love and Sex
- The Body, Gender, and Identity
- The Individual and Cultural Identity
- Power
- Science, Technology, and the Environment

It would be possible to describe virtually every work of art in terms of these themes, which represent universal concerns that all creative people, in all cultures and at all times, have sought to explore and understand. If different cultures and different eras have inevitably addressed them differently, the quest to understand the world and our place in it is common to us all.

Chapter 21
Spiritual Belief

Learning Objectives

21.1 Compare the ways that different faiths have attempted to access spiritual states, and describe the role of art in these practices.

21.2 Outline some of the difficulties faced by various religions in giving their deities human form, and describe some strategies for overcoming these problems.

21.3 Characterize sacred space.

21.4 Explain why abstraction is particularly suitable for representing spiritual matters.

In 1768, when Captain James Cook sailed on the *Endeavour* from Plymouth, England, to explore the uncharted waters of the South Pacific, one of the most distinctive art forms that Cook and his crew encountered was tattooing, a word derived from *tatau*, the Tahitian term for the practice. One of Cook's crew, Sydney Parkinson, a young draftsman on board to record botanical species, captured the tattooed face of a Maori warrior during the voyage (**Fig. 21-1**). The Maori, who first inhabited the islands of New Zealand in about 900 CE, had imported the practice from the Polynesian islands to the north.

Tattooing is an aspect of complex sacred and ritual traditions found throughout the Pacific Islands. The islanders believed that many individuals, places, and objects were imbued with *mana*, a spiritual substance that is the manifestation of the gods on earth and that instills great power upon whomever or whatever carries it. Chiefs, considered descendants of the gods, were supposedly born with considerable quantities of *mana*, nobility with less, and commoners with almost none. A person might increase his or her *mana* by skillful or courageous acts, or by wearing certain items of dress, including tattoos. Thus, the warrior depicted by Parkinson possesses considerable *mana*.

Among the Maori—whose own name for tattooing is *ta moko*—the most sacred part of the body was the head, and so it was the most appropriate place for a tattoo. All high-ranking Maori were tattooed, including women (although less elaborately), and the first tattoos were inscribed during the rituals marking the passage into adulthood. As here, they generally consisted of broad, curving, parallel lines from nose to chin, spiral forms on the cheeks, and broad, parallel lines between the bridge of the nose and the ears following the curve of the brow. Their design mirrors the human form and is meant to celebrate it. The design was almost always bilaterally symmetrical, but each one was so distinctive that, after coming in contact with Western practice, many Maori began signing documents with them. The tattoo artist possessed great skill—and thus considerable *mana*. Using a bone chisel, the tattoo artist cut deeply into the skin. Pigment made from burnt Kauri gum or burnt vegetable caterpillars was then pushed into the cuts by tapping, the sound of which, "ta-ta," gives the process its name.

The Maori thought of the tattoo as art. For them, the first artists were the Maori gods, but over time the gods designated certain distinguished humans, possessing large quantities of *mana*, as *tohunga*, a word that literally

Fig. 21-1 Sydney Parkinson, *Portrait of a Maori*, 1769. Wash drawing, 15½ × 11⅝ in., later engraved and published as Plate XVI in Parkinson's *Journal*, 1773. British Library, London.

means "expert," but in common usage designates a priest. The gods, it was believed, used these *tohunga* as their agents to create the art that they, the gods, wished to be used in rituals and worship. The tattoo artist was, thus, *tohunga ta moko*.

Since the earliest times, the artist's ability to create has been associated with Creation itself—with the unknown forces believed to have fashioned the world in the first place. Artists depict deities, create ritual objects, and design and decorate sacred spaces. Art in itself represents a higher realm of experience, which communicates the possibility that even higher realms might exist.

Connecting with Spirits and the Divine

How have different faiths attempted to access spiritual states, and what is the role of art in these practices?

The spiritual life of many of the world's peoples is informed by the belief that the forces of nature are inhabited by living spirits, a kind of polytheistic faith known as animism. Other polytheistic faiths, such as Hinduism, hold that the divine takes multiple forms, represented by multiple gods and goddesses, although there may be a single divine source of being. In the world's monotheistic faiths—Judaism, Christianity, and Islam, in particular—one God is the creator and transcendent power of the world. Nontheistic faiths such as Buddhism do not have deities, but followers cultivate a spiritual practice that will allow them to ultimately experience transcendence. Art plays multiple roles in the attempt to connect with the spirit world and attain spiritual states of being.

We have some understanding of how the ancient San people of Africa attempted to connect with the spirits residing in nature through the rock art that survives in open-air caves below the overhanging stone cliffs atop the hills of what is now Matobo National Park in Zimbabwe, some of which dates back as far as 5,000–10,000 years (**Fig. 21-2**). A giraffe stands above a group of smaller giraffes crossing a series of large, white, lozenge-shaped forms with brown rectangular centers, many of them overlapping one another. To the right, six humanlike figures are joined hand in hand, probably in a trance dance. For the San people, whose current belief systems can be traced back almost as far as the rock art, prolonged dancing activates *num*, a personal energy or potency that the entire community can acquire. Led by a shaman, a person thought to have special ability to communicate with the spirit world, the dance encourages the *num* to heat up until it boils over and rises up through the spine to explode, causing the dancers to enter into a trance. Sweating and trembling, the dancers variously convulse or become rigid. They might run, jump, or fall. The San believe that, in many instances, the dancer's spirit leaves the body, traveling far away, where it might enter into battle with supernatural powers. At any event, the trance imbues the dancer with almost supernatural agency. The dancers' *num* is capable of curing illnesses, making game available for hunters, or controlling the weather.

Fig. 21-2 Wall painting with giraffes, zebra, eland, and abstract shapes, San people, Inanke Cave, Matobo National Park, Zimbabwe, before 1000 CE.
Photo: Christopher and Sally Gable © Dorling Kindersley.

Fig. 21-3 Kachina doll (Maalo), Hopi culture, late 19th century. Wood, pigment, feathers, fiber, and string, height 11½ in. The Brooklyn Museum of Art.
Museum Expedition 1904, Museum Collection Fund, 04.297.5604. Image courtesy of Brooklyn Museum of Art.

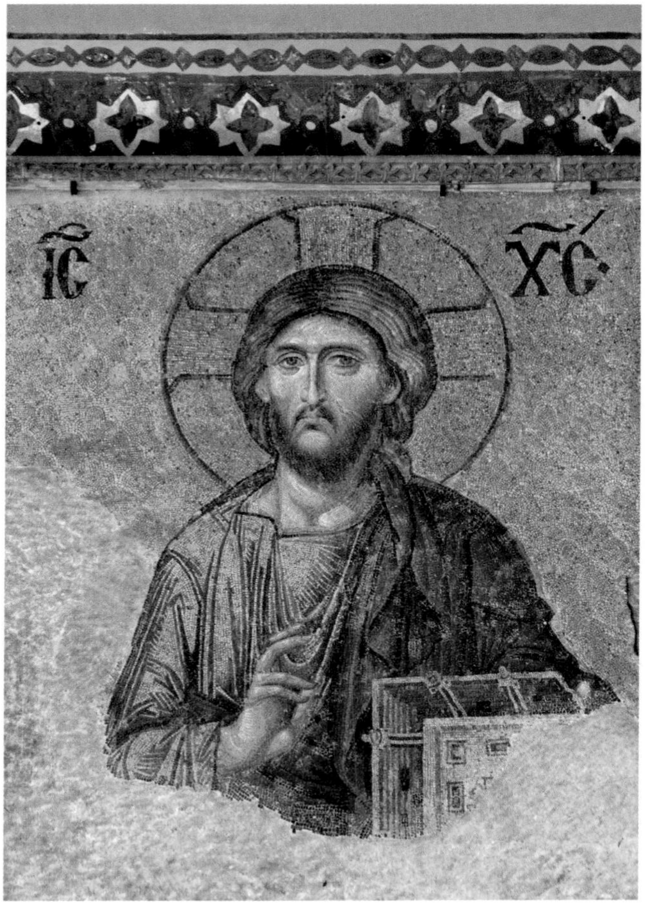

Fig. 21-4 *Christ*, from *Deësis* mosaic, 13th century. Hagia Sophia, Istanbul.
Photo: Ayhan Altun/Altunimages.

The concept of animism is also central to the spiritual lives of the Pueblo peoples of the American Southwest, who have maintained the active practice of their ancient religious rites and ceremonies, which they have chosen not to share with outsiders. Most, for instance, do not allow their ceremonial dances to be photographed. These dance performances tell stories that relate to the experiences of the Pueblo peoples, from planting, hunting, and fishing in daily life to the larger experiences of birth, puberty, maturity, and death. Still other stories explain the origin of the world, the emergence of a particular Pueblo people into the world, and their history. Most Pueblo people believe that they originated in the womb of Mother Earth and, like seeds sprouting from the soil in the springtime, were called out into the daylight by their Sun Father. This belief about origins is embodied in a type of narrative known as an emergence tale, a form of creation myth.

At the heart of the Zuni emergence tale is a moment when, to the dismay of their parents, many children are transformed into water-creatures—turtles, frogs, and the like—and the Hero Twins instruct the parents to throw these children back into the river. Here they become kachinas or katcinas, deified spirits. The Pueblo believe that kachina spirits manifest themselves in performance and dance. Masked male dancers impersonate the kachinas, taking on their likeness as well as their supernatural character. Through these dance visits, the kachinas, although always "nearby," can exercise their powers for the good of the people. The nearly 250 kachina personalities embody clouds, rain, crops, animals, and even ideas such as growth and fertility. Although kachina figurines are made for sale as art objects, particularly by the Hopi, the actual masks worn in ceremonies are not considered art objects by the Pueblo people. Rather, they are thought of as active agents in the transfer of power and knowledge between the gods and the men who wear them in dance. This particular kachina (**Fig. 21-3**) appeared during Angi'wa (a series of Night Dances), and is an agent for rain and good crop yield. (Kachina dolls made for sale, by contrast, are considered empty of any agency, power, or even significance.)

While not thought to be invested with power by God, the icons, or images, that adorned the walls, and sometimes ceilings, of Byzantine Orthodox churches beginning in the seventh century CE were believed to help the faithful communicate with the divine. The *Christ* from the *Deësis* mosaic in Hagia Sophia in present-day Istanbul (**Fig. 21-4**; see also Fig. 17-5) is one of many important icons that decorate the church. In the words of the sixth-century Byzantine poet Agathias: "The mortal

Fig. 21-5 Frontispiece, *Diamond Sutra*, from Cave 17, Dunhuang, printed in the ninth year of the Xiantong Era of the Tang dynasty, 868 CE. Ink on paper, woodblock handscroll. British Library, London.

man who beholds the image directs his mind to a higher contemplation. . . . The eyes encourage deep thoughts, and art is able by means of colors to ferry over the prayer of the mind." Thus, the icon was in some sense a vessel of prayer directed to the saint—or, in this case, Christ—and even offered the viewer its protection.

The idea that an image could play a role in spiritual practice developed in Buddhism as well. In the early stages of the religion's development, it was believed to be impossible to represent the Buddha since he had already passed to nirvana. Instead, his presence was symbolized by such things as his footprints, the banyan tree beneath which he achieved enlightenment, the wheel (representing *dharma*, the Wheel of Law), or elephants, symbols of mental strength. Eventually, however, representations of the Buddha evolved and sometimes served, like Christian icons, to direct the mind to higher levels of contemplation. The representation of the Buddha in the frontispiece of the *Diamond Sutra* (**Fig. 21-5**; see also Fig. 10-2) is an invitation to contemplate the writings within, which consist of a collection of the Buddha's sayings or aphorisms—concise thoughts expressed in a memorable way. In the **sutra**, the Buddha—who is an enlightened being but not a god—has finished his customary walk with his *bhikshus*, or monks, to beg for food, and he sits down to rest. His disciple the Elder Subhuti comes forth and asks him a question: "World-honored One, if good men and good women seek the Consummation of Incomparable Enlightenment, by what criteria should they abide and how should they control their thoughts?" In the print, Subhuti can be seen kneeling in the lower left corner. What follows is a dialogue in which the Buddha addresses the nature of perception, the point being that our limited understanding of reality and enlightenment—our attachment to the world of mere appearances—blinds us to higher truths. At the end of the sutra, the Buddha thus reminds Subhuti:

> Thus shall ye think of all this fleeting world:
> A star at dawn, a bubble in a stream;
> A flash of lightning in a summer cloud,
> A flickering lamp, a phantom, and a dream.

As such, the Buddha warns Subhuti about the dangers of trusting in the world of appearances, and by extension the dangers of trusting in representation in art. The Buddha's representation in the *Diamond Sutra* print is itself "a flickering lamp, a phantom, and a dream."

Giving Gods Human Form

What are the difficulties the faithful have in representing their deities, and what strategies do they employ to overcome these problems?

The ancient Greeks did not question artistic representations of their religious universe; indeed, they installed sculptures of the gods in temples and monuments and worshiped them as cult images or idols. The Greek gods thought like humans, acted like humans, and spoke like humans in the many myths of their lives and adventures that explained natural phenomena and human history. Each Greek city-state traced its origins to a particular founding god—Athena for Athens, Zeus for Sparta. Sacred sanctuaries were dedicated to others. Unlike the Hebrew God, the Greek gods present humans with no clear principles of behavior, and the priests and priestesses who oversaw the rituals dedicated to them produced no scriptures or doctrines. The gods watched over the individual at birth, nurtured the family, and protected the city-state. They controlled the weather, the seasons, health, marriage, longevity, and the future, which they could foresee. Aside from their immortality, there was nothing special about them except their power, which was enormous, sometimes frighteningly so. But the Greeks believed that as long as they did not overstep their bounds and try to compete with the gods—the sin of hubris, or pride—the gods would protect them.

While variously identified as either Zeus, king of the Greek gods, or as Poseidon, god of the sea, the nearly 7-foot-high bronze statue in the Archeological Museum in Athens (**Fig. 21-6**; see also Fig. 3-24) reveals a great deal about how the Greeks thought of their gods. For all their gods' foibles, in representing them, the Greeks did assume that they were physically perfect. This god is well proportioned and powerfully athletic. He represents, in this sense, something all Greeks could seek to emulate, as they did in the athletic competition that they held every four years for nearly 1,000 years beginning in 776 BCE—the Olympic Games.

The Christian idea that Jesus was the Son of God made flesh found multiple styles of expression in works

Fig. 21-6 ***Zeus*, or *Poseidon*, ca. 460 BCE.** Bronze, height 6 ft. 10 in. National Archaeological Museum, Athens.
Ministry of Culture Archeological Receipt Fund, 15161. © Marie Mauzy.

Fig. 21-7 Raphael, *The Alba Madonna*, ca. 1510. Oil on panel transferred to canvas, diameter 37¼ in., framed 4 ft. 6 in. × 4 ft. 5½ in. National Gallery of Art, Washington, D.C.
Andrew W. Mellon Collection, 1937.1.24. Photo © 1999 Board of Trustees, National Gallery of Art. Photo: José A. Naranjo.

of art that variously focused on Jesus' divine or human nature. In *The Alba Madonna* (**Fig. 21-7**; see also Fig. 8-9), Raphael perfectly balances both aspects of Jesus' being. The baby Jesus holds up the cross as if it were a toy for John the Baptist to see, but, of course, its significance is far greater than that. It is as if they know what they cannot know at this moment—that is, Jesus' future sacrifice. The baby's nudity suggests, of course, his innocence, even as his look suggests his wisdom. But perhaps more than anything else, the reflective gaze of the Virgin captures the viewer's imagination, as if we have caught her literally in the moment, thinking of a future about which she can only know intuitively—a real mother, worrying about her child's future as all mothers must.

Less than a decade after Raphael painted *The Alba Madonna*, at the start of what would become known as the Protestant Reformation, Ulrich Zwingli instituted a program of iconoclasm in which churches in Zurich were purged of all imagery on the grounds that images provoked at least the potential for idolatry. Such works were also seen as the embodiment of the Catholic taste for material, rather than spiritual, well-being. Outraged at the pomp, expense, and seeming excess with which the Vatican was decorating Rome, Zwingli used the authority of the prohibition against worship of false idols in the Ten Commandments to argue that art's appeal to the senses rather than the intellect was contrary to proper religious practice and unbecoming to the dignity of any place of worship.

A depiction of a church dedicated to St. Bavo, in Haarlem (**Fig. 21-8**), painted by Pieter Saenredam shows a typical Dutch Reformed interior stripped of all furnishings, its walls whitewashed by Calvinist iconoclasts. A single three-tiered chandelier hangs from the ceiling above three gentlemen whom Saenredam includes in the composition in order to establish the physical and, more important, spiritual vastness of the medieval church's interior. This stripped-down, white space is meant to reflect the purity and propriety of the Reformed Church and its flock.

The Islamic faith shares with certain Protestant sects and Judaism a belief that God (Allah) is never to be represented in human form. In Islamic art there is a distinct preference for the word over and above the representational image, but representation of humans and animals is only prohibited in religious writings and architecture, where it has the potential to be associated with idolatry. Allah is referenced only in calligraphy by any one of his 99 names—*al-Malik* (the King), *al-Rahim* (the Exceedingly Merciful), and so on. For instance, the center of the star from a calligraphic scroll containing verses

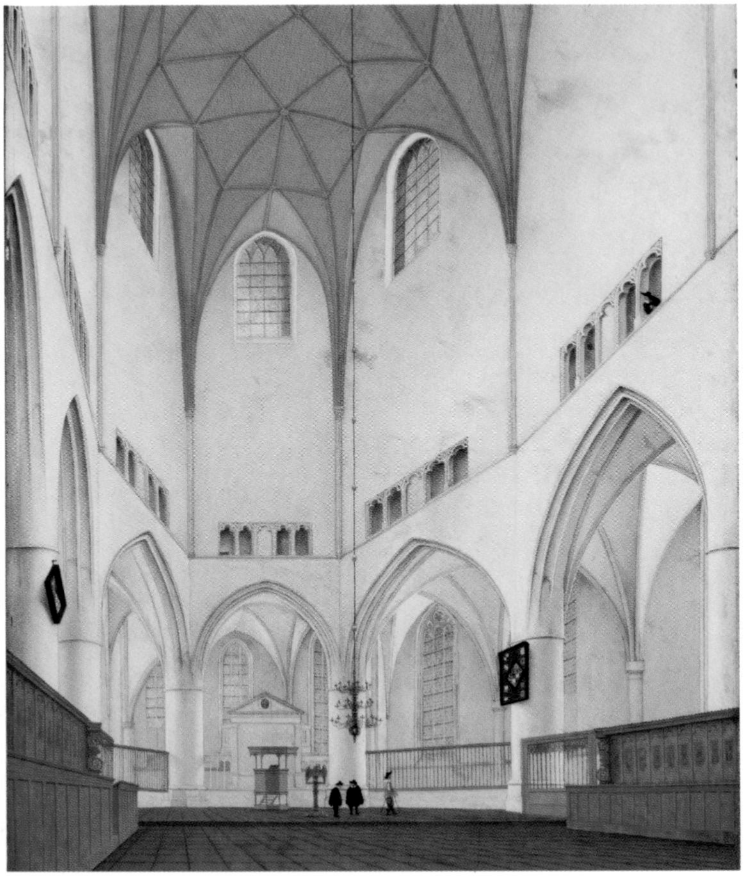

Fig. 21-8 Pieter Saenredam, *Interior of the Choir of St. Bavo's Church at Haarlem*, 1660. Oil on panel, 27⅞ × 21⅝ in. Worcester Art Museum, Worcester, Massachusetts.
Charlotte E.W. Buffington Fund, 1951.29. Bridgeman Images.

Fig. 21-9 Calligraphic scroll (detail), Syria or India, 14th–15th centuries. Ink, watercolor, and gold on paper, full scroll 14⅜ in. wide, 26 ft. 3 in. long. The al-Sabah Collection, Dar al-Athar al-Islamiyyah, Kuwait.

from the Qur'an, sayings of the Prophet, invocations, and proverbs features the name *al-Shafi* (the Healer) (**Fig. 21-9**). The expressive potential of calligraphy as an art form is evident in this elegant work.

Sacred Space

What are the characteristics of sacred space?

To enter a sacred space is to find oneself in a place where the normal concerns of daily life are suspended, or at least temporarily held in abeyance. Architects and artists have responded to the challenge of creating this unique environment and investing it with symbols of the faith.

The Kaaba

The act of pilgrimage, in which the faithful make a spiritual journey to a sacred space, is common to many of the world's religions. Practitioners of the Muslim faith are required, if their circumstances allow, to participate at least once in their lives in the annual pilgrimage to Mecca (in Saudi Arabia) known as the Hajj. During the last month of the Islamic calendar, Muslims from around the world gather to perform a series of rituals over a five-day period in their holy city. In undertaking the Hajj, pilgrims demonstrate their willingness to leave behind everything in their lives for the sake of God.

One of the rituals of the Hajj is to walk seven times around the Kaaba (**Fig. 21-10**). Situated in the center of the Haram Mosque in Mecca, the Kaaba ("cube") defines

Fig. 21-10 The Kaaba, center of the Haram Mosque, Mecca, Saudi Arabia. © Ahmed Jadallah/Reuters/Corbis.

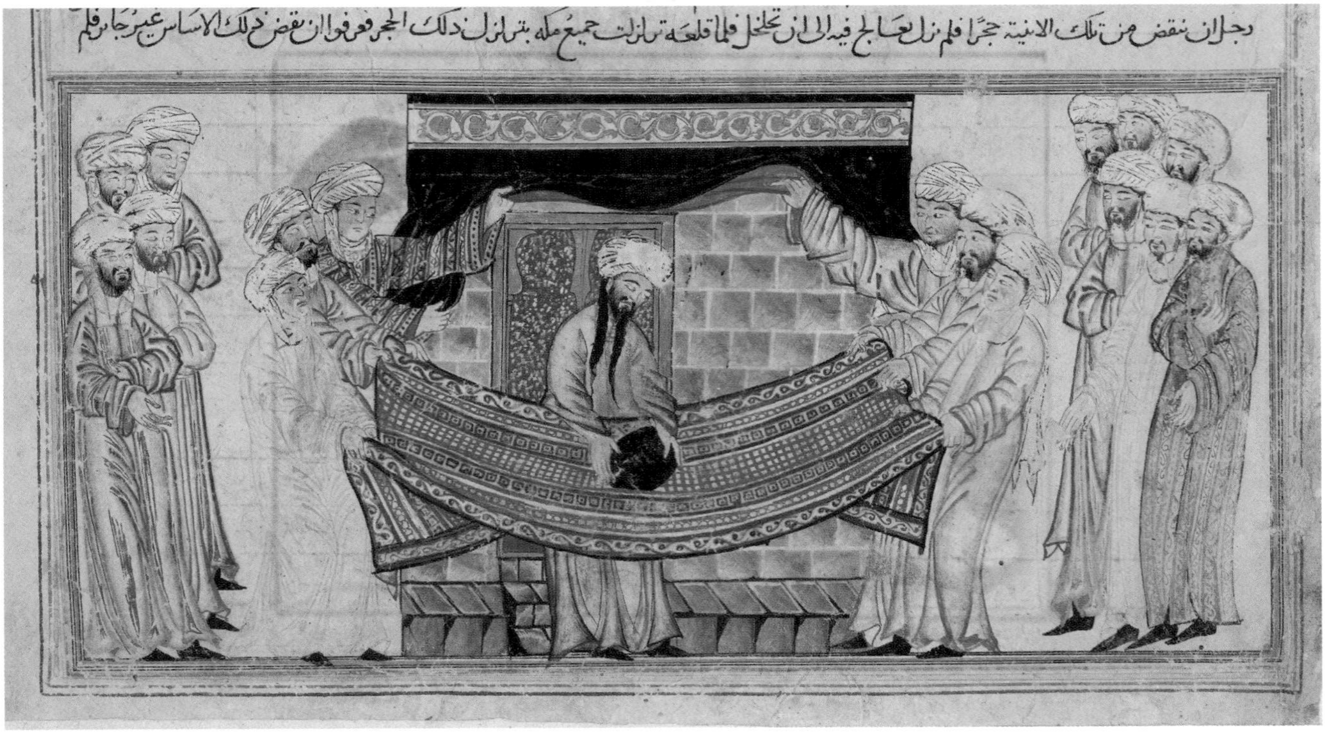

Fig. 21-11 ***Muhammad Placing the Black Stone on His Cloak*****, from Rashid al-Din's** ***Jami al-Tawarikh (Universal History)*****, copied and illustrated at Tabriz, Iran, 1315.** Illuminated manuscript, $5\frac{1}{8} \times 10\frac{1}{4}$ in. University Library, Edinburgh.

a sacred space. Muslims believe it is their place of origin, the site of the first "house of God," built at God's command by the biblical Abraham and his son Ismael, the ancestors of all Muslims. It is the physical center of Muslim life, around which all things turn and to which all things in the universe are connected, symbolic of the cosmos itself. For this reason, Muslims face in the direction of the Kaaba during their daily prayers as well.

Although among Sunni Muslims representation of the Prophet Muhammad has always been forbidden, beginning in the thirteenth and fourteenth centuries, images of Muhammad began to appear widely in illustrated manuscripts, many of Shia origin. One such illustration—*Muhammad Placing the Black Stone on His Cloak*, from Rashid al-Din's *Jami al-Tawarikh* (*Universal History*) (**Fig. 21-11**)—depicts a key story in the history of the Kaaba and the Muslim faith. The Kaaba holds a sacred Black Stone, probably a meteorite, which reportedly "fell from Heaven." Workers who were rebuilding the Kaaba were preparing to replace the sacred stone inside, and a quarrel broke out among the principal Arab tribes regarding who would have the privilege of laying the stone. Everyone agreed that the first passerby would do the honor. That passerby turned out to be Muhammad, who placed the stone on his cloak and then gave a corner of the cloak to the head of each tribe to carry into the building. The story establishes Muhammad as a political as well as a spiritual leader, and, perhaps more important, as a prophet capable of uniting the diverse elements of Arab culture.

A Japanese Shrine

The fulfillment of spiritual life through pilgrimages to sacred spaces is a practice common to many of the world's religions. In Japan, the three sacred shrines of Kumano, south of Osaka, all considered places of physical healing and depicted in a hanging scroll dating from around 1300 (**Fig. 21-12**), were connected together by a pilgrimage route with so many people visiting Kumano that the pilgrimage became popularly known as the "Procession of Ants." The shrines are actually about 80 miles apart: The one at the bottom of the scroll is in the mountains of the Kii Peninsula in a cypress forest, the middle one is on the eastern coast of the peninsula, and the top one is near a famous waterfall that can be seen to its right. These three shrines are among the most important examples of the Japanese fusion of the indigenous Shinto religion and

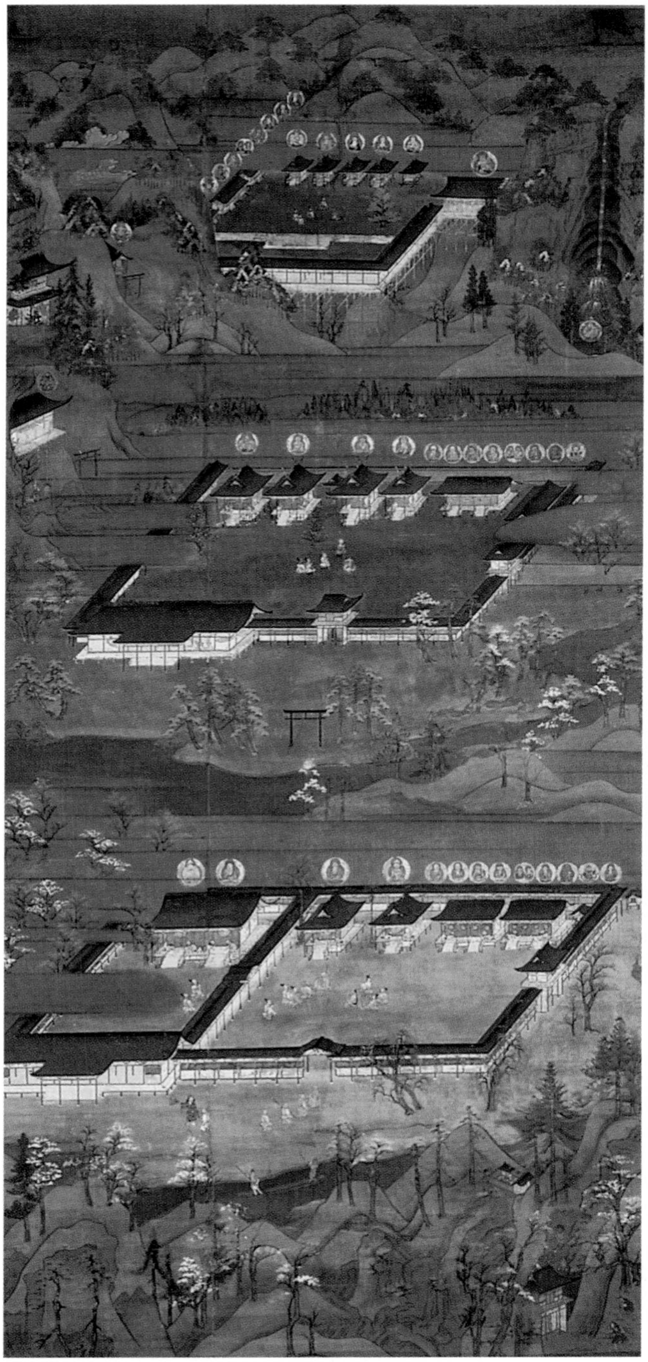

Fig. 21-12 *Kumano Mandala*, Kamakura period, ca. 1300. Hanging scroll, ink and color on silk, 4 ft. 4¼ in. × 24¼ in. The Cleveland Museum of Art.
John L. Severance Fund, 1953.16. Photo © Cleveland Museum of Art.

Buddhism, which arrived in Japan in the sixth century CE. According to the *Kojiki*, or *Chronicles of Japan*, a collection of myths and stories compiled in about 700 CE, the islands that constitute Japan were formed by two *kami* (Shinto gods)—Izanagi and his consort, Izanami. In Shinto, trees, rocks, water, and mountains—especially Mount Fuji, the volcano just outside Tokyo, which is said to look over the country as its protector—are all manifestations of the *kami*, which, like kachinas in Pueblo culture, are the spirits that are embodied in the natural world. Even the natural materials with which artists work, such as clay, wood, and stone, are imbued with the *kami* and are to be treated with the respect and reverence due to a god. The Kumano shrines are dedicated to the *kami* of the three Kumano mountains, Hongu, Shingu, and Nachi.

The Hindu Pilgrimage Place

In the Hindu religion, pilgrimages to sacred spaces, of which there are literally thousands, are especially important to spiritual life, and have become increasingly so over time. In fact, in 2013, the *Kumbh Mela* festival at Allahabad, celebrated approximately every twelfth year (its timing is determined by the movement of the planet Jupiter around the sun), marked the largest gathering of people in one place in history. Approximately 100 million pilgrims came to bathe at the "Sangam"—the confluence of the holy rivers Ganga, Yamuna, and the Sarasvati, a river described in ancient Hindu texts, but long since lost or perhaps even simply mythical.

Although many pilgrimage sites include elaborate temples and shrines, such as the Kandariya Mahadeva Temple in Khajuraho in central India (**Fig. 21-13**; see also Fig. 17-24), it is the location itself that is first and foremost sacred. The *Silpa Shastra*, a text dating from the end of the first millennium, outlines the procedures for choosing a temple site. The ground upon which a temple sits was first chosen because it seemed a site appropriate for a god to take up residence, with the proximity of

Fig. 21-13 Kandariya Mahadeva Temple, Khajuraho, Madhya Pradesh, India, Chandella dynasty, ca. 1025–50.
© Neil Grant/Alamy.

water, source of all fruitfulness, a priority. Although the landscape at Khajuharo has changed dramatically since medieval times, tradition has it that the 84 original temples in the region were set next to 84 different lakes with 84 wells dedicated to watering the sacred groves that surrounded them. Before the temple could be built, the ground had to be purified by planting and harvesting the site for two seasons and then allowing cows—sacred in Indian culture—to graze the fields.

Approaching the temple, pilgrims would first walk around it, barefoot, in prayer, symbolically approaching the peaks of the Himalayas, the home of the gods. Upon entering the temple, they would circle the inner sanctum—the *garbhagriha*, or "womb chamber," containing the *lingam* (phallus) of Shiva, once again in prayer. In total darkness, but alight in prayer, they believe they make eye contact with Shiva, and so receive divine blessing.

The Pilgrimage Church

Throughout the Middle Ages, it was likewise customary for Christians to go on religious pilgrimages to holy places or sites containing sacred objects. People believed that their prayers for forgiveness, healing, fertility, or anything else would have a better chance of being fulfilled if they were able to get physically close to a holy object, person, or site. The Church of St. Sernin, in Toulouse, France (**Fig. 21-14**; see also Fig. 14-19), housed the relics—the bones, clothing, or other possessions of a Christian saint or martyr—of Saturninus (St. Sernin). The latter was the first bishop of Toulouse, who, in 250 BCE, when Rome still controlled southern France, had died when he was roped to a bull and dragged down the main street of Toulouse (then known as Tolosa) for refusing to worship the Roman gods. In the eleventh century, the church became a major stopping point for Christians making a pilgrimage to Santiago de Compostela in the northwest corner of the Iberian Peninsula, which housed the bones of St. James.

Fig. 21-14 Nave, St. Sernin, Toulouse, France, ca. 1080–1120.
© Bildarchiv Mondheim GmbH/Alamy.

Perhaps because it was closer to northern Europeans than either Jerusalem or Rome, Santiago de Compostela was by far the most popular site of pilgrimage in the eleventh through thirteenth centuries. It had also developed a reputation as a site for miracles, and by the mid-twelfth century, a *Pilgrim's Guide to Santiago de Compostela* had appeared. Written in Latin, probably by monks in southern France, it describes and illustrates the towns and monuments on the major pilgrimage routes through France and Spain. St. Sernin was the second stop along the southernmost route.

The Native American Mission Church

The sacred spaces of many contemporary Native American cultures are more complex. Despite Spain's program to convert Native Americans to Christianity in the sixteenth century, the Native American cultures of the Southwest never comfortably assimilated Western religion. In August 1680, the Pueblo peoples of present-day New Mexico and Arizona simultaneously revolted under the leadership of a San Juan Indian named Popé. They killed 21 of the province's 33 Franciscan friars and 308 Spanish settlers, including men, women, and children. Survivors fled south to El Paso del Norte.

Not until 1692 would the Spanish reassert control of the region, but by then they had learned their lesson. They formally recognized the Pueblos' rights to their lands, and they abandoned their attempt to force Christianity upon the population. As a result, the Pueblo peoples today still retain the greater part of their pre-Conquest culture. But interestingly, since 1692, the two traditions, native and Christian, have stood side by side, especially in terms of mission architecture and decoration, resulting in the creation of a composite and syncretic style—that is, a style that combines different cultural practices and principles.

The decorative program of the Church of San José at Old Laguna Pueblo, the first church to be rebuilt after the Reconquest of 1699–1706, is a case in point (**Fig. 21-15**). The altar and ***retablo***, or altarpiece ensemble, are the

Fig. 21-15 The Laguna Santero, *Retablo* and high altar of the Church of San José, Old Laguna Pueblo, New Mexico, ca. 1780–1810.

work of an artist known as the Laguna Santero, an itinerant Mexican artist who created altar ensembles from the 1780s to about 1810, not only at Laguna but also at Acoma, Zia, Santa Ana, and Pojoaque Pueblos, and for churches in Santa Cruz de la Cañada and Santa Fe. (A *santero* is a New Mexico artist whose carvings and paintings depict saints, angels, or other religious figures.) The high altar at Laguna is decorated with floral motifs—which may have once covered the walls to both right and left of the altar as well—probably meant to replicate the European woven tapestries found in the wealthier cathedrals to the south. The carved wooden *retablo* behind the high altar consists of four spiraling columns, topped by a painting of the Holy Trinity. In the center of the columns is St. Joseph (San José), the patron saint of the church, holding the Christ Child in one arm. To the left is St. John Nepomuk, sainted for refusing to violate the secrecy of the confessional, and, to the right, St. Barbara, patron saint of those who work with explosives, and hence associated with thunder and lightning. Attached to the top of the *retablo* and extending above the altar is a buffalo hide, painted with a sun on the left, a moon on the right, and between them a rainbow and stars. Extending from the sun are zigzag lines that culminate in a triangular head, symbol of the Pueblo deity, the Horned Water Snake, god of lightning and rain. At each side of the altar are three mountains set beneath an overarching rainbow. Each possesses the eyes and mouth of a kachina (see Fig. 21-3). They echo the Holy Trinity at the top of the *retablo*, who stand beneath the rainbow on the buffalo hide above, each figure being backed by a triangular green halo. Thus Pueblo and Christian traditions are unified in the design, and this syncretic impulse is underscored not only by the Pueblo designs which run the length of the nave but also by the fact that the Christ Child in St. Joseph's arms carries a green peyote button.

Spirituality and Abstraction

How is abstraction particularly suited to representing spirituality?

One of the more powerful scared spaces in the United States is the Rothko Chapel in Houston, Texas (**Fig. 21-16**), which is simultaneously a nondenominational sanctuary and an all-enveloping work of art. The work was commissioned by Houston philanthropists John and Dominique de Menil. In conversations with the French Dominican friar Father Marie-Alain Couturier, who had taken them on a tour of churches in France, the decoration of which he was himself largely responsible for—at Vence, the Chapel of the Rosary designed by Henri Matisse in 1948–51, and Le Corbusier's Chapel of Notre Dame du Haut of 1954, among others—the de Menils came to believe in the importance of commissioning religious works from avant-garde artists.

Fig. 21-16 Mark Rothko, Rothko Chapel, Houston, Texas, opened 1971.

The Rothko Chapel consists of 14 paintings—three triptychs and five single panels were painted between 1964 and 1967 expressly for the octagonal building designed to house them. The north, east, and west walls display the triptychs, probably intended by Rothko to evoke the standard three panels of Renaissance altarpieces, while single paintings occupy the other five walls. The north triptych, across from the twin entrances, and the four corner panels at first appear to be a monochrome black, but as the light from a baffled skylight above changes in the chapel—as clouds pass by, or as the sun moves across the sky—the surfaces reveal richly layered browns and plums. The south panel and the east and west triptychs each consist of a sharp-edged black rectangle on a brown field. The scale of these paintings is intentionally large. Although the dimensions vary, all 14 panels are over 14 feet high. "The reason I paint [large pictures]," Rothko explained in 1951, "is precisely because I want to be very intimate and human. To paint a small picture is to place yourself outside your experience, to look upon an experience as a stereopticon view or reducing glass. However you paint the larger picture, you are in it. It isn't something you command."

Rothko had long believed that his paintings offered people something akin to a "religious experience" (see Fig. 20-23). He thought of the painting, and the chapel even more so, as an imaginative space into which the viewer was invited to enter. And because that space was abstract—because there was no recognizable object for the viewer to grasp—the imaginative possibilities offered by contemplating it were totally open-ended. "A picture lives by companionship," Rothko had stated as early as 1947, "expanding and quickening in the eyes of the sensitive observer."

The belief that abstraction could offer the viewer a religious experience was first articulated by the German Expressionist painter Wassily Kandinsky early in the twentieth century. One of the artist's most important early experiences occurred in 1889, before he had determined to be a painter, when he was on an ethnographic research trip to what was then the remote village of Vologda, north of Moscow. There, he found himself standing in the icon, or "red" ("red" is synonymous with "beautiful" in Old Russian), corner of a local peasant's home:

> They taught me to move within the picture, to live in the picture. I still remember how I entered the living room for the first time and stood rooted to the spot before this unexpected scene. . . . The "red" corner [was] thickly, completely covered with

> painted and printed pictures of the saints. . . . I felt surrounded on all sides by painting, into which I had thus penetrated. The same feeling had previously lain dormant within me, quite unconsciously, when I had been in the Moscow churches, and especially in the main cathedral of the Kremlin.

Such religious feeling was, Kandinsky believed, possible to replicate in painting, as he came to argue in a small book called *Concerning the Spiritual in Art*, published in 1910 as the Blue Rider group was forming. The aim of the book, Kandinsky explained, "was to awaken [the] capacity for experiencing the spiritual in material and in abstract phenomena." Thus the picture was a sort of sacred space that induced in viewers the same feelings they might experience when entering a church or standing in the "red" corner of a peasant's home. It was a space outside of everyday life, a precinct that opened toward the eternal rather than the everyday.

It is not difficult to imagine entering into his 1913 painting *Composition VII* (**Fig. 21-17**; see Fig. 20-7 for a much smaller study of it). At 6½ by almost 12 feet, the viewer feels as surrounded as Kandinsky did standing in the Vologda icon corner. Colors explode around us—suggesting cosmic forces at battle with one another, as if we are immersed in the moment of biblical Apocalypse, just before the moment of rebirth. Kandinsky called such paintings "Compositions" in order to invoke a kind of musical abstraction, the very inarticulate feelings that music can produce in the imagination. "Color," he wrote in *Concerning the Spiritual in Art*, "is the keyboard, the eyes are the hammers, the soul is the piano with many strings. The artist is the hand that plays, touching one key or another purposively, to cause vibrations of the soul."

In 1985–86, Brice Marden, a good deal of whose work, he admits, was deeply influenced by the paintings in the Rothko Chapel, which he first saw in 1972, began a series of paintings based on the poems of the ninth-century Buddhist hermit Cold Mountain, or Han Shan. He was particularly moved by an edition of Cold Mountain's poems published by the Copper Canyon Press in Port Townsend, Washington, in which the original Chinese poems appear on the left-hand page, and their translations on the right. Chinese is written in vertical columns top to bottom, going right to left. On each page there were four vertical couplets, and this grid structure appealed to him. In essence, he adapted this calligraphic structure to the flow of a kind of restrained Jackson Pollock-like line. The final paintings are meant

Fig. 21-17 Wassily Kandinsky, *Composition VII*, 1913. Oil on canvas, 6 ft. 6½ in. × 9 ft. 11⅛ in. Tretyakov Gallery, Moscow, Russia.

to reflect something of the spiritual reverence for nature Marden found in the Buddhist poems (**Fig. 21-18**). "In the poems," Marden has explained,

> they're constantly talking about these monks wandering in the mountains and they're meditating and [seeking] the achievement of truth. You know, you cross this bridge, and it's a very tricky stone bridge high in the Tiantai mountains. You cross the bridge and that's where the immortals are living. This painting evolved so that there was a sort of arc. That's why it's called *Cold Mountain (Bridge)*.

The painting, in other words, represents a kind of spiritual quest, a striving that might ultimately lead to enlightenment.

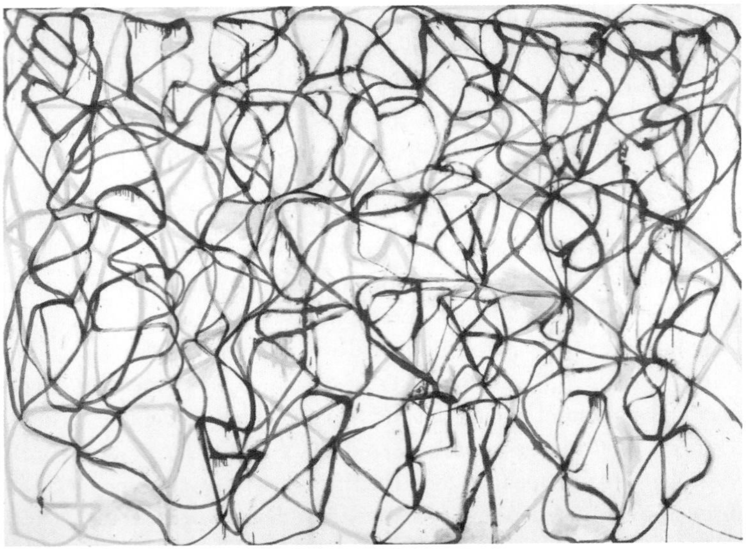

Fig. 21-18 Brice Marden, *Cold Mountain 6 (Bridge)*, 1989–91. Oil on linen, 9 × 12 ft. San Francisco Museum of Modern Art.
Purchase through a gift of Phyllis Wattis. 99.367. © 2015 Brice Marden/Artists Rights Society (ARS), New York.

THE CRITICAL PROCESS

Thinking about Art and Spiritual Belief

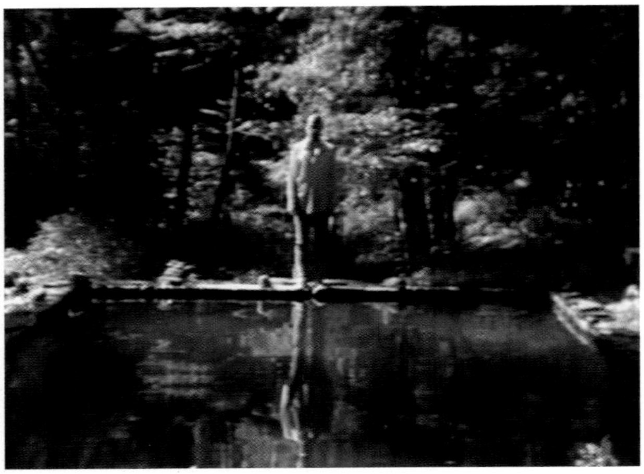

Fig. 21-19 Bill Viola, *The Reflecting Pool*, 1977–79.
Four stills. Video, color, mono sound, 7 min.
Bill Viola Studio LLC. Photo: Kira Perov.

In an interview with Raymond Bellour in 1985, Bill Viola explained that, in *The Reflecting Pool* (**Fig. 21-19**; see also Fig. 11-41),

> *I was trying to get at the original notion of baptism in a way—a process of cleansing or clearing away, and the idea of breaking through illusion. Water is such a powerful, obvious symbol of cleansing, and also of birth, rebirth, and even death. . . . There is also the suggestion of the events of this world as being illusory, or transient, since they are visible as reflections on the surface of the water. The direct reality is never perceived.*

How does it compare to the philosophical position expressed by the Buddha in the *Diamond Sutra* (see Fig. 21-5)?

Viola explores similar themes in his *Room for St. John of the Cross* (**Fig. 21-20**; see also Figs. 6-17 and 6-18). In prison, St. John wrote *The Dark Night of the Soul*, which describes, in John's words, "the method followed by the soul in its journey upon the spiritual road to the attainment of the perfect union of love with God, to the extent that is possible in this life." The book consists almost entirely of a line-by-line, sometimes word-by-word exposition of the poem of eight stanzas that opens it. It begins:

One dark night
fired with love's urgent longing
—ah, the sheer grace!—
I went out unseen,
my house being now all stilled.

How might this quest compare to *The Reflecting Pool*? Can you see any similarities between it and the Buddhist quest that is the subject of Brice Marden's *Cold Mountain 6 (Bridge)*?

Fig. 21-20 Bill Viola, *Room for St. John of the Cross*, 1983. Video/sound installation. Museum of Contemporary Art, Los Angeles.
Bill Viola Studio LLC. Photo: Kira Perov.

Thinking Back

21.1 Compare the ways that different faiths have attempted to access spiritual states, and describe the role of art in these practices.

The spiritual life of many of the world's peoples is informed by a polytheistic belief that the forces of nature are inhabited by living spirits, while monotheistic faiths believe in one God as the creator and transcendent power of the world. Nontheistic faiths such as Buddhism cultivate a spiritual practice. What forces of agency inform the tattoo practices of the Maori? How does *num* work in the rituals of the San peoples? How does animism inform the kachinas of the Pueblo peoples of the American Southwest? What agency does the Russian Orthodox icon possess? How do the Buddhist teachings in the *Diamond Sutra* challenge the world of appearances?

21.2 Outline some of the difficulties faced by various religions in giving their deities human form, and describe some strategies for overcoming these problems.

How did the Greeks portray their gods? How did the Catholic Church justify representations of Christ? During the Protestant Reformation, churches first in Switzerland and then across Europe were purged of all religious imagery. How did the iconoclasts responsible justify their actions? What varying positions do various Muslim faithful take in regard to representing God? The Prophet Muhammad?

21.3 Characterize sacred space.

Sacred space is a space in which the normal concerns of daily life are suspended or, at least, held in abeyance. What is the Kaaba and in what ways is it a sacred space? How does the *Kumano Mandala* reflect the Shinto religion? What primarily defines the sacred spaces of the Hindu religion? Why, in the Middle Ages, were the pilgrimage churches considered especially important sacred spaces? How do the *retablo* and altarpiece in the Church of San José at Old Laguna Pueblo in New Mexico reflect a syncretic notion of sacred space?

21.4 Explain why abstraction is particularly suitable for representing spiritual matters.

Large, abstract paintings like those of Rothko, Kandinsky, and Marden all possess the power to envelop the viewer in their space. In some sense, as Kandinsky understood, such paintings are themselves sacred spaces. Why and how do they depend on the viewer—what Rothko calls the "sensitive observer"—to bring their spiritual potential to life?

Chapter 22
The Cycle of Life

Learning Objectives

22.1 Describe how depictions of pregnancy cause us to reflect on our own humanity.

22.2 Outline some of the narratives suggested by images of youth and aging.

22.3 Discuss some of the ways in which an awareness of our own mortality is reflected in art.

22.4 Outline some of the ways in which burial practices reflect a belief in the afterlife.

In Tibetan Buddhism, the continuing cycle of life—from birth into the world, to death, and then rebirth, once again into the world, a cycle one can only be liberated from through enlightenment—is traditionally imaged by a *thangka*, or painting, of the *Bhavacakra*, or Wheel of Life (**Fig. 22-1**). According to legend, this cycle, or *samsara* as it is known, was originally drawn by the Buddha himself. The Wheel is held in the jaws of Yama, the Lord of Death, and by extension the Lord of the Wheel—a Buddhist deity whose origins can be traced back to Hinduism. At the Wheel's center are three symbolic creatures, each biting the other's tail in an endless circle: a pig, who represents ignorance, a snake, representing envy and hatred, and a red cock, who stands for lust and greed. These are the basic evils that poison the soul, and whoever chooses to live in their clutches will follow the dark side, depicted in the half-circle on the right side of the next ring surrounding the center, opposite the light half-circle depicting the path to bliss. The large areas between the spokes of the wheel depict the six different levels of existence into which one might be reborn. At the top is a sort of paradise on earth, the home, for instance, of bodhisattvas, mortals imbued with divine spirit but who have not yet attained nirvana. At the bottom is hell—a world of sexual depravity, violence, and subjection, but not a world without hope, for, by atoning for one's sins, rebirth into a different level of existence is possible. Moving down the Wheel on the right is, first, the world of demigods who, despite the fact that they live in prosperity, are constantly at war with each other, driven by jealousy and envy. Below that, just above hell on the left, is a world of unbridled desire filled with those whose appetites cannot be quenched, the so-called hungry ghosts. Moving down the Wheel on the left is, first, the world of humans, who are seen striving for spiritual attainment despite their ignorance. Beneath the human world is the world of animals, oppressed by the fact that they are devoured by others and must serve as beasts of burden. The outer ring of the Wheel depicts the journey of a single person through the stages of life, showing in detail how, through cause and effect, we are subject to the continual suffering of birth, life, and rebirth. The entire Wheel of Life, then, represents the possibility of transforming suffering by understanding how we, as individuals, must transform ourselves if enlightenment can ever be won. But, perhaps above all, it represents the constant state of change that is the cycle of life itself, the very impermanence of existence.

Fig. 22-1 *Thangka* depicting *Bhavacakra* (Wheel of Life), Bhutan, 15th–17th century. Mineral colors with organic matter. Private collection.

Photograph by John C. Huntington. Courtesy of the Huntington Photographic Archive at Ohio State University.

Birth

How do depictions of pregnancy cause us to reflect on our own humanity?

The impermanence of being that is captured in the Wheel of Becoming could be said to begin with birth itself. In the narrow coastal plain between the Pacific Ocean on the west and the snow-capped peaks and high grasslands of the Andes mountains which on the east capture rainfall from the Pacific Ocean, creating rivers that drop quickly to the sea across one of the most arid deserts in the world, Moche culture flourished for a thousand years, from about 200 BCE to 800 CE. Theirs was a world of enormous contrast and unpredictable fluctuation in the weather brought on by what we now call El Niño, the climatic event that today occurs every two to seven years, characterized by a warming of surface waters that dramatically reduces the upwelling of cold, nutrient-rich water off the western coast of South America, causing die-offs of plankton and, in turn, the fish that were a staple of the Moche diet. The coastal river valleys in which the Moche lived were essentially long ribbons of oases that cut through the arid desert coastline. In these river basins, they built irrigation systems, canals and ditches that diverted virtually every drop of water from the mountains into their fields. These fields were, in turn, fertilized with extremely rich seabird droppings (guano) collected along the Pacific shoreline.

As we have seen (see Fig. 18-22), the Moche were master potters, depicting almost every aspect of Moche life in their distinctive stirrup-spouted bottles (the enormous number of which suggest, again, the importance of water to the culture). They were the first potters in the Americas to produce clay objects from molds (many of the figurines that sit atop their vessels were made in molds), thus allowing the potters to reproduce the same objects again and again. That said, the portraits of people, especially rulers, that sit atop the vessels are so individualized that they seem to have been modeled from life. This scene (**Fig. 22-2**), although offering a surprisingly realistic depiction of childbirth, may well symbolize larger notions of fertility and regeneration. Found in a burial chamber, it seems to underscore the fragility of the Moche existence, the cycle of life and death that—like the contrast between the river valleys and desert wastelands in which they lived, and the coming and going of the fish as a consequence of cyclical weather patterns—defined their lives.

The connection of birth to the cyclical patterns of nature was clear to Leonardo da Vinci, and the miracle of the fetus in the womb led him to produce—along with other precisely drawn dissections of the human body

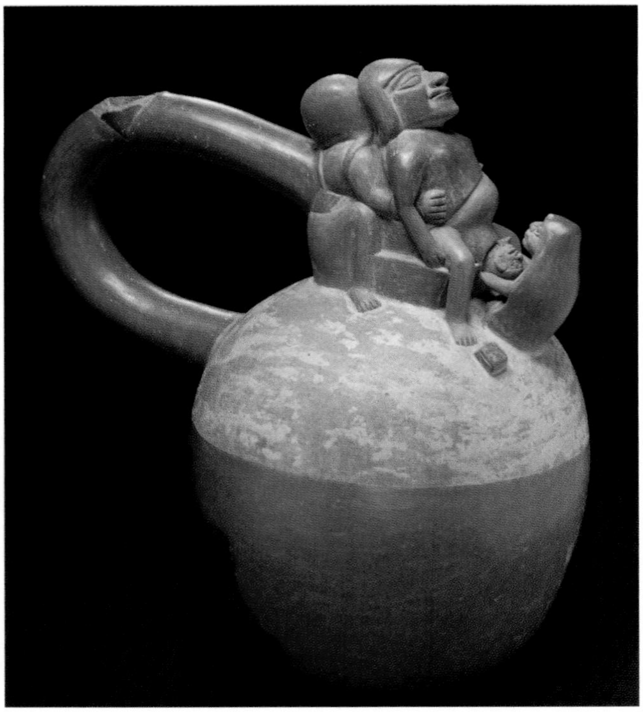

Fig. 22-2 Vessel with birth scene, Peru, Moche culture, 0–700 CE. Pottery, height 8¾ in. (spout broken off the handle). Ethnologisches Museum, Staatliche Museen zu Berlin.

dating from between 1510 and 1513—the famous anatomical study of an embryo illustrated here (**Fig. 22-3**). For Leonardo, the human body was closely akin to the earth itself:

> As man has in him bones the supports and framework of his flesh, the world has its rocks the supports of the earth; as man has in him a pool of blood in which the lungs rise and fall in breathing, so the body of the earth has its ocean tide which likewise rises and falls every six hours, as if the world breathed; as in that pool of blood veins have their origin, which ramify all over the human body, so likewise the ocean sea fills the body of the earth with infinite springs of water.

Thus, in some sense, whatever Leonardo was studying (and he studied almost everything—natural phenomena like wind, storms, and the movement of water; anatomy and physiology; physics and mechanics; music; mathematics; plants and animals; geology; and astronomy, to say nothing of painting and drawing), he was, at some level, also studying himself. Surely, in the embryo, he saw reflected his own origins.

We are probably likewise meant to identify with the depictions of Adam and Eve in Jan van Eyck's *Ghent Altarpiece* (see Fig. 1-21). Both figures are portrayed with a clarity and a realism that are astonishing. We can see almost every strand of Eve's hair as it flows over her

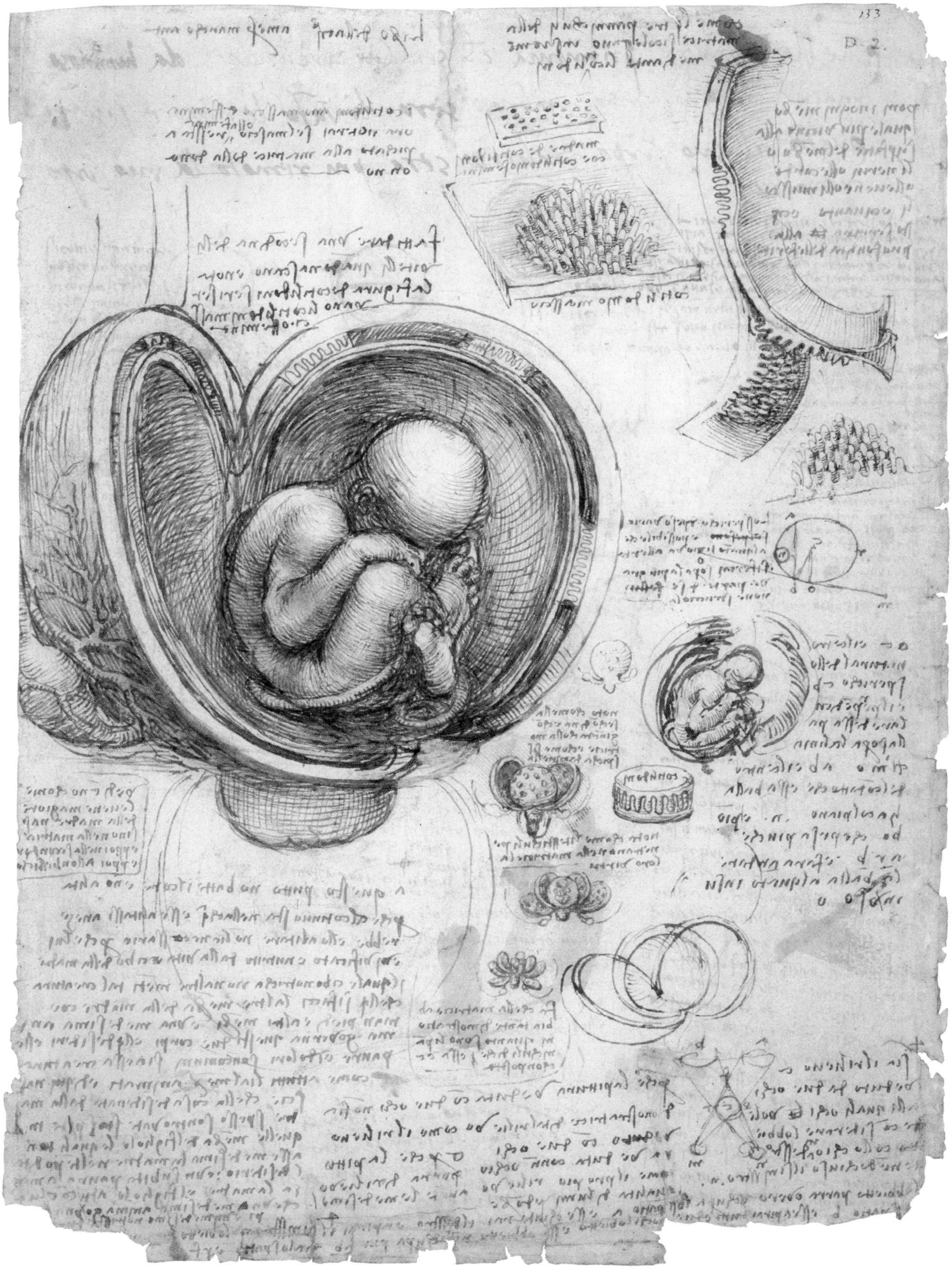

Fig. 22-3 Leonardo da Vinci, *Embryo in the Womb*, ca. 1513. Pen and brown ink, 11¾ × 8½ in. The Royal Collection.

shoulder (**Fig. 22-4**), while the nudity of the pair seems pure flesh. Note how Eve's left shoulder and Adam's toes seem to extend out of the picture plane as if to enter our space, a suggestion intensified when these two side panels are turned in toward the middle, as they almost always were, since the wall against which van Eyck's ensemble was placed is smaller than the fully extended altarpiece.

Eve's protruding belly has usually been understood as a representation of the preferred female body-type of the age—most agree that her posture suggests her fertility rather than her actual pregnancy (compare, for instance, the bride in van Eyck's *Giovanni Arnolfini and His Wife*; see Fig. 2-17). But art historian Linda Seidel has recently argued that she is pregnant indeed:

> In Gen. 3:16, God mandates that Eve will suffer the anguish of pain in childbirth, a situation to which Jan's near life-sized figure alludes with exceptional bluntness. The dark line that vertically bisects Eve's belly corresponds anatomically to the juncture between abdominal muscle plates that is known as the linea alba. As these plates spread apart during pregnancy to accommodate the expanding uterus, the line darkens, a phenomenon usually observed around the fourth month of pregnancy.

Thus, she stands in marked contrast to the shriveled fruit she holds in her hand—full of seed and ripe, although, simultaneously, in the vulnerability of her nakedness, forecasting the pain of childbirth and the suffering of humankind after the Fall.

Fig. 22-4 Jan van Eyck, *Eve* panel from *The Ghent Altarpiece*, ca. 1432. Oil on panel, 7 ft. × 12¾ in. Church of St. Bavo, Ghent, Belgium.

Youth and Age

What kinds of narratives are suggested by images of youth and aging?

In an 1887 article in *Harper's New Monthly Magazine*, the great American novelist Henry James found a similarly disquieting suggestiveness in a painting by the young American painter John Singer Sargent, who was, at the time, living in France. Sargent had been commissioned in 1882 by the expatriate couple Edward Darley Boit and Mary Louisa Cushing Boit to paint their four daughters in the foyer of their Paris apartment (**Fig. 22-5**). In the foreground, Julia, the youngest child, aged four, sits on the floor with her doll between her legs. To the left, facing the viewer forthrightly, but gazing just to the viewer's left, is Mary Louisa, aged eight. In the shadows of the doorway, Jane, aged 12, looks directly at us, while Florence, the eldest, aged 14, leans, as if unwilling to cooperate with the painter, against one of two enormous

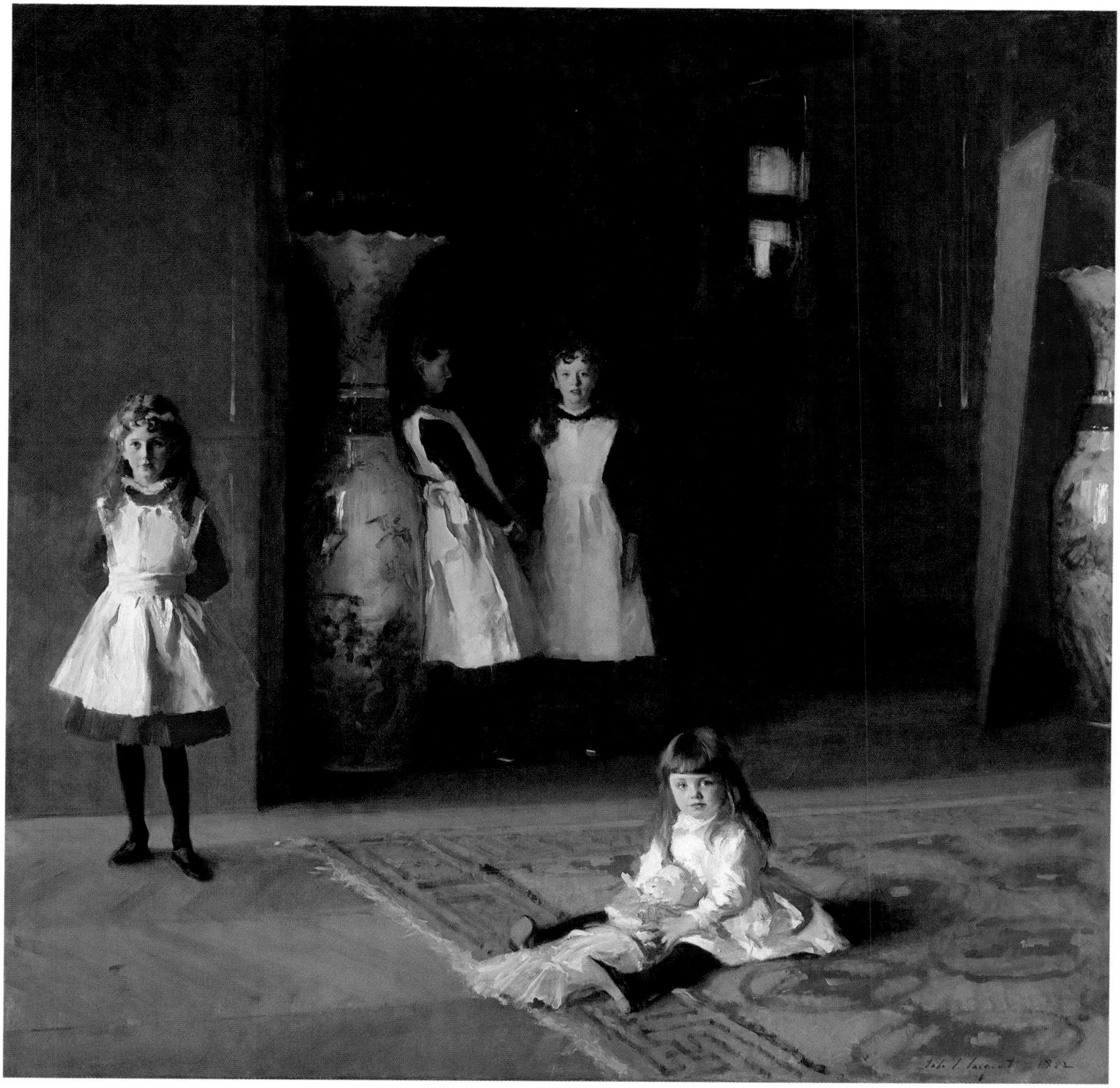

Fig. 22-5 John Singer Sargent, *The Daughters of Edward Darley Boit*, 1882. Oil on canvas, 7 ft. 3⅜ in. × 7 ft. 3⅜ in. Museum of Fine Arts, Boston.
Gift of Mary Louisa Boit, Julia Overing Boit, Jane Hubbard Boit, and Florence D. Boit in memory of their father, Edward Darley Boit, 19.124.

Chinese vases that lend the scene something of an "Alice in Wonderland" effect.

James first described this painting as "a rich, dim, rather generalized French interior (the perspective of a hall with a shining floor, where screens and tall Japanese vases shimmer and loom), which encloses the life and seems to form the happy play-world of a family of charming children." But gradually he came to perceive in the work the same mysterious depth that he tried to convey in his own fiction—"the sense," he called it, "of assimilated secrets." The giant vases—the girls' mother had inherited a considerable fortune from her family's trade with China—loom over the scene as if to assert an uneasy authority. More disturbing, perhaps, is the red screen, which seems to slash into the space like a bloody knife. There is, as well, a real sense of disconnection among Sargent's subjects. At least at some level, the painting is a parable of the coming of

Fig. 22-6 Nicholas Nixon, *The Brown Sisters*, 1976. Gelatin silver print, 7 11/16 × 9 5/8 in. Museum of Modern Art, New York.

age of young women in late nineteenth-century society, moving from the innocence of youth to the privacy and alienation of adolescence—and suggesting an adult life that in fact turned out to be as withdrawn as the existence depicted in the painting itself. None of the girls ever married. Florence, the eldest, became an avid golfer—one of the first young women in America to take up the sport. She died in 1919 at the age of 51. Her sister Jane was in and out of mental institutions her entire life, suffering from anger and depression, until her death at age 85 in 1955. The two youngest daughters, Julia and Mary Louisa, lived together in Newport, Rhode Island, until Julia died in 1945 at age 71. Mary Louisa passed away in 1969 at age 91, alone.

It is within the family, of course, that the process of aging—the cycle of life—is most evident to us all. This is the real subject of Nicholas Nixon's ongoing series of photographs depicting his wife, Bebe Brown Nixon, and her three sisters (**Figs. 22-6** and **22-7**). Each year, beginning in 1975, when the four women ranged in age from 15 to 25, Nixon has made a black-and-white photograph of the four, always showing them arranged in the same order from left to right: Heather, Mimi, Bebe, and Laurie. Although he shoots any number of exposures, he has printed only one photograph each time. By 2013, he had created a series of 38 photographs that reveal not only the gradual aging process of the sisters, but, he suggests, the ever-changing dynamics of the relationships among them. Yet one of the most fascinating aspects of the series is the commitment of the women to sustain the project, not least now, as they age, with the prospect of their—or the photographer's—eventual demise. The series is not only a testament to time's relentless force, but to the power of family, and love, to endure and sustain us all, as if in spite of time itself. The power of the image to endure may, Nixon's work suggests, in fact lie at the heart of every family's commitment to documenting in photography its history, even as the family is transformed and irrevocably changed by its very history.

The feminist, activist, and artist Suzanne Lacy has continually addressed the issue of aging in American society since 1976, when she staged a performance called *Inevitable Associations* at the American Theater Convention in the lobby of the Biltmore Hotel in Los Angeles. The hotel was, at the time, undergoing a renovation that the Los Angeles media had compared to a "facelift" for an "aging dowager." Lacy's performance was staged in three booths. In the first, a young woman passed out copies of the news articles Lacy and her collaborators considered offensive. In the second, a surgeon's assistant handed out pamphlets showing women before and after their plastic surgeries. Throughout the day, Lacy, in the third booth, was slowly aged by a Hollywood make-up artist. In the lobby opposite Lacy, old women dressed in black began to arrive and seat themselves in ten red chairs. As Lacy's make-up was completed, the tenth old woman arrived, and the ten women surrounded Lacy and dressed

Fig. 22-7 Nicholas Nixon, *The Brown Sisters, Truro, Massachusetts*, 2011. Gelatin silver print, 17 15/16 × 22 5/8 in. Museum of Modern Art, New York.

her in black as well. Finally, the group posed together and dispersed into the crowd. The next day, three of the older women, seated on the same red chairs within three circles of spectators, described their lives since turning 60. While the work clearly critiqued ageism in American society, the performance also empowered its senior participants by allowing them to actively engage with the issues.

One of the most visually spectacular of Lacy's works on this theme is *Whisper, the Waves, the Wind* (**Fig. 22-8**), a performance tableau in which 154 women over the age of 65 proceeded through an audience of 1,000 people and down steep stairs to two beach coves situated back to back in La Jolla, California, to sit around white cloth-covered tables and talk about their lives, their relationships, their hopes, and their fears. In the middle of the performance, the audience was invited onto the beach to listen close at hand. The piece was motivated by several salient facts: By the year 2020, one in five people in the United States will be over 65; this population will be predominantly female and single; and today women account for nearly 75 percent of the aged poor. For Lacy, the performance reinforced the strong spiritual and physical beauty of older women: "They reminded me of the place where the ocean meets shoreline. Their bodies were growing older, wrinkled. But what I saw was the rock in them; solid, with the presence of the years washing over them." By isolating the women on a beach—a symbolic line of demarcation and transition—separated from those who need to hear them, Lacy underscores their isolation. In doing so, she also represents the experience of aging in America, the experience of being caught between the culture's compassion for the aging and its willingness to ignore them. The image of these women, in white, in this setting, also helps us to understand the beauty of their aging, a fact that we might otherwise ignore, eliciting not only our admiration but also a certain hope for our own endurance, the dignity of our own maturation. Finally, the stark contrast between the orderliness and "civilized" quality of the tables on the beach and the natural "wildness" of the shoreline suggests the power of the human imagination to transform our prejudices through art.

Fig. 22-8 Suzanne Lacy, *Whisper, the Waves, the Wind*, 1984. Site photograph of a performance in the *Whisper Projects*.
Courtesy of Suzanne Lacy.

Contemplating Mortality

What are some of the ways in which an awareness of our own mortality is reflected in art?

The inevitable fact of death has, from the earliest times, both troubled and fascinated the human imagination. Sometime around 7400 BCE, for instance, at Çatalhöyük (also known as Chatal Huyuk) in central Turkey, a permanent village began to take shape that would flourish for nearly 1,200 years. At one point or another, as many as 3,000 people lived here in close proximity to one another in rectangular houses made of mud bricks held together with plaster. The rows of windowless houses that composed the village, the walls of which rose as high as 16 feet, must have served a defensive purpose, but they also contained what archeologists have come to view as an extraordinary sense of communal history. Their interior walls and floors were plastered and replastered, then painted and repainted with a white lime-based paint, again and again over hundreds of years. Beneath the floors of some—but not all—of the houses were burials, averaging about six per house, but sometimes rising to between 30 and 62 bodies. For reasons that are not entirely clear, from time to time, these bodies were exhumed, and the skulls of long-deceased ancestors were removed, and then reburied in new graves or in the foundations of new houses as they were built and rebuilt. Whatever the rationale for such ceremonies, they could not have helped but create a sense of historical continuity in the community.

Çatalhöyük was first extensively excavated from 1958 by Sir James Mellaart, who concluded that the village's culture was matrilineal, based in no small part on his discovery of a number of female figurines, including a clay sculpture of a seated woman (**Fig. 22-9**), who represented, he believed, a fertility or mother goddess. Found in a grain bin—evidence of the community's growing agricultural sophistication—she sits enthroned between two felines, perhaps in the process of giving birth. But Ian Hodder of Cambridge University, who took up excavations of the site in 1993, after a nearly 30-year hiatus, has recently concluded that she is something other than a fertility goddess. In 2005, he wrote:

> There are full breasts on which the hands rest and the stomach is extended in the central part. There is a hole in the top for the head which is missing *[the head shown in the photograph here is a modern addition]*. As one turns the figurine around one notices that the arms are very thin, and then on the back of the figurine one sees a depiction of either a skeleton or the bones of a very thin and depleted human. The ribs and vertebrae are clear, as are the scapulae and the main pelvic bones. The figurine can be interpreted in a number of ways—as a woman turning into an ancestor, as a woman associated with death, or as death and life conjoined. . . . Perhaps the importance of female imagery was related to some special role of the female in relation to death as much as to the roles of mother and nurturer.

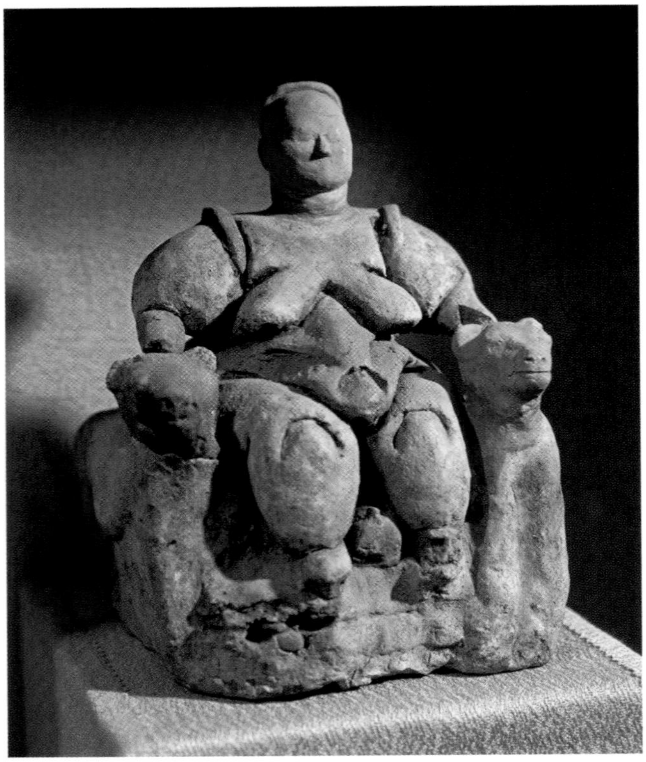

Fig. 22-9 Woman seated between two felines, Çatalhöyük, Turkey, ca. 6850–6300 BCE. Terra cotta, height 4⅝ in. Museum of Anatolian Civilizations, Ankara.
akg-image/De Agostini Picture Lib./M. Seemuller.

Supporting Hodder's theories is a burial of a deceased woman who holds in her arms the plastered and painted skull of a male.

From the front, the Çatalhöyük woman appears to be an image of fecund fullness, but from the rear she seems to be caught in the throes of death, as her body submits to the process of decay and decomposition. It is as if, in Çatalhöyük, it was well understood that death lurks behind life. This was, in fact, the motivation for depictions of the decaying body in the Japanese art of *kusozu*, "painting of the nine stages of a decaying corpse," popular from the thirteenth through the nineteenth century. The subject itself is derived from a traditional Buddhist text, the *Discourse on the Great Wisdom*, which dates from the early fifth century. The text argues that contemplation of the nine stages of a decaying corpse allows one to overcome love of the body and, by extension, carnal desire, and thus come ever closer to enlightenment, and it sets out the canonical sequence of nine stages in the process. Traditionally, the portrayal of the nine stages of decomposition begins with a pre-death portrait of the subject—in Kobayashi Eitaku's 16-foot *kusozu* handscroll, a loosely robed courtesan (**Fig. 22-10**). Here, she is meant to represent the very carnal desire that the subsequent images are designed to thwart, and in this she is similar to the frontal view of the Çatalhöyük woman. To move through the handscroll, from the bloating of the corpse to its decomposition and, in the seventh stage, also illustrated here, its consumption by animals and birds, is, in effect, like moving behind the Çatalhöyük woman to see her eviscerated body.

Such fascination with death and the contemplation of our own mortality has perhaps never been more all-consuming than it was in the fourteenth century when the bubonic plague, or Black Death, wreaked havoc on the Western world (see Chapter 18). Within months of rats infected with the plague arriving in Sicily, the disease spread northward, through the ports of Venice, Genoa, and Pisa, across Italy, southern France, and eastern Spain.

The lasting psychological effects of the epidemic cannot be overstated, amounting to a growing social obsession with death itself. A good example is the Book of Hours—a private prayer book containing a calendar, services for the canonical hours, and sometimes special prayers—commissioned by Bonne of Luxembourg, wife of the dauphin of France, from her court illuminator, Jean Le Noir, at some point probably not long before her own death from the plague

Fig. 22-10 Kobayashi Eitaku, two scenes from the handscroll *Body of a Courtesan in Nine Stages of Decomposition*, 1870s. Ink and color on silk, 10 in. × 16 ft. 5½ in. The British Museum, London.

2008,3033.1.

Fig. 22-11 Jean Le Noir, pages with *The Three Living* (left) and *The Three Dead* (right), from the *Psalter and Hours of Bonne of Luxembourg, Duchess of Normandy*, before 1349. Grisaille, color, gilt, and brown ink on vellum, $5\frac{3}{16} \times 7\frac{11}{16}$ in. opened. Metropolitan Museum of Art, New York.

Cloisters Collection, 1969.86 © 2015. Image copyright Metropolitan Museum of Art/Art Resource/Scala, Florence.

in 1348 (**Fig. 22-11**). On the left-hand page, three horsemen contemplate three cadavers in increasing states of decay on the right-hand page. One horseman brings a handkerchief to his nose to fight off the stench. The cadavers address the horsemen: "What you are we were and what we are you will be!" The artist's depiction of the human body in decay is astonishingly realistic—especially in light of the Church ban on performing autopsies. As in Japanese *kusozu*, by making us confront death, the artist is determined to bring us face to face with the ultimate truth of things.

But since the plague destroyed people and not possessions, the enormous decrease in population resulted in a corresponding increase in per capita wealth, and those who survived invested in religious art—chapels and hospitals, altarpieces and votive statues—in gratitude for being spared or in the hope of preventing future infection. Painters and sculptors turned their attention to the representation of the sufferings of Christ, the sorrows rather than the joys of the Virgin, and the miracles of the saints.

These images of *The Three Living* and *The Three Dead* in the *Psalter and Hours of Bonne of Luxembourg* are an example of what is known as a ***memento mori*** (literally, in Latin, "remember that you will die"), an image that invites viewers to contemplate their own mortality, the vanity of their earthly pursuits, and the transient nature of all their earthly possessions and desires. One of the classic expressions of this sentiment—which is in fact a directive to lead a virtuous, even ascetic life—is Nicolas Poussin's *The Shepherds of Arcadia* (**Fig. 22-12**). Three shepherds have come upon a tombstone in Arcadia, a region on the

Fig. 22-12 Nicolas Poussin, *The Shepherds of Arcadia* (a.k.a. *Et in Arcadia Ego*), 1638–39. Oil on canvas, $33\frac{1}{2} \times 47\frac{5}{8}$ in. Musée du Louvre, Paris.

Inv. INV7300. Photo © Musée du Louvre, Dist. RMN-Grand Palais/Angèle Dequier.

Greek Peloponnese that was celebrated during the Renaissance as a kind of idyllic landscape, an area of unspoiled and harmonious wilderness as yet untouched by civilization. The trio are evidently attempting to come to grips with the stone's significance. The shepherd at the left leans casually upon the grave as if wholly unaware of its meaning. The second shepherd, in blue, kneels before it and points at its inscription, *"Et in Arcadia ego"*—"Even in Arcadia, there am I," even as he casts his shadow across it. This shadow, of course, represents his "shade," or spirit, and unwittingly he thus begins to reveal the inscription's meaning. The third shepherd turns toward the female figure standing at the right, as if to say, "I think I understand." She rests her hand on his back as if to comfort him in his new knowledge. Just who this female figure is has been a matter of some scholarly debate, but since the shepherds are in Arcadia it seems reasonable to suggest that she is Athena, the Greek goddess of wisdom and the one figure in the painting who fully understands the inscription's meaning: "Even in such a blessed place as Arcadia, I, Death, hold sway."

Vanitas paintings such as *Still Life with Lobster* by Jan de Heem (**Fig. 22-13**; see also Fig. 9-16) are also examples of the *memento mori* tradition. In seventeenth-century Holland, lobster was a luxury foodstuff (see Chapter 9); considered in the light of the *memento mori* tradition, its inclusion in such a scene is especially poignant, for lobsters are kept alive until the moment they are dropped into boiling water and cooked for about 15 minutes. Their bright red color, such a prominent feature of de Heem's composition, results from their being boiled. In fact, still-life painting as a genre is tied particularly closely to the *memento mori* tradition. The French name for still life is *nature morte*, "dead nature" (see the introduction to Part 2). Likewise, in Italian, the genre's name is *natura morta*. The origins of the name date back to the habit of fifteenth-century Italian painters and miniaturists of recording their observations of birds and beasts in model-books for later use in finished paintings for their aristocratic patrons—scenes depicting the courtly hunting culture of the era. Their models were not, of course, live animals, but dead specimens.

Fig. 22-13 Jan de Heem, *Still Life with Lobster*, late 1640s. Oil on canvas, 25⅛ × 33¼ in. Toledo Museum of Art, Toledo, Ohio. Purchased with funds from the Libbey Endowment. Gift of Edward Drummond Libbey, 1952.25. Photo: Photography Incorporated, Toledo.

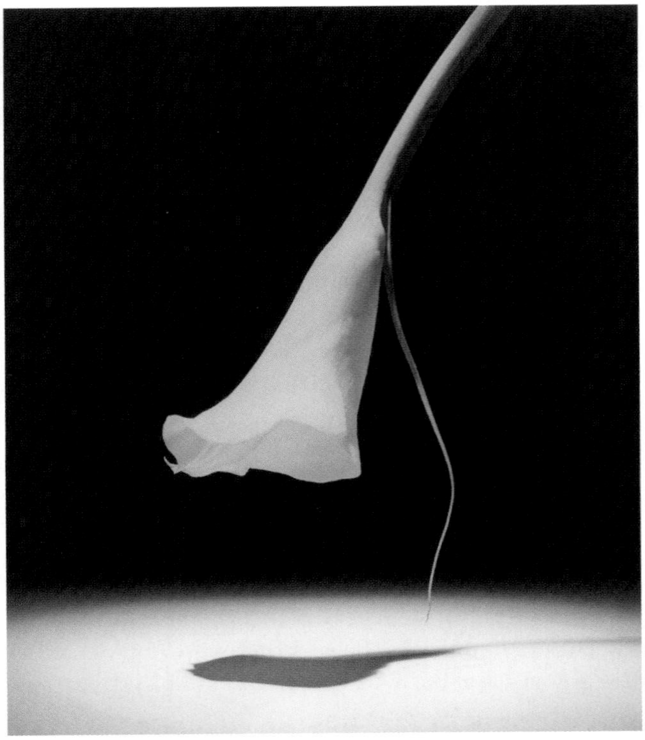

Fig. 22-14 Robert Mapplethorpe, *Calla Lily*, 1986. Gelatin silver print, 19¼ × 19⅜ in. Solomon R. Guggenheim Museum, New York.

Gift, 93.4302.

Still-life arrangements of flowers—often single stems—were among Robert Mapplethorpe's favorite subjects. *Calla Lily* (**Fig. 22-14**) was shot in 1986, the same year that Mapplethorpe was diagnosed with AIDS. The HIV/AIDS contagion swept through the art world rather like the Black Death had once swept through Europe. Between 1985 and 1990, it is safe to say that everyone in the arts knew someone who had died or was dying of AIDS. In light of this it is somewhat surprising that very few people recognized that Mapplethorpe's flower photographs were *memento mori*. *Calla Lily*, for instance, is lit in a manner reminiscent of Rembrandt's *The Three Crosses* (see Fig. 3-7), and the shadow its drooping form casts upon the table below recalls the shadow that the kneeling man in Poussin's *The Shepherds of Arcadia* casts upon the tombstone's inscription. In its stark black-and-white contrast, Mapplethorpe invokes the battle for life in the midst of the dark surround of death, a spiritual strength in the face of AIDS.

Burial and the Afterlife

What are some ways in which burial practices reflect belief in the afterlife?

Perhaps because works of art and architecture are themselves acts of imagination that seem to transcend the bounds of daily experience, offering us evidence of a seemingly innate human ability to exceed our own limitations, they have traditionally been associated with burial sites and the possibility of an afterlife in some other realm, a realm with which we might in some way communicate.

The ancient Egyptians' belief in the afterlife was a direct reflection of their understanding of the cycle of seasonal change and return. Nearly every year, before dams were built upstream in the twentieth century, torrential rains caused the Nile River to rise dramatically. Most years, from July to November, the ancient Egyptians could count on the Nile flooding their land. When the river receded, deep deposits of fertile silt covered the valley floor. Fields would then be tilled, and crops planted and tended. If the flooding was either too great or too minor, especially over a period of years, famine could result. The cycle of flood and sun, devastation and renewal, made Egypt one of the most productive cultures in the ancient world—and one of the most stable.

The great pyramids at Giza (**Fig. 22-15**; see also Fig. 14-2) are expressions of this sense of cyclical return. Egyptian culture was dedicated to providing a home for the *ka*, that part of the human being that defines personality and that survives life on earth after death (see Chapter 16). The pyramids were the largest of the resting places designed to house the *ka*. When a king died in the royal palaces on the east bank of the Nile, his body was transported across the river to a valley temple on the west bank. After a ritual ceremony, it was carried up the causeway to the temple in front of the pyramid where another ritual was performed—the "opening of the mouth," in which priests "fed" the deceased's *ka* a special meal. The body was then sealed in a relatively small tomb deep in the heart of the pyramid, from which ran two airshafts oriented to specific stars, including Sirius, the brightest star in the night sky. The relationship between the various sides of the structure suggests that the Egyptians understood and made use of the mathematical value π (pi). All of this has led to considerable theorizing about "the secret of the pyramids." One theory is that the pyramids' sides represented the descending rays of the sun god Re, whose cult was particularly powerful at the time the pyramids were built (see Chapter 16). Another is that the three pyramids are aligned to reflect the three stars that form the belt of the constellation Orion. In any case, it was in the heavens that the *ka* of the king was reborn.

The elaborate burial process was not meant solely to guarantee survival of the king's *ka*. It also prepared him for a "last judgment," which was routinely illustrated in Books of Going Forth by Day (now also called Books of the Dead), collections of magical texts or spells buried with the deceased to help them survive the ritual of judgment. The moment of judgment

Fig. 22-15 Pyramids of Menkaure (ca. 2470 BCE), Khafre (ca. 2500 BCE), and Khufu (ca. 2530 BCE). Original height of Pyramid of Khufu 480 ft., length of each side at base 755 ft.

is depicted in one such Book of Going Forth by Day, a papyrus scroll created for an otherwise anonymous man known as Hunefer (**Fig. 22-16**). The scene reads from left to right in a continuous pictorial narrative. To the left, Anubis, overseer of funerals and cemeteries, leads Hunefer into the judgment area with his right hand while in his left he carries an *ankh*, symbol of eternal life. Hunefer's heart, which has the form here of a small pot, is next weighed against the ostrich feather as Ammit, the vile "Eater of the Dead," part crocodile, part lion, and part hippopotamus, looks on. In this image, Hunefer passes the test—not surprising, given that the work is dedicated to ensuring that Hunefer's *ka* survive in the afterlife. Finally, the sky god Horus, usually pictured as a hawk, an *ankh* in his left hand, leads Hunefer to Osiris, god of goodness,

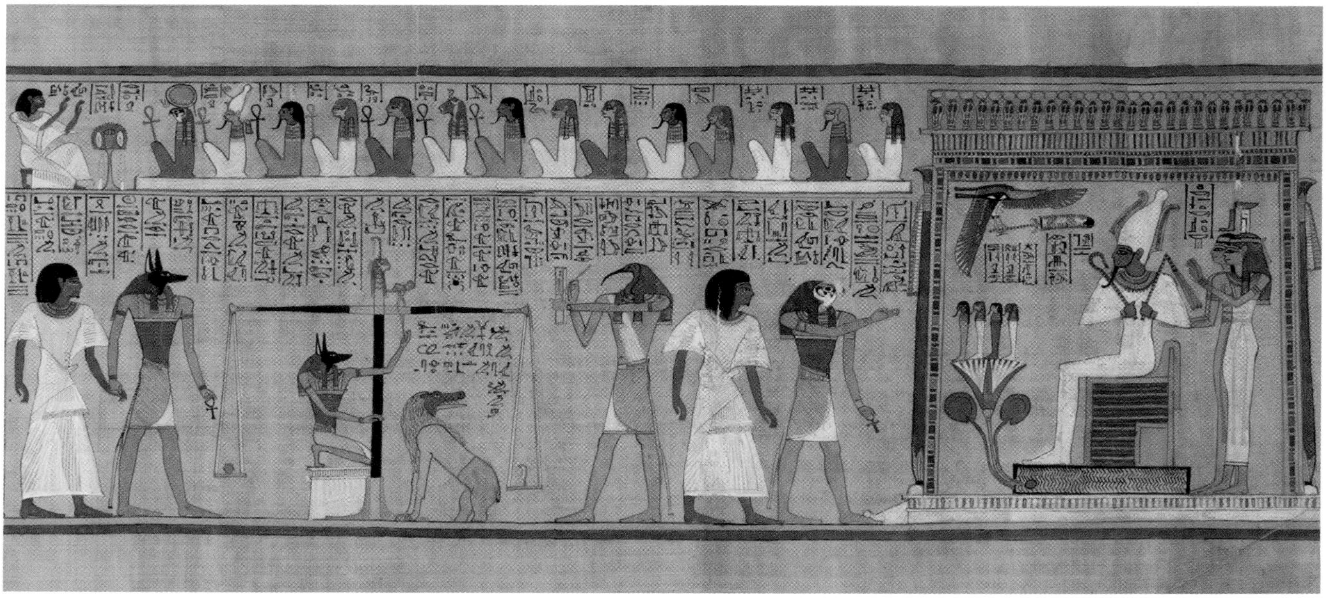

Fig. 22-16 *Last Judgment of Hunefer by Osiris*, from a Book of Going Forth by Day in his tomb at Thebes, Dynasty 19, ca. 1285 BCE. Painted papyrus scroll, height 15⅝ in. The British Museum, London.

vegetation, and death, who is seated under a canopy and who oversaw this moment of judgment.

Like the Egyptian pyramids, the Temple of Inscriptions at Palenque, in the present-day Mexican state of Chiapas, was the final resting place of a king, K'Inich Janab Pacal, who ruled for 67 years and died in 683 CE. Inscribed with the history of the Palenque kings, the Temple of Inscriptions was erected over his grave and rises in nine steps, representing nine levels of the Mayan Underworld where the souls of the dead finally came to rest.

In 1952, Alberto Ruz, a Mexican archeologist, discovered the entrance to the tomb of Lord Pacal hidden under large stone slabs in the floor of the shrine at the top of the pyramid. Ruz had to clear away the passage down to Pacal's tomb, at the very base of the structure, which had been back-filled with stone debris. A small tube connected the tomb with the upper level, thus providing the dead king with an eternal source of fresh air. Pacal himself was buried in a large uterus-shaped sarcophagus, the lid of which represents Pacal falling off the Wacah Chan, the great tree that connects the Upperworld, the Middleworld, and the Underworld (**Fig. 22-17**). Since the sarcophagus weighs over 5 tons, it was surely put in place before the Pyramid of Inscriptions was built above it, though it well may not have contained the body of Pacal when it was constructed. The tree on the lid is encircled by a double-headed serpent, signifying the royal lineage of the deceased. The king was believed to be the embodiment of the Wacah Chan, and when he stood at the top of a pyramid in ritual activity, he was seen as linking the three layers of the universe in his own person. During such rituals, the king would let his own blood in order to give sustenance to the spiritual world. Some scholars now believe that the Wacah Chan can actually be read astronomically as the Milky Way, along which the spirit of the dead travel before being reborn into a new life.

Fig. 22-17 Cast of sarcophagus cover of K'Inich Janab Pacal, died 683 CE, from the Temple of Inscriptions, Palenque, Mexico. Limestone, 12 ft. 6 in. × 7 ft. National Anthropological Museum, Mexico.
Art Archive/National Anthropological Museum Mexico/Gianni Dagli Orti.

As both the Egyptian pyramids and the Mayan Temple of Inscriptions suggest, cultures often treat the death of their rulers with special, memorial architecture. In Greek culture, those who were most distinguished in life were believed to pass on to a special place, a paradise known as the Elysian Fields, where humans enjoy an afterlife comparable to that of the gods. Its first mention in Greek literature is in Homer's *Odyssey*, where it is named as the resting place of Menelaus, husband of Helen. But it was the Roman poet Virgil's description that would most influence later eras—"a land of joy, the green pleasaunces and happy seats of the Blissful groves" (*Aeneid* 6:637–39)—and hence the French would call the broad and tree-lined avenue that Marie de' Medici, wife to King Henri IV, ordered built in 1616 the "Champs-Elysées" (*champs* is French for "fields"). And it is in this context that the cemetery as we today know it came into being.

Before the nineteenth century, most burial sites in Europe and America were in grounds adjoining churches—which is to say, in the middle of cities and towns. But by the middle of the eighteenth century, many of these urban cemeteries were almost literally exploding with corpses. Many people, who by then possessed at least a rudimentary understanding of infection, argued that these urban cemeteries were a breeding ground for disease. On December 1, 1780, a cellar wall on the Rue de la Ferronnerie, next to the Cemetery of the Holy Innocents in the area of Paris today known as Les Halles, burst, releasing noxious gases and fluids into the streets, and the cemetery was permanently closed. As for the dead, they were reburied in catacombs dug from ancient quarries beneath the city streets, today a tourist site.

This vast removal of the dead amounted to a banishment of the specter of death from the daily life of the city, culminating finally, in 1804, with Napoleon's Imperial Decree on Burials. Henceforth, burial was banned within the city. Each corpse would have an individual plot, permanent if space allowed, in one of four garden environments outside the city proper—among them, the bucolic Père Lachaise Cemetery (**Fig. 22-18**), which even today attracts

Fig. 22-18 After Pierre Courvoisier, *View of Père Lachaise Cemetery from the Entrance*, 1815. Color engraving. Bibliothèque des Arts Décoratifs, Paris.
Archives Charmet/Bridgeman Images.

Parisian strollers to its hills and paths. It was envisioned that in these new Elysian Fields, with their wandering paths and panoramic views, children would periodically scatter flowers, and before long it did indeed become routine for the living to place flowers upon the graves of the deceased. America soon adopted the idea, first, in 1831, at Mount Auburn Cemetery in Cambridge, Massachusetts, and then, in 1842, at Greenwood Cemetery in Brooklyn. Thus, the idea of the cemetery as a kind of landscape garden, as we know it today, was born.

The individual graves in these cemetery gardens are often decorated with elaborately sculpted gravestones—a way for the living to honor their dead forebears. In Mexican culture, the dead are remembered with *ofrendas* (Spanish for "offerings"), temporary altars generally created for the annual Mexican *Dia de los Muertos* (Day of the Dead) celebration. These constructions mediate between the living and the dead, whose spirits are brought back through the *ofrendas* and remembered by living relatives. In 1984, the year after actress Dolores del Rio, who worked for five decades in both Hollywood and the Mexican cinema, died at the age of 78, Amalia Mesa-Bains created *An Ofrenda for Dolores del Rio* (**Fig. 22-19**). Mesa-Bains has explained her *ofrenda* this way:

> With a career in both the American and Mexican cinema, Dolores symbolized a universal yet particularly Mexican beauty to a generation of Chicanos. In her position as an accepted beauty in both cultures, Dolores gave meaning and power to a generation of Chicanos suffering rejection because of the accepted Anglo standard of beauty. This altar gratefully acknowledges the power of her mythic beauty and her contribution to *Nuestra Cultura*. The objects on the altar are a gesture symbolizing her glamour, elegance and *corazon* [heart].

Through this *ofrenda*, Mesa-Bains honors and remembers someone who both inspired and affirmed her own life as an artist.

Fig. 22-19 Amalia Mesa-Bains, *An Ofrenda for Dolores del Rio*, 1984, revised 1991. Mixed-media installation including plywood, mirrors, fabric, framed photographs, found objects, dried flowers, and glitter, dimensions variable; as seen here, approx. 8 × 6 × 4 ft. Smithsonian American Art Museum, Washington, D.C.
Museum purchase through the Smithsonian Institution Collections Acquisition Program, 1998.161. © 2015. Photo Smithsonian American Art Museum/Art Resource/Scala, Florence. © 2015 Amalia Mesa-Bains.

THE CRITICAL PROCESS

Thinking about the Cycle of Life

In 2013, choreographer Stephen Petronio asked artist Janine Antoni (see Fig. 4-24) if she would be interested in doing the visuals for his new dance, *Like Lazarus Did*, a collaboration detailed in the art21 *Exclusive* segment "Janine Antoni: Collaborating with Stephen Petronio." The work was inspired by themes of birth, death, and resurrection—the themes that are the subject of this chapter. These are echoed in composer Son Lux's score, which combines electronic minimalism with African-American spirituals and texts, including, in a call-and-response sequence featuring Lux's recorded voice and a full choir, Sojourner Truth's famous exhortation, "Where did your Christ come from? From God and a woman," from her 1851 address to the Women's Convention in Akron, Ohio, "Ain't I a Woman?" The title of the piece comes from a similar call-and-response: "I wanna die," Lux sings, and the chorus replies, "Like Lazarus did." What is the reference to Lazarus?

Watching Petronio's troupe rehearse, Antoni was moved to offer him something in counterpoint to the exuberance and complexity of the dance itself—her own stillness. For the hour-long duration of the performance, she lay completely still, a caged light bulb in her left hand, suspended above the audience in a helicopter stretcher, contemplating her own body and her own death, for hanging above her were replicas of her own body parts—lungs, arm bones, spine, legs, torso. As the audience entered the theater, with Antoni already in place, they were given small cards with, on one side, a photograph of Antoni's hand holding her light, and, on the other, the question "Should I look among the living / Should I look among the dead / If I'm searching for you?" And in fact the major tension of the work turned out to be the dynamic relationship between Antoni's deathlike lack of movement and the continuous flowing movement of Petronio's dancers.

As Petronio was creating the piece, his pregnant cousin was sending him sonograms of her baby, and Petronio decided to base the final number in the work, a solo for dancer Nick Sciscione, on the fetal body positions he found in the sonograms—a quiet but transcendent moment of rebirth to conclude the piece. Antoni suggested that it would be wonderful if Sciscione could perform the work in honey, which both looks and feels like amniotic fluid. This was, of course, impossible to do on stage, but after the conclusion of the dance's tour, Petronio and Antoni collaborated on a 14-minute video of Sciscione moving in a honey-coated tube, which they called *Honey Baby* (**Fig. 22-20**). How does *Honey Baby*, segments of which can be seen in the art21 video, reflect the larger themes of *Like Lazarus Did*? How does the video reflect the cycle of life as a theme?

Fig. 22-20 Janine Antoni and Stephen Petronio, *Honey Baby*, 2013. Still. Video, 14 min. Edition of 10 and 4 AP. Performer: Nick Sciscione. Videographer: Kirsten Johnson. Composer: Tom Laurie. Editor: Amanda Laws.
Courtesy of the artists and Luhring Augustine, New York.

Thinking Back

22.1 Describe how depictions of pregnancy cause us to reflect on our own humanity.

The Moche vessel depicting a birth might also reflect larger notions of rebirth and regeneration. How might it relate to the environmental circumstances of the Moche homeland? For Leonardo da Vinci, the human body was analogous to the earth itself. How, in studying the embryo, did he see his own origins? In Jan van Eyck's depiction of Eve in *The Ghent Altarpiece*, we are meant to see both the promise of birth and the suffering of humankind. How does art historian Linda Seidel argue that Eve is pregnant in van Eyck's painting?

22.2 Outline some of the narratives suggested by images of youth and aging.

John Singer Sargent's *Daughters of Edward Darley Boit* is a portrait of four young girls, but how does it also suggest the process of aging and its consequences? What is the theme of Nicholas Nixon's *The Brown Sisters*? How does Suzanne Lacy critique the American cultural approach to aging?

22.3 Discuss some of the ways in which an awareness of our own mortality is reflected in art.

From the earliest times, the inevitable fact of death has both troubled and fascinated the human imagination. The citizens of Çatalhöyük, in ancient Turkey, buried their dead beneath the floors of their homes, and periodically unearthed them and reburied them again. How does the woman of Çatalhöyük reflect the community's sense of the presence of death in life? What is the Japanese art of *kusozu*? What was the impact of the Black Death on Western consciousness? What makes Nicolas Poussin's *The Shepherds of Arcadia* a *memento mori*? How does Robert Mapplethorpe's *Calla Lily* serve as a *memento mori*?

22.4 Outline some of the ways in which burial practices reflect a belief in the afterlife.

The annual cycle of flood and sun—the inundation of the Nile River Valley that deposited deep layers of silt, followed by months of sun in which crops could grow in the fertile soil—helped to define Egyptian culture. Can you describe this belief in terms of cyclical harmony? Most surviving Egyptian art and architecture is devoted to burial and the afterlife, the cycle of life, death, and rebirth. The pyramids at Giza are especially dedicated to this cycle. What particular aspect of Egyptian spiritual life do they embody? What is the *ka*? What are the Books of Going Forth by Day? How is the tomb of Pacal in the Temple of Inscriptions at Palenque similar to the Egyptian pyramids? What is the Wacah Chan? Before the nineteenth century most burial sites in Europe and America were in churchyards—that is, in the center of cities and towns. But when, on December 1, 1780, a cellar wall on the Rue de la Ferronnerie alongside the Cemetery of the Holy Innocents in Paris burst, releasing noxious gases and fluids into the streets, that cemetery was not only closed, but a new rural cemetery was inaugurated, led by the creation of the Père Lachaise Cemetery in Paris. How does Père Lachaise reflect the tradition of the Elysian Fields, which stretches back to the Greeks? What is an *ofrenda*? How does Amelia Mesa-Bains's *Ofrenda for Dolores del Rio* reflect the actress's impact on Chicano culture?

Chapter 23
Love and Sex

Learning Objectives

23.1 Describe how the tension between physical and spiritual love manifests itself in different cultures.

23.2 Explain some of the different ways in which desire has been imaged.

23.3 Discuss the kiss as an image of desire.

Since his teens, the sculptor Auguste Rodin had been haunted by Dante's *Divine Comedy*, and by the *Inferno* in particular, a vision of Hell composed of nine descending rings of sinners undergoing punishment, each more gruesome than the one before it. Led by the Roman poet Virgil, Dante descends into the first circle of sinners and there encounters the lovers Paolo and Francesca, murdered by Francesca's husband and Paolo's brother, Giancotto, for committing adultery. Their illicit love was motivated, they tell Dante, by reading Chrétien de Troyes's medieval romance *Lancelot*, the story of the knight Lancelot's love for Guinevere, the wife of the legendary King Arthur. When Rodin began work on *The Gates of Hell* in 1880 (see Fig. 7-29), it was to the *Inferno* that he turned for inspiration, and Paolo and Francesca, forever condemned to unreconciled love, doomed to touch each other but never consummate their feelings, were among his first subjects (the pair are at the bottom of the left-hand door).

Rodin was probably attracted to their story because it explores the twin capacities of love and lust, the ennobling power of love that can simultaneously unleash the destructive forces of unbridled passion and sexual desire. In *The Gates*, the couple flies forward, as in Dante's poem, "swept together . . . on the wind." But soon after starting work on *The Gates*, Rodin conceived of depicting a different moment, before their murder, when they read of Guinevere being kissed by Lancelot. As Francesca tells Dante:

> he who is one with me alive and dead [Paolo]
> breathed on my lips the tremor of his kiss. . . .
> That day we read no further.

In *The Kiss* (*Le Baiser*) (**Fig. 23-1**), only the fact that the man still holds a book in his left hand alludes to the original story. Rodin transforms the couple into every man and every woman—love personified, and erotic love at that—even as he transforms marble into flesh. There is no more enduring theme in art than this mysterious coupling of love and sex, transcendent emotion and carnal desire.

Physical and Spiritual Love

How does the tension between physical and spiritual love manifest itself in different cultures?

Almost all cultures have struggled to resolve the tension between mere physical desire and the higher orders of feeling associated with more spiritual ideas of love. In

Fig. 23-1 Auguste Rodin, *The Kiss* (*Le Baiser*), 1888–89. Marble, 5 ft. 11½ in. × 44¼ in. × 46 in. Musée Rodin, Paris. Inv. S.1002. © Vanni Archive/Art Resource, New York.

his *Republic*, for instance, the Greek philosopher Plato argued that sex should be permitted only for purposes of procreation. Anything that encouraged emotional and sensory feelings over and against the exercise of reason and the pursuit of ideal beauty, he believed, was potentially a danger to the well-being of the state. Various forms of this attitude have survived in Western culture to the present day. But in other cultures sex and physical passion are something to be celebrated.

Sexuality in the Hindu World

One of the most important figures in the Hindu pantheon of gods is Shiva, the destroyer (see Fig. 17-22). He embodies the world's cyclical rhythms—hence his role as Lord of the Dance—and since the cyclical destruction of the world is followed by its new creation, he is a positive force, possessing the reproductive powers that led him to be represented as a *lingam* (phallus), often carved in stone on temple grounds or at shrines. But one of the most popular representations of him among Nepalese Hindus shows him seated with his wife, Uma (**Fig. 23-2**). Uma tenderly places her hand on the inside of his thigh as he draws her to him with his left hand. In her left hand, Uma holds a lotus, symbol of divine purity, but a parrot, symbol of physical passion, is pecking at it. Thus, physical and spiritual love are conjoined, just as the joyful harmony between male and female, Shiva and Uma, represents the ultimate oneness and harmony of the universe.

A wall of even more erotic sculptures rises alongside the *garbhagriha*, or "womb chamber" in which rests the *lingam* of Shiva, at Kandariya Mahadeva Temple in Khajuraho (**Fig. 23-3**; see also Figs. 17-24 and 21-13). Its placement seems purposeful, since sculptures depicting other aspects of daily life cover many other walls of the temple. These sculptures probably represent the idea of *kama*—meaning "desire" or "longing," usually but not exclusively sexual—the satisfaction of which is one of the four goals of human life in Hindu tradition. Sex, in this tradition, is a process of enjoyment (reflected in the faces of Shiva and Uma in the eleventh-century Nepalese sculpture), and it manifests itself as a general feeling of well-being before, during, and after the act itself. In the

Fig. 23-2 *Shiva Seated with Uma (Uma-Maheshvara)*, Nepal (Kathmandu Valley), Thakuri dynasty, 11th century. Copper alloy, height 11⅛ in. Metropolitan Museum of Art, New York.

Samuel Eilenberg Collection, Ex Coll.: Columbia University, Purchase, Rogers Fund, 1987.218.1. © 2015. Image copyright Metropolitan Museum of Art/Art Resource/Scala, Florence. Photo: Maggie Nimkin.

Fig. 23-3 Erotic couples on wall of Kandariya Mahadeva Temple, Khajuraho, India, ca. 1000 CE.
Height of sculptures approx. 39 in.

harmony of the male and female principles, it represents the harmony of the cosmos.

Eros and the Idea of Love in Ancient Greece

For the ancient Greeks, the idea of *eros*—the source of our word "erotic"—embodies the same conjoining of physical and spiritual love that the Hindus in Nepal saw in the sculptural representations of Shiva and Uma. For them, love is, ideally, ennobling—the loved one becomes virtuous by being loved. They further distinguished between Common Love, which is simply physical, and Heavenly Love, which is also physical but is generated only in those who are capable of rational and ethical development. Indeed, for Socrates, *eros* comes to be defined as more than just interpersonal love; it is also desire—something akin to the Hindu *kama*. It is a desire with which the Greek personification of the idea, the youthful, winged god Eros, can smite any mortal by shooting them with an arrow from his bow. Socrates defines it as the desire for something it lacks, and what *eros* lacks and needs is beauty. The purpose of love, then, according to Socrates, is to give birth to beauty "in both body and mind," and, finally, to attain insight into the ultimate Form of Beauty.

The high tone of this philosophical approach to love is at distinct odds with the less refined aspects that also find expression in ancient Greek culture, namely in the drinking and sexual license that the Greeks associated with Dionysus, the god of wine and intoxication. As early as the sixth century BCE, groups of men regularly celebrated Dionysus, coming together for the enjoyment of dance, music, and wine. Sexual license was the rule of the day. By the time that Socrates was arguing for beauty in "both body and mind," Dionysiac festivals were ubiquitous throughout Greece. There were seven each year in Athens alone, during which monumental phalli stood in the streets, and public drunkenness, sexual license, and unbridled revelry were the norm. The Greeks well understood that love and sex were intertwined in highly complex ways, that the two were in some sense compatriots, as they are represented in the sculpture of *Dionysus and Eros* at the Naples Archaeological Museum (**Fig. 23-4**), a Roman copy of a type created by the Greek sculptor Praxiteles (see Fig. 12-11). The arms of Dionysus are a restoration, as is most of the torso of Eros. Dionysus' left hand probably rested on Eros' head originally, and Eros probably carried a bow and arrow. The sculpture suggests that the two are closer than one might think—or closer than Socrates suggests. In fact, the god Eros is cunning, unmanageable, and sometimes cruel to the point of mocking those who are struck by his arrows. He toys with his victims, inducing confusion and even frenzy in their hearts.

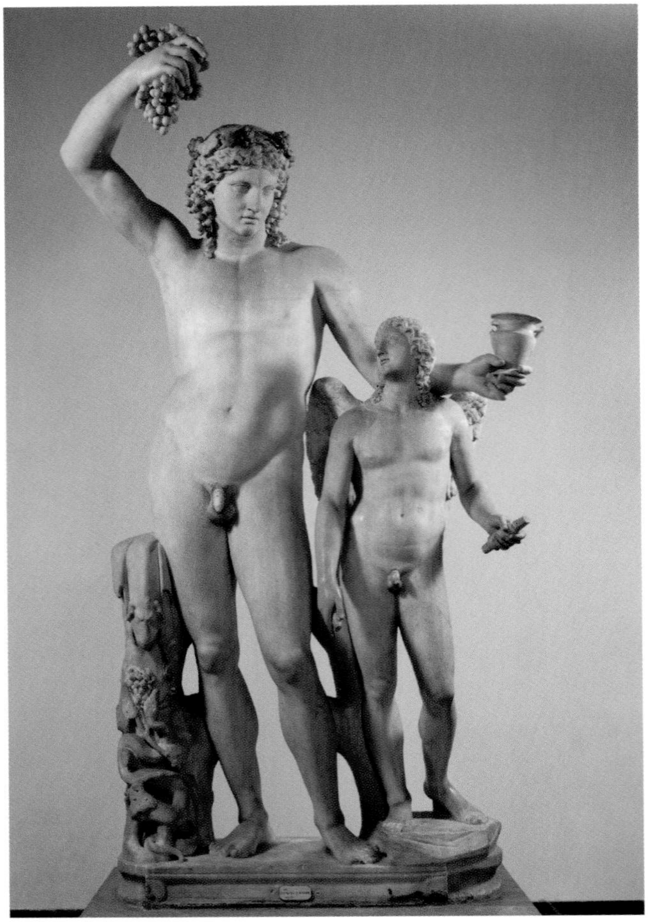

Fig. 23-4 ***Dionysus and Eros*, Roman copy of a statue attributed to Praxiteles, 2nd century CE.** Marble. National Archaeological Museum, Naples.

A Persian Tale

By the twelfth century, what would prove a long-standing tradition of storytelling associated with love between man and woman as a cosmic force for harmony and justice had taken hold in Persia. In many of these tales, the woman plays a role similar to the Greek god Eros. She cunningly toys with her lover, confusing and manipulating him. But as with the Greek *eros*, the pursuit of the beautiful, often in the form of a beautiful woman or, sometimes, a beautiful man is an allegory for, or figurative representation of, the pursuit of the beauty that is God. One of the most popular of these tales was the "Seduction of Yusuf and Zulaykha," a retelling of the biblical story of Joseph and the wife of Potiphar, Zuleika, which is also included in the Qur'an as the story of Yusuf and Zulaykha.

In the story, Zulaykha builds a palace with seven rooms, each decorated with an erotic painting of herself and Yusuf, in order to seduce the beautiful youth, who has sworn, in the firm knowledge that carnal knowledge and true happiness are wide apart, that his love for Zulaykha is purely spiritual. As Zulaykha leads the unsuspecting Yusuf from room to room, she locks each door behind her. When they reach the last room, she throws herself on Yusuf, who flees as each of the seven doors miraculously opens before him. The palace and its decorations stand for the temptations of the material world with its seven habitable climatic regions. Yusuf's beauty, which Zulaykha mistakenly sees as physical rather than spiritual, is comparable to the beauty of God, and his faith in the all-seeing God unlocks the doors to allow his escape, and Zulaykha bemoans her loss.

The illustration by Bihzad of Zulaykha desperately grasping at the fleeing Yusuf's coat (**Fig. 23-5**) depicts the palace as almost labyrinthine in its complexity, a complexity that is probably meant to reflect the war of feelings and emotions that each of the story's protagonists

Fig. 23-5 Bihzad, *The Seduction of Yusuf*, from a copy of Sadi's *Bustan* ("Orchard"), prepared for Sultan Husayn Mirza at Herat, Persia (present-day Afghanistan). 1488.
Ink and color on paper, 11⅞ × 8⅔ in. National Library, Cairo.
akg-image/Erich Lessing.

faces. The sumptuous tilework, the carpets, the delicate woodwork, all add to the physical beauty of the image. And the interplay of the perspectival renderings of the staircases and balconies, with the flat two-dimensional patterning of the decoration, contributes to the sense of instability that characterizes the entire scene.

The Medieval Courtly Love Tradition

Yusuf's brand of love as something purely spiritual and ennobling would make its way to Europe, by way of Islamic culture in Andalusian Spain, particularly in the tradition of "courtly love" championed in the poetry of the troubadours whose work had a tremendous influence on the French court, beginning in the twelfth century. The troubadour poets—most of them men, though a few were women—usually accompanied themselves on a lyre or lute, and in their poems they can be said to have "invented" romantic love as we know it today—not the feelings and emotions associated with love, but the conventions and vocabulary that we use to describe it. As in almost all the traditions we have discussed so far, the primary feeling is one of desire or longing, of a knight or nobleman for a woman (usually unattainable because married or of a higher status), or, when the troubadour was a woman—a trobairitz—the reverse. Thus, to love is to suffer, to wander aimlessly, unable to concentrate on anything but the mental image of the beloved, to lose one's appetite, to lie sleepless at night—in short, to give up life for a dream. There was, in addition, a quasi-religious aspect to courtly love. Recognizing that he is beset by earthly desires, the lover sees his ability to resist these temptations and rise above his own base humanity as evidence of his spiritual purity. Finally, in the courtly love tradition, the smitten knight or nobleman must be willing to perform any deed to win his lady's favor. In fact, the loyalty that he once conferred upon his lord in the feudal system is, in courtly love, transferred to his lady (who is often, in fact, his lord's wife), as the scenes on a jeweled twelfth-century casket make clear (**Fig. 23-6**). At the left, a lady listens, rather sternly, as a troubadour poet expresses his love for her. In the center is a knight, sword in one hand and key to the lady's heart in the other. On the right, the knight kneels before the lady, his hands

Fig. 23-6 Casket with scenes of courtly love, from Limoges, ca. 1180. Champlevé enamel, 3⅝ × 8½ × 6⅜ in.
The British Museum, London.
1859,0110.1. © Trustees of British Museum.

shaped in a heart; a rope around his neck, held by the lady, signifies his fidelity to her.

The Privatization of Sex in the West

The idea of the lover trying to resist his earthly desires and rise above his base humanity by performing heroic acts of self-denial was, of course, consistent with the Western Church's dim view of passion and, especially, its categorization of lust as one of the seven deadly sins. In fact, it could be argued that the Church forced sex in the Western world to go underground. It became a private matter. Certainly nothing like the wall of erotic couples at the Kandariya Mahadeva Temple in India—a decidedly public space—could be tolerated in the West. This is not to say that erotic imagery disappeared—it simply disappeared from public view. A painting like Bronzino's *An Allegory with Venus and Cupid* (**Fig. 23-7**; see also Fig. 18-28) was commissioned by the court in Florence, Italy, for the private apartments of François I

Fig. 23-7 Bronzino, *An Allegory with Venus and Cupid*, ca. 1540–50. Oil on wood, approx. 5 ft. 1 in. × 4 ft. 8¾ in. National Gallery, London.

of France. The king's taste for paintings of an erotic nature was well known. The work was intended not only to appeal to this taste but also to demonstrate Florentine intellectual cleverness through an allegory that required unraveling. Here, Venus (Aphrodite to the Greeks) and her son, the adolescent Cupid (Eros to the Greeks), engage in an incestuous embrace. Venus holds the golden apple in her hand, the reward judged to be hers by Paris when he chose her as the most beautiful of the goddesses, thus inaugurating the events that would lead to the Trojan War.

The governing theme of the painting is Luxuria (Sensual Indulgence). At the top right, pulling back the blue curtain to reveal the perverse relationship between mother and son, is Time, with an hourglass on his back. He is helped by Truth at the top left. The exact meaning of the figures behind the two illicit lovers is ambiguous. Below Truth is Envy, or perhaps the so-called "French disease," the illness we know today as syphilis, which first appeared in epidemic proportions in Italy after the French invaded in 1494. At the right is Folly, who is about to throw rose petals over mother and son. Behind him is Pleasure, who extends a honeycomb to the couple, but note that her body is that of a dragon whose tail curves below Folly's feet. The work, like the style of *vanitas* painting that would develop in the Netherlands at about the same time (see Fig. 22-13), seems to offer an admonition about the short-lived rewards of erotic love. And yet, of course, Bronzino's painting celebrates erotic love even as it warns against it.

Imaging Desire

What are some of the different ways in which artists have imaged desire?

In 1975, the film critic Laura Mulvey published an essay, "Visual Pleasure and Narrative Cinema," that would subsequently become famous as the first feminist critique of Hollywood film. For Mulvey, women in cinema reflect a "traditional exhibitionist role" in which they are "simultaneously looked at and displayed, with their appearance coded for strong visual and erotic impact." This, she says, is "the magic of the Hollywood style," which "arose, not exclusively, but in one important aspect, from its skilled and satisfying manipulation of visual pleasure. Unchallenged, mainstream film coded the erotic into the language of the dominant patriarchal order." However accurate a critique of Hollywood film, the principles of display that Mulvey outlines have been, as she suggests, "traditional" in Western art since at least the ancient Greeks, and they were especially important to nineteenth-century painters of an Orientalist bent (see Chapter 26). Eugène Delacroix's *Odalisque* (**Fig. 23-8**; see also Fig. 19-13) was painted to be looked at and enjoyed for its visual and erotic impact. In his book *Ways of Seeing*, John Berger famously distinguishes between being naked and being nude: "To be naked is to be oneself. To be nude is to be seen naked by others and yet not recognized for oneself." The figure in Delacroix's *Odalisque* is not a person; she is an object of desire. She could in fact be said to be the

Fig. 23-8 Eugène Delacroix, *Odalisque*, 1845–50. Oil on canvas, 14⅞ × 18¼ in. Fitzwilliam Museum, University of Cambridge, England.
Bridgeman Images.

Fig. 23-9 Pablo Picasso, *Les Demoiselles d'Avignon*, 1907. Oil on canvas. 8 ft. × 7 ft. 8 in. Museum of Modern Art, New York.

Digital image, Museum of Modern Art, New York/Scala, Florence. © 2015 Estate of Pablo Picasso/Artists Rights Society (ARS), New York.

very image of desire, which of course remains unfulfilled because its object is unattainable. She remains, forever, an image—and a fantasy. Nevertheless, Delacroix's painting is structured as if it were a private space into which the viewer has been admitted. Its subject's eyes are half-closed, her lips slightly parted, as if intoxicated by the hashish in the hookah beside her or the act of sex itself—or both. The scabbard of a *yatagan*—a Turkish sword—lies at her feet, a symbol of male power unsheathed.

It is worth comparing Delacroix's *Odalisque* to Pablo Picasso's *Les Demoiselles d'Avignon* (**Fig. 23-9**; see also Fig. 1-13). As threatening as Picasso's painting is stylistically, it has much in common with the Delacroix. At the very center of Delacroix's painting, covered with a bit of sheet, are the nude's genitalia. The same is true of the Picasso. At the very center of the painting, at the intersection of the two diagonals that have been drawn on the image, is a semi-transparent cloth covering the central nude's sexual organs (**Fig. 23-10**). That crossing point is

Fig. 23-10 Line analysis of Pablo Picasso, *Les Demoiselles d'Avignon*, 1907.

Digital image, Museum of Modern Art, New York/Scala, Florence. © 2015 Estate of Pablo Picasso/Artists Rights Society (ARS), New York.

also at the vertical center of the painting. Picasso's image of desire is, however, far more ambivalent that Delacroix's. His prostitutes, in effect, invite the viewer into the painting, into the private space of the brothel, even as they turn, in their African masks, to frighten the viewer away. Just as the central nude's genitalia are covered by a sheet at once transparent and opaque, *Les Demoiselles* both attracts and repulses the viewer. And it images desire in terms very similar to Jenny Holzer's maxim: "Protect me from what I want" (see Fig. 26-22).

The Voyeur

If the gaze of the viewer is implicit in both the Delacroix and the Picasso paintings, it is often made explicit in depictions of the voyeur, a figure who might best be described as desire personified. The illicit gaze of the voyeur is, for instance, the subject of Jean-Honoré Fragonard's famous painting *The Swing* (**Fig. 23-11**), which suggests an erotic intrigue between two lovers, a conspiracy emphasized by the sculpture of Cupid to the

Fig. 23-11 Jean-Honoré Fragonard, *The Swing*, 1767. Oil on canvas, 32⅝ × 26 in. Wallace Collection, London.

left, holding his finger to his mouth as if to affirm the secrecy of the affair. The painting's subject matter was in fact suggested by another artist, Gabriel-François Doyen, who was approached by the baron de Saint-Julien to paint his mistress "on a swing that a bishop would set going. You will place me," the baron instructed, "in such a way that I would be able to see the legs of the lovely girl, and better still, if you want to enliven your picture, a little more." Doyen declined the commission but suggested it to Fragonard.

Much of the power of the composition lies in the fact that the viewer shares, to a degree, the voyeuristic pleasures of the reclining lover. The entire image is charged with an erotic symbolism that would have been commonly understood at the time. For instance, the lady on the swing lets fly her shoe—the lost shoe and naked foot being a well-known symbol of lost virginity. The young man reaches toward her, hat in hand—the hat that in eighteenth-century erotic imagery was often used to cover the genitals of a discovered lover. Even more subtly, and ironically, the composition echoes the central panel of Michelangelo's Sistine Ceiling, *The Creation of Adam* (see Fig. 5-24). The male lover assumes Adam's posture, and the female lover God's, although she reaches toward Adam—to bring him to life, as it were—with her foot, not her hand.

Somewhat surprisingly, in Korea, not long after Fragonard painted *The Swing*, a very similar image of a beautiful woman on a swing was created by Sin Yunbok, an employee of the Korean court's Bureau of Painting. He could hardly have known of the Fragonard, but the near-simultaneity of the paintings' creation underscores the theme's imaginative power. Sin Yunbok's painting (**Fig. 23-12**) depicts a group of seven

Fig. 23-12 Sin Yunbok, *Women on Tano Day*, Joseon dynasty, Korea, late 18th–early 19th century.
Ink and colors on paper, 11⅛ × 13⅞ in. Gansong Museum of Art, Seoul.
akg-images/VISIOARS.

Fig. 23-13 Fulani (Wodaabe) men at a *gerewol*, southern Niger, 1980s.

gisaeng—lower-class women whose beauty and artistic accomplishments gave them access to the company of upper-class gentlemen—on Tano Day, a festival celebrated in the countryside on the fifth day of the fifth month of the lunar calendar to commemorate the start of summer and the promise of a bountiful harvest. The activities of men and women were segregated, men engaging in wrestling matches, and women in swing competitions. Traditionally women also washed their hair in stream water boiled with sweetly scented leaves of sweet flag, or calamus, believed to make one's hair shiny. As one *gisaeng* climbs onto the swing, revealing her undergarments in a fashion remarkably close to the girl in Fragonard's painting, four other *gisaeng* bath in the stream in various states of undress. The standing figure turns to gaze provocatively downstream in the direction of the viewer, whose own voyeuristic presence at the scene is underscored by the two monks spying on the women from behind a rock at the top left of the painting.

An African Festival

As both Sin Yunbok's painting and the Greek Dionysiac festivals suggest, sexual license often permeates the festival atmosphere. In Africa, the Fulani of southern Niger annually celebrate a week-long *gerewol* festival at the end of the rainy season in September when the nomadic Wodaabe cattle herders, who consider themselves superior to all other Fulani peoples, gather at the southern edge of the Sahara before heading south into their dry-season pastures. The Wodaabe men (**Fig. 23-13**) paint their faces in such a way as to stress their height, the whiteness of their eyes and teeth, and the beauty of their noses. They decorate themselves with feathers, jewelry, and elaborate embroidered panels, and then they engage in a competitive line dance, sometimes for hours on end, designed to show off their physical strength and endurance. The entire celebration is, in effect, a male beauty contest—in contrast to Hollywood cinema, the male is the object of the female gaze here.

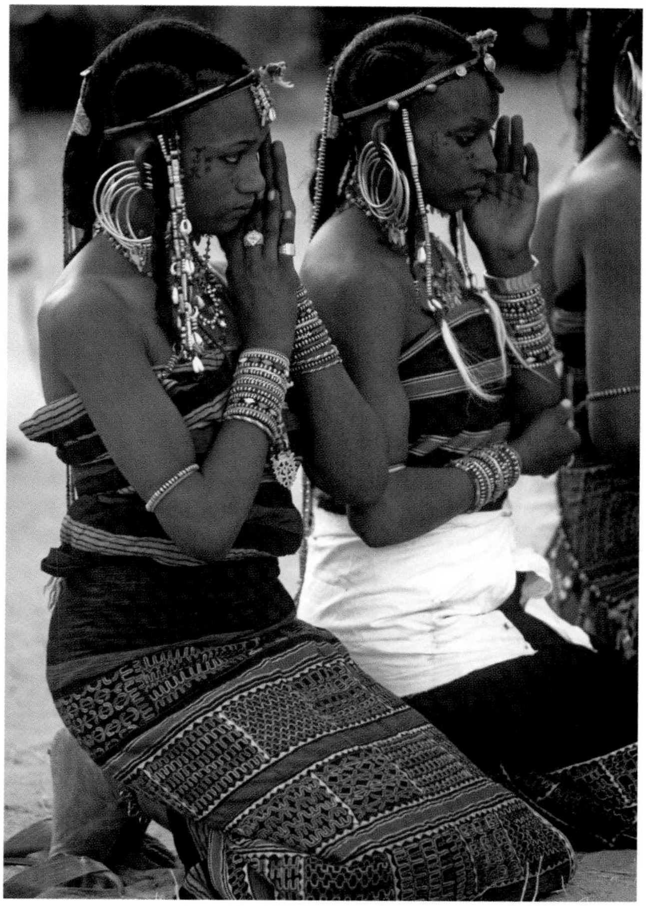

Fig. 23-14 Fulani (Wodaabe) women at a *gerewol*, southern Niger, 1980s.
© Robert Estall photo agency/Alamy.

Fig. 23-15 Constantin Brancusi, *The Kiss*, 1916. Limestone, 23 × 13¼ × 10 in. Philadelphia Museum of Art.
Louise and Walter Arensberg Collection, 1950. © 2015. Photo Philadelphia Museum of Art/Art Resource/Scala, Florence. © 2015 Artists Rights Society (ARS), New York/ADAGP, Paris.

The women (**Fig. 23-14**), themselves adorned in multicolored wires, beads, and brass, act as judges, pretending to avert their gaze, even as the object of the entire ritual is for each woman to choose a champion and take him as her lover. In fact, during the festival, both men and women are free to set aside their marriage vows. The *gerewol* is at once a celebration of male and female beauty and a frank acceptance of sexual attraction, tied as it is to procreation and the creation of healthy and beautiful children.

Kisses

How does the kiss function as an image of desire?

As Auguste Rodin's *The Kiss* demonstrates (see Fig. 23-1), the evocation of touch is one of the most powerful ways to image desire, and, as the sculpture also demonstrates, the kiss is one of the most powerfully suggestive of all types of touch. In the early 1900s, Constantin Brancusi worked for a month in the studio of Rodin, but he soon abandoned the master's approach. For one thing, Rodin employed his assistants to help him cast or carve his sculptures—this was Brancusi's job in Rodin's studio—but, in creating his own art, Brancusi wanted to work with his own hands, carving the stone himself because, he felt, only then could he understand and communicate with his material, which, to him, was a living entity. And instead of the realism that Rodin championed, Brancusi sought to arrive at a more abstract and, to his mind, universal approach to form and subject matter.

Thus, Brancusi's *The Kiss* (**Fig. 23-15**) can be thought of as something of a response to Rodin's work of the same name. The sculpture exists in several versions; the version reproduced here is the artist's fourth rendering of it in stone. It insists on its origins as a single block of stone—a single block divided in half down the middle by an incised line, the female body differentiated from the male by the simple roundness of her breast. This verticality is countered by the two horizontal bands of the lovers' arms, which reach around each other in a grip that seems to visually cement the two together. Their eyes are rendered in profile, yet they merge to form one Cyclopean eye, topping the graceful arch defined by their hairlines. This is an image of two becoming one, a solid stone born of their embrace.

Created the same year as Brancusi's *The Kiss*, Francis Picabia's "kiss," in the Dada painting *Machine Tournez*

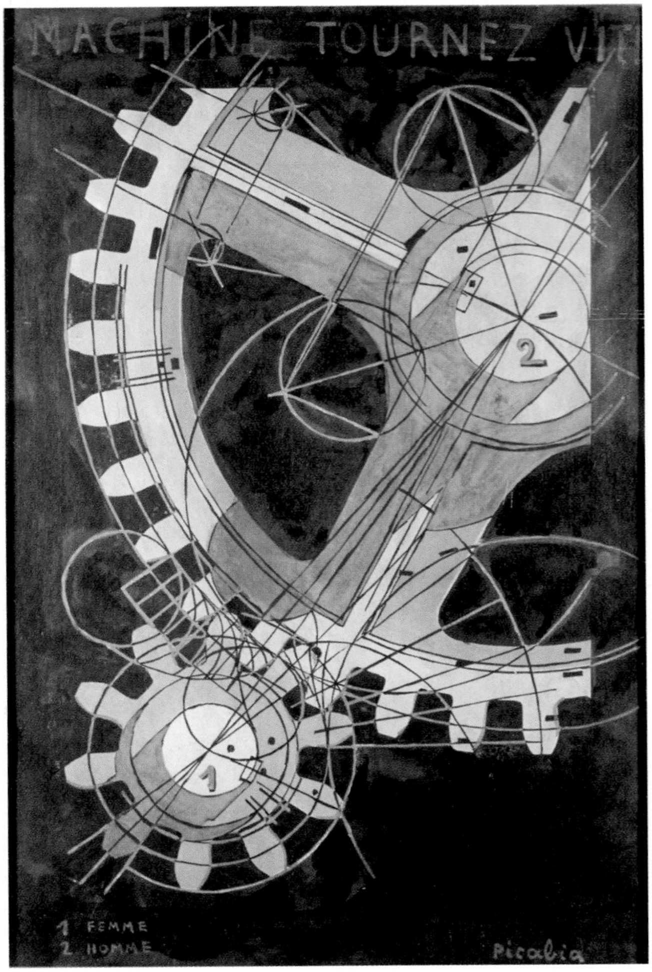

Fig. 23-16 Francis Picabia, *Machine Tournez Vite* (*Machine Turn Quickly*), 1916. Tempera on paper, 19¼ × 12⅝ in. Private collection.

Bridgeman Images. © 2015 Artists Rights Society (ARS), New York/ ADAGP, Paris.

Fig. 23-17 Andy Warhol, *Kiss*, 1963. 16 mm film, black-and-white, silent, approx. 54 min. Museum of Modern Art, New York. The Andy Warhol Foundation for the Visual Arts Film Preservation Program. F553.

© 2015 Andy Warhol Museum, Pittsburgh, PA, a museum of Carnegie Institute. All rights reserved. Film still courtesy of Andy Warhol Museum.

Vite (*Machine Turn Quickly*) (**Fig. 23-16**), takes on a completely different character. This "kiss"—or is it more than that?—is rendered as the coupling of two cogs in a machine. The smaller cog is labeled "1" and the larger "2." A key at the bottom left of the painting explains:

1. Femme [Woman]
2. Homme [Man]

Sexual encounter is reduced to a mere mechanical interaction, a prototypical Dadaesque reaction to the horrors of World War I (see Chapter 20). Here, human interaction is devoid of any emotion. In the face of the realities of the war, "love" is but a sham, a sacrifice to the machinery of civilization itself.

Such cynicism is not unique to Dada. In many ways, Andy Warhol's experiments in film anticipate Laura Mulvey's critique of cinema a decade later. *Kiss* (**Fig. 23-17**) is a 54-minute silent film consisting of a series of shorter films of different couples kissing—men and women, women and women, men and men—at excruciating length. If the film begins by arousing a certain voyeuristic expectation, that expectation soon collapses into an almost comic display of couples grinding mouth against mouth, slobbering now and again, gasping for air—all in total silence. Warhol desexualizes the event by making it go on and on. And the viewer, recognizing that this is all going nowhere, comes to understand that this film is not about kissing, but about monotony, boredom, and time.

Warhol had shown men kissing in *Kiss* 40 years before Banksy first stenciled his *Kissing Coppers* (**Fig. 23-18**; see also Fig. 20-45) on the wall of the Prince Albert pub in Brighton, U.K. But Banksy's work challenged macho stereotypes in a way that Warhol's film did not, and, perhaps more important, humanized the very authority figures charged with enforcing laws prohibiting graffiti. Law enforcement is "disarmed."

Iñigo Manglano-Ovalle's *Le Baiser/The Kiss* (**Fig. 23-19**) is set at Mies van der Rohe's icon of modernist architecture on the Fox River in Plano, Illinois, the Farnsworth House (see Fig. 14-40). The house

Fig. 23-18 Banksy, *Kissing Coppers*, ca. 2005. Spray paint on wall, various sites, Brighton and London, U.K.

was commissioned by Chicago physician Dr. Edith Farnsworth in 1946 as a weekend getaway, but by the time it was finished, what had begun as a close personal relationship with the architect, quite possibly a romantic one, had turned to litigation. Manglano-Ovalle's piece, filmed on site in Plano, is about estrangement, and not just that of the Farnsworth/Mies relationship. In the video, Manglano-Ovalle himself is washing the house's windows. Inside, a young woman with headphones on is spinning disks. When the camera is outside looking in, Manglano-Ovalle explains, "it is always miked to the sound of the squeegee on the glass. The squeegee squeaks and sarcastically kisses the building." When the camera is inside looking out, the score is "an ethereal electronic music which is a single moment of a guitar solo by the band Kiss, and the nano-second is stretched to make the sound piece." At one level, he says, the piece is simply about visiting a shrine of modern architecture: "I was trying to figure out a way to touch the building." In this sense, it is about the attraction that contemporary artists like Manglano-Ovalle feel for modernism itself even as they reject it. But it is also about the relationship between the window-washer and the girl inside, irrevocably separated by the modernist glass wall. In this sense, it is remarkably close in feel to Picasso's *Les Demoiselles d'Avignon*, an image of both attraction and repulsion as the two figures are unable to navigate the barriers that separate them—literally the glass wall, but figuratively the divisions of social class.

Fig. 23-19 Iñigo Manglano-Ovalle, *Le Baiser/The Kiss*, 2000. Video still, video installation and projection, aluminum structure, dimensions variable.

THE CRITICAL PROCESS
Thinking about Love and Sex

Fig. 23-20 Barbara Kruger, *Untitled (I shop therefore I am)*, 1987. Photographic silkscreen/vinyl, 9 ft. 3 in. × 9 ft. 5 in. Courtesy of Mary Boone Gallery, New York.

Western culture has cultivated the idea of desire most thoroughly in advertising, which has used the human body to confuse consumers about just what it is they are buying—the product or its sexual allure. But it is consumer culture itself that provokes advertising's sexual strategies, as Barbara Kruger's billboard-size testament to the power of consumer culture attests (**Fig. 23-20**). Kruger first worked as a page designer at *Mademoiselle*, published by Condé Nast, which also publishes *Vogue*, *Vanity Fair*, *Glamour,* and *Condé Nast Traveler* among about 15 other magazines, all dedicated to the attractions of image and status. Kruger's work reminds us just how thoroughly we are defined by how we look, what we wear, and what we buy. We no longer think (Kruger's poster is a play on René Descartes's famous dictum, "I think therefore I am"), we consume.

Almost from its earliest days, advertising has understood it has the power to so transform us. Jan Toorop's salad-oil poster (**Fig. 23-21**; see also Fig. 15-13) underscores one of the most prominent ways in which sex sells. Toorop's poster is double-edged—that is, the two women in it are engaged in a completely traditional female endeavor, preparing a salad, and yet their flowing gowns and abundant hair (which fill every corner of the image) suggest a kind of self-indulgent narcissism. As one sits dressing the salad, the other lifts her hands and eyes upward, as if the preparation of the salad were some quasi-religious rite. What do you make of the fact that there are no males in the image? To whom is this advertisement addressed? How might this poster be viewed as more politically advanced than not? In other words, what does it suggest about the independence of these two figures from the traditional roles that they simultaneously fulfill?

Fig. 23-21 Jan Toorop, Poster for *Delftsche Slaolie* (Delft Salad Oil), 1894. Dutch advertising poster. Digital image, Museum of Modern Art, New York/Scala, Florence.

Thinking Back

23.1 Describe how the tension between physical and spiritual love manifests itself in different cultures.

Physical love is frankly acknowledged as an important part of life in the Hindu religion. What is its spiritual side from the Hindu point of view? Plato defines *eros* as something more than just interpersonal love; it is the desire for something one lacks—that is, "beauty in both mind and body." But Dionysiac festivals offered a different side of *eros*. What were their characteristics? How does Bronzino's *An Allegory with Venus and Cupid* reflect conflicting attitudes about the nature of *eros*? How does the relationship between Yusuf and Zulaykha in the Persian tale reflect the tension between physical and spiritual love? Romantic love could be said to have originated in the courtly love poetry of the troubadour poets in southern France in the late Middle Ages. What are some of the characteristic features of a romantic courtship? In what ways is courtly love similar to that of Yusuf and Zulaykha? The Western Church's dim view of passion and, especially, its categorization of lust as one of the seven deadly sins could be said to have forced sex in the Western world to go underground. How does Bronzino's *An Allegory with Venus and Cupid* reflect this trend to remove sex from the public sphere?

23.2 Explain some of the different ways in which desire has been imaged.

Like women in Hollywood cinema, traditional paintings of reclining nudes are coded for strong visual and erotic impact. How does John Berger's distinction between the naked and the nude help us understand this? How is desire imaged in Pablo Picasso's *Les Demoiselles d'Avignon*? How does voyeurism inform Jean-Honoré Fragonard's *The Swing*, and what erotic symbolism informs the painting? How is the viewer implicated in the voyeurism of Sin Yunbok's *Women on Tano Day*? In the Fulani *gerewol* festival, the male dancers submit themselves to the female gaze. How do the dancers compare to women in Hollywood cinema?

23.3 Discuss the kiss as an image of desire.

How would you compare Constantin Brancusi's *The Kiss* to Rodin's? What accounts for the cynicism of Francis Picabia's *Machine Tournez Vite* (*Machine Turn Quickly*)? How does Andy Warhol's film *Kiss* subvert the eroticism of the act? What social issues are raised by Banksy's *Kissing Coppers* and Iñigo Manglano-Ovalle's *Le Baiser/The Kiss*?

Chapter 24
The Body, Gender, and Identity

Learning Objectives

24.1 Explain why "beautiful" is an ambiguous word in reference to the body.

24.2 Discuss some of the factors that have motivated artists to use their own bodies in works of art.

24.3 Differentiate between biological sex and gender, and discuss some of the ways in which identity is constructed.

The **selfie** has become one of the most popular forms of photography ever. Literally millions and millions of them inhabit Instagram. (In 2014, the Android app boasted 200 million users. On the day the author looked, Justin Bieber's Instagram account contained over 1,700 posts, a great many of them selfies, and had nearly 20 million followers.) The art critic Jerry Saltz recently argued that selfies are a "new visual genre—a type of self-portraiture formally distinct from all others in history. Selfies have their own visual autonomy." Taken at arm's length from the subject, they are closely cropped, and any photograph that shows both hands of the subject cannot, by definition, be a selfie—except for the selfie taken in a mirror, in which case the presence of the cell phone defines it. They can be narcissistic, but narcissism is usually a private affair—the self admiring the self—and selfies are a profoundly public form. They express who we think we are, and the more of them that fill our Instagram account, the more people can see the range of our being. They rarely achieve the high-art look of a posed photograph, let alone a self-portrait in painting. But the best of them possess a remarkable sense of presence. In this example by professional photographer Laura Knapp (**Fig. 24-1**), her bug-eyed expression—as if the flash on her camera phone delayed for a second, then surprised her—offers an almost comic contrast to her evening dress, necklace, and lipstick. Unlike most selfies, this one takes advantage of some high-art principles of composition and design—most notably the complementary color contrast between red and green, the repetition of forms between her chin and her necklace, the play of light and dark, and the symmetrical balance of the whole. But it is, above all, the sense of surprise that draws us to it. It's funny. And this sense that we are seeing Laura Knapp, at this moment, in all her pre-date anxiety, is the selfie's most important quality. As Saltz says, selfies are "an instant visual communication of where we are, what we're doing, who we think we are, and who we think is watching." They capture our complex sense of the contemporary self—our bodies, our gender, and our identities—that is the subject of this chapter.

The Body Beautiful

Why is "beautiful" an ambiguous term when referring to the body?

The human body has always inspired a love for the beautiful, but different eras and cultures have defined what constitutes a beautiful human body in all

Fig. 24-1 Laura Knapp, *Selfie*, 2014. Digital color photograph, dimensions variable.

Fig. 24-2 *Woman* (formerly a.k.a. the *Venus of Willendorf*), Lower Austria, ca. 25,000–20,000 BCE. Limestone, height 4½ in. Naturhistorisches Museum, Vienna.
akg-image/Erich Lessing.

kinds of ways—long-legged and slender or plump and voluptuous, petite and demure or athletic and aggressive. The body of the *Woman* from Willendorf (**Fig. 24-2**; see also Fig. 16-2) is typical of the earliest depictions of the human body, with its pendulous breasts, wide hips, swollen belly, and clearly delineated genitalia. This suggests that what was most valued about the body in prehistoric times was its ability to sustain itself for some period of time without food, and thus its ability to nourish a child at the same time. But archeologist Clive Gamble has recently argued that this body-type served as a form of nonverbal communication among groups of ancient peoples widely scattered across what is today the European continent. He suggests that, whenever groups of these hunter-gatherers met up, as they must occasionally have done when tracking game, these easily portable female statues served as signs suggesting the amicability of the hunters bearing them (it is doubtful that many, if any, of these groups shared a common language). These figurines, in other words, were invitations to interact and, in all likelihood, mate. They thus encoded a system of shared values—about the body, about sexuality, and about survival.

Many cultures have notions of beauty far different from our own. In the lower reaches of the Niger River, in a region that was once tropical rainforest but that has now been largely cleared for farming, the Igbo people have created large display figures called *ugonachomma*—literally, "the eagle seeks out beauty"—depicting beautiful young women (**Fig. 24-3**). While not what we in the West might call a "realistic" depiction of the female form, the sculpture, carved as a centerpiece for a competitive dance, embodies all the attributes of beauty that the Igbo profess. The exaggerated length of her neck reflects the Igbo preference for long necks. As the mirror in her hand suggests, she is a triumph of cosmetic artistry. Her face is painted white, which reflects not only the Igbo preference for light-colored skin but also the practice of washing dark skin with a chalk solution in order to highlight the intricate designs—applied with indigo (*uli*)—that cover her body. Keloidal scars, cut into the skin of young women before marriage, lead down her torso to her navel, which is itself distended, another Igbo sign of beauty. This figure originally held an umbrella in her left hand, which, like the mirror, signified her wealth and prestige.

In Igbo culture, the *ugonachomma*'s beauty is paired with a different sort of beauty possessed by

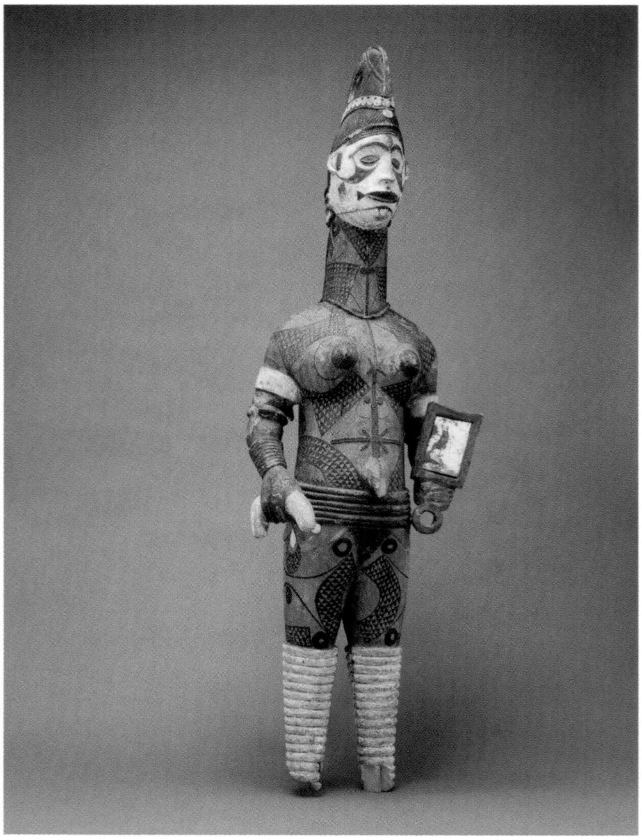

Fig. 24-3 *Ugonachomma* display figure, Igbo, Nigeria. Wood, pigment, mirror, height 50 in. Seattle Art Museum.
Photo: Paul Maciapia.

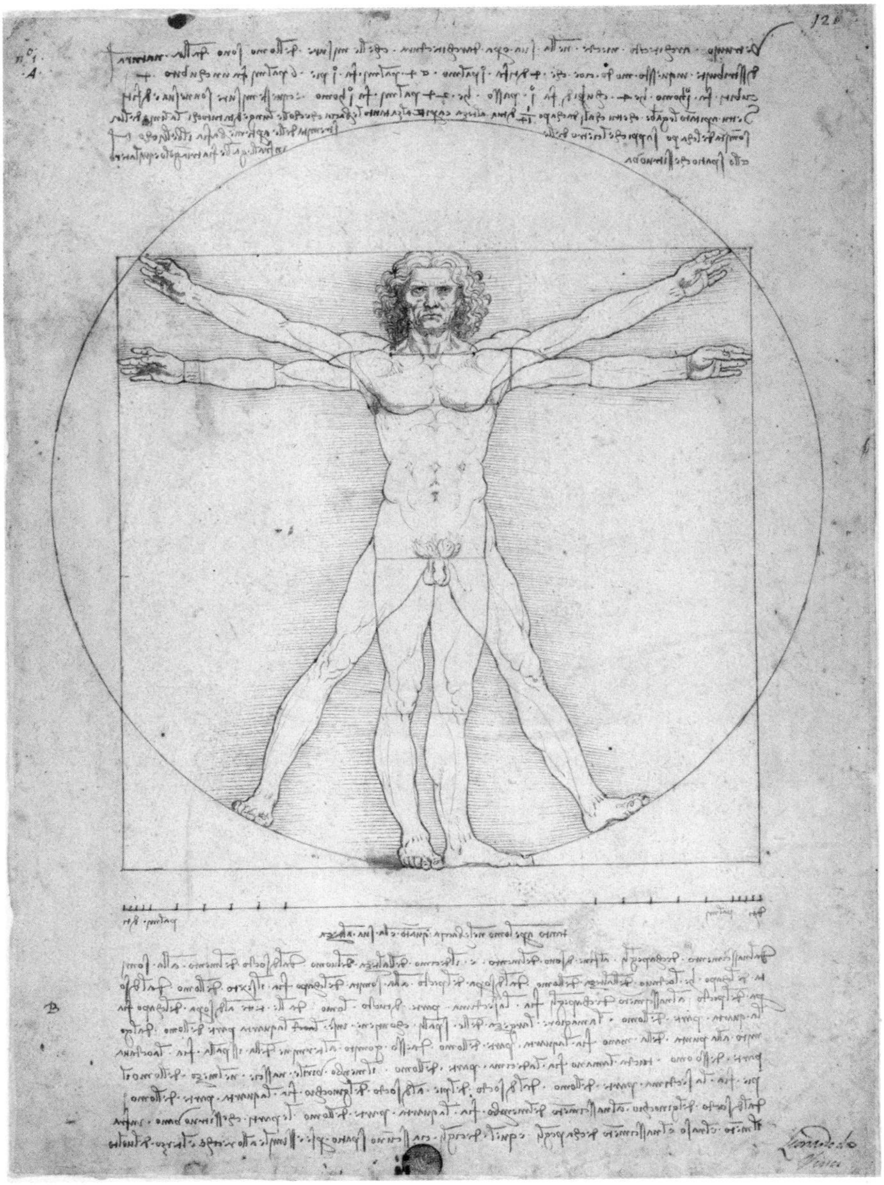

Fig. 24-4 Leonardo da Vinci, *Study of Human Proportion: The Vitruvian Man*, ca. 1492. Pen-and-ink drawing, 13½ × 9⅝ in. Gallerie dell'Accademia, Venice.
CAMERAPHOTO Arte, Venice.

men who have achieved titled status in the community. Known as "the eagle strengthens kinship," the titled man is also the "eagle" who seeks out the *ugonachomma*'s beauty. Indeed, the beautiful maiden is often praised by being called the eagle's "kola," a reference to the rare, light-colored kola nut that is integral to every Igbo ceremony. The *ugonachomma* possesses "the power of beauty," while the titled man possesses "the beauty of power."

If the Igbo *ugonachomma* strikes the Western eye as anything but beautiful, that is perhaps the case because, in the West, we have come to value "right" proportion as an absolute standard of beauty, a standard for which the *ugonachomma* has no regard. Leonardo's *Study of Human Proportion: The Vitruvian Man* (**Fig. 24-4**; see also Fig. 7-1) is based on the idea that the human body is beautiful in direct relation to its perfect proportions. It is an homage to the Roman author Vitruvius, whose notions of ideal proportion were, in turn, indebted to the Greek sculptor Polyclitus, who, in the fifth century BCE, wrote a now-lost text about proportion, known as the *Canon*. In Polyclitus' system, the ideal human form was determined by the height of the head from the crown to the chin. The head was one-eighth the total height, the width of the shoulders was one-quarter the total height, and so on, each measurement reflecting these ideal proportions. For Polyclitus, these relations resulted in the work's *symmetria*, the origin of our word "symmetry," but meaning, in Polyclitus' usage, "commensurability," or "having a common measure." Thus, the ideal figure reflects a higher mathematical order and embodies the ideal harmony between the natural world and the intellectual or spiritual realm.

For Vitruvius, whose acquaintance with Polyclitus' *Canon* provides our only firsthand account of the original, the circle and square were the ideal shapes. Polyclitus' proportion was the geometrical equivalent of Pythagoras' music of the spheres, the theory that each planet produced a musical sound, fixed mathematically by its velocity and distance from Earth, which harmonized with those produced by other planets and was audible but not recognized on Earth. Thus, according to Vitruvius, if the human head is one-eighth the total height of an idealized figure, then the human body itself fits into the ideal musical

Fig. 24-5 Peter Paul Rubens, ***The Disembarkation of Marie de' Medici at the Port of Marseilles on November 3, 1600*** **(detail), 1621–25.** Oil on canvas, 13 × 10 ft. Musée du Louvre, Paris.
akg-image/Erich Lessing.

interval of the octave, the interval that gives the impression of duplicating the original note at a higher or lower pitch. Such balance, harmony, and symmetry are the very definition of Classical beauty.

In the seventeenth century, Peter Paul Rubens likewise turned to Classical Greek sculpture as the model for his own notions of the beautiful body. But, as a painter, Rubens was not so concerned with the form of the body, but rather with the materiality of the body's flesh, as is suggested by the contrast between the three naiads, or water nymphs, at the bottom center of his *Disembarkation of Marie de' Medici at the Port of Marseilles on November 3, 1600* (**Fig. 24-5**; see also Fig. 19-3), and the two Greek gods, Neptune and Triton, beside them. The distinct difference in skin color underscores a crucial difference in the quality of their flesh. The male bodies are defined by their musculature—and they are in keeping with the Vitruvian model promulgated by Leonardo. But the female bodies are defined by soft bulges and rolls—the word "meaty" comes to mind. Rubens's conception of the female body beautiful was, in other words, quite different from the Greeks'. Where the suggestion of movement had been realized in antiquity by clinging drapery, Rubens renders it in wrinkles and folds of skin. Where, in marble especially, skin is rendered as a smooth, idealized surface—consider Rodin's *The Kiss* (*Le Baiser*) (see Fig. 23-1)—in Rubens's hands, skin is textured, plump, carnal. As Kenneth Clark puts it in his book *The Nude: A Study in Ideal Form*, "Rubens wished his figures to have weight." And for Rubens this weight could be rendered best in oil paint, with the sensual feel of the brush on canvas, as if it were touching the very flesh it painted. In this, he could be said to inaugurate an approach to painting the beautiful body that results two centuries later in the nudes of Delacroix (see Fig. 23-8).

Performance: The Body as Work of Art

What are some of the factors that have motivated artists to use their own bodies in their work?

Among the earliest artists to actively use their body in an artwork itself was Carolee Schneemann. In 1963, the Icelandic, Paris-based painter Erró photographed her in an action in which her body became part of the painting titled *Eye Body: 36 Transformative*

Actions (**Fig. 24-6**). Schneemann developed the piece quite consciously as a rebuttal to Abstract Expressionist painting: "Using my body as an extension of my painting-constructions challenged and threatened the psychic territorial power lines by which women, in 1963, were admitted to the Art Stud Club, so long as they behaved enough like the men, and did work clearly in the traditions and pathways hacked out by the men."

Schneemann built an environment consisting of four large panels that were, at the time, a series of works-in-progress, paintings that were themselves radical departures from traditional painting, rivaled at the time only by Robert Rauschenberg's combine-paintings (see Fig. 9-33)—assemblages that included motorized umbrellas, a pile of fur, paint, shattered glass, transparent plastic, live garter snakes, a cow skull, a plaster-covered dress form, and various tools. Into this environment Schneemann inserted her own body. She describes the event:

> Covered in paint, grease, chalk, ropes, plastic, I establish my body as visual territory. Not only am I an image-maker, but I explore the image value of flesh as material I choose to work with. The body may remain erotic, sexual, desired, desiring, and yet still be votive—marked and written over in a text of stroke and gesture discovered by my creative female will.

Fig. 24-6 Carolee Schneemann, *Eye Body: 36 Transformative Actions*, December 1963. Paint, glue, fur, feathers, garter snakes, glass, plastic, with the studio installation *Big Boards*.

Photographs by Icelandic artist Erró, on 35 mm black and white film. Courtesy of Carolee Schneemann.

In a very real sense, Schneemann's work possesses a therapeutic drift, for her action was designed to begin to address the rift—both sexual and psychological—between men and women in the art world and beyond.

This sense of the importance of art intervening in the social dynamic was shared by the German performance artist Joseph Beuys. In 1974, Beuys flew to New York wrapped in a cocoon of felt. He was taken by ambulance to the René Block Gallery on East Broadway where he shared a fenced-in gallery space for three days with a wild coyote. The piece was called *I Like America and America Likes Me* (**Fig. 24-7**). The felt cocoon was a reference to his own myth of origin: When serving as a fighter pilot in the German Luftwaffe during World War II, he claimed to have been shot down in the dead of winter over the Crimea, where he was saved by a band of Tatars who wrapped him in animal fat and felt to nurse his body back to heath. It now seems likely that this story is untrue, but symbolically it reminds us of Beuys's principal theme, near-death and rebirth through healing, a process that he found impossible to communicate without such fables, and which he saw as central to the possibility of meaningful political behavior since, from his point of view, all of Western society was essentially a wounded body.

Fig. 24-7 Joseph Beuys, *I Like America and America Likes Me*, 1974. Performance, René Block Gallery, New York, duration three days.

Photo: Caroline Tisdale. Courtesy of Ron Feldman Fine Arts, New York.

Fig. 24-8 Kimsooja, *A Beggar Woman—Mexico City*, 2000. Single-channel video projection, silent, 8 min. 50 sec. loop. Courtesy of Kimsooja Studio.

In *I Like America and America Likes Me*, Beuys takes one of his most common performance roles, that of a wounded shaman, or mystical healer. The coyote was chosen to join him because it is the most adaptable of all native species and because in many Native American creation myths it is the coyote that teaches human beings how to survive. Over the course of the three days, Beuys would occasionally speak with the coyote, perform shamanistic rituals around the space, and sleep on a pile of hay that was originally meant for his four-legged companion, while the coyote slept on two large pieces of felt that were intended to serve as Beuys's bed. Each day copies of the *Wall Street Journal* arrived, representing the destructive forces of materialism that Beuys, the shaman, had come to America to heal. In the manner of a painting contained by a frame, Beuys's performance was framed by the gallery space. Like Jackson Pollock's paintings (see Figs. 6-12 and 6-13), where the drips and sweeps of paint on canvas record Pollock's actions as a painter and document them, the photographs of Beuys's work record his actions as an artist and similarly document them.

In her video work, Korean artist Kimsooja uses her body to investigate the human condition in all its frailty. *A Beggar Woman* (**Fig. 24-8**) was inspired when Kimsooja saw an old woman begging in the main square of Mexico City, the Zócalo. Seated on the ground, wrapped in upon herself, she put out her hand asking for money. "I was so struck by that action," Kimsooja explains in the art21 *Exclusive* video "Kimsooja: '*A Beggar Woman*' and '*A Homeless Woman*,'" and I wanted to question for myself again what that action really means." So she adopted the same pose as the old woman, and put out her hand to beg. When, finally, a man came up and gave her money, she suddenly felt completely vulnerable, and she began to cry. Similarly, she has lain down in the street as if she were a homeless person sleeping. "My body," she says, "becomes like a storm on the street." The videos are structured so that we can, in turn, identify with Kimsooja. They are shot from the rear, showing only her back. She becomes like a figure with its back to us in a landscape painting (see Fig. 19-16, Casper David Friedrich's *Monk by the Sea*, for comparison), a stand-in for us all.

Gender and Identity

How do biological sex and gender differ, and how has this difference been explored in the arts?

Gender does not refer to one's biological sex, and traditional gender roles probably have more to do with social expectations than any biological imperative. In the last half of the twentieth century, the feminist movement challenged the gender stereotypes imposed on women, and it was followed soon after by the lesbian, gay, bisexual, and transgender (LGBT) community's exploration of gender's enormous complexities. What both the feminist movement and the LGBT community have taught us is that identity is something constructed, not given.

Constructing Female Identity

A case can be made that we are constructions created out of the media imagery that inundates our world, and no artist has exploited the power of the media to define us to greater effect than Cindy Sherman. Beginning in the late 1970s, Sherman began to take photographs of herself as if they were stills from unknown Hollywood films. (She describes how she goes about setting up her shoots in the art21 *Exclusive* segment "Cindy Sherman: Mannequins and Masks.") Although they were not enactments of any actress playing a role in an actual film, these *Untitled Film Stills* were immediately recognizable. The fact that we can identify almost all of the stereotypes that inform these photographs—and, in fact, the pleasure of Sherman's work can be said to reside in our ability to ascribe certain "personalities" to each image—demonstrates just how deep-seated our "knowledge" of female identity really is. What we know is what the movies have given us.

In 1981, *Artforum* magazine commissioned Sherman to create a series of color photographs. Inspired by the size of the magazine, Sherman decided to make a series of double-spreads imitating *Playboy* centerfolds (**Fig. 24-9**; see also Fig. 20-41). They violate the viewer's expectations by revealing, instead of the female body, a depth of character and emotion. Speaking of these works, Sherman explains:

> In content I wanted a man opening up the magazine to suddenly look at it with an expectation of something lascivious and then feel like the violator that they would be. Looking at this woman who is perhaps a victim. I didn't think of them as victims at the time. . . . But I suppose. . . . Obviously I'm trying to make someone feel bad for having a certain expectation.

Some critics objected to the series, arguing that Sherman was reaffirming teenage stereotypes, but Sherman argued that she was simply revealing how pervasive and "readable" such stereotypes are. Nonetheless, fearing that the photographs might be misunderstood, *Artforum* never published them.

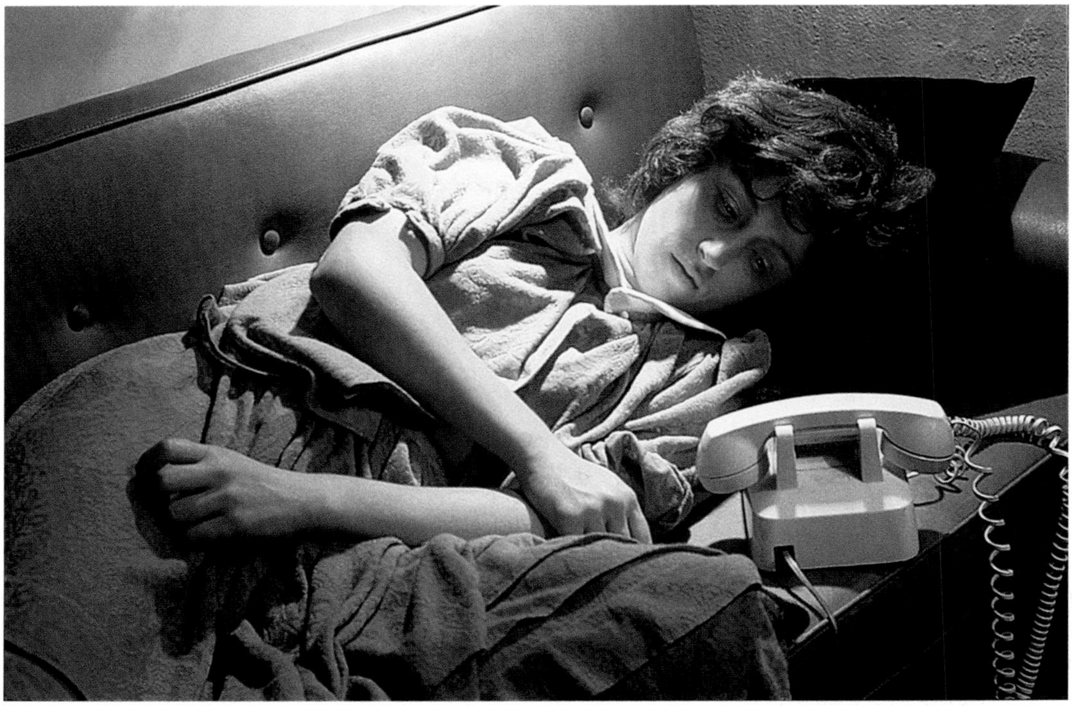

Fig. 24-9 Cindy Sherman, *Untitled #96*, 1981. Chromogenic color print, 24 in. × 4 ft.
Courtesy of the artist and Metro Pictures, New York.

Fig. 24-10 Andy Warhol, *Marilyn Monroe*, 1967. Silkscreen print, 37½ × 37½ in. Chazen Museum of Art, University of Wisconsin–Madison.

Robert Gale Doyon Fund and Harold F. Bishop Fund Purchase. 1978-252. Image courtesy Chazen Museum of Art. © 2015 Andy Warhol Foundation for the Visual Arts, Inc./Artists Rights Society (ARS), New York.

It is fair to say that the stereotypes that Sherman reveals are, by and large, the product of the male gaze as film historian Laura Mulvey describes it (see Chapter 23). Andy Warhol's repeated depictions of Marilyn Monroe (**Fig. 24-10**; see also Fig. 10-30), with their garish, almost violent colors, address this same idea. Toward the end of her life, Marilyn Monroe, born Norma Jeane Mortenson, commented on her stardom: "My popularity," she said, "seems almost entirely a male phenomenon." It was, in other words, men who defined her—from Hugh Hefner, publisher of *Playboy* magazine, who first featured her in a centerfold spread in 1953, to her husbands, baseball player Joe DiMaggio and playwright Arthur Miller, to President John F. Kennedy, with whom she had a secret affair. In the movies she usually played "the humiliating stereotype of a dumb blonde: depersonalized, sexual, even a joke," as feminist author Gloria Steinem puts it in her book *Marilyn: Norma Jeane*. Steinem goes on to point out: "Acting, modeling, making a living more from external appearance than from internal identity—these had been Marilyn's lifelines out of poverty and obscurity." But, in the end, her suicide in 1962 suggests that, without an identity that seemed to her authentic, her life had become meaningless. In these terms, Monroe has become something of a feminist icon, the very embodiment of the fate of female identity in a male-dominated culture.

Of course, the usual fate of women has been to assume the identity of "wife." But if, historically, "wife" is one of the most common identities that women have assumed, courtesan is another, both identities prescribed by the dominant male cultures in which women have historically found themselves. Titian's *Venus of Urbino* (**Fig. 24-11**; see also Fig. 18-11) may well represent both. As a Venetian painter, Titian would have been well

Fig. 24-11 Titian, *Venus of Urbino*, 1538. Oil on canvas, 47 in. × 5 ft. 5 in. Galleria degli Uffizi, Florence.
© Studio Fotografico Quattrone, Florence.

acquainted with Venice's so-called "honest courtesans," who were among the city's most educated citizens and who—unlike ordinary prostitutes, who sold only their sexual favors—were highly sophisticated intellectuals who gained access to the city's aristocratic circles as well. "Thou wilt find the Venetian Courtesan a good Rhetorician and an elegant discourser," wrote one early seventeenth-century visitor to the city. Although subject to the usual public ridicule—and often blamed, together with the city's Jews, for any troubles that might befall the republic—they were understood by writers of the day to be more products of men's own shortcomings and desires than willful sinners in their own right. This group of courtesans, in fact, dominated the Venetian literary scene. Many of their poems transform the clichés of courtly love poetry into frankly erotic metaphors, undermining the superior position of men in Italian society.

A similar differentiation of roles developed during the Edo period in Japan—from 1625 to 1868—when the geisha and courtesans of the Yoshiwara pleasure district were continually celebrated in prints such as Suzuki Harunobu's *Two Courtesans, Inside and Outside the Display Window* (**Fig. 24-12**; see also Fig. 10-7). Each possessed a distinct identity in relation to her clients. Courtesans were essentially high-class prostitutes, while geisha were primarily entertainers, technically forbidden to compete with the courtesans in the sexual arena. The *tayu*, the highest-ranking courtesans, were renowned for their beauty and often attained celebrity status. And, like the geisha, they were highly trained in the arts. They were poets, musicians, calligraphers, and skilled sexual partners, all in one. Their artistic cultivation in some sense legitimized their trade—their clients found themselves in the company of not merely a prostitute but a culturally refined sensibility.

But their identity was in some measure as made-up as their powdered faces. Most were sold into prostitution at a young age in the hope that, in return for the financial benefit they brought to the family, they would live a more comfortable life and perhaps even receive an education. In fact, the girls had to pay back the money given their parents and were essentially indentured slaves imprisoned in the Yoshiwara district for as long as 20 years. They dreamed, of course, of becoming famous *tayu*, but the likelihood of ever attaining that rank was slim at best.

Well into the nineteenth century, the possibilities for women to define themselves in terms other than those

Fig. 24-12 Suzuki Harunobu, *Two Courtesans, Inside and Outside the Display Window*, Japanese, Edo period, about 1768–69. Woodblock print (*nishiki-e*), ink and color on paper, $26\frac{3}{8} \times 5\frac{1}{16}$ in. Museum of Fine Arts, Boston.

Fig. 24-13 Édouard Manet, *The Gare Saint-Lazare*, 1873. Oil on canvas, 36¾ × 45⅛ in. National Gallery of Art, Washington, D.C.

Gift of Horace Havemeyer in memory of his mother, Louisine W. Havemeyer 1956.10.1. Photo © Board of Trustees, National Gallery of Art, Washington, D.C.

imposed upon them by men were extremely limited, as Édouard Manet suggests in *The Gare Saint-Lazare* (**Fig. 24-13**). His model is Victorine Meurent. She had already appeared several times, most notably in *Le Déjeuner sur l'herbe* (see Fig. 19-24) and *Olympia* (see Fig. 1-15). Here she assumes a role very different than those she played in *Le Déjeuner sur l'herbe* and *Olympia*. The little girl is the daughter of Manet's friend Alphonse Hirsch, in whose garden the scene is set; she gazes through the fence at the tracks, obscured by the smoke of a passing train, in the new train station of Saint-Lazare. The painting is a study in contrasts. The little girl is dressed in white with blue trim, while the older woman, posed here as her mother, or perhaps her nanny, is in blue with white trim. The one sits, regarding us; the other stands, gazing through the fence railing. The nanny's hair is down, the little girl's up. The nanny's angular collar is countered by the soft curve of the little girl's neckline. The black choker around the one's neck finds its way to the other's hair. The older woman sits with her puppy on her lap, an ironic symbol of contentment. The little girl is eating grapes (beside her on the ledge), which have bacchanalian associations. The older escapes into her novel, perhaps a romantic one, while the younger looks out at the trains leaving the station, possibly dreaming of adventure. And both are literally fenced in. Manet's painting suggests that the little girl will grow up into the woman beside her, implicitly portraying the limits of women's possibilities in nineteenth-century French society.

Constructing Male Identity

It stands to reason that if female identity is not essential but socially constructed, the same should hold true for men. One of the first artists to address this theme was Richard Prince, who during the late 1970s had lived with Cindy Sherman in New York. By 1980—the year that horse-riding Hollywood hero Ronald Reagan was elected president—Prince had taken to photographing advertisements of cowboys, specifically the Marlboro Man, a practice that he has continued down to the present day (**Fig. 24-14**). Prince recognized that Philip Morris Co. was not so much selling cigarettes as it was an image—the smoker as the independent, rough-and-tumble hero. Thus, in rephotographing the original ads, Prince underscored the inauthenticity of the ad campaign itself. One of the underlying themes of this image is that the Marlboro cowboy, apparently riding free on the range, is symbolically galloping headlong toward his death. And as Prince well understood, in identifying with the image, the American male was mistaking dependence for independence.

In the catalogue to the exhibition *Richard Prince: Spiritual America*, at the Guggenheim Museum in New York

Fig. 24-14 Richard Prince, *Untitled (Cowboy)*, 1989. Chromogenic print, 4 ft. 2 in. × 5 ft. 10 in. Metropolitan Museum of Art, New York.
Purchase, Horace W. Goldsmith Foundation Gift through Joyce and Robert Menschel and Jennifer and Joseph Duke Gift, 2000.272. © 2015. Image copyright Metropolitan Museum of Art/Art Resource/Scala, Florence. © Richard Prince.

in 2007–08, novelist Annie Proulx described the particular appeal of Prince's cowboys:

> The clothing is important. There is, in the world, no costume so flattering and male as a cowboy getup: the tight jeans that show off thigh muscles and crotch, leather or woolly chaps with the cutout front that enhances the wearer's sexuality, fancy boots that make him look taller and leaner and that sound a solid footstep often enriched by the ring of spurs, the hat that dignifies the most foolish face, disguises a receding hairline, and adds more height, the leather vest casually open, the brilliantly colored shirt and contrasting silk neck rag, all add up to drama and indicate quick motion, masculine beauty, the work ethic, and a little danger. It is the clothing that attracts us to the cowboy.

It is the clothing, and the fact that he wears it, as Proulx explains, "against a backdrop of the most spectacular scenery in North America, both desert and mountain range." The cowboy's is an image to which most, if not all, American males aspired in the 1940s and 1950s—in the age, that is, of the great American cowboy films—and his is an image that still holds some ascendancy in the popular imagination, as the Marlboro Man attests.

Mel Bochner's *Win!* (**Fig. 24-15**), commissioned by the Dallas Cowboys for their stadium in Arlington, Texas, addresses another side of American male identity.

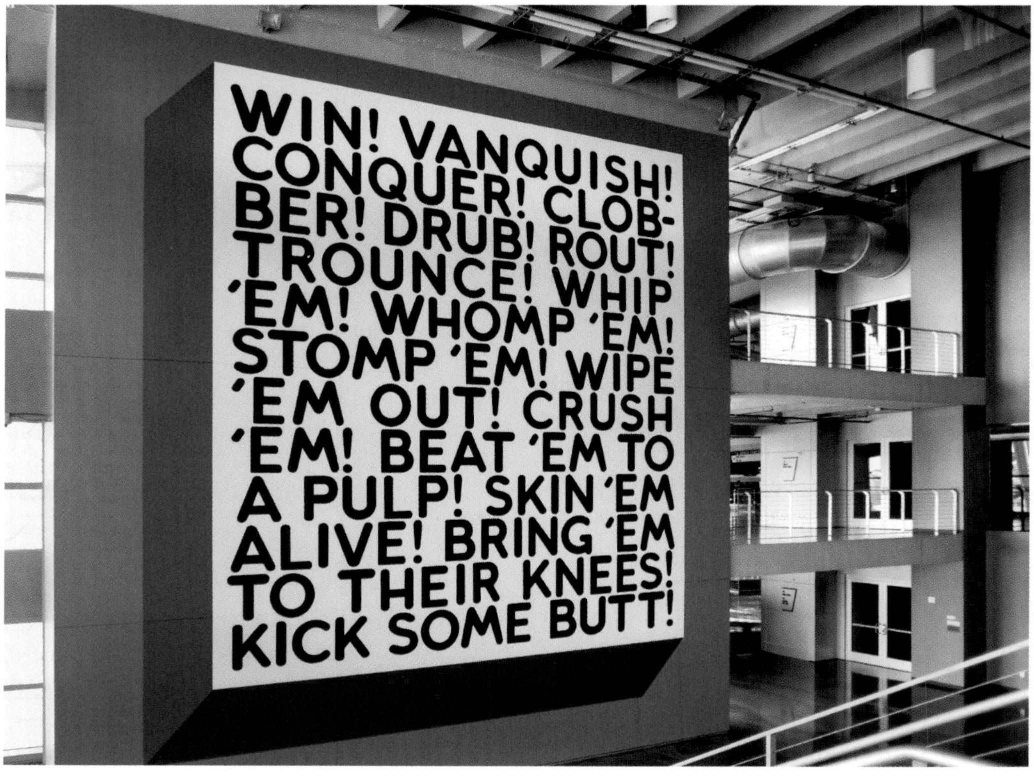

Fig. 24-15 Mel Bochner, *Win!*, 2009. Acrylic on wall, 38 ft. 2 in. × 33 ft. 3 in. Located in Northeast Monumental Staircase, AT&T Stadium (formerly Dallas Cowboys Stadium), Arlington, Texas.
Photo: James Smith/Dallas Cowboys.

It subtly challenges the macho culture of professional football—and its fanbase—even as it seems to celebrate it. As one of the pioneers of conceptual art during the 1960s, Bochner became interested in the relationship between words and their visual display and began a series of "thesaurus paintings" which delve more deeply than one might expect into the cultural implications of words like "Money," "Die," "Useless," "Obscene," and "Sputter." *Win!* is one of his most recent works in the ongoing series. By the time one finishes reading the painting, the violence that underscores the game of football is manifest—and appears alarmingly closer to war than sport.

The gay rights movement would play a dramatic role in challenging American attitudes about the nature of masculinity. In the early hours of Saturday morning, on June 28, 1969, police officers entered a gay nightclub in New York's Greenwich Village called the Stonewall Inn, more or less expecting to close the establishment down for lack of a liquor license. But the Inn's patrons reacted violently, throwing garbage cans, bricks, beer cans, and bottles at the windows and what a reporter for the *Village Voice* called "a rain of coins" at the police. Very soon after, the Inn was on fire. Rioting continued until about 4 AM, and nightly for several days thereafter. A year later, the first ever Gay Pride parade was staged to celebrate the events of June 1969.

The struggle for equal rights for gay people continues, of course, to this day. Sixteen years after Stonewall, in 1985, Andy Warhol conceived of his book *America*, a collection of his Polaroid photographs, at least in part as a means to "out" America, to show it its own gay side. At the very heart of the book is a "Physique Pictorial," showing male bodybuilders. Early on he includes a portrait of himself in drag, just one of many he shot in the early 1980s. There is an image of a Gay Pride parade. And then there are the portraits of gay celebrities, such as Liberace (with punk star John Sex), Keith Haring, and Robert Rauschenberg.

Warhol also includes a portrait of Lance Loud (**Fig. 24-16**). Loud has quite evidently constructed his own image out of the Classical nude as realized in Leonardo's *Study of Human Proportions: The Vitruvian Man* (see Fig. 24-4). Loud was the first reality-TV star. Born in 1951, he grew up in Eugene, Oregon, before moving to Santa Barbara for his teenage years. He discovered Warhol in his early teens, became his pen pal, and then, as a young man, moved to New York. When he was 22, in 1973, PBS featured the William C. Loud family—Mom and Dad, Bill and Pat (who incidentally separated and divorced on the show), and their five children, Delilah, Kevin, Grant, Michele, and Lance—in a 12-hour documentary series entitled *An American Family*. It chronicled the day-to-day lives of the family for seven months, and it attracted 10 million viewers. As a *Newsweek* cover story proclaimed in March 1973, the show torpedoed the fantasy of the American family embodied in shows like *The Brady Bunch*. Lance's forthright homosexuality spurred a national controversy, especially after he appeared on *The Dick Cavett Show* and other talk shows, and as it became apparent that he was inspiring countless other gay and lesbian Americans to acknowledge their own sexuality. By 1978, Lance had started the band The Mumps, a rock band that played weekly at CBGB's and Max's in New York; Warhol's photograph is of Lance Loud the rock star—yet another media model for the male. American attitudes about masculinity and male identity were in a state of transition, and sexual stereotypes were being challenged as never before.

Fig. 24-16 Andy Warhol, *Lance Loud*, from *America*, 1985. Black-and-white photograph.

Challenging Gender Identity

In 1862, Manet painted his favorite model, the same Victorine Meurent who would appear 11 years later as a nanny in *The Gare Saint-Lazare* (see Fig. 24-13), this time in the costume of an *espada*—the matador in a bullfight (**Fig. 24-17**). Meurent worked for Manet, in effect, as a performance artist, assuming this role, then that, for over a decade. Most telling, Manet has no qualms about

Fig. 24-17 Édouard Manet, *Mademoiselle V . . . in the Costume of an Espada,* 1862. Oil on canvas, 5 ft. 5 in. × 4 ft. 2¼ in. Metropolitan Museum of Art, New York.

H. O. Havemeyer Collection, Bequest of Mrs. H. O. Havemeyer, 1929.100.53. © 2015. Image copyright Metropolitan Museum of Art/Art Resource/Scala, Florence.

drawing attention, by simply titling the painting as he has, to the fact that his female model is dressed in male clothing. Indeed, at the Salon of 1863, Manet exhibited this painting along with *Young Man in the Costume of a Majo* and *Le Déjeuner sur l'herbe* as a triptych. In the former, his younger brother Gustave donned the same trousers and bolero that Meurent wears here, and in the latter Gustave posed for the male figure on the right. Seen together, they self-consciously challenged the assumptions of Realist painting. These were paintings constructed using models who played parts interchangeably from painting to painting. They clearly had very little to do with Realism, then such an important style in French painting (see Chapter 19). In fact, Meurent stands in the bullring in a space radically and illogically disconnected from the scene behind her, where a bullfight takes place not drawn from life but from a series of 33 prints by Francisco Goya, *The Tauromaquia*, published in 1816 (**Fig. 24-18**). Manet insists that his paintings are fictions. By extension, so is identity.

Cross-dressing is a strategy for announcing that one's biological sex is not necessarily coincident with one's gender identity. In the early 1920s, and then on and off for the rest of his career, Marcel Duchamp dressed and signed works of art under the name Rrose Sélavy

Fig. 24-18 Francisco Goya, *The Tauromaquia: The Spirited Moor Gazul is the First to Spear Bulls according to the Rules,* 1816. Etching, 9⅞ × 13⅞ in.

© 2015. Photo Art Resource/Scala, Florence.

(**Fig. 24-19**). The name is a pun: *Eros, c'est la vie* ("Eros, that's life"). Puns, of course, are linguistic expressions of semantic doubling and ambiguity. They are at once the same and different. They model, in other words, the sameness and difference in the simultaneity of different biological and gender identities. This is the same point Duchamp makes by adding a mustache to Leonardo's *Mona Lisa* in the work punningly titled *L.H.O.O.Q.* (see

Fig. 24-19 Man Ray, *Marcel Duchamp as Rrose Sélavy,* ca. 1920–21. Gelatin silver print, 8½ × 6¹³⁄₁₆ in. Philadelphia Museum of Art.

Samuel S. White 3rd and Vera White Collection, 1957. © 2015. Photo Philadelphia Museum of Art/Art Resource/Scala, Florence. © 2015 Man Ray Trust/Artists Rights Society (ARS), New York/ADAGP, Paris.

Fig. 24-20 Eleanor Antin, *My Kingdom Is the Right Size*, from the series *The King of Solana Beach*, 1974.
Photograph mounted on board, 6 × 9 in.
Courtesy of Ronald Feldman Fine Arts, New York.

Fig. 20-11). Here, in Man Ray's photograph of Duchamp, Rrose wears the hat and fur-trimmed coat of Germaine Everling, the soon-to-be second wife of Francis Picabia (see Fig. 23-16). The hands in the photograph are Everling's as well, and their distinct femininity adds to the illusion. Or, Duchamp seems to ask, is it really an illusion after all?

Beginning in the early 1970s, Eleanor Antin began assuming a series of personae designed to allow her to explore dimensions of her own self that might otherwise have remained hidden. One of the earliest of these personae was the King—a medieval knight errant, decked out in a false beard, a velvet cape, lacy blouse, and leather boots, who would wander the streets of "his" kingdom, the small town of Solana Beach, just north of San Diego, California, conversing with his "subjects" (**Fig. 24-20**). "The usual aids to self-definition," Antin wrote the same year as this performance piece, "sex, age, talent, time, and space—are merely tyrannical limitations upon my freedom of choice." Here she explores the possibilities of being not merely male, but a powerful male—something wholly at odds with her diminutive physical presence. "I took on the King," Antin further explained, "who was my male self. As a young feminist I was interested in what would be my male self . . . he became my political self."

Shigeyuki Kihara is an artist of Japanese/Samoan extraction who resides in New Zealand as a transgender woman—a biological male who lives as a woman—the word for which among the Samoan peoples, for whom the "third gender" has historically held a place as not only socially acceptable but also widely practiced, is *fa'a fafine*. Kihara's work is directly inspired by nineteenth- and early twentieth-century photographs of Samoan islanders taken by non-Samoans whose assumptions about the lives of their subjects were deeply tainted by the same sorts of ideas that drew painter Paul Gauguin to the South Seas during the same era—the dream of a "primitive" culture of unity, peace, and naked innocence far removed from the turmoil of "civilized" life (see Fig. 19-33). *Ulugali'i Samoa: Samoan Couple* (*ulugali'i* is Samoan for "married couple") (**Fig. 24-21**) is a recreation of one of these colonial photographs, which were, in fact, distributed worldwide as postcards. But as a result of the impact of Christian missionaries in the islands, by the time these postcards were circulating throughout the West as part of a burgeoning trade in pornography, the Samoans themselves most usually dressed themselves in Western clothing. The photographers required their adolescent Samoan models to expose their breasts in order to satisfy the same fantasies that so appealed to Gauguin.

Kihara has posed herself as the woman in this photograph, bare-breasted, holding a plaited fan (a traditional status symbol), and wearing a bark cloth dress, traditionally made throughout the Pacific Islands from the paper mulberry tree. The male is similarly attired and holds a fly whisk, like the fan, a status symbol. Around his neck he wears a *ulafala*, a red lei crafted from the fruit of the pandanus tree and normally worn by a high-ranking Samoan *tulafale* (orator chief). As in nineteenth-century photographs, the couple is posed in the studio in front of an array of tropical foliage as if in a natural setting. Kihara further undermines this construction of "authentic" island identity by digitally superimposing her own face, now made-up with a wig and mustache, on the body of the male. The photograph challenges accepted notions of identity at every level—in terms of gender roles, colonial assumptions about Samoan culture, and even the reality of the photographic image itself.

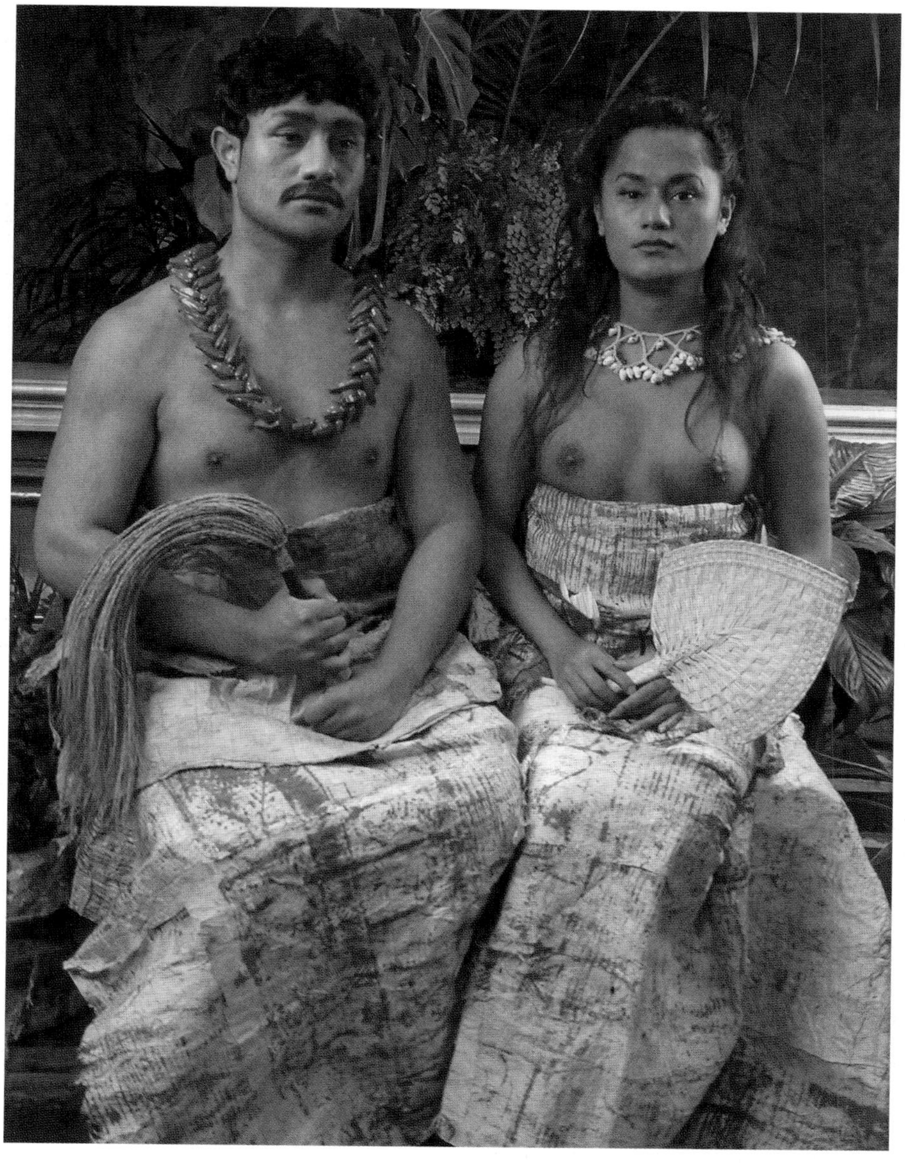

Fig. 24-21 Shigeyuki Kihara, *Ulugali'i Samoa: Samoan Couple*, 2004–05. PC-type photograph, 31½ × 23⅗ in. Edition of 5. Metropolitan Museum of Art, New York.

THE CRITICAL PROCESS

Thinking about the Body, Gender, and Identity

In 1961, when she was just 12 years of age, the Cuban-born artist Ana Mendieta and her 14-year-old sister were sent, along with 14,000 other Cuban children, to the United States through the "Operation Peter Pan" program jointly run by the United States government and Catholic charities. Her politically prominent family feared reprisals from Fidel Castro's Communist revolution. She lived, at first, in refugee camps and other institutions, until she finally entered foster home networks in Iowa. It was not until 1966 that she was reunited with her mother and younger brother, and not until 1979 that her father joined them, finally having been released from prison for his role in the Bay of Pigs invasion.

Mendieta never fully recovered from the trauma of separation, not merely from her family but from her native land. In Iowa, she felt she had no sense of self, no identity. As a graduate painting student at the University of Iowa, she addressed this issue directly by transplanting the beard of fellow student Morty Sklar to her own face. The immigration of the beard reenacted, in terms of gender, her own removal from Cuba to Iowa. The beard did not "belong," although she claims that, when she saw it on her face, it seemed to have become "natural," quite likely a reference to the "naturalization" process undertaken by foreign immigrants.

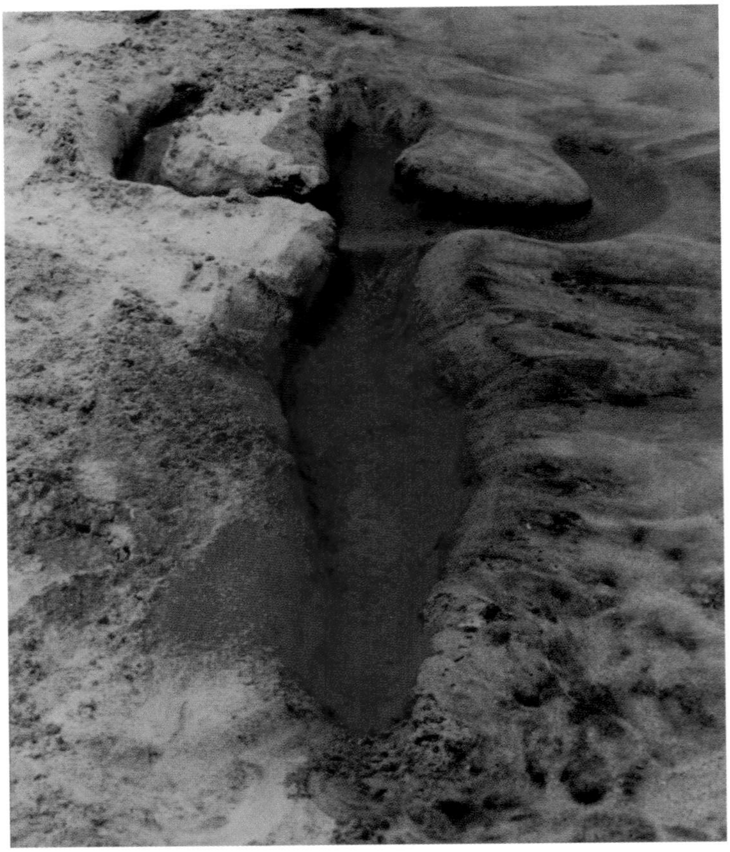

Fig. 24-22 Ana Mendieta, *Untitled*, 1976. From *Silueta Works in Mexico*, 1973–77. Color photograph from a suite of 12, 19⅜ × 26⁹⁄₁₆ in. Museum of Contemporary Art, Los Angeles.

Purchased with a grant provided by Judith Rothschild Foundation. © Estate of Ana Mendieta Collection, LLC. courtesy of Galerie Lelong, New York.

Soon after graduating, she journeyed to Mexico and felt a connection to the land that she had not experienced since leaving Cuba. There, she began to place her silhouette—*silueta* in Spanish—onto and into the earth itself. In the action illustrated here (**Fig. 24-22**), she formed a *silueta* on the beach at La Ventosa, Mexico, filling it with red tempera that was ultimately washed away by the ocean waves. "I am overwhelmed," she would later write, "by the feeling of having been cast from the womb (nature). . . . Through my earth/body sculptures, I become one with the earth. . . . The after-image of being encompassed within the womb is a manifestation of my thirst for being."

But the image is not merely a bodily imprint in the sand. It is simultaneously the image of a broad-handled knife, and a bloody knife at that. This is a reference to the African-Cuban religion of *Santería*, specifically to the *orisha* (a spirit or deity who is one manifestation of God) Ogun, the fierce warrior and inventor of the knife who defends his *Santería* followers against injustice. It is he who gives the initiate the authority to use the knife in animal sacrifice, a required part of any initiation into the religion since, without blood sacrifice, the *orishas* are not present and the consecration would thus be illegitimate.

How does the double meaning of Mendieta's *silueta* reflect her own sense of identity? Her image on the beach was soon washed away by the tide. What does this suggest to you about her sense of her own body? Why is the beach—the zone between land and sea—a particularly apt place to put a *silueta*?

Thinking Back

24.1 Explain why "beautiful" is an ambiguous word in reference to the body.

Different eras and different cultures have defined what constitutes a beautiful body in different ways. Prehistoric peoples apparently valued a body-type characterized by pendulous breasts, wide hips, and a swollen belly. How has archeologist Clive Gamble explained the preponderance of these female figurines? How does the *ugonachomma* figure reflect the values of the Igbo people? For the ancient Greeks, the beautiful body was determined by how closely it conformed to ideal proportions. How did they think these proportions reflected larger universal truths? How did Peter Paul Rubens define the beautiful body?

24.2 Discuss some of the factors that have motivated artists to use their own bodies in works of art.

Why did Carolee Schneemann incorporate herself into the work *Eye Body*? German performance artist Joseph Beuys saw himself as a shaman, healing social and political divisions. What division was he trying to heal in *I Like America and America Likes Me*? What motivated Kimsooja to work in the street as if she were a beggar?

24.3 Differentiate between biological sex and gender, and discuss some of the ways in which identity is constructed.

Contemporary artists like Cindy Sherman have argued that female identity has been largely constructed by the media, movies in particular. How do Sherman's many self-portraits in a wide variety of roles support this assertion? What, from Andy Warhol's point of view, were the consequences of this role-playing for Marilyn Monroe? Historically, women were relegated to two principal roles—wife and courtesan. How do these roles reflect the imposition of male power? How does the *Venus of Urbino* mediate between both? What is the difference between a geisha and a courtesan? What possibilities for women in nineteenth-century French society does Édouard Manet's *The Gare Saint-Lazare* suggest?

Male identity is as socially constructed as female identity. What sense of self does the Marlboro Man suggest in Richard Prince's work? How does Mel Bochner's *Win!* reflect yet another media model? How has the gay rights movement changed American attitudes about masculinity?

One's given biological sex may differ from one's gender, the culturally learned social roles with which one identifies. Cross-dressing is a strategy for announcing that one's biological sex is not necessarily coincident with one's gender identity. How did Manet use it to underscore the difference between his art and the dominant Realist style? Why did Marcel Duchamp and Eleanor Antin choose to dress as the opposite sex? How does Shigeyuki Kihara address wider questions of colonial power through her examination of gender identity?

Chapter 25
The Individual and Cultural Identity

Learning Objectives

25.1 Define nationalism and describe how the arts have been used to construct and critique national identities.

25.2 Describe how the visual signs of class inform works of art.

25.3 Discuss racial identity as it manifests itself in African-American art.

Gender plays an important role in the formation of identity (see Chapter 24). But identity is determined by other factors as well—by ethnic and class distinctions, as well as social and political allegiances to community and state. Almost all African cultures, for instance, emphasize the well-being of the group over the individual, a conviction invoked, guaranteed, and celebrated by the masked dance. In the face of European challenges to the integrity of African cultures, dance has become, in fact, an especially important vehicle in maintaining cultural identity and continuity.

The masked dance is a ritual activity so universally practiced from one culture to the next across West Africa that it could be called the focal point of the region's cultures. It unites the creative efforts of sculptors, dancers, musicians, and others. Originally performed as part of larger rituals connected with stages in human development, the passing of the seasons, or stages of the agricultural year, the masked dance in recent years has become increasingly commercial—a form of entertainment disconnected from its original social context. This modern photograph of the *banda* mask being used by the Baga Mandori people who live on the Atlantic coastline of Guinea is unique, however, in capturing an actual *banda* dance (**Fig. 25-1**). The *banda* mask dance is normally performed at night, with only torches for illumination, but in 1987 villagers agreed, for the sake of creating a photographic record, to begin the performance at dusk. The photographs taken that evening by Fred Lamp, curator of African art at the Yale University Art Gallery, are the only extant photographs of an actual *banda* performance.

The *banda* mask is a sort of amalgam of different creatures, combining the jaws of a crocodile, the face of a human, the elaborate hairstyle of a woman, the body of a serpent, the horns of an antelope, the alert ears of a deer, and, rising between the horns, the tail of a chameleon. The *banda* mask dance is generally performed at initiations, harvest ceremonies, and funerals, and is renowned for its spectacular acrobatics, with the wearer spinning high in the air and low to the ground, as if in defiance of the enormous weight of the mask itself. The choreography of the dance actually involves the dancer spinning madly while holding the headdress aloft, then twirling the mask in a series of figure eights, at last dashing it down to the ground before returning it to his head, all in one seamless burst of movement.

The *banda* mask, finally, is believed to possess **agency**. That is, it helps to effect change—the transformation (as symbolized by the chameleon's tail) from adolescence to adulthood, from fall to winter, from life to death. And it embodies the collective consciousness of the group—a shared sense of identity—by drawing the community into its celebratory dance.

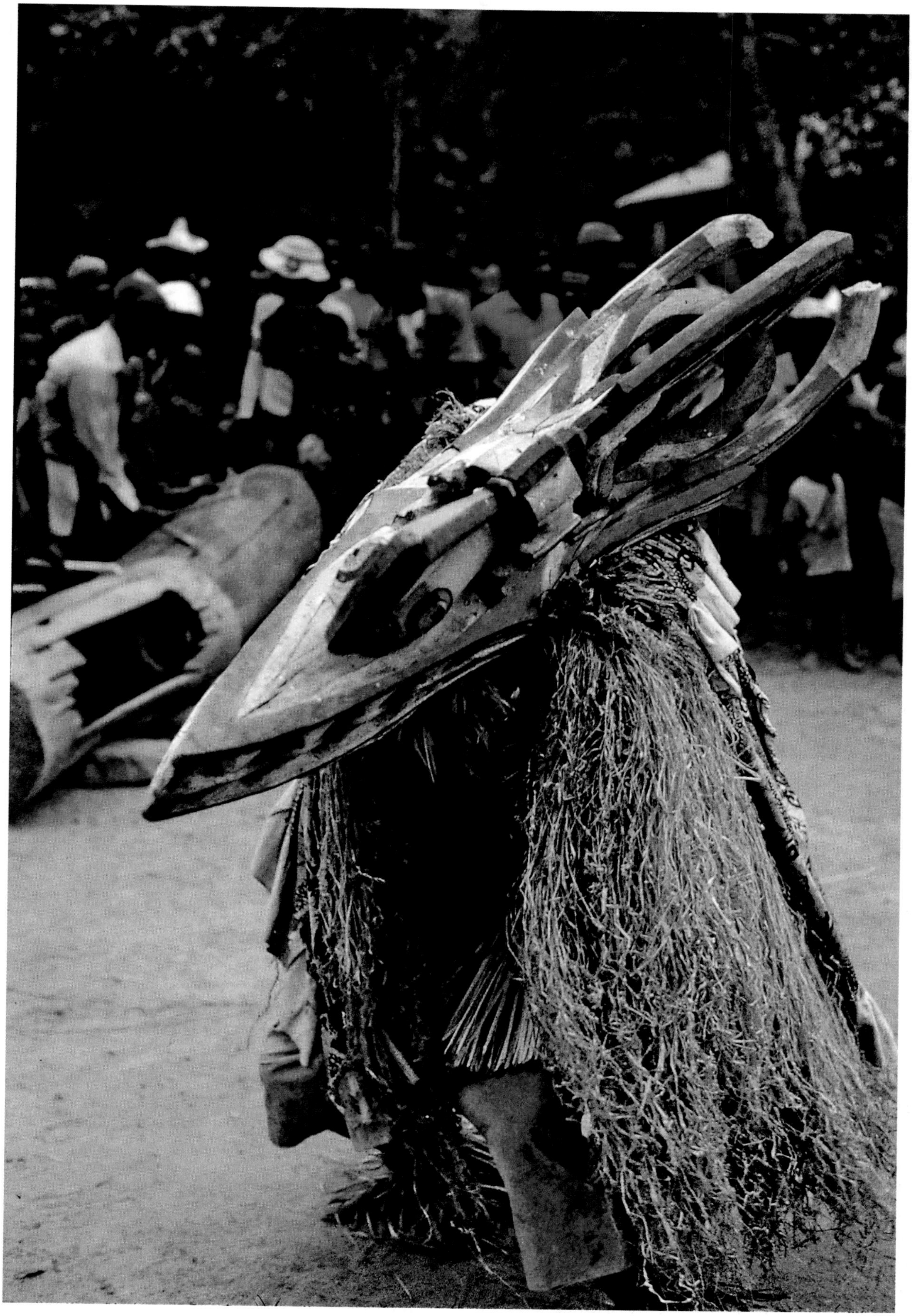

Fig. 25-1 ***Banda*** **dance, Baga Mandori, Guinea, 1987.**
Photograph courtesy of Frederick John Lamp.

Nationalism and Identity

What is nationalism and how have the arts been used to construct and critique national identities?

Throughout the nineteenth century, and into the twentieth, peoples around the world increasingly began to define themselves as part of larger groups. One of the most important factors contributing to this was nationalism. Nationalists claimed that people sharing the same language, historic experience—often embodied in folk-songs, folk-poetry, and folk-dances passed down through the generations—and very often ethnic identity made up a nation.

National Identity in Europe and America

Nationalism was closely tied to the idea of throwing off the yolk of monarchs and rulers—to the idea, inspired by the French Revolution of 1789, of self-determination, not of the individual, but of a "people." One of the great artistic expressions of this sentiment is Eugène Delacroix's *Liberty Leading the People* (**Fig. 25-2**; see also Fig. 19-19). After the defeat of Napoleon in 1815, the monarchy in France had been restored. But the rule of the new king, Charles X, was tenuous, and, when, in the spring of 1830, he called for new elections, liberals demanding substantial reforms and freedoms won a large majority in a legislative body called the Chamber of Deputies. On July 25, 1830, Charles responded by dissolving the Chamber, reinstituting censorship of the press, and restricting the right to vote to the wealthiest men. The next day, rioting erupted as workers took to the streets, erected barricades, and confronted royalist troops. In the following days, 1,800 people died. Soon after, Charles abdicated the throne and left France for England. In his place, the Chamber of Deputies named the duke of Orléans, Louis-Philippe, king of their new constitutional monarchy.

Fig. 25-2 Eugène Delacroix, *Liberty Leading the People*, 1830. Oil on canvas, 8 ft. 6⅜ in. × 10 ft. 8 in. Musée du Louvre, Paris.
Louvre-Lens, France/Bridgeman Images.

Liberty Leading the People is Delacroix's response to these events. A bare-breasted Lady Liberty, symbolic of freedom's nurturing power, strides over a barricade, the *tricolor* flag of the Revolution in hand, accompanied by a young street ruffian waving a pair of pistols. On the other side is a middle-class gentleman in top hat and frock coat, and beside him, in a smock, a man of the working class wielding a saber. Another worker, dressed in the colors of the Revolution, grasps at Liberty's feet. The whole triangular structure of the composition rises from the bodies of two French royalist guards, both stripped of their shoes and one of his clothing by the rioting workers. To the middle-class liberals who had fomented the 1830 revolution, the painting was frighteningly realistic. The new king, Louis-Philippe, ordered that it be purchased by the state and then promptly put it away so that its celebration of the commoners would not prove too inspiring. In fact, the painting was not seen in public again until 1848, when Louis-Philippe was himself deposed by yet another nationalist revolution. But the painting boldly asserts the principles of nationalist identity—all classes of people coming together to demand their shared rights under the flag of nationhood and the nurturing figure of Liberty.

Nationalist sentiment in the United States was tied, almost paradoxically, to the country's self-definition as the home of rugged individuals able to fend for themselves in the frontier wilderness. John Gast had essentially illustrated this sense of American national identity in his popular painting *American Progress* (**Fig. 25-3**). Pushing westward by train, covered wagon, stagecoach, and on foot, the frontiersmen are inspired by the allegorical figure of Progress, trailing a telegraph wire from her left hand and clutching a schoolbook in the other. At the top right of the painting is Manhattan, the twin towers of the Brooklyn Bridge, construction of which had begun in 1869, visible on the shores of the East River. At the top left is Puget Sound, as painted by Albert Bierstadt around the same time (see Fig. 2-6). And as Progress moves westward, she brings with her the light of civilization. Native Americans, bear, and buffalo are driven off to the margins.

Writing about American national identity in 1893—several years after the U.S. Census Bureau had

Fig. 25-3 John Gast, *American Progress*, 1872. Oil on canvas, 20¼ × 30¼ in. Private collection.
Photo © Christie's Images/Bridgeman Images.

proclaimed the frontier closed—historian Frederick Jackson Turner argued that the frontier had produced a "dominant individualism," men "of coarseness and strength . . . acuteness and inquisitiveness, [of a] practical and inventive turn of mind . . . [with] restless and nervous energy . . . [and the] buoyancy and exuberance which comes with freedom." From the beginning, he continued, this "frontier individualism . . . promoted democracy." Yet he also warned that

> the democracy born of free land, strong in selfishness and individualism, intolerant of administrative experience and education, and pressing individual liberty beyond its proper bounds, has its dangers as well as its benefits. Individualism in America has allowed a laxity in regard to governmental affairs which has rendered possible the spoils system and all the manifest evils that follow from the lack of highly developed civic spirit. In this connection may be noted also the influence of frontier conditions in permitting lax business honor, inflated paper currency and wildcat banking.

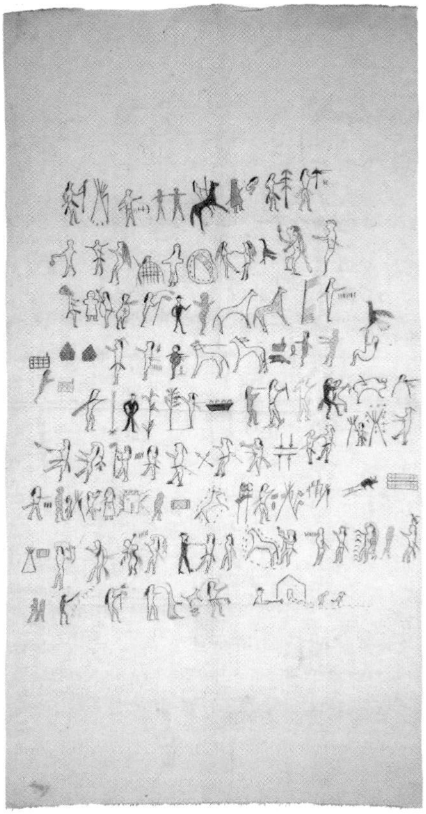

Fig. 25-4 Sioux winter count, ca. 1900. Muslin, wax crayon, 69¼ × 35¼ in. The John and Marva Warnock Collection, Los Altos, California.
Photo courtesy of Splendid Heritage.

Turner articulated here the seminal American myth and the source of the country's nationalist spirit. True or false, his "frontier thesis," as it came to be known, affirmed the role that most people thought individualism would have to play if the nation were to continue to progress forward and meet the challenge of its increasing global presence.

Native American Tribal History and Identity

Of course, the very "frontier individualism" that Turner saw as promoting the American sense of self was also responsible for the destruction of the Native American populations. Native Americans self-identify as a group insofar as they can trace their ancestry to pre-contact peoples. But, today, the Federal government recognizes 566 different Native American tribes, speaking 250 different languages. While they share the common history of their conquest, the songs, stories, and dances that have been passed down through the generations are largely unique to each.

Unlike almost all other Native American tribes in North America, the Native Americans of the Great Plains recorded their history in copious detail, painting images in relatively flat, semi-abstract images on buffalo-hide robes, the exterior hides of teepees, shields, and muslin cloths. In these designs, humans are generally stick figures, and events are described in selective detail. They served as memory aids that would help the owner in relating his family's history through the traditional art of storytelling. Some tribes, particularly the Lakota Sioux and Kiowa, recorded family or band history in what is known as a "winter count" (**Fig. 25-4**). Marking the passing of the years in winters—the Lakota designated a year as the time elapsed from first snowfall to first snowfall—tribal artists created pictographic images, one for each year, which would, in effect, stir the collective memory of what else had happened in the year. They then arranged the pictographs in a pattern, often circular, reading from the center outward, but also in linear designs as seen here, reading from left to right in the first row, then right to left in the second, and so on.

This particular winter count covers the years 1776 to 1879. As the buffalo disappeared in the last decades of the nineteenth century, Plains artists turned to drawing on cloth. This winter count was probably copied to muslin cloth from an original count on hide. White men are depicted in black, wearing hats, and sometimes bearded. Their first appearance in this winter count is in the middle of the third row, followed immediately by a drawing of a pox-covered figure—note, however, that the first pox-covered figures occur in the top row, in about 1780. One of the most interesting figures in this winter count is at the end of the sixth row—a teepee surrounded by crosses representing stars. The winter-count year is 1833–34, when, on November 12, 1833, the Leonid meteor shower occurred. The winter count ends with the image of a white man firing a gun at two wounded figures running from a house. Three years after the Cheyenne and Lakota had joined forces in the Great Sioux War, the Cheyenne chief Morning Star, known to the Lakota as Dull Knife, was captured and confined at Fort Robinson, Nebraska. This last image documents the attempted escape of Dull Knife and his followers on January 8, 1879, when most of the Cheyenne, chiefly women and children, were killed by Federal troops. The winter count is thus both an image of a tribal nation's history and testimony to its demise.

National Identity in China and Japan

While in Europe nationalism did not really take hold until the nineteenth century, in Asia nationalist sentiment had already been long established, stretching back as far as the Qin dynasty in China when Qin Shihuangdi first built the Great Wall to discourage nomads from the north from invading (see Fig. 16-33). When, in fact, the Chinese were conquered by Mongol nomads from the steppes north of China in the thirteenth century, many of the scholar-painters of the Chinese court, exiled themselves, conscientiously sought to keep traditional values and arts alive by cultivating earlier styles in both painting and calligraphy. A symbolic vocabulary of resistance arose: orchids, which flourish without soil around their roots, symbolized the theft of Chinese soil by invaders (see Fig. 18-13); bamboo, as painted here by Ke Jiusi in the manner of the eleventh-century master Wen Tong (**Fig. 25-5**), represented flexibility, the quality that allows it to bend but not break; pine, which can grow in poor, rocky soil, and stays green even in the worst of the winter, signified cultural survival; and plum, which blooms in winter despite the harsh conditions in which it finds itself, stood for perseverance in the face of adversity. During the Yuan dynasty of the Mongol conquerors, these became the very symbols of Chinese national identity.

After the Mongol invaders were expelled in 1368, China managed to keep all foreigners—whom they called *fanqui*, or "foreign devils"—at bay. By the eighteenth century, as demand for Chinese tea and spices rose worldwide, foreign ships were admitted only to Canton (present-day Guangzhou), and traders were confined to a narrow strip of land where they lived and did business. The Japanese were even more protective of their identity. In the late sixteenth and early seventeenth centuries, threatened in particular by the growing influence of Christianity brought by

Fig. 25-5 Ke Jiusi, *Bamboo, after Wen Tong*, Yuan dynasty, 1343. Hanging scroll, ink on silk, 42⅜ × 18¾ in. Metropolitan Museum of Art, New York.
ex coll.: C. C. Wang Family, Gift of Oscar L. Tang Family, 2006.571. © 2015. Image copyright Metropolitan Museum of Art/Art Resource/Scala, Florence.

Jesuit and Franciscan friars, the emperors pursued an increasingly isolationist foreign policy. Christianity, even as practiced by foreigners, was banned altogether in 1614. In 1635, the Japanese were forbidden to travel abroad, and in 1641 foreign trade was limited to the Dutch, who were confined to a small area in Nagasaki harbor, and the Chinese, who were confined to a quarter within the city of Nagasaki itself. Japan would remain sealed from foreign influence until 1853, when the American commodore Matthew Perry sailed into Edo Bay with four warships and a letter from the president of the United States urging the Japanese to receive the American sailors. The following year, Japan formally reopened its ports to the world.

But a strong sense of national identity was firmly established, and it resulted, in the first half of the twentieth century, in an aggressive nationalism designed to assert Japan's preeminence in Asia. In 1931, Japan invaded Manchuria, then Shanghai a year later, and the rest of China in 1937. The air attack on Pearl Harbor, Hawaii, on December 7, 1941, was, of course, the blow that set off World War II in the Pacific.

This penchant for nationalist feeling in Japan, which by the 1980s had begun to reemerge with Japan's rise as a commercial powerhouse built on technological innovation, inspired Yanagi Yukinori to create an installation titled *Hinomaru Illumination (Amaterasu and Haniwa)* (**Fig. 25-6**). The space is filled with rows of replica *haniwa* figures—the terra-cotta sculptures topped with images ranging from fish, birds, and monkeys, to women, falconers, and warriors in armor—that date back to the fifth and sixth centuries and that were used to decorate tombs, sometimes by the thousands. The figures face a hypnotic, radiating neon version of the Japanese flag, the *hinomaru,* "circle of the sun," which is, in turn, linked to the Japanese imperial family, whom the Japanese believe is descended from the Shinto sun goddess, Amaterasu. The *haniwa* here represent the Japanese people who blindly pay obeisance to those in power.

Fig. 25-6 Yanagi Yukinori, *Hinomaru Illumination (Amatersau and Haniwa)*, 1993. Neon, neon transformer, programming circuit, painted steel, and *haniwa* figures; dimensions variable. Installation at the Museum of Art, Kochi, Japan.
Courtesy of Miyake Fine Art, Tokyo and Yanagi Studio.

Class and Identity

How do the visual signs of class inform our understanding of works of art?

In industrialized societies in particular, economic status played as large a role as anything else in determining a person's identity. Often uprooted from their ethnic or national roots—as they migrated looking for work, or as they were forced out of their traditional neighborhoods—people came to identify themselves in terms of class.

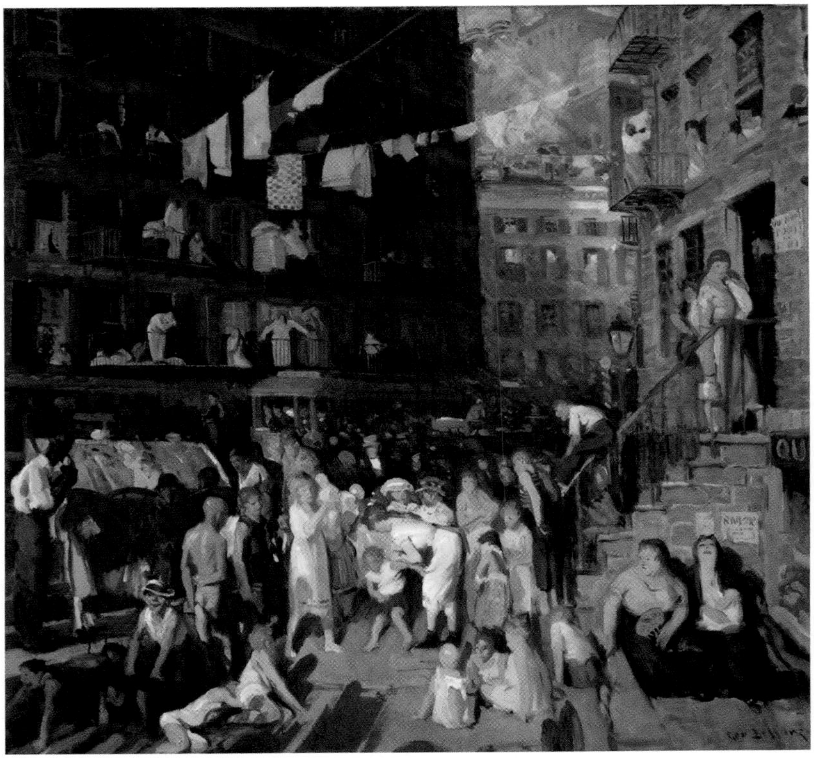

Fig. 25-7 George Bellows, *Cliff Dwellers*, 1913. Oil on canvas, 40³⁄₁₆ × 42¹⁄₁₆ in. Los Angeles County Museum of Art.
Los Angeles County Fund. 16.4. Image courtesy of LACMA.

Marking Class

Visual clues often allow us to determine a person's class. By 1913, when George Bellows painted the two works illustrated here—the first, *Cliff Dwellers* (**Fig. 25-7**), in May of that year, and the second, *A Day in June* (**Fig. 25-8**), a month later—New York City was one of the most class-conscious cities in the world. Fully three-quarters of the city's population was foreign-born, having arrived via Ellis Island, which opened in 1892. Italians, Germans, Poles, and waves of Jews from Hungary, Romania, Russia, and Eastern Europe sought the unlimited opportunities they believed were to be found in America. Living side by side with these working-class immigrants were fully one-third of the nation's millionaires, wealthy industrialists, ambitious merchants, and sometimes flagrantly corrupt politicians. *Cliff Dwellers* represents the former, *A Day in June* the latter. The cramped space of the one contrasts dramatically with the open space of the other. The body language in the paintings is entirely different. In *Cliff Dwellers*, bodies bulge in loose-fitting, ill-kempt garments; children play leapfrog and lounge in the street; at the center of the scene, a woman bends over to spank her child, who has presumably caused the child held high by the young woman in white to the left to cry. The women in *A Day in June* are, by way of contrast, elegant and erect, presumably corseted, the children tidy, well behaved, even graceful. Painted one right after the other, the paintings might best be viewed as a sort of essay on class, and given that a lithograph based on *Cliff Dwellers*, ironically titled *Why Don't They All Go to the Country for Vacation?*, appeared in the socialist magazine *The Masses* in August, it may be that the class Bellows finds least sympathetic is the one with all the wealth.

Fig. 25-8 George Bellows, *A Day in June*, 1913. Oil on canvas, 36½ × 48 in. Detroit Institute of Arts.
Detroit Museum of Art Purchase, Lizzie Merrill Palmer Fund, 17.17. Photo © 2015, Detroit Institute of Arts.

Similar class divisions defined Paris in the second half of the nineteenth century, divisions that are particularly

Fig. 25-9 Pierre-Auguste Renoir, *Bal du Moulin de la Galette*, 1876. Oil on canvas, 4 ft. 3½ in. × 5 ft. 9 in. Musée d'Orsay, Paris.
Bridgeman Images.

apparent if we compare two paintings of 1876, Pierre-Auguste Renoir's *Bal du Moulin de la Galette* (**Fig. 25-9**; see also Fig. 19-30) and Edgar Degas's *The Glass of Absinthe* (**Fig. 25-10**; see also Fig. 19-26). Every Sunday afternoon, crowds gathered at the Moulin de la Galette, a dance hall set in an enclosed courtyard beneath a windmill near the top of the butte of Montmartre, on the still relatively rural north side of Paris. The women in the painting are all actually neighborhood working-class girls—seamstresses, florists, milliners, daughters of workers. We know this because Renoir's friend Georges Rivière, depicted wearing a straw hat and seated in the lower right corner of the picture, wrote a lengthy account of its creation. But Renoir masks their origins, dressing them in the bright fashions of the day and bringing them into the world of his intellectual friends as if they belonged there. Everyone is equally at ease—carefree, young, and happy.

Renoir's painting seems almost utopian beside Degas's, which every viewer of the day would have recognized as a depiction of a working-class couple. Where Renoir's painting is outdoors and open, its figures dappled in sunlight, sharing the day in conversation, Degas's is indoors and closed-in, its figures isolated in their thoughts. The light flooding through the curtains reflected in the mirror behind them may be that of morning, since the drink beside the male is a "mazagran"—a hangover remedy made of cold black coffee and seltzer

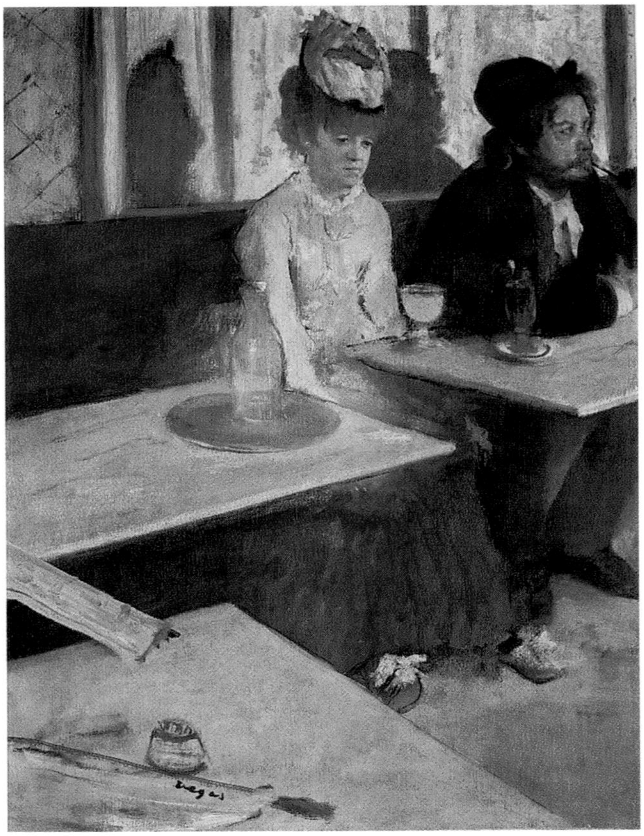

Fig. 25-10 Edgar Degas, *The Glass of Absinthe*, 1875–76. Oil on canvas, 36 × 27 in. Musée d'Orsay, Paris.
Photo Scala, Florence.

water. But it is the glass of absinthe in front of the female that tells the tale. Absinthe was a working-class drink, consumed at all hours, and laced with wormwood, believed to be a highly addictive and psychosis-inducing drug. It was described by Alfred Delvau in his 1862 *Anecdotal History of the Cafés and Cabarets of Paris* as "a terrible and frightening drink . . . [that] makes you lose your footing right away. . . . It sticks immense wings on your shoulders and you leave for a country without horizon and without frontier, but also, without poetry and without sun." And it was undeniably the major source of alcoholism among the working class. By the end of the century, its consumption by volume totaled nearly 3.5 million gallons compared to 2.16 million gallons for all other liquors combined. By contrast, in Renoir's painting, the foreground group appears to be drinking a red liquor of some kind, perhaps red wine, but maybe the apéritif Dubonnet, which was becoming popular at the time. Whatever the case, the drink marks the class.

One of the favorite subjects of the *ukiyo-e* printmakers in nineteenth-century Japan (see Chapter 10) was the landscape print, and, together with Hokusai's *Thirty-Six Views of Mount Fuji* (see Fig. 7-21), the most important of these is a series by Utagawa Hiroshige called *The Fifty-Three Stations of the Tokaido*. Some 300 miles long, the Tokaido (literally, the "Eastern Sea Road") was the main road linking the old imperial capital of Japan, Kyoto, where the emperor lived, and Edo, present-day Tokyo, where the Shogun, or military leader of the country, resided. Along the road were 53 stations, offering travelers food and lodging. Although Hiroshige's series is most renowned for its landscape views, it also offers the viewer an almost complete compendium of Japanese social classes and an essay on class division. The ostensible subject of *Hamamatsu: Winter Scene* (**Fig. 25-11**) is the famous castle at Hamamatsu, the 29th station on the road, but it is just visible across the barren winter rice paddies to the right, above the well-dressed traveler who stands smoking a pipe in the foreground. Hiroshige's real subject is, in fact, this figure and his relation to the others. On the left, four *kumosuke*, unskilled laborers who served as freelance porters on the highway, warm themselves by a fire, removing their robes to reveal their loincloth underclothing. To the right, a peasant woman carrying a child on her back approaches the group. The placement of the tree in the center of the print is crucial, for it not only divides city, on the right, from farm, on the left—the urban from the rural—it marks the class division so

Fig. 25-11 Utagawa Hiroshige, *Hamamatsu: Winter Scene*, plate 30 from *The Fifty-Three Stations of the Tokaido*, Hoeido edition, 1831–34. Woodblock print, $9\frac{7}{8} \times 14\frac{3}{4}$ in. Ashmolean Museum, Oxford, U.K.
Art Archive/Ashmolean Museum.

evident in the print. Hiroshige printed some 30 different editions of this series, but the one illustrated here, known as the Hoeido edition, is by far the most famous.

Place and Displacement

The broad, open avenues that converge on the Place de l'Europe in Gustave Caillebotte's painting of the scene (**Fig. 25-12**; see also Figs. 4-18 and 4-19) were the result of what has come to be known as the **Haussmannization** of Paris. In July 1853, Napoleon III chose Baron Georges-Eugène Haussmann to supervise a daunting task—planning the modernization of Paris by destroying the old city and rebuilding it anew. Napoleon III and Haussmann shared a dream: to rid Paris of its medieval character, transforming it into the most beautiful city in the world. By 1870, their reforms were largely completed, resulting in improved housing and sanitation, and increased traffic flow, all of which encouraged growth in the city's shopping districts.

But the vast renovation served another important purpose as well: to prevent the possibility of uprisings like that depicted in Delacroix's *Liberty Leading the People* (see Fig. 25-2) from ever happening again. By widening the streets, Haussmann made it harder for ordinary people to build barricades. By extending long, straight boulevards across the capital, on the other hand, he made it easier for the military to move troops and artillery rapidly within the city. And he integrated each project into a larger-scale city-planning strategy. After demolishing the labyrinth of ancient streets and dilapidated buildings that were home to the rebellious working class—25,000 buildings between 1852 and 1859, and after 1860 another 92,000—the government installed enormous new sewer lines before extending impressively wide boulevards, the so-called *grands boulevards*, atop them.

The wholesale destruction of working-class neighborhoods throughout Paris was the price the city paid for this transformation. Almost all of the new, less expensive housing for workers was erected on the outskirts of the city, and many residents of the demolished areas were subsequently moved to new working-class suburbs. The working-class exodus to the outskirts of Paris resulted in a city inhabited almost exclusively by the bourgeoisie and upper-class citizens

Fig. 25-12 Gustave Caillebotte, *Place de l'Europe on a Rainy Day*, 1876–77. Oil on canvas, 82½ × 108¾ in. The Art Institute of Chicago.

of the type strolling toward the viewer in Caillebotte's painting. To further facilitate the exodus of the working class, Haussmann banned large-scale industry (as opposed to artisan workshops) from the city. By the last quarter of the nineteenth century, Paris became a city of leisure, a city of the good life, surrounded by a ring of industrial and working-class suburbs, and it remains so to the present day.

Since the early 1980s, Beijing has undergone a transformation similar to Haussmann's transformation of Paris in the 1850s and 1860s. In an effort to radically modernize the city, the traditional working-class houses (*siheyuan*) have been destroyed and tiny alleyways (*hutong*) (**Fig. 25-13**) widened into boulevards as the Chinese capital has transformed itself into an international metropolis. The main driver of the modernization of Beijing has been the migration of the Chinese people from rural farms and communities into urban centers, which has happened at a rate unprecedented in human history. In 1950, only 13 per cent of the population lived in cities; today, nearly half the population are urban dwellers.

Zhang Dali's graffiti works, a series of profiles of his own head called *Dialogue and Demolition*, are a reaction

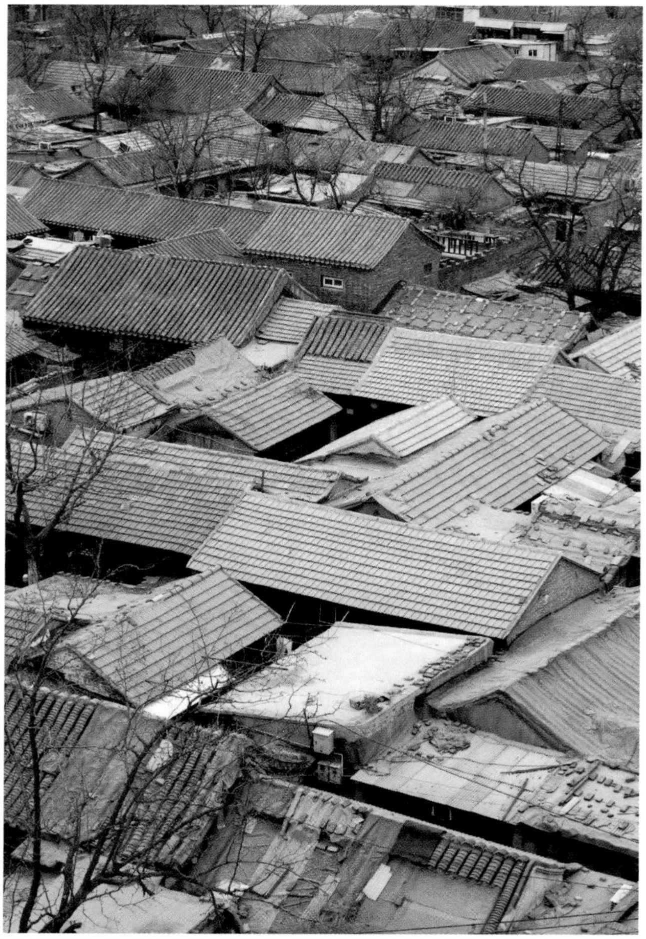

Fig. 25-13 Aerial view of an old *hutong* area, Beijing.
© Radius Images/Corbis.

Fig. 25-14 Zhang Dali, *Dialogue and Demolition No. 50*, 1998. Photograph, 23⅝ × 35⅜ in. Klein Sun Gallery, New York. Courtesy of Klein Sun Gallery, Zhang Dali.

to this process of modernization. Between 1995 and 1998, he created over 2,000 of these images around the city on walls and bridges scheduled for demolition. The two profiles shown here (**Fig. 25-14**), one drawn on the wall, the other chiseled out, are metaphors for the individual's place in society and the loss of that place in the onslaught of demolition. Zhang outlines a space that becomes a nonspace, literally a hole in the wall. Sprayed on the wall in between the two profiles are the tags "AK-47" and "18K," the first a reference to the Soviet assault weapon that represents, to Zhang, the violence being perpetrated upon the city and its inhabitants, and the second a reference to 18-carat gold, a symbol for the economic driver of capitalism that is, in the end, responsible for the destruction of the traditional city. The word "Dialogue" in his title goes back to 1989 and the massacre in Tiananmen Square on June 4 when hundreds—perhaps thousands—of protesting students were killed by government troops. It was a word used repeatedly by the students in their protests, a call for communication between the authorities and the protestors that never took place. The irony, of course, is that the desire for dialogue remains unfulfilled.

Racial Identity and African-American Experience

How has racial identity manifested itself in African-American art?

Since biblical times, Western culture has tended to associate blackness with negative qualities and whiteness with positive ones, and it is understandable that people might take offense at this association. In *"Race"ing*

Fig. 25-15 Nikolai Buglaj, *"Race"ing Sideways*, 1991. Graphite and ink, 3 × 40 in.

Sideways (**Fig. 25-15**), Nikolai Buglaj has drawn 13 racers, conceived as mannequins in an installation, tied for the lead in a race no one seems intent on winning. From left to right, their skin color changes from white to black, even as their clothing changes from black to white, a double version of the traditional "value" scale. But what "values" are at stake here? The runners are moving forward uniformly, all equally "making progress." But this equality is an illusion. Left to right, our "values" change. They reveal themselves to be governed by questions of class (clothing color, i.e., "white collar," "blue collar") and race (skin color). And we understand that Buglaj's drawing is a stinging indictment of the lack of progress we have made in race and class relations in this country. For Buglaj, perceptual illusion replicates cultural illusion.

Double Consciousness and the Great Migration

And progress—or the lack thereof—has been the driving force of the Civil Rights Movement since the beginning of the twentieth century. The philosophical roots of the movement reach back to the turn of the century and the work of black historian and sociologist W. E. B. Du Bois, whose book *The Souls of Black Folk*, first published in 1903, proposed that the identity of African Americans was fraught with ambiguity:

> [America] yields him no true self-consciousness. . . . One ever feels his two-ness,—an American, a Negro; two souls, two thoughts, two unreconciled strivings; two warring ideals in one dark body, whose dogged strength alone keeps it from being torn asunder.
>
> The history of the American Negro is the history of this strife—this longing to attain self-conscious manhood, to merge his double self into a better and truer self. . . . He simply wishes to make it possible for a man to be both a Negro and an American, without being cursed and spit upon by his fellows, without having the doors of Opportunity closed roughly in his face.

When, in 1909, the National Association for the Advancement of Colored People (NAACP) was founded to advance the rights of blacks, Du Bois became editor of its magazine, *The Crisis*. His sense of the double consciousness informing African-American experience (a double consciousness that informs the very term "African American") was often expressed in the magazine's pages.

In the years before the outbreak of World War I, nearly 90 percent of all African Americans lived in the South, three-quarters of them in the rural South. Impoverished after a boll weevil infestation ruined the cotton crop, and threatened especially by the rise of white terrorists like the Ku Klux Klan, whose membership reached some 4 million by the early 1920s, blacks flooded into the North, where there was a huge demand for labor once the war began. From 1915 through 1918, as war raged in Europe, between 200,000 and 350,000 Southern blacks moved north in what came to be called the Great Migration. In the course of a mere 90 days early in the 1920s, 12,000 African Americans left Mississippi alone. An average of 200 left Memphis every night. Displaced from the rural South to the urban North, transformed from field hands into industrial laborers, these migrants faced a real crisis in self-definition.

This Great Migration was later celebrated in a series of 60 paintings by the African-American artist Jacob Lawrence, who moved to Harlem in 1924 at the age of seven, into a cultural community so robust, and so new, that the era has come to be known as the Harlem Renaissance. Lawrence was trained as a painter at the Harlem Art Workshop, and completed the *Migration* series when he was just 23 years old (**Fig. 25-16**). It won him immediate fame. In 1942, the Museum of Modern Art in New York and the Phillips Collection in Washington, D.C. each bought 30 panels. That same

Fig. 25-16 Jacob Lawrence, *The Migration of the Negro, Panel No. 60: And the Migrants Kept Coming*, 1940–41. Casein tempera on hardboard panel, 18 × 12 in. Museum of Modern Art, New York.

Gift of Ms. David M. Levy, 28.1942.30. Digital image, Museum of Modern Art, New York/Scala, Florence. © 2015 Jacob and Gwendolyn Knight Lawrence Foundation, Seattle/Artists Rights Society (ARS), New York.

year, Lawrence became the first black artist to be represented by a prestigious New York gallery—the Downtown Gallery. Throughout the series, Lawrence's figures are almost faceless, two-dimensional silhouettes: They possess almost no individuality. Rather, they represent the race itself, the shared humanity (or inhumanity) of what it means to be a black person in America.

Lawrence's flat figures probably owe much to the work of the leading visual artist in New York City in the 1920s, Aaron Douglas, a native of Topeka, Kansas, who arrived in Harlem in 1925 with a Bachelor of Fine Arts degree from the University of Nebraska, where he had been the only black student in his class. *Aspiration* (**Fig. 25-17**) celebrates many of the same themes as Lawrence's *Migration* series, depicting the progression out of slavery, represented by the shackled arms that rise up out of the bottom of the painting, out of the South, and toward the promise of the industrial North.

But, as Douglas well knew, the realization of such aspirations was hard won. The jazz clubs that were so much at the center of African-American culture in Harlem were, in fact, restricted to white customers—blacks could only enter as performers or waiters. Access to satisfactory housing was extremely limited as whites created de facto white-only neighborhoods. Except in Harlem, landlords in New York City were unwilling to rent to black tenants: In 1920, a one-room apartment in Harlem rented to whites for $40 and to blacks for between $100 and $125. These high rental expenses led to extreme population density—in 1920s Harlem, there were over 215,000 people per square mile (by way of comparison, today there are fewer than 70,000 people per square mile in all Manhattan island).

The jobs to which Aaron Douglas's silhouette figures are aspiring were slow in coming. At the outset of World War II, A. Philip Randolph had organized a march on Washington "for jobs in national defense and equal integration in the fighting forces." Ten thousand blacks were scheduled to march on July 1, 1941, prompting President Roosevelt to issue Executive Order 8802 on June 25, banning discriminatory hiring practices in the defense industry and the Federal government.

But the Civil Rights Movement really gathered momentum soon after, on December 1, 1955, when Rosa Parks was arrested in Montgomery, Alabama, for refusing to move to the Negro section of a bus. Dr. Martin Luther King, then pastor of the Dexter Avenue Baptist Church in Montgomery, called for a boycott of the municipal bus system in protest. The

Fig. 25-17 Aaron Douglas, *Aspiration*, 1936. Oil on canvas, 5 × 5 ft. Fine Arts Museums of San Francisco.

Photo © Fine Arts Museums of San Francisco. Art © Heirs of Aaron Douglas/Licensed by VAGA, New York.

boycott lasted over a year. In November 1956, the U.S. Supreme Court declared that the segregation of buses violated the Fourteenth Amendment. A Federal injunction forced Montgomery officials to desegregate their buses, and Dr. King and a white minister rode side by side in the front seat of a city bus, setting the stage for a decade of liberation and change that reached across American society.

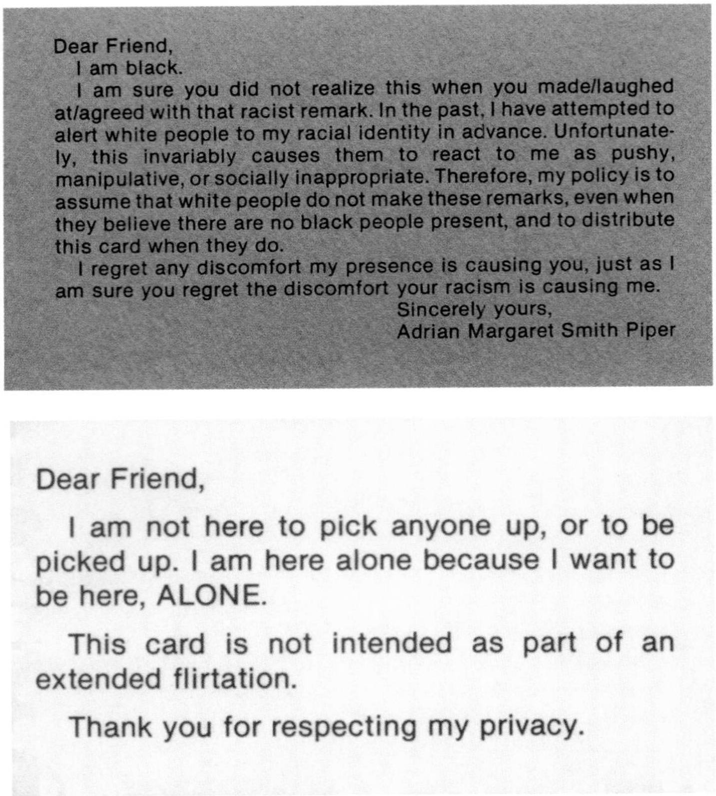
Dear Friend,
I am black.
I am sure you did not realize this when you made/laughed at/agreed with that racist remark. In the past, I have attempted to alert white people to my racial identity in advance. Unfortunately, this invariably causes them to react to me as pushy, manipulative, or socially inappropriate. Therefore, my policy is to assume that white people do not make these remarks, even when they believe there are no black people present, and to distribute this card when they do.
I regret any discomfort my presence is causing you, just as I am sure you regret the discomfort your racism is causing me.
Sincerely yours,
Adrian Margaret Smith Piper

Dear Friend,
I am not here to pick anyone up, or to be picked up. I am here alone because I want to be here, ALONE.
This card is not intended as part of an extended flirtation.
Thank you for respecting my privacy.

Fig. 25-18 Adrian Piper, *My Calling (Card) #1 (for Dinners and Cocktail Parties)*, 1986–90 (top). *My Calling (Card) #2 (for Bars and Discos)*, 1986 (bottom). Performance props: business cards with printed text on cardboard, 3½ × 2 in. Indiana University. Gift of John P. Bowles, 2006.558, 2006.559. Photo: Michael Cavanagh and Kevin Montague. © APRA Foundation Berlin.

New African-American Identities

Since the 1960s, the "double consciousness" that W. E. B. Du Bois articulated over a century ago has multiplied into a more plural and diverse set of consciousnesses as attested by the "calling cards" of artist and philosopher Adrian Piper (**Fig. 25-18**). As a woman with African ancestry frequently mistaken for "white," racist remarks were made in her presence. Similarly, when she attended social events unaccompanied, men assumed that she was "available." The calling cards were designed to rebuke the offenders, and she considered the occasions on which she was driven to hand them out as, in words she sometimes used as a sort of subtitle to the cards, "Reactive Guerilla Performances for Dinner and Cocktail Parties." As a product of both the Civil Rights and feminist movements, Piper's identity was now triple—she was a woman, an American, and racially mixed, and none of these identities rested easily with the others.

The complexities of African-American identity took a new turn in 2001 when curator Thelma Golden's exhibition *Freestyle* at the Studio Museum in Harlem introduced the phrase "Post-Black" into the discussion, by which she meant artists who were first and foremost artists and only secondarily black. The youngest artist in the show was Rashid Johnson, whose mother taught African history and African-American history at Northwestern University as he was growing up. "I grew up enveloped in this kind of Afro-centric conversation," Johnson explains in the art21 *New York Close Up* segment "Rashid Johnson Makes Things to Put Things On":

> We celebrated Kwanzaa. My mother wore dashikis and had an afro. But the thing that I think is most interesting to me is that one day they just weren't wearing dashikis any more, and there were no more afros. And we weren't celebrating Kwanzaa any more. That transition from Afro-centrism . . . to your parents becoming essentially just like middle-class soccer moms . . . is why humor has become so interesting to me.

Johnson's shelflike sculpture *Souls of Black Folk* (**Fig. 25-19**)—"a thing to put things on"—embodies just this "Post-Black" sensibility. It is composed of 100 green-spined copies of W. E. B. Du Bois's *Souls of Black Folk*. In the middle of the central panel, composed of black soap and wax—black soap is an African skincare product used for nurturing sensitive skin—is the golden logo of Sigma Pi Phi, the first African-American Greek-lettered fraternity, a secret society perhaps better known simply as "the Boulé." Sitting on small shelves across the work, dishes of shea butter evoke Johnson's first trip to West Africa, at age 18, where he saw Ashanti warriors slathering it over themselves because it made them so slippery that their enemies could not grab them. Overlooking the whole shrine is the cover of jazz trumpeter Miles Davis's 1986 album *Tutu*, named for South African archbishop Desmond Tutu. The gold "space rocks" that

Fig. 25-19 Rashid Johnson, *Souls of Black Folk*, 2010. Black soap, wax, books, vinyl, brass, shea butter, plants, space rocks, mirrors, gold paint, stained wood, 9 ft. 6 in. × 10 ft. 4¾ in. × 24⅛ in.

flank Davis's image refer to the cosmic, quite literally "far-out," music of Sun Ra. All in all, the work suggests not just the history of African-American culture, but, more than a little irreverently, the vast array of "things" that have come to compose Johnson's and the culture's identity.

THE CRITICAL PROCESS

Thinking about the Individual and Cultural Identity

Flags were not commonly used as symbols of national identity until the eighteenth century. The French *tricolor* that Liberty hoists above her head in Delacroix's *Liberty Leading the People* (see Fig. 25-2) was designed in 1794 to symbolize the French Revolution, but it was banned by the monarchy after the defeat of Napoleon and replaced by a white flag, to symbolize purity and royal authority. After the July Revolution depicted in Delacroix's painting, the *tricolor* was permanently restored as the French national flag.

Every American knows the probably apocryphal story of Betsy Ross, George Washington, and the origins of the "Stars and Stripes." Ross did make American flags, but there were many other versions. On June 14, 1777, Congress resolved that "the Flag of the United States be 13 stripes alternate red and white," and that "the Union be 13 stars white in a blue field representing a new constellation." The 13 stripes were understood to represent the original 13 colonies, but Congress did not stipulate a pattern for the stars, and different arrangements were used until 1912, when an official arrangement of the 48 stars representing the states was adopted.

Americans came to identify closely with their flag, especially after the adoption of Francis Scott Key's "Star-Spangled Banner" as the national anthem in 1931. One of the most controversial works of art that has ever addressed the politics that surround the American flag is Dread Scott's *What Is the Proper Way to Display a U.S. Flag?* (**Fig. 25-20**), which consisted of a 34 × 57-inch American flag draped on the floor beneath photographs of flag-draped coffins and South Koreans burning the flag. It was first displayed on February 20, 1989 in an installation at the Art Institute of Chicago consisting of works of art by 66 students who were members of minority groups. Beneath the photos was a ledger in which viewers were asked to record their opinions. The problem was not only that the flag was on the floor, but that it was difficult to write in the ledger without stepping on it. Thus, the flag became a barrier to the freedom of expression it was meant to defend. Viewers had to choose which they revered more—the flag or freedom of speech.

Angry veterans wearing combat fatigues protested the exhibit soon after it opened, waving American flags, singing the national anthem, and carrying signs saying, "The American flag is not a doormat." The opposition centered not only on the fact that Scott had placed a real flag—not the representation of one—on the floor, an act that violated a certain sense of decorum, but also on the suggestion that people should walk on it. Scott responded by noting that he had purchased the flag at a store for $3.95. It had been made in Taiwan.

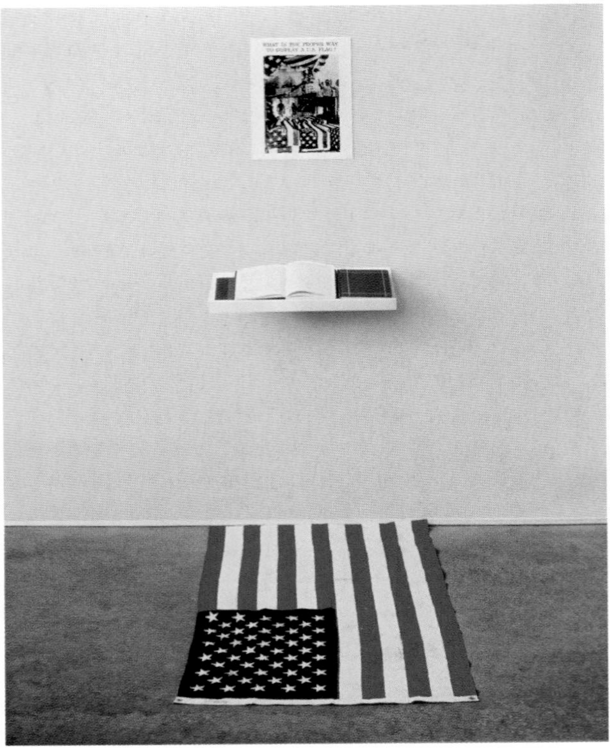

Fig. 25-20 Dread Scott, *What Is the Proper Way to Display a U.S. Flag?*, 1988. Gelatin silver print, U.S. flag, book, pen, shelf, audience, 6 ft. 8 in. × 10 ft. 8 in. × 5 ft.

How does this work both invoke and challenge the concept of nationalism? What myths or assumptions do you believe Scott was trying to debunk? It is important to know that Scott is African American, and that his name is a reference to Dred Scott, the enslaved African American who unsuccessfully sued for his freedom and that of his wife and two daughters in 1857. Why do you think Dread Scott the artist has changed the spelling of his first name? And how does this work address issues of African-American identity?

Thinking Back

25.1 Define nationalism and describe how the arts have been used to construct and critique national identities.

Nationalism is the belief that people who share the same language, historic experience, and very often ethnic identity make up a nation. What class distinctions are evident in Eugène Delacroix's *Liberty Leading the People*, and why was King Louis-Philippe of France wary of the painting? In the United States, the lure of the frontier created strong nationalist sentiments. How did Frederick Jackson Turner respond to the individualism that the frontier inspired? How did Native Americans define their own sense of self in response to this frontier individualism? Both China and Japan protected their sense of national identity by allowing foreigners only meager access to their countries. How did the Chinese react to control of their country by Mongol invaders during the Yuan dynasty? How did Yanagi Yukinori react to Japanese nationalism?

25.2 Describe how the visual signs of class inform works of art.

A person's class also determines identity. How did George Bellows distinguish between upper- and lower-class New Yorkers in his paintings? How do class divisions manifest themselves in Impressionist painting? How does Hiroshige demonstrate class division in his print *Hamamatsu: Winter Scene?* In France, the process known as "Haussmannization" transformed Paris. What is Haussmannization? How did it affect the working class? How does contemporary Chinese society, as reflected in Zhang Dali's graffiti practice, embody some of the same tensions as Haussmann's Paris?

25.3 Discuss racial identity as it manifests itself in African-American art.

The lack of progress toward equality has played a large role in determining African-American identity. W. E. B. Du Bois argued that African Americans had a "double" sense of identity. What was the Great Migration? How did it affect African-American identity? How was that identity expressed in the work of Jacob Lawrence and Aaron Douglas? How did Adrian Piper express her "triple" identity? In what ways is Rashid Johnson's work an example of "Post-Black" identity?

Chapter 26
Power

Learning Objectives

26.1 Describe some of the means by which rulers have asserted their power in art.

26.2 Discuss some of the issues surrounding power as it affects women.

26.3 Define colonialism and outline some of the ways that artists have addressed it.

26.4 Explain how the museum wields power.

In 2009, British photographer Edmund Clark was given access to the Guantanamo Bay detention facility at the U.S. Naval Base in Cuba as part of a larger project to explore three notions of "home": the homes of the American community stationed on the base; the complex of camps in which detainees are housed; and the homes where those detainees who have been released now live. Clark explains:

> The series' disjointed narrative aims to convey the sense of disorientation and dislocation central to the daily experience of incarceration at Guantanamo, and to explore the legacy of disturbance such experiences leave in the minds and memories of these men, as the viewer is asked to jump from prison camp detail to domestic still life, from life outside to the naval base and back again; from light to dark.

Camp Five, Detainee's Cell (**Fig. 26-1**) shows the kind of cell that Omar Deghayes, one of the released detainees who are the focus of Clark's project, remembers well. When Deghayes was transferred to Camp Five, he was, he says,

> held in isolation in a stark, white, concrete cell. It was a difficult place. It was very cold with the air conditioning always turned up high; the cell was painted a bright white and harshly lit; and the lights were kept on all the time, which was especially painful after I was injured when an Emergency Response Force guard gouged one of my eyes. There was a flap that the guards lifted from the outside to look in, but I could never see out through it.

Deghayes, a Libyan citizen who had had legal residency status in the United Kingdom since childhood, was arrested in Pakistan in 2002 and transferred to the Guantanamo detention center that same year, when the facility received its first "unlawful combatants" (as opposed to "prisoners of war," a distinction allowing the U.S. to ignore the Geneva Conventions). He was released on December 18, 2007, never having been charged with any crime, but blinded in one eye.

Deghayes's description of the conditions in which he lived in Camp Five reflect the mechanisms of power that the British philosopher and social theorist Jeremy Bentham devised, in 1791, for his ideal prison, the Panopticon (**Fig. 26-2**), a circular building with a surveillance house at its center, allowing a single guard to observe all the inmates. In his book *Discipline and Punish: The Birth of the Prison*, the great French historian

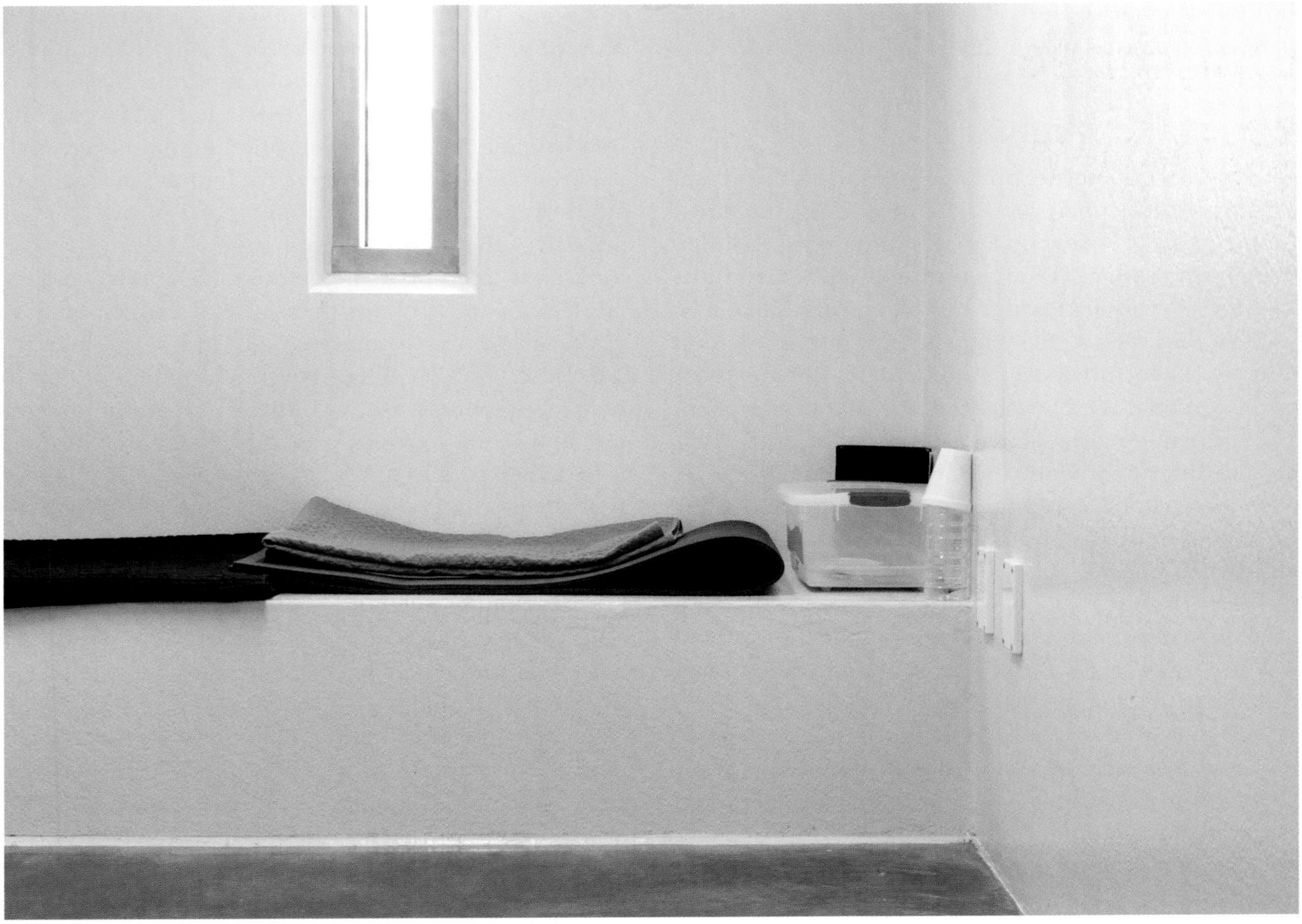

Fig. 26-1 Edmund Clark, *Camp Five, Detainee's Cell*, from the series *Guantanamo: If the Light Goes Out*, Guantanamo Bay detention facility, Cuba, 2009. Chromogenic color print, 4 × 5 ft.

Michel Foucault outlined its major effect, which was "to induce in the inmate a state of conscious and permanent visibility that assures the automatic functioning of power." It is this condition of visibility and the power that it exercises that is the subject of this chapter. No ruler is truly all-seeing but art can help foster that illusion. No country can realistically exercise control over any other except by representing itself as so strong that the other must of necessity feel weak and dependent. And in these relations of power, the museum of course also exercises its authority to tell us what we can or should see.

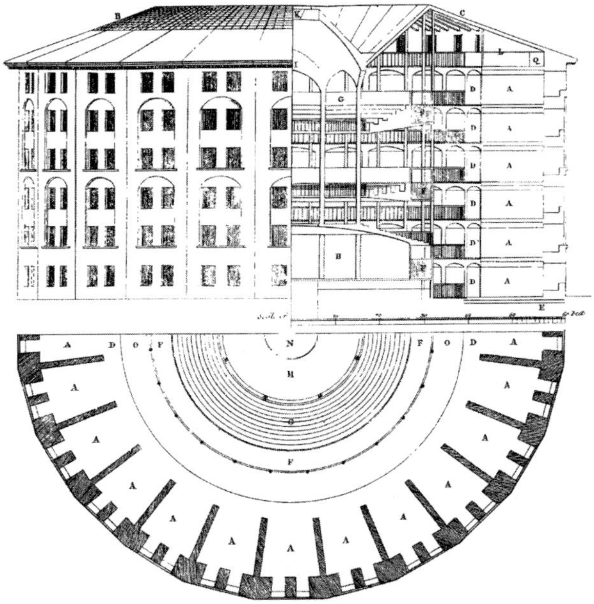

Fig. 26-2 Jeremy Bentham, *A General Idea of a Penitentiary Panopticon*, drawn by Willey Reveley, 1791. From *The Works of Jeremy Bentham*, vol. IV (Edinburgh: William Tait, 1838–43), pp. 172–73.

Representing Rulers

By what means have rulers asserted their power in art?

Power is inherent in rule. It can, of course, be used for good, or it can be abused. But power can only be wielded effectively if those over whom it lords accept and respect it.

Rulers have, as a result, consistently turned to art to portray themselves in as positive a light as possible.

Power and Might

Rulers in every culture and age have used the visual arts to broadcast their power. In the ninth century BCE, for instance, the Assyrian king Ashurnasirpal II built a magnificent capital at Kalhu (present-day Nimrud), on the Tigris River, surrounded by nearly 5 miles of walls, 120 feet thick and 42 feet high. A surviving inscription tells us that Ashurnasirpal invited 69,574 members of the upper classes to celebrate the city's dedication. The entire population of the region, of all classes, probably did not exceed 100,000, and thus many guests from throughout Mesopotamia and farther away must have been invited. The size of the capital, the huge number of guests, were all calculated to underscore the king's power.

Alabaster reliefs decorated many of the walls of Ashurnasirpal's palace complex, including a depiction of *Ashurnasirpal II Killing Lions* (**Fig. 26-3**; see also Fig. 16-8). These reliefs were specifically designed to celebrate and underscore for all visitors to Ashurnasirpal's palace the military prowess of the Assyrian army and their king. They are thus a form of cultural propaganda, celebrating the kingdom's achievements even as they were meant to intimidate its potential adversaries. In fact, the Assyrians were probably the most militant civilization of ancient Mesopotamia, benefactors of the invention of iron weaponry. By 721 BCE, the Assyrians had used their iron weapons to conquer Israel, and by the middle of the seventh century BCE, they controlled most of Asia Minor from the Nile Valley to the Persian Gulf.

When the emperor Qin Shihuangdi was buried in about 210 BCE, he chose to assert his military might, which he surely believed would continue in the afterlife, by burying an army of more than 6,000 ceramic infantrymen in pits surrounding his tomb (**Fig. 26-4**; see also Fig. 12-12). These ceramic figures are a demonstration of extraordinary authority and power. The assembly of this army required a workforce of literally thousands. Each figure is composed of a variety of prefabricated parts: a plinth, or base, legs, a torso, separate arms, two hands (themselves made of smaller, individual units), and a head. There were three kinds of plinth, two types of leg sets, eight different torsos and eight different heads, to which distinctive individual features were added such as hairstyles, mustaches, and different types of ears and noses. Each individual was then separately painted in a wide variety of basic color schemes. So many different combinations were available that it is almost impossible to find any two figures that look alike. This modular form of mass production must have required a bureaucracy of extraordinary skill. This bureaucracy would have needed to oversee not only the assembly of the final figures, but the production of each modular unit, including its modeling in clay, and its firing in kilns at temperatures of between 950 and 1,000 degrees Fahrenheit. The kilns themselves would have had to be built, and the vast quantity of firewood necessary to fire the figures at such temperatures could not have come from local sources alone.

Almost 1,800 years later, Napoleon Bonaparte conceived of his official state art program with the same aim of asserting his power and might by celebrating major events by commissioning paintings, sculpture, and architecture. The paintings and sculptures were prominently

Fig. 26-3 *Ashurnasirpal II Killing Lions*, from the palace complex of Ashurnasirpal II, Kalhu (modern Nimrud, Iraq), ca. 850 BCE. Alabaster, height approx. 39 in. The British Museum, London.

Fig. 26-4 Tomb of Emperor Qin Shihuangdi, 221–206 BCE. Painted ceramic figures, life-size.
© O. Louis Mazzatenta/National Geographic.

displayed in public settings and the architecture was situated at important junctions in Paris. All were meant to present the physically small but extremely ambitious man as hero and leader of France or to remind the public of his efforts on their behalf.

Jacques-Louis David (see Figs. 3-20 and 19-9) established himself as one of Napoleon's favorite artists when he painted *Napoleon Crossing the Saint-Bernard* (**Fig. 26-5**). Here he depicts Napoleon on horseback leading his troops across the pass at Saint-Bernard in the Alps in 1800, about to cross into Italy and take control of Piedmont and Lombardy. In its clearly drawn central image and its emphasis on right angles (consider Napoleon's leg, the angle of his pointing arm to his body, the relation of the horse's head and neck, and the angle of its rear legs), the painting is fully Neoclassical (see Chapter 19). In the background, as is typical of David, is a more turbulent scene as Napoleon's troops drag a cannon up the pass. In the foreground, inscribed on the rocks, are the names of the only generals who ever crossed the Alps into Italy: Hannibal, whose brilliance in defeating the Romans in the third century BCE Napoleon sought to emulate; Karolus Magnus (Charlemagne), the great Frankish Holy Roman emperor; and Napoleon himself.

Fig. 26-5 Jacques-Louis David, *Napoleon Crossing the Saint-Bernard*, 1800–01. Oil on canvas, 8 ft. 11 in. × 7 ft. 7 in. Musée National du Château de la Malmaison, Rueil-Malmaison, France.
Photo © RMN-Grand Palais (musée des châteaux de Malmaison et de Bois-Préau)/Gérard Blot.

Actually, Napoleon did not lead the crossing of the pass but accompanied his rearguard, mounted on a mule led by a peasant. David's work is pure propaganda, designed to create a proper myth for the aspiring leader. Though still four years from crowning himself emperor, his intention to unite Europe and rule it are made clear in his identification with Charlemagne. Napoleon was boldly creating a myth that is probably nowhere better expressed than by the great German philosopher Georg Wilhelm Friedrich Hegel in a letter of October 13, 1806: "I have seen the emperor, that world soul, pass through the streets of the town on horseback. It is a prodigious sensation to see an individual like him who, concentrated at one point, seated on a horse, spreads over the world and dominates it."

No image captures Napoleon's sense of himself better than the 1806 portrait by David's student Jean-Auguste-Dominique Ingres of *Napoleon on His Imperial Throne* (**Fig. 26-6**). In this commission from Napoleon, Ingres depicts him as a monarch who embodies the total power of his country. Ingres combines two well-known frontal images of the deities Jupiter, or Zeus, and God the Father with the imperial attributes of the historical emperors Charlemagne and Charles V of Spain. The Jupiter image was a lost sculpture known only in a gemstone replica but attributed to Phidias, the master of the Greek Golden Age. The God the Father image was in Jan van Eyck's *Ghent Altarpiece* (see Fig. 1-22), which Napoleon had taken from Ghent during his Prussian campaign and installed in the Louvre. Ingres establishes the emperor's identification with Charlemagne by the sword beneath his left forearm and the ivory hand of justice, both of which were believed to have originally belonged to Charlemagne. And he evokes the Habsburg Holy Roman emperor Charles V of Spain through the scepter in Napoleon's right hand, thus symbolically uniting France and Austria for the first time since Charlemagne's reign in the early Middle Ages. Like David's *Napoleon Crossing the Saint-Bernard*, Ingres's painting is a conscious act of propaganda, cementing in the public mind the image of the emperor as nearly godlike in his power and dominion. The David and Ingres portraits underscore the fact that Napoleon understood quite well the ability of art to move and control the popular imagination.

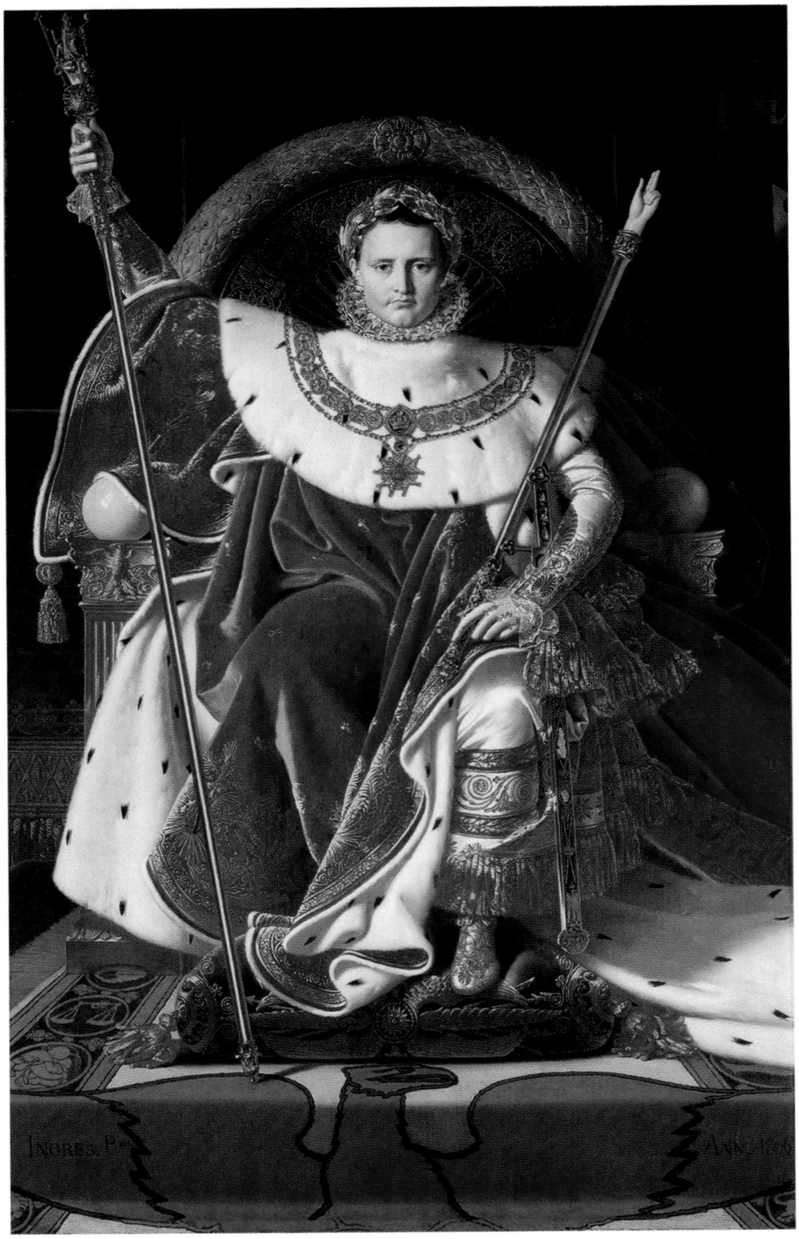

Fig. 26-6 Jean-Auguste-Dominique Ingres, *Napoleon on His Imperial Throne*, 1806. Oil on canvas, 8 ft. 6 in. × 5 ft. 4 in. Musée de l'Armée, Paris. akg-image/Erich Lessing.

The Imperial Gaze

Perhaps the single most powerful figure in the ancient world was Alexander the Great, who was born in Macedonia in 356 BCE and who, by the time he was 30 years old, had conquered all of Egypt and the Middle East, and pushed eastward as far as the Indian Punjab across the Indus River. He had marched over 11,000 miles without a defeat, destroyed ancient empires, and founded over 70 cities, naming many after himself. His was the largest empire ever known.

Even during his lifetime, but especially after his death, sculptures celebrating the youthful hero

Fig. 26-7 ***Alexander the Great*, head from a Pergamene copy ca. 200 BCE of a statue, possibly after a 4th-century BCE original by Lysippus.** Marble, height 16⅛ in. Archeological Museum, Istanbul.
akg-image/Erich Lessing.

Fig. 26-8 Lin Chunhua, *Chairman Mao en Route to Anyuan*, 1967. Screenprint after an original oil painting, 7 ft. 2½ in. × 5 ft. 10¼ in.
Photo © GraphicaArtis/Bridgeman Images.

abounded, almost all of them modeled on originals sculpted by Lysippus, whom Alexander hired to do all his portraits. Alexander is easily recognizable—his disheveled hair long and flowing, his gaze intense and melting, his mouth slightly open, his head alertly turned on a slightly tilted neck (**Fig. 26-7**). His eyes look past us, as if he is looking beyond the present to greater things—a look that might best be called the "imperial gaze." Lysippus has dramatized his hero. That is, he did not merely represent Alexander as naturalistically as possible, he also animated him, showing him in the midst of action. In all likelihood, he idealized him as well. The creation of Alexander's likeness was a conscious act of propaganda. Early in his conquests, the young hero referred to himself as "Alexander the Great," and Lysippus' job was to embody that greatness.

Lysippus' rendering of Alexander's gaze is the first instance of a look that appears again and again throughout the history of rulers and their representation—even, for instance, in modern China. *Chairman Mao en Route to Anyuan* (**Fig. 26-8**), painted by Lin Chunhua at the beginning of the Cultural Revolution, shows the 29-year-old Mao striding to the site of a 1922 miners' strike in Jiangxi province where he would organize the miners in their fight to free themselves from their essentially feudal and impoverished lives. Mao's wife, Jiang Qing, loved the painting so much that she encouraged its reproduction throughout China. Over 900 million posters were printed, making it the most reproduced painting in history. The youthful Mao's visage, the determination of his gaze as he seems to peer beyond the moment and into the future, into history, into his destiny, is very much like Alexander's. Mao strides forward into the future of his country, just as, the poster seems to say, every Chinese citizen must.

Women and Power

How has the issue of power affected women?

The vast majority of world cultures—though by no means all—are patriarchies; that is, they are social systems in which males predominantly hold power. As the concept of "fatherhood" came to be firmly rooted in the human imagination—it seems likely that throughout the Paleolithic era the role of the father in procreation was barely, if at all, understood—and, secondly, as the Ice Age waned and migrating peoples came into increasing contact, resulting in more and more conflict as they sought to secure food, males increasingly came to dominate societies.

In ancient Rome, the patriarchal structure of society was codified. Every male member of the poorer classes—craftspeople, merchants, and laborers, known as plebeians—chose for his patron a member of the patrician class, the landowning aristocrats who served as priests, magistrates, lawyers, and judges. Indeed, most patricians were themselves clients of some other patrician of higher status whose duty it was to represent the plebeian in any matter of law and provide an assortment of assistance in other matters, primarily economic. This paternalistic relationship—which we call patronage—reflected the family's central role in Roman culture. The *pater*, "father," protected not only his wife and family but also his clients, who submitted to his patronage. In return for the *pater*'s protection, family and client equally owed the *pater* their total obedience—which the Romans referred to as *pietas*, "dutifulness." So embedded was this attitude that when, toward the end of the first century BCE, the republic declared itself an empire, the emperor was called *pater patriae*, "father of the fatherland."

The first emperor to serve as *pater patriae* was Augustus, and he quickly addressed what he considered to be a crisis in Roman society—the demise of family life. Adultery and divorce were commonplace. There were more slaves and freed slaves in the city than citizens, let alone aristocrats. And family size, given the cost of living in the city, was diminishing. He reacted by criminalizing adultery and passed several other laws to promote family life. Men between the ages of 20 and 60 and women between the ages of 20 and 50 were required to marry. A divorced woman was required to remarry within six months, a widow within a year. Childless adults were punished with high taxes or deprived of inheritance. The larger an aristocrat's family, the greater his political strength. It is no coincidence that when Augustus commissioned a large monument to commemorate his triumphal return after establishing Roman rule in Gaul and restoring peace to Rome, the *Ara Pacis Augustae* (Altar of Augustan Peace), he had its exterior walls on the south decorated with a retinue of his own large family, a model for all Roman citizens, in a procession of lictors (the class of citizens charged with guarding and attending to the needs of magistrates), priests, magistrates, senators, and other representatives of the Roman people (**Fig. 26-9**).

Art historians believe that the *Ara Pacis Augustae* represents a real event, perhaps a public rejoicing for Augustus' reign (it was begun in 13 BCE when he was 50), or the dedication of the altar itself, which occurred on his wife Livia's fiftieth birthday in 9 BCE. The realism of the scene is typically Roman. A sense of spatial depth is created by depicting figures farther away from us in low relief and those closest to us in high relief—so high,

Fig. 26-9 Imperial Procession (detail), south frieze, *Ara Pacis Augustae*, Rome, 13–9 BCE. Marble, width approx. 35 ft.

Fig. 26-10 ***Theodora and Her Attendants*****, San Vitale, ca. 547.** Mosaic, 8 ft. 8 in. × 12 ft. CAMERAPHOTO Arte, Venice.

in fact, that the feet of the nearest figures project over the architectural frame into our space. This technique would have encouraged viewers—the Roman public—to feel that they were part of the same space as the figures in the sculpture itself. The Augustan peace is the peace enjoyed by the average Roman citizen, the Augustan family a metaphor for the larger family of Roman citizens.

The *Ara Pacis Augustae* is preeminently a celebration of family. Three generations of Augustus' family are depicted in the relief. It also demonstrates the growing prominence of women in Roman society. Livia is depicted holding Augustus' family together, standing between her stepson-in-law, Marcus Agrippa, and her own sons, Tiberius and Drusus. Livia became a figure of idealized womanhood in Rome. She was the "female leader" of Augustus' programs of reform, a sponsor of architectural projects, and a trusted advisor to both her husband and son. While Livia enjoyed greater power and influence than most, Roman women possessed some rights of citizenship, although they could not vote or hold public office. Still, married women retained their legal identity. They controlled their own property and managed their own legal affairs. Elite women modeled themselves after Livia, wielding power through their husbands and sons.

Livia was by no means the only wife of a famous ruler to assert her power. The power of the empress Theodora of Constantinople was at least comparable to that of her husband Justinian. Indeed, in the two mosaics depicting Theodora and Justinian in Ravenna (see Figs. 17-7 and 17-8), the golden halo surrounding Theodora's head is considerably larger than that encircling Justinian's, and she wears far more elaborate jewelry (**Fig. 26-10**)—a large crown hung with a strand of pearls (believed to protect the wearer from disease), and a wide collar of gold embroidery and jeweled cloth. Where Justinian's cloak is plain, hers is embroidered with the three Magi who brought gifts to the infant Jesus, just as she brings a huge golden chalice studded with jewels as an offering to Christ. She is further distinguished from Justinian by being centered beneath a fluted shell canopy, which serves to accentuate her halo.

In 532, when fights between rival gangs in Constantinople briefly caused the emperor Justinian to consider abandoning the city, Theodora persuaded him to stay: "If you wish to save yourself, O Emperor," she is reported to have counseled, "that is easy. For we have much money, there is the sea, here are the boats. But think whether after you have been saved you may not come to feel that you would have preferred to die." The empress's words were recorded in the *Anekdota*, or *Secret History*, of Procopius of Caesarea. Though the latter was Justinian's official historian, this work was a scathing, deceitful, and almost certainly apocryphal account of Justinian and Theodora's rule that was not intended for publication in the author's lifetime—hence its "secret" status. Procopius evidently harbored much ill will toward his employers. He attacks the emperor and empress on moral grounds, particularly citing the lowness of their origins and the baseness of their behavior, and he quite evidently sees himself as their superior. His description of Theodora creates an entirely different identity for the empress than is depicted in the Ravenna mosaic. Justinian comes off as little better than a common thief, Theodora as a nymphomaniac. But Procopius does not come off particularly well himself. His account of the couple seems to have been provoked by the fact that the two enjoyed a union of mutual respect and apparently equal status. Theodora represented a nexus of power—not simply female but evidently more ruthless and far less easygoing than her husband—that did not fit a conventional understanding of women's place in society, a place Theodora sought constantly to improve. She shut down brothels in the capital, intervened on behalf of wronged women, and influenced the passage of many laws to improve the status of women in the empire. In Procopius' ranting we can recognize the level of invective that many public figures have endured throughout Western history.

In Nigeria, among the Yoruba people, who live at the eastern end of the West African forests, near the Niger River, the highest-ranking woman is called *Iyalode*, or "mother of all." The culture is patriarchal in structure; nevertheless, although rare, there are instances of Yoruba women serving as chief, and the *Iyalode* position is one of particular power, as this *elefon* helmet mask suggests (**Fig. 26-11**). The *elefon* are the ancestral emperors of the Yoruba city of Oyo, and this mask was meant to evoke them in dance. Like most African masks, it was worn by a male, and the mask proper—its bottom quarter—is male. But the top three-quarters consist of a representation of an *Iyalode* as chief. She carries a fly whisk in one hand and wears a tall conical crown and a necklace of large coral beads—all symbols of a Yoruba chief. In her left hand, she holds the upside-down figure of another woman. This gesture represents the power of the *Iyalode* to exercise discipline over women who have erred. The *Iyalode* also represented the collective interests of women before the king. But perhaps most important here is that the *Iyalode* stands upon the head of a male, thus exercising her power over him as well.

One of the primary focuses of the contemporary feminist movement has been, of course, to address the imbalance of power that exists between men and women. In her *Kitchen Table Series*, a collection of 20 photographs and 14 short texts made in 1990, Carrie Mae Weems explores the dynamics of what is, arguably, the most female of places, the domestic space of the kitchen. As she puts it in the art21 *Exclusive* video "Carrie Mae Weems: 'The Kitchen Table Series,'" the kitchen is where "the battle around the family, the battle around monogamy, the battle around polygamy, the battle between the

Fig. 26-11 *Elefon* helmet mask, Yoruba culture, Nigeria, after 1900. Wood, height 4 ft. 3½ in. The University of Iowa Museum, Stanley Collection.

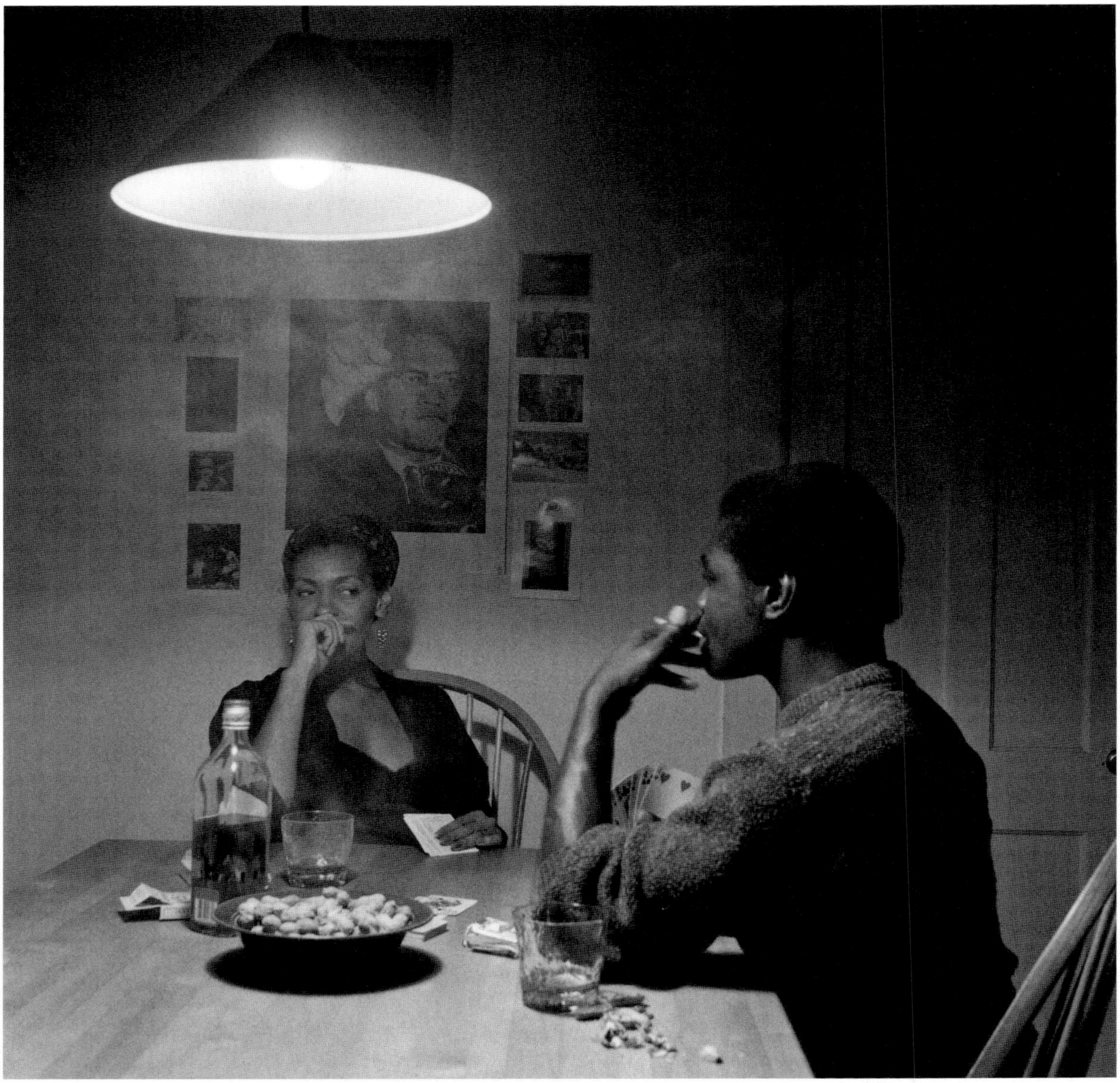

Fig. 26-12 Carrie Mae Weems, *Untitled (Man Smoking/Malcolm X)*, from *The Kitchen Table Series*, 1990.
Gelatin silver print, 27¼ × 27¼ in.

sexes is going to be played out." In *Untitled (Man Smoking/Malcolm X)* (**Fig. 26-12**), the battle is being played out as a game of cards over a bowl of peanuts, a pack of cigarettes, and a bottle of whiskey. The image is, in effect, a compendium of the African-American experience, ranging from the peanuts, positioned directly under the harsh bright light of the lamp, which refer to one of the two (with cotton) primary crops worked by enslaved Africans—and later, under Jim Crow, their indentured heirs—in the American South, to the poster of Malcolm X, the great African-American Muslim minister and civil rights activist who inaugurated the Black Power movement. As Weems explains in the art21 video, "Women hold the key to the bedroom and the key to the generations, while men of course hold the key to power." Her project, she says, is to begin to find a way "to alter the domestic space, the social living arrangement"—to achieve some new balance of power.

Power, Race, and the Colonial Enterprise

What is colonialism and how have artists addressed it?

The peanuts in Carrie Mae Weems's *Untitled (Man Smoking/Malcolm X)* carry a greater weight than just their reference to slavery in the United States. As Weems well knows, the peanut originated in South America, where Spanish and Portuguese conquistadors first discovered it and took it back to Europe. The Portuguese then introduced it to Africa, where it was used to feed captured slaves on their journey in slave ships across the Atlantic, and, ultimately, enslaved Africans brought it to plantations in the U.S. South. The peanut is, in other words, a symbol of not just the African diaspora, but of colonial power in general.

One of the most compelling examples of colonial power in Mexican art is *casta* painting. Because of the almost total absence of European women in the Americas during the sixteenth century, the Spanish conquistadors turned to other women for sexual partners. Very soon there were large numbers of people of variously mixed race, called *castas* or castes. The most common *castas* were *mestizo* (Spanish-Indian), *mulatto* (Spanish-black), *zambo* (black-Indian), and then later, in the seventeenth century, *castizo* (a light-skinned *mestizo*) and *morisco* (a light-skinned *mulatto*). By the eighteenth century, as growing numbers of Filipinos and other Asian populations arrived in Mexico (generally as slaves), and as the various castes themselves intermingled, a new term came into the language to indicate racial indeterminacy, *tente en el aire*, "hold yourself in the air." By the end of the century, fully one-quarter of the population was of mixed race.

This situation gave rise to the distinct genre of family portrait that is ***casta* painting** (**Fig. 26-13**). By and large, *casta* paintings exist in sets of 16, recording the process of race-mixing in the Americas. Each portrays a man and a woman of different races with one or two of their children, and each is titled with a sort of equation, as in the image illustrated here—a Spaniard plus a black equals a *mulatto*. These *casta* paintings are generally arranged hierarchically, with pure-blooded Spanish or *criollo* (descendants of pure-blooded Spanish born in Mexico) parents producing equally pure-blooded offspring

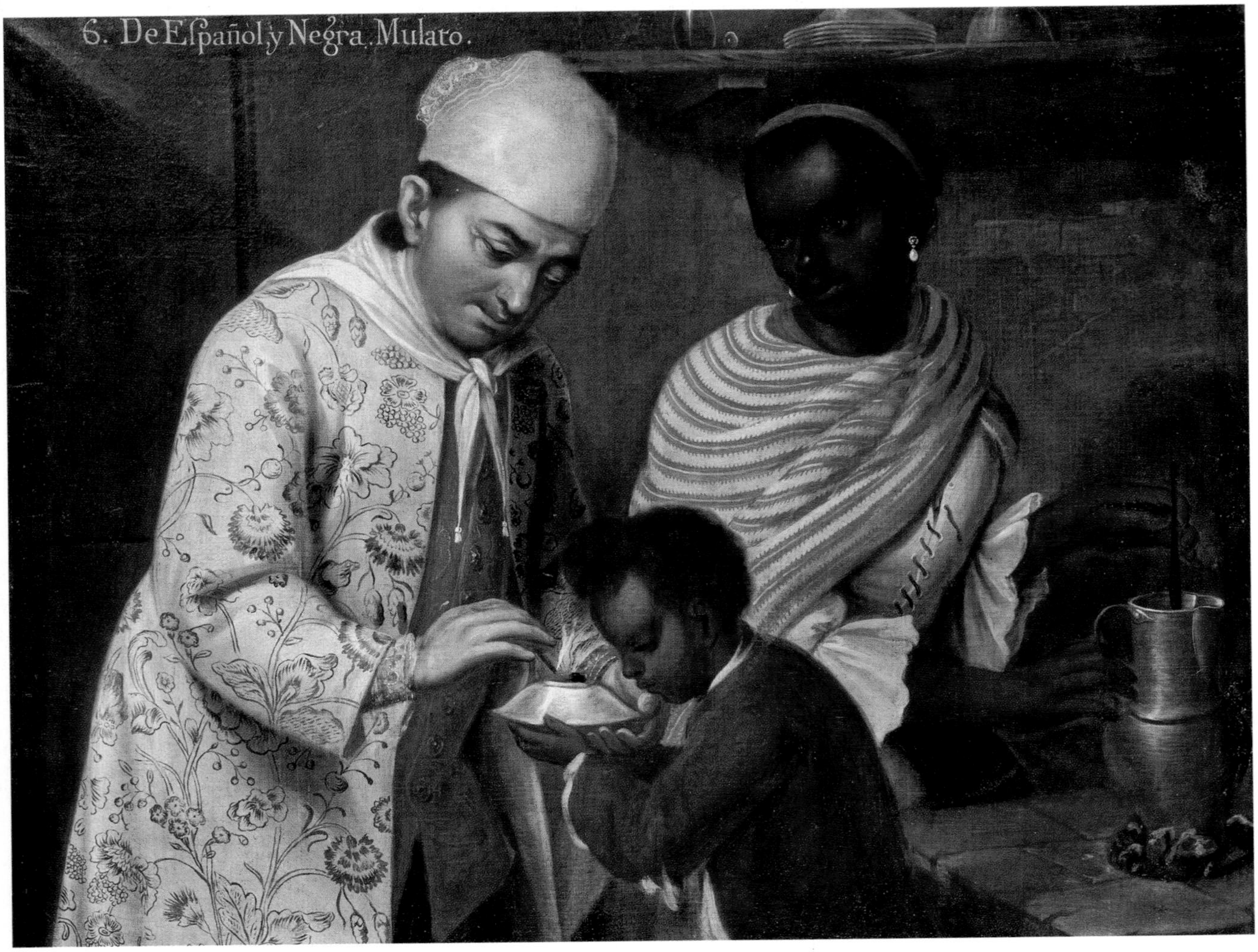

Fig. 26-13 Attributed to José de Alcíbar, *From Spaniard and Black, Mulatto* (*De Español y Negra, Mulato*), ca. 1760. Oil on canvas, 31 × 38¼ in. Denver Art Museum, Gift of Jan and Frederick R. Mayer Collection, 2014.217.
Photo courtesy of Denver Art Museum.

Fig. 26-14 Shahzia Sikander, *The Last Post*, 2010. Still. HD video animation, 10 min.
Courtesy of the artist.

placed first in order. The offspring of black parents were at the bottom, and Indians variously in the middle. The painting reproduced here is positioned, as inscribed at the top left, in sixth place in the hierarchical scale (so high, despite the black mother, because of the Spanish father). The Spaniard's African wife is making hot chocolate at the stove, while his *mulatto* son brings him a brazier to light his cigarette. The social difference between father and son is highlighted by the distinct difference in the richness of their clothing—the father wears a chintz coat, imported from India. While it is clear that the *casta* paintings are indicative of the Spanish obsession with racial genealogy and a genuine interest in the dynamics of racial intermixing—never before so readily apparent—that obsession was at least partly based on the Spanish nobility's insistence on affirming its own position at the top of the ladder.

Shahzia Sikander's video animation *The Last Post* (**Fig. 26-14**), which she discusses in the art21 *Exclusive* video "Shahzia Sikander: 'The Last Post,'" explores colonial trade relations between the British East India Company and China in the nineteenth century. The East India Company was established in 1600, with the idea of pursuing trade in India and China. By 1757, the Company effectively ruled India, but India was seen as the stepping-stone to the larger markets in China, whose silks, porcelains, and teas were highly valued throughout Europe and America. More important to the British than these wares was the opium trade. In order to compensate for the gold and silver spent on the purchase of tea, porcelains, and silks, the British East India Company began selling the Chinese large quantities of opium, which it grew in India. Produced at a very low cost, opium was a very profitable trade item for the British. Unfortunately for the Chinese, opium addiction rapidly became a severe social problem. In 1839, after the emperor's son died an opium-related death, the Chinese moved to ban the drug.

The British responded by declaring war and subsequently crushed China, attacking most of its coastal and river towns. In the resulting Treaty of Nanjing, China ceded Hong Kong to Britain and paid an indemnity of 21 million silver dollars (roughly equivalent to $2 billion today). Chinese ports and markets were opened to Western merchants, and by 1880, the import of cheap machine-made products resulted in the collapse of the Chinese economy. It would not recover for over a century.

The central character in Sikander's video is an East India Company Man who travels throughout India and then ventures into China. The title refers to the bugle call that signals the end of the day, but that is also used to commemorate soldiers who die in war. The moment illustrated here, as the Company Man explodes into a thousand pieces, suggests a future in which Western influence in China and the Indian subcontinent has ended, as would indeed come to pass in the years after World War II.

Fig. 26-15 William Kentridge, *History of the Main Complaint*, 1996. Still. Film, 35 mm, shown as video, projection, black and white, and sound (mono), 5 min. 50 sec.

Courtesy Marion Goodman Gallery, New York. © Goodman Gallery 2006. All rights reserved.

William Kentridge's stop-motion video work (**Fig. 26-15**; see also Fig. 8-23) is a direct reflection of European colonial adventuring in Africa. By the 1880s, France was extracting phosphates from Morocco, Belgium gems, ivory, and rubber from the Congo, and Britain diamonds from South Africa. In this way, Europe's African colonies became primarily focused on producing large quantities of raw materials—a commodity-based export economy that left most Africans in dire poverty. The social dislocation created by the South African diamond mines lies at the heart of Kentridge's work.

The diamond mines required huge amounts of labor, and native Africans supplied it. Between 1871 and 1875, an estimated 50,000 Africans arrived every year at the diamond mines, replacing roughly the same number who left each year. Laborers lived in closed compounds designed to control theft but that were actually nearer in character to prisons. Workers left the compound each morning and returned to it each evening after work, when they were searched for diamonds hidden on their persons. These European-designed structures were also a sure way to control potentially unruly Africans. They also effectively separated black Africans from local white residents, an enforced separation that in many respects marks the beginning of South African apartheid (literally "separateness" in Afrikaans, the dialect of Dutch spoken by Afrikaners), the social legacy of which is Kentridge's subject. When, in *History of the Main Complaint*, the comatose Soho Eckstein hits an African woman with his car as he drives down the highway, he is, in effect, rehearsing the entire history of apartheid in South Africa, the history of which he comes to recognize as his own. As he sees the figure leaning over the body in the road, his own face is reflected in the rear-view mirror, as if his eyes are looking backward, into the past. He is, in this moment, the very heir of Cecil Rhodes, whose De Beers Mining Company in Kimberley, South Africa, founded in 1880, once controlled as much as 80 percent of the world's diamonds.

Yinka Shonibare, MBE, has addressed the British colonial enterprise directly in a monumental work made in 2010 for the Fourth Plinth in London's Trafalgar Square, *Nelson's Ship in a Bottle* (**Fig. 26-16**). (The Fourth Plinth Project was inaugurated in 1998 to place a temporary artwork on the otherwise empty plinth each year.) At the Battle of Trafalgar on October 21, 1805, Admiral Lord Nelson led a fleet of 27 ships against a combined fleet of 33 French and Spanish ships west of Cape Trafalgar on the southwest coast of Spain. Nelson's decisive victory, during which he was mortally wounded, resulted in the Royal Navy enjoying unchallenged supremacy of the seas in the nineteenth century, and set the stage for Britain's subsequent colonial adventuring.

Shonibare's sculpture is a 1:30 scale model of Lord Nelson's ship HMS *Victory*, fitted with sails made of his trademark printed fabric (see Fig. 13-28),

Fig. 26-16 Yinka Shonibare MBE, *Nelson's Ship in a Bottle*, Fourth Plinth, Trafalgar Square, London, 2010. Glass bottle stopped with a cork containing a ship with printed fabric sails, length 15 ft. 5 in., diameter 9 ft. 2¼ in.

Courtesy of James Cohan Gallery, New York and Shanghai © Yinka Shonibare MBE. All Rights Reserved, DACS/ARS, New York 2015.

material created by English and Dutch designers, manufactured in Europe, exported to Africa, and then remarketed in the West as authentic African design. Today it is in the collection of the Royal Naval Museum; as installed in Trafalgar Square, named in honor of Nelson's victory, it faced Nelson's Column in the center of the square, atop which stands a statue of Nelson himself. In the art21 *Exclusive* video "Yinka Shonibare MBE: 'Nelson's Ship in a Bottle,'" the Nigeria-raised Shonibare explains, "When I first came to Britain, I learned that being black meant that you were supposed to be somewhat inferior. I didn't quite understand that concept at all. But of course now I understand it better in the context of colonialism and slavery." Nelson's ship was in some sense the harbinger of that concept, but *Nelson's Ship in a Bottle*, made over 200 years later by a Nigerian who in 2005 was made a Member of the Order of the British Empire (MBE), an honorary title he now adds with a certain irony to his name, suggests that the result of Britain's imperial adventuring has been the creation of one of the most culturally and ethnically diverse cities in the world.

Slavery—the trafficking of human beings—is one of the most perverse and disturbing consequences of the colonial era, and it proves to be a subtle, but pervasive subtext in depictions of the nude in nineteenth-century art. One of the things that viewers found most disturbing about Édouard Manet's *Olympia* (see Fig. 1-15) was that her gaze seemed to dominate the viewer, reversing the traditional relations of power that define the male's relation to the courtesan, and by extension the master–slave relationship as well.

The colonial enterprise in the Middle East is cemented in the traditional relations of power that *Olympia* seems to overthrow, and it is the subject of a book written in 1978 by Edward Said, then a professor of English and comparative literature at Columbia University, which is titled simply *Orientalism*. At the most basic level, his title was meant to evoke a long-standing academic discipline in the West that had focused on "the Orient." What struck Said about Western studies of the region was that Orientalist scholarship seemed to be an "institution for dealing with the Orient—dealing with it by making statements about it, authorizing views of it, describing it, by teaching it, settling it, ruling over it: in short, Orientalism was a Western style for dominating, restructuring, and having authority over the Orient." Orientalism, in other words, was a way of inscribing a certain identity on the Middle East.

For Said, the Orientalist style is particularly inscribed in Western paintings of the odalisque—a female slave or concubine in a Turkish harem—such as Ingres's *Grande Odalisque* (**Fig. 26-17**; see also Fig. 19-12). Such paintings exploit the deep-seated Western male belief in and envy of the Orientalist male dominance of the

Fig. 26-17 Jean-Auguste-Dominique Ingres, *Grande Odalisque*, 1814. Oil on canvas, 35¼ in. × 5 ft. 3¾ in. Musée du Louvre, Paris.

Inv. RF1158. Photo © RMN-Grand Palais (musée du Louvre)/Thierry Le Mage.

female in the harem. Here is a field of play over which the Western male might gaze unperturbed by the strictures of the Western moral order. For, in fact, before such a painting, the viewer, always implicitly male, might indulge his most libidinous dream even as he maintained the decorum of his position—he was, after all, simply enjoying great art.

In Said's terms, the position of the viewer in front of such works is a position of mastery. He controls the situation with his gaze. His is a look of cultural superiority, strength, and domination. His gaze is, in short, an exercise in power that still exerts its authority throughout the world, and its continuing power is the subject of Moroccan-born artist Lalla Essaydi. Her work is about the impact of the Western gaze on Arab culture, and it is specifically about the ways in which Orientalist nineteenth-century painting has inscribed itself on Arab women. If she appreciates the fact that the Western Orientalist painters admired the beauty that they discovered in the Arab world, she cringes at their presentation of women. The title of her series of photographs *Les Femmes du Maroc* (*The Women of Morocco*) is an explicit reference to a famous painting by Eugène Delacroix, *Les Femmes d'Alger* (*The Women of Algiers*), a depiction of three Algerian concubines and their servant, while *La Grande Odalisque* (**Fig. 26-18**) is a direct reference to Ingres's painting of the same name (see Fig. 26-17). In all the photographs in the series, Essaydi covers her model and the space surrounding her with Arab calligraphy. The model melds with the space, a fact that is, in fact, implied by the word "harem." The word derives from the Arabic *haram* or *haraam*, a word that means both "a sacred inviolable space" or "sanctuary" and "sinful." It is this tension, this complexity, that Essaydi's photographs exploit. The texts that cover everything are written in henna, a traditional dye used for body decoration in Arab culture, and they originate with a personal story from Essaydi's youth. But in the course of inscribing the story on the walls, and the clothing and body of the model—a process which can take several months—the texts take on the character of a dialogue with the model, a sort of journal documenting both Essaydi's story and the stories of the women she photographs. In this sense, the women are no longer Western stereotypes, but real people with real stories to tell, a reality emphasized here by the dirt on the feet of the model—she walks on real ground.

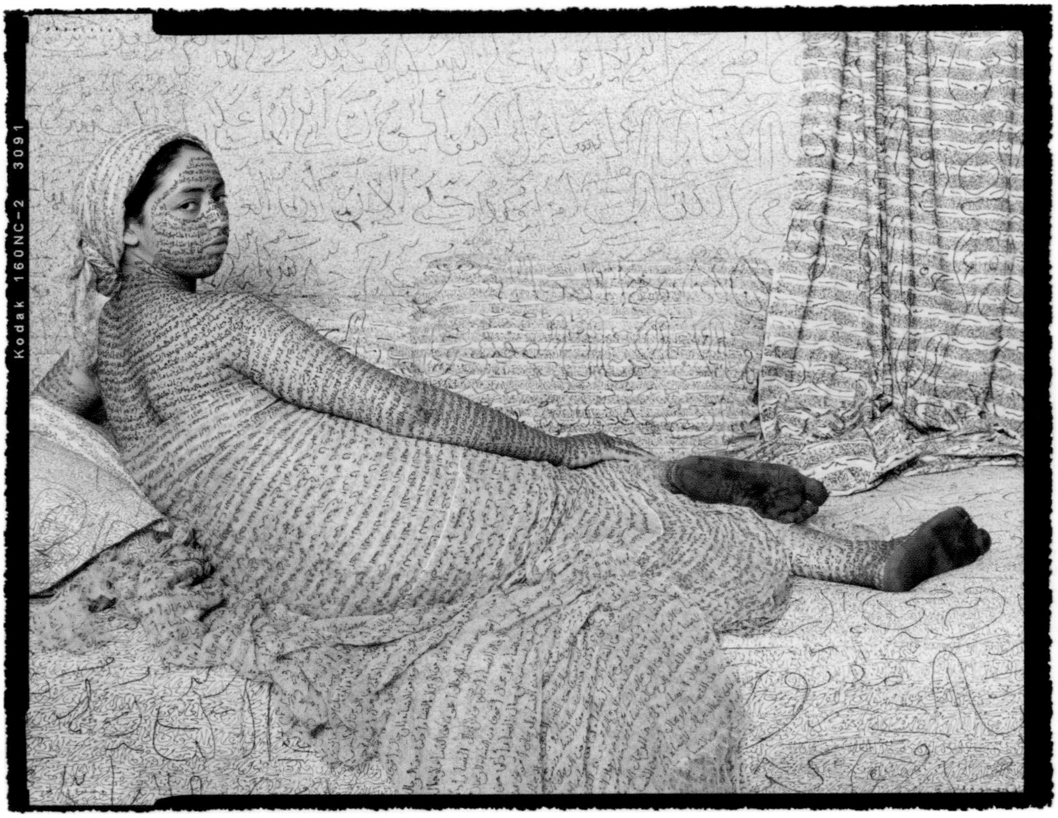

Fig. 26-18 Lalla Essaydi, *La Grande Odalisque*, from the series *Les Femmes du Maroc* (*The Women of Morocco*), 2008. Photograph, C-print.
Courtesy of Edwynn Houk Gallery, New York.

The Power of the Museum

How has the museum wielded power as an institution?

Homi Bhaba, a great student of contemporary global culture, has reminded us of the "artifactual" consequences of Western colonization in an essay exploring the connection between contemporary culture and its colonial heritage. "The great remains of the Inca or Aztec world are the debris . . . of the Culture of Discovery," he writes. "Their presence in the museum should reflect the devastation that has turned them from being signs in a powerful cultural system to becoming the symbols of a destroyed culture." This headdress (**Fig. 26-19**), presented by Cortés to the Holy Roman emperor Charles V as that of the Aztec king Motecuhzoma and now in the Museum of Ethnology in Vienna, is a case in point (that this was actually Motecuhzoma's is doubtful, but it is genuinely Aztec). Consisting of 450 green tail feathers of the quetzal bird, blue feathers from the cotinga bird, beads, and gold, it is a treasure of extraordinary beauty and can be appreciated in purely aesthetic terms, as the museum presents it. Yet as Homi Bhaba points out, "It seems appropriate . . . [to make] present in the display of art what is so often rendered unrepresentable or left unrepresented—violence, trauma, dispossession." In other words, Bhaba believes that the headdress's history, the tale of Cortés and his betrayal of Motecuhzoma, should enter into the museum display.

Museums have great power to control not only what we see but how we see it. Even the way they arrange their collections reveals their prejudices. Commenting on these arrangements in the art21 *Exclusive* video "Kerry James Marshall: On Museums," Marshall points out that, as an African-American artist,

> at some point you become acutely aware of your absence in the whole historical timeline that develops this kind of narrative of mastery. . . . The

Fig. 26-19 Feather headdress worn by Aztec priests representing deities, 16th century.
Feathers, gold appliqué, and fiber net, 45⅝ in. × 5 ft. 8⅞ in. Weltmuseum, Vienna.
Bridgeman Images.

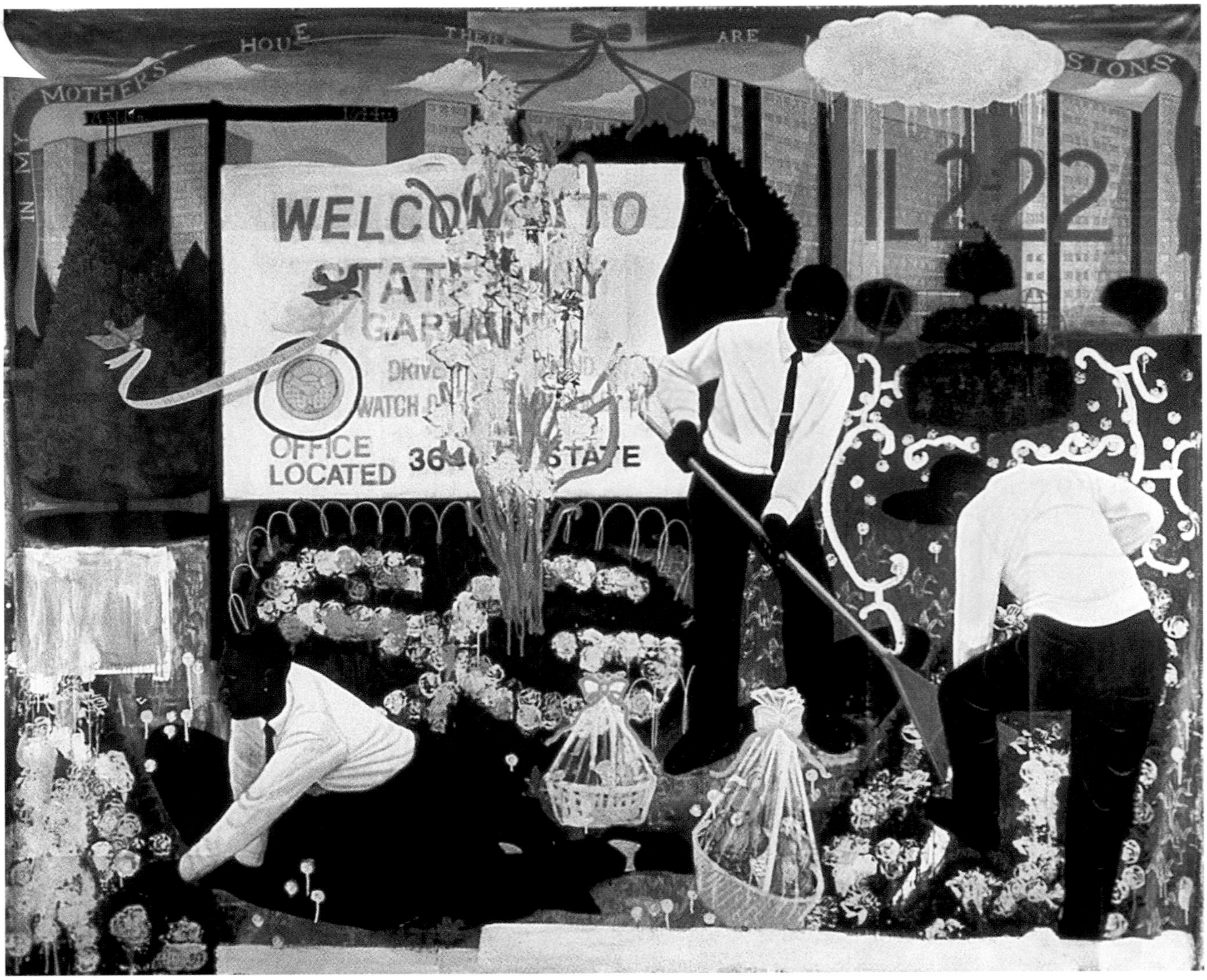

Fig. 26-20 Kerry James Marshall, *Many Mansions*, 1994. Acrylic and collage on unstretched canvas, 9 ft. 6 in. × 11 ft. 3 in.
Courtesy of Jack Shainman Gallery, New York.

> people who make the "best stuff," they are all Europeans. And where do other people start to come into the field? Well, only after they had been dominated and colonized by Europeans. And then what do they start to do? They start to do what the Europeans were doing.

Marshall, in fact, admits that in his paintings of the Chicago housing projects like *Many Mansions* (**Fig. 26-20**; see also Fig. 20-39) he himself turned to Europeans for his inspiration: "My model for them was the genre of pastoral painting that extends from Giorgione's *Tempest* [see Fig. 18-10] to Édouard Manet's *Déjeuner sur l'herbe* [see Fig. 19-24]." But if he began with European models, he quickly added his own distinctive elements. The paintings, he says,

> are overabundant, particularly lush, particularly rich in surface and mark making; they have very opulent color. In them, the sky is always just a little too bright a blue; the sun is always beaming just a little too gaily; there are bluebirds of happiness and flowers bursting out all over the place, and the people occupy the space very casually.

The paintings, in other words, purvey a sense of false optimism, even though Marshall says, "the world of the people who inhabit the projects is still filled with incredible hope and possibility." What Marshall brings to his pastoral landscapes is, in fact, that sense of incredulity. In turn, his paintings challenge the museum's sense of history by offering the viewer an alternative kind of space in the canvas itself, one not normally seen on the museum's walls.

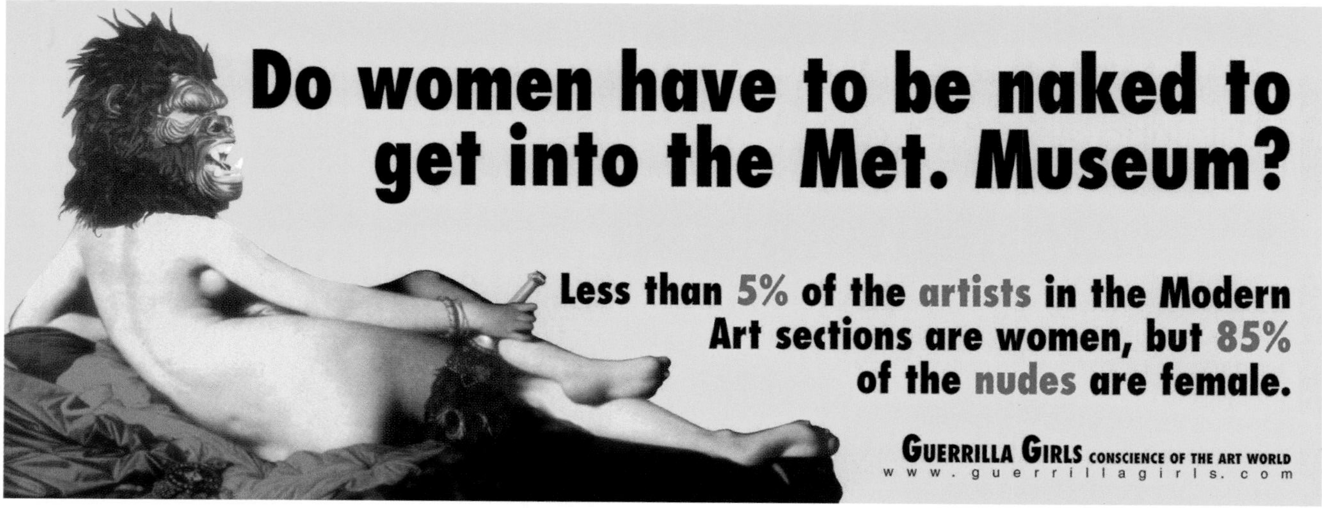

Fig. 26-21 Guerrilla Girls, *Do Women Have to Be Naked to Get into the Met. Museum?*, 1989. Poster.

Up until the 1990s, it was very difficult for women to enter the art world. Very few museums exhibited their work, and they were extremely underserved by the gallery system. In 1985, an anonymous group of women who called themselves the Guerrilla Girls began hanging posters in New York to draw attention to the problem (**Fig. 26-21**). The figure in this poster is a parody of Jean-Auguste-Dominique Ingres's *Grande Odalisque* (see Fig. 26-17), and it draws specific attention to the sexist collecting practices of the Metropolitan Museum in New York. In another poster, the Guerrilla Girls listed the specific galleries who represented less than 1 woman for every 10 men. Yet another poster asked: "How Many Women Had One-Person Exhibitions at NYC Museums Last Year?" The answer:

Guggenheim 0
Metropolitan 0
Modern 1
Whitney 0

One of the Guerrilla Girls' most daring posters was distributed in 1989. It asked, "When racism & sexism are no longer fashionable, what will your art collection be worth?" It listed 67 women artists and pointed out that a collection of works by all of them would be worth less than the auction value of any one painting by a famous living male artist. Its suggestion that the value of the male artists' work might be drastically inflated struck a chord with many.

By the late 1990s, the situation had changed somewhat. Many more women were regularly exhibited in New York galleries and their work was given more major retrospectives. But, internationally especially, women continued to get short shrift. Where a retrospective by a major male artist—Robert Rauschenberg, for instance—might originate in New York at the Guggenheim and travel to international venues around the world, most retrospectives of women artists remained much more modest—a single nontraveling show at, say, the New Museum in New York or the Los Angeles County Museum of Art. Indeed, in 2012, when the auction house Christie's made $388 million at its sale of contemporary art in New York, the male-to-female ratio of artists represented was five-to-one—seemingly a distinct improvement. However, the proceeds on the work by women artists added up to only $17 million—less than 5 percent of the total, a fact that suggests that work by women remains undervalued in the art world.

THE CRITICAL PROCESS

Thinking about Power

Jenny Holzer's text-based artworks have appeared on electronic LED billboards, silkscreen paintings, posters, T-shirts, coffee mugs—virtually anywhere print might usually appear. She is famous, particularly, for aphorisms that twist clichés into powerful and disturbing truths—"Truisms," she calls them: "Protect me from what I want," "Abuse of power should come as no surprise." The power of language—not the spoken word, but language in the visual field—could be said to be her subject.

In 2008–09, Holzer mounted a one-person show, first at the Museum of Contemporary Art in Chicago, and then at the Whitney Museum of American Art in New York, titled *PROTECT PROTECT*. It featured work from her own writings from 1977 to 2001, as well as later work featuring texts from U.S. government sources, including plans for the Iraq and Afghanistan Wars, the testimony of victims and witnesses to U.S. actions in the Middle East, and statements by detainees at the Guantanamo Bay detention facility in Cuba.

The title of Holzer's show is entirely ambiguous. It simultaneously evokes her famous Truism "Protect me from what I want" and the ostensible political rationale for the invasion of Iraq (to protect the world from Saddam Hussein's weapons of mass destruction). It also suggests the necessity of protecting ourselves from those who would ostensibly protect us. In *Thorax* (**Fig. 26-22**), text scrolls by on multiple thin screens in seductive purple–blue colors arranged in a tower that is an abstracted reproduction of the human thorax, the region of the body from the neck to the diaphragm that protects the heart and the lungs behind the ribcage. The text of this work comes from conflicting descriptions of an incident in which an Iraqi combatant was killed by American forces. The power of the text is deliberately at odds with the beauty of the color. Why do you suppose Holzer uses such lush color to present her horrific texts? Does color possess a certain power in its own right? How would you compare Holzer's work to Edmund Clark's photograph *Camp Five, Detainee's Cell*, reproduced at the beginning of this chapter? In the art21 *Exclusive* video "Jenny Holzer: Writing and Difficulty," Holzer speaks of the difficulty of creating these pieces. Why do you think she found it difficult? How do these works address questions of power?

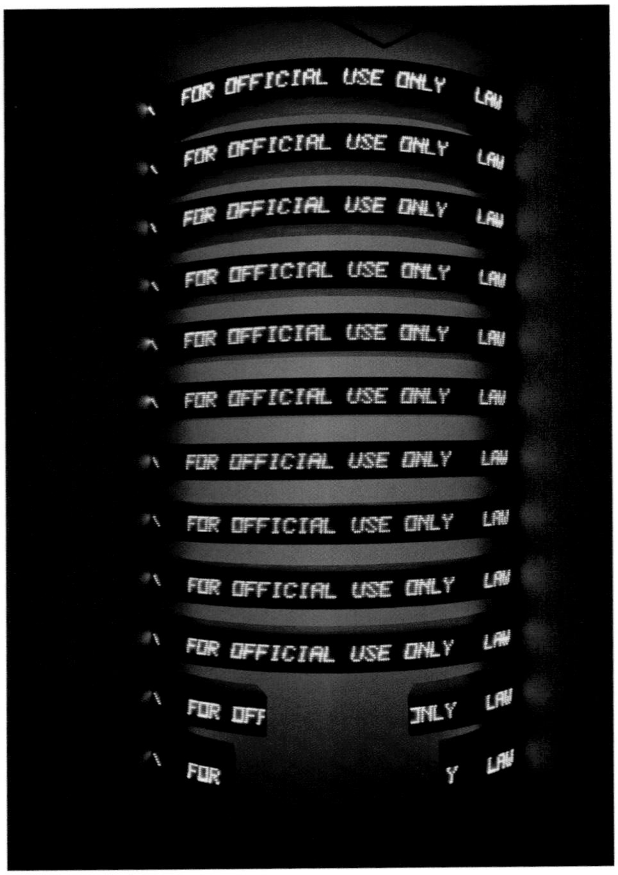

Fig. 26-22 Jenny Holzer, *Thorax*, 2008. Twelve double-sided, curved electronic LED signs with white diodes on front and red and blue diodes on back, 8 ft. 8¼ in. × 4 ft. 10⁵⁄₁₆ in. × 37⅛ in. Text: U.S. government documents. The Broad Art Foundation, Santa Monica.

Thinking Back

26.1 Describe some of the means by which rulers have asserted their power in art.

From the court of the Assyrian king Ashurnasirpal to Qin Shihuangdi in China and the government of Napoleon Bonaparte, art has been created to underscore the leader's power. All three leaders recognized the propagandistic potential of art. How does Jean-Auguste-Dominique Ingres's *Napoleon on His Imperial Throne* create an image of the emperor that is almost godlike? What is the "imperial gaze"?

26.2 Discuss some of the issues surrounding power as it affects women.

The vast majority of world cultures are patriarchies, and in ancient Rome this arrangement was codified in the Roman practice of patronage, in which the patrician "father" looked after the plebeians under his care as he would his own family. After the advent of the Roman Empire, the emperor—the first of whom was Augustus—was called *pater patriae*, "father of the fatherland." How did Augustus' wife, Livia, exercise a certain power in light of Roman patriarchy? In Constantinople, Justinian's empress, Theodora, exercised considerable power herself. How is her power, relative to that of her husband, the emperor Justinian, reflected in the mosaics at Ravenna? Why do you think Procopius so objected to her power? What is remarkable about the *elefon* mask depicting an *Iyalode* from the Yoruba culture? How does Carrie Mae Weems address the issue of power in African-American family life?

26.3 Define colonialism and outline some of the ways that artists have addressed it.

Colonialism is the exercise of power by the West over Africa, India, Asia, and the Americas. How do *casta* paintings reflect the colonial enterprise? What was the East India Company and what power did it exercise that Shahzia Sikander objects to particularly? What are the origins of apartheid in South Africa, and how does William Kentridge's *History of the Main Complaint* reflect that history? How does Yinka Shonibare MBE address colonialism? What is "Orientalism" and how has Lalla Essaydi responded to it?

26.4 Explain how the museum wields power.

Museums have wielded power by constructing histories that leave important information and/or artists out. What does Homi Bhaba object to? Kerry James Marshall? Since the 1980s, the Guerrilla Girls have protested the art world's lack of acknowledgment of women artists. What is the situation today?

Chapter 27

Science, Technology, and the Environment

Learning Objectives

27.1 Describe how technological innovation is reflected in the arts.

27.2 Describe some of the ways that artists have helped to shape public perception of the environment.

27.3 Explain how some artists have approached the landscape and environment from a longer or deeper point of view.

From a superficial point of view, art and science seem to be opposite poles of human endeavor: Art creates imaginative spaces designed to evoke an emotional response in the viewer, while science seeks a rational, objective, and quantifiable description of the real world. But both artists and scientists are acutely sensitive to the events and phenomena of existence, and both are dedicated to illuminating the nature of reality. An artist like Leonardo da Vinci was, in fact, equal parts painter, engineer, anatomist, botanist, and, arguably, psychologist. In his book *Art and Physics: Parallel Vision in Space, Time, and Light*, Leonard Shlain points out that words like "'volume,' 'space,' 'mass,' 'force,' 'light,' 'color,' 'tension,' 'relationship,' and 'density' are descriptive words that are heard repeatedly if you trail along with a museum docent. They also appear on the blackboards of freshman college physics lectures." Artists have traditionally responded to discoveries in science and mathematics, and, especially, the technological advances these discoveries have made possible.

In the nineteenth century, the development of the railroad transformed not only manufacturing by bringing both raw materials to producers and products to consumers faster, but also our very way of seeing. In 1834, there were approximately 762 miles of track in the United States. A decade later that number had grown by 5½ times to 4,311 miles. By 1854, the new number had tripled to 15,675 miles. And, by January 1, 1864, the amount of completed railway had grown to 33,860 miles—some 44-fold growth in the space of 30 years. This was in itself a profound technological achievement. But perhaps more important, in the 60-year span from 1800 to 1860, the introduction of train travel introduced the human eye to the perception of speed.

For all its play with linear and atmospheric perspective, J. M. W. Turner's *Rain, Steam, and Speed—The Great Western Railway* (**Fig. 27-1**; see also Fig. 5-4) is also a commentary on this transformation. The bridge that the train speeds across (**Fig. 27-2**) was a technological marvel. Designed by Isambard Kingdom Brunel, engineer for the Great Western Railway, it carried the railway across the River Thames on two brick arches. It was, in its day, the widest and flattest bridge in the world, and made it possible for the train to achieve the speeds it did. The engine is probably *The Firefly*, which could achieve speeds of 70 m.p.h., and which, in 1844, when Turner painted this, traveled the approximately 200 miles from London to Exeter in 270 minutes.

Fig. 27-1 J. M. W. Turner, *Rain, Steam, and Speed—The Great Western Railway*, 1844. Oil on canvas, 33¾ in. × 4 ft. The National Gallery, London.
akg-image/National Gallery, London.

Earlier, when humans traveled on horseback or foot, their eyes had been trained to concentrate on the near-at-hand. Suddenly, humans were traveling at a speed of at least 25 m.p.h.—by the 1830s, trains had been built that were capable of traveling at regular speeds of 60 m.p.h.—and the eye had to dismiss the near-at-hand, which had become a blur, and focus instead on the distant landscape. The domain of vision was turned now to the horizon. In Turner's painting, all detail of the near-at-hand has disappeared. And if the first words of his title—*Rain, Steam*—refer to the effects of atmosphere on vision, the third word, *Speed*, refers to the transformation of the act of seeing by technology.

Fig. 27-2 Isambard Kingdom Brunel, Maidenhead Railroad Bridge, 1840. Two spans, each 128 ft.
© Peter Lane/Alamy.

Technology and the Arts

How is technological innovation reflected in the arts?

Developments and innovations in architecture—from the Eiffel Tower (see Fig. 14-25) to the development of the skyscraper with its steel-and-reinforced-concrete construction (see Fig. 14-41) to the architectural response to environmental change—have consistently been driven

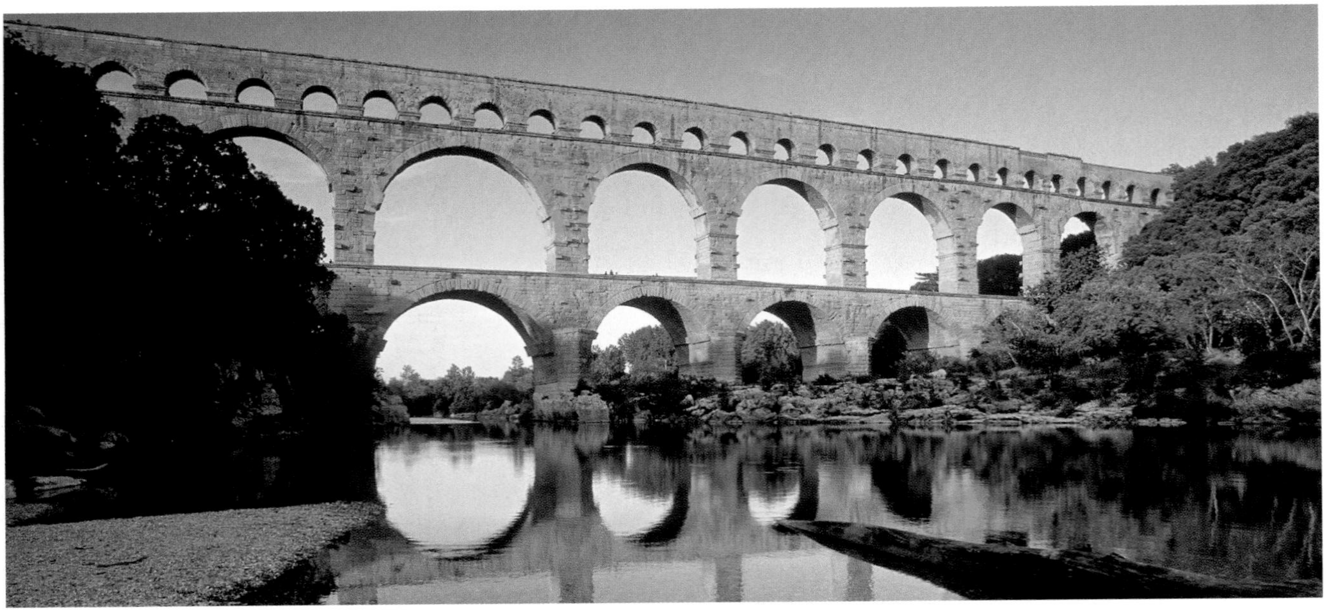

Fig. 27-3 Pont du Gard, near Nîmes, France, late 1st century BCE–early 1st century CE. Height 164 ft.
© Walter Bibikow/Getty Images.

by scientific and technological advances. The Pont du Gard (**Fig. 27-3**; see also Fig. 14-13), for instance, is one of the great technological feats of Roman times. The water that the aqueduct transported to the city of Nîmes originated in the springs of the Fontaine d'Eure some 12 miles to the north of the city. The aqueduct itself is some 31 miles long with an elevation drop of, astonishingly, only 56 feet over its entire length. Gravity is, in fact, all that propelled the water, and the Pont du Gard itself drops only 0.98 inches across its 1,181-foot length. The aqueduct delivered some 200 million liters of water a day, and the water took some 27 hours to flow from the source to the city. At 164 feet in height, the Pont du Gard is, furthermore, the highest aqueduct span that the Romans ever built.

One of the most remarkable architectural and engineering feats of modern times is Kansai International Airport in Osaka, Japan (**Fig. 27-4**). In the late 1980s, when architect Renzo Piano (see Fig. 1-18) was hired to design the airport terminal, there was insufficient land available in or near Osaka to accommodate the airport and its complex infrastructure, so a team of Japan's leading engineers created an artificial island in Osaka Bay. Three miles offshore, the island platform is anchored to the ocean floor in 130 feet of bedrock. These pilings—more than 1,000 of them—extend upward through 65 feet of mud and another 65 feet of water, each equipped with sensors to monitor settling that can be accounted for and corrected by hydraulic jacks. The curved roof of the terminal itself is a series of arcs designed so that they rotate around an axis centered 10 miles beneath the Earth's surface, giving it an unparalleled ability to withstand earthquakes. Indeed, in the 1995 earthquake that essentially destroyed Kobe across Osaka Bay, the airport was virtually unscathed. The terminal itself is a mile long, its sightlines

Fig. 27-4 Renzo Piano Building Workshop, Aerial view of Kansai International Airport, Osaka, Japan, 1988–94. © Fondazione Renzo Piano. © KIAC.
Photo: Kawaetsu.

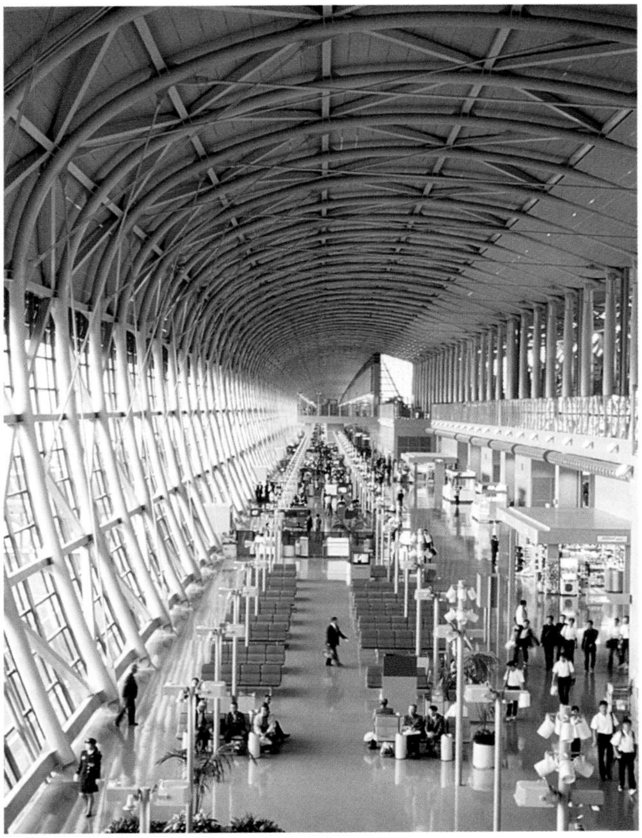

Fig. 27-5 Renzo Piano Building Workshop, International departures lounge, Kansai International Airport, Osaka, Japan, 1988–94. © Fondazione Renzo Piano.
Photo: Shunji Ishida.

uninterrupted down its entire length (**Fig. 27-5**). Ocean breezes are conveyed under the roof into the terminal, stirring large mobiles that give witness to the movement of air and wind throughout the space. Over 42 gates can accommodate up to 100,000 travelers a day.

The technologies associated with modeling clay into bowls, pots, and plates, first by stacking and coiling, then by throwing them on a potter's wheel (in use in the Middle East and China by 3000 BCE), have remained remarkably consistent (see Chapter 13). It is a simple step from forming clay pots and firing them to modeling clay sculptural figures and submitting them to the same firing process. Examples of clay modeling can be found in some of the earliest Paleolithic cave sites, but these Paleolithic sculptures were never fired. One of the most interesting examples of Neolithic fired-clay figurines is the work of the so-called Nok people who lived in what is now Nigeria. We do not know what the Nok called themselves—they are identified instead by the name of the place where their artifacts were discovered. In fact, we know almost nothing about the Nok. We do not know how their culture was organized, what their lives were like, or what they believed. But while most Neolithic peoples in Africa worked in materials that were not permanent, the Nok fired clay figures of animals and humans that were approximately life-size.

These figures were first unearthed early in the twentieth century by miners over an area of about 40 square miles. Carbon-14 and other forms of dating revealed that some of these objects had been made as early as 800 BCE and others as late as 600 CE. Little more than the hollow heads have survived intact, revealing an artistry based on abstract geometrical shapes (**Fig. 27-6**). In some cases, the heads are represented as ovals, and in others, as cones, cylinders, or spheres. Facial features are combinations of ovals, triangles, graceful arches, and straight lines. Holes in the eyes and nose may have been used to control temperature during firing. These heads were probably shaped with wet clay and then, after firing, finished by carving details into the hardened clay. Some scholars have argued that the technical and artistic sophistication of works by the Nok and other roughly contemporaneous groups suggests that it is likely there are older artistic traditions in West Africa that have not as yet been discovered. Certainly, farther to the east, in the sub-Saharan regions of the Sudan, Egyptian culture had exerted considerable influence for centuries, and it may well be that Egyptian technological sophistication had worked its way westward.

One of the most remarkable periods of innovation in the ceramic arts occurred in England in the last half of the eighteenth century. There, a group known as the Lunar Society gathered each month on the night of the full moon (providing both light to travel home by and the name of

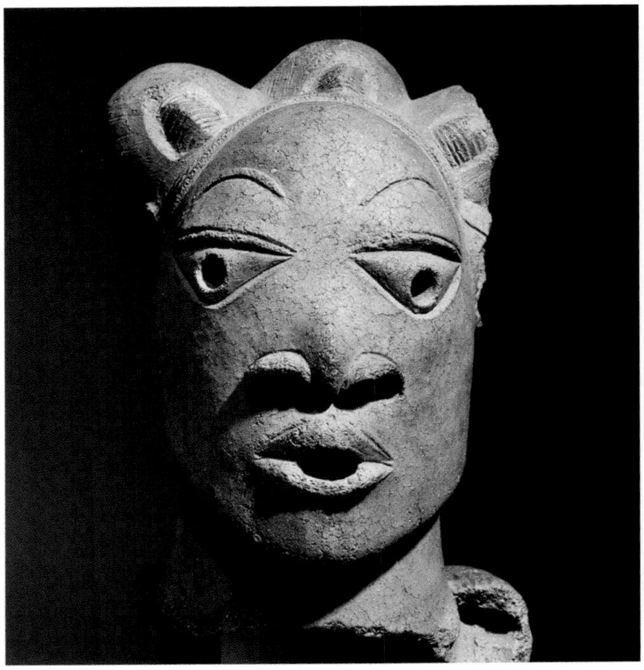

Fig. 27-6 Nok head, ca. 500 BCE–200 CE. Terra cotta, height $14\frac{3}{16}$ in. National Museum, Lagos, Nigeria.
Werner Forman Archive/National Museum, Lagos, Nigeria, location: 02.

the Society). Its members included prominent manufacturers, inventors, and naturalists. Among them were Matthew Boulton, whose world-famous Soho Manufactory produced a variety of metal objects, from buttons and buckles to silverware; James Watt, inventor of the steam engine, who would team with Boulton to manufacture it; Erasmus Darwin, whose writings on botany and evolution anticipate by nearly a century his grandson Charles Darwin's famous conclusions; William Murdock, inventor of gas lighting; Benjamin Franklin, who was a corresponding member; and Josiah Wedgwood, Charles Darwin's other grandfather and the inventor of mass manufacturing at his Wedgwood ceramics factories. From 1765 until 1815, the group discussed chemistry, medicine, electricity, gases, and any and every topic that might prove fruitful for industry. It is fair to say that the Lunar Society's members inaugurated what we think of today as the **Industrial Revolution**. The term itself was invented in the nineteenth century to describe the radical changes in production and consumption that were transforming the world.

Wedgwood opened his first factory in Burslem, Staffordshire on May 1, 1759, where he began to produce his highly durable cream-colored earthenware (**Fig. 27-7**; see also Fig. 13-3), which quickly became the favorite of Queen Charlotte, wife of King George III, and led, in 1762, to Wedgwood's appointment as royal supplier of dinnerware. Wedgwood's production process was unique. Instead of throwing individual pieces and shaping them by hand—heretofore the only way ceramic ware had been produced, even in China, where, 2,000 years earlier, the workers making the hundreds of ceramic warriors guarding the tomb of Qin Shihuangdi (see Fig. 12-12) had molded all the figures by hand—he cast liquid clay in molds and then fired it. The speed of production was thus greatly increased, even more so as patterns were mechanically printed on the finished china. Queen's Ware, as it came to be known, was soon made available to mass markets in both Europe and America, and Wedgwood's business flourished. It is an exemplary product of the Industrial Revolution—a product created on new machinery in new factories, thus creating a supply of consumer goods unprecedented in history and answering an extraordinary, and ever-increasing, demand for everyday items, from toys, furniture, kitchen utensils, and china, to silverware, watches, and candlesticks.

Fig. 27-7 Josiah Wedgwood, Queen's Ware dinner service (detail), ca. 1790. Private collection.
Photo © Christie's Images/Bridgeman Images.

Art and Environmental Understanding

How have artists helped to shape public perception about the environment?

In the nineteenth century, as painters turned more and more to the landscape as a source of inspiration in their pursuit of the Romantic sublime and the beautiful (see Chapter 19), they sometimes found themselves confronted by a sense of progress that threatened to overwhelm nature itself. In the stump, they saw the destruction of the forest; in the farm, the end of great grasslands; in mining, the scarification of the land itself; and in industry, the darkening of the very skies with smoke. Nature was at risk and, as the twentieth century came and went, this risk became more and more apparent. Artists have often helped the public come to understand just what is at stake in these changes.

Nature and Industry

In April 1859, the painter Albert Bierstadt joined the expeditionary force of Colonel Frederick W. Lander, a military engineer employed by the United States government to survey a proposed rail route through the South Pass of Wyoming. When the largest of the works that Bierstadt developed from sketches on that expedition, *The Rocky Mountains, Lander's Peak* (**Fig. 27-8**), was exhibited at the New York Metropolitan Fair in 1864, it thrilled the public, which associated the very size of the canvas with the great wealth of natural resources that the West seemed to offer the nation—the California Gold Rush of 1848–55 may have been history, but at that very moment, vast quantities of silver were about to be discovered in the mountains of Colorado. And the painting brought Lander's name and his survey to the attention of all. Lander's expedition was among the first of a series of forays that, by 1867, would cause Congress to authorize the study of the geological structures and mineral resources along the route of the transcontinental railroad. In the year Lander set out, the value of industrial products outstripped the

Fig. 27-8 Albert Bierstadt, *The Rocky Mountains, Lander's Peak*, 1863 (detail). Oil on canvas, 6 ft. 1½ in. × 10 ft. ¾ in. Metropolitan Museum of Art, New York.

value of agricultural products in the nation's economy for the first time.

Two years later, in May 1869, John Wesley Powell, professor of geology at Illinois State Normal University, led an expedition of nine men, in three small boats, into the canyonlands of the Green and Colorado Rivers on a trip fraught with hardships. Powell and five other members of the original crew survived the journey, emerging from the Grand Canyon on August 13, 1869. Powell subsequently made many more journeys to the region in 1870, 1871, 1872, and 1873. On the last, he was accompanied by Thomas Moran, whose paintings of Yellowstone had so moved Congress that they had declared it the world's first national park in 1872.

Fig. 27-9 *Noon-Day Rest in Marble Canyon*, after an original sketch by Thomas Moran, from J. W. Powell, *Exploration of the Colorado River of the West and its Tributaries*, 1875. Wood engraving, 6½ × 4⅜ in. The New York Public Library, New York. New York Public Library.

In 1875, the Government Printing Office published Powell's *Exploration of the Colorado River of the West and its Tributaries*, illustrated with over 30 works by Moran (**Fig. 27-9**; see also Fig. 10-14). The first half of the book is in large part a diary of the first expedition, but the second is a geological description of the physical features of the Colorado River canyons, including geological cross-sections showing features such as the strata of sandstones, shales, and limestones composing the Uinta mountains; long discussions and cross-section diagrams of the geological formations exposed in the Grand Canyon, including faults; and a long discourse on erosion. "We have looked back unnumbered centuries into the past," Powell concludes, "and seen the time when the schists in the depths of the Grand Cañon were first formed as sedimentary beds beneath the sea. . . . Thus ever the land and sea are changing; old lands are buried, and new lands are born, and with advancing periods new complexities of rock are found; new complexities of life evolved."

In 1871, the geologist Ferdinand Vandeveer Hayden led an expedition, consisting of a botanist, a zoologist, a mineralogist, a meteorologist, and a team of topographers, to the still largely unexplored region of Yellowstone to determine if the land held any potential for mineralogical or other development. As amazed as he was by what he saw, Hayden assured Congress that the Yellowstone region was unsuitable for farming, ranching, or mining, and warned of the dire consequences if they did not protect its geological wonders from private development.

In fact, industry was already having a dramatic impact on the environment worldwide. Industrialization was powered by fossil fuels, first by coal and then, in the first decade

Fig. 27-10 Thomas Anshutz, *Steamboat on the Ohio*, ca. 1896. Oil on canvas, 27¼ in. × 4 ft. ¼ in. Carnegie Museum of Art, Pittsburgh.
Patrons Art Fund: Gift of A. W. Mellon Educational and Charitable Trust. 57.36.

of the twentieth century, by oil and gas, all three of which tended to be used mostly to generate electricity. In London, coal smoke from industry famously combined with fog to create what was called "the Big Smoke." In 1873, smog killed over 700 people in London in a single week.

In the late nineteenth and early twentieth centuries, in the roughly 90 miles down the Ohio River from Pittsburgh, Pennsylvania to Wheeling, West Virginia, great steel mills and other heavy industry arose along the river banks due both to the abundance of nearby coal resources and to the ease of river transportation. Thomas Anshutz's *Steamboat on the Ohio* (**Fig. 27-10**) is testimony to this change. On the near bank, youthful swimmers frolic in the water. Across the river, a factory belches smoke. The contrast could not be more stark—the dark rowboat versus the bright steamship, the two nude boys standing vertically in opposition to the two tall smokestacks on the ship, a spot of red on the near bank, a bank of red dominating the far shore.

By the early decades of the twentieth century, the smoke associated with industrial growth in the Ohio Valley caused heavy fogs to form, coating buildings with soot. But when Joseph Pennell, one of the most innovative American printmakers of the period, depicted Pittsburgh itself (**Fig. 27-11**), his feelings about what he saw were ambiguous:

> Way down below the level road on which I stood, way on the opposite side of the river, Pittsburgh lies a dark, low mass, hemmed in by its rivers, lorded by its hills; in the hollow the smoke hangs so dense often I could not see the city at all, but once in a while a breeze falls on the town, and the great white skyscrapers come forth from the thick, black cloud, and the effect is glorious—the glorification of Work, for Pittsburgh is the work-city of the world.

Pollution seemed the inevitable consequence of labor and jobs—and was, it seemed at the time, worth the price.

Fig. 27-11 Joseph Pennell, *Pittsburgh, No. II*, 1909. Etching. The Cleveland Museum of Art.
Bequest of James Parmelee, 1940.782. Photo © Cleveland Museum of Art.

Contemporary photographer LaToya Ruby Frazier's work is testament to the fact that it is not worth the price. Frazier was born in 1982 in Braddock, Pennsylvania, a community 5 miles east of Pittsburgh that in the 1920s was a thriving steel town of some 20,000 people—by and large unskilled African-American steelworkers who arrived from the South during the Great Migration. But as the steel industry in the United States collapsed in the 1970s and 1980s, so did Braddock. Today, its population is just over 2,000. For over a decade Frazier has been photographing her family. Her original intention was to make a kind of family album that defied the stereotypes of poor, African-American families so prevalent in the media. But when, in 2009, her grandmother, with whom she was extremely close, died of pancreatic cancer and diabetes, she began to think about environmental degradation in the Braddock community and its impact on those still living there. In the art21 *New York Close Up* segment "LaToya Ruby Frazier Makes Moving Pictures," she describes *Self-Portrait (March 10 AM)* (**Fig. 27-12**), the first image resulting from this new awareness:

Fig. 27-12 LaToya Ruby Frazier, *Self-Portrait (March 10 AM)*, 2009. Gelatin silver print, 20 × 16 in.

> *Self-Portrait (March 10 AM)* was shot after I'd buried my grandmother in Pittsburgh and I felt like more than my soul went with her. . . . It became important for me to look at why we're dying. I've always been in the shadow of the steel mill . . . and if you live in proximity to the mill, you're really breathing in toxins. . . . My family happens to only be a springboard to talking about issues of class, health care, and environmental racism.

Frazier not only understands that the environment impacts the body—Braddock has the highest rates of infant mortality, asthma, and cancer in the country—but also that it is African Americans who are left to live in these degraded places. She has been particularly impressed by Mike Davis's 2006 book *Planet of Slums*, and sees in his description of Albania and Bulgaria in the 1980s and 1990s a situation analogous to Braddock: "Simultaneously," Davis writes, "there has been massive neglect, disinvestment, even abandonment of the crucial district infrastructures and factory-based social services, and as a result, older apartment blocks—indeed whole neighborhoods, and some entire cities—have regressed to slum conditions." Braddock is this place as well, and it represents, in miniature, a global condition.

Environmental Catastrophe

Most natural disasters are the product of humanity's tampering with the environment. The collapse or malfunction of manmade systems has inspired an apocalyptic vision that is the subject of a number of video and sculpture installations created over the course of the last decade by Matthew Ritchie (see Fig. 3-1). In the art21 *Exclusive* video "Matthew Ritchie: Apocalypse," he wonders, "What

Fig. 27-13 Matthew Ritchie, three stills from *The Iron City*, 2006. Continuous video loop with interactive audio, 1½ hours.

© Matthew Ritchie, Image Courtesy of Andrea Rosen Gallery, New York.

happened to that idea of a better world? . . . You think about apocalypse. That's the logic that the world will end and another is the world will be perfect. We seem to have ended up with just the one where it's just going to get worse and worse." In his animated video *The Iron City* (**Fig. 27-13**), the world is inundated by flood—at once evocative of the biblical flood and the great tsunami that overwhelmed Thailand in 2004. Through a round aperture evoking the porthole of a ship or the lens of a camera, the viewer is caught up in a fury of waves and debris. Bridges, piers, boats, and cargo containers are washed away. What are recognizably the NASA launch vehicle Saturn V's engine nozzles float by—another "leap for mankind" doomed to extinction. If Ritchie's vision is bleak, he also believes that out of destruction the possibility of beginning again arises.

Certainly no one caused the earthquake that resulted in the disastrous tsunami and subsequent nuclear power plant meltdown in Fukushima, Japan, in 2011. But the power plant's inability to survive the natural disaster, according to an independent Japanese commission, was wholly predictable. The culpability of the Japanese power companies and government regulators was the subject of a project by the Japanese six-person artist collective Chim↑Pom (the name is derived from the slang word *chimpo*, meaning "cock" or "prick"). Within a couple of months of the disaster, they had mounted an exhibition in Tokyo, the centerpiece of which was *Radiation-Exposed Flowers Harmony* (**Fig. 27-14**). The piece consisted of flowers and plants collected within a 20-mile radius of the Fukushima power plant, and then, with the aid of flower artist Junichi Kakizaki, transformed into a giant, monstrous *ikebana*. Japanese *ikebana* is more than simply what the West thinks of as flower arranging; it is the art of creating a living thing in which humanity's closeness to nature is celebrated and revered. In Chim↑Pom's installation, a Geiger counter sat beside the flowers, always reading a low level of radioactivity, and before the exhibition was over, the flowers had begun to rot.

Fig. 27-14 Chim↑Pom, in collaboration with Junichi Kakizaki, *Radiation-Exposed Flowers Harmony*, 2011. Flowers, plants, mixed media.

Photo: Kei Miyajima. Courtesy of MUJIN-TO Production, Tokyo. © Chim↑Pom.

Fig. 27-15 Alan Montgomery, *Deepwater Horizon*, 2011. Oil on canvas and print media, 18 × 15 in.
Courtesy of the artist.

Alan Montgomery's *Deepwater Horizon* (**Fig. 27-15**) is named for the oil spill in the Gulf of Mexico that flowed unabated from the Deepwater Horizon drilling rig operation for three months in 2010. By the time the flow was checked, an estimated 4.9 million barrels of crude oil had been released into the Gulf, killing scores of birds and fish, fouling wetlands and beaches, and destroying the economy of a region just barely recovering from the effects of Hurricane Katrina. Montgomery's painting is part of a series entitled *Sweetcrude*—literally, oil that has low levels of sulfur and hydrogen, and is thus much easier to refine, but, in Montgomery's view, the word reverberates with double meanings. His painting reflects this duality, luscious and painterly on the one hand, but reflecting the tragedy of the disaster on the other. The palm at the lower right seems to disintegrate before our eyes. At the top center, a bird's head rises above the incoming waves. And at the bottom left, a fallen angel struggles to even stand. In the very center, the painting becomes almost totally abstract, black with traces of color, like oil consuming color, beyond Montgomery's ability to articulate it.

In late August 2005, Hurricane Katrina made landfall along the coast of the Gulf of Mexico from Florida to Texas, causing the deaths of 1,836 people either during the hurricane or in the flooding that followed it. Most severely damaged was the city of New Orleans, where the levee system designed by the U.S. Army Corps of Engineers disastrously failed. Nearly 80 percent of the city was under water, and the government's response, directed by the Federal Emergency Management Agency (FEMA), was anything but immediate.

Three months after Katrina struck, acclaimed African-American filmmaker Spike Lee, together with cameraman Cliff Charles, made the first of eight trips to New Orleans, where they conducted interviews and shot footage for a film that would turn out to be four hours long by the time it ran on HBO in 2006. *When the*

Fig. 27-16 Spike Lee (director and producer), *When the Levees Broke: A Requiem in Four Acts*, 2006. Still. Film, 4 hrs.

Levees Broke: A Requiem in Four Acts (**Fig. 27-16**) won three Emmy Awards, a Peabody Award for excellence in broadcasting, and was included in the 2008 Whitney Biennial, an exhibition at New York's Whitney Museum of American Art designed to highlight leading new trends in American art every two years. Lee and his team spoke with nearly 100 people, including Louisiana governor Kathleen Blanco; New Orleans mayor Ray Nagin; local residents Phyllis Montana LeBlanc, Kimberly Polk, and Shelton "Shakespeare" Alexander; activists like Reverend Al Sharpton; journalists like CNN's Soledad O'Brien; and the musicians Wynton Marsalis, Terence Blanchard, and Kanye West. In the film, these interviews are intercut with photographs of and news stories about the disaster itself—FEMA director Michael Brown on CNN discounting reports that thousands were living like refugees inside the Superdome; President George W. Bush himself telling Brown, in all sincerity, "You're doing a heck of a job"; and Secretary of State Condoleezza Rice shopping for shoes in New York and taking in the Broadway musical *Spamalot* even as New Orleans was being inundated. The whole is a rapid-paced montage that even at its considerable length captivated museum-goers at the Whitney Biennial. In the end, the film's major theme is, in fact, very close to LaToya Ruby Frazier's indictment of Braddock, Pennsylvania: The inadequacy of the relief effort in New Orleans is a direct reflection of the indifference and prejudice of a country to those predominantly black and poor citizens whom it deems more or less expendable—another example of environmental racism.

One of the more stunning revelations of environmental racism associated with Katrina resulted from artist/activist Mel Chin's visit to the city soon after the hurricane. "I remember standing in the ruins of the Ninth Ward," Chin recounts in the art21 *Exclusive* video "Mel Chin: 'Paydirt,'" "and realizing as a creative individual that I felt hopeless and inadequate. And I was flooded by this terrible insecurity that being an artist was not enough to deal with the tragedy that was before me." But upon reflection he came to realize that "the disaster was in the soil before the disaster." What was in the soil was lead. It turns out that New Orleans is the second most contaminated city in the country, and that there is a proven connection between elevated levels of lead, which is a neurotoxin, in the blood and learning disabilities, lower-than-average intelligence, and violent behavior later in life when children reach adulthood.

Chin saw his first duty as an artist to be the abatement of lead in the soil of New Orleans. He thus

Fig. 27-17 Mel Chin, *Operation Paydirt/Fundred Dollar Bill Project*, 2006–ongoing.
Courtesy of the artist.

conceived of *Operation Paydirt/Fundred Dollar Bill Project* (**Fig. 27-17**), an ongoing collaboration, initiated by himself, between schoolchildren—those most affected by lead poisoning—and scientists. At the core of the project is a creative campaign advancing public education and community engagement through the creation of "fundreds"—original, personal interpretations of $100 bills hand-drawn by children from around the country—with the goal of raising $300 million in symbolic cash, representing the real $300 million price tag for lead abatement in New Orleans. Once Chin's goal is reached, he plans to deliver the fundreds to Congress—a populist plea for government funding. Indeed, the necessary technology is in place. In a protocol called TLC

(Treat-Lock-Cover), lead-contaminated soil is treated with a phosphate derived from fish bones, Apatite II. This phosphate binds to lead, neutralizing its toxicity. Implementation of the protocol is already under way in New Orleans and West Oakland, California. In May 2014, *Operation Paydirt* was given an award by the U.S. Department of Housing and Urban Development's Office of Healthy Homes and Lead Hazard Control for Best Community Engagement Initiative.

Among the most troubling of environmental disasters is climate change, a direct result of pollution and greenhouse gas emissions. In her preface to the catalogue of the 2010 workshop-exhibition *Rising Currents: Projects for New York's Waterfront* (see Fig. 14-8), Dr. Judith Rodin, president of the Rockefeller Foundation, began by noting:

> For millions of people around the world, the consequences of climate change will become increasingly evident and increasingly devastating. Higher temperatures will create more droughts and lead to the spread of heat-related diseases. Harsher storms will lead to flooding and the loss of crops and safe drinking water. All of this, taken together, will mean the destruction of homes, jobs, food, and—tragically—lives.

A series of three sculptures by artist Maya Lin (best known for having designed the Vietnam Veterans' Memorial in Washington, D.C.) calls attention to this same state of affairs, although more obliquely. Titled *Disappearing Bodies of Water*, the work consists of layers of white Vermont Danby marble carved to represent the diminution of three bodies of water between 1980 and today—Lake Chad, the Aral Sea, and the Arctic Sea ice mass (**Fig. 27-18**). The shape of each layer of marble is derived from satellite images of the shrinking bodies of water taken over the course of the last 33 years, the top layer representing the most recent expanse of the water's surface. The three pieces thus represent both physical and temporal change. As Lin says in the art21 *Exclusive* video "Maya Lin: Disappearing Bodies of Water," the

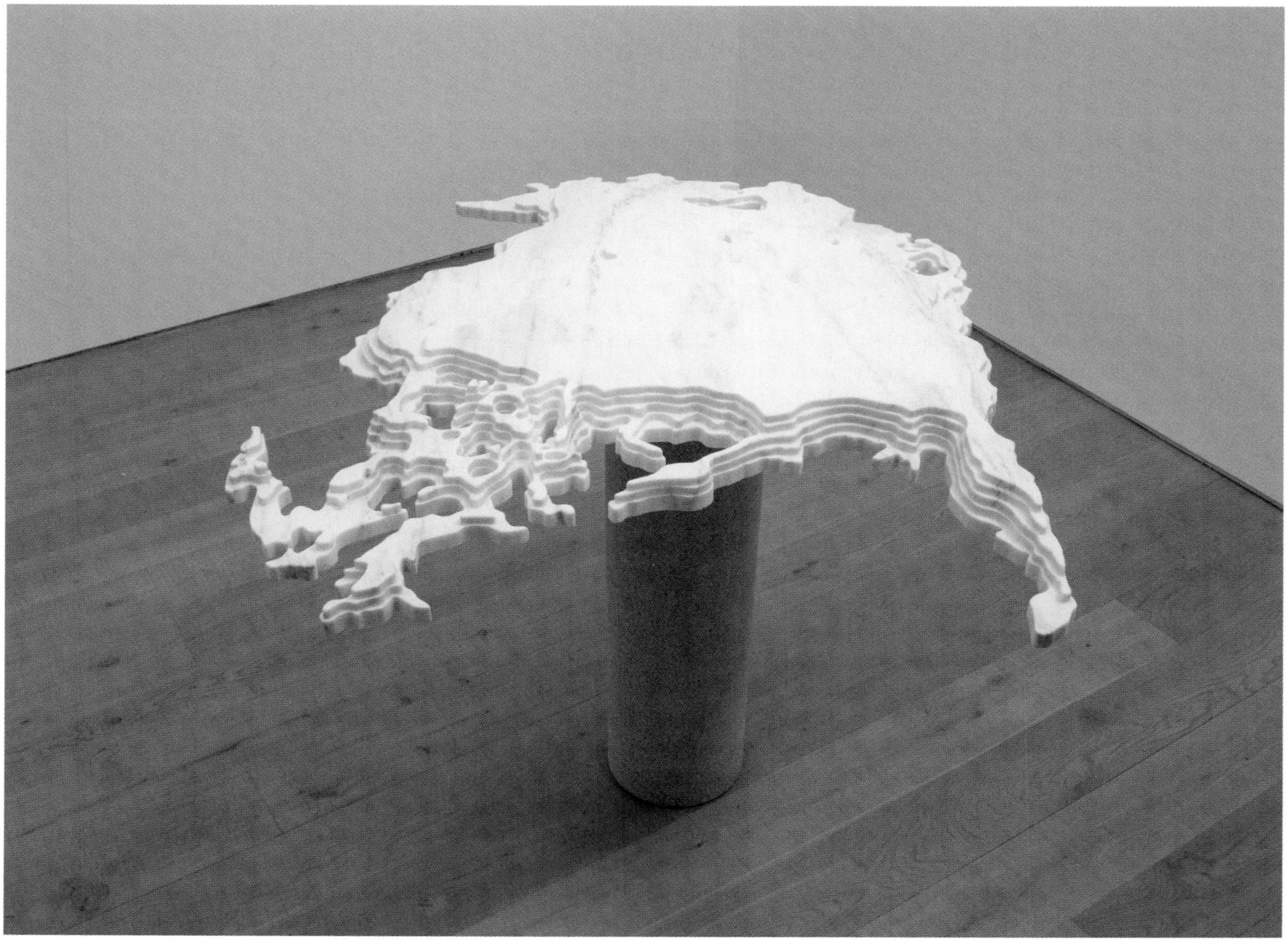

Fig. 27-18 Maya Lin, *Disappearing Bodies of Water: Arctic Ice*, 2013. Vermont Danby marble, granite base, 4 ft. × 46 in. × 4 ft. 4 in. Edition 1 of 3 + 1 AP.

Fig. 27-19 Mary Mattingly, *Triple Island*, 2013. Three interlocking buoyant platforms with gardens, livestock, and functional shelter spaces.
Courtesy of the artist.

works are designed to facilitate "the discussion of what we are doing to the environment."

In light of what seems like almost inevitable ecological doom, artist Mary Mattingly has created projects designed to show us how we might survive, and fundamental to her vision is her conviction that humanity must reduce its footprint on the planet. In 2009, in her *Waterpod Project*, she and three crew members lived aboard a 30-by-100-foot barge that drifted through New York's waterways for five months, docking at sites throughout the city's five boroughs so that citizens could explore it and consider its possibilities. Fitted out with living quarters, a greenhouse, a windmill, and a chicken coop, it was completely self-sustaining.

In late July 2013, Mattingly took up residence in her *Triple Island* (**Fig. 27-19**) on a barren stretch of Manhattan waterfront facing the East River that had served as a collection site for destroyed and abandoned automobiles after Hurricane Sandy. It consisted of a living space, a community garden, and a greenhouse, each on its own separate 16-by16-foot island, and each constructed on floatable 55-gallon drums should the river rise as it did during the hurricane of October 2012. Like the *Waterpod Project*, *Triple Island* was designed to be self-sustaining, depending on regenerative natural systems, such as composting, rainwater collection, and localized power sources, including a solar power system. Several different volunteers lived in the space across the four months to November 2013. "On the one hand," Mattingly explains in the art21 *New York Close Up* segment "Mary Mattingly's Waterfront Development," "I want *Triple Island* to be sculptural. And on the other hand, it really needs people to exist in the space to come alive." If the sculpture is a prototype and catalyst for alternative methods of agriculture and housing in the face of an apocalyptic future, it is possible, Mattingly's project suggests, to live off the grid even on the densely populated Lower East Side of Manhattan. Thus, the work is also symbolic of a kind of optimism about how people can come together in a collaborative, grassroots way to survive.

Fig. 27-20 Don Gray, *Stone #2*, from the series *Nine Stones*, 2009. Oil on panel, 23 × 23 in.

Art, the Environment, and the Longer View

How have artists come to appreciate the landscape and environment from a longer or deeper point of view?

One day in 2009, as painter Don Gray was getting out of his car in a small gravel parking lot at a nature preserve in the Grande Ronde Valley in northeastern Oregon, his attention was drawn to the basalt boulders evenly spaced around the edge of the space. Although they were entirely ordinary—and, in terms of the geology of the Columbia River Plateau, abundant to the point of composing almost the entire upper mantle of the region—Gray was suddenly struck by their presence. In fact, he realized that this stone, the product of one of the largest-ever "flood" lava flows, in which magma flows out of vents in the earth's crust rather than erupting, occurring some 15 to 17 million years ago, connected the present moment to the remote past at a scale that was virtually unimaginable. He began to think of the stones as part of a larger "living organism," in the manner that the indigenous peoples of the region think of the entire earth as a living organism. "It occurred to me," he says, "that the only reason we think of a rock as inanimate is because its lifespan is unimaginably longer than our own. I sensed the life in these stones as metaphors of the living earth." Gray decided to paint a "portrait" of each stone, resulting in a series of paintings titled *Nine Stones* (**Fig. 27-20**). The play of light in the paintings conveys a sense of time passing in the present, which contrasts dramatically with the gradual transformation of the landscape of the Grande Ronde Valley over millions of years, but this longer or deeper view into the history of the landscape and environment has interesting implications for artists as they contemplate the world that surrounds them.

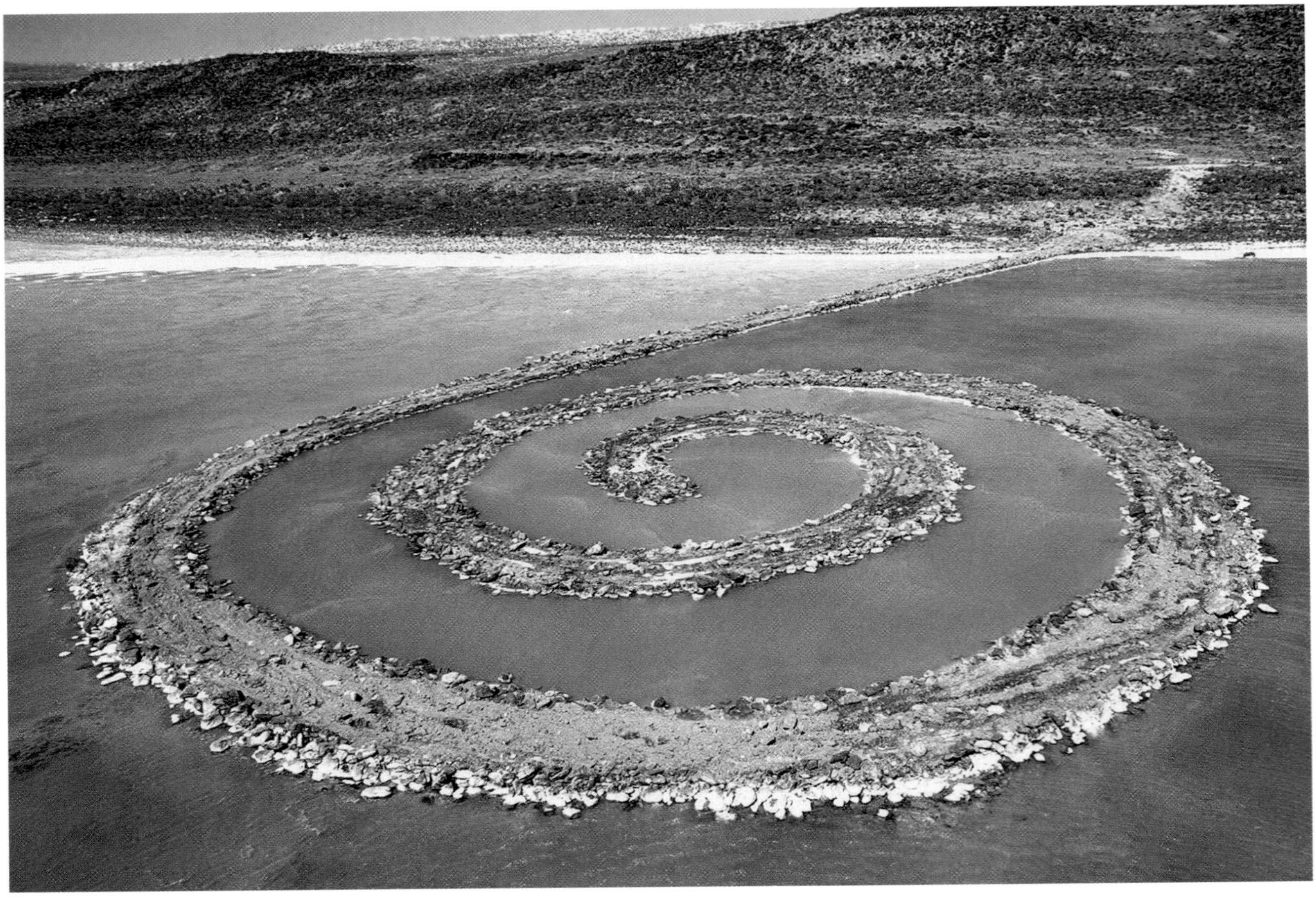

Fig. 27-21 Robert Smithson, *Spiral Jetty*, Great Salt Lake, Utah, April 1970. Black rock, salt crystals, earth, red water (algae), 3 ft. 6 in. × 15 ft. × 1,500 ft.

Collection: Dia Art Foundation, New York. Courtesy James Cohan Gallery, New York and Shanghai. Art © Holt Smithson Foundation/ Licensed by VAGA, New York.

Robert Smithson was first attracted to the site of *Spiral Jetty* (**Fig. 27-21**; see also Fig. 12-26) when he saw a number of abandoned oil rigs, dilapidated piers and shacks, and "countless bits of wreckage" at Rozel Point, just south of where he would come to build *Spiral Jetty* itself. "A great pleasure arose," he wrote, "from seeing all those incoherent structures. This site gave evidence of a succession of man-made systems mired in abandoned hopes." In other words, they represented the forces of human-induced environmental entropy.

Entropy was first demonstrated in the middle of the nineteenth century in the second law of thermodynamics which shows that, when energy is transformed from one form to another, some irrecoverable loss (entropy) occurs. For Smithson, the Humpty Dumpty nursery rhyme is "a nice succinct definition of entropy": Once he has had his great fall, all the king's men cannot put Humpty together again. In his essay "A Tour of the Monuments of Passaic, New Jersey," which appeared in *Artforum* in December 1967, Smithson provides another demonstration of entropy:

> Picture in your mind's eye the sand box divided in half with black sand on one side and white sand on the other. We take a child and have him run hundreds of times clockwise in the box until the sand gets mixed and begins to turn grey; after that we have him run anti-clockwise, but the result will not be a restoration of the original division but a greater degree of greyness and an increase in entropy.

In a 1971 interview, conducted after *Spiral Jetty* was completed, Smithson explained the work this way:

> The main objective is to make something massive and physical enough so that it can interact with those things [climate and its changes] and go through all kinds of modifications. If a work has sufficient physicality, any kind of natural change would tend to enhance the work. Geology has its own kind of entropy, that has to do with sediment mixtures. Sediment plays a part in my work. . . . I'm interested in collaborating with entropy.

Spiral Jetty collaborates with entropy by providing a place where, over time, the human works will inevitably succumb to the persistence of natural processes.

But most human interventions in the landscape are not as benign as Smithson's. As the year 2008 was drawing to a close, not a month before Barack Obama would be inaugurated the 44th President of the United States, the outgoing administration of President George W. Bush put 150,000 acres of public land in the Utah's red-rock country up for auction with the intention of opening otherwise pristine wilderness lands to oil and gas exploration. Posing as a bidder, University of Utah student Tim DeChristopher bid for and won 14 parcels, consisting of some 22,000 acres of land near Arches National Park and Labyrinth Canyon, worth $1.8 million. But DeChristopher had no money, a fact that soon became apparent. He was escorted out of the auction by Federal agents and taken into custody. He was subsequently indicted, on April 1, 2009, on two felony counts for violation of the Federal Onshore Oil and Gas Leasing Reform Act and making false statements.

As he awaited trial, his situation came to the attention of Los Angeles-based artist Andrea Bowers, whose work since the late 1990s has focused on nonviolent civil disobedience. *United States v. Tim DeChristopher* (**Fig. 27-22**) is a 16-minute video that alternates between pans across the sometimes stunning desert landscape of the red-rock country, relatively close-up shots of DeChristopher telling his story, and Bowers herself, at first a tiny speck in the distance, walking into the foreground, carrying a slate on which she writes the number of the particular parcel of land behind her that DeChristopher had tried to purchase. Bowers's intrusion into the video footage is crucial, because it helps to establish the vast scale of the space behind her, which, in the flatness of the screen, seems otherwise almost dimensionless, and it underscores just how much land DeChristopher's activism aimed to preserve.

DeChristopher was convicted on both counts in July 2011, sentenced to two years in prison (he served 21 months), and ordered to pay a $10,000 fine. But DeChristopher's actions had drawn attention to what Secretary of the Interior Ken Salazar, soon after DeChristopher's arrest, determined to be an illegal sale, citing the Bureau of Land Management's violation of environmental laws protecting air quality and historic preservation. The sale of 77 of the original 116 parcels was voided. DeChristopher's was a political act, and Bowers's video an equally political work of art, both of which take a long view of the necessity of preserving the planet.

Fig. 27-22 Andrea Bowers, *United States v. Tim DeChristopher*, 2010. Single-channel HD video, color with sound, 16 min. 15 sec. looped. Utah Museum of Fine Arts.
Courtesy of Susanne Vielmetter, Los Angeles Projects.

THE CRITICAL PROCESS

Thinking about Science, Technology, and the Environment

Since 2005, New York artist David Brooks has worked as a volunteer field team member with conservation biologist Dr. Nathan Lujan in Ecuador, Peru, and Venezuela, studying the evolution of the local armored catfish populations. Their association is documented in the art21 *New York Close Up* segment "David Brooks Is in His Element." Dr. Lujan studies small changes in the tooth structure of the catfish, of which there are over 850 known species. In Brooks's words, seeing these changes is "almost like witnessing evolution itself." Thus, for Brooks, "to look at things that exist in sort of biological spheres through deep-time scenarios is actually quite a fantastic, wondrous experience."

Brooks's sense of "deep" biological time goes a long way toward explaining his sculpture *Imbroglios (A Phylogenetic Tree, from Homo Sapiens to Megalops Atlanticus)* (**Fig. 27-23**). The piece is a three-dimensional representation of a phylogenetic tree, a creation of Western science designed to diagram evolutionary relationships between species. As is usual practice, *Homo sapiens*—humans, of course—stands at the top of the tree in its rightful place as viewer. At the bottom of the tree is *Megalops atlanticus*, the Atlantic tarpon. Between the two, however, is the structure of a genetic tree that remains unpopulated and blank. The question Brooks raises is this: What is the relationship between the tarpon and humankind?

As it turns out, the tarpon is a close relative of the very first predatory fish that evolved in the sea. It is a sort of living fossil. It also actually breathes air through a bladder that opens when it surfaces—a habit that announces its presence to its own major predator, inshore sport fishermen who relish the fight with a fish that can weigh up to 200 pounds in waters just a few feet deep.

If it is hard to imagine the genetic connection between the tarpon and *Homo sapiens*, then does Brooks's installation suggest some other kind of connection? What does he mean by titling his work *Imbroglios*? While not extinct, tarpon populations have dramatically dwindled over the course of the last century. What, in "deep" biological time, has evolved, or not?

Fig. 27-23 David Brooks, *Imbroglios (A Phylogenetic Tree, from Homo Sapiens to Megalops Atlanticus)*, 2012. Fiberglass, gelcoat, MDF, pencil, hardware, 5 × 12 × 21 ft.

Thinking Back

27.1 Describe how technological innovation is reflected in the arts.

What transformation of human vision did J. M. W. Turner respond to in his painting *Rain, Steam, and Speed*? Developments and innovations in architecture, such as the Pont du Gard, have consistently been driven by scientific and technological advances. What technological feat is represented by Kansai International Airport? What technological innovation was used by the Nok to create their sculptural figures? What advances to ceramic production did the Industrial Revolution introduce?

27.2 Describe some of the ways that artists have helped to shape public perception of the environment.

The expeditionary forces of Colonel Frederick W. Lander and geologist Ferdinand Vandeveer Hayden in the nineteenth century were designed to study the geological structures and mineral resources of the American West. What did Hayden's survey find? What was the outcome of his expedition? How did the geologist John Wesley Powell react to the Grand Canyon?

Industry has had an enormous impact on the environment. From the outset, the industrial development of the Ohio Valley, from Pittsburgh to Wheeling, West Virginia, was seen as a mixed blessing. How did Thomas Anshutz and Joseph Pennell convey their ambivalence? Why is contemporary photographer LaToya Ruby Frazier anything but ambivalent?

Spike Lee and Mel Chin have reacted to Hurricane Katrina and its devastating impact on New Orleans in different ways. What point of view, however, do they share? In the face of climate change, and the massive environmental changes that it suggests, art has taken an increasingly apocalyptic turn. What do Matthew Ritchie and the Japanese collective Chim↑Pom have in common? A common theme running through this art is the need to educate the broader public. What do Maya Lin and Mary Mattingly share in these terms?

27.3 Explain how some artists have approached the landscape and environment from a longer or deeper point of view.

Many artists take a longer view of the environment. What did the artist Don Gray see in the basalt rocks of the Grande Ronde Valley? What is entropy? What examples did Robert Smithson use to define it? What is the nature of the politics behind Andrea Bowers's *United States v. Tim DeChristopher*? How does her video convey the scale of DeChristopher's activism?

The Critical Process

Thinking Some More about the Chapter Questions

CHAPTER 1 Andy Warhol's *Race Riot*, 1963.

Warhol seems most interested in the second traditional role of the artist: to give visible or tangible form to ideas, philosophies, or feelings. He is clearly disturbed by the events in Birmingham. By depicting the attack on Martin Luther King, Jr., in the traditional red, white, and blue colors of the American flag, he suggests that these events are not just a local issue but also a national one. Thus, to a certain degree, he also reveals a hidden truth about the events: All Americans are implicated in Bull Connor's actions. Perhaps he also wants us to see the world in a new way, to imagine a world without racism. The second red panel underscores the violence and anger of the scene. As horrifying as the events are, it is possible to imagine a viewer offended not by the police actions but by Warhol's depiction of them, his willingness to treat such events as "art."

CHAPTER 2 Two Representations of *Treaty Signing at Medicine Lodge Creek.*

Taylor's version of the events is the more representational by traditional Western standards, Howling Wolf's the more abstract. But Howling Wolf's version contains much more accurate information. Taylor's scene could be anywhere. In contrast, by portraying the confluence of Medicine Lodge Creek and the Arkansas River, Howling Wolf describes the exact location of the signing ceremony. Taylor focuses his attention on the U.S. government officials at the center of the picture, but relegates the Native Americans present to the periphery. From Taylor's ethnocentric perspective, the identities of the Native Americans present are of no interest. In contrast, Howling Wolf's aerial view shows all those present, including women, equally. Each person present is identified by the decoration of the dress and tipis. Women are valued and important members of the society. Their absence in Taylor's work suggests that women have no place at important events. In fact, it is possible to argue that Taylor's drawing is about hierarchy and power, while Howling Wolf's is about equality and cooperation.

CHAPTER 3 *Zeus*, or *Poseidon*, ca. 460 BCE, and Robert Mapplethorpe's *Lisa Lyon*, 1982.

In the Greek bronze, the submission of the male body to the discipline of geometry is especially evident in the definition of the god's chest and stomach muscles, which have been sculpted with great attention to detail, and in the extraordinary horizontality of the outstretched left arm. Lyon presents herself to the viewer in the same terms. Rather than a passive object of display, Lyon is an active athlete. By presenting herself in this way, Lyon asserts the power of the female and implicitly argues that the female body has been "conditioned" not so much by physical limitations as by culture.

CHAPTER 4 Isaac Julien's *Ten Thousand Waves*, 2010.

Three different means of representing space co-exist in Julien's work: the viewer experiences his work in two, three, and four dimensions. If the invention of linear perspective in the fifteenth century provided artists with the means to represent three-dimensional space convincingly on a two-dimensional surface, then Julien's multi-screen video projections, which are individually two-dimensional, suggest the possibility of representing four-dimensional space—that is, a space–time continuum—in the three-dimensional setting of the gallery. The viewer moves among these spaces in a kind of flow, as the figures in the videos migrate from one space to another, and as we migrate among them. Time is experienced as flux, change. The image lacks stability. In this way, Julien might be said to capture the speed and instability of modern life itself. And, as we follow the different stories—from pre-Revolutionary Shanghai to Fujian Province, to Mao's Cultural Revolution, to present-day China—the linear flow of time collapses so that we feel all of these different historical times simultaneously, just as the digital present collapses time and space into a new global present.

CHAPTER 5 Katharina Grosse's *Cincy*, 2006.

The free-flowing color of Grosse's work stands in stark contrast to the geometrical linearity of the building with its gray concrete and black aluminum-paneled facade. As if in defiance of Hadid's refinement, Grosse has piled dirt, itself painted in iridescent greens and yellows, beneath the column centered in the lobby windows. The exuberance of her gestures is to Hadid's building as Delacroix's study for *The Death of Sardanapalus* (see Fig. 3-23) is to Jacques-Louis David's study for the *The Death of Socrates* (see Fig. 3-21).

CHAPTER 6 Bill Viola's *Room for St. John of the Cross*, 1983.

The simple geometric architecture of the small cell contrasts dramatically with the wild natural beauty of the scene on the large screen. The former is closed and contained, classically calm, the latter open and chaotic, romantically wild. The former is still and quiet, the latter active and dynamic. The larger room, lit only by the screen image, seems dark and foreboding. The cell, lit by a soft yellow light, seems inviting. Time is a factor in terms of our experience of the work. If we approach the cell, our view of the screen is lost. When we stand back from the cell, the rapid movement on the screen disrupts our ability to pay attention to the scene in the cell. The meditative space of the cell stands in stark contrast to the turbulent world around it. And yet the cell represents captivity, the larger room freedom, both real freedom and the freedom of imaginative flight.

CHAPTER 7 Claude Monet's *The Railroad Bridge, Argenteuil*, 1874.

Monet uses one-point linear perspective to create the bridge. A grid-like geometry is established where the bridge's piers cross the horizon and the far riverbank. The wooden support structure under the bridge echoes the overall structure of grid and diagonals. In this the picture is classical. But countering this geometry is the single expression of the sail, a curve echoed in the implied line that marks the edge of the bushes at the top right. A sense of opposition is created by the alternating rhythm of light to dark established by the bridge's piers and in the complementary color scheme of orange and blue in both the water and the smoke above. The almost perfect symmetrical balance of the painting's grid structure is countered by the asymmetrical balance of the composition as a whole (its weight seems to fall heavily to the right). There are two points of emphasis, the bridge and the boat. We seem to be witness to the conflicting forces of nature and civilization.

CHAPTER 8 Frank Auerbach's *Head of Catherine Lampert VI,* 1979–80.

The energy of both sitter and artist is captured not only in the quick, almost furious movement of Auerbach's line but also in the almost three-dimensional sense of depth of the image resulting from repeated erasures and redrawing. As in Delacroix's drawing for *The Death of Sardanapalus* (see Fig. 3-23), this suggests the volatility of his sitter's personality but, just as in his final painting Delacroix presents Sardanapalus in quiet acceptance of the chaos surrounding him, Auerbach, especially in the white planes of Lampert's face and the apparently unerased certainty with which he has drawn her nose, presents her not just in repose, but as possessing a certain steadfastness, which might be said to mirror her willingness to return again and again to pose for the artist.

CHAPTER 9 Fred Tomaselli's *Airborne Event,* 2003.

Almost by definition, the medium of collage, which Tomaselli can be said to take almost to new heights, suggests the artificiality of our perceived environment, a world in which almost all visual experience is constructed and manipulated by others, a world in which our "highs" are no longer naturally, but instead artificially, induced. If in Fra Andrea Pozzo's *The Glorification of St. Ignatius* (see Fig. 9-7) St. Ignatius soars toward heaven, in the contemporary world, Tomaselli suggests, such religious transcendence is increasingly only attainable by artificial (i.e., drug-induced) means.

CHAPTER 10 Andy Warhol's *Marilyn Monroe,* 1967, and *San Francisco Silverspot,* 1983.

Marilyn Monroe died a suicide in 1963, as much an endangered species as the Silverspot butterfly: a human being whose identity had been stripped, reducing her to an "image," whose real personality and humanity meant almost nothing to anyone. But Warhol understands that being transformed into a media image might have its positive effects as well: that where Monroe was destroyed by Hollywood image-making, the Silverspot might be saved. His color makes Monroe and the butterfly garish, but it draws attention to the plight of both. And both are images that challenge their viewers to change, images that confront our collective indifference.

CHAPTER 11 Jeff Wall's *A Sudden Gust of Wind (after Hokusai),* 1993.

The greatest transformation is that the pastoral world of the Hokusai print has been replaced by what appears to be an industrial wasteland. The businessmen, of course, have created this landscape. No mountain could be seen in Wall's work, even if there were one. The sky is thick with what appears to be pollution. There is nothing spiritual about this place. Wall's photograph is like a "still" from a motion picture. It implies that we are in the midst of a story. But what story? How can we ever know what is "really" happening here? Knowing that Wall has completely fabricated the scene, we recognize that, in fact, nothing is "really" happening here. Wall's is a world of complete illusion, in which meaning flies away as surely as the papers on a sudden gust of wind.

CHAPTER 12 Christo's *Over the River, Project for the Arkansas River, State of Colorado,* 2010.

Because viewers' experiences of *Over the River* will change depending on their point of view—above it, below it, at different points down the river—it is a kind of sculpture in-the-round. As in Anish Kapoor's *Cloud Gate* (see Fig. 12-22), viewers can experience the piece both from outside and inside it, and it is designed, like *Cloud Gate,* to direct viewers' attention to the larger environment that surrounds it. But unlike Kapoor's, Christo's piece is temporary. For him, the debate surrounding its installation—especially the questions it forces the community to confront about the nature of art and aesthetic experience—are paramount. And the work will live on, perhaps more powerfully than if it were permanent, as a kind of legend—"Once upon a time. . . ."

CHAPTER 13 Institute for Figuring, *Crochet Coral Reef* project, 2005–ongoing.

In Western culture, geometry and mathematics have traditionally been considered male domains (see the Greek treatment of the male body; see Fig. 4-29). But, of course, it is males who have largely controlled political and economic power as the Great Barrier Reef has succumbed to their environmental policies—or their environmental indifference. Crochet is transformed here into an act of political commentary and community protest. The work is a visual record of its time and place, but one of ominous portent.

CHAPTER 14 Taos Pueblo, 1000–1450, and Moshe Safdie's Habitat, 1967.

The walls of Safdie's Habitat abut the walls of adjoining units, as in Native American pueblos, just as Safdie also uses the roofs of units to provide outdoor living space for the unit above. Safdie's Habitat is, however, decidedly modern in its look, creating a sense of visual variety absent in Native American pueblo design. This variety is made possible by technological advancements, specifically the use of reinforced concrete and steel cable construction techniques. Like Le Corbusier's Domino Housing Project, Safdie's design is modular and almost infinitely expandable, both sideways and upward. Any combination of windows and walls can be hung on the frame. Internal divisions can be designed in an endless variety of ways. It differs from Le Corbusier's Project in the variety of elevations it presents to the viewer despite the uniformity of its parts, creating a sense of the individuality of each unit within the broader community.

CHAPTER 15 Mika Tajima's *A Facility Based on Change,* 2011.

In its focus on the uniformity and sterility of Herman Miller's Action Office, Tajima's critique of its modernist aesthetic implicitly valorizes a more open, pluralistic, and freeform workplace—a workplace that might be called postmodern. The geometrical regularity of modernism is a necessary byproduct of the manufacturing process, which by definition makes the same thing, in assembly-line fashion, again and again. While a single example of such a product might be thought of as "beautiful," as it proliferates into a vast sea of office uniformity, it loses its appeal. One can imagine the workplace literally moving out of the "office" into a mobile, digital environment. Such versatility is, of course, the concept driving Knoll's Toboggan Chair (see Fig. 15-1), but one can imagine a work environment filled with these chairs quickly looking just as sterile and monotonous as Herman Miller's Action Office.

CHAPTER 20 Olafur Eliasson's *The Weather Project,* 2003.

The questions raised by Eliasson's work about the function of art today and the place of the museum will only be answered in the future, through your own experiences. But they invite you, as a viewer and participant in the world of art, to consider such questions every time you visit a museum or gallery. The idea is to end by asking questions, not answering them: Why am I here, in the museum? you should wonder. Why does it matter? What have I learned about who we are as humans? Why am I drawn to this space? to this work? to this line, or color, or form?

CHAPTER 21 Bill Viola's *The Reflecting Pool,* 1977–79.

In *The Mérode Altarpiece* (see Fig. 9-14), Mary's role as a vessel for the Incarnation of God is embodied in the water pot that hangs in the niche above the Archangel Gabriel's head. Water is, of course, associated with the womb, the source of life itself. As Viola hangs above the pool, he assumes a fetal position, suggesting the immanence of his own rebirth. In the *Diamond Sutra* (see Fig. 21-5), the Buddha is shown in dialogue with his disciple, the Elder Subhuti, in which the Buddha addresses the nature of perception, the point being that our limited understanding of the nature of reality and enlightenment—our attachment to the world of mere appearance—blinds us to higher truths. This is precisely the point of Viola's *The Reflecting Pool*: We see the outside world reflected in the pool, but our vision is unable to penetrate the surface to see what lies in its depths. The quest to see below the surface of things is comparable, in Christianity, to St. John of the Cross' "journey upon the spiritual road" to the union of love with God, a private journey in darkness seeking light, in turn comparable to the achievement of truth through meditation described by Cold Mountain and imaged, abstractly, in Brice Marden's painting *Cold Mountain 6 (Bridge)* (see Fig. 21-18).

CHAPTER 22 Janine Antoni and Stephen Petronio's *Honey Baby*, 2013.

Lazarus is Lazarus of Bethany, a town near Jerusalem, who, as told in chapter 11 of the Gospel of St. John, was restored to life by Jesus four days after his death, and this miracle represents, for John, Jesus' power over even the greatest of humanity's enemies—death itself. In the video *Honey Baby*, which grew out of Antoni and Petronio's collaboration, they recreated the last segment of *Like Lazarus Did*, but in a uterine-like sculptural space that freed dancer Nick Sciscione from the constraints of the stage. They wanted to create a piece "where one could not quite feel gravity," Antoni explains. "Having had a child," Antoni says, "it's miraculous that a body can grow another body, that one body grows from the nutrients of another body." It is that miracle—the cycle of life as one life begets another—that *Honey Baby* celebrates.

CHAPTER 23 Jan Toorop's poster for *Delftsche Slaolie*, 1894.

Toorop's poster, made in the last decade of the nineteenth century, embodies the ambiguous place in which women found themselves as the twentieth century approached, as their domestic roles confronted their sensual beings. They simultaneously represented purity and sexuality (or at least the possibility of both). The male (the man of the house?) is the implicit viewer of this scene, but these women are oblivious to his presence, suggesting the growing independence of women. In fact, the poster possesses very real lesbian overtones. But, especially in the context of food and its preparation—i.e., the gratification of appetite—the poster is designed to sell self-indulgence.

CHAPTER 24 Ana Mendieta's *Silueta Works in Mexico*, 1973–77.

Mendieta possesses a certain double identity—at once Cuban, with the attendant identification with *Santería* traditions, and American, with the attendant identification with, among other things, the intellectual traditions of graduate education in art and art history at the University of Iowa. But she is equally alienated from her own self-identification with nature, and her works are something of an attempt to reunify herself with the natural world. Her *silueta* at the beach, soon overcome by wave action and obliterated, actually ties her to the rhythms of the sea, and by extension nature. The beach is a zone that mediates between two opposites. As the *silueta* disappears, it is, in this sense, an image of sacrifice that ties her back to *santería* as well.

CHAPTER 25 Dread Scott's *What Is the Proper Way to Display a U.S. Flag?*, 1988.

Perhaps nothing evokes nationalist feeling more than the flag itself, but the photographs of flag-draped coffins and the image of South Koreans burning the American flag on the wall are purposefully inflammatory. Is the sacrifice of soldiers in the service of their country noble or foolish? Were the South Koreans justified in their antipathy toward the United States? These are, of course, the questions that Scott is asking the public to address in the ledger beneath the photograph. But, he asks further, what is more important to you, your right to free speech or your respect for the flag—both of which are sources of nationalist sentiment? In other words, Scott presents us with choices in this work that make us uncomfortable—choices we might even "dread." Scott, of course, also knew that the audience for his work would be composed of a great many white people, and if they were to label his work "unAmerican," as many would, then, he asks, where does that position him as an African American?

CHAPTER 26 Jenny Holzer's *Thorax*, 2008.

Holzer's use of lush color draws us into the work to confront issues with which we might otherwise be uncomfortable. In that sense, color exercises power over the viewer in a way that paradoxically the stark, white, concrete cell does in Edmund Clark's *Camp Five, Detainee's Cell* (see Fig. 26-1). But the regular and repetitive order defines both in formal terms and suggests the regimen of discipline that is at work. Holzer's difficulty lies in the fact that she, too, must confront what she abhors, and in so doing wrest power from it.

CHAPTER 27 David Brooks's *Imbroglios*, 2012.

Brook's phylogenetic tree suggests not so much the connection of *Homo sapiens* to the emergence of mammals out of the sea eons ago as it does the place of predatory behavior in the genetic make-up of so many species. An imbroglio, after all, is a difficult situation often complicated by misunderstanding, disagreement, or bitterness, and as we hunt the fish to the point of extinction, how likely are we to check our predatory instincts? The continuation of predatory behavior undermines the very idea of evolution. Have we really "evolved" so much? Are we more like tarpons than we might think?

Glossary

Words appearing in *italics* in the definitions are also defined in the glossary.

absolute symmetry Term used when each half of a composition is exactly the same. (page 134)

abstract In art, the rendering of images and objects in a stylized or simplified way, so that though they remain recognizable, their formal or expressive aspects are emphasized. Compare both *representational* and *nonobjective art*. (page 33)

Abstract Expressionism A painting style of the late 1940s and early 1950s, predominantly American, characterized by its rendering of expressive content by *abstract* or *nonobjective* means. (page 507)

acropolis The elevated site above an ancient Greek city, conceived as the center of civic life. (page 335)

acrylic A plastic resin that, when mixed with water and pigment, forms an inorganic and quick-drying paint *medium*. (page 203)

actual weight As opposed to *visual weight*, the physical weight of material in pounds. (page 134)

additive process (1) In color, the fact that when different *hues* of colored light are combined, the resulting mixture is higher in key than the original hues and brighter as well, and as more and more hues are added, the resulting mixture is closer and closer to white. (2) In sculpture, the process in which form is built up, shaped, and enlarged by the addition of materials, as distinguished from *subtractive* sculptural processes, such as carving. (pages 101, 274)

adobe A mixture of earth, water, and straw formed into sundried mud bricks. (page 334)

aerial perspective See *atmospheric perspective*. (page 89)

aesthetic Our sense of what is beautiful. (page 10)

afocal Without any focal points. (page 141)

agency The capacity of a thing to exert power or act in the world. (page 605)

ambulatory A covered walkway, especially around the *apse* of a church. (page 418)

amphitheater A building type invented by the Romans (literally meaning a "double theater"), in which two semicircular theaters are brought face to face. (page 338)

analogous colors Pairs of colors, such as yellow and orange, that are adjacent to each other on the *color wheel*. (page 102)

anamorphic Referring to a drawing that presents a distorted image which appears in natural form when viewed at a raking angle. (page 14)

animation In film, the process of sequencing still images in rapid succession to give the effect of live motion. (page 260)

animism The belief in the existence of souls and the conviction that nonhuman things can also be endowed with a soul. (page 19)

apartheid Literally "separateness" in Afrikaans, the dialect of Dutch spoken by Afrikaners, apartheid was the enforced separation of black and white residents of South Africa until 1994. (page 178)

aperture The opening that determines the quantity of light admitted by a camera lens. (page 250)

apse A semicircular recess placed, in a Christian church, at the end of the *nave*. (page 340)

aquatint An *intaglio* printmaking process in which the acid bites around powdered particles of resin, resulting in a *print* with a granular appearance. The resulting *print* is also called an aquatint. (page 230)

arbitrary color Color that has no *realistic* or natural relation to the object that is depicted, as in a blue horse or a purple cow, but that may have emotional or expressive significance. (page 112)

architrave In architecture, the lintel, or horizontal, weight-bearing beam, that forms the base of the *entablature*. (page 336)

Art Deco A popular art and design style of the 1920s and 1930s associated with the 1925 Exposition Internationale des Arts Décoratifs et Industriels Modernes in Paris and characterized by its integration of organic and geometric forms. (page 371)

Art Nouveau The art and design style characterized by undulating, curvilinear, and organic forms that dominated popular culture at the turn of the century, and that achieved particular success at the 1900 International Exposition in Paris. (page 369)

assemblage An *additive* sculptural process in which various and diverse elements and objects are combined. (page 286)

asymmetrical balance Balance achieved in a composition when neither side reflects or mirrors the other. (page 136)

atmospheric perspective A technique, often employed in landscape painting, designed to suggest three-dimensional space in the two-dimensional space of the picture plane, and in which forms and objects distant from the viewer become less distinct, often bluer or cooler in color, and contrast among the various distant elements is greatly reduced. (page 89)

auteurs Film directors who are considered the "authors" of their work. (page 260)

avant-garde From the French, "advance guard," or "vanguard"—those whose innovations are in advance of their time. (page 23)

balance The even distribution of weight, either *actual weight* or *visual weight*, in a composition. (page 134)

balloon-frame Another name for *wood-frame* construction that came into usage because early skeptics believed that houses built in this manner would explode like balloons. (page 343)

Baroque A dominant style of art in Europe in the seventeenth century, characterized by its theatrical, or dramatic, use of light and color, by its ornate forms, and by its disregard for classical principles of composition. (page 464)

barrel vault A masonry roof constructed on the principle of the arch, that is, in essence, a continuous series of arches, one behind the other. (page 337)

basilica In Roman architecture, a rectangular public building, entered through one of the long sides. In Christian architecture, a church loosely based on the Roman design, but entered through one of the short ends, with an *apse* at the other end. (page 420)

Bauhaus A German school of design, founded by Walter Gropius in 1919 and closed by Hitler in 1933. (page 374)

bilateral symmetry Term used when the overall effect of a composition is one of *absolute symmetry*, even though there are clear discrepancies side to side. (page 134)

binder In a *medium*, the substance that holds *pigments* together. (page 165)

buon fresco See *fresco*. (page 185)

burin A metal tool with a V-shaped point used in *engraving*. (page 225)

burning A photographic technique that increases the exposure to areas of the print that should be darker. Compare *dodging*. (page 251)

burr In *drypoint* printing, the ridge of metal that is pushed up by the *engraving* tool as it is pulled across the surface of the plate and that results, when inked, in the rich, velvety *texture* of the drypoint *print*. (page 227)

calligraphy Handwriting as a form of art. (page 30)

calotype The first photographic process to use a negative image. Discovered by William Henry Fox Talbot in 1841. (page 243)

canon (of *proportion*) The "rule" of perfect proportions for the human body as determined by the Greek sculptor Polyclitus in a now lost work, known as the *Canon*, and based on the idea that each part of the body should be a common fraction of the figure's total height. (page 147)

cantilever An architectural form that projects horizontally from its support, employed especially after the development of *reinforced concrete* construction techniques. (page 347)

capital The crown, or top, of a *column*, upon which the *entablature* rests. (page 336)

Carolingian art European art from the mid-eighth to the early tenth century, given impetus and encouragement by Charlemagne's desire to restore the civilization of Rome. (page 428)

cartoon As distinct from common usage, where it refers to a drawing with humorous content, any full-size drawing, subsequently transferred to the working surface, from which a painting or *fresco* is made. (page 163)

cast iron A rigid, strong construction material made by adding carbon to iron. (page 342)

cast shadow In *chiaroscuro*, the shadow cast by a figure, darker than the shadowed surface itself. (page 94)

***casta* painting** A distinct genre of family portrait that records the process of race-mixing in the Americas. (page 628)

casting Pouring molten material into a mold and allowing it to harden. (page 283)

ceramics Objects formed out of clay and then hardened by *firing* in a very hot oven, or *kiln*. (page 282)

chiaroscuro In drawing and painting, the use of light and dark to create the effect of three-dimensional, *modeled* surfaces. (page 93)

chinoiserie Literally "all things Chinese," a style of art based on Chinese designs popular in Europe in the eighteenth century. (page 476)

cire-perdue See *lost-wax process*. (page 283)

civilizations Social, economic, and political entities distinguished by their ability to express themselves through images and, later, written language. (page 394)

closed palette See *palette*. (page 110)

close-up See *shot*. (page 258)

coiling A method of *ceramic* construction in which long, rope-like strands of clay are coiled on top of one another and then smoothed. (page 305)

collage A work made by pasting various scraps or pieces of material—cloth, paper, photographs—onto the surface of the *composition*. (page 205)

colonnade A row of *columns* set at regular intervals around the building and supporting the base of the roof. (page 335)

color wheel A circular arrangement of *hues* based on one of a number of various color theories. (page 101)

column A vertical architectural support, consisting of a *shaft* topped by a *capital*, and sometimes including a base. (page 336)

combine-painting Robert Rauschenberg's name for his works of high-relief collage. (page 208)

complementary colors Pairs of colors, such as red and green, that are directly opposite each other on the *color wheel*. (page 104)

composition The organization of the formal elements in a work of art. (page 37)

connotation The meaning associated with or implied by an image, as distinguished from its *denotation*. (page 189)

Constructivism A Russian art movement, fully established by 1921, that was dedicated to *nonobjective* means of communication. (page 373)

Conté crayon A soft drawing tool made by adding clay to graphite. (page 169)

content The meaning of an image, beyond its overt *subject matter*; as opposed to *form*. (pages 30, 37)

contour lines The perceived lines that mark the border of an object in space. (page 49)

contrapposto The disposition of the human figure in which the hips and legs are turned in opposition to the shoulders and chest, creating a counter-positioning of the body. (page 281)

core of the shadow The darkest area on a form rendered by means of *modeling* or *chiaroscuro*. (page 94)

cornice The upper part of the *entablature*, frequently decorated. (page 336)

cross-cutting In film technique, when the editor moves back and forth between two separate events in increasingly shorter sequences in order to heighten drama. (page 258)

cross-hatching Two or more sets of roughly parallel and overlapping lines, set at an angle to one another, in order to create a sense of three-dimensional, *modeled* space. See also *hatching*. (page 96)

crossing In a church, where the *transepts* cross the *nave*. (page 340)

Cubism A style of art pioneered by Pablo Picasso and Georges Braque in the first decade of the twentieth century, noted for the geometry of its forms, its fragmentation of the object, and its increasing abstraction. (page 496)

Dada An art movement that originated during World War I in a number of world capitals, including New York, Paris, Berlin, and Zurich, which was so antagonistic to traditional styles and materials of art that it was considered by many to be "anti-art." (page 501)

daguerreotype One of the earliest forms of photography, invented by Louis Jacques Mandé Daguerre in 1839, made on a copper plate polished with silver. (page 242)

De Stijl A Dutch art movement of the early twentieth century that emphasized abstraction and simplicity, reducing form to the rectangle and color to the *primary colors*—red, blue, and yellow. (page 372)

delineation The descriptive representation of an object by means of *outline* or *contour* drawing. (page 167)

denotation The direct or literal meaning of an image, as distinguished from its *connotation*. (page 189)

diagonal recession In perspective, when the lines recede to a *vanishing point* to the right or left of the *vantage point*. (page 75)

didacticism An approach to making art emphasizing its ability to teach and, particularly, elevate the mind. (page 189)

dodging A photographic technique that decreases the exposure of selected areas of the print that the photographer wishes to be lighter. Compare *burning*. (page 251)

dome A roof generally in the shape of a hemisphere or half-globe. (page 338)

drums The several pieces of stone used to construct a *column*. (page 334)

drypoint An *intaglio* printmaking process in which the copper or zinc plate is incised by a needle pulled back across the surface, leaving a *burr*. The resulting *print* is also called a drypoint. (page 227)

earthenware A type of *ceramic* made of porous clay and fired at low temperatures that must be *glazed* if it is to hold liquid. (page 306)

earthworks *Environments* that are out-of-doors. (page 279)

editing In filmmaking, the process of arranging the sequences of the film after it has been shot in its entirety. (page 257)

edition In printmaking, the number of *impressions* authorized by the artist made from a single master image. (page 214)

elevation The side of a building, or a drawing of the side of a building. (page 336)

embossing In metalworking, the raised decoration on the surface of an object. The reverse of *repoussé*. (page 322)

embroidery A traditional fiber art in which the design is made by needlework. (page 316)

encaustic A method of painting with molten beeswax fused to the support after application by means of heat. (page 184)

engraving An *intaglio* printmaking process in which a sharp tool called a *burin* is used to incise the plate. The resulting *print* is also called an engraving. (page 225)

en plein air (also "*plein-air* painting") A French expression meaning "in the open air," used specifically to refer to the act of painting outdoors. (page 197)

entablature The part of a building above the *capitals* of the *columns* and below the roof. (page 336)

entasis The slight swelling in a *column* design to make the column appear straight to the eye. (page 334)

environments Sculptural spaces that are large enough for the viewer to move around in. (page 279)

etching An *intaglio* printmaking process in which a metal plate coated with wax is drawn upon with a sharp tool down to the plate and then placed in an acid bath. The acid eats into the plate where the lines have been drawn, the wax is removed, and then the plate is inked and printed. The resulting *print* is also called an etching. (page 225)

Expressionism An art that stresses the psychological and emotional content of the work, associated particularly with German art in the early twentieth century. See also *Abstract Expressionism*. (page 498)

extreme close-up See *shot*. (page 258)

Fauves The artists of the early twentieth century whose work was characterized by its use of bold *arbitrary color*. Their name derives from the French word meaning "wild beasts." (page 498)

figure-ground relation The relationship between a work of art (the figure) and the surface upon which the work is made (the ground). (page 68)

firing The process of baking a *ceramic* object in a very hot oven, or *kiln*. (page 282)

flashback A narrative technique in film in which the editor cuts to episodes that are supposed to have taken place before the start of the film. (page 258)

fluting The shallow vertical grooves or channels on a *column*. (page 334)

flying buttress On a Gothic church, an exterior arch that opposes the lateral thrust of an arch or vault, as in a *barrel vault*, arching inward toward the exterior wall from the top of an exterior *column* or pier. (page 341)

focal point In a work of art, the center of visual attention, often different from the physical center of the work. (page 140)

foreshortening The modification of perspective to decrease distortion resulting from the apparent visual contraction of an object or figure as it extends backward from the picture plane at an angle approaching the perpendicular. (page 79)

form (1) The literal *shape* and *mass* of an object or figure. (2) More generally, the materials used to make a work of art, the ways in which these materials are used in terms of the formal elements (line, light, color, etc.), and the *composition* that results. (page 37)

fresco Painting on plaster, either dry (*fresco secco*) or wet (*buon*, or true *fresco*). In the former, the paint is an independent layer, separate from the plaster proper; in the latter, the paint is chemically bound to the plaster, and is integral to the wall or support. (page 185)

fresco secco See *fresco*. (page 185)

frieze The part of the *architrave* between the *entablature* and the *cornice*, often decorated. (page 276)

frontal An adjective used to describe any object meant to be seen from the front. (page 276)

frontal recession In perspective, when the lines recede to a *vanishing point* directly across from the *vantage point*. (page 75)

frottage The technique of putting a sheet of paper over textured surfaces and then rubbing a soft pencil across the paper. (page 120)

full shot See *shot*. (page 258)

functional objects Items intended for everyday use. (page 300)

Futurism An early twentieth-century art movement, characterized by its desire to celebrate the movement and speed of modern industrial life. (page 70)

genres In film, a style having a particular content, such as Westerns, Romances, and so on. (page 260)

gesso A plaster mixture used as a *ground* for painting. (page 188)

giornata Literally, "a day's work," the area a *fresco* painter is able to complete in a single sitting. (page 187)

glazing In *ceramics*, a material that is painted on a ceramic object that turns glassy when fired. (page 303)

Gothic A style of architecture and art dominant in Europe from the twelfth to the fifteenth century, characterized, in its architecture, by features such as *pointed arches*, *flying buttresses*, and a verticality symbolic of the ethereal and heavenly. (page 431)

gouache A painting *medium* similar to *watercolor*, but opaque instead of transparent. (page 200)

green architecture An architectural practice that strives to build more environmentally friendly and sustainable buildings. (page 331)

grid A pattern of horizontal and vertical lines that cross each other to make uniform squares or rectangles. (page 56)

groin vault A masonry roof constructed on the arch principle and consisting of two *barrel vaults* intersecting at right angles to each other. (page 338)

ground A coating applied to a canvas or printmaking plate to prepare it for painting or *etching*. (pages 184, 225)

Happenings Spontaneous, often multimedia, events conceived by artists and performed not only by the artists themselves but often by the public present at the event as well. (page 296)

hatching An area of closely spaced parallel lines, employed in drawing and *engraving*, to create the effect of shading or *modeling*. See also *cross-hatching*. (page 96)

Haussmannization The modernization of Paris in the mid-nineteenth century by Baron Georges-Eugène Haussmann. (page 610)

Hellenism The culture of ancient Greece. (page 409)

high (*haut*) relief A sculpture in which the figures and objects remain attached to a background plane and project off of it by at least half their normal depth. (page 276)

highlights The spot or one of the spots of highest key or value in a picture. (page 94)

hue A color, as found on a *color wheel*. (page 101)

humanism A belief in the unique value and capacity of human beings to act individually and collectively in meaningful ways. (page 446)

hypostyle space A large interior space characterized by many closely spaced columns supporting the roof. (page 424)

iconoclasts Literally "image breakers," those who, taking the Bible's commandment against the worship of "graven" images literally, wished to destroy images in religious settings. (pages 32, 421)

iconography The study or description of images and symbols. (page 39)

impasto Paint applied very thickly to canvas or support. (page 53)

implied line A line created by movement or direction, such as the line established by a pointing finger, the direction of a glance, or a body moving through space. (page 50)

impression In printmaking, a single example of an *edition*. (page 214)

Impressionists The painters of the Impressionist movement in nineteenth-century France whose work is characterized by the use of discontinuous strokes of color meant to reproduce the effects of light. (page 488)

Industrial Revolution Radical changes in production and consumption during the late eighteenth and nineteenth centuries that transformed society. (page 642)

infrastructure The systems that deliver services to people—water supply and waste removal, energy, transportation, and communications. (page 359)

installations *Environments* that are indoors. (page 279)

intaglio Any form of printmaking in which the line is incised into the surface of the printing plate, including *aquatint*, *drypoint*, *etching*, *engraving*, and *mezzotint*. (page 224)

intensity The relative purity of a color's *hue*, and a function of its relative brightness or dullness; also known as *saturation*. (page 101)

intermediate colors The range of colors on the *color wheel* between each *primary color* and its neighboring *secondary colors*; yellow–green, for example. (page 101)

International Style A twentieth-century style of architecture and design marked by its almost austere geometric simplicity. (page 351)

in-the-round See *sculpture in-the-round*. (page 278)

investment In *lost-wax casting*, a mixture of water, plaster, and powder made from ground-up pottery used to fill the space inside the wax lining of the mold. (page 284)

iris shot In film, a *shot* that is blurred and rounded at the edges in order to focus the attention of the viewer on the scene in the center. (page 258)

ka In ancient Egypt, the individual spirit of the deceased. (page 281)

keystone The central and uppermost *voussoir* in an arch. (page 337)

kiln An oven used to bake *ceramics*. (page 282)

kinetic art Art that moves. (page 122)

kiva In Anasazi culture, the round, covered hole in the center of the communal plaza in which all ceremonial life took place. (page 330)

line A mark left by a moving point, actual or implied, and varying in direction, thickness, and density. (page 48)

linear perspective See *one-point linear perspective* and *two-point linear perspective*. (page 75)

linocut A form of *relief* printmaking, similar to a *woodcut*, in which a block of linoleum is carved so as to leave the image to be printed raised above the surface of the block. The resulting *print* is also known as a linocut. (page 222)

lithography A printmaking process in which a polished stone, often limestone, is drawn upon with a greasy material; the surface is moistened and then inked; the ink adheres only to the greasy lines of the drawing; and the design is transferred to dampened paper, usually in a printing press. (page 232)

load-bearing In architecture, construction where the walls bear the weight of the roof. (page 334)

local color As opposed to optical color and *perceptual color*, the actual *hue* of a thing, independent of the ways in which colors might be mixed or how different conditions of light and atmosphere might affect color. (page 111)

long shot In film, a *shot* that takes in a wide expanse and many characters at once. (page 258)

lost-wax process A bronze-casting method in which a figure is molded in wax and covered with clay; the whole is fired, melting away the wax and hardening the clay, and the resulting hardened mold is then filled with molten metal. (page 283)

low (*bas*) relief A sculpture in which the figures and objects remain attached to a background plane and project off of it by less than one-half their normal depth. (page 276)

Mannerism The style of art prevalent especially in Italy from about 1525 until the early years of the seventeenth century, characterized by its dramatic use of light, exaggerated perspective, distorted forms, and vivid colors. (page 461)

mass Any solid that occupies a three-dimensional volume. (page 69)

matrix In printmaking, the master image. (page 214)

medium Plural form, media (1) Any material used to create a work of art. (2) In painting, a liquid added to paint that makes it easier to manipulate. (pages 101, 134)

medium shot See *shot*. (page 258)

megaliths From the Greek *meaga* meaning "big," and *lithos*, meaning "stone." A huge stone used in prehistoric architecture. (page 395)

memento mori From the Latin "remember that you will die," an image that invites viewers to contemplate their own mortality. (page 556)

metalpoint A drawing technique, especially silverpoint, popular in the fifteenth and sixteenth centuries, in which a stylus with a point of gold, silver, or some other metal was applied to a sheet of paper treated with a mixture of powdered bones (or lead white) and gumwater. (page 165)

mezzotint An *intaglio* printmaking process in which the plate is ground all over with a *rocker*, leaving a *burr* raised on the surface that if inked would be rich black. The surface is subsequently lightened to a greater or lesser degree by scraping away the burr. The resulting *print* is also known as a mezzotint. (page 230)

mihrab A niche set in the wall of a *mosque* indicating the direction of Mecca. (page 424)

minbar A stepped pulpit for a preacher on the *qibla* wall of a *mosque*. (page 424)

Minimalism A style of art, predominantly American, that dates from the mid-twentieth century, characterized by its rejection of expressive content and its use of "minimal" formal means. (page 509)

mixed media The combination of two or more *media* in a single work. (page 204)

modeling In sculpture, the shaping of a form in some plastic material, such as clay or plaster; in drawing, painting, and printmaking, the rendering of a form, usually by means of *hatching* or *chiaroscuro*, to create the illusion of a three-dimensional *form*. (page 94)

modernism Generally speaking, the various strategies and directions employed in twentieth-century art—*Cubism, Futurism, Expressionism*, etc.—to explore the particular formal properties of any given *medium*. (page 506)

monochromatic A color composition limited to a single *hue*. (page 110)

monotype A printmaking process in which only one *impression* results. (page 234)

montage In film, the sequencing of widely disparate images to create a fast-paced, multifaceted visual impression. (page 258)

mosaic An art form in which small pieces of tile, glass, or stone are fitted together and embedded in cement on surfaces such as walls and floors. (page 421)

mosque In Islam, the place of worship. (page 424)

naturalism A brand of representation in which the artist retains apparently realistic elements but presents the visual world from a distinctly personal or subjective point of view. (page 35)

nave The central part of a church, running from the entrance through the *crossing*. (page 340)

negative shape *or* space Empty space, surrounded and shaped so that it acquires a sense of form or volume. (pages 68, 72)

Neoclassicism A style of the late eighteenth and early nineteenth centuries that was influenced by the Greek Classical style and that often employed Classical themes for its subject matter. (page 477)

nonobjective art Art that makes no reference to the natural world and that explores the inherent expressive or aesthetic potential of the formal elements—line, shape, color—and the formal *compositional* principles of a given *medium*. Also known as nonrepresentational art. (page 33)

oculus A round, central opening at the top of a *dome*. (page 339)

odalisque A female slave or concubine in a Turkish harem. (page 14)

oil paint A medium using linseed oil as a *binder* that became particularly popular beginning in the fifteenth century. (page 193)

one-point linear perspective A version of *linear perspective* in which there is only one *vanishing point* in the *composition*. (page 75)

open palette See *palette*. (page 110)

optical painting (Op Art) An art style particularly popular in the 1960s in which line and color are manipulated in ways that stimulate the eye into believing it perceives movement. (page 124)

order In Classical architecture, a style characterized by the design of the *platform*, the *column*, and its *entablature*. (page 336)

original print A *print* created by the artist alone and that has been printed by the artist or under the artist's direct supervision. (page 214)

outline The edge of a shape or figure depicted by an actual line drawn or painted on the surface. (page 49)

pagoda A multistoried structure of successively smaller, repeated stories, with projecting roofs at each story, functioning as a temple or sacred building. (page 438)

palette Literally, a thin board, with a thumb hole at one end, upon which the artist lays out and mixes colors, but, by extension, the range of colors used by the artist. In this last sense, a *closed* or *restricted palette* is one employing only a few colors and an *open palette* is one using the full range of *hues*. (page 102)

pan In film, a *shot* in which the camera moves across the scene from one side to the other. (page 258)

pastel (1) A soft crayon made of chalk and pigment; also, any work done in this *medium*. (2) A pale, light color. (page 170)

pattern A repetitive motif or design. (page 56)

pencil A drawing tool made of graphite encased in a soft wood cylinder. (page 169)

pendentive A triangular section of a masonry hemisphere, four of which provide the transition from the vertical sides of a building to a covering *dome*. (page 421)

perceptual color Color as perceived by the eye. Compare *local color*. (page 111)

performance art A form of art, popular especially since the late 1960s, that includes not only physical space but also the human activity that goes on within it. (page 296)

perspective The way in which the picture plane—the flat surface of the canvas—functions as a window through which a specific scene is presented to the viewer. (page 66)

photogenic drawing With the *daguerreotype*, one of the first two photographic processes, invented by William Henry Fox Talbot in 1839, in which a negative image is fixed to paper. (page 242)

photomontage A collage consisting entirely of photographs (page 205)

photorealistic A drawing or painting so realistic in appearance that it appears to be a photograph. (page 33)

pigments The coloring agents of a *medium*. (page 165)

planographic printmaking process Any printmaking process in which the *print* is pulled from a flat, planar surface, chief among them *lithography*. (page 232)

platform The base upon which a *column* rests. (page 336)

pointed arch An arch that is not semicircular but rather rises more steeply to a point at its top. (page 341)

pointillism A style of painting, championed by Georges Seurat in particular, consisting of small points of pure colors, juxtaposed with one another, in the belief that they might mix together in the viewer's eye—so that a dot of blue next to a dot of yellow might produce the effect of green. (page 107)

polychromatic A color composition consisting of a variety of *hues*. (page 110)

Pop Art A style arising in the early 1960s characterized by emphasis on the forms and imagery of mass culture. (page 508)

porcelain A type of *ceramic* fired at the highest temperature that becomes virtually translucent and extremely glossy in finish. (page 306)

positive shapes The figure in a *figure-ground relation*. (page 68)

post-and-lintel construction A system of building in which two posts support a crosspiece, or lintel, that spans the distance between them. (page 334)

Post-Impressionism A name that describes the painting of a number of artists, working in widely different styles, in France during the last decades of the nineteenth century. (page 490)

postmodernism A term used to describe the willfully plural and eclectic art forms of contemporary art. (page 154)

primary colors The *hues* that in theory cannot be created from a mixture of other hues and from which all other hues are created—namely, in *pigment*, red, yellow, and blue, and in refracted light, red–orange, green, and blue–violet. (page 101)

print Any one of multiple *impressions* made from a master image. (page 212)

proof A trial *impression* of a *print*, made before the final *edition* is run, so that it may be examined and, if necessary, corrected. (page 214)

proportion In any composition, the relationship between the parts to each other and to the whole. (page 147)

qibla The wall of a *mosque* that, from the interior, is oriented in the direction of Mecca, and that contains the *mihrab*. (page 424)

radial balance A circular composition in which the elements project outward from a central core at regular intervals, like the spokes of a wheel. (page 138)

realism Generally, the tendency to render the facts of existence, but, specifically, in the nineteenth century, the desire to describe the world in a way unadulterated by the imaginative and idealist tendencies of the *Romantic* sensibility. (page 33)

rebars Steel reinforcement bars used in *reinforced concrete*. (page 350)

registration In printmaking, the precise alignment of *impressions* made by two or more blocks or plates on the same sheet of paper, used particularly when printing two or more colors. (page 222)

reinforced concrete Concrete in which steel reinforcement bars, or *rebars*, are placed to both strengthen and make concrete less brittle. (page 350)

relief (1) Any sculpture in which images and forms are attached to a background and project off it. See *low relief* and *high relief*. (2) In printmaking, any process in which any area of the plate not to be printed is carved away, leaving only the original surface to be printed. (pages 216, 276)

Renaissance The period in Europe from the fourteenth to the sixteenth century, characterized by a revival of interest in the arts and sciences that had been lost since antiquity. (page 444)

repetition See *pattern* and *rhythm*. (page 150)

replacement process A term for casting, by, for instance, the *lost-wax process*, in which wax is replaced by bronze. (page 284)

repoussé In metalworking, a design realized by hammering the image from the reverse side. (page 322)

representational art Any work of art that seeks to resemble the world of natural appearance. (page 33)

restricted palette A selection of colors limited in its range of *hues*. (page 110)

retablo A frame, usually ornate, enclosing decorated panels, paintings, and other revered objects rising above and behind an altar. (page 540)

rhythm An effect achieved when shapes, colors, or a regular *pattern* of any kind is repeated over and over again. (page 150)

rocker A sharp, curved tool used in the *mezzotint* printmaking process. (page 230)

Rococo A style of art popular in the first three-quarters of the eighteenth century, particularly in France, characterized by curvilinear forms, *pastel* colors, and light, often frivolous subject matter. (page 475)

Romanesque art The dominant style of art and architecture in Europe from the eighth to the twelfth century, characterized, in architecture, by Roman precedents, particularly the round arch and the *barrel vault*. (page 429)

Romanticism A dramatic, emotional, and subjective art arising in the early ninteenth century in opposition to the austere discipline of *Neoclassicism*. (page 479)

round arch A curved, often semicircular architectural form that spans an opening or space built of wedge-shaped blocks, called *voussoirs*, with a *keystone* centered at its top. (page 336)

salons During the *Rococo* period, social and artistic gatherings held by society hostesses on particular days of the week. (page 474)

sans serif A type of letterform that does not possess the small lines at the end of the letter's main stroke, characteristic of *serif type*. (page 373)

saturation See *intensity*. (page 101)

scale The comparative size of an object in relation to other objects and settings. (page 144)

scarification Decorative effects made by scarring the body. (page 441)

sculpture in-the-round As opposed to *relief*, sculpture that requires no wall support and that can be experienced from all sides. (page 277)

secondary colors *Hues* created by combining two *primary colors*; in *pigment*, the secondary colors are traditionally considered to be orange, green, and violet; in refracted light, yellow, magenta, and cyan. (page 101)

selfie A self-portrait made on a cameraphone, taken at arm's length and closely cropped. (page 582)

serif type Letterforms that have small lines at the end of the letter's main stroke. (page 373)

serigraphs Also known as *silkscreen* prints, in which the image is transferred to paper by forcing ink through a mesh; areas not meant to be printed are blocked out. (page 233)

shade A color or *hue* modified by the addition of another color, resulting in a *hue* of a darker value, in the way, for instance, that the addition of black to red results in maroon. (page 93)

shadow The unlighted surface of a form rendered by *modeling* or *chiaroscuro*. (page 94)

shaft A part of a *column*. (page 336)

shape A two-dimensional area, the boundaries of which are measured in terms of height and width. More broadly, the *form* of any object or figure. (page 66)

shell system In architecture, one of the two basic structural systems, in which one basic material both provides the structural support and the outside covering of a building. (page 333)

shot In film, a continuous sequence of film frames, including a *full shot*, which shows the actor from head to toe, a *medium shot*, which shows the actor from the waist up, a *close-up*, showing the head and shoulders, and an *extreme close-up*, showing a portion of the face. Other shots include the *long shot*, the *iris shot*, the *pan*, and the *traveling shot*. (page 258)

silkscreen Also known as a *serigraph*, a print made by the process of serigraphy. (page 233)

simultaneous contrast A property of *complementary colors* when placed side by side, resulting in the fact that both appear brighter and more intense than when seen in isolation. (page 104)

sinopie The *cartoon* or underpainting for a *fresco*. (page 168)

site-specific An *installation* designed for a particular place in such a way that the space is transformed by its presence. (page 279)

sizing An astringent crystalline substance called alum brushed onto the surface of paper so that ink will not run along its fibers. (page 219)

skeleton-and-skin system In architecture, one of the two basic structural systems, which consists of an interior frame, the skeleton, that supports the more fragile outer covering of the building, the skin. (page 333)

slab construction A method of *ceramic* construction in which clay is rolled out flat, like a pie crust, and then shaped by hand. (page 304)

slip Liquid clay used in decorating *ceramic* objects. (page 305)

solvent A thinner that enables paint to flow more readily and that also cleans brushes; also called *vehicle*. (page 184)

spectrum The colored bands of visible light created when sunlight passes through a prism. (page 100)

springing The lowest stone of an arch, resting on the supporting post. (page 339)

star In the popular cinema, an actor or actress whose celebrity alone can guarantee the success of a film. (page 258)

states In *etching*, each of the stages in the printmaking process. (page 212)

stippling In drawing and printmaking, a pattern of closely placed dots or small marks employed to create the effect of shading or *modeling*. (page 224)

stoneware A type of *ceramic* fired at high temperature and thus impermeable to water. (page 306)

stopping out In *etching*, the application of varnish or *ground* over the etched surface in order to prevent further etching as the remainder of the surface is submerged in the acid bath. (page 227)

storyboards Panels of rough sketches outlining the shot sequences of a film. (page 260)

stupa A large, mound-shaped Buddhist shrine. (page 416)

stylobate The base, or *platform*, upon which a *column* rests. (page 148, 336)

subject matter The literal, visible image in a work of art, as distinguished from its *content*, which includes the *connotative*, symbolic, and suggestive aspects of the image. (page 30)

sublime That which impresses the mind with a sense of grandeur and power, inspiring a sense of awe. (page 481)

subtractive process (1) In color, the fact that, when different *hues* of colored *pigment* are combined, the resulting mixture is lower in key than the original hues and duller as well, and as more and more hues are added, the resulting mixture is closer and closer to black. (2) In sculpture, the process in which form is discovered by the removal of materials, by such means as carving, as distinguished from *additive* sculptural processes, such as *assemblage*. (pages 101, 274)

support The surface on which the artist works—a wall, a panel of wood, a canvas, or a sheet of paper. (page 183)

Surrealism A style of art of the early twentieth century that emphasized dream imagery, chance operations, and rapid, thoughtless forms of notation that expressed, it was felt, the unconscious mind. (page 502)

sutra An aphorism or collection of aphorisms in Buddhism. (page 534)

symbols Images that represent something more than their literal meaning. (page 39)

symmetrical When two halves of a *composition* correspond to one another in terms of size, shape, and placement of forms. (page 134)

tapestry A special kind of *weaving*, in which the *weft* yarns are of several colors that the weaver manipulates to make a design or image. (page 316)

technologies Technologies, literally, are "words" or "discourses" (from the Greek *logos*) about a "techne" (from the Greek word for art, which in turn comes from the Greek verb *tekein*, "to make, prepare, or fabricate"). In art, then, any medium is a techne, a means of making art. (page 159)

technology The materials and methods available to a given culture. (page 328)

tempera A painting *medium* made by combining water, pigment, and, usually, egg yolk. (page 188)

temperature The relative warmth or coolness of a given *hue*; hues in the yellow–orange–red range are considered to be warm, and hues in the green–blue–violet range are considered cool. (page 102)

tenebrism From the Italian *tenebroso*, meaning murky, a heightened form of *chiaroscuro*. (page 94)

tensile strength In architecture, the ability of a building material to span horizontal distances without support and without buckling in the middle. (page 333)

tesserae Small pieces of glass or stone used in making a *mosaic*. (page 421)

texture The surface quality of a work. (page 116)

time and motion The primary elements of temporal media, linear rather than spatial in character. (page 116)

tint A color or *hue* modified by the addition of another color, resulting in a hue of a lighter value, in the way, for instance, that the addition of white to red results in pink. (page 93)

transept The crossarm of a church that intersects, at right angles, with the *nave*, creating the shape of a cross. (page 340)

traveling *or* tracking shot In film, a *shot* in which the camera moves back to front or front to back. (page 258)

triptych An artwork made of three panels which may be hinged together so that the side segments (or wings) fold over the central area. (page 20)

triumphal arches Roman arches designed for triumphant armies to march through, usually composed of a simple *barrel vault* enclosed within a rectangle, and enlivened with sculpture and decorative engaged *columns*. (page 412)

trompe l'oeil A manner of two-dimensional representation in which the appearance of natural space and objects is recreated with the intention of fooling the eye of the viewer, who may be convinced that the subject actually exists in three-dimensional space. (page 7)

truss In architecture, a triangular framework that, because of its rigidity, can span much wider areas than a single wooden beam. (page 343)

tunnel vault See *barrel vault*. (page 337)

tusche A greasy material used for drawing on a *lithography* stone. (page 233)

two-point linear perspective A version of *linear perspective* in which there are two (or more) *vanishing points* in the *composition*. (page 77)

tympanum The semicircular arch above the lintel over a door, often decorated with sculpture. (page 430)

ukioy-e The Japanese term for a type of popular art depicting everyday life. (page 217)

vanishing point In *linear perspective*, the point on the horizon line where parallel lines appear to converge. (page 75)

vanitas A tradition of still-life painting, especially popular in northern Europe in the seventeenth century, reminding the viewer of the frivolous quality, or vanity (*vanitas* in Latin), of human existence. (pages 57, 195)

vantage point In *linear perspective*, the point where the viewer is positioned. (page 75)

vehicle See *solvent*. (page 184)

visual weight As opposed to *actual weight*, the apparent "heaviness" or "lightness" of a shape or form. (page 134)

voussoir A wedge-shaped block used in the construction of an arch. (page 337)

warp In *weaving*, the vertical threads, held taut on a loom or frame. (page 316)

wash Large flat areas of ink or *watercolor* diluted with water and applied by brush. (page 175)

watercolor A painting *medium* consisting of *pigments* suspended in a solution of water and gum arabic. (page 198)

weaving A technique for constructing fabrics by means of interlacing horizontal and vertical threads. (page 316)

weft In *weaving*, the loosely woven horizontal threads, also called the *woof*. (page 316)

wet-plate collodion process A photographic process, developed around 1850, that allowed for short exposure times and quick development of the print. (page 244)

wood engraving Actually a *relief* printmaking technique, in which fine lines are carved into the block, resulting in a *print* consisting of white lines on a black ground. The resultant print is also called a wood engraving. (page 221)

woodcut A *relief* printmaking process, in which a wooden block is carved so that those parts not intended to print are cut away, leaving the design raised. The resultant *print* is also called a woodcut. (page 216)

wood-frame A true *skeleton-and-skin* building method, commonly used in domestic architecture to the present. (page 342)

woof See *weft*. (page 316)

Zone System A framework for understanding exposures in photography developed by Ansel Adams, where a zone represents the relation of the image's (or a portion of the image's) brightness to the value or tone that the photographer wishes it to have in the final print. Thus each picture is broken up into zones ranging from black to white with nine shades of gray in between—a photographic gray scale. (page 249)

Credits

Preface p. 3: Peter Eleey, "The Exploded Drive-In," in Klaus Biesenbach and Peter Eleey, *Doug Aitken: Sleepwalkers*, Museum of Modern Art: New York, 2007, 94, 128. Courtesy Peter Eleey, New York.

Chapter 1 p. 6: Cai Guo-Qiang, personal statement released after 2008 Olympics, quoted in Trong Gia Nguyen, "Cai Guo-Qiang Responds to Olympics fireworks 'Controversy,'" art21 magazine, August 22, 2008; p. 7: Jasper Johns, quoted in Michael Crichton, *Jasper Johns*, Abrams: New York, 1977, 28. Nelson Goodman, *Languages of Art*, Harvester Press: Brighton, 1977; p. 13: Pablo Picasso, quoted in C. Rhodes, *Primitivism and Modern Art*, © Thames and Hudson: London, 1994; p. 14: Mia Mask, *Divas on Screen: Black Women in American Film*, University of Illinois Press: Champaign, IL, 2009, 61; p. 15: Antonin Proust, quoted in Alexander Sturgis, Rebels and Martyrs: *The Image of the Artist in the Nineteenth Century*, Yale University Press: New Haven, CT, 2006, 122; p. 18: Renzo Piano, 1998 Laureate, *The Pritzker Architecture Prize*, 7; p. 22: Louis Sirkin, quoted by Isabel Wilkerson, "Trouble Right Here in Cincinnati: Furor Over Mapplethorpe Exhibit." *New York Times*, March 29, 1990. Judge David J. Albanese of Cincinnati, quoted in *The Washington Post*, September 7, 1990, B5. Robert Sobieszek, quoted in Elizabeth Hess, "Art on Trial: Cincinatti's Dangerous Theater of the Ridiculous," *Village Voice*, October 23, 1990; p. 23: Chris Ofili, from an interview by Marcelo Spinelli, *Brilliant! New Art from London*, exh. cat. Minneapolis: Walker Art Center, March 23, 1995, 67; p. 24: Richard Serra, *Writings/Interviews*, University of Chicago Press, 1994.

Chapter 2 p. 28: Harold Rosenberg, "Interview with Willem de Kooning," *Artnews* 71, September 1972; p. 32: The Prophet Muhammad, *Qur'an*, Chapter 19, Book 24, Hadith no. 5246. Exodus 20:4–5, *The Holy Bible*, King James Version, 1665; p. 35: Don Eddy, "George D. Green," New York, 2010; p. 36: Wolf Kahn, quoted in Justin Spring, *Wolf Kahn*, Abrams: New York, 2011, 73. © Wolf Kahn, licensed by VAGA, New York, www.vagarights.com; p. 37: Kazimir Malevich, trans. Howard Dearstyne, *The Non-Objective World: The Manifesto of Suprematism*, Dover Publications: New York, 2003 [1926]; p. 38: Beatriz Milhazes, quoted in Carol Kino, "Modern Motifs, With Echoes of Brazil," *New York Times*, Oct. 6, 2008. Beatriz Milhazes, transcribed from "Video portrait of Beatriz Milhazes," produced by Philip Dolin & Molly Bernstein, 2008, Particle Productions for the James Cohan Gallery, New York; p. 43: Marvel Comics: from "X-Men" series, by Marvel Comics, New York.

Chapter 3 p. 48: Matthew Ritchie, from narrative accompanying his image, "A Glorious Martyrdom Awaits Us All at the Hands of Our Tender and Merciful God," art21, 2003. Matthew Ritchie, quoted in Wesley Miller, "Matthew Ritchie | Apocalypse," art21 magazine, August 21, 2008; p. 53: Vincent van Gogh, letter to brother Theo, quoted in Alfred H. Barr, Vincent van Gogh, Psychology Press: New York, 1967, 32. Vincent van Gogh, quoted in Alfred H. Barr, *Vincent van Gogh*, Psychology Press: New York, 1967, 166; p. 54: Vincent van Gogh, quoted in Ronald Pickvance, *Van Gogh in Arles*, Metropolitan Museum of Art: New York, 1984, 102, 103, 126; p. 59: From introduction, in wenda gu, "the divine comedy of our times: a thesis on united nations art project & its time and environment," 1995 © gu wenda, used by permission; p. 60: Hung Liu, transcribed from "A World of Art: Works in Progress: Hung Liu," a 24-minute video produced by Henry Sayre for Annenberg/CPB, 1996. © Hung Liu; p. 61: Hung Liu, artist's statement on the occasion of her 1995 solo exhibition, "The Last Dynasty," at the Steinbaum Krauss Gallery, New York. Hung Liu, transcribed from "A World of Art: Works in Progress: Hung Liu," a 24-minute video produced by Henry Sayre for Annenberg/CPB, 1996. © Hung Liu.

Chapter 4 p. 66: Julie Mehretu, interview by Susan Sollins, "To Be Felt as Much as Read," art21, May 2013; p. 70: Filippo Marinetti, "Le Futurisme" (The Futurist Manifesto), *Le Figaro*, February 20, 1909. Filippo Marinetti, *Le Figaro*, February 1909, quoted in Robert Jay Lifton and Nicholas Humphrey, *In a Dark Time*, Harvard University Press, 1984, 78. Filippo Marinetti, from "Futurist Manifestos," edited and introduced by Umbro Apollonio. Futurismo © 1970 Verlag M.DuMont Schauberg, Cologne and © 1970 Gabriele Mazzolta Editore, Milan. English translation © 1973 Thames & Hudson Ltd., London; p. 81: Janine Antoni, Interview "'Touch' and 'Moor,'" art21; p. 84: Carol Diehl, originally published in *Art in America*, April 2005. Courtesy BMP Media Holdings, LLC; p. 85: Feng Mengbo, quoted in Carolina A. Miranda, "Let the Games Begin," *ArtNews*, April 2011. By permission of Caroline A. Miranda.

Chapter 5 p. 88: Carlos Cruz-Diez, *Cromosaturación*, "About." Courtesy The Museum of Fine Arts, Houston; p. 91–92: J. Turner, quoted in J. Ziff, "'Backgrounds, an Introduction of Architecture and Landscape:' a Lecture by J. M. W. Turner," *Journal of the Warburg and Courtauld Institutes*, XXVI, 1963, 145; p. 93: Genesis 1:1–4, *The Holy Bible*, King James Version, 1665; p. 104: Romare Bearden, "Rectangular Structure in My Montage Paintings," in *Leonardo*, vol. 2, Pergamon Press: Oxford, 1969, 16; pp. 108–109: Originally published in Robert Storr, Chuck Close, et al., *Chuck Close*, pp. 93–94, New York: The Museum of Modern Art, 1998. © 1998, The Museum of Modern Art, New York; p. 110: Transcribed from the video "Brice Marden on the Dylan Painting," January 2007. © 2015 Brice Marden / Artists Rights Society (ARS), New York. Used by permission; p. 112: From "Bonnard: The Late Paintings," by Sasha M. Newman. © 1984 by Centre Georges Pompidou, Paris. Additional material © 1984 by The Phillips Collection, Washington, D.C. and the Dallas Museum of Art. Reprinted by kind permission of Thames & Hudson Ltd, London; p. 113: Vincent van Gogh, September 8, 1888, letter to his brother, Theo, in Mark Roskill (ed.), *The Letters of Vincent Van Gogh*, Touchstone: New York, 1997 [1927], 289. Wassily Kandinsky, quoted in Peter Selz, *German Expressionist Painting*, University of California Press: Berkeley, CA, 1974, 230. Wassily Kandinsky, quoted in Paul Overy, *Kandinsky: The Language of the Eye*, Praeger Publishers: New York, 1969.

Chapter 6 p. 116: Phillip K Smith III, in "Lucid Stead" Project Statement—Phillip K. Smith III, 2013. Courtesy the artist & Royale Projects: Contemporary Art; p. 126: Rudy Burckhardt, quoted in Carter Ratcliff, *The Fate of a Gesture: Jackson Pollock and Postwar American Art*, Farrar, Straus and Giroux: New York, 1996, 1–2; pp. 126–127: Jackson Pollock, "My Painting," 1947, quoted in William Slattery, *Lieberman, An American Choice: The Muriel Kallis Steinberg Newman Collection*, Metropolitan Museum of Art: New York, 1981, 62; p. 127: Rudy Burckhardt, quoted in Carter Ratcliff, *The Fate of a Gesture: Jackson Pollock and Postwar American Art*, Farrar, Straus and Giroux: New York, 1996. Jackson Pollock, quoted in Nancy Jachec, *Jackson Pollock: Works, Writings, Interviews*, Ediciones Poligrafa: Barcelona, 2011. Hans Namuth, in Hans Namuth and Barbara Rose (ed.), *Pollock Painting*, Agrinde: New York, 1980. Jackson Pollock, written on the back of a photo of himself taken in his studio, late 1940s; p. 128: Grace Ndiritu, excerpted from *The Essential Art of African Textiles: Design Without End September 30, 2008–April 5, 2009*. Copyright © 2000–2014 by The Metropolitan Museum of Art, New York. Reproduced by permission.

Chapter 7 p. 140: Andrea Palladio in Andrea Palladio, trans. Robert Tavernor and Richard Schofield, *The Four Books of Architecture*, MIT Press: Cambridge, MA, 1997. From Witold Rybczynski, *The Perfect House: A Journey with the Renaissance Master Andrea Palladio*, Scribner: New York, 2002, 225; p. 144: Do-Ho Suh, quoted in Thelma Golden, Susan Sollins, and Marybeth Sollins, *Art in the Twenty-First Century*, Abrams: New York, 2003, 43; p. 152: Jacob Lawrence, quoted in Susan E. Strickler and William Hutton, *American Paintings*, Toledo Museum of Art, 1979, 78; p. 153: From "Laylah Ali: Portraiture, Performance, and Violence," art21 interview. Laylah Ali, transcribed from the art21 *Exclusive* video "Newspaper Clippings."; p. 155: From Robert Venturi, Denise Scott Brown, and Steven Izenour, *Learning from Las Vegas: The Forgotten Symbolism of Architectural Form*, MIT Press: Cambridge, MA, 1977. "As I Walked Out One Evening," copyright © 1940 and renewed 1968 by W. H. Auden; from W. H. AUDEN COLLECTED POEMS by W. H. Auden. Used and reprinted by permission of Random House, an imprint and division of Random House LLC, and of Curtis Brown, Ltd. All rights reserved. Any third party use of this material, outside of this publication, is prohibited. Interested parties must apply directly to Random House LLC and Curtis Brown, Ltd. for permission.

Chapter 8 p. 162: Savonarola, from his sermons on the psalm *Quam bonus*, in Carmen Bambach, *Drawing and Painting in the Italian Renaissance Workshop: Theory and Practice, 1300–1600*, 83. © Cambridge University Press 1999, reproduced with permission; p. 166: From Leonardo da Vinci, "Treatise on Painting," in D. Summers, *Michelangelo and the Language of Art*, Princeton University Press, 1981, 74; p. 169: Vija Celmins, from an audio program accompanying the MoMA exhibition *Tempo*, June 29 to September 9, 2002. © 2002 The Museum of Modern Art, New York; p. 170: *Vija Celmins: Drawing as Thinking*, exhibition brochure 1999. By kind permission of Anthony d'Offay, London; p. 172: Sandy Brooke, personal communication with the artist; pp. 172–173: Sandy Brooke, personal communication with the artist; p. 175: Henri Matisse, quoted in Muriel Silberstein-Storfer and Mablen Jones, *Doing Art Together: The Remarkable Parent-Child Workshop of The Metropolitan Museum of Art*, Simon and Schuster: New York, 1982, 146; p. 177: Whitfield Lovell and Lucy R. Lippard, *The Art of Whitfield Lovell: Whispers from the Walls*, Pomegranate: Portland, OR, 2003, 54; p. 179: Marjane Satrapi, from her graphic novel *Persepolis*, trans. Henry M. Sayre; p. 180: Catherine Lampert, "Introduction, Frank Auerbach," *1986 Exhibition Catalogue*, The British Council: London, 8. Isabel Carlisle in Catherine Lampert, Norman Rosenthal, and Isabel Carlisle, *Frank Auerbach: Painting and Drawings 1954–2001*, Royal Academy of Arts: London, 2001, 62.

Chapter 9 p. 193: Julie Green, in correspondence with the author; p. 197: Transcribed from "Close Encounters with Josephine Halvorson," a segment of art21's *New York Close Up* series, 2012; pp. 197–198: Transcribed from "Rackstraw Downes in 'Balance'," art21 *Exclusive* segment, season 6, 2012; p. 200: John Marin in Ruth Fine, *John Marin*, National Gallery of Art: Washington, DC, 1990, 126; p. 203: Helen Frankenthaler, quoted in Barbara Rose, *Helen Frankenthaler*, Abrams: New York, 1972, 54; pp. 203–204: The exhibition brochure for Jeremy Deller's *English Magic* installation in the British Pavilion for the 2013 Venice Biennale, British Council: London, 2013; p. 208: Marjorie Perloff and Charles Junkerman, *John Cage: Composed in America*, University of Chicago Press, 1994, 172. Branden Wayne Joseph and Robert Rauschenberg, *Random Order: Robert Rauschenberg and the Neo-avant-garde*, MIT Press: Cambridge, MA, 2003, 108.

Chapter 10 p. 220: Vincent van Gogh, quoted in Henry M. Sayre, *The Humanities: Culture, Continuity and Change*, Volume II, *1600 to the Present*, Second Edition, Pearson eTextbooks, 984; p. 227: Genesis 1:3, *The Holy Bible*, King James Version, 1665; p. 231: "Jane Dickson: an Interview by Claudia Gould," *The Print Collector's Newsletter*, Volumes 17–18, 1986, 204; pp. 234–235: Maurice Prendergast, quoted in Hedley Howell Rhys, *Maurice Prendergast, 1859–1924*, Museum of Fine Arts, Boston and Harvard University Press, 1960, 14; p. 235: Maurice Prendergast's brother, quoted in Van Wyck Brooks, "Anecdotes of Maurice Prendergast," *Magazine Art*, 31, October 1938.

Chapter 11 p. 238: Catherine Opie, quoted in Faye Hirsch, "Lake Cure: Q+A with Catherine Opie." Originally published in ArtinAmericaMagazine.com, July 2011, Courtesy BMP Media Holdings, LLC; p. 241: Quoted in Jonathan Green, *American Photography: A Critical History 1945 to the Present*, Abrams: New York, 1984, 132; p. 242: Paul Delaroche, nineteenth century; p. 244: *William Henry Fox Talbot: Photographs from the J. Paul Getty Museum*, Getty Publications, 2002, 84. Julia Margaret Cameron, quoted in Sylvia Wolf, Julia Margaret Cameron, Stephanie Lipscomb, et al., *Julia Margaret Cameron's Women*, Yale University Press, 1998, 38; p. 245: Timothy O'Sullivan, quoted in Robert Hirsch, *Seizing the Light: A Social History of Photography*, McGraw-Hill Education: New York, 2008, 86; pp. 246–247: *Alfred Stieglitz: Photographs from the J. Paul Getty Museum*. J. Paul Getty Museum Getty Publications, 1995, 20; p. 249: Henri Cartier-Bresson, quoted in Henry M. Sayre, *Writing about Art*, Pearson/Prentice Hall: Upper Saddle River, NJ, 2006, 53; p. 250: Ansel Adams, quoted in Sandra Forty, *Ansel Adams: in the National Archives*, TAJ Books: Charlotte, NC, 2006, 7; p. 251: Ansel Adams, quoted in David Wyatt, *Five Fires: Race, Catastrophe, and the Shaping of California*, Oxford University Press, 1997, 128–129; pp. 252–253: From Jerry Uelsmann, "Random Thoughts on Photography," quoted in James L. Enyeart and Jerry N. Uelsmann: *Twenty-five Years: A Retrospective*, New York Graphic Society/ Little Brown: Boston/ New York, 1982 [1962], 37. © Jerry N. Uelsmann; p. 253: Jerry Uelsmann, in "Maker of Photographs: Jerry Uelsmann," conversations and emails with Robert Hirsch, 2001–2002; p. 256: Eleanor Antin, quoted in a press release of January 24, 2008 for Eleanor Antin exhibition "Helen's Odyssey." Courtesy of Ronald Feldman Fine Arts, New York; p. 258: Sergei Eisenstein, quoted in Sergei Eisenstein and Jay Leyda (ed. and trans.), *The Film Sense*, Harcourt, Brace & World: New York, 1947, 32; pp. 259–260: Al Jolson, quoted in Donald Crafton, *The Talkies: American Cinema's Transition to Sound, 1926–1931*, University of California Press: Berkeley, CA, 1999, 109; p. 264: From William Wegman, *Rage and Depression* video (transcription), courtesy of the artist; p. 267: Excerpt from William J. Mitchell, *E-topia: "Urban Life, Jim—but Not as We Know It,"* MIT Press: Cambridge, MA, 1999, 32, 33, 41; p. 268: Bill Viola, *Reasons for Knocking at an Empty House: Writings 1973–1994*, Thames and Hudson: New York, 1995, 242. Luke 1:31. Scripture quotation taken from the New English Bible, copyright © Cambridge University Press and Oxford University Press, 1961, 1970. All rights reserved; p. 269: Bill Viola, from a video documenting a recreation of Jacopo Pontormo's 1528 painting *The Visitation*, quoted in Amelia Jones (ed.), *A Companion to Contemporary Art Since 1945*, Wiley: New York, 2009, 119.

Chapter 12 p. 274: Transcribed from the art21 *Exclusive* video, "Sarah Sze: Improvisation," 2012; p. 279: Quoted from "Ernesto Neto by Bill Arning," an interview published in *BOMB* magazine, issue 70, Winter 2000. @BOMBmagazine, New Art Publications, and its Contributors. All rights reserved. *BOMB* can be read at www.bombmagazine.org; p. 280: Michelangelo, quoted in Victoria J. Marsick and Karen E. Watkins, *Facilitating Learning Organizations: Making Learning Count*, Gower: Aldershot, 17; p. 283: R. E. Bradbury, quoted in Kate Ezra, *Royal Art of Benin: The Perls Collection in the Metropolitan Museum of Art*, Metropolitan Museum of Art: New York, 31; p. 288: Jeff Koons: *Art Changes Every Day*, interview with Susan Sollins, art21, 2014; p. 291: Anish Kapoor, quoted in Mary Joe Hughes, *The Move Beyond Form: Creative Undoing in Literature and the Arts Since 1960*, Palgrave Macmillan: New York, 44; p. 296: Allan Kaprow, quoted in Donna M. Binkiewicz, *Federalizing the Muse: United States Arts Policy and the National Endowment for the Arts, 1965–1980*, University of North Carolina Press, 2004, 136. Jackson Pollock, quoted in Douglas Kahn, *Noise, Water, Meat: A History of Sound in the Arts*, MIT Press: Cambridge, MA, 1999 [1958]; p. 297: Marina Abramović, quoted in Adrian Heathfield and Hugo Glendinning (eds.), *Live: Art and Performance*, Routledge: New York, 2004.

Chapter 13 p. 300: From Anni Albers, Preface, *On Weaving*, Dover: New York, 2003 [1965], 15. Ann Hamilton, *the event of a thread*, artist's statement, 2012–2013. Courtesy Ann Hamilton Studio; p. 302: Josiah

Wedgwood's catalogue, quoted in Richard Tames, *Josiah Wedgwood*, Osprey: Oxford, 1997, 9; p. 308: Luke 22:19, *The Holy Bible*, King James Version, 1665. Julie Green, originally published in *Ceramics Monthly* (www.ceramicsmonthly.org), "Last Supper" by Megan Fizell, September 2011, 42–45. Reproduced with permission. Copyright, the American Ceramic Society; p. 311: Abbot Suger, quoted in Crosby, Sumner McKnight, Jane Hayward, et al., *The Royal Abbey of Saint-Denis in the Time of Abbot Suger (1122–1151)*, Metropolitan Museum of Art: New York, 1981, 105; p. 312: Dale Chihuly, quoted in Robert Bersson, *Responding to Art: Form, Content, & Context*, McGraw-Hill: New York, 2003. Fred Wilson in "Chandelier Mori, (Speak of Me as I Am)," detail, art21, 2003; p. 313: Fred Wilson in "Drip Drop Plop," art21, 2001; p. 314: Fred Wilson, quoted in Glenn Harper, *Interventions and Provocations: Conversations on Art, Culture, and Resistance*, SUNY: New York, 1998, 101; p. 315: Fred Wilson and Lisa Graziose Corrin (ed.), *Mining the Museum: An Installation*, New Press, 1994; p. 316: Wendy Weitman, *Kiki Smith: Prints, Books & Things*. © 2003 The Museum of Modern Art, New York; p. 319: Clay Lohmann, personal communication with the author; p. 320: Magdalena Abakanowicz, quoted in Fred Kleiner, *Gardner's Art through the Ages: The Western Perspective*, vol. 2, 776; pp. 320–321: Yinka Shonibare, quoted in *New Art Examiner* 28: Chicago, Pennsylvania, and Washington, D.C. New Art Associations, 2000, xlix; p. 323: Benvenuto Cellini, quoted in John Addington Symonds (trans.), *The Life of Benvenuto Cellini*, Phaidon Press: New York, 1995; p. 324: Chris Burden, quoted in Fred Hoffman, Lisa Le Feuvre, Paul Schimmel, et al., *Chris Burden*, Thames & Hudson: London, 2007, 120.

Chapter 14 p. 331: From Obie Bowman's website, www.searanchescape.com/ob-bowman.html. Extract reprinted by kind permission of Obie Bowman, Architect, FAIA; p. 332: Eric Bunge and Mimi Hoang, quoted in *Rising Currents: Projects for New York's Waterfront*, Museum of Modern Art: New York, 2010, 100; p. 342: Guy de Maupassant, quoted in Neil Leach, *Rethinking Architecture: A Reader in Cultural Theory*, Routledge: New York, 2005, 164; p. 345: C. R. Ashbee, quoted in Bruce Smith and Yoshiko Yamamoto, *The Beautiful Necessity*, Gibbs Smith: Layton, UT, 2004, 92; p. 348: Frank Lloyd Wright, quoted in *Software Development*, 9, 1–6, Miller Freeman, Incorporated, 2001, 7; p. 349: Frank Lloyd Wright, quoted in Robert Pogue Harrison, *Forests: The Shadow of Civilization*, University of Chicago Press, 2009, 234; p. 350: Alfred H. Barr, Jr., quoted in Christopher Wilk and Marcel Breuer, *Marcel Breuer, Furniture and Interiors*, Museum of Modern Art: New York, 1981, 11. Le Corbusier, *Towards a New Architecture*, Courier Corporation: Chelmsford, MA, 2013 [1927], 2, 4; p. 354: Frank Gehry, quoted in Bob de Wit and Ron Meyer, *Strategy: Process, Content, Context: An International Perspective*, Cengage Learning EMEA, 2010, 88; p. 356: Frederick Law Olmsted, quoted in Silvia Barry Sutton (ed.), *Civilizing American Cities: Writings on City Landscapes*, Perseus Books: New York, 1997; p. 358: Frederick Law Olmsted, quoted in Albert Fein, *Frederick Law Olmsted and the American Environmental Tradition*, George Braziller: New York, 1972. Frederick Law Olmsted, quoted in Silvia Barry Sutton (ed.), *Civilizing American Cities: Writings on City Landscapes*, Perseus Books: New York, 1997.

Chapter 15 p. 364: Owen Jones, quoted in Harry Francis Mallgrave, *Modern Architectural Theory: A Historical Survey, 1673–1968*, Cambridge University Press, 2005, 171. William Morris, quoted in Bradley J. Macdonald, *William Morris and the Aesthetic Constitution of Politics*, Lexington: Lanham, MD, 1999; p. 365: William Morris, quoted in Charles Harvey and Jon Press, *William Morris: Design and Enterprise in Victorian Britain*, Manchester University Press, 1991, 42; p. 366: William Morris, quoted in A. H. R. Ball (ed.), *The Earthly Paradise*, Cambridge University Press, 1931; pp. 366–367: William Morris, quoted by his daughter May Morris in *The Collected Works of William Morris*, vol. 15, *The Roots of the Mountains*, Longman: London, 1912, xv–xvi, xxii–xxiii; p. 367: William Morris, quoted in Ruth Kinna, *William Morris: The Art of Socialism*, University of Wales Press: Cardiff, 2000; p. 368: Frank Lloyd Wright, quoted in Edgar Kaufmann and Ben Raeburn, *Frank Lloyd Wright: Writings and Buildings*, Meridian Books: New York, 1960, 102. Frank Lloyd Wright, "In the Cause of Architecture," in Robert Twombly (ed.), *Frank Lloyd Wright, Essential Texts*, W. W. Norton: New York, 2009 [1908], 89; p. 371: Le Corbusier, *L'Esprit Nouveau* (The New Spirit), 1925, quoted in Tom Dewey, *Art Nouveau, Art Deco, and Modernism: A Guide to the Styles, 1890–1940*, Mississippi Museum of Art, 1983 [1925]. Le Corbusier, *L'Esprit Nouveau* (The New Spirit), 1925, quoted in Victor Arwas, *Art Deco*, Abrams: New York, 46; p. 372: Le Corbusier, *L'Esprit Nouveau* (The New Spirit), 1925, quoted in Victor Arwas, *Art Deco*, Abrams: New York, 49; p. 374: Henri Mouron, *A.M. Cassandre*, Schirmer Mosel Production, 1984. © MOURON. CASSANDRE. Lic 2015-13-02-02 www.cassandre.fr. Walter Gropius, quoted in Victor Arwas, *Art Deco*, Abrams: New York, 1980, 49; p. 375: Marcel Breuer, quoted in Christopher Wilk and Marcel Breuer, *Furniture and Interiors*, Museum of Modern Art: New York, 1981, 37. Walter Gropius, quoted in Anton Kaes, Martin Jay, and Edward Dimendberg, *The Weimar Republic Sourcebook*, University of California Press: Berkeley, CA, 1994. Walter Gropius, quoted in Vassiliki Kolocotroni, *Modernism: An Anthology of Sources and Documents*, University of Chicago Press, 1998; p. 378: Raymond Loewy, quoted in Jeffrey Meikle, *Twentieth Century Limited: Industrial Design In America 1925–1939*, Temple University Press, 2010; p. 380: Eero Saarinen, address about Charles Eames (1960), quoted in Robin Schuldenfrei (ed.), *Atomic Dwelling: Anxiety, Domesticity, and Postwar Architecture*, Routledge: New York, 2012; p. 382: From Andrea Branzi, "New Design and New Qualities," trans. Antonino Mazza, in Christina Ritchie and Loris Calzolari, *Phoenix: New Attitudes in Design, Phoenix: Toronto, 1984*, 14–15. © Antonino Mazza. This work is protected by copyright and the making of this copy was with the permission of Access Copyright. Any alteration of its content or further copying in any form whatsoever is strictly prohibited unless otherwise permitted by law; p. 385: April Greiman, quoted in Josh Smith, "Design Discussions: April Greiman on Technology," an *idsgn* blog interview, September 10, 2009. By kind permission of April Greiman. April Greiman, in Liz Farrelly and April Greiman, *Floating Ideas Into Time and Space*, Watson-Guptill: New York, 1998; p. 386: Letter from Barack Obama to Shephard Fairey, www.obeygiant.com/headlines/check-it-out#more-628.

Chapter 17 p. 422: Justinian, quoted in Cyril Mango, *The Art of the Byzantine Empire, 312–1453: Sources and Documents*, Prentice Hall: Englewood Cliffs, NJ, 1972; p. 430: From Erwin Panofsky and Gerda Panofsky-Soergel (eds. & trans.), *Abbot Suger on the Abbey Church of Saint-Denis and Its Art Treasures*, 2nd edition, Princeton University Press, 1979, 101; p. 431: Abbot Suger, quoted in Sumner McKnight Crosby, Jane Hayward, et al., *The Royal Abbey of Saint-Denis in the Time of Abbot Suger (1122–1151)*, Metropolitan Museum of Art: New York, 1981, 105.

Chapter 18 pp. 446–447: From Giovanni Pico della Mirandola, "Oration on the Dignity of Man," 1486, in Ernst Cassirer, Paul Oskar Kristeller, John Herman Randall Jr. (eds.), and E. Livermore Forbes (trans.), *The Renaissance Philosophy of Man*, University of Chicago Press,1948, 3–4; p. 447: Matthew 22:21, *The Holy Bible*, King James Version, 1665; p. 456: Shen Zhou, original translation in Richard Edwards, *The Field of Stones: A Study of the Art of Shen Chou (1427–1509)*, Freer Gallery of Art, Smithsonian Institution: Washington, DC, 1962, 40; p. 464: Francesco Borromini, quoted in Horst Woldemar Janson and Anthony F. Janson, *History of Art: The Western Tradition*, Prentice Hall: Upper Saddle River, NJ, 2004; pp. 464–465: Saint Teresa, in James Christian, *Philosophy: An Introduction to the Art of Wondering*, Cengage Learning: Stamford, CT, 2011.

Chapter 19 p. 484: Gustave Courbet, quoted in Maurizio Sanzio Viano, *A Certain Realism: Making Use of Pasolini's Film Theory and Practice*, University of California Press: Berkeley, CA, 1993; pp. 486–487: Maxime du Camp, in *Revue des Deux Mondes*, 1863, quoted in George Heard Hamilton, *Manet and His Critics*, Yale University Press: New Haven, CT, 1986, 43; p. 488: Théodore Duret, quoted in Carla Rachman, *Monet A&I*, Phaidon Press: New York, 1997 [1878]; p. 490: Georges Rivière, quoted in Barbara Ehrlich White, *Impressionism in Perspective*, Prentice Hall: Englewood Cliffs, 1978, 8.

Chapter 20 p. 496: Louis Vauxcelles, quoted in Paul van der Grijp, *Art and Exoticism: An Anthropology of the Yearning for Authenticity*, LIT

Verlag Münster, 2009, 149; p. 498: Maurice Denis, quoted in Russell T. Clement, *Les Fauves: A Sourcebook*, Greenwood Publishing Group: Westport, CT, 1994, xii; p. 499: Wassily Kandinsky, quoted in Peter Selz, *German Expressionist Painting*, University of California Press: Berkeley, 1957, 176. Wassily Kandinsky, *Concerning the Spiritual in Art*, University of Rochester Press, 1911. Franz Marc, quoted in Pier Carlo Santini, *Modern Landscape Painting*, Phaidon Press: New York, 1972, 50; p. 500: Umberto Boccioni, "The Plastic Foundations of Futurist Sculpture and Painting," Lacerba, 1913, quoted in Lawrence Rainey, Christine Poggi, and Laura Wittman (eds.) *Futurism: An Anthology*, Yale University Press: New Haven, CT, 2009, 142; p. 502: Marcel Duchamp, quoted in Irina D. Costache, *The Art of Understanding Art: A Behind the Scenes Story*, John Wiley & Sons: Hoboken, NJ, 2012. André Breton, quoted in Shireen K. Lewis, *Race, Culture, and Identity: Francophone West African and Caribbean Literature and Theory from Négritude to Créolité*, Lexington: Lanham, MD, 2006, 5; p. 504: Emiliano Zapata and Pancho Villa, quoted in Thomas Fleming, *Thomas Fleming*, Marshall Cavendish, 2007, 54; p. 506: Lee Krasner, quoted in Gijs Van Hensbergen, *Guernica: The Biography of a Twentieth-Century Icon*, Bloomsbury: London, 2005; p. 508: Willem de Kooning, quoted in Mark Stevens, Willem De Kooning, and Annalyn Swan, *De Kooning: An American Master*, A. A. Knopf: New York, 2004. Mark Rothko, quoted in Christopher Butler, *Pleasure and the Arts: Enjoying Literature, Painting, and Music*, Oxford University Press, 2014, 124; p. 510: Gerhard Richter, in *Gerhard Richter: Paintings*, exhibition catalogue, Museum of Contemporary Art: Chicago, 1988. From documenta 7 catalogue, courtesy of Museum Fridericianum Veranstaltungs-GmbH. © Gerhard Richter 2015; p. 511: From "Interview with Hans Ulrich Obrist," in Hans Ulrich Obrist and Dietmar Elger (eds.), *Gerhard Richter—Writings 1961–2007*, Distributed Art Publishers: New York, 2009, 527. From Robert Storr, *September: A History Painting by Gerhard Richter*, Tate Publishing: London, 2010, 8–9. Elizabeth Murray, transcribed from art21 *Exclusive* video "Bop," 2002. Elizabeth Murray: "'Bop' and the Process of Painting," art21 interview, 2003; p. 513: Jimmie Durham, *A Certain Lack Of Coherence: Writings on Art and Cultural Politics*, Kala Press, 1993, 9; p. 516: From Aldona Jonaitis, *Art of the Northwest Coast*, University of Washington Press / Douglas & McIntyre: Vancouver, 2006; pp. 518–519: Louis Agassiz, quoted in Henry Louis Gates, Jr. and D. Yacovone (eds.), *Lincoln on Race and Slavery*, Princeton University Press, 2009, xxiii; p. 519: Carrie Mae Weems, audio interview for "MoMA 2000: Open Ends," The Museum of Modern Art and Acoustiguide, Inc. © 2000 The Museum of Modern Art, New York; p. 520: John 14:2, *The Holy Bible*, King James Version, 1665; p. 521: Enrique Chagoya, quoted in Lois Fichner-Rathus, *Understanding Art*, Cengage Learning: Stamford, CT, 2012; p. 523: Raymond Pettibon, transcription of the words at the bottom of his painting *Untitled*, 2003. © The Artist, courtesy Sadie Coles HQ. London; p. 524: Banksy, *Wall and Piece*, Random House: London, 2006; p. 525: Jonathan Bailey, e-mail message to Jennifer Allora and Guillermo Calzadilla, quoted in Lisa D. Freiman, Carrie Lambert-Beatty, and Yates McKee, *Gloria: Allora & Calzadilla*, Indianapolis Museum of Art, 2011, 45, n55. Courtesy of the artists. Phil Collins to Suzanne Weaver, quoted in Lisa D. Freiman, Carrie Lambert-Beatty, and Yates McKee, *Gloria: Allora & Calzadilla*, Indianapolis Museum of Art, 2011, 45, n55. Phil Collins, quoted in Suzanne Weaver (ed.), Bruce Hainley, Liz Kotz, and Simon Reynolds, *Phil Collins: "The World Won't Listen,"* Dallas Museum of Art, 2008, 65; p. 526: Olafur Eliasson, quoted in Ismail Soyugenc and Richard Torchia (eds.), *Olafur Eliasson: Your Colour Memory*, Arcadia University Art Gallery: Glenside, PA, 2006, 82.

Chapter 21 p. 542: Mark Rothko, from "A Symposium on How to Combine Architecture, Painting, and Sculpture," *Interiors*, 110, 10, May 1951, 104, quoted in Kristine Stiles (ed.), *Theories and Documents of Contemporary Art: A Sourcebook of Artists' Writings*, University of California Press: Berkeley, 1996, 26. © 2015 Kate Rothko Prizel & Christopher Rothko / Artists Rights Society (ARS), New York. Mark Rothko, "Statement," *Tiger's Eye*, 1, 2, December 1947, 44, quoted in Charles Harrison and Paul Wood (eds.), *Art in Theory 1900–1990: An Anthology of Changing Ideas*, Blackwell: Oxford, 1992, 565; pp. 542–543: Wassily Kandinsky, "Reminiscences/ Three pictures," 1913, quoted in Kenneth C. Lindsay and Peter Vergo (eds.), *Kandinsky: Complete Writings on Art* vol 1, Da Capo Press: New York, 1994 [1982], 368–369. Copyright © Mar 22, 1994, Peter Vergo. Reprinted by permission of Da Capo Press, a member of the Perseus Books Group; p. 543: Wassily Kandinsky, quoted in H. W. Janson and Anthony F. Janson, *History of Art*, 5th edition, Prentice Hall: Englewood Cliffs,1995, 912; p. 544: From the San Francisco Museum of Modern Art video, "Brice Marden on Cold Mountain," 2000. © 2015 Brice Marden / Artists Rights Society (ARS), New York. From Raymond Bellour and Bill Viola, "An Interview with Bill Viola," *October*, 34, Autumn 1985, 91–119, 94. By kind permission of Bill Viola. From Kieran Kavanaugh and Otilio Rodriguez Copyright (trans.), *The Collected Works of St. John of the Cross*, © 1964, 1979, 1991 by Washington Province of Discalced Carmelites: ICS Publications 2131 Lincoln Road, N.E. Washington, D.C. 20002-1199 U.S.A. www.icspublications.org.

Chapter 22 p. 550: From Linda Seidel, "Adam and Eve: Shameless First Couple of the Ghent Altarpiece," *Different Visions: A Journal of New Perspectives on Medieval Art*, 1, September 2008, 13; p. 553: From *Whisper, the Waves, the Wind*, a film and performance by Suzanne Lacy, 1994, 34. Used by kind permission; p. 561: Amalia Mesa-Bains, quoted in *Galería Posada, Ofrendas*, October 7–November 17, 1984, La Raza Bookstore and Galería Posada: Sacramento, CA, 1984, 2. Used by kind permission of Dr. Amalia Mesa-Bains, Professor Emerita, California State University, Monterey Bay.

Chapter 23 p. 564: From THE DIVINE COMEDY by Dante Alighieri, translated by John Ciardi. Copyright 1954, 1957, 1959, 1960, 1961, 1965, 1967, 1970 by the Ciardi Family Publishing Trust. Used by permission of W. W. Norton & Company, Inc; p. 572: From John Berger, *Ways of Seeing*, Penguin: New York, 1973, 54; p. 575: From Hugh Honour and John Fleming, *A World History of Art* 7th edition, Laurence King: London, 2005, 614; p. 579: From the art21 segment, Iñigo Manglano-Ovalle, in "Ecology," 2007.

Chapter 24 p. 582: From "Art at Arm's Length: A History of the Selfie," *New York Magazine*, February 3, 2014. Used by permission; p. 586: From Kenneth Clark, *The Nude: A Study in Ideal Form*, Princeton University Press, 1972, 144; p. 587: From Carolee Schneemann, *Imaging Her Erotics: Essays, Interviews, Projects*, MIT Press: Cambridge, MA, 2002, 55; p. 588: Kimsooja, transcribed from art21 *Exclusive* videos "Kimsooja: 'A Beggar Woman' and 'A Homeless Woman'," 2009; p. 589: Cindy Sherman, originally published in InterviewMagazine.com, November 2008, Courtesy BMP Media Holdings, LLC; p. 590: From Gloria Steinem, *Marilyn: Norma Jeane*, MJF Books: New York, 1997, 15, 22; p. 593: From Glenn O'Brien, interview with Annie Proulx in Nancy Spector, Richard Prince, catalogue to the exhibition *Richard Prince: Spiritual America*, 285. Originally published in *Richard Prince* © 2007 The Solomon R. Guggenheim Foundation, New York. Used by permission; p. 598: Ana Mendieta, quoted in John Perrault, "Earth and Fire: Mendieta's Body of Work," in Petro Barreras del Rio and John Perrault (eds.) *Ana Mendieta: A Retrospective*, New Museum of Contemporary Art: New York, 1987, 10.

Chapter 25 p. 609: From Alfred Delvau, *Histoire anecdotique des cafés et cabarets de Paris* (Anecdotal History of the Cafés and Cabarets of Paris), Paris, 1862, as quoted in Robert L. Herbert, *Impressionism: Art, Leisure, & Parisian Society*, Yale University Press, New Haven, CT, 1988, 74; p. 613: From A. Phillip Randolph, "Call to Negro America to March on Washington for Jobs and Equal Participation in National Defense," *Black Worker*, May 1941, 14. Courtesy of A. Philip Randolph Institute; p. 614: Transcribed from the art21 *New York Close Up* segment "Rashid Johnson Makes Things to Put Things On," 2013.

Chapter 26 p. 618: From Edmund Clark, "Introduction," in *Guantanamo: If the Light Goes Out*, Dewi Lewis Publishing: Stockport, 2010. By kind permission of Edmund Clark. From Omar Deghayes, "You're Famous Now," in Edmund Clark, *Guantanamo: If the Light Goes Out*, Dewi Lewis, Stockport, 2010. By kind permission of Edmund Clark; p. 619: From *Discipline and Punish: The Birth of the Prison* by Michel Foucault. English Translation copyright © 1977 by Alan Sheridan (New York: Pantheon). Originally published in French as *Surveiller et Punir: Naissance de la prison*. Copyright © 1975 by Editions Gallimard. Reprinted by permission of Editions Gallimard; p. 633: From Homi K. Bhabha, "Postmodernism/ Postcolonialism," in Robert S. Nelson and Richard Shiff, *Critical Terms for Art History*, 2nd ed., University of Chicago Press, 2003, 450, 321; pp. 633–634: Transcribed from the art21 *Exclusive* video "Kerry James Marshall: On Museums," 2008; p. 634: KERRY JAMES MARSHALL, text by Kerry James Marshall. Copyright © 2000. Used by permission of Harry N. Abrams, Inc., New York. All rights reserved.

Chapter 27 p. 638: From Leonard Shlain, *Art and Physics: Parallel Visions in Space, Time and Light*, William Morrow: New York, 1991, 20; p. 644: From John Wesley Powell, *Exploration of the Colorado River of the West and Its Tributaries*, Government Printing Office: Washington, D.C., 1875, 214; p. 645: From Joseph Pennell, *Joseph Pennell's Pictures of the Wonder of Work*, J. B. Lippincott: Philadelphia, 1916; p. 646: Transcribed from the art21 *New York Close Up* video "LaToya Ruby Frazier Makes Moving Pictures," 2012. Mike Davies, *Planet of Slums*, Verso/ New Left Books: London and New York:, 2006, 167; p. 647: Transcribed from art21 *Exclusive* video "Matthew Ritchie: Apocalypse," 2008; p. 649: Transcribed from art21 *Exclusive* video "Mel Chin: Paydirt," 2008; p. 651: From *Rising Currents: Projects for New York's Waterfront*, Museum of Modern Art: New York, 2011, 9; p. 652: Transcribed from art21 *Exclusive* video "Maya Lin: Disappearing Bodies of Water," 2013. Transcribed from art21 *New York Close Up* video "Mary Mattingly's Waterfront Development," 2014; p. 653: Don Gray, quoted in exhibition statement, "Stone," The Nightingale Gallery, Eastern Oregon University: La Grande, OR, 2012; p. 654: From Robert Smithson, "The Spiral Jetty," in Jack Flam (ed.), *Robert Smithson: Collected Writings*, Berkeley: University of California Press, 1996, 146. © Estate of Robert Smithson/ Licensed by VAGA, New York, NY, www.vagarights.com; p. 656: Transcribed from art21 *New York Close Up* video "David Brooks Is in His Element," 2013.

Index

Page numbers in *italics* refer to figure/illustration.

A

Abakanowicz, Magdalena
Backs in Landscape, 319–320, *320*
Abramoviæ, Marina
The House with the Ocean View, 297, *297*
Imponderabilia, 297, *297*
Absolute symmetry, 134
Abstract art, 33. *See also* Art
Abstract Expressionism, 507
and American modernism, 506–508
Abstraction
and spirituality, 542–544
Abstraction, Porch Shadows (Strand), 82, *82*, 247
Acropolis, 335
The Acropolis, Athens, 408, *408*
Acrylic resins, 203
Action Office, 388
Active seeing, 7–8
Actual texture, 118, *119*, 121
Actual weight, 134
Adams, Ansel
Moonrise, Hernandez, New Mexico, *250*, 251
Additive processes, 101, *101*, 274
Adler company, 375
Adobe bricks, 334
Adobe Photoshop, 386
The Adoration of the Magi (Tiepolo), *174*, 175
Aegean cultures, 404–407
Aesthetic pleasure, 10
Afocal art, 141
Africa, cultures of, 441–442
African-American art. *See also* Art
iconography of heroism in, 42–43
racial identities in, 611–615
Whispers from the Walls, 177, *177*
African-American artists. *See also* Artists
Catlett, Elizabeth, 223, *223*
Johnson, Rashid, 614
Lawrence, Jacob, 613
Lovell, Whitfield, 177, *177*
Piper, Adrian, 614
Ringgold, Faith, 8, *8*
Thomas, Mickalene, 14, *14*
African-Americans
racial identities in art of, 611–615
African art. *See also* Art
banda mask, 600, *601*
dancing mask, 38, *38*, 600, *601*
feast-making spoon *(Wunkirmian)*, 72, *72*
sculpture, 12, 17
textiles, 127
African artists. *See also* Artists
Anatsui, El, 150, *151*
Kentridge, William, 177–178, *178*
Kwei, Kane, 16–17, *17*
Samba, Chéri, 50–52, *51*
African art of the encounter, 461
African festival, 576–577
Afterglow I (Kahn), 36, *36*
After the Bath, Woman Drying Herself (Degas), *170*, 170–171
Agassiz, Louis, 518
Agathias, 533
Agree, James
Let Us Now Praise Famous Men, 247
Agriculture, 394
a-ha, 160, *161*
Ahearn, John
Homage to the People of the South Bronx: Double Dutch at Kelly Street 1: Frieda, Jevette, Towana, Stacey, 285–286, *286*
Airborne Event (Tomaselli), 210, *210*
Airflow, Chrysler, 377, *377*, 378
Air Liner Number 4 (Bel Geddes and Koller), *377*, 377–378
Aitken, Doug
Sleepwalkers, 3
Ai Weiwei
Han Dynasty Urn with Coca-Cola Logo, 517, *517*
Ajitto (Mapplethorpe), 22, *22*
Akhenaten, 399
Alabama Tenant Farmer's Kitchen (Washstand with View into Dining Area of Burroughs' Home, Hale County, Alabama) (Evans), *247*, 247–248
The Alba Madonna (Raphael), 166–167, *166–167*, 536, *536*
Albers, Anni, 300
Wall hanging, 317, *317*
Alcíbar, José de, *From Spaniard and Black, Mulatto (De Español y Negra, Mulatto)*, 628, *628*
Aldus Pagemaker, 386
Alexander the Great, *215*, 409, 622, *623*
Algorithm (Allora and Calzadilla), *524*, 524–525
al-Hadid, Diana
Nolli's Orders, 512, *512*
Ali, Laylah
Untitled, *152*, 152–153
The Allegory of Painting (The Painter and His Model as Klio) (Vermeer), *158*, 159
Allora, Jennifer
Algorithm, *524*, 524–525
Altarpieces
The Ghent Altarpiece (Van Eyck), 19–20, *19–20*, 548
Maestà ("Majesty") *Altarpiece* (Duccio), 75, *75*
American artists
Manglano-Ovalle, Iñigo, 579
Rauschenberg, Robert, 635
Weems, Carrie Mae, 518–519, 626–628
American Art News, 23
American Modern dinnerware (Wright), *378*, *378*
American modernism, 506
and Abstract Expressionism, 506–508
American Progress (Gast), 603, *603*
Amida Buddha sculpture, 43, *43*. *See also* Sculptures
Amiens Cathedral, 340, *340*
Amphitheater, 338, *338*
Anagamas, 304
An Allegory with Venus and Cupid (Bronzino), 463, *463*, *571*
Analogous color schemes, 102
Anamorphic projection, 14
Anatsui, El, 150, *151*
Between Earth and Heaven, *151*
Andre the Giant Has a Posse (Fairey), 386
The Angel Appearing to the Shepherds (van Rijn), *226*, 227
Angkor Wat, Cambodia, 436, *436*
Animation, 260
Animism, 19, 532, 533
An-My Lê
29 Palms: Night Operations III, *248*, 248–249
Annie G., Cantering, Saddled (Muybridge), 240, *240*
Annunciation and Visitation, 433, *433*
The Annunciation (The Mérode Altarpiece) (Campin), *194*, 194–195
Annunciation of the Death of the Virgin from Maestà Altarpiece (Duccio), *75*, 75–76
An Ofrenda for Dolores del Rio (Mesa-Bains), 561, *561*
Anshutz, Thomas, *Steamboat on the Ohio*, 645, *645*
Antenna Design, 362
Anthemius of Tralles, 420, *420*, *421*
Antin, Eleanor
Constructing Helen, 256, *256*
Minetta Lane-A Ghost Story, 291–292, *292*
My Kingdom Is the Right Size, 596, *596*
Antoni, Janine
Honey Baby, 562, *562*
Touch, 81, *81*
Antony, Mark, 398
Apache tribes, 330
Apartheid, 178
A Pastoral Landscape (Claude), 469, *469*
Aperture, 250
Apollinaire, Guillaume, 107
Apollo Belvedere, 39, *39*, 478
Apoxyomenos (The Scraper), 409, *409*
Apple Corporation, 382, 383
Apple iPhone, 386, *386*

Apse (Romanesque architecture), 340
Aquatint, 230–231
Archaiologia, 404
Archeological Museum, Athens, 535
Archer, Frederick, 244, 249
Arches, 336–341
Architectural Record, 346
Architecture
and actual weight, 133
community life and, 356–361
early technologies, 333–341
eighteenth and nineteenth century environment and, 328–333
Greek, 148
green, 17, 331–332
Indian, 186
infrastructure and, 359
Islamic religious, 32
and light, 88
modern and contemporary technologies, 342–356
Rasin Building, 132–133, *133*
Renaissance, 137
Romanesque, 429–430
Rosenthal Center for Contemporary Art, 114, *114*
suburbia and, 358–359
technological innovations in, 639–642
Villa La Rotonda, 138–140, *139*
Architrave, 336
Arch of Titus, *413*
Arens, Egmnt C., *378*
Aristotle, 409, 452
Armor *(yoroi), 440,* 441
Armory Show, 23–24
Arringhiera, 26
Art, 10
Assyrian king and, 320
Baroque, 464–470
body as work of, 586–588
Byzantine, 420–424
Carolingian, 428–429
ceramic, 641–642
in China, 436–439, 455–457
chinese kings and, 620
colonialism in, 627–632
contemporary, 510–525
earliest, 394–396
early Christian, 420–424
environmental catastrophe in, 645–652, 646–652
environmental understanding and, 642–652
French power in, 620–622
Gothic, 431–433
Greece power in, 622
in historical context, 391
imbalance of power and, 626–627
in India, 433–436
in Japan, 439–441, 455–457
kinetic, 122
meaning of, 37–38
Mesopotamian, 396–397
in Mexico, 457–461, 628
narratives in, 122–123, *123*
nature, 642–646
nature and industry, 642–645
racial identities in, 611–615
Romanesque, 340, 429–430
rulers power in, 619–622
in South America, 457–461
technological innovations in, 638–642
themes of, 529
time and motion, 116
value in, 20–26
visual signs of class in, 607–611
visual weight, 134
Art and Physics: Parallel Vision in Space, Time, and Light (Shlain), 638
Art Deco, 371. *See also* Art Moderne
Artforum, 589
Art history/periods
Cubism, 496–498
earliest art, 394–396
eighteenth and nineteenth century, 472–492
Fauvism, 498
Futurism, 500
German Expressionism, 498–499
Minimalism, 508–509
of Native Americans, 604–605
politics and painting, 504–506
Pop Art, 508–509
Renaissance, 444–446
Rococo, 474–476
Roman, 410–414
Surrealism, 500–504
Art in America, 84
Artistic Culture in America (Bing), 369
Artistic value, 21–23
Artists. *See also specific artists*
African-American, 633–634
American, 635
creative process, 10
German, 587–588
imaging desire, 572–574
Korean, 588
longer/deeper view of environment, 653–655
modern, 82–85
roles of the, 10–20
scale and proportion, 146–147
shaping public perception of environment, 642–646
using own bodies, 582–588
value in art, 20–26
women (*See* Women artists)
The Artist's Mother (Seurat), 169, *169*
Art market
contemporary art and, 521–525
Art Moderne, 371. *See also* Art Deco
Artnews, 126
Art Nouveau movement, 364, 368, 369–370
The Art of Painting (Vasari), 182, *183*
Art of the Northwest Coast (Jonaitis), 516
Art parks, 294–295
Arts and Crafts Exhibition Society, 366
Arts and Crafts Movement, 364–368
Aryans, 401. *See also* Vedic people
Aryan tribesmen, 433
A Scythed Chariot, Armored Car and Pike (da Vinci), 451, *451*
Ashbee, C. R., 345
Ashoka, 416
Ashurnasirpal II Killing Lions, 620, *620*
Asia
developments in, 414–416
Aspiration (Douglas), *613,* 613–614
Assemblage, 286–289
Assumption and Consecration of the Virgin (Titian), 50, *51*
Assurnasirpal II, 397
Assurnasirpal II Killing Lions, 397, *397*
Assyrians, 397
Astaire, Fred, 133
Astra Construction, 494
Asymmetrical balance, *136,* 136–138
At daylight the miserable man was carried to an oak . . . (Gonzales-Day), 15–16, *16*
Athena Parthenos, 408
Atheneum (Meier), 356, *357*
Athens (Cartier-Bresson), 249, *249*
"Atlas" Slave (Michelangelo), 280, *280*
Atmospheric (aerial) perspective, 89–92, *90*
Auerbach, Frank
Head of Catherine Lampert VI, 180, *180*
Augustus, 414
Augustus of Primaporta, 411, *411*
Aurelius, Marcus, 414
Auteurs, 260
Avant-garde, 23–25
Avenue of the Dead, 458, *458*

B

Backs in Landscape (Abakanowicz), 319–320, *320*
Bacon, Francis
Three Studies of Lucian Freud, 20–21, *21*
Bailey, Jonathan, 525
Baker, Josephine, 94
Balance
asymmetrical, 136–138
defined, 134
radical, 138–140
symmetrical, 134–136
Bal du Moulin de la Galette (Renoir), *489,* 489–490, 608, *608*
Balla, Giacomo, 500
Dynamism of a Dog on a Leash, 500, *500*
Ballet Mécanique (Léger), 257, *257*
Balloon-frame construction, 343. *See also* Wood-frame construction
Bamboo (Ke Jiusi), *605,* 605
Banana Flower (O'Keeffe), 168, *168*
Banda mask dance, 600, *601*
Banksy
Banksy: Wall and Pieces, 524
Kissing Coppers, 524, *524*
Banksy Locations & Tours: A Collection of Graffiti Locations and Photographs in London, England (Bull), 524
Banksy: Wall and Pieces (Banksy), 524
Barack Obama "Hope" Poster (Fairey), 386, *387*
Barber Shop (Lawrence), 150–152, *151,* 153
Bardon, Geoff, 37
Baroque art, 464–470
Barr, Alfred H., Jr., 350

Barrel vault, 337–338, *337-338*, 340, 412
Barrel-vaulted gallery, Colosseum, Rome, 338, *338*
Barrie, Dennis, 21–22
Barron, Steve, 160
Basel School of Arts and Crafts, 381
Basilica, 420
The Basket of Apples (Cézanne), *46*, 47
Basquiat, Jean-Michel, 204
Charles the First, *42*, 42–43
iconographic images by, 42–43
Bath (Cassatt), 221, *221*
Bathers (Fragonard), 475, *475*
The Bathers (Seurat), 491, *491*
Batman: The Dark Knight Returns (Miller), 178
Battle of Anghiari (da Vinci), 451
Battle of Cascina (Michelangelo), 451
Battleship Potemkin (Eisenstein), 258, *258*
Bauhaus, 374–376
Bauhaus 1 cover (Bayer), *376*
Bauhaus magazine, *376*
Bayer, Herbert
Bauhaus 1 cover, *376*
Universal Alphabet, 376
Beard, Richard, 243
Bearden, Romare
She-ba, *103*, 103–104
Beat the Whites with the Red Wedge (Lissitzky), 373
Beethoven
Ode to Joy, 525
A Beggar Woman-Mexico City (Kimsooja), 588, *588*
Bel Geddes, Norman, 377
Air Liner Number 4, *377*, 377–378
Horizons, 378
Belgian artists
Magritte, René, 502
Bellows, George
Cliff Dwellers, 607, *607*
A Day in June, 607, *607*
Benito, Edouardo, 371
Vogue magazine cover, 371
Bent-Corner Chest (Kook), 324–325, *325*
Bentham, Jeremy, *A General Idea of a Penitentiary Panopticon*, 618, *619*
Berliner Platze (Mehretu), 66–67, *67*
Bernini, Gianlorenzo, 464
The Cornaro Family in a Theater Box, 464, *465*
David, 122, *123*
The Ecstasy of St. Theresa, 464, *465*
St. Peter's basilica colonnade, 464, *464*
Beta Ghiorghis (House of St. George), Lalibela, 442, *442*
Between Earth and Heaven (Anatsui), *151*
Beuys, Joseph
I Like America and America Likes Me, 587–588, *587*
Bhikshus, 534
Bierstadt, Albert
Puget Sound on the Pacific Coast, 33, *33*, 35–36, 603
The Rocky Mountains, Lander's Peak, 642, *643*
Bihzad of Zulaykha, 569, *569*
Bilateral symmetry, 134
Bilongo, 18
Bing, S., 369
Artistic Culture in America, 369
The Birch (Gladu), 344, *345*
Birchler, Alexander
Detached Building, *128*, 129, *129*
Bird carved from soapstone, Great Zimbabwe, 442, *442*
Bird Skeleton (Smith), 212, *213*
Birnbaum, Dara
Technology/Transformation: Wonder Woman, 263, *263*
The Birth of a Nation (Griffith), 257–258
Birth of Venus (Cabanel), 256, *256*
The Birth of Venus (Botticelli), 449–450, *450*
Black Death, 446, 555. *See also* Bubonic plague
Black Face and Arm Unit (Jones), 93, *93*
Black Flag, 523
Black Gold, 150
Black Lines (Schwarze Linien) (Kandinsky), 113, *113*
Black Lung (Lohmann), 319, *319*
"Black Paintings," 482
The Black Pirate, 260
Black Square (Malevich), 37, *37*
Blaxploitation films, 14
Blériot, Louis, 494
Blizzard Entertainment, 129
Blue Rider group, 498–499, 543
Boccaccio, 444
Boccioni, Umberto, 500
Development of a Bottle in Space, 71, *71*
Development of a Bottle in Space Through Color, 71
Development of a Bottle in Space Through Form, 71
Table + Bottle + House, 70, *70*
Unique Forms of Continuity in Space, 500, *500*
Bochner, Mel
Win!, 593, *593*
Bodhisattva, Ajanta, India, 185–187, *186*
Body
beautiful, 582–586
as work of art, 586–588
Body of a Courtesan in Nine Stages of Decomposition (Eitaku), 555, *555*
Bohr, Niels, 500
Boit, Edward Darley, 550
Boit, Mary Louisa Cushing, 550
Bologna, Giovanni
Capture of the Sabine Women, 278, *278*
Bonaparte, Napoleon, 478
Bonheur, Rosa
Plowing in the Nivernais, 485, *485*
Bonnard, Pierre, 369
The Terrace at Vernon, 112, *112*
Book of Genesis, 93
Book of Hours, 555
Book of Lamentations, 418
Book of Revelation, 474
Bop (Murray), 511, *511*
Borromini, Francesco
San Carlo alle Quattro Fontane facade, 464, *465*
Boston Common at Twilight (Hassam), 138, *138*
Botticelli, Sandro, 449
The Birth of Venus, 449–450, *450*
Primavera, 192, *192*
Boucher, François
Le Chinois galant, 476, *476*
Boulevard des Capucines (Monet), 488
Bowers, Andrea
United States v. Tim DeChristopher, 655, *655*
Bowman, Obie
Brunsell Residence, California, 331, *331*
Bradbury, R. E., 283
Bradley, David P.
Indian Country Today, 514, *514*
Brady, Mathew, 244–245
The Brady Bunch, 594
Brahmans, 433
Brandard, R., 225
Branzi, Andrea, 382
Braque, Georges, 199, 371, 372
Houses at l'Estaque, 496, *496*
Violin and Palette, 497, *497*
Breton, André, 502, 507
Breuer, Marcel
Armchair, Model B3, 375
Bridge over a Pool of Water Lilies (Monet), *490*
Bringing the War Home (Eisenstein), 205
British National Trust, 345
Bronze Age Aegean peoples, 404
Bronze-casting technology, 402
Bronzino
An Allegory with Venus and Cupid, 463, *463*, 571, *571*
Brooke, Sandy
Fate and Luck: Eclipse, *172*, 172–173
Brookhart, Theodore, *378*
Brooks, David, *Imbroglios (A Phylogenetic Tree, from Homo Sapiens to Megalops Atlanticus)*, 656, *656*
Brown, Denise Scott, 155, 512
Brown, Robert, 124
Brownian motion, 124
The Brown Sisters (Nixon), 552, *552*
The Brown Sisters, Truro, Massachusetts (Nixon), 552, *552*
Brueghel, Jan, the Elder
Flowers in a Blue Vase, 56, *57*
The Brueghel Series: A Vanitas of Style (Steir), 56–57, *57*
Bruguera, Tania, 19, *19*
Brunelleschi, Filippo, 276, 432, 447
Sacrifice of Isaac, 277, *277*
Bubonic plague, 444, 446. *See also* Black Death
The Bucket List (Crabb), 209
Budd, Ralph, 377
Buddhism, 418, 433, 436, 439, 534, 539
Diamond Sutra, 214, *214*
iconography representing, 43
Buddhist Path of Life, 416
Buddhist wall paintings, 438
Buglaj, Nikolai
"Race"ing Sideways, 611–612, *612*
Bulfinch, Charles
Harrison Gray Otis House, 344, *344*

Bull, Martin
Banksy Locations & Tours: A Collection of Graffiti Locations and Photographs in London, England, 524
Bunge, Eric, 332
New Aqueous City, 332, *333*
Buon fresco, 185
Burckhardt, Rudy, 126–127
Burden, Chris
Shoot, 263, *263*
Urban Light, 324, *324*
The Burghers of Calais (Rodin), 285, *285*
Burial at Ornans (Courbet), 484, *484*
The Burial of Count Orgaz (El Greco), *463,* 463–464
Burin, 225
Burj Khalifa (Smith), *355,* 355–356
Burke, Edmund
Inquiry into the Origin of Our Ideas of the Sublime and the Beautiful, 481
Burlington Railroad, 377
Burlington *Zephyr, 376,* 376–377
Burne-Jones, Sir Edward, 367
Burnet, Thomas
Sacred Theory of the Earth, 10
Burning, 251
Burroughs, William S., 513
Burton, F. C., 323
Byzantine art, 420–424, *420–423,* 625, *625*
Byzantine Orthodox churches, 533

C

Cabanel, Alexander
Birth of Venus, 256, *256*
Cadillac Fleetwood, General Motors, 379, *379*
Caesar, Julius, 414
Cai Guo-Qiang, 4–6, *5*
Footprints of History: Fireworks Project for the Opening Ceremony of the 2008 Beijing Olympic Games, 4–5, *5,* 8
Project to Extend the Great Wall of China by 10,000 Meters: Project for Extraterrestrials No. 10, 4, *5,* 15
Transient Rainbow, 100, *100*
Cahokia Mounds State Historic Site, Illinois, 403–404, *404*
Caillebotte, Gustave
Place de l'Europe on a Rainy Day, 77, *77, 610,* 610–611
Cai Lun, 162
Calatrava, Santiago
Port Authority Trans Hudson (PATH) station, 359, *359*
Calder, Alexander
Untitled, 122
California Institute of Technology, 376
Calla Lily (Mapplethorpe), 558, *558*
Callicrates, 408
Calligraphic scroll (detail), Syria or India, 537, *537*
Calligraphy, 30–31
The Calling of St. Matthew (Caravaggio), 465–466, *466*
Calotype, 243
Calvary (Samba), 50–52, *51*
Calzadilla, Guillermo
Algorithm, 524, 524–525
Cameron, Julia Margaret, 244
Portrait of Thomas Carlyle, 244, *244*
Camp Five, Detainee's Cell (Clark), 618, *619*
Campin, Robert
The Annunciation (The Mérode Altarpiece), 194, 194–195
The Canon, 147, 585
Cañon City, 298
Cantilever, 347
Cao Fei
RMB City, in *Art in the Twenty-First Century,* 270, *270*
Capital, 336
Corinthian, 336
Doric, 336
Ionic, 336
Capture of the Sabine Women (Bologna), 278, *278*
Cara Grande, 104, *104*
Carambola (Milhazes), 37–38, *38*
Caravaggio, 465–466
The Calling of St. Matthew, 465–466, *466*
Carlisle, Isabel, 180
Carlyle, Thomas, 244, *244*
Carnival on the Boulevard des Capucines (Monet), 488, *489*
Carolingian art, 428–429
Carrà, Carlo, 500
Carracci, Annibale
Landscape with Flight into Egypt, 468, *468*
Carter, Linda, 263
Cartier-Bresson, Henri
Athens, 249, *249*
Carved relief sculpture, 276
Carving, 280–282
Cassandre, A. M.
L'Intrans poster, 374, *374*
Cassatt, Mary, 220
Bath, 221, *221*
The Coiffure, 96, *96*
light/dark contrasting by, 98–99, *98–99*
In the Loge (At the Français, a Sketch), 98–99, *98–99*
The Map (The Lesson), 227, *227*
Young Mother, Daughter, and Son, 171, 171–172
Casta painting, *628,* 628–629
Casting, 283–286
Cast iron, 342
Cast-iron construction, 342
Cast shadow, 94
Catholic League for Religious and Civil Rights, 23
Catlett, Elizabeth
Sharecropper, 223, *223*
CBS, 382
Cedi, Anang, 16
Cellini, Benvenuto
Saltcellar: Neptune (Sea) and Tellus (Earth), 323, *323*
Celmins, Vija
Untitled (Ocean), 169, 169–170
Central Chinese Television building (Koolhaas and Scheeren), 353, *353*
Century of Progress Exposition, 377
Ceramic arts, 641–642
Ceramic bowl, 476, *476*
Ceramics, 282, 303–310
coiling, 305
as politics, 308–309
porcelain, 306–310
potter's wheel, 305–306
slab construction, 304–305
Cézanne, Paul, 490
The Basket of Apples, 46, 47
The Large Bathers, 492, *492*
Mme. Cézanne in a Red Armchair, 84, *84*
Mont Sainte-Victoire and the Viaduct of the Arc River Valley, 492, *492*
Still Life with Cherries and Peaches, 491, 491–492
Chagoya, Enrique
Crossing I, 520–521, *521*
Chairman Mao en Route to Anyuan (Chunhua), 623, *623*
Chalk and charcoal paintings, 167–169
Chan Buddhism, 457
Chaplin, Charlie, 259, *259*
Charles the First (Basquiat), *42,* 42–43
Chaucer, Geoffrey, 367
The Works of Geoffrey Chaucer Newly Augmented, 367
Chauvet, Jean-Marie, 392
Chauvet Cave, 392
Chauvet cave painting, 392, *393*
Cheng Sixiao, *Ink Orchids,* 455, *455*
Cherokee Indian Nation, 43
Chesneau, Ernest, 489
Chez le Père Lathuille (Manet), 488, *488*
Chiaroscuro, 93–94, *94*
Chihuly, Dale, 311
Mille Fiori, 311–312, *312*
Chim↑Pom (Kakizaki), 647, *647*
Chin, Mel
Operation Paydirt/Fundred Dollar Bill Project (Mel Chin), 649–651, *650*
China
art in, 436–439, 455–457
national identities in, 605–606
Chine-collé, 228
Chinese art. *See also* Art
Dunhuang, 9
national identities in, 605–606
Chinese artists. *See also* Artists
Cai Guo-Qiang, 4–6, *5,* 8, 10, 15, 100, *100*
Cao Fei, 270, *270*
Feng Mengbo, 84–85, *85*
Hung Liu, 12, 58, *58, 60,* 60–61, *61*
Liang Kai, 175, *175*
Shen Zhou, 456, *456*
Chinese Buddhist monks, 436
Chinese culture, 402
Chinoiserie, 476
Christ, from *Deësis* mosaic, *421,* 533, *533*
Christian art in Europe, 427–433
Carolingian art, 428–429
Gothic art, 431–433
Romanesque art, 429–430
Christianity, 418, 420, 532

Christian religion
foreshortening in art depicting, 79, *79*
light/dark in art depicting, *90*
line/linear perspective in art depicting, *75*, 75–76
oil painting depicting, *194*, 194–195
principles of design in art of, 138, *139*
use of patterns, 148–150, *149*
Christian Roman Empire, 422
Christo
Over the River, Project for the Arkansas River, State of Colorado, 298, *298*
Chromosaturation (Cruz-Diez), 88, *89*
Chrysler, P., 378
Chrysler *Airflow*, 377, *377*, 378
Chrysler Salon, N. Y. C., *377*
Chuck Close, 108
Chung, Maggie, 86
Chunhua, Lin
Chairman Mao en Route to Anyuan, 623, *623*
Church of St. Sernin, 540, *540*
Cincy (Grosse), 114, *114*
Cinématographe, 240
Cire-perdue, 283. *See also* Lost-wax process
Citizen Kane, 260
Civilization (Clark), 39
Civilizations, 394
Egyptian, 397–400
Great River Valley, 400–402
Greek, 407–410
Claerbout, David
Sections of a Happy Moment, 267, *267*, 273
Clark, Edmund
Camp Five, Detainee's Cell, 618, *619*
Clark, Kenneth, 586
Civilization, 39
The Nude: A Study in Ideal Form, 586
Class
and identities, 607–611
marking, 607–610
place and displacement, 610–611
Claude (Claude Lorrain)
A Pastoral Landscape, 469, *469*
Clay ceramics, 282
Clemenceau, Georges, 124
Cleopatra, 398
Cleopatra Jones, 14
Cliff Dwellers (Bellows), 607, *607*
Climate, and architecture, 330–331
Close, Chuck, 107, 108–109, *108–109*
Stanley II, *108–109*
Closed/restricted palette, 110
Close-up, 258
Cloud Gate (Kapoor), 291, *291*
Coatlicue, 459, *459*
The Coiffure (Cassatt), 96, *96*
Coiling, 305
Cold Mountain 6 (Bridge) (Marden), 544, *544*
Cole, Henry, 364
Coleridge, Samuel, 479
Colin, Paul
Figure of a Woman, 94, *94*
Collage, 205–207
political, 206–207
The Collected Works of William Morris, 366
Collins, Phil
The World Won't Listen, 525, *525*
Cologne Cathedral, Germany, 432, *432*
Colonialism in art, 627–632
Colonnade, 335
Color
and digital photography, 251–256
emphasis and focal point created using, 141–144
in fluorescent light, 88
intermediate, 101
light and, 88, *89*
local, 111
perceptual, 111
primary, 101
representational use of, 111–112
schemes, 102–107
secondary, 101
symbolic, 112–113, *113*
vocabulary, 100–102
Color and Information (Winters), 84, *85*
Color wheel, 101
Colossal Buddha, Bamiyan, 436, *437*
Colossal head, Olmec culture, 403, *403*
Colosseum, Rome, 338, *338*
Columbus, Christopher, 450, 455, 457–458
Column, 336
Column of Trajan, 412–414, *413*
Combine-painting, 208
The Communist Manifesto (Marx), 485
Community life, and architecture, 356–361
Complementary color schemes, 104
Complex societies in the Americas, 402–404
Composition, 37
Composition VII (Kandinsky), *498*, 499, 543, *543*
Computer and new media, 267–270
Concerning the Spiritual in Art (Kandinsky), 499, 543
Connor, Bull, 26
Connotation, 189
Considering Mother's Mantle (McCoy), 294, *294*
Constable, John, 10
The Hay Wain, 479–480, *480*
Constantine, 414, 420
Constructing Helen (Antin), 256, *256*
Construction
cast-iron, 342
frame, 342–345
load-bearing, 334
post-and-lintel, 334–336
steel-and-reinforced-concrete, 345–356
Constructivism, Russian, 373
Contamination (Contaminação) (Vasconcelos), 321, *321*
Conté, Nicholas-Jacques, 169
Conté crayon, 169
Contemporary art, 510–525
cross-fertilization in, 510–525
global present, 513–518
identity, media, and the art market, 521–525
plurality of styles, 510–513
revisioning history, 513–518, 518–521
Content, 30, 37
Contour lines, 49–50
Contrapposto, 281
Contrast
of light and dark, *92*, 92–93, 96–97, *97*
simultaneous, 104
Cook, James, 530
Coram, Thomas
View of Mulberry House and Street, 330, *330*
Core of the shadow, 94
Corinthian capital, 336
The Cornaro Family in a Theater Box (Bernini), 464, *465*
Cornice, 336
Coronation of the Virgin (Quarton), 135, *135*, 141
Corps de Dame (Dubuffet), *173*, 173–174
Cortés, Hernán, 459, 461, 521, 633
Courbet, Gustave
Burial at Ornans, 484, *484*
"Courtly love" tradition, *570*, 570–571
Couturier, Marie-Alain, 542
Crabb, Ron
The Bucket List, 209, *209*
The Craft and Art of Clay, 306
Craft media
ceramics, 303–310
fiber, 313–321
functional objects, 300
glass, 310–313
metal, 321–324
overview, 300
wood, 324–326
Crafts as fine art, 302–303
The Craftsman, 345, 368
Crane, Walter, 366
Crawford, Thomas
Statue of Freedom, 524
The Creation of Adam (Michelangelo), 102, *102*, 575
Creative process, 10
Cribbed roof construction of a kiva, 331, *331*
Crichton, Michael, 267
The Crisis, 612
Criss-Crossed Conveyors-Ford Plant (Sheeler), 247, *247*
Critical thinking, 10
Crochet Coral and Anemone Garden, 326, *326*
Crochet Coral Reef project, 326, *326*
Cross-cutting, 258
Cross-dressing, 595
Cross-hatching, 96
Crossing (Romanesque architecture), 340
Crossing I (Chagoya), 520–521, *521*
Crux (Hill), 264, *264*
Cruz-Diez, Carlos
Chromosaturation, 88, *89*
Crystal Palace, 364, *364*, *365*
Cubism, 371, 496–498
Cultural conventions, 39
Cultural identities, 616
Culture
Aegean, 404–407
of Africa, 441–442
iconography representing, 39–43
light/dark contrast reflecting, 96–97, *97*
Mesopotamian, 396–397
words and images in, 30–32
Culture Wars, 21–23

Cut with the Kitchen Knife Dada through the Last Weimar Beer Belly Cultural Epoch of Germany (Höch), 206, *207*
Cycle of life
birth, 548–550
burial and the afterlife, 558–561
contemplating mortality, 554–558
youth and age, 550–553

D

Dada, 500–504
and Surrealism, 500–504
Daguerre, Louis-Jacques-Mandé
Le Boulevard du Temple, 242, 242–243
Daguerreotype, 242, *242*
Dalí, Salvador, 502
The Persistence of Memory, 502, *502*
Dali, Zhang
Dialogue and Demolition No. 50, 611, *611*
Dan Flavin Art Institute, Bridgehampton, NY, 88, *89*
Daniel Guggenheim Fund for the Promotion of Aeronautics, 376
Dante Alighieri, 444
Dark Sailor, 150
The Daughters of Edward Darley Boit (Sargent), 550–551, *551*
Daumier, Honoré
Fight between Schools, Idealism and Realism, 485, *485*
Rue Transnonain, 232, 232–233
David (Bernini), 122, *123*
David (Donatello), *446,* 446–447
David (Michelangelo), *25,* 25–26
David, Jacques-Louis
The Death of Marat, 477, *477*
Death of Socrates, 62, 62–63
Napoleon Crossing the Saint-Bernard, 621, *621*
da Vinci, Leonardo, 447
atmospheric perspective by, 89–92, *90*
Battle of Anghiari, 451
Embryo in the Womb, 548, *549*
The Last Supper, 76, 185, 451
Madonna and Child with St. Anne and Infant St. John the Baptist, 163, 163–164
Madonna of the Rocks, 90, 91, 92
Mona Lisa, 451, *451*
A Scythed Chariot, Armored Car and Pike, 451, *451*
Study for a Sleeve, 164, *164*
Study of a Woman's Head or of the Angel of the Vergine delle Rocce, 165, *165*
Study of Human Proportion: The Vitruvian Man, 132, *133,* 134, 585, *585,* 594
A Day in June (Bellows), 607, *607*
The Day of the Gods (Mahana no Atua) (Gauguin), 490–491, *491*
The Dead Christ (Mantegna), 79, *79*
Dead Flower (Yoshitomo Nara), 49, *49*
de Alvarado, Pedro, 459
The Death of Marat (David), 477, *477*
Death of Socrates (David), *62,* 62–63
de Chirico, Giorgio, 502
Melancholy and Mystery of a Street, 502, *502*
de Cormont, Renaud, 341
de Cormont, Thomas, 341
de Durán, Diego
History of the Indies of New Spain, 459, *459*
Deepwater Horizon (Montgomery), 648, *648*
Degas, Edgar, 220
After the Bath, Woman Drying Herself, 170, 170–171
The Glass of Absinthe, 487, *487*
Degas, Edgar, *The Glass of Absinthe,* 608, *608*
de Heem, Jan
Still Life with Lobster, 195, 195–196, 557, *557*
de Heusch, Luc, 30
de Kooning, Willem
North Atlantic Light, 28–29, *29,* 30, 36
Woman and Bicycle, 507, 507–508
Delacroix, Eugène, 572
Liberty Leading the People, 483, *483, 602,* 602–603, 610, 616
Odalisque, 478–479, *479*
Study for The Death of Sardanapalus (David), *63,* 63–64, 180
de La Tour, Georges
Joseph the Carpenter, 141, *141*
Delaunay, Robert, 107
L'Équipe de Cardiff (The Cardiff Team), 494, *495*
Premier Disque, 107
Delaunay, Sonia, 107, 110
Prismes Electriques (Electric Prisms), 110
Delineation, 167
Deliverance (DiBenedetto), 74, *74*
Deller, Jeremy
English Magic, 203
de Luzarches, Robert, 341
de Maupassant, Guy, 342
de Medici, Catherine, 328
de Menil, Dominique, 542
de Menil, John, 542
Dennis, Thomas, 325, *325*
Denotation, 189
Deodorant, 264
The Deposition (van der Weyden), 448, *448*
Der Blaue Reiter ("The Blue Rider") artists, 498
Der Lauf der Dinge (The Way Things Go) (Weiss and Fischli), 266, *266*
Design
modern Avant-Gardes and, 371–374
in the modernist era, 371–376
in nineteenth century, 364–370
organic, 376–387
since 1980, 381–388
streamlining, 376–381
Design, principles of
balance as, 134–140
emphasis and focal point, 140–144
overview of, 132–134
pattern, repetition, and rhythm, 148–153
scale and proportion, 144–148
unity and variety, 153–155
Design profession
Art Deco movement in, 371
Art Nouveau movement in, 369–370
Arts and Crafts Movement in, 364–368
Avant-Gardes movement in, 371–374
Bauhaus movement in, 374–376
since 1980, 381–388
Streamlining movement in, 376–381
Desired image
kissing as, 577–579
painting, 572–577
De Stijl movement, 372
Detached Building (Birchler and Hubbard), *128,* 129, *129*
de Toulouse-Lautrec, Henri, 369
Detroit Institute of Arts, 504
de Troyes, Chrétien
Lancelot, 564
Development of a Bottle in Space (Boccioni), 71, *71*
Development of a Bottle in Space Through Color (Boccioni), 71
Development of a Bottle in Space Through Form (Boccioni), 71
Dharmachakra mudra, 438
Diagonal recession, 75
Dialogue and Demolition No. 50 (Dali), 611, *611*
Diamond, William, 25
Diamond Sutra, from Cave 17, Dunhuang, 214, *214,* 534, *534*
Dias, Bartholomeu, 455
DiBenedetto, Steve
Deliverance, 74, *74*
The Dick Cavett Show, 594
Dickson, Jane
Stairwell, 231, *231*
Dickson, W. K. Laurie, 240
Didacticism, 189
Die Brücke ("The Bridge") artists, 498
Die grossen blauen Pferde (The Large Blue Horses) (Marc), 499, *499*
Diehl, Carol, 84
Digital space, 84–85
Dine, Jim
Toothbrushes, 233, *233*
Dionysus and Eros
sculpture of, 568, *568*
Disappearing Bodies of Water: Arctic Ice (Lin), *651,* 651–652
The Disasters of War (Goya), 482
Discipline and Punish: The Birth of the Prison (Foucault), 618
Discobolus (The Discus Thrower) (Jianguo), 529
Discourse on the Great Wisdom, 554
The Disembarkation of Marie de' Medici at the Port of Marseilles on November 3, 1600 (Rubens), 474, *475*
Distortions of space, 77–79, *78*
Divas on Screen, 14
Divine Comedy (Dante), 152, 564
"Divine frenzy," 452
Djingareyber Mosque, Timbuktu, 425, *426*
Dobson, Tamara, 14
Dodging, 251
Does It Make Sense? (Design Quarterly) (Greiman), 384, *384*
Do-Ho Suh
Public Figures, 144, *145*
Dome of the Rock, Jerusalem, 418, *419*
Dome of the Rock's ambulatory, 418

Domes, 336–341
Domino Housing Project (Le Corbusier), 372
Donatello, *David, 446,* 446–447
Dong Qichang, 456
Don't Name Fish after Friends (Green), *192,* 192–193
Doric capital, 336
Doryphoros (The Spear Bearer) (Polyclitus), 147, *147,* 412
Douglas, Aaron
  Aspiration, 613, 613–614
Downes, Rackstraw
  Presidio in the Sand Hills Looking East with ATV Tracks and Water Tower, 197, 197–198
Doyen, Gabriel-François, 575
Draftsman Drawing a Female Nude (Dürer), *78,* 78–79
Drawing
  dry media, 165–173
  innovative media, 175–179
  liquid media, 173–175
  materials, 165–175
  preparatory sketches to works of art, 160–164
Dreyfuss, Henry, 43
Drift No. 2 (Riley), 124, *125*
Drip Drop Plop (Wilson), 312, *312*
Drive-by Shooting: April Greiman Digital Photography (Greiman), 385, *385*
Drums, 334
Dry media, 165–173. *See also* Media
  chalk and charcoal, 167–169
  graphite, 169–170
  metalpoint, 165
  oilsticks, 172–173
  pastel, 170–172
Drypoint, 227
Dubuffet, Jean
  Corps de Dame, 173, 173–174
Duccio
  Annunciation of the Death of the Virgin from Maestà Altarpiece, 75, 75–76
  Maestà ("Majesty") *Altarpiece,* 75, *75*
Duchamp, Marcel, 507
  Fountain, 501, *501*
  L.H.O.O.Q., 501, *501*
  Nude Descending a Staircase, 23, *23*
The Duchess of Polignac (Vigée-Lebrun), 475, *475*
Duco, 202
Dunhuang, 8–9
Dürer, Albrecht, 198, 454
  Draftsman Drawing a Female Nude, 78, 78–79
  Self-Portrait, 454, *454*
Duret, Théodore, 488
Durham, Jimmie
  Headlights, 513, *513*
Durrington Wells, 395
Dylan, Bob, 382
The Dylan Painting (Marden), 110, *110*
Dynamism of a Dog on a Leash (Balla), 500, *500*

E

The Eagle Has Landed (Voulkos), *304,* 304–305
Eames, Charles, Side chair, 379–380, *380*
Eames, Ray, Side chair, 379–380, *380*
Earl, Harley, 379
Early architectural technologies, 333–341
  arches, vaults, and domes, 336–341
  load-bearing construction, 334
  post-and-lintel construction, 334–336
Early Christian art, 420–424
Early Renaissance, 446–450
EarthCloud (Higby), 307, *307*
Earthenware, 306
Earthworks, 279, 292–294
Eastman, George, 240
The Ecstasy of St. Theresa (Bernini), 464, *465*
Eddy, Don, 35
Ede, Chris, 387
  illustration for Clear Channel Online Music & Radio, 387
Edgeworth, Maria, 243
Edison, Thomas, 240, 369
Editing, 257
Edition, 214
Egeria Handing Numa Pompilius His Shield (Kauffmann), 477, *477*
Egyptian civilization, 397–400
Egyptian culture, 398
Egyptian raised reliefs, 276
Eiffel, Gustave, 342
  Eiffel Tower, 342, *342*
Eighteenth and nineteenth century art history, 472–492
  China and Europe, 476
  cross-cultural contact, 476
  Impressionism, 488–490
  Neoclassicism, 477–479
  Post-Impressionism, 490–492
  Poussin *versus* Rubens, 474
  Realism, 483–488
  Rococo, 474–476
  Romanticism, 479–483
Einstein, Albert, 500
Eisen, Kesai, 220
Eisenstein, Sergei
  Battleship Potemkin, 258, *258*
  Bringing the War Home, 205
Eitaku, Kobayashi
  Body of a Courtesan in Nine Stages of Decomposition, 555, *555*
Elder Subhuti, 534
Eleey, Peter, 3
Elefon helmet mask, Yoruba culture, 626, *626*
Elevation (Greek temple), 336
  capital, 336
  column, 336
  entablature, 336
  platform, 336
  shaft, 336
  stylobate, 336
El Greco
  The Burial of Count Orgaz, 463, 463–464
Eliasson, Olafur
  Suney, 73, *73*
  The Weather Project, 526, *526*
El Niño, 460, 548
Elysian Fields, 560, 561
Embossing, 322
Embroidered *rumal,* 316–317, *317*
Embroidery, 316
Embryo in the Womb (da Vinci), 548, *549*
Emperor Qin Shihuangdi, tomb of, 282, *282*
Emphasis and focal point, 140–144
Encaustic, 184
Endeavour, 530
English Arts and Crafts Movement, 368
English Civil War, 43
English Magic (Deller), 203
Engraving, 225
Enlightened One, 416
Entablature, 336
  architrave, 336
  cornice, 336
  frieze, 336
Entasis, 334
Enter the Rice Cooker (Shimomura), 234, *234*
Environment, 279
  and architecture, 328–333
  catastrophe in arts, 645–652
  from deeper/longer point of view, 653–655
  green architecture, 331–332
  impact of climate, 330–331
  science, technology and, 656
  site-specific, 279
  understanding, 642–652
Eros
  ancient Greece love and, 568
Erosion and Strip Farms East Slope of the Tehachapi Mountains (Garnett), 120–121, *121*
Escamilla, Isidro
  Virgin of Guadalupe, 122–123, *123*
Essaydi, Lalla
  La Grande Odalisque, 632, *632*
E.T., 261
Etching, 225–227
Etruscan art, 411
Europe
  national identities in, 602–604
Evans, Sir Arthur, 405
Evans, Walker
  Roadside near Birmingham, Alabama, 241, *241*
Eve panel, from *The Ghent Altarpiece* (van Eyck), 550, *550*
Ever Is Over All (Rist), 523, *523*
Exhibition of the Society of Independent Artists, 501
Exploration of the Colorado River and Its Tributaries (Powell), 644, *644*
Exploration of the Colorado River of the West (Powell), 222, *222*
Exposition Internationale des Arts Décoratifs et Industriels Modernes, 370, 371
Expressionism, 499. *See also* German Expressionism
Expressive qualities of line, 52–53, 56–59
Extreme close-up, 258
Eye Body: 36 Transformative Actions (Schneemann), 587, *587*

F

Fairbanks, Douglas, 259, 260
Fairey, Shepard
  Andre the Giant Has a Posse, 386
  Barack Obama "Hope" Poster, 386, *387*

Fallen (Hammond), 102–103, *103*
Fantasia, 260
Farm Security Administration (FSA), 247
Farnsworth House (Mies van der Rohe), 351, *351*
Fate and Luck: Eclipse (Brooke), *172*, 172–173
Fauves, 498
Fauvism, 498
Favrile glassware, 369
Feast-making spoon *(Wunkirmian)*, 72, *72*
Fellini, Federico, 260
Female identities, 589–592
Feng Mengbo
Game Over: Long March, 84–85, *85*
Fervor (Neshat), 96–97, *97*
Fiber, 313–321
The Fickle Type (Utamaro), *218*, 218–219
Fight between Schools, Idealism and Realism (Daumier), 485, *485*
Figure-ground relation, 68
Figure of a Woman (Colin), 94, *94*
Film, 257–261
Fine art
crafts as, 302–303
Finiguerra, Maso
Youth Drawing, 162, *162*
Firdawsi
Shahnamah, *31*, 31–32
Firing, of material, 282
First Crusade, 425, 426
First Surrealist Manifesto, 502
First Temple of Hera, Italy, 334, *335*
Fischli, Peter
Der Lauf der Dinge (The Way Things Go), 266, *266*
Five Pillars of Islam, 425
Flag (Johns), *7*, 7–8
The Flagellation of Christ (Piero della Francesca), 448, *449*
Flâneur, 15
Flashback, 258
Flavin, Dan, 88, *89*
Fleischer, Max, 160
Florence Cathedral (Santa Maria del Fiore), 432, *432*
Flowers in a Blue Vase (Brueghel), 56, *57*
Fluorescent light, 88, *89*
Fluting, 334
Flying buttresses, 341, *341*
Flying Horse Poised on One Leg on a Swallow, 416, *416*
Focal point and emphasis, 140–144
Footprints of History: Fireworks Project for the Opening Ceremony of the 2008 Beijing Olympic Games (Cai Guo-Qiang), 5–6, *5*
Ford, Edsel B., 504
Ford, Henry, 247
Ford, logo of, 381, *381*
Foreshortening, *79*, 79–81
Form, 37–38
Forty-Two-Line Bible (Gutenberg), 215, *215*
Fountain (Duchamp), 501, *501*
Four Books on Architecture (Palladio), 140
Four Darks in Red (Rothko), 508, *508*
Foxy Brown, 14
Fragonard, Jean-Honoré, 574
Bathers, 475, *475*
Fragonard, *The Swing*, 574, *574*
Frame construction, 342–345
Frankenthaler, Helen
The Bay, *202*, 202–203
Frankl, Paul T.
Skyscraper, 371
Fränzi Reclining (Heckel), *216*, 216–217
Frazier, LaToya Ruby, *Self-Portrait*, 646, *646*
French Academy, 474
French artists
David, Jacques-Louis, 62, 477, 621
Delacroix, Eugène, 63–64, 180, 478–479, 483, 572–574, 602–603, 616
Doyen, Gabriel-François, 575
Manet, Édouard, 14–15, 220, 486–489, 592, 594–595, 631, 634
French Revolution, 472, 477, 478, 485
Fresco, 184–188
Fresco secco, 185
Freud, Lucian, 20
Freud, Sigmund, 20
Friedrich, Caspar David
Monk by the Sea, *481*, 481–482, 588
Frieze, 276
Frisius, Gemma, 241, *241*
From Spaniard and Black, Mulatto (De Español y Negra, Mulatto) (Alcíbar), 628–629, *628*
Frontal recession, 75
Frontal relief sculpture, 276
Frottage, 120
Full shot, 258
Functional objects, 300
Funerary mask (Mask of Agamemnon), 406
Futurism, 70, 500

G

Gable, Clark, 260
Gaffney, Vince, 395
Galeries de l'Art Nouveau, 369
Gamble, Clive, 584
Game Over: Long March (Feng Mengbo), 84–85, *85*
Ganges River Valley, 401
Garbhagriba, 435
Garbhagriha, 566
García, Antonio López
New Refrigerator, 196, *196*
Garcia, Mannie, 387
Gardner, Alexander
A Harvest of Death, Gettysburg, Pennsylvania, July 1863, 245, *245*
Gardner's Photographic Sketchbook of the War, 245, *245*
The Gare Saint-Lazare (Édouard), 592, *592*
Garnett, William A.
Erosion and Strip Farms East Slope of the Tehachapi Mountains, 120–121, *121*
Garrard, Mary D., 182
Gast, John
American Progress, *603*, 603–604
The Gates of Hell (Rodin), 152, *152*, 153, 564
Gauguin, Paul, 490
The Day of the Gods (Mahana no Atua), 490–491, *491*
Gautama, Siddhartha, 416. *See also* Shakyamuni Buddha
Gay rights movement, 593
Gehry, Frank, 133, *133*, 154–155
Guggenheim Museum Bilbao, *354*, 354–355, *355*
Guggenheim Museum Bilbao, North Elevation, 354, *354*
Gender, line associated with, 64
Gender identities
challenges in, 594–597
challenging, 594–597
female, 589–592
male, 592–594
General Electric, 382
A General Idea of a Penitentiary Panopticon (Bentham), 618, *619*
General Motors
Cadillac Fleetwood, 379, *379*
Genres, 260
Gentileschi, Artemisia
Judith and Maidservant with the Head of Holofernes, 94, *95*, 96, 141
Self-Portrait as the Allegory of Painting, 182–183, *183*, 210
Geometric Backyards, New York (Strand), 82, *82*
Geometric sans serif fonts, 373
Gerewol festival, 576–577
Géricault, Théodore
The Raft of the Medusa, 482, *483*
German artists
Beuys, Joseph, 587–588
German Expressionism, 498–499. *See also* Expressionism
German Lutheran Church, 356
Gesso, 188
The Ghent Altarpiece (Van Eyck), 19–20, *19–20*, 32, 548, *550*, 622
Ghiberti, Lorenzo, 276
Sacrifice of Isaac, 277, *277*
Ginn, Greg, 523
Ginzer (Smith), 212, *213*
Giorgione
The Tempest, 453, *453*
Giornata, 187
Giotto
Lamentation, 187, *187*
Madonna and Child Enthroned, 188–189, *189*, 192
Giovanni Arnolfini and His Wife Giovanna Cenami (Van Eyck), 39–41, *40*, 550
Girl before a Mirror (Picasso), *503*, 503–504
Gislebertus, *Last Judgment*, 430, *430*
Giuliani, Rudolph W., 23
Gladiators (Rosler), 205, *205*
Gladu, Christian
The Birch, 344, *345*
Glass, 310–313
The Glass of Absinthe (Degas), 487, *487*, 608, *608*
Glazing, 303
The Glorification of St. Ignatius (Pozzo), 188, *188*, 210
Gober, Robert
Untitled, 289, *289*
God Bless America (Ringgold), 8, *8*

Goddess
Evans, Arthur, 405–406
images found at Palace of Minoson Crete, 405
Minoans and, 405–406
Snake, 405, *405*
worship, 435
The Goddess, 86
Goddess of Democracy, Tiananmen Square, 529
The Goddess Durga Killing the Buffalo Demon, Mahisha (Mahishasuramardini), 435, *435*
The Gold Rush, 259, *259*
Gone with the Wind (Menzies, art director), 260, *261*
Gonzales-Day, Ken
At daylight the miserable man was carried to an oak . . . , 15–16, *16*
Lynching in the West: 1850-1935, 16
Searching for California Hang Trees, 16, *16*
A Good Day for Cyclists (Tynan), 203
Goodman, Nelson, 7
Gordon, Daniel, 254
Gordon, Douglas
24 Hour Psycho, 258–259, *259*
Gorman, Pat, 383
Go Shirakawa, 440
Gothic art, 431–433
Goya, Francisco
The Tauromaquia, 595, *595*
Goya y Lucientes, Francisco de
The Disasters of War, 482
Saturn Devouring One of His Sons, 482, *482*
Grainstack (Sunset) (Monet), 111, *111*, 123
Grainstacks (Monet), 499
Grande Odalisque (Ingres), 478–479, *479*, 631, *631*, 635
Grands Projets, 328
Graphite paintings, 169–170
Graven images, 32
Gray, Don
Stone #2, 653, *653*
Great Buddha at Nara, 439
Great Depression, 507
Great Exhibition of 1851, 364
Great River Valley civilizations, 400–402
Great Serpent Mound, Ohio, 294, *294*
The Great Stupa, Sanchi, 416, *416*
Great Sun, 404
Great Wall of China, 414, *414*
The Great Wave off Kanagawa (Hokusai), 146, *146*, 219
Great Wild Goose Pagoda at Ci'én Temple, *438*, 439
Great Zimbabwe walls/towers, 442
Greek art
sculptures, 39, *39*
Greek artists
El Greco, *463*, 463–464
Polyclitus, 147, 409, 585
Greek civilization, 407–410
Greek culture, 407
Greek Peloponnese, 557
Green, George
marooned in dreaming: a path of song and mind, 34–35, *34–35*
Green, Julie
Don't Name Fish after Friends, 192, 192–193
The Last Supper, 308–309, *308–309*
Green architecture, 17, 331–332
energy efficiency and solar orientation, 332
integration and compatibility with the natural environment, 331–332
recycled, reusable, and sustainable materials, use of, 332
smaller buildings, 331
The Greeting (Viola), 268–269, *268–269*
Gregory the Great, 428
Greiman, April, 383
and design technology, 384–385
Does It Make Sense? (Design Quarterly), 384, *384*
Drive-by Shooting: April Greiman Digital Photography, 385, *385*
Guardrail to Sevilla, 385
madeinspace.la website, screen capture, 384, *384*
Something from Nothing, 385
Grey Area, 66
Grid, 56
Grier, Pam, 14
Griffith, D. W.
The Birth of a Nation, 257–258
Gris, Juan, 205, *205*
Groin vaults, *337*, 338, 341
Gropius, Walter, 374
Grosman, Tatyana, 233
Grosse, Katharina
Cincy, 114, *114*
Grounds, 184, 225–226
hard, 225
soft, 225–226
Guantanamo Bay Detention Facility, 618
Guardrail to Sevilla (Greiman), *385*
Guernica (Picasso), 505, *505*
Guggenheim Museum Bilbao (Gehry), *354*, 354–355, *355*, 592
Guggenheim Museum Bilbao, North Elevation (Gehry), 354, *354*
Guide (Smith), 316, *316*
Guidobaldo della Rovere, Duke of Urbino, 454
Guitar, Sheet Music, and Wine Glass (Picasso), 497, *497*
Guo Si, 439
Guo Xi
Early Spring, 438, 439
Gursky, Andreas
Ocean II, 254–256, *255*
Gutenberg, Johannes, 162, 214–215
Forty-Two-Line Bible, 215, *215*

H

Haas, Richard, 7
Habitat (Safdie), *360*, 360–361
Haboku Landscape (Sesshu Toyo), 457, *457*
Hadid, Zaha, 114, *114*
Hajj, 537
Halvorson, Josephine
Carcass, 196–197, *197*
Hamilton, Ann, 300
the event of a thread, 300, *301*
Hammond, Jane
Fallen, 102–103, *103*
Hammurabi, 397
Han dynasty, 414–415
Han Dynasty Urn with Coca-Cola Logo (Ai Weiwei), 517, *517*
Happenings, 296
Harket, Morten, 160
Harmony in Red (The Red Room) (Matisse), 83, *83*, 128
Harmony Society, 356
Harper's New Monthly Magazine, 550
Harry Potter, 261
Harunobu, Suzuki
nishiki-e calendars, 217
Two Courtesans, Inside and Outside the Display Window, 217, *217*, 591, *591*
A Harvest of Death, Gettysburg, Pennsylvania, July 1863 (O'Sullivan and Gardner), 245, *245*
Hassam, Childe
Boston Common at Twilight, 138, *138*
Hatching, 96
Hatsu-Yume (First Dream), 265
Hausmann, Raoul, 206
Haussmannization, 610
Havemeyer, H. O., 171
Hayden, Ferdinand Vandeveer, 644
The Hay Wain (Constable), 479–480, *480*
Headlights (Durham), 513, *513*
Head of a King (Oni), 441, *441*
Head of an Oba, 283, *283*
Head of a Satyr (Michelangelo), 96, *96*
Head of Catherine Lampert VI (Auerbach), 180, *180*
Hearst, William Randolph, 260
Heckel, Erich, 498
Fränzi Reclining, 216, 216–217
Hellenism, 409
Hellenistic Age, 409
Hellenistic Empire, 410
Hellenistic realism, 409
Helms, Jesse, 21
Hepworth, Barbara
Two Figures, 72, *72*
Heraclitus, 453
Herman Miller Company, 380, 388
Herman Miller Research Corp., 388
Hermes and Dionysus (Praxiteles), 281, *281*
Herodotus, 407
Heroism, 43
Higby, Wayne
EarthCloud, 307, *307*
Lake Powell Memory-Seven Mile Canyon, 307, *307*
Highlights, 94
High relief figures, 276
High-relief sculptures, 276
High Renaissance, 450–454
Hijra, 424
Hill, Gary
Crux, 264, *264*
Hinduism, 401, 433, 434, 532, 546
Hindu *kama,* 566–568
Hindu pilgrimage places, 539–540
Hindus sexuality
erotic sculptures in temples and, 566–568

Hinomaru Illumination (Yukinori), 606, *606*
Hippocrates, 407
Hiratsuka, Yuji
Miracle Grow Hypnotist, 228, *229*
Hiroshige, Utagawa
Hamamatsu: Winter Scene, 609, *609*
Moon Pine, Ueno, *80*, 80–81
One Hundred Views of Edo, *80*, 80–81
Hirshhorn Museum, 517
History of the Indies of New Spain (de Durán), 459, *459*
History of the Main Complaint (Kentridge), 178, *178*, 630, *630*
Hittites, 397
Hoang, Mimi, 332
New Aqueous City, 332, *333*
Höch, Hannah
Cut with the Kitchen Knife Dada through the Last Weimar Beer Belly Cultural Epoch of Germany, 206, *207*
Study for "Cut with the Kitchen Knife Dada through the Last Weimar Beer Belly Cultural Epoch of Germany," 206, *206*
Hodder, Ian, 554
Hofmann, Armin
Poster for *Giselle, Basler Freilichtspiele*, 381, *381*
Hokusai
The Great Wave off Kanagawa, 146, *146*, 219
Shunshuu Ejiri, 271–272, *272*
The Holy Family with a Kneeling Monastic Saint (Sirani), 173, *173*
The Holy Virgin Mary (Ofili), 22, *23*
Holzer, Jenny, *Thorax*, 636
Homage to the People of the South Bronx: Double Dutch at Kelly Street 1: Frieda, Jevette, Towana, Stacey (Ahearn), 285–286, *286*
Homer
The Iliad, 406, 411
Odyssey, 406, 560
Homer, Winslow
A Wall, Nassau, *198*, 198–199
Honey Art Dreaming (Tjakamarra), *36*, 36–37
Honey Baby (Antoni and Petronio), 562, *562*
Hopper, Edward
Nighthawks, 507, *507*
The Horde (Ernst), 120, *120*
Horizons (Bel Geddes), 378
House Beautiful magazine, 368
Household (Kaprow), 296, *296*
Houses at l'Estaque (Braque), 496, *496*
Houses on the Hill, Horta de Ebro (Picasso), *496*, 497
The House with the Ocean View (Abramoviæ), 297, *297*
Hubbard, Teresa
Detached Building, *128*, 129, *129*
Hue, 101, *101*
Hulsenbeck, Richard, 206
Human form
giving Gods, 535–537
Humanism, 446
Hundreds of Birds Admiring the Peacocks (Yin Hong), 456, *456*
Hundred Years' War, 285
Hung Liu
Relic 12, 58, *58*, 60
Three Fujins, 61, *61*
Virgin/Vessel, *60*, 60–61
The Hunt of the Unicorn, VII: The Unicorn in Captivity, 313, *313*
Hurricane Katrina, 648
Hypostyle space, 424

I

Ice Age, 394
Iconoclasts, 421
Iconography, 39–43
Ictinos, 408
Idea of beauty, 10
Identities
African-American, 611–615
contemporary art and, 521–525
gender, 582–598
individual and cultural, 616
nationalism and, 602–606
visual signs of class and, 607–611
I Do Not Know What It Is I Am Like, 265
Iliad (Homer), 406, 411
I Like America and America Likes Me (Beuys), *587*, 587–588
Illustrator, 386
Il Magnifico, 449
Image of desire
kiss as, 577–579
Imaging desire
artists, 572–574
kiss function as, 577–579
Imbroglios (A Phylogenetic Tree, from Homo Sapiens to Megalops Atlanticus) (Brooks), 656, *656*
I'm Learning to Fly!! (Rae), 513, *513*
Impasto, 53
Imperial gaze, 622–623
Implied line, 50–52
Imponderabilia (Abramoviæ and Ulay), 297, *297*
Impression, 214
Impressionism, 488–490
Impressionists, 488
Impression-Sunrise (Monet), *488*, 488–489
Inca stone wall of the Coricancha, *460*, 460–461
InDesign, 386
India
art in, 433–436
Indian Country Today (Bradley), 514, *514*
Individual identities, 616
Industrial Revolution, 302, 642
Industry in arts, 642–645
Indus Valley civilizations, 400–402
Infrastructure, 359
Ingres, Jean-Auguste-Dominique
Grande Odalisque, 478–479, *479*, 631, *631*
Mme. Rivière, 147, *147*
Napoleon on His Imperial Throne, 622, *622*
Ink Orchids (Cheng Sixiao), 455, *455*
Inquiry into the Origin of Our Ideas of the Sublime and the Beautiful (Burke), 481
Installation art, 290–292
Installations, 279
Institute For Figuring
Crochet Coral Reef project, 326, *326*
Insurrection! (Our Tools Were Rudimentary, Yet We Pressed On) (Walker), 208, *208*
Intaglio printmaking technique, 224, *224*
Intaglio processes, 224–231
aquatint, 230–231
drypoint, 227
engraving, 225
etching, 225–227
mezzotint, 230–231
Intensity, 101, *101*
Interior of the Choir of St. Bavo's Church at Haarlem (Saenredam), 536, *536*
Intermediate colors, 101
International Museum of Photography, 22
International Style, 351
Internet, 381
In the Loge (At the Français, a Sketch) (Cassatt), 98–99, *98–99*
Inventory of Slaves and Livestock (Will), 314, *314*
Investment, 284
Ionic capital, 336
iPhone, Apple, 386, *386*
Iris shot, 258
The Iron City (Ritchie), 647, *647*
Iron Maiden, 179
Isidorus of Miletus, 420, *420*, *421*
Islamic Taliban, 438
Islam/Islamic culture, 418, 433, 441, 532
iconographic image interpretation by, 41
Muslim culture and, 424–427
rise of, 424–427
Italian Renaissance, 453, 454
Iyoba (queen mother) mask, 461, *461*
Izenour, Steven, 155, 512

J

Jackson, Michael, 179
James, Henry, 550
Jami al-Tawarikh (Universal History) (Rashid al-Din), *538*
Japan
art in, 439–441, 455–457
national identities in, 605–606
Japanese art
printmaking as, 609–610
technological innovations in, 638–642, *640*, *641*
Japanese artists. *See also* Artists
Hiroshige, Utagawa, *80*, 80–81
Murakami, Takashi, 48
Utamaro, Kitagawa, 218–219, *219*, 221, *221*
Japanese shrine, 538–539
Japonaiserie: The Courtesan (After Kesai Eisen) (van Gogh), 220, *220*
Jar (Martinez), 305, *305*
The Jazz Singer, 259
Jeanneret, Pierre
Villa Savoye, Poissy-sur-Seine, France, 350, *350*
Jefferson, Thomas, 478
Monticello, 478
Jewish Temple of Solomon, 418
Jianguo, Sui
Discobolus (The Discus Thrower), 529
John C. Hench Division of Animation and Digital Arts, 160

Johns, Jasper
Flag, *7*, 7–8
Johnson, Philip, 351
Johnson, Rashid, *Souls of Black Folk*, 614–615, *615*
John the Baptist, 446
Jolson, Al, 259
Jonaitis, Aldona, 516
Art of the Northwest Coast, 516
Jones, Ben
Black Face and Arm Unit, 93, *93*
Jones, Owen, 364
Jorge, Seu, 3
Joseph the Carpenter (de La Tour), 141, *141*
Judaism, 418, 532
The Judgment of Paris (Raimondi), 487, *487*
Judith and Maidservant with the Head of Holofernes (Gentileschi), 94, *95*, 96, 141
Julien, Isaac
Ten Thousand Waves, 86, *86*
July Revolution, 483
Jurassic Park (Crichton), 267
Justinian and His Attendants, 422, *423*, *625*, 625–626
Just in Time (Murray), 155, *155*

K

Kaaba, *537*, 537–538
Kachina doll (Maalo), 533, *533*
Kahlo, Frida
Las Dos Fridas (The Two Fridas), 136, *136*
Kahn, Adam
Brockholes Visitor Center, Preston, 332, *332*
Kahn, Wolf
Afterglow I, 36, *36*
Kakizaki, Junichi, Chim↑Pom, 647, *647*
Kami (Shinto gods), 439, 539
Kanak culture, 18
Kandariya Mahadeva Temple, Khajuraho, 435, *435*, *539*, 539–540, 566, *567*
Kandinsky, Wassily, 498, 499, 507, 542–543
Black Lines (Schwarze Linien), 113, *113*
Concerning the Spiritual in Art, 499, 543
Sketch I for "Composition VII," 498, 499, 543, *543*
Kansai International Airport, *640*, 640–641, *641*
Kapoor, Anish
Cloud Gate, 291, *291*, 298
Kaprow, Allan
Household, 296, *296*
Kauffmann, Angelica
Egeria Handing Numa Pompilius His Shield, 477, *477*
Kaufmann, Lillian, 348–349
Keats, John, 479
Ke Jiusi
Bamboo, *605*, 605
Kelly, Ellsworth
Brier, 50, *50*
Three Panels: Orange, Dark Gray, Green, 67–68, *68*
Kelmscott Press, 366
Kente cloths, 150, *150*
Kentridge, William, 177–178, *178*
History of the Main Complaint, 178, *178*, 630, *630*
Keystone, 337
Khamseh (Quintet), *32*
Khan, Kublai, 439, 455
Khmer monarchy, 436
Khomeini, Ayatollah, 179
"Kids in America," 179
Kihara, Shigeyuki
Ulugali'i Samoa: Samoan Couple, 596–597, *597*
Kiln, 282
Kimsooja
A Beggar Woman-Mexico City, 588, *588*
Kinetic art, 122
King, Martin Luther, Jr., 26
King Charles I of England, 43
King Henri IV, 474, 560
King Khafre statue, 399, *399*
King Louis VI, 431
King Louis VII, 311
King Minos, 404–405
King Narmer, 398
Kirchner, Ernst, 498
The Kiss (Brancusi), 577, *577*
The Kiss (Le Baiser), 564
The Kiss (Picabia), 577–578, *578*
The Kiss (Rodin), 577, 586
The Kiss (Warhol), 578, *578*
Kissing Coppers (Banksy), 524, *524*, 578, *579*
Kiva, 330
Knapp, Laura, 582
Knoll's Toboggan chair, 362, *363*
Koberger, Anton, 215
Kodak, 240, 254
Koetsu, Hon'ami
Raku Tea Bowl, 304, *304*
Kojiki (Chronicles of Japan), 439, 539
Koklova, Olga, 10, 503
Koko the Clown, 160
Koller, Otto
Air Liner Number 4, 377, 377–378
Kollwitz, Käthe
Self-Portrait, Drawing, *168*, 168–169
Koolhaas, Rem, 352
Koons, Jeff, 517
Puppy, *288*, 288–289
Korean artists
Kimsooja, 588
Kouros (The Kritios Boy), 281, *281*
Kraakporselein, *306*
Krasner, Lee
Untitled, 506, *506*
Kruger, Barbara, 580
Untitled (We won't play nature to your culture), *522*, 522–523
kshatriyas, 433
Ku Klux Klan, 258
Kumano Mandala, 538, *539*
Kumbh Mela festival, 539
Kwakwaka'wakw pictograph (Nicholson), 515, *515*
Kwakwaka'wakw pictograph (Wilson), 515, *515*
Kwei, Kane, 16–17, *17*

L

La Chahut (The Can-Can) (Seurat), *106*, 107, 491
Lacy, Suzanne, 552
Inevitable Associations, 552
Whisper, the Waves, the Wind, 553, *553*
La Dolce Vita, 260
Lady of Dai with Attendants, 415, *415*
La Grande Odalisque (Essaydi), 632, *632*
Laguna Santero, 541, *541*
Lake Powell Memory-Seven Mile Canyon (Higby), 307, *307*
Lalibela, 442
Lamentation (Giotto), 187, *187*
Lancelot (de Troyes), 564
Lance Loud (Warhol), 594, *594*
Landscapes
atmospheric perspective in, *91*, 91–92
representational *versus* abstract, 35–37, *36*
Landscape with Flight into Egypt (Carracci), 468, *468*
Landscape with St. John on Patmos (Poussin), 474, *474*
The Laocoön Group, 410, *410*, 478
Lapatin, Kenneth
Mysteries of the Snake Goddess, 405
La Pittura, 182
La Revue Nègre, 94
The Large Bathers (Cézanne), 492, *492*
L'Arroseur Arrosé (Waterer and Watered), 240, *240*
Las Dos Fridas (The Two Fridas) (Kahlo), 136, *136*
Las Meninas (The Maids of Honor) (Velázquez), 142–143, *143*
L'Association Mensuelle, 232
Last Judgment (Gislebertus), 430, *430*
The Last Judgment (Michelangelo), 462, *462*
Last Judgment of Hunefer by Osiris, 559, *559*
The Last Post (Sikander), 629, *629*
The Last Supper (da Vinci), 76, 185, 451
The Last Supper (Green, Julie), 308–309, *308–309*
Law Code of Hammurabi, 397
Lawler, Louise
Pollock and Tureen, 154, *154*
Lawrence, Jacob
Barber Shop, 150–152, *151*, 153
The Migration of the Negro, Panel No. 60: And the Migrants Kept Coming, 612–613, *613*
You can buy bootleg whiskey for twenty-five cents a quart, 200, *200*
Learning from Los Vegas (Venuri, Brown & Izenour), 155, 512
Le Baiser/The Kiss (Manglano-Ovalle), 578, *579*
Le Boulevard du Temple (Daguerre), *242*, 242–243
Le Brun, Charles, 474
Le Chinois galant (Boucher), 476, *476*
Le Corbusier
Domino Housing Project, 350, *350*, 372
L'Esprit Nouveau (The New Spirit), 371
Pavillon de l'Esprit Nouveau, 371, 374

Towards a New Architecture, 350
Villa Savoye, Poissy-sur-Seine, France, 350, *350*
Le Déjeuner sur l'herbe (Luncheon on the Grass) (Manet), *486,* 486–487
Léger, Fernand, 507
Ballet Mécanique, 257, *257*
Leigh, Vivien, 260
Le Journal, 497
Le Noir, Jean, 555
The Three Dead, 555–556, *556*
The Three Living, 555–556, *556*
L'Équipe de Cardiff (The Cardiff Team) (Delaunay), 494, *495*
Les Demoiselles d'Avignon (Picasso), 10, 12–13, *12–13,* 18, 503, 573
Leslie's Illustrated Gazette, 44, *44*
L'Esprit Nouveau (The New Spirit) (Le Corbusier), 371
Les Très Riches Heures du Duc de Berry (Limbourg Brothers), 444, *445*
Le Sun, 9
Let Us Now Praise Famous Men (Agee), 247
Lewis and Clark Expedition of 1804-05, 7
LeWitt, Sol, 53, 509
Wall Drawing #146A: All two-part combinations of arcs from corners and sides, and straight, not straight, and broken lines within a 36-inch (90 cm) grid, 509, *509*
Wall Drawing No. 681 C, 56, *56*
L.H.O.O.Q. (Duchamp), 501, *501*
Liang Kai
The Poet Li Bo Walking and Chanting a Poem, 175, *175*
Liberty Leading the People (Delacroix), *483,* 483–484, *602,* 602–603, 610, 616
Li Bo, 175
Libyan Sibyl (Michelangelo), 190–191, *190–191*
Lichtenstein, Roy, 508
Oh, Jeff . . . I Love You, Too . . . But . . . , 508, *508*
Light
architecture using, 88
atmospheric (aerial) perspective using, 89–92, *90, 91*
chiaroscuro, 93–94
color and, 88, *89*
dark contrasting with, *92,* 92–93, 96–97, *97*
emphasis and focal point created using, 141–144
fluorescent, 88, *89*
Limbourg Brothers, 444
Les Très Riches Heures du Duc de Berry, 444, *445*
Lin, Maya
Disappearing Bodies of Water: Arctic Ice, 651, 651–652
Lindbergh, Charles, 494
Lindisfarne Gospels, 148–150, *149*
Line
contour, 49–50
expressive qualities of, 52–53, 56–59
gender associated with, 64
implied, 50–52
orientation, 62–64
outline, 49
qualities of, 52–53, 56–59
varieties of, 48–52
Linear perspective, 75–77
Lingam (phallus), 434, 435, 566
Linocut, 222–223
L'Intransigeant, 374, *374*
L'Intrans poster (Cassandre), 374, *374*
Lion Gate, Mycenae, Greece, 334, *334*
Liquid media, 173–175. *See also* Media
pen and ink, 173–174
wash and brush, 175
Liquor Headmaster, 150
Lissitzky, El
Beat the Whites with the Red Wedge, 373
Lithography, 232–233
Little Liber (Turner), 230, *230*
Lives of the Painters (Vasari), 163
Live-Taped Video Corridor (Nauman), 262, *262*
Load-bearing construction, 334
Load-bearing walls, 334
Local color, 111
Lockheed
P-38 Lightning fighters, 379, *379*
Loewy, Raymond, 378
The Lofty Message of the Forests and Streams (Guo Si), 439
Lohmann, Clay
Black Lung, 319, *319*
Long shot, 258
The Lord of the Rings, 261
Los Angeles Freeway Interchange, 359
Lost-wax casting process, 283, *284*
Lost-wax process, 283. *See also Cire-perdue*
Lott, Willie, 480
Louisa, Julia, 552
Louisa, Mary, 552
Louis XIII, 328
Louis XIV, 472
Louis XIV, King of France (Rigaud), 472, *473*
Love
beautiful body and, 582–586
and *eros* in ancient Greece, 568
medieval courtly tradition, 570–571
Persian tale about, 568–570
physical and spiritual, 564–572
Lovell, Whitfield
Whispers from the Walls, 177, *177*
Low relief figures, 276
Low-relief sculptures, 276
Lucas, George, 261
Lucid Stead (Smith), 116, *116*
Lumière, August, 240
Lumière, Louis, 240
Lynching in the West: 1850-1935 (Gonzales-Day), 16
Lyon, Lisa, 64, *64,* 108
Lysippus, 409

M

Machiavelli, Niccolò, 447
Machine Tournez Vite (Machine Turn Quickly) (Picabia), 577–578, *578*
Macintosh computer, Apple Corporation, 383, 386, *386*
Maclure, William, 356
MacPaint, 386
MacWrite, 386
Made in Space (Greiman), *384,* 384–385
Mademoiselle V . . . in the Costume of an Espada (Manet), 594, *595*
Maderno, Carlo, 464
St. Peter's basilica nave/ façade, 464, *464*
Madness Is a Part of Life (Neto), 279, *279*
Madonna and Child Enthroned (Giotto), 188–189, *189,* 192
Madonna and Child with St. Anne and Infant St. John the Baptist (da Vinci), *163,* 163–164
Madonna of the Rocks (da Vinci), *90,* 91, 92
Maestà ("Majesty") *Altarpiece* (Duccio), 75, *75*
Magritte, or The Object Lesson, 30
Magritte, René, 502
The Treason of Images, 30, *30*
Maidenhead Railroad Bridge, Brunel, 639, *639*
Maidens and Stewards, 276, *276*
Male identities, 592–594
Malevich, Kazimir
Black Square, 37, *37*
The Non-Objective World, 37
Man, Controller of the Universe (Rivera), 504, *504*
Mana, 530
Manet, Édouard, 220
Chez le Père Lathuille, 488, *488*
The Gare Saint-Lazare, 592, *592*
Le Déjeuner sur l'herbe, 592, 595
Le Déjeuner sur l'herbe (Luncheon on the Grass), 486, 486–487
Mademoiselle V . . . in the Costume of an Espada, 594, *595*
Olympia, 14, 15, *15,* 486, 592
Young Man in the Costume of a Majo, 595
Manhattan Design, 383
Mannerism, 461–464
Mansion at Parlange Plantation, Louisiana, 344, *344*
Mantegna, Andrea
The Dead Christ, 79, *79*
Manuscripts
Les Très Riches Heures du Duc de Berry (Limbourg Brothers), 444, *445*
The Mérode Altarpiece (Campin), 448
Man with Big Shoes, 78, *78*
Many Mansions (Marshall), 519–520, *520,* 634, *634*
Mao Zedong, 85
The Map (The Lesson) (Cassatt), 227, *227*
Mapplethorpe, Robert, 21–22
Ajitto, 22, *22*
Calla Lily, 558, *558*
Lisa Lyon, 64, *64*
Marc, Franz, 499
Die grossen blauen Pferde (The Large Blue Horses), 499, *499*
Marcel Duchamp as Rrose Sélavy (Ray), 595, *595*
Marden, Brice, 543–544
Cold Mountain 6 (Bridge), 544, *544*
The Dylan Painting, 110, *110*
Marey, Étienne-Jules, 24
Marilyn Monroe (Warhol), 236, *236,* 590, *590*

Marilyn: Norma Jeane (Steinem), 590
Marin, John
Untitled (The Blue Sea), 199, 199–200
Marinetti, Filippo, 500
Marooned in dreaming: a path of song and mind (Green), 34–35, *34–35*
Marshall, Chan, 3
Marshall, Kerry James, 518
Many Mansions, 519–520, *520*
Marshall, Kerry James, *Many Mansions,* 634, *634*
Martel, Charles, 425
Martinez, Julián
Jar, 305, *305*
Martinez, María
Jar, 305, *305*
Marvel Comics, 43
Marx, Karl, 487
The Communist Manifesto, 485
Masaccio
The Tribute Money, 447, *447,* 448
Mass
defined, 69
vs. shape, 67–69
Massachusetts Institute of Technology, 376
Massachusetts Museum of Contemporary Art (Mass MoCA), 509
Matisse, Henri, 499, 542
Harmony in Red (The Red Room), 83, *83,* 128
innovative drawing, 175–177
Matisse: The Fabric of Dreams, His Art and His Textiles, 128
Venus, 176, 177
Woman with a Hat, 498, *498*
Matisse: The Fabric of Dreams, His Art and His Textiles (Matisse), 128
Matrix, 214
Matte painting, 209
Mattingly, Mary, *Triple Island,* 652, *652*
Maus: A Survivor's Tale (Spiegelman), 178
Mazu, 86
McCarthy, Joseph, 7
McCoy, Karen
Considering Mother's Mantle, 294, *294*
Media, 134
contemporary art and, 521–525
dry, 165–173
encaustic, 184
fresco, 184–188
liquid, 173–175
mixed, 204–209
oil paint, 193–198
synthetic, 202–204
tempera, 188–193
watercolor and gouache, 198–201
Medium intensity, 101
Medium shot, 258
Megaliths, 395
Mehretu, Julie
Berliner Platze, 66–67, *67*
Mural, 144, *144*
Meier, Richard
Atheneum, 356, *357*
Meissonier, Ernest
Memory of Civil War (The Barricades), 484, *484*
Melancholy and Mystery of a Street (de Chirico), 502, *502*
Mellaart, Sir James, 554
Memento mori, 193, 556, 557
Memory of Civil War (The Barricades) (Meissonier), 484, *484*
Memphis Group, 382
Mendieta, Ana
Untitled (Silueta Series, Mexico), 598, *598*
Menkaure with a Woman, 280, 281
Menzies, William Cameron, 260, *261*
The Mérode Altarpiece (Campin), 448
Mesa-Bains, Amalia
An Ofrenda for Dolores del Rio, 561, *561*
Mesoamerican culture, 403, 458
Mesopotamian culture, 396–397
Metal, 321–324
Metalpoint, 165
Metalwork, from Mining the Museum: An Installation by Fred Wilson (Wilson), 315, *315*
The Metamorphosis of Plants (von Goethe), 317
Metro-Goldwyn-Mayer (MGM), 259
Mexican Revolution, 504
Mexico
art in, 457–461
Mezzotint, 230–231
Michelangelo, 447, 450
"Atlas" Slave, 280, *280*
Battle of Cascina, 451
The Creation of Adam, 102, *102,* 575
David, 25, 25–26
Head of a Satyr, 96, *96*
The Last Judgment, 462, *462*
Libyan Sibyl, 190–191, *190–191*
Pietà, 118, *118*
Study for the Libyan Sibyl, 190, *190*
Middle Ages, 444, 447, 540
Mies van der Rohe, Ludvig
Farnsworth House, 351, *351*
Seagram Building, 351, *351*
The Migration of the Negro, Panel No. 60: And the Migrants Kept Coming (Lawrence), 612–613, *613*
Mihrab, 425
Milhazes, Beatriz
Carambola, 37–38, *38*
Mille Fiori (Chihuly), 311–312, *312*
Miller, Frank, 178
Miluniæ, Vlado, 133, *133,* 154–155
Mimosoidea Suchas, Acacia (Talbot), 242, *242*
Minbar, 424
Minetta Lane-A Ghost Story (Antin), 291–292, *292*
Ming dynasty, 456
Minimalism, 508–509
Minkisi, 18
Minkonde figures, 18–19
Minoan culture, 404–407
Minoan peoples, 404–407
Miracle Grow Hypnotist (Hiratsuka), 228, *229*
The Miracle of the Slave (Tintoretto), 463, *463*
Miró, Joan
Painting, 503, *503*
Mississippian cultures, 294, 403–404
Mississippian peoples, 404
Mitterrand, François, 328
Mixed media, 204–209
collage and photomontage, 205–207
painting beyond the frame, 208–209
Mme. Cézanne in a Red Armchair (Cézanne), 84, *84*
Moche culture, 459–460, *460,* 548, *548*
Moche Lord with a Feline, 460, *460*
Modeling, 94, *94,* 282
Modern and contemporary architectural technologies, 342–356
cast-iron construction, 342
frame construction, 342–345
steel-and-reinforced-concrete construction, 345–347
Modern Avant-Gardes movement, 371–374
Modernism, American, 506
Moeslinger, Sigi, 362
Mogao caves, 9, *9*
Molten bronze, 284
Molten wax, 284
Mona Lisa (da Vinci), 451, *451*
Mondrian, Piet, 507
Monet, Claude
Boulevard des Capucines, 488
Bridge over a Pool of Water Lilies, 490
Carnival on the Boulevard des Capucines, 488, *489*
Grainstack (Sunset), 111, *111,* 123
Grainstacks, 499
Impression-Sunrise, 488, 488–489
The Railroad Bridge, Argenteuil, 156, *156*
Water Lilies, Morning: Willows, 124, *124*
Monks Mound, of Cahokia Mounds State Historic Site, Illinois, *404*
Monk by the Sea (Friedrich), *481,* 481–482, 588
Monochromatic paintings, 110
Monogram (Rauschenberg), 208–209, *209*
Monotypes, 234–235
Montage, 258, *258*
Montgomery, Alan, *Deepwater Horizon,* 648, *648*
Monticello, 478
Mont Sainte-Victoire and the Viaduct of the Arc River Valley (Cézanne), 492, *492*
Moon Pine, Ueno (Utagawa Hiroshige), *80,* 80–81
Moonrise, Hernandez, New Mexico (Adams), *250,* 251
Morisot, Berthe
Reading, 490, *490*
Morris, May, 366
Morris, William, 364–366
Morris Adjustable Chair, *366*
Morris & Co., 365, 367, 372
Mosaic glass bowl, 310, *310*
Mosaics, 421
Mosque, 96, 424–427, 537, *537*
Motion, 116. *See also* Movement
Brownian, 124
and visual art, 121–122, *122*
Moussa, Mansa, 425
Movement. *See also* Motion
and gesture, 166–167
illusion of, 124, *125*
Movement (Marey), 24
Mr. Smith Goes to Washington, 260
MTV logo, 383, *383*

Muhammad Placing the Black Stone on His Cloak, from *Jami al-Tawarikh (Universal History),* 538, *538*
Mujer Pegada Series (Neri), 118, *119*
Mummification, 398
Mummy Portrait of a Man, 184, *184*
Murakami, Takashi, 48
Mural (Mehretu), 144, *144*
Mural on Houston Street, SoHo, Manhattan, New York (Scharf), 204, *204*
Murray, Elizabeth
Bop, 511, *511*
Just in Time, 155, *155*
Museum as power, 633–635
Museum of Modern Art, New York City, 3, 332, 379
Guerrilla Girls, daring posters by, 635, *635*
Museum power
as symbols of destroyed culture, 633–635
Muslim Empire, 423, 425
The Mustard-Seed Garden, 218
Muybridge, Eadweard
Annie G., Cantering, Saddled, 240, *240*
Mycenaean culture, 406
My Kingdom Is the Right Size (Antin), 596, *596*
"My Painting," 126
Mysteries of the Snake Goddess (Lapatin), 405

N

Namban painting, 457, *457*
Namuth, Hans, 127
Naples Archeological Museum, 568
Napoleon Crossing the Saint-Bernard (David), 621, *621*
Napoleonic Wars, 169
Natchez people, 404. *See also* Mississippian peoples
National Endowment for the Arts (NEA), 21, 24
National identities
chinese, 605–606
in Europe and America, 602–604
flags as, 616
Japanese, 606
Native Americans, 604–605
National Palace Museum, Taipei, 476
Native American artists
Nicholson, Marianne, 515
Wolf, Howling, 44–45
Native American Mission Church, 540–542
Native Americans
art history and identities of, 604–605
tribes, 604–605
Natural disasters photographs, 646–652
Naturalism, 35
Nature in arts, 642–645
Nature morte, 47
Nauman, Bruce
Live-Taped Video Corridor, 262, *262*
Nave (Romanesque architecture), 340
Nave, Reims Cathedral, *73*
Nawa, Kohei
PixCell-Deer 24, 517–518, *518*
Ndiritu, Grace
Still Life: White Textiles, *128,* 128–129
Negative space, 72–73
Nelson's Ship in a Bottle (Shonibare), *630,* 630–631
Neoclassicism, 477–479
Neolithic cultures, 394–395
Neolithic painted pottery, 395
Neolithic tribal people, 402
Nepalese Hindus, 566
Nepalese sculpture, *566*
sex and, 566–568
Neri, Manuel
Mujer Pegada Series, 118, *119*
Neshat, Shirin, 96–97, *97*
Fervor, 96–97, *97*
Rebellious Silence, 30, *30*
Women of Allah, 30
Neto, Ernesto
Madness Is a Part of Life, 279, *279*
TorusMacroCopula, 279, *279*
Nevelson, Louise
Sky Cathedral, 287, *287,* 288
New Aqueous City (Bunge), 332, *333*
New Aqueous City (Hoang), 332, *333*
New Book of Insects (Yoshimaro), 220
New Refrigerator (García), 196, *196*
New Stone Age, 394
New York Close Up, 197, 388
New York Evening Mail, 33
New York's Central Park (Olmsted), 356, *357*
New York's Central Park (Vaux), 356, *357*
New York University, 376
Nicholson, Marianne
Kwakwaka'wakw pictograph, 515, *515*
Night Attack on the Sanjo Palace, 440, *440*
The Night Café (van Gogh), 112–113, *113,* 490
Night Chrysanthemum (Steir), *92,* 93, 123
Nighthawks (Hopper), 507, *507*
Nike of Samothrace, 409, *409,* 500
Nike relief, 408, *408*
Nishiki-e calendars, 217
Nixon, Nicholas
The Brown Sisters, Truro, Massachusetts, 552, *552*
Nkonde, 19
No. 32, 1950 (Pollock), 126–127, *126–127,* 141
Nok head artistry, 641, *641*
Nolde, Emil, 498
Nolli, Giambattista, 512
Nolli's Orders (al-Hadid), 512, *512*
Nonobjective art, 33
The Non-Objective World (Malevich), 37
Noon-Day Rest in Marble Canyon from *Exploration of the Colorado River of the West* (Powell), 222, *222*
North Atlantic Light (de Kooning), 28–29, *29,* 30, 36
No Sign of the World (Ritchie), 48, *49*
No Title (The bright flatness) (Pettibon), 523, *523*
Nouvel, Jean
Torre Agbar, 353, *353*
The Nude: A Study in Ideal Form (Clark), 586
The Nuremberg Chronicle (Schedel), 215, *215*
Nu-Wa, 58–59

O

Ocean II (Gursky), 254–256, *255*
O'Connor, John, 22–23
Octavian (Roman general), 398
Oculus, 339
Odalisque (Delacroix), 478–479, *479, 572*
Odalisques, 14, *15*
Ode to Joy (Beethoven), 525
Odyssey (Homer), 406, 560
The Odyssey (Homer), 406
The Office: A Facility Based on Change (Propst), 388
Office for Metropolitan Architecture (OMA), 352
Ofili, Chris, 21
The Holy Virgin Mary, 22, *23*
Oh, Jeff . . . I Love You, Too . . . But . . . (Lichtenstein), 508, *508*
Oil paintings, 193–198
Oilsticks paintings, 172–173
O'Keeffe, Georgia
Banana Flower, 168, *168*
Purple Hills near Abiquiu, 506, 507
Oldenburg, Claes, 508
Ole, Scheeren, 353
Olinsky, Frank, 383
Olmsted, Frederick Law
New York's Central Park, 356, *357*
Olmsted, Vaux & Co., 358
Olympia (Manet), 14, 15, *15,* 486
Olympic Games, 406–407, 494, 535
180 Farben (180 Colors) (Richter), 105, *105,* 107
One Hundred Views of Edo (Utagawa Hiroshige), *80,* 80–81
One-point linear perspective, 75, *75*
On Weaving (Albers), 300
The Open Door (Talbot), 243, *243*
Open palette, 110
Operation Paydirt/Fundred Dollar Bill Project (Chin), 649–651, *650*
Opie, Catherine
Untitled #13 (Spring), 238, *239*
Optical painting, 124
Oregon Historical Society, 7
Organic design, 376–387
Orientalism, 631
Original print, 214
Orozco, José Clemente, 202, 504
O'Sullivan, Timothy
A Harvest of Death, Gettysburg, Pennsylvania, July 1863, 245, *245*
Othello: The Moor of Venice (Shakespeare), 312
Outline line, 49
Over the River, Project for the Arkansas River, State of Colorado (Christo), 298, *298*

P

Pacal, K'Inich Janab, 560, *560*
Pahlavi, Shah Mohammed Reza, 179
Paik, Nam June
Video Flag, 262, *262*
The Painted Hills (Alvis), *250,* 251
Painters
David, Jacques-Loui, 621
Ingres, Jean-Auguste-Dominique, 622
Venetian, 590–591
Painting (Miró), 503, *503*

Paintings
  Bellows, George, 607
  classes of, 607–611
  Delacroix's, *572*, 572–573
  desired image, 572–577
  encaustic, 184
  fresco, 184–188
  luxuria (sensual indulgence), 572
  media, 183–193
  mixed media, 204–209
  oil, 193–198
  overview, 182–183
  Picasso's, *573*, 573–574
  places in, 610–611
  politics and, 504–506
  Renoir, Pierre-Auguste, 489–490, 608–609
  sex in, 571–572
  synthetic media, 202–204
  tempera, 188–193
  vanitas, 572
  watercolor and gouache, 198–201
Palace Museum, Beijing, 476
Palette, 102
  closed or restricted, 110
  open, 110
Palette of King Narmer, 398, *398*
Palladio, Andrea
  Four Books on Architecture, 140
  Villa La Rotonda, 138–140, *139*
Pan, 258
Panathenaic Procession, 276
Pancho Villa, 504
Paris Illustré, 220, *220*
Paris-Journal, 489
Parker, Charlie, 42
Parkinson, Sydney, 530
  Portrait of a Maori, 530, *531*
Parrhasius, 182
Parthenon, 10, 148, *148*
The Passing, 265
Pastel paintings, 170–172
Pattern, 56, 148–153
Patterson, Michael, 160
Pavillon de l'Esprit Nouveau (Le Corbusier), 371, 374
Pax Romana, 414
Paxton, Joseph, 364
Pegasus Vase (Wedgwood), *302*, 303
Pei, I. M., 328
  Glass Pyramid, *329*
Peloponnesian War, 409
Pen and ink, 173–174
The Pencil of Nature (Talbot), 244
Pendentives, 421
Pennell, Joseph, *Pittsburgh, No. II,* 645, *645*
Perceptual color, 111
Performance art, 296
  as living sculpture, 295–297
Pericles, 408
Perry, Matthew C., 220
Persepolis (Satrapi), 178–179, *179*
Persian griffin bracelet, 322, *322*
Persian Wars, 407
The Persistence of Memory (Dalí), 502, *502*
Perspective, 66
  atmospheric (aerial), 89–92, *90*
  distortions of space and, 77–79, *78*
  foreshortening, *79*, 79–81
  linear, 75–77
  one-point linear, 75, *75*
  two-point linear, 77
Petrarch, 444
Petronio, Stephen, 562
  Honey Baby, 562, *562*
Pettibon, Raymond
  No Title (The bright flatness), 523, *523*
Pharaohs, 398
Phidias, 408
Philip, King of Macedon, 409
Philip IV, King of Spain (Velázquez), 142, *142*
Philip of Macedon, 410
Philosophers
  British, 618, 620
Photogenic drawing, 242, *242*
Photographers
  British, 618
Photographic print, 249–251
Photographic space, 82
Photography
  color and digital, 251–256
  computer and new media, 267–270
  early history and formal foundations of, 241–251
  and film, 257–261
  form and content, 246–249
  Mapplethorpe, 64, *64*
  photographic print, 249–251
  selfies, 582
  video art, 261–266
Photomontage, 205–207
Photorealistic art, 33
Physical Love, 564–572
Piano, Renzo, *17*, 17–18
Picabia, Francis, *Machine Tournez Vite (Machine Turn Quickly)*?, 577, *578*
Picasso, Pablo, 199, 371, 372, 496
  Girl before a Mirror, 503, 503–504
  Guernica, 505, *505*
  Guitar, Sheet Music, and Wine Glass, 497, *497*
  Houses on the Hill, Horta de Ebro, 496, 497
  Les Demoiselles d'Avignon, 10, 12–13, *12–13,* 18, 503
  Seated Bather (La Baigneuse), 10, *11*, 20
Pickford, Mary, 259
The Picnic (Prendergast), 235, *235*
Pico della Mirandola, Giovanni, 446–447
Piero della Francesca
  The Flagellation of Christ, 448, *449*
Pietà (Michelangelo), 118, *118*
Pilchuck Glass School, 311
Pilgrimage church, 540
Pilgrim's Guide to Santiago de Compostela, 540
Pink Chrysanthemum (Steir), *92*, 93, 123
Pinocchio, 260
Piper, Adrian, *My Calling (Card),* 614, *614*
Pittsburgh, No. II (Pennell), 645, *645*
PixCell-Deer 24 (Nawa), 517–518, *518*
Place de l'Europe on a Rainy Day (Caillebotte), 77, *77*, 610, *610*
Planet of Slums (Davis), 646
Planographic printmaking process, 232
Platform, 336
Plato, 408, 452
Platonic Academy of Philosophy, 449
Playboy magazine, 379, 590
Pleasure Pillars (Sikander), 517, *517*
Pleasure Point (Rubins), *290*, 290–291
Plein-air painting, 111
Plowing in the Nivernais (Bonheur), 485, *485*
The Poet Li Bo Walking and Chanting a Poem (Liang Kai), 175, *175*
Poet on a Mountaintop (Shen Zhou), 456, *456*
Pointed arch, 341, *341*
Political visions, 25–26
Politics
  painting and, 504–506
Pollock, Jackson, 124, 507
  No. 32, 1950, 126–127, *126–127*, 141
Pollock and Tureen (Lawler), 154, *154*
Polo, Marco, 455
Polychromatic paintings, 110
Polyclitus, 409
  Doryphoros (The Spear Bearer), 147, *147*
Pont du Gard, Nîmes, France, 337, *337*, 359, 640, *640*
Pop Art, 508–509
Pope Julius II, 190, 450
Pope Leo III, 428
Popular cinema, 259–261
Porcelain, 306–310
Portrait of a Boy, 410
Portrait of a Maori (Parkinson), 530, *531*
Portrait of Mnonja (Thomas), 14, *14*, 15
Portrait of Queen Mariana (Velázquez), 142, *142*
Portuguese Warrior Surrounded by Manillas, Nigeria, 461, *461*
Poseidon (or *Zeus*) Greek bronze, 64
Post-and-lintel construction, 334–336
Poster for *Giselle, Basler Freilichtspiele* (Hofmann), 381, *381*
Post-Impressionism, 490–493
Postmodernism, 154
Potter's wheel, 305–306
Pottery wheel-throwing, 306, *306*
Poussin, Nicolas, 474
  Landscape with St. John on Patmos, 474, *474*
  The Shepherds of Arcadia (a.k.a. *Et in Arcadia Ego*), 556, *556*
Powell, John Wesley
  Exploration of the Colorado River and Its Tributaries, 644, *644*
  Exploration of the Colorado River of the West, 222, *222*
Power
  imperial gaze and, 622–623
  museum, 633–635
  museum as, 633–635
  rulers art, 619–622
  women and, 623–627
Pozzo, Fra Andrea
  The Glorification of St. Ignatius, 188, *188*, 210
Praxiteles
  Hermes and Dionysus, 281, *281*
Prehistoric peoples, 392

Prendergast, Maurice
The Picnic, 235, *235*
Preparatory sketches, 160–164
Presidio in the Sand Hills Looking East with ATV Tracks and Water Tower (Downes), *197,* 197–198
Primary colors, 101
Primavera (Botticelli), 192, *192*
Prince, Richard, *Untitled (Cowboy),* 592, *593*
Print, 212
Printmaking
earliest uses, 214–215
intaglio processes, 224–231
lithography, 232–233
monotypes, 234–235
overview, 212, *213*
relief processes, 216–223
silkscreen, 233–234
Prismes Electriques (Electric Prisms) (Delaunay), *110*
Privatization of sex, *571,* 571–572
Problème d'eau. Où trouver l'eau? (The Water Problem. Where to Find Water?) (Samba), 516, *516*
"Procession of Ants," 538
Project to Extend the Great Wall of China by 10,000 Meters: Project for Extraterrestrials No. 10 (Cai Guo-Qiang), 4, *5,* 15
Proofs, 214
Prophet Muhammad, 32, 418, 425, 538
Proportion and scale, 144–148
Propst, Robert, 388
The Office: A Facility Based on Change, 388
Protestantism, 464
Protestant Reformation, 536
Proust, Antonin, 15
Psalter and Hours of Bonne of Luxembourg, Duchess of Normandy, 556, *556*
Public Figures (Do-Ho Suh), 144, *145*
Public opinion, 23–25
Puget Sound on the Pacific Coast (Bierstadt), 33, *33,* 35–36, 603
Pugin, A. W. N., 364
Puppy (Koons), *288,* 288–289
Purple Hills near Abiquiu (O'Keeffe), *506,* 507
Purse cover, 427–428, *428*
Puryear, Martin
Self, 69, *69*
Untitled IV, 69, *69*
Pyramid of the Sun, 458, *458,* 459–460
Pyramids of Khafre, 330, *330,* 558, *559*
Pyramids of Khufu, 330, *330,* 558, *559*
Pyramids of Menkaure, 330, *330,* 558, *559*

Q

Qibla, 425
Qin Shihuangdi, 414
Qin Shihuangdi Tomb, 620–621, *621*
QuarkXPress, 386
Quarton, Enguerrand
Coronation of the Virgin, 135, *135,* 141
Queen Nefertiti bust, 399, *399*
Queen's Ware dinner service (Wedgwood), 302, *302*

R

"Race"ing Sideways (Buglaj), 611–612, *612*
Race Riot (Warhol), 26–27, *27*
Racial identities
in African-American art, 611–615
in art, 627–632
"Rackstraw Downes: Texas Hills," 197
Radical balance, 138–140
Rae, Fiona
I'm Learning to Fly!!, 513, *513*
The Raft of the Medusa (Géricault), 482, *483*
Rage and Depression (Wegman), 264, *264*
The Railroad Bridge, Argenteuil (Monet), 156, *156*
Raimondi, Marcantonio
The Judgment of Paris, 487, *487*
Rain, Steam, and Speed-The Great Western Railway (Turner), 91, *91,* 638, *639*
Raku Tea Bowl (Koetsu), 304, *304*
Raphael, 450
The Alba Madonna, 166–167, *166–167,* 536, *536*
The School of Athens, 452, *452*
Rashid al-Din
Jami al-Tawarikh (Universal History), *538*
Rasin Building, 132–133, *133*
Rauschenberg, Robert, 587, 594
at Guggenheim, 635
Monogram, 208–209, *209*
Ray, Man, *Marcel Duchamp as Rrose Sélavy,* 595, *595*
Reading (Morisot), 490, *490*
Realism, 33, 483–488
Rebars, 350
Recession, 75
Reckinger, Candace, 160
Reconstruction drawing, *343*
Red and Blue Chair (Rietveld), *372,* 373, 375
Red-figure calyx-krater, 303, *303,* 306
The Reflecting Pool (Viola), 544, *544*
Reims Cathedral, France, *73,* 432, *433,* 444
Reinforced concrete, 350
Relative value, 92
Relic 12 (Hung Liu), 58, *58,* 60
Relief-printing technique, 216, *216*
Relief processes, 216–223
linocut, 222–223
woodcut, 216–221
wood engraving, 221–222
Relief sculpture, 276–277
Religion
Buddhism (*See* Buddhism)
Christian (*See* Christian religion)
Rembrandt van Rijn
The Resurrection of Christ, *467,* 467–468
Renaissance, 444–446, 557
Renaissance art
early Renaissance, 446–450
Gothic *versus,* 444
high Renaissance, 450–454
Renoir, Pierre-Auguste
Bal du Moulin de la Galette, *489,* 489–490, 608, *608*
Repetition, 148–153
Replacement process, 284
Repoussé, 322
Representational art
defined, 33
Republic (Plato), 566
The Resurrection of Christ (Rembrandt van Rijn), *467,* 467–468
Retablo of Church of San José, 540–542, *541*
Rhythm, 148–153
Richard I, King of England, 425
Richter, Gerhard
180 Farben (180 Colors), 105, *105,* 107
September, 510, *510*
Rietveld, Gerrit
Red and Blue Chair, *372,* 373, 375
Rigaud, Hyacinthe
Louis XIV, King of France, 472, *473*
Riley, Bridget
Drift No. 2, 124, *125*
Ringgold, Faith
God Bless America, 8, *8*
Tar Beach, *318,* 318–319
We Flew Over the Bridge: The Memoirs of Faith Ringgold, 319
Rising Currents: Projects for New York's Waterfront, 332
Rist, Pipilotti
Ever Is Over All, 523, *523*
Ritchie, Matthew
The Iron City, 647, *647*
No Sign of the World, 48, *49*
Ritual disk *(bi),* 402, *402*
Rivera, Diego, 202, 504
Man, Controller of the Universe, 504, *504*
River valley societies
in China, 400–402
in India, 400–402
Rivière, Georges, 490
Rizzoli International, 108
RMB City, in *Art in the Twenty-First Century* (Cao Fei), 270, *270*
Roadside near Birmingham, Alabama (Evans), 241, *241*
Robert Mapplethorpe Foundation, 22
Rockefeller, Nelson A., 504–505
The Rocky Mountains, Lander's Peak (Bierstadt), 642, *643*
Rococo art, 474–476
Rodin, Auguste, 564
The Burghers of Calais, 285, *285*
The Gates of Hell, 152, *152,* 153
The Three Shades, 152, *152*
Rogers, Ginger, 133
Roman art, 410–414
art history of, 410–414
patriarchal structure of, 624
Roman Empire, 394, 410
Romanesque architecture, 429–430
apse, 340
crossing, 340
nave, 340
transepts, 340
Romanesque art, 429–430
Romanization, 428
Roman Pantheon
exterior, 339, *339*
interior, 339, *339*
Romantic individualism, 482

Romanticism, 479–482
Room for St. John of the Cross (Viola), 130, *130*, 544, *545*
Room No. 2 (popularly known as the *Mirrored Room*) (Samaras), 141, *141*, 144
Roosevelt, Franklin D., 507, 613
Roosevelt, Teddy, 23
Rosenthal Center for Contemporary Art, 114, *114*
Rose window, south transept, Chartres Cathedral, 138, *139*
Rosler, Martha
Gladiators, 205, *205*
Rothko, Mark
Four Darks in Red, 508, *508*
Rothko Chapel, 542, *542*, 543
Round arch, *336*, 337, 432
Royal Academy of Painting and Sculpture, 474
Rubens, Peter Paul, 10, 198
Disembarkation of Marie de' Medici at the Port of Marseilles on November 3, 1600, 474, *475*, 586, *586*
Rubins, Nancy
Pleasure Point, 290–291, *290*
Rubin vase, *68*, 68–69
Rue Transnonain (Daumier), *232*, 232–233
Rumals, 316
Rushing Brook (Sargent), 200, *201*
Ruskin, John, 364
The Stones of Venice, 364
Russell, John, 54
Russian Constructivism, 373
Russolo, Luigi, 500
Ruz, Alberto, 560
Rybczynski, Witold, 140

S

Saarinen, Eero, 379
Tulip Pedestal furniture, *380*, 380–381
TWA Terminal, John F. Kennedy International Airport, 352, *352*
Saarinen, Eliel, 379
Sacred space
Hindu pilgrimage places, 539–540
Japanese shrine, 538–539
Kaaba, 537–538
Native American Mission Church, 540–542
pilgrimage church, 540
Sacred Theory of the Earth (Burnet), 10
Sacrifice of Isaac (Brunelleschi), 277, *277*
Sacrifice of Isaac (Ghiberti), 277, *277*
Saenredam, Pieter
Interior of the Choir of St. Bavo's Church at Haarlem, 536, *536*
Safdie, Moshe
Habitat, *360*, 360–361
Saffarzadeh, Tahereh, 30
Salons, 474
Saltcellar: Neptune (Sea) and Tellus (Earth) (Cellini), 323, *323*
Samarangana Sutra Dhara, 186
Samaras, Lucas
Room No. 2 (popularly known as the *Mirrored Room*), 141, *141*, 144
Samba, Chéri
Calvary, 50–52, *51*
Problème d'eau. Où trouver l'eau? (The Water Problem. Where to Find Water?), 516, *516*
Samsara, 546
San Carlo alle Quattro Fontane facade (Borromini), 464, *465*
Sanctuary of the mosque at Córdoba, Spain, 427, *427*
San Francisco Silverspot, from the series *Endangered Species* (Warhol), 236, *236*
Santa Costanza, Rome, 420, *420*
San Vitale, Ravenna, 422, *422*
Sargent, John Singer, 550
The Daughters of Edward Darley Boit, 550–551, *551*
Sargent, Singer
Rushing Brook, 200, *201*
Satrapi, Marjane
Persepolis, 178–179, *179*
Saturation, 101, *101*
Saturn Devouring One of His Sons (Goya), 482, *482*
Savonarola, Girolamo, 163, 450
Scale and proportion, 144–148
Scarification, 441
Scharf, Kenny
Mural on Houston Street, SoHo, Manhattan, New York, 204, *204*
Schedel, Hartmann
The Nuremberg Chronicle, 215, *215*
Schimmel, Paul, 523
Schneemann, Carolee, *Eye Body: 36 Transformative Actions*, 586–587, *587*
The School of Athens (Raphael), 452, *452*
Sciscione, Nick, 562
Scott, Dread, *What Is the Proper Way to Display a U.S. Flag?*, 616, *616*
Scrolls of Events of the Heiji Period, 440, *440*
Sculptures
and actual weight, 134
additive processes, 274
art parks, 294–295
assemblage, 286–289
carving, 280–282
casting, 283–286
earthworks, 292–294
environments, 279
erotic, 566–568
forms of sculptural space, 276–279
Greek, 39, *39*, 585, 622
installations, 290–292
in-the-round, 277–279
modeling, 282
movement as characteristic of, 122, *123*
and patterns, 150, *151*
performance art as living, 295–297
relief, 276–277
representing *kama*, 566
Shonibare's, 630–631
subtractive processes, 274
time and motion depicted in, 122, *123*
Seagram Building (Mies van der Rohe), 351, *351*
Searching for California Hang Trees (Gonzales-Day), 16, *16*
Searle, William, 325, *325*
Seated Bather (La Baigneuse) (Picasso), 10, *11*, 20
Secondary colors, 101
Second Crusade, 425
Second Temple of Jerusalem, 418
Sections of a Happy Moment (Claerbout), 267, *267*, 273
Seduction of Yusuf and Zulaykha, 568–570, *569*
Seeing
active, 7–8
process of, 6–7
Selected Works 1976-1981, 265
Self (Puryear), 69, *69*
Selfies, 582, *583*
Self-Portrait (Dürer), 454, *454*
Self-Portrait (Frazier), 646, *646*
Self-Portrait, Drawing (Kollwitz), *168*, 168–169
Self-Portrait as the Allegory of Painting (Gentileschi), 182–183, *183*, 210
Senefelder, Alois, 232
Sensation: Young British Artists from the Saatchi Collection, 22
September (Richter), 510, *510*
Serif type fonts, 373
Serigraphs, 233–234
Serigraphy, 234
Serra, Richard
Tilted Arc, *24*, 24–25
Sesshu Toyo, *Haboku Landscape*, 457, *457*
Seurat, Georges, 490
The Artist's Mother, 169, *169*
The Bathers, 491, *491*
La Chahut (The Can-Can), *106*, 107, 491
Severini, Gino, 500
Sex. *See also* Love
African festival and, 576–577
hindus, 566–568
privitization of, 571–572
voyer and, 574–576
Sexual license, 568
Sforza, Ludovico, 450
Shadow, 94
Shaft, 336
Shahnamah (Firdawsi), *31*, 31–32
Shakespeare
Othello: The Moor of Venice, 312
Shaktism, 435
Shakyamuni Buddha, 416. *See also* Gautama, Siddhartha
Shang dynasty, 402
Shape
vs. mass, 67–69
negative shapes, 68
positive shapes, 68
Sharecropper (Catlett), 223, *223*
Shaving a Boy's Head (Utamaro), 221, *221*
She-ba (Bearden), *103*, 103–104
Shell system, 333
Shen Zhou, *Poet on a Mountaintop*, 456, *456*
The Shepherds of Arcadia (a.k.a. *Et in Arcadia Ego*) (Poussin), 556, *556*
Sherman, Cindy
Untitled #96, 522, *522*
Sherman, Cindy, *Untitled #96*, 589, *589*
She-Wolf, 411, *411*

Shimomura, Roger
Enter the Rice Cooker, 234, *234*
Shinto, 439
Ship in a Storm (Turner), 230, *230*
Shiva as Lord of the Dance (Nataraja), 434, *434*
Shonibare, Yinka
Nelson's Ship in a Bottle, 630, 630–631
Victorian Couple, 320, *320*
Shoot (Burden), 263, *263*
Shoshone tribes, 330
Shots, 258
Shudras, 433
Shunshuu Ejiri (Hokusai), 271–272, *272*
Side chair (Eames), 379–380, *380*
Sikander, Shahzia
Pleasure Pillars, 517, *517*
Sikander, Shahzia, *The Last Post,* 629, *629*
Silkscreens, 233–234
Silpa Shastra, 539
The Silver Streak, 377
Simultaneous contrast, 104
Simultanism, 494, 496
Sinopie, 168
Sioux winter count, *604,* 604–605
Siquieros, David Alfaro, 202, 504
Sirani, Elisabetta
The Holy Family with a Kneeling Monastic Saint, 173, *173*
Site-specific environments, 279
Skeleton-and-skin system, 333
Sketch I for "Composition VII" (Kandinsky), *498,* 499
Skidmore, Owings & Merrill, 355, 356
Sky Cathedral (Nevelson), 287, *287,* 288
Skyscraper (Frankl), 371
Slab construction, 304–305
Slavery, 407
Sleepwalkers (Aitken), 3
Smith, Adrian
Burj Khalifa, *355,* 355–356
Smith, Kiki
Bird Skeleton, 212, *213*
Ginzer, 212, *213*
Guide, 316, *316*
Smith, Phillip K., III
Lucid Stead, 116, *116*
Smithson, Robert
Spiral Jetty, 293–294, *293,*654, *654*
Smithson, Robert, *Spiral Jetty, 654,* 654–655
Smithsonian Institution, 517
Snake Goddess (Priestess), 405–406, *405*
Snow Storm: Steamboat off a Harbor's Mouth (Turner), 225, *225*
Snow White and the Seven Dwarfs, 260
Sobieszek, Robert, 22
Social commentary
words and images in, 30–32
Solvents, 184
Something from Nothing (Greiman), 385
Son Lux, 562
Sottsass, Ettore
"Carlton" Room Divider, 382, *382*
The Souls of Black Folk (Du Bois), 612, 614
Souls of Black Folk (Johnson'shelflike sculpture), 614, *615*
South America
art in, 457–461
The Sower (van Gogh), 54–55, *55*
Space
digital, 84–85
distortions of, 77–79, *78*
negative, 72–73
in painting, 83–84
photographic, 82
three-dimensional, 74–81
Spanish artists
El Greco, *463,* 463–464
Spanish Civil War, 505
Spencer, Platt Rogers, 382
Spiegelman, Art, 178
Spiral Jetty (Smithson), 293–294, *293, 654,* 654
Spiritual belief
giving Gods human form, 535–537
sacred space, 537–542
Spirits and the divine, connecting with, 532–534
spirituality and abstraction, 542–544
Spirituality
and abstraction, 542–544
Spiritual Love, 564–572
Spouted Ritual Wine Vessel *(Guang),* 402, *402*
Springing, 339
Spruce Tree House, 330, *331*
Stagecoach, 260
Stairwell (Dickson), 231, *231*
Stanley II (Close), *108–109*
The Starry Night (van Gogh), 52–53, *53,* 490
Star Wars, 261
Statue of Freedom (Crawford), 524
St. Augustine of Canterbury, 428
Steamboat on the Ohio (Anshutz), 645, *645*
Steel-and-reinforced-concrete construction, 345–356
The Steerage (Stieglitz), *246,* 246–247
Steinem, Gloria, *Marilyn: Norma Jeane,* 590
Steir, Pat
The Brueghel Series: A Vanitas of Style, 56–57, *57*
Night Chrysanthemum, 92, 93, 123
Pink Chrysanthemum, 92, 93, 123
Stele of Hammurabi, 397
St. Elsewhere, 382
Stewart, Jimmy, 260
Stickley, Gustav, 344
The Craftsman, 368
Stieglitz, Alfred
The Steerage, 246, 246–247
Still Life: White Textiles (Ndiritu), *128,* 128–129
Still Life with Cherries and Peaches (Cézanne), *491,* 491–492
Still Life with Eggs and Thrushes, from Villa of Julia Felix, 185, *185*
Still Life with Lobster (de Heem), *195,* 195–196, 557, *557*
Still Life with Lobster (Vallayer-Coster), *140,* 141
Stippling, 224
St. Matthew, from *Lindisfarne Gospels,* 428, *429*
St. Matthew from *Gospel Book of Charlemagne,* 429, *429*
Stone #2 (Gray), 653, *653*
Stonehenge, 395, *395,* 396
Stonehenge Hidden Landscapes Project, 395
The Stones of Venice (Ruskin), 364
Stoneware, 306
Stopping out, 227
Storr, Robert, 511
Storyboards, 260
St. Patrick, 422, 427
St. Peter's basilica, 464, *464*
Strand, Paul
Abstraction, Porch Shadows, 82, *82,* 247
Geometric Backyards, New York, 82, *82*
"Streamliner" Meat Slicer, *378*
St. Sernin, Toulouse, 340, *340*
Stuart, James
Greek orders, from *The Antiquities of Athens,* 336, *336*
Study for a Sleeve (da Vinci), 164, *164*
Study for "Cut with the Kitchen Knife Dada through the Last Weimar Beer Belly Cultural Epoch of Germany" (Höch), 206, *206*
Study for The Death of Sardanapalus (Delacroix), *63,* 63–64, 180
Study for the Libyan Sibyl (Michelangelo), 190, *190*
Study of a Woman's Head or of the Angel of the Vergine delle Rocce (da Vinci), 165, *165*
Study of Human Proportion: The Vitruvian Man (da Vinci), 132, *133,* 134, 138, 585, *585,* 594
Stupa, 416
Stylobate, 148, 336
Subject matter, 30
Sublime, 481
A Subtlety (Walker), 144, *145,* 146, 155
Subtractive processes, 101, *101,* 274
Suburbia, 358–359
A Sudden Gust of Wind (Wall), *271,* 271–272
Suger, Abbot, 311
Sullivan, Louis H., 345
Bayard-Condict Building, 345–346, *346*
Suney (Eliasson), 73, *73*
Surrealism, 502
Dada and, 500–504
Sutherland, Donald, 3
The Swing (Fragonard), 574, *574*
Swinton, Tilda, 3
Symbolic color, 112–113, *113*
Symbols, 39–43
furniture of estate, 41
Symbol Source-book: An Authoritative Guide to International Graphic Symbols (Dreyfuss), 43
Symmetrical balance, 134–136
Synthetic media, 202–204
Sze, Sarah
Triple Point (Pendulum), 274, *275*

T

The Table (Gris), 205, *205*
Table + Bottle + House (Boccioni), 70, *70*
Taimina, Daina, 326
Tajima, Mika, 388
A Facility Based on Change, 388, *388*
Taj Mahal, Agra, India, *134,* 135
"Take On Me," 160, *161*

Talbot, William Henry Fox
Mimosoidea Suchas, Acacia, 242, *242*
The Open Door, 243, *243*
The Pencil of Nature, 244
Tang dynasty, 438
Tanguy, Yves, 507
Taos Pueblo apartment, 360
Tapestry, 316
Tar Beach (Ringgold), *318*, 318–319
Tattooing, 530
The Tauromaquia: The Spirited Moor Gazul Is the First to Spear Bulls according to the Rules (Goya), 595, *595*
Taylor, John
Treaty Signing at Medicine Creek Lodge, 44, *44*
Technology, 328
in art, 638–642
Tempera, 188–193, 196
Temperature, color, 102
The Tempest (Giorgione), 453, *453*
Ten Commandments, 32
Tenebrism, 94
Tenebroso, 94
Ten Physiognomies of Women (Utamaro), *218*, 218–219
Tensile strength, 333
Tension
between physical and spiritual love, 566–568
Ten Thousand Waves (Julien), 86, *86*
Teotihuacán, Mexico, 458, *458*
The Terrace at Vernon (Bonnard), 112, *112*
Tesserae, 421
Texture
actual, 118, *119*, 121
defined, 116
visual, 120–121, *120*, *121*
Thangka depicting Bhavacakra (Wheel of Life), Bhutan, 546, *547*
Theodora and Her Attendants, San Vitale, 422, *423*, *625*, 625–626
Third Crusade, 425
Thomas, Mickalene, 254
Portrait of Mnonja, 14, *14*, 15
Thorax (Holzer), 636
The Three Crosses (van Rijn), 52, *52*
The Three Dead (Le Noir), 555–556, *556*
Three-dimensional space, 74–81
Three Fujins (Hung Liu), 61, *61*
Three-Legged Buddha (Zhang Huan), 295, *295*
The Three Living (Le Noir), 555–556, *556*
Three Panels: Orange, Dark Gray, Green (Kelly), 67–68, *68*
The Three Shades (Rodin), 152, *152*
Three Studies of Lucian Freud (Bacon), 20–21, *21*
Tibetan Buddhism, 546
Tiepolo, Giovanni Battista
The Adoration of the Magi, *174*, 175
Tiffany, Louis Comfort, 369
Tiffany and Co., 369
Tile mosaic, *mihrab*, 424, 425, *425*
Tilted Arc (Serra), *24*, 24–25
Time, 116
based media, 128–129, 271–272
seeing over, 124
and visual art, 121–122, *122*
Tintoretto
The Miracle of the Slave, 463, *463*
Titanic, 261
Titian
Assumption and Consecration of the Virgin, 50, *51*
Venus of Urbino, 454, *454*, 590
Tjakamarra, Old Mick
Honey Art Dreaming, *36*, 36–37
Todaiji temple, Nara, 439, *439*
Tohunga, 530, 532
Tomaselli, Fred
Airborne Event, 210, *210*
Toorop, Jan, 370
Salad-oil poster, 580, *580*
Toothbrushes (Dine), 233, *233*
To Raise the Water Level in a Fish Pond (Zhang Huan), 295–296, *296*
"Toreador" fresco, 404, *405*
Torre Agbar (Nouvel), 353, *353*
Torso of a "priest-king" from Mohenjodaro, 401, *401*
TorusMacroCopula (Neto), 279, *279*
Touch (Antoni), 81, *81*
Towards a New Architecture (Le Corbusier), 350
Tracking shot, 258
Trail of Tears, 43
Transepts (Romanesque architecture), 340
Transient Rainbow (Cai Guo-Qiang), 100, *100*
Traveling, 258
Treaty Signing at Medicine Creek Lodge
Taylor, John, 44, *44*
Wolf, Howling, *44*, 44–45
The Tribute Money (Masaccio), 447, *447*, 448
Triple Island (Mattingly), 652, *652*
Triple Point (Pendulum) (Sze), 274, *275*
Triptych, 20
Triumphal arches, 412
Trojan War, 406, 410
Trompe-l'oeil architectural murals, 7
Truss, 343, *343*
Truth and Reconciliation Commission, 178
Tulip Pedestal Furniture (Saarinen), *380*, 380–381
Tunnel vault, 337, *337*
Turner, Joseph Mallord William, 479
Little Liber, 230, *230*
Rain, Steam, and Speed-The Great Western Railway, 91, *91*, 638, *639*
Ship in a Storm, 230, *230*
The Upper Falls of the Reichenbach, 479–481, *481*
Tusche, 233
Tutankhamun Hunting Ostriches from His Chariot, 322, *322*
Tutu, Desmond, 178
24 Hour Psycho (Gordon), 258–259, *259*
29 Palms: Night Operations III (An-My Lê), *248*, 248–249
Twilight, 261
Two Courtesans, Inside and Outside the Display Window (Harunobu), 217, *217*, 591, *591*
Two Figures (Hepworth), 72, *72*
Two-point linear perspective, 77
Tympanum, 430, *430*, 432
Tynan, Sarah
A Good Day for Cyclists, 203
Typography
geometric sans serif fonts, 373
serif type styles, 373

U

Udagawa, Masamichi, 362
Uelsmann, Jerry
Untitled, 252–253, *252–253*
Ugonachomma (the eagle seeks out beauty), 584–585, *584*
Ukiyo-e print, 217, 218–219, *218–219*, 222, 228, 234, 609
Ulay
Imponderabilia, 297, *297*
Ulugali'i Samoa: Samoan Couple (Kihara), 596–597, *597*
Unique Forms of Continuity in Space (Boccioni), 500, *500*
United States
national identities in, 603–604
United States v. Tim DeChristopher (Bowers), 655, *655*
Unity and variety, 153–155
Universal, 259
Universal Limited Art Editions (ULAE), 233
University of Michigan, 376
Untitled (Ali), *152*, 152–153
Untitled (Calder), 122
Untitled (Krasner), 506, *506*
Untitled (Uelsmann), 252–253, *252–253*
Untitled (Cowboy) (Prince), 592, *593*
Untitled (Man Smoking/Malcolm X) (Weems), 627, *627*
Untitled (Ocean) (Celmins), *169*, 169–170
Untitled (We won't play nature to your culture) (Kruger), *522*, 522–523
Untitled #13 (Spring) (Opie), 238, *239*
Untitled #96 (Sherman), 522, *522*, *589*, 589–590
Untitled IV (Puryear), 69, *69*
Untitled (The Blue Sea) (Marin), *199*, 199–200
Untitled (Silueta Series) (Mendieta), 598, *598*
Upanishads, 433
The Upper Falls of the Reichenbach (Turner), 479–481, *481*
Urban Light (Burden), 324, *324*
U.S. Air Force, 379
Utamaro, Kitagawa
The Fickle Type, *218*, 218–219
Shaving a Boy's Head, 221, *221*
Ten Physiognomies of Women, *218*, 218–219

V

Vaishayas, 433
Vallayer-Coster, Anna
Still Life with Lobster, *140*, 141
van der Weyden, Rogier
The Deposition, 448, *448*
Van Eyck, Jan
Eve panel, from *The Ghent Altarpiece*, 550, *550*
The Ghent Altarpiece, 19–20, *19–20*, 32
The Ghent Altarpiece, 548
Giovanni Arnolfini and His Wife Giovanna Cenami, 39–41, *40*, 550
van Gogh, Vincent
Japonaiserie: The Courtesan (After Kesai Eisen), 220, *220*

The Night Café, 112–113, *113*
The Night Café, 490
The Sower, 54–55, *55*
The Starry Night, 52–53, *53,* 490
Vanishing point, 75
Vanitas paintings, 57, 195–196, 557, 572
van Rijn, Rembrandt
The Angel Appearing to the Shepherds, 226, 227
The Three Crosses, 52, *52*
van Ruisdael, Jacob
View of Haarlem from the Dunes at Overveen, 469, *470*
Vantage point, 75
Vasari, Giorgio
The Art of Painting, 182, *183*
Lives of the Painters, 163
Vasconcelos, Joana
Contamination (Contaminação), 321, *321*
Vaults, 336–341
Vaux, Calvert
New York's Central Park, 356, *357*
Vedas, 433
Vedic caste system, 433
Vedic people, 401. *See also* Aryans
Vehicle, 184
Velázquez, Diego, 468
Las Meninas (The Maids of Honor), 142–143, *143*
Philip IV, King of Spain, 142, *142*
Portrait of Queen Mariana, 142, *142*
Venturi, Robert, 155
Venuri, Robert, 512
Venus (Matisse), *176,* 177
Venus of Urbino (Titian), 454, *454,* 590
Venus of Willendorf, 394, *394,* 584, *584. See also Woman*
Vermeer, Johannes
The Allegory of Painting (The Painter and His Model as Klio), 158, 159
Woman Holding a Balance, 137, *137*
Vessel with birth scene, 548, *548*
Victorian Couple (Shonibare), 320, *320*
Video art, 261–266
Video Flag (Paik), 262, *262*
Video Flag X (Chase Manhattan Bank collection), 262
Video Flag Y(The Detroit Institute of Arts), 262
Video Flag Z (Los Angeles County Museum of Art), 262
Viewers
vantage point of, 75
View of Haarlem from the Dunes at Overveen (van Ruisdael), 469, *470*
View of Mulberry House and Street (Coram), 330, *330*
View of Père Lachaise Cemetery from the Entrance, 560–561, *561*
Vigée-Lebrun, Marie-Louise-Élisabeth
The Duchess of Polignac, 475, *475*
Vignon, Pierre-Alexandre
La Madeleine, Paris, 478
Village Voice, 594
Villa La Rotonda (Palladio), 138–140, *139*
Viola, Bill
The Greeting, 268–269, *268–269*
The Reflecting Pool, 265, 265–266
The Reflecting Pool, 544, *544*
Room for St. John of the Cross, 130, *130,* 544, *545*
The Visitation, 268–269, *268–269*
Violin and Palette (Braque), 497, *497*
Virgil, 444, 560, 564
Virgin of Guadalupe (Escamilla), 122–123, *123*
Virgin/Vessel (Hung Liu), *60,* 60–61
Vishnu Puranas, 434
Visigoths, 423, 427
The Visitation (Viola), 268–269, *268–269*
Visual arts, 28. *See also* Art
and motion, 121–122, *122*
rulers power in, 619–623
and time, 121–122, *122*
Visual communication
selfies and, 582
Visual conventions, 44–45
Visual literacy
on iconography, 39–43
words and images in, 30–32
"Visual Pleasure and Narrative Cinema," (Mulvey), 572
Visual texture, 120–121, *120–121*
Visual weight, 134
Vogue magazine cover (Benito), 371
Voisin, Charles, 494
Voisin, Gabriel, 494
von Goethe, Johann Wolfgang, 93
The Metamorphosis of Plants, 317
von Richthofen, Manfred, 505
von Richthofen, Wolfram, 505
Voulkos, Peter
The Eagle Has Landed, 304, 304–305
Voussoirs, 337
The Voyeur, 574–576

W

Wacah Chan, 560
Wailing Wall, 418
Walker, Emery, 366
Walker, Kara, 518
Insurrection! (Our Tools Were Rudimentary, Yet We Pressed On), 208, *208*
A Subtlety, 144, *145,* 146, 155
Wall, Jeff
A Sudden Gust of Wind, 271, 271–272
A Wall, Nassau (Homer), 198, *198*
Wall Drawing #146A: All two-part combinations of arcs from corners and sides, and straight, not straight, and broken lines within a 36-inch (90 cm) grid (LeWitt), 509, *509*
Wall Drawing No. 681 C (LeWitt), 56, *56*
Wall hanging (Albers), 317, *317*
Wall paintings, 532, *532*
Wall Street Journal, 588
Walt Disney, 260
Walter, Marie-Thérèse, 503
Warhol, Andy, 508
Lance Loud, 594, *594*
Marilyn Monroe, 236, *236,* 590
Race Riot, 26–27, *27*
San Francisco Silverspot, from the series *Endangered Species,* 236, *236*
Warner Brothers, 259
War of the Worlds (Wells), 260
Warp, 316
The Warrior Vase, 406, *406*
Wash and brush, 175
Watercolor and gouache, 198–201
Water Lilies, Morning: Willows (Monet), 124, *124*
Water tank, Mohenjo-Daro, Indus Valley, 401, *401*
Wayne, John, 260
Wayne, June, 233
Ways of Seeing (Berger), 572
The Weather Project (Eliasson), 526, *526*
Weaver, Suzanne, 525
Weaving, 316
Webb, Philip, 364, 366
Wedgwood, Josiah, 366
Pegasus Vase, 302, *302*
Queen's Ware dinner service, 302, *302, 642, 642*
Weems, Carrie Mae, 518
Untitled (Man Smoking/Malcolm X), 627, *627*
You Became a Scientific Profile & A Negroid Type, from *From Here I Saw What Happened and I Cried,* 518–519, *519*
We Flew Over the Bridge: The Memoirs of Faith Ringgold (Ringgold), 319
Weft (woof), 316
Wegman, William
Rage and Depression, 264, *264*
Weiss, David
Der Lauf der Dinge (The Way Things Go), 266, *266*
Wells, H. G., 260
Wenda Gu, 58
Wertheim, Christine, 326
Wertheim, Margaret, 326
Western culture, 407
Western Empire, 420, 423
Wet-plate collodion photographic process, 244
What Is the Proper Way to Display a U.S. Flag? (Scott), 616, *616*
When the Levees Broke: A Requiem in Four Acts, 647–648, *648*
Whisper, the Waves, the Wind (Lacy), 553, *553*
Whispers from the Walls (Lovell), 177, *177*
Wilde, Kim, 179
Will, Caleb Goodwin
Inventory of Slaves and Livestock, 314, *314*
Wills, Childe Harold, 382
Wills-Wright, Tom
Burj Al-Arab, Dubai, 356, *356*
Wilson, Fred
Drip Drop Plop, 312, *312*
Metalwork, from Mining the Museum: An Installation by Fred Wilson, 315, *315*
Wilson, Mollie
Kwakwaka'wakw pictograph, 515, *515*
Wilson, Ted, 93
Win! (Bochner), 593, *593*
Wind-tunnel testing, 377
Winters, Terry
Color and Information, 84, *85*
The Wizard of Oz, 260, 523
Wodaabe men, *576,* 576–577

Wodaabe women, 576–577, *577*
Wolf, Howling
  Treaty Signing at Medicine Creek Lodge, 44–45, *45*
Woman, 394, *394. See also Venus of Willendorf*
Woman and Bicycle (de Kooning), *507,* 507–508
Woman Holding a Balance (Vermeer), 137, *137*
Woman on a Bridge, 318, 318–319
Woman with a Hat (Matisse), 498, *498*
Womb chamber. *See Garbhagriha*
Women
  art power, 623–627
  female identities in art and, 589–592
  feminist movement and, 521–522, 589, 626–627
  Iranian, 29
  line associated with, 64, *64,* 587
  power and, 623–627
  representations of, 9, 264
  as rulers, 625
  suffrage, 170
Women artists. *See also* Artists
  Ali, Laylah, *152,* 152–153
  An-My Lê, *248,* 248–249
  Antin, Eleanor, 256, *256*
  Antoni, Janine, 81, *81*
  Brooke, Sandy, *172,* 172–173
  Bruguera, Tania, 19, *19*
  Cassatt, Mary, 96, *96,* 98–99, *98–99, 171,* 171–172, 220, 221, *221,* 227, *227*
  Catlett, Elizabeth, 223, *223*
  de Heem, Jan, *195,* 195–196
  Eames, Ray, 380, *380*
  Essaydi, Lalla, 632
  Greiman, April, 383, 384–385, *384–385*
  Höch, Hannah, 206, *206,* 207
  Holzer, Jenny, 636
  Kihara, Shigeyuki, 596–597
  Lacy, Suzanne, 552
  Mendieta, Ana, 598
  Murray, Elizabeth, 155, *155*
  Ndiritu, Grace, *128,* 128–129
  Nicholson, Marianne, 515
  O'Keeffe, Georgia, 168, *168*
  Opie, Catherine, 238, *239*
  Palladio, Andrea, 138–140, *139*
  Riley, Bridget, 124, *125*
  Rosler, Martha, 205, *205*
  Sherman, Cindy, 589
  Sirani, Elisabetta, 173, *173*
  Smith, Kiki, 212, 213
  Vallayer-Coster, Anna, *140,* 141
  Van Eyck, Jan, 19–20, *19–20,* 32, 39–41, *40*
  Walker, Kara, 144, 145, *145,* 155, 208, *208*
Wonder Woman, 263
Wood, 324–326
Woodcut, 216–221
Wood engraving, 221–222
Wood-frame construction, 342–343, *343. See also* Balloon-frame construction
Words and images, relationship of, 30–32
Wordsworth, William, 479
"Workaday furniture," 366
The Works of Geoffrey Chaucer Newly Augmented (Chaucer), 367, *367*
World Mountain, 416
World of Warcraft, 129, *129*
World War I, 371, 372, 500–501
World War II, 379
The World Won't Listen (Collins), 525, *525*
Wright, Frank Lloyd, 345, 346, 368, 370
  Drawing for *Fallingwater, 348,* 348–349
  Fallingwater, 348–349, *349*
  Robie House, 346–347, *347*
Wright, Orville, 494
Wright, Russel
  American Modern dinnerware, 378, *378*
Wunkirles, 72
Wu Yonggang, 86

X

X Portfolio, 21

Y

Yin Hong
  Hundreds of Birds Admiring the Peacocks, 456, *456*
Yoshitomo Nara
  Dead Flower, 49, *49*
You Became a Scientific Profile & A Negroid Type, from *From Here I Saw What Happened and I Cried* (Weems), 518–519, *519*
You can buy bootleg whiskey for twenty-five cents a quart (Lawrence), 200, *200*
Young Mother, Daughter, and Son (Cassatt), 171, *171*
Youth Drawing (Finiguerra), 162, *162*
Yukinori, Yanagi
  Hinomaru Illumination, 606, *606*
Yunbok, Sin, 574
  Women on Tano Day, 575, *575*

Z

Zagwe, 442
Zapata, Emiliano, 504
Zealy, J. T., 518
Zen Buddhism, 441, 457
0.10: The Last Futurist Exhibition of Paintings, 37
Zeus (Poseidon), 535, *535*
Zeus (Poseidon) Greek bronze, 64
Zeuxis, 182
Zhang Huan
  To Raise the Water Level in a Fish Pond, 295–296, *296*
  Three-Legged Buddha, 295, *295*
Zhang Qian, 415–416
Zhu Shixing, 436
Zhu Yuanzhang, 455
Ziggurat, 396
Zone System, 249–250
Zwingli, Ulrich, 536